lonely planet

Indonesia

Sumatra
p511

Kalimantan
p609

Sulawesi
p663

Maluku
p419

Papua
p465

Java
p57

Nusa Tenggara
p315

Bali
p207

David Eimer, Paul Harding, Ashley Harrell, Trent Holden,
Mark Johanson, MaSovaida Morgan, Jenny Walker, Ray Bartlett,
Loren Bell, Jade Bremner, Stuart Butler, Sofia Levin,
Virginia Maxwell, Ryan Ver Berkmoes

PLAN YOUR TRIP

BARONG DANCE (P270), BALI

VIANY BRANDS/SHUTTERSTOCK ©

GUNUNG BROMO (P192), JAVA

AKTUREY/SHUTTERSTOCK ©

ON THE ROAD

Contents

ON THE ROAD

COOKING COURSE (P771), BALI

EDMUND LOWE PHOTOGRAPHY/SHUTTERSTOCK ©

Contents

UNDERSTAND

SURVIVAL GUIDE

COVID-19

We have re-checked every business in this book before publication to ensure that it is still open after the COVID-19 outbreak. However, the economic and social impacts of COVID-19 will continue to be felt long after the outbreak has been contained, and many businesses, services and events referenced in this guide may experience on-going restrictions. Some businesses may be temporarily closed, have changed their opening hours and services, or require bookings; some unfortunately could have closed permanently. We suggest you check with venues before visiting for the latest information.

6

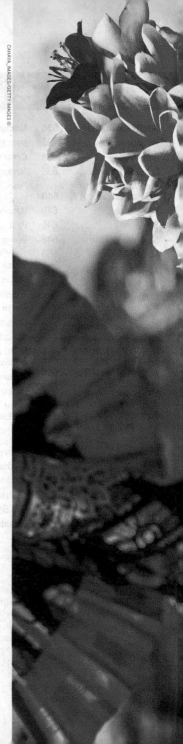

Right: Balinese
Legong dancer
(p270)

WELCOME TO

Indonesia

Gliding across the Banda Sea, from one stunning island to another, temple-hopping around Yogyakarta, beach-bumming in Bali and Nusa Tenggara, bar- and club-hopping in Jakarta, wishing I had more time to explore the jungles of Kalimantan or wind my way through Sulawesi's mountains. Indonesia is so vast and varied that it's impossible to be bored here. And then there are the people, an astonishing mix of races and cultures and all welcoming you with a smile and hello. What's not to love?

By David Eimer, Writer

For more about our writers, see p832

Indonesia

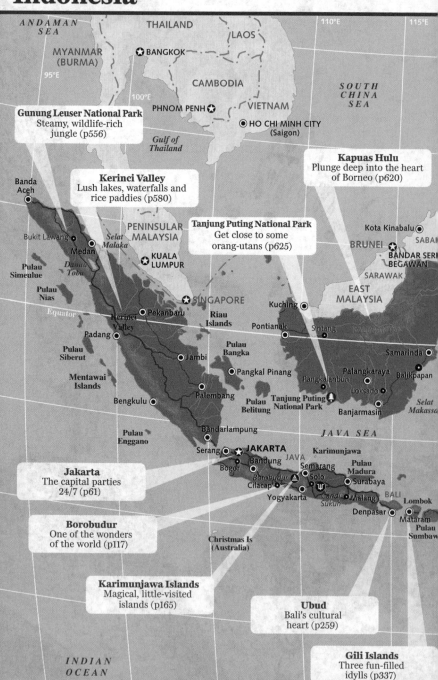

Gunung Leuser National Park
Steamy, wildlife-rich jungle (p556)

Kerinci Valley
Lush lakes, waterfalls and rice paddies (p580)

Kapuas Hulu
Plunge deep into the heart of Borneo (p620)

Tanjung Puting National Park
Get close to some orang-utans (p625)

Jakarta
The capital parties 24/7 (p61)

Borobudur
One of the wonders of the world (p117)

Karimunjawa Islands
Magical, little-visited islands (p165)

Ubud
Bali's cultural heart (p259)

Gili Islands
Three fun-filled idylls (p337)

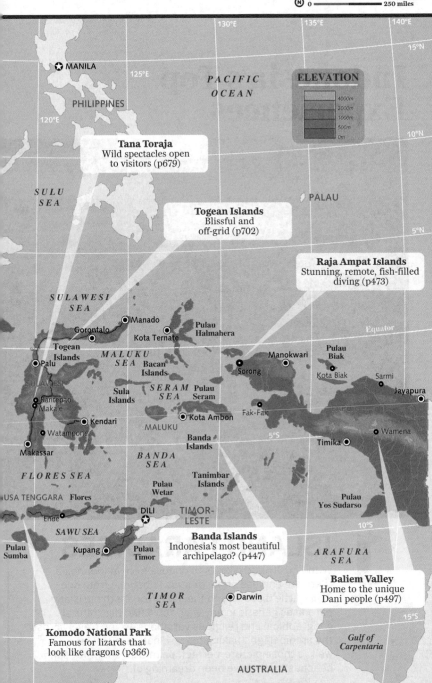

Tana Toraja
Wild spectacles open
to visitors (p679)

Togean Islands
Blissful and
off-grid (p702)

Raja Ampat Islands
Stunning, remote, fish-filled
diving (p473)

Banda Islands
Indonesia's most beautiful
archipelago? (p447)

Baliem Valley
Home to the unique
Dani people (p497)

Komodo National Park
Famous for lizards that
look like dragons (p366)

ELEVATION

4000m
2000m
1000m
500m
0m

0 — 500 km
0 — 250 miles

PACIFIC
OCEAN

MANILA

PHILIPPINES

120°E

125°E

130°E

135°E

140°E

15°N

10°N

5°N

SULU
SEA

PALAU

SULAWESI
SEA

Manado
Gorontalo
Kota Ternate

Pulau
Halmahera

Equator

Togean
Islands

Palu

MALUKU
SEA

Bacan
Islands

Manokwari

Pulau
Biak

Kota Biak

Sarmi

Jayapura

SULAWESI

Rantepao
Makale

Sula
Islands

SERAM
SEA

Pulau
Seram

Sorong

Fak-Fak

Kendari

Kota Ambon

MALUKU

Wamena

Watampone

Banda
Islands

5°S

Timika

Makassar

BANDA
SEA

Tanimbar
Islands

FLORES SEA

Pulau
Yos Sudarso

USA TENGGARA Flores

Ende

Pulau
Wetar

DILI

TIMOR-
LESTE

10°S

SAWU SEA

Kupang

Pulau
Timor

ARAFURA
SEA

Pulau
Sumba

TIMOR
SEA

Darwin

15°S

Gulf of
Carpentaria

AUSTRALIA

Indonesia's Top Experiences

1 ISLAND PARADISES

With 17,000-odd islands to choose from in Indonesia, there are endless opportunities to bounce from one idyllic little discovery to the next. Nor are these island paradises generic in any way. You'll find big cultural, geographical and religious variations as you travel across the archipelago, making for fascinating journeys, as well as those picture-perfect, palm-fringed, white-sand beaches that you've been dreaming of.

Above: Togean Islands (p702)

Gili Islands

One of Indonesia's greatest joys is hopping on a fast boat from busy Bali and arriving on one of the irresistible Gili Islands. Think sugar-white sand, bathtub-warm, turquoise waters teeming with sharks, rays and turtles and wonderful beach resorts and bungalows. p337

Right: Gili Trawangan (p340)

Banda Islands

The Banda Islands offer a rich and intoxicating cocktail of history, culture and raw natural beauty. Draped in jungle and clove and nutmeg trees, fringed with white-sand beaches and surrounded by clear blue seas and pristine reefs, this remote archipelago is a wonder. p447

Above: Pulau Run (p456)

Togean Islands

Almost smack on the equator, the blissful, off-grid Togean Islands are an unadulterated vision of the tropics: blinding white-sand beaches, majestic coral reefs, a smattering of fishing villages, homestay digs and a jungly interior packed with wildlife. p702

Above: Jetty, Togean Islands

2

ORANG-UTANS & DRAGONS

Indonesia is one of the most biodiverse environments on Earth and a great place for animal adventures. The undoubted stars of the show are the orang-utans of Borneo and Sumatra – the only places on the planet where these great apes can be found in the wild – and Komodo dragons, the world's largest lizards.

Tanjung Puting National Park

The African Queen meets jungle safari in this ever-popular national park in southern Kalimantan, where you can get up close to Asia's largest ape, the orang-utan, and also cruise the jungle aboard your own private *klotok*. p625

Above: Orang-utan (p626)

Komodo National Park

Indonesia's best-known national park features hulking mountainous islands blanketed in savannah and patrolled by Komodo dragons. There's also big nature beneath the water's surface here, including lots of sharks and manta rays. p366

Above: Komodo dragon (p367)

Gunung Leuser National Park

This vast expanse of steamy tropical jungle draped across the mountains and valleys of northern Sumatra is paradise for both naturalists and adventure travellers. Come here to hike in search of lethargic orang-utans. p556

Above top: Thomas's leaf monkey, Gunung Leuser National Park

3 TEMPLE HOPPING

Indonesia isn't as well known for temples as its neighbours, yet you'll find some of the region's most ancient and beautiful ones here. Borobudur is a must-see and one of the most important Buddhist sites in the world. Java and Bali are also home to stunning, sometimes hidden away, temples that serve as reminders of both Indonesia's cultural and religious diversity and its long history.

Pura Luhur Batukau

On the slopes of Gunung Batukau and surrounded by forest, Pura Luhur Batukau is one of Bali's most important temples: a misty, remote place steeped in ancient spirituality. p297

Below: Sculpture, Pura Luhur Batukau

ARTIE PHOTOGRAPHY (ARTIE NG)/GETTY IMAGES ©

Borobudur

The breathtaking Borobudur Temple complex is a stunning and poignant epitaph to Java's Buddhist heyday in the 9th century and a highlight of any visit to Indonesia. p117

Above: Buddha, Borobudur Temple (p118)

Prambanan

Comprising the remains of some 244 temples, this enormous World Heritage–listed 9th-century wonder near Yogyakarta in Java is the largest Hindu temple in Indonesia and one of Southeast Asia's major attractions. p143

Right: Prambanan Temple (p144)

4 CULTURE & CLUBS

Above: Legong dance (p270)

Java and Bali are especially rich in culture, but fine music, dance, theatre, painting, puppetry and artisan crafts can be found throughout Indonesia. Yogyakarta and Solo are hubs of traditional Javanese culture, while Ubud on Bali has become known as a cultural centre thanks to the movie and book *Eat, Pray, Love*. For contemporary music and clubs head to Jakarta, home to some of Southeast Asia's best nightlife.

Balinese Dance

Enjoying a Balinese dance performance is a highlight of a visit to Indonesia's most famous holiday island. The haunting sounds, elaborate costumes, careful choreography and light-hearted comic routines add up to great entertainment. p270

Ubud

The artistic heart of Bali, Ubud exudes a compelling spiritual appeal. There are art galleries galore, nightly dance performances and any number of cultural events to enjoy. p271

Jakarta Nightlife

One of Southeast Asia's best-kept party secrets, Jakarta has everything from superstylin' lounges frequented by the oh-so-beautiful crowd, to low-key bars, alt-rock music venues and pumping electronic dance music clubs. p78

5 OUTDOOR ADVENTURES

Indonesia offers countless opportunities for hiking – or travelling by boat – through some of the most spectacular landscapes you'll ever see. Bali and Java offer treks manageable for anyone reasonably fit, but if you really want to get away from it all you can dive into remote mountain valleys inhabited by minority peoples, trek through remote rainforests or navigate rivers that seem to wind forever through the jungle.

HIDJRI AZIM/SHUTTERSTOCK ©

GUDKOV ANDREY/SHUTTERSTOCK ©

Kerinci Valley

High in the mountains, Kerinci Valley is a photogenic landscape of lakes, forests, waterfalls, lush rice paddies and traditional villages that's perfect for off-grid adventures. p580

Above top: Tea plantation, Kerinci Valley

Baliem Valley

Trekking in the Baliem Valley is the highlight of a trip to Papua for most visitors and takes you into the world of the Dani, a mountain people whose traditional culture still stands proud. p497

Above: Dani tribesperson (p501)

Tana Toraja

Tana Toraja in southern Sulawesi offers beautiful valleys and rice terraces, coffee plantations, timeless villages and fascinating Torajan architecture and culture. p679

Above: Batutumonga (p688), Tana Toraja

6 UNDERSEA LIFE

GEORGETTE DOUWMA/GETTY IMAGES ©

HANS GERT BROEDER/GETTY IMAGES ©

Raja Ampat Islands

These remote islands off Papua's northwest tip are a diver's dream. The coral is pristine and there are fish of every size, shape and hue you can imagine. The snorkelling is fine as well. p473

Pulau Bunaken

The water around Pulau Bunaken is more beautiful than you could imagine: 300 types of coral, 3000 species of fish, to say nothing of armchair-sized turtles, dolphins and dugong. p713

Pulau Weh

This island off the northern tip of Sumatra has easy offshore access to an aquarium-like wonderworld of colourful fish and marine life. p547

Top left: Hawksbill turtle, Pulau Misool (p475)
Left: Nembrotha kubaryana, or variable neon slug, Pulau Bunaken (p713)

With so many islands and so much coral, Indonesia offers wonderful possibilities for diving and snorkelling. This is also one of the cheapest places to dive in Southeast Asia. The Raja Ampat Islands are the jewel in the crown – home to the greatest diversity of marine life on the planet – but you'll find stunning drop-offs, eye-popping coral and endless fish all across the archipelago.

7 LITTLE-SEEN BEACHES

With 17,000-plus islands, you're never too far from a beach in Indonesia. In fact, there are so many seductive strips of sand that the hard part is deciding which one to go to. Some places – Bali and the Gili Islands – draw the party crowd. But there are hundreds of beaches where your footprints will be the first for a while. Here are three lesser-known favourites.

Karimunjawa Islands

Around 90km off the north coast of Central Java, the Karimunjawa Islands are a group of 27 coral-fringed beauties with some of the finest beaches in all of Indonesia. p165

Below: Pantai Tanjung Gelam (p166), Karimunjawa Islands

Banyak Islands

This chain of largely unin-habited sandy dots fringed by pristine coral reefs has Sumatra's best beaches: all sugary white sand and crystal clear waters. It's the perfect place to play *Cast Away*. p553

Above: One of the Banyak (Many) Islands

Rote

Just southwest of West Timor, laid-back and little-visited Rote has mile after mile of powdery white-sand beaches, some with epic surf, with hardly anyone on them. p403

Right: Rote

8 INDONESIA ON A PLATE

ARIYANI TEDJO/SHUTTERSTOCK ©

Above: *Nasi campur* (p773) with side dishes

Indonesia's food scene is better than ever. World-class restaurants abound on Bali and in the major cities, and there are now excellent eateries even in remote regions such as Maluku, Flores and West Timor. Indonesian cuisine reflects the country's multicultural history and there are many regional variations, but you'll find *nasi campur* – literally 'mixed rice' but essentially the dish of the day – everywhere you go.

Bali Asli

The ultra-fresh *nasi campur* at this restaurant and cooking school in East Bali might be the best you'll ever taste. But all the Balinese and Indonesian dishes on offer here are bursting with flavour. p290

Nusa

Perhaps Jakarta's finest upmarket Indonesian restaurant, the menu at stylish Nusa changes nightly depending on what the chefs source from the best local markets and suppliers. p76

Historia

Eat your way around the archipelago at this hip Jakarta restaurant with a menu of dishes from across Indonesia. The Javanese noodles and grilled chicken satay are superb. p75

9 UNDER THE VOLCANO

There are around 400 volcanoes in Indonesia and almost a third of them are active, but that doesn't mean you can't climb them for stunning summit sunrises. Some – such as Gunung Api in the Banda Islands – can be scaled in an arduous three hours or so. Others require overnight treks. Frequent eruptions mean that you'll need to check the current activity status of any volcano before ascending.

Gunung Rinjani

Dominating the northern half of Lombok, the active Gunung Rinjani (3726m) is Indonesia's second-tallest volcano. Sacred to Hindus and Sasaks, it's one of the most popular peaks to climb. p327

Above top: Gunung Rinjani

Gunung Krakatau

One of the world's most infamous and volatile volcanoes, Krakatau is still highly active. If it's rumbling, you won't be allowed to climb it. p606

Above left: Gunung Krakatau erupting

Gunung Agung

Prone to frequent eruptions – the last in 2019 – Gunung Agung can be climbed in a tough four to six hours. The reward is tremendous views across Bali. p280

Above: Gunung Agung

10 CATCHING A WAVE

TRUBAVIN/SHUTTERSTOCK ©

JOHN SEATON CALLAHAN/GETTY IMAGES ©

Kuta Beach

Kuta Beach is where surfing began in Asia and tourism started in Bali. Unlike many of Indonesia's prime surf sites, this is a good spot for beginners and there's lots of surf infrastructure. p217

Mentawai Islands

You'll find some of the world's best waves off Sumatra's Mentawai Islands. There are dozens of legendary breaks and consistent surf all year round. p565

G-Land

East Java's Plengkung – better known to surfers as G-Land – is one of the world's premier surf spots with consistently perfect waves and long rides. p201

Left top: Surfing (p42), Kuta Beach
Left: Surfers, Mentawai Islands
(p565)

Indonesia is a surfer's paradise. You can catch waves all across the archipelago with new breaks being discovered every year. Bali attracts the crowds but Java, Nusa Tenggara and Sumatra – arguably the hottest surf spot in Indonesia right now – offer superb waves, too. There are surf schools and board rental at the most popular sites on Bali and Java, so you've got no excuse for not getting wet.

Need to Know

For more information, see Survival Guide (p783)

Currency
rupiah (Rp)

Language
Bahasa Indonesia

Visas
Visas are not hard to obtain, but the most common – 30 days – is short for such a big country. Even the 60-day visa can feel restrictive.

Money
ATMs and money changers are widespread across Indonesia's cities and tourist areas. In remote areas, ATMs don't always work and rates of exchange are often poor.

Mobile Phones
Cheap SIM cards and internet calling make it easy to call from Indonesia at reasonable prices.

Time
Western Indonesian Time (GMT/UTC plus seven hours); Central Indonesian Time (GMT/UTC plus eight hours); Eastern Indonesian Time (GMT/UTC plus nine hours).

When to Go

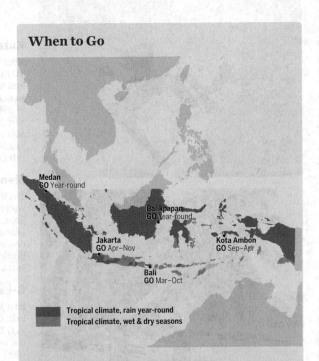

Medan
GO Year-round

Balikpapan
GO Year-round

Jakarta
GO Apr–Nov

Kota Ambon
GO Sep–Apr

Bali
GO Mar–Oct

Tropical climate, rain year-round
Tropical climate, wet & dry seasons

High Season
(Jul & Aug)

➡ Tourist numbers surge across Indonesia, from Bali to Sulawesi and beyond.

➡ Room rates can spike by 50%.

➡ Dry season except in Maluku and Papua, where it is rainy.

Shoulder
(May, Jun & Sep)

➡ Dry season outside Maluku and Papua.

➡ Best weather in Java, Bali and Lombok (dry, not so humid).

➡ You can travel more spontaneously.

Low Season
(Oct–Apr)

➡ Wet season in Java, Bali and Lombok (and Kalimantan flowers).

➡ Dry season (best for diving) in Maluku and Papua.

➡ Easy to find deals and you can travel with little advance booking (except at Christmas and New Year).

Useful Websites

Inside Indonesia (www.inside indonesia.org) News and thoughtful features.

Jakarta Globe (https://jakarta globe.id) Top-notch national English-language newspaper.

Jakarta Post (www.thejakarta post.com) Indonesia's original English-language daily.

Tiket.com (www.tiket.com) A convenient way for foreigners to purchase flights with their credit cards. Download the app.

Lonely Planet (www.lonely planet.com/indonesia) Destination information, hotel bookings, traveller forum and more.

Important Numbers

Mobile phones are everywhere in Indonesia now; numbers usually start with 08 and don't require an area code.

Indonesia country code	☏62
International call prefix	☏001/017
International operator	☏102
Directory assistance	☏108
Police	☏110/112
Fire	☏113
Ambulance	☏118

Exchange Rates

Australia	A$1	11,250Rp
Canada	C$1	11,640Rp
Euro zone	€1	17,440Rp
Japan	¥100	13,400Rp
New Zealand	NZ$1	10,390Rp
UK	UK£1	20,138Rp
US	US$1	14,567Rp

For current exchange rates, see www.xe.com.

Daily Costs

Budget: Less than 500,000Rp

➡ Simple rooms: less than 200,000Rp

➡ Cheap street meals: less than 40,000Rp

➡ Local transport such as bemos: from 5000Rp

Midrange: 500,000–2,000,000Rp

➡ Double rooms with air-con: 300,000–800,000Rp

➡ Cheap flights to shorten distances: from 500,000Rp

➡ Guides and meals in restaurants, each 250,000–800,000Rp

Top End: More than 2,000,000Rp

➡ Stay at resorts or boutique properties in remote places: more than 850,000Rp

➡ Flights and cars with drivers to get around: 500,000–1,000,000Rp

➡ Special tours for activities such as diving; top restaurants on Bali: more than 1,000,000Rp

Opening Hours

The following are typical opening hours across Indonesia.

Banks 8am to 3pm Monday to Friday, to 1pm Saturday

Government offices Generally 8am to 4pm Monday to Thursday, to noon Friday

Post offices 8am to 2pm Monday to Friday (in tourist centres, main post offices are often open longer and/or on weekends)

Restaurants 8am to 10pm

Shopping 9am or 10am to 5pm; larger shops and tourist areas to 8pm; many closed Sunday

Arriving in Indonesia

Soekarno-Hatta International Airport (Jakarta) Jakarta is the primary entry point to Indonesia, but most people merely change planes here before continuing on to their final destination. If staying in Jakarta, you can reach your hotel by taxi (220,000Rp, 45 minutes to two hours), train (70,000Rp, 45 minutes) or bus (40,000Rp, 45 minutes to two hours).

Ngurah Rai International Airport (Denpasar) Bali is the only airport with significant international service apart from Jakarta. Prepaid 24-hour taxis are available to all parts of Bali. It's 80,000Rp for Kuta, 130,000Rp for Seminyak and 300,000Rp for Ubud.

Getting Around

Transport in Indonesia takes many forms.

Boat Slow and fast boats link the many islands, but beware of rogue operators with dodgy safety standards.

Bus Buses of all sizes travel almost everywhere cheaply and slowly.

Car Rent a small car for US$30 a day (Bali), get a car and driver from US$60 a day.

Motorbike Rent one for as little as 70,000Rp a day.

Becak Motorbike with sidecar; Indonesia's version of a tuk tuk.

Ojek Get a cheap ride on the back of a motorbike. Used everywhere.

Taxi Fairly cheap in cities, can be pricey in tourist areas.

For much more on **getting around**, see p796

PLAN YOUR TRIP NEED TO KNOW

First Time Indonesia

For more information, see Survival Guide (p783)

Checklist

➡ Make sure your passport is valid for at least six months.

➡ It's easiest to apply for a 60-day visitor visa in your home country.

➡ Organise travel insurance, diver's insurance and an international driving permit.

➡ Get a medical check-up and clearance if you're planning to dive.

➡ Inform your bank and credit-card company of your travel plans.

What to Pack

➡ Sunscreen and insect repellent; both are hard to find outside tourist areas.

➡ Earplugs for the mosque and traffic wake-up calls.

➡ A torch (flashlight).

➡ A sarong – it's a fashion statement, blanket, beach mat, sheet, mattress cover, towel and shade from the sun.

➡ Phone adaptor.

Top Tips for Your Trip

➡ Check the weather before you decide when and where to go: Indonesia is so vast that the different regions have their own weather patterns.

➡ Avoid visiting during Ramadan: many places will shut down or are booked solid, and much of the population is on the move.

➡ Flights are inexpensive and flying between destinations not only saves time, but is more convenient and comfortable.

➡ Hop on board the local transport: it's cheap and a good way to hang out with people.

➡ If you're heading off the beaten track take plenty of cash: ATMs don't always work and you often can't change money.

What to Wear

Light, loose-fitting clothes are the most comfortable in the tropical heat. If you're trekking in the jungle, or hiking up volcanoes and to higher elevations, bring sturdy footwear, rain gear and a jacket or fleece. When visiting temples or mosques, wear clothes that cover shoulders, elbows and knees. Bring something smart if you're planning on fine dining or hitting the nightlife in Jakarta or Bali.

Sleeping

Accommodation in Indonesia ranges from the very basic to the super-luxurious. It's wise to reserve well in advance in the most touristed areas, especially if you're visiting during the peak months of July, August and December.

Hotels Often excellent in tourist destinations. Standards drop quickly elsewhere.

Guesthouses Can range from boutique-style to simple family-run operations.

Hostels Generally found in the most visited places: Jakarta, Bali, Flores, Gili Islands.

Homestays Often the only option in remote areas.

Camping Possible in national parks and on some multiday hikes.

Villas High-end villas are a popular choice in Bali.

Safety

Security in touristed areas increased after the 2002 and 2005 Bali bombings but has since been relaxed. The odds you will be caught up in such a tragedy are low. Luxury hotels that are part of international chains tend to have the best security, though they also make the most tempting targets, as shown in Jakarta in 2003 and 2009. Suicide bombers did strike a bus terminal in East Jakarta in 2017, killing three policemen, and churches in Surabaya were targeted in May 2018 in attacks that killed 28 people, but such incidents remain rare.

Bargaining

Many everyday purchases in Indonesia require bargaining. Accommodation has a set price, but this is usually negotiable in the low season. Bargaining can be an enjoyable part of shopping, so maintain your sense of humour and keep things in perspective. As a general rule, if prices are displayed, prices are fixed; if not, bargaining may be possible.

Tipping

Tipping is not generally practised across much of Indonesia, but in popular tourist destinations like Bali a small gratuity for services is now expected.

Restaurants (Bali) 10% is the standard tip now.

Hotels Most midrange and all top-end hotels and restaurants add 21% to the bill for tax and service (known as 'plus plus').

Taxis, Massages & Porters A tip of 5000Rp to 10,000Rp is appreciated.

Hindu temple in Bali (p207)

DAVIDEANGELINI/SHUTTERSTOCK ©

Etiquette

Places of worship Be respectful. Remove shoes and dress modestly when visiting mosques; wear a sash and sarong at Bali temples.

Body language Use both hands when handing somebody something. Don't display affection in public or talk with your hands on your hips.

Clothing Avoid showing a lot of skin, although many local men wear shorts. Don't go topless if you're a woman (even in Bali).

Photography Before taking photos of someone, ask – or mime – for approval.

Eating

Indonesia has many eating options. Usually, you only need to reserve in advance at high-end places in the big cities or tourist destinations.

Restaurants Found in cities and tourist destinations.

Rumah makan Literally 'eating house' and less formal than restaurants.

Warung Simple open-air joints that often specialise in one particular dish.

Street vendors The locals choice for basic noodle and soup dishes.

Markets Fantastic for fresh fruit.

Month by Month

TOP EVENTS

Galungan & Kuningan, dates vary

Pasola, February & March

Idul Fitri, May

Tana Toraja Funeral Festivals, July & August

Ubud Writers & Readers Festival, October

January

The near-perfect temperatures in Bali draw many Europeans searching for warmth.

🎎 Gerebeg

Java's three most colourful festivals are held annually in Yogyakarta at the end of January and April and the beginning of November. Huge numbers of people in traditional dress march in processions with garish floats, all to the tune of gamelan music. (p127)

February

It's the dry season in the east. This is a good time to hit dive and snorkel sites in Maluku and Papua, where the waters will be especially clear.

🎎 Pasola

Nusa Tenggara's biggest festival: vividly dressed teams of horsemen engage in mock, though sometimes bloody, battles in West Sumba. Often coincides with Nyale in Lombok, a huge fishing festival celebrated by the Sasaks.

🎎 Cap Goh Meh

Dragons and lions dance on Chinese Lunar New Year in ethnic communities across Indonesia. Some of the most colourful are in Singkawang, where these creatures dance alongside seemingly possessed Chinese and Dayak holy men during Kalimantan's biggest Chinese Lunar New Year celebration. (p619)

March

The rainy season is tailing off in Java, Bali and western Nusa Tenggara, and this is a good time to visit Indonesia as crowds are few and options are many.

🎎 Nyepi

Bali's major Hindu festival, Nyepi, celebrates a new year on the religious calendar. It's marked by inactivity – to convince evil spirits that Bali is uninhabited. The night before sees community celebrations with *ogoh-ogoh*, huge papier-mâché monsters that go up in flames. March or early April.

May

The weather in Java and Bali is ideal, but in the eastern parts of the Indonesian archipelago the rainy season is set to start.

🎎 Waisak

A key festival for Indonesia's Buddhists, Waisak commemorates the birth, enlightenment and death of the Gautama Buddha. Thousands of worshippers gather at Java's Borobudur temple complex on the first full moon of May. (p120)

🎎 Idul Fitri

Idul Fitri is the traditional end of Ramadan, the Muslim month of fasting, and this huge weeklong holiday sees tens of millions of people travelling to their home villages or holidaying in places like Bali. Avoid travelling if possible. The date is slightly earlier each year.

June

A relaxed time in Indonesia that sees few crowds anywhere. June tends to be very hot around much of the archipelago, but the dry season is just around the corner.

 Danau Sentani

The Danau Sentani festival features spectacular traditional dances and chanting as well as boat events, music, crafts and more. A highlight of Papua's north, it centres on lakeside Kalkhote, near Sentani town. (p489)

Danau Toba Festival

This week-long festival in mid-June features canoe races on Sumatra's famus crater lake as well as Batak cultural performances. (p532)

July

Visitor numbers are high in Bali and other areas popular with tourists. July is often the coolest and driest time of the year outside Maluku and Papua, where it is the rainy season.

Tana Toraja Funeral Festivals

A Sulawesi highlight and an excellent reason to visit the island. Held during July and August, the ceremonies often shock first-time visitors. Toraja working throughout the country return home for celebrations and funeral rituals. (p682)

August

Independence Day on 17 August sees parades and celebrations in Jakarta and across the country. You'll see school kids practising

their marching in the prior weeks. Bali gets busy with Australians escaping winter.

Erau Festival

Every August thousands of Dayaks from across Kalimantan attend the Erau festival in Tenggarong, a vast intertribal party punctuated by traditional dances, ritual ceremonies and other events. It draws folk dancers worldwide; plan ahead to reserve space. (p649)

☆ Bidar Races

Spectacular *bidar* (canoe) races are held on South Sumatra's Sungai Musi in Palembang every 17 August and 16 June (the city's birthday). There is also a dragon-boat festival in Padang in July or August. Up to 60 rowers power these boats. (p598, p561)

Baliem Valley Festival

A celebration of indigenous culture in Papua's Baliem Valley, with mock 'tribal fighting', full traditional regalia, dance and music. The festivities take place over two days during the second week of August. (p499)

September

The driest month of the year on Kalimantan and so perfect for orang-utan spotting.

October

A good month for travel with few crowds and many good deals. It's the start of rainy season in Java and Bali.

🏃 Ubud Writers & Readers Festival

This Ubud festival brings together scores of writers and readers from around the world in a celebration of writing – especially that which touches on Bali. Its reputation grows each year. (p263)

☆ Madura Bull Races

Bull racing is the major sport on Pulau Madura, off Java. Teams compete throughout the year to make the finals held annually in Pamekasan. These competitions feature over 100 racing bulls and legions of fervent fans. Note, the festival is associated with animal-welfare issues.

November

It's the rainy season across western Indonesia. But it's perfect weather for diving in Maluku and Papua.

December

Popular tourist areas are very busy from the week before Christmas through New Year's. It's prime time for diving in areas such as Maluku's Banda Islands.

Galungan & Kuningan

One of Bali's major festivals, Galungan celebrates the death of the legendary tyrant Mayadenawa. Over 10 days the gods come to earth for the festivities. Barong (mythical lion-dog creatures) prance through temples and villages. Locals rejoice with family feasts. The date changes each year.

Itineraries

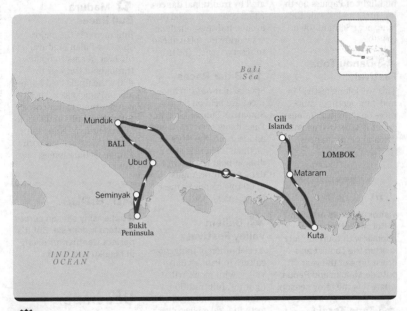

2 WEEKS: Beaches, Bars, Bodies & Bliss

Mix the offbeat with the sublime in Indonesia's heart of tourism.

Start in Bali, acclimatising in the resorts, clubs and shops of **Seminyak**. Dose up on sun at the beach, then explore the perfect little beaches and surf breaks of the **Bukit Peninsula**.

Head north to immerse yourself in the 'other' Bali – the culture, temples and rich history of **Ubud**. Take a cooking course, unwind at a spa, wander the rice paddies and see Bali's famous traditional dance. Then escape to the misty mountains for treks to waterfalls amid coffee plantations in and around **Munduk**.

Next is Lombok. Take the ferry from Bali's port town of Padangbai to Lombok's launching pad of Lembar. Head to **Kuta** for mellow vibes amid the wonderful beaches of south Lombok. Then potter through the rice fields and Hindu temples around **Mataram**.

Ferry from Bangsal to the deservedly celebrated **Gili Islands**, where seamless beaches, translucent water and vivid reefs beg for snorkelling. Or if time's short, catch a fast boat directly to the Gilis from Bali.

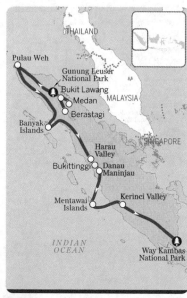

3 WEEKS The Java Jaunt

Indonesia's most populous island mixes the nation's future and past with natural beauty.

Begin in **Jakarta** and wrap your senses around the dizzying smells, sounds, sights and people of Indonesia's teeming capital. Linger long enough to binge on Bintang beer and splurge in the city's shops, then head to **Batu Karas** for classic laid-back beach vibes or go for the resorts of nearby **Pangandaran**.

After you've worshipped the sun for a week or so, catch the train to **Yogyakarta**, Java's cultural capital. Dabble in batik, amble through the *kraton* (walled city palace) and part with your rupiah at the vibrant markets. A day trip to majestic **Borobudur** is a must.

From Yogyakarta, journey to the laid-back city of **Solo**, via the enigmatic temples of **Prambanan**. From there, visit **Malang** and its cluster of nearby Hindu temples. Then head into the clouds at awesome **Bromo-Tengger-Semeru National Park**, spending a night on the lip of Tengger crater. Finally, hike to the magnificent turquoise sulphur lake of **Kawah Ijen** on the Ijen Plateau

6 WEEKS Sumatra

Sumatra is big and you'll have to hustle to fully appreciate its myriad natural charms within visa constraints.

Start your explorations in **Medan**, then head out of town to **Bukit Lawang** to see the island's famous residents, the orangutans. It's a short jaunt from here to **Berastagi**, a laid-back hill town amid volcanoes.

Head northwest to Ketambe for truly wild orang-uatan encounters in **Gunung Leuser National Park**. Then take a bus to Banda Aceh, from where it's a short boat ride to world-class diving at **Pulau Weh**. Take a bus along the coast south (or fly) and venture off the west coast to the **Banyak Islands**, a surfing and beach paradise. Back ashore, follow the Trans-Sumatran Hwy south to **Bukittinggi**, a good base for exploring the cultures and beauty of the **Harau Valley** and **Danau Maninjau**.

More surf, sand and underwater joy await at the **Mentawai Islands**. Next, head inland to the volcanic **Kerinci Valley** and Kerinci Seblat National Park for remote jungle villages. Finally, head far south to **Way Kambas National Park**, where the highlights include elephants. From here, it's easy to catch the Java ferry.

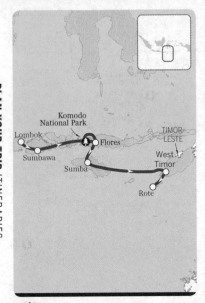

6 WEEKS Nusa Tenggara

Lombok is well-known to visitors and Flores is also popular, but the island province of Nusa Tenggara holds many more surprises.

Head east from **Lombok**. Admire the beautiful coastline and surf breaks such as Maluk and Pantai Lakey that dot **Sumbawa**. Catch the ferry to **Flores**, where Labuan Bajo is the fast-growing hub for exploring nearby **Komodo National Park**. Enjoy dragons and small, beautiful island beaches.

Flores is a rugged volcanic island with thriving ancient cultures and dramatic terrain, which is increasingly explored via the fast-improving Trans-Flores Hwy. Visit Bajawa to explore volcanoes and villages, then use mountainside Moni as a base for visiting the vivid waters at Kelimutu. Savour the lovely beaches near Paga.

Now take a ferry south to isolated and timeless **Sumba**, where superb beaches such as Waikabubak and Tambolaka are starting to attract visitors. After indulging in sun and isolation, fly to Kupang in **West Timor**. Visit entrancing ancient villages like None, Boti and Temkessi in the surrounding areas to the east, then jump over to **Rote** for relaxed beach vibes.

4 WEEKS The Great East

Papua is the launching pad for this route through some of Indonesia's most exotic and beautiful territory. You can do it in 30 days with judicious use of flights; otherwise take your time for the full land and sea adventure.

Start at the transport hub of **Jayapura**. But you'll only be there long enough to charter a boat to visit the magnificent **Danau Sentani**, a 96.5-sq-km lake with 19 islands perfect for inland island-hopping.

Back on dry land, take to the air to get to the beautiful **Baliem Valley**, rich in culture and hike-worthy mountain scenery, jumping-off point for treks into the little-explored Yali Country, and home to the Dani people, an ethnic group whose members have eschewed most modern things and live a traditional life. Enjoy mountain views from a thatched hut.

Fly to **Nabire** via Jayapura and spot whale sharks off the coast – you can even swim with them. Then fly up for some idle island time on **Pulau Biak**. Next it's a flight to **Sorong**, a base for trips out to the **Raja Ampat Islands** – a paradise for divers and snorkellers, with Indonesia's most abundant and varied marine life.

8 WEEKS Indonesia's Island Core

Explore two of Indonesia's greatest concentrations of islands in these little-visited regions.

In **Makassar** pause amid the pandemonium for excellent seafood. But don't overdo it, as you want to be fully alive for the elaborate funeral ceremonies in **Tana Toraja**, a nine-hour bus trip from Makassar. From here, another long bus ride takes you to the mountain-lake town of **Tentena**, from where you can access the ancient megalithic statues of **Lore Lindu**. A four-hour shared-car journey whisks you to **Ampana**, where you take a ferry to the amazing, beguiling **Togean Islands** for days of island-hopping between iconic beaches.

Tearing yourself away, boat to **Gorontalo**, then board a bus or plane to **Manado** and take a boat to laid-back **Pulau Bunaken**. Fly from Manado to **Pulau Ternate**, which is as pretty a tropical island paradise as you'll find. From there, fly onto **Kota Ambon** on Maluku's Pulau Ambon. Pause only briefly, then take the fast ferry to the crystalline seas, multicoloured reefs and empty beaches of the **Banda Islands**. Finally make the jaunt by boat southeast to the **Kei Islands**, for perfect beaches.

6 WEEKS Postcards Come to Life

Mysterious rivers of unfathomable length that wind through the jungle are the avenues via which travellers can discover Kalimantan's incredible diversity of life, including orang-utans.

Unassuming **Pangkalan Bun** is the entry point to this excursion – it's the launching pad for trips into glorious **Tanjung Puting National Park**, one of the prime places for spotting orang-utans. Scan the canopy for their amber bodies from the upper deck of a *klotok* (houseboat) as it drifts down the beautiful Sungai Sekonyer.

From Pangkalan Bun, fly or take the overnight bus to colourful **Banjarmasin**. Make sure to visit its animated floating markets, one of the most photogenic sights in Kalimantan. Detour for some hiking and bamboo rafting in the remote hills around **Loksado**. From Banjarmasin, travel overland to **Samarinda** and make an expedition along **Sungai Mahakam**. Several days upstream will land you in the river's western reaches, which are peppered with semi-traditional Dayak villages and preserved forests. Travel back to the coast and head north to primitive, teardrop-shaped **Pulau Derawan** and its offshore underwater wonders.

Off the Beaten Track

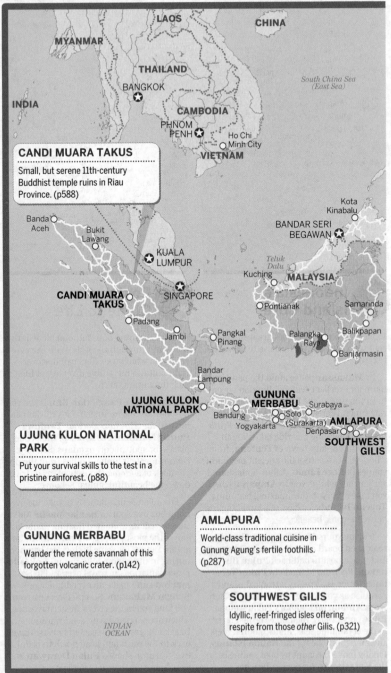

CANDI MUARA TAKUS

Small, but serene 11th-century Buddhist temple ruins in Riau Province. (p588)

UJUNG KULON NATIONAL PARK

Put your survival skills to the test in a pristine rainforest. (p88)

GUNUNG MERBABU

Wander the remote savannah of this forgotten volcanic crater. (p142)

AMLAPURA

World-class traditional cuisine in Gunung Agung's fertile foothills. (p287)

SOUTHWEST GILIS

Idyllic, reef-fringed isles offering respite from those *other* Gilis. (p321)

0 ——— 1,000 km
0 ——— 500 miles

BOGANI NANI WARTA-BONE NATIONAL PARK

This remote national park offers both rare species and ancient burial sites buried deep within the forests. (p708)

PULAU HALMAHERA

The largest island in Maluku but also one of the least-visited, Halmahera offers beaches and volcanoes, little-seen dive sites and the chance to venture into one of Indonesia's most remote national parks. (p431)

MANILA

PHILIPPINES

Sulawesi
Sea

Gorontalo

Palu

Makale

Makassar

Kota
Ternate **PULAU HALMAHERA**

**BOGANI NANI
WARTABONE
NATIONAL PARK**

Manokwari
Sorong
Kota Biak

Jayapura

Kota
Ambon

Fak-fak

**PULAU
TANIMBAR
KEI**

Timika

Wamena

KOROWAI

PAPUA
NEW
GUINEA

DILI

Kupang

PULAU TANIMBAR KEI

This idyllic island has superb white-sand beaches ringed by tranquil turquoise sea and a complete lack of tourist infrastructure. Find a homestay with the friendly locals and let the days drift by. (p462)

AUSTRALIA

KOROWAI

Visit the world's most talented tree-house builders in super-remote Papua. (p509)

Gili Meno (p34

Plan Your Trip

Outdoor Adventures

Indonesia's volcanic archipelago geography creates a thrilling range of adventure opportunities. The many seas offer superb diving and snorkelling, and some of the world's most famous waves for surfers. On land, its string of dramatic volcanoes, wildlife-filled jungles and rushing rivers are an adventurer's delight.

Best Experiences

Best Beach

The beaches of South Lombok (p331), especially those that line the bays around Kuta (Lombok, not Bali), are stunning and worthy of the trip.

Best Diving

The Raja Ampat Islands (p473) are on many a diver's bucket list, and with good reason: the wealth and variety of marine life is nothing short of astonishing. Sumatra's Pulah Weh is good too.

Best Surfing

Tough competition, but we say Sumatra for its pure perfection and consistency. The Mentawais (p565) and Nias (p536) are home to some of the world's most legendary waves.

Best Hiking & Trekking

The Baliem Valley (p497) draws acolytes from around the world for hikes among some of the world's most unique cultures.

Best Wildlife-Watching

Kalimantan's Tanjung Puting National Park (p625): anchor along one of its iconic rivers and watch orang-utans go about their business just metres away.

Beaches

With 17,000-plus islands, Indonesia has a lot of beaches. These range from the wildly popular beaches on south Bali to those for hardcore party people on the Gili Islands, and literally hundreds more where your footprints will be the first of the day.

Pantai is 'beach' in Bahasa Indonesia.
Note that sunscreen can be hard to find outside major tourist areas.

Bali

Fabled for its beaches, Bali actually pales in comparison to scores of other islands in Indonesia. What the island does have is a thriving beach culture, with surfing and places to imbibe, ranging from the dead simple to the hipster-luxe. Locals and visitors alike pause on west-facing beaches at sunset.

Kuta Beach (p217) This is the original draw for tourists, with a golden-sand arc sweeping past Canggu to the northwest. Its beach breaks are good for both beginners and experienced surfers.

Bukit Peninsula (p239) Bali's southern tip has famous surf spots and beaches such as Bingin and Padang Padang that feature little pockets of bright sand below limestone cliffs. The east side has reef-protected strands, such as the one at Nusa Dua.

East Bali (p278) A long series of open-water beaches begins north of reef-protected Sanur. Waves pound volcanic sand that ranges from a light grey to charcoal black.

Java

Beaches near cities in Java can be very busy on weekends, but venture a little further and you'll find some great sand.

Batu Karas (p112) A simple village with two great beaches and a classic laid-back vibe.

Southeast of Yogyakarta (p138) Explore this beautiful coastline, a succession of alluring golden-sand coves divided by craggy headlands (but skip Parangtritis, which is not in the same league).

Karimunjawa Islands (p165) Some 27 islands compose this offshore marine park, which gets very few visitors. It has some of the finest beaches in Indonesia.

Watu Karang (p189) East Java's finest patch of white sand, worshipped by beach-lovers and surfers alike.

Maluku

The fine beaches here have barely been discovered.

Banda Islands (p447) Maluku's best beaches are all in the Bandas. Charter a boat from Bandaneira and enjoy exquisite empty beaches on Pulau Hatta, Pulau Ai and Pulau Run (Rhun). The best of the Banda bunch is Pulau Neilaka, more a white sandbar than an island.

Kei Islands (p457) Sugary Pasir Panjang is ground zero for beach lounging. The petroglyph-swathed cliffs and mind-bending scenery at Ohoidertawun are also worth consideration. Rent a bike and make the two-hour trek to the stunning, remote and drop-dead-gorgeous beaches of Pantai Ohoidertutu. Otherwise charter a boat from Pulau Kei Kecil to Pantai Ngurtavur's blinding white sandbar.

Nusa Tenggara

Nusa Tenggara is probably the region of Indonesia with the most beaches awaiting discovery.

Gili Islands (p337) The Gilis are easily reached from Bali and Lombok, and you can snorkel right off the blinding white sands. Gili Trawangan has one of the country's most vibrant party scenes.

Lombok (p316) Head south for the pristine white-sand islands of Gili Asahan and the north coast of Gili Gede. Kuta is an immense series of one spectacular beach or bay after another. Get there, rent a motorbike and explore.

Sumbawa (p355) In west Sumbawa the best beaches are south of Maluk in Rantung and north in Jelenga. In the east, head to the Lakey area.

Flores (p368) Head to the islands off Labuan Bajo and you'll find bliss, especially on Pulau Sebayur and Pulau Kanawa. Pantai Merah on Komodo Island is famous for its sublime pink-sand beaches. The Seventeen Islands Marine Park off the Riung coast also has a dozen remote islands with epic and empty white-sand beaches to laze upon.

Rote (p403) The main beach in Nemberala town is beautiful enough, but the beaches just get wider and whiter the further south you travel. Ba'a is the most beautiful of the bunch. We also enjoy the empty sugary beaches on nearby islands Pulau Do'o and Pulau Ndao.

Balangan Beach, Bukit Peninsula (p239)

Papua

While Papua's better known for its diving and hiking, word is getting out fast about its islands ringed with powdery white sand.

Raja Ampat Islands (p473) There are some divine and empty beaches here, but due to the high cost of reaching the area they tend to be enjoyed mainly as a secondary activity by people who are diving and/or snorkelling.

Pulau Biak (p492) The Padaido Islands (p495) off Pulau Biak have some decent beaches that are not too hard to reach.

Sumatra

The best beaches on this huge island are actually on tiny islands offshore.

Banyak Islands (p553) Banyak means 'many', and it's true there are many fine beaches among the 99 islands in this remote and seldom-visited chain off Aceh.

Mentawai Islands (p565) Overshadowed by its reputation as a legendary surf destination, this island chain also features insanely beautiful beaches.

Pulau Bintan (p591) A gem in the Riau Islands, this island has some fine beaches where you can live the tropical fantasy in a hut.

WHEN TO GO

There are vast variations in the weather across the huge swath of islands that is Indonesia. Generally, dry season in Java, Bali, Lombok and Sumatra is May to September, while Maluku and Papua have their best weather from October to April. But exceptions are the rule, especially as the seasons increasingly become confused with changing weather patterns. You'll want to research any location you plan to visit carefully if the weather will play a role in your enjoyment.

Cycling, Gili Meno (p348)

Cycling

Cycling in Indonesia is booming. Lowland towns such as Yogyakarta and Solo in Java teem with bikes, and bicycles are gaining popularity in Bali. Lombok has good roads for cycling.

Bali

Bike tours are available across the island. Some are simple downhill jaunts through rice fields while others are much more adventurous.

Java

Yogyakarta is a big cycling centre; pedal out to see the Prambanan Temple (p144). Bikes are also for rent at Borobudur, while Solo is another good place to join a bike tour.

Sumatra

Cycling the languid streets of Danau Toba (p529) is a great way to explore the island. On Danau Maninjau (p577) you can pedal around the crater lake.

Nusa Tenggara

Bicycles are available for hire on the Gili Islands; Trawangan (p340) is best suited for exploration.

Diving

With so many islands and so much coral, Indonesia offers wonderful possibilities for diving and is regarded as one of the cheapest places to do so in Southeast Asia.

Bali

Indonesia's tourist hub has a plethora of excellent dive shops, schools and operators.

Nusa Penida (p257) Serious diving that includes schools of manta rays and 2.5m sunfish.

Pulau Menjangan (p307) Spectacular 30m wall off a small island. Good for divers and snorkellers of all skills and ages.

Tulamben (p292) A popular sunken WWII freighter lies right off the shore.

SAFETY GUIDELINES FOR DIVING

Before embarking on a scuba-diving or snorkelling trip, consider the following points to ensure a safe and enjoyable experience:

➡ Ensure you possess a current diving certification card from a recognised scuba-diving instruction agency.

➡ Be sure you are healthy and feel comfortable diving.

➡ Obtain reliable information about physical and environmental conditions at the dive site. Ask your operator or guide detailed questions.

➡ Dive only at sites within your realm of experience and engage the services of a certified dive instructor.

➡ Check your equipment thoroughly beforehand. In much of Indonesia, the equipment (if it's available) may not be in top condition. Bali is your best bet for finding reliable equipment for hire.

Java

While the island isn't known for its diving, there are some spots if you look.

Karimunjawa Islands (p165) These islands have some dive sites, including a century-old Norwegian wreck dive.

Kalimantan

Kalimantan has a growing number of dive resorts with house reefs and fast boats to access islands.

Derawan Archipelago (p657) Features a diverse range of sites: Pulau Derawan has excellent macro diving; Pulau Sangalaki is famous for mantas; Pulau Maratua has sharks, rays and barracuda.

Maluku

Diving has great promise here but is mostly undeveloped.

Banda Islands (p447) Seasonal dives can explore lava flow off Pulau Gunung Api, or the wonderful coral-crusted walls off Pulau Hatta, Pulau Ai and Pulau Run.

Pulau Ambon (p435) Something of a dive mecca. There are reef dives outside the bay off the Ambon coast, but most divers come here for the excellent muck diving on the slopes within Teluk Ambon.

Pulau Halmahera (p431) One of several untapped dive sites in North Maluku; get in touch with local guide Firman (p434) for tips on dive sites.

Nusa Tenggara

A vast range of diving opportunities awaits. Major destinations have land-based dive shops. For untapped dive sites, bring your own buoyancy control devices, regulators and computers (tanks are usually accessible) and explore Rote, Sumbawa and Sumba.

Gili Islands (p337) Among the best places to get certified worldwide; accessible reefs are within a 10-minute boat ride.

Lombok (p316) If you get lucky, you can see schooling hammerheads at Blongas, usually in mid-September.

Flores (p368) World-class sites within the Komodo National Park (p366); in peak season up to 50 liveaboards ply these waters.

Alor Archipelago (p390) Crystalline waters and arguably the most pristine reefs in Indonesia, and you'll have the sites almost all to yourself.

Pulau Moyo (p359) Pristine, colourful coral with plunging walls and a huge variety of marine life.

Papua

Bring your own equipment to ensure you get the most out of the journey.

Raja Ampat Islands (p473) Among the best in the world for the diversity and quantity of marine life. It's a remote area and quite expensive. Most divers head out on liveaboard boats for one- to two-week cruises, or stay at the handful of dive resorts.

Nabire (p495) Head out to dive with whale sharks; nearby is a coral reef home to giant clams, seahorses and a multitude of sharks.

Pulau Biak (p492) Take the plunge to explore a famous US WWII seaplane wreck.

Top: Diving, Raja
Ampat Islands (p473)

Bottom: Coral,
Komodo National Park
(p366)

DON MAMMOSER/SHUTTERSTOCK ©

FABIO LAMANNA/SHUTTERSTOCK ©

Snorkelling, Banda Islands (p447)

Snorkelling

For many, there's bliss to be found in the simplicity of snorkelling beautiful waters right off the beaches. Most dive operators will let snorkellers hitch a ride on trips, but don't expect much in the way of decent masks and fins outside the most popular sites. Bring your own if you're picky. There are also some wonderful free-diving outfits.

Bali

Bali is ringed by good snorkelling sites that are easily reached.

Pulau Menjangan (p307) A steady current takes you right along the edge of the beautiful 30m coral wall.

Tulamben (p292) A popular sunken WWII freighter is easily reached right offshore.

Amed (p289) This coastline along east Bali has plenty of colourful coral and fish directly off the beach.

Java

Java has some healthy coral reefs that make for good low-key snorkelling spots.

Karimunjawa Islands (p165) This archipelago has a number of islands fringed by colourful corals.

Baluran National Park (p205) An offshore site featuring a drop with plenty of fish and corals.

Kalimantan

Derawan Archipelago (p657) Features some of the country's best snorkelling; head to its outer islands, as reefs around Pulau Derawan are damaged.

Maluku

There are plenty of accessible coral gardens on the many islands here.

Banda Islands (p447) Can be snorkelled, though you'll need to free dive a bit to get the best views of the drop-offs. You might see turtles and sharks off Pulau Hatta.

Lease Islands (p443) These rarely visited islands, with wonderful clear waters, offer great snorkelling, including off uninhabited Pulau Molana.

Nusa Tenggara

Nusa Tenggara has the best selection of snorkelling sites in the country. You can

Sulawesi

New dive areas are opening up, but favourites such as Bunaken are popular for a reason.

Pulau Bunaken (p713) Part of a large marine park, this island, which is easily reached from Manado, offers all sorts of diving.

Pantai Bira (p673) Varied marine life, including groupers, rays and occasional whale sharks, and colourful corals.

Lembeh Strait (p719) Muck diving at its finest; a weird and wonderful world of bizarre critters awaits discovery between Pulau Lembeh and Bintung.

Sumatra

Despite the diving potential on Mentawai and Banyak Islands, both remain the domain of surfers.

Pulau Weh (p547) One of Indonesia's best diving locations is this small coral-ringed island with 20 dive sites featuring an incredible wealth of marine life. It continues to grow in popularity, while retaining its laid-back charm

RESPONSIBLE DIVING

The popularity of diving puts immense pressure on many sites. Consider the following tips when diving and help preserve the ecology and beauty of Indonesia's reefs.

➡ Avoid touching living marine organisms with your body or dragging equipment across the reef. Never stand on coral.

➡ Be conscious of your fins. The surge from heavy fin strokes near the reef can damage delicate organisms. When treading water in shallow reef areas, take care not to kick up clouds of sand. Settling sand can easily smother delicate reef organisms.

➡ Practise and maintain proper buoyancy control. Major damage can be done by divers descending too fast and colliding with the reef.

➡ Don't collect coral or shells.

➡ Ensure that you collect all your rubbish and any litter you find as well. Plastics in particular are a serious threat to marine life.

➡ Don't ever feed the fish.

➡ The best dive operators will require that you adhere to these points.

snorkel all the Moyo and Alor dive sites and share a boat with the divers.

Gili Gede (p321) Head to the southeast coast to visit Gili Layar and Gili Rengit to swim among masses of tropical fish and thriving, colourful coral.

Komodo (p364) The best snorkel sites are around Pulau Kanawa, Pulau Sebayur and off Pantai Merah.

Papua

Divers aren't the only ones having fun here.

Raja Ampat Islands (p473) Many superb snorkelling sites are reachable just by walking off a beach or taking a boat. Dive resorts and homestays all offer snorkelling.

Nabire (p495) Snorkel with whale sharks.

Padaido Islands (p495) Great snorkelling with lots of colourful coral, caves, long walls and plenty of big fish and turtles.

Sulawesi

Sulawesi has a large number of great snorkelling sites.

Pulau Bunaken (p713) Great for snorkelling for many of the same reasons that it's a good dive location.

Togean Islands (p702) Given the challenges in reaching these idyllic little gems, it's nice that there's good underwater action once you get here.

Sumatra

The best snorkelling is around the little islands offshore. Rudimentary day trips are available, but travellers are advised to bring their own snorkelling gear.

Banyak Islands (p553) The stunning gin-clear waters of the Banyaks have to be seen to be believed, with a heap of tropical fish, turtles and deep-sea creatures.

Pulau Weh (p547) This island off the northern tip of Sumatra has easy offshore access to an aquarium-like wonderworld of colourful fish and marine life.

Surfing

Indonesia lures surfers from around the globe, many with visions of empty palm-lined beaches, bamboo bungalows and perfect barrels peeling around a coral reef. The good news is that mostly the dreams come true, but just like anywhere else, Indonesia is subject to flat spells, onshore winds and crowding (particularly on Bali). A little research and preparation go a long way.

There are usually boards for rent (but don't expect great quality), and surf schools are located at the major surf sites.

Bali

Despite the crowds, Bali remains a surfer's paradise, with some of the best tubes in the world. Breaks are found right around the south side of the island, and there's a large infrastructure of schools and board-rental places.

Kuta Beach (p217) Where surfing came to Asia. Generally a good place for beginners (unless it's pumping), with long, steady breaks.

Bukit Peninsula (p239) From Bali's largest sets at Ulu Watu and Padang Padang to world-class breaks at Balangan and Bingin, this is one of Indo's best surf spots.

Keramas (p282) Right-hand break that's fast, powerful and hollow. The world pro comp is held here, and it also has the novelty of night surfing under lights.

Medewi (p313) Famous point break with a ride right into a river mouth.

Nusa Lembongan (p253) The island is a mellow scene for surfers who come for the right-hand breaks known as Shipwrecks and Lacerations, and the less challenging leftie at Playgrounds.

Java

Java is still being explored by surfers, who find new breaks every year. Its popular breaks at G-Land, Cimaja, Batu Karas and Pacitan have surf schools and shops.

G-Land (p201) One of the world's best left-handers, G-Land is a holy grail for expert surfers. With consistently perfect waves and long rides, it's worthy of all the hype.

SURF INFO ONLINE

Bali Waves (www.baliwaves.com) Surf reports, including webcams of top spots.

Magic Seaweed (www.magicsea weed.com) Popular and respected for reliable surf reports and forecasts.

SurfAid International (www.surf aidinternational.org) Surfer-run aid organisation.

Gone to Get Salty (www.gonetoget salty.com) Useful guide offering a heap of tips and covering the practicalities of planning where to go and securing accommodation.

Surf Travel Company (www.surf travel.com.au) Australian outfit with camps, yacht charters, destination information, surfer reviews and more.

Cimaja (p95) A popular surf spot at Pelabuhan Ratu. The fabled Ombak Tujuh break is off a pebble beach.

Pulau Panaitan (p89) Some of Indonesia's most photogenic but dangerous waves; experts only.

Batu Karas (p112) One of several good breaks around Pangandaran, a popular surf spot off the southern coast of Central Java.

Pacitan (p188) This town on a beautiful little horseshoe bay rewards surfers who make the trek.

Nusa Tenggara

You could spend years exploring – and discovering! – places to surf in Nusa Tenggara.

Lombok (p316) South Lombok is a surf utopia. There are numerous breaks from Ekas to Gerupuk to Kuta, all of which can be accessed from Kuta. Tanjung Desert (Desert Point) is more of a surf camp, and it's also legendary.

Sumbawa (p355) Jelenga (Scar Reef) and Maluk are among the greatest and most overlooked surf breaks in the world. Surfers regularly descend here to surf Supersuck, which offers one of the best barrels anywhere.

Rote (p403) T-Land is the legendary left, but there are hollow waves in Bo'a Bay as well.

Sumba (p405) West Sumba has the best breaks, but it's not set up for tourists. You'll have to hire a car, drive into remote villages and paddle out on sight and feel.

Sumatra

Arguably Indonesia's hottest surf region; newish areas such as Telo are attracting surfers in the know and further areas are opening up all the time.

Mentawai Islands (p565) Surfing is huge business in the Mentawais, where you'll find some of the world's best waves. Everything's here, from simple losmen (budget accommodation) and luxury resorts to seven- to 10-day all-inclusive trips on surf boats. Primo breaks include Macaronis, Lance's Right and Pitstops.

Pulau Nias (p536) Another legendary spot for surfers in search of the perfect wave, this low-key spot is most famous for its right-hander Keyhole in Sorake Beach. Its west coast is also packed full of sublime breaks, as is the Telo Islands (p540) just south – a region that's really starting to take off.

Krui (p601) Word's certainly out about the pumping waves found off the coast in South Sumatra,

Surfing at Padang Padang (p241), Bukit Peninsula

but it's still yet to attract mobs; not unlike other Sumatra secret spots Banyaks (p553) and Simeulue (p552).

Whitewater Rafting

Some of the rivers tumbling down Indonesia's volcanic slopes draw adventure operators and thrill-seeking tourists.

Bali

Two reputable operators are Mason Adventures (p214) and Bio (p214); both offer rafting, river boarding and tubing.

Sungai Ayung Features 33 Class II to III rapids, which are fun and suitable for all levels.

Sungai Telagawaja Rafting trips take on this scenic and wild stretch of river near Muncan in east Bali.

Java

Java probably has Indonesia's best whitewater rafting.

Sungai Citarak (p94) Churns out Class II to IV rapids.

Green Valley (p112) Located near Pangandaran; you can skip a raft altogether and go 'body rafting' in a life jacket.

Kalimantan

Loksado (p639) The bamboo rafting here is more of a relaxing paddle than an adrenaline rush.

Sulawesi

Sungai Sa'dan (p685) Lures adventure junkies to tackle its 20-odd rapids (some up to Class IV).

Tana Toraja (p679) Rafting agents in Rantepao organise trips down its canyon.

Minahasa (p718) Combine rafting rapids with wildlife-watching.

Sumatra

Bukit Lawang (p521) Finish off your sweaty jungle trek with an enjoyable wet 'n' wild river journey down fun rapids.

Hiking

Setting off on foot in Indonesia offers limitless opportunities for adventure and exploration, from volcanic peaks with celestial dawn views to remote jungle treks; you can leave civilisation behind.

Bali

Bali is very walkable. No matter where you're staying, ask for recommendations, and set off for discoveries and adventures.

Gunung Agung (p280) Sunrises and isolated temples on Bali's most sacred mountain; however in 2018 it was off limits due to its series of eruptions.

Gunung Batur (p301) This volcano's otherworldly scenery almost makes you forget about the hassles.

Munduk (p295) Lush, spice-scented waterfall-riven landscape high in the hills.

Sidemen Road (p280) Rice terraces and lush hills; comfy lodgings for walkers.

Taman Nasional Bali Barat (p309) A range of hikes through alternating habitats of jungle, savannah and mangroves.

Ubud (p259) Beautiful walks between one hour and one day through rice, river-valley jungles and ancient monuments.

Java

Java has some great walks. Guides are always available at national park offices or via guesthouses. Tents and sleeping bags can be rented at Semeru. Organised hikes can be set up in Kalibaru (to Merapi) and Malang (to Semeru; p179).

Gunung Bromo (p192) One of three volcanic cones (one active) that emerge from an eerie caldera. A must-see sight; however, expect mass crowds due to its popularity.

Gede Pangrango National Park (p96) Waterfalls and the nearly 3000m-high Gunung Gede, an active volcano, are the highlights.

Gunung Lawu (p153) On the border of Central and East Java, this 3265m mountain is dotted with ancient Hindu temples.

Gunung Semeru (p195) It's a tough three-day trek to the top of Java's tallest peak (3676m), which is nearly always volcanically active.

Ijen Plateau (p196) Surrounded by scenic coffee plantations and misty jungle, this blockbuster volcano is most famous for the eerie 'blue fire' that illuminates its sulphurous crater lake.

Kalimantan

The jungles of Borneo remain seemingly impenetrable in vast areas, and that's all the more reason for intrepid trekkers to set out on a trail.

Cross-Borneo Trek (p613) This uber-choice of Kalimantan treks is best undertaken by contacting either De'Gigant Tours (p645) in Samarinda or Kompakh (p621) in Putussibau and going from there. No one should try to organise it by themselves.

Loksado (p639) A real-life adventure park with dozens of rope and bamboo bridges across streams amid thick jungle.

Gunung Besar (p639) The highest peak in the Meratus mountain range, Besar (1901m) is accessed via a three- to four-day hike from Loksado.

Maluku

Gunung Api (p454) Head up this perfectly formed volcanic cone (656m) on a quite arduous three-hour self-guided trek.

Gunung Api Gamalama (p429) Tick off this active volcano from your list by climbing to its crater peak (1721m) for stunning views on an eight-hour return trek.

Nusa Tenggara

Lombok and Flores are both easily accessible and home to some top hikes.

Gunung Tambora (p361) Make it to the top of this 2772m volcano, famed for its 1815 eruption, still the most powerful eruption on record.

Gunung Rinjani (p327) Indonesia's second-tallest volcano is on Lombok. The standard trek is three to four days; it begins near a sacred waterfall, skirts lakes and hot springs, and culminates with sunrise on one of two peaks.

Flores (p368) Enjoy hikes to remote villages only accessible by trail, the most interesting of which is the trek to Wae Rebo in the Manggarai region. You can also climb Gunung Inerie in the Bajawa area, or hike to the remote Pauleni Village near Belaragi.

Papua

Trekking is the reason for many people to visit Papua.

Baliem Valley (p497) World-class trekking: great hiking in wonderful mountain scenery among friendly, traditional people. It's possible to sleep most nights in villages; some simpler routes don't require guides or porters.

Top: Traveller at the base of Gunung Bromo (p192)

Bottom: Camping with views of Gunung Rinjani (p327)

MUHD FUAD ABD RAHIM/SHUTTERSTOCK ©

Korowai region (p509) Tough jungle trekking in an area populated by ex-headhunters who live in tree houses. You'll need a well-organised, expensive guided trip.

Carstensz Pyramid & Gunung Trikora (p496) You'll need mountaineering skills to climb the two highest mountains in Oceania. Both involve high altitudes and camping in a cold climate. Organise through specialist agencies.

Yali Country (p506) Make your way around Kosarek for fascinating encounters with locals dressed in traditional rattan hoops, penis gourds, grass skirts, and accessories made of boar tusks, cassowary feathers and orchid fibres.

Sulawesi

The region around Tana Toraja could occupy months of trekking.

Tana Toraja (p679) Beautiful valleys and fascinating Torajan architecture and culture are highlights. Good guides are readily available in Rantepao.

Mamasa (p693) West of Tana Toraja, this 59km trek linking Tana Toraja and Mamasa is a three-day treat.

Tomohon (p717) Hike up to Gunung Lokon's crater lake.

Sumatra

Unsurprisingly, this vast island offers a huge range of overland adventures.

Mentawai Islands (p565) Famous for its hunter-gatherer tribes, the Mentawais still have dense, untouched jungle that you can penetrate by longboat on river journeys. Local guides will take you to their isolated abodes.

Berastagi (p525) A cool retreat from steamy Medan. Easy treks include volcanoes.

Bukittinggi (p572) You can meander through tiny villages, climb volcanoes or head off into the jungle for the three-day trek to Danau Maninjau.

Kerinci Seblat National Park (p582) Dense rainforest, high mountains and rare animals such as Sumatran tigers and slow lorises are the highlights of treks through Sumatra's largest park.

Gunung Leuser National Park (p556) Trek in search of orang-utans in Bukit Lawang and Ketambe.

Around Bengkulu (p585) Truly get off the beaten track by trekking to waterfalls, volcanoes and hot springs and by overnighting in local villages.

Watching Wildlife

Indonesia's wildlife is as diverse as everything else about the archipelago. Great apes, tigers, elephants and monkeys – lots of monkeys – plus one mean lizard are just some of the more notable critters you may encounter.

SAFETY GUIDELINES FOR HIKING

Before embarking on a hiking trip, consider the following points to ensure a safe and enjoyable experience.

➡ Pay any fees and obtain any permits required by local authorities.

➡ Be sure you are healthy and feel comfortable walking for a sustained period.

➡ Obtain reliable information about physical and environmental conditions along your intended route.

➡ Be aware of local laws, regulations and etiquette about wildlife and the environment.

➡ Walk only in regions and on trails/tracks within your realm of experience.

➡ Be aware that weather conditions and terrain vary significantly from one region, or even from one trail or track, to another. Seasonal changes and sudden weather shifts can significantly alter any trail or track. These differences influence what to wear and what equipment to carry.

➡ Ask before you set out about the environmental characteristics that can affect your walk, and how experienced local walkers deal with these considerations.

➡ Strongly consider hiring a guide. Indonesia has many good guides who have invaluable local knowledge.

Orang-utan, Tanjung Puting National Park (p625)

Bali

Other than prevalent macaque monkeys and an occasional monitor lizard, Bali has limited wildlife encounters (with the exception of a night out in Kuta).

Taman Nasional Bali Barat (p309) Excellent for birdwatching, and also has multiple species of deer, monkey, wild pig and buffalo.

Java

The national parks are home to a huge range of animals and birds – and usually guides ready to lead you.

Ujung Kulon National Park (p88) Extremely rare one-horned Javan rhinoceros and leopard live among the Unesco-listed rainforest.

Alas Purwo National Park (p200) You may spot various deer, peacocks and even a leopard or two.

Baluran National Park (p205) Head out on a 4WD safari to spot wild oxen and other large animals amid natural grasslands.

Meru Betiri National Park (p199) Home to a vast range of wildlife, including leopards and the intriguing giant squirrel.

Kalimantan

Kalimantan is mostly about jungle river trips to experience wildlife such as orang-utans.

Tanjung Puting National Park (p625) The orang-utan spotting is superb and you'll also see all manner of birds and reptiles.

Gunung Palung National Park (p624) Search for wild orang-utans, gibbons, sun bears and lots of birds at this park near Sukudana.

Maluku

Maluku remains a relatively untapped birder paradise. It's worth the effort and cash to access the national parks of Seram and Halmahera.

Aketajawe-Lolobata National Park (p435) You can stalk Wallace's standard-winged bird of paradise in this eastern Halmahera reserve.

Nusa Tenggara

This vast collection of islands has one real star.

Komodo National Park (p366) First and foremost is the area's namesake endemic species: the

A GUIDE TO GUIDES

A guide can make or break your trip. Some travellers report disappointing trips with cheap guides, but high fees alone don't guarantee satisfaction. Here are some tips for choosing a guide.

➡ Meet the guide before finalising any trip. (If you're dealing with a tour agency, insist on meeting the guide you'll travel with, not the head of the agency.)

➡ Quiz the guide about the itinerary. That can begin by email, WhatsApp or telephone, and will also provide a sample of their ability in your language. (Be aware that guides using email may have a helper handling correspondence.) Listen to their ideas, and see if they listen to yours.

➡ Guides usually offer package prices and should be able to roughly itemise trip costs. Be clear on what's included in the package, particularly regarding transport and food.

➡ Some guides offer the option of charging you only their fee (250,000Rp to 800,000Rp per day) while you pay other expenses directly.

➡ Find out what you'll need from the guide, such as water.

➡ For ambitious treks in places such as Papua, you may need to hire porters to help carry your food and water, in addition to a guide.

Komodo dragon. But there are also slow-screeching flocks of flying foxes roosting on mangrove islands in the park.

Seventeen Islands Marine Park (p381) Near Riung you can find barking deer, wild water buffalo and rich bird life.

Papua

Papua is fantastic birdwatching territory, including for birds of paradise. It's more difficult to find other Papuan wildlife, including exotic marsupials such as tree kangaroos, cuscus and sugar gliders, though some expert local guides can help.

Raja Ampat Islands (p473) Birds of paradise and many other species cause birdwatchers to flock here.

Pegunungan Arfak (p484) Thickly forested mountains hide all manner of birds.

Wasur National Park (p507) It's fairly easy to spot wallabies and deer here.

Danau Habbema (p504) Cuscus, birds of paradise and sometimes tree kangaroos are found near this isolated lake.

Sulawesi

Tarsiers are all the rage among Sulawesi wildlife spotters.

Tangkoko-Batuangas Dua Saudara Nature Reserve (p720) Your best bet to see tarsiers is here with a guide.

Lore Lindu National Park (p697) Tarsiers, birds of paradise, monkeys and more are found in this protected area.

Sumatra

Large mammals such as elephants, orangutans and Sumatran tigers have homes amid the still untrodden tracts of wilderness here.

Gunung Leuser National Park (p556) Famous for orang-utans but also home to monkeys, Sumatran elephants, tigers and rhino.

Kerinci Seblat National Park (p582) Birds abound, and in the seldom-visited Ladeh Panjang region there's even a form of bear, as well as tigers.

Way Kambas National Park (p604) Elephant-watching and birdwatching trips, as well as habitat for the rare Sumatran rhino and tiger.

Rock Climbing & Canyoning

While it's still an emerging scene, there are reputable operators offering climbing, canyoning, abseiling and spelunking. Gear is provided, but serious climbers will want to bring their own.

Bali

Ubud Based in Mas, outside Ubud, Adventure & Spirit (p214) offers very popular canyoning day trips out to central Bali that combine abseiling, swimming, jumping, climbing and ziplining through scenic gorges and waterfalls.

Nusa Lembongan

Flores (p368) Head to the Cunca Wulang Cascades around Labuan Bajo for 7m jumps off waterfalls into swimming holes.

Sumatra

One of Indonesia's more well-known spots for rock-climbers.

Harau Valley (p579) The area is popular for rock climbing and hikes. Guides can be arranged here.

Sulawesi

Minahasa (p718) Outside Tomohon, this scenic area is gaining recognition for its adventure activities, including abseiling, canyoning and 60m drops from Tekaan Telu waterfall.

Water Sports

Surfing isn't the only way to catch a wave in Indo these days; kitesurfing is fast catching on as a popular water sport. For something more relaxing, jump in a sea kayak for a paddle around.

Java

Banyuwangi (p203) For those with their own gear, Pulau Tabuhan gets some good winds for kitesurfing. It hosts the Tabuhan Island Pro in August.

Bali

Sanur (p246) The best spot in Bali for kitesurfing. Rip Curl has set up shop, and offers kitesurfing lessons and equipment hire, as well as windsurfing and stand-up paddleboarding.

Nusa Tenggara

Pantai Lakey & Hu'u (p361) One of the world's top 10 kitesurfing destinations; the season runs from July to November.

Kuta (p331) Several operators offer lessons and rental.

Komodo National Park (p366) Glide through the park on a guided kayak tour from Labuan Bajo.

Sumatra

Aceh (p541) From May to September, Lampu'uk on Aceh's west coast is popular for kitesurfing. Lhoknga is the best place to head.

Banyak Islands (p553) Jump in a sea kayak to explore dozens of tropical islands.

Papua

Raja Ampat Islands (p473) Rent a kayak with or without a guide to explore pristine waters.

Plan Your Trip
Family Travel

Want a great way to improve your Indonesia trip? Bring the kids!
Parents say that they see more because children are so quickly
whisked into everyday life across this child-loving archipelago.
Natural barriers break right down as locals open their arms – and
lives – to children.

Best Regions for Kids

Bali

The island at the heart of Indonesian tourism is
ideal for kids. There are beautiful beaches, many
with gentle surf, plus great spots for first-time
snorkellers and surfers. Cool temples of Indiana
Jones ilk dot the island, and there are dozens of
child-friendly hotels and resorts.

Nusa Tenggara

Lombok is a slightly more adventurous version of
Bali but is still easy for families and has gorgeous
beaches in the south. Of the Gilis (where no one
ever got lost), Air combines a relaxed vibe with
activities, hotels and restaurants that are great
for kids. Flores offers amazing wildlife at Komodo
National Park.

Java

Batu Karas is a wonderful and safe beach. The
easy hiking around Gunung Bromo is a good
choice for families. More remote, the beaches and
offshore islands in Karimunjawa delight families,
while kids lap up the mysteries of Borobudur and
Prambanan.

Indonesia for Kids

Travel outside cities requires patience,
hardiness and experience – for both parents and kids. Most Indonesians adore
children, especially ones touring their
country; however, children may find the
constant attention overwhelming. In the
experience of some visitors, travelling
in Indonesia is, in fact, easier with kids
because locals are more helpful than they
would be if you were travelling alone as
an adult.

You will need to learn your child's age
and sex in Bahasa Indonesia – *bulau*
(month), *tahun* (year), *laki-laki* (boy) and
perempuan (girl). In conversations with
locals, you should make polite enquiries
about the other person's children, present
or absent.

Children's Highlights
Outdoor Activities

Bali (p221) Good for surfing and snorkelling and
has classes geared to kids.

Pulau Bunaken, Sulawesi (p713) Offers fabulous
snorkelling where you can see dolphins, flying fish
and more in the wilds of Sulawesi.

Bukit Lawang, Sumatra (p521) River tubing and
gentle jungle hikes with a good chance of spotting
orang-utans.

Animal-Spotting

Ubud Monkey Forest, Ubud (p262) The primates here never cease to delight.

Camp Leakey, Kalimantan (p626) Board a river trip to the province's best venue for families and the place to spot orang-utans.

Komodo National Park, Nusa Tenggara (p366) It's easy to see the fearsome dragons safely at this popular park.

Cultural Exchange

Temkessi, West Timor (p402) Children can make friends with their peers in the ancient villages of this area.

Putussibau, Kalimantan (p621) The communal living in the longhouses of the Kapuas Hulu region helps kids quickly make friends with their Dayak counterparts.

Yogyakarta, Java (p122) A classic destination for Indonesian school kids, and yours will enjoy its myriad cultural attractions as well.

Planning

Kid-friendly facilities are generally limited to Bali, which caters well to holidaying families. Elsewhere you will find Indonesia very hit or miss in terms of specifically catering to children, even as it warmly welcomes them.

What you bring from home and what you source in Indonesia largely depends on where you're going and what you'll need. As always, you can get most things you might need on Bali (or to a certain extent Lombok, Jakarta and Yogyakarta), but there is the trade-off of tracking down what you need and simply adding it to your luggage.

For very young children, the dilemma is to bring either a backpack carrier or a pram/stroller. If you can, bring both. Prams are tough going on uneven or non-existent footpaths, but are worthwhile in south Bali and other developed areas.

➡ Children's seats for cars are rare and, where they exist, sometimes low quality.

➡ Sunscreen and mosquito repellent are difficult to find on Bali and nonexistent elsewhere.

➡ Baby wipes, disposable nappies (diapers) and baby formula are all readily available in cities and big towns but seldom elsewhere.

➡ Bali has a ready supply of babysitters (and lots of nightlife to divert parents). Elsewhere you will be providing the childcare.

➡ Nappy-changing facilities usually consist of the nearest discreet, flat surface.

➡ Breastfeeding in public is acceptable in areas such as Bali, Papua and Sumatra away from

STAYING SAFE

The sorts of facilities, safeguards and services that Western parents regard as basic may not be present. Places with great views probably have nothing to stop your kids falling over the edge, that gorgeous beach may have perilous surf, swimming pools are never fenced etc. Health standards are low in Indonesia compared to the developed world, but with proper precautions, children can travel safely.

➡ A major danger to kids – and adults for that matter – is traffic, and bad pavement and footpaths in busy areas.

➡ Check conditions carefully for any activity. Just because that rafting company sells tickets to families doesn't mean they accommodate the safety needs of children.

➡ Consider the health situation carefully, especially with regards to malaria and dengue fever.

➡ Rabies is a major problem, especially on Bali. Keep children away from stray animals, including cats, dogs and monkeys.

➡ As with adults, contaminated food and water present the most risks; children are more at risk from sunstroke and dehydration.

➡ Pharmaceutical supplies can usually be purchased in larger cities.

Pura Luhur Ulu Watu (p242)

Aceh, but virtually unseen in Maluku, Sulawesi and Kalimantan. In parts of West Java and the conservative islands of Nusa Tenggara it's inappropriate. Take your cue from local mothers.

➡ Hotels and guesthouses often have triple and family rooms, plus extra beds can be supplied on demand. Baby beds and highchairs, however, are uncommon.

➡ Hotel staff are usually very willing to help and improvise, so always ask if you need something for your children.

➡ Larger resorts often have special programs and facilities for kids that include lots of activities during the day and evening.

➡ Bring binoculars so young explorers can zoom in on wildlife, rice terraces, temples, world-class surfers and so on.

➡ With widespread 4G data and wi-fi, a smartphone or tablet is handy so children can tell those at home about everything they're missing and have an easy escape from the trip itself.

Regions at a Glance

Indonesia's 17,000-plus islands are dominated by a few large ones. Sumatra, Java and Sulawesi are diverse places that have swaths of untouched land. Kalimantan and Papua are part of even larger islands and offer plenty of opportunity for serious adventure and exploration. Java remains the heart of the country historically, culturally and economically. Nusa Tenggara and Maluku comprise hundreds of islands, from ever-more-popular Lombok to the relative isolation of the Banda Islands. Although small in size, Bali figures large for visitors, drawing half of Indonesia's tourists. As always, your biggest consideration will be managing the time on your visa.

Java

Culture
Volcanoes
Temples

Javanese culture fuses animist, Buddhist and Hindu influences with both mystic traditions and orthodox Islamic practices. Monuments, mosques and temples that reflect this spiritual complexity exist alongside a spectacular tropical landscape spiked with smoking volcanoes.

p57

Bali

Culture
Nightlife
Surfing

The rich culture of Bali is matched by its myriad attractions for visitors: excellent dining and nightlife, hundreds of good places to stay, famous beaches, epic surfing, alluring shopping and a gracious welcome.

p207

Nusa Tenggara

Surfing
Diving
Culture

Whether you're here for waves, or to dive deep underwater or into ancient cultures, Nusa Tenggara offers gifts unmatched. From Lombok to Timor via Flores you will be tempted, blessed and satiated, yet left hungry for more.

p315

Maluku

Diving
Culture
Beaches

Empires vied to control the precious spices of these diverse, beautiful islands. Push past their present-day isolation to discover brilliant coral gardens, jungle-swaddled volcanoes, crumbling colonial mansions and a history as rich as it is troubled.

p419

Papua

Diving & Snorkelling
Hiking
Tribal Culture

Remote Papua is an adventurer's fantasy. From high mountain valleys and snaking jungle rivers to translucent coastal waters teeming with life, it offers superb trekking and world-class diving among proud tradition-steeped indigenous peoples.

p465

Sumatra

Wildlife
Hiking
Surfing

Sumatra is one big, steamy, jungle-covered adventure where you can go from surfing some of the world's best waves and snorkelling amid pristine reefs to trekking through dense rainforest in search of orangutans or ascending active volcanoes.

p511

Kalimantan

River Journeys
Diving
Wildlife

Bisected by countless rivers, Borneo's legendary rainforest attracts wildlife enthusiasts and hardened trekkers. Dayak longhouses preserve the rich communal culture of a forgotten era, while the underwater paradise of the Derawan Archipelago draws in-the-know divers.

p609

Sulawesi

Culture
Diving
Hiking

Wind your way through this crazy-shaped island of elaborate funeral ceremonies. Take trails through terraced rice fields and tarsier-filled jungles to coasts of abundant corals, thriving underwater fauna and cultures that revolve around the sea.

p663

On the Road

AT A GLANCE

POPULATION
140 million

**MOST ACTIVE
VOLCANO**
Gunung Merapi
(p141)

**BEST PLACE TO
BUY BATIK**
Solo (p146)

BEST CHEAP EATS
Historia (p75)

BEST BEACH
Watu Karang (p189)

WHEN TO GO
May
Spectacular Waisak
processions to mark
the birth of the Bud-
dha in Borobudur.

Jun
Perhaps the perfect
month for travel, with
clear skies and few
crowds.

Aug
Independence Day
brings a riot of colour
as towns and villages
are bedecked with
flags.

Gunung Bromo (p192)
SSPHOTOGRAPHY/GETTY IMAGES ©

Java

The heart of the nation, Java is a complex island of great antiquity: this, after all, is where ancient Java Man stood upright and walked abroad. As such, Java – the most populated island on earth – is defined primarily by people. Human ingenuity has left the island sprinkled with ancient treasures, such as the temples of Borobudur and Prambanan. It has also shaped a culture that resonates in modern life, as expressed through the artistic traditions of Yogyakarta and Solo, and contributes to the modern dynamism of the Indonesian capital, Jakarta. Java's megacities may be crowded and gridlocked but they have a restless energy that is magnetic.

People have shaped the natural landscape, too, giving it an urban texture that runs in slithers through the pea-green paddy fields. Add in nature's splendours – smoking volcanoes, rainforest and white-sand beaches – and Java becomes irresistible.

History

Java has a history of epic proportions and a record of human habitation that extends back 1.7 million years to when 'Java Man' roamed the riverbanks. Waves of migrants followed, moving down through Southeast Asia.

Early Javanese Kingdoms

Blessed with exceptional fertility from its mineral-rich volcanic soil, Java has long played host to intensive *sawah* (wet-rice) agriculture.

With agrarian stability small principalities emerged, including the Hindu Mataram dynasty, in the 8th century, with worship centred on the god Shiva. Hinduism co-existed with Buddhism for centuries, and the massive Hindu Prambanan complex was constructed within a century of Borobudur, the world's biggest Buddhist monument.

Mataram eventually fell, perhaps at the hands of the Sumatra-based Sriwijaya kingdom. The Javanese revival began in AD 1019 under King Airlangga, a semi-legendary figure who formed the first royal link with Bali.

Early in the 13th century, the legendary Ken Angrok briefly succeeded in uniting much of Central and East Java, and Javanese culture flourished. With the emergence of the much-celebrated Majapahit kingdom, ruling from Trowulan, came the first Javanese trading nation. This kingdom traded with China and most of Southeast Asia, and grew to claim sovereignty over the entire Indonesian archipelago.

Islamic Kingdoms

Islamic influence grew in Java in the 15th and 16th centuries, and Muslim military incursions into East Java forced many Hindu-Buddhists eastwards to Bali. By the 17th century, the Muslim kingdoms of Mataram and Banten were the only two powers in Java left to face the arrival of the Dutch.

Dutch Period

As the Dutch set up camp in Batavia (Jakarta), Banten remained a powerful force, but civil war within the royal house led to its eventual collapse.

The Mataram Sultanate also became plagued by infighting, and following three Javanese Wars of Succession, the last in 1746, the Dutch split the kingdom, creating the royal houses of Solo and Yogyakarta.

Resistance to Dutch influence continued, erupting in the anti-Dutch Java War (1825–30), but the colonists prevailed and subsequently Javanese courts became little more than ritual establishments, overseen by a Dutch *residen* (governor).

Java Today

Java still rules the roost when it comes to political and economic life in Indonesia. It has the bulk of the country's industry, is easily its most developed island, and has over the years received the lion's share of foreign investment.

The economic crisis of the late '90s hit hard, when huge numbers of urban workers lost their jobs and rioters targeted Chinese communities. But Java bounced back relatively quickly, and enjoyed a period of comparative stability and growing prosperity in the early 21st century. Glittering shopping malls and a boom in the tech business are the most obvious signs of Java's steady (if unspectacular) modernisation.

Bali apart, Java is the most outward-looking island in Indonesia, and its literate, educated population is the most closely connected to the rest of the world. Extraneous influences matter here, and Java is the most Westernised island in the country, as well as the corner of the nation most influenced by radical pan-Islamic ideology. While most Javanese are moderate Muslims, there's an increasingly vocal conservative population (as well as tiny numbers of fanatics prepared to cause death and destruction in the name of jihad). The Bali bombers all came from Java, and Java-based terrorists targeted foreign investments in Jakarta in 2003 and 2004, as well as several international hotels in 2009. The Surabaya church bombings in 2018 were a tragic reminder that, after a relatively peaceful decade, Isis-inspired terrorism has not been wholly eradicated.

Despite this resurgence in terrorism, and despite recent earthquakes and volcanic eruptions and the slowdown in economic growth since 2012, the Javanese look to the future with optimism. Thanks to an upsurge in foreign travel, people are increasingly prosperous and cosmopolitan. But as the island develops apace, pressing environmental issues (including pollution and the floods that threaten Jakarta most years) present an increasing threat. Infrastructure woes – inadequate highways and waste management, and a lack of investment in train and metro networks – also hamper growth. This makes the slide in the rupiah and economic struggles more predictable than surprising.

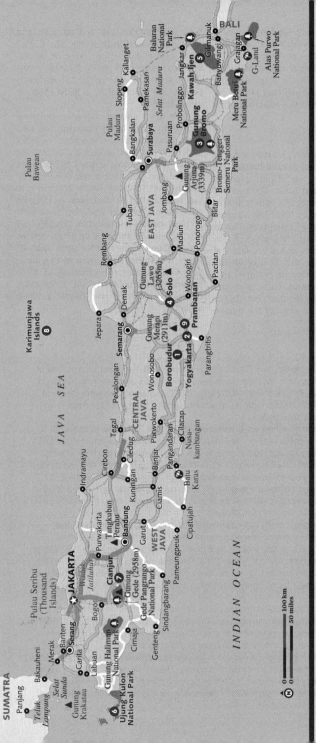

Java Highlights

1 Borobudur Temple (p118)
Enjoying this ancient Buddhist temple at sunrise.

2 Yogyakarta (p122)
Exploring Java's golden age in its dynamic cultural capital.

3 Gunung Bromo (p192)
Plodding through a moonscape of ash and spectacular vistas.

4 Solo (p146) Touring the cottage industries in this city of batik.

5 Kawah Ijen (p196) Hiking to the crater lake with strong-armed sulphur miners.

6 Ujung Kulon (p88)
Exploring this magnificent national park.

7 Cianjur (p97) Meeting the locals via a community tourism project.

8 Karimunjawa Islands (p165) Island-hopping in a patchwork of turquoise seas.

9 Prambanan (p144)
Cycling through rural roads from Yogyakarta to the exquisite Hindu temples of this ancient temple complex.

Corruption has long hindered fairness and growth in Java, with poverty and unemployment persisting and a growing disparity between the megacity elite and their rural counterparts. This is a problem the nation's political leaders will need to resolve if Java is to live up to the optimism of its people.

Culture

Javanese culture is a complex interaction of traditions arising from ancient animist beliefs and overlaid by the religious precepts of both Hinduism and Islam. The result of these diverse influences is a culture that is unified by monotheistic belief but nuanced with a strong sense of mysticism. This is exemplified in modern life through a tangible respect for ghosts and benevolent and malevolent spirits, as well as a sensitivity to magic. Some believe, for example, that magic power is concentrated in amulets and heirlooms (especially the Javanese dagger known as the kris), in parts of the human body, such as the nails and the hair, and in sacred musical instruments. The *dukun* (faith healer and herbal doctor or mystic) is still consulted by many Javanese when illness strikes, and *jamu* (herbal medicine) potions are widely taken to boost libido or cure ailments.

As in many ancient cultures, refinement and courtesy are highly regarded, and loud displays of emotion, coarseness, vulgarity and flamboyant behaviour are considered *kasar* (bad manners; coarse). Being *halus* (refined), on the other hand, is integral to Hindu court tradition, which still exists in the heartland of Central Java. In contrast with Islam, the court tradition has a hierarchical world view, based on privilege and often guided by the gods or nature spirits. It contributes to the notable Javan indirectness – a trait that stems from an unwillingness to make others feel uncomfortable. It is considered impolite to point out mistakes and sensitivities, or to directly criticise authority.

JAVA MAN

Charles Darwin's *On the Origin of Species* (1859) spawned a new generation of naturalists in the 19th century, and his theories sparked acrimonious debate across the world. Ernst Haeckel's *The History of Natural Creation* (1874) expounded Darwin's theory of evolution and surmised that primitive humans had evolved from a common ape-man ancestor, the famous 'missing link'.

One student of the new theories, Dutch physician Eugene Dubois, went to Java in 1889 after hearing of the uncovering of a skull at Wajak, near Tulung Agung in East Java. Dubois worked at the dig, uncovering other fossils closely related to modern humans. In 1891, at Trinil in East Java's Ngawi district, Dubois unearthed an older skullcap, along with a femur and three teeth he later classified as originating from *Pithecanthropus erectus*, a low-browed, prominent-jawed early human ancestor, dating from the Middle Pleistocene epoch. His published findings of 'Java Man' caused such a storm in Europe that Dubois buried his discovery for 30 years.

Since Dubois' findings, many older examples of *Homo erectus* (the name subsequently given to *Pithecanthropus erectus*) have been uncovered in Java. The most important and most numerous findings have been at Sangiran, where in the 1930s Ralph von Koenigswald found fossils dating back to around one million BC. In 1936, at Perning near Mojokerto, the skull of a child was discovered and was purported to be even older. Most findings have been along Sungai Bengawan Solo (Bengawan Solo River) in Central and East Java.

Geochronologists have now dated the bones of Java's oldest *Homo erectus* specimens at 1.7 million years, but also postulate that the youngest fossils may be less than 40,000 years old. This means that *Homo erectus* existed in Java at the same time as *Homo sapiens*, who arrived on the island some 60,000 years ago, and reignites the debate about whether humankind evolved in Africa and migrated from there, or whether humans evolved on several continents concurrently. Those interested in learning more should pick up a copy of Carl Swisher, Garniss Curtis and Roger Lewin's extremely readable book, *Java Man*, or pay a visit to the excellent Sangiran Museum (p146), which charts the history of humankind.

TOP FIVE JAVA READS

➡ *A Shadow Falls: In the Heart of Java* by Andrew Beatty. Based on sustained research in a remote Javanese village, this cultural study examines the conflict between mystic Javanese traditionalists and orthodox Islam.

➡ *Jakarta Inside Out* by Daniel Ziv. A collection of humorous short stories tackling the vibrant underbelly of Indonesia's capital.

➡ *The Religion of Java* by Clifford Geertz. A classic book on Javanese religion, culture and values. It's slightly dated (it was based on research conducted in the 1950s) but is nonetheless a fascinating read.

➡ *Javanese Culture* by Koentjaraningrat. One of the most comprehensive studies of Javanese society, history, culture and beliefs. This excellent reference book covers everything from Javanese toilet training to kinship lines.

➡ *Raffles and the British Invasion of Java* by Tim Hannigan. An excellent, authoritative account of the brief period of British rule, and the role of Sir Thomas Stamford Raffles, in the early 19th century.

Java has three main ethnic groups, each speaking their own language and practising Islam: the Javanese of Central and East Java (where *halus* is taken very seriously); the Sundanese of West Java; and the Madurese from Pulau Madura (who have a reputation for blunt-speaking and informality). Small communities of Hindus remain, including the Tenggerese of the Bromo area and the Badui of West Java, whose religion retains many animist beliefs. Even metropolitan Jakarta identifies its own polyglot tradition in the Betawi, the name for the original inhabitants of the city.

ⓘ Getting There & Around

AIR

Jakarta has numerous international and domestic connections. Other useful international gateways in Java include Surabaya, Solo, Bandung, Yogyakarta and Semarang. Domestic flights can be very convenient and affordable: Jakarta, Yogyakarta, Bandung and Surabaya are all well connected to the neighbouring islands of Bali, Sumatra and Lombok; if your time is short, it's worth booking a few internal flights to cut down on those hours on the road.

SEA

Ferries run around the clock between East Java and Bali, heading from Ketapang harbour in Banyuwangi to Gilimanuk in West Bali. There's also a 24-hour ferry servicing Sumatra, running between the West Javanese port of Merak to Bakauheni in South Sumatra.

Both Jakarta and Surabaya have harbours with weekly **Pelni** (🖉 021-2188 7000; www.pelni. co.id) passenger ferry services to destinations such as Kalimantan and Sulawesi.

BUS

Java has a comprehensive bus network, which connects with the neighbouring islands of Sumatra to the west, Bali to the east and Nusa Tenggara beyond. Java's road network suffers from narrow roads and increasing traffic volume so journeys across the island tend to be slow and tedious.

TRAIN

Java has a fairly punctual and efficient rail service running right across the island. In general, train travel tends to offer better comfort than bus journeys. Timetables and reservations are available online at www.kereta-api.co.id; the website is in Bahasa Indonesia but Google Translate helps make sense of the information for non-native speakers. Another useful booking site is www.traveloka.com. Unfortunately, rail network capacity is limited (many of the lines are single track) and demand often exceeds supply. During holiday periods, trains are always booked weeks or months ahead.

JAKARTA

📱 021 / POP 10.7 MILLION

One of the world's greatest megalopolises, Jakarta is a dynamic and vibrant city. Its chaotic charm and juxtapositions can be found on every street.

An organism unto itself, Jakarta is a town in the midst of a very public metamorphosis and, despite the maddening traffic, life here is lived at speed, driven by an industriousness and optimism that's palpable. With this fast-developing pace come challenges. It's no oil painting, yet beneath the new high-rises, relentless concrete, gridlocked

Jakarta

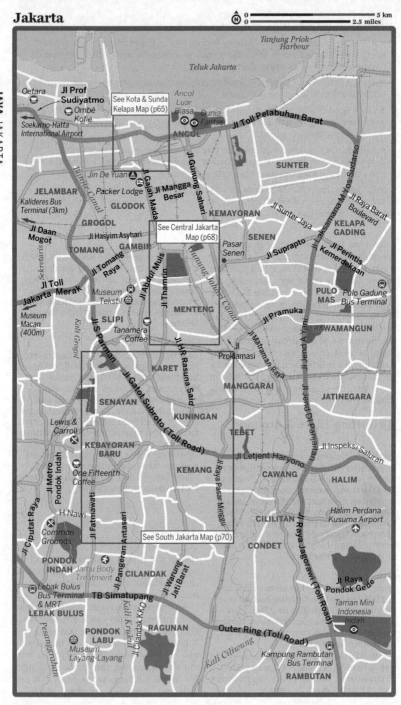

N 0 — 5 km
0 — 2.5 miles

Tanjung Priok Harbour

Teluk Jakarta

Oetara
Jl Prof Sudiyatmo
Ombé Kofie
Soekarno-Hatta International Airport

Ancol Luar Biasa
See Kota & Sunda Kelapa Map (p65)
Dunia Fantasi
ANCOL

Jl Toll Pelabuhan Barat

SUNTER

Jl Raya Barat Boulevard

Kali Besar Canal
Jin De Yuan
Packer Lodge
Jl Gajah Mada
Jl Mangga Besar
Jl Gunung Sahari

JELAMBAR
Kalideres Bus Terminal (3km)
GLODOK
GROGOL

KEMAYORAN
Jl Sunter Jaya

KELAPA GADING

Jl Daan Mogot
Jl Hasyim Asyhari
TOMANG
GAMBIR

See Central Jakarta Map (p68)

Jl Abdul Muis
Pasar Senen
SENEN
Jl Suprapto
Jl Perintis Kemerdekaan

Sekretaris
Jl Tomang Raya
Museum Tekstil
Jl Thamrin

Gunung Jahang Canal

PULO MAS
Pulo Gadung Bus Terminal

Jl Toll Jakarta Merak

Jl S Parman

Museum Macan (400m)

Kali Grogol

SLIPI
Tanamera Coffee
MENTENG
Jl HR Rasuna Said
Jl Pramuka
RAWAMANGUN

Jl Gatot Subroto (Toll Road)

Jl Proklamasi
Jl Mataram Raya
Jl Jend DI Panjaitan
Jl Jend A Yani

KARET

MANGGARAI
JATINEGARA

SENAYAN
Lewis & Carroll

KUNINGAN

Jl Inspeksi Saluran

KEBAYORAN BARU

TEBET

Jl Letjent Haryono
CAWANG
HALIM

Jl Metro Pondok Indah
One Fifteenth Coffee
KEMANG

Jl Raya Pasar Minggu

CILILITAN
Halim Perdana Kusuma Airport

H Nawi

CONDET

Jl Ciputat Raya
Common Grounds

Jl Fatmawati
See South Jakarta Map (p70)

Jl Raya Jagorawi (Toll Road)

PONDOK INDAH
Jamu Body Treatment
CILANDAK

Jl Pangeran Antasari

Jl Warung Jati Barat

Jl Raya Pondok Gede

Lebak Bulus Bus Terminal & MRT
LEBAK BULUS

TB Simatupang

Taman Mini Indonesia Indah

Kali Krukut

PONDOK LABU
Museum Layang-Layang

PONDOK LABU

RAGUNAN

Outer Ring (Toll Road)

Kali Cilandak KKO

Pesanggrahan

Kali Ciliwung

Kampung Rambutan Bus Terminal

RAMBUTAN

streets, smattering of slums and a persistent blanket of smog, Jakarta has plenty of pleasant surprises, including a world-class food and coffee scene. Its citizens – even the poorest among them – remain good-natured and positive, and compared to many world capitals, crime levels are low.

From the steamy, potent streets of Chinatown and Glodok to Kota's vestiges of a colonial past, the old city is the prequel to Jakarta's development. The newer Merdeka Square is where Indonesia presents the face it wants the world to see: bold and confident. Further south, luxurious mega-developments are plopped next to humble neighbourhoods, with pockets of emerging art scenes and bohemian coffee shops. Across the city it's possible to rub shoulders with Indonesia's future leaders and thinkers in sleek restaurants and rooftop bars. Hedonists can go clubbing and drinking 'till dawn, much to the dismay of the current administration.

History

No one would have picked the site of Jakarta for what is today one of the world's most populous cities. It's a swampy plain where rivers drain into the ocean. But thanks to a port that proved vital during the Dutch colonial era, it became the funnel for commerce and wealth for the entire archipelago. It has seen every dramatic moment leading up to the Indonesia of today and remains the country's heart, if not its soul.

Dutch Rule

At the beginning of the 17th century, the Dutch and English jostled for power in the city, and in late 1618 the Jayakartans, backed by the British, besieged the Vereenigde Oost-Indische Compagnie (VOC) fortress. The Dutch managed to fend off the attackers until May 1619 when, under the command of Jan Pieterszoon Coen, reinforcements stormed the town and reduced it to ashes. A stronger shoreline fortress was built and the town was renamed 'Batavia' after a tribe that once occupied parts of the Netherlands in Roman times. It soon became the capital of the Dutch East Indies.

Within the walls of Batavia the prosperous Dutch built tall houses and pestilential canals in an attempt to create an Amsterdam in the tropics. By the early 18th century, the city's population had swelled, boosted by both Javanese and Chinese eager to take advantage of Batavia's commercial prospects.

By 1740 ethnic unrest in the Chinese quarters had grown to dangerous levels and on 9 October violence broke out on Batavia's streets. Between 5000 and 10,000 Chinese were massacred. A year later Chinese inhabitants were moved to Glodok, outside the city walls. Other Batavians, discouraged by severe epidemics between 1735 and 1780, also moved, and the city began to spread far south of the port. In 1808, the government moved south to today's Lapangan Banteng, where the large buildings continue in service of the Indonesian government today.

Post Independence

By 1900, great wealth from the coffee and sugar trade was flowing through Batavia and the population was 116,000. Most of the residents still lived in poverty, however, as the Dutch reserved education and other opportunities for a small minority of people. Dutch colonial rule came to an end with the Japanese occupation in 1942 and the name 'Jakarta' was restored. On 17 August 1945 Sukarno and Hatta declared Indonesia's independence in Jakarta. When the Japanese left at the end of WWII, the Dutch returned and tried again at colonial rule. But it was too late, and after much bloodshed, a peace agreement paved the way for the Indonesian flag to rise over Istana Merdeka palace on 27 December 1949.

During the 1950s and into the 1960s, Sukarno tried to turn Jakarta into his ideal of a modern city. The worst slums were cleared from the centre of the city as a few became wealthy from oil money and other revenues from the booming economy. This all changed, however, with the economic collapse of 1997. The capital quickly became a political battleground and the epicentre of protests demanding Suharto's resignation.

Jakarta erupted in days of rioting as thousands took to the streets and looted malls. The Chinese were hardest hit, with shocking tales of rape and murder emerging after the riots.

The City Today

To the surprise of many, Indonesia's nascent democracy thrived. After a period of parliamentary and governmental wrangling, the nation's first direct presidential elections were held in 2004. A centrist, Susilo Bambang Yudhoyono (SBY), won and was re-elected with more than 60% of the vote five years later. In 2014, the popular governor of Jakarta, Joko Widodo, ran for president against a candidate representing the political old guard and won.

The next Jakarta governor took office with what seemed to be significant handicaps. Basuki Tjahaja Purnama (universally called Ahok) is Christian and Chinese – not obvious attributes for leading the capital region of the world's largest Muslim nation. He catered to the enormous needs of millions at the bottom of the economy and he took on corruption in an effective manner.

Ahok's opposition teamed up with hardline Muslim groups to accuse Ahok of blasphemy and as a result a new Jakarta governor, Anies Baswedan, took office in 2017; he made various attempts to clean up the city before the Asian Games in 2018, including putting a giant nylon net over polluted and foul-smelling rivers to minimise the stench. After considering the Asian Games a great success, the city was on a high, and the authorities put in a bid for the 2032 Olympics.

Since then, Jakarta has continued on a familiar path: scores of Indonesians arrive in hopes of finding opportunity and greatly outpace official efforts to accommodate them, the water is still polluted despite clean-up efforts, new upscale mall and hotel projects are underway, and traffic and pollution remain at critical levels.

⊙ Sights

Despite its nooks of fun and culture, to the uninitiated Jakarta can feel overwhelming. Kota is where the main attractions are easily found. Here live the vestiges of old Batavia, the colonial Dutch city of the 18th century. There are plenty of museums and places to stroll as you survey the city's efforts to reclaim its past even as it plans for the future. Just south, Glodok is the heart of old Chinatown, a busy, compact and vibrant area with temples and markets.

⊙ Kota & Glodok

There are three main zones of sights, all close to each other. Taman Fatahillah (p64) anchors the colonial sights that extend north and west. Kota Railway Station is a hub for the bank museums and the nearby **Gereja Sion** (Map p65; Jl Pangeran Jayakarta) FREE church. Just south, Glodok is compact and perfectly walkable.

★**Taman Fatahillah** SQUARE
(Map p65; btwn Jl Stasiun & Jl Pintu Besar Utara) Kota's central cobblestone square, surrounded by imposing Dutch colonial buildings, is Jakarta's most attractive location and a popular gathering spot for tourists and locals. The stately bell-towered former town hall (1627) now houses the excellent Jakarta History Museum, while the former Palace of Justice (1866) building has been transformed into the Museum Seni Rupa Dan Keramik (p66), showcasing traditional and contemporary Indonesian artists. Also here is Museum Wayang, featuring the best *wayang* (flat wooden puppets) collection in Java.

★**Museum Bank Indonesia** MUSEUM
(Map p65; ☎021-2600 1588; www.bi.go.id/en/tentang-bi/museum; Pintu Besar Utara 3; admission 5000Rp; ☻8am-3.30pm Tue-Thu, 8-11.35am & 1-3.30pm Fri, 8am-4pm Sat & Sun) This museum presents an engaging and easily consumed history of Indonesia from a loosely financial perspective, in a grand, expertly restored, neoclassical former bank headquarters that dates from the early 20th century. All the displays (including lots of zany audiovisuals) are slickly presented, with exhibits about the spice trade and the financial meltdown of 1997 (and subsequent riots), as well as a gallery dedicated to currency, with notes from every country in the world.

Jin De Yuan BUDDHIST TEMPLE
(Vihara Dharma Bhakti Temple; Map p62; Jl Kemenangan; ☻dawn-dusk) FREE This large Chinese Buddhist temple compound dates from 1755, and even though it was mostly destroyed by fire in 2015, it remains one of the most atmospheric and important in the city. The main structure has an unusual roof crowned by two dragons eating pearls, while the interior is richly adorned with Buddhist statues, ancient bells and drums, and some wonderful calligraphy. Dense incense and candle smoke wafts through the rooms.

Jakarta History Museum MUSEUM
(Museum Sejarah Jakarta, Museum Kesejarahan Jakarta; Map p65; ☎021-692 9101; Taman Fatahillah; adult/student/child 5000/3000/2000Rp; ☻9am-5pm Tue-Sun) The Jakarta History Museum is housed in the old town hall of Batavia, a stately whitewashed Dutch colonial structure that was once the epicentre of an empire. This bell-towered building, built in 1627, served the administration of the city

Kota & Sunda Kelapa

Kota & Sunda Kelapa

and was also used by the city law courts. Inside, it has a collection of artefacts and an impressive 10m painting depicting the attempted siege of Batavia by the Mataram forces in 1628.

Museum Wayang MUSEUM
(Puppet Museum; Map p65; ☏021-692 9560; Taman Fatahillah; adult/child 5000/2000Rp; ⏰9am-4.30pm Tue-Sun; 🚼) This puppet museum has one of the best collections of *wayang*

(flat wooden puppets) in Java and its dusty cabinets are full of a multitude of intricate, eerie and beautiful characters from across Indonesia, as well as China, Vietnam, India, Cambodia and Europe. The building itself dates from 1912. Ask about the occasional free *wayang* performances.

Museum Bank Mandiri   MUSEUM
(Map p65; Jl Pintu Besar Utara; 15,000Rp; ☺9am-3.30pm Tue-Thu, 9-11.30am & 1-3.30pm Fri, 9am to 6.30pm Sat & Sun) FREE One of two bank museums within a block of each other might have you scratching your head, but it's worthwhile popping in to explore the behind-the-scenes inner workings of a bank, and the interior of this fine 1930s art deco structure.

Museum Seni Rupa Dan Keramik   GALLERY
(Museum of Fine Arts & Ceramics; Map p65; ☑021-690 7062; Taman Fatahillah; adult/child 5000/2000Rp; ☺9am-5pm Tue-Sun) Built between 1866 and 1870, the former Palace of Justice building is now a fine arts museum. It houses a vast collection of historic Indonesian and Chinese ceramics and Majapahit terracottas, along with contemporary and abstract works by prominent Indonesian artists. Pause and relax in the palm-shaded grounds.

Petak Sembilan Market   MARKET
(Pasar Kemenangan; Map p65; Jl Kemenangan; ☺dawn-dusk) Be sure to wander down the narrow Kemenangan Market/Petak Sembilan Market off Jl Pancoran, lined with atmospheric temples and crooked houses with red-tiled roofs. It's an assault on the senses, with skinned frogs and live bugs for sale next to vast piles of produce. Stalls extend down even narrower neighbouring alleys.

Kali Besar   CANAL
(Map p65; Jl Kali Besar Barat) The Kali Besar is an 18th-century canal built along the Ciliwung River, connecting the port to the old city of Batavia. It once thrived with commerce, and boats shuttled goods to and from the port. Almost 300 years ago it was lined with houses of Batavia's rich and famous. Today you can still see vestiges of this era in buildings in various stages of restoration and decay along the canal.

Sunda Kelapa   PORT
(Map p65; Jl Maritim Raya) A kilometre north of Taman Fatahillah (p64), the old port of Sunda Kelapa still sees the magnificent Makassar schooners *(pinisi)*. In some respects the dock scene here has barely changed for centuries, with porters unloading cargo from sailing ships by hand and trolley, though it's far less busy today. There is a more modern main harbour to the right of here, where fancy yachts are docked.

Syahbandar Menara   HISTORIC BUILDING
(Watchtower; Map p65; off Jl Pakin; adult/child incl Museum Bahari 5000/2000Rp; ☺7.30am-4.30pm, to 5pm Fri) Just before the entrance to the maritime museum is an atmospheric harbourmaster watchtower, built in 1839 to sight and direct traffic to the port. Views include the unappealing landfill and polluted water, but you can still take in some of old Batavia and the chaotic scenes below. Entry includes a visit to the Museum Bahari.

Museum Bahari   MUSEUM
(Maritime Museum; Map p65; ☑021-669 3406; Jl Pakin 1; adult/student/child 5000/2000Rp/free; ☺7.30am-4.30pm Sat-Thu, to 5pm Fri) Near Jakarta's historic port are several 17th-century VOC (Vereenigde Oost-Indische Compagnie; the Dutch East India Company) warehouses that comprise the Museum Bahari. This is a good place to learn about the city's maritime history, with a sprawling series of galleries covering everything from nautical legends and famous explorers to WWII history in the archipelago. Also included in the price is the 1839 Syahbandar Menara observation tower, just before the entrance to the maritime museum.

◉ Central Jakarta

If a centre for this sprawling city had to be chosen, then Merdeka Square (Lapangan Merdeka) would be the bullseye, with the national monument (Monas) being the dart. This huge grassy expanse is home to the first president of Indonesia's gift to the nation (Monas), and is surrounded by good museums and some fine colonial-era buildings. This part of Jakarta is not about atmospheric streets or peculiar sights; rather it's the political centre and where the nation makes a statement about its stature and prominence.

★ Merdeka Square   SQUARE
(Lapangan Merdeka; Map p68; Jl Merdeka Selatan) It is here that Jakartans come to take a breather from the traffic. The figurative centre of Jakarta, Merdeka Square (*merdeka* means independence) is actually a trapezoid

measuring almost 1 sq km. In the 19th century, the Dutch called it Koningsplein (Kings Square) and it became a focal point for the city after they moved the government here from old Batavia (Kota). It's always had an important role in local life. The main entrance is on the south side.

★ Museum Nasional   MUSEUM
(National Museum; Map p68; ☑021-386 8172; www.museumnasional.or.id; Jl Medan Merdeka Barat 12; admission 10,000Rp; ◎8am-4pm Tue-Fri, to 5pm Sat & Sun) The National Museum is the best of its kind in Indonesia and an essential visit. The enormous collection begins around an open courtyard of the 1862 building, which is stacked with magnificent millennia-old statuary including a colossal 4.5m stone image of a Bhairawa king from Rambahan in Sumatra, who is shown trampling on human skulls. The ethnology section is superb, with Dayak puppets and wooden statues from Nias sporting beards (a sign of wisdom) plus some fascinating textiles.

Over in a spacious modern wing there are four floors with sections devoted to the origin of humankind in Indonesia, including a model of the Flores 'hobbit'. There's also a superb display of gold treasures from Candi Brahu in Central Java: glittering necklaces, armbands and a bowl depicting scenes from the Ramayana. At the back of the courtyard, look for the architectural collection with models of some of the extraordinary structures from across the archipelago. Nearby, the textile collection (koleksi tekstil) has beautiful fabrics including koffo from Sulawesi, an intricate woven cloth with rich gold threads.

The Indonesian Heritage Society (www. heritagejkt.org) organises free English tours of the museum at 10am on Tuesday, Wednesday, Thursday and Saturday, with an additional tour on Thursday at 1.30pm. Tours are also available in French, Japanese and Korean and at other times; consult the website for the latest schedule.

★ Galeri Nasional   GALLERY
(National Gallery; Map p68; ☑021-3483 3954; www.galeri-nasional.or.id; Jl Medan Merdeka Timur 14; ◎9am-4pm Tue-Sun) **FREE** Over 1700 works of art by foreign and Indonesian artists are part of the National Gallery collection. While only a few works are on display at any time, there are also large spaces for regular – and well-curated – special exhibits. The centre-piece of the sprawling palm-shaded complex is an 1817 Dutch building.

There's a small open-air cafe that offers a wonderful respite from pounding the local pavement pondering monuments. Visitors must check their bags into a cloakroom.

Istana Merdeka   PALACE
(Independence Palace; Map p68; Jl Medan Merdeka Utara) The presidential palace (one of six in Indonesia) stands to the north of Merdeka Square. It was built in 1879 and was Sukarno's official residence during his reign, although Suharto spurned it. On 27 December 1949, the Dutch flag was lowered for the last time and the red-and-white flag of independent Indonesia was raised. Hundreds of thousands of Indonesians gathered to witness the event and chant merdeka (freedom).

Masjid Istiqlal   MOSQUE
(Independence Mosque; Map p68; Jl Veteran I; ◎4am-11pm) **FREE** The striking, modernist Masjid Istiqlal is adorned by patterned geometric grates on the windows. Completed in 1978, it's the largest mosque in Southeast Asia, with five levels representing the five pillars of Islam. Its dome is 45m across and its minaret tops 90m. Non-Muslim visitors are welcome. You have to sign in first and robe up (men should cover their legs, women their legs and arms). Once suitably dressed you'll be directed to a gallery overlooking the main hall.

Monumen Irian
Jaya Pembebasan   MONUMENT
(Irian Jaya Liberation Monument; Map p68; Lapangan Banteng) The twin towers of this monument with a dodgy provenance soar over grassy Lapangan Banteng (p69) and are topped by a sculpture of a man breaking his chains. It dates to the Sukarno era and was designed as anti-Imperialist propaganda, even as Indonesia took over Irian Jaya (Timor and Papua) despite local protests in 1963. These days some call it the 'Freedom Monument'.

Monumen
Nasional   MONUMENT
(Monas, National Monument; Map p68; Merdeka Sq; adult/student/child 15,000/8000/4000Rp; ◎lift 8am-4pm & 5.30-8pm) Ingloriously dubbed 'Sukarno's final erection', the 132m-high National Monument (aka Monas), which rises into the shroud of smog and towers over Merdeka Square, is both Jakarta's principal

Central Jakarta

N 0 ━━━━━━ 500 m
0 ━━━━━━ 0.25 miles

Kota (3km)

32

Sawah
Besar

Jl Hayam Wuruk
Jl Gajah Mada
Jl Batu Ceper Raya
Jl Batu Tulis Raya
17
Jl Ceylan
Jl Pintu Air V
Kemayoran
Jl Bungur Besar

Jl Dr Sutomo

Jl Ir H Juanda
Jl Veteran
Juanda
Jl Antara
Jl Pos
Jl Budi
Utomo
Jl Gn Sahari Raya

Jl Majapahit
Jl Veteran 3
Jl Veteran
20
6
22
5
Jl Gedung Kesenian
Jl Banteng Timur
Jl Katedral
Jl Syahrir U

Jl Tanah Abang 81
4
GAMBIR
Jl Medan Merdeka Utara
7
Jl Banteng
Selatan

Jl Tanah
Abang 2
Jl Medan Merdeka Barat
3
Merdeka Square
(Lapangan Merdeka)
8
Jl Perwira
Jl Pejambon
Jl Abdul Rachman
Saleh Raya
Jl Kalilio
Jl Senen Raya 3
Jl Pasar Senen

**Museum
Nasional**
Jl Abdul Muis
Jl Tanah Abang Timur
Gambir
Jl Medan Merdeka Utara
1 *Galeri
Nasional*
Jl Senen Raya
28

*Merdeka
Square*
2 P
Jl Medan Merdeka Selatan
US Embassy
Jl Prapatan
Jl Kwitang

Jl Budi Kemuliaan

Jl Thamrin
Jl Kebon Sirih Raya
Jl Menteng
Jl Jaksa
Jl Wahid Hasyim
Jl Menteng Raya
Sungai Krukut

See Jalan Jaksa Area Map (p74)
Gondangdia
Jl Johar
Jl Cikini 6
21

Jl Sunda
9
*French
Embassy*
Jl Gereja Theresia
Jl Sunda
15
Jl Cut Nyak Dien
CIKINI
24
*Cikini
Hospital*

Jl Kebon Kacang 11
Jl Yusuf Adi winata
18
Jl Cokroaminoto
Jl Teuku Umar
Jl Dr Sam Ratulangi
Jl Cikini Raya

Jl Kebon Kacang Raya
11 29
26
12
25
Jl Sultan Syahrir
Jl Prof Mohammad Yamin SH
16
10 14
Jl Raden
Saleh Raya

23
German Embassy
19
MENTENG
Jl Teuku Cik Ditiro
Jl
Pegangsaan
Timur

30
Jl Kusuma Atmaja
Jl Surnenep
Jl Imam Bonjol
Jl Taman
Suropati
Cikini
27
Jl Surabaya

*Sudirman
Station*
Jl Sumardi
Jl Sunda
Kelapa
Jl Diponegoro

13

Central Jakarta

landmark and the most famous architectural extravagance of the former president. Begun in 1961, Monas was not completed until 1975, when it was officially opened by Suharto. The monument is constructed from Italian marble and topped with a sculpted flame, gilded with 50kg of gold leaf.

Entrance to the monument is via an underground tunnel below the huge terrace; follow the crowds. You'll have to purchase a magnetic-strip entrance card for an additional 35,000Rp – though it's redeemable against public transport and some other museums. Tickets to the top usually sell out, so to avoid disappointment aim to get here before noon weekdays (and 9am weekends) for the first session, or around 6pm for the evening session.

The lift to the top of the monument leaves every hour, and there's capacity for 600 at the top. If you'd rather not queue, you can just walk up to the goblet – the first platform on the monument – for a lower view over the square. A section in the base is devoted to a small **history museum** with dioramas of notable moments in Indonesian history.

Note that from Monday to Thursday the entrance/exit point is only from the southwest and northwest gates.

Lapangan Banteng   SQUARE
(Banteng Square; Map p68; btwn Jl Banteng Timur & Jl Katedral) Just east of Merdeka Square, Lapangan Banteng is surrounded by some of Jakarta's best colonial architecture. It was first designed by the Dutch in the early 19th century, when it was called Waterlooplein. It has basketball courts, football pitches and a children's play area.

⊙ South & West Jakarta

Jakarta's sprawling south has vast *kampung* (the traditional villages where most Jakartans live) punctuated by islands and ribbons of glitz, wealth and bohemian hang-outs. Malls as flashy as any in the world and posh hotels anchor huge office developments. Amid this are neighbourhoods with real personalities, like captivating Kemang with its array of restaurants, ubercool coffee houses and trendy boutiques. After dark, some of Jakarta's legendary clubs still party the night away. West Jakarta is home to a couple of interesting museums, including the new contemporary art museum.

⭐ **Museum Macan**   MUSEUM
(Museum of Modern & Contemporary Art in Nusantara; ☑ 021-2212 1888; www.museummacan.org; Jl Panjang Raya 5, Kebon Jeruk; exhibitions 50,000-100,000Rp; ⊗ 10am-6pm Tue-Sun) This museum

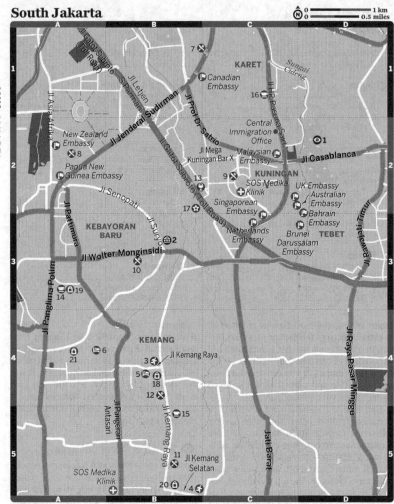

is Indonesia's first modern and contemporary art museum and an exciting cultural development for the city. It was built to house the private art collection of businessman Haryanto Adikoesoemo, who has amassed some 800 works by Indonesian artists. Touring exhibitions have included Anish Kapoor, Ai Weiwei, Jeff Koons and Yayoi Kusama.

★ **Museum Layang-Layang** MUSEUM
(Kites Museum of Indonesia; Map p62; 📞 021-765 8075; Jl H Kamang 38; 15,000Rp; ⊘9am-4pm; 👪) Families will love Jakarta's kite museum, located in a quiet backstreet in Pondok Labu, South Jakarta. Inside a traditional

Indonesian house, complete with courtyard, there's a collection of around 600 kites. A 10-minute educational video explains the different styles and origins of kite flying (and that it probably all started in Indonesia). The impressive range of kites includes a 3D giant horse and cart, dragon, ship and lion fish, plus 2D kites made of bamboo and banana-tree leaves.

RUCI Art Space & Cafe GALLERY
(Map p70; 📞 021-7279 9769; http://ruciart.com; Jl Suryo Blok S 49; ⊘gallery 11am-7pm, cafe 10am-midnight Mon-Thu, to 1am Fri & Sat) RUCI Art Space has become a favourite on the

South Jakarta

city's burgeoning art scene. Occupying an industrial space in the hip neighbourhood of Senopati, the gallery hosts regular solo and group exhibitions from local contemporary artists. Work ranges from painting and photography to installation art. A large cafe is attached, decorated with designer furniture and selling drinks (coffee from 30,000Rp), mains (noodle and rice dishes from 55,000Rp, tacos from 35,000Rp) and desserts (milk fritters, panna cotta, cinnamon banana fritters from 35,000Rp).

**Taman Mini
Indonesia Indah** AMUSEMENT PARK
(Beautiful Indonesia Miniature Park; Map p62; ☑021-8779 2078; www.tamanmini.com; Jl Raya Taman Mini; 15,000Rp; ⊙7am-10pm; ☝) This 100-hectare park has full-scale traditional houses for each of Indonesia's provinces, with displays of regional handicrafts and clothing, and even a mini-scale Borobudur. Museums, theatres and an IMAX cinema are scattered throughout the grounds, which all command additional entrance fees (from 20,000Rp to 140,000Rp). Other attractions include a small water park, space exploration museum and an atrium with more than 760 species of birds from around Indonesia. Free cultural performances are staged in selected regional houses.

It's advisable to hire a Grab (p83) car, Go-Jek (p84) motorbike or bicycle (25,000Rp per hour) within the park as the place is enormous. You can easily spend hours roaming around here.

Museum Tekstil MUSEUM
(Textile Museum; Map p62; www.museumtekstil jakarta.com; Jl Aipda K S Tubun 2-4; adult/child 5000/2000Rp, batik class 40,000Rp; ⊙9am-4pm Tue-Sun) Very much a worthwhile visit if you've any interest in weaving and fabrics, this museum houses a collection of around 2000 precious textiles, including hundreds of batik pieces, both antique and contemporary, lots of looms and a garden containing plants used for natural dyes. It's about 2km southwest of Merdeka Square, and not easily reached by public transport. Ask about classes to study batik.

Jakarta War Cemetery CEMETERY
(Map p70; www.ogs.nl; Jl Menteng Pulo Raya; ⊙8am-5pm) **FREE** During WWII, thousands of people were made prisoners of war and killed in and around Jakarta. Early victories by the Japanese killed scores of troops from colonial Dutch military as well as the British Commonwealth. After the war, the Dutch and the UK, on behalf of the Commonwealth, established this cemetery to bring together the deceased from across Indonesia. It's a beautiful and serene place. The staff keep gates locked to avoid vandalism, but will unlock the gates for visitors.

🏃 Activities

Swimming, yoga, massage and walking tours are the main activities in Jakarta. However, Jakarta adventure companies also offer day trips further afield. It's possible to go diving and snorkelling at the Thousand Islands, off Jakarta's north shore, or go rafting and hiking four hours' south of Jakarta, if you're desperate to escape the city smog.

Gudang-Gudang Yoga Studio
YOGA

(Map p70; ☑021-718 0173; www.gudanggudangyoga.com; Jl Kemang Timur 88; drop-in classes 110,000Rp; ☺8am-4pm) Get away from the urban hustle and bustle at this one-of-a-kind yoga studio and sanctuary of peace. Experienced yogis and beginners are welcome at a range of classes that include vinyasa, Jivamukti and other meditations. Classes in the traditional Javanese *joglo* hut are particularly atmospheric – with the soothing sounds of a water fountain. There's a cafe next door.

Bersih Sehat Menteng
MASSAGE

(Map p74; ☑021-390 0204; www.bersihsehat.com; 1st fl, Jl KH Wahid Hasyim 106; 1hr massage 170,000Rp; ☺10am-9pm) The hygienic and elegant massage and sauna facilities and professional masseurs at this spa are highly recommended. Find it in the complex behind the small Warung Ngalam (p76) restaurant.

Jamu Body Treatment
SPA

(Map p62; ☑021-765 9691; www.jamutraditionalspa.com; Jl Cipete VIII/94B, Cipete; massage & treatments from 170,000Rp; ☺9am-7pm) An elegant spa in South Jakarta that uses *jamu* (Indonesian herbs with medicinal and restorative properties) for its treatments. Choose from scrubs, masks, wraps, reflexology, and warm stone and Balinese massages.

Bike Rental
CYCLING

(Map p65; Taman Fatahillah; per 30min 20,000Rp; ☺9am-sunset) Ride around Kota on a brightly coloured, big-tyred Dutch-style bike. You can't miss the stands set up on various edges of the square. The rental fee includes the use of a broad-brimmed straw hat. Let the selfies commence!

⌦ Tours

★ Jakarta Walking Tour
WALKING

(http://jakartawalkingtour.com; tours from €40) Offers a wide range of customisable tours geared towards food, markets, the old neighbourhood of Kota and much more. The price includes pick-up at your hotel. Walks are not long and include transport where necessary between scattered venues (eg the food tour).

Hidden Jakarta Tours
TOURS

(☑0812 803 5297; www.realjakarta.blogspot.com; per person US$50) Hidden Jakarta offers tours of the city's traditional *kampung*, the urban villages of the poor. These warts-and-all tours take you along trash-choked riverways, into cottage-industry factories and allow you to take tea in residents' homes. Minimum two people.

Other Side of Jakarta
WALKING

(☑0812 8108 8277; 3hr tour per person 700,000Rp) Friendly local guide Yuda offers tours of the Glodok area covering sights like the Sunda Kelapa (p66) old harbour, Taman Fatahillah (p64) square, Museum Bahari (p66) and the watchtower, **Jembatan Kota Intan** (Kota Intan Bridge; Map p65; Jl Kali Besar) old bridge and more. He'll do a custom trip depending on your interests, but his tours require booking with a few days' notice.

City Tour Bus
TOURS

(Peta Bus Wisata; www.transjakarta.co.id; ☺9am-5pm Mon-Sat, noon-7pm Sun) **FREE** Ride around central Jakarta on free double-decker tour buses courtesy of the city's government. Run by Transjakarta, the buses offer a DIY experience as there's no narration. Still, you can't beat the price or the view. There are numerous stops, including those at Plaza Indonesia (p81), Museum Nasional (p67), National Monument (p67) and Museum Bank Indonesia (p64).

✲ Festivals & Events

Independence Day
CULTURAL

(Hari Kemerdekaan; ☺17 Aug) Indonesia's independence is celebrated; the parades in Jakarta are the biggest in the country.

Djakarta Warehouse Project
MUSIC

(www.djakartawarehouse.com; Jakarta International Expo Centre, Kota Tua; tickets from 1,600,000Rp; ☺Dec) Running over two days at the Jakarta International Expo Centre, the largest annual festival of electronic dance music in Asia has around 90,000 attendees annually. Previous acts include Roger Sanchez, David Guetta, Skrillex and Tiësto. Certain Islamic groups disapprove of the festival, believing it promotes immoral behaviour. The venue may have to change, but for now the beat goes on.

Indonesian Dance Festival
DANCE

(http://indonesiandancefestival.id; ☺early Nov) Features contemporary and traditional performances at the Taman Ismail Marzuki (p80).

Car Free Day PARADE
(www.infocarfreeday.net; Jl Sudirman & Jl Thamrin; ⊙6-11am Sun) FREE An initiative to reduce pollution in Indonesia's capital and combat fossil fuel emissions has become a real community event. Five kilometres along Jakarta's main thoroughfares are closed to all private vehicles for five hours every Sunday. People come out in their thousands to promenade, cycle, roller skate and enjoy the fume-free stretch of city.

Jakarta Fair FAIR
(www.jakartafair.co.id; Jakarta International Expo Centre, Kota Tua; ⊙Jun) Marks the establishment of the city in 1527. As well as being celebrated with fireworks around the city, the Jakarta Fair combines commerce and culture with thousands of exhibitors and hundreds of performances. It's held for a month at the Jakarta International Expo complex in Kemayoran.

🛏 Sleeping

🛏 Jalan Jaksa Area

While it's not a backpacker's haven any more, there's one particularly good hostel in this neighbourhood, plus a variety of very good midrange and top-end hotels. Like the area itself, none is overly hectic.

Konko Hostel HOSTEL $
(Map p74; 021-391 1127; https://konko-hostel. com; Jl Kebon Sirih Raya 03/03; dm/s/d 123,000/280,000/300,000Rp; ✳@🛜) With crisp sheets and fresh paint, Konko is the stylish new kid on the block. Near the city's main sights, it has dorms sleeping four, six and 12 people, plus privates with small desks and en suites. There are reading lights for every bed, plus communal areas including a cosy beanbag TV lounge, a gym and a yoga space.

Hotel Dreamtel HOTEL $$
(Map p74; 021-392 8728; www.dreamteljakarta. com; Jl Johar 17-19; d/tr incl breakfast from 525,000/622,500Rp; P✳🛜) Great location and reasonable prices are just two of the attributes of this high-rise midrange gem. Clad in dark colours, the 87 rooms are large and feature many amenities like fridges, safes, tea- and coffee-making facilities, and hairdryers. Bathrooms have large, all-glass showers.

★**Artotel Thamrin** DESIGN HOTEL $$$
(Map p68; 021-3192 5888; www.artotel indonesia.com; Jl Sunda 3; r incl breakfast from 833,000Rp; P✳🛜) You can't miss this building – it's covered in an enormous pink, white and black illustration. Eight Indonesian artists were each given one floor of this hip hotel and told to go wild. The results are striking. As well as the decorative murals – ranging from cartoonish to graffiti to minimalist chic – rooms feature luxe furnishings, large comfy beds and oodles of amenities.

★**Kosenda Hotel** BOUTIQUE HOTEL $$$
(Map p74; 021-3193 6868; www.kosendahotel. com; Jl KH Wahid Hasyim 127; r from 720,000Rp; P✳🛜) Hip but not overbearing, minimalist and modern but comfortable. The rooms aren't huge but they are very clean and tastefully designed with built-in desks, floating beds and glass-box baths. There's a great lounge with reading material of the *Monocle* ilk. The breakfast buffet is lovely, and there's a cool 24-hour restaurant (p77) in the lobby, a gym, and a superb bar (p79).

🛏 Cikini & Menteng

South of Merdeka Square, the adjoining neighbourhoods of Cikini and Menteng are Jakarta at its genteel best. Many streets are tree lined and even the canals seem relatively clean. Cikini's main drag, Jl Cikini Raya, is lined with good cafes and restaurants. Menteng has Jakarta's commercial spine, the major road of Jl Thamrin, and its top-end hotels and malls.

★**Capsule Hotel Old Batavia** HOSTEL $
(Map p68; 021-390 5123; http://capsulehotel oldbatavia.jakartahotels.site; Jl Cikini Raya 60Z; dm 125,000-135,000Rp, r 260,000Rp; @🛜) Hidden in a quiet alley, adjacent to the Six Degrees hostel, the dorms here are capsule-style with personal reading lights and lockers for your belongings. Private rooms have en-suite bathrooms. Some rooms are windowless. There's a family atmosphere, and the lovely staff will shake your hand and remember your name when you check in; they're helpful with local info too.

★**Six Degrees** HOSTEL $
(Map p68; 021-314 1657; www.jakarta-back packers-hostel.com; Jl Cikini Raya 60B-C, Cikini; dm 110,000-150,000Rp, d incl breakfast with/without bathroom 300,000/260,000Rp; ✳@🛜) Run by a helpful and friendly team, with good

Jalan Jaksa Area

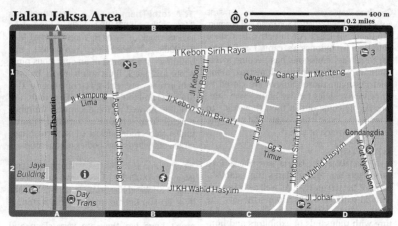

Jalan Jaksa Area

info on the local Cikini area (just south of Merdeka Square), Six Degrees rightfully remains popular with travellers. There's a relaxed, sociable atmosphere, a pool table and TV room, kitchen, and roof garden complete with bar and outdoor gym. Clean dorms sleep between four and 10 people, and privates have small desks.

★ **Hotel Indonesia Kempinski**   HOTEL $$$
(Map p68; ☑ 021-2358 3800; www.kempinski.com; Jl Thamrin 1; r 2,500,000-5,000,000Rp; 🅿 ❋ @ 🛜 ☷) Formerly *the* Hotel Indonesia, Jakarta's original luxury hotel will be forever linked to the Suharto era. Now renovated and reimagined, it still delivers the glamour. Rooms are a decent size with tasteful rugs, neutral tones, sumptuous baths, glass desks, ergonomic desk chairs, wood furnishings, quality linens and firm beds. Kids enjoy the Little VIP Playground.

Grand Hyatt Jakarta   HOTEL $$$
(Map p68; ☑ 021-2992 1234; https://jakarta.grand.hyatt.com; Jl Thamrin 28-30; r from 3,300,000Rp; ❋ @ 🛜 ☷) This huge prominent hotel dominates its landmark location. It's the upscale centre of commercial Jakarta, and glitzy malls are nearby. Rooms are decorated in light-coloured textiles, wood and

marble. Bathrooms have separate tubs and showers. There's a plethora of public services (including a palm-tree-flanked swimming pool and a 575m running track), plus six eateries.

🛏 Other Areas

★ **Packer Lodge**   HOSTEL $
(Map p62; ☑ 021-629 0162; www.thepacker lodge.com; Jl Kermunian IV 20-22; dm/s/d incl breakfast from 140,000/200,000/275,000Rp; ❋ 🛜) This boutique hostel in Glodok offers hip, Ikea-chic environs and plenty of amenities close to Kota. Choose among the four- and eight-bed dorms where the bunks are curtained pods with electrical outlets, lights and USB charger. There are also very reasonably priced singles and doubles with and without bathrooms, decorated with inspirational travel motifs. There's a spacious common kitchen.

★ **Wonderloft Hostel**   HOSTEL $
(Map p65; ☑ 021-2607 2218; www.wonderloft.id; Jl Bank 6; dm/d incl breakfast from 105,000/ 260,000Rp; ❋ @ 🛜) Well located for the sights and sounds around colonial Kota, this is a lively hostel with cheerful staff and a social set-up. In the evenings the lobby is

abuzz with backpackers playing pool, beer in hand, to go with darts, foosball and a kitchen busy with guests cooking. Dorms have icy air-con and beds with curtains, power points and lamps.

★ Amaris Hotel
La Codefin Kemang
HOTEL $$

(Map p70; ☑021-719 1516; http://amarishotel.com; Jl Kemang I 3-5; r incl breakfast from 460,000Rp; [P][❄][🛜]) Gaudy like a billboard, the bright primary colours splashed on the exterior continue on the inside of this jazzy chain. Around 100 rooms have small windows, TVs and wooden floors; some have city views. The hotel restaurant serves simple Indonesian meals. All the basics are here, but the hotel's best feature is its location in the heart of Kemang.

★ Shangri-La Jakarta
HOTEL $$$

(Map p68; ☑021-2922 9999; www.shangri-la.com; Jl Jendral Sudirman; r from 1,700,000Rp; [P][❄][@][🛜][🏊]) This enormous posh hotel with a grand marbled-floor lobby and lavish grounds manages to feel like a park in the middle of Jakarta. There is a range of activities for children, including the Sunday Kids' Zone and the Aqua Playground. The hundreds of rooms have soothing grey decor; some have tubs with views of the city.

Dharmawangsa
HOTEL $$$

(Map p70; ☑021-725 8181; www.the-dharmawangsa.com; Jl Brawijaya Raya 26; r from 3,100,000Rp; [❄][@][🛜][🏊]) One of the city addresses, this fancy five-star hotel exudes style and class, with 100 huge rooms (all with balconies) surrounded by landscaped gardens and fountains. The hospitality is particularly good – each guest has access to 24-hour private butler service. The restaurants and leisure facilities – including two pools, a fine spa, and squash and tennis courts – are also outstanding.

✖ Eating

✖ Kota & Glodok

★ Historia
INDONESIAN $

(Map p65; ☑021-690 4188; www.facebook.com/HistoriaJakarta; Jl Pintu Besar Utara 11; mains 35,000-60,000Rp; ⊙10am-9pm Mon-Fri, to 10pm Sat & Sun; 🛜) Served in a hip Kota warehouse with soaring ceilings, big art murals and a retro-industrial vibe, Historia's dishes hail from around the archipelago. Try bandeng

goreng sambal (grilled milkfish with steamed rice and Balinese sambal), sate ayam (grilled chicken satay with rice and peanut sauce), bakmie godog Jawa (Javanese noodles with a spicy broth) and plenty of tasty mixed-rice dishes.

Pantjoran Tea House
CAFE $

(Map p65; ☑021-690 5904; Jl Pintu Besar Selatan 1; mains 30,000-90,000Rp; ⊙9am-9pm) One of the first buildings restored as part of the government program to revitalise the Old Town, this pie-shaped 1928 beauty makes a good first impression for Glodok visitors. Aside from the many types of tea on offer, there's a long list of Indonesian and Chinese meals (from nasi goreng and dumplings to carp with sweet-and-sour sauce).

Café Batavia
INTERNATIONAL $$

(Map p65; ☑021-691 5531; www.cafebatavia.com; Jl Pintu Besar Utara 14; mains 58,000-278,000Rp; ⊙9am-midnight Sun-Thu, to 1am Fri & Sat; 🛜) This 200-year-old building overlooking Kota's old Dutch quarter pulls crowds. It certainly looks the part, with its classy bistro styled with colonial decor, old parlour floors, marble tabletops and art deco furnishings. There are better places to eat around the square, but for ambience you've hit the jackpot. The large menu offers Asian and Western dishes, and an old-world bar for cocktails.

✖ Central Jakarta

Restoran Sari Minang
INDONESIAN $

(Map p68; ☑021-3483 4524; Jl Ir H Juanda 4; mains 20,000-50,000Rp; ⊙8am-midnight; [❄]) The veteran waiters at this Padang-style eatery have been serving diners since 1968. It's cafeteria style with faded red chairs and fluorescent lighting, but it's immensely popular. Try the spicy curries and cool off in the air-con.

✖ South Jakarta

Mie Chino Pasar Santa
INDONESIAN $

(Map p70; Pasar Santa, Jl Cipaku I; mains from 18,000Rp; ⊙noon-8pm Tue-Sun) The hipster haven of Pasar Santa (p81) has a charming little independent market on the top floor. Here, stalls sell food that stems from the culinary dreams of young chefs. This no-frills joint has only three things on the menu – meatballs, dumplings and unbelievably tasty bowls of chicken and mushroom noodles. Believe us, they must be tried.

★ Blue Terrace
HEALTH FOOD $$

(Map p70; ☑ 021-251 0888; www.ayana.com/jakarta/ayana-midplaza-jakarta/eat-and-drink/venues/blue-terrace; Ayana Midplaza Hotel, Jl Jenderal Sudirman Kav 10-11; mains from 65,000Rp; ⏱7am-9pm) Counteract some of Jakarta's toxins at Blue Terrace, which crafts beautifully presented dishes for the health conscious. The menu is chock full of colourful salads and mains, all delicately arranged and many garnished with edible flowers. The seared yellow fin tuna with quinoa, beetroot, capsicum, roasted cherry tomato, quail egg and pesto dressing is simply divine.

★ Din Tai Fung
CHINESE $$

(Map p70; ☑ 021-5790 1288; www.dintaifung.co.id; Plaza Senayan Arcadia, Jl New Delhi 9; 4/6/10 dumplings from 42,000/58,000/90,000Rp; ⏱10.30am-10pm Mon-Thu, 10.30am-11pm Fri, 10am-11pm Sat, 10am-10pm Sun; ❄🔊) This branch of the Michelin-starred Taiwanese dumpling restaurant, one of many in Jakarta, is well hidden and has a relaxing ambience. It specialises in *xiaolongbao* (steamed dumplings), plus other exceptionally executed dumplings and dishes. Order delicious *ji-aozi* fried dumplings, plus roast duck, crispy fried chicken with chilli, and black pepper tenderloin beef with garlicky green beens.

★ Loewy
FRENCH $$

(Map p70; ☑ 021-2554 2378; www.loewyjakarta.com; Jl Lingkar; mains 85,000-250,000Rp; ⏱7.30am-1am Mon-Fri, 9am-1am Sat & Sun; 🔊) One of Jakarta's best eats is this casual 1940s Paris–meets–New York bistro located right in the middle of the busiest business district. It serves classic French brasserie (French onion soup or steak frites) and Asian fare (Indonesian short ribs and Hainan chicken). However, it's after dark when Loewy really comes alive, with its **bar** (cocktails from 110,000Rp; ⏱7.30am-1am Mon-Fri, 9am-2am Sat, 9am-1am Sun) staffed by top mixologists.

Lara Djonggrang
INDONESIAN $$

(Map p68; ☑ 021-315 3252; www.tuguhotels.com; Jl Teuku Cik Ditiro 4; mains 80,000-130,000Rp; ⏱11am-1am; 🔊) It's easy to think you've stumbled across an enchanting lost temple at Lara Djonggrang. Its dimly lit, incense-filled space is decorated with traditional furnishings – dark-wood chairs, red tablecloths and Indonesian sculptures and art. Imperial Indonesian dishes are tasty and beautifully presented with a smorgasbord of colour. Interestingly, the bar was actually created from part of a 200-year-old temple.

J Sparrow's Bar & Grill
SEAFOOD $$

(Map p70; ☑ 021-5010 1819; www.jsparrows.com; Noble House Bldg, 2 Jl Dr Ide Anak Agung Gde Agung; ⏱10am-1am Sun-Thu, 11am-2am Fri & Sat) A nautical art deco interior, bespoke cocktails and an excellent seafood menu make J Sparrow's one of the most stylish places in central Jakarta to grab dinner and drinks. Expect fresh sea produce including lobster and Cajun prawns, plus meat dishes such as lamb chops and tri-tip beef. Vintage cocktails include New York sours and gin fizzes. A live band performs on Wednesdays.

Queen's Head
BRITISH $$

(Map p70; ☑ 021-719 6160; www.queenshead jakarta.com; Jl Kemang Raya 18C; mains 85,000-235,000Rp; ⏱11.30am-1am Sun-Tue, to 2am Wed-Sat) Seminyak meets Islington in this popular lounge-pub that combines Balinese style with hip geometric design and a modern take on British pub fare. Fish and chips, roasted pork belly, seafood red curry, beef pie and freshly baked bread are some of the options. There's an outdoor area and the bar serves top cocktails well into the early hours.

★ Nusa
INDONESIAN $$$

(Map p70; ☑ 021-719 3954; www.nusagastronomy.com; Jl Kemang Raya 81; lunch dishes 75,000-170,000Rp, 8-course set dinner menu 850,000Rp; ⏱11am-3pm & 6-11pm Tue-Sat; 🅿) Inside this grand old 1920s colonial house is one of Jakarta's best upmarket Indonesian restaurants. The menu changes nightly depending on what the chefs source from the best local markets and suppliers. Expect creative inspiration and nuanced flavours. Note that as the restaurant is halal, no alcohol is served. Food styling is elegant; many tables overlook the back garden.

✕ Jalan Jaksa Area

Warung Ngalam
INDONESIAN $

(Map p74; ☑ 021-391 2483; Jl KH Wahid Hasyim 106; mains 20,000-45,000Rp; ⏱9am-10pm) A warung (food stall) for a new age, this narrow, open-sided cafe with single seating serves up delicious Indonesian dishes with a panoply of Asian influences. Patrons swoon for crispy duck, fried tofu, fish-head soup, homemade noodles and more. Vegetables are fresh and varied. Expect to wait for a seat around lunchtime.

★ **Waha Kitchen** ASIAN $$

(Map p74; ☑ 021-3193 6868; www.wahakitchen. com; Kosenda Hotel, Jl KH Wahid Hasyim 127; mains 68,000-148,000Rp; ⊗24hr) A fittingly fashionable bistro occupies the lobby of the designer Kosenda Hotel, with a 24-hour bar and a menu of modern Asian. Food appears to be served with a Western palate in mind, with classic but well-executed dishes like spicy seafood noodles, Hainanese chicken rice, black pepper beef and salted egg yolk fried prawns.

Shanghai Blue 1920 CHINESE, INDONESIAN $$

(Map p74; ☑ 021-391 8690; www.tuguhotels. com; Jl Kebon Sirih Raya 77-79; dishes 58,000-108,000Rp; ⊗11am-11pm) Dine like you've time travelled to 1920s Shanghai in an atmospheric room loaded with tapestries, wood carvings, red lanterns and flamboyant furnishings (some rescued from an old Batavia teahouse). Standouts from the menu include crab-stuffed lychee, fried Shanghai street dumplings, and roasted duck marinated in 12 spices and served with hoisin sauce.

✗ Cikini & Menteng

★ **Kunstkring Paleis** INDONESIAN $$

(Map p68; ☑ 021-390 0899; www.tuguhotels. com; Jl Teuku Umar 1; mains 68,000-488,000Rp; ⊗5pm-midnight) High tea or cocktails? You can have both, plus a divine Indonesian dinner in between at this alluring re-imagined Dutch colonial mansion, once Batavia's fine arts centre (it showed works by Van Gogh, Picasso, Chagall and Gauguin after it opened in 1914). Exhibitions continue today.

★ **Plataran Menteng** INDONESIAN $$

(Map p68; ☑ 021-2962 7771; www.plataran.com; Jl Cokroaminoto 42; ⊗11am-10pm) This excellent restaurant in a grand, old, light-and-airy mansion has plenty of ambience. There's a live pianist, birdcages and reminders of a bygone era but it's not stuffy or pretentious. Asian fusion with Indonesian flavours is done well. Try the nasi goreng four ways, pad Thai, shrimp vermicelli, grilled chicken skewers, or roasted duck, mangosteen and curry sauce.

★ **Tjikini** INDONESIAN $$

(Map p68; ☑ 021-3193 5521; http://tjikini.com; Jl Cikini Raya 17; mains 55,000-190,000Rp; ⊗7am-11pm; ☎) On one of the best coffee strips in Jakarta, this appealing cafe has an alluring

vintage style with bentwood chairs and tiled floors. Coffee drinks are superb; the menu has creative takes on Indonesian fare and flavoursome noodles.

★ **OKU** JAPANESE $$$

(Map p68; ☑ 021-2358 3896; www.kempinski. com; Hotel Indonesia Kempinski, Jl Thamrin; mains 140,000-1,350,000Rp; ⊗noon-3pm & 6-10.30pm; ☎) Inside Hotel Indonesia Kempinski (p74), OKU is an outstanding Japanese dining experience. Its Zen-like minimalist dining room allows the food to stand out. Chef Kazumasa Yazawa serves up modernised Japanese cuisine, but don't mistake this for fusion. Standout dishes include the extraordinary wagyu with macadamia nuts and black garlic miso, Japanese hot pot and sashimi cuts. Reservations recommended.

★ **Por Que No** TAPAS $$$

(Map p68; ☑ 021-390 1950; http://porqueno. co.id; 5th fl, Jl Cokroaminoto 91; dishes 45,000-260,000Rp; ⊗noon-midnight Tue-Thu & Sun, to 2am Fri & Sat; ☎) A tucked-away, uberhip rooftop tapas bar with terrace in the De Ritz Building in Menteng, this spot is popular with those in the know. Try the grilled and sliced tenderloin, deep-fried dory, mozzarella balls, calamari in its own ink and prawns sautéed with chilli and garlic. Best to save room for a dessert of churro ice-cream sandwiches.

✗ Other Areas

★ **Common Grounds** CAFE $$

(Map p62; ☑ 021-7592 0880; www.common grounds.co.id; 3rd fl, Jl Metro Pondok Indah; mains from 75,000Rp, coffee from 30,000Rp; ⊗10am-10pm) Common Grounds is a pioneer of Melburnian third-wave coffee culture in Jakarta. Its award-winning baristas brew fine coffees roasted in-house, while the kitchen churns out a range of excellently prepared international comfort dishes such as smashed avocado on toast, huevos rancheros with rendang, chicken and waffles, Thai beef salads and breakfast burritos.

★ **Lewis & Carroll** CAFE $$

(Map p62; ☑ 0812 1381 8465; www.lewisand carrolltea.com; Jl Bumi 4, Kebayoran Baru, Jakarta Selatan; dishes 55,000-125,000Rp; ⊗8am-10pm) There are more than 70 types of artisanal tea on offer at Lewis & Carroll. The tea lounge serves locally sourced teas with names like Batavia Grey and Java Jewels. If you don't know where to start, the fragrant loose-leaf teas are presented in trays of test tubes that you can smell before ordering.

Drinking & Nightlife

If you're expecting the capital of the world's largest Muslim country to be a sober city with little in the way of drinking culture, think again. Bars are spread throughout the city. You'll find rooftop lounge bars, pubs serving excellent meals and clubs partying through the night. And cafe culture has really taken off in the last few years.

Nightlife can be found in Central Jakarta south towards Jl Jaksa and in the big hotels along Jl Thamrin. The many food stalls at the southwest corner of Merdeka Square stay open well into the evening for nonalcoholic refreshments. Alternatively there's a cafe at the Museum Nasional (p67), another **cafe** (Map p68; ☑ 0812 237 1314; Jl Katedral 1; coffee from 20,000Rp; ⊙ 7am-8pm Mon-Fri, to 1pm Sat) next to the post office and a good **cupcake cafe** (Map p68; ☑ 021-384 5777; Jl Batu Tulis Raya 50; cupcakes from 35,000Rp; ⊙ 8am-8pm).

 Kota & Glodok

★ Acaraki
COFFEE

(Map p65; www.acaraki.com; Gedung Kerta Niaga 3, Kota Tua, Jl Pintu Besar Utara 11; jamu from 18,000Rp; ⊙ 10am-10pm) Hidden in a renovated building near Taman Fatahillah (p64), Acaraki is the coolest cafe in the area. It's decorated with exposed brickwork and an enormous wicker lampshade. It serves coffee, plus the traditional Indonesian medicinal drink *jamu* (herbal infusions of roots, bark, flowers, seeds, leaves and fruits, believed to have many health benefits); flavours include aromatic ginger.

★ Colosseum Club
CLUB

(Map p65; ☑ 021-690 9999; http://colosseum. id; Jl Kunir 7; from 80,000Rp, event prices vary; ⊙ 10pm-5am Wed-Sat) Next to the 1001 Hotel, this vast club with a huge dance floor and a 16m-high roof is the venue for what's easily one of the most impressive lighting systems in the world. Trance, house, retro and foam are just some of the elements of the spectacle. Somewhat upscale, there's still a hint of sleaze around the edges.

 South Jakarta

★ Dragonfly
CLUB

(Map p70; ☑ 021-520 6789; www.ismaya.com/ dragonfly; Jl Jendral Gatot Subroto Kav 23, Graha BIP; drinks from 80,000Rp; ⊙ 9pm-4am Wed, Fri & Sat) In the most unlikely of locations (the lobby of an office building), you'll find this top stop for visiting DJs to Jakarta. Lights are projected onto Dragonfly's mesmerising tunnel-shaped interior, there's a bar at the club's centre and the DJ booth is at the far end. Dragonfly attracts affluent revellers, plus a few insalubrious types. The dress code is strict.

★ Filosofi Kopi
COFFEE

(Map p70; ☑ 021-7391 0939; http://filosofikopi. id/store; Jl Melawai 6; coffee from 22,000Rp; ⊙ 11am-11pm Mon-Fri, 7am-11pm Sat & Sun; 🛜) Immortalised by the Indonesian coffee-lover's movie *Filosofi Kopi* (the film itself was shot here), this busy cafe does a range of local coffees prepared using siphon, V-60, Aeropress and Vietnam drip. It's a cool little space with exposed brick and illustrations on the walls and is a good spot for a break if you've been shopping at nearby Blok M (p81).

One Fifteenth Coffee
COFFEE

(Map p70; ☑ 021-7179 1733; www.1-15coffee.com; Jl Kemang Raya 37; coffee from 26,000Rp, dishes 37,000-180,000Rp; ⊙ 7am-9pm; 🛜) This Indonesian Barista Championship–winning small chain, named after the perfect water-to-coffee ratio, is known for its minimalist style and exceptional coffee. Kemang Raya's branch is no exception, with simple grey decor and wooden chairs. The coffee is flavoursome and the food perfectly executed. We love the shakshuka with merguez sausage, goat's cheese, baked eggs and flatbread.

St Ali Jakarta
COFFEE

(Map p70; ☑ 021-5290 6814; www.stali.com.au/ jakarta; Setiabudi Bldg 2, Jl HR Rasuna Said, Lippo Kuningan; coffee from 35,000Rp, flights 130,000Rp; ⊙ 7am-8pm; 🛜) Getting onboard South Jakarta's burgeoning third-wave coffee scene is acclaimed Melbourne roaster St Ali. As well as Indonesian coffees, it does African single-origin pour-overs prepared at its designated brew bar, and offers tasting flights if you want to sample a few. Enjoy your chosen brew on a communal work bench or stall.

🍷 Cikini & Menteng

★ Tanamera Coffee
COFFEE

(Map p62; ☑ 021-5797 3798; www.tanamera coffee.com; Jl Sudirman 52-53, SCBD; coffee from 30,000Rp; ☺ 7am-10pm; 🛜) A contender for Jakarta's best cup of coffee is this third-wave roaster that offers a range of single-origin beans from around Indonesia. It now has numerous branches, but still sources its beans directly from farmers to ensure fair trade and quality, and all offer V60 pour-overs or espresso machine coffees, along with tasty breakfasts.

Bakoel Koffie
CAFE

(Map p68; www.bakoelkoffie.com; Jl Cikini Raya 25; dishes 30,000-70,000Rp; ☺ 9am-midnight Mon, 8am-midnight Tue-Sun; 🛜) Occupying a fine old colonial building dating to 1878, this elegant art-deco-style cafe has twirling ceiling fans, marble-top round tables and vintage weighing scales and clocks. It serves strong coffee using beans from across the archipelago. Cakes, breakfasts and local dishes like nasi goreng and *bubur ayam* (Jakarta-style chicken with spicy peanut sauce) can also be ordered.

Cloud Lounge
LOUNGE

(Map p68; ☑ 021-2992 2450; www.cloudjakarta. com; 49th fl, The Plaza, Jl Thamrin; mains from 130,000Rp, cover varies; ☺ dining 6.30-11pm, lounge 4pm-2am Sun-Thu, to 3am Fri & Sat) Gourmet bites in a decadent dining room, flaming cocktails, an indoor-outdoor lounge with views of the entire city from the 49th floor of the Plaza tower – this hip spot is a mainstay on Jakarta's upscale night scene. Meals range from pasta and rice dishes to wagyu rib-eye. While 360-degree views are lure enough, there are also rotating DJs.

Immigrant
CLUB

(Map p68; ☑ 021-2992 4126; www.immigrant -jakarta.com; 6th fl, Plaza Indonesia, Jl Thamrin 28-30; mains from 80,000Rp, cover varies; ☺ 11am-1am Sun-Tue, to 4am Wed-Sat) By day this is a stylish art deco dining lounge high atop the trendy Plaza Indonesia (p81) mall. At night, the adjacent club serves crafted cocktails and imported wines and hosts top DJs (who mix R&B, hip hop and bubblegum rock). It attracts a glamorous local and expat crowd. Happy hour runs 4pm to 10pm with 25% off selected drinks.

🍷 Other Areas

★ Awan
BAR

(Map p74; ☑ 021-3193 6868; www.awanlounge. com; Kosenda Hotel, Jl KH Wahid Hasyim 127; ☺ 5pm-1am Sun-Thu, to 2am Fri & Sat) Set on the top floor of Kosenda Hotel, this lovely rooftop garden bar manages to be both understated and dramatic. There's a vertical garden, ample tree cover, plenty of private nooks flickering with candlelight and a vertigo-inducing glass skylight that plummets nine floors down.

Oetara
COFFEE

(Map p62; ☑ 0813 1485 5500; www.facebook. com/oetara.coffee; Jl Pluit Karang Barat 25A; menu items 45,000- 75,000Rp, coffee from 25,000Rp; ☺ 8am-10pm Mon-Fri, 9am-10pm Sat & Sun; 🛜) Cool, laid-back, bright neighbourhood coffee shop with marble tabletops, vintage chairs, tiled walls, hardwood floors and a chrome cage over the serving counter. All-day food options include organic granola, sesame chicken yakisoba salad, Mediterranean-style couscous and prawn-curry pasta. The coffee is super smooth. Nice terrace area too.

Ombé Kofie
COFFEE

(Map p62; ☑ 0811 175 1269; Jl Pluit Sakti 117; coffee from 30,000Rp; ☺ 8am-4.45pm Mon-Sat, 10am-4.45pm Sun; 🛜) In an affluent north Jakarta suburb, this cool little neighbourhood cafe offers pour-over coffees using beans sourced from across the archipelago. Patrons can sit on a stool at the bar and wax lyrical with the passionate baristas about all things java.

One Fifteenth Coffee
CAFE

(Map p62; ☑ 0812 9000 2128; www.1-15coffee.com; Jl Dr Kusuma Atmaja 79; ☺ 7am-9pm) Offering a glimpse into Jakarta's affluent class is this uberslick cafe. It was one of the city's first places to embrace the third-wave scene, using Indonesian and Ethiopian single-origin beans prepared using techniques such as Chemex, Kalita wave, Aeropress, V60, cold brew and French press.

☆ Entertainment

Compared to other large cities, Jakarta has fewer opportunities to enjoy live music and cultural performances. For jazz and classical music, watch for listings at top-end restaurants, hotel lounges or special events. However, the cinema experience is quite

JAKARTA FOR CHILDREN

On Jakarta's bayfront, **Ancol Luar Biasa** (Dreamland; Map p62; ☑ 021-2922 2222; www.ancol.com; Jl Pantai Indah; basic admission 25,000Rp; ⊗ 24hr; 🚼), the people's 'Dreamland', is a landscaped recreation complex popular with families. It has worn amusement rides, and sporting and leisure facilities, including bowling, but it gets crowded on weekends. Prime attractions include the **Pasar Seni** (art market), which has cafes, craft shops and art exhibitions.

The park also includes the **Gondola** (www.ancol.com/id/destinasi/gondola; Ancol Luar Biasa; Mon-Fri 55,000Rp, Sat & Sun 65,000Rp; ⊗ 11am-6pm Mon-Fri, 10am-6pm Sat, 9am-6pm Sun; 🚼) and the **Atlantis Water Adventure** (☑ 021-2922 2222; www.ancol.com; Ancol Luar Biasa; Mon-Fri 120,000Rp, Sat & Sun 175,000Rp; ⊗ 8am-6pm Mon-Fri, 7am-6pm Sat & Sun; 🚼) water-park complex, where there's a wave pool, water slides and a slide pool, plus artificial beaches. There's also the **Epic Cable Park** (Ancol Luar Biasa; 2hr incl equipment 300,000Rp; ⊗ 10am-6pm) wakeboarding course and the huge **Dunia Fantasi** (Fantasy Land; Map p62; ☑ 021-6471 2000; www.ancol.com; Ancol Luar Biasa; Mon-Fri 200,000Rp, Sat & Sun 295,000Rp; ⊗ 10am-6pm Mon-Fri, 9am-8pm Sat & Sun; 🚼) fun park, which includes various rides from roller coasters to bumper cars and big swings. There's also an 'Eco Park' with a deer enclosure and a zipline.

Marine mammal lovers be warned – **Seaworld Ancol** (www.ancol.com), with its controversial marine-life shows, lives here too (scientific studies are now providing incontestable evidence that keeping cetaceans in captivity for public entertainment is harmful to the animals).

The park is huge and taxis operate inside; if you plan on walking, give yourself enough time to get from one attraction to another. A free shuttle can be caught to and from the main attractions inside the park. If you want to stay and do it all again the following day, there's a **Mercure** (☑ 021-640 6000; Ancol Luar Biasa; r from 950,000Rp; 🅿 ❄ @ 🛜 ☲) hotel inside the park.

---

something: VIP multiscreen venues show Hollywood blockbusters in English (with Indonesian subtitles) and tickets are very cheap.

Taman Ismail Marzuki   PERFORMING ARTS
(TIM; Map p68; ☑ 021-3193 7530, 021-230 5146; http://tamanismailmarzuki.jakarta.go.id; Jl Cikini Raya 73) Jakarta's premier cultural centre has a great selection of cinemas, theatres and exhibition spaces. Performances (such as Sundanese dance and gamelan music events) are always high quality and the complex has a cafeteria too. Check the website for upcoming events.

CGV Grand Indonesia   CINEMA
(Map p68; ☑ 021-2358 0484; www.cgv.id; level 8, Grand Indonesia West Mall, Jl Thamrin 1; regular tickets 50,000Rp, gold/velvet class from 100,000Rp/220,000Rp) If you've never had a VIP cinema experience, this is the place to do it. Gold class has a premium lounge, reclining chairs and waiter service (you can buy drinks and snacks from your chair), while velvet class has actual beds, which fit two people. The complex also has virtual-reality headset booths and regular screens.

Kinosaurus Jakarta   CINEMA
(Map p70; www.kinosaurusjakarta.com; Jl Kemang Raya 8B; tickets 50,000Rp; ⊗ screenings usually 7pm & 9.30pm Fri, 4.30pm & 7pm Sat & Sun) Walk through the Aksara bookshop, then rub shoulders with Jakarta's artistic community at this hidden cinema, which hosts independent short and fringe films from around Indonesia and the world. Most are either in English or have English subtitles, but there are exceptions. Check the website for details of upcoming movies.

Nautilus   LIVE MUSIC
(Map p70; ☑ 021-2277 1888; www.fourseasons.com/jakarta/dining/lounges/nautilus-bar; Four Seasons Hotel, Capital Pl, Jl Jendral Gatot Subroto Kav 18, Kuningan Barat; cocktails from 175,000Rp; ⊗ noon-1am) Nautilus is a bold, classic European-versus-Asian-bling drinking lounge at the Four Seasons hotel. Upon entering, you're drawn to the striking mural of the historic Sunda Kelapa (p66) port behind the bar. There's live music (ranging from singers to jazz musicians, soul musicians and pianists) between 6pm and 9pm Tuesday to Saturday.

🛍 Shopping

Besides the gaggle of enclosed malls, South Jakarta has oodles of interesting shops. As always, you'll find a fine selection for browsing along the streets of Kemang. For bargains, check out the huge buildings filled with vendors at **Blok M** (Map p70; 📞 021-726 0170; http://malblokm.com; Jl Melawi; ⊙ 10am-10pm), plus the hip booths at Pasar Santa.

🛍 South Jakarta

★ Aksara
BOOKS

((ak.'sa.ra); Map p70; 📞 021-719 9288; www. facebook.com/AksaraStore; Jl Kemang Raya 8; ⊙ 10am-10pm) A wide selection of books (many in English) plus fine stationery and writing accessories make this hip hang-out a must-stop for anyone interested in words on paper. There's a small cafe serving coffee and cakes, plus a workshop offering various creative classes including sessions in pottery and art (enquire within about schedules).

★ dia.lo.gue artspace
ART

(Map p70; 📞 021-719 9671; https://dialogue-art space.com; Jl Kemang Selatan 99; ⊙ 10am-10pm; 🛜) Contemporary art exhibitions, stylish designer goods, books, old travel posters and good coffee all come together in this chic space. Bare concrete and glass are an ideal backdrop for the captivating variety here. Those who want to hang out longer stop at the trendy cafe on site – it serves brekkie, pasta, Asian plates and other mains (dishes 49,000Rp to 80,000Rp).

★ Pasar Santa
MARKET

(Map p70; Jl Cipaku I; ⊙ daily, hours vary) On the 2nd floor of a rundown old-school mall you'll find Jakarta's hipster entrepreneurs. Dozens of individual booths sell everything from retro psychedelic clothing and vinyl to handmade jewellery, cakes, skateboards and micro-roasted coffee. Many stalls don't open till after lunch, so aim to come around 3pm. The food vendors are another reason to visit, including tasty noodles at Mie Chino (p75).

Tulisan
GIFTS & SOUVENIRS

(Map p70; 📞 021-7278 0235; www.tulisan.com; ground fl, City Walk, Darmawangsa Sq, Jl Darmawangsa 9; ⊙ 9am-9pm) Tulisan is an Indonesian accessories label that specialises in brightly coloured illustrated prints and is best known for its playful canvas tote bags. The flagship store is a wonderful place for gifts, stocking a plentiful selection of quirky wall-hangings, illustrated paper goods, homewares and other oddities. Every single product is handcrafted.

🛍 Cikini & Menteng

★ Bartele Gallery
MAPS

(Map p68; 📞 021-2993 8997; www.bartelegallery. com; Mandarin Oriental Hotel, Jl Thamrin; ⊙ 11am-8pm) On the 1st floor of the Mandarin Oriental Hotel, a treasure trove of antique maps awaits at this compact shop. Prints, some dating back 500 years, are also displayed. Look for originals drawn by explorers to document their discoveries. Photos from the 19th century and a smattering of antiques round out your visit.

Pasar Jl Surabaya
MARKET

(Map p68; Jl Surabaya; ⊙ 8am-5pm) Jakarta's famous street market is in Menteng. It has woodcarvings, furniture, textiles, jewellery, old vinyl records and many (dubious) antiques from nautical memorabilia to vintage kitchen items. Bargain like crazy.

Plaza Indonesia
MALL

(Map p68; www.plazaindonesia.com; Jl Thamrin 28-30; ⊙ 10am-10pm; 🛜) This high-end mall is centrally located and offers a wide selection of stores, including leading Indonesian boutiques and the likes of Cartier and Louis Vuitton. In the basement there's an excellent, inexpensive food court. It rivals the Grand Indonesia mall nearby for top-end cred.

Grand Indonesia
MALL

(Map p68; www.grand-indonesia.com; Jl Thamrin; ⊙ 10am-10pm) This luxury mall contains a plethora of upscale fashion outlets, plus high-street favourites like Uniqlo and Zara. There are also a number of good local and international restaurants, and a multiscreen cinema. It sprawls over eight marble-clad floors.

🛍 Other Areas

Pasar Senen Jaya
MALL

(Map p68; 📞 021-422 2525; Jl Pasar Senen; ⊙ 7am-5pm) The mall to the masses, this huge complex has myriad shops and vendors selling just about every day-to-day item imaginable. Cheap shoes, batik clothes, homewares, toys – the list goes on and on. In the mornings, throngs of bakers on the southeast side sell fresh sweets.

ℹ Information

DANGERS & ANNOYANCES

Although some foreign embassies warn against travel to Indonesia, and especially Jakarta, overall there's little risk for travellers. For such a huge city with obvious social problems, it is surprisingly safe.

➡ Exercise more caution after dark late at night in Glodok and Kota, where there are some seedy clubs and bars.

➡ Robberies by taxi drivers have been known to take place, so always opt for reputable firms and app-booking services such as the citywide Bluebird group, Grab or Go-Jek.

➡ Jakarta's buses and trains can be crowded, particularly during rush hours, and this is when pickpockets ply their trade.

MEDIA

Jakarta Globe (www.thejakartaglobe.com) Originally printed as an excellent daily newspaper, with 48 pages of stylish layout, quality reporting and illuminating features, but it's now solely online. The Jakarta coverage is still good though.

Jakarta Post (www.thejakartapost.com) English-language broadsheet with news, views and cultural content.

MEDICAL SERVICES

Cikini Hospital (Map p68; ☑ emergency 021-3899 7744, urgent care 021-3899 7777; www.rscikini.com; Jl Raden Saleh Raya 40) Caters to foreigners and has English-speaking staff.

SOS Medika Klinik (Map p70; ☑ 021-750 5980, emergency 021-750 6001; www.internationalsos.co.id/sos-medika/cipete; Jl Puri Sakti 10, Cipete; ☺ 24hr emergency treatment, clinic 7am-10pm) Offers English-speaking GP appointments, dental care, and emergency and specialist healthcare services. Also has a clinic in **Kuningan** (Map p70; ☑ 021-5794 8600; www.internationalsos.com; 2nd fl, Menara Prima Bldg, Jl Dr Ide Anak Agung Gde Agung, Kuningan; ☺ 8am-6pm Mon-Fri, to 2pm Sat).

POST

Smaller branches are common. International service is somewhat reliable.

Main Post Office (Gedung Pos Ibukota; Map p68; Jl Gedung Kesenian I; ☺ 7.30am-7pm Mon-Fri, to 1pm Sat)

TOURIST INFORMATION

Jakarta Visitor Information Office (Map p74; ☑ 021-316 1293, 021-315 4094; www.jakarta-tourism.go.id; Jl KH Wahid Hasyim 9; ☺ 8am-4pm) Private, very helpful tourism agency. Staff can book tours, flights and hotels (helpful as transport providers often require a local bankcard). Also has a desk at the airport.

WEBSITES

What's New Jakarta (www.whatsnewjakarta.com) Good general-interest site featuring events and openings around town.

Living in Indonesia (www.expat.or.id) Geared at longer-term visitors; everything from restaurant reviews and visa information to chat rooms.

Jakarta.go.id (www.jakarta-tourism.go.id) The Jakarta City Government Tourism Office's official site; listings including transport and events.

JakChat (www.jakchat.com) English-language forums where you can discuss everything from bars to politics.

Jakarta 100 Bars (www.jakarta100bars.com) A no-holds-barred website that trolls through Jakarta's ever-changing nightlife action.

Lonely Planet (www.lonelyplanet.com/indonesia/jakarta) Destination information, hotel bookings, traveller forum and more.

ℹ Getting There & Away

Jakarta is the main international gateway to Indonesia. It's a hub for domestic and international flights as well as train services from across Java. Though train travel is the preferred choice for many, bus routes also radiate out in all directions, and there are even some boat services.

Flights, cars and tours can be booked online at lonelyplanet.com/bookings.

AIR

Soekarno-Hatta International Airport (CGK; www.soekarnohatta-airport.co.id; Tangerang City) is 35km west of the city centre. All international flights and most domestic flights operate from CGK. Surging passenger numbers mean that it can get chaotic, so give yourself plenty of time for formalities.

There are three terminals, each with a full range of facilities, such as ATMs, information desks and exchange counters. It's vital to confirm which terminal your flight will depart from as terminals are not close to each other. A free shuttle service operates between the three terminals.

Terminal 1 The hub for many domestic flights.

Terminal 2 Used for both international and domestic flights.

Terminal 3 The hub for international flights.

Halim Perdana Kusuma Airport (HLP; www.halimperdanakusuma-airport.co.id) is 11km south of Jakarta's Cikini district. It has a limited domestic service.

BOAT

Pelni shipping services operate on sporadic schedules to ports all over the archipelago. The **Pelni ticketing office** (Map p68; ☑ 021-162; www.pelni.co.id; Jl Gajah Mada 14; ⊙ 8am-4.30pm Mon-Fri) is 1.5km northwest of the Monumen Nasional in central Jakarta.

Pelni ships all arrive at and depart from Pelabuhan Satu (dock No 1) at Tanjung Priok, 13km northeast of the city centre. Transjakarta *koridor* (busway lines) 10 and 12 provide a direct bus link. Single fares start at 2000Rp; routes and bus arrivals vary wildly depending on traffic. A Grab from central Jakarta costs around 50,000Rp, a taxi starts from around 80,000Rp.

BUS

The city's main bus terminals are **Kampung Rambutan** (Map p62; Rambutan) (serving all Java and beyond, reached via Transjakarta bus line 7); **Pulogadung** (Jl Raya Bekasi; ☎) (for Sumatra among other destinations, reached via bus lines 2 or 4); **Lebak Bulus** (Map p62; Jl Lebak Bulus Raya) (for Yogya and Semarang, reached via bus line 8) and **Kalideres** (Jl Daan Mogot) (of less use to visitors). All are a long way from the city centre. The Transjakarta busway (p84) to these terminals uses bus lanes; a car journey can take hours in traffic. Tickets (some including travel to the terminals) for the better buses can be bought from agencies (like www.redbus.id/en or www.easybook.com). Note that train travel is a faster, safer, more comfortable and often cheaper option.

MINIBUS

Door-to-door *travel* minibuses (shared cars or vans) are not a good option in Jakarta because it can take hours to pick up or drop off passengers in the traffic jams. Unless you've the patience of a saint, take a train, plane or bus.

Day Trans (Map p74; ☑ 0855 855 6767, 021-2967 6767; www.daytrans.co.id; Jl Thamrin; ⊙ 6am-8pm) minibuses to Bandung (110,000Rp, hourly); keep an eye out for sales on its website.

CAR & MOTORCYCLE

Renting a car via **Grab** (www.grab.com) is a good option for the day if you're exploring outside the city limits (it's around 700,000Rp for the whole day including petrol). Toll roads radiate out from Jakarta; these are much faster but cost extra on top of your pre-paid fee. Go-Jek (p84) motorcycles are also a cheap option and may take you beyond the city limits. Negotiate with your driver.

TRAIN

Jakarta's four main train stations are quite central. Schedules (www.kereta-api.co.id) run to cities around Jakarta and across Java, and train travel is the most convenient way to leave the city. You can also book via booking agencies Tiket (https://en.tiket.com) and Traveloka (www.traveloka.com/en), and can even get a train–ferry–bus connection to Bali. Fares are cheap, so it can be worth buying the best available class of service.

Gambir (Map p68; Jl Medan Merdeka Timur 1) is the most convenient and important of Jakarta's train stations. It's on the eastern side of Merdeka Square, a 15-minute walk from Jl Jaksa. It handles express trains to Bandung, Yogyakarta, Solo, Semarang, Malang and Surabaya. It is a well-run and modern facility with full services and a good place to buy tickets. **Jakarta Kota** (Map p65; Jl Asemka) is an art deco gem in its namesake neighbourhood. It has limited services and commuter trains to greater Jakarta areas and Bogor. **Pasar Senen** (Map p62; Jl Bungur Besar) to the east mostly has economy-class trains to the east and south. **Tanah Abang** (THB; Jl Jati Baru Raya) has economy trains to the west.

To Bandung

There are frequent services from Gambir to Bandung along a scenic hilly track, but be sure to book in advance (especially on weekends and public holidays). Comfortable Argo Parahyangan services depart daily (economy/executive from 100,000/140,000Rp, 3¼ hours) between 5.05am and 11.20pm.

To Bogor

Commuter trains leave from Jakarta Kota station to Bogor (6000Rp to 16,000Rp, one hour) roughly hourly. All trains are horribly crowded during rush hours.

To Yogyakarta & Solo

From Gambir there are several daily exclusive-class trains (285,000Rp to 450,000Rp, 7½ to eight hours) to Yogyakarta, leaving between 8am and 9.15pm; some continue to Solo, one hour further on.

To Surabaya

There are three daily exclusive-class trains between Gambir station and Surabaya (375,000Rp to 500,000Rp, nine to 10½ hours) and three economy trains from Pasar Senen (105,000Rp to 270,000Rp, 11¼ hours).

ⓘ Getting Around

TO/FROM THE AIRPORTS

Soekarno-Hatta International Airport (CGK) A toll road links CGK to the city; the journey takes 45 minutes to two hours depending on traffic and the final destination. Taxis cost around 220,000Rp to central Jakarta. A new train service (one way 70,000Rp, 45 minutes, every 20 minutes from 6.20am to 11.20pm)

JAVA JAKARTA

running from the airport to **BNI City Station** (Sudirman; Map p68; www.railink.co.id; Jl Stasiun Sudirman Baru) in central Jakarta is now complete. Otherwise Damri buses run to major train stations and cost 40,000Rp.

Halim Perdana Kusuma Airport (HLP) Not served well by public transport. A taxi to central Jakarta costs 120,000Rp. At the time of research, planning was underway for an express train to connect CGK with HLP.

BUS

Transjakarta is a network of air-conditioned buses that run on reserved busways (designated lanes that are closed to all other traffic). They are the quickest way to get around the city.

One of the most useful routes is *koridor* (busway line) 1, which runs north to Kota, past Monas and along Jl Sudirman. Stations display maps (www.transjakarta.co.id/peta-rute).

Most busways have been constructed in the centre of existing highways, and stations have been positioned at roughly 1km intervals. Access is via elevated walkways and each station has a shelter. Fifteen *koridor* are up and running.

Fares cost 3500Rp to 9000Rp, which covers any destination in the network (regardless of how many *koridor* you use). Payment is via a stored-value card (40,000Rp, including 20,000Rp credit), which is available from station ticket windows. Note that you can share the card with others, so there's no need to purchase more than one if travelling in a group.

Most buses run from 5am to 10pm and are often very crowded. Also during rush hour, some vehicles are diverted onto the busways, which clogs progress.

There are seven 24-hour bus services – *koridor* 1, 9, 3, 2, 5, 8 and 10. Their frequency is (in theory) between 30 minutes and 60 minutes, traffic permitting.

Schedules vary greatly – it's best to leave extra time for every journey. Buses very rarely run to schedule, due to traffic.

CAR & MOTORCYCLE

➔ Major international car-rental firms have offices at the airport and in the city.

➔ Most people opt for a car with a driver, who can navigate Jakarta's chaotic and poorly marked streets. These can be arranged through your hotel (from 500,000Rp to 700,000Rp per day) or via the Grab (p83) app. Fuel, but not tolls or parking, is included in the price.

➔ In an effort to curb the sclerotic traffic, cars with odd and even licence plate numbers are banned from entering the city on alternative days.

➔ With suitable bravery, you can hop on a motorcycle and join Jakarta's traffic, but it is not for the inexperienced. A better option is to grab a **Go-Jek** (☏ 021-725 1110; www.go-jek.com) or Grab (p83) bike. Both companies operate an app-based *ojek* (motorbike) service and provide helmets. A short ride will be about 25,000Rp.

TAXI

Ride-hailing companies Grab and Gojek both offer a reliable and remarkably cheap means of getting around town, either by air-conditioned car or motorbike taxi (helmet provided). Order and manage your rides through the apps.

Standard taxis are also inexpensive. All are metered and flagfall is 7500Rp, costing around 300Rp for each subsequent 100m after the first kilometre. By far the safest and most reliable taxis are run by **Blue Bird** (☏ 021-794 1234; www.bluebirdgroup.com); they can be found cruising, at cab stands and at many hotels. Order one using its handy app.

Tipping is greatly appreciated.

TRAIN

The **Jakarta MRT** (☏ 021-390 6454; www.jakartamrt.co.id) runs along a spine in the north from Kampung Bandan (via Jl Thamrin and Blok M) to Lebak Bulus in the south. The first section of the **Jakarta LRT** (www.lrtjakarta.co.id) runs from East Jakarta to the north of the city, a route more suitable for local commuters than tourists.

TUK-TUK

Tuk-tuks are everywhere in central Jakarta. They're often a little faster than other modes of transport, due to being able to negotiate small gaps in the traffic. However, they can be inconvenient to use, as fares need to be negotiated, and tourists can end up paying more than the price of a metered taxi.

THOUSAND ISLANDS

☏ 021 / POP 21,000

A string of 130 palm-fringed islands in the Jakarta Bay, the Thousand Islands (Pulau Seribu) offer white-sand beaches and calm, clear seas (aside from the islands closest to the mainland, which are plagued by trash). Although they're hardly a match for many of Indonesia's other dream isles, they're certainly a welcome break from the polluted air of Jakarta. Most visitors to the archipelago are concrete-jungle-fleeing Jakartans and expats, and because of this, the Thousand Islands are expensive by Indonesian standards.

Several islands have been developed into resorts with bungalows and water sports. Pulau Pramuka is the group's district centre, but most people live on Pulau Kelapa. Pulau Panjang has the only airstrip on the islands.

You can book island trips at Ancol Marina, which sits within a large resort and amusement-park complex, or book via the Jakarta Visitor Information Office (p82).

🛏 Sleeping

It's wise to book all accommodation in advance as getting from one island to another to check out different hotels is difficult and costly.

**Tiger Islands Village
& Eco Resort**   RESORT $$$
(☑0878 8234 1314, 0812 9753 1395; www.pulau
macan.com; Pulau Macan; cabins per person incl full board from 2,229,000Rp) 🏊 A couple of glittering tropical dots in the ocean host this delightful, upmarket eco-resort. This beachside retreat uses recycled rainwater, solar panels and nature-friendly products. It may not be cheap, but the experience and location are special, and there is good snorkelling offshore.

Pulau Bidadari Resort   RESORT $$$
(☑021-6471 3173; www.pulaubidadariecoresort.
com; Pulau Bidadari; s/d per person incl full board from 985,000/1,605,000Rp) The closest of the resorts to Jakarta and handy as a base for visiting other nearby islands such as Pulau Kahyangan, Pulau Kelor (which has the ruins of an old Dutch fort) or Pulau Onrust (where the remains of an 18th-century shipyard can be explored). Otherwise, the beaches are filthy and the simple cottages run-down. It can be booked directly at Ancol Marina.

❶ Getting There & Away

The resorts have daily speedboats from Jakarta's **Ancol Marina** (☑021-6471 1822; Taman Impian Jaya Ancol) for guests and day trippers, usually leaving between 8am and 11am and returning between 2pm and 5pm, with additional services on weekends. Some are just a 30-minute ride away, but the furthest islands take around two hours or more to reach. Return day-trip rates to the resorts with lunch include Pulau Bidadari (400,000Rp) and Pulau Macan (750,000Rp).

Locals will ferry you from one island to the next (but this can be pricey). Most islands are small enough to easily explore on foot and some have bikes for hire.

WEST JAVA

Many tourists only experience the lush, volcanic panoramas of West Java (Jawa Barat) through the murky window of a lumbering bus or train, but this dramatic, diverse region has plenty to detain the inquisitive traveller who enjoys breaking away from the standard Java traveller circuit. Historically, it's known as Sunda, and its people and language are Sundanese.

West Java stretches from the remote islands of the Ujung Kulon National Park (last Javan home of the one-horned rhino) in the west to the sweeping beaches of Pangandaran in the east. In between, you can visit the infamous offshore volcano of Krakatau; surf in the chilled coastal resorts, Cimaja and Batu Karas; experience local culture in Cianjur; and stroll through Bogor's lush botanical gardens. It's also the most densely populated region in the entire country, and road travel can be exasperatingly slow going as a result.

❶ Getting There & Away

Jakarta is, needless to say, the main entry point to the wonders of West Java. Flights come into Jakarta from across the country and across the world. Bandung offers a (marginally) less chaotic entry point with a fair few domestic and international flights using this city's airport.

A romantic way of arriving in West Java is by boat, and there are frequent ferries linking Java and Sumatra as well as Pelni ships leaving Jakarta for distant Indonesian dots.

Banten

☑0254 / POP 10,000

Once set on the edge of a lush network of rice fields, the fishing town of Banten was a great maritime capital, where the Dutch and English first landed in Java to secure trade and struggle for economic supremacy. After many years floating in obscurity, Banten and surrounding towns (including nearby sprawling Serang) are today becoming major ports and virtual Jakarta suburbs. If nothing else Banten is a perfect example of warp-speed, globalised development, as what's left of this once ever-green breadbasket gets gobbled up, one shovelful at a time.

The chief landmark of Banten is the 16th-century mosque **Mesjid Agung** (Jl Masjid Agung Banten) **FREE**, which was once a good example of early Islamic architecture; its great white octagonal minaret was

West Java

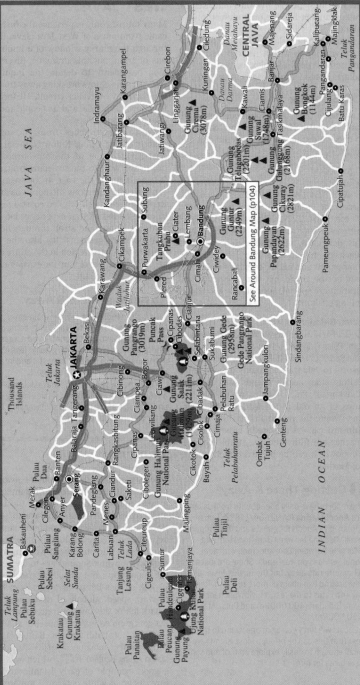

See Around Bandung Map (p104)

reputedly designed by a Chinese Muslim. More recent renovations however, means it no longer carries quite the same historical gravitas.

❶ Getting There & Away

Take a bus from Jakarta's Kalideres bus terminal to Serang (30,000Rp, 1½ hours), 10km south of Banten, from where a minibus (12,000Rp, 20 minutes) will drop you near the Mesjid Agung.

Merak

📞 0254

Right on the northwestern tip of Java, Merak is an ugly port town and the terminus for ferries shuttling to south Sumatra. For decades there's been talk of a bridge connecting Java and Sumatra here, and in 2007 the ambitious project finally got the go-ahead only for the idea to be shelved again in 2014 before any construction work had started. So, for the foreseeable future, travel between the two islands will continue to be by boat – a far more romantic way of arriving or departing Java, we think. Merak is 140km from Jakarta.

❶ Getting There & Away

The **bus terminal** and **train station** are at the **ferry dock**.

Ferries to Bakauheni in Sumatra depart every 30 minutes, 24 hours a day. Foot passengers pay 15,000Rp and cars are 350,000Rp. The journey takes about two hours. Fast boats (41,000Rp, 45 minutes) also make this crossing, but they don't run in heavy seas. The through-buses to Bandarlampung are the easiest option.

Frequent buses make the run between Merak and Jakarta (100,000Rp to 130,000Rp, 2½ hours). Most go to the capital's Kalideres bus terminal, but buses also run to/from Jakarta's Pulo Gadung and Kampung Rambutan. Other buses run all over Java, including Bogor (150,000Rp) and Bandung (160,000Rp to 200,000Rp). For Labuan (30,000Rp), a change at Cilegon is required.

There are also infrequent trains (7000Rp) to Jakarta, which have economy-class carriages only.

Carita

📞 0253 / POP 7000

An easy trip from Jakarta and other massive West Java urban areas, Carita is a different world, with rising jade hills clumped with palms and laced with green rivers. The sandy beach crashes with one small (and very inconsistent) surf break, **Karang Bolong**, and the area is popular with weekenders from Jakarta. However, despite the easy appeal to frazzled city types, most travellers give the place a miss unless they're headed to Krakatau or the Ujung Kulon National Park.

⭐ Tours

Virtually everyone in town is peddling a Krakatau tour. Travel agencies, including **Java Rhino** (📞 0812 1275 2333; www.krakatoatour.com; Jl Raya Carita), can organise trips. Check your tour boat first as waves can be rough, and make sure it has a radio and life-jackets on board.

Day trips to Krakatau start at 2,500,000Rp after bargaining. Trips to Ujung Kulon start at 6,250,000Rp for a three-day tour.

🛏 Sleeping & Eating

Most of the hotels are aimed more at domestic tourists, and quality can seem quite low compared to similar-priced places elsewhere in Java. Rates increase on weekends by about 20% at most places.

Sunset View HOTEL $
(📞 0253-801 075; www.augusta-ind.com; Jl Raya Carita; r with fan from 225,000Rp, with air-con 295,000Rp; ❋🛜❄) This centrally located hotel on the inland side of the coastal road offers large, clean rooms. The restaurant downstairs serves Indonesian grub. Rates rise by about 20% at weekends.

Archipelago HOTEL $$$
(📞 0253-880 888; www.archipelago-carita.com; Jl Raya Carita Km10; r from 600,000Rp, cottages from 1,500,000Rp; ❋🛜❄) Nest in a cool Torajan-style cottage or smaller, modern 'Jakarta rooms' right on the beach; this is the nicest choice in Carita. It has a beautiful pool (though not as nice as the huge natural one out front!) and views of fishing platforms, but no restaurant. Rates rise around 25% at weekends.

❶ Getting There & Away

To get to Carita from Jakarta, take a bus to Labuan and then an *angkot* to Carita (10,000Rp to 15,000Rp). On weekends allow extra time for the journey.

GUNUNG KRAKATAU

On 22 December 2018, Gunung Krakatau blew its top. In fact it erupted so forcefully it blew itself almost out of existence. According to the Indonesian Centre for Volcanology, the original 338m-high volcano is now reduced to only 110m and is no longer visible from the Java mainland. The collapse of the cone into the sea triggered a massive tsunami, killing over 200 people in the Sunda Strait, between Java and Sumatra. The victims were taken by surprise as tsunami warnings are generally generated by an earthquake, not by the disintegration of landmass.

Of course, this is not the first time Krakatau has erupted. Located 50km from the West Java coast and 40km from Sumatra, the volcanic mass has been volatile for the past two centuries. Regarded by 17th- and 18-century mariners as a mere nautical landmark in the narrow Selat Sunda, the volcano sprang to life in the 19th century with an eruption (on 27 August 1883) so explosive that on the island of Rodriguez, more than 4600km to the southwest, a police chief reported hearing the booming of heavy guns. On that occasion, Krakatau sent up a column of ash 80km high and threw into the air nearly 20 cubic kilometres of rock. Ash fell on Singapore 840km to the north and on ships as far as 6000km away; darkness covered Selat Sunda from 10am on 27 August until dawn the next day.

Even more destructive were the great ocean waves Krakatau triggered. A tsunami more than 40m high swept over the nearby shores of Java and Sumatra, and the wave's passage reached Aden (on the Arabian Peninsula). Coastal Java and Sumatra were devastated: 165 villages were destroyed and more than 36,000 people were killed. The following day a telegram sent to Singapore from Batavia (160km east of Krakatau) reported odd details such as 'dizzy' fish that were easy to catch; for three years ash clouds circled the earth, creating spectacular sunsets.

Throughout the 20th century, the inner cone called Anak Krakatau, meaning 'Child of Krakatau', grew at the rate of 7m per year through fits and starts of lava flow. The astonishing return of life to the devastated islands has been the subject of intense scientific study. Not a single plant was found on Krakatau a few months after the 1883 event, but a century later the vegetation appeared undisturbed. It remains to be seen how much of the flora and fauna will have survived the current eruption, but it seems clear that Krakatau's role in reshaping the landscape of the straits is not over yet.

Labuan

☑ 0253 / POP 49,200

The dreary little port of Labuan is merely a jumping-off point for Carita or for Ujung Kulon National Park, but it is home to the helpful **Labuan PHKA office** (☑ 0253-801731; www.ujungkulon.org; Jl Perintis Kemerdekaan 51; ◎ 8am-4pm Mon-Fri), located 2km north of town towards Carita (look for the rhino statue).

The **Tanjung Lesung Bay Villas** (☑ 021-572 7345; http://tanjunglesung.com; cottages from 800,000Rp) is an inviting resort with individual cottages, all of which are a little different from one another, although wooden furnishings and colourful flourishes are universal. Some rooms have cool, semi-outdoor showers. Perhaps more of a highlight than the rooms are the gardens loaded with coconut trees that centre around a pool and the delicious beach out front (reasonable snorkelling too).

It's not actually in Labuan itself, but on the opposite side of the horseshoe bay to the south and about a 40km drive from Labuan town itself. Ideally you need private transport to get there from Labuan.

Frequent buses depart from Kalideres bus terminal in Jakarta for Labuan (50,000Rp, 3½ hours). Regular buses also operate between Labuan and Bogor (50,000Rp, four hours). *Angkots* for Carita (5000Rp, 30 minutes) leave from the market, 100m from the Labuan bus terminal.

Ujung Kulon National Park

On the remote southwestern tip of Java, this Unesco World Heritage–listed **national park** (www.ujungkulon.org; 150,000-225,000Rp) has remained an outpost of prime rainforest and untouched wilderness, virgin beaches and healthy coral reefs. Relatively inaccessible, Indonesia's first national park is visited by few people, but it is one of the most rewarding in all Java.

The national park also includes the nearby island of Panaitan (where Captain James Cook anchored *HMS Endeavour* in 1771) and the smaller offshore islands of Peucang and Handeuleum. Much of the peninsula is dense lowland rainforest and a mixture of scrub, grassy plains, swamps, pandanus palms and long stretches of sandy beach on the west and south coasts.

Most people visit Ujung Kulon on a tour organised through an agency, but it's also possible to head to Tamanjaya village and access the park from there or to make arrangements directly through the park office in Labuan.

☞ Tours

Tours can be set up in Tamanjaya itself, with the park office in Labuan or via more expensive Carita tour agencies. Basically you can either walk or boat it into the park; there are no roads. Either way, you must have a guide.

Factor in food costs (around 50,000Rp per day, per person), your guide (150,000Rp per day) and tent rental (around 100,000Rp per trip). Bring along lightweight food, such as packaged noodles, and drinking water if you are hiking; otherwise food can be organised by tour operators or the park wardens. Supplies are available in Tamanjaya, but in Sumur and Labuan there is far more choice. Boat trips are much more expensive as the boat hire costs from 3,000,000Rp per day depending on boat type and destination.

If you'd rather get organised in advance, book through the park office in Labuan. A three-day/two-night all-inclusive tour costs about 8,000,000Rp (for two people). This includes return road and sea transport on a wooden boat, accommodation inside the national park, snorkelling, canoeing, hiking and meals. You'll pay double for a much more comfortable and faster speedboat.

Surf packages are also available to Panaitan; Bali-based **Surf Panaitan** (☏0852 1644 8250; www.surfpanaitan.com) charges from US$900 for a seven-day trip.

🏃 Activities

Few corners of Java offer such potential for truly wild, off-the-beaten-track jungle hiking and beach lounging, but you need to be well prepared.

A three-day hike across to the west coast via beaches and river crossings and on to

Pulau Peucang is very popular, but there are decent alternatives, including a route that takes in good coastal scenery and the lighthouse at Tanjung Layar, the westernmost tip of mainland Java. Or, for wildlife viewing, you can set up a series of day hikes in Tamanjaya.

Pulau Peucang, which can only be reached by chartered boat, is one of the more popular destinations in the park thanks to it having good accommodation. Peucang also has beautiful white-sand beaches and coral reefs on its sheltered eastern coast (snorkelling gear is available).

Pulau Handeuleum, which is ringed by mangroves, is less commonly visited. It has some Timor deer but doesn't have Peucang's attractions. Canoes can be hired (50,000Rp) for the short cruise up a jungle river.

Large **Pulau Panaitan** is more expensive to reach but has some fine beaches and hiking. It's a day's walk between the PHKA posts at Legon Butun and Legon Haji, or you can walk to the top of Gunung Raksa, topped by a Hindu statue of Ganesh. Panaitan is a legendary surfing spot, with breaks including the infamous One Palm Point, a left-hand barrel that spins over a sharp reef.

🛏 Sleeping

Advance bookings are recommended for Pulau Peucang and Handeuleum, particularly at weekends; contact the Labuan PHKA office. Within the park, you can camp or stay at the primitive huts for a small fee.

Tamanjaya village, the main gateway to the park, has budget accommodation and guides.

Sunda Jaya Homestay   GUESTHOUSE **$**
(☏0818 0618 1209; http://sundajaya.blogspot. com; Tamanjaya; r per person 150,000-200,000Rp; meals 30,000-50,000Rp; 🛜) This Tamanjaya guesthouse was orginially built by the World Wildlife Fund and has four simple, clean rooms, each with two single beds and mosquito nets. Bathrooms are shared. Good meals are offered and there's free tea and coffee. The genial owner is an expert on the national park and can organise guides and supplies.

★ Niki Peucang Lodge   LODGE **$$**
(☏0811 6112 772; Pulau Peucang; d full board from 549,000Rp; ❄) If you want to get away from it all, this wonderful spot is the place to come. Surprisingly smart given its remote location, it has a good restaurant and absolute peace

UJUNG KULON'S CLAIMS TO FAME

Ujung Kulon is best known for two things: surfing and being the last refuge of the one-horned Javan rhinoceros.

The one-horned Javan rhinoceros was once the most widespread of Asian rhino species, occurring across a great swath of SE Asia, India and China. Due to persecution, poaching and habitat loss, it's today one of the globe's most critically endangered large mammals – there are estimated to be between 55 and 61 remaining, all right here.

Numbers are thought to be stable and the rhinos are breeding; however, they are an extremely rare sight. You are far more likely to come across *banteng* (wild cattle), wild pigs, otters, deer, squirrels, leaf monkeys, gibbons and big monitor lizards. Leopards also live in the forest and crocodiles in the river estuaries. Green turtles nest in some of the bays and the bird life is excellent.

Not all visitors to the park come for the wildlife, though. Panaitan Island is home to several incredible surf breaks. Best known of these is the infamous **One Palm Point**. At first glance, this mesmerising left-hander, which barrels in perfect form for hundreds of metres down the side of the island, appears to be the world's most perfect wave. And 99% of the time there's barely another surfer around, and that's because this beauty comes with a very severe sting in its tail. Even at high tide, the wave breaks over razor-sharp, live coral in water depths that can be measured in centimetres. The wave itself is so long and fast that it's almost impossible to outrun it, with the result that you *will* get violently thrown across that reef. This is one surf spot that is reserved only for the absolute best surfers and even then most people wear full wetsuits and helmets for safety. There are other waves here as well, but almost all of them are equally unforgiving. Do not even consider coming here to surf unless you are of a very high standard.

and quiet. The attractive, air-conditioned bungalows offer hot-water bathrooms and comfortable beds.

There are some divine stretches of sand nearby, wild jungle walks, and barking deer, monkeys and wild boar frequently wander in and out of view of the lodge. The deer sometimes even go for a paddle in the sea!

Pulau Handeuleum Lodge　　　LODGE $$
(www.ujungkulon.org; Pulau Handeuleum; r 250,000Rp) Set in a coconut grove, this lodge has been recently renovated and has six simple double rooms with fans. There's a kitchen, but you must bring your own food, as the island has no other dining options. You also must charter a boat from Tamanjaya (3,500,000Rp, one hour) to get here.

❶ Information

The Labuan PHKA office (p88) is a useful source of information. You pay your entry fee when you enter the park, at the park office in Tamanjaya or on the islands. Hikers should try to pick up a copy of the excellent (but rarely available) *Visitor's Guidebook to the Trails of Ujung Kulon National Park* (50,000Rp) from the park office.

The best time to visit Ujung Kulon is in the dry season (April to October), when the sea is generally calm and the reserve less boggy. Malaria has been reported in Ujung Kulon.

❶ Getting There & Away

From Labuan there's one direct bus to Tamanjaya (50,000Rp, 3½ hours) daily at noon. There are also hourly *angkots* as far as Sumur (35,000Rp, two hours) until around 4pm. From Sumur, an *ojek* to Tamanjaya is about 30,000Rp.

The road between Sumur and Tamanjaya is usually in very poor shape, particularly during rainy season.

You may also charter a boat to get here from Carita, Labuan or Sumur. Given the long stretch of open sea, fork out for a decent one. Speedboats are double the price of the wooden relics but worth it. Surf tours use their own transport.

Bogor

📱 0251 / POP 1.1 MILLION

'A romantic little village' is how Sir Thomas Stamford Raffles described Bogor when he made it his country home during the British interregnum. As an oasis of unpredictable weather – it is credited with 322 thunderstorms a year – cool, quiet Bogor was the chosen retreat of colonials escaping the stifling, crowded capital.

Things have changed a little since then, and today the long arm of Jakarta reaches the whole way to Bogor, meaning this satellite city experiences the overspill of the capital's perennial traffic and air-quality problems. Despite the relentless pull of 'development', the world-class botanical gardens that sit right in the heart of the city would still put a smile on the face of any old colonialists and more than justify a day trip from Jakarta. The city is also a handy base for a number of interesting attractions in the nearby green and lush countryside.

Remember to pack an umbrella!

◎ Sights

★ Kebun Raya
GARDENS

(Great Garden; www.krbogor.lipi.go.id; admission 26,000Rp; ⊚ 8am-4.30pm) At the heart of Bogor are the fabulous botanical gardens, known as the Kebun Raya; the city's green lung covers 87 hectares. Everyone loves the Orchid House with its exotic and delicate blooms, but there are more than 15,000 species of plant here including 400 different kinds of palm (don't miss the footstool palm, which tops out at an impressive 25m). There are lots of graceful pandan trees and some huge agave and cacti in the Mexican section.

To avoid Bogor's infamous thunderstorms, try to visit as early in the day as you can and allow at least half a day to enjoy Kebun Raya. Just relaxing on one of the grand lawns with a book is as much an attraction as the horticulture. Look out also for monitor lizards, exotic bird life and deer.

Governor-General Raffles first developed a garden here, and the spacious grounds of the Istana Bogor (Presidential Palace) were expanded by Dutch botanist Professor Reinwardt, with assistance from London's Kew Gardens, and officially opened in 1817.

Near the main entrance of the gardens is a small memorial, erected in memory of Governor-General Raffles' first wife Olivia Raffles, who died in 1814 and was buried in Batavia. There is also a cemetery near the palace with Dutch headstones, including the tomb of DJ de Eerens, a former governor-general.

Crowds flock here on Sunday, but the gardens are quiet at most other times. Don't miss the delightful Grand Garden Café (p93), the perfect spot for lunch.

Pasar Bogor
MARKET

(cnr Jl Otto Iskandardinata & Jl Suryakencana; ⊚ 6am-1pm) Jl Suryakencana, steps from the garden gates, is a whirlwind of activity as shoppers spill en masse from within the byzantine concrete halls of Pasar Baru onto the street. Inside, the morning market is awash with all manner of produce and flowers, meat and fish, second-hand clothes and more. Hot, sweltering and loud, it's a hell of a browse. Dive into the barter and trade, and experience Bogor.

Gong Workshop
FACTORY

(☑0251-832 4132; Jl Pancasan 17) FREE In business for around 200 years, this family-run operation is one of the few remaining gongsmiths in Java, where you can see gamelan instruments smelted over a charcoal fire by hand. It's a fascinating insight into what goes into producing such beautiful music. A few pricey gongs and *wayang golek* puppets are on sale.

Istana Bogor
HISTORIC BUILDING

In the northwestern corner of the botanical gardens, the summer palace of the president was formerly the opulent official residence of the Dutch governors-general from 1870 to 1942. Today, herds of white-spotted deer roam the immaculate lawns and the building contains Sukarno's huge art collection, which largely focuses on the female figure. The palace is only open to groups (minimum 10) by prior arrangement, and children are not allowed inside. Contact the tourist office (p93) for more information.

☞ Tours

Tours of Bogor can be arranged through the tourist office (p93) for around 200,000/350,000Rp per half-/full day. The tours take in a working-class *kampung* (neighbourhood) and various cottage industries, including the gong factory and tofu factory. Speak to the office about hiking trips into Halimun National Park. Prices are around 1,000,000Rp per person for trips to the nearby Gunung Salak, an active volcano.

🛏 Sleeping

Bogor has a good choice of accommodation, including all the national and international chain hotels. There are also a number of budget guesthouses that offer more character as well as local info and tours.

Cendana Mulia Hostel Bogor
HOSTEL $

(☑0812 866 2795, 0251-857 1445; Jl Cendana Mulia 9; dm/r incl breakfast with shared bathroom from 100,000/160,000Rp; ❋ 🛜) In a quiet residential street to the north of town is this popular, chilled-out hostel. The whole place

Bogor & Kebun Raya

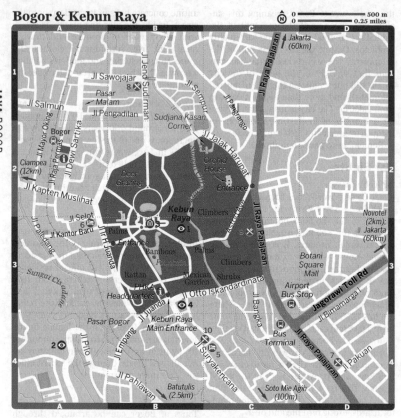

Bogor & Kebun Raya

is spotless, the staff are super-friendly and
the little garden is a pleasant place to sit
and chat to other travellers. Prices go up by
10,000Rp to 20,000Rp on weekends, while
in low season you can expect significant
discounts.

Tom's Homestay　　　　　　GUESTHOUSE **$**
(☑ 0877 7046 7818; www.tomshomestay.com;
Jl Selot 32; r incl breakfast 120,000Rp; 🛜)
Offering a great local experience is this
character-filled family home, whose owner
has lived here his entire life and is a wealth
of knowledge on what to do in the area. In
a faded colonial building, the three rooms
are basic and have shared bathrooms, but
they're spacious and there's a back verandah to relax on while looking into the
jungle-like backyard. It's a 10-minute walk
from the train station.

101 HOTEL **$$**

(☑0251-756 7101; www.the101hotels.com; Jl Suryakencana 179-181; r incl breakfast from 718,000Rp; P❀@🛜🏊) Relatively sleek, with a parlour-floor lobby and a nice pool area, this hotel rises like a shark fin above the city, looming over the red roof tiles and domed mosques. Set close to the gardens and the morning market, rooms have tiled floors, flat-screens and accent walls, which complete the tastefully modern, minimalist decor. Many have balconies.

Savero Golden Flower HOTEL **$$**

(☑0251-835 8888; www.golden-flower.co.id; Jl Raya Pajajaran 27; r from 391,000Rp; P❀🛜🏊) Built in a colonial mansion style, this glossy upmarket hotel is blessed with a perfect location looming over the botanical gardens. Despite the sumptuous appearance, however, the beige and white rooms aren't huge, though they have a certain class, with rain showers and plush linen. The standard of service is high, and it's still fairly new and clean.

 Eating

Soto Mie Agih INDONESIAN **$**

(☑0251-832 8038; Jl Suryakencana 313; mains 25,000-50,000Rp; ☉8am-8pm) Specialising in *soto mie* (a rich noodle soup), this simple place does such a roaring trade that you might have to queue for a table. Word is that the *soto mie* tastes so much better than elsewhere because pork is added to many of the dishes (so some Indonesians avoid it for religious reasons).

De' Leuit INDONESIAN **$$**

(☑0251-839 0011; www.deleuit.co.id; Jl Pakuan III; mains 43,000-112,000Rp; ☉10am-9pm; 🛜🅿) The most happening eatery in Bogor. There's seating on three floors beneath a soaring, pyramid-shaped thatched roof, though the best tables are on the first two levels. It does exciting variations on the standard *sate* (satay), mixed rice, fried *gurame* (fish) and fried chicken, as well as a variety of local veggie dishes.

⭐**Grand Garden Café** INTERNATIONAL **$$**

(☑0251-857 4070; Kebun Raya; mains 45,000-200,000Rp; ☉9am-11pm; 🛜) The cafe-restaurant in the botanical garden is a wonderfully civilised place for a bite or a drink, with sweeping views down to the water-lily ponds. It's a little pricey (especially as you need to pay the 25,000Rp entry fee, though

it's free after 4pm), but the tasty international and Indonesian food, cold beer and sublime setting make it an essential stop.

It was here that Indonesian President Joko met Barack Obama during the latter's visit in 2017. Their table remains a popular selfie spot.

Doea Tjangkir INDONESIAN **$$**

(☑0251-754 7385; www.doeatjangkir.com; Jl Sawojajar 40; mains 40,000-65,000Rp; ☉10am-10pm) Dress smart for this classy upmarket restaurant, located inside a painstakingly restored colonial building. The menu consists primarily of expertly crafted modern Javanese cuisine, but it also has a few European classics such as steak and chips. You can eat inside among the faded portraits of old colonial types or out on the garden terrace.

Kentjana CHINESE **$$**

(Resto Kencana; ☑0251-833 0698; Jl Suryakencana 143; dishes 35,000-120,000Rp; ☉noon-10pm) A tasteful, soulful Chinese diner with a wonderful *mapo tofu* on the menu (the tofu was among the silkiest we've ever had), along with a number of ethnic Chinese Indonesian dishes. All served up in a gold and red room decked out with Chinese lanterns and artfully arranged black-and-white photos of yesteryear Bogor. The house sambal rocks.

ℹ **Information**

PHKA Headquarters (Jl Ir H Juanda 15; ☉7am-2.30pm Mon-Thu, to 11am Fri) The official body for the administration of all of Indonesia's wildlife reserves and national parks; located next to the main garden gates.

Tourist Office (☑0816 195 3838; Jl Dewi Sartika 51; ☉8am-6pm) The friendly team here can help out with basic queries about the region, provide a city map and also offer excellent, well-priced tours.

BCA Bank (Jl Ir H Juanda 28; ☉8am-4pm Mon-Sat) Has an ATM accepting foreign Visa cards.

ℹ **Getting There & Away**

BUS

Every 15 minutes or so, buses depart from Jakarta's Kampung Rambutan bus terminal (10,000Rp to 15,000Rp, one hour) for Bogor's **bus station** (Jl Raya Pajajaran), located in the centre of town.

Buses depart frequently to Bandung (air-con, 70,000Rp, 3½ hours), Pelabuhan Ratu (55,000Rp, three hours) and Labuan (50,000Rp, four hours). For Cianjur (25,000Rp to 30,000Rp, two hours), white minibuses (called *colt*) depart regularly from the bus station. Door-to-door *travel* minibuses go to Bandung for 100,000Rp.

Damri buses head direct to Jakarta's Sukarno-Hatta International Airport (standard/deluxe 55,000/75,000Rp, two to three hours) every 40 minutes from 2am to 8.30pm from **Jl Raya Pajajaran**.

CAR

The tourist board can recommend car drivers to explore the region around Bogor; rates start at 500,000Rp per day.

TRAIN

Train is by far the most enjoyable (and fastest) way of travelling between Bogor and Jakarta. Express trains (6000Rp to 16,000Rp, one hour) connect Bogor with the capital roughly every hour, though try to avoid travelling during rush hour. Economy trains are more frequent, but they are packed with people – some clinging to the roof.

🛈 Getting Around

Green *angkot* minibuses (3000Rp) shuttle around town, particularly between the bus terminal and train station. *Angkot* 03 does a counterclockwise loop of the botanical gardens on its way to Jl Kapten Muslihat, near the train station. *Angkot* 06 gets you to the bus terminal from the train station.

Becak are banned from the main road encircling the gardens. Taxis are rare in Bogor.

Around Bogor

With lush forests, rugged, hilly landscapes, white-water rapids and few international tourists, Bogor's outskirts are full of natural thrills for those who are after an easy escape from the surrounding urbanity.

👁 Sights

Gunung Halimun
National Park   NATIONAL PARK

(✎park office 0266-621256; www.halimunsalak. org; Jl Raya Cipanas, Kabandungan; 250,000Rp) This mixed-use national park is home to small swatches of primary rainforest, but also includes plantations such as the Nirmala Tea Estate. The park's best feature is the rich montane forest in the highland regions around Gunung Halimun (1929m), its tallest peak. The scenery is ravishing and there's a lot of wildlife (though most of it is hard to see), including langurs and gibbons as well as profuse bird life. Several happy days could be spent hiking here.

The most popular walk is a half-day hike taking in three waterfalls.

ArusLiar Adventure (Map p70; ✎021-2270 7917; www.arusliar.co.id; 3rd fl, Jl Kemang Raya 31; rafting per person from 225,000Rp; ⏰9am-6pm Mon-Fri) is a recommended local operator running hiking trips in the park and white-water rafting in the peripheral areas. Otherwise, speak to the staff at the tourist office in Bogor (p93) about setting up a trip.

The usual access (you need your own transport) is through Cibadak on the Bogor–Pelabuhan Ratu road, from where you turn off to Cikadang and then on to the Nirmala Tea Estate. Rainfall in the park is between 4000mm and 6000mm per year. Most of this falls from October to May, when a visit is more or less out of the question. There is a helpful park office on the eastern edge of the village of Kabandungan.

🛏 Sleeping & Eating

⭐ Lodges Ekologika
on Portibi Farms   FARMSTAY $$

(✎0812 8211 8850; www.portibi.com; huts $10, bungalows US$45-65, r US$66; meals per day $40) 🌿 Set on the terraced slopes of Gunung Salak (2211m), this organic farm and gourmet kitchen has developed a reputation for imaginative meals crafted from ingredients grown on its 14 hectares. Most guests stay in charming rooms and bungalows built from reclaimed teak, glass and polished concrete, and blessed with magnificent views (with cheap and simple bamboo huts available for backpackers).

Whatever their budget, most guests spend their downtime in the Pacifist Cannibal Lounge. It is here, on the ground floor of the main house, where the owner, a recovering American academic, mixes original cocktails behind a curved reclaimed-timber bar, while the sound system thumps out classic punk anthems and neo-classic hip-hop beats.

But above all, the family-style meals are the thing. Think homemade ravioli, steamed barramundi, tempe tacos folded in housemade tortillas, and colourful salads, which are among the best we've ever had. Though it attracts mostly midrange customers, backpackers can take advantage of special midweek rates (all-inclusive US$30), though you'll be crashing in a hut. Advance bookings are obligatory.

Cimaja

☑ 0266

Cimaja is an attractive, low-key surf resort some 100km south of Bogor, with a good choice of accommodation and several decent and reasonably quiet surf spots (though none attain the epic standards that can be found elsewhere in the archipelago). There's also a mystical quality to the place. After a long sunset session, as you wander back through the rice fields along the canals, you'll hear the ethereal calls to prayer filter through the palms and feel far from Java's teeming cities. All up, the slow pace and oceanic air makes for an exhilarating change that will appeal even to non-surfers.

To get here, you have to pass through the large, unlovely resort of Pelabuhan Ratu; Cimaja is 8km further west. There are a couple of banks with ATMs in Cimaja, and several more in Pelabuhan Ratu.

◉ Sights & Activities

The main beach is a stony affair, but attractive enough. It's often pounded by crashing surf and the swimming can be treacherous. Take extreme care. For a sandy beach you'll have to head west for a kilometre or so to **Karang Hawu** (Sunset Beach), a broad strip of dark sand.

About 3km north of Pantai Karang Hawu are the **Cipanas hot springs**. Boiling water sprays into the river, and you can soak downstream where the hot and cold waters mingle. It is a very scenic area, with lush forest upstream and a waterfall, though it's crowded on weekends.

Mostly, though, Cimaja is all about the surf. In general, the wave quality isn't as high as in more famous surf areas of Indonesia, but as every surfer knows, even an average Indonesian surf spot is probably 10 times better than your home break!

Some of the better-known waves include Cimaja Point, which is a long, walled-up right point with rare cover-up sections. It's the most consistent and crowded wave. Indicator Point, which is just outside Cimaja Point, fires at high tide when there's a big swell, but it's only for experienced surfers. Karang Hawu has a sectiony beach break that is good for beginners.

There are other spots tucked away along the coastline either side of Cimaja. Some of these are very good waves indeed.

Diving, fishing, rafting and motorcycling trips can also be organised through your guesthouse, and so can surf lessons. They cost about 150,000Rp per day (excluding soft board rental, which is another 100,000Rp).

🛏 Sleeping & Eating

Cimaja is very quiet during the week and fills up at weekends and during holidays, when prices rise by around 20% at many places.

Cimaja Homestay HOMESTAY $

(☑ 0858 4615 9092; http://cimajahomestay.com; Jl Raya Cisolok; s/d 200,000/250,000Rp; ✹ 🤶) Set in the rice fields a short way back from the main surf break is this sky-blue, concrete-block homestay, tended by lovely English-speaking staff who offer four sparkling tiled rooms. Surfboards are available for rent.

★ Nurda's LODGE $$

(☑ 0813 1475 9937; www.cimajapoint.com; Jl Raya Cisolok; r 150,000-400,000Rp; ✹ 🤶) This surf lodge is set in large grassy grounds just back from the main surf break and with views out over the waves. Rooms are tiled, modern and spacious, though not especially imaginative. The restaurant is the most creative in town and serves fish and tempe burgers, chicken schnitzel, and grilled and fried seafood complete with lots of surf talk.

Sadly, some of the rooms have been tainted by smokers.

Cimaja Square BUNGALOW $$

(☑ 0266-644 0800; http://cimajasquare.com; Jl Raya Cisolok; bungalows 150,000-400,000Rp; ✹ @ 🤶) Attractive thatched roof, brick and wood cottages, all of good size and built over the rice paddies make this a tranquil and endearing choice. It's a five-minute stroll from the main point break. The bathrooms can be mosquito sanctuaries.

At the decent in-house **restaurant** (☑ 0266-644 0800; www.cimajasquare.com; Jl Raya Cisolok; mains 40,000-60,000Rp; ⊙ 7am-9pm) you not only get solidly prepared and presented international dishes (think pasta, burgers, pizza, seafood and some standard Indonesian dishes) at this open-to-all hotel restaurant, but also a good atmosphere and a mix of international surfers and travellers eating, knocking back a few Bintangs and playing pool.

ℹ Getting There & Away

To reach Cimaja, you first need to get to Pelabuhan Ratu. Buses run throughout the day from Bogor (air-con/normal 55,000/35,000Rp, three to four hours) to Pelabuhan Ratu. There is no direct access to or from Jakarta. You have to get to Bogor first.

Some buses continue on from Pelabuhan Ratu to Cimaja. These are supplemented by regular *angkot* (5000Rp, 30 minutes, but expect to pay more if you have surfboards with you), which run about every 20 minutes. Some *angkot* then go on to Cisolok, past Sunset Beach.

Motorbikes can be hired for 60,000Rp per day from locals in Cimaja, and surfboard racks are available.

Cibodas

📞 0263 / POP 142,500

Home to the famous Kebun Raya Cibodas, a botanical garden where nature always seems to be one step ahead of the gardeners' pruning blades, Cibodas and its cool air are popular with weekending city folk, although it features on the itineraries of only a few foreign visitors.

Cibodas, like most of West Java, is swelling beyond its original skin. Once a relatively prosperous yet simple tea and market town, with nice homes dotting the green hills, now it has gleaming malls, fashion outlets and upmarket lodgings serving weekenders from nearby cities. The road from Jakarta and Bogor climbs in elevation, through a sprawling hill resort known as the Puncak to a height of 1490m before descending to Cibodas. Note that at the weekend and during holidays the traffic along this route is almost gridlocked.

Visitors must pay 2000Rp to enter Cibodas village.

◉ Sights

Kebun Raya Cibodas   GARDENS

(📞 0263-520 448; www.krcibodas.lipi.go.id; per person 16,500Rp, car 16,000Rp; ⊙ 8am-5pm) The stunning gardens of Kebun Raya Cibodas are an extension of the Bogor botanical gardens. Spread over the steep lower slopes of Gunung Gede and Gunung Pangrango at an altitude of 1300m to 1440m, these lush gardens are among the dampest places in Java. The Dutch tried to cultivate quinine here (its bark is used in malaria medication), though the East Javan climate proved more suitable.

⌂ Sleeping

Bali Ubud Guesthouse   GUESTHOUSE $

(📞 0263-512 051; Jl Kebun Raya; r from 240,000Rp) About 4km south of the entrance to Kebun Raya Cibodas, this Balinese-owned place has attractive rooms with balconies that enjoy spectacular valley views. The restaurant here also makes the most of the views, serving good Western and Indonesian food, and cold Bintang. However, they do keep pit-bull dogs here, which can be off-putting for some.

ℹ Getting There & Away

The turn-off to Cibodas is on the Bogor–Bandung Hwy, a few kilometres west of Cipanas. Buses running between these two cities will drop you off at the turn-off. The gardens are 5km from the main road. *Angkot* run from the roadside in Cipanas up to the gardens and the entrance to the Gede Pangrango National Park (5000Rp, 10 minutes).

Gede Pangrango National Park

In every way the highlight of the Gede Pangrango National Park is the climb to the peak of the volcanically active Gunung Gede (2958m). From the top of Gede on a clear day you can see Jakarta to the north, or, more enticingly, the sensuous south coast of Java.

Because it's close to Jakarta, this is an extremely popular mountain to climb. Numbers are restricted and during peak holiday season there may be a waiting list. At other times you can normally just rock up and trek the next day.

🏃 Activities

There are a number of different walking trails within the park. The majority are fairly long and are better suited to those who don't mind getting muddy and scratched by jungle thorns. **Park authorities** (📞 0263-512776; www.gedepangrango.org; per person weekday/weekend 22,500Rp/27,500Rp) can advise on routes and supply guides.

Gunung Gede   TREKKING

The thick, jungled slopes of the 2958m Gunung Gede volcano offer one of the most exciting and challenging treks in West Java. The 10km hike right to the summit takes at least 12 hours there and back, so you should start as early as possible and take warm clothes (night temperatures can drop to 5°C), food, water and a torch (flashlight). Most hikers leave by 2am to reach the summit in the early morning before the mists roll in.

❶ Getting There & Away

For 5000Rp *angkot* run from Cibodas to the park entrance, which is right next to the entrance for the Kebun Raya Cibodas. There is a charge of 3000Rp for every vehicle entering the national park and 1000Rp per vehicle occupant.

Cianjur

✍ 0263 / POP 161,500

A market town that's famed throughout Java for the quality of its rice, Cianjur is enveloped by shimmering green paddy fields. However, it's no tourist town; instead, it's a sprawling urban settlement with little charm that just serves as a base to explore the area's fine walking trails, hillside villages and attractive countryside.

The town (which is more an amalgamation of villages) has few attractions, but instead serves as a popular base to explore the attractive surrounds.

The **Sarongge Valley** (✍ 0857 5976 8683; ⊙ 9am-2pm Mon-Thu & Sat) FREE green-tea plantation and processing factory lies 20km north of Cianjur. The site also includes a silkworm farm and flower farms. Near town, there's also **Jhon** (✍ 0263-264 444; https://the jhons.com; 30,000Rp, additional charges for other activities; ⊙ 8am-9pm Mon-Fri, to 10pm Sat & Sun), a leisure complex with three pools, paintballing, boating and other activities. It's around 3km northwest of the town centre.

🛏 Sleeping

SL Guesthouse HOMESTAY $
(Chill Out Guest House; ✍ 0813 2172 9004, 0877 1458 5454; www.cianjuradventure.com; Jl Arwinda Km 0.5; r incl full board 300,000Rp; 🖳) Set in the joyful and inviting middle-class family home of Yudhi Suryana, here guests sleep in private or shared rooms with curtained-off beds and a shared bathroom. It's starting to show its age a bit, but there's a large yard usually bustling with family members (and other guests). Rates include three tasty meals and strong local coffee, and free laundry too.

Best part: Yudhi arranges a handful of delightful tours (p98) in the region. He also arranges bus and train tickets, and books private transport.

The guesthouse is actually around 10km northeast of Cianjur and very complicated to find without some local knowledge. The best bet is simply to phone and ask them to explain how to get there.

🍴 Eating

The Cianjur region is famous for its sweet, spicy cuisine, and there are several delicious dishes unique to the area. Be sure to try the local *lontong* (sticky rice with tofu in a delicious, sweet coconut sauce); there are several warungs on Jl Dewisartika that specialise in this dish. Look out for some of the best beef *sate* in Java, locally known as *marangi*, which is available in many places across town. Other local specialities include delicious *batagor* (crispy tofu) and *pandan wangi* rice, which is fragrantly flavoured short-grain rice that's often cooked with lemon grass and spices.

Lotek LP INDONESIAN $
(✍ 0263-264 554; Jl Juanda 28; meals 10,000-20,000Rp; ⊙ 6.30am-10pm) A scruffy storefront Sundanese diner run by a charming *ibu* who mixes a fine gado gado (14,000Rp), plus authentically sweet and sticky *sate marangi* (5000Rp per stick).

Ikan Bakar Cianjur SEAFOOD $$
(✍ 0263-263 392; Jl Dr Muwardi 143; mains 35,000-80,000Rp; ⊙ 9am-10pm) A local institution with gurgling fountains, a koi pond entryway and a soaring tiled roof in the indoor-outdoor dining area. Choose your fish from the freshwater tanks – they have gurame or nila, which they butterfly and grill, pan fry whole, or cook in turmeric soup.

❶ Getting There & Away

From Jakarta the easiest – if not necessarily fastest – way to Cianjur is via a daily minibus (125,000Rp, three hours) organised through the SL Guesthouse. The minibus will pick you up from any Jakarta area hotel, but be warned that this zig-zagging around Jakarta collecting clients can add hours to the journey.

Otherwise, buses leave Jakarta's Kampung Rambutan every 30 minutes to Cipanas (40,000Rp, two hours) and Cianjur (50,000Rp, three hours). On weekends (when traffic is terrible around Puncuk Pass) buses are routed via Jonggol (add an extra hour to your journey and an extra 10,000Rp to your tab). Buses to and from Bandung (normal/air-con

DON'T MISS

LIVE LIKE A LOCAL
....

Author Yudhi Suryana (who for years lived in New Zealand) has been building the tourism industry in Cianjur, one guest at a time. Through his homestay, the Chill Out Guest House (p97), and through his rare agenda of treks and driving tours, his goal is to offer independent travellers a slice of authentic Sundanese life.

There are several different tours and activities, including one to Cangling, a **floating village** (per person 175,000Rp) on a nearby lake, with a fish-farming economy, and to a local school in town. The profusion of plastic around the floating village can be disappointing, but there is no doubt that you're seeing real Javanese life up close – with all its charms and challenges.

However, the most popular trip is the **traditional village tour** (200,000Rp per person, lunch included). Guests will take local *angkot* transport from the centre of Cianjur into the hills, where you'll follow a concrete *gang* (footpath) until it flakes away into earth. The 90-minute hike, past elegantly terraced rice fields and stands of clove, cardamom and guava trees, eventually leads to Kampung Gombong where you will have lunch at a wonderful braided bamboo home.

The whole village is filled with homes that, for the moment at least, remain far from asphalt roads and are served by small shops and tiny lanes that only the brave and knowledgeable can navigate with a motorbike. Lunch is prepared over an open flame in the kitchen. After lunch you can have a massage and a nap before the lazy and beautiful wander back to the asphalt streets. This is the perfect antidote to those contagious urban blues so common in West Java.

Yudhi arranges airport pick-ups and drop-offs, as well as bus and train tickets to or from Jakarta, Bandung or Yogyakarta.

20,000/30,000Rp, two hours) run every half hour.

There are buses to Bogor from Cianjur (weekday/weekend 25,000/35,000Rp, 1½ to two hours) and the highway by Cipanas every 20 minutes. The **bus station** is at the eastern end of town but many of the buses that are just passing through town will drop off and pick up passengers anywhere along the main road through town.

Bandung
022 / POP 2.6 MILLION

Bandung is a city of punks and prayer, serious religion and serious coffee. Here are teeming markets and good shopping, thriving cafes in reclaimed colonial Dutch relics, palpable warmth and camaraderie on street corners, and traffic everywhere you look. Almost everything great and terrible about Indonesia can be found in Bandung. You may cringe at the young teens smoking and the systemic poverty, and nod with respect at the city's thriving art, shopping and cafe scene. Yes, Bandung has everything, except nature, and after the bottle-green hills of Cibodas, the sprawling bulk of Bandung is quite the urban reality check. But even if the local mountains are cloaked in smog, the city does make a good base for day trips to the surrounding countryside – high volcanic peaks, hot springs and tea plantations are all within reach.

◉ Sights

There are some fine Dutch art deco structures to admire on Jl Jenderal Sudirman and Jl Asia Afrika, two of the best being the **Prama Grand Preanger** (022-423 1631; www.pramahotels.com; Jl Asia Afrika 181; r/ste from 550,000/2,277,000Rp; ✸ 🛜 🏊) and the Savoy Homann Hotel (p101), both of which have imposing facades. In the north of the city, **Villa Isola** is another wonderful Dutch art deco structure.

★ Selasar Sunaryo
Art Space   GALLERY
(022-250 7939; www.selasarsunaryo.com; Jl Bukit Pakar Timur 100; ⊙10am-5pm Tue-Sun) **FREE** Just outside town in the pretty rural district of Ciburial is this sleek contemporary art gallery. It exhibits both Indonesian and international artists in both an impressive permanent exhibition and monthly changing shows in its four galleries. There's also an attractive cafe here set under a protruding tree.

Villa Isola NOTABLE BUILDING
(Bumi Siliwangi; ☑0813 2245 3101, 022-201316; Jl
Dr Setiabudhi 229; ☺interior visits by appointment)
FREE Around 7km north of the centre, Villa Isola is a landmark art deco building, a
four-storey villa built by a Dutch media bar-
on in the 1930s as a private residence. It's
now the University of Education's administrative offices. This curvaceous architectural
masterpiece is in excellent condition; from
its balconies there's a fine perspective of
Bandung. It's possible to enter the building
if you call ahead.

Governor's Residence NOTABLE BUILDING
(off Jl Kebon Kawung) One of Bandung's most
beautifully restored period buildings,
though you can only gaze at it from behind
the railings.

**Bandung Institute
of Technology** UNIVERSITY
(ITB; www.itb.ac.id/en; Jl Ganeca) Opened in
1920, the ITB was the first university open
to Indonesians – Sukarno studied here, and
it has a reputation for political activism. In
1998, in the lead-up to Suharto's downfall,
up to 100,000 students rallied daily. Set in
spacious grounds, the complex contains
some bizarre hybrid Indo-European architecture. Visit the art gallery (admission free;
opens on request) as its fine-arts school is
internationally famous.

🏃 Activities

Bersih Sehat MASSAGE
(☑022-426 0765; Jl Sultan Tirtayasa 31; ☺10am-
10pm) This is an excellent massage and
treatment salon. Rates are reasonable with a
one-hour body massage costing 130,000Rp.
A 90-minute treatment with a massage and
lulur scrub costs just 150,000Rp.

👉 Tours

English-speaking **Enoss** (☑0852 2106 3788;
enoss_travellers@yahoo.com) is a good-natured
freelance tour guide who runs one-day tours
(395,000Rp per person) of the sights to the
north and south of the city. The tours get
you away from the more predictable touristy
locations. He can also set up trips to Pangandaran (800,000Rp) via Garut.

🛏 Sleeping

Bandung offers quality accommodation
across all budgets: there are a few good hostels, funky well-priced business hotels and

classy historical digs. Luxury hotels offer
online discounts, so shop around.

⭐Buton Backpacker Lodge HOSTEL $
(☑022-423 8958; www.buton-backpacker-lodge
-id.book.direct; Jl Buton 14A; dm/r incl breakfast
110,000/250,000Rp; ❇🛜) A brilliant central
boutique hostel with well-designed eight-
bed pod dorms, which provide more privacy
than the traditional bunk-bed-style dorms
(though you do feel a little like you're sleeping in a coffin...). There are also colourful,
smart single and double rooms, some of
which have shared bathrooms. Great communal spaces, a spread of traditional Sundanese food for breakfast and friendly staff
round out the deal.

Attic HOSTEL $
(☑0857 7690 5080; Jl Juanda 130; incl breakfast
dm 120,000Rp, d with private/shared bathroom
250,000/200,000Rp; ❇🛜) While it's a tad out
of the way, 4km north of the city, the Attic remains one of Bandung's best budget options.
It's run by a friendly crew, who are helpful
in assisting with local travel info and offer
tours in the area. The dorms and private
rooms are basic, but spotlessly maintained,
and they have comfortable beds.

Popular Hostel HOSTEL $
(☑0811 8581 888, 022-426 0600; Jl Braga 45; dm/
s/d incl breakfast 150,000/150,000/200,000Rp;
❇🛜) In the heart of the action is this
well-established but institutional-feeling
hostel, located up a flight of scruffy marble
stairs from Jl Braga. Bunks are set up in two-
bed, six-bed and 16-bed arrangements. All
dorms are air-conditioned and come with
lockers and wi-fi, and the individual reading
lights are a nice touch.

**Summerbird
Boutique Hotel** BOUTIQUE HOTEL $$
(☑022-603 0228; www.summerbirdhotel.com; Jl
Kesatriaan 11; d from 519,000Rp; ❇🛜) When the
rooms go by names such as Vintage Choco-
late Flavor or Scandanavian Milk (whatever
that might be?), you know you're going to be
staying somewhere hip. And this pleasing-
ly styled 28-room hotel certainly delivers.
It even describes itself as 'Instagramable'!
Despite the varying decor schemes, all
rooms are modern, comfortable and have a
countryside charm.

There's an equally cool cafe attached to it
and great staff. It's a few minutes' walk from
the train station on a quieter street.

Bandung

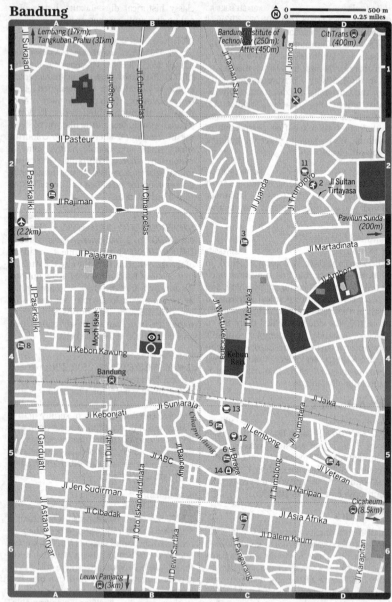

favehotel Braga HOTEL $$
(📞022-8446 8222; www.favehotels.com/en; Jl Braga 99, Braga City Walk Entertainment Complex; r from 370,000Rp; ❈ 🛜) Part of a reliable national chain, this bright and bold design hotel is a good central choice that lands you in the heart of all the nightlife action. Here you can expect a stylish, air-conditioned room with cable TV for under US$30.

101 HOTEL $$
(📞022-426 0966; www.the101hotels.com; Jl Juanda 3; r incl breakfast from 780,000Rp; 🅿❈🛜🏊) Part of a small national chain; the 101's re-

Bandung

claimed wood-panelled facade dripping with vines is cool, as is the Sino-Portuguese tile in the lobby and groovy lounge spaces. The jazzy rooms are just as attractive, with blonde-wood furnishings and checkerboard tile floors, though they aren't huge. It's set in the leafy north.

★ **Savoy Homann Hotel**   HISTORIC HOTEL **$$**
(☑022-423 2244; www.savoyhomannbandung. com; Jl Asia Afrika 112; r/ste from 583,000/ 930,000Rp; ❋@🛰❋) Dating back to 1921, this wonderful-looking hotel has a superb sweeping facade and a palm-tree-filled atrium, while the impressively large and bright rooms and communal areas retain real art deco class, with period lighting and stylish details galore. Promo deals are available on the website.

Tama Boutique Hotel   DESIGN HOTEL **$$$**
(☑022-426 4888; www.tama-boutique.com; Jl Rajiman 5; r/ste incl breakfast from 950,000/ 1,200,000Rp; ❂🛰) An unusual 'building block' exterior gives way to a contemporary, Japanese-influenced design hotel with floor-to-ceiling wall murals, wooden furnishings and low, comfortable beds. All of which help to make this one of the more eye-catching Bandung hotels. Continuing with the Far Eastern feel, there's also a decent in-house Korean restaurant with great rooftop views.

✖ Eating

Bandung is renowned throughout Java for its cuisine and for having great places to eat. And for many visitors, eating out is a Bandung highlight. In the centre, Jl Braga has a strip of cafes and restaurants. Many of Bandung's most exclusive places are concentrated in the north of town. For cheap eats check out the night warungs on Jl Cika-

pundung Barat, across from the *alun-alun* (main public square).

Hangover   PUB FOOD **$**
(Jl Braga 47; dishes 20,000-50,000Rp; ❂11am-2am Mon-Thu, to 3am Fri & Sat, to 1am Sun) A busy pub restaurant, with classic rock and blues on the stereo and a comforting range of updated Western and Indo classics emerging from the kitchen. It does meatballs with fried rice, oxtail soup, chicken burgers and a delicious hot salty tofu. And it serves icy-cold beer, of course, which goes well with the big TV screens showing sport.

Plenty of foreign tourists and expats stop by, but the music can be too loud for easy conversation.

Kiosk   INDONESIAN **$**
(Jl Braga, Braga City Walk; meals 15,000-50,000Rp; ❂10am-10pm; 🛰) This mini food court on the ground floor of the Braga City Walk is ideal for mixing with locals and sampling some unusual snacks from *kaki lima* (street vendor) style stalls. Order a *lotek* (Sundanese salad) or a noodle dish. Drinks include juices – try the *sirsak* (soursop) – cold beers and iced coffees.

Paviliun Sunda   INDONESIAN **$$**
(☑022-426 7700; Jl Martadinata 97; mains 40,000-100,000Rp; ❂8am-11pm) A classy restaurant serving modern, well-presented Sundanese food, including fresh fish and *karedok* (salad of long beans and bean sprouts in a spicy sauce). The fried or barbecued fish, which comes with a variety of interesting sides and sauces served on banana-leaf plates, is delicious.

EATBOSS Dago   INTERNATIONAL **$$**
(☑022-253 1222; www.eatboss.co.id; Jl Juanda 72; mains 40,000-125,000Rp; ❂9am-11pm; 🛰)

A modern chain restaurant blessed with bright colours and a terrific design. Serves standard Indonesian dishes as well as pasta and burgers. Portions are big and cheap, though not of the highest quality.

 Drinking & Nightlife

After dark Jl Braga is the place to be, with small bars, pool halls, karaoke lounges and live-music venues. Up in north Bandung, the well-heeled head to places along Jl Juanda, and students converge on Jeans St aka Jl Cihampelas (though there are few bars here).

★**Wiki Koffee** CAFE

(☑ 022-4269 0970; Jl Braga 90; coffee from 19,000Rp; ☺ 7am-midnight; ☜) The best place for coffee on Jl Braga is this smoky cafe set in a restored old storefront and tastefully decorated with vintage furniture, art and fresh-cut flowers. This is where the hip, young and cute collide in intimate corners and at table-and-chair arrangements that feel like your living room.

It does a small food menu (mains 22,000Rp to 25,000Rp), with sweet snacks like waffles and salty ones like fried chicken wings. But it's mostly a hangout spot with good coffee. Hence the long wait for a table.

Cups Coffe & Kitchen CAFE

(☑ 022-426 5092; Jl Trunojoyo 25; coffee 15,000-20,000Rp, snacks 40,000-50,000Rp; ☺ 7am-10pm Sun-Thu, to 11pm Fri & Sat; ☜) A polished-concrete atrium cafe with orchids hung on the wall, smoke in the air and mostly Western snacks and sandwiches on the menu. Fish and chips, Caesar salad, burgers and hot dogs are all here for the ordering, but coffee is its thing. That's what draws Bandung's creative class for all-day work-and-sip sessions.

Roempoet BAR

(Jl Braga 80; ☺ noon-2am Mon-Thu, to 3am Fri-Sun) Intimate bar with live bands (mainly playing covers most nights) and a social vibe. Sizzling *sate* is also served.

 Entertainment

Bandung is a good place to see Sundanese performing arts; however, performance times are haphazard – check with the Tourist Information Centre for the latest schedules.

★**ASTI Bandung** PERFORMING ARTS

(☑ 022-731 4982; www.isbi.ac.id; Jl Buah Batu 212, Kampus STSI Bandung) In the southern part of the city about 3km from the centre, this is a school for traditional Sundanese arts – music, dancing and *pencak silat* (martial arts). There are frequent good performances, some of which are held in a breezy outdoor setting.

Events are not widely advertised online, so you might be better popping past and enquiring as to what's on and when.

Saung Angklung PERFORMING ARTS

(☑ 022-727 1714; www.angklung-udjo.co.id; Jl Padasuka 118; adult/child under 12yr 75,000/50,000Rp; ☺ 10.30am-5pm) Hosts enjoyable, if not entirely authentic, *angklung* (bamboo musical instrument) performances daily in a Sundanese cultural centre that also features dance events and ceremonial processions. It's around 10km northeast of the city centre.

Shopping

With glitzy malls and factory outlets, shopaholics love Bandung. Bandung's celebrated Jeans St (Jl Cihampelas) has masses of cheap clothing stores. Jl Cibaduyut, in southwest Bandung, is to shoes what Jl Cihampelas is to jeans. Check out Jl Braga for antiques, art and curios. Jl Trunojoyo, in the leafy north end, offers the hippest, trendiest styles and shoppers.

Kayu Solid ART

(☑ 022-426 0577; Jl Braga 29; ☺ 10am-6pm) The coolest showroom on Jl Braga displays the artistry of nature. The medium here is huge slabs of tropical wood, minimally treated and displayed like fine art. Admire the wonders of teak, jackfruit, rosewood and many others. None of it is cheap, but it's still a better deal than in Jakarta.

TRAINS FROM BANDUNG

DESTINATION	COST (RP)	DURATION (HR)	FREQUENCY (DAILY)
Jakarta (Gambir)	80,000-250,000	3¼	10
Surabaya	190,000-460,000	11-13½	3
Yogyakarta	165,000-370,000	7¼-8½	6

If you're looking for that one-of-a-kind dining room or coffee table, it has the goods. Staff can arrange shipping.

Pasar Jatayu MARKET
(Jl Arjuna; ⊙8am-6pm) Search this flea market for collectables hidden amid the junk.

ℹ Getting There & Away

AIR
Bandung's **Husein Sastranegara airport** (☏150 138; http://huseinsastranegara-airport. co.id) is 4km northwest of town, and is fast becoming an important international and domestic transport hub. It's a key hub for AirAsia (www.airasia.com), with connections to Kuala Lumpur, Singapore and domestic cities, including Denpasar. Lion Air (www.lionair.co.id) flies to Banjarmasin, Batam, Denpasar, Surabaya and Yogyakarta. Garuda (www.garuda-indonesia. com) and Citilink (www.citilink.co.id) connect to Denpasar and Surabaya.

It costs around 50,000Rp to the airport by taxi from the city centre.

BUS
Five kilometres south of the city centre, **Leuwi Panjang bus terminal** (Jl Sukarno Hatta) has buses west to places such as Cianjur (normal/air-con 20,000/30,000Rp, two hours), Bogor (air-con 80,000Rp, 3½ hours) and to Jakarta's Kampung Rambutan bus terminal (60,000Rp to 70,000Rp, three hours). Buses to Bogor take at least an hour longer on weekends due to traffic.

On the city's eastern outskirts, **Cicaheum bus terminal** (Jl Nasution) serves Cirebon (normal/air-con 40,000/100,000Rp, four hours, hourly), Garut (normal/air-con 25,000/30,000Rp, two hours, every 40 minutes), Pangandaran (normal/air-con 65,000/80,000Rp, six hours, hourly), Wonosobo (90,000Rp, nine to 10 hours) and Yogyakarta (120,000Rp to 250,000Rp, 10½ to 12 hours). Note that the traffic around the Cicaheum terminal can be so clogged it can take almost as long to reach the bus station as it does to get the bus to wherever you're going!

CitiTrans (☏022-251 4090, 0804 1111 000; www.cititrans.co.id; Jl Dipatiukur 53) offers luxury shuttle-bus service to the Jakarta airport (180,000Rp, five hours), departing hourly.

TRAIN
Bandung Station is centrally located, 1km northwest of the *alun-alun*.

ℹ Getting Around

Bandung is a fiendishly difficult city to negotiate on public transport, and few travellers bother as taxi rates are reasonable. Stick to the ever-reliable Bluebird taxis, as well as Grab and Go-Jek. A taxi to the airport costs around 50,000Rp.

Angkot run from Stasiun Hall (St Hall), on the southern side of the train station, to Dago, Ledeng and other destinations; fares cost from 5000Rp. City buses (called Damri) run from west to east down Jl Asia Afrika to Cicaheum bus terminal, and from the train station to Leuwi Panjang bus terminal.

North of Bandung

Hot springs bubble up from the earth and are piped into tubs at the soothing resorts north of Bandung.

◉ Sights & Activities

Tangkuban Prahu VOLCANO
(Mon-Fri 200,000Rp, Sat & Sun 300,000Rp; ⊙info centre 7am-5pm) This volcanic crater, 30km north of Bandung, has a flat, elongated summit that resembles an upturned boat *(prahu)*. It's a huge attraction and certainly a spectacular sight, but also a major tourist trap. If you do decide to go, try to aim for early in the day as by noon the mist starts to roll in. Expect forceful guides trying to sell you overpriced souvenirs. Many foreign visitors find it pricey and not worth the hassle.

It's possible to circumnavigate most of the caldera on foot, but as wannabe guides can be aggressive and tourists have been robbed, there are better places for a highland walk.

Gracia Spa HOT SPRINGS
(☏0260-724 9997; www.graciaspa.com; 35,000Rp; ⊙7am-11pm) Eight kilometres northeast of Tangkuban Prahu in the village of Ciater, Gracia Spa is a natural hot spring set in gorgeous grounds on the lower slopes of the volcano. The springs have been developed in an upmarket way and are kept clean. There are three large pools, expensive villa accommodation and a spa and a restaurant, and it's very quiet midweek.

Sari Ater Hot Spring Resort HOT SPRINGS
(☏0260-471 700; www.sariater-hotel.com; spring access 20,000-70,000Rp; ⊙24hr) This is the village of Ciater's main attraction. Although they're quite commercialised, the pools are among the best of the hot springs around Bandung. Plush but overpriced rooms (from 900,000Rp), villas and permanent upmarket 'safari' tents (from 950,000Rp) are available here. The pools can get insanely busy on weekends.

Around Bandung

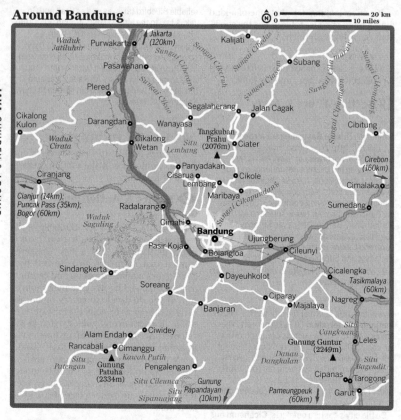

0 — 20 km
0 — 10 miles

Ciwidey & Around

☑ 022 / POP 26,000

The mountains surrounding the small farming town of Ciwidey, south of Bandung, offer magnificent scenery, a rolling evergreen landscape of neatly cropped tea bushes, clumps of tropical forest and misty hilltops. Although there are no standout tourist attractions, the area is ideal for gentle explorations and is well off the standard backpacker trail. The cooler climate is an attraction in itself, and the area lends itself to the growing of more temperate fruits. It can sometimes seem as if every second house has a strawberry patch.

Although the area is seldom visited by international travellers, it's very popular with people from Bandung and Jakarta. This means that it can initially be a struggle to get here through the endless Bandung suburbs and traffic, even on weekdays.

On weekends, when Jakartans descend en masse – well, you've been warned.

◉ Sights

Ciwidey itself has few attractions but does have minimarts and hotels. You really need your own set of wheels to properly get the most out of this area. It's easy to combine Kawah Putih, Kawah Rengganis and Situ Patengan into a fun day trip as they are all close to one another and within 50km of Ciwidey. Touring this region by public transport is possible but a pain. Most travellers explore the area on a tour from Bandung.

Kawah Rengganis   HOT SPRINGS

(30,000Rp) Lovely Kawah Rengganis (also known as Kawah Cibuni) is a pretty, isolated river fed by hot springs and surrounded by billowing steam from volcanic vents. It's off the main tourist path and is wonderful for bathing. You have to park by the road and walk for a few minutes up to the pools; villagers here ask visitors for a 50,000Rp donation to visit their land. It's best to avoid wearing skimpy swimwear when bathing here.

Kawah Putih
LAKE

(Indonesians/foreigners 20,000/50,000Rp) Sulphur mists swirl around the deadened and burnt black trees that line the shores of the acid-water volcanic lake of Kawah Putih (or white lake).

It's a mesmerising and slightly eerie sight that is popular with domestic tourists and well worth the short drive from Ciwedey. If you want a closer look at the hypnotic turquoise lake waters pay 10,000Rp to walk out along the wooden pontoon.

Situ Patengan
LAKE

(20,000Rp) Situ Patengan is a pretty lake buried into the folds of mountains carpeted in tea estates and remnant patches of forest. It's a popular stop with local tourists and has tearooms and boat trips catering to the Sunday crowds. For the best view of the lake, head out onto the deck of the ridiculously tacky beached boat. It's 18km southwest of Ciwedey and best reached by private transport.

🛏 Sleeping & Eating

Malabar
Tea Village
HISTORIC HOTEL $$

(📞 0853 2037 1164; Banjarsari, Pangalengan; r Mon-Fri from 325,000Rp, Sat & Sun from 475,000Rp) It's hard to beat this idyllically situated colonial guesthouse, located at an altitude of 1500m in a working tea plantation near the town of Pangalengan. The simple, clean rooms, each with a front porch and Dutch-era furnishings, make it a great place to kick back for a few days.

Saung Gawir
INDONESIAN $$

(📞 0812 2113 3664; Jl Raya Ciwidey; meals 30,000-90,000Rp; ⊙ 9am-5pm) This restaurant-strawberry farm has startling valley views from its roadside perch in Alam Endah. Ignore the tour groups, pick a table and soak up the quintessential Javanese scenery as you feast on authentic local cuisine (don't miss the excellent grilled carp). And, of course, it would be rude not to buy some berries while you're here.

Bandung to Pangandaran

Heading southeast from Bandung, the road passes through rolling hills and stunning volcanic peaks, skirting – at a safe distance – the particularly explosive Gunung Papandayan (2622m). This is the Bandung–Yogyakarta road as far as Banjar; the Bandung–Yogyakarta train line passes through Tasikmalaya and Banjar, but not Garut. After the choked streets of Jakarta and Bandung, these quieter back roads are a pleasure. If you're in a private vehicle, it pays to slow down here. Take the time to pause in small roadside villages or veer off down jungle-fringed back lanes, creating adventures as you go.

Garut & Cipanas

📞 0262 / POP 126,000

The pretty village of Cipanas makes a tranquil base for a day or two exploring volcanic scenery and soaking away any travelling tensions in a hot-spring bath or pool. Six kilometres to the south is Garut, a once-lovely spa town that's now become a featureless sprawl and leatherware centre that you'll need to pass through to get to Cipanas.

The region is famed for its *dodol* – a confectionery of coconut milk, palm sugar and sticky rice. The Picnic brand is the best, and it is possible to visit the **factory** (📞 0811 203 5689; www.dodolpicnicgarut.com; Jl Pasundan 102; ⊙ 8.30am-2pm) in Garut where it's made.

🛏 Sleeping

Cipanas has a good choice of places to stay; all are strung along Jl Raya Cipanas, the resort's single road. Many of the flashier hotels have swimming pools heated by the springs; if you're staying at a cheaper option, it's possible to use the pools for a minimal fee (10,000/5000Rp per adult/child). Prices rise on weekends.

Kampung Sumber Alam
RESORT $$

(📞 0262-238000; www.resort-kampungsumber alam.com; r 570,000-3,750,000Rp; ❄ @ 🏊) Water, water everywhere at this upmarket resort with attractive thatch-and-timber bungalows built around and over water-lily ponds complete with croaking frogs. If you prefer your swimming a little more chlorinated, there's a large and impressive pool complex. It's popular with Indonesian families, particularly at weekends, though

HIKING GUNUNG PAPANDAYAN

Twin-peaked Gunung Papandayan, 28km southwest of Garut, is one of the most active volcanoes in West Java. Papandayan exploded in 1772, a catastrophe that killed more than 3000. It erupted again in 2002, and thousands were forced to flee when pyroclastic flows devastated the area. Papandayan is periodically closed to visitors, so check first with locals before setting out.

The impressive bubbling yellow **Kawah Papandayan** (100,000Rp) is just below the peak and clearly visible from the Garut valley on clear mornings. From the car park it is an easy half-hour walk to the crater, which is riddled with bubbling mud pools, steam vents and crumbling sulphur deposits. Take care – keep well to the right when ascending through the crater.

Consider hiring a guide (around 350,000Rp per day, but many will allow bargaining) from the PHKA office, as the car-park area is generally full of cowboys. For fine views, go early in the morning before the clouds roll in. Gunung Papandayan's summit is a two-hour walk beyond the crater, and there are fields of Javan edelweiss near the top.

Craters to the west of Garut that can be visited are Kawah Darajat, 26km away, and Kawah Kamojang, 23km away, the site of a geothermal plant that has defused the once spectacular geyser activity and replaced it with huge pipes. Sigh, progress.

To get here, take a Cikajang minibus and get off at the turn-off on the outskirts of Cisurupan (10,000Rp), where you can catch a waiting ojek (40,000Rp one way, 13km).

---

note that the call to prayer from the nearby mosque is enthusiastic.

Tirtagangga Hotel HOTEL **$$**
(☑0262-232549; http://tirtaganggahotel.com; Jl Raya Cipanas 130; r Mon-Fri from 680,000Rp, Sat & Sun from 950,000Rp; ✳️🛜🏊) A large, somewhat sterile but well-run hotel offering good-value rooms with wood-panelled walls, modern decor and generous bathrooms, many with tubs fed with hot-spring water. The huge pool is surrounded by palm trees, and the restaurant serves authentic Indonesian food.

ℹ Getting There & Away

Garut is connected with Bandung (25,000Rp, three hours) and also Pangandaran (55,000Rp, four to five hours). Angkot connect Garut with Cipanas very regularly.

Pangandaran

☑0265 / POP 52,200

Situated on a narrow isthmus, with a broad stretch of sand on either side and a thickly forested national park on the nearby headland, Pangandaran is West Java's premier beach resort. It's built up, especially toward the south end where a jumble of concrete block towers stand shoulder to shoulder across the channel from the national park. Yet for most of the year, Pangandaran is a quiet, tranquil place to enjoy walks along the beach or through the forest. Of course,

on weekends and during peak holiday times, the town fills up to the point where you can hardly see empty sand for all the humanity.

Sadly, sections of the beach are littered with plastic and flotsam, especially during peak tourist time, and are in dire need of a clean-up.

A 6000Rp admission charge is officially levied at the gates on entering Pangandaran.

⊙ Sights

**Pangandaran
National Park** NATIONAL PARK
(Taman Nasional Pangandaran; weekday/weekend 215,000/315,000Rp; ⊙7am-5pm) This national park, which takes up the entire southern end of Pangandaran, is a wild expanse of dense forest. Within its boundaries live porcupines, *kijang* (barking deer), hornbills, monitor lizards and various species of monkey. Small bays within the park also enclose pretty tree-fringed beaches, so bring your bathers. The park is divided into two sections: the recreation park and the jungle. Due to environmental degradation, the jungle is usually off limits.

Well-maintained paths allow the recreation park to be explored, passing small caves (including Gua Jepang, which was used by the Japanese in WWII), the remains of a Hindu temple, Batu Kalde, and a nice beach on the eastern side. English-speaking guides hang around both entrances and charge around 350,000Rp (per group of four) for a three-hour walk on a weekday and 400,000Rp at weekends. Longer hikes are also possible.

Pangandaran's best swimming beach, white-sand **Pasir Putih**, lies on the western side of the national park. It's a thin stretch of soft sand fronted by a reef that's pretty well thrashed, though plenty of fish still live, eat and love there. You can swim over here from the southern end of the main resort beach if the surf is not too rough, but take care of rip currents and the steady stream of boats that shuttle people back and forth (per person 40,000Rp return). They will not be looking for you. The beach stretches to a point that gets a reasonable wave (it's very shallow and not suited to learners) when the swell is big. On calm days, the swim out to the point is peaceful and devoid of boat traffic. The large marooned ship here is an illegal Antarctic toothfish fishing vessel that was sunk by the ministry of Maritime Affairs as a monument to the government's efforts in fighting illegal fishing. However, it's supposed to sit upright, not toppled over as it is now.

Note that many tourists take advantage of a scam whereby boat operators will ferry you over to the park in their boats allowing you to avoid paying the park entry fees. The park authorities are already starved of money to properly preserve the park, so consider the morals of your actions before taking advantage of this.

At sunset, huge fruit bats emerge from the forest. They fly down the length of Pangandaran's beach but have to evade local boys who patrol with barbed-wire kites. Few are trapped this way, but every now and then a bat's wing will get caught on a kite string and the creature will be brought crashing to the ground in a fit of squeals, before being dispatched to the cooking pot.

🏃 Activities

The beach is wide and long, and relentlessly pummelled by a heavy swell that doesn't make for great swimming, as dangerous rips swirl (listen to the lifeguards!). But it is a great place to get out on a board or learn how to ride (surf lessons can be easily arranged).

Mas Rudin   ADVENTURE
(📞 0813 8005 6724; www.pangandaran-guide.com; Jl Pantai Barat, Nanjungsari Shopping Centre) Mas Rudin is a tremendous local guide who operates out of MM Books (p110) and offers fair

prices on a range of tours. His website has a wealth of information.

Pangandaran Surf   SURFING
(📞 0265-639436; Mini Tiga Homestay, off Jl Pamugaran Bulak Laut) The friendly staff from Pangandaran Surf are all lifesavers, speak English and understand local conditions. Board hire runs about 75,000Rp per day, and lessons are 250,000Rp per day. It operates out of Mini Tiga Homestay.

🍽 Tours

Many guesthouses sell day tours taking in sights and activities in and around the town (Green Canyon, Green Valley, and various home-industry visits). Tours (from 350,000Rp per person) normally include transport and entry fees as well as a simple lunch.

There are also tours to Paradise Island, an uninhabited nearby island with good beaches (including a 5km white-sand beach) and waves.

🛏 Sleeping

The principal area for budget or independent travellers is the main beach, where guesthouses are dotted along a grid of quiet lanes just inland from the shore. Most cheaper places have cold-water-only bathrooms.

Expect to pay 15% to 30% more at some places on weekends and holidays.

Many places have flexible prices that are dependent on demand, so you might get a good deal on weekdays outside the main holiday periods.

Pangandaran has a tightly controlled becak union. All hotels have to pay commission to the becak driver who takes you to your accommodation, so if you walk in on your own without a trailing becak driver, you'll be in a better bargaining position.

Mini Tiga Homestay   GUESTHOUSE $
(📞 0265-639436, 0878 2639 3801; www.minitiga homestay.weebly.com; off Jl Pamugaran Bulak Laut; s/d incl breakfast with fan 136,000/150,000Rp, with air-con from 148,000/185,000Rp; 🛜) Long-standing and superb-value backpackers with 13 clean, spacious rooms with nice decorative touches – including bamboo walls and batik wall hangings. All have en suite bathrooms and Western toilets. There are plenty of nooks and crannies in which to hide away with a book, and a small garden space with tables where you can talk with fellow travellers.

Pangandaran

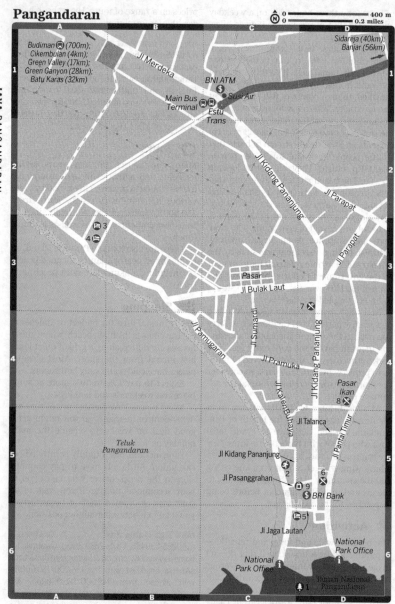

Budiman (700m);
Cikembulan (4km);
Green Valley (17km);
Green Canyon (28km);
Batu Karas (32km)

Sidareja (40km);
Banjar (56km)

Jl Merdeka

BNI ATM
Susi Air
Main Bus
Terminal
Estu
Trans

Jl Kidang Pananjung

Jl Parapat

Jl Parapat

Pasar

Jl Bulak Laut

7

Jl Sumardi

Jl Pamugaran

Jl Pramuka

Jl Kidang Pananjung

Pasar
Ikan
8

Jl Kalen Buhaya

Jl Talanca

Jl Pantai Timur

Teluk
Pangandaran

Jl Kidang Pananjung
2
Jl Pasanggrahan
9
BRI Bank
6

5
Jl Jaga Lautan

National
Park Office

National
Park Office

Taman Nasional
Pangandaran
1

Bale'Ku

HUT **$**

(☎ 0813 2270 2692; Jl Sadiproyo, Desa Wonoharjo;
d incl breakfast from 175,000Rp) And now for
something totally different... Down a maze
of tracks through the rice fields, this guesthouse represents back-to-nature simplicity.

Built entirely from wood and bamboo (but
with solid floors), the main communal area
is on raised stilts above a pond, while the
rooms, each of which has an en suite bathroom, are set among the rice fields.

Pangandaran

★ **Adam's Homestay** HOTEL **$$**
(☏ 0813 2146 1636, 0265-639396; off Jl Pamugaran Bulak Laut; r incl breakfast 350,000-488,000Rp; ❄🛜🏊) Pangandaran's most creative guesthouse is a wonderfully relaxed and stylish place with artistically presented rooms (many with balconies, beamed ceilings and outdoor bathrooms) spread around a luxurious pool and landscaped verdant Balinese garden bursting with exotic plants, lotus ponds and birdlife. There's good international and local food available, including wonderful breakfasts cooked by German owner, Kirsten.

**Nyiur Indah
Beach Hotel** BOUTIQUE HOTEL **$$**
(☏ 0265-639380; http://nyiurindahbeach.hotel. mypangandaran.com; Jl Pamugaran 46; r from 675,000Rp; ❄🛜🏊) Taking centre stage at this low-rise boutique hotel is an artistic multi-level pool complex lined with water-spouting Balinese statues. The sizeable rooms have high-end tile floors and linens, shuttered windows, wood furnishings, wall-mounted flat-screens, day beds, built-in desks and lovely bathrooms. It's more popular with middle-class holidaying Javanese than foreigners, and we think it's all the better for it.

 Eating

Pangandaran is famous for its excellent seafood, and by far the best place to sample it is in the pasar ikan (fish market).

Green Garden Cafe INDONESIAN **$**
(Jl Kidang Pananjung 116; mains 20,000-35,000Rp; ⊗8am-10pm; 🍴) Run by welcoming owners Asep and Rini, this popular, unassuming warung has been cooking great local dishes since 1997. Try the delicious *batagor* (crispy tofu), which is fried in cassava flour and served with spicy peanut sauce, or the

evening charcoal seafood barbecue, all washed down superbly with a cold beer.

It's recently undergone a refurb, but still with little evidence of a garden!

Brillo Pizza PIZZA **$**
(☏ 0812 2280 1742; Desa Cikembulan; pizzas 50,000-100,000Rp; ⊗noon-9.30pm) Pangandaran might have lots of fabulous seafood, but sometimes you just need something, well, less healthy... And this fun pizzeria a few kilometres out of town to the west fulfills such needs. Thin-based, wood-fired pizzas come with a variety of toppings, and you can enjoy them eating alfresco in the pretty garden.

Pasar Ikan SEAFOOD **$$**
(Fish Market; Jl Pantai Timur; fish around 90,000Rp; ⊗8am-10pm) Pangandaran's terrific fish market consists of more than a dozen large, open-sided restaurants just off the east beach. Karya Bahari is considered the best – which is why it's so crowded – but all operate on exactly the same basis. The fresh seafood here is so good it could probably entice a mermaid to the table.

Chez Mama Cilacap INDONESIAN **$$**
(☏ 0265-630098; Jl Kidang Pananjung 197; mains 30,000-75,000Rp; ⊗8am-10.30pm Sun-Thu, to 11pm Fri & Sat) One of the oldest restaurants in Pangandaran, the French-Indonesian-run Mama Cilacap has a large, airy thatched dining room and twirling ceiling fans. It offers a huge range of Indonesian specialities, but it's most famous for its fresh seafood, which you can choose from the cooler.

🍷 **Drinking & Nightlife**

★ **Bamboo Beach Café** BAR
(☏ 0813 1350 7272; Jl Pamugaran, Kampung Turis 1; ⊗8am-late) This old favourite has upped sticks and moved further along the beach (alongside a number of other warungs), but the beach-bum vibe and sunset sea views

are just as good as before and it remains the perfect place to scout the swell with a cold Bintang in hand. With luck, someone will grab a guitar and start strumming.

It's 4.5km west of town, and around 20,000Rp by Grab taxi or 10,000Rp by motorbike to get here.

🛍 Shopping

MM Books   BOOKS

(☑ 0813 8005 6724; Jl Pantai Barat, Nanjungsari Shopping Centre; ⊗ 8.30am-8.30pm) Sells a wide range of secondhand Western titles from a roadside shop stacked floor to ceiling with English, Dutch, French, German and Spanish titles (and probably a few other languages!). The proprietor, Mas Rudin (p107), is one of the best and most trustworthy guides in town.

ℹ Information

MONEY

BNI ATM (Jl Merdeka; ⊗ 8am-4pm Mon-Sat) There's a second branch on Jl Bulak Laut.

BRI Bank (Jl Kidang Pananjung; ⊗ 8am-4pm Mon-Sat) Changes cash dollars and major brands of travellers cheques.

TOURIST INFORMATION

Tickets and information for the Pangandaran National Park are available from offices on **Jl Pantai Timur** (Jl Pantai Timur; ⊗ 7am-5pm) and **Jl Pangandaran** (Jl Pangandaran; ⊗ 7am-5pm).

ℹ Getting There & Away

Pangandaran can be a frustratingly slow and complicated place to get to. The nearest train station is in Sidareja, 41km away, which is serviced by direct trains from Jakarta (130,000Rp, 8½ hours), Bandung (60,000Rp, five hours) and Yogyakarta (105,000Rp, three hours). Speak to Mas Rudin (p107) about organising train tickets. You'll need to pay a 6000Rp tourist levy upon entering town.

AIR

Susi Air (☑ 0800 122 7874; www.susiair.com; Jl Merdeka 312; ⊗ 8am-7pm Mon-Fri) flies daily to Pangandaran airstrip (20km west of town) from Jakarta's Halim Perdana Kusuma airport (824,000Rp, one hour). Double-check your bookings before departure.

BUS

Most *patas* (express) buses to Jakarta and Bandung leave from the **main bus terminal** (Jl Merdeka), 1.5km north from the beach and tourist centre. The **Budiman** (☑ 0265-339854; www.budimanbus.com) bus depot, about 2km

west of Pangandaran along Jl Merdeka, also has regular departures, but most swing by the main terminal too.

Buses run to Bandung (around 80,000Rp, six hours) roughly every hour and to Jakarta's Kampung Rambutan bus terminal (around 100,000Rp, eight to nine hours). To Bandung, there are also **Sari Harum** (☑ 0265-639513, 0265-607 7065) door-to-door *travel* minibuses (100,000Rp, six hours, two daily).

Budiman runs minibus services to Yogyakarta (90,000Rp, nine hours, five daily), while **Estu Trans** (☑ 0812 2679 2456; www.estutrans. co.id) has minibuses (140,000Rp, nine hours) leaving at 7am and 6.30pm. Both leave from the main bus terminal.

From the main bus terminal there are hourly buses to both Banjar (40,000Rp, 2½ hours) and Sidareja (30,000Rp, two hours) for train connections.

CAR

Travel agencies rent minibuses with drivers for about 900,000Rp per day including driver and petrol. The most popular trip is a three-day tour to Yogyakarta, usually via Wonosobo for the first night, Dieng for sunrise, then on to Borobudur. You'll reach Yogyakarta via Prambanan on the final day.

TRAIN

The nearest stations are Sidareja and Banjar. As the overland trip by bus to Yogyakarta takes a punishing eight or nine hours, train travel, which is normally faster and certainly more comfortable, makes a lot of sense. From Sidareja there are two daily trains (140,000Rp to 320,000Rp, 3½ hours). Agents in Pangandaran organise combined minibus to Sidareja station and economy/business/exclusive train tickets for 250,000/375,000/475,000Rp; minimum two people. Or you could save some rupiah by catching a local bus to Sidareja (25,000Rp), and another bus to the station (10,000Rp; though you'll have to wait until the bus is full until it leaves) and buying a train ticket there (avoiding commission), but there's a risk of not getting a seat on the train once you arrive in Sidareja.

Banjar station, 65km away, is a better bet if you're heading to Jakarta (68,000Rp, nine hours) and Bandung (140,000Rp to 320,000Rp, three to four hours).

Travel agents and hotels can help with travel arrangements and tickets on all routes.

ℹ Getting Around

Pangandaran's brightly painted becak (bicycle-rickshaws) start at around 10,000Rp and require heavy negotiation; expect to pay around 20,000Rp from the main bus terminal to the

OFF THE BEATEN TRACK

BACKWATER BOATING TO CILACAP

For an off-beat 'make your own' kind of adventure, it's possible to travel along jungle-fringed backwaters by boat eastwards from Pangandaran, via Majingklak harbour to Cilacap on the Citandui River, but there are no scheduled connections, so you'll have to charter your own *compreng* (wooden boat). Boatmen in Majingklak will do the three-hour trip for a minimum of 600,000Rp (depending on boat type). Alternatively, you can call ahead through a tour agent in Pangandaran to Kalipucang harbour and organise a boat from there for the same price.

Wherever you begin, you will motor up a lazy green river, with low-rise jungled hills on both sides, passing through estuaries and meandering around islands thick with scrub. You will pass a series of riverside villages and wooden-boat harbours, slip through narrow channels into the mangroves where troops of monkeys maraud and solitary cranes meditate beneath a powder-blue sky. Toward the end you'll even pass Nusakambangan Prison Island where some of the so-called Bali 9 were executed by firing squad in the surrounding jungle. As you approach, the prison has the spooky isolated setting of a horror movie, then you round a bend and enter Cilacap's major industrial port, with fiery smokestacks coming from Indonesia's largest petrol refinery. Just like that, you're back in 'civilisation'.

From Cilacap there are direct buses to Yogyakarta (60,000Rp, five hours).

main beach area. Grab and Gojek ride-share taxis and motorbikes both operate in town, and offer the cheapest and most reliable option. Bicycles can be rented for 20,000Rp per day, and motorcycles cost around 70,000Rp per day.

Around Pangandaran

The scenic coastline around Pangandaran has some terrific surf beaches, forests, lagoons, fishing villages and a recreational park or two. It's a joy to explore by motorbike. Hotels and travel agencies can set up guided trips.

West of Pangandaran

Ciokoto   VILLAGE
(☑ 0823 1909 8199; Jl Raya, Km12; ⊙ 8am-4pm)
Surrounded by other small villages and roads lined with palm trees and paddy fields, the tiny village of Ciokoto is the site of a large *wayang golek* workshop, where high-quality puppets are for sale (from 600,000Rp). It's fascinating watching the carvers bring the wood to life, and while they're working, they will probably tell stories about each puppet.

Karang Tirta   LAGOON
Karang Tirta is a lagoon set back from the beach with *bagang* (fishing platforms). It's 16km from Pangandaran and 2km south of the highway.

🏃 Activities

Green Canyon   BOATING
(Cujang Taneuh; per boat from 200,000Rp; ⊙ 7.30am-4pm Mon-Thu, 1-4pm Fri, 7am-4pm Sat & Sun) The number-one tour from Pangandaran (or Batu Karas) is to Green Canyon where, as the name suggests, green comes in fifty shades. Boats buzz up the jungle-fringed, emerald river from a small marina to a waterfall and a beautiful canyon where there's fun swimming (though the current is often strong here). Locals take good care of the river and you won't see any plastic rubbish; keep an eye out to spot monitor lizards en route.

Boatmen work on a return-trip schedule of just 45 minutes, which only gives you about 15 minutes to swim and explore the narrowest and most beautiful part of the canyon. If you want to motor further upstream or stay longer you'll have to pay an extra 100,000Rp for each additional 30 minutes.

Many tour operators in Pangandaran run trips here for around 300,000Rp and include 'countryside' excursions to make a full-day tour.

To get here yourself, arrange transport to the Green Canyon river harbour (where you can hire a boat) on the highway, 1km before the turn-off to Batu Karas. The entrance is clearly signposted at several points along the highway.

Green Valley
SWIMMING

(Sungai Citumang; entrance 15,000Rp, body rafting from 125,000Rp; ◷ 8am-5pm) Reached by a rough inland road from the village of Cipinda (8km from Pangandaran; look out for the sign Citumang), this attraction involves an easy riverside walk from a dam to a small but beautiful gorge called Green Valley. You can swim in the gorge and there are cliff jumps for the brave (or foolhardy).

Batu Karas
☑ 0265 / POP 3000

The idyllic fishing village and surfing hotspot of Batu Karas, 32km west of Pangandaran, is one of the most enjoyable places to kick back in West Java. It's as pretty as a picture – a tiny one-lane fishing settlement, with two beaches separated by a wooded promontory.

The main surfing beach is the smaller one, and it's a sweet bay tucked between two rocky headlands. The other is a long arcing black-sand number packed with pontoon fishing boats that shove off each night looking for fresh catch in the tides. There's good swimming, with sheltered sections that are calm enough for a dip, but many visitors are here for the breaks, and there's a lot of surf talk.

On weekends, however, it can become inundated with domestic tourists. The best time to surf and relax here is midweek.

🏃 Activities

Batu Karas is one of the best places in Indonesia to learn how to surf. It's also a classic longboard spot. The Point (at the end of the main surf beach) is perfect for beginners and longboarders with paddle-in access from the beach, and has slow, peeling waves over a sandy bottom. Its sheltered position means it needs a fairly decent-sized swell to even start showing. Other waves include the Reef, a faster, more consistent and slightly more hollow righthander a 10-minute walk up the beach from the Point; and Bulak Bender, a more challenging righthander in the open ocean that's a 40-minute ride away by bike or boat.

🛏 Sleeping

In recent years Batu Karas's popularity has taken off as more guesthouses have opened, but the village still retains a low-key, relaxed charm. You can take your pick between rustic homestays and more upmarket resort-style hotels.

Bonsai Bungalow
GUESTHOUSE $

(☑ 0812 2197 8950; Jl Pantai Indah; r with fan/air-con 200,000/250,000Rp; ◉) An upgrade from the other beach bungalows is this laid-back choice across the road from the beach, with spartan rooms with attached bathroom, a porch to hang out on and an option of air-con. There's no food here, but beer can be arranged.

Pondok Cowet
GUESTHOUSE $

(☑ 0821 4167 5977; www.pondokcowet.com; Jl Jumleng; r Mon-Fri from 200,000Rp, Sat & Sun from 250,000, villa from 750,000Rp; ❀ ☎) Tucked down a dirt road 50m from the main fishing beach and in a garden filled with tropical flowers and fruit trees (guests can pick their own fruit), this attractive option offers cool brick-house cabins and rather creative modern rooms with a mosaic of floor-to-ceiling glass, exposed brick walls, pebbled bathroom floors and cow-print blankets.

★ Ermaja's Pavilion
BOUTIQUE HOTEL $$

(☑ 0811 235 003; r from 400,000Rp; ☎) Not your average backpackers' beach shack, Ermaja's Pavilion is a stunningly converted colonial building set in landscaped gardens, where the rooms feature delicate Indonesian artworks and antiques, freestanding semi-open-air bathtubs, iron beds and teak furnishings, and each room has a tiled terrace replete with embroidered cushions and elegant vases bulging with foliage. It's a short walk from the beach.

★ Villa Monyet
BOUTIQUE HOTEL $$

(☑ 0822 6000 0079; www.villamonyetjava.com; r incl breakfast from 400,000Rp; ☎) Topped with domed, thatched roofs, the seven imaginatively designed rooms at this well-run mini resort are scattered through leafy grounds. Each room has wooden furnishings and marine-inspired decor, and some have terraces with strategically positioned hammocks. The friendly owners throw frequent seafood barbecue nights and there's always a fun-loving crew staying.

🍴 Eating

L-Pari
INTERNATIONAL $

(☑ 0822 6023 7802; BK Homestay; mains 20,000-50,000Rp; ◷ 7am-10pm; ☎) A tourist-driven kitchen serving international and local favourites. It does a tasty fish curry and reasonable pasta and fish and chips, and even mixes guacamole in season. All served in a stylish open-faced dining room dotted with sumptuous booths and decorated with photos printed on wood depicting the local groms (young surfers). Prices are reasonable.

Beach Corner INDONESIAN $
(☑0852 2140 1544; mains 15,000-40,000Rp; ⊙7am-10pm) Plonked directly on the sand at the edge of the surf beach is this aptly named warung, serving Indonesian and Western mains, cold beer and strong Javanese coffee. It also has two basic rooms (double 150,000Rp) with sublime sea views.

Bayview Seafood SEAFOOD $$
(mains 50,000-80,000Rp; ⊙11am-late Fri-Sun) On the main junction as you enter the village, and open only on weekends, this Indo-German *ikan bakar* (grilled fish) joint offers a range of seafood dishes. Choose your protein from the cooler, and it'll be grilled, sautéed or fried up. Pair yours with the *karedok* (cabbage salad with spicy peanut dressing).

❶ Getting There & Away

There's no public transport to Batu Karas, but it can be reached from the Pangandaran bus terminal by taking a bus to Cijulang (20,000Rp) then an *ojek* the remaining distance for 25,000Rp to 40,000Rp. Or you can hire a motorbike in Pangandaran (per day 70,000Rp) and drive yourself, or book a private car transfer (300,000Rp). Otherwise you could chance your luck with a Grab taxi, which is around 100,000Rp drop off from Pangandaran.

CENTRAL JAVA

As home to the great world-class monuments of Borobudur and Prambanan, this is the must-see region of Java. Jakarta may be the nation's capital, but the Javan identity is at its strongest here, in the island's historic heartland. This is where Java's first major Indian-inspired civilisation originated and it served as the stronghold of the great Islamic sultanates centred on the *kraton* (walled city palaces) of Yogyakarta and Solo. Today, Central Java (Jawa Tengah) remains the province where the island's cultural traditions are most readily observable.

Although Central Java has a reputation for having a short fuse when contending with religious and political sentiments, it's a relaxed, easy-going province for visitors. Yogyakarta (at the centre of its own quasi-independent 'special region' stretching from the south coast to Gunung Merapi) and Solo,

just 65km to the northeast, are Java's most interesting cities. But even Semarang, the province's busy, maritime capital, has some charm.

❶ Getting There & Away

Central Java is well serviced by public transport, with an excellent rail network linking the main cities of Semarang and Yogyakarta with the capital, Jakarta, and cities in the east of Java, including Surabaya. Luxury buses and less comfortable minibuses connect most small towns. The south coast is less accessible but car hire with a driver is easily arranged.

Wonosobo

☑0286 / POP 700,000 / ELEV 781M

Bustling Wonosobo is the main gateway to the Dieng Plateau. At 900m above sea level in the central mountain range, it has a pleasant, almost temperate climate and attracts visitors from the hotter lowlands. While it lacks any obvious sights, it is nonetheless an attractive place with a large *alun-alun* and a typical rural town market. With a selection of comfortable accommodation options, Wonosobo makes a good base for exploring the region, including the Dieng Plateau, which is just over an hour away and served by regular buses.

🛏 Sleeping

★**Pondok Bamboo** GUESTHOUSE $$
(☑0818 948 495; sendangsaribamboo@gmail.com; Jl Raya Dieng Km7; r incl breakfast 400,000Rp; P⊜) This delightful guesthouse, at the top of the tiny village of Kalikuning, has three chalets with bamboo fixtures and fittings within the family acreage. But the main attraction isn't the rooms, the beautiful rural location or the quaintness of the village – rather it's the genuine emphasis on family hospitality. Meals are possible (lunch or dinner 30,000Rp) but private transport is required.

Duta Homestay HOMESTAY $$
(☑0286-321674, 0813 9337 9954; Jl Rumah Sakit III; d incl breakfast 200,000-300,000Rp; P✳🛜) Located 3km from the bus station, this guesthouse has been hosting travellers for years. The attractive rooms are arranged around a beautiful walled garden and the new additions sport elaborately carved facades with traditional wooden doorways. The entire house is decorated with interesting memorabilia, collected by the owner's mother.

Central Java

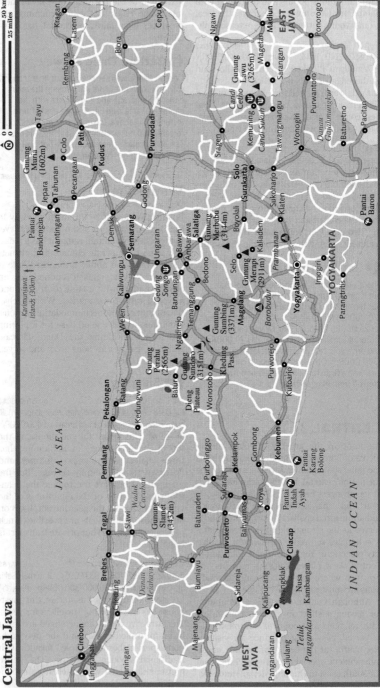

Gallery Hotel Kresna HISTORIC HOTEL $$$
(📞 0286-324111; www.kresnahotelwonosobo.com; Jl Pasukan Ronggolawe 30; r/exec deluxe incl breakfast 650,000/825,000Rp; ✳@�✽) Built as a retreat for Dutch planters, the Kresna dates from 1921 and retains a certain colonial charm with stained-glass windows and polished floors. Sadly little investment has been made to maintain standards and rooms are old fashioned and poorly serviced. Staff are delightful, however, and facilities include a grand restaurant, pleasant bar, pool table and a large pool.

🍴 Eating & Drinking

**Basement Café
and Resto** INTERNATIONAL $
(📞 0286-322992; Jl Jenderal A Yani 137; mains 35,000Rp, large Bintang 48,000Rp; ⊗1-11pm) Live music every Saturday (7.30-10pm) has helped to establish this stylish basement bar and restaurant as a popular gathering point for locals and foreigners. In the heart of town, it serves local dishes and simple international fare, but coffee is its trump card – delicious brews served with home-baked gingerbread.

Dieng INDONESIAN $
(📞 0286-321266; Jl Sindoro 12; meals 15,000-40,000Rp; ⊗8am-7pm; 🍴) Occupying a Dutch colonial building, this restaurant comes into its own at lunchtime, when busloads of tourists pile in for the buffet-style lunch on route to Dieng. Available dishes include *mie goreng* (fried noodles), *rendang* (beef coconut curry), soups, fried chicken and shrimp, as well as a range of vegetarian and tofu dishes. Early evening the food is a tad retro!

De Koffie CAFE
(Jl Mayor Kaslam 29; ⊗2-10pm) This lively venue hosts live bands each Saturday (7pm) and has a friendly youthful vibe. Mains cost around 22,500Rp.

ⓘ Information

BNI Bank (Bank Negara Indonesia; Jl Jenderal A Yani; ⊗8am-4pm Mon-Sat)

ⓘ Getting There & Away

Wonosobo's main **Mendolo Bus Terminal** (Jl Raya Kertek) is 4km out of town on the Magelang road.

There are buses connecting Wonosobo with Yogyakarta (60,000Rp, four hours), Jakarta (150,000Rp, 10 to 12 hours), Borobudur (25,000Rp, three hours) and Magelang

(15,000Rp, 40 minutes) until about 4pm. There are also services to Surabaya (185,000Rp, 10 hours) and Bandung (88,000Rp, 8½ hours, at 6pm).

Hourly buses go to Semarang (45,000Rp, four hours), passing through Ambarawa (35,000Rp, 2½ hours).

Frequent buses to Dieng (25,000Rp, one hour) leave throughout the day (the last at 5pm) and continue on to Batur; you can catch them on Jl Rumah Sakit, 100m from Duta Homestay (p113).

Sumber Alam (📞 0286-321589; www.sumber alam.co.id) has door-to-door minibuses to Yogyakarta (60,000Rp, 3½ hours) via Borobudur (50,000Rp, 2½ hours).

Dieng Plateau

📞 0286 / POP LESS THAN 3000 / ELEV 2085M

The lofty volcanic plateau of Dieng (Abode of the Gods), a fertile landscape laced with terraced potato and tobacco fields, is home to some of the oldest Hindu architecture in Java. More than 400 temples, most dating from the 8th and 9th centuries, originally covered this 2000m-high plain, but they were abandoned and forgotten and only rediscovered in 1856 by the archaeologist Van Kinsbergen.

These squat, simple temples, while of great archaeological importance, can be slightly underwhelming for non-experts. Rather, Dieng's striking scenery, which comes into its own during and just after the rainy season, is the main reason to make the long journey to this region.

A word of warning: the area has become popular with local coach tours and unfortunately this has contributed to the despoliation of some sights, particularly Kawah Sikidang. Those who have seen active crater lakes elsewhere may want to give Kuwah Sikidang a miss.

⊙ Sights & Activities

The temples and the main natural sights can easily be visited in one day on foot. An early start, before the afternoon mists roll in, is worthwhile as the waters of Telaga Warna (Coloured Lake) are most striking in sunlight.

A pleasant three- or four-hour walk begins at the Arjuna Complex (p116), near to Dieng village, and loops along the road to Candi Bima (p116), Kawah Sikidang (p117) (Crater) and Telaga Warna (p116). The latter can be circumnavigated or viewed from the nearby hilltop before returning to the village.

Pandering to the local obsession with selfie photographs, it can at times feel as if the whole plateau is being exploited as a stage set for photo opportunities. This means that many of the natural sights are now littered with swings and giant lettering, heart-shaped selfie frames and other tourist paraphernalia. While this has some cultural interest, it may disappoint those going in search of wild nature. Ubiquitous litter is a further issue.

★ Telaga Warna   LAKE
(Coloured Lake; Mon-Fri 107,500Rp, Sat & Sun 157,500Rp; ⊘7am-5pm) Ringed by highland forest and steep-sided vegetable terraces, this lake is renowned for its exquisite colour. Ranging from a delicate turquoise to a rich cobalt blue, the hue of the water is determined by the sulphur deposits that bubble up from the depths. A trail circumnavigates both Telaga Warna and neighbouring Telaga Pengilon, paved in concrete for most of the way. The lakeside offers lots of secluded spots for a picnic and opportunities to hike along paths through neighbouring terraces.

Ratapan Angin   VIEWPOINT
(Dieng Plateau Theatre; 30,000Rp; ⊘5am-6pm) For a spectacular perspective of Telaga Warna, it's worth climbing the hill above the lake. Called Ratapan Angin (and signposted as Dieng Plateau Theatre), this established viewpoint is accessible by car for around 500m, but the remaining half kilometre to the hilltop is via a steep path. At the top, enterprising locals have built a variety of selfie stations, including a rope bridge and swings, none of which mar the view, which is particularly striking around sunset.

Candi Bima   HINDU TEMPLE
FREE Proudly sitting atop its own processional staircase, Candi Bima is unique in Java, with *kudu* (sculpted heads) peering from each alcove of this elaborately carved temple. It lies around halfway along a walking tour of the central plateau, and sits at the junction with Kawah Sikidang.

Gunung Sikunir   VIEWPOINT
South of Dieng village, the main attractions are the sunrise viewpoint of Gunung Sikunir, 1km past Sembungan village, and the shallow lake of **Telaga Cebong**. Views from Sikunir are spectacular, stretching

across Dieng and east as far as Merapi and Merbabu volcanoes on a clear day. To reach the hill in time for sunrise, start at 4am from Dieng. It's a one-hour walk to Sembungan and another 30 minutes to the top of the hill. Guides charge around 150,000Rp per person.

Kawah Sileri   LAKE
Kawah Sileri, 2km off the main road and 6km from Dieng village, is a smoking crater with a hot lake that makes a fascinating sight from the hill above. The sheltered viewpoint is accessible by car – if anyone can be persuaded to drive there! The funnels of sulphuric steam rising from the cauldron below, and the strewn ash across the hillside, give witness to the angry nature of this active site.

Arjuna Complex   HINDU TEMPLE
(incl Candi Gatutkaca & Kawah Sikidang 30,000Rp; ⊘7am-6pm) The five main Shiva temples that form the Arjuna Complex are clustered together in the middle of the Dieng Plateau. In common with other temples in the area, they are named after *wayang* (Javanese puppet theatre performance) heroes from the Mahabharata epic: Arjuna, Puntadewa, Srikandi, Sembadra and Semar. With mouth-shaped doorways and bell-shaped windows, some still attract acts of worship including the burning of incense. Raised paths link the temples as the area is often waterlogged in the rainy season.

Museum Kailasa Dieng   MUSEUM
(5000Rp; ⊘8am-3pm) This museum displays an array of Hindu statues and cultural artifacts in two buildings. It is perhaps of only passing interest but there are a few gems, including a statue of Shiva's carrier, Nandi the bull (with the body of a man and the head of a bull), a headless image of Shiva and an animist gargoyle sporting an erection. All displays are in Bahasa Indonesia.

Kawah Candradimuka   LAKE
Nine kilometres from Dieng village is the pleasant 1.5km trail through fields to Kawah Candradimuka. A spur of the trail branches off to two lakes: Telaga Nila (a longer, two-hour walk) and Telaga Dringo. Just a few hundred metres past the turn-off to Kawah Candradimuka is Sumur Jalatunda. This well is in fact a deep hole some 100m across with vertical walls plunging to bright-green waters. Only the well is accessible by car.

Sembungan VILLAGE

South of the geothermal station, the paved road leads to Sembungan, which, at 2300m, is said to be the highest village in Java. Potato farming has made this large community relatively wealthy. It is a worthwhile destination as part of a hike to the neighbouring viewpoint of Gunung Sikunir, which lies a further half hour from the village.

Kawah Sikidang LAKE

(incl Arjuna Complex & Candi Gatutkaca 30,000Rp) This volcanic crater with steaming vents and bubbling mud ponds is a major local tourist attraction, marked by rows of warung food stalls and strategically positioned selfie stations. This isn't the place to commune with nature, however fascinating the flopping mud pools and whistling vents of steam, not least because quad-bike routes and the inevitable litter have spoilt the site. Nonetheless, for the nascent vulcanologist, it makes a reasonable first introduction to an eruptive landscape.

Gunung Prau HIKING

A popular, steep, three-hour guided trek to Gunung Prau (2565m) begins from Dieng village at 3am in order to catch the sunrise on the summit. The top isn't a defined peak but a rolling savannah with views of five volcanoes and eight mountains. Several outfitters offer the trek. Losmen Budjono charges 250,000Rp.

🛏 Sleeping & Eating

Dieng's dozen or more guesthouses are notoriously poor value. Spartan conditions, semi-clean rooms and cool or lukewarm water are the norm. The village is tiny and most accommodation is on the main road. Staying in Wonosobo, which has better facilities, provides a more comfortable alternative.

Food isn't Dieng's strong point, although Losmen Budjono musters tasty favourites and a cold beer! While in town it's worth trying the local herb, *purwaceng*. It is often served as tea or with coffee and is said to warm the body in cold weather.

Losmen Budjono GUESTHOUSE $

(☑0286-642046, 0852 2664 5669; www.losmen budjono.com; Jl Raya Dieng, Km26; r with shared/private bathroom 100,000/200,000Rp; 🕿) Located near the Wonosobo junction, this simple, sociable guesthouse has been hosting backpackers for years and has a certain ramshackle charm with basic, clean, economy rooms. The friendly, orderly restaurant downstairs (mains 12,000Rp to 25,000Rp) sports tablecloths and lace curtains and rustles up a mean egg and chips – the latter sourced from locally grown potatoes.

Homestay Arjuna HOMESTAY $

(☑0813 9232 9091; Jl Telaga Warna; r 200,000-250,000Rp) Rooms in this friendly family home are pretty and clean with floral bedspreads, painted walls and hot-water bathrooms. Some access a terrace onto the road with a view of verdant farmland beyond. There's a koi pond in the lobby, basic meals on offer, and free drinking water for reusable bottles. The call to prayer is also crystal clear!

Homestay Flamboyan HOMESTAY $$

(☑0813 2760 5040, 0852 2744 3029; www.flamboyandieng.com; Jl Raya Dieng 40; s/d 200,000/350,000Rp; 🕿) One of three homestays on this corner offering simple but reasonable lodging. All rooms have private bathrooms (*mandi* style), high ceilings and basic furnishings, cheered up with jolly bedspreads.

❶ Information

The **BRI Bank** (Jl Raya Dieng), near Hotel Gunung Mas, has an ATM and changes US dollars.

❶ Getting There & Away

Dieng is 26km from Wonosobo, which is the usual access point by bus (20,000Rp, 45 minutes to one hour). Most travellers visit Dieng on a day tour and travel agents, including Jogja Trans (p127) in Yogyakarta, charge 650,000Rp per car (maximum five people) with a stop at Borobudur on the return journey.

Borobudur

☑0293 / POP 113,150 / ELEV 270M

Together with Angkor Wat in Cambodia and Bagan in Myanmar, Borobudur ranks as one of the great cultural icons of Southeast Asia. Looming above a patchwork of bottle-green paddy fields and slivers of tropical forest, this colossal Buddhist monument has survived volcanic eruptions, terrorist attack and the 2006 earthquake. The last caused considerable damage, but thankfully this most enigmatic of temples has remained undiminished in scale and beauty.

Borobudur is at the centre of an attractive assembly of traditional rice-growing *kampung* (villages), ringed by volcanic peaks. Called the Garden of Java by locals, the region, with its rural homestays and guesthouses, scattered temples and tradition of honey and tofu production, warrants at least an overnight stay. For those who find Borobudur's bucolic charms a delightful antidote to the urban experience of nearby Yogyakarta, there are plenty of reasons to extend a visit, including engaging with the local culture through cooperative tours.

History

Little is known about the early history of Borobudur except that it was built some time between AD 750 and 850, during the Sailendra Dynasty. A huge workforce must have been required to hew, transport and carve the 60,000 cubic metres of stone in constructing the temple, but the details remain as vague as the monument's name, which possibly derives from the Sanskrit words 'Vihara Buddha Uhr', meaning 'Buddhist Monastery on the Hill'.

Borobudur was abandoned soon after its completion – partly due to a decline in Buddhism and partly due to a shift of power from Central to Eastern Java – and for centuries it lay forgotten. It was only in 1815, when Sir Thomas Stamford Raffles governed Java, that the site was cleared and the scale and skill of the monument's construction was revealed.

Restoration of the temple began in the early 20th century under the Dutch. Over the years, the supporting hill around which Borobudur is constructed became waterlogged and the whole stone mass started to subside. A US$25-million Unesco-sponsored restoration project was undertaken between 1973 and 1983 to stabilise the monument. This involved taking most of it apart, stone by stone, adding new concrete foundations, inserting PVC and a lead drainage system, and then putting it back together again.

In 1991 Borobudur was declared a World Heritage Site.

◉ Sights

★ **Borobudur Temple**   BUDDHIST TEMPLE
(☑0811 268 8000; www.borobudurpark.com; adult 350,000Rp, student or child under 10yr 210,000Rp, sunrise or sunset adult/student/child 475,000/400,000/250,000Rp, combination with Prambanan Temple 630,000/378,000Rp, guided tour per hour 1-10 people 150,000Rp; ⊙ 6am-5.15pm, sunrise 4am, sunset 5.15pm) Dating from the 8th and 9th centuries, and built from two million blocks of stone, Borobudur is the world's largest Buddhist temple and one of Indonesia's most important cultural sites. The temple takes the form of a symmetrical stone stupa, wrapped around a hill and nestled in a compound of trimmed lawns fringed with tropical hardwoods. Remarkable for the detail of the stone carving, this beautiful monument looks particularly enigmatic at dawn and dusk – a sight worth the extra entry fee.

Borobudur was conceived as a Buddhist vision of the cosmos. Rising from a square base, it comprises a series of square terraces topped by three circular platforms, linked by four stairways that thread through carved gateways to the summit. Viewed from the air, the structure resembles a 3Dl tantric mandala (symbolic circular figure) through which Buddhist pilgrims could thread a path from the everyday, represented in stone relief, towards a contemplation of nirvana at the monument's crowning stupa.

Paralleling the spiritual journey towards enlightenment, the 2.5km of narrow corridors lead past rich sequences of stone reliefs that can be read as a textbook of early Javanese culture and Buddhist doctrine. The main entry point is via the eastern gateway; from here a clockwise rotation around the lower terraces reveals a carnal world of passion and desire; some friezes here are deliberately hidden by an outer covering of stone, but they are partly visible on the southern side of the monument. Bad deeds are punished through lowly reincarnation, while good deeds are rewarded by reincarnation as a higher form of life.

Nearly 1460 narrative panels and 1212 decorative panels grace the monument's six terraces and a guide can help bring this pageant – the ships and elephants, musicians and dancing girls, warriors and kings – to life. Some sequences are played out over several panels. On the third terrace, for example, the dream of Queen Maya, involving a vision of white elephants with six tusks, is represented as a premonition that her son would become a Buddha, and the sequence crescendos in the birth of Prince Siddhartha and his attainment of enlightenment. Many other panels are related to Buddhist concepts of cause and effect or karma.

MAKING THE MOST OF BOROBUDUR

As one of Indonesia's great heritage sights, Borobudur receives large volumes of tourists at all times of the day and the crowds can be particularly intense at weekends. Even at sunrise and sunset, many visitors are willing to pay the surcharge to enter at these times in the vain hope of some peace and quiet in the temple compound. Visiting with the desire to have the temple to yourself, therefore, is likely to lead to only one thing: disappointment.

Rather than trying to dodge the crowds, there's some merit in embracing the site for what it is – a festival of happy tourism, good-natured jostling in the company of fellow visitors, and ducking below the masonry to assist in inauthentic selfies that show an empty site. With this approach, the site takes on a new relevance, in which school trips and family groups, in-country tourists and pilgrims provide at least part of the interest and offer a valuable opportunity to learn more about Indonesia today. This is particularly the case as foreigners are invariably asked to pose for a photo with Indonesian tourists, offering the perfect excuse to strike up a conversation.

If you're determined on some solitude, then it's worth being creative in how you seek it out. Thanks to the nature of the site, it's perfectly possible to find some space to enjoy a moment of calm reflection even at the busiest times of day. Most visitors head straight up to the top of the monument, take a few photos and descend via the opposite staircase. By taking the slow route to the top, however, and walking clockwise around each of the six terraces, there is bound to be a section of priceless carving overlooked by your fellow visitors in their pursuit of the summit. This approach also allows for a greater sense of anticipation on reaching the top terrace with its distinctive stupa.

Another good way to enjoy Borobudur is to take a horse and cart around the perimeter. The 20-minute circuit suggests lots of vantage points of the whole temple, which adopts different moods at different times of the day. There's a small hill with some shade 100m or so directly south of the temple, where you can escape the heat and contemplate the monument in relative peace.

Little guidance is needed to feel the impact of the upper platforms with their multiple images of the Buddha. A total of 432 seated statues and 72 further images (many now headless) adorn the latticed stupas on the top three terraces. The very top platform is circular, signifying the eternal. Whatever one's beliefs, the view from the monument's summit, especially on a humid day when mist rises from the surrounding paddy fields, is sublime – and made all the more spectacular if anticipated by slowly ascending through each of the terraces in turn.

Admission to the temple includes entrance to the **Karmawibhangga Museum**, featuring 4000 original stones and carvings from the temple, and the **Borobudur Museum**, with more relics, interesting photographs and gamelan performances at 9am and 3pm. The Museum Kapal Samurrarska (p120) houses a full-size replica of an 8th-century spiceship, which was remarkably designed and built based on an image depicted in one of the panels that adorn Borobudur Temple.

Tickets for the temple, which include a free audio guide, can be purchased online. A combined Borobudur–Prambanan ticket is only valid for two days and does not include the sunrise or sunset surcharge. Families take note that even high school children need to show a student ID card (or a letter from the school) to get the student discount rate.

★ **Mendut Temple & Monastery**   BUDDHIST TEMPLE
(Jl Mayor Kusen 92; admission 20,000Rp; ⊙ 6am-5.30pm) This exquisite temple, around 3.5km east of Borobudur, may look insignificant compared with its mighty neighbour, but it houses the most outstanding statue in its original setting of any temple in Java. The magnificent 3m-high figure of the Buddha is flanked by Bodhisattvas: Lokesvara on the left and Vairapana on the right. The Buddha is also notable for his posture: he sits Western-style with both feet on the ground. Admission includes entry to Candi Pawon (p120), a Buddhist temple, 2km west.

Candi Pawon BUDDHIST TEMPLE

(3500Rp, incl entry to Mendut Temple & Monastery; ☺8am-4pm) In a pretty neighbourhood of tiled-roofed houses, around 1.5km east of Borobudur, this small solitary temple is similar in design and decoration to the Mendut Temple (p119). Sharing the characteristics of other Central Javanese temples, with a broad base and pyramidal roof, it is adorned with elaborately carved relief panels. Pot-bellied dwarfs pouring riches over the entrance to this temple suggest that it was dedicated to Kuvera, the Buddhist god of fortune.

Museum Kapal Samurrarska MUSEUM

(Borobudur site; incl film 25,000Rp) This museum, dedicated to the importance of the ocean and sea trade in Indonesia, houses an 18m wooden outrigger, a replica of a boat depicted on a stone panel at Borobudur Temple. This boat sailed first to Madagascar and then on to Ghana in 2003, retracing 1000 ancient Javanese trading links and highlighting the original spice trade with Africa.

👉 Tours

Kaleidoscope of Java (p127) is an excellent Yogyakarta agency that operates fascinating tours of the Borobudur region. For cultural interest, locally based Jaker is highly recommended.

★ Jaker TOURS

(☑0293-788845; jackpriyana@yahoo.com.sg; Lotus II Homestay, Jl Balaputradewa 54; ☺3-4hr village hike 150,000-175,000Rp) 🏃 Most members of this group of local guides were born in the area and provide expert local knowledge, usually in fluent English. Tours vary seasonally, but typically cover Selogriyo (rice terraces and a small Hindu temple), tofu and pottery villages, a large batik workshop and hilltop Setumbu for sunrise views of the Borobudur monument.

✨ Festivals & Events

Festival of Borobudur CULTURAL

Around June, the colourful Festival of Borobudur features Ramayana-style dance, folk-dancing competitions and handicraft exhibitions, while offering visitors the opportunity for white-water rafting and other activities in and around the town.

Waisak RELIGIOUS

The Buddha's birth, his enlightenment and his reaching of nirvana are all celebrated on the full-moon day of Waisak. A great procession of saffron-robed monks travels from Mendut to Pawon and on to Borobudur, where candles are lit and flowers strewn about as offerings, followed by praying and chanting. This holiest of Buddhist events attracts thousands, and usually falls in May.

🛌 Sleeping

Rajasa Hotel & Restoran GUESTHOUSE $

(☑0293-788276; Jl Badrawati II; r incl breakfast with fan & cold water 250,000Rp, with air-con & hot water 400,000Rp; ✳🛜) A deservedly popular, welcoming guesthouse with rooms that face rice fields (through railings) about 1.5km south of the bus terminal. A family room sleeps four (450,000Rp). This traditional residence has a lovely restaurant (mains 25,000Rp to 35,000Rp) with Javanese specialties, vegetarian dishes and cold beer. Wi-fi is restricted to the lobby.

Lotus II Homestay GUESTHOUSE $$

(☑0293-788845; jackpriyana@yahoo.com.sg; Jl Balaputradewa 54; r incl breakfast 250,000-500,000Rp; ✳@🛜) This popular, friendly guesthouse is owned by one of the founders of Jaker, so reliable local information in fluent English can be expected here. The spacious rooms are attractively furnished and some have delightful views of the neighbouring rice fields. The rear balcony is perfect for breakfast, afternoon tea and an evening beer.

★ Rumah Boedi BOUTIQUE HOTEL $$$

(☑0293-559498; www.rumahboediborobudur. com; Tingal, Wanurego; r from 990,000Rp; ✳🛜) Set in a magnificent garden of mature hardwoods, abundant creepers and outrageous sprigs of orchids, this boutique hotel (3km east of the monument) offers a magical rural retreat and spa. Contemporary rooms with water features are set within their own secret gardens while the lounge occupies a giant open-sided pavilion. The restaurant offers authentic local dishes cooked by the village chef.

Saraswati Borobudur HOTEL $$$

(☑0293-788843; saraswatiborobudur@yahoo.co. id; Jl Balaputradewa 10; r incl breakfast 1,300,000-3,850,000Rp; 🅿♨✳@🛜🏊) This striking hotel, with its sprays of gorgeous orchids in the marble foyer, is worth considering as one of the few quality hotels within walking distance of the monument. Among the many services in this elegant, colonial-style hotel

WORTH A TRIP

VILLAGES AROUND BOROBUDUR

Borobudur sits in a large bowl-shaped valley ringed by mountains and volcanoes that the locals call *mahagelan* – the giant bracelet. Within that jagged edge lies a classic Javanese landscape of old villages and fertile rice fields that have yet to succumb to the urban sprawl of Java's nearby megacities.

While most visitors to Borobudur arrive on a day trip from nearby Yogyakarta, those who are able to stay a little longer are rewarded with the simple pleasures of rural life – delicious fresh food, clean air and restful sleep punctuated only by the occasional chirping frog. Locals have understood the attraction of this antidote to the urban experience, and offer rural retreats ranging from homestays to forest resorts. They also organise visits to nearby villages, each of which specialises in a particular cottage industry.

Two villages within this rural idyll are of particular interest to the visitor. The small community of **Karang**, which lies 3km west of Borobudur, is famous for making tofu. There are several kitchens in the village, each producing around 50kg of *tahu* daily using traditional methods, cooking with coconut oil over a wood fire. Nearby **Nglipoh**, meanwhile, is a ceramics centre that locals claim has been making clay pots for more than 1000 years and everyone in the village is involved in their production in some way. Today production centres mostly on *ibu* (cooking vessels), although glazed ashtrays and other pots are for sale too.

are airport transfer (350,000Rp for up to four people), massage (300,000Rp per hour) and village tours (from 300,000Rp).

Eating

Most hotels and guesthouses have restaurants; Rajasa Hotel is a good choice for moderately priced Javanese specialities, while fine dining at the Patio is offered in a colonial setting with wonderful views.

For inexpensive local fare, there are several warungs outside the monument entrance.

Alea Coffee Shop   CAFE **$**
(☑ 0812 8080 2956; Jl Balaputradewa 58; mains 17,000-35,000Rp; ⊙ 7am-9pm; 🛜) This tranquil cafe and art gallery, with outdoor decking overlooking rice paddies, is a great spot for Javanese coffee and a cold beer. Or roll up at night for Indonesian dishes under the fairy lights.

It also offers accommodation (doubles 350,000Rp), plus cycling tours (250,000Rp) of local villages.

★ Patio   INTERNATIONAL **$$$**
(☑ 0293-788888; www.plataranborobudur.com; Plataran Borobudur Resort & Spa, Jl Dusun Kretek, Karangrejo; mains 60,000-300,000Rp; ⊙ 7am-11pm) For a magical hilltop setting enhanced by traditional music, this vintage restaurant, 4km west of Borobudur, is hard to match. Eat in the formal dining room or

out on the terrace with views of the monument. Local dishes are served with modern international flair and there's an extensive wine list.

ℹ Information

The **tourist information centre** (☑ 0293-788266; www.borobudurpark.com; Jl Balaputradewa 1; ⊙ 6am-5.30pm) is a useful resource. In addition, hotels and guesthouses make it a point to advise their guests on local opportunities for spa treatments, Javanese massages, trips to local villages and other attractions. There is a **BNI Bank ATM** (Jl Medang Kamulan; ⊙ 8am-4pm Mon-Sat) near the temple entrance.

ℹ Getting There & Away

Day tours of Borobudur are easily arranged in Yogyakarta, which lies just 42km to the southeast. Otherwise buses leave Yogyakarta's Jombor bus terminal (30,000Rp to 40,000Rp, 1¼ hours, every 30 minutes to one hour) for Borobudur. The last buses to/from Borobudur are at around 3pm to 4pm.

Buses leave the Borobudur terminal to Magelang (10,000Rp, every hour, 30 minutes) until 4pm.

Grab and Go-Jek both operate in Borobudur, making it easy to get around. Renting a bicycle, however, is a more enjoyable option; try **Wisata Sepeda** (☑ 0812 296 2533, 0856 4188 6006; Jl Balaputradewa 38; per day 15,000-150,000Rp; ⊙ 6am-7pm).

ⓘ Getting Around

In Borobudur, becak (bicycle-rickshaws) cost between 10,000Rp and 15,000Rp anywhere in the town. Bicycles (30,000Rp for 12 hours) and motorbikes (75,000Rp to 100,000Rp) can be hired from most hotels.

Yogyakarta

☑ 0274 / POP 430,000 / ELEV 110M

If Jakarta is Java's financial and industrial powerhouse, Yogyakarta is its soul. Central to the island's artistic and intellectual heritage, Yogyakarta (pronounced 'Jogjakarta' and called Yogya, 'Jogja', for short) is where the Javanese language is at its purest, the arts at their brightest and its traditions at their most visible.

Fiercely independent and protective of its customs – and still headed by a sultan, whose *kraton* (walled city palace) remains the hub of traditional life – contemporary Yogya is nevertheless a huge urban centre (the entire metropolitan area is home to over 3.3 million) complete with malls, fast-food chains and traffic jams, even as it remains a stronghold of batik, gamelan and ritual.

Put it all together and you have Indonesia's coolest, most liveable and lovable city, with street art, galleries, coffee shops and abundant cultural attractions. It's also a perfect base for visiting Indonesia's most important archaeological sites, Borobudur and Prambanan, along with nearby Mt Merapi volcano.

History

Yogyakarta owes its establishment to Prince Mangkubumi, who in 1755 returned to the former seat of Mataram and built the kraton of Yogyakarta. He took the title of sultan and created the most powerful Javanese state since the 17th century.

Yogya has always been a symbol of resistance to colonial rule; it was the heart of Prince Pangeran Diponegoro's Java War (1825–30) and became the capital of the republic from 1946 until independence in 1949.

When the Dutch occupied Yogya in 1948, the patriotic sultan locked himself in the *kraton* and let rebels use the palace as their headquarters. The Dutch did not dare move against the sultan for fear of arousing the anger of millions of Javanese, who looked upon him almost as a god. As a result of the sultan's support of the rebels, Yogya was granted the status of a special region when independence finally came.

◉ Sights

Most sights of interest are concentrated in and around the *kraton* in central Yogya and along, or just off, the main street, Jl Malioboro.

As well as historical landmarks and museums, there are plenty of venues to explore Yogya's thriving contemporary art culture; the *Jogya Art Map* from **Kedai Kebun Forum** (Map p124; www.kedaikebun.com; Jl Tirtodipuran 3; ⊘ 11am-11pm Wed-Mon) helps navigate these.

◉ The Kraton & Around

The historic *kraton* area harbours most of Yogya's most important buildings and tourist attractions. The area is best explored on foot. While it springs from historic roots, the neighbourhood is no sleepy relic, making it a fascinating part of town to wander through.

★ Kraton   PALACE

(Map p124; ☑ 0274-373321; Jl Rotowijayan, Blok 1; admission 15,000Rp, camera 1000Rp, guided tour by donation; ⊘ 8.30am-1.30pm Sat-Thu, to 12.30pm Fri, closed national holidays) Beside the southern *alun-alun* (main square), Yogya's enormous *kraton* (palace) is the cultural and political heart of this fascinating city. Effectively a walled city, this complex of pavilions and residences is home to around 25,000 people and encompasses a market, shops, cottage industries, schools and mosques. Around 1000 of the inhabitants are employed by the resident sultan. Although it's technically part of the *kraton*, there's a separate entrance (and ticket) for the Pagelaran Pavilion (p125), overlooking the northern *alun-alun*.

The *kraton* comprises a series of luxurious halls, spacious courtyards and pavilions built between 1755 and 1756, with European flourishes, such as Dutch-influenced stained glass, added in the 1920s. There were originally separate entrances to the *kraton* for men and women, marked by giant male and female dragons (although it's hard to determine which are which!). Although this segregation is no longer practised, an appreciation of history runs deep here, and the palace is attended by dignified elderly retainers, who wear traditional Javanese dress. The innermost complex is off limits as the current sultan still resides here, but visitors can enter some of the surrounding courtyards. Alas, the treasures of the palace are poorly displayed, but it remains a fascinating place to wander.

At the centre of the *kraton* is the reception hall, the **Bangsal Kencana** (Golden Pavilion). With a fine marble floor, intricately decorated roof, stained-glass windows and columns of carved teak, it makes a suitably imposing statement for the reception of foreign dignitaries. The gifts from some of these illustrious visitors, including European monarchy, are housed within two little **museums** in the same courtyard complex. Interesting exhibits here also include gilt copies of the sacred *pusaka* (heirlooms of the royal family) and gamelan instruments, the royal family tree, old photographs of grand mass weddings and portraits of the former sultans of Yogya. A modern memorial building dedicated to the beloved Sultan Hamengkubuwono IX, with photographs and some of his personal effects, occupies some side rooms.

Outside the *kraton,* in the centre of the northern square, there are two sacred *waringin* (banyan trees). In the days of feudal Java, white-robed petitioners would patiently sit here, hoping to catch the eye of the king. In the *alun-alun kidul* (southern square), two similar banyan trees are said to bring great fortune to those who can walk blindfolded between them without mishap; on Friday and Saturday nights the youth of Yogya attempt this feat to a chorus of laughter from friends.

Daily **performances** in the *kraton's* inner pavilion are included in the price of the entrance ticket. Currently, there's gamelan on Monday and Tuesday (10am to noon), *wayang golek* (puppetry) on Wednesday (9am to noon), classical dance on Thursday (10am to noon), Javanese poetry readings on Friday (10am to 11.30am), leather puppetry on Saturday (9am to 1pm) and Javanese dance on Sunday (11am to noon).

★**Taman Sari**   PALACE
(Map p124; Jl Taman; admission 15,000Rp, camera 3000Rp; ◎9am-3pm) This once-splendid pleasure park of palaces, pools and waterways, built between 1758 and 1765, functioned as the playground of the sultan and his entourage. It's said that the sultan had the Portuguese architect of this elaborate retreat executed, to keep his hidden pleasure rooms secret. Today the complex is in ruins, damaged by Diponegoro's Java War and an earthquake in 1865, but enough has been restored to recapture its former glory.

Surrounding Taman Sari is a fascinating residential district of traditional Javanese houses, each of which seems to be vying for the most gorgeous bloom or vine, or for the most vocal songbird. The area is home to a

---

YOGYA IN...

Two Days

Start the day by visiting the Kraton and enjoying a traditional performance of gamelan, *wayang* or dance, then spend the afternoon exploring the *kampung* (neighbourhood) surrounding the sultan's palace and the nearby Taman Sari. In the evening stroll the narrow streets of the traditional Sosrowijayan area with its many restaurants.

On the second day, wander down Jl Malioboro scouting for batik bargains, or meander through Yogya's main market, Pasar Beringharjo (p125). Take a becak (bicycle-rickshaw) ride to Kota Gede (p126) to search for silver, then spend the evening idling along Jl Prawirotaman. Alternatively, head to Mediterranea (p131) in Jl Tirtodipuran for dinner and have a nightcap at one of the many neighbouring bars.

Four Days

After two days exploring Yogya, it's time to wander further afield. Rise early to catch the sunrise at the incomparable Buddhist temple of Borobudur (p118), before exploring the verdant countryside and fascinating villages around the monument. Consider staying overnight at one of the town's rural retreats.

Keep day four aside for Prambanan (p144), the Hindu masterpiece on the other side of the city; it's fun to make a whole day of it by cycling there via some of the minor outlying temples.

Yogyakarta

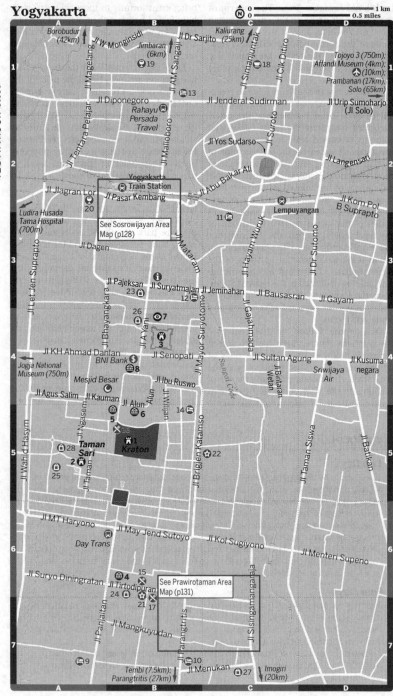

Borobudur (42km)
Jl W Monginsidi
Jimbaran (6km)
Jl Dr Sarjito
Kaliurang (25km)

19

13

Jl AM Sangaji
Jl Magelang
Jl Simanjuntak
Jl Cik Ditiro

18

Tojoyo 3 (750m);
Affandi Museum (4km);
Prambanan (17km);
Solo (65km)

Jl Diponegoro
Rahayu Persada Travel
Jl Jenderal Sudirman
Jl Urip Sumoharjo (Jl Solo)

Jl Tentara Pelajar
Jl Malioboro
Jl Suroto
Jl Yos Sudarso
Jl Langensari

Yogyakarta Train Station
20
Jl Jlagran Lor
Jl Pasar Kembang
Jl Abu Bakar Ali
Lempuyangan
Jl Kom Pol B Suprapto

Ludira Husada Tama Hospital (700m)

See Sosrowijayan Area Map (p128)

11

Jl Dagen
Jl Mataram
Jl Hayam Wuruk
Jl Dr Sutomo

Jl Let Jen Supprapto

Jl Pajeksan
23
Jl Suryatmajan
Jl Jeminahan
Jl Bausasran
Jl Gayam

12

26

7

Jl Bhayangkara
Jl A Yani
3
Jl Mayor Suryotomo
Jl Gajahmada

Jl KH Ahmad Dahlan
BNI Bank
8
Jl Senopati
Jl Sultan Agung
Jl Kusuma-negara

Jogja National Museum (750m)

Mesjid Besar
Jl Ibu Ruswo
Sungai Code
Jl Bintaran Wetan
Sriwijaya Air

Jl Agus Salim
Jl Kauman
Jl Alun
5
6
Jl William
14

Jl Wahid Hasym
Jl Ngasem
16
1
Kraton
22
Jl Brigjen Katamso
Jl Taman Siswa
Jl Batikan

Taman Sari
28
2
25
Jl Taman

Jl MT Haryono
Jl May Jend Sutoyo
Jl Kol Sugiyono
Jl Menteri Supeno

Day Trans

Jl Suryo Diningratan
4
15
Jl Tirtodipuran
24
21
17

See Prawirotaman Area Map (p131)

Jl Panjaitan
Jl Mangkuyudan
Jl Parangtritis
Jl Sisingamangaraja

9
10
27
Jl Menukan

Tembi (7.5km);
Parangtritis (27km)
Imogiri (20km)

0 ——— 1 km
0 ——— 0.5 miles
N

Yogyakarta

community of around 2000 residents, some of whom have set up shop in their front room, selling crafts or offering coffee and snacks.

In the middle of this district, via a labyrinth of small lanes, there's a unique **underground mosque** with a central open-to-the-sky atrium accessed via an Escheresque stairway. It's become a popular place for a selfie, and watching locals queue for the privilege of posing on the central stair is part of the experience.

Sono-Budoyo Museum MUSEUM
(Map p124; ☑ 0274-376775; www.sonobudoyo. com; Jl Pangurakan 6; 10,000Rp; ⊙ 8am-3.30pm Tue-Thu, Sat & Sun, to 2.30pm Fri) This treasure chest is one of the best museums in Yogya. It is only small but is home to a first-class collection of Javanese art, including *wayang kulit* puppets, *topeng* (masks), kris and batik. The courtyard houses some Hindu statuary and artefacts from further afield, including superb Balinese carvings. Wayang kulit (p133) performances are held here.

Benteng Vredeburg FORT
(Independence Struggle Museum; Map p124; Jl A Yani, Jl Margo Mulyo 6; 10,000Rp; ⊙ 8am-4pm Mon-Fri) The old Dutch fort, with its impressive moat, is a popular destination for school outings, as it communicates Indonesia's recent history through engaging dioramas in the former barrack rooms.

Pasar Beringharjo MARKET
(Map p124; Jl A Yani; ⊙ 9am-5pm) Yogya's main market is a lively and fascinating place to visit. Batik, catering for tourist tastes and mostly of the inexpensive *batik cap* (stamped batik) variety, is sold here, but the warungs (food stalls), fruit and vegetable stalls and *rempah rempah* (spice) stands crowded towards the rear of the ground floor prove that this is still a traditional meeting point for vendors. The market is at its most atmospheric early in the morning.

Pagelaran Pavilion HISTORIC BUILDING
(Bangsal Pagelaran; Map p124; Jl Alun-Alun Utara; admission 7000Rp, camera 2000Rp; ⊙ 8.30am-2pm) Due to a schism in the ruling royal family, there is a small portion of the *kraton*, overlooking the northern *alun-alun*, that is walled off from the main part of the palace complex. Entrance to this area, which encompasses several halls containing dioramas, historical royal photos and horse carriages, is with a separate ticket. The main attraction here is **Siti Hinggil**, a pavilion used for the coronation of the sultans – and for the inauguration of President Sukarno in 1949.

Museum Kareta Kraton MUSEUM
(Map p124; Jl Rotowijayan; 5000Rp, photography 1000Rp; ⊙ 9am-4pm) This wonderful old carriage house exhibits the opulent chariots of the sultan. The leather-upholstered and intricately painted carriages tell their own

tales, with crowns and dragons, gold-leaf emblems and painted landscapes.

Jogja National Museum GALLERY
(☑ 0274-586105; www.jogjanationalmuseum.com; Jl Amri Yahya 1; ☉ 10am-9pm) FREE Yogyakarta's premier contemporary art gallery is located within a brutalist concrete block that was built as an art faculty back in the 1950s. Today it exhibits diverse shows by Indonesian artists that change monthly; the useful website lists details of forthcoming exhibitions.

◉ Eastern Yogyakarta

The east of the city encompasses the silver village of Kota Gede and is the location of several museums.

Kota Gede AREA
In 1582, Kota Gede was made the first capital of the Mataram kingdom, the founder of which, Panembahan Senopati, is buried in a tomb here. Today, the area is an upmarket suburb of Yogyakarta and the hub of Yogya's famous silver industry. Kota Gede is 5km southeast of Jl Malioboro (Sosrowijayan), from where it's reachable by bus 3A. A becak costs around 50,000Rp.

Affandi Museum GALLERY
(☑ 0274-562593; www.affandi.org; Jl Laksda Adisucipto 167; adult/student/child under 6yr 100,000/50,000Rp/free, camera 20,000-30,000Rp; ☉ 9am-4pm) One of Indonesia's most celebrated artists, Affandi (1907–90) lived and worked in a wonderfully quirky self-designed riverside studio, about 6km east of the centre. Today it's the Affandi Museum, a must for any self-respecting art lover. It has an extensive collection of his abstract paintings, the expressionist style of which features distinctive brush strokes reminiscent of Van Gogh.

Tombs of Mataram Kotagede TOMB
(Jl Masjid Mataram; admission by donation; ☉ sacred tomb 10am-1pm Tue-Fri, closed during Ramadan) The 16th-century founder of the Mataram kingdom, Panembahan Senopati, is buried in the small graveyard of an old mosque located in the suburb of Kota Gede. It is the last resting place of other royals too and the entire site has a sense of reverent peace about it. The buildings here resemble Balinese temple structures and represent an interesting combination of architectural styles. Mandatory sarongs are provided

(donation required) at the entrance to the inner tomb complex.

🏃 Activities

Animal Friends Jogja VOLUNTEERING
(AFJ; www.facebook.com/animalfriendsjogja) Volunteers can work for this not-for-profit animal welfare organisation caring for rescued animals. As well as running an animal shelter, it campaigns on issues ranging from banning the dog-meat industry to contesting dolphin circuses.

🎓 Courses

Yogya offers a variety of courses, ranging from cooking demonstrations to language classes in Bahasa Indonesia.

HS Silver JEWELLERY MAKING
(☑ 0274-375107; www.hssilver.co.id; Jl Mondorakan 1; 2hr course 250,000Rp; ☉ 8am-5.30pm) An introductory course in the delicate art of silversmithing – a traditional cottage industry in Yogya – is available here. Participants are shown how to design and fashion this valuable metal into a ring that can be taken home as part of the course fee.

Alam Bahasa Indonesia LANGUAGE
(☑ 0851 0389 5187, 0851 0900 1577; www.alam bahasa.com; Jl Sarirejo, Maguwoharjo; per hr 138,700Rp) One-on-one and small-group Bahasa Indonesia language study from a professional school, with student discounts offered. Two hours minimum. Skype lessons also available.

👉 Tours

Agents on Jl Prawirotaman and in the Sosrowijayan area offer a host of tour options at similar prices. Typical day tours are Dieng; Gedung Songo and Ambarawa; Prambanan; Borobudur and Parangtritis; and Solo and Candi Sukuh.

Longer tours, such as to Gunung Bromo and on to Bali and Bromo/Ijen (from 900,000Rp for three days and two nights), are also offered. Tours depend on the number of people (a minimum of two to four is often necessary).

Operators also arrange cars with a driver, with rates starting at 500,000Rp per day and increasing to 1,000,000Rp for 24-hour trips, including the driver's expenses.

★ Via Via Tours TOURS
(Map p131; ☑ 0274-372874, 0274-386557; www.via viajogja.com; Jl Prawirotaman I 30; ☉ 8am-11pm)

This famous cafe-restaurant (p132) offers many creative tours in Yogya and across central and eastern Java. Bike and motorbike tours include a back-road trip to Prambanan (135,000Rp); there are also food-tasting tours (from 275,000Rp), city walks (150,000Rp) and even a *jamu* (herbal medicine) and massage tour (300,0000Rp). Yoga classes (60,000Rp) take place morning (9am or 9.30am) and evening (6.30pm).

★ Kaleidoscope of Java   TOURS
(Map p131; ☑ 0812 2711 7439; www.kaleidoscope ofjavatour.com; Gang Sartono 823, Rumah Eyang; day trip 350,000Rp) Fascinating tours of the Borobudur region run by Atik and her Dutch husband Coen. The day trip from Yogya involves visits to Borobudur, Pawon and Mendut temples, along with a fascinating insight to West Javanese culture and traditions. Tours include a cooking class, meals and transport, but not the entrance fee to the temples. Sunrise trips to Borobudur are also possible.

Jogja Trans   TOURS
(☑ 0274-439 8495, 0816 426 0124; www.jogjatrans holiday.com) Good all-rounder for tours to destinations in Central Java and beyond, including day trips to the Dieng volcanic plateau and its Hindu temples.

Great Tours   TOURS
(Map p128; ☑ 0821 3656 3231, 0274-583221; www. greattoursjogja.com; Jl Sosrowijayan 29; ◉ 8am-8pm) Operates tours in Yogya and across Java, including to the volcanoes (Bromo, Ijen, Dieng, Merapi), as well as chartered transport to destinations throughout Central Java.

★☆ Festivals & Events

Art Jog   ART
(www.artjog.co.id; ◉ May) Sponsored by the Tourist Board, this annual contemporary art festival, held in May, features a wide range of local shows and international exhibitions. Running since 2007, most of the events are held at Jogja National Museum.

There's a good website giving the festival schedule and opening times.

Gerebeg   CULTURAL
There are three Gerebeg festival that occur each year, featuring Java's most colourful and grand processions. In traditional court dress, palace guards and retainers, not to mention large floats of decorated mountains of rice, make their way during each of these

festivals to the main **mosque** (Grand Mosque; Map p124; off Jl Alun-Alun Utara), west of the *kraton,* to the sound of prayer and gamelan music. The dates change each year, so contact the tourist information centre (p136) for an exact schedule.

Jogja Art Weeks   ART
(www.jogjaartweeks.com; ◉ mid-Apr–Aug) Running over several months, this festival features hundreds of events hosted in galleries and art spaces around the city. The exhibitions, music performances, poetry recitals and film screenings are advertised around town. Check the website for dates and schedules of events.

🛏 Sleeping

Yogya has Java's best range of hostels, guesthouses and hotels, many offering excellent value for money. During the high season – July, August and Christmas and New Year – it's necessary to book ahead.

🛏 Sosrowijayan Area

This area is very popular with backpackers, as most of Yogya's cheap guesthouses are in the souk-like maze of *gang* (alleys) within this traditional neighbourhood. But the best part about staying in this virtual *bule* (foreigner) ghetto is that those little lanes spill out onto Jl Sosrowijayan and are within a short stroll of the more authentic Jl Malioboro.

Andrea Hotel   GUESTHOUSE $
(Map p128; ☑ 0274-563502; www.andreahotel jogja.wordpress.com; Gang II 140, Sosrowijayan; incl breakfast s/d with fan & shared bathroom 160,000/175,000Rp, r with fan & private bathroom 175,000Rp, s/d with air-con from 230,000/260,000Rp; ☀🔊) The Andrea is a charming little guesthouse with tasteful rooms fitted with stylish fixtures and good-quality beds. Even the rooms without en suite have a bathroom allocated for private use. The Andrea's claim to fame is its 'celebrated terrace', a slim verandah at street level from where to watch the Sosrowijayan world go by.

Tiffa   GUESTHOUSE $
(Map p128; ☑ 0274-512841; tiffaartshop@yahoo .com; Jl Sosrowijayan GT I/122; s/d with fan 150,000/175,000Rp, with air-con 175,000/ 200,000Rp; ☀🔊) A tidy little losmen owned by a hospitable family, with a handful of smallish, quirky and charming rooms, each

JAVA YOGYAKARTA

Sosrowijayan Area

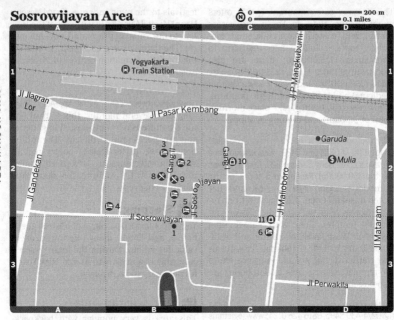

with private *mandi* (Indonesian bath). There's a communal balcony for breakfast and Javanese coffee.

Dewi Homestay   HOMESTAY **$**
(Map p128; ☑ 0274-516014; dewihomestayjogja@ gmail.com; Jl Sosrowijayan 115; r incl breakfast with fan/air-con 200,000/250,000Rp; ❈ 🛜) This attractive, long-running homestay has lots of character, with a shady garden decorated with driftwood and dotted with interesting mementos collected by the owner. Rooms are charming and spacious, and many have four-poster beds draped with mosquito nets. At reception there's a book exchange and cold Bintang in the fridge.

★1001 Malam   HOTEL **$$**
(Map p128; ☑ 0274-515087; www.1001malam hotel.com; Sosrowijayan Wetan I/57, Gang II; d incl

breakfast from 600,000Rp; ❈🛜) A beautiful Moroccan-style hotel, a short stroll from Jl Malioboro, complete with hand-carved wooden doorways and a delightful Moorish courtyard bristling with lipstick palms (with red trunks) and trailing vines. The rooms are quite plain compared to the flourish of the common areas, but they are comfortable enough and livened up with murals on the walls. Low season brings 50% discounts.

★Pyrenees Jogja   DESIGN HOTEL **$$**
(Map p128; ☑ 0274-543299; www.pyreneesjogja. com; Jl Sosrowijayan 1; r incl breakfast 620,000-820,000Rp; ❉❈🛜) This stylish addition to Sosrowijayan marks the beginning of this classic budget thoroughfare. The steel and glass design maximises the light in the tall, narrow building, and koi carp, swimming in a pond in the foyer, bring some splashes

of colour to the monotone chic. Rooms are comfortable and elegant and there's an attractive (licensed) rooftop lounge.

Bladok Hotel
GUESTHOUSE $$

(Map p128; ☎ 0274-523832, 0274-560452; www. bladok.web.id; Jl Sosrowijayan 76; incl breakfast s/d with fan from 170,000/265,000Rp, with air-con 360,000/495,000Rp; ✳❄🛜🏊) This attractive, well-run guesthouse, on the main thoroughfare in Sosrowijayan, benefits from a greater sense of space than lodgings hidden in the lanes. In a classic Indonesian building with whitewashed walls and tiled roof, rooms are arranged around a central courtyard with a plunge pool and waterfall and have tiled floors and crisp, fresh linen. The cafe-restaurant serves European food.

🛏 Prawirotaman Area

This attractive area has both tasteful budget options and some lovely midrange guesthouses. Plenty have pools and the choice of restaurants is excellent, but it is something of a tourist enclave within an Indonesian city.

Rumah Eyang
GUESTHOUSE $

(Map p131; ☎ 0812 2711 7439; www.kaleidoscope ofjavatour.com; Gang Sartono 823, off Jl Parangtritis; dm 85,000Rp, r incl breakfast from 220,000Rp; ✳🛜) Rooms are simple and comfortable in this attractive suburban house, but the real benefit here is that Atik, the Javanese author-owner-tour-guide, is a font of knowledge about the region and offers great tours (p127) to Borobudur. Atik's warm welcome makes this a top choice for an authentic Javanese experience.

Abrabracadabra
HOSTEL $

(Map p124; ☎ 0819 1630 8777, 0857 2792 6925; Jl Minggiran Baru 19; incl breakfast dm from 60,000Rp, d from 200,000Rp; 🛜🏊) Offering a warm welcome, this tiny, arty and original hostel is one of a kind. The communal area, which has a kitchen for guest use, straddles a small plunge pool surrounded by tropical vines. Fan-cooled rooms are individually decorated in styles including street art, jungle room and junkyard-industrial, while the dorms offer privacy with curtains and power points. They have a cool treehouse room too, if you're seeking an added quirk.

Via Via
GUESTHOUSE $

(Map p131; ☎ 0274-374748; www.viaviajogja.com; Prawirotaman 3/514A; dm from 80,000Rp, d incl breakfast from 220,000Rp; ✳🛜🏊) Part of the expanding Via Via empire, this guesthouse enjoys a quiet side-street location not far from its cafe-restaurant (p132) of the same name. It has seven stylish rooms with high ceilings and semi-open bathrooms, as well as two air-conditioned dorms. Out back there's a garden and a swimming pool, which features a wall mural by renowned local street artist, Anagard.

★Adhisthana
BOUTIQUE HOTEL $$

(Map p131; ☎ 0274-413888; www.adhisthana hotel.com; Jl Prawirotaman II 613; dm/r incl breakfast from 150,000/450,000Rp; @🛜🏊) Featuring an intriguing juxtaposition of colonial house and designer hotel, the facade of this elegant option is strikingly decorated with a fun collection of window shutters. Boutique touches include designer sofas and furnishings, a pool edged with palm trees and a large 24-hour coffee shop.

★Greenhost
BOUTIQUE HOTEL $$

(Map p131; ☎ 0274-389777; www.greenhosthotel. com; Jl Prawirotaman II 629; r incl breakfast from 650,000Rp; ✳@🛜🏊) This raw, natural-wood and polished-concrete structure hung with vines is a terrific boutique hotel. The lobby is the ground floor of a dramatic atrium, and its lemongrass-scented rooms offer polished-concrete floors and raw-wood furnishings. In the lobby there's an indoor saltwater pool, and stylish restaurant rustling up seasonal farm-to-table cuisine – including veggies grown on its rooftop.

In-house spa treatments, cooking classes (per person 150,000Rp) and bicycle hire (per day 10,000Rp) are also available.

Dusun Jogja Village Inn
HOTEL $$$

(Map p124; ☎ 0274-373031; www.jvidusun.co.id; Jl Menukan 5; r incl breakfast from 765,000Rp; ✳🛜🏊) This fine hotel with its distinctive bamboo facade brings a sense of the rural into the heart of the city. Most of the luxurious rooms have ample balconies overlooking a beautiful tropical garden and large kidney-shaped pool. It's a 10-minute walk from the restaurants of Prawirotaman, although the hotel's own open-air restaurant is hard to beat.

🛏 City Centre

Laura's Backpackers 523
HOSTEL $

(Map p124; ☎ 0812 2525 6312, 0812 2525 6319; www.laurasbackpackers523.weebly.com; Jl Hansip Karnowaluyo 523; dm incl breakfast 95,000Rp; ✳🛜) Located down a narrow street in an appealing neighbourhood, this popular hotel spills over two sites. The main building has a leafy courtyard that doubles as a vegetarian cafe. Gender-segregated dorms have curtains for privacy, air-conditioning, power points and lamps. Staff are very friendly and an excellent source of local info. They can arrange bike hire and tours for guests.

★**Phoenix Hotel** HISTORIC HOTEL **$$$**
(Map p124; ☑0274-566617; www.accorhotels.com; Jl Jenderal Sudirman 9-11; r incl breakfast from 1,300,000Rp; P✿❄☀@🛜≋) Right in the heart of the city, this historic hotel is easily the best in its class and is a Yogya landmark. Dating back to 1918, it's been sensitively converted to incorporate modern facilities. Rooms are gorgeous, and it's worth paying a little extra for those with balconies overlooking the pool. There's an excellent bar and restaurant with Indonesian-themed buffets.

★**Meliã Purosani** LUXURY HOTEL **$$$**
(Map p124; ☑080 8234 1953; www.melia.com; Jl Suryotomo 31; r incl breakfast from 1,200,000Rp; P✿❄☀@🛜) This centrally located luxury hotel is set in a tropical garden of soaring palms, mature frangipani and carp ponds. Rooms here are comfortable and spacious and most overlook the garden. Excellent Javan specialities appear on the buffet or à la carte for breakfast, lunch and dinner. Gamelan performances in the foyer and themed buffets make this a popular top-end choice.

🛏 **Outskirts**

Omah Jegok Homestay GUESTHOUSE **$**
(☑0821 3374 9524; www.omahjegok.weebly.com; Jl Plataran, Kashian; r incl breakfast from 165,000Rp; 🛜) One for cat and dog lovers, this arty homestay run by Animal Friends Jogja (p126) doubles as a shelter for rescued animals. It's a basic setup with only a couple of rooms (no air-con) in a forested residential area on the confluence of two small rivers, 5km from downtown Yogya. It costs 50,000Rp to get here by taxi.

See You Soon! Hostel HOSTEL **$**
(Map p124; ☑0274-287 2350; www.seeyousoonhostel.com; Jl Sawojajar 25-29A; dm 90,000Rp; ❄@🛜) Along a side street in an appealing local neighbourhood, this delightful hostel is run by a young, friendly team. It's a compact setup with a six-bed dorm (mixed gender) configured like a doll's house with bunk beds and curtains for privacy. Downstairs has a small kitchen, computer and TV lounge, and bicycles for rent.

★**d'Omah** BOUTIQUE HOTEL **$$$**
(☑0274-368050; www.yogyakartaaccommodation.com; Jl Parangtritis Km8.5, Tembi; r incl breakfast & afternoon tea from 1,350,000Rp; ❄@🛜≋) About 8km south of Yogya, surrounded by rice fields, this tasteful hotel occupies traditional Javanese buildings with a lily pond in the main courtyard. The rooms are grouped in villa-like compounds, each with a pool, and the grounds are a delight to explore, graced as they are with artworks and fringed by rural vistas. It's especially lovely at night, lit by torchlight.

🍴 **Eating**

Yogya is a great place to eat out, with street food and local restaurants offering the city's distinctive jackfruit and chicken dishes. For excellent restaurants catering to a Western palate, two streets, Jl Prawirotaman and adjacent Jl Tirtodipuran, offer the world on a plate.

🍴 **Sosrowijayan Area**

Superman II Resto INTERNATIONAL **$**
(Map p128; Gang 2; mains 25,000-75,000Rp; ☺9am-9pm; 🛜) Just like the movie, the sequel is better than the original, and Superman II has now stolen the show. At this open-air restaurant offering tasty Western favourites, there's a miniature banana grove with random rabbits and chickens – for curiosity, apparently, rather than for the pot.

Bedhot Resto INDONESIAN **$**
(Map p128; ☑0274-512452; Gang II; mains 25,000-50,000Rp; ☺8am-11pm; 🛜🍴) One of the most popular hang-outs in Sosrowijayan is this double-storey warung that does tasty Indonesian and international food that's a cut above the usual tourist fare. Cold beer, fresh juices and wi-fi make it the perfect place to while away an afternoon.

🍴 **Prawirotaman Area**

Bu Ageng INDONESIAN **$**
(Map p124; ☑0274-387191; Jl Tirtodipuran 13; mains 13,000-32,000Rp; ☺11am-11pm Tue-Sun) Traditional Javanese dishes including *eyem penggeng* (chicken simmered in spiced coconut cream) are served in this tasteful interior space with wood columns and a bamboo-mat ceiling, with twirling fans.

Prawirotaman Area

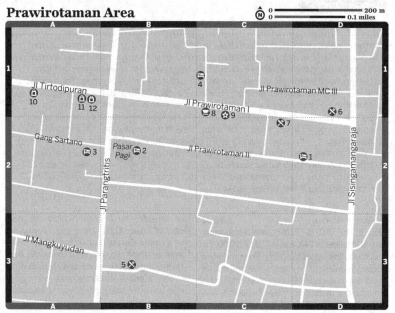

Prawirotaman Area

Favourites include beef tongue, smoked fish, beef stewed in coconut milk and durian bread pudding.The *kampung* chicken is truly free-range, lean, flavourful and not that meaty. Bone-sucking required!

Tempo del Gelato   GELATO **$**
(Map p131; ☎ 0274-373272; www.facebook.com/tempogelato; Jl Prawirotaman I 43; small/medium/large 20,000/40,000/60,000Rp; ⊙10am-11pm) This stone-and-glass cafe is a delightful venue for Italian ice cream. Flavours on rotation include ginger, *kemangi* (lemon basil), dragon fruit, 'hot and spicy', lemongrass and green tea, among more familiar favourites. At the time of research it was moving across

the road into its new colossal, brown-brick building location.

Milas   VEGETARIAN **$**
(Map p131; ☎ 0851 0142 3399; Jl Prawirotaman IV 127; dishes 18,000-45,000Rp; ⊙3-10pm Tue-Fri, noon-10pm Sat & Sun; ☑ 🖈) 🍃 Offering a surprise haven from the traffic, this secret garden of a restaurant is part of a project centre for street youth. It focuses on meat-free cooking including Indonesian mains, burgers, sandwiches, salads and desserts. There's an excellent choice of juices, smoothies and coffee, plus a store selling handmade, organic products.

DON'T MISS

YOGYA'S STREET FOOD

In the evening, street-food vendors line the northern end of Jl Malioboro; here you can try Yogya's famous *ayam goreng* (deep-fried chicken soaked in coconut milk) and dishes such as *sambal welut* (spicy eel) and *nasi langgi* (coconut rice with tempe). Many students head here in the evening to snack on *oseng oseng*, which is a kind of mini *nasi campur* (rice with a bit of everything) and only costs 5000Rp to 10,000Rp. It's a lot of fun with impromptu *lesahan* seating (traditional style of dining on straw mats) and young Indonesians strumming their guitars into the small hours. Complemented by the clip-clop of the horse carts and the whirring clank of the *becak* mob, Jl Malioboro is that different world – that open doorway into the Indonesian way of life.

During daylight hours look out for Yogya's famous *gudeg*, a jackfruit curry served with chicken, egg and rice, which is served from stalls all over town. Recommended spots include the string of eateries along Jl Wilijan (500m east of the *kraton*) or the rooftop restaurant above Hamzah Batik (p134).

★ **Mediterranea** BISTRO **$$**
(Map p124; ☎0274-371052; www.restobykamil. com; Jl Tirtodipuran 24A; mains 47,000-220,000Rp; ⊗8.30am-11pm; 🛜) This lively French-owned kitchen is a delight in every sense and comes highly recommended by expats. Everything is homemade, including crusty baguettes and croissants, ice cream, crème brûlée, along with the pasta and popular wood-fired pizzas. For breakfast it cooks up egg-and-bacon rolls (a rarity in Java). Icy, well-priced mojitos (50,000Rp) are another reason to drop by.

✖ New Section

Via Via INTERNATIONAL **$$**
(Map p131; ☎0274-386557; www.viaviajogja.com; Jl Prawirotaman I 30; mains 27,000-65,000Rp; ⊗7am-11pm; 🛜) Via Via is always full with travellers enjoying a menu of global cuisine including Indian and Middle Eastern dishes, homemade pastas, burgers and sandwiches on home-baked bread. The Indonesian meal of the day is always worth a look, too.

✖ Other Areas

Tojoyo 3 INDONESIAN **$**
(Jl Urip Sumoharjo 133; dishes 4000-12,500Rp; ⊗4-10.30pm) This brightly lit, local-style restaurant specialises in turmeric-rubbed, fried chicken. Dishes are impossibly cheap and improbably good. Little wonder all the tables and benches are generally packed with locals. It's set on a commercial strip east of Jl Malioboro.

Gadri Resto INDONESIAN **$$**
(Map p124; ☎0274-373520; Jl Rotowijayan 5; mains 34,000-110,000Rp; ⊗9am-9pm) This restaurant is touched by royalty as it's located just outside the *kraton,* within the residence of Prince Gusti Jaryo Haju Joyouksumo, a son of the current sultan. Many of his favourite dishes are on offer, including *nasi campur* among other rice and chicken dishes. The family's antiques and belongings make an interesting backdrop to standard fare.

🍸 Drinking & Nightlife

Sakapatat Social House BAR
(Map p124; ☎0274-523723; www.sakapatat.com; Jl Pakuningratan 34; ⊗4pm-1am; 🛜) A little out of the way in a residential area north of town is this hip, contemporary Belgian-owned gastropub. It has several local beers on tap along with Belgian beers and a large menu of mocktails. Choose from the leafy beer garden or atmospheric interior with exposed brick. There's a menu of Belgian fries and tasty burgers using homemade buns.

Taphouse PUB
(Map p124; ☎0812 2444 2255; www.facebook. com/taphouse.jogja; Jl Jlagran Lor 18; ⊗7pm-2am; 🛜) A good spot for a beer, this atmospheric bar is set within a crumbling, stylised, ruined-brick courtyard. It's a sprawling, eclectic space with bench tables and beanbags on the grass. There's a big screen showing movies and sports, a menu of pub food and a lengthy drinks list. Live music and DJs entertain punters most nights from 10pm.

Ruang Seduh COFFEE
(Map p131; Jl Prawirotaman I/16; ⊗8am-10pm; 🛜) A must for coffee enthusiasts, this tiny cafe feels more like a laboratory with its frosty white decor and high-tech coffee-brewing station installed with digital gadgetry. It

serves a range of Indonesian single-origin coffees (25,000Rp), all painstakingly prepared and up there with the best in town.

Awor Gallery & Coffee COFFEE
(Map p124; ☑0274-292 4679; www.awor-gallery.com; Jl Simanjuntak 2; ⊗9am-midnight) One for those who take their coffee seriously. Grab a stool at the counter and watch aficionado baristas painstakingly prepare Indonesian coffees as an exact science, using V60, Kalita Wave, Aeropress, siphon or traditional *tubruk* (unfiltered coffee) methods. It has smart decor, a menu of contemporary cafe fare and art on the walls.

☆ Entertainment

Yogya is a key centre for traditional Javanese performing arts. Dance, *wayang* (shadow-puppet performance) or gamelan is performed every morning at the railway station or the kraton (p122). Check with the tourist office (p136) for current listings and any ongoing special events (such as the Ramayana ballet in town or, even more spectacularly, at Prambanan, p146).

Jl Sosrowijayan is something of a live-music hub with casual venues often rocking with local beats – albeit mainly cover bands. For original local indie bands, check out what's coming up at Jogja National Museum (p126).

Sono-Budoyo Museum PUPPET THEATRE
(Map p124; ☑0274-385664; Jl Pangurakan 6; admission 20,000Rp, camera 3000Rp; ⊗8-10pm Mon-Sat) Popular two-hour performances held most nights; the first half-hour involves the reading of the story in Javanese, so most travellers skip this and arrive later.

Ramayana Ballet Purawisata DANCE
(Map p124; ☑0274-375705, 0274-371333; www.purawisata-jogja.rezgo.com; Jl Brigjen Katamso; adult/child 5-10 yrs 300,000/150,000Rp; ⊗8pm) Nightly traditional dance performances of the Ramayana at 8pm, which go on for around 1½ hours. You can dine here and watch the show (600,000Rp). To watch the show without dinner, if booked a month in advance, costs 220,000Rp.

Asmara Art & Coffee Shop LIVE MUSIC
(Ascos; Map p124; ☑0274-422 1017; www.facebook.com/asmaracoffee; Jl Tirtodipuran 22; ⊗5pm-1am Mon-Sat; ☎) It calls itself an art and coffee shop, but this split-level grungy venue is more like a restaurant and bar. Frequent live bands play here from 9pm. Regulars include a really good reggae band on Thursday, and there's a fun, mixed crowd every night. Locals call it 'Ascos'.

K Meals LIVE MUSIC
(Map p131; ☑0274-287 1790; Jl Prawirotaman I 20; ⊗9am-1am) A fairly standard pub, but worth dropping in for the live music. Bands play

---

THE YOGYA SCENE

It may look quiet and conservative by day, but at night Yogya becomes a very different beast. With art-gallery openings, all-night dance parties by the riverside or on nearby beaches, DJs, live bands, MCs and ska punk, there's an edge to the city that make it a hard place to leave.

The following sites, posted by arts organisations, galleries or bands, feature upcoming events.

Krack Studio (www.facebook.com/KrackStudio)

IndoArtNow (www.facebook.com/indoartnow)

LifePatch (www.facebook.com/lifepatch)

Kedai Kebun Forum (www.kedaikebun.com)

Yes No Klub (www.facebook.com/yesnoklubyk)

Senyawa (www.facebook.com/senyawamusik)

Zoo (www.facebook.com/zooindonesia)

Jogja Noise Bombing (www.facebook.com/jogjanoisebombingpeople)

Dub Youth (www.facebook.com/DubyouthOfficial)

D.I.G. Project (www.facebook.com/doingrouproject)

EnergyRoom (www.facebook.com/energyroom)

from 8pm and feature acoustic music on Mondays, the Top 40 on Tuesdays, classic rock on Wednesdays, the blues on Thursdays, and reggae on Fridays and Saturdays.

🔒 Shopping

Yogyakarta is famed for its crafts. These range from the cheap and cheerful souvenirs of Jl Malioboro and adjoining Jl Sosrowijayan, to exquisite hand-waxed batik and the meticulous silverwork of Kota Gede (p126).

In common with rival city Solo, Yogya is famous for batik. There is a huge variety on offer from inexpensive cotton prints, produced in industrial quantity for the tourist trade and sold at outlets along Jl Malioboro, to the refined hand-waxed textiles, the patterns of which have been developed over centuries.

Most of the batik workshops and several large showrooms are to be found along Jl Tirtodipuran, south of the *kraton*. Many of these workshops, such as Batik Plentong and Batik Winotosastro, give free guided tours of the batik process from 9am to 3pm.

As a word of warning, some of these workshops give commission to those who bring in potential shoppers and this can lead to a rather aggressive approach by touts around key tourist areas.

Although a few antiques can be found in the shops and markets, be aware that dealers spend an inordinate amount of time ageing puppets, masks and all manner of other goods in the pursuit of antiquity.

Jl Tirtodipuran and Jl Prawirotaman have stores selling artefacts and furniture from all over Indonesia. Prices are generally inflated – bargaining is expected.

🔒 Around Jl Malioboro & Jl Sosrowijayan

OXX DESIGN
(Map p128; www.oxenfree.net; Jl Sosrowijayan 2; ⊙2-10pm) This is a small concept store, which stocks a diverse selection of cool, contemporary art, indie clothing, handmade jewellery, accessories and hats.

Lucky Boomerang Bookshop BOOKS
(Map p128; ✆0274-895006, 0878 6169 8307; Gang I 67, Jl Sosrowijayan 1; ⊙11am-8pm) Secondhand guidebooks and fiction, maps and books on Indonesia in various languages,

along with underground zines, postcards and souvenirs.

Hamzah Batik CLOTHING
(Map p124; ✆0274-588524; Jl A Yani 9; ⊙8am-9pm) A cheap and cheerful place to browse for souvenirs, including ready-made clothes from machine-produced batik, leatherwork, batik bags, *topeng* (wooden masks used in funerary dances) and *wayang golek* (3D wooden puppets). The store has a rooftop restaurant, good for local specialities.

Batik Keris CLOTHING
(Map p124; www.batikkeris.co.id; Jl A Yani 71; ⊙9am-8pm) One of many Batik Keris outlets in Java selling excellent-quality batik at fixed prices. Best for traditional styles – men's shirts start at about 200,000Rp for printed batik and climb to 1,700,000Rp for hand-waxed fabric.

🔒 Around Jl Prawirotaman & Jl Tirtodipuran

Voice of Jogya CLOTHING
(Map p124; ✆0878 3888 3079; www.voiceofjogja. com; ⊙8am-5pm) Within the labyrinthine alleyways of Taman Sari's (p123) palace walls, this cool clothing store was set up by a local designer, whose T-shirts blend Yogya youth culture with contemporary, indie flair.

Prices start around 150,000Rp.

Batik Winotosastro ARTS & CRAFTS
(Map p131; ✆0274-375218; www.winotosastro. com/batik; Jl Tirtodipuran 54; ⊙9am-5pm) With free guided tours of batik production before 3pm, this outlet caters mainly for tour groups but that is not a complaint. Their commitment to the art and culture of hand-produced batik has made them a well-respected brand.

Via Via GIFTS & SOUVENIRS
(Map p131; www.viaviajogja.com/fair-trade-shop; Jl Prawirotaman 30; ⊙8am-11pm) 🌿 Via Via is a great place to pick up a fair-trade souvenir. With an interesting range of locally made, sustainable crafts and accessories, as well as organic coffee, spices, Indonesian books and postcards, this is a shop with soul.

Batik Plentong ARTS & CRAFTS
(Map p131; ✆0274-373777; www.batikplentong. com; Jl Tirtodipuran 48; ⊙8am-5.30pm) Batik Plentong gives free guided tours of the batik process in the attached workshop (8am to 4pm). Prices reflect visits from tour groups,

but the quality is high with an emphasis on beautiful hand-waxed batik.

Gong ARTS & CRAFTS
(Map p131; ☑0274-385367; gong56jogja@yahoo.com; Jl Tirtodipuran 56; ⊗8am-10pm) A hole-in-the-wall storefront with an exciting collection of authentic antique wooden puppets and masks from across the archipelago, though most are from Java. Some are 50 years old. To the discerning collector this is a treasure chest.

Doggyhouse Records MUSIC
(Map p124; ☑0274-378002; www.doggyhouserecords.com; Jl Nogosari 1; ⊗10am-9pm Tue-Sat) The recording studio of local label Doggyhouse Records has a small shop selling CDs and vinyl of local bands; anything from heavy metal to dub reggae. It's a good spot to get the lowdown on the local scene.

Lana Gallery ART
(Map p124; ☑0877 3929 3119; Jl Menukan 276; ⊗9am-8pm) Sells contemporary art by new and emerging artists from across the archipelago, many of them graduates of Yogya's fine arts school.

Chocolate Monggo FOOD
(Map p124; ☑0812 2684 1339; www.chocolatemonggo.com; Jl Tirtodipuran 10; ⊗8am-10pm) Established by a Belgian expat in 2005 to introduce his handmade chocolates to local markets, this chocolaterie has since expanded into a factory with cafes across Java. This attractive cafe-shop in the heart of Tirtodi-puran offers truffles and other tasty samples while customers sip their coffee, and there's a factory tour for those interested in the art of chocolate making.

🛍 Kota Gede District

The suburb of Kota Gede (p126) specialises in silver, although it can be found all over town. Fine filigree work is a Yogya speciality and the big workshops produce some very attractive jewellery, boxes, bowls, cutlery and miniatures. There are dozens of smaller silver shops on Jl Kemesan and Jl Mondorakan (two of the main routes through Kota Gede) for more modest pieces.

Guided tours of the process, with no obligation to buy, are available at the large factories. Most shops are closed on Sunday.

HS Silver JEWELLERY
(☑0274-375107; www.hssilver.co.id; Jl Mondorakan 1; ⊗8am-5.30pm) Established in 1950, this well-regarded silver shop occupies the same traditional premises and has a workshop onsite. Free tours illustrate the complexity of working on filigree designs and would-be silversmiths can try their hand at making a ring during a course (p126). The shops sells some beautiful work, including jewellery and ornaments, all of which is made onsite. Discounts available.

Tom's Silver JEWELLERY
(☑0274-372818; Jl Ngeski Gondo 60; ⊗10am-5pm) With an extensive selection of hand-crafted silverware and some superb large

---

ACCESSIBILITY IN CENTRAL JAVA

In Yogyakarta, **Difa City Tour** (☑082 328 016 326; difacitytour.com), known locally as Difa-Jek – a combination of the Indonesian words for 'disabled' and 'motorcycle taxi' – is a motorcycle taxi service aimed specifically at people with disabilities that employs only drivers with physical impairments of their own. Their specially designed three-wheeled motorbikes are all fitted with sidecars that can accommodate a wheelchair.

Borobudur (p118) and Prambanan (p144) temples are both partially accessible: although there are stairs to get onto the temples themselves, it's possible to get right to the foot of the temples by wheelchair. The Sultan's palace (kraton; p122) is mostly wheelchair-accessible.

SRAT (Solo Raya Accessible Tourism for All) was founded recently by local disability activists to advocate for better access for tourists to Solo and Yogyakarta. Tourists can ask for advice at solorayaaccessibletourism@gmail.com.

Hyatt Regency (☑274 869 123; www.hyatt.com/en-US/hotel/indonesia/hyatt-regency-yogyakarta/yogya; Jl Palagan Tentara Pelajar, Yogyakarta) has three accessible rooms. Other hotels claim to have accessible rooms but it would be wise to check their facilities and configuration before you book.

For more information see p784.

ℹ️ BATIK BANDITS

Batik salesmen strike up conversations, pretending to be guides, and take the hapless visitor to a 'fine-art student exhibition' or a 'government store', when in fact there are no such official shops or galleries in town. Some of these salesmen hang around the *kraton*, where they tell would-be visitors that the *kraton* is closed or there are no performances. This is generally a prelude to an invitation to a 'royal' batik showroom instead.

The tourist board receives hosts of complaints about these on-commission hustlers and it's having some effect. Approaches are now more discreet and the hard sell in store has vanished to the point of leaving the genuine customer clueless about what to buy.

pieces, Tom's also has a workshop where the labour-intensive process of working silver is demonstrated.

MD Moeljodihardjo
Silver Works
JEWELLERY

(✆ 0274-375063; Jl Kemasan, Kota Gede; ⊗ 8am-3pm Mon-Sat) Rings, bracelets, earrings and other silver items are sold at this workshop outlet. It's down a small alley off the main street.

ℹ️ Information

DANGERS & ANNOYANCES

→ Yogya is a safe city but smooth-talking batik salesmen can be an irritation.

→ Some becak drivers are in on the scam, offering 'special rates' of 1200Rp for one hour with an obligatory visit to a batik showroom.

MEDICAL SERVICES

Ludira Husada Tama Hospital (✆ 0813 9203 6945, 0274-530 5300; www.rsludirahusada tama.com; Jl Wiratama 4; ⊗ 24hr)

MONEY

BNI Bank (Map p124; ✆ 0274-376287; Jl Trikora 1; ⊗ 8am-4pm Mon-Sat) is opposite the main post office. **Mulia** (Map p128; ✆ 0274-547688; www.muliamoneychanger.co.id; Jl Maliboro 60, Inna Garuda Hotel; ⊗ 7am-7pm Mon-Fri, to 3pm Sat & Sun) has the best money-changing rates in Yogya, and changes euros, pounds, Australian, Canadian and US dollars, and Swiss francs.

TOURIST INFORMATION

Yogyakarta's **tourist information office** (Map p124; ✆ 0274-566000; www.visitingjogja.com/en; Jl Maliboro 16; ⊗ 8am-8pm Mon-Thu, to 7pm Fri & Sat, 9am-2pm Sun; 🛜) is the country's best organised, with delightful, helpful staff, free maps and good transport information. A number of publications (including a calendar of events and a great map) are available, and there's a booking service for transport, local attractions and performances.

Yogyes.com (www.yogyes.com) is an excellent portal to the city and Central Java.

TRAVEL AGENCIES

Great Tours (p127) is good for sunrise tours, bus and minibus tickets, chartered transport and tours to Borobudur, Bromo and Ijen. Other reliable companies are Angkasa Trans (p138) and Jogja Trans (p127).

ℹ️ Getting There & Away

AIR

Yogyakarta Adisucipto International Airport (www.yogyakartaairport.com; Jl Raya Solo, Km 9) has international connections to Singapore and Kuala Lumpur, plus many domestic connections.

AirAsia (✆ 0804 133 3333; www.airasia.com) flies to Singapore, KL, Jakarta, Medan and Bali. **Garuda** (Map p128; ✆ 0274-558474; www.garuda-indonesia.com; Jl Maliboro 60, Hotel Inna Garuda) links Yogya with Balikpapan, Bali and Jakarta. **Lion Air** (✆ 021-6379 8000; www.lionair.co.id) flies to Bali, Lombok, Jakarta, Bandung, Surabaya, Balikpapan and Banjarmasin. **Sriwijaya Air** (Map p124; ✆ 0274-414777; www.sriwijayaair.co.id; Jl Sultan Agung 54) flies to Balikpapan, Jakarta and Surabaya.

It's worth noting that Solo's Adi Sumarmo International Airport (p152) also has international and domestic flights and is only around 60km from Yogya.

BUS

Yogya's main bus terminal, **Giwangan** (Jl PS Giwangan Lor), is 5km southeast of the city centre; buses 3A, 3B, 4A, 4B, 7, 10 and 11 connect the bus terminal with Yogyakarta train station and Jl Maliboro. Buses run from Giwangan to points all over Java, and also to Bali. Luxury buses are well worth the extra expense for long trips. Although it's cheaper to buy tickets at the bus terminal, it's much more convenient to book online or through ticket agents along Jl Mangkubumi, Jl Sosrowijayan or Jl Prawirotaman. These agents can also arrange hotel pickups.

For Prambanan (3500Rp, 40 minutes), Trans Jogja bus 1A leaves regularly from Jl Maliboro.

Buses to/from Borobudur (from 30,000Rp, 1¼ hours, every 30 minutes) depart from the **Jombor Bus Terminal** (Jl Magelang), 6km north from Yogya's town centre. This terminal can be reached with Trans Jogja bus 2A, 2B, 5B, 5A, 8 and 9.

MINIBUS

Minibuses run to all major cities from Yogya. Prices are similar to air-conditioned buses. Journeys of more than four hours can be cramped – trains and buses offer more comfort. Due to traffic patterns, it's much faster to get to Solo, Surabaya or Probolinggo by train.

Sosrowijayan and Prawirotaman agents sell tickets or they can be bought direct from the minibus companies; these include **Rahayu Persada** (Map p124; ☑ 0274-544258; Jl Diponegoro 15), **Joglosemar** (☑ 0274-623700; www.joglosemarbus.com; Jl Magelang Km7), **DayTrans** (Map p124; ☑ 0274-385990; www.daytrans.co.id; Jl MT Haryono 1) and Sumber Alam (p115). Destinations served include Semarang (60,000Rp to 85,000Rp, four hours), Solo (55,000Rp), Surabaya (90,000Rp), Malang (120,000Rp) and Wonosobo (70,000Rp, 3½ hours) for Dieng. For Pangandaran (90,000Rp, seven to nine hours), **Budiman Bus** (www.budimanbus.com) has five services daily, while **Estu Trans** (☑ 0812 2679 2456, 0274-668 4567; Jl Wates Km4.5) has a departure at 9am and 8pm (from 85,000Rp).

TRAIN

The centrally located **Yogyakarta Train Station** (www.kai.id/ticket.com; Jl Pringgokusuman) – commonly known as Tugu station – handles most long-distance destinations. Economy-class trains also depart from and arrive at Lempuyangan station, 1km to the east, including the morning trains to Probolinggo and Banyuwangi.

ⓘ Getting Around

ARRIVING IN YOGYAKARTA

Yogyakarta Adisucipto International Airport Situated 10km east of the centre, the airport is very well connected to the city by public transport. Bus 1A (3500Rp) connects the airport with main street, Jl Malioboro. *Pramek* trains stop at the airport's Maguwo station. Rates for taxis from the airport to the city centre are currently fixed at 150,000Rp.

Giwangan Bus Terminal Located 5km southeast of the city centre, the bus terminal is connected to Yogyakarta Train Station and Jl Malioboro by bus 3B.

Yogyakarta Train Station Centrally located, the city's main train station is a short walk from Jl Malioboro or a 35,000Rp to 50,000Rp taxi ride to most other parts of town.

BECAK

Yogyakarta has an oversupply of becak (bicycle-rickshaws) and their owners tend to be

TRANSPORT FROM YOGYAKARTA

Bus

DESTINATION	FARE (RP)	DURATION (HR)	FREQUENCY
Bandung	125,000–220,000	10	3 daily
Borobudur	30,000–40,000	1½	every 30min to 1 hour
Denpasar	320,000–350,000	19	2-3 daily
Jakarta	120,000–250,000	12	10-12 daily
Surabaya	140,000–200,000	7	10 daily

Train

DESTINATION	FARE (RP)	DURATION (HR)	FREQUENCY
Bandung	80,000–650,000	7-8½	6 daily
Banyuwangi	94,000–450,000	11½-14	2 daily
Jakarta	160,000–1,000,000	7½-9¾	20 daily
Malang	170,000–445,000	7-8	6 daily
Probolinggo	70,000–360,000	8-9½	4 daily
Sidareja (for Pangandaran)	88,000–340,000	2½-3¾	6 daily
Solo	32,000–450,000	1	numerous
Surabaya	70,000–450,000	4¼-6¼	12 daily

BROMO BY PUBLIC TRANSPORT

All kinds of buses are available to Gunung Bromo and these often continue on to Bali. As a rule of thumb, the smaller the bus, the less enjoyable the experience, as the route is inescapably long. It takes around 13 hours to Bromo and a minimum of 20 hours to Bali.

For those determined on the minibus option to Bromo (from 180,000Rp) there are a couple of scams to be aware of. Some operators, for example, terminate short of Cemoro Lawang (perhaps after a mysterious 'breakdown'), dropping passengers off at an undesirable hostel on the mountain ascent. Purchasing a ticket from a reliable agent such as Great Tours (p127), or online through Easy Book (www.easybook.com), and checking up-to-date information with other travellers on Lonely Planet's Thorn Tree forum (www. lonelyplanet.com/thorntree) can help avoid such skulduggery.

Bromo can also be reached by train via Probolinggo, departing Yogyakarta train station several times daily (70,000Rp to 315,000Rp, 8½ to nine hours). From Probolinggo, there's a shuttle bus or a taxi to Cemoro Lawang (the gateway village for Mt Bromo) costs around 400,000Rp.

a little aggressive for business. Nonetheless, these are a fun way to get around. Watch out for drivers who offer cheap hourly rates, unless you want to do the rounds of all the batik galleries that offer commission. A short trip costs about 20,000Rp to 30,000Rp.

Gojek and Grab both offer inexpensive motorcycle taxis, which are perfect for short trips if travelling solo.

BICYCLE
Bikes can be hired from many hotels. They cost from 25,000Rp to 30,000Rp for 24 hours (with a 10,000Rp deposit). Bikes should always be locked, even in rural suburbs.

BUS
Yogya's reliable bus system, Trans Jogja, consists of modern air-conditioned buses running from 6am to 9pm on 11 routes around the city and as far away as Prambanan. The terminal for these buses is at **Condong Catur** (☑ 0813 9277 7937; Jl Anggajaya 1). Tickets cost 3500Rp per trip. Trans Jogja buses only stop at the designated bus shelters. Bus 1A is a very useful service, running from Jl Malioboro past the airport to Prambanan. The tourist office has route maps.

CAR & MOTORCYCLE
Travel agencies on Jl Sosrowijayan and Jl Prawirotaman rent out cars with a driver for trips in the Yogya region for 500,000Rp to 600,000Rp per day including petrol. Few drivers speak English, but it can still be an excellent way to explore the area. One reliable company is **Angkasa Trans** (☑ 0878 3850 9123, 0812 1594 7241; 500,000Rh per 12hr day in Yogya, from 950,000Rp per 24hr day in Central Java), another is Jogja Trans (p127).

Motorbikes cost around 50,000Rp to 90,000Rp per day and a deposit is generally required.

TAXI
Ride-sharing apps Gojek and Grab are the cheapest, quickest and safest way to get around town. Metered taxis are also cheap, costing 15,000Rp for short trips; **Blue Bird** (☑ 0274-641 1234; www.bluebirdgroup.com) is considered the most reliable.

South Coast

The south coast of Central Java consists of a series of attractive sandy coves punctuated by volcanic headlands and pounded by the full force of the Indian Ocean. The coastline was once an isolated corner of Java with few facilities, but now that electricity finally extends along the shore, it is becoming a popular weekend destination for those escaping the traffic of cities such as Yogyakarta and Solo. Midweek, however, Java's southern seaside remains a quiet and peaceful spot.

The main coast road winds through rolling hills, past fields of peanuts and cassava, and through fields of flowers grown solely as selfie backdrops (2000Rp per pose!). Small lanes lead off this road to exposed bays, where the open sea is rough and angry, and swimming is only advisable in selected, sheltered spots.

Inland, the ancient tombs of Imogiri make for a fascinating side-trip.

❶ Getting There & Away
Yogyakarta is connected by public transport to Parangtritis, the main (but not very attractive) resort on the south coast. Buses from Yogyakarta's Giwangan bus terminal, which pass along Jl Parangtritis at the end of Jl Prawirotaman, leave throughout the day for the one-hour journey

(9000Rp). The last bus back from Parangtritis leaves at around 6pm.

Other than this connection, there is no public transport to the beaches east of this resort. A taxi costs around 350,000Rp to 500,000Rp in one direction from Yogya, but it's not always easy to find a return ride. It's better to organise a pickup before leaving the city or hire a car and driver for the duration of your visit (around 1,000,000Rp per 24 hours).

Imogiri

A royal graveyard cresting a hilltop 20km south of Yogyakarta, Imogiri was first built by Sultan Agung in 1645 to serve as his own mausoleum. Since then it has become something of an A-list cemetery for royalty. There are three major courtyards: the central one contains the tombs of Sultan Agung and succeeding Mataram kings; and the other two are dedicated to the sultans of Solo and Yogyakarta.

Pilgrims from across Central Java journey to the **tomb of Sultan Agung** (10,000Rp; ☉10am-1pm Mon & Sun, 1.30-4pm Fri). To enter the tombs, which are traditionally accessed via a daunting 500 steps, Javanese court dress is obligatory, hired and wrapped at the entrance (2000Rp – and not washed after the previous overheated wearer). Shoes must be removed to enter the complex – punishing for those unused to walking on hot stones. Despite such minor challenges, this atmospheric spot is worth the climb, if only to witness others in earnest prayer.

❶ Getting There & Away

To get to Imogiri (10,000Rp, 40 minutes), it's possible to take an *angkot* to Panggang and ask to be let off at the *makam* (graves). *Angkot* and buses (5000Rp) from Yogyakarta stop at the car park, from where it is about 500m to the base of the hill and the start of the steps. For more reliable transport, a taxi from Yogyakarta costs 300,000Rp including waiting time.

Indrayanti & Krakal Bay

Tiny Indrayanti lies at the eastern end of a string of dramatic, cliff-edged bays, at the point where the main coast road turns inland. With miles of empty beach to explore and headlands to clamber round, it makes a perfect pause in a busy itinerary of Javan travel. A few people assemble here at weekends and it can even be busy during public holidays – just enough life, in other words,

to save the lonesome traveller from going stir crazy.

Neighbouring Krakal Bay, with its broader sweep of sand, attracts day-trippers who come to eat seafood at the cluster of small restaurants fringed along the high tide.

◉ Sights

Pantai Indrayanti   BEACH
(Pulang Syawal; 10,000Rp; ☉dawn-11pm) Around 65km from the city, this beach is pounded by a less frenetic sea than at other points along the coast south of Yogya. There's not much to do here other than paddle in the shallows, but, with a couple of guesthouses and a seafood restaurant, it still makes for a pleasant spot to while away a day or two. Giant boulders frame the beach's eastern end, while a series of golden sandy beaches head west, skipping towards the sunset.

🛏 Sleeping & Eating

Royal Joglo   CABIN $$
(☎0813 2525 3300; theroyaljoglo@yahoo.com; Krakal Bay; r with breakfast Mon-Fri 458,000Rp, Sat & Sun 569,000Rp; ❈🌐) This smart little *joglo*-style guesthouse, with a polished front step, is within walking distance of Krakal Beach. Accommodation is in attractive cabins with small porches and Javanese tiled roofs. There are only four rooms, but a further four are being built. Communicating in English is a bit of a challenge.

Cemara Udang   INN $$
(☎0823 2821 0384; Pantai Indrayanti; r incl breakfast & cold-water shower 400,600-500,000Rp; Ⓟ❈) At the west end of Indrayanti beach, this friendly little guesthouse is a simple but delightful place to stay. The sound of the waves pounding the beach opposite is the only interruption to the tranquility of the spot. Top-floor rooms, with wooden furnishings, have views across the road and out to sea. There's a 10% discount offered on weekdays.

Indrayanti Resto   SEAFOOD $
(☎0878 3962 5215; Pantai Indrayanti; mains 15,000-60,000Rp) The tiny ocean-facing Indrayanti restaurant serves the catch of the day. With tables sunk in the sand, it's a pleasant spot to watch the sun go down. A small shop alongside sells some surprisingly fashionable (given the minimal nature of the facilities here) beachwear and accessories.

Warung Makan
Mampir Dahar   INDONESIAN $
(Krakal Bay; meals 20,000-40,000Rp) In the middle of Krakal Bay there's a stretch of sand fringed with simple, sea-facing restaurants such as this, all of which serve more or less the same fare. Fish, squid and prawn dishes cost around 25,000Rp, while lobster or crab is 50,000Rp.

❶ Getting There & Away

To reach the area, it's best to organise transport in advance. There's no public transport connecting Indrayanti and Krakal Bay, but it's possible to walk the 2.5km between the two along the quiet country road.

Kukup

You can smell the seaweed from 500m inland at this small beach with its distinctive pavilion out at sea. That's because seaweed is the mainstay of local industry: women, in particular, harvest the livid green weed from perilous rock pools at the turn of the tide; and this nutritious vegetable crops up in many local dishes or is turned into delicious *peyek,* seaweed crackers.

The rocks make for interesting investigation, but swimming is not advisable here. That doesn't stop the beach being crowded at the weekend, and in fact Kukup is one of the most visited areas on this stretch of the south coast, outside the big resort of Parangtritis. Attracting a mostly local crowd, Kukup offers a great way to meet the Javanese enjoying their leisure as they stroll the half-kilometre inland strip of souvenir stalls. Vendors sell shells and cotton clothing and rustle up instant seafood delights.

Kukup and Krakal Bay can only be reached by private transport, which is best arranged from Yogya.

Pantai Kukup   BEACH
(10,000Rp; ⊙ dawn-midnight) This sweeping stretch of coast, an hour's drive from Yogya, is home to the important cottage industry of seaweed collection. Locals bent double over the rock pools are a familiar sight and there is a strong and delicious smell of ozone, more often associated with cold Atlantic coastal zones. The seaweed (*peyek*) is deep fried and sold in warungs along the approach to the beach. As can be gauged from the number of stalls here, it gets busy at weekends.

A paved coastal path threads along the cliff edge to a derelict concrete pavilion out at sea: a bracing vantage point from which to admire the rough sea gouge crabs from the rock pools and fling them back onto land. Swimming is advised only with caution here and at neighbouring **Drini Beach** (famed for an islet joined by a sandbar to the shore).

Penginapan Kukup Indah   GUESTHOUSE $
(☑ 0878 3966 5441; Pantai Kukup; r 100,000-300,000Rp; ❀) There's not too much to commend this basic guesthouse except that it is within a five-minute walk of the beach. Still, it's clean and well managed and some rooms have air-con. There's no food served here, but plenty of warungs sell rice or noodles with fried fish and seaweed crackers on the amble towards the sea.

Inessya Resort   RESORT $$
(☑ 0812 8321 6600; Jl Ke Puncak Timur; f 1,500,000Rp; ❀) A fun hilltop getaway, this small hotel's best asset is a modest infinity pool with a fantastic 180-degree view of the Indian Ocean. Swimming towards the pool's edge feels like taking a stroke towards Australia. The enormous family room here sleeps eight in four double beds – great for a group of friends looking for a cosy retreat from Yogya.

Kaliurang & Kaliadem

☑ 0274 / ELEV 871M

Kaliurang, 25km north of Yogyakarta, is the nearest hill resort to the city and a major gateway to Gunung Merapi. At 900m, it has a cool, refreshing climate. In fact, during the rainy season, Kaliurang often sits in a thick bank of clouds, but on clear days the views of Merapi are magical.

There are two museums in the area, both worth exploring, and with a couple of choice places to stay, Kaliurang offers a delightfully refreshing escape from the heat and congestion of the Yogya plain.

On the way into the village of Kaliadem (3000Rp entry fee), there is the somewhat ghoulish spectacle of homes destroyed in Merapi's 2010 eruption, in which over 300 people died. Though the area is condemned, many lifelong residents have returned to reclaim their homes. Enterprising locals have turned the disaster into an opportunity by running off-road excursions to the lava flow.

◉ Sights

Merapi Volcano Museum   MUSEUM
(☑0274-896498; www.mgm.slemankab.go.id; Jl Kaliurang Km 25.7, Kaliurang; admission 10,000Rp; ⊙8am-3pm Tue-Thu, Sat & Sun, to 2.30pm Fri) This impressive museum is located in a striking angular structure that resembles a volcano. Exhibits dedicated to Merapi include a scale model, which demonstrates eruptions from the 18th century until today and how they altered the mountain's shape. There are vintage seismometers on display, along with a motorbike excavated from molten ash. There's an earthquake simulator, a cinema screening the story of the 2010 eruption (10,000Rp) and profiles covering volcanoes of Indonesia and the world.

Gunung Merapi
National Park   NATIONAL PARK
(Taman Nasional Gunung Merapi; Jl Kaliurang Km22.6; incl insurance Mon-Fri 151,000Rp, Sat & Sun 226,000Rp; ⊙8am-4pm) From Kaliurang, there are two entrances to this national park, set on the shoulders of volcanic Gunung Merapi. The more developed entrance on Jl Kaliurang is surrounded by a dozen warungs and offers a more dramatic approach as cliffs loom over a ribbon road. Both gates access just a few kilometres of trails, which lead to caves where Japanese soldiers hid during WWII, and two different hilltop views of Merapi.

Maps at the park entrance delineate the areas open for exploration. Only the foolhardy step beyond the limits: in a sudden eruption, lava can flow down the mountain at 300km/h. A 15-minute walk to the Promojiwo viewpoint offers vistas of Merapi, past a forest incinerated in the 2010 eruption. A roughly 3km hike to Puncak Plawangan offers better views.

Ullen Sentalu   MUSEUM
(☑0274-895161; www.ullensentalu.com; Jl Boyong Km 25, Kaliurang; adult/child incl tour 100,000/60,000Rp; ⊙8.30am-4pm Tue-Fri, to 5pm Sat & Sun) The Ullen Sentalu museum is a surprise find on the slopes of Merapi. Set within a contemporary space, it includes extensive gardens and a unique collection that centres on the royal family and their stories. There are wonderful artefacts to admire, including some priceless batik, Javanese oil paintings and local sculpture, exhibited in rooms connecting underground chambers. Visits are only possible as part of a guided tour, lasting one hour and departing every 15 minutes. Photography is not permitted.

☞ Tours

Belantara Adventure   ADVENTURE
(☑0852 2736 6130; Jl Bebeng, Kaliadem; jeep tours 150,000Rp, 1/2hr motorbike tours 50,000/150,000Rp) One of several outfitters on the main road above town offering off-road jeep tours (maximum four people) to a village that was decimated by the 2010 eruption. Motorbike tours on 150cc bikes are also possible, with boots, helmets and gloves provided.

⌂ Sleeping

★Vogels Hostel   HOSTEL $
(☑0274-895208; Jl Astamulya 76, Kaliurang; dm 50,000Rp, bungalow with shared/private bathroom & hot water 150,000/250,000Rp; 🛜) Housed in a faded but charming art deco structure built in 1926, Vogels is a backpacker institution that's barely changed since it opened in 1978 – even the prices have stayed pretty much the same! Rooms have retro furnishings and lots of character and this is undoubtedly the best address for hikers. There are cosy bungalows at the rear.

The owner, Christian Awuy, is an authority on Merapi and its many moods and has been guiding hikers into the national park for decades. Aged over 70 and now about to retire, he's training up the next generation to take on the mantle – not easy given the volatility of the landscape.

Vogels has a veritable library of information, with books and maps on the area, and popular hikes on the shoulders of Merapi are organised from here. The most popular hike (five hours, 350,000Rp per person including professional English-speaking guide and food; excluding park entrance fee) starts out at 4am with a briefing and film and ascends to a good viewpoint for sunrise. Five-hour birdwatching tours begin at 5am with chances to spot green parrots and kingfishers, macaques and deer.

The restaurant (mains 15,000Rp to 30,000Rp) offers the best food in town, including dishes from Sulawesi, Western classics and a fantastic selection of coffee beans. Beer can be arranged too.

★The Cangkringan
Jogja Villas & Spa   RESORT $$$
(☑0274-447 8653; www.cangkringan-villa.com; Jl Raya Merapi Golf, Kaliadem; r from 919,000Rp,

HIKING GUNUNG MERAPI & GUNUNG MERBABU

Few of Southeast Asia's volcanoes are as evocative, or as destructive, as Gunung Merapi (Fire Mountain). Towering 2911m over Yogyakarta, Borobudur and Prambanan, this immense peak is a threatening, disturbingly close presence for thousands. Indonesia's most active volcano, Merapi has erupted frequently over the past century; the massive 2010 eruption killed 353 and forced the evacuation of 360,000 more. Every year, offerings from Yogya's *kraton* (palace) are made to appease the mountain's foul temper. Placid neighbouring Gunung Merbabu (3144m), by contrast, has lain dormant for centuries. With a population density of 700 people per sq km, both mountains support hundreds of fascinating small communities (at Selo and Kaliurang, for example, both of which offer accommodation and organise hiking tours).

Merapi is frequently declared off limits to visitors. But if conditions permit, climbing the cone is possible in the dry season (April to September). In 2018, following a number of minor eruptions, the top of Merapi was off limits, leading to greater interest in climbing Merbabu.

Gunung Merapi

During quiet periods, hikers hoping to reach the summit of Gunung Merapi by dawn set off at 1am from New Selo (1600m). This is a suburb of the main village of Selo high on the shoulder of Gunung Merapi and clearly marked by a giant selfie station spelling out the name of the community. A gathering of warungs and stalls marks the trailhead, from where it takes around three to four hours to climb to the summit. While it's a tough, demanding walk, it's manageable by anyone with a reasonable level of fitness. Some choose to leave at 5am for the trip to the summit and catch sunrise on the trail instead. Proper footwear is essential. The trail eventually leads to a rocky, chilly campsite at 2500m on the third plateau (known as Pasar Bubrah) that some tours use as a last staging post.

If conditions are favourable, the final ascent is very tough, past billowing vents and through loose volcanic scree and sand. A guide for this part is essential. On clear days the views from the summit, deep into the 500m-wide crater from the rim, are sublime.

The danger of the rim, with its freezing winds and unstable terrain, can't be overemphasised. Merapi can suddenly explode into action at any time, but assuming access to the cone is open, treks to the top can be organised from Selo (guides cost 500,000Rp per person).

There is a fee to enter the national park (p141) surrounding Gunung Merapi. For up-to-date Merapi information and hiking accounts, consult www.gunungbagging.com.

Gunung Merbabu

While it doesn't perhaps have the same thrill as climbing an active volcano, the hike to the top of Gunung Merbabu has the best view of the action if truculent Merapi kicks off. Even on a calm day, views of its conical dome from the safe vantage point of Merbabu make this tough (but not technically challenging) ascent worthwhile.

The summit of Merbabu is not a peak as such but a dimpled plateau, covered with beautiful grassy savannah. The route passes through forest and low vegetation above the treeline, becoming steep and often very windy towards the summit. Ascents are generally made over two days with an overnight at a basic base camp.

Trips usually include the price of a guide (500,000Rp per group), porter (200,000Rp per person per day) and a tent and sleeping bag (150,000Rp). Food can be provided and cooked by the porter, but this isn't included in the price.

Several villages on the shoulder of Merbabu act as base camps for the ascent and are signposted from the road to Selo. Each village charges a small entrance fee (around 5000Rp) to help maintain their impossibly tiny mountain roads.

villa from 1,200,000Rp; P ⊖ ❄ 🛜 🏊) This contemporary spa and villa complex is graced by an elegant *joglo* lobby, beautifully landscaped garden and 19 sumptuous villas with marble-inlaid floors. Some of these share small pools, while a honeymoon suite boasts its own private swimming pool (2,000,000Rp). Noise from the street is a minor gripe.

Surrounded by flowering bougainvillea and sweet-smelling frangipani, the restaurant is open to nonresidents.

ⓘ Getting There & Away

There is no reliable or convenient transport directly to Kaliurang or Kaliadem, but taxis (from 200,000Rp one way) and tours cover this area from Yogyakarta.

Tours, with a company such as **Discover Your Indonesia** (www.discoveryourindonesia.com; hiking tours per person from 450,000Rp, minimum 2 people), include sunrise and a hike on Gunung Merapi, starting at around 450,000Rp.

Selo

🗹 0274 / POP UNDER 3000 / ELEV 1640M

The authentic little village of Selo is set on and between the slopes of two volcanoes, and stitched together with tobacco fields and vegetable plots. It's a picturesque spot with the tiled roofs of village houses running down the steep slopes of Gunung Merapi like a lava flow. Most visitors simply zip in after dark, to climb Gunung Merapi or Merbabu and view the epic sunrise, which is a pity because the villages here are a delight to wander around in their own right.

Guides (500,000Rp per person) can be easily arranged for the Merapi climb in Selo (some 50km west of Solo) but it's best to reserve ahead. Contact the Selo Guide Association. If the Merapi summit is off-limits, dormant Merbabu can be climbed safely at any time and offers gorgeous savannah vistas from the top.

🏃 Activities

Selo Guide Association   HIKING
(🗹 0878 3632 5955) Guides from this association can be easily arranged for the Gunung Merapi or Merbabu volcano climbs (500,000Rp return), but it's best to reserve ahead.

🛌 Sleeping & Drinking

Ratri Homestay   GUESTHOUSE $
(🗹 0276-320073; Jl Desa Samiran, Kampung Samiran; d/tr incl breakfast & hot-water bathroom 150,000/250,000Rp; 🛜) At the foot of the road to New Selo, this helpful guesthouse has a number of simple but reasonably comfort-able rooms arranged around a balconied terrace. The rooms are painted in wild colours and even the outside walls and an abandoned car got a lick of paint in the decorating frenzy.

One- or two-hour 'soft hikes' are organised from here and the guesthouse hosts tour agencies for more major hiking trips from Yogya.

Homestay Selo   HOMESTAY $
(www.homestaymerapi.com; Jl Jarakan, Kampung Damandiri; r incl breakfast 165,000Rp) 🍴 One of a number of homestays that are clustered along 'Homestay Street', this friendly enterprise at the top of the street is part of a village cooperative. All the pretty hostelries in the cooperative offer the same services for the same price, and all sport beautiful traditional Javanese flourishes (tiled roofs, gorgeous gardens) that make it hard to choose between them.

Warung Damandiri   COFFEE
(Jl Jarakan, Kampung Damandiri; coffee 10,000Rp; ⏰8am-6pm) With unrivalled views across the gorgeous little village of Selo, towards the looming, brooding presence of Gunung Merapi, this open-air coffee shop boasts free wi-fi and an 'I love Merapi' selfie station. The landlady rustles up fried banana fritters sprinkled with local cheese (3500Rp) and Javanese coffee. Packets of locally grown Arabica beans are also on sale (6500Rp).

ⓘ Getting There & Away

Selo can be reached from Solo by taking a bus to Boyolali, which stops at Selo en route (16,000Rp, two hours). From Yogyakarta, take a Magelang bus to Blabak (9000Rp, one hour) and an *angkot* or bus to Selo (6000Rp). A private car from Yogya is around 450,000Rp one way.

Prambanan

Best visited as a day trip from Yogya, the spectacular temples of Prambanan, set in the plains of Central Java, are the best surviving examples of Java's extended period of Hindu culture. With nearby Borobudur, they are one of the top highlights of Southeast Asia.

All the temples in the Prambanan area were built between the 8th and 10th centuries AD, when Java was ruled by the Buddhist Sailendras in the south and the Hindu Sanjayas of Old Mataram in the north.

The two dynasties were united by the marriage of Hindu Rakai Pikatan and the Buddhist Sailendra princess, Pramodha-vardhani. This may explain why a number of temples, including those of the Prambanan temple complex and the smaller Plaosan group, reveal both Shivaite and Buddhist elements in architecture and sculpture. But Prambanan is a Hindu site first and fore-most, and the wealth of sculptural detail on the great Shiva temple here is the nation's most outstanding example of Hindu art.

⊙ Sights

★ **Prambanan Temple** HINDU TEMPLE
(☑ 0274-496402; www.borobudurpark.com; Jl Raya Yogya–Solo; adult/student & child under 10yr 350,000/210,000Rp, combination with Borobudur 630,000/378,000Rp, guide per hour 150,000Rp; ⊙ 6am-5.15pm) Comprising the remains of some 244 temples, World Heritage–listed Prambanan is Indonesia's largest Hindu site and one of Southeast Asia's major at-tractions. The highlight is the central com-pound, where eight main and eight minor temples are assembled on a raised platform – an architectural crescendo of carved ma-sonry and staircases, the high note of which is Candi Shiva Mahadeva. Prambanan sits within a large park dotted with lesser tem-ples – a day is needed to do the site justice.

Extended over two centuries, building at Prambanan commenced in the middle of the 9th century – around 50 years after Boro-budur. Little else is known about the early history of this temple complex, although it's thought that it may have been built by Rakai Pikatan to commemorate the return of a Hindu dynasty to sole power in Java. The whole Prambanan Plain was abandoned

when the Hindu-Javanese kings moved to East Java and, in the middle of the 16th century, a great earthquake toppled many of the temples. Prambanan remained in ruins for years, its demise accelerated by treasure hunters and locals searching for building materials. While efforts were made in 1885 to clear the site, it was not until 1937 that re-construction was first attempted. Most tem-ples have now been restored to some extent, and, like Borobudur, Prambanan was listed as a Unesco World Heritage Site in 1991.

Prambanan suffered extensive damage in the 2006 earthquake. Although the main temples survived, hundreds of stone blocks collapsed or were cracked (479 blocks in the Shiva temple alone). Today the main struc-tures have been restored, but a lot of work remains to be done and parts of the complex are still off limits.

In the main courtyard, **Candi Shiva Ma-hadeva**, dedicated to Shiva, is not only the largest of the temples but also the finest. The main spire soars 47m high and the temple is lavishly carved. The 'medallions' that deco-rate its base have a characteristic Pramba-nan motif – small lions in niches flanked by *kalpatura* (trees of heaven) and a menag-erie of stylised half-human, half-bird *kin-nara* (heavenly beings). The vibrant scenes carved onto the inner wall of the gallery encircling the temple are from the Ramaya-na – they tell how Lord Rama's wife, Sita, is abducted and how Hanuman, the monkey god, and Sugriwa, the white-monkey gener-al, eventually find and release her.

The temple's interior comprises a main chamber at the top of the eastern stairway with a four-armed statue of Shiva the De-stroyer. The statue is notable for the fact

---

❶ MAKING THE BEST OF PRAMBANAN

The main sights are clustered around Prambanan Temple, which naturally enough tends to attract the biggest crowds – and for good reason: the temple complex, on a raised platform above the plain, is spectacular at any time of day or season.

But Prambanan is far from the only worthwhile sight in the area and often the lesser-known temples, such as **Candi Sojiwan** (Candi Sajiwan; Jl Tulung Tamanmartani; 10,000Rp; ⊙ 8am-5pm), **Candi Sari** (off Jl Raya Yogya–Solo; 10,000Rp; ⊙ 8am-3pm) and **Candi Kalasan** (Jl Raya Yogya–Solo; 10,000Rp; ⊙ 8am-5pm) (one of the oldest temples on the Prambanan plain) which have a delicate and unassuming beauty of their own, are overlooked. Walking around their fallen masonry without a cast of thousands is one of the special privileges of this area.

Golf carts and horse-drawn carriages connect the main temple complex at Pramba-nan with the lesser-known structures that are scattered across the extensive temple grounds. Temples outside the park area can be reached by bicycle or taxi.

that this mightiest of Hindu gods stands on a huge lotus pedestal, a symbol of Buddhism. In the southern cell is the potbellied and bearded Agastya, an incarnation of Shiva as divine teacher; in the western cell is a superb image of the elephant-headed Ganesha, Shiva's son and the god of knowledge. Ganesha's right hand, usually holding his ivory tusk, was broken off in the earthquake. In the northern cell, Durga, Shiva's consort, can be seen killing the demon buffalo. Some people believe that the Durga image is actually an image of the Slender Virgin, who, legend has it, was turned to stone by a man she refused to marry. She is still an object of pilgrimage and her name is often used for the temple group.

Candi Vishnu touches 33m and sits just north of Candi Shiva Mahadeva. The temple's impressive reliefs tell the story of Lord Krishna, a hero of the Mahabharata epic, while a four-armed image of Vishnu the Preserver crowns the inner sanctum. **Candi Brahma** is Candi Vishnu's twin temple. South of Candi Shiva Mahadeva, it is carved with the final scenes of the Ramayana. The spectacular mouth doorway is noteworthy and the inner chamber contains a four-headed statue of Brahma, the god of creation.

The park surrounding Prambanan contains a number of lesser-known temples, including the Buddhist temple **Candi Sewu**. Dating from around AD 850, it comprises dozens of outer shrines, decorated with stupas. Originally it was surrounded by four rings of 240 smaller 'guard' temples, leading to its name 'Thousand Temples'. Outside the compound stood four sanctuaries at the points of the compass, of which **Candi Bubrah**, now reduced to its stone foundation, is the most southern. The renovated main temple has finely carved niches around the inner gallery, which would once have held bronze statues. To reach Candi Sewu, hire a bike (20,000Rp) or take the toy train or golf cart (20,000Rp) that shuttle visitors back and forth from the exit of Prambanan's main temple site; failing that, it's a pleasant 20-minute walk from the main complex through semi-shaded parkland.

Tickets for Prambanan can be purchased online. Options include a combined Prambanan–Kraton Ratu Boko package and a Prambanan–Borobudur discount ticket. Note that the latter is only valid for two days and doesn't cover the extra surcharge to visit at sunrise or sunset.

Candi Sambisari TEMPLE

(Jl Candi Sambisari; 10,000Rp; ⊙7am-5pm) This Shiva temple, possibly the latest temple at Prambanan to be erected by the Mataram dynasty, was discovered by a farmer in 1966. Excavated from under ancient layers of protective volcanic ash and dust, it lies almost 6m below the level of the surrounding fields and is remarkable for its perfectly preserved condition. The inner sanctum of the temple is dominated by a large lingam and yoni (stylised penis and vagina), typical of Shiva temples.

Plaosan Temples TEMPLE

(3000Rp; ⊙6am-5pm) Built around the same time as the larger Prambanan temple group, the Plaosan temples combine both Hindu and Buddhist religious symbols in their elaborate temple carving. **Plaosan Lor** (Plaosan North) comprises two restored, identical main temples, surrounded by some 126 small shrines and solid stupas, most of which are now just a jumble of stone. **Plaosan Kidul** (Plaosan South) has more stupas and the remnants of a temple, but little renovation work has been done.

Kraton Ratu Boko RUINS

(Palace of King Boko; www.borobudurpark.com; Jl Piyungan–Prambanan; adult/child under 10yr 362,500/217,500Rp, combination ticket with Prambanan 630,000Rp; ⊙6am-5.15pm) Kraton Ratu Boko is a partly ruined Hindu palace complex dating from the 9th century. Perched on a hilltop overlooking Prambanan, it is believed to have been the central court of the mighty Mataram dynasty. There's a large gateway and the platform of Candi Pembakaran (the Royal Crematorium), as well as a series of bathing places staggered on different levels leading down to the village. The sunset view over the Prambanan Plain is magnificent.

☞ Tours

Java Heritage Tour CYCLING

(✆0819 1553 4286; www.javaheritagetour.com; 359,000Rp per person) Providing a lovely way to set the splendours of Prambanan within their rural context, this 2½-hour cycle tour from Candi Sambisari follows small lanes and introduces elements of cultural interest along the route. Entrance to temples is not included in the price, but a free shuttle back from Prambanan is available for those too weary to cycle back to Yogyakarta.

JAVA PRAMBANAN

☆ Entertainment

★ Ramayana Ballet
DANCE

(☑ 0274-496408, 0811 268 8000; www.borobudur park.com; tickets from 125,000Rp; ⊙ 7.30-9pm Tue, Thu & Sat) Held at the outdoor theatre just west of the main Prambanan temple complex, the famous Ramayana Ballet is Java's most spectacular dance-drama troupe. The story of Rama and Sita takes place three nights a week; from May to October it is performed on the open-air stage (weather permitting), while other times it's held indoors.

❶ Getting There & Away

The temples of Prambanan can be visited from Yogyakarta, 17km to the southwest. From Yogyakarta, take TransJogja bus 1A (3600Rp, 40 minutes) from Jl Malioboro. From Solo, buses take 1½ hours and cost 25,000Rp. It's also possible to reach Prambanan by taking a train to Maguwo station (near Yogyakarta airport). From here, the TransJogja bus 1A stops at Prambanan.

For an interesting cycle route along backstreets, join the Java Heritage Tour (p145). This starts at Candi Sambisari and leads along rural lanes past Kraton Ratu Boko to Prambanan.

Hiring a motorcycle allows for a combined trip to Kaliurang. From Kaliurang, instead of going back to the main Yogyakarta–Solo road, take the 'Solo Alternatif' route signposted in the village of Pakem, about halfway between Yogyakarta and Kaliurang. From there the road passes through some beautiful countryside, before joining the highway just before Prambanan's main entrance.

Solo

☑ 0271 / POP 555,300 / ELEV 95M

Arguably the heartland of Javanese identity and tradition, Solo (officially known as Surakarta) has a distinct character determined by the city's long and distinguished past. As a seat of the great Mataram empire, it competes with its great rival, Yogyakarta, as the hub of Javanese culture. In contrast with its more contemporary and cosmopolitan neighbour, however, conservative Solo is less interested in courting foreign tourists, resulting in a refreshingly authentic urban experience.

Few visitors stay more than one night, which is a pity as there is much to explore. With backstreet *kampung* (neighbourhoods) and an elegant *kraton* (walled city palace), traditional markets and gleaming malls, Solo has plenty of attractions. It's also an excellent place to experience traditional performing arts, as it attracts students and scholars to its renowned music and dance academies.

With a magnificent batik museum, Solo is arguably the best place to buy batik clothing. Batik cloth here is elevated to an art form.

History

Following the sacking of the Mataram court at Kartosuro in 1742, Sultan Pakubuwono II established his new court near the Solo river in 1745. His heir, Pakubuwono III, lost half of the kingdom to the court of Yogyakarta, but a later descendent, Pakubuwono X (1893– 1938), revived the city's fortunes. Eschewing the pointless business of fighting rival royals, he invested instead in culture and Solo remains today a centre of the arts.

Dithering over opportunities to play a positive role in the revolution, Solo was sidelined after WWII as Yogyakarta became the seat of the new independent government. So it remained until, in 1998, rioters brought the city to national attention with the systematic looting and burning of shopping centres and the targeting of Chinese-owned businesses. Solo continues to be associated with violent radicalism, with links to extremist groups such as Jemaah Islamiah, but this is barely evident in a city coming to terms with modernity.

⊙ Sights

★ House of Danar Hadi
MUSEUM

(☑ 0271-713140; Jl Slamet Riyadi 261; admission 35,000Rp; ⊙ 9am-4pm, showroom to 9pm) Danar Hadi is one of the world's finest batik museums. The handpicked favourites from the owner's private collection (1078 pieces from a collection of 11,000) are magnificently displayed on wooden trellises throughout 11 rooms of this grand old colonial building. An obligatory guided tour, helpfully tailored to the visitor's time and interest, covers the highlights among the antique and royal pieces on display. A demonstration of the craft is included in the tour and there's a shop. No photography.

★ Sangiran Museum of Ancient Man
MUSEUM

(Kebayanan II, Krikilan; 11,500Rp; ⊙ 8am-4pm Tue-Sun) With the largest collection of *Homo erectus* fossils in the world (the bones of 70 individuals), Sangiran is an important ar-

TRADITION & DISASTER

Solo is a deeply superstitious city and many of its citizens are acutely observant of Javanese and Islamic ritual. So when the *kraton* (palace) ignited in flames on 1 January 1985, many locals saw it as a consequence of the incumbent sultan Pakubuwono XII's lack of observance of tradition. For years he'd been lax with his ceremonial duties, and his alleged womanising was the talk of the town. The sultan had also taken to living the high life in Jakarta, rather than presiding over court life in Solo.

Firefighters responding quickly to the blaze found their engines could not fit through the main gateway, which was thought to be sacred, and initially refused to smash through it. Around 60% of the palace subsequently burned to the ground.

To appease deeply felt Javanese customs, a purification ceremony was performed. The head of a tiger, snake, buffalo and deer were buried, and tons of ashes were returned to the coast to quell the wrath of Nyai Loro Kidul, the Queen of the South Seas, whose influence over the tragic events was seen to be pivotal by many. General Benny Murdani, who investigated the fire, was eager to counter these locally held superstitions, stating 'reporters will *not* reach their own conclusions. The reason for the fire was an electrical short circuit'.

When Pakubuwono XII died in 2004, he left 37 children from six wives and mistresses, but no clear heir. Pakubuwono XIII eventually assumed the throne after years of family infighting.

chaeological excavation site. This was where 'Java Man' *(Pithecanthropus erectus)* was unearthed by a Dutch professor in 1936 – a discovery celebrated in this excellent museum, Krikilan's only attraction. On display are skulls (one of *Homo erectus*), various pig and hippopotamus teeth, and fossil exhibits, including mammoth bones and tusks. Large dioramas suggest the fossils' prehistoric context.

Radya Pustaka Museum   MUSEUM
(Jl Slamet Riyadi 275; 3000Rp; ⊙9am-2pm Tue-Sun) This small museum occupies a grand old Javanese building. Dating back to 1890, it is the second-oldest museum in the whole of Indonesia and contains a valuable collection of local and Dutch literature. More accessible for the casual visitor are the cabinets of gamelan instruments, jewelled kris (traditional daggers), puppets and *wayang beber* (scrolls that depict *wayang* stories).

Kraton Surakarta   PALACE
(Kraton Kasunanan; ☑0271-656432; Jl Sidikoro; admission 15,000Rp, photography 3500Rp, guide 50,000Rp; ⊙9am-2pm Mon-Fri, to 3pm Sat & Sun) Once the hub of an empire, today the Kraton Surakarta, established in 1745, is a faded symbol of a bygone era. It's worth a visit, but much of the *kraton* was destroyed by fire in 1985. Many of the inner buildings were rebuilt, but today the allure of this once-majestic palace has somewhat

vanished and its structures are left bare and unloved – though restorations will hopefully improve things. The main sight for visitors is the Sasono Sewoko museum.

Mangkunegaran Palace   PALACE
(Istana Mangkunegaran; www.puromangkunegaran.com; Jl Ronggowarsito; admission 20,000Rp; ⊙8am-3pm Mon-Wed, Fri & Sat, to 2.30pm Thu & Sun) Built in 1757, the Mangkunegaran Palace in the centre of Solo is still a royal residence. Some rooms are dedicated to a delightful palace museum devoted to the personal collection of Mangkunegara VII. On display are gold-plated dresses for royal dances, a superb mask collection, jewellery and a few oddities, including huge Buddhist rings, a stuffed Javanese leopard and tiger, and gold genital covers. The worthwhile, mandatory guides mostly speak English (a tip of 30,000Rp plus is appreciated).

🏃 Activities

Jaladara Steam Train   RAIL
(☑0856 4200 3322; large/small group per person 150,000/360,000Rp; ⊙9am-11.30am) Running only when chartered, and trundling through the heart of the city, the Jaladara train offers a fun morning excursion. Built in Germany in 1896, the train sports carriages with vintage wooden fittings. The trip (with an English-speaking guide) starts at Purwosari train station, 3km west of the centre, and stops for a visit to a Kampung Batik Kauman

Solo (Surakarta)

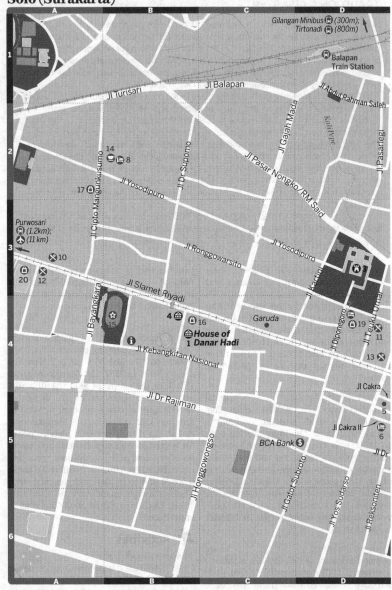

(p152) batik workshop before terminating at Sangkrah train station.

☞ Tours

Jogja Trans (p127), in nearby Yogyakarta, offers excellent tours of Solo. For a more lo-

cal perspective, guesthouses and freelance guides offer city, regional and bike tours. Check with the Solo tourist office (p152).

Miki Tours   TOURS

(☑0271-665352; Jl Yos Sudarso 17) This travel agent offers tours to the countryside around

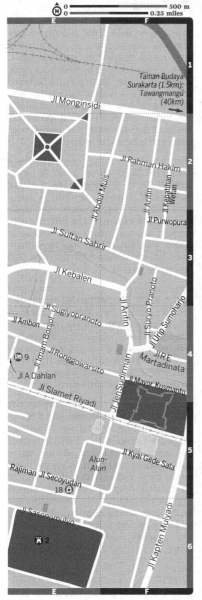

| 0 | 500 m |
| 0 | 0.25 miles |

Solo (Surakarta)

🛏 Sleeping

Cakra Homestay   HOMESTAY **$**
(✆0878 3636 3686, 0271-634743; Jl Cakra II 15; r incl breakfast with shared/private bathroom from 125,000/175,000Rp, r with air-con & private bathroom from 200,000Rp; ❄☎🏊) Although the rooms are simple, this atmospheric old homestay, in a magnificent timbered building between Solo's two palaces, scores highly for those interested in Javanese culture. There's a gamelan room with occasional free performances and a lovely, palm-shaded pool. Shared bathrooms are Western- and *mandi*-style. Wi-fi access is in public areas only.

★**Warung Baru Homestay**   GUESTHOUSE **$**
(✆0271-656369, 0812 268 7443; off Jl Ahmad Dahlan; r incl breakfast with fan/air-con from 100,000/150,000Rp; ❄☎) Hidden down a

Solo, including Candi Sukuh (p153), Candi Cetho (p154) and **Astana Giribangun** (Jl Astana Giribangun, Dengkeng, Girilayu; admission by donation; ⊙8am-5pm) (475,000Rp, minimum two people).

small *gang* (alley) off Jl Ahmad Dahlan, this unique guesthouse, run by a delightful, charismatic owner, offers four exceptional-value rooms in her heavy-timbered Javanese home. The more expensive rooms have hot water and bathtubs. Breakfast is offered in the little restaurant (p150) around the corner, which doubles as an old-school travellers' haunt.

Popular tours from here include a bicycle route (to see *arak* palm wine production and rice and gamelan factories) from 9am to 2pm and a one-day batik course from 9am to 4pm; both cost 100,000Rp. Day trips by car to Candi Cetho and other nearby attractions cost 450,000Rp (up to four people).

★ **Roemahkoe** HISTORIC HOTEL $$
(☑ 0271-714024; www.roemahkoe.com; Jl Dr Rajiman 501; standard/deluxe d incl breakfast from 450,000/970,000Rp; ❋ ⬤) This beautiful historical hotel, occupying an old batik workshop, has been stylishly renovated with 14 rooms featuring wood panelling and art deco windows. Deluxe rooms come with marble baths, quaint platforms for climbing into bed and mahogany furniture. The highly recommended restaurant, Laras, occupies a leafy courtyard of water features.

There are examples of batik for sale in an inner pavilion.

★ **Rumah Turi** BOUTIQUE HOTEL $$
(www.rumahturi.com; Jl Srigading II 12, Turisari; r incl breakfast from 360,000Rp; tr 600,000Rp; ❋ ⬤) A reimagined property draped with plants; there is no other hotel quite like this deconstructed lodge, where the restaurant is lit with bare bulbs and the vertical gardens are a work of art. Standard rooms sport unique designer desks, but are otherwise rather basic – the deluxe rooms are a better bet. It's the sprigs of imaginative garden, however, that steal the show.

Omah Sinten Heritage Hotel BOUTIQUE HOTEL $$
(☑ 0271-641160; www.omahsinten.net; Jl Diponegoro 34-54; r from 520,000Rp; P ❋ ⬤) Better known for its restaurant, this hotel offers a few delightful rooms in the vintage, brick Javanese building. With high ceilings, ceramic tiled floors, tasteful wood furniture and exposed brick in the bathrooms, guests are offered a step back in time accompanied by modern convenience.

✗ Eating

Nasi Liwet Wongso Lemu INDONESIAN $
(Jl Teuku Umar; meals 12,000-30,000Rp; ⊙ 4pm-1am) Solo street dining at its best, this evening-only stall, run by an *ibu* (mother; older woman) clothed in traditional batik, specialises in *nasi liwet*: coconut-flavoured rice served on a banana leaf topped with shredded chicken, chicken liver (optional), egg, turmeric-cooked tofu and special seasonings. Tables are set up with pickled vegetables and tofu fried in turmeric.

Warung Baru INTERNATIONAL $
(☑ 0271-656369; Jl Ahmad Dahlan 23; mains 15,000-20,000Rp; ⊙ 7am-9pm; ✎) A classic backpackers' hangout, the Baru is also a good spot to try local Solonese specialities such as *nasi liwet* (coconut-milk rice with chicken and egg), along with vegetarian dishes, home-baked black rice bread, Indian curries and the usual Western fare. Cold beer is also on offer.

Adem Ayem INDONESIAN $
(☑ 0271-712891; Jl Slamet Riyadi 342; mains 15,000-35,000Rp; ⊙ 6am-10pm) This huge canteen-like restaurant, with swirling colonial-style fans and photos of ye olde Surakarta, doesn't look much from the outside, but it attracts local diners by the dozen. The attraction? Wonderful chicken dishes, souped, fried or served up *gudeg* (jackfruit curry) style.

★ **Omah Sinten** INDONESIAN $$
(☑ 0271-641160; www.omahsinten.net; Jl Diponegoro 34-54; mains 35,000-62,000Rp; ⊙ 7am-11pm; ⬤) Sharing space with a heritage hotel is this attractive restaurant offering home-style Solonese specialities. While the menu makes good reading, giving the history of the dishes, the atmosphere is quite formal, with live classical Javanese music attracting locals on an official night out. It's a lovely spot, though, with a koi pond and convenient location opposite Mangkunegaran Palace.

Soga FUSION $$
(☑ 0271-727020; www.sogaresto.com; Jl Slamet Riyadi 261; mains 40,000-115,000Rp; ⊙ 10am-10pm; ⬤) This stylish Indonesian and fusion restaurant is part of the Danar Hadi complex (p146), next to the batik museum and showroom. Mains include meat and pasta dishes, steaks and chops. It comes into its own on busy nights, when laughter and the hum of

conversation provide atmosphere in the elegant but brightly lit dining room.

Laras
INDONESIAN $$

(☑ 0271-714024; www.roemahkoe.com; Roemahkoe Hotel, Jl Dr Rajiman 501; mains from 45,000Rp; ⊘ 7am-10pm; 🛜) This delightful restaurant is inside a former batik factory, currently occupied by the Roemahkoe heritage hotel. It's particularly evocative at night, when candlelit, and on Saturday, when a gamelan orchestra plays on a platform in the open-sided pavilion. Specials include *selat Solo* (a local sliced-beef salad served with a boiled egg).

Ralana
INDONESIAN $$

(☑ 0271-765 0333; Jl Slamet Riyadi 301; mains 30,000-130,000Rp; ⊘ 10am-10pm Sun-Fri, to midnight Sat) Most notable for the setting in a restored Dutch colonial compound (with some puzzling modern touches such as a ceiling of umbrellas), this enormous restaurant encompasses a courtyard hosting live bands every night except Thursday, and private dining rooms dominated by large artworks. The menu includes the usual Indonesian and international staples with some fun departures.

🍸 Drinking & Nightlife

Nota Bene
COFFEE

(☑ 0822 2999 2322; www.instagram.com/notabene bistro; Jl Srigading II 16; ⊘ 10am-10pm Mon-Fri, to 11pm Sat & Sun) This fresh, white-painted cafe sells a range of local Javanese coffees in a hip, air-conditioned space on the ground floor. There's also a pleasant open-air lounge upstairs serving Indonesian and Western fusion food. The 'special coffees', including Kopi Pak Bambang, are delicious.

☆ Entertainment

Solo is an excellent place to see traditional Javanese performing arts, with performances taking place at Mangkunegaran Palace (p147) on Wednesdays (10am until noon) and Kraton Surakarta (p147) on Sundays at 1pm. Most hotels provide more information on 'what and where'.

★ Sriwedari Theatre
THEATRE

(R Maladi Stadium, Jl Slamet Riaydi; 10,000Rp; ⊘ performances 8-10pm Tue-Sat) The theatre in this vacant plot (formerly an amusement park now undergoing redevelopment) is the unlikely venue of one of the best shows in

Java! Traditional dance performances by Solo's esteemed and long-running *wayang orang* (masked dance-drama) troupe involve hundreds of magnificently costumed participants and a full gamelan orchestra.

🛍 Shopping

Solo is one of Indonesia's main textile centres. Distinctive, beautiful batik is produced in Solo and workshops around town sell both batik fabric and items of clothing made from this labour-intensive material. Cheaper items are made with block-print, but many fabrics in the high-end workshops are still handcrafted. Most showrooms sell fixed-price items but it's possible to bargain in smaller outlets.

A wide range of other cotton and silk fabrics are also produced in Solo. Other items for sale include traditional kris – the ceremonial dagger, worn unusually on the back, tucked into the waistband. Kris sport a variety of finely crafted blades, some of which are serpentine rather than straight. The wooden sheaths are often wrapped in silver and the handles are like giant polished bean pods, crafted from a local hardwood. While it is no problem exporting one of these magnificent pieces, note that not all countries allow them to be imported.

Street vendors at the eastern side of the *alun-alun*, near Kraton Surakarta, sell a wonderful assortment of polished semiprecious stones, some of them set into rings and pendants. Finer jewellery, meanwhile, decorates the windows of goldsmiths on Jl Dr Rajiman (Secoyudan), which runs along the southern edge of the *alun-alun*.

Gems and antiques are found in a covered market near Kraton Surakarta (p147) while two big malls, **Solo Grand Mall** (☑ 0271-725111; www.solograndmall.com; Jl Slamet Riyadi; ⊘ 9am-9pm) and **Paragon Mall** (☑ 0271-727306; www.solo-paragon.com; Jl Cipto Mangunkusumo; ⊘ 10am-10pm; 🛜), are handy for more everyday supplies.

★ Pasar Triwindu
MARKET

(Windujenar Market; Jl Diponegoro; ⊘ 9am-4pm) Solo's flea market is the place to search for antiques including *wayang* puppets, old batik and ceramics, as well as clocks, vinyl records, coins and vintage cameras. It's a fun place to root around, and a specialist shop near the main entrance sells newly crafted and heirloom kris.

BEAUTIFUL BATIK

Batik is at its most exquisite in Solo, where the tradition of batik production dates back centuries and is expressive of the most refined court traditions. At the House of Danar Hadi (p146) museum, which houses over 1000 priceless pieces collected by the owner of this esteemed batik workshop, it is easy to be seduced by the beauty of the designs. Some designs are formalised as part of traditional costume, signifying courtesan or servant, others are free-flowing creations that reveal Chinese, Indian and Arab influences. All are products of intense labour. The *batik tiga negeri,* or three-cities batik, for example, is moved from town to town to allow for washing in distinct local waters, each of which contributes to the subtlety of the colours involved. Other designs require painstaking 'painting' of repeated forms (dots, floral motifs, complex patterns) and an eye for negative space: batik is a reductive, seven-step process, with wax applied to prevent colour taking when the fabric is washed, so the artist must plan multiple colourways meticulously.

Batik Danar Hadi (p151) and **Batik Keris** (☑0271-643292; www.batikkeris.co.id; Jl Yos Sudarso 62; ⊙9am-8pm) give demonstrations in the art of hand-producing these beautiful fabrics, some of which are sold in the showrooms in traditional lengths of 2.5m by 1m.

But not all batik is produced as part of a wholesale industry. Much fabric still derives from cottage industries and two suburbs of Solo in particular are renowned for their batik-making prowess. Thriving family-run workshops can be found, for example, in the narrow lanes of **Kampung Batik Kauman**, just south of Jl Slamet Riyadi. Centred around Jl Cakra (one of the main backpacker districts), most of the workshops occupy Dutch-era relics and make for some wonderful photo opportunities. Another batik 'village' is found within **Kampung Batik Laweyan**, south of the Roemahkoe (p150) hotel, which itself was once a batik workshop. Residents in both areas welcome visitors and are eager to sell a piece or two.

Batik Danar Hadi CLOTHING
(www.danarhadibatik.com; Jl Slamet Riyadi 261; ⊙9am-7pm) Danar Hadi is an important Solonese batik manufacturer and sells an extensive collection through this beautiful showroom. Styles include traditional Javanese shirts for men, sarongs and exquisite scarves for women and some interesting women's clothing with a more Western cut in batik, or designed in printed silk.

Pasar Klewer MARKET
(Jl Secoyudan; ⊙8am-5pm) This bustling textile market burned down in a fire in 2015 and has been rebuilt in more or less the same location. Selling all manner of cloth and ready-made clothes, there are some bargains to be had, particularly for cotton goods.

❶ Information

Maps, brochures and information on cultural events are available at the **Tourist Office** (☑0271-716501; Jl Slamet Riyadi 275; ⊙7.30am-4pm Mon-Sat, to 2pm Sun) and a few tours are on offer. There are many banks in town with ATMs including **BCA Bank** (cnr Jl Dr Rajiman & Jl Gatot Subroto; ⊙8am-3pm Mon-Fri).

❶ Getting There & Away

AIR

Solo's **Adi Sumarmo International Airport** (☑0271-780715; www.adisumarmo-airport.com/en; Jl Bandara Adi Sumarmo) has regular flights to Jakarta and Surabaya, along with Bali, Sumatra, Sulawesi and Kalimantan.

BUS

The **Tirtonadi Bus Terminal** (Jl Ahmad Yani) is 3km from the centre of the city. Buses leave here for destinations such as Yogyakarta (20,000Rp to 25,000Rp, 1½ hours, hourly) and Prambanan (15,000Rp to 20,000Rp, 1½ hours), Semarang (35,000Rp, 3¼ hours) and Surabaya (60,000Rp to 75,000Rp, five hours). A door-to-door shuttle bus to Yogyakarta is 70,000Rp. There's also a minibus to Bromo (200,000Rp, daily 10am).

The neighbouring **Gilingan Minibus Terminal** (Jl Ahmad Yani) has express air-con minibuses to Semarang and Surabaya.

TRAIN

Solo is located on the main Jakarta–Yogyakarta–Surabaya train line and most trains stop at **Balapan** (☑0271-714039; Jl Monginsidi 112), the principal train station.

Yogyakarta is best reached by train from Solo. Prambanan is also easily accessible – via a train to Maguwo station near Yogyakarta's airport and bus 1A to the temple.

Getting Around

Air-conditioned Batik Solo Trans buses connect Adi Sumarmo International Airport, 10km northwest of the centre, with Jl Slamet Riyadi (25,000Rp). A taxi costs around 100,000Rp; **Kosti Solo Taxis** (☎027-185 6300) are reliable, but, as everywhere, Grab and Gojek are cheaper and easier.

Taxis cost about 25,000Rp from the train station or bus terminal into the centre.

Guesthouses can arrange bicycle/motorcycle hire from around 15,000/75,000Rp per day.

Gunung Lawu

Towering Gunung Lawu (3265m), lying on the border of Central and East Java, is one of the holiest mountains in Java. Hindu temples dot the slopes and each year thousands of pilgrims seek spiritual enlightenment by climbing the peak.

History has it that when Majapahit fell to Islam, the Hindu elite all fled east to Bali; Javanese lore, by contrast, claims that Brawijaya V, the last king of Majapahit, went west. Brawijaya's son, Raden Patah, was the leader of Demak and led the conquering forces of Islam against Majapahit; rather than fight his own son, Brawijaya retreated to Gunung Lawu to seek spiritual enlightenment. There he achieved nirvana as Sunan Lawu, and today pilgrims come to the mountain to seek his spiritual guidance or attain magic powers.

The area surrounding Gunung Lawu is very attractive, with rice, tea and potato fields covering the mountain slopes in neat terraces.

Sights

The unique temples on Gunung Lawu – some of the last Hindu temples built in Java before the region converted to Islam – are a fascinating mixture of styles and incorporate elements of fertility worship. The most famous temple on the slopes of the mountain is beautiful Candi Sukuh.

★Candi Sukuh HINDU TEMPLE

(admission 25,000Rp; ⏲7am-5pm) In a magnificent position 900m above the Solo plain with fine views of Gunung Lawu, Candi Sukuh is one of Java's most enigmatic and striking temples. It's not a large site, but it's beautifully proportioned with a truncated pyramid of rough-hewn stone. Fascinating reliefs and Barong statues decorate the facade. It's clear that a fertility cult was practised here: several explicit carvings have led to Sukuh being dubbed the 'erotic' temple. It's a quiet, isolated place with a potent atmosphere.

Built in the 15th century during the declining years of the Majapahit kingdom, Candi Sukuh seems to have nothing whatsoever to do with other Javanese Hindu and Buddhist temples. The origins of its builders and strange sculptural style (with crude, squat and distorted figures carved in the *wayang* style found in East Java) remain a mystery and it seems to mark a reappearance of the pre-Hindu animism that existed 1500 years earlier.

A large stone lingam and yoni mark the entrance gateway. Flowers are still often scattered here, as locals maintain that these symbols were used to determine whether a wife had been faithful, or a wife-to-be was still a virgin. Any woman wearing a sarong and jumping across the lingam had to keep the sarong firmly wrapped: if it fell off, her infidelity was proven. Other interesting cult objects include a monument depicting Bima, the Mahabharata warrior hero, with Narada, the messenger of the gods, both in a stylised womb. Another monument depicts Bima passing through the womb at his birth. In the top courtyard, three enormous flat-backed turtles stand like sacrificial altars. A 2m lingam once topped the pyramid, but it was removed by Sir Thomas Stamford Raffles in 1815 and now resides in the National Museum in Jakarta.

Sarongs are required (available for a small donation at the entrance).

TRAINS FROM SOLO

DESTINATION	FARE (RP)	DURATION (HR)	FREQUENCY (DAILY)
Jakarta	250,000-1,000,000	8¼-11	5-7
Surabaya	88,000-300,000	3¾-5½	6-8
Yogyakarta	from 32,000	1	19

Virtually all travellers arrive here on a tour from Solo or Yogyakarta or come by private taxi. For those determined to use public transport, a bus bound for Tawangmangu from Solo stops in Karangpandan (20,000Rp). From here a Kemuning minibus (6000Rp) stops at the turn-off to Candi Sukuh, from where it's a steep half-hour walk uphill (2km) to the site. For around 80,000Rp, ojek will take you to both Sukuh and Cetho. A return Grab taxi from Solo will set you back about 300,000Rp.

Candi Cetho   TEMPLE

(25,000Rp; ⊙7am-5pm) Candi Cetho (pronounced 'Cheto') is spread over terraces rising up the misty hillside, on the northern face of Gunung Lawu at around 1400m. Thought to date from around 1350, the *candi* (temple) closely resembles a Balinese temple in appearance, though it combines elements of Shivaism and fertility worship. The entrance is marked by temple guardians and there's a striking platform with a turtle head and a large lingam on the upper terrace.

The temple, which rises spectacularly through six tiers of narrow gateways and processional steps, remains a focus of active worship. Balinese and Javanese Hindus visit Candi Cetho to pray and give offerings regularly. Indeed, the villagers who live just below the temple form one of Java's last remaining Hindu populations. The third tier attracts the most offerings of fruit, flowers and incense. Temple sarongs are mandatory, for a small donation, for those in Western dress.

There are several homestays in the village, with simple rooms available for around 120,000Rp per night. Few visitors tend to stay the night, however, as Cetho is usually included in the temple tours from Solo and Yogyakarta.

🛏 Sleeping

Sekar Tanjung Homestay   HOMESTAY $

(☎0813 2934 6500; Jl Trengguli, Gumeng; r 150,000Rp; P) Within a half-hour walk of Candi Cetho, this homestay is brand new. As such the stark concrete block that comprises this simple lodging looks somewhat raw. That said, the rooms are comfortable with sprung mattresses, interior bathrooms, TV, tea and hot water. The big draw, however, is the views – 180 degrees of emerald fields descending to the Solo plain.

Sukuh Cottage   HOTEL $$

(☎027-1702 4587; www.sukuh-cottages-and-res tauran.business.site; Kemuning; r incl breakfast 400,000Rp; ☞) Just before Sukuh temple – and enjoying the same exquisite views – this rural hotel has attractive rooms and villas built from natural materials and dotted around a gorgeous garden full of orchids. There's an elevated viewing platform and restaurant. Reserve ahead. , as the lodge often gets booked out by tour in high season.

🍽 Eating & Drinking

Bale Branti   TEAHOUSE $

(Jalan Kaliondo 1, Kemuning; mains from 20,000Rp, tea from 15,000Rp; ⊙9am-7pm) This attractive teahouse is set in an authentic *joglo* (traditional Javanese house), with over a dozen wood tables shaded by parasols edging tea terraces. It's a good place to try the local brew or have lunch. The *nasi campur* rice comes with generous side dishes.

Ndoro Donker   TEAHOUSE

(Jl Afedling Kemuning 18, Kemuning; ⊙9am-6pm) Named after the first tea mogul of Java and set in the 19th-century home on his original plantation, this teahouse teems with visitors at the weekend, enjoying the cooler air after Solo. Food is available (mains 10,000Rp to 60,000Rp) and there's a splendid shop

---

HIKING GUNUNG LAWU

The village of Cemoro Sewu, 10km east of Tawangmangu, is the starting point for the hike to the summit of Gunung Lawu. Mystics and holidaying students make the night climb throughout the year, especially on Saturdays. On the 1 Suro, the start of the Javanese new year, thousands of pilgrims trek to the summit to meditate before sunrise.

For the best chance of witnessing a clear sunrise, it's best to start early the night before – by 10.30pm at the latest. It's a long, steady six-hour hike, but one of the easiest mountains in Java to tackle. While the stony path is clearly marked and has handrails in places, it's still best to bring a torch. Sign in at the PHKA (Perlindungan Hutan dan Konservasi Alam; the Directorate General of Forest Protection and Nature Conservation) post before starting the climb (admission to walk 20,000Rp).

attached, selling tea from local plantations and a range of biscuits and tinned boiled sweets from Europe.

❶ Getting There & Away

It is difficult to visit Gunung Lawu by public transport, so almost all travellers heading out this way either take a tour from nearby Solo or hire a car with a driver (from 500,000Rp for 12 hours for up to four people). A standard tour, offered through travel agents and hotels in Solo, includes Candi Sukuh, Candi Cetho and Astana Giribangun and costs around 500,000Rp per person for a minimum of two people.

Tawangmangu

☑ 0271 / POP 43,000 / ELEV 1194M

Tawangmangu, a sprawling hill resort on the western side of Gunung Lawu, is a popular weekend retreat for wealthy Solonese. It's a pleasant enough place to escape the city heat and for a hike or two in the hills, but it's best visited as a day trip from Solo or as part of a visit to Gunung Lawu.

◉ Sights

Grojogan Sewu   WATERFALL

(160,000Rp; ☺ 8am-4pm) This 100m-high waterfall, about 3km from town, is a favourite playground for monkeys (as is the parking area). It is reached by a long flight of steps down a hillside, but the chilly, dirty swimming pool isn't inviting.

From the bottom of the waterfall, a trail leads along a good track to Candi Sukuh (p153), a 2½-hour walk away. Some Solo guides offer other treks in the area. Horses can be hired for the one-hour round trip through the woodland for 150,000Rp.

⌖ Sleeping

Hotel Bintang   HOTEL $

(☑ 0271-696269; www.hotelasiasolo.co.id; Jl Raya Lawu; r incl breakfast Mon-Fri 225,000Rp, Sat & Sun 250,000Rp; ❈ 🛜) An uninspiring modern hotel on the main street with three floors of rooms of varying quality. Newer, sleeker rooms on the riverside have dark-wood furniture, LCD TV and stylish lighting. Not much English is spoken but staff are helpful. There's a minimart, a cafe-restaurant and unfortunate karaoke on weekends.

❶ Getting There & Away

Buses travel to Solo (10,000Rp to 15,000Rp) regularly. The entrance to the waterfall com-

VILLAGE OF KEMUNING

The small tea-farming village of Kemuning makes a pleasant gateway to Candi Sukuh and Candi Cetho, with a few teahouses with good kitchens and one rather alluring guesthouse (p154). The whole village becomes a selfie vantage point at the weekend and some enterprising locals have capitalised on this by providing various novel frames for that all-important shot.

plex is a 3km walk uphill along the main street through town, with an obvious left turn at the sign.

North Coast

Central Java's north coast doesn't feature on many travellers' itineraries, except as a gateway to the Karimunjawa Islands, but this steamy strip of land is not without charm. For many centuries the coast was a major trading post for merchants from Arabia, India and China, and multiculturalism continues to flourish today in the cuisine and architecture of the region.

Merchants brought more than just material wealth to the region and in fact Islam entered Java through the north coast in the 15th and 16th centuries, as evidenced by the tombs of the country's great saints, which are located here.

Central Java's capital is not Yogya, as many assume, but Semarang, a rapidly growing metropolis and major shipping centre. This often-overlooked city has lots of interesting sights and an old quarter that is currently being renovated.

The north coast can resemble a continuous strip of urbanisation, hemmed in on either side by fields. These slivers of development that run from city to city encompass sights of local interest, rather than major must-sees, but are fascinating nonetheless. Sights include a train station museum (p161) at Ambarawa and Java's oldest mosque (p162) in Demak.

The north coast has a strong craft tradition and cottage industries define many of the small rural towns and villages in the region. Pekalongan is celebrated for its batik, while Jepara is a major centre for wooden furniture.

JAVA NORTH COAST

ⓘ Getting There & Away

The north coast is well connected with other parts of mainland Java by public transport, while flights and ferry rides connect Semarang and Jepara with the Karimunjawa Islands. As the home of the original railway network, this part of Java takes pride in its trains.

Semarang

📞 024 / POP 1.3 MILLION / ELEV 7M

Steamy Semarang, with its giant port, rapidly developing city centre and affluent outskirts, is home to a large Chinese population whose influence on local life is evident in the city's culture and cuisine. The inner core of the city dates back to the Dutch colonial period and many of the fine old buildings from this era are being renovated. When complete, this old quarter will no doubt become the focus of a visit for most travellers.

Much of the city's dynamism, however, is centred not on resurrecting past glories but on celebrating current success. This can be sensed in the giant new malls and wealthy business hotels around Simpang Lima (Five Ways) square. Indeed, Semarang is the provincial capital of Central Java and – perhaps more than Solo and Yogyakarta, the cities favoured by tourists – offers an authentic travel experience for those looking to understand Java today.

◉ Sights

★ Old City
AREA

(Outstadt; around Jl Jenderal Suprapto) Semarang's atmospheric old quarter, often referred to by its Dutch name, the Outstadt, is well worth investigating. Until recently, most of the area's colonial buildings were abandoned as city authorities focused on new-builds rather than shoring up past legacies. Today, however, a revived interest in the area with its obvious potential for tourism has led to a new investment, and coffee shops, stylish restaurants and other attractions now occupy the tastefully renovated townhouses.

While it is fair to say that the revival project has some way to go, there are still worthwhile attractions here including **Gereja Blenduk** (Jl Jenderal Suprapto) `FREE` church. Built in 1753, this elegant church with its large cupola forms the centre of the old quarter around which are a number of delightful places to eat. A street market sells a few modestly priced antiques and memorabilia and there's a well-respected modern

art space, the **Semarang Gallery** (📞 024-355 2099; www.galerisemarang.com; Jl Taman Srigunting 5-6; admission 10,000Rp; ⊙ 10am-4.30pm). The old city is prone to flooding and during the rainy season some of the backstreets are impassable.

Lawang Sewu
HISTORIC BUILDING

(Jl Pemuda; adult/student or child 10,000/5000Rp; ⊙ 7am-9pm) Semarang's most famous landmark, Lawang Sewu ('Thousand Doors'), comprises two colossal colonial buildings that were one of the headquarters of the Indonesian railways during the Dutch era. The structures are sparsely used with only the occasional exhibit (mostly about the railway system) on view. Nevertheless, the empty corridors, where clerks and engineers once worked, have their own interest, with features including stained glass and a magnificent marble staircase.

Gedung Batu
TEMPLE

(Sam Po Kong Temple; 📞 024-760 5277; Jl Simongan 129, Bongsari; admission free to worshippers, viewing compound 10,000Rp, temples 30,000Rp; ⊙ 9am-6pm) This huge Chinese temple complex, 5km southwest of the city centre, comprises three main temple buildings and many smaller structures that date back to 1724, although built on earlier foundations. Most of the elegant, red-painted structures are Indo-Chinese in style, with tiered pagoda-style roofs.

Gedung Batu lies around 30 minutes from central Semarang, reached by taking the Damri bus 2 from Jl Pemuda to Karang Ayu (a suburb west of central Semarang) followed by an *angkot* (minibus) to the temple.

Chinatown
AREA

(south of Jl Jenderal Suprapto) Semarang's Chinatown is well worth investigating, particularly around the riverside Gang Lombok. With temples, pagodas, shop houses, jade jewellers, pharmacists, fortunetellers and food stalls, the area illustrates the depth of the connection between China and this port city. The focus of the entire community is the **Tay Kak Sie Temple** (Gang Lombok), dating back to 1746, with its huge drums and incense-clouded interior.

Simpang Lima
SQUARE

While Jl Pemuda, Semarang's premier boulevard in Dutch times, remains an important artery and shopping street, Simpang Lima is the sociable hub of modern Semarang. This grassy 'square' is surrounded by cine-

JAMU – A HERBAL REMEDY

Semarang is known for its *jamu*, a herbal medicine produced from a variety of ingredients such as honey, leaves, seeds and bark. Said to have a number of health benefits for the liver and intestines, it has also been associated with enhancing the libido. Some claim that the medicine dates back hundreds of years and even read some of the stone panels at Borobudur, with their hints of pestle and mortar and masseuse, as descriptive of its production. The sight of women selling bottled forms of this medicine, sweetened with honey and carried in open-weave baskets, was once common. Now the herbal remedy is more likely dispensed in tablet form.

Although *jamu* didn't originate from here, Semarang has acquired a name for its production thanks to two large manufacturers, both of which house small museums and offer tours. **Jamu Nyonya Meneer** (☏024-658 2529; Jl Raya Kaligawe, Km4; ☉museum 10am-3.30pm Sun-Fri) FREE is near the bus terminal, while **Jamu Jago** (☏024-747 5172; www.jago.co.id; Jl Setia Budi 179, Srondol Kulon; ☉8am-3pm Mon-Sat) FREE is 6km south of the city on the Ambarawa road.

ma complexes and modern malls. Crowds congregate here in the evenings and wander past shops displaying consumer items that remain beyond the reach of many, though this doesn't seem to dent their enthusiasm for the bright lights of the big city.

Ronggowarsito Museum MUSEUM
(☏024-760 2389; Jl Abdulrachman Saleh 1, Kalibanteng Kulon; 10,000Rp; ☉8am-3pm) This large provincial museum houses an interesting collection of antiquities, crafts including batik and *wayang* puppets, and assorted fossils and curios collected from all over Central Java. The most interesting exhibit is a recycled stone panel from the Mantingan mosque (near Jepara) – one side shows Islamic motifs, while the reverse shows the original Hindu-Buddhist scene. It's approximately 2km before the airport.

🛏 Sleeping

Sleep & Sleep HOSTEL $
(☏0813 1010 0456; Jl Imam Bonjol 15-17; sleep capsule 39,000Rp) For those on a tight budget, this centrally located hostel, comprising 'sleep capsules' with lockers, offers clean compartments along serviced corridors with minimal privacy. A new concept in Semarang, it remains to be seen whether the accommodation will live up to its billing. Those with a pioneering spirit (or an economy train to catch from Poncol) might find it worth a try.

★ Novotel Semarang HOTEL $$
(☏024-356 3000; www.accorhotels.com; Jl Pemuda 123; r from 700,000Rp; ❉@🛜☒) In a good location between the old city and Simpang Lima, this smart business-oriented hotel

has an outdoor pool, a gym and spa. Rooms are contemporary, spacious and comfortable, many with city views. There are two cafe-restaurants and the lavish breakfast buffet covers multiple cuisines with egg and noodle stations.

Tjiang Residence GUESTHOUSE $$
(☏024-354 0330; Jl Gang Pinggir 24; d incl breakfast 315,000Rp; ❉🛜) In the heart of Chinatown, a short stroll from the Tay Kak Sie temple, this budget hotel is a character-filled choice with a red facade and Chinese screened windows. The corridors have an unfortunate damp smell, but the tiny rooms are fresh and neat with wood floors, Ikea-chic desks and flat-screen TVs.

Gumaya Tower Hotel HOTEL $$$
(☏024-355 1999; www.gumayatowerhotel. com; Jl Gajah Mada 59-61; r incl breakfast from 1,550,000Rp; ❉@🛜☒) Towering over the city, this luxury hotel offers understated, well-designed rooms at good-value prices. Rooms come with large LCD TVs, fast wi-fi and gorgeous bathrooms with tubs. There's an infinity pool, and panoramic city views from the top-deck bar. Popular with business travellers.

🍴 Eating

Semarang's large Chinese population is reflected in the local cuisine. At night, Simpang Lima hosts dozens of *kaki lima* (food carts) serving snacks and meals in traditional *lesahan* fashion (on straw mats). There is also an extensive food court on the 4th floor of the Plaza Simpang Lima. Don't leave town without trying the local speciality, *wingko*.

Semarang

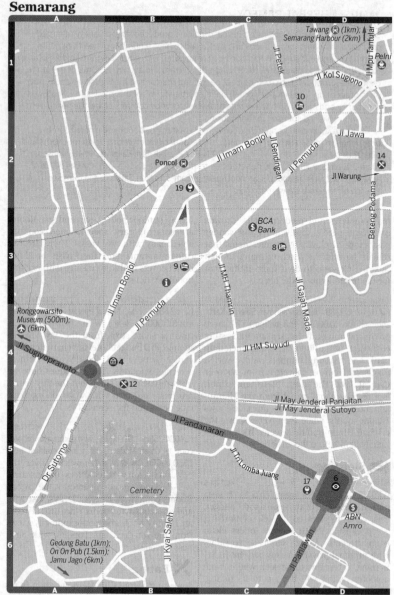

★ **Toko Wingko Babad** BAKERY **$**
(☏024-354 2064; Jl Cendrawasih 14; cakes
5300Rp; ⊙7am-7pm) A wonderful, anachronistic bakery and store that hasn't changed
in half a century. The delicious *wingko* (coconut cakes served warm) are the signature
treats of this veritable old city institution,
served plain or flavoured with jackfruit,
chocolate, banana or durian. The jackfruit is
especially addictive.

TekoDeko CAFE **$**
(☏024-354 4501; Jl Jenderal Suprapto 44, Kota
Lama; mains 25,000-50,000Rp; ⊙9am-10pm) A

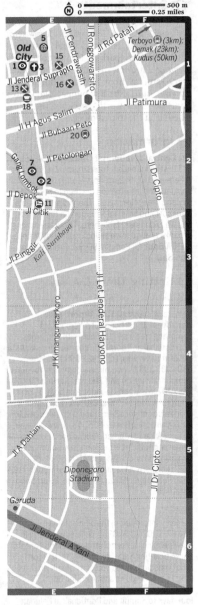

Semarwis Night Market   CHINESE $
(Jl Warung; meals 18,000–40,000Rp; ⊙5–11pm
Fri-Sun) Fine Chinese-style noodles and
babi sate (pork satay) are local favourites
at this weekend market. The sociable atmosphere is helped along by a bit of low-
key karaoke, fortune-telling and flirting
young couples.

★ Holliday Restaurant   CHINESE $$
(☑024-841 3371; Jl Pandanaran 6; mains 27,000–
110,000Rp; ⊙7am–11pm; ☑) It's easy to see why
this two-storey restaurant is permanent-
ly packed: the food is exceptionally good!
Earning the unreserved recommendation of
the local Chinese population, the restaurant
attracts large parties to its circular tables
even on a weekday. Dishes of super-fresh
seafood, including jellyfish and lobster, and
hot plates of bean curd are among the local
favourites.

Spiegel   FUSION $$
(Jl Jenderal Suprapto 34; mains from 60,000Rp;
⊙10am–midnight; ☎) Housed in a converted old general store (circa 1895) and once

fun tiled coffee house in a restored old relic,
this cafe brews up espresso coffee, pots of
tea and sandwiches. Pastas and nasi goreng
(fried rice) are on offer too. There's a small
shop selling homemade fare and a great
rooftop sundeck.

patronised by Dutch colonists, Spiegel has become a pivotal point of the old quarter. The island bar serves up tasty cocktails, and marble tables set the stage for fusion dishes that combine local flavours with international favourites. The attached designer boutique sells sumptuous printed silk clothing for women.

Ikan Bakar Cianjur INDONESIAN $$

(☑ 024-356 2333; www.ibcgroup.co.id; Jl Jenderal Suprapto 19; meals 55,000-100,000Rp; ⊙10am-10pm) Occupying a sensitively restored building (Semarang's former courthouse), this character-filled restaurant with its yellow roof tiles sports art deco chandeliers, antique tiles and soaring ceilings. A wide choice of snacks and seafood meals are served here, but most locals come for the house speciality – *gurame* and *nila* fish (from 88,000Rp), which arrives souped, fried or grilled.

🍸 Drinking & Nightlife

★ Hero Coffee CAFE

(☑ 0856 4153 7333; Jl Kepodang 33, Purwodinatan; ⊙8am-1am) This delightful cafe is one of several popping up in the old city area. Housed in a beautifully restored colonial terrace, with a pink awning and wrought-iron details, it features international favourites including toasted sandwiches and fried sliced potatoes. The homely interior is a winner, with giant murals, wooden tables and colourful plates, and there's an assortment of home-bakes for sale.

E Plaza CLUB

(☑ 024-845 2293; www.eplaza.co.id; Jl Ruko Gajahmada Lantai II 29, off Simpang Lima, Gajahmada Plaza; ⊙noon-3am) Semarang can be lacking when it comes to nightlife, but this popular complex, right by the Simpang Lima square, contains an upmarket club, cinema and lounge bar. It draws a young energetic crowd and is a good bet for a night out. The club entrance fee is 50,000Rp.

On On Pub PUB

(☑ 024-355 6556; www.ononpub.com; Jl Tanjung 1; ⊙5pm-midnight Mon-Fri, to 1am Sat, 11am-midnight Sun) A classic expat hang-out in the centre of town, this pub sells ice-cold draught Bintang as well as decent international food, including the famous OMG sausage!

☆ Entertainment

TBRS Cultural Centre PUPPETRY

(☑ 024-831 1220; Jl Sriwijaya 29, Tegalwareng; ⊙6am-midnight) For traditional entertainment, this leafy park (a former zoo) holds *wayang orang* theatre performances every Saturday from 7pm to midnight, and *wayang kulit* (shadow-puppet play) most Thursdays. It's worth checking the latest schedule at the tourist office.

ℹ Information

The **Central Java Tourist Office** (☑ 024-351 5451; www.indonesia-tourism.com/central-java; Jl Pemuda 147; ⊙9am-4pm Mon-Fri) has useful booklets and information devoted to both the city and the entire region. There is also reliable transport and hotel information on the Karimunjawa Islands available here. There are dozens of banks around town including a handy branch of **BCA Bank** (Jl Pemuda 90-92; ⊙8am-4pm Mon-Sat).

ℹ Getting There & Away

AIR

Semarang's **Ahmad Yani Airport** (www.ahmadyani-airport.com; Jl A Yani 1, Kota Semarang) is a transport hub with numerous international and domestic connections. **AirAsia** (☑ 24hr call centre 021-2927 0999, toll free 0804 133 3333; www.airasia.com) flies to Kuala Lumpur (Malaysia) and Jakarta. **Garuda** (☑ 024-351 7007; www.garuda-indonesia.com; Jl Jenderal A Yani 142) and **Citilink** (www.citilink.co.id) also connect Semarang with Jakarta. **Lion Air** (☑ airport office 024-761 4315; www.lionair.co.id; Jl A Yani 1, Ahmad Yani Airport) connects Semarang with Jakarta, Bandung, Batam and Banjarmasin and **Sriwijaya Air** (☑ 024-841 3777; www.sriwijayaair.co.id; Jl Mt Haryono 719, Ruko Peterongan Plaza A6) flies to Jakarta and Surabaya.

BOAT

For ferry information, the office of **Pelni** (☑ 024-354 6722, 024-354 0381, call centre 021-162; www.pelni.co.id; Ferry Terminal, Jl Mpu Tantular 25; ⊙ticketing 8am-5pm Mon-Thu, to noon Fri & Sat) has timetables you can consult after its ticket sales windows shut (around 5pm). There are economy and 1st-class boats every three or four days to Sampit and Pontianak in Kalimantan. Prices and schedules change frequently so check with Pelni near to your departure date.

BUS

Semarang's **Terboyo bus terminal** (www.bosbis.com; Jl Terminal Terboyo) is 4km east of town, just off the road to Kudus. Air-con minibuses also travel to destinations across the island, including Wonosobo (60,000Rp), Solo (50,000Rp), Yogyakarta (70,000Rp) and Surabaya (from 55,000Rp for economy). Agents for luxury buses and air-conditioned minibuses include **Rahayu** (024-354 3935; Jl Let Jenderal Haryono 9; ⊙7am-8pm) and **Nusantara Indah** (024-355 4981; Jl Sudirman 75).

TRAIN
Semarang lies on the main north coast Jakarta–Cirebon–Surabaya train route. **Tawang** (024-354 4544; www.entiket.com; Jl Taman Tawang 1) is Semarang's main station for all exclusive- and business-class services. Economy-class trains depart from Semarang's **Poncol** (www.entiket.com; Jl Imam Bonjol, Purwosari) train station.

ⓘ Getting Around

City buses charge a fixed 3000Rp fare and terminate at the Terboyo bus terminal. Buses 1, 2 and 3 run south along Jl Pemuda to Candi Baru. Short becak rides cost around 8000Rp; a ride of more than 3km costs around 15,000Rp. Semarang has plenty of metered taxis, including **Bluebird** (024-670 1234).

Semarang's Ahmad Yani Airport is 6km west of the city centre. Taxis into town cost from 35,000Rp (there's an official desk at arrivals), and around 40,000Rp when returning to the airport using the taxi meter.

Ambarawa
0298 / POP 58,000 / ELEV 481M
The market town of Ambarawa, 28km south of Semarang, is of interest to trainspotters as the home of the excellent Ambarawa Train Station Museum. The town was once the site of a Japanese internment camp, where up to 15,000 Europeans were held during

WWII – a monument and park commemorate the spot. Today, the town is a jolly place with neatly painted tree trunks and forests of flags around Independence Day.

Ambarawa has hotels, or the Mesa Stila Resort in an old coffee plantation in the nearby foothills makes for a highly memorable experience.

◉ Sights

Ambarawa Train
Station Museum   MUSEUM
(Museum Kereta Api Ambarawa; 0298-591035; www.internationalsteam.co.uk/ambarawa/museum; Jl Stasiun 1; adult/child 3-12 yrs 10,000/5000Rp; ⊙8am-5pm) Fans of vintage railways will love this museum, located in the premises of the old Koening Willem I station, a couple of kilometres outside of town on the road to Magelang. The station opened in 1873 and still sports a tiled passenger terminal, old clocks, conductor offices filled with vintage typewriters and ticket windows stocked with telegraph machines. The stars of the show, however, are the 22 turn-of-the-century steam engines.

🛏 Sleeping

★Mesa Stila Resort   HERITAGE HOTEL $$$
(0298-596333; www.mesahotelsandresorts.com/mesastila; Jl Losari, Rw 3, Pingit; villa from 2,600,000Rp; P❄✳@🛜🏊) Nestled in a 22-hectare coffee plantation, the Mesa Stila Resort is one of Indonesia's most magical hotels. At an altitude of 900m, the forest gives way to inspiring vistas from the villa-style rooms and a classically conical volcano looms over the neatly trimmed lawns and

TRANSPORT FROM SEMARANG
Bus

DESTINATION	FARE (RP)	DURATION (HR)
Jepara	60,000	2½
Kudus	50,000	1¼
Pekalongan	65,000	3
Wonosobo	60,000	2½
Yogyakarta	70,000	4

Train

DESTINATION	FARE (RP)	DURATION (HR)	FREQUENCY
Jakarta	from 220,000	6	10 daily
Pekalongan	from 40,000	1¼	6 daily

red-tiled *joglos*. It's some 12km southwest of Ambarawa; a taxi from town (60,000Rp) passes beautiful rice terraces.

ℹ Getting There & Away

Ambarawa can be reached by public city bus (Transjateng) from Semarang (3500Rp, one hour). There are several services to Yogyakarta (50,000Rp, three hours) via Magelang; the last bus leaves at around 6pm.

Demak

☑ 0291 / POP 27,500 / ELEV 12M

Demak, 25km east of Semarang, marks the point at which it is claimed that Islam was introduced into Java. As the capital of the island's first Islamic state, it was from here that the Hindu Majapahit kingdom was conquered and much of Java's interior converted.

The town's economic heyday has now passed and even the sea has retreated several kilometres, leaving this former port landlocked. But the role this small town once played has not been forgotten and the old mosque here is highly revered. In a lingering sense of the town's illustrious past, Demak is locally regarded as one of the most beautiful and well-tended in Java; indeed, the streets are litter-free, the tree trunks painted in harmonious two-tone colours, and even the *andong* (cart) horses are adorned with extra-elaborate headdress feathers.

COTTAGE INDUSTRIES

This part of Central Java is home to a number of key craft industries. Intricately carved *jati* (teak) and mahogany furniture and relief panels are on display at shops and factories all around Jepara, but the main carpentry centre is in fact the village of **Tahunan**, 4km south of Jepara on the road to Kudus.

Brightly coloured, Sumba-style ikat (a kind of woven cloth), using traditional motifs, are woven and sold in the village of **Troso**, situated 14km south of Jepara and 2km off the main road. Unusually for Java, men predominantly do the weaving. **Pecangaan**, 18km south of Jepara, produces rings, bracelets and other jewellery from monel (stainless-steel alloy).

Buses from either Semarang or Kudus (both 10,000Rp) stop right outside the great mosque.

Mesjid Agung   MOSQUE

(Jl Sultan Fattah, Bintoro) FREE Demak's venerable Mesjid Agung (circa 1466), notable for its triple-tiered roof, is Java's oldest mosque and one of the archipelago's foremost Muslim pilgrimage sites. Legend has it that it was built from wood by the *wali songo* (nine holy men) in a single night. Four main pillars in the central hall were originally made by four of the Muslim saints, and one pillar, erected by Sunan Kalijaga, is said to be made from scraps of timber magically fused together.

Kudus

☑ 0291 / POP 95,000 / ELEV 52M

Kudus takes its name from the word *al-Quds* – the Arabic name for Jerusalem. Founded by the Muslim saint Sunan Kudus and with a venerable mosque dating from the 16th century, it remains an important pilgrimage site. Despite its strong Muslim identity, and in common with much of Java, Kudus retains links with a Hindu past and the slaughter of cows is still forbidden here.

The town is moderately attractive, with an elongated main street dominated by a huge tobacco factory. This is where the first *kretek* (clove cigarettes) were produced, and today Kudus is still a stronghold of *kretek* production – there are said to be 25 factories in the town and panniers of green leaves seem to be bulging from every truck in the dry season. Sukun, a manufacturer outside of town, still produces *rokok klobot* (clove tobacco rolled in corn leaves).

◉ Sights

Kudus retains a delightful old quarter, or Kauman, with narrow streets where merchants in small kiosks sell religious souvenirs, dates, prayer beads and caps. On Fridays, men dressed in white robes and women in *jilbab* (head coverings) of all hues make their way on foot to pray at the Mesjid Al-Manar.

★ Sunan Kudus Tomb   TOMB

(Mesjid al-Manar, Jl Menara 3-5, Kauman; donations welcome) From the courtyards behind the *mesjid* (mosque), a palm-lined path leads to the imposing tomb of the Muslim saint Sunan Kudus, shrouded behind a curtain of lace. The narrow doorway, draped with heavy gold-embroidered curtains, leads to an inner chamber and the grave. It makes a particularly impressive sight when lit up at night, and energised by the faith of pilgrims. A generous sense of welcome is extended to curious non-Muslims.

Mesjid Al-Manar MOSQUE
(Al-Aqsa Menera; Jl Menara 3-5, Kauman) This beautiful old mosque, built in 1549 by Sunan Kudus, is famous for its red-brick *menara* (minaret). This minaret may have originally been the watchtower of a Hindu temple – the curiously squat form and flared sides of the mosque certainly have more in common with Balinese temples than with traditional Islamic architecture. Inside the main prayer hall, Muslim worshippers pray in the shadow of a Hindu-style brick gateway, a fascinating juxtaposition of Javanese religious heritage.

🛏 Sleeping

Wisma Karima Hotel GUESTHOUSE $
(☑ 0852 9170 5111; Jl Museum Kretek Jati Kulon 3; r incl breakfast 65,000-120,000Rp; ❄) Just off the highway on the south side of town, this guesthouse is run by a welcoming family and has nine rooms, some quite spacious and with air-con, but all a little old-fashioned. No English is spoken.

Hotel Kenari Asri HOTEL $$
(☑ 0291-446200; Jl Kenari II; r incl breakfast 350,000-500,000Rp, ste 700,000Rp; ❄ 🛜) This decent, two-storey hotel sports a rather grand entrance and has serviceable and clean (if rather small) rooms with functioning air-con. Some rooms smell heavily of smoke. The hotel has two strong assets though: the staff, who speak English, are especially hospitable; and the kitchen musters an excellent breakfast.

🍴 Eating & Drinking

★ Soto Bujatmi JAVANESE $
(☑ 0291-446170; Jl Wahid Hasyim 43; bowl of soto kudus 14,000Rp; ⊙ 7am-9.30pm) This is the very best place to try the famed chicken soup of Kudus. Cooks stir up cauldrons of the brew over a log-fired oven and diners pack round simple tables decorated with jars of rice crackers. *Soto kudus* is served with optional extras, such as *sate* (satay) comprising entrails and cow-skin. Bean-curd wafers are another accompaniment to the broth.

SOUP FOR THE SOUL

Kudus is famed for its delicious *soto kudus*, a rich chicken soup, which is served with a variety of entrails and crackers. Depending on the amount of turmeric used, it can range from pale brown to bright yellow and is flavoured with lots of garlic. The other delicacy in town is *Jenang kudus*, a sweet made of glutinous rice, brown sugar and coconut.

Sari Lembur Kuring INDONESIAN $
(☑ 0291-439770; Jl Agil Kusumadya 35; mains 18,000-50,000Rp; ⊙ 9am-10pm) A large, pleasant restaurant complete with a koi pond, offering tasty Sundanese and Javanese food under a shady pagoda. It's popular with local families enjoying a night out.

ⓘ Information

The **HSBC Bank** (Jl Ahmed Yani 9; ⊙ 8am-4pm Mon-Sat) has an ATM, and there are several more on Jl Ahmed Yani beside the Taman Bojana food complex.

ⓘ Getting There & Away

Kudus is on the main Semarang–Surabaya road. The bus terminal is around 4km south of town. City minibuses run from behind the bus terminal to the town centre (5000Rp), or take a becak. Buses go from Kudus to Demak (20,000Rp, 50 minutes) and Semarang (30,000Rp, 1½ hours). Buses to Jepara (35,000Rp, 1¼ hours) leave from the Jetak subterminal, 4km west of town (5000Rp by minibus).

Jepara

☑ 0291 / POP 20,000 / ELEV 9M

Famed as Java's best woodcarving centre, Jepara has a long history of furniture production, which has contributed greatly to its evident prosperity. The town's fortunes inevitably wax and wane with the fashion for 'brown goods' (wood furniture) but dozens of furniture showrooms continue to make a living from the industry. Contemporary styles are possible to spot among the more ubiquitous heavy carved panels designed for the home market.

With the decline in demand from international furniture outlets, there are fewer resident expats in town, but Jepara still hosts buyers from all over the world. As a result, this is one of the more cosmopolitan towns in rural Java.

The town's broad avenues and small *gangs* (alleys) lined with homes that open onto back-door canals, together with the nearby beaches, make it a tranquil spot to take a break from the road. Jepara is also a major gateway to the Karimunjawa Islands.

◎ Sights

Market Apung
CANAL

(cnr Jl Suprapto & Jl Pesajen) This character-filled fish and produce market is housed in some old Dutch godowns (warehouses) on a bridge close to the sea. The main attraction is really the assemblage of old fishing boats sheltering in the canal alongside. Near sunset, it's a riot of colour.

Museum RA Kartini
MUSEUM

(☑ 0291-591169; Jl Wolter Monginsidi; 3000Rp; ⊙ 8am-4pm) On the north side of Jepara's attractive *alun-alun*, this museum is dedicated to one of Indonesia's most celebrated women. One room is devoted to Kartini and contains portraits and memorabilia of this pioneer of women's rights and her family. Other rooms contain assorted archaeological findings, including a yoni and lingam,

local art and artefacts, such as fine wood-carvings and ceramics. There's also a 16m skeleton of a whale. Troso weaving is for sale in the gift shop (from 130,000Rp).

Pantai Bandengan
BEACH

(Tirta Samudra; Jl Raya Tirta Samudra) Jepara has some fine white-sand beaches, including Pantai Bandengan, 7km northeast of town. It's one of the best beaches on the north coast – an arc of gently shelving white sand, which is beautiful at sunset. The main public section is littered, but just a short walk along this gives way to clean sand, clear water and safe swimming. A bemo (minibus; 5000Rp) to here can be hailed from Jl Pattimura in Jepara.

Pantai Kartini
BEACH

(Permandian; Jl AE Suryani; adult/child 10,000/5000Rp; ⊙ 24hr) Close to the ferry port, this is Jepara's most popular beach. With funfair rides, souvenir stalls, tethered goats, shell shops and mosques, it's a good place to relax in the company of locals on leave. Boats are available for rent (from around 180,000Rp return) to nearby **Pulau Panjang**, which has excellent white-sand beaches. Permandian also has the **Kura Kura Ocean Park** (admission 12,500Rp, open 9am to 4pm); occupying a giant turtle-shaped concrete structure, it contains a modest aquarium.

🛏 Sleeping

Nusantara
HOTEL $

(☑ 0291-1426 0610; nstrhotel@gmail.com; Jl Kolonel Sugiono 20; r 180,000Rp; ❋ 🛜) A beautifully carved wooden boat and an attractive pergola distinguish the outside of this otherwise ordinary hotel. The air-con is somewhat under-functioning and the mosquitoes take revenge at night, but the friendly staff ensure guests are up in time for the early-morning ferry and are helpful in arranging transport around town. Rooms are clean and comfortable if cramped.

Bayfront Villa
INN $$

(☑ 0821 3634 6151; www.bayfronthotel.blogspot.com; Jl Universitas Diponegoro, Teluk Awur; r/ste from 550,000/950,000Rp; ❋ 🛜 🌊) This attractive hotel on a clean, narrow stretch of beach offers a handful of homely rooms, set around a delightful pool. The upper rooms open onto a common terrace with sea views. There is also a little bar on the beach.

KARTINI: AN INDO ICON

Raden Ajeng Kartini, a writer, feminist and progressive thinker, was born in 1879, the daughter of the *bupati* (regent) of Jepara. She grew up in the *bupati*'s residence, on the eastern side of the *alun-alun*, excelled at school and learnt to speak fluent Dutch by the age of 12. It was in this residence that Kartini spent her *pingit* ('confinement' in Javanese), when girls from 12 to 16 are kept in virtual imprisonment and forbidden to venture outside the family home. Kartini later used her education to campaign for women's rights and to petition against colonialism, before dying at the age of 24 just after the birth of her first child. A national holiday is held on 21 April, known as Kartini Day, in recognition of her pioneering work for women's rights, and a museum in the heart of town is dedicated to her life and work. Traditional local Troso weaving is for sale in the museum gift shop (from 130,000Rp).

Ocean View Residence HOTEL $$
(☑ 0291-429 9022; www.facebook.com/oceanview jepara; Jl Tegalsambi, Tahunan; r standard/superior/ deluxe incl breakfast 770,000/875,000/900,000Rp; ❄ 🛜 🏊) Down a narrow lane that zigzags through backstreets, this modernist beachside resort comprises 23 rooms and attracts a youthful clientele. Deluxe rooms represent the best value, with full kitchens, ocean views and some interesting artwork on the walls. The sunset barbeque from 4pm to 8pm (15,000Rp) is popular, although the loud music somewhat spoils the ambience.

🍴 Eating

Pondok Rasa INDONESIAN $
(☑ 0291-591025; Jl Pahlawan II; mains 25,000-85,000Rp; ⊗ 9am-9pm Sat-Thu; 🖉) Just across the river from the *alun-alun*, Rasa is a traditional Javanese restaurant with a pleasant garden setting and Indonesian food served *lesahan* (traditional way of dining on straw mats) style. There's lots of choice for vegetarians.

★ Yam-Yam SEAFOOD $$
(☑ 0291-598755; Jl Pantai Karang Kebagusan, Km5; mains 25,000-78,000Rp; ⊗ 8am-11pm) This stylish beachfront restaurant is the indisputable top choice in Jepara. Dining is in the garden, around a pool or on tables so close to the sea that the fish almost swim up to the plate. Candlelight lends romance to the evening, while the thatched brick-house kitchen delivers the catch of the day with delicious lemon dressing, tender steaks, Thai dishes and Italian favourites.

ℹ️ Information

The **tourist office** (☑ 0291-591169; www.go jepara.com; Jl AR Hakim 51; ⊗ 7.30am-2.30pm Mon-Fri, 8am-2pm Sat & Sun) is in the western part of town. It has very helpful staff and runs a particularly informative website.

ℹ️ Getting There & Away

Frequent buses make the trip from Jepara to Kudus (35,000Rp, 1¼ hours) and Semarang (from 50,000Rp, 2½ hours). A few buses also go to Surabaya (105,000Rp, 6½ hours), but Kudus has more connections.

ℹ️ Getting Around

Taxis are plentiful and charge similar prices. A fare within the town centre costs around 12,000Rp, including to the Kartini harbour for boats to Karimunjawa.

Karimunjawa Islands

The dazzling offshore archipelago of Karimunjawa, a marine national park, consists of 27 coral-fringed islands – only five of which are inhabited. Most islanders are Javanese but there are a few Bugis and Madurese families, who make a living from fishing, seaweed cultivation and, increasingly, tourism. Lying about 90km north of Jepara, the islands are a tropical haven of white-sand beaches, turquoise seas and relaxed retreats.

Holidaying Indonesians account for most of the visitors here, although a growing number of foreign travellers now brave the rough seas (which can occur at any time of year) for a few days of R&R. Independent travellers head almost exclusively for the main island, Pulau Karimunjawa; this lush, mountainous little landmass, ringed with coral reefs, is home to most of the archipelago's facilities and the only town of any size, also named (somewhat confusingly) Karimunjawa.

👁 Sights

★ Pantai Annora BEACH
(East Coast, Pulau Karimunjawa; 5000Rp) This public beach on the east coast of Pulau Karimunjawa is the gateway to the island's most exquisite ocean view. A rough path leads along the headland to a series of stunning vistas, where the sea appears as a patchwork of interlacing blues from deep indigo to aquamarine. A couple of simple swings at the end of the promontory give the best vantage point, but go soon: developers have their eye on the spot.

Mangrove Boardwalk NATIONAL PARK
(North Coast, Pulau Karimunjawa; 155,000Rp; ⊗ 8am-5pm) A boardwalk leads through the mangrove swamps that typify the coastal fringe of Pulau Karimunjawa and other islands in the archipelago. This unique habitat is home to a number of birds including kingfishers and a variety of waders. A tiered hide halfway along the boardwalk provides a perfect vantage point for birdwatching. Interpretative boards in English explain the different mangrove species that make up this intriguing landscape. Watch out for the red crosses on the boardwalk indicating rotten timbers!

Pantai Batu Topeng BEACH
(West Coast, Pulau Karimunjawa; parking 5000Rp; 🅿) There's cold beer on the go at the tiny

beach bar, or *mie goreng* (fried noodles) rustled up in a basic warung, at this friendly little beach. Even when a gale whips up a cappuccino of an ocean on the east coast, the west coast is invariably flat white with long slow rollers sliding into the shore.

Bukit Love
VIEWPOINT

(Love HIll; West Coast, Pulau Karimunjawa; 10,000Rp) This hillside viewpoint is a favourite selfie station for locals, complete with a giant white love heart framing the view. With a wonderful vantage on the sinking sun, strategically positioned behind a coconut palm, this venue boasts a variety of perfect spots to capture the day's end – including a thatched hut and a hilltop bar.

Pantai Tanjung Gelam
BEACH

(Sunset Beach; West Coast, Pulau Karimunjawa; admission incl parking 5000Rp; P) This beautiful beach is hemmed with palm trees and, beyond the lilac and emerald water, white horses charge across a coral reef. Small warungs serve basic noodles and people gather here to watch the sunset.

Activities

★Dunia Bintang Tour & Travel
DIVING

(World Star; ☑ 0822 2111 4504; www.karimunjawapackage.com; Jl Jenderal Sudirman, Karimunjawa Town, Pulau Karimunjawa; island hopping with 2 snorkelling sites incl equipment & lunch 200,000Rp; ☺8am-9pm) Dunia Bintang is run by a delightful Karimun-British couple. They organise diving (the most popular dive site focuses on a 100-year-old Norwegian wreck that plunges to 25m), snorkelling and island-hopping trips in boats with a maximum of 17 on board. They can also advise about the current ferry schedule.

Salma Dive Shop
DIVING

(Karimunjawa Dive Centre; ☑0852 2533 3677; www.karimunjawadivecentre.com; Pulau Karimunjawa; 2-dive package with equipment per person 875,000Rp; ☺6am-midnight) This dive centre comes recommended by resident expatriates. It offers a two-dive package, available only with a minimum of two people. Also offers rental of a range of equipment, including masks and fins, wetsuits and underwater cameras.

Festivals & Events

★Independence Day Carnival
CARNIVAL

(Alun-Alun, Karimunjawa Town, Pulau Karimunjawa; ☺Aug) Every year, costumed islanders from across Palau Karimunjawa congregate in the main town to celebrate Independence Day. Tiny tots dress up in police uniforms, beauty queens grace Ramayana-style chariots and young men cross-dress as women in this pageant of colour and dance. The parade makes a couple of laps of the tiny town centre, before assembling for prize-giving in the *alun-alun*.

Sleeping

Accommodation is limited so it's important to book well in advance, particularly if staying over on a Saturday night or during peak holiday times. Many hotels offer package deals that include transport from Jepara or Semarang.

Other than the places listed here, all on Pulau Karimunjawa, guests can stay on Pulau Menyawakan, where the **Kura Kura Resort** (☑in Semarang 024-7663 2510; www.kurakuraresort.com; Pulau Menyawakan; half board s/d US$225; ☺May-Oct; ❋ ☎ ☂) offers a luxury escape with sea-view cottages and private pools. The island is reached by the resort's own plane.

Bodhi Tree Hostel
GUESTHOUSE $

(☑ 0812 3922 2203; Jl Diponegoro, Karimunjawa Town, Pulau Karimunjawa; r with shower & air-con incl breakfast 350,000Rp, mixed dm 90,000-100,000Rp) This tastefully decorated guesthouse caters largely for budget travellers in eight-person dorms, but has some attractive rooms with air-con too. In the heart of town, guests can either eat in or stroll out for warung fare in the nearby *alun-alun*.

Coco Huts
BUNGALOW $$

(☑0812 3556 3136; www.cocohutskarimunjawa.com; Jl Danang Jaya, East Coast, Pulau Karimunjawa; r incl breakfast 300,000-600,000Rp; ☎) Owned by a well-known German footballer-turned-commentator and his brother, who were born in Indonesia, this hotel comprises a series of wooden cottages with traditional tiled roofs on a steep inland hillside.

Hotel Escape
HOTEL $$

(☑0813 2574 8481; www.escapekarimun.com; Jl Danang Jaya, South Coast, Pulau Karimunjawa; r incl breakfast from 300,000Rp; ❋☎) A five-minute walk from the ferry terminal, this two-storey brick lodge is right by the sea. There's no beach as such, but a wide lawn shaded by coconut palms gives a pleasant sense of space. Rooms are no-nonsense, and modern and simple fare is available in the restaurant.

MAKING THE MOST OF KARIMUNJAWA ISLANDS

Most visitors to the islands are immediately seduced by the relaxed atmosphere and the most activity they are likely to muster is a stroll from room to sea and back. For those willing to tear themselves away from the beach, however, the main island offers some fun activities.

Scooter Touring

Biking around the main island of Pulau Karimunjawa by scooter is a popular pastime, with stops possible at various beauty spots along the way. The mountainous terrain doesn't lend itself to first-time bikers, although many give it a go regardless; rental prices are generally 75,000Rp per day.

Island Hopping

The most popular activity from the main island of Pulau Karimunjawa is island hopping, which involves a half- or whole-day boat trip with opportunities to swim, snorkel on the reef and land on one or two nearby deserted tropical islands. The uninhabited islands of Menjangan Besar and Menjangan Kecil both have magnificent sweeping white sands and offshore snorkelling, and are within easy reach of Pulau Karimunjawa.

Chartering a boat costs 1,500,000Rp for a half day for two people or 1,700,000Rp for a full day. Hotel owners often ring round to muster a group, saving costs for their guests. For a place in a boat (maximum 15 people), it costs 175,000Rp for a half day or 225,000Rp for a full day.

As a marine park, many parts of Karimunjawa – including Pulau Burung and Pulau Geleang – are officially off limits (although this protected status is unfortunately not always strictly enforced). It helps if visitors respect the off-limits zone to minimise the negative impact of increased tourism.

Swimming & Snorkelling

It's not necessary to put out to sea to enjoy the crystal-clear water surrounding Palau Karimunjawa: two excellent beaches with snorkelling opportunities lie just a 7km ride by motor scooter from the island's main town.

There's a modest fee for parking at these sandy beaches – Batu Topeng (p165) and Pantai Tanjung Gelam – which helps to keep them clean of litter that washes up. A handful of warungs and bars, set up beneath the coconut trees, collect an assembly of like-minded souls at sunset.

Diving

The reefs around many of the islands offer decent diving. The most popular dive site centres on a 100-year-old Norwegian wreck that plunges to 25m. Dives can be organised through Dunia Bintang Tour & Travel and Salma Dive Shop.

Hiking & Birdwatching

While it's hard to pull yourself away from the shore, park rangers can help organise a hike up Pulau Karimunjawa's 600m peak, Gunung Gendero, and guesthouses can usually arrange this on behalf of their guests.

On the north coast of the island there's a circuit of wooden walkways (p165), which allow an exploration of the extensive mangroves that fringe Pulau Karimunjawa (just mind the rotten slats!). At dawn and dusk it's a haven for birds and there's a multi-tiered hide on the edge of the grove for excellent birdwatching.

The ugly concrete access road is unfortunate. Trips and bike rental available.

★ **Breve Azurine**　　　　　　　RESORT $$$
(☑ 0297-319 1059;　www.breveazurine.com;　Jl Danang Jaya, RT 4, East Coast, Pulau Karimunjawa; r incl breakfast from 2,280,000Rp; ✱ @ 🛜 ☲) With

a private beach, this gorgeous hillside resort offers a genuine island welcome. Rustic cottages with open-air bathrooms have magnificent sea views or there's a main lodge with a hardwood verandah that serves as the common area. The restaurant is nested above a tropical garden and candlelit suppers can be arranged under the rustling palms.

Transfers from the jetty are included in the tariff, and the use of kayaks and snorkelling gear is free. A helpful service desk organises island-hopping, hiking and diving excursions for those who just can't sit still.

✗ Eating

Most visitors eat either at their lodging or at a neighbouring hotel, but there are extra options in the main town of Karimunjawa, where a growing number of restaurants and bars offer typical Indonesian dishes and grilled fish. Standard international fare such as pizzas is also available and the odd cafe is making an appearance.

Cafe Amore   INTERNATIONAL $
(JI Sutomo, Karimunjara Town, Pulau Karimunjawa; mains 25,000Rp; ☺4-10pm; 🛜) Occupying a lovely spot among reconstructed wooden *joglo* fronting the marina, this atmospheric restaurant, with its palm-tree garden and mowed lawns, is a perfect place for a sundowner. Food is served after 7pm.

Night Market   INDONESIAN $
(Alun-Alun, JI Diponegoro, Karimunjawa Town, Pulau Karimunjawa; meals 50,000Rp; ☺6-9pm) A local favourite for dinner is the night market on the *alun-alun* in the centre of Karimunjawa town. Over a dozen stalls offer tasty *ikan bakar* (grilled fish), grilled corn, fried bananas, fresh juice and more. Diners sit *lesahan*-style on a mat on the grass field.

Eat & Meet   INTERNATIONAL $$
(📞0297-319 1103; JI Sutomo, Karimunjawa Town, Pulau Karimunjawa; burgers 70,000Rp; ☺4-11pm) A very popular restaurant in the middle of town, Eat & Meet brings out delicious thin-crust pizzas from an on-site oven. Interesting local dishes include marinated fish wrapped in a banana leaf (65,000Rp), but most travellers are attracted by the burgers and familiar Western favourites.

ℹ Information

The Semarang tourist office (p160) can help with practicalities.

There's a BRI ATM in the village that takes MasterCard, but it can run out of money, so bring ample cash.

ℹ Getting There & Away

Flights and ferries connect the mainland of Java with Pulau Karimunjawa (the main island). Vio-lent weather between December and February, and high winds at any time of year, can disrupt travel, but in calm weather both function on schedule most of the time. Ferries are more frequently cancelled due to weather than flights.

It's vital to book transport well ahead, especially on weekends and during high season.

AIR
It is possible to reach Pulau Karimunjawa by air from both Semarang (650,000Rp, 40 minutes, every Tuesday, Wednesday and Thursday) and Surabaya (600,000Rp, 1½ hours, every Tuesday and Thursday) with Nam Air (www.sriwijayaair.co.id) or **Air Fast** (📞0215-200696; www.airfastindonesia.com). Planes with Air Fast are tiny and seat just 12, so book ahead. The flight itself can be an adventure, but if winds are calm it's a magical ride.

BOAT
Karimunjawa's boat connections are fairly reliable, and there are links from both Semarang and Jepara. Check all schedules with the Semarang tourist office, which can also book tickets and make reservations.

At the time of research, from Jepara's Kartini harbour, the Express Bahari boat (executive class 230,000Rp, two hours) sailed to Pulau Karimunjawa on Mondays, Tuesdays and Fridays at 9am and Saturdays at 10am, returning on Mondays at noon, Wednesdays at 11am, Saturdays at 7am and Sundays at 11am. The Siginjai (economy 150,000Rp) sails from Jepara on Monday, Wednesday, Friday and Saturday at 7am, but takes four to six hours. Be warned, economy tickets are cheaper but they are also below deck in often-choppy seas, where seasickness is more common than not – never pleasant.

ℹ Getting Around

From Pulau Karimunjawa, it costs 1,500,000Rp to charter a wooden boat for a half-day trip. Hiring a moped (from 65,000Rp per day) is a good way to get around the main island's 22km of reasonable roads for those who know how to manage a hill start.

EAST JAVA

East Java (Jawa Timur) is a wild, rolling region of dizzying peaks, smoking volcanoes and unspoilt panoramas. Dotted across this landscape you'll discover ancient temples being swallowed by a riot of vegetation, national parks where growls, barks, and squawks echo from the undergrowth, and stunning beaches with world-class surfing.

East Java

For most visitors, though, East Java is all about raw volcanic power and the landscapes created by these unpredictable mountains of fire. Nowhere is more synonymous with this than the sublime Bromo-Tengger Massif region, with its puffing volcanic giants and inspiring sunrises. Further east, the Ijen Plateau, with its crater lake and brave sulphur miners, is equally captivating.

Nature hasn't got it all its own way in East Java, though. The regional capital, Surabaya, is a booming, fast-paced city, which constantly excites, while smaller Malang, which is ringed by ancient Hindu temples, seems somehow more laid-back and genteel.

ⓘ Getting There & Away

The main gateway to the region is the booming city of Surabaya. The busy airport here receives flights from across Indonesia as well as international flights from surrounding Southeast Asian nations. Malang also has good flight connections with other Indonesian cities.

One of the most popular ways to arrive in or leave East Java is by taking one of the frequent ferries running between Bali and Banyuwangi.

Frequent trains link Surabaya with cities in central and western Java. There are also a few daily trains between Malang and Yogyakarta. All bigger towns in East Java have good bus connections with cities elsewhere in Java.

Surabaya

☑ 031 / POP 2.84 MILLION

Surabaya is like a bottle of wine: it gets better the more you get to know it. Give it time and you'll discover that Surabaya has many quixotic corners of interest. Its historic Arab Quarter is a fascinating labyrinth of lanes, and the city has one of Indonesia's biggest Chinatowns and some impressive, though disintegrating, Dutch buildings.

Having said all this, initial impressions aren't likely to be great. Polluted, congested and business-driven, Surabaya isn't a pedestrian-friendly city. Just crossing the eight-lane highways that rampage through the centre is a challenge in itself, and against the calm of rural East Java, it is pandemonium writ large.

For most foreign visitors, the city is merely a transport hub. For locals, Surabaya is closely linked to the birth of the Indonesian nation, as it was here that the battle for independence began. To them, Surabaya is Kota Pahlawan (City of Heroes).

◉ Sights

Exploring north Surabaya from a sightseeing bus is a lot of fun, and also free. The House of Sampoerna has a Surabaya Heritage Track, a tram-style bus that leaves the factory three times daily (Tuesday to Sunday) to take in the sights of Chinatown and the Arab Quarter, plus visit cottage industries (such as a noodle factory). The route changes from time to time; check the website for details. It's essential to book in advance, particularly on weekends.

In 2018 a series of terrorist bomb attacks hit Surabaya, which left 25 people dead (including the suicide bombers – some of whom were children). At the time of research, the city was calm and there were no specific warnings about visiting.

◉ Old City

Even though much of Surabaya's historic centre is literally falling to pieces, the old city easily wins the Most Attractive Neighbourhood prize. With crumbling Dutch architecture – including the stunning old **governor's residence** (Jl Gubernur Suryo 7) – a souk-like Arab Quarter and strong Chinese influences, it's by far the most atmospheric part of Surabaya to explore.

From the old city you can head north to the Kalimas harbour, where brightly painted *pinisi* (Makassar or Bugis schooners) from Sulawesi and Kalimantan unload their wares.

◉ Arab Quarter

A warren of narrow lanes, Surabaya's Arab Quarter has the atmosphere and appearance of a Middle Eastern medina, with stalls selling prayer beads, *peci* (black Muslim felt hats) and other religious paraphernalia. All alleys lead to the **Mesjid Ampel** (Jl Ampel Suci) FREE, the most sacred mosque in Surabaya. Behind the mosque pilgrims chant and present rose-petal offerings at the grave of Sunan Ampel (1401–81 AD), one of the nine saints credited with introducing Islam to Java.

House of Sampoerna MUSEUM
(☑ 031-353 9000; Jl Taman Sampoerna; ◎ 9am-6pm) FREE Undoubtedly the city's best-presented attraction, the House of Sampoerna is home to one of Indonesia's most famous *kretek* cigarette manufacturers (now owned by US giant Altria, formerly Philip

Morris). Whatever you think about the tobacco industry, this factory and museum make a fascinating place to visit. The building itself is a wonderful 19th-century Dutch structure, originally an orphanage but later converted into a theatre (indeed, Charlie Chaplin once dropped by).

◉ Chinatown

East of Jembatan Merah is Surabaya's Chinatown, with hundreds of small businesses and warehouses. Becak and hand-pulled carts are still the best way to transport goods through the crowded, narrow streets. **Pasar Pabean** is a sprawling, darkly lit market, where you can buy everything from Madurese chickens to Chinese crockery.

Further east, near the canal, the stunningly atmospheric **Kong Co Kong Tik Cun Ong temple** (Klenteng Hong Tiek Hian Temple; Jl Dukuh) is primarily Buddhist, but has a variety of Confucian and Taoist altars if you can see them through the plumes of incense smoke.

Jembatan Merah BRIDGE
Originally the old city was divided along ethnic lines, with Europeans on the west side of the Kali Mas river and Chinese, Arabs and Javanese on the east bank. Jembatan Merah is a famous bridge that connected the two halves of the city; it also saw fierce fighting during Indonesia's battle for independence. Jl Jembatan Merah, running parallel to the canal, is a grungy replica of Amsterdam, but worthy (although run-down) examples of Dutch architecture can be seen here.

◉ Other Areas

Masjid al Akbar MOSQUE
(Jl Masjid Agung Timur I) FREE Perhaps the most impressive modern mosque in Indonesia. You'll probably get a glimpse of Masjid al Akbar's magnificent array of bulbous watery-turquoise-tiled domes as you exit the city. Staff are happy to show visitors around and will accompany you up the elevator to the top of the freestanding ottoman-style minaret, which offers spectacular views.

Monumen Kapal Selam LANDMARK
(☑031-549 0410; Jl Pemuda; 15,000Rp; ⊘8am-10pm) Surabaya's foremost stretch of renovated waterside real estate centres on the iron hulk that is *Pasopati*, a massive Russian submarine commissioned into the Indonesian navy in 1962. You can poke around

the horribly cramped interior, peek through the periscope and even climb into the torpedo tubes. It's in a small landscaped park near a couple of cafes popular with young smoochers.

🛏 Sleeping

There are a few options, but for a city its size Surabaya lacks decent budget places. High-standard, low-priced midrange accommodation choices are everywhere, and there are also some excellent deals available in the luxury-hotel sector, with rooms starting at US$40 for four-star hotels.

The Hostel HOSTEL $
(☑0812 3517 4233; https://the-hostel-home-for-backpackers.business.site; Jl Simpang Dukuh 38-40; dm incl breakfast 120,000Rp; ❄🛜) The simplicity of its name is perhaps reflective of its genius. Rather than bells and whistles, it sticks to the basic principles of what tourists want: cleanliness, comfortable dorm beds, friendly management and a convenient location. Hence it gets rave reviews across the board. The one small niggle is that there are a *lot* of beds in each dorm.

Hotel Paviljoen HOTEL $
(☑031-534 3449; www.hotelpaviljoen.com/id; Jl Genteng Besar 94-98; r incl breakfast with fan/aircon from 148,000/198,000Rp; ❄🛜) A respite from Surabaya's manic streets, this venerable Dutch colonial villa (c 1917) retains a twinkle of charm and grandeur. Rooms are basic and spartan, but they're clean and have some lovely touches, including Mediterranean-style shuttered windows. The location could not be better. Pay the extra rate for the bigger room and hot water. Staff can arrange tours of the region. Each evening street food stalls set up here out the front.

Artotel HOTEL $$
(☑031-568 9000; www.artotelindonesia.com; Jl Dr Soetomo 79–81; r from 400,000Rp; 🅿❄🛜) Someone went to town when they designed this aggressively artsy hotel. We love the foyer area with its melting wax-like columns, the graffiti in the public areas and the cartoon-like art in the bedrooms. Best thing is that all the artworks were produced by emerging local talent. Comfortable, clean and good value.

MaxOne Hotel@Tidar DESIGN HOTEL $$
(☑031-9900 1877; www.maxonehotels.com; Jl Tidar 5; d from 330,000Rp; ❄🛜) What Surabaya lacks in budget guesthouses, it makes up

Surabaya

N 0 ⎯⎯⎯⎯⎯ 500 m
0 ⎯⎯⎯⎯⎯ 0.25 miles

Tanjung
Perak
Harbour
(2.5km)

1

18

*House of
Sampoerna*

Kalimas Harbour
(2.5km)

**ARAB
QUARTER**

5

Jl Ampel Suci

Jl Nyamplungan

Jl Rajawali

Jl Kasuari

Jl Panggung

7

Jl Kertopaten

CHINATOWN

3

Jl Kembang Jepun

4

Jl Merak

Jl Krem Barat

Jl Sikatan

Jl Veteran

Jl Jembatan
Merah

Jl Samudra

Jl Waspada

Jl Kapasan

Jl Indrapura

Jl Kebon Rojo

Jl Setasiun Kota

Jl Pahlawan

Kota

Pelni

Jl Dupak

Jl Cepu

Pasar Turi

Jl Tembaan

Jl Pasar Besar

Jl Jagalan

Jl Pengheta

Jl Bubutan

Kali Mas

Jl Penelel

Jl Ngaglik

Jl Grogol

Jl Undaan Kulon

Jl Undaan Wetan

Jl Kusuma Bangsa

Jl Kamboja

17

13

Jl Geteng Kali

Jl Raya Jaksa

Jl Ambengan

11

Jl Tunjungan

Jl Embong Malang

10

Jl Genteng Besar

16

9

12

Jl Walikota Mustajab

*Tunjungan
Plaza*

21

Jl Kaliasin Pompa

2

Jl Yos Sudarso

15

20

Jl Pemuda

6

Gubeng

Jl Pangtima Sudirman

Jl Basuki Rahmat

Jl Embong Cermie

Jl Sonokembang

Jl Kayun

Mercure (900m);
Masjid al Akbar (8km)
(15km)

8

Jl Sumatra

19

14

Jl Raya Gubeng

Surabaya

for in cool, arty and affordable chain hotels. One such example is this reliable budget chain, which is decked out with plenty of colour and flair. Rooms come equipped with comfortable beds, cable TV, fast wi-fi and icy air-con. It also has a cool rooftop bar (p174), smart restaurants, and room service if you want a night in.

★ Hotel Majapahit
Surabaya HISTORIC HOTEL $$$
(☑031-545 4333; www.hotel-majapahit.com; Jl Tunjungan 65; r/ste from 1,066,000/1,275,000Rp; ✳@🛎🏊) This landmark colonial hotel exudes class and heritage, with colonnaded courtyards, fountains, verdant greenery and a gorgeous pool area (though it's located on a busy road, so some background traffic noise bleeds into the scene). Rooms, some with private terraces overlooking the gardens, are beautifully presented with paintings of old Indoneisa on the walls and lots of polished-wood furnishings.

Bumi Surabaya HOTEL $$$
(☑031-531 1234; www.bumisurabaya.com; Jl Basuki Rahmat 106-128; r from 1,200,000Rp; 🅿✳🛎🏊) A self-styled 'city resort'; the rooms at this former Hyatt are all conservative stately elegance, but the gardens are an explosion of tropical vegetation and dazzling flowers. There's also a fab swimming pool, which is the ideal place to end a day after exploring Surabaya's sticky streets.

✖ Eating

You won't be left hungry in Surabaya – there's a huge array of eating options. Local dishes include *rawon*, a thick, black beef

soup that tastes better than it sounds. For cheap eats, Pasar Genteng (p174) has good night warungs. Late-night munchies can also be had at the offshoot of Jl Pemuda, opposite the **Plaza Surabaya** (Jl Pemuda 33-37; ⊘10am-9.30pm), which buzzes with **foodstall** (off Jl Pemuda; mains 10,000-20,000Rp; ⊘8am-late) activity around the clock.

BU Kris INDONESIAN $
(☑031-561 1010; Jl Abdul Wahab Siamin; mains 30,000-60,000Rp; ⊘10.30am-10pm) With simple tiled walls, plastic-coated menus and chipped tables piled with plates of food, it's not the looks that bring crowds of noisy locals to eat at this renowned classic, but the food. BU Kris is famous for its *iga penyet*, a traditional dish of beef ribs with sambal. You'll struggle to find anywhere that does it better.

Soto Ambengan
Pak Sadi Asli INDONESIAN $
(☑031-532 3998; Jl Ambengan 2; soup 24,000Rp; ⊘8am-10pm) This dimly lit dive, filled with locals, is the original location of a chain of *soto ayam* warungs with branches across Surabaya. Short on noodles, long on shredded chicken, the broth brims with oil and turmeric and beautifully marinates the meat. Drop in a dollop of the fine sambal and you'll feel nourished and satisfied. A local legend.

Ahimsa Vegan Lounge VEGETARIAN $
(☑031-535 0466; Jl Kusuma Bangsa 80; dishes 10,000-25,000Rp; ⊘8am-10pm; 🖉) An elegant, upmarket vegetarian restaurant owned by a welcoming Indo-Chinese family, who serve delicious rice dishes (try *nasi hainan*, a

mixed rice platter), salads and soups, including a vegetarian *bakso*. No MSG is used. As for the muzak...

Pasar Genteng
MARKET $

(Jl Genteng Besar; mains around 8000Rp; ⊙7am-9pm) For cheap eats, Pasar Genteng has a few good night warungs.

Tanamera Coffee
INTERNATIONAL $$

(☑031-9909 5000; www.tanameracoffee.com; Jl Taman Sampoerna; mains 45,000-240,000Rp; ⊙10am-6pm; 🐉) This cafe is adjacent to the House of Sampoerna (p170) museum and occupies a gorgeous colonial structure complete with stained-glass windows and brash and diverse art works – a memorable spot for a meal or quality single-origin coffees. The menu features gourmet versions of local and Western classics, including nasi goreng, burgers and steaks, along with fusions such as spaghetti rendang.

★ De Soematra 1910
EUROPEAN $$$

(☑031-501 0666; www.de-soematra.com; Jl Sumatera 75; mains 65,000-110,000Rp; ⊙11.30am-10pm) Put on your posh frock to come to this highly regarded restaurant. It's set inside a renovated colonial mansion with 6m-high ceilings, chandeliers and carved wooden drinks counters (with sherry decanters, of course). The food, which is modern Italian, is as memorable as the setting and includes treats such as mushroom cappuccino with lace truffle oil, and pan-fried baby lobster.

★ Citrus Lee
FUSION $$$

(☑031-561 5192; Jl Kutai 12; mains 400,000-600,000Rp; ⊙6-10pm Tue-Sun) At Citrus Lee the food is art, and every dish is delicately painted onto a plate. The chef-owner trained in Paris, and the French influence seeps into many of his dishes. For most people menu highlights are the starters (think foie gras with shrimps), or the steaks – which are easily the best in the city.

Drinking & Nightlife

Though Surabaya does not have much of a drinking culture, if you look hard enough, you'll find restaurants, bars and clubs that serve alcoholic drinks and have live music.

Loveshack Skybar
ROOFTOP BAR

(☑031-9900 1877; MaxOne Hotel@Tidar, 7th fl, Jl Tidar 5; ⊙5pm-1am Mon-Sat, to midnight Sun; 🐉) On the top floor of the designer MaxOne hotel is this cool rooftop bar that's the perfect spot to enjoy a balmy evening with a cold drink in hand. There's live music most nights and a menu of international and Indonesian cuisine (mains 35,000Rp to 63,000Rp).

Colors
PUB

(☑031-503 0562; Jl Sumatera 81; ⊙from 5pm) Popular with all, this large upmarket pub-club, which has been going for years, has live music and a DJ every night. There's a full bar, but drinks are expensive. It doesn't get going until after 9pm.

Shopping

Tunjungan Plaza
MALL

(Jl Basuki Rahmat; ⊙10am-10pm) A virtual city within a city, the massive, multi-layered, multi-building Tunjungan Plaza is easily one of the city's biggest and best shopping malls. It covers a whopping 16 hectares!

ⓘ Information

Tourist Information Centre (☑031-534 0444; Jl Gubernur Suryo 15; ⊙8am-8pm Mon-Sat, to 3pm Sun) Has helpful English-speaking staff, and can offer plenty of leaflets, a map of the city and also a file with good details about backpacker accommodation and up-to-date transport schedules and prices.

Jl Pemuda has plenty of banks, as does Tunjungan Plaza.

ⓘ Getting There & Away

AIR

Surabaya Juanda International Airport (www.surabayaairport.com) is Indonesia's third busiest and is used by more than 20 airlines. There are international connections to cities in Asia and numerous domestic flights.

BOAT

Surabaya is an important port and a major transport hub for ships to the other islands. Boats depart from Tanjung Perak harbour; bus P1 from outside Tunjungan Plaza heads here. There's no fixed schedule, but Pelni ships sail to Makassar in Sulawesi roughly twice a week (economy/1st class from 272,000/846,000Rp), Pontianak in Kalimantan roughly every 10 days (economy 326,000Rp), and Jakarta weekly (economy 240,000Rp). Head to the **Pelni ticket office** (☑031-329 3197, national 021-162; www.pelni.co.id; Jl Pahlawan 112; ⊙8am-5pm Mon-Sat) for more information.

BUS

Surabaya's main bus terminal, called **Purabaya** (or Bungurasih), is 13km south of the city centre. It's reasonably well organised, and computer monitors display bus departure times; however, watch out for pickpockets. Crowded Damri city buses (bus P1) run between the bus terminal and the Jl Tunjungan/Jl Pemuda intersection in the city centre. A metered taxi costs around 70,000Rp, and an online taxi around 50,000Rp.

Buses from Purabaya head to points all over Java, Madura and Bali. Most buses on long-distance routes, such as to Solo, Yogyakarta, Bandung and Denpasar, are night buses that leave in the late afternoon or evening. Bookings can be made at Purabaya bus terminal and travel agencies in the city centre (expect a mark-up). The most convenient bus agents are those on Jl Basuki Rahmat.

All buses heading south of Surabaya on the toll road get caught up in heavy traffic around the Gembol junction. During rush hour this can add an hour to your journey.

Due to horrendous traffic jams, trains are a much better option than buses.

MINIBUS

Door-to-door *travel* minibuses are not normally a good way of travelling from Surabaya. The city is so big that you can spend two hours just collecting passengers from their hotels and homes before you even get started. Destinations and sample fares include Malang (100,000Rp), Solo (140,000Rp), Yogyakarta (150,000Rp) and Semarang (150,000Rp to 160,000Rp). Try the agencies along Jl Basuki Rahmat.

TRAIN

From Jakarta, trains taking the fast northern route via Semarang arrive at the **Pasar Turi train station** (031-534 5014) southwest of Kota train station. Trains taking the southern route via Yogyakarta, and trains from Banyuwangi, arrive at **Gubeng train station** (031-503 3115). Gubeng train station is much more central and sells tickets for all trains. There are only very infrequent, very slow economy-class trains to Malang.

🛈 Getting Around

ARRIVING IN SURABAYA
Surabaya Juanda International Airport
Bluebird taxis cost around 100,000Rp to/ from the city centre, including toll-road fees. Damri buses (25,000Rp) run from the airport to Purabaya bus terminal; from there, change to the P1 bus to the city centre or the A2 bus to the Gubeng train station. Both cost 5000Rp.

Purabaya Bus Terminal Accessed by Damri city buses (bus P1) from Jl Tunjungan/Jl Pemuda intersection in the city centre. A taxi costs around 60,000Rp.

Gubeng Train Station Centrally located, so a taxi to the centre (around 50,000Rp) or walking to your accommodation is your best bet.

Pasar Turi Train Station Walk to Jl Bubutan. From there take a Damri bus to the city centre. By taxi it's around 35,000Rp to 55,000Rp to the centre.

TRANSPORT FROM SURABAYA
Bus

DESTINATION	FARE (RP; ECONOMY/AIR-CON)	DURATION (HR)
Banyuwangi	46,000/95,000	7
Kudus	28,000/85,000	8
Malang	8500/30,000	2-3
Probolinggo	20,000/30,000	2½
Semarang	35,000/90,000	9
Solo	31,000/75,000	7½
Sumenep	19,000/68,500	4½

Train

DESTINATION	FARE (RP)	DURATION (HR)	FREQUENCY (DAILY)
Banyuwangi	56,000-200,000	6¼-7¼	4
Jakarta	150,000-500,000	9-11¼	6
Probolinggo	29,000-275,000	2	6
Semarang	49,000-360,000	3½-4	8
Solo	100,000-350,000	3¾-4½	6-8
Yogyakarta	100,000-300,000	4¼-5¼	8

BUS

Surabaya has an extensive city bus network, with normal buses (6000Rp) and *patas* buses (express; 5000Rp per journey). Watch out for pickpockets, as buses can be crowded. One of the most useful services is the *patas* P1 bus, which runs from Purabaya bus terminal into the city along Jl Basuki Rahmat. In the reverse direction, catch it on Jl Tunjungan.

TAXI

Surabaya has air-conditioned metered taxis and online taxis such as Grab, Go-Jek and Uber. Flag-fall is 7500Rp; reckon on around 25,000Rp for a trip of around 4km. **Bluebird taxis** (☑ 031-372 1234; www.bluebirdgroup.com) are the most reliable and can be called in advance. They also make long-haul trips to Malang and beyond.

Trowulan

One of the great archaeological sites of East Java, Trowulan is a beautiful collection of soaring 13th-century red-brick temples spread over manicured grounds. Every bit as impressive as many better-known Javanese temple complexes, Trowulan is thought to have once been the capital city of the Majapahit Empire. Despite the site's great historical importance, it's almost criminally overlooked by many time-pressed foreign visitors. However, it's easy to make a day trip from Surabaya or even slot a visit in as you travel between that city and the Bromo area.

History

Trowulan was once the capital of the largest Hindu empire in Indonesian history. Founded by Singosari prince Wijaya in 1294, it reached the height of its power under Hayam Wuruk (1350–89), who was guided by his powerful prime minister, Gajah Mada. During this time, Majapahit received tribute from most of the regions encompassing present-day Indonesia and even parts of the Malay Peninsula.

Its wealth was based on its control of the spice trade and the fertile rice-growing plains of Java. The religion was a hybrid of Hinduism – with worship of the deities Shiva, Vishnu and Brahma – and Buddhism, but Islam was tolerated, and Koranic burial inscriptions found on the site suggest that Javanese Muslims resided within the royal court. The empire came to a catastrophic end in 1478 when the city fell to the north-

coast power of Demak, forcing the Majapahit elite to flee to Bali and opening Java up to the Muslim conquest.

Sir Thomas Stamford Raffles, the great British explorer and governor-general of Java, was the first Westerner to encounter Trowulan in 1815, and though it was choked in forest, he described the ruins as 'this pride of Java'.

◎ Sights

The ruins are scattered over a large area around the modern village of Trowulan, 12km from Mojokerto. The Majapahit temples were mainly built from red-clay bricks that quickly crumbled. This means that many have been rebuilt and are relatively simple, but they do give a good idea of what was once a great city. As the temples are spread over a such a large area, it's best to either hire a becak or come in a car.

Some of the most interesting ruins include the gateway of **Bajang Ratu**, with its strikingly sculpted kala heads; the **Tikus Temple** (Queen's Bath – used for ritual bathing and cleansing); and the 13.7m-high **Wringinlawang Gate**. The **Pendopo Agung** is an open-air pavilion built by the Indonesian army. Two kilometres south of the pavilion, the **Troloyo cemetery** is the site of some of the oldest Muslim graves found in Java, the earliest dating from AD 1376.

Trowulan is refreshingly hawker-free, though as there's a distinct lack of information on site, you may want to hire a freelance guide (there's often one waiting at the museum). Expect to pay around 100,000Rp for a half-day.

Close to the Trowulan site is a modern, but interesting, giant sleeping **Buddha statue** (3000Rp).

★ Trowulan Museum   MUSEUM

(☑ 0321-494313; 50,000Rp, incl entry to ruins; ◐ 8am-4pm Mon-Fri) One kilometre from the main Surabaya–Solo road, the impressive Trowulan Museum houses superb examples of Majapahit sculpture and pottery from East Java. Pride of place is held by the splendid statue of Kediri's King Airlangga as Vishnu astride a huge Garuda, taken from Belahan. It should be your first port of call for an understanding of Trowulan and Majapahit history, and it includes descriptions of the other ancient ruins in East Java.

❶ Getting There & Away

Trowulan can be visited as a day trip from Surabaya, 60km to the northeast. From Surabaya's Purabaya bus terminal, take a Jombang bus (14,000Rp, 1½ hours), which can drop you at the turn-off to the museum; a becak tour of the sites will cost around 50,000Rp for a half-day excursion after bargaining.

Hiring a private car and driver in Surabaya for a day trip to the site costs around 500,000Rp.

Pulau Madura

⟋ 0328 / POP 3,630,000

The flat, sun-blasted and deeply traditional island of Madura may now be connected to Java by Indonesia's longest bridge, but the character of the people and scenery feel like somewhere far away in time and geography.

Traditional culture is strong (the sarong and *peci* are the norm), the people are deeply Islamic (virtually all children attend religious schools called *pesantren)* and the island is famous for the colourful pageantry of its popular annual bull races.

Madura's southern side is lined with shallow beaches and cultivated lowland, while the northern coast alternates between rocky cliffs and great rolling sand-dune beaches, the best of which is at Lombang. At the extreme east are a tidal marsh and vast tracts of salt around Kalianget. The interior is riddled with limestone slopes, and agriculture is limited. Sumenep is the main town, and unless the bull races are on, it attracts few tourists.

◉ Sights & Activities

There are many fine villas along the route between Sumenep and Kalianget. About halfway between the two towns are the ruins of a Dutch fort dating from 1785, and a cemetery. The Kalianget region is a centre for salt production – you'll see great mounds of the white powder piled up for export if you pass by in the dry season.

Fishing villages such as **Ambunten** and **Tanjung Bumi** and their brightly painted *perahu* (boats) dot the north coast. The coast is lined with beaches; few are particularly wonderful, though the turquoise shallows do make a stunning contrast with the wind-rattled, white-stone shore. Pantai Lombang, 30km northeast of Sumenep, has stunning white sands. Locals harvest tree saplings for the bonsai market and sell coconuts to visitors. At **Labuhan Mangrove**

Educational Park (Labuhan; ◷ 7.30am-6pm) **FREE** a raised wooden walkway runs through the forest, allowing you look for some of the unusual birds, insects, fish and, hopefully, mudskippers that rely on mangroves.

Buses link all the towns and villages along the north coast.

❶ Getting There & Away

Wings Air (www.lionair.co.id) has daily flights between Surabaya and Sumenep. The flight takes 35 minutes.

Buses go directly from Surabaya's Purabaya bus terminal via Bangkalan and Pamekasan through to Sumenep (normal/*patas* 40,000/60,000Rp, four hours) roughly every hour. Buses also run to Sumenep (passing through Surabaya) from Banyuwangi (via Probolinggo), Malang, Semarang and Jakarta.

From East Java there's a daily **ferry** (⟋ 0328-663054) from Jangkar harbour (near Asembagus) to Kalianget (60,000Rp, five to six hours) in Madura. At research time it departed Jangkar at 1pm and from Kalianget at 8am. Schedules are weather dependent and change regularly; contact the Sumenep tourist office (p178) to check times. Buses run from Situbondo to Jangkar. To get to Kalianget, take minibus 'O' (3000Rp, 20 minutes) from Sumenep.

Sumenep

⟋ 0328 / POP 101,000

Sumenep, in the far east of the island, is a sleepy, refined town, with a Mediterranean air and quiet, lazy streets. By mid-afternoon the whole town seems to settle into a slow, collective siesta. With dozens of crumbling villas and a fine *kraton* (walled city palace) and mosque, it is easily Madura's most interesting town.

◉ Sights

Kraton PALACE
(10,000Rp; ◷ 7am-2pm Mon-Sat) Occupied by the present *bupati* (regent) of Sumenep, the grand *kraton* and its **Taman Sari** (Pleasure Garden; 2000Rp; ◷ 7am-5pm) date back to 1750. The bathing pools once used by the royal women are still here, though they're no longer in use. There's also a small **museum** (2000Rp incl in Taman Sari entry; ◷ 7am-5pm) with an interesting collection of Madurese furniture, stone sculptures and *binggel* (heavy silver anklets worn by Madurese women). All were possessions of Madurese royals once upon a time.

Sumenep

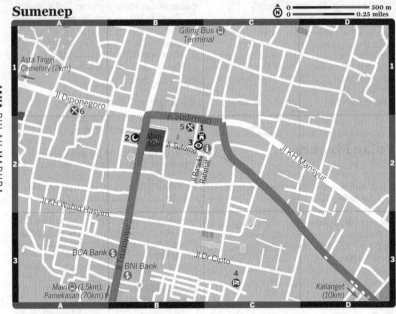

Sumenep

Mesjid Jamik　　　　　　　　　　MOSQUE
(Alun-Alun; ⊘ 24hr) FREE Looking more like
an extravagant city gateway than a mosque,
Sumenep's 18th-century Mesjid Jamik is
notable for its three-tiered Meru-style roof,
Chinese porcelain tiles and ceramics.

Asta Tinggi Cemetery　　　　　CEMETERY
(⊘ 24hr) The tombs of the royal family are at
the Asta Tinggi Cemetery, which looks out
over the town from a peaceful hilltop 3km
northwest of the centre. The main royal
tombs are decorated with carved and brightly painted panels; two depict dragons said to
represent the colonial invasion of Sumenep.
At weekends there's often a crowd of locals
here paying their respects.

🛏 Sleeping & Eating

There are plenty of good, inexpensive eateries. Be sure to order the local speciality *sate
kambing* (goat satay), which is often served
with raw shallots and rice cakes. *Soto madura,* a spicy soup with nuts, lemon grass and
beef, is another speciality. Good places to try
these dishes include **Rumah Makan Kartini**
(☑ 0328-662431; Jl Diponegoro 83; mains 12,000-
20,000Rp; ⊘ 8am-9pm) and **Rumah Makan
17 Agustus** (☑ 0328-662255; Jl Sudirman 34;
mains from 14,000-25,000Rp; ⊘ 8am-8pm).

Hotel C-1　　　　　　　　　　HOTEL $
(☑ 0328-674368; Jl Sultan Abdurrahman; r
125,000-400,000Rp; ✳🛜) The smartest place
in town, this modern hotel has a good selection of simple rooms decorated with
hand-carved wooden furniture. It's clean,
mattresses are springy and the linen is fresh.
It's about 2km southeast of the centre.

ⓘ Information

Tourist Office (☑ 0328-667148, 0817 933
0648; kurniadi@consultant.com; Jl Sutomo 5;
⊘ 7am-3.30pm Mon-Fri) Run by enthusiastic

and knowledgeable staff, who can help out with most matters relating to both Sumenep and the island.

BCA (Jl Trunojoyo; ⊗8am-4pm Mon-Sat) and **BNI** (Jl Trunojoyo; ⊗8am-4pm Mon-Sat) banks are on Jl Trunojoyo; both offer currency exchange.

🛈 Getting There & Away

Sumenep's main **bus terminal** is on the southern side of town, a 10,000Rp becak (bicycle rickshaw) ride from the centre. Buses leave roughly hourly until 4pm for Surabaya's Purabaya bus terminal (normal/*patas* 40,000/60,000Rp, four hours) and big cities across Java, including Malang. Bus agents along Jl Trunojoyo sell tickets. The **Giling bus terminal** for *angkots* heading north is right near the stadium, a short walk or becak ride from the centre. From Giling, minibuses go to Lombang, Slopeng, Ambunten and other north-coast destinations.

Malang

☑0341 / POP 887,450

With leafy, colonial-era boulevards and a breezy climate, Malang moves at a far more leisurely pace than the regional capital, Surabaya. It's a cultured city with several important universities, and is home to a large student population. The central area is not too large and is quite walkable.

Established by the Dutch in the closing decades of the 18th century, Malang earned its first fortunes from coffee, which flourished on the surrounding hillsides. Today the city's colonial grandeur is quickly disappearing behind the homogenous facades of more modern developments, but there's still much to admire for now.

With a number of Hindu temples and sights outside the city, Malang makes an ideal base to explore this intriguing corner of East Java.

◎ Sights

The interior of the busy *alun-alun* (main public square) in front of Hotel Tugu Malang is a lovely and lively park, with a monument at the centre of a pond that is afloat with hundreds of lotus blossoms and surrounded by gorgeous spreading trees.

Across the main Surabaya road from the downtown area, the hazy, mystical and imposing silhouette of Mt Semeru looms over the wide avenue that is Jl Semeru. Gotta love symmetry.

Hotel Tugu Malang   MUSEUM

(☑0341-363891;   www.tuguhotels.com/hotels/malang; Jl Tugu III; tour per person incl meal 115,000Rp; ⊗9am-9pm) Malang's most impressive museum isn't actually a museum at all, but a hotel: the boutique, four-star Hotel Tugu Malang (p180), a showcase for its owner, arguably Indonesia's foremost collector of Asian art and antiquities. English-speaking tours are available all day, but aim for evening for candlelight ambience; it's complimentary for guests staying here, while admission for nonguests is redeemable against restaurant orders.

The exhibits include 10th-century ceramics, jade carvings from the 13th century, Ming dynasty porcelain, Qing dynasty wood carvings and even the complete facade of a Chinese temple.

Jalan Besar Ijen   AREA

Malang has some wonderful colonial architecture. Just northwest of the centre, Jl Besar Ijen is Malang's millionaires' row, a boulevard lined with elegant whitewashed mansions from the Dutch era. Many have been substantially renovated, but there's still much to admire. On Sunday mornings it's closed to traffic and a market is set up along here; in late May it becomes the setting for the city's huge Malang Kembali festival.

Pasar Bunga   MARKET

(⊗7am-5pm) The flower market, Pasar Bunga, is pleasantly sited around a river valley and is the place to stroll in the morning.

🎯 Tours

Malang is a good place to set up a tour to Bromo; these are usually on the route that runs via Tumpang. Costs depend on numbers and transport, but two/three/four people can expect to pay about 850,000/750,000/650,000Rp per person for a sunrise tour in a 4WD (they usually leave at 1.30am). Options to continue the trip on to Ijen and then Ketapang harbour (for Bali) are also popular.

Trips to southern beaches and temples around Malang are also possible. If you want to create your own itinerary, a day's car hire (with driver) starts at around 600,000Rp.

Wijaya Travel (☑0341-325118; Jl Pajajaran 7) is a reliable agency that can arrange shuttles to Solo, Yogyakarta and Probolinggo.

Helios Tours by Smartine Travel TOURS

(☑ 0853 3404 4000, 0341-351801; www.helios tour.net; Jl Suropati 27; ⊙ 8am-8pm) A well-organised operator with an incredible number of tour options, from standard day trips to Bromo to hardcore trekking expeditions to Gunung Semeru. Staff are switched-on and deal with lots of travellers. The three-day tours to the turtle-nesting grounds at Sukamade beach (3,449,000Rp) are a great way of visiting a little-known corner of Java.

Jona's Homestay TOURS

(☑ 0341-324678; Jl Sutomo 4) The owners of this homestay can organise tours to Bromo and around Malang; they also rent scooters to guests.

🎎 Festivals & Events

Malang Kembali CULTURAL

Held in late May, Malang Kembali celebrates *ludruk,* an old-time music-hall tradition that was very popular in Java in the last century. Jl Besar Ijen, home to many wonderful old Dutch villas, is closed to traffic for five days, and there's street theatre, live music, shows, and actors in period costumes. You can also taste traditional food and drinks.

🛏 Sleeping

Kampong Tourist HOSTEL $

(☑ 0341-345797; www.kampongtourist.com; Hotel Helios, Jl Pattimura 37; s/d/tr dm 70,000/125,000/155,000Rp, gazebo s/d 145,000/ 170,000Rp; 🛜) On the rooftop of Hotel Helios are these comfy dorm beds (and interestingly include double and triple-sized beds), along with bamboo gazebo-style rooms. Its bar-cafe is a good spot for a meal and a cold beer with commanding city views.

Huize Jon Hostel HOSTEL $

(☑ 0818 386 300; Jl Majapahit; dm 70,000Rp; ❄🛜) This hostel gets the basics right. There's an immaculate, bright dorm featuring 14 pod-style beds with individual curtains giving a little extra privacy. The communal bathrooms are just as good, and there's an atmospheric downstairs communal area where it's easy to find travel buddies. Staff organise cheap Bromo and Ijen trips that get great feedback.

Jona's Homestay HOMESTAY $

(☑ 0341-324678; Jl Sutomo 4; r from 150,000Rp; ❄🛜) This long-running homestay in a colossal colonial villa is run by a sweet family.

The location in an affluent neighbourhood is also convenient and quiet. Even though the rooms are aged, it's still comfortable enough if you get the right room – some are definitely better than others, so ask to see a few before settling in.

A basic breakfast is available, as is cheap beer. It hires bicycles and scooters and runs Bromo tours.

Same Hotel HOTEL $$

(☑ 0341-303 1999; Jl Pattimura 19; r incl breakfast from 375,000Rp; ❄🛜) With its rather grand colonnaded Italianate facade and sparkling lobby, the strangely named Same Hotel flirts with tackiness. Fortunately, thanks to low prices and subtler-looking rooms that are also quiet, clean and comfortable, we'd say this is one of Malang's better choices. Also comes with professional staff, fast wi-fi, cable TV, room service and inclusive buffet breakfast.

Hotel Helios HOTEL $$

(☑ 0341-362 741; Jl Pattimura 37; r with fan/air-con 200,000/350,000Rp; ❄🛜) Helios has steadily upgraded the quality and prices of its accommodation in recent years. Behind the flash reception you'll find a selection of bright, clean, comfortable rooms grouped around a rear garden (and cafe). Most rooms have a flat-screen TV, high ceiling and modern bathroom. The economy options are tiny and spartan. Helios Tours is based here.

Hotel Sahid Montana HOTEL $$

(☑ 0341-362751; www.sahidhotels.com; Jl Kahuripan 9; r from 350,000Rp) A tiled, three-star indoor-outdoor inn serving mostly domestic tourists. Rooms are set on three floors around a garden gurgling with fountains. It's a decent enough choice, and is popular with tour groups, but it doesn't have a lot of character.

★ Hotel Tugu Malang BOUTIQUE HOTEL $$$

(☑ 0341-363891; www.tuguhotels.com; Jl Tugu III; r from 1,360,000Rp; ❄@🛜🏊) For a real flavour of what Java has to offer, this remarkable luxury hotel, loaded with local character and genuine hospitality, sets the standard. It manages to be both laid-back and elegant.

🍴 Eating

In town there are a number of decent warungs serving tasty Indonesian dishes. For cheap eats head for Jl Agus Salim, which comes alive at night with local specialities

Malang

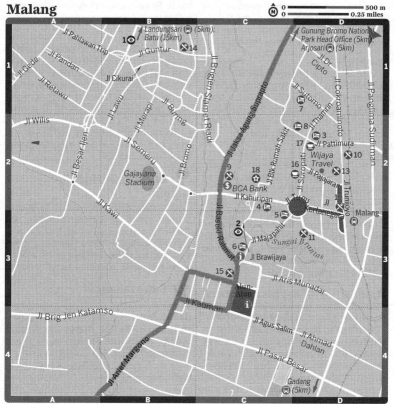

Malang

⦿ Sights
Hotel Tugu Malang	...........................(see 5)
1	Jalan Besar Ijen	......................................B1
2	Pasar Bunga	....C3

☯ Activities, Courses & Tours
Helios Tours	.... (see 3)
Jona's Homestay	..............................(see 7)

🛏 Sleeping
3	Hotel Helios	....D2
4	Hotel Sahid Montana	............................C2
5	Hotel Tugu Malang	.................................C3
6	Huize Jon Hostel	...................................C3
7	Jona's Homestay	.....................................D1
Kampong Tourist	.... (see 3)
8	Same Hotel	....D2

✴ Eating
9	Agung Resto	....C2
10	Bebek Gong	....D2
11	Inggil	....D3
12	Kertanegara	....D2
Melati	....(see 5)
13	Mie Tomcat	....D2
14	The Library	....B1
15	Toko Oen	....C3

🍸 Drinking & Nightlife
16	Ben House	....D2
17	Legi Pait	....D2

🎭 Entertainment
18	Taman Rekreasi Senaputra	..................C2

such as *nasi rawon* (beef soup served with fried onion and rice) and *bakso malang* (meatball soup served with noodles and grilled fish).

Bebek Gong INDONESIAN $
(☏ 0341-365055; Jl Cokroaminoto 2D; dishes 17,000–23,000Rp; ☺ 11am-10pm) A dressed-up warung dangling with lovely rattan lanterns

and lined with bamboo wallpaper, serving fried chicken and duck meals to the Malang masses. Platters come with raw cabbage and long beans on the side. Rice is 5000Rp extra.

Agung Resto
INDONESIAN $

(✆ 0341-357061; Jl Basuki Rahmat 80; mains 10,000-18,000Rp; ⊙ 8am-9pm) This cheerful spot with plastic chairs and tables has tasty, inexpensive local food, including *martabak* (pancake-like meat, egg and vegetable dish), rice and fish dishes, plus great juices.

Toko Oen
INTERNATIONAL $

(✆ 0341-364052; Jl Basuki Rahmat 5; mains 28,000-67,000Rp; ⊙ 8am-9.30pm) Boasting an imposing 1930 art deco frontage, Toko Oen is a throwback to ye olde days, with rattan furniture, waiters in starched whites, and Sinatra on the stereo. It serves middling Indonesian fare and cheap steaks, but it's the ice cream that, for some reason, is renowned among Indonesians. Don't expect much. It's all about the atmosphere here.

★ Melati
INDONESIAN, INTERNATIONAL $$

(✆ 0341-363891; www.tuguhotels.com; Hotel Tugu Malang, Jl Tugu III; mains 40,000-120,000Rp; ⊙ 24hr; ❖) The Tugu hotel's poolside restaurant is a romantic setting for a meal, with attentive staff to guide you through the delicious Indonesian and Chinese Peranakan options. It also does a damn fine *rijsttafel* (selection of Indonesian dishes served with rice). International mains such as pasta and grilled meats are also excellent. The wine list rocks, as does the selection of cocktails.

★ The Library
INTERNATIONAL $$

(✆ 0341-355487; Jl Baluran 2; mains 30,000-50,000Rp; ⊙ 8am-11pm Sun-Fri, to midnight Sat) With industrial-chic furnishings, shelves of books and graffiti wall art, this eye-catching cafe-restaurant, which is super-popular with local students, serves light Western-style meals such as Treasure Island, a delicious mix of salmon with mango salsa. It's renowned for its coffee, smoothies and breakfasts, including runny poached eggs on toast. Also has decent burgers and pasta.

Inggil
INDONESIAN $$

(✆ 0341-332110; Jl Gajahmada 4; mains 22,000-43,000Rp; ⊙ 10am-10pm) The delightfully eccentric Inggil is as much a museum or art gallery as a restaurant. Walls are lined with old photos, dozens of *wayang kulit* puppets stare vacantly at you as you tuck into the excellent traditional Javanese dishes, and if

you're lucky, a gamelan orchestra will provide a musical accompaniment.

Kertanegara
INDONESIAN $$

(✆ 0341-366203; www.kertanegararesto.com; Jl Kertanegara I; mains 25,000-80,000Rp; ⊙ noon-11pm; ✆) Occupying a large corner plot, this upmarket place has a garden terrace, strung with oh-so-many Christmas lights. Its enormous menu offers flavoursome European, Indonesian and Chinese food, with quite a good choice for vegetarians, and lots of seafood. Has occasional live music featuring syrup-voiced crooners.

🍷 Drinking & Nightlife

Legi Pait
COFFEE

(✆ 0822 3081 5835; Jl Pattimura 24; ⊙ 7am-1pm & 4-11pm Fri-Wed; ❖) A popular hang-out for the young and cool of Malang is this corner cafe with stained-wood furnishings. It serves a wide range of local coffees and infusions, juices and meals to an indie soundtrack.

☆ Entertainment

Taman Rekreasi Senaputra
PERFORMING ARTS

(Jl Brawijaya; 7000Rp, children 13yr & under 6000Rp; ⊙ 8am-4pm) Malang's cultural and recreational park has a hectically busy swimming pool and children's playground and some quirky events. *Kuda lumping* (horse trance) dances (7000Rp) are performed every Sunday morning at 10am.

The dancers ride rattan 'horses' then fall into a trance, writhing around on the ground with their eyes bulging. Still in a trance-like state, they perform assorted masochistic acts without any apparent harm, such as eating glass. The spectacle will not be to everyone's taste. On a more sober note, *wayang kulit* (shadow puppet) shows are regularly held here (usually on the fourth Sunday of the month); the tourist office has the latest schedule.

ℹ Information

Malang has plenty of banks; most are congregated along Jl Basuki Rahmat, including **BCA** (Jl Basuki Rahmat; ⊙ 8am-4pm Mon-Sat).

Gunung Bromo National Park Head Office (✆ 0341-491828; tn-bromo@malang.wasantara .net.id; Jl Raden Intan 6; ⊙ 7.30am-4pm Mon-Fri) A short way north of the city centre. Plenty of info on routes to and from the park.

Tourist Information Office (✆ 0341-346231; Jl Basuki Rahmat; ⊙ 8am-4pm) Helpful tourist office.

Tourist Information Kiosk (Alun-Alun; ⊙ 8am-4pm) This small kiosk is staffed by students.

⊙ Getting There & Away

Due to dangers driving on the sandy volcanic road, the shortcut to Bromo via the easterly route from Malang is only permissable for those who've signed up with a 4WD tour. If that's you, you're in for a treat as the route is spectacular. If you have your own vehicle, you'll need to take the much longer and less interesting northerly route via Probolinggo.

For a reliable taxi company, use **Citra** (🕿 0341-490555).

BUS & ANGKOT

Malang has three bus terminals. **Arjosari** (Jl Teluk Mandar) , 5km northeast of town, is the main one with regular buses to Surabaya, Probolinggo and Banyuwangi. Long-distance buses to Solo, Yogyakarta, Denpasar and even Jakarta mostly leave in the early evening. Minibuses (called *angkot* or *mikrolet* locally) run from Arjosari to nearby villages such as Singosari and Tumpang.

Gadang bus terminal is 5km south of the city centre, and sends buses along the southern routes to destinations such as Blitar (25,000Rp, two hours).

Buses depart **Landungsari bus terminal**, 5km northwest of the city, to destinations west of the city, such as Batu (10,000Rp, 40 minutes).

Plenty of door-to-door travel companies operate from Malang, and hotels and travel agencies can book them. Wijaya Travel (p179) is a reliable agency and can arrange shuttles to Solo, Yogyakarta and Probolinggo.

Abimanyu Travel (🕿 0812 3007 1652, 0341-304 1382) has minibuses to Surabaya (100,000Rp) that will drop you off at hotels in Surabaya or at the airport (thus saving the long haul from Surabaya's bus terminal).

TRAIN

Malang Train Station (Jl Trunojoyo 10) is centrally located but not well connected to the main network. There are daily trains to Yogy-

akarta (170,000Rp to 445,000Rp, seven hours) via Solo, Surabaya (35,000Rp to 60,000Rp, two hours), Probolinggo (58,000Rp, three hours) and Banyuwangi (62,000Rp, 7¾ hours), from where you can hop on a ferry to Bali.

⊙ Getting Around

Grab and Gojek online taxis and motorbikes offer a cheap means of getting around town.

Mikrolet (small minibus taxis) run all over town. Most buzz between the bus terminals via the town centre. These are marked A–G (Arjosari to Gadung and return), A–L (Arjosari to Landungsari) or G–L (Gadang to Landungsari). Trips cost 4000Rp; or 8000Rp if you have a large bag.

Around Malang

The lush, palm-dappled rice and corn fields around Malang are scattered with evocative Hindu and Buddhist ruins, making for a fun half-day road trip.

⊙ Sights

The Singosari temples lie in a ring around Malang and are mostly funerary temples dedicated to the kings of the Singosari dynasty (AD 1222–92), the precursors of the Majapahit kingdom.

Candi Singosari   TEMPLE
(Jl Kertanegara 148; admission by donation; ⊙ 7.30am-4pm) Situated right in the village of Singosari, 12km north of Malang, this temple stands 500m off the main Malang–Surabaya road. One of the last monuments erected to the Singosari dynasty, it was built in 1304 in honour of King Kertanegara, the fifth and last Singosari king, who died in 1292 in a palace uprising.

Candi Kidal   TEMPLE
(Jl Candi Kidal; admission by donation; ⊙ 7am-noon & 1-4pm) Set in the village of Kidal, west of Tumpang, with houses rising all around,

BUSES FROM MALANG

DESTINATION	FARE (RP)	DURATION (HR)	FREQUENCY
Banyuwangi	70,000	7	11am & 10pm
Denpasar	140,000 incl ferry	12	6pm
Jember	23,000-40,000	4½	every 90min
Probolinggo	40,000	2½	every 10min 5am-5pm
Solo	110,000	10	8am & 7pm
Surabaya	20,000-25,000	2½-3	hourly
Yogyakarta	150,000	11	8am & 7pm

Around Malang

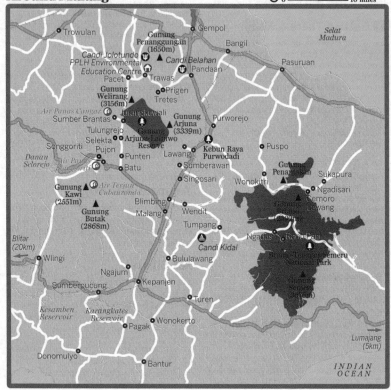

this graceful temple was built around 1260 as the burial shrine of King Anusapati (the second Singosari king, who died in 1248). Now 12m high, it originally topped 17m and is an example of east Javanese architecture. Its slender form has pictures of the Garuda (mythical man-bird) on three sides, plus bold, glowering *kala* (demonic faces often seen over temple gateways).

Candi Sumberawan BUDDHIST TEMPLE

(admission by donation; ☺ 7.30am-4pm) This small, squat Buddhist stupa lies in the terraced, cultivated foothills of Gunung Arjuna, about 5km northwest of Singosari. It was built to commemorate the 1359 visit of Hayam Wuruk, the great Majapahit king. Within the temple grounds are a lingam stone and the crumbling remains of additional stupa, along with the remains of recent offerings.

But what makes the temple really special is the approach. You'll walk from the main village road – a checkerboard of tarps layered with drying corn – down a 400m dirt path, which parallels a canal, and through rice fields until you reach the ruins. Young men use the canal for bathing, so don't be surprised to see a naked body or two en route to the stupa. In Javanese culture it's polite to avert your eyes – the boys will duck down into the water in fits of giggles as you pass. Opposite the temple is a spring – the source of the gurgling canal – where locals go to cool off on sweltering weekends.

Take an *angkot* (5000Rp) from Singosari *pasar* (market) on the highway to Desa Sumberawan, then walk 500m down the road to the canal and the dirt path.

Candi Jago TEMPLE

(Jajaghu; Jl Wisnuwardhana; admission by donation; ☺ 7.30am-4pm) Along a small road near the market in Tumpang, 22km from Malang, Candi Jago was built between 1268 and

1280 and is thought to be a memorial to the fourth Singosari king, Vishnuvardhana. The temple has some interesting decorative carving from the Jataka and the Mahabharata, in the three-dimensional style of *wayang kulit* (shadow-puppet play), which is typical of East Java.

Purwodadi

A few kilometres north of Lawang on the road to Surabaya, the **Kebun Raya Purwodadi** (☑ 0343-615 033; admission 25,000Rp, tours 15,000Rp; ☉ 7.30am-4pm) are expansive dry-climate botanical gardens. The 85 hectares are beautifully landscaped and contain over 3000 species, including 80 kinds of palm, a huge fern collection, a Mexican section, myriad orchids and many varieties of bamboo. The garden office to the south of the entrance has a map and leaflets. Air Terjun Cobanbaung is a high waterfall next to the gardens.

The gardens are easily reached; take any bus from Malang to Surabaya and ask to be dropped off at the entrance.

Gunung Arjuna-Lalijiwo Reserve

This wild and little-known reserve includes the dormant volcano Gunung Arjuna (3339m), the semi-active Gunung Welirang (3156m) and the Lalijiwo Plateau on the northern slopes of Arjuna. Experienced and well-equipped hikers can walk from the resort town of Tretes to Selekta in two days, but you need a guide to go all the way. Alternatively, you can climb Welirang from Tretes or Lawang.

To get to the start of the hikes, take a bus to Pandaan (18,000Rp) from Malang or Surabaya and then a minibus to Tretes (10,000Rp).

Gunung Penanggungan

The remains of no fewer than 81 temples, dating from the 10th to 16th centuries, are scattered over the slopes of Gunung Penanggungan (1650m). This sacred Hindu mountain is said to be the peak of Mt Mahameru, which according to legend broke off and landed at its present site when Mt Mahameru was transported from India to Indonesia.

Historically this was a very important pilgrimage site for Hindus, and a few Javanese mystics, meditators and Hindus still visit the mountain today. Pilgrims make their way to the top of the mountain and stop to bathe in the holy springs adorned with Hindu statuary. The two main bathing places are **Candi Jolotundo** and **Candi Belahan**, the best examples of remaining Hindu art. Both are difficult to reach.

A minibus from Pandaan (south of Surabaya) to Trawas, the village that serves as base camp for the mountain, costs 8000Rp.

🏃 Activities

PPLH Environmental Education Centre OUTDOORS
(☑ 0321-681 8752; www.pplhselo.or.id; bungalows from 485,000Rp) In a stunning setting on the evergreen western slopes of Penanggungan, the PPLH Environmental Education Centre is a supremely relaxing and interesting place. It's mainly set up to teach groups about the merits of organic agriculture, composting and garbage management, but it has eight

---

HIKING GUNUNG WELIRANG & GUNUNG ARJUNA

It's a hard, five-hour walk (17km) to the very basic huts used by the Gunung Welirang sulphur collectors. Hikers usually stay overnight here in order to reach the summit before the clouds roll in around mid-morning. Bring your own camping gear, food and drinking water (or hire it all at the PHKA post for around 200,000Rp per day), and be prepared for freezing conditions. From the huts it's a 4km climb to the summit. Allow at least six hours in total for the ascent, and 4½ hours for the descent.

The trail passes Lalijiwo Plateau, a superb alpine meadow, from where a trail leads to Gunung Arjuna, the more demanding peak. From Arjuna, a trail leads down the southern side to Junggo, near Selekta and Batu. It's a five-hour descent from Arjuna this way; a guide is essential.

Get information from the **PHKA post** (☑ 081 2178 8956; Jl Wilis 523; ☉ 8am-5pm Mon-Sat) at the entrance to the park. Guides can be hired here for 300,000Rp to 400,000Rp per day; allow two days to climb one mountain and three days for both.

simple, comfortable cottages with outdoor bathrooms that can be rented by tourists.

There's an organic restaurant and the meals get rave reports. School groups pass through from time to time, disturbing the tranquillity somewhat, but most of the time it's very peaceful. Expert guides can be hired for hikes (about 200,000Rp per day), and they'll gladly explain about plants used for herbal medicines. To get there, take a Trawas-bound minibus (8000Rp) from Pandaan and an *ojek* (20,000Rp) from Trawas.

Batu

📍 0341 / POP 190,000

Batu, 15km northwest of Malang, is a large hill resort on the lower reaches of Gunung Arjuna, and is surrounded by volcanic peaks. It's a popular weekend destination for locals, but few foreigners visit, which is a real shame as the scenery is gorgeous and the climate more forgiving than that in much of Java. All up, it makes for a relaxing couple of days' stay.

👁 Sights

Songgoriti   HOT SPRINGS
(20,000Rp; ⊙ 8am-9pm) Songgoriti, 3km west of Batu, has well-known hot springs and a small, ancient Hindu temple on the grounds of the Hotel Air Panas Songgoriti. The temple, which dates back to the 9th century, was once much larger, and today all you see is the very top part. Most of the temple is thought to be buried below.

Nearby, Pasar Wisata is a tourist market selling mostly apples, bonsai plants and volcanic stone mortars and pestles, which make for an unusual and surprisingly light-weight souvenir.

Sumber Brantas   VILLAGE
The small village of Sumber Brantas, far above Selekta resort, and in a gorgeous misty mountain setting, is at the source of the Sungai Brantas (Brantas River). From here you can walk 2km to **Air Panas Cangar** (admission 10,500Rp, car 5000Rp; ⊙ 7.30am-5pm), hot springs high in the mountains surrounded by forest and mist.

Air Terjun Cubanrondo   WATERFALL
(10,000Rp; ⊙ 7.30am-5pm) The tall and narrow single waterfall of Air Terjun Cubanrondo drops off the cliffs 5km southwest of Songgoriti.

🏃 Activities

Selekta   SWIMMING
(35,000Rp; ⊙ 7.30am-5pm) Selekta, a small resort 5km further up the mountain from Batu and 1km off the main road, is home to the Pemandian Selekta, a large swimming-pool complex set in landscaped gardens. Other 'highlights' include some terrifying plastic dinosaurs, a giant fish tank, something mysteriously called a 'Dad Boat' and a giant lion's mouth you can walk into.

🛏 Sleeping & Eating

Accommodation is available in Batu, Songgoriti and all along the road to Selekta. Songgoriti and Selekta are small, quiet resorts; Batu has the best facilities but is more built-up. Add around 25% to prices for weekend rates.

Kampung Lumbung   LODGE $$$
(📍 0851 0444 4142; www.grahabunga.com; Jl Ir Sukarno; r weekday/weekend from 550,000/ 650,000Rp, cottage weekday/weekend from 1,000,000/1,200,000Rp; 🛜🏊) 🅿 A wonderful eco-hotel where the complex resembles a traditional village and all the buildings make good use of recycled wood and solar power. There's excellent local food in the restaurant. The natural environment is sublime here: the climate is refreshing and the air is fresh. It's 1km south of central Batu.

Hotel El Royale Kartika Wijaya   HISTORIC HOTEL $$$
(📍 0333-338 2999; www.kartikawijaya.com; Jl Panglima Sudirman 127; r incl breakfast from 1,100,000Rp; 🛜🏊) An imposing colonial residence in sweeping grounds dotted with palms, lawns and tennis courts. The rooms are bright, spacious and filled with wicker furnishings, and the service is impressive. The walk-in room rates (quoted here) make it overpriced, but by booking online you can often secure heavily discounted room rates.

Warung Bethania Batu   INDONESIAN $
(📍 0341-591 158; Jl Diponegoro 103; mains 24,000-65,000Rp; ⊙ 10.30am-9pm) This bamboo-walled restaurant with unusual tree-trunk furnishings and pictures of past clients on the walls, is the best-known place in Batu for fried fish and chicken. Both are served with delicious sides of fresh salads and sambals.

❶ Information

There are several banks with ATMs along Jl Panglima Sudirman.

❶ Getting There & Away

From Malang's Landungsari bus terminal take a Kediri bus or a *mikrolet* (small taxi) to Batu (10,000Rp, 40 minutes). *Mikrolet* connect Batu's **bus terminal** (Jl Dewi Sartika) with the centre via Panglima Sudirman.

From the bus terminal, *mikrolet* run to Selekta (3000Rp, 20 minutes) and Sumber Brantas (6000Rp, 45 minutes). *Mikrolet* turn off to Sumber Brantas at Jurangkuwali village. For Air Panas Cangar, walk 2km straight ahead from Jurangkuwali.

You'll find plenty of *ojek* around Batu to get you to all of these destinations.

South-Coast Beaches

The coast south of Malang has some good beaches, but facilities are limited. **Sendangbiru** is a picturesque fishing village separated by a narrow channel from **Pulau Sempu**. This island nature reserve has a couple of lakes, Telaga Lele and Telaga Sat, both ringed by jungle. Boats can be hired (around 200,000Rp return) to get you to Sempu. Take your own provisions.

A few kilometres before Sendangbiru, a rough track to the left leads 3km to **Tambakrejo**, a small fishing village with a sweeping sandy bay, which (despite the surf) is generally safe for swimming.

Balekambang is best known for its picturesque Hindu temple on the small island of Pulau Ismoyo, connected by a footbridge to the beach. Balekambang is one of the most popular beaches and is crowded on weekends. There are basic guesthouses in the village.

Minibuses from Malang's Gadang bus terminal travel to Sendangbiru (25,000Rp, two hours), past the turn-off to Tambakrejo. For Balekambang, buses run direct from Malang for 15,000Rp.

Blitar

✐ 0342 / POP 132,000

A low-key provincial city, Blitar is off the standard Javan tourist trails, but with several compelling sights in the vicinity, a hotel worth travelling for and a quiet and gentle atmosphere, Blitar is well worth a visit. The town makes a good base for visiting the Panataran temple complex and the spectacular active volcano of Gunung Kelud. It's also the home of Indonesia's first president, Sukarno; his memorial is worth checking out.

❍ Sights

Makam Bung Karno   MONUMENT
(Jl Sukarno 152; 3000Rp, incl museum entry; ⏱7am-11pm) At Sentul, 2km north of the town centre, former president Sukarno's grave is marked by a massive black stone and an elaborate monument of columns and murals depicting his achievements. Sukarno (or Bung Karno) is widely regarded as the father of the Indonesian nation, although he was only reinstated as a national hero in 1978. Despite family requests that he be buried at his home in Bogor, Sukarno was buried in an unmarked grave next to his mother in Blitar.

🛏 Sleeping & Eating

★**Tugu Sri Lestari**   HISTORIC HOTEL $$
(☎0342-801 766; www.tuguhotels.com; Jl Merdeka 173; r incl breakfast from 490,000Rp, Sukarno ste incl breakfast 3,700,000Rp; ❋☎) There's a real sense of history throughout this hotel, which is in a converted Dutch colonial building dating from the 1850s. The rooms in the principal building are incredibly atmospheric, with high ceilings and grand teak beds; those in the modern extension at the rear are neat and functional.

Waroeng Tugu Blitar   INDONESIAN $
(☎0342-801 766; www.tuguhotels.com; Jl Merdeka 173; mains 32,000-78,000Rp; ⏱8am-10pm; ✐) With an elegant colonial ambience, the in-house restaurant of the Tugu Sri Lestari is a fine place to delight in well-presented, upmarket versions of such local specialities as *udang swarloka* (deep-fried shrimp balls), *tahu kembang jenar* (crispy tofu stuffed with mushrooms, bean sprouts and bamboo shoots) and *nasi kare ayam ny oei* (chicken cooked in yellow curry served with rice).

Bu Mamik   INDONESIAN $
(☎0342-806 634; Jl Kalimantan 11; mains 7500-32,000Rp; ⏱10am-9pm) Tasty *ayam bakar* (grilled chicken) is what brings droves of locals to this quaint, stilted indoor-outdoor restaurant with carved columns and twirling fans.

VISITING GUNUNG KELUD

With a plunging crater and steaming vents and in a near-permanent state of growl, Gunung Kelud (1731m) is one of Java's most active and rewarding volcanoes to visit. An eruption in 1919 killed 5000 people, while one in 2007 sent smoke 2.5km into the air and created a 250m-high cone within the caldera. The volcano erupted again in February 2014 and the resulting ash smothered buildings across East and Central Java.

When Kelud is calm, you can access a viewpoint ridge. To do this, drive to the car park below the mountain and then take a motorbike taxi (25,000Rp) to just short of the summit. From there, it's a brief walk to the viewpoint. Repairs to access roads were ongoing at the time of research.

Entrance to Gunung Kelud is controlled at a gateway 10km before the summit because of the active nature of the beast. The volcano's grumpy temperament means that it's not always safe to visit. Hotels in Blitar will be able to give the latest on the status of the volcano.

Around 30km directly north of Panataran, Kelud is not accessible by public transport. The easiest way here is to hire a car or *ojek* from Blitar. After bargaining, the latter will do a half-day return trip via Panataran for around 120,000Rp.

ⓘ Information

There are several banks in town, including **BCA Bank** (Jl Merdeka; ⊙8am-4pm Mon-Sat).

ⓘ Getting There & Away

Regular buses run from Blitar to Malang (25,000Rp, 2½ hours) and Surabaya (50,000Rp, 4½ to five hours), as well as Solo (120,000Rp, six hours). The **bus terminal** is 4km south of town along Jl Kenari (3000Rp by *angkot* from the centre). *Angkudes* run from the western end of Jl Merdeka to Panataran temple for 6000Rp, passing close to Makam Bung Karno; you'll have to walk the last 300m or so.

Blitar has a few useful train connections, with three daily services heading to both Solo (160,000Rp to 465,000Rp, 4½ hours) and Yogyakarta (160,000Rp to 465,000Rp, five to 5½ hours).

Hiring a car and driver makes a lot of sense to see the sights; the Hotel Tugu Blitar can organise this for from 550,000Rp per day. Or hire an *ojek* for much less at around 100,000Rp.

Panataran

The **Hindu temples** (admission by donation; ⊙7am-5pm) at Panataran (locally called 'Penataran') are the largest intact Majapahit temples, and the finest examples of ancient East Javanese architecture and sculpture. Construction began in 1197, during the Singosari dynasty, with building work continuing for another 250 years. Most of the important surviving structures date from the great years of the Majapahit kingdom during the 14th century.

Around the base of the first-level platform, the comic-strip carvings tell the story of a test between the fat, meat-eating Bubukshah and the thin, vegetarian Gagang Aking.

Further on is the small Dated Temple, so called because of the date '1291' (AD 1369) carved over the entrance. On the next level are colossal serpents snaking endlessly around the Naga Temple, which once housed valuable sacred objects.

At the rear stands the triple-tiered Mother Temple, its lowest panels depicting stories from the Ramayana. Behind is a small royal *mandi* with a frieze depicting lizards, bulls and dragons around its walls.

Three hundred metres southeast of the turn-off to the Panataran Hindu temples, the **Museum Panataran** (admission by donation; ⊙8am-2pm Tue-Thu, Sat & Sun, to 11am Fri) has an impressive collection of statuary from the complex, but labelling is poor.

Entry is by donation; 10,000Rp should be suitable. There's a 3000Rp parking fee if coming by car.

Pacitan

✆ 0357 / POP 54,000

A long way from anywhere, the small south-coast town of Pacitan lies on a horseshoe bay ringed by rocky cliffs. It's a beach resort with limited accommodation and a few fresh seafood restaurants. For a long time very few foreigners ever made it here. Today, thanks to the discovery of some epic surf spots in the town's vicinity an ever-increasing number of foreign surfers are passing through.

Non-surfing tourists remain rare, but the stunning coastline here offers much tourist potential.

The blonde beach at Pacitan itself is set in a rather dramatic bay shaped like a stemless wine glass. The natural harbour to the west is set against the towering jungled cliffs, and there's a series of decent beach peaks as the beach meanders east toward a reasonable point break.

If you make an off-season visit during the week, you've a good chance of having a virtually deserted beach to yourself.

🏃 Activities

Pantai Ria Teleng SURFING
Pantai Ria Teleng, 4km or so from town at the eastern end of the bay, has golden sand and good surfing conditions for beginners as the waves break over a sandy bottom. Surfboards and bodyboards can be hired here, and there are lifeguards. Swimming is possible when the seas are calm.

🛏 Sleeping

Harry's Ocean House GUESTHOUSE $
(☑0878 9514 5533; Pancer Beach; dm 40,000Rp, hut without bathroom 50,000Rp, r with fan/air-con 90,000/110,000Rp, cottages 150,000-250,000Rp; ❄) This friendly and buzzing place has four styles of frills-free rooms on offer: dorms, a bamboo hut, concrete rooms and stilted wooden cottages with arched roofs. The property is on a back road, inland from the beach. It has another branch in nearby Watu Karung.

Arya Homestay GUESTHOUSE $
(☑0812 5201 2388; Jl Teleng Ria 2; r 200,000Rp; ☎) Simple, fan-cooled tiled rooms come with high slanted ceilings and friendly management. It's on the inland road and just a moment's walk from the beach.

ℹ Information

There are several banks with ATMs on Jl Jend Sudirman.

ℹ Getting There & Away

Buses run to Pacitan from Solo (60,000Rp, 4½ hours) and also from Ponorogo (22,000Rp, 2½ hours) via a scenic road. From Ponorogo, direct buses go to Blitar (35,000Rp, three hours).

Direct travel minibuses (70,000Rp, three hours) connect Yogyakarta with Pacitan; call **Aneka Jaya** (☑0357-883048; Jl Agus Salim).

There's very little public transport around Pacitan. Motorbikes with surfboard racks can be rented from some Pacitan guesthouses (50,000Rp to 80,000Rp per day).

Watu Karang
☑0357
Stunning Watu Karang, about 13km southwest of Pacitan, is an evocative fishing village with an arc of fine white sand and turquoise water offshore. For years the village was virtually unknown to tourists, but then in 2009 the international surf media lifted the lid on two epic surf spots in the bay here, and since then increasing numbers of surfers have been heading to Watu Karang.

If you're not a surfer then you're going to be in the minority, but the gorgeous beach is easily one of the best in East Java, and with increasingly good accommodation, Watu Karang makes for a charmed spot to chill out for a few days.

This is also agate country, and hawkers sell reasonably priced polished stones and rings.

Watu Karang is not served by public transport; you'll need to hire a car in Pacitan or arrange transport with your guesthouse.

◎ Sights

At Punung village, on the Solo road 17km north of Watu Karang, is the turn-off to some magnificent limestone caves. **Gua Putri** is 2km from the highway, and the much more impressive **Gua Gong**, 8km away, is the largest and most spectacular cave system in the area.

The turn-off to the more famous **Gua Tabuhan** (Musical Cave) is 4km north on the highway beyond Punung, and then another 4km from there. This huge limestone cavern was a refuge for prehistoric humans 50,000 years ago. Pay the resident musicians here and they'll strike up an impressive 'orchestral' performance by striking rocks against stalactites, each in perfect pitch, and echoing pure gamelan melodies. You must hire a guide and a lamp. There's no easy way of getting here by public transport, so you'll need to find a car and driver in Watu Karang.

🏃 Activities

Watu Karang has two surf spots – one a left and one a right. Both waves are short, sharp, hollow and extremely heavy. This is

WHALE-SHARK TOURS

Each year between January and March (the start of the season is better than the end) an annual migration causes quite a stir in Probolinggo. Twenty or more whale sharks, some measuring up to 8m, gather in the shallow seas off Pantai Bentar, 8km east of town. Boats take camera-toting local tourists on trips to see these marine giants, the world's largest fish (a harmless plankton feeder). In Javanese they're known as *geger lintang* ('stars on the back'), a reference to the starlike spots these sharks can be identified by. Boats only charge 15,000Rp or so per person, providing there are enough passengers. As the sea is usually murky, snorkelling is seldom rewarding. Sightings are far from guaranteed, with even boat operators admitting to only a 50/50 chance of seeing them. If you're determined to see one in Java, it's best to allow for two days of boat excursions.

expert-only surf country. The waves here are especially suited to bodyboarders, and Watu Karang is now considered one of the planet's best bodyboard spots.

Sleeping

Watukarung Prapto Homestay　　HOMESTAY $
(☑ 0853 2675 7012; r from 200,000Rp; ❋ 🛜) Behind a terracotta-roofed family house is a series of wooden cabin rooms, which, though spartan, are polished clean and have good mattresses and attached bathrooms. The family that runs the place will quickly adopt you as one of their own.

Pasir Putih　　HOMESTAY $
(☑ 0852 8102 3187; s/d 175,000/250,000Rp; ❋🛜) One of the best homestays in the village, Pasir Putih offers modern rooms with private bathrooms and patios overlooking the beach. Chuck in a royal welcome from the owner and tasty home cooking and you're onto a winner.

Istana Ombak　　RESORT $$$
(www.istanaombak.com; Jl Kerapu Milak 151; all-inclusive surf packages from 1,500,000Rp; 🛜🏊) The original Watu Karang surf camp is a stunner, with comfortable thatched cottages and villas, wi-fi and satellite TV. Peer over

the side of the cool, blue infinity pool and you can watch the waves explode down the reef. It offers solid local surf intel and spectacular family-style dinners, not to mention direct access to the beach.

❶ Getting There & Away

Infrequent buses run between Pacitan and Watu Karang. The journey takes around an hour. Most places to stay will arrange transfers from either Pacitan town or, easier, direct from Yogyakarta (around 600,000Rp)

Probolinggo

📞 0335 / POP 220,800
For most travellers, Probolinggo is a bustling, featureless transit point in the fertile plains on the route to Gunung Bromo. You probably won't want or need to hang around here long, but the innovative tourist information people might try to change your mind.

◉ Sights

Candi Jabung　　HINDU TEMPLE
(Paiton; ⊘ 6am-6pm) **FREE** This rarely visited but worthwhile 14th-century, red-brick Majapahit temple is thought to be a funerary site for Majapahit royalty. The base of the 16m-high temple has pictures of animals and scenes of daily life carved into it, although most of these are quite badly eroded.

Sleeping & Eating

★ Clover Homestay　　HOTEL $
(☑ 0335-449 3483; Jl Mawar Merah 8; r incl breakfast from 150,000Rp) By far the best place to stay in Probolinggo, Clover is a smart and colourful 29-room hotel, where the small and spotless rooms have deep purple or hazy-blue walls and decent hot-water bathrooms. It's a good place to connect with other Bromo-bound travellers, and we love the dining room/communal hang-out with frilly oriental umbrellas.

Waserda HQQ　　INDONESIAN $
(Jl Bengawan Solo 68; mains 20,000Rp; ⊘ 5am-9pm) This humble warung is run by a sweet wife-and-husband team, who cook up delicious East Javanese dishes such as *nasi pecel* (rice with a spicy peanut sauce, spinach and bean sprouts), *nasi rawon* (beef soup served with rice) and *mie Jawa* (stir-fried noodles), as well as a delicious slow-cooked

rendang (beef coconut curry). The strong Javanese coffee will blow your socks off.

Sumber Hidup CHINESE, INDONESIAN $
(Jl Dr Saleh II; mains 16,000-30,000Rp; ⊘8am-10pm) Large restaurant on the main strip that serves good Chinese food and Indonesian dishes. Doubles as an ice-cream parlour.

ⓘ Information

DANGERS & ANNOYANCES

Probolinggo's bus terminal has a poor reputation among travellers. It's by no means dangerous, it's just that the numerous touts aren't always totally honest about onward transport.

The main scam involves overcharging for bus tickets. Some reputable-looking ticket agents ask for double (or more) the standard price. You can check departure times and prices on the monitor in the waiting area, or head to Toto Travel. Unless it's a holiday (when you might want to book ahead) often the best thing to do is find the bus you need, and pay the fare onboard.

Also, when travelling to Probolinggo, make it clear to the ticket collector that you want to be dropped off at the Bayuangga bus terminal; we've received emails from travellers complaining of being left at random travel agents and charged exorbitant fares for bus tickets.

Thieves are common on the buses in East Java, especially on buses departing from Probolinggo.

If arriving by train, beware of tour agencies who are offering free transport rides to Cemoro Lawang; this will inevitably involve heading to their office where they will attempt to sell you their tour package.

TOURIST INFORMATION

Tourist Information Centre (☑0335-432420; Jl Mansyur; ⊘8am-4pm) Staff can organise city tours and can hook you up with local schools that are looking for English speakers to help students; you only need to spare an hour or two of your time. It's located by the train station.

ⓘ Getting There & Away

BUS

Probolinggo's **Bayuangga bus terminal** is located about 5km from town on the road to Gunung Bromo. There are TV monitors here with bus departure information. Buses to Banyuwangi, Bondowoso and Surabaya depart frequently; most transport to Denpasar is between 7pm and 11pm. If want to make an advance reservation, head to the helpful **Toto Travel** (☑0335-443 8267, 0822 3224 4088; www.facebook.com/tototravelprobolinggo; Bayuangga Bus Terminal), where the owners speak English fluently.

Angkot run to/from the main street and the train station for 5000Rp.

MINIBUS

Gunung Bromo minibuses leave from a stop just outside Probolinggo's Bayuangga bus terminal, heading for Cemoro Lawang (35,000Rp, two hours) via Ngadisari until around 4pm; but they won't leave until they have 10 to 15 passengers. Overcharging tourists is common on this route. Late-afternoon buses charge more to Cemoro Lawang (50,000Rp to 100,000Rp) when fewer passengers travel beyond Ngadisari. Make sure your bus goes all the way to Cemoro Lawang when you board.

TAXI

Taxis and freelance car drivers meet trains and wait for business at the bus station. A trip to Cemoro Lawang costs around 400,000Rp to 500,000Rp after bargaining; more later in the day.

TRAIN

About 2km north of town, the train station is 6km from the bus terminal. Probolinggo is on the Surabaya–Banyuwangi line. There are three daily trains to Yogyakarta (95,000Rp to 315,000Rp, 8½ to nine hours); four to six daily exclusive- and business-class trains to Surabaya (29,000Rp to 275,000Rp, two hours), and around five daily trains travelling east to Banyuwangi (27,000Rp to 160,000Rp, 4¼ to five hours)

Angkot D (5000Rp) connects the train station with the bus terminal.

BUSES FROM PROBOLINGGO

DESTINATION	FARE (RP; ECONOMY/AIR-CON)	DURATION (HR)
Banyuwangi	40,000/50,000	5
Bondowoso	20,000/35,000	2½
Denpasar	120,000/180,000	11
Jember	20,000/30,000	2½
Malang	20,000/30,000	2½
Surabaya	20,000/30,000	2½-3
Yogyakarta	100,000/150,000	10-11

Gunung Bromo & Bromo-Tengger-Semeru National Park

☑ CEMORO LAWANG 0335 /
ELEV CEMORO LAWANG 2217M

A lunarlike landscape of epic proportions and surreal beauty, the volcanic Bromo region is one of Indonesia's most breathtaking sights. Rising from the guts of the ancient Tengger caldera, Gunung Bromo (2392m) is one of three volcanoes to have emerged from a vast crater, stretching 10km across. Flanked by the peaks of Kursi (2581m) and Batok (2440m), the smouldering cone of Bromo stands in a sea of ashen, volcanic sand, surrounded by the towering cliffs of the crater's edge. Just to the south, Gunung Semeru (3676m), Java's highest peak and one of its most active volcanoes, throws its shadow over the whole scene.

The vast majority of independent travellers get to Bromo via the town of Probolinggo and stay in Cemoro Lawang, where facilities are good. There are other options in villages on the road up from Probolinggo. Additional approaches via Wonokitri and Ngadas are possible.

Gunung Bromo

Gunung Bromo is unforgettable. It's not the mountain itself, but the sheer majesty of the experience: the immense size of the entire Tengger crater, the supernatural beauty of the scenery and the dramatic highland light that will saturate your brain with tranquility – for at least a little while.

Virtually all tours are planned to enable you to experience the mountain at sunrise. This is when the great crater is at its ethereal best and colours are most impressive. But visibility is usually good throughout the day in the dry season (June to September), even though the slopes below Cemoro Lawang may be covered in mist. Later in the day you'll also avoid the dawn crowds – things get especially busy during holiday periods. In the wet season it's often bright and clear at dawn but quickly clouds over.

It's a short, enjoyable hike to Bromo from Cemoro Lawang. The 3km (40-minute) 'trail' wanders down the crater wall and across the eerie Laotian Pasir (Sea of Sand) to the slopes of Bromo. White stone markers are easy to follow during the day but can be more elusive in the dark. Make sure you climb the right cone; Bromo has a stone staircase. Some hikers, disoriented in the dark, have attempted to climb neighbouring Batok. If you're lucky you will share the rim with groups of Balinese or Javanese Hindu pilgrims who have come to pray to one of the three most sacred mountains in Hindu lore and make offerings in the hopes of satisfying the volcano and the gods.

After ascending the 253 steps, you'll come face to face with the steaming, sulphurous guts of the volcano. There are sweeping views back across the Laotian Pasir to the lip of the crater and over to Batok and the Hindu temple (open only on auspicious days in the pilgrim calendar) at its base.

Mercifully, there's little of the tacky commercialism (bar the odd souvenir seller) that besmirches many Indonesian scenic spots, though there is ample plastic litter on the rim (please pack your bottles and trash out). The local Tengger people may press you into accepting a horse ride across the crater bed, but there's no serious hassle. No matter how many folks are gathered on the rim, it's still easy to connect spiritually with this sacred peak if you wander around the lip of the Bromo cone, away from the main viewing point.

History

Unsurprisingly, the eerie landscape of Bromo and its neighbouring volcanoes has spawned countless myths and legends. It is said that the Tengger crater was originally dug out with just half a coconut shell by an ogre smitten with love for a princess.

But Bromo is of particular religious significance to the Hindu Tengger people who still populate the massif. They first fled here to escape the wave of Islam that broke over the Majapahit kindgom in the 16th century. The Tengger believe that Bromo once fell within the realm of the childless King Joko Seger and Queen Roro Anteng, who asked the god of the volcano for assistance in producing an heir. The god obliged, giving them 25 children, but demanded that the youngest, a handsome boy named Dian Kusuma, be sacrificed to the flames in return. When the queen later refused to fulfil her promise, the young Dian sacrificed himself to save the kingdom from retribution.

🏃 Activities

The classic Bromo tour offered by all hotels and guides in Cemoro Lawang (and other villages) involves pick-up at around 3.30am and a 4WD journey up to the neighbouring peak of Gunung Penanjakan (2770m). This viewpoint offers the best vistas (and photographs) of the entire Bromo landscape, with Gunung Semeru puffing away on the horizon. However, at the time of research this viewpoint was closed in order to allow it time to recover from the absolute pounding it has received from tens of thousands of visitors. There was no information on when (or if) it might re-open. For the moment drivers are taking clients to other viewpoints. After sunrise, 4WDs head back down the steep lip of the crater and then over the Laotian Pasir (Sea of Sand) to the base of Bromo. It's usually easy to hook up with others for this tour to share costs. Private jeeps cost 600,000Rp, but sometimes you can negotiate a cheaper price. If you pay for a single seat, expect to be crammed in with four or five others, though the price (125,000Rp) is right.

Alternatively, it's a two-hour hike to the top of Gunung Penanjakan, the so-called second viewpoint, from Cemoro Lawang. But King Kong Hill – perched just 20 minutes beyond the first viewpoint, and also on Penanjakan, set on a ledge jutting out from the main trail – has even better views than the top. From here, looking toward the west, you'll see Bromo bathed in that dawn light, along with Gunung Batok, with Gunung Semeru photobombing from behind. It can take up to an hour to reach it, but it's a stunning walk. Just up from the village, the slopes are planted with scallions, potatoes and cauliflower. You won't see them in the dark, but they make a lovely vista on the easy downhill stroll. Trekkers can also take an interesting walk across the Laotian Pasir to the village of Ngadas (8km), below the southern rim of the Tengger crater. From here, motorbikes and 4WDs descend to Tumpang, which is connected by regular buses to Malang.

🎊 Festivals & Events

In September, Jiwa Jawa (p194) lodge hosts a jazz festival, Gunung Jazz (www.jazzgunung. com) with performances from international and domestic artists held in the open-air hotel grounds.

Kasada RELIGIOUS
The wrath of Bromo is appeased during the annual Kasada festival, when Tenggerese Hindus come to Bromo to make peace with the mountain, and pray for health and good harvests. During this time, local daredevils descend into the crater and use nets to

---

TIPS FOR VISITING BROMO

➜ Bromo's popularity means that during high season (July, August, Indonesian holidays and the Christmas period) and weekends, the two main viewpoints can get very crowded between sunrise and the early morning. Organised tours all follow the same schedule and on the busiest days there can be a couple of hundred people lined up along these viewpoints all desperate to get the perfect selfie as the sun rises... Consider visiting Gunung Penanjakan and the Bromo crater at other times of day.

➜ There are two entry posts as you drive uphill toward Cemoro Lawang and into Taman Nasional Bromo-Tengger-Semeru. The first will charge a mere 10,000Rp entrance fee, but the second is the real ticket. And that ticket costs 220,000Rp (Monday to Friday) and 350,000Rp (Saturday and Sunday). Steep? Yes, but worth it.

➜ Walking from Cemoro Lawang to the Bromo crater only takes around 40 minutes to one hour, and enables you to take in the scenery and get your boots dusty in the grey volcanic sands of the Laotian Pasir (Sea of Sand); face masks are recommended, and can be purchased from vendors.

➜ At any time of year it's cold in the early morning and temperatures can drop to single digits or near-freezing. Guesthouses rent out jackets for around 40,000Rp.

➜ The lip of the crater in Cemoro Lawang (between the Cemara Indah hotel and Lava View Lodge) has lots of viewing spots where you can savour Bromo's superb scenery away from the crowds.

➜ If you're unlucky and cloudy weather curtails your views of Bromo, drop by the gallery at the Jiwa Jawa hotel to see what you've missed. And then stay another day and hope that the skies clear.

attempt to catch offerings (money, food and even live chickens) thrown down by others above.

It's a risky business and is as dangerous as it sounds – every few years someone slips and the volcano claims another victim. The festival takes place on the 14th day of the Kasada month in the traditional Hindu lunar calendar. Dates change each year, but for the next couple of years, it's likely to fall in June.

🛏 Sleeping & Eating

Accommodation in the Bromo area is notoriously poor value for money. Given its proximity to Bromo, the village of Cemoro Lawang is the most convenient place to stay, and offers a choice of rudimentary guesthouses or overpriced hotels. Around 5km eastwards towards Probolinggo is another enclave of guesthouses that also has some OK spots.

CEMORO LAWANG

Bromo Otix Guesthouse GUESTHOUSE $
(☑0852 5773 6209; Cemoro Lawang; r with shared/private bathroom 150,000/200,000Rp) A cut above the rest of the Cemoro Lawang competition, the Bromo Otix has three classes of rooms. Those in the new front block are smart, brightly painted and have attached bathrooms with warm water. Those in the rear blocks are older and have shared bathrooms but are still well kept. The staff are friendlier than in most nearby guesthouses.

Lava View Lodge HOTEL $$
(☑0812 4980 8182, 0335-541009; Cemoro Lawang; r/bungalows from 700,000/800,000Rp; 🛜) This well-run hotel is 500m along a side road on the eastern side of the village. As it's almost on the lip of the crater, you can stumble out your door to magnificent Bromo views. The wooden rooms and bungalows are comfortable enough, though they lack the wow factor you'd expect for this price. Staff are friendly.

Cafe Lava Hostel HOTEL $$
(☑0335-541020, 0812 3584 1111; www.cafelava.lavaindonesia.com; Cemoro Lawang; d/tr/f incl breakfast from 450,000/750,000/900,000Rp; ✴🛜) With a sociable vibe thanks to its restaurant (p194) and attractive layout (rooms are scattered down the side of a valley), this is first choice for most travellers, despite steep prices and fairly low quality. Economy

rooms are very small and gloomy, but they're neat and have access to a shared verandah and clean communal bathrooms fitted with hot showers.

Cafe Lava Resto INDONESIAN $
(☑0335-541020; Cafe Lava Hostel, Cemoro Lawang; mains 25,000-48,000Rp; ⏱7.15-10am & 12.30-9pm; 🛜) Attached to the Cafe Lava Hostel, this is about the best place to eat around the volcano, though that's not saying much. It has a menu of Indonesian classics, as well as some seasonal mushroom dishes, to go with a few Western and Chinese options and cold Bintang. There's a breakfast buffet in the mornings (50,000Rp).

NGADISARI & WONOTORO

Yoschi's Hotel GUESTHOUSE $$
(☑0813 3129 8881, 0335-541018; www.hotelyoschi.com; Wonokerto St 117, Km2; r incl breakfast with shared/private bathroom 300,000/540,000Rp, cottages from 1,020,000Rp; @🛜) This rustic place has lots of character, with bungalows and small rooms dotted around a large, leafy garden compound. However, most lack hot water (there's a shared hot shower next to the men's toilet) and cleanliness standards could be better. A huge restaurant serves up pricey Western and Indonesian food (subject to a stiff 20% service charge). It's 4km below Bromo just below the village of Ngadisari.

Jiwa Jawa HOTEL $$$
(☑0335-541193; www.jiwajawa.com; Ngadisari; r incl breakfast from 1,800,000Rp, ste from 4,700,000Rp; 🛜) An ultra-modern mountain lodge, this excellent place has stylish though compact rooms with beautiful photo art on the walls, quality mattresses, floor-to-ceiling windows and the best bathrooms you've ever seen on the side of an exploding volcano. You'll also love the elevated cafe-restaurant, which has sweeping views over villages and vegetable fields.

ℹ Information

Information about trails and mountain conditions is available from the PHKA posts in Cemoro Lawang and the southern outskirts of Wonokitri. Both extend their opening hours during busy periods. The park's official office is located in Malang. There are PHKA posts in **Cemoro Lawang** (☑0335-541038; Cemoro Lawang; ⏱8am-3pm Tue-Sun) and **Wonokitri** (☑0335-357 1048; Wonokitri; ⏱8am-3pm Tue-Sun).

There's a BNI ATM close to the crater lip in Cemoro Lawang.

❶ Getting There & Away

Probolinggo is the main gateway to Bromo. From Probolinggo there are public minibuses to Cemoro Lawang (35,000Rp to 40,000Rp, two hours) at the foot of Bromo, but they only leave when they're full (15 people). Mornings are the best time to try and get one of these. Otherwise, there are shuttles run by tour operators for around 60,000Rp to 100,000Rp. A privately rented vehicle from Probolinggo is likely to cost in the region of 450,000Rp to 600,000Rp return, with an overnight stop. These private vehicles are not allowed to take visitors down into the caldera, so you will have to pay for a place in a jeep like everyone else from Cemoro Lawang (or you can walk around the Bromo sights). For the return trip you can try to take the public minibus (which again, have no set schedules, but normally leave around 8am to 10am). Otherwise there's a shuttle (50,000Rp to 60,000Rp) that leaves around 9.30am to Probolinggo, from where you can catch long-distance buses (p138) to Yogyakarta and Denpasar.

Gunung Semeru

Part of the huge Tengger Massif, the classic cone of Gunung Semeru is the highest peak in Java, at 3676m. Also known as Mahameru (Great Mountain), it is looked on by Hindus as the most sacred mountain of all and the father of Gunung Agung on Bali.

Semeru is one of Java's most active peaks and has been in a near-constant state of eruption since 1818 – it exploded as recently as March 2009. At the time of research the mountain was open to hikers, but periodically officials will warn against attempting the summit due to volcanic acitivity.

Trekking tours from Malang usually take two (or sometimes three) days to get to the summit and back. Expect to pay around 750,000Rp per person, per day for a three-day, two-night hike including all supplies, transport, meals and an English-speaking guide.

To hike the peak independently, take an *angkot* (10,000Rp, 45 minutes) from Malang's Arjosari bus station to Tumpang. Here you can charter an *ojek*/4WD (around 80,000/600,000Rp) to Ranu Pani village, the start of the trek. There are several homestays (200,000Rp to 350,000Rp per person including meals) in Ranu Pani (2109m). Good ones include **Pak Tasrip** and **Pak Tumari**, both of which serve meals and can organise guides (150,000Rp per day), tents and sleeping bags (which are essential).

HIKING GUNUNG SEMERU

➡ Semeru is a highly active volcano, and its status changes rapidly – check with the national-park office in Malang, locally in Ranu Pani village and also online at www.gunungbagging.com.

➡ Because several hikers have died of heart attacks climbing Semeru, officially you're supposed to have a health certificate to confirm that you should be able to make it there and back. These are best obtained in Malang in advance, but are not always requested.

➡ Nights on the mountain are bitterly cold (often near-freezing) and inexperienced climbers have died of exposure. Make sure you have adequate gear and clothing.

➡ The best time of year to make the climb is May to October when you have a decent chance of clear skies and dry weather.

Hikers *must* register with the **PHKA post**, which is towards the lake in Ranu Pani. It will have the latest information about conditions – you may not be able to access the summit and may only make it as far as the Arcopodo campsite. You may be asked to produce a health certificate. Expect to pay a small fee for a climbing permit and entrance for the national park (weekday/weekend 217,500/317,500Rp).

Rangers will direct you to the trailhead for Semeru. The route is lined with markers for some distance and passes three shelters, so it's difficult to get lost. You'll pass pretty Ranu Kumbolo, a crater lake (2400m), 13km or 3½ hours from Ranu Pani. The trail then crosses savannah before climbing to Kalimati (three hours), at the foot of the mountain. From Kalimati it is a steep climb of around an hour to Arcopodo, where there is a flattish campsite.

From Arcopodo, it is a short, steep climb to the start of the volcanic sands, and then a tough three-hour climb through loose scree to the peak. Semeru explodes every half hour and the gases and belching lava make the mountain dangerous – stay away from vents. On a clear day, there are breathtaking views of Java's north and south coasts, as well as vistas of Bali. To see the sunrise, it is necessary to start at about 1.30am for the summit.

Bondowoso

📱 0332 / POP 69,780

Bondowoso, suspended between the highlands of Tengger and Ijen, is the gateway to Bromo and Ijen and home to some of the island's best *tape*, a tasty, sweet-and-sour snack made from boiled and fermented cassava. It's mainly a transit and market town, and tours to Ijen can be organised here.

🛏️ Sleeping & Eating

Palm Hotel   HOTEL $$

(📞 0332-421 201; www.palm-hotel.net; Jl A Yani 32; r incl breakfast with fan & cold shower 225,000Rp, with air-con from 364,000Rp; 🅿️🛜🏊) Just south of the huge, grassy *alun-alun* (main public square), this aging hotel has a large, heat-busting pool that makes it a great escape from Java's punishing humidity. Take your pick from simple and somewhat tatty fan-only options with cold-water *mandi* or larger air-conditioned rooms that show a minimalist design influence.

ℹ️ Getting There & Away

To get to Ijen there are many (cramped) minibuses to Sempol (around 30,000Rp, 2½ to 3½ hours), a gateway village for those tackling the volcano; all leave Bondowoso's **bus terminal** (Jl Imam Bonjol) before 1pm. From Sempol you can take an *ojek* (50,000Rp) to Pos Paltuding, the starting point for treks to Ijen. Otherwise Palm Hotel can arrange trips for 750,000Rp.

Other destinations from Bondowoso include Jember (7000Rp, one hour), Probolinggo (25,000Rp to 35,000Rp, two hours) and Surabaya (normal/air-con 38,000/70,0000Rp, five hours).

Ijen Plateau

The fabled Ijen Plateau is a vast volcanic region dominated by the three cones of Ijen (2368m), Merapi (2800m) and Raung (3332m). Virtually everyone comes purely for Ijen – to hike up to its spectacular sulphur crater lake, and to experience the unworldly sight of its 'blue fire' phenomenon.

However, the rest of the area is also worth exploring, and its sweeping vistas combined with a temperate climate make the plateau a great base for a few days. Threaded with streams and gurgling with hot springs, it's a beautiful, forested alpine area, with rubber and clove groves, cloud-soaked passes and evocative shade-grown coffee plantations.

Along with the plantations and their company *kampung* (villages), there are a few isolated settlements.

⊙ Sights

★ Kawah Ijen   LAKE

(Mon-Fri 100,000Rp, Sat & Sun 150,000Rp) The Ijen plateau's most extraordinary sight is the magnificent turquoise sulphur lake of Kawah Ijen. A night hike to the crater in which the lake boils will introduce you to blue fire, spectacular scenery and a group of men with what must be one of the world's most unusual jobs. Pay entry fees at the PHKA post.

Kebun Balawan   PLANTATION

(📞 0823 3262 8342) FREE Visits to this coffee plantation include a wander through coffee groves and an informal tour of the plantation's factory. It also has thermal pools and a gushing thermal waterfall (5000Rp) set amid lush jungle. Arrange a visit through the Catimor Homestay in Kalisat village.

🏃 Activities

The starting point for the trek to the crater is the **PHKA post** (weekdays/weekends 100,000/150,000Rp; motorbikes/cars 5000/10,000Rp; ⊙24hr) at Pos Paltuding, which can be reached from Bondowoso or Banyuwangi. Sign in and pay your entry fee here. The steep 3km path up to the observation post (where there's a teahouse) takes just over an hour. From the post it's a further 30-minute walk to the lip of the wind-blasted crater and its stunning views.

From the crater rim, an extremely steep, gravelly path leads down to the sulphur deposits and the steaming lake. Most climbers make the effort to set out in the middle of the night in order to witness the stunning and eerie spectacle of its 'blue fire', which blazes on the shore of the crater lake. Only visible in the darkness of night (generally best viewed before 4am – which is when most people arrive to coincide with sunrise), this phenomenon of glowing electric-blue flame is explained through the combustion of sulphurous gases, an effect seen only in a few places on earth (Iceland is another). Although park authorities don't prevent tourists descending into the crater, signs warn against doing so. Should you chose to, the walk down takes around 30 minutes; the path is slippery in parts and the sulphur fumes towards the bottom can be

KAWAH IJEN'S SULPHUR GATHERERS

Buried deep into a steep-sided crater at 2148m above sea level, Kawah Ijen is renowned for its sulphur 'miners' (more accurately 'gatherers'). Each night these men brave clouds of noxious gases and devil-dancing sulphurous blue flames to dig hunks of yellow sulphur out of the ground surrounding the lake and carry it off to processing centres lower down the mountain. Most of the 300 men involved in this activity have minimal safety equipment and do nothing more than tie a wet piece of cloth around the mouth and nose to protect them from the highly dangerous sulphur clouds that swirl around the lake. These DIY miners then spend the next six-or-so hours scurrying back down the volcano with 60kg to 80kg loads on their backs.

It's arduous work that pays very little (around 800Rp per kilo), and yet the nonstop, physical exertion keeps the collectors incredibly fit. Few report health problems despite breathing great lungfuls of sulphurous fumes virtually every day of their lives. The sulphur collected is used for cosmetics and medicine, and is added to fertiliser and insecticides.

Despite the hardships of their job, the miners are a cheery lot and are happy to be photographed for a small fee (indeed most of them probably now make a significant proportion of their income from tourism rather than from mining).

overwhelming. Expect burning lungs and streaming eyes if you do make it to the bottom. Take great care – a French tourist fell and died here some years ago. A gas mask is a very good idea, and they are available for hire for 50,000Rp at Pos Paltuding; make sure you test it works before setting off. Children and those with respiratory illnesses should avoid making the descent into the crater.

Close to the lakeshore, you can be certain that at some point you will find yourself enveloped in a gas cloud. Even with a gas mask, this can be quite distressing. Breathing can be difficult, eyes can sting painfully and visibility can be dramatically reduced. The important thing is not to panic. Try to quickly but calmly move away from the lakeshore and out of the cloud. Bringing along a guide (100,000Rp to 150,000Rp) from the PHKA post is highly recommended. Finally, a note on camera equipment. The sulphur gases are highly corrosive. Unprotected camera equipment (especially more sensitive SLRs) can quickly malfunction if exposed to the gases for too long. Keep your electronic equipment sealed up in a plastic bag as much as possible.

Back at the lip of the crater, where the air will suddenly feel wonderfully rich and clean, turn left for the climb to the highest point (2368m) and magnificent views at sunrise, or keep walking counterclockwise for even more expansive vistas of the lake. On the other side of the lake, opposite the vent, the trail disappears into crumbling vol-

canic rock and deep ravines. Do not attempt to cross this.

The ideal time to make the Kawah Ijen hike is in the dry season between April and October. However, while the path is steep, it's usually not too slippery, so the hike is certainly worth a try in the rainy season if you have a clear day.

Ijen is highly volatile, and although its last major eruption was in 1936, the crater is frequently closed when volcanic activity increases. Check with hotels in surrounding towns as to the current status.

🛏 Sleeping & Eating

Catimor Homestay   LODGE **$**
(☑ 0823 3262 8342; catimor_n12@yahoo.com; Blawan; r 200,000-400,000Rp; 🖥🏊) This budget lodge has an excellent location in the Kebun Balawan coffee plantation, close to hot springs and a waterfall. Rooms are divided between its original wooden Dutch planters lodge (c 1894), which features a decrepit yet wildly atmospheric sitting area, or better maintained and cleaner rooms around its sparkling, chilly pool and hot tub (from 4pm).

★ Jiwa Jawa Ijen   BOUTIQUE HOTEL **$$$**
(☑ 0628-1130 3818; www.jiwajawa.com; r/ste incl breakfast from 1,960,000/2,660,000Rp; 🖥🏊) There couldn't be a greater contrast between the hellish landscapes of the Kawah Ijen crater and this boutique hotel, which snuggles away under banana and palm trees, and offers hypnotic views over the countryside

from its designer viewing platform. The rooms are smart and well equipped, and quality art and Javanese handicrafts can be found throughout.

Ijen Resort HOTEL **$$$**
(☎0815 5810 4576, 0819 3764 6004; www.ijendiscovery.com; Dusun Randuagung; r/ste from 2,133,000/2,646,500; ❄📶≋) This top-end resort, set in fertile grounds, has beautiful rooms with stone or timber floors, open-air bathrooms and attractive furnishings. From the figure-eight infinity pool, you can admire views out over the rice terraces to distant brooding volcanoes. If you can afford it, the resort is an ideal place to while away a few days in blissful peace.

★ **Java Banana** FUSION **$$**
(Jiwa Jawa; ☎0628-1130 3818; www.jiwajawa.com; mains 65,000-195,000Rp; ⏲8am-10pm) Set off the road up to Ijen from Banyuwangi, this restaurant, inside the upmarket Jiwa Jawa (p197) hotel, is a stunner, with a massive ground-floor gallery and an outdoor amphitheatre with spectacular volcano views. The menu is ambitious. Expect mains such as parrotfish in Mediterranean ragu, quail salad, and a nori-crusted rack of lamb.

ℹ Getting There & Away

It is possible to travel nearly all the way to Kawah Ijen by public transport, but most visitors charter transport. Both access roads are narrow, winding and slow going, although the Banyuwangi road has been improved and is the fastest route to the PHKA post at Pos Paltuding (1¼ hours).

FROM BONDOWOSO

From Wonosari, 8km from Bondowoso towards Situbondo, a rough, potholed road runs via Sukosari and Sempol to Pos Paltuding. It's normally passable in any high-clearance vehicle, but sometimes a 4WD is necessary. Sign in at the coffee-plantation checkpoints (around 5000Rp) on the way. Hotels in Bondowoso can arrange day tours to Ijen for around 750,000Rp.

By public transport, several *angkot* (small minibuses) run from Bondowoso to Sempol (40,000Rp, 2½ hours), most in the late morning, but there's a final one at noon. If passengers want to continue on to Pos Paltuding, drivers will sometimes do so, though foreigners are regularly overcharged on this route. Alternatively *ojek* in Sempol charge around 50,000Rp one way. At Pos Paltuding, there are usually a few drivers to take you back.

FROM BANYUWANGI

The Banyuwangi–Ijen road was in good condition at the time of research, though it has been known to be impossibly rutted in the past. Check locally for current conditions before setting off. There's no public transport all the way from Banyuwangi to Pos Paltuding, which is a sparsely populated region.

The best option is to take a tour with one of the better Banyuwangi hotels; these cost from 200,000Rp to 300,000Rp per person, depending on the vehicle and whether entry fees, guides and a packed breakfast are included. Another option is to organise a 4WD (800,000Rp per vehicle) through the Banyuwangi tourist office. Chartering an *ojek* from Banyuwangi to Ijen is possible for around 200,000Rp (including a wait of four hours). *Ojek* drivers hang around the Ketapang Ferry Terminal (p204) and at Banyuwangi's Sri Tanjung Bus Terminal (p204), or ask at your guesthouse.

Heading back down the mountain, from Pos Paltuding to Banyuwangi, *ojek* charge around 100,000Rp for a one-way ride.

Kalibaru

☎0333 / POP 5000

The picturesque road from Jember to Banyuwangi winds around the foothills of Gunung Raung, through rainforest, and up to the small hill town of Kalibaru (428m).

The village itself is not much to look at, but those few hundred metres of altitude give it a more benign climate than many parts of Java. The town makes a good base from which to visit the plantations around Glenmore to the east, or the smaller, more easily visited plots of coffee and cloves to the north of Kalibaru train station.

The area has many coffee plantations, and guides can be hired (100,000Rp) for group tours to see rubber tapping and processing, as well as cacao and coffee processing.

☞ Tours

Margo Utomo Resort offers several tours, including ones to spice and coffee plantations and longer trips to Meru Betiri and Alas Purwo National Parks. On the plantation visits English-speaking guides will show you around a totally organic estate, which has a butterfly park; peppercorn, cinnamon and nutmeg trees; and vanilla and cacao plants. Also on offer are 4WD trips to surrounding villages that take in a waterfall and a cacao factory. Contact the hotel in advance about joining a tour.

🛏 Sleeping & Eating

Kendi Villas   BOUTIQUE HOTEL **$$**
(☑ 0878 5523 4338; https://kendi-villas-and-spa
-id.book.direct; Jl Putri Gunung 99; r incl breakfast
from 415,000Rp; ❄ 🛜 🏊) A small and modern
resort-style place with friendly management
and tile-floored individual cottages lined
up alongside an inviting pool. Rooms have
splashes of modern art on the walls. There's
a gazebo in the garden next to a stream and
with views over the mountains.

Margo Utomo Eco Resort   HOTEL **$$**
(☑ 0333-897700; www.margoutomo.com; Jl Lapan-
gan 10; r incl breakfast 550,000Rp; @ 🏊) This
classy former plantation enjoys a resplendent garden, bursting with shrubs and
flowers (all neatly labelled). The gardens
definitely outclass the cottages, which are
pricey considering their simplicity, but they
are tasteful and have charm. All have ceiling
fans. Follow the path and you'll find a 20m
pool at the rear of the grounds.

Kalibaru Cottages   BUNGALOW **$$**
(☑ 0333-897333; www.kalibarucottages.com; r incl
breakfast 390,000-620,000Rp; ❄ 🛜 🏊) A large,
well-run resort boasting expansive, mani-
cured grounds with a T-shaped pool fringed
by palm trees. Faux-traditional cottages are
spacious and have semi-open-air showers.
The restaurant is a bit pricey. It's 4km west
of town on the Jember road. Staff can organ-
ise good local tours of plantations and cot-
tage industries.

❶ Getting There & Away

Buses running between Jember (15,000Rp, one
hour) and Banyuwangi (25,000Rp, three hours)
can drop you near the hotels. The train station
is in the village centre; Kalibaru is on the main
Banyuwangi–Jember–Probolinggo–Surabaya
train line.

Jember

☑ 0331 / POP 332,000

Jember is a large city and service centre for
the surrounding coffee, cacao, rubber, cotton
and tobacco plantations. It's relatively clean,
with a futuristic mosque that looks like a
flying saucer by its *alun-alun* (main pub-
lic square), but there's no reason to linger.
If you plan to go to Meru Betiri, you could
drop by the Meru Betiri National Park Office
(p200), which has accommodation details
and background information on the park.

🛏 Sleeping & Drinking

Jember has a reasonable selection of places
to stay in all price bands. There's live music
every evening at the Aston Jember Hotel. If
you don't like the groove, you can at least
drown your sorrows with a beer.

Aston Jember Hotel   BUSINESS HOTEL **$$**
(☑ 0331-423888; www.astonhotelsinternational.
com; Jl Sentot Prawirodirjo 88; r from 418,285Rp;
❄ 🛜 🏊) Wooden floors, funky wallpaper,
floor-to-ceiling windows, thick mattresses and an impressive swimming pool that
nearly encircles half the hotel. This modern,
business hotel is as good as things get in
Jember, and it makes for a very comfortable
overnight stay. Decent breakfast spread.

❶ Getting There & Away

Jember has an excess of transport terminals.
The main one, **Tawung Alun** (or Terminal Jember), 6km west of town, has buses to Banyuwangi (35,000Rp, four hours) and Kalibaru
(15,000Rp, one hour), and economy buses to
Denpasar, Solo and Yogyakarta. *Angkot* run from
here to Terminal Arjesa, which serves Bondowoso (10,000Rp, 45 minutes).

There are also subterminals to the east (for
Banyuwangi) and south (for Watu Ulo). Jember
is also located on the Surabaya–Banyuwangi
train line; the station is in the town centre.

Meru Betiri National Park

The Meru Betiri National Park, covering 580
sq km between Jember and Banyuwangi districts, is an area of magnificent coastal rainforest and abundant wildlife, making it one
of Java's finest parks. It's famous as having
been one of the last refuges of the Java tiger,
now almost certainly extinct. Meru Betiri is
very difficult to access (often impossible in
the rainy season), which keeps the number
of visitors to a trickle, but the park authorities are actively trying to promote tourism.

The future of the park is under threat on
several fronts. Illegal loggers, farmers and
hunters encroach on its territory. Mining
companies, and illegal miners, are also eyeing up the park after significant gold deposits were found here.

⊙ Sights & Activities

Wildlife, found mostly in the mountain forests, includes leopards, wild boars, monkeys,
banteng, black giant squirrels, civets, retic-
ulated pythons (the world's longest snake)

and Javanese eagles. You're sure to see a lot of monkeys, monitor lizards and hornbills – maybe even the rhinoceros hornbill, which emits a bark-like honk.

Trails are limited in the park and a guide (100,000Rp) is necessary. There are good coastal walks, but sadly there's quite a bit of trash around, on the beach and inland. For the really adventurous, it's possible to make a three-day traverse of the park on foot.

Rajegwesi, at the entrance to the park, is on a large bay with a sweeping beach and a fishing village. Past the park entrance the road climbs, giving expansive views over spectacular Teluk Hijau (Green Bay), with its cliffs and white-sand beach. A trail leads 1km from the road down to Teluk Hijau, or it is about a one-hour walk east from Mess Pantai.

Permisan Bay
BEACH

The best beach by far in the park is at Permisan Bay, an almost sausage-shaped bay with calm waters and a small island in the middle. It's a half-day hike from Sukamade. You can camp on the beach, but bring everything you might need with you as you'll almost certainly be all alone.

Sukamade Turtle Beach
WILDLIFE RESERVE

The park's major attraction is the protected turtle beach at Sukamade, one of Indonesia's most important turtle-spawning grounds, where several species come ashore between October and April to lay their eggs. You've a good chance of seeing a turtle here; green turtles and olive ridleys are the most common. Giant leatherbacks used to be seen between December and February, but sightings are rare these days.

Mess Pantai arranges night turtle-watching trips (150,000Rp per person). Rangers gather up the eggs shortly after they are laid and rebury them in a fenced-off zone in order to stop wild pigs digging up and eating all the eggs.

🛏 Sleeping & Eating

There are guesthouses on the Sukamade plantation and in Rajegwesi, but these are some distance from the beach. There are basic meals available in villages fringing the park, but it's best to bring food with you.

Mess Pantai
BUNGALOW $

(☑ 033-133 5535; r with shared/private bathroom 150,000/250,000Rp) Set among patches of forest and agricultural land 700m behind

Pantai Sukamade, Mess Pantai is a basic but peaceful place to stay in the park. Unfortunately, any romance the place might have is countered by the generally run-down state of the rooms and piles of rubbish... If you can, bring a tent and camp deeper in the park.

ⓘ Information

The park is wet for much of the year as the coastal mountains trap the rain. Visit in the dry season from April to October, because the road into the park fords a river, which easily floods. Even in the dry season you may have to wade across the river and walk into the park.

The park's **office** (☑ 0331-321530; www.meru betiri.id; Jl Sriwijaya 53; ⊗ 8am-3pm Sun-Fri) in Jember has plenty of information; entrance to the park costs 150,000Rp.

ⓘ Getting There & Away

Meru Betiri can be a tough place to reach, even by 4WD. Roads are rough and you have to ford rivers in some places. The most direct way to Sukamade from Banyuwangi or Jember is to first take a bus to Jajag, then a minibus to Pesangga-ran (12,000Rp, one hour), where you'll probably have to change and get in another to Sarongan (10,000Rp, around one hour), a small town with warungs and stores where you can stock up on supplies. Drivers in Sarongan will try their hardest to get you to charter a 4WD. Ojeks to Sukamade (around 120,000Rp) can be arranged here, but generally only in the dry season; during the wet season the rivers are impassable. Otherwise, you'll have to get a truck ('taxi' in these parts), as the ojek don't run to a fixed schedule. This should cost 30,000Rp, though foreigners are routinely overcharged. The truck has no problem with swollen rivers unless there is severe flooding. If you can't find any onward transport to the park from Jajag, an ojek from there to Sukamade will cost around 250,000Rp. It's a painfully long journey of nearly 60km.

Alas Purwo National Park

Occupying the the remote Blambangan Peninsula on the southeastern tip of Java, Alas Purwo has spectacular beaches, good opportunities for wildlife-spotting, and savannah, mangrove and lowland monsoon forests. Apart from day-trippers and surfers, the park gets few visitors.

Alas Purwo means First Forest in Javanese: according to legend, this is where the earth first emerged from the ocean. Many soul-searchers and mystics flock here during the month of Suro, which marks the Javanese New Year. These pilgrims meditate in caves and pray to Nyai Loro Kidul. Pura Giri Selokah, a Hindu temple in the park, also attracts pilgrims, especially during Pagerwesi, the Hindu New Year.

The huge surf at Plengkung – aka G-Land, on the isolated southeastern tip of the peninsula – is home to one of the best left-hand waves in the world, with perfect barrels reeling for hundreds of metres over a shallow reef, and there are surfers aplenty.

◎ Sights & Activities

Alas Purwo is dominated by lowland coastal forest, but there are few trails by which to explore it. As a result, vast expanses of the eastern park are untrammelled.

You can use Trianggulasi as a base for some interesting short walks. The white-sand beach here is beautiful, but swimming is usually dangerous.

Sadengan   WILDLIFE RESERVE

Down a spur that branches from the main road just after the Hindu temple, Sadengan grazing ground has the largest herd of *banteng* (wild cattle) in Java. Keep an eye out for the birds hopping along their backs in a search for ticks and other insects, and lovely herons often glide into the frame. *Kijang* (deer) and peacocks can also be seen here from the viewing tower. This beautiful meadow, backed by rolling, forested hills, is a 2km walk from Trianggulasi.

Ngagelan   BEACH

The turtle hatchery at Ngagelan is set in a protected, fenced-off plot behind the beach, where rangers who have collected the eggs keep them piled and dated under the brown sand, shielding them from birds and other predators. The beach itself, where four species of turtles nest – including greens and leatherbacks – is wide, majestic and 18km long. You can see the light-brown sand arc along the coast all the way to G-Land. You can't swim here, though, as the rip tide is all powerful.

Turtles emerge from the sea under the cover of night, and after they lay their eggs, the rangers gather them and place them in the hatchery where they will gestate for 50 days before hatching and seeking the sea. To get here, it's a 6km drive from Rowobendo through lowland forest along a rough road, or a 7km walk along the beach at low tide from Trianggulasi. A ranger will gladly show you around, but he won't speak much English.

Gua Istana & Gua Padepokan   CAVE

From Pancur, a trail heads 2km inland through some good forest to Gua Istana, a small cave, and another 2km further on to Gua Padepokan. Both contain Hindu shrines.

🏄 Activities

G-Land   SURFING

(Plengkung) Plengkung, known in surfing circles as G-Land or just Grajagan, is one of the planet's premier surfing spots, and home to three seasonal surf camps. When conditions are good, the left-hander here – which can be further broken down into several often distinct sections, each with its own name and mood – barrels for hundreds of metres over a razor-sharp, shallow reef. This is very much experts-only surf territory, though there are also some beginner waves over a sand-bar bottom.

When it's firing, there can be 100 people in the water, which sounds overwhelming, but the mob usually strings out to manageable numbers as heads seek waves that suit their skill set. The surf camps offer transport to the waves from a small marina that's easy to find in the shallows. Swimmers can swim east along the reef from here, though low tide is quite low, so you may need to pick your way through the reef when you come in.

The surf camps are all set about 500m apart from one another in different coves. Bobby's (p203) has the more dramatic setting and offers pagodas and hammocks on the beach. G-Land Jack's (p202) is the furthest up the point. G-Land Joyo's (p202) has a long bench on a rocky outcrop, along with lounges oriented toward the waves and the sunset beyond. Oh yes, those sunsets are absolutely magical!

You are in a raw and wild part of the world now. There are leopards often caught on game cameras, and one ranger swears he once saw a tiger with her cub. The jungled coastline certainly looks like something out of *Jurassic Park*. No wonder G-Land is the stuff of surf legend.

Joyo's Fishing Trips   FISHING

(www.g-land.com; G-Land; half-day US$60) Joyo's offers fishing trips thanks to resident surfer and fisherman Mick Burke, who has lived here for 11 seasons and takes folks 2km offshore to his favourite fishing spots, searching for amberjack, Spanish mackerel and dogtooth tuna. He and his guests rarely return empty handed.

ⓘ GRAJAGAN BEACH

For surfers wanting to avoid the high-end costs of staying in G-Land (Plengkung), an alternative is to base yourself outside the national park at Grajagan Beach. Located around 40km northwest across the bight from G-Land (or 52km south of Banyuwangi), here surfers can instead access the waves by chartering a fishing boat for the day.

Get in touch with Ropik, a friendly local who offers boat trips to G-Land, the cost of which can be split among four people; also, given it doesn't make landfall, you won't have to pay national-park fees. You'll lose valuable surf time commuting to G-Land each day, so consider other, lesser, surf spots around the village itself. Plus you'll get a more authentic slice of Indonesia than is possible at the surf-bubble resorts at G-Land itself.

For accommodation your best bet is Wana Wisata, located directly on the black sandy beach. The cafe next door isn't always open, but Wana Wisata's manager can arrange beers and barbecue fish.

To get to here, you can catch a Jember-bound bus from Banyuwangi to Benculuk (10,000Rp), from where you can arrange a minibus or *ojek* (passenger motorcycle) to Grajagan (50,000Rp to 75,000Rp).

☞ Tours

There are three surf camps at Plengkung (G-Land): Bobby's, G-Land Joyo's and G-Land Jack's. The surfing packages usually include boat transfers from Bali, accommodation and meals. Though it is possible to make your way here under your own steam, it's important to book ahead to make sure the camps have room for you. There is no other place to stay.

Grajagan Surf Charter   SURFING
(☑ 0813 5808 0565, 0853 3092 9851; kenrofish72@gmail.com; 4-person boat trip 1,500,000Rp) Based outside the national park is this boat-charter option that makes trips to G-Land from Grajagan Beach, about 45km northwest from Alas Purwo. Owner Ropik speaks good English, and can arrange fishing and eco trips to the mangroves. He's also a good source for local surf spots.

🛌 Sleeping & Eating

National-park campsites are dusty and lack shelter from the wind and the road. We don't recommend them.

The G-Land (Plengkung) surf camps usually have three-night minimums, but if you arrive with your own transport, you may be able to negotiate a single night or two. Contact them in advance to check, though.

From Trianggulasi, the nearest warung (meals 10,000Rp) is at Pancur, where there are also simple rooms (100,000Rp per person). In the G-Land surf resorts carb-heavy meals are included in the price, as is a beer or two.

Wana Wisata   GUESTHOUSE $
(☑ 0821 4397 3873; Grajagan Beach; ⊗ r with fan/air-con from 200,000/250,000Rp; ❄) Not actually in G-Land but over the bay in Grajagan Beach (outside the national park) is this laid-back losmen, which overlooks an attractive black-sand beach. The spartan fan rooms are around the back with no views, so it's worth upgrading to the beach-facing bungalows if you're seeking added comforts such as air-con. Only very basic English is spoken.

G-Land Jack's Surf Camp   SURF CAMP $$$
(☑ bookings in Bali 0361-472 9102; http://g-land jacksurfcamp.com; G-Land; 3-night package cottage fan/air-con US$550/725) With its prime location in front of (arguably) the best part of the reef, plus a multi-level watch tower for sundown beers and wave-watching, Jack's (formally known as Raymond's) is a classic. Accommodation is in three levels of comfortable wooden bungalows. In the cheapest rooms, you might be sharing with another guest. Meals, transfers and beers included in the price.

G-Land Joyo's Surf Camp   SURF CAMP $$$
(☑ 0822 4725 1148; bookings in Bali 0819 9992 5777; www.g-land.com; 3 nights incl food & transport from Bali from US$625; ❄ 🛜) Joyo's has steadily upped its game over the years. It has good-quality thatched wooden bungalows with fan or air-conditioning, a large-screen TV for sports, pool tables, internet access and table tennis. It also offers free yoga, as well as fishing trips, and the crew who run the place are a blast. Price includes all meals and a free ration of three beers per day.

Bobby's Surf Camp SURF CAMP $$$
(☑ bookings in Bali 036-175 5588; www.grajagan. com; G-Land; 3-night packages US$640; ❋ @ 🛜)
Right opposite the waves, this attractive camp has three standards of bungalow in shady grounds with a restaurant and bar. It has beach volleyball, ping-pong and pool tables, and boat and fishing trips can be arranged. Set back from the beach, in the jungle, the best nests are the two-storey stilted teak cottages in the trees.

ℹ Information

The usual park entry is by road, via the village of Pasar Anyar, which has a large **national park office** (☑ 033-341 0857; ⊗ 7.30am-4pm Mon-Fri) and interpretive centre. Stop by to check on park accommodation and campsites; alternatively, check with the head office in Banyuwangi. You can also just show up cold, though you should book in with one of the surf camps if you intend to spend the night.

The actual gateway to the park is 10km south along a bad road at Rowobendo where you need to pay your admission fee (10,000Rp per car, 150,000Rp per person). From here it's 2.5km to Trianggulasi.

ℹ Getting There & Away

Alas Purwo is a pain to get to by public transport. The best way here is to hire a motorbike or car in Banyuwangi; the access roads are poor but usually doable.

By bus, you need to get to Brawijaya bus terminal in Banyuwangi, from where there are buses to Kalipahit (15,000Rp, 1½ hours). Then take an *ojek* for around 80,000Rp to the park office in Pasar Anyar to check on accommodation, before pushing on to the park. The 12km road from Pasar Anyar to Trianggulasi is badly potholed but is flat and negotiable by car.

If you're going only for the surf, then speedboat transfers from Bali are generally included in surf-camp fees.

Banyuwangi

☑ 0333 / POP 116,000

Java's land's end is a pleasant, growing city, home to a large number of Osig people, whose roots reach back centuries in southeast Java. Most travellers simply pass through on their way to or from Bali by ferry, but the city does make a reasonable and comfortable base to explore the Ijen Plateau and other national parks along the east coast, and there are a couple of reasonable beaches in the vicinity. The town takes pride in its appearance and is a multiple winner of the 'Cleanest Town in Indonesia' award.

Point of clarification: the ferry port for Bali, the bus terminal and the train station are all some 8km north of town in Ketapang, though all transport states 'Banyuwangi' as its destination.

⊙ Sights

Pulau Tabuhan ISLAND
A droplet of creamy white sand, topped with a tuft of scrub, this tiny island set offshore from Java, nearly halfway to Bali, is surrounded by a ring of turquoise shallows with a deep blue drop-off about 50m from shore. You'll see bait balls, schools of tropical fish and some coral structures. The water is aquarium clear, and from the beach the volcanoes and mountains from Java and Bali are spread out in all directions.

Though the winds can rip (there's a reason an annual kite-surf contest is held here), it's possible to camp. If you do, you're likely to have the place to yourself. Unfortunately, not all island visitors are as considerate to the environment as we know you will be, and there can be quite a lot of rubbish at times. To get here, take a taxi or *ojek* to the Rumah Apung port, north of the ferry terminal, and hire a boat from there. It's 400,000Rp to 500,000Rp with bargaining for a round trip.

Blambangan Museum MUSEUM
(Jl A Yani; ⊗ 8am-4pm Mon-Thu, to 11am Fri) FREE
Located in the same building as the tourist office, this small museum is devoted to culture from the area, with batik and traditional costumes, ceramics and curios. Labelling is a bit hit and miss, but the museum turns up the odd dusty piece of interest.

Hoo Tong Bio Chinese Temple TEMPLE
(Jl Ikan Gurami 54; ⊗ 6am-10pm) One of the few sights in Banyuwangi is this dragon-encrusted temple, built in 1784. It's well worth a peek.

✯ Festivals & Events

Banyuwangyi Festival CULTURAL
The Banyuwangyi Festival is a two-month series of music, arts, culture and sporting events organised by the stellar tourist office, and is held on weekends in August and September. The Jazz Festival is one such event; it's held at the Jiwa Jawa amphiteatre (p198) on the slopes of Ijen.

🍴 Sleeping & Eating

Banyuwangi has decent, well-priced accommodation including some boutique-style places. The town is also becoming an increasingly popular base from which to visit Ijen Plateau (p196). For cheap eats, there are warungs on the corner of Jl MT Haryono and Jl Wahid Haysim. Being on the coast, there are some good seafood options too.

Green Ijen Homestay   GUESTHOUSE $

(📱 0823 3255 5077; greenijen@gmail.com; Jl Opak 7; r incl breakfast with shared bathroom & fan/aircon 125,000/200,000Rp; ❄🛜) Easily one of Banyuwangi's best budget choices is this relaxed, lime-green guesthouse, tucked down a residential street in town. Rooms are both spotless and comfortable. It's run by Johan, who's very helpful and is clued up with all the local tourist info. It's also the place to arrange good-value Ijen volcano tours (per person 200,000Rp, excluding entrance ticket) to see the 'blue flame'.

★ Bangsring Breeze   BOUTIQUE HOTEL $$$

(📱 0823 3126 4847; www.bangsringbreeze.com; Jl Raya Situbondo Km17; r from 1,580,000Rp; 🅿❄🛜⊞) Simply one of the finest hotels in eastern Java. Each of the five rooms here have been individually and tastefully designed – think high ceilings, wood floors, throw rugs, stained driftwood furnishings, Buddhist and Hindu statues and fine art. There's a gorgeous pool overlooking the sea and Bali's Menjangan island, and a spectacular volcano rising behind the property.

Hotel Ketapang Indah   HOTEL $$$

(📱0333-422 280; www.ketapangindahhotel.com; Jl Gatot Subroto; d incl breakfast from 720,000Rp; ❄@🛜⊞) This lovely resort-style hotel is a peaceful place to stay. Its huge, well-kept rooms and traditional-style cottages are dotted around a sprawling tropical garden, shaded with coconut palms and extending to the sea. The 18m pool is big enough for laps, and has a small bar for pool-side cocktails. It's 2km south of the ferry terminal.

Warung Bik Ati   INDONESIAN $

(📱0333-423 165; Jl A Yani 83; mains 27,000Rp; 🕘9am-9pm) For over 70 years Bik Ati has been perfecting its house special, *nasir-awon* (black beef soup with rice). The secret to the taste is the inclusion of keluak seeds, which (and you might prefer to read this after your meal...) contain cyanide. Fortunately the preparation method ensures that the cyanide all leeches out safely. We lived to tell the tale anyway.

Ikan Bakar Pesona   SEAFOOD $

(Jl Sudarso 147; dishes 13,000-45,000Rp; 🕘1-10pm) A classic Indonesian fish house where the tablecloths are sealed in plastic to easily wipe down the Makassar-style shrapnel after a serious feast. Famous for 10 flavours of crab (get yours Padang style), it also does grilled fish six different ways. Prices are fair and the food is delicious.

ℹ Information

Alas Purwo National Park (📱0333-428675; Jl Brawijaya; 🕘7.30am-3pm Mon-Thu, to 11am Fri) Head office 2km south of the town centre.

Banyuwangi Tourist Office (📱0333-424172; Jl A Yani 78; 🕘7am-4pm Mon-Thu, to 11am Fri) Helpful staff who speak Dutch and some English, and can organise tours.

ℹ Getting There & Away

AIR

Banyuwangi's tiny Blimbingsari airport is 9km south of the centre. There's no public transport to the airport; a taxi will cost around 50,000Rp.

BOAT

The **Ketapang Ferry Terminal** is around 8km north of town. Ferries depart around the clock for Gilimanuk (one hour, every 45 minutes) in Bali. The ferry costs 33,000Rp for passengers (or 6500Rp if you already have an e-card); through-buses between Bali and Java include the fare in the bus ticket. It's 51,000Rp for a motorbike and 159,000Rp for a car (including four passengers). Note that Bali is one hour ahead of Java time.

BUS

Banyuwangi has two bus terminals. The **Sri Tanjung terminal** is 3km north of Ketapang ferry terminal, 11km from the centre. Buses from here head along the north coast road to Baluran (12,000Rp, one hour), Probolinggo (normal/patas 36,000/60,000Rp, five hours) and Surabaya (54,000/90,000Rp, seven hours). Buses to Denpasar (40,000/70,000Rp, five hours) include the ferry trip.

Brawijaya terminal (also known as Karang Ente), 4km south of town, covers buses along the southern highway to Kalibaru (15,000/22,000Rp, two hours) and Jember (35,000Rp, three hours).

TRAIN

The main Banyuwangi train station is just a few hundred metres north of the ferry terminal. Trains head to Probolinggo (29,000Rp to

245,000Rp, 4¼ to five hours, five daily), Surabaya (56,000Rp to 250,000Rp, 6¼ to 7¼ hours, four daily) and Yogyakarta (94,000Rp, 13 to 14 hours, two daily, 6.30am and 11.05am).

Baluran National Park

Baluran National Park once harboured a diverse range of ecosystems in a 250-sq-km chunk of northeastern Java; though lately development has severely impacted the park, it remains a magical place to visit. Extensive grasslands still cover parts of the park, providing grazing for *banteng* (wild cattle), various deer and water buffalo, and the savannah-like terrain is vaguely reminiscent of East Africa.

⊙ Sights

Baluran is home to hundreds of Timor deer and *banteng,* plus sambar deer, *muntjac* deer, two species of monkey and wild boars. Bird life is also excellent, with green peafowl, red and green jungle fowl, hornbills, white-bellied woodpeckers and bee-eaters all easy to spot.

Pantai Bama   BEACH
Fringed by mangroves, the sandy cove of Bama is 4km north of Bekol. It's a popular weekend retreat for local families, but usually peaceful at other times. Canoes (40,000Rp) and snorkelling gear (60,000Rp) can be hired.

Watch out for the cheeky long-tailed macaques here, who are not averse to violently mugging you for any food you might be carrying (if they do get too close for comfort, rangers advise that lifting up a stick as if readying to hit them will see them scarper).

⚡ Activities

Bekol   HIKING
From the PHKA office on the highway, it's 14km down a flat gravel track to Bekol. The friendly rangers here look after a couple of lodges and can act as guides (150,000Rp per half-day). You don't need a guide to hike along a well-maintained trail to Pantai Bama (1½ hours), which follows a riverbank where deer are common.

On the hill above the guesthouses at Bekol, there is a viewing tower that provides a panoramic view over a 300-hectare clearing. *Banteng* and deer can be seen here, and wild dogs can sometimes be seen hunting, usually in the early morning.

🛏 Sleeping

Most visitors tend to come as part of a day trip, so accommodation is often available, but it pays to book ahead in the peak June-to-August holiday period.

Park Bungalow   BUNGALOW $
(r 100,000-400,000Rp) The park has limited bungalow accommodation. Pantai Bama is the preferred location as you're right on the beach and it's better set up for visitors. There is accommodation available in concrete bungalows and a warung for cheap meals (mains 9000Rp to 22,000Rp) and drinks. The rooms are functional, but perfectly comfortable and the views over a beach bookended with mangroves is perfect.

Rosa's Ecolodge   GUESTHOUSE $$
(☑0815 7443 5105; www.rosasecolodge.com; Ds Sidomulyo RT 03/03; r incl breakfast 450,000Rp; ✳ @) Rosa's spacious rooms have woven bamboo walls, private bathrooms and shady front porches. The place is geared towards guests who join its Baluran tours (750,000Rp), and priority is given to groups during busy times. It's on the northern edge of the park in the village of Sumberwaru. Buffet-style meals of tasty Javanese food are served here.

ℹ Information

You'll find the **PHKA office** (☑0823 3221 3114, 0333-461936; http://balurannationalpark.web.id; Wonorejo; ⊙7.30am-4pm) on the coastal highway in the village of Wonorejo, between Surabaya and Banyuwangi. Guides can be booked for around 250,000Rp per day. Entrance costs 150,000Rp on a weekday and 225,000Rp on weekends and holidays. An extra 10,000Rp is charged for a car.

Baluran can be visited at any time of the year, but the dry season (June to November) is usually the best time because the animals congregate near the waterholes at Bekol and Bama.

ℹ Getting There & Away

A regular stream of Surabaya–Banyuwangi buses all pass right by the almost hidden park entrance. From Banyuwangi it's a one-hour journey (10,000Rp). Coming from the west, Baluran is four hours from Probolinggo. PHKA rangers at the entrance can arrange an *ojek* (around 40,000Rp) to take you the next 12km to Bekol; the road is in pretty good shape and should be passable by most cars. A 4WD is not necessary.

JAVA BALURAN NATIONAL PARK

AT A GLANCE

⭐

POPULATION
4.3 million

OLDEST TEMPLE
Pura Besakih (p281)

BEST BEACH
Kuta Beach (p217)

BEST SEAFOOD
Sardine (p233)

BEST YOGA
Yoga Barn (p263)

📅

WHEN TO GO
Jul, Aug & Dec
High season is Bali's busiest and buzziest time. Book ahead for rooms.

May, Jun & Sep
Often the best weather: slightly cooler and drier; less crowded.

Jan–Apr, Oct & Nov
Low season makes spontaneous travel easy. Things go quiet for the Nyepi festival.

Pura Ulun Danu Bratan (p293)
PLATONGKOH/GETTY IMAGES ©

Bali

Impossibly green rice terraces, pounding surf, enchanting Hindu temple ceremonies, mesmerising dance performances, ribbons of beaches and truly charming people: there are as many images of Bali as there are flowers on the island's ubiquitous frangipani trees.

This small island looms large for any visit to Indonesia, and no other place is more visitor-friendly. Hotels range from surfer dives to lavish retreats in the lush mountains. You can dine on local foods bursting with flavours fresh from the markets or let world-class chefs take you on a global culinary journey. From a cold Bintang beer at sunset to an epic night of clubbing, your social whirl is limited only by your fortitude.

Small in size doesn't mean homogenous: manic Kuta segues into glitzy Seminyak; the artistic swirl of Ubud is a counterpoint to misty hikes amid volcanoes; and mellow beach towns such as Bingin, Amed and Pemuteran lie dotted along the coast.

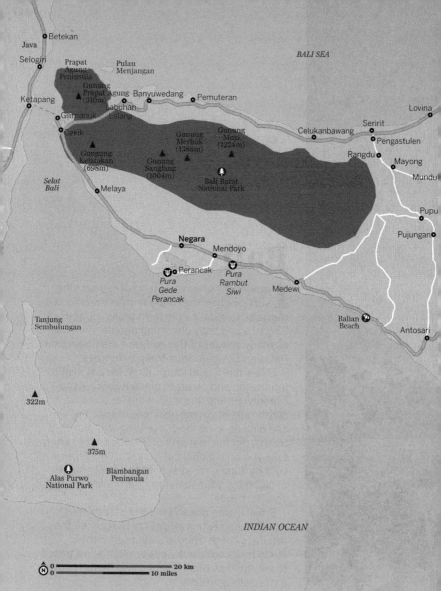

Bali Highlights

1 **Bukit Peninsula** (p239) Surfer-watching on great white sands.

2 **Sybaritic Spas** (p263) Indulging the body, mind and soul with sumptuous treatments in Ubud.

3 **Nusa Penida** (p258) Feeling small diving alongside manta rays.

4 **Ubud** (p259) Centering your spirit in Bali's artistic heart.

5 **Kuta** (p225) Raving in the manic clubs of Bali's most legendary scene.

Kubutambahan
Yeh Sanih
Sangsit
Pacung
Singaraja
Pura Maduwe Karang
Tejakula
Sukasade
Sawan
Sembirenteng
Gunung Penulisan (1745m)
Tembok
Gitgit
Catur
Penulisan
Gunung Batur (1717m)
Songan
Tianyar
Pura Ulun Danu Bratan (Candikunung)
Gunung Catur
Kintamani
Batur
Toya Bungkah
Kubu
Candikuning
Penelokan
Danau Batur
Gunung Abang (2152m)
Tulamben
Bedugul
Gunung esong 60m)
Gunung Batukau (2276m)
Pacung
Gunung Agung (3142m)
Culik
Amed
Aas
Kayuanbua
Besakih
Pura Besakih
Tirta Gangga
Gunung Seraya (1175m)
ra Luhur Batukau
Jatiluwih
Petang
Kayubihi
Pampatan
Rendang
Muncan
Penebel
Pujung
Tampaksiring
Pura Kehen (Bangli)
Iseh
Amlapura
Ujung
Marga
Payangan
Bangli
Bukit Jambul
Sideman
Tenganan
Gili Trawangan (35km); Lembar (Lombok) (60km)
Sangeh
Ubud ② ④
Pejeng
Semarapura (Klungkung)
Pura Goa Lawah
Candidasa
Tabanan
Mengwi
Mas
Pura
nah Lot
Sempidi
Celuk
Sukawati
Lebih
Kusamba
Padangbai
Selat Lombok
Kediri
Batuan
Selat Badung
Batubulan
Ketewel
Canggu
Denpasar
Nusa Lembongan
Seminyak ⑦
Sanur
Jungutbatu
Lembongan
Ped
Sampalan
Legian
Kuta ⑤
Benoa Harbour
Pura Sakenan (Pulau Serangan)
Toyapakeh
Karangsari
Jimbaran ⑧
Tanjung Benoa
Nusa Ceningan
③
Bukit Mundi (529m)
Semaya
adang adang
Bingin
Nusa Dua
Nusa Penida
⑥
① **Bukit Peninsula**
Lombok (40km)
⑨
Pecatu
ra Luhur lu Watu
INDIAN OCEAN

---

⑥ **Padang Padang** (p241) Tackling fabled surf breaks.

⑦ **Seminyak** (p226) Chic shopping, hotels and restaurants shatter island clichés.

⑧ **Jimbaran** (p240) Getting wrist-deep in platters of fresh prawns.

⑨ **Pura Luhur Ulu Watu** (p242) Ambling around oceanside shrines and sacred

sites along the limestone precipice.

⑩ **Tulamben** (p292) Snorkelling in a wild underwater world.

History

There are few traces of Stone Age people in Bali, although it's certain that the island was populated very early in prehistoric times – fossilised Homo erectus remains from neighbouring Java have been dated to as early as 250,000 years ago. The earliest human artefacts found in Bali are stone tools and earthenware vessels dug up near Cekik in west Bali, which are estimated to be 3000 years old.

When Islam swept through Java in the 12th century, the rulers of the Hindu Majapahit kingdom moved to Bali while the priest Nirartha established temples, including Rambut Siwi, Tanah Lot and Ulu Watu. In the 19th century, the Dutch formed alliances with local princes and eventually conquered the island. Westerners began celebrating Balinese arts in the 1930s; surfers arrived in the 1960s. As tourism has boomed, Bali's unique culture has proved to be remarkably resilient.

Hindu Influence

Java began to spread its influence into Bali during the reign of King Airlangga (1019–42), or perhaps even earlier. At the age of 16, when his uncle lost the throne, Airlangga fled into the forests of western Java. He gradually gained support, won back the kingdom once ruled by his uncle and went on to become one of Java's greatest kings. Airlangga's mother had moved to Bali and remarried shortly after his birth, so when he gained the throne, there was an immediate link between Java and Bali. It was at this time that the courtly Javanese language known as Kawi came into use among the royalty of Bali; the rock-cut memorials seen at Gunung Kawi, near Tampaksiring, provide a clear architectural link between Bali and 11th-century Java.

After Airlangga's death, Bali remained semi-independent until Kertanegara became king of the Singosari dynasty in Java two centuries later. Kertanegara conquered Bali in 1284, but the period of his greatest power lasted a mere eight years, until he was murdered and his kingdom collapsed. The great Majapahit dynasty was then founded by his son, Wijaya. With Java in turmoil, Bali regained its autonomy, and the Pejeng dynasty rose to great power. Temples and relics of this period can still be found in Pejeng, near Ubud.

Dutch Dealings

In 1597 Dutch seamen were among the first Europeans to appear in Bali. Setting a tradition that has prevailed to the present day, they fell in love with the island and when Cornelius de Houtman, the ship's captain, prepared to set sail from the island, two of his crew refused to come with him. At that time Balinese prosperity and artistic activity, at least among the royalty, was at a peak, and the king who befriended de Houtman had 200 wives and a chariot pulled by two white buffalo, not to mention a retinue of 50 dwarfs, whose bodies had been bent to resemble the handle of a kris (traditional dagger). By the early 1600s, the Dutch had established trade treaties with Javanese princes and controlled much of the spice trade, but they were interested in profit, not culture, and barely gave Bali a second glance.

In 1710 the 'capital' of the Gelgel kingdom was shifted to nearby Klungkung (now called Semarapura), but local discontent was growing; lesser rulers were breaking away, and the Dutch began to move in using the old strategy of divide and conquer. In 1846 the Dutch used Balinese salvage claims over shipwrecks as a pretext to land military forces in northern Bali, bringing the kingdoms of Buleleng and Jembrana under their control. Their cause was also aided by the various Balinese princes who had gained ruling

OFFERINGS TO THE GODS

No matter where you stay, you'll witness women making daily offerings around their family temple and home, and in hotels, shops and other public places. You're also sure to see vibrant ceremonies, where whole villages turn out in ceremonial dress, and police close the roads for a spectacular procession that can stretch for hundreds of metres. Men play the gamelan (traditional Balinese and Javanese orchestral music) while women elegantly balance magnificent tall offerings of fruit and cakes on their heads.

There's nothing manufactured about what you see. Dance and musical performances at hotels are among the few events 'staged' for tourists, but they do actually mirror the way Balinese traditionally welcome visitors, whom they refer to as *tamu* (guests). Otherwise, it's just the Balinese going about their daily life as they would without spectators.

NYEPI

This is Bali's biggest purification festival, designed to clean out all the bad spirits and begin the year anew. It falls around March or April according to the Hindu *caka* calendar, a lunar cycle similar to the Western calendar in terms of the length of the year. Starting at sunrise, the whole island literally shuts down for 24 hours. No planes may land or take off, no vehicles of any description may be operated, and no power sources may be used. Everyone, including tourists, must stay off the streets. The cultural reasoning behind Nyepi is to fool evil spirits into thinking Bali has been abandoned so they will go elsewhere.

For the Balinese, it's a day for meditation and introspection. For foreigners, the rules are more relaxed, so long as you respect the 'Day of Silence' by not leaving your residence or hotel. If you do sneak out, you will quickly be escorted back to your hotel by a stern *pecalang* (village police officer).

As daunting as it sounds, Nyepi is actually a fantastic time to be in Bali. Firstly, there's the inspired concept of being forced to do nothing. Catch up on some sleep, or if you must, read, sunbathe, write postcards, play board games...just don't do anything to tempt the demons! Secondly, there are colourful festivals the night before Nyepi.

interests on Lombok and were distracted from matters at home, unaware that the wily Dutch would use Lombok against Bali.

In 1894 the Dutch, the Balinese and the people of Lombok collided in battles that would set the course of history for the next several decades.

With the north of Bali long under Dutch control and the conquest of Lombok successful, the south was never going to last long. Once again it was disputes over the ransacking of wrecked ships that gave the Dutch an excuse to move in. In 1904 after a Chinese ship was wrecked off Sanur, Dutch demands that the rajah of Badung pay 3000 silver dollars in damages were rejected, and in 1906 Dutch warships appeared at Sanur. This event led to the *puputan* (an honourable but suicidal option when faced with an unbeatable enemy) where nearly 4000 Balinese died.

Independence

In 1942 the Japanese landed unopposed in Bali at Sanur (most Indonesians saw the Japanese at first as anticolonial liberators). The Japanese established headquarters in Denpasar and Singaraja, and their occupation became increasingly harsh for the Balinese. When the Japanese left in August 1945 after their defeat in WWII, the island was suffering from extreme poverty. The occupation had fostered several paramilitary, nationalist and anticolonial groups that were ready to fight the returning Dutch.

In August 1945 just days after the Japanese surrender, Sukarno, the most prominent member of the coterie of nationalist activists, proclaimed the nation's independence. It took four years to convince the Dutch that they were not going to get their great colony back. In a virtual repeat of the *puputan* nearly 50 years earlier, Balinese freedom fighters led by the charismatic I Gusti Ngurah Rai (namesake of the Bali airport) were wiped out by the Dutch in the battle of Marga in west Bali on 20 November 1946. The Dutch finally recognised Indonesia's independence in 1949 – though Indonesians celebrate 17 August 1945 as their Independence Day.

At first, Bali, Lombok and the rest of Indonesia's eastern islands were grouped together in the unwieldy province of Nusa Tenggara. In 1958 the central government recognised this folly and created three new governmental regions from the one, with Bali getting its own and Lombok becoming part of Nusa Tenggara Barat.

Culture

Ask any traveller what they love about Bali and, most times, 'the people' will top their list. Since the 1920s, when the Dutch used images of bare-breasted Balinese women to lure tourists, Bali has embodied the mystique and glamour of an exotic paradise.

For all the romanticism, there is a harsher reality. For many Balinese, life remains a near hand-to-mouth existence, even as the island prospers due to tourism and the middle class grows. And the idea of culture can sometimes seem misplaced as overzealous touts test your patience in their efforts to make a living.

But there's also some truth to this idea of paradise. There is no other place in the world

WHAT'S IN A NAME?

Far from being straightforward, Balinese names are as fluid as the tides. Everyone has a traditional name, but their other names often reflect events in each individual's life. They also help distinguish between people of the same name, which is perhaps nowhere more necessary than in Bali.

Traditional naming customs seem straightforward, with a predictable gender nonspecific pattern to names. The order of names, with variations for regions and caste, is:

First-born Wayan (Gede, Putu)

Second-born Made (Kadek, Nengah, Ngurah)

Third-born Nyoman (Komang)

Fourth-born Ketut (or just Tut, as in 'toot')

Subsequent children reuse the same set, but as many families now settle for just two children, you'll meet many Wayans and Mades.

Castes also play an important role in naming and have naming conventions that clearly denote status when added to the birth order name. Bali's system is much less complicated than India's.

Sudra Some 90% of Balinese are part of this, the peasant caste. Names are preceded by the title 'I' for a boy and 'Ni' for a girl.

Wesya The caste of bureaucrats and merchants. Gusti Bagus (male) and Gusti Ayu (female).

Ksatria A top caste, denoting royalty or warriors. I Gusti Ngurah (male) and I Gusti Ayu (female), with additional titles including Anak Agung and Dewa.

Brahman The top of the heap: teachers and priests. Ida Bagus (male) and Ida Ayu (female).

Traditional names are followed by another given name – this is where parents can get creative. Some names reflect hopes for their child, as in I Nyoman Darma Putra, who's supposed to be 'dutiful' or 'good' (dharma). Others reflect modern influences, such as I Wayan Radio who was born in the 1970s, and Ni Made Atom who said her parents just liked the sound of this scientific term that also had a bomb named after it.

Many are given nicknames that reflect their appearance. For example, Nyoman Darma is often called Nyoman Kopi (coffee) for the darkness of his skin compared with that of his siblings. I Wayan Rama, named after the Ramayana epic, is called Wayan Gemuk (fat) to differentiate his physique from his slighter friend Wayan Kecil (small).

like Bali, not even in Indonesia. Being the only surviving Hindu island in the country with the largest Muslim population in the world, Bali's distinctive culture is worn like a badge of honour by a fiercely proud people. After all, it's only in the last century that 4000 Balinese royalty, dressed in their finest, walked into the gunfire of the Dutch army rather than surrender and become colonial subjects.

True, development has changed the landscape and prompted endless debate about the displacement of an agricultural society by a tourism-services industry. And the upmarket spas, clubs, boutiques and restaurants in Seminyak and Kerobokan might have you mistaking hedonism, not Hinduism, for the local religion. But scratch the surface and you'll find that Bali's soul remains unchanged.

The island's creative heritage is everywhere you look, and the harmonious dedication to religion permeates every aspect of society, underpinning the strong sense of community. There are temples in every house, office and village, on mountains and beaches, in rice fields, trees, caves, cemeteries, lakes and rivers. Yet religious activity is not limited to places of worship. It can occur anywhere, sometimes smack-bang in the middle of peak-hour traffic.

Religion

Bali's official religion is Hindu, but it's far too animistic to be considered in the same vein as Indian Hinduism. The Balinese worship the trinity of Brahma, Shiva and Vishnu, three aspects of the one (invisible) god, Sanghyang Widi, as well as the *dewa* (ancestral gods) and village founders. They also worship gods of earth, fire, water and mountains; gods of fertility, rice, technology and books; and demons who inhabit the world underneath the ocean. They share the Indian belief in karma and reincarnation, but much less emphasis is attached to other Indian customs. There is no 'untouchable caste', arranged marriages are very rare, and there are no child marriages.

The most sacred site on the island is Gunung Agung, home to Pura Besakih and frequent ceremonies involving anywhere from hundreds to sometimes thousands of people. Smaller ceremonies are held across the island every day to appease the gods, placate the demons and ensure balance between *dharma* (good) and *adharma* (evil) forces.

Islam is a minority religion in Bali; most followers are Javanese immigrants, Sasak people from Lombok or descendants of seafaring people from Sulawesi.

Most muslims on Bali practise a moderate version of Islam, as in many other parts of Indonesia. They generally follow the Five Pillars of Islam; the pillars decree that there is no god but Allah and Muhammad is His prophet; that believers should pray five times a day, give alms to the poor, fast during the month of Ramadan and make the pilgrimage to Mecca at least once in their lifetime. However, in contrast to other Islamic countries, Muslim women are not segregated, head coverings are not compulsory (although they are becoming more common) and polygamy is rare. A stricter version of Islam is beginning to spread from Lombok, which in turn is being influenced by ultra-conservative Sumbawa.

Temples

Every village in Bali has several temples, and every home has at least a simple house-temple. The Balinese word for temple is *pura*, from a Sanskrit word literally meaning 'a space surrounded by a wall'. Similar to a traditional Balinese home, a temple is walled in – so the shrines you see in rice fields or at 'magical' spots such as old trees are not real temples. These simple shrines or thrones often overlook crossroads, to protect passers-by.

All temples are built on a mountains–sea orientation, not north–south. The direction towards the mountains, *kaja*, is the end of the temple, where the holiest shrines are found. The temple's entrance is at the *kelod*. *Kangin* is more holy than the *kuah,* so many secondary shrines are on the *kangin* side. *Kaja* may be towards a particular mountain – Pura Besakih in east Bali is pointed directly towards Gunung Agung – or towards the mountains in general, which run east–west along the length of Bali.

An Island of Artists

It's telling that there is no Balinese equivalent for the words 'art' or 'artist'. Until the tourist invasion, artistic expression was exclusively for religious and ritual purposes, and was almost always done by men. Paintings and carvings were used purely to decorate temples and shrines, while music, dance and theatrical performances were put on to entertain the gods who returned to Bali for important ceremonies. Artists did not strive to be different or individual as many do in the West; their work reflected a traditional style or a new idea, but not their own personality.

That changed in the late 1920s when foreign artists began to settle in Ubud; they went to learn from the Balinese and to share their knowledge, and helped to establish art as a commercial enterprise. Today, it's big business. Ubud remains the undisputed artistic centre of the island, and artists come from near and far to draw on its inspiration, from Japanese glass-blowers to European photographers and Javanese painters.

Galleries and craft shops are all over the island; the paintings, stone carvings and woodcarvings are stacked high on floors and

BALI CULTURE

BALI WEBSITES

Bali Advertiser (www.baliadvertiser.biz) Bali's expat journal with insider tips and good columnists.

Bali Discovery (www.balidiscovery.com) Excellent weekly summary of news and features, plus hotel deals.

Bali Paradise (www.bali-paradise.com) Compendium site of info and links.

The Beat Bali (http://thebeatbali.com) Comprehensive listings for nightlife, music and events.

Coconuts Bali (https://coconuts.co/bali) Local news and occasional features.

Lonely Planet (www.lonelyplanet.com/bali) Destination information, hotel bookings, traveller forum and more.

BALI TOURS

Standardised organised tours are a convenient and popular way to visit a few places in Bali. There are dozens and dozens of operators who provide a similar product and service. Much more interesting are specialised tour companies that can take you far off the beaten track, offer memorable experiences and otherwise show you a different side of Bali. You can also easily arrange your own custom tour.

Aaranya Wildlife Odysseys (in Australia 1300 585 662; www.aaranya.com.au; prices vary) Wildlife-focused tours of Bali led by prominent field researchers and biologists.

Adventure & Spirit (0853 3388 5598; www.adventureandspirit.com; from US$110) This professional operator offers popular canyoning day trips to central Bali involving abseiling, swimming, jumping, climbing and zip-lining among scenic gorges and waterfalls.

Archipelago Adventure (0851 0208 1769, mobile 0812 3850517; www.archipelago -adventure.com; adult/child from US$55/45) Offers a range of tours, including ones on Java. In Bali, there are rides around Jatiluwih and Danau Buyan, and mountain biking on trails from Kintamani.

Bali Bike-Baik Tours (0361-978052; www.balibike.com; tours from 500,000Rp) Tours run downhill from Kintamani. The emphasis is on cultural immersion and there are frequent stops in tiny villages and at rice farms.

Bali Eco Cycling (0361-975557; www.baliecocycling.com; adult/child from US$50/30) Tours start at Kintamani and take small roads through lush scenery south to Ubud; other options focus on rural culture.

Bio (0361-270949; www.bioadventurer.com; adult/child from 950,000/850,000Rp) Get closer to the water on an individual river board or a tube. Tours go to west Bali.

JED (Village Ecotourism Network; 0361-366 9951; www.jed.or.id; tours US$75-150) Organises very highly regarded tours of small villages, some overnight. Often needs volunteers to improve its services and work with the villagers.

Mason Adventures (Bali Adventure Tours; 0361-721480; www.masonadventures.com; Adventure House, Jl Ngurah Rai Bypass; rafting trips from 695,000Rp) A large-scale adventure-tour company that runs rafting trips along Sungai Ayung (Ayung River) near Ubud, as well as jungle trekking and buggies, mountain biking and helicopter tours.

Sobek (0361-729016; www.balisobek.com; rafting from US$52) Offers well-regarded rafting trips on both the Sungai Ayung and Sungai Telagawaja.

Suta Tours (0361-462666, 0361-466783; www.sutatour.com; prices vary) Arranges the standard tours as well as trips to cremation ceremonies and special temple festivals, market tours and other custom plans.

---

will trip you up if you're not careful. Much of it is churned out quickly, and some is comically vulgar (you're not thinking of putting that 3m-high vision of a penis as Godzilla in your entryway, are you?) but there is also a great deal of extraordinary work.

Balinese Dance

There are more than a dozen different dances in Bali, each with rigid choreography, requiring high levels of discipline. Most performers have learnt through painstaking practice with an expert. No visit is complete without enjoying this purely Balinese art form; you will be delighted by the many styles, from the formal artistry of the Legong to crowd-pleasing antics in the Barong. One

thing Balinese dance is not is static. The best troupes, such as Semara Ratih in Ubud, are continually innovating.

You can catch a quality Balinese dance performance at any place where there's a festival or celebration, and you'll find exceptional performances in and around Ubud. Performances are typically at night and last about 90 minutes, and you'll have a choice of eight or more performances a night.

With a little research and some good timing, you can attend performances that are part of temple ceremonies. Here you'll see the full beauty of Bali's dance and music heritage in its original context. Performances can last several hours. Absorb the hypnotic music and the alluring moves of the performers as well as the rapt attention of the crowd. Music, theatre and dance courses are also available in Ubud.

With the short attention spans of tourists in mind, many hotels offer a smorgasbord of dances – a little Kecak, a taste of Barong and some Legong to round it off. These can be pretty abbreviated, with just a few musicians and a couple of dancers.

ℹ Information

DANGERS & ANNOYANCES
Hawkers & Touts

Many visitors regard hawkers and touts as *the* number one annoyance in Bali. Visitors are frequently, and often constantly, hassled to buy things. The worst places for this are Jl Legian in Kuta, Kuta Beach, the Gunung Batur area, Lovina and the temples at Besakih and Tanah Lot. And the cry of 'Transport?!?' that's everywhere. Many touts employ fake, irritating Australian accents ('Oi! Mate!').

Use the following tips to deflect attention.

→ Completely ignore touts/hawkers.

→ Don't make any eye contact.

→ A polite *tidak* (no) actually encourages hawkers.

→ Never ask the price or comment on the quality of their goods unless you're interested in buying.

Swimming

Kuta Beach and those to the north and south are subject to heavy surf and strong currents – always swim between the flags. Trained lifeguards are on duty, but only at Kuta, Legian, Seminyak, Nusa Dua and Sanur. Other beaches can have strong currents, even when protected by reefs.

Be careful when swimming over coral and never walk on it. It can be very sharp and coral cuts are easily infected. In addition, you are damaging a fragile environment.

Water pollution is a problem, especially after rain. Swim far away from any open streams you see flowing into the surf, including the often foul and smelly ones at Double Six Beach and Seminyak Beach. The seawater around Kuta is commonly contaminated by run-off.

ℹ Getting There & Away

AIR

Although Jakarta, the national capital, is the gateway airport to Indonesia, there are also many direct international flights to Bali. **Ngurah Rai International Airport** (http://bali-airport. com), just south of Kuta, is the only airport in Bali. It is sometimes referred to internationally as Denpasar or on some internet flight-booking sites as Bali.

International airlines flying to and from Bali have myriad flights to Australia and Asian capitals. The present runway is too short for planes flying nonstop to/from Europe.

Domestic airlines serving Bali from other parts of Indonesia change frequently.

BUS

The **Mengwi bus terminal** (Jl Mengwi-Mengwitani) is 12km northwest of Denpasar, just off the main road to west Bali. Many long-distance buses to/from Denpasar's Ubung bus terminal (p253) also stop here.

When travelling to/from south Bali, you can save time using this terminal rather than the one in Denpasar. Metered taxis are available and fares should be 150,000Rp to 200,000Rp.

The ferry crossing from Bali is included in the services offered by numerous bus companies, many of which travel overnight to Java. It's advisable to buy your ticket at least one day in advance from a travel agent or at the terminals in Denpasar (Ubang) or Mengwi. Note that flying can be almost as cheap as the bus.

Fares vary between operators; it's worth paying extra for a decent seat (all have air-con). Destinations include Yogyakarta (350,000Rp, 20 hours) and Jakarta (500,000Rp, 24 hours). You can also get buses from Singaraja in north Bali.

SEA

Pelni (www.pelni.co.id), the national shipping line, operates large boats on infrequent long-distance runs throughout Indonesia. For Bali, Pelni ships stop at the harbour in Benoa. Schedules and fares are found on the website. You can enquire and book at the **Pelni ticket office** (☑ 0361-763963, 0623 6175 5855; www.pelni. co.id; Jl Raya Kuta 299; ☺ 8am-noon & 1-4pm Mon-Fri, 8am-1pm Sat) in Tuban.

You can reach Java, just west of Bali, via the ferries that run between Gilimanuk in west Bali and Ketapang (Java), and then take a bus all the way to Jakarta.

Public car ferries travel slowly between Padangbai and Lembar on Lombok. There are also fast boats from various ports in Bali to the Gilis and Lombok.

ℹ Getting Around

The best way to get around is with your own transport, whether you drive, hire a driver or cycle. This gives you the flexibility to explore places that are otherwise inaccessible.

BICYCLE

Many people tour the island by *sepeda* (bike) and many visitors use bikes around towns and for day trips.

There are plenty of bicycles for rent in tourist areas, but many are in poor condition. Ask at your accommodation. Prices start from 30,000Rp per day. Note that traffic conditions mean that riding a bike is not for the meek.

BOAT

Fast boats linking Bali with Nusa Lembongan, Lombok and the Gili Islands have proliferated, especially as the latter places have become more popular.

BUS

Tourist buses are economical and convenient ways to get around. You'll see signs offering services in major tourist areas. Typically a tourist bus is an eight- to 20-passenger vehicle. Service is not as quick as with your own car and driver but it's far easier than trying for public bemos and buses.

Kura-Kura Bus (Map p222; ☑ 0361-757070; www.kura2bus.com; Jl Ngurah Rai Bypass, ground fl, DFS Galleria; rides 20,000-80,000Rp, 3-/7-day pass from 150,000/250,000Rp; ☎) This innovative expat-owned tourist-bus service covers important areas of south Bali and Ubud. Buses have wi-fi and run during daylight and early evening, from every 20 minutes to over two hours. Check schedules online or with the app. There are eight lines and the hub is the DFS Galleria duty-free mall.

Perama (☑ 0361-751170; www.peramatour. com) The major tourist-bus operator. It has offices or agents in Kuta, Sanur, Ubud, Lovina, Padangbai and Candidasa.

CAR & MOTORCYCLE

Renting a car or motorbike can open up Bali for exploration but can also leave you counting the minutes until you return it; driving conditions can be harrowing at certain times and south Bali traffic is often awful. But it gives you the freedom to explore back roads and lets you set your own schedule.

Most people don't rent a car for their entire visit but rather get one for a few days of meandering.

Motorbikes are a popular way of getting around – locals ride pillion almost from birth. A family of five all riding cheerfully along on one motorbike is called a Bali minivan.

Rentals cost around 60,000/350,000Rp per day/week. This should include minimal insurance for the motorcycle but not for any other person or property. Some have racks for surfboards.

Think carefully before renting a motorbike. It is dangerous and every year visitors go home with lasting damage – this is no place to learn to ride. Helmet use is mandatory.

In heavily developed parts of Bali, Go-Jek is a popular mobile application that allows you to order on-demand motorcycle rides (in addition to just about anything you'd like delivered to you). Note that you must have an Indonesian SIM card, and it may be hard to get picked up

---

ⓘ HIRING A VEHICLE & DRIVER

An excellent way to travel anywhere around Bali is by hired vehicle, allowing you to leave the driving and inherent frustrations to others. If you're part of a group, it can make sound economic sense as well.

It's easy to arrange a charter: just listen for one of the frequent offers of 'transport?' in the streets around the tourist centres. Approach a driver yourself or ask at your hotel, which is often a good method, because it increases accountability. Also consider the following:

➡ Although great drivers are everywhere, it helps to talk with a few.

➡ Get recommendations from other travellers.

➡ You should like the driver and their English should be sufficient for you to communicate your wishes.

➡ Costs for a full day should average 500,000Rp to 800,000Rp.

➡ The vehicle, usually a late-model Toyota Kijang seating up to seven, should be clean.

➡ Agree on a route beforehand.

➡ Make it clear if you want to avoid tourist-trap restaurants and shops.

➡ On the road, buy the driver lunch (they'll want to eat elsewhere, so give them 20,000Rp) and offer snacks and drinks.

➡ Many drivers find ways to make your day delightful in unexpected ways. Tip accordingly.

or dropped off in heavily touristed areas due to territory rivalries between local drivers.

TAXI

Metered taxis are common in south Bali and Denpasar (but not Ubud). They are essential for getting around and you can usually flag one down in busy areas. They're often a lot less hassle than haggling with drivers offering 'transport!'

➡ The best taxi company by far is **Blue Bird Taxi** (☑ 0361-701111; www.bluebirdgroup. com), which uses blue vehicles with a light on the roof bearing a stylised bluebird. Drivers speak reasonable English and use the meter at all times. Many expats will use no other firm. Blue Bird has a slick app that summons a taxi to your location just like Uber. Watch out for fakes – there are many. Look for 'Blue Bird' over the windscreen and the phone number.

➡ Taxis are fairly cheap: Kuta to Seminyak can be 80,000Rp.

➡ Avoid any taxis where the driver won't use a meter, even after dark when they claim that only fixed fares apply.

➡ Other taxi scams include lack of change, 'broken' meter, fare-raising detours and offers for tours, massages, prostitutes etc.

KUTA & SOUTHWEST BEACHES

The swathe of south Bali hugging the amazing ribbon of beach that runs north almost from the airport is the place many travellers begin and end their visit to the island.

In Seminyak and Kerobokan there is a bounty of restaurants, cafes, designer boutiques, spas and the like that rivals anywhere in the world, while Kuta and Legian are the choice for rollicking all-night clubbing, cheap souvenir singlets and carefree family holidays. North around Canggu is Bali's most exciting region, where great beaches vie with enticing cafes and compelling nightlife.

Renowned shopping, all-night clubs, fabulous dining, cheap beer, sunsets that dazzle and relentless hustle and bustle are all part of the experience. But just when you wonder what any of this has to do with Bali – the island supposedly all about spirituality and serenity – a religious procession appears and shuts everything down. And then you know the answer.

Kuta & Legian

☑ 0361 / POP 46,660

Loud and frenetic, Kuta and Legian are the epicentre of mass tourism in Bali. The grit and wall-to-wall cacophony have become notorious through often overhyped media reports of tourists behaving badly.

Although this is often the first place many visitors hit in Bali, the region is not for everyone. Kuta has ugly narrow lanes jammed with cheap cafes, surf shops, incessant motorbikes and an uncountable number of T-shirt vendors and bleating offers of 'massage'. Flash new shopping malls and chain hotels show that Kuta's allure may continue to grow.

Legian appeals to a slightly older crowd (some say it's where Kuta people go after they get married). It's equally commercial and has a long row of family-friendly hotels close to the beach.

◎ Sights

Kuta and Legian's main appeal is, of course, the beach. Take a walk on this sweep of sand north from the airport to Kerobokan and beyond.

★ Kuta Beach   BEACH

(Map p222) Tourism in Bali began here and is there any question why? Low-key hawkers will sell you soft drinks and beer, snacks and other treats, and you can rent surfboards, lounge chairs and umbrellas (negotiable at 10,000Rp to 20,000Rp), or just crash on the sand. The sunsets are legendary.

Legian Beach   BEACH

(Map p222) An extension north from Kuta Beach, Legian Beach is quieter thanks to the lack of a raucous road parallel to the beach and fewer people.

Double Six Beach   BEACH

(Map p222) The beach becomes less crowded as you go north from Legian until very popular Double Six Beach, which is alive with pickup games of football and volleyball all day long. It's a good place to meet partying locals. Watch out for water pollution after heavy rains.

Bali Sea Turtle Society   HATCHERY

(Map p222; ☑ 0811 388 2683; www.baliseaturtle. org; Kuta Beach; ⊙ site 24hr, turtle releases 4.30pm Apr-Oct) The Bali Sea Turtle Society is a conservation group working to protect olive

South Bali

ridley turtles. It's one of the more responsible turtle hatcheries in Bali, and re-releases turtle hatchlings into the ocean from Kuta Beach. Join the queue to collect your baby turtle in a small plastic water bath, pay a small donation, and join the group to release them. Signs offer excellent background info.

Dream Museum Zone
MUSEUM

(Map p222; ☑ 0361-849 6220; www.facebook.com/dmzbali/; Jl Nakula 33X; 110,000Rp, child under 3 free; ☉ 9am-10pm; ⊕) Fun for the whole family, this museum features a collection of around 120 interactive life-size murals that come to life – or rather, can be viewed in 3D – once photographed. It's divided into 14 sections so you can take your pick from Indonesia, Jurassic Park, Egypt and others.

Activities

Pro Surf School
SURFING

(Map p222; ☑ 0361-751200; www.prosurfschool.com; Jl Pantai Kuta 32; lessons per day from 675,000Rp) Right along Kuta Beach, this well-regarded school has been getting beginners standing for years. It offers all levels of lessons, including semiprivate ones, plus gear and board rental. There are dorm rooms (from 150,000Rp), a pool and a cool cafe.

Waterbom Park
WATER PARK

(Map p220; ☑ 0361-755676; www.waterbom-bali.com; Jl Kartika Plaza; adult/child from 535,000/385,000Rp; ☉ 9am-6pm) This watery amusement park covers 3.8 hectares of landscaped tropical gardens. It has assorted water slides (a couple of dozen in total, including the 'Climax'), swimming pools, a FlowRider surf machine and a 'lazy river' ride. Other indulgences include a food court, a bar and a spa.

Jamu Traditional Spa
SPA

(Map p222; ☑ 0361-752520, ext 165; www.jamu traditionalspa.com; Jl Pantai Kuta, Alam Kul Kul; 1hr massage from 350,000Rp; ☉ 9am-7pm) In serene surrounds at a resort hotel you can enjoy a massage in rooms that open onto a pretty garden courtyard. If you've ever wanted to be part of a fruit cocktail, here's your chance – treatments involve tropical nuts, coconuts, papayas and more, often in fragrant baths.

Sleeping

Kuta, Legian and Tuban have hundreds of places to stay. Tuban and Legian have mostly midrange and top-end hotels – the best places for budget accommodation are Kuta and southern Legian. Almost every hotel has air-con and a pool. Dozens of generic midrange chain hotels are appearing throughout the area. Many are very inconveniently located.

Any place west of Jl Legian won't be more than a 10-minute walk to the beach.

★ Hotel Ayu Lili Garden
HOTEL $

(Map p222; ☑ 0361-750557; ayuliligardenhotel@yahoo.com; off Jl Lebak Bene; r with fan/air-con from 195,000/250,000Rp; ⊛ ☎ ⊛) In a *relatively* quiet area near the beach, this vintage family-run hotel has 22 bungalow-style rooms. Standards are high and for a little but extra you can add amenities such as a fridge.

Sri Beach Inn
GUESTHOUSE $

(Map p222; ☑ 0361-755897; Gang Legian Tewngah; r with fan/air-con from 200,000/350,000Rp; ⊛ ☎) Follow a series of paths into the heart of old Legian; when you hear the rustle of palms overhead, you're close to this guesthouse in a garden with five rooms. More money gets you hot water, air-con and a fridge. It offers cheap monthly rates.

★ Kuta B&B Plus
GUESTHOUSE $

(KBB; Map p222; ☑ 0818 568 364; www.kutabnb.com; Jl Pantai Kuta 1E; dm/r from 100,000/250,000Rp; ⊛ ☎) There are nine comfortable rooms in this fine guesthouse on a busy Kuta corner – it has all the basics. It's a 10-minute walk from the beach and a 10-minute ride from the airport. It has a wonderful rooftop with views over the Kuta skyline; nightlife is close too.

★ Puri Damai
GUESTHOUSE $$

(Map p222; ☑ 0361-730665; www.puridamai.com; Jl Werkudara; apt 1-/2-bedroom US$70/140; ⊛ ☎ ⊛) An elegant choice tucked away near Double Six Beach, this exquisite little hotel is run by Made, the doyen of the Made's Warung empire. The 12 units are sizeable apartments with full kitchens, dining and living areas, terraces and balconies. The compact compound is lush and the furniture is relaxed tropical.

Jayakarta Hotel
RESORT $$

(Map p222; ☑ 0361-751433; www.jayakartahotels resorts.com; Jl Pura Bagus Taruna; r incl breakfast 1,100,000-2,400,000Rp; ⊛ @ ☎ ⊛) The Jayakarta fronts a long and shady stretch of beach. The palm-shaded grounds, several pools and various restaurants make it a favourite with groups and families. Hair-braiders by the pool give kids that holiday look. The 331 rooms are large and in two- and three-storey blocks. Wi-fi not in all rooms.

Kuta, Legian & Seminyak

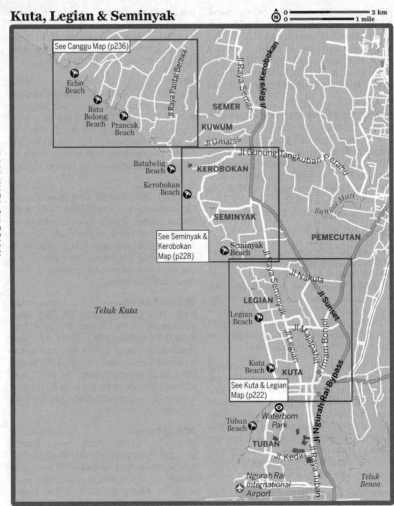

★ **Un's Hotel** HOTEL $$
(Map p222; ☑ 0361-757409; www.unshotel.com; Jl Benesari; r with fan/air-con 380,000/490,000Rp; ❄@🛜🏊) A hidden entrance sets the tone for the secluded feel of Un's, a two-storey place with bougainvillea spilling over the pool-facing balconies. The 30 spacious rooms in a pair of blocks (the southern one is quieter) feature antiques and comfy cane loungers. It's close to the beach.

Double-Six RESORT $$$
(Map p222; ☑ 0361-730466; www.double-six.com; Double Six Beach 66; r incl breakfast from 3,900,000Rp; ❄🛜🏊) A colossus five-star re-

sort, Double-Six takes a leaf out of the Vegas book of extravagance. Fronted by a luxurious 120m pool, the 146 spacious rooms all overlook the beach, and have 24-hour butler service, and TVs in the bathrooms; some rooms have balcony hot tubs. It has an enormous rooftop bar (p225), plus several restaurants including the noted Plantation Grill (p224).

Bali Mandira Beach Resort HOTEL $$$
(Map p222; ☑ 0361-751381; www.balimandira.com; Jl Padma 2; r US$150-360; ❄🛜🏊) Gardens filled with bird-of-paradise flowers set the tone at this 191-room, full-service resort with four-storey blocks and individual gar-

den units. Cottages have updated interiors, and the bathrooms are partly open-air. A dramatic pool at the peak of a stone ziggurat (which houses a spa) offers sweeping ocean views, as does the cafe.

Stones
RESORT $$$

(Map p222; ☑0361-300 5888; www.stoneshotel bali.com; Jl Pantai Kuta; r incl breakfast from US$110; ❄☏☱) Looming across the road from Kuta Beach, this vast resort boasts a huge pool, a vertical garden and 308 rooms in five-storey blocks. The design is hip and contemporary, and high-tech features abound. It's one of the growing number of megahotels along this strip and affiliated with Marriott. Some rooms have bathtubs on the balcony.

✗ Eating

There's a profusion of dining options here. Cheap tourist cafes with Indonesian standards, sandwiches and pizza are ubiquitous.

Find laid-back travellers' cafes by wandering the *gang* and looking for crowds. For quick snacks and 4am beers, 24-hour Circle K stores are everywhere. Beware of big-box restaurants on Jl Sunset. Heavily promoted, they suffer from traffic noise and are aimed at tourists.

★ Pisgor
INDONESIAN $

(Jl Dewi Sartika; treats from 2000Rp; ⊙10am-10pm) All sorts of goodness emerges from the ever-bubbling deep-fryers at this narrow store-front near the airport. The *pisang goreng* (banana fritters) are not to be missed and you can enjoy more esoteric fare such as *ote-ote* (vegetable cakes). Get a mixed bag and munch away with raw chillies for extra flavour.

Kuta Night Market
INDONESIAN $

(Map p222; Jl Blambangan; mains 15,000-25,000Rp; ⊙6pm-midnight) This is an enclave of stalls and plastic chairs. It bustles with locals and tourism workers chowing down on hot-off-the-wok treats, grilled goods and other fresh foods.

Warung Nikmat
INDONESIAN $

(Map p222; ☑0361-764678; Jl Bakung Sari 6A; mains 20,000-40,000Rp; ⊙8am-9pm) This long-running Javanese favourite is known for its array of authentic Indonesian dishes, including beef *rendang* (curry), *perkedel* (fritters), prawn cakes, *sop buntut* (oxtail soup) and various curries and vegetable dishes. Get there before 2pm for the best selection.

BALI KUTA & LEGIAN

BALI FOR KIDS

Best Beaches

Kuta Beach (p217) Surf schools.

Sanur Beach (p246) Kids will get their kicks in the gentle surf.

Batu Bolong Beach (p235) Where the cool kids of all ages hang out.

Best Water Fun

Pulau Menjangan, north Bali (p307) The best snorkelling on the island.

Rice fields walks, Ubud (p259) For something different, walk amid muddy water filled with ducks, frogs and other fun critters.

Best Frolicking

Bali Treetop Adventure Park, Candikuning (p294) Kids can make like monkeys.

Waterbom Park, Tuban (p219) A huge aquatic playground.

Best for Animals

Ubud Monkey Forest, Ubud (p262) Monkeys and temples!

Bali Bird Park, south of Ubud (p275) Amazing birds and reptiles.

Dolphin watching, Lovina (p302) Boat rides to see dolphins on Bali's north coast.

Best Cool Old Things

Tirta Empul, north of Ubud (p275) Kids will love the *Indiana Jones*–like pools at the ancient water palace and park.

Kuta & Legian

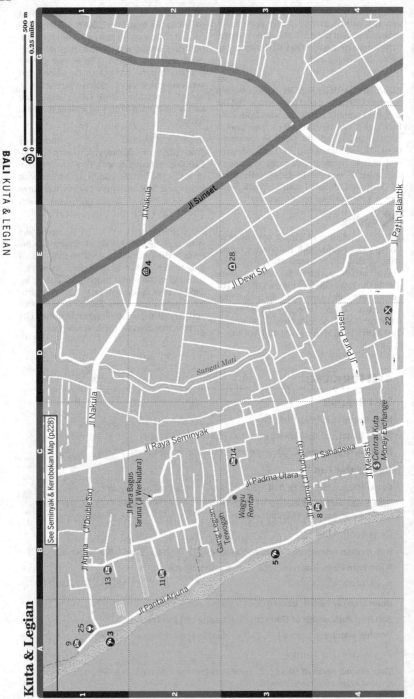

See Seminyak & Kerobokan Map (p228)

Jl Sunset

Jl Nakula

Jl Dewi Sri

Sungai Mati

Jl Nakula

Jl Raya Seminyak

Jl Pura Puseh

Jl Patih Jelantik

Jl Arjuna (Jl Double Six)

Jl Pura Bagus Taruna (Jl Werkudara)

Jl Padma Utara

Jl Sahadewa

Jl Melasti

Central Kuta Money Exchange

Gang Legian Tewogah

Wagru Rental

Jl Padma (Jl Yudistra)

Jl Pantai Arjuna

500 m
0.25 miles

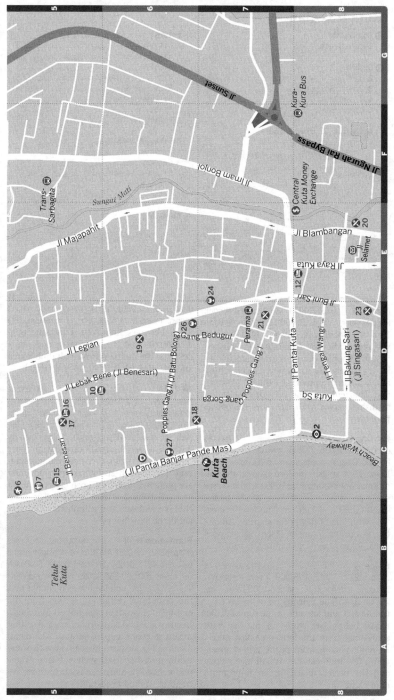

Kuta & Legian

★**Poppies Restaurant** INDONESIAN $$
(Map p222; ☑0361-751059; www.poppiesbali.com;
Poppies Gang I; mains 50,000-135,000Rp; ☺8am-
11pm; 🛜) Opening its doors in 1973, Poppies
was one of the first restaurants established
in Kuta (Poppies Gang I is even named after
it). It's popular for its elegant garden setting
and a menu of upmarket Balinese, Western
and Thai cuisine. The *rijsttafel* (selection
of dishes served with rice) and seafood is
popular.

Fat Chow ASIAN $$
(Map p222; ☑0361-753516; www.fatchowbali.com;
Poppies Gang II; mains from 65,000Rp; ☺9am-
11pm; 🛜) A stylish, modern take on the traditional open-fronted cafe, Fat Chow serves
Asian-accented fare at long picnic tables,
small tables and lounges. The food is creative, with lots of dishes for sharing. Among
the favourites: crunchy Asian salad, pork
buns, Tokyo prawns and authentic pad Thai.

Balcony INTERNATIONAL $$
(Map p222; ☑0361-757409; www.thebalcony
bali.com; Jl Benesari 16; mains 50,000-170,000Rp;
☺6am-11pm) The Balcony has a breezy trop-
ical design and sits above the din of Jl Be-
nesari below. Get ready for the day with
something from the long breakfast menu.
At night choose from pasta, grilled meats
and a few Indo classics. It's all nicely done
and the perfect place for an impromptu
date night.

Kopi Pot CAFE $$
(Map p222; ☑0361-752614; www.kopipot.com; Jl
Legian; mains from 43,000Rp; ☺7am-11pm; 🛜)
Shaded by trees, Kopi Pot is a favourite, popular for its coffees, milkshakes and many
desserts. The multilevel, open-air dining area
and bar sits back from noxious Jl Legian.

★**Take** JAPANESE $$
(Map p222; ☑0361-759745; www.take.rama
restaurantsbali.com; Jl Patih Jelantik; mains
70,000-300,000Rp; ☺11am-midnight; 🛜) Flee
Bali for a relaxed version of Tokyo just by
ducking under the traditional curtain over
the doorway at this ever-expanding restau-
rant. Hyper-fresh sushi, sashimi and more
are prepared under the keen eyes of a team
of chefs behind a long counter. The head
chef is a stalwart at the Jimbaran fish mar-
ket in the early hours.

Plantation Grill MODERN AUSTRALIAN $$$
(Map p222; ☑0361-734300; www.plantationgrill
bali.com; 4th fl, Double-Six Hotel, Double Six Beach
66; mains 200,000-850,000Rp; ☺6pm-midnight)
The gaudy sign outside leaves no doubt that
this posh hotel restaurant springs from the
empire of Australian chef Robert Marchetti.
Inside you'll find a luxurious tropical setting
meant to evoke a 1920s fantasy. The menu
features big steaks and seafood with some
wildly priced specials such as lobster Ther-
midor (855K!). Sling bar is an intimate retreat for a fantasy cocktail.

♀ Drinking & Nightlife

Sunset on the beach is popular, with a drink at a sea-view cafe or beachside beer vendor. Later, the legendary nightlife action heats up. Many spend the early evening at a hipster joint in Seminyak before working their way south to oblivion. Stylish Seminyak clubs are popular with gay and straight crowds. Kuta and Legian have a mixed crowd.

★ Velvet
BAR

(Map p222; ☑ 0361-846 4928; Jl Pantai Kuta, Beachwalk, level 3; ☺ 11am-late) The sunset views can't be beat at this large terrace bar and cafe at the beach end of the Beachwalk mall. It morphs into a club after 10pm Wednesday to Sunday. Grab a lounger for two.

Bounty
CLUB

(Map p222; Jl Legian; ☺ 10pm-3am) Set on a faux sailing boat amid a mini-mall of food and drink, the Bounty is a vast open-air disco that pumps all night to hip-hop, techno, house and party tracks. Foam parties, go-go dancers, drag shows and cheap shots add to the rowdiness.

★ Double-Six Rooftop
BAR

(Map p222; ☑ 0361-734300; www.doublesixrooftop.com; Double Six Beach 66; ☺ 3-11pm; ☏) An infinity pool, suave lounges, a commanding location and tiki torches: this ostentatious bar above the Double-Six hotel could be the villain's lair from an alt universe Bond film. Amazing sunset views are best enjoyed from the circular booths – the minimum 1,000,000Rp spend to reserve one is redeemable against food, and perfect for groups. Drinks are pricey.

Cocoon
CLUB

(Map p222; ☑ 0361-731266; www.cocoon-beach.com; Jl Arjuna; ☺ 10am-midnight) A huge pool with a view of Double Six Beach anchors this sort-of high-concept club (alcohol-branded singlets not allowed!), which has parties and events around the clock. Beds, loungers and VIP areas surround the pool; DJs spin theme nights.

Engine Room
CLUB

(Map p222; ☑ 0361-755188; www.engineroombali.com; Jl Legian 89; ☺ 6pm-4am) Open to the street, this lurid club features go-go dancers in cages as a come-on. As the evening progresses almost everyone dances and clothing gets shed. It's a wild party, with four hedonistic venues playing music that includes hip-hop, trap and rap.

🛍 Shopping

Kuta has a vast concentration of cheap, tawdry shops (top-selling souvenirs include penis-shaped bottle openers), and flashy surf-gear emporiums. As you head north along Jl Legian, the quality improves and you start finding cute boutiques, especially near Jl Arjuna (which has wholesale fabric, clothing and craft stores, giving it a bazaar feel). Continue into Seminyak for absolutely fabulous shopping.

★ Luke Studer
SPORTS & OUTDOORS

(Map p222; ☑ 0361-894 7425; www.studersurfboards.com; Jl Dewi Sri 7A; ☺ 9am-8pm) Legendary board-shaper Luke Studer works from this large and glossy shop. Short boards, retro fishes, single fins and classic longboards are sold ready-made or custom-built.

Joger
GIFTS & SOUVENIRS

(☑ 0361-752523; www.jogerjelek.com; Jl Raya Kuta; ☺ 10am-8pm) This Bali retail legend is the most popular store in the south. Mobs of Indonesian tourists come for doe-eyed plastic puppies or one of thousands of T-shirts bearing wry, funny or simply inexplicable phrases (almost all are limited edition). In fact the sign out front says 'Pabrik Kata-Kata', which means 'factory of words'. Warning: conditions inside the cramped store are insane.

ℹ Information

DANGERS & ANNOYANCES

The streets and *gang* are usually safe but there are many annoyances. Touts offer prostitutes, Viagra and other tawdry diversions. You'll also grow weary of the cloying cries of 'massage?' and other dubious offers. But your biggest irritation will likely be the sclerotic traffic.

There are ongoing reports of injuries and deaths among tourists and locals due to *arak* (colourless, distilled palm wine) being adulterated with methanol, a poisonous form of alcohol. Avoid free cocktails and any offers of *arak*.

POLICE
Tourist Police Station (☑ 0361-224111; 170 Jl Kartika; ☺ 24hr)

Tourist Police Post (Map p222; ☑ 0361-784 5988; Jl Pantai Kuta; ☺ 24hr) A second tourist police office right across from the beach; the officers have a gig that is sort of like a Balinese *Baywatch*.

MONEY
Central Kuta Money Exchange (Map p222; ☑ 0361-762970; www.centralkutabali.com; Jl Raya Kuta 168; ☺ 8am-6pm) This trustworthy

place deals in numerous currencies. Has many locations, including a branch in **Legian** (Map p222; Jl Melasti; ⊗8.30am-9pm) and counters inside some Circle K convenience stores.

POST

Postal agencies that can send mail are common. **Main Post Office** (Map p222; ☑ 0361-754012; Jl Selamet; ⊗7am-2pm Mon-Thu, to 11am Fri, to 1pm Sat) On a little road east of Jl Raya Kuta, this small and efficient post office is well practised in shipping large packages.

❶ Getting There & Away

A minivan from the airport costs 200,000Rp to Tuban, 250,000Rp to Kuta and 260,000Rp to Legian. When travelling to the airport, get a metered taxi for savings. A motorbike taxi will usually cost about half of a regular taxi.

BUS

For public buses to anywhere in Bali, you'll have to go to the appropriate terminal in Denpasar first. Tourist shuttles are widely advertised on backstreets.

Perama (Map p222; ☑ 0361-751551; www. peramatour.com; Jl Legian 39; ⊗7am-10pm) is the main tourist shuttle-bus operation in town; it may do hotel pick ups and drop-offs for an extra 10,000Rp (confirm with staff when making arrangements). It usually has at least one bus a day to destinations including Lovina (125,000Rp, 4½ hours), Padangbai (75,000Rp, three hours) and Ubud (60,000Rp, 1½ hours).

Trans-Sarbagita (Map p222; ☑ 0811 385 0900; Jl Imam Bonjol; 3000Rp; ⊗5am-9pm), Bali's public bus service, has four routes that converge on the central parking area just south of Istana Kuta Galleria. Destinations include Denpasar, Sanur, Jimbaran and Nusa Dua.

Kuta is a hub for the highly useful Kura-Kura tourist bus (p216) service.

❶ Getting Around

The hardest part about getting around south Bali is the traffic. Besides using taxis, you can rent a motorbike (60,000Rp per day, or less for long-term rental), often with a surfboard rack, or a bike – just ask at the place you're staying or the reputable **Wagyu Rental** (Map p222; Jl Padma Utara; per day 60,000Rp; ⊗8am-6pm) in Kuta. One of the nicest ways to get around the area is by foot along the beach.

TAXI

In traffic, a taxi ride from Kuta into Seminyak can top 150,000Rp and take more than 30 minutes; walking the beach will be quicker.

Seminyak

☑ 0361 / POP 6140

Fabulous Seminyak is the centre of life for hordes of the island's expats, many of whom own boutiques, design clothes, surf, or do seemingly nothing at all. It may be immediately north of Kuta and Legian, but in many respects, not the least of which is its intangible sense of style, Seminyak feels almost like it's on another island.

It's a dynamic place, home to scores of restaurants and clubs and a wealth of creative, designer shops and galleries. World-class hotels line the beach, and what a beach it is – as wide and sandy as Kuta's but less crowded.

Seminyak seamlessly merges with Kerobokan, which is immediately north – in fact the exact border between the two is as fuzzy as most other geographic details in Bali. You could easily spend your entire holiday in Seminyak.

❍ Sights

Seminyak's sights are almost entirely related to consumption. After the beach and its temples, simply strolling the main strips and pausing to people-watch can be richly rewarding – and entertaining.

★**Pantai Seminyak**   BEACH
(Map p228) A lounger and an ice-cold Bintang on the beach at sunset is simply magical. A good stretch can be found near Pura Petitenget, and it tends to be less crowded than further south in Kuta.

Pura Petitenget   HINDU TEMPLE
(Map p228; Jl Petitenget) This is an important temple and the scene of many ceremonies. It is one of a string of sea temples that stretches from Pura Luhur Ulu Watu on the Bukit peninsula north to Pura Tanah Lot in western Bali. Petitenget loosely translates as 'magic box'; it was a treasured belonging of the legendary 16th-century priest Nirartha, who refined the Balinese religion and visited this site often.

The temple is renowned for its anniversary celebrations on the Balinese 210-day calendar. It is right next to Pura Masceti.

BIASA ArtSpace   GALLERY
(Map p228; ☑ 0361-730308; www.biasagroup. com; Jl Raya Seminyak 34; ⊗9am-9pm) FREE Founded in 2005, BIASA ArtSpace showcases the work of up-and-coming Indonesian

and international artists. The gallery has a line-up of rotating exhibitions in a variety of art forms, from painting and photography to sculpture and installation art. The upper floor houses a mini library and a restoration studio.

🏃 Activities

Seminyak's spas (and those of Kerobokan) are among the best in Bali and offer a huge range of treatments, therapies and pleasures.

★ Jari Menari   SPA
(Map p228; ☑0361-736740; www.jarimenari.com; Jl Raya Basangkasa 47; massages from 435,000Rp; ☺9am-9pm) Jari Menari is true to its name, which means 'dancing fingers': your body will be one happy dance floor. The all-male staff use massage techniques that emphasise rhythm. It also offers massage classes (from US$170).

Prana   SPA
(Map p228; ☑0361-730840; www.pranaspabali.com; Jl Kunti 118X; massages from 510,000Rp; ☺9am-10pm) A palatial Moorish fantasy that is easily the most lavishly decorated spa in Bali, Prana offers everything from basic hour-long massages to facials and all manner of beauty treatments.

Surf Goddess   SURFING
(☑0858 997 0808; www.surfgoddessretreats.com; per week incl private room from US$2495) Surf holidays for women that include lessons, yoga, meals and lodging in a posh guesthouse in the backstreets of Seminyak.

Seminyak Yoga Shala   YOGA
(Map p228; ☑0361-730498; www.seminyakyogashala.com; Jl Basangkasa; classes from 140,000Rp) No-nonsense yoga studio with daily classes in several styles including ashtanga, Mysore and yin yang.

🛏 Sleeping

Seminyak has a wide range of accommodation, from world-class beach resorts to humble hotels hidden on backstreets. This is also the start of villa-land, which runs north from here through the vanishing rice fields beyond Canggu. For many, a private villa with its own pool is a holiday dream.

Oodles of midrange chain hotels across south Bali add Seminyak to their names even when they're as far away as Denpasar.

Raja Gardens   GUESTHOUSE $$
(Map p228; ☑0361-934 8957; www.jdw757.wixsite.com/rajagardens; off Jl Camplung Tanduk; r from 600,000Rp; ❋🖥🌊) Here since 1980, this old-school guesthouse has spacious, grassy grounds with fruit trees and a quiet spot located almost on the beach. The eight rooms are fairly basic but there are open-air bathrooms and plenty of potted plants. The large pool is a nice spot to lounge by, and it's generally a mellow place.

Sarinande   HOTEL $$
(Map p228; ☑0361-730383; www.sarinandehotels.com; Jl Sarinande 15; r incl breakfast 630,000-680,000Rp; ❋🖥🌊) The 26 excellent-value rooms here are in older two-storey blocks set around a small pool; the decor is a bit dated but everything is well maintained. Amenities include fridges, satellite TV and DVD players, and there's a cafe. The beach is a three-minute walk away.

★ Samaya   VILLA $$$
(Map p228; ☑0361-731149; www.thesamayabali.com; Jl Kayu Aya; villa from US$725; ❋🖥🌊) Understated yet cultured, the Samaya is one of the best bets for a villa right on the beach in south Bali. It boasts 52 villas in a luxurious contemporary style, each featuring a private pool. Some units are in a compound away from the water. The food, from breakfast onwards, is superb.

★ Oberoi   HOTEL $$$
(Map p228; ☑0361-730361; www.oberoihotels.com; Jl Kayu Aya; r incl breakfast from 4,600,000Rp; ❋@🖥🌊) The beautifully understated Oberoi has been a refined Balinese-style beachside retreat since 1971. All accommodation options have private verandahs, and as you move up in price, additional features include walled villas, ocean views and private pools. From the cafe that overlooks the almost-private sweep of beach to the numerous luxuries, this is a place to spoil yourself.

Casa Artista   GUESTHOUSE $$$
(Map p228; ☑0361-736749; www.casaartistabali.com; Jl Sari Dewi 17; r incl breakfast US$175-195; ❋🖥🌊) You can literally dance for joy at this cultured guesthouse where the owner, a professional tango dancer, offers lessons. The 12 compact rooms, with names such as Passion and Inspiration, are in an elegant two-storey house surrounding a pool. Some have crystal chandeliers; breakfast is served on your patio.

Seminyak & Kerobokan

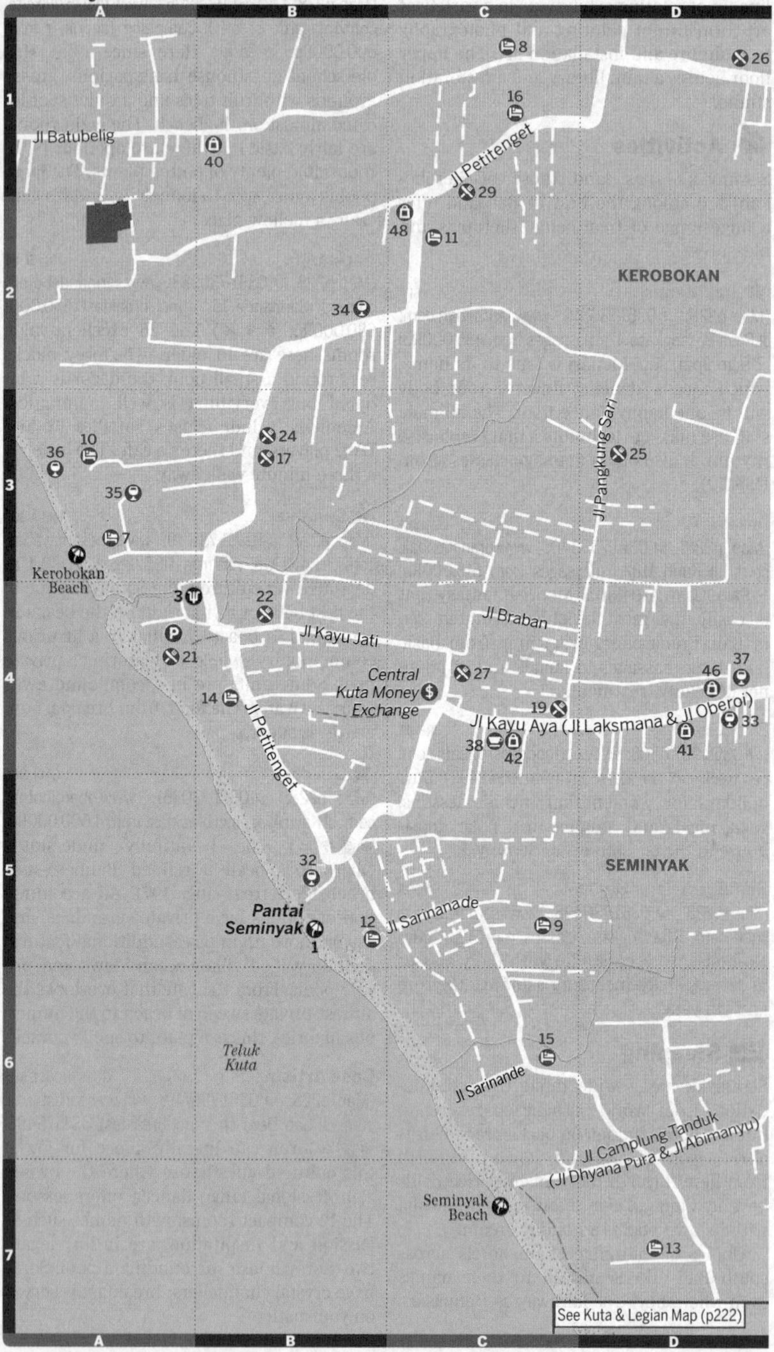

Jl Batubelig
40
8
16
26
Jl Petitenget
29
48
11
KEROBOKAN
34
10
36
24
17
Jl Pangkung Sari
25
35
7
Kerobokan Beach
3
22
Jl Braban
Jl Kayu Jati
P
21
Central Kuta Money Exchange
27
14
Jl Petitenget
19
46
37
Jl Kayu Aya (Jl Laksmana & Jl Oberoi)
38
42
41
33
32
SEMINYAK
Pantai Seminyak
1
12
Jl Sarinanade
9
15
Teluk Kuta
Jl Sarinande
Jl Camplung Tanduk (Jl Dhyana Pura & Jl Abimanyu)
Seminyak Beach
13
See Kuta & Legian Map (p222)

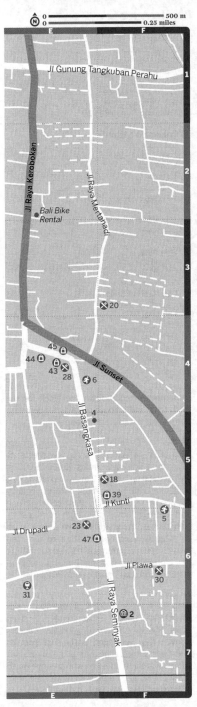

✗ Eating

Jl Kayu Aya is the focus of Seminyak eating (despite the hokey nickname 'Eat St') but there are great choices for every budget virtually everywhere. Note that some restaurants morph into clubs as the night wears on. Conversely, some bars and clubs also have good food. Meanwhile, you're never far from top-notch coffee as Seminyak has a thriving cafe culture.

Warung Ibu Made INDONESIAN $

(Map p228; Jl Basangkasa; mains from 15,000Rp; ⏱7am-7pm) The woks roar almost from dawn to dusk amid the constant hubbub on this busy corner of Jl Raya Seminyak, where several stalls cook food fresh under the shade of a huge banyan. Refresh yourself with the juice of a young coconut.

Café Moka CAFE $

(Map p228; ☎0361-731424; www.cafemokabali. com; Jl Basangkasa; treats 15,000-35,000Rp; ⏱7am-10pm; ❄) Enjoy French-style baked goods (fresh baguettes!) at this popular bakery and cafe. Many escape the heat and linger here for hours over little French treats. The bulletin board spills over with notices for villa rentals.

Warung Taman Bambu BALINESE $

(Map p228; ☎0361-888 1567; Jl Plawa 10; mains from 28,000Rp; ⏱10am-10pm; 🛜) This classic warung may look simple from the street but the comfy tables are – like the many fresh and spicy dishes on offer – a cut above the norm. There's a small stand for *babi guling* (spit-roast pig) right next door.

★ Sisterfields CAFE $$

(Map p228; ☎0361-738454; www.sisterfieldsbali. com; Jl Kayu Cendana 7; mains 85,000-140,000Rp; ⏱7am-10pm; 🛜) Trendy Sisterfields does classic Aussie breakfasts such as smashed avocado, and more-inventive dishes such as salmon Benedict and maple-roasted-pumpkin salad. There are also hipster faves such as pulled-pork rolls and shakshuka poached eggs. Grab a seat at a booth, the counter or in the rear courtyard. There are several other good places for coffee nearby.

Motel Mexicola MEXICAN $$

(Map p228; ☎0361-736688; www.motelmexicola bali.com; Jl Kayu Jati 9; mains from 60,000Rp; ⏱11am-1am) Not your average taqueria, Motel Mexicola is an extravaganza that channels a tropical version of a nightclub. The huge space is decked out in kitschy neon

Seminyak & Kerobokan

and palm trees. Food is secondary to drinks: soft corn tortilla tacos filled with tempura prawn or shredded pork, along with meaty mains. Cocktails, served in copper kettles, are a treat on a balmy evening.

★ **Ginger Moon**   ASIAN **$$**
(Map p228; ☑0361-734533; www.gingermoon bali.com; Jl Kayu Aya 7; mains 65,000-195,000Rp; ☺noon-11pm; 🛜🚼) Australian chef Dean Keddell presides over an appealing, airy space, with carved wood and palms. The Asian fusion menu features a 'Best of' list of favourites, served in portions designed for sharing and grazing. Top picks include cauliflower pizza and a special chicken curry. There's a good kids' menu.

Nalu Bowls   HEALTH FOOD **$$**
(Map p228; ☑0812 3660 9776; www.nalubowls.com; Jl Drupadi; 60,000-80,000Rp; ☺7.30am-6pm) Inspired by Hawaii's culture and tropical ingredients, this chain of acai bowl establishments has made a big splash in Bali. The flagship Seminyak restaurant occupies just a small bar downstairs from Shelter Cafe, but the line

sometimes extends down the block for the fresh fruit and smoothie bowls topped with homemade granola and bananas.

★ **Shelter Cafe**   AUSTRALIAN **$$**
(Map p228; ☑0813 3770 6471; www.sheltercafe bali.com; Jl Drupadi 1; mains 45,000-85,000Rp; ☺7.30am-6pm; 🛜) This second-storey, back-alley cafe brims daily with the beautiful people of Seminyak, their coffee strong and their acai bowls piled high (prepared by Nalu Bowls, the acai bar downstairs). With an extensive menu of healthy fare, it's a top brunch spot in Seminyak. It's also something of a cultural hub, hosting things like pop-up fashion stores and parties on weekends.

La Lucciola   FUSION **$$$**
(Map p228; ☑0361-730838; Jl Petitenget; mains 120,000-400,000Rp; ☺9am-11pm) A sleek beachside restaurant with good views across a lovely lawn and sand to the surf from its 2nd-floor tables. The bar is popular with sunset-watchers, most of whom move on to dinner here. The menu is a creative melange of international fare with Italian flair.

🍸 Drinking & Nightlife

Like your vision at 2am, the division between restaurant, bar and club blurs in Seminyak. Although it lacks massive clubs where you can greet the dawn (or vice versa), stalwarts can head south to the rough edges of Kuta and Legian in the wee hours.

Numerous bars line Jl Camplung Tanduk, though noise-sensitive locals complain if things get too raucous.

La Favela   BAR
(Map p228; ☑0812 4612 0010; www.lafavela.com; Jl Kayu Aya 177X; ⊘5pm-3am; 🛜) An alluring, mysterious entry seduces you into full bohemian flair at South Bali's most popular nightspot. Themed rooms lead you on a confounding tour from dimly lit speakeasy cocktail lounges and antique dining rooms to graffiti-splashed bars. Tables are cleared after 11pm to make way for DJs and a dance floor, which sees upwards of 8000 people partying on weekends. It's equally popular for its garden **restaurant**.

Red Carpet Champagne Bar   BAR
(Map p228; ☑0361-737889; www.redcarpetchampagnebar.com; Jl Kayu Aya 42; ⊘1pm-4am) Choose from more than 200 types of champagne at this over-the-top glam bar on Seminyak's couture strip. Waltz the red carpet and toss back a few namesake flutes while contemplating a raw oyster and displays of frilly frocks. It's open to the street (but elevated, darling) so you can gaze down on the masses.

★ Revolver   CAFE $$
(Map p228; ☑0851 0088 4968; www.revolverespresso.com; off Jl Kayu Aya; mains 55,000-140,000Rp; ⊘7am-midnight; ❄🛜) Wander down a tiny *gang* and push through narrow wooden doors to reach this matchbox coffee bar that does an excellent selection of brews. There are just a few tables in the creatively retro room that's styled like a Wild West saloon; nab one and enjoy tasty fresh and creative meals for breakfast and lunch.

Ku De Ta   CLUB
(Map p228; ☑0361-736969; www.kudeta.net; Jl Kayu Aya 9; ⊘8am-late; 🛜) Ku De Ta teems with Bali's beautiful people (including those whose status is purely aspirational). Scenesters perfect their 'bored' look over drinks during the day while gazing at the fine stretch of beach. Sunset brings out crowds, who dine on eclectic fare at tables. The music throbs with increasing intensity through the night. Special events are legendary.

La Plancha   BAR
(☑0878 6141 6310; www.laplancha-bali.com; off Jl Camplung Tanduk; ⊘9am-11pm) The most substantial of the many beach bars along the beach walk south of Jl Camplung Tanduk, La Plancha has its share of ubiquitous brightly coloured umbrellas and beanbags on the sand, plus a typical beach menu (pizzas, noodles etc). DJs and beach parties take over after sunset.

Bali Joe   GAY & LESBIAN
(Map p228; ☑0361-300 3499; www.balijoebar.com; Jl Camplung Tanduk 8; ⊘8pm-3am; 🛜) One of several lively LGBTIQ venues along this strip. Drag queens and go-go dancers rock the house nightly.

🛍 Shopping

Seminyak has it all: designer boutiques (Bali has a thriving fashion industry), retro-chic stores, slick galleries, wholesale emporiums and family-run workshops.

The best shopping starts on Jl Raya Seminyak at Bintang Supermarket and runs north through Jl Basangkasa. The retail strip branches off into Jl Kayu Aya and Jl Kayu Jati while continuing north on Jl Raya Kerobokan into Kerobokan.

★ Ashitaba   ARTS & CRAFTS
(Map p228; ☑0361-737054; Jl Raya Seminyak 6; ⊘9am-9pm) Tenganan, the Aga village of east Bali, produces the intricate and beautiful rattan items sold here. Containers, bowls, purses and more (from 50,000Rp) display the very fine weaving.

Thaikila   CLOTHING
(Map p228; ☑0361-731130; www.thaikila.com; Jl Kayu Aya; ⊘9am-9pm) 'The dream bikini of all women' is the motto of this local brand that makes a big statement with its tiny wear. The swimwear is French-designed and made right in Bali. If you need something stylish for the beach, come here.

★ Drifter Surf Shop   FASHION & ACCESSORIES
(Map p228; ☑0361-733274; www.driftersurf.com; Jl Kayu Aya 50; ⊘9am-11pm) High-end surf fashion, surfboards, gear, cool books and brands such as Obey and Wegener. Started by two savvy surfer dudes, the shop stocks goods noted for their individuality and high quality.

Souq   HOMEWARES
(Map p228; ☑0822 3780 1817; www.souqstore.co; Jl Basangkasa 10; ⊘8am-8pm) The Middle East meets Asia at this glossy high-concept store

BALI SEMINYAK

with Bali-designed housewares and clothing. It has a small cafe with healthy breakfast and lunch choices, plus good coffee and cold-pressed juices. It carries the 'Madame Camille' line of beautiful fashion accessories from Canggu's It Was All A Dream.

★ Bamboo Blonde
CLOTHING

(Map p228; ☑0361-731864; www.bambooblonde. com; Jl Kayu Aya 61; ☺10am-10pm) Shop for frilly, sporty or sexy frocks and formal wear at this cheery designer boutique (one of 11 island-wide). All goods are designed and made in Bali.

★ Theatre Art Gallery
ARTS & CRAFTS

(Map p228; ☑0361-732782; Jl Raya Seminyak; ☺9am-8pm) Specialises in vintage and reproduction *wayang* puppets used in traditional Balinese theatre. Just looking at the animated faces peering back at you is a delight.

Lucy's Batik
TEXTILES, CLOTHING

(Map p228; ☑0361-736098; www.lucysbatikbali. com; Jl Basangkasa 88; ☺9.30am-9pm) Great for both men and women, Lucy's is a good spot to shop for the finest batik. Shirts, dresses, sarongs and bags are mostly handwoven or hand-painted. It also sells fabric.

Sandio
SHOES

(Map p228; ☑0361-737693; www.facebook.com/ sandio.bali; Jl Basangkasa; ☺10am-8pm) Shoes and sandals at great prices. Replace the one you lost riding your scooter.

❶ Information

DANGERS & ANNOYANCES

Seminyak is generally more hassle-free than Kuta and Legian. But it's worth reading up on the warnings, especially on surf and water pollution.

MONEY

ATMs can be found along all the main roads.
Central Kuta Money Exchange (Map p228; www.centralkutabali.com; Jl Kaayu Aya, Seminyak Sq; ☺8.30am-9.30pm) Reliable currency exchange.

❶ Getting There & Away

The Kura-Kura tourist bus (p216) has a route linking Seminyak with Umalas in the north and Kuta in the south, however it runs infrequently.

Metered taxis are easily hailed. A trip from the airport with the airport taxi cartel costs about 250,000Rp; a regular taxi to the airport costs about 150,000Rp. You can beat the traffic, save the ozone and have a good stroll by walking along the beach; Legian is about 15 minutes away.

Kerobokan

☑0361 / POP 13,815

Continuing seamlessly north from Seminyak, Kerobokan combines some of Bali's best restaurants and shopping, lavish lifestyles and still more beach. Glossy new resorts mix with villa developments.

🛏 Sleeping

Bali's blight of generic midrange chain hotels has also infected Kerobokan. Otherwise you'll find good-value choices amid sybaritic villa hotels, plus some excellent beach resorts.

M Boutique Hostel
HOSTEL $

(Map p228; ☑0361-473 4142; www.mboutique hostel.com; Jl Petitenget 8; dm from 125,000Rp; ❄@🛜🏊) A contemporary choice for flashpackers, M Boutique's beds are capsule dorms, which come with the benefit of privacy. Each has shutter blinds, a drop-down table, a reading light and an electrical plug. The lawn and small plunge pool add charm.

Villa Bunga
HOTEL $$

(Map p228; ☑0361-473 1666; www.villabunga.com; Jl Petitenget 18X; r 500,000-550,000Rp, apt from 600,000Rp; ❄🛜🏊) An excellent deal in the heart of Kerobokan, this hotel has 13 rooms set in two-storey blocks around a small pool. Rooms are small but modern and have fridges.

Brown Feather
GUESTHOUSE $$

(Map p228; ☑0361-473 2165; www.brownfeather. com; Jl Batu Belig 100; r 500,000-800,000Rp; ❄🛜🏊) On the main road, but backing onto rice paddies, this small hotel exudes a Dutch-Javanese colonial charm. Rooms mix simplicity with old-world character, such as wooden writing desks and washbasins made from old Singer sewing machines. For rice-field views, go for room 205 or 206. There's a small pool and free bicycle rental, too.

Grand Balisani Suites
HOTEL $$

(☑0361-473 0550; www.balisanisuites.com; Jl Batu Belig; r US$85-220; ❄🛜🏊) Location! This elaborately carved complex is right on popular Batu Belig Beach. The 96 rooms are large and have standard teak furniture plus terraces (some also have great views). Wi-fi is limited to public areas.

★ Katamama
BOUTIQUE HOTEL $$$

(Map p228; ☑0361-302 9999; www.katamama. com; Jl Petitenget 51; r from 3,500,000Rp; ❄🛜🏊) The same architectural derring-do that makes Potato Head much copied is on display at the club's hotel. However here the details are lavish and artful. Designed by Indonesian Andra Matin, it has 57 suites in a confection of Javanese bricks, Balinese stone and other indigenous materials. There are huge windows, lavish seating areas and private terraces and balconies.

★**Alila Seminyak** RESORT $$$
(Map p228; ☑0361-302 1888; www.alilahotels. com; Jl Taman Ganesha 9; r from 3,100,000Rp; ❄🛜🏊) This sprawling resort has a prime position right at the junction of Seminyak and Kerobokan beaches (and nightlife). The 240 rooms come in various flavours. The cheapest have garden views, but as you rise up through the rate card you get beach views and more space. The colour scheme is a sandy palette of beige and tan.

🍴 Eating

Kerobokan boasts some of Bali's best restaurants, whether budget or top end.

★**Warung Sulawesi** INDONESIAN $
(Map p228; ☑0821 4756 2779; Jl Petitenget 57B; mains from 35,000Rp; ⊙10am-8pm) Find a table in this quiet family compound and enjoy fresh Balinese and Indonesian food served in classic warung style. Choose a rice, then pick from a captivating array of dishes that are always at their peak at noon. The long beans are yum!

Warung Sobat SEAFOOD $
(☑0361-731256; Jl Pengubengan Kauh 27; mains 37,000-100,000Rp; ⊙11am-10.30pm; 🛜) Set in a bungalow-style large open-sided brick space, this old-fashioned restaurant excels at fresh Balinese seafood with an Italian accent (lots of garlic!). Prices are extraordinary, as you can see from the value-minded expats who pack the place every night.

Gusto Gelato & Coffee GELATO $
(Map p228; ☑0361-552 2190; www.gusto-gelateria.com; Jl Raya Mertanadi 46; gelato from 25,000Rp; ⊙10am-10pm; ❄🛜) Bali's best gelato is made fresh throughout the day, with unique flavours such as rich Oreo, surprising and delicious tamarind and *kamangi* (lemon basil). The classics are here as well.

Biku FUSION $
(Map p228; ☑0361-857 0888; www.bikubali. com; Jl Petitenget 888; mains 40,000-95,000Rp; ⊙8am-11pm; 🛜🚼) Housed in a 150-year-old teak *joglo* (traditional Javanese house), wild-

ly popular Biku retains the timeless vibe of its predecessor. The menu combines Indonesian and other Asian with Western influences in a cuisine Biku calls 'tropical comfort food'. The burgers get rave reviews as do the desserts. Be sure to book ahead. There's a good kids' menu.

It's also popular for high tea (11am to 5pm; 110,000Rp per person). It can be served Asian-style – with samosa, spring rolls etc, and green or oolong tea – or traditional – with cucumber sandwiches etc.

★**Sangsaka** INDONESIAN $$
(Map p228; ☑0812 3695 9895; www.sangsaka bali.com; Jl Pangkung Sari 100; mains 80,000-180,000Rp; ⊙6pm-midnight Tue-Sun) On a Kerobokan backstreet, this casual restaurant serves well-nuanced versions of Indonesian dishes drawn from across the archipelago. Many are cooked over various types of charcoal, which vary depending on the origin of the dish. The dining area is done up in the usual vintage-wood motif, with just a touch more polish than usual. It has a good bar.

★**Saigon Street** VIETNAMESE $$
(Map p228; ☑0361-897 4007; www.saigonstreet bali.com; Jl Petitenget 77; mains 50,000-175,000Rp; ⊙11am-1am; 🛜) Modern, vibrant and packed, this Vietnamese restaurant lures in the buzzing masses with its swanky neon decor. Creative Vietnamese dishes include peppery betel leaves filled with slow-cooked octopus, and there's an impressive rice-paper roll selection, along with curries, *pho* (rice-noodle soup) and grilled meats cooked on aromatic coconut wood. Cocktails include the 'bang bang' martini, a chilled bit of boozy splendour. Book ahead.

★**Sardine** SEAFOOD $$
(Map p228; ☑0811 397 8111; www.sardinebali. com; Jl Petitenget 21; mains 160,000-350,000Rp; ⊙11.30am-4pm & 6-11pm; 🛜) Seafood fresh from the famous Jimbaran market is the star at this elegant yet intimate, casual yet stylish restaurant. It's in a beautiful bamboo pavilion, with open-air tables overlooking a private rice field. The inventive bar is a must and stays open until 1am. The menu changes to reflect what's fresh. Booking is vital.

🍺 Drinking & Nightlife

Some of Kerobokan's trendier restaurants have stylish bar areas that stay open late, while the beach club Mrs Sippy (p234) is the daytime drinking hotspot.

Potato Head
CLUB

(Map p228; ☑ 0361-473 7979; www.ptthead.com; Jl Petitenget 51; ⊙10am-2am; 🐾) Bali's highest-profile beach club is one of the best. Wander up off the sand or follow a long drive off Jl Petitenget and you'll find much to amuse, from an enticing pool to restaurants like the swanky Kaum and zero-waste Ijen, plus a pizza garden, lots of lounges and patches of lawn for chillin' the night away under the stars.

★ Mrs Sippy
CLUB

(Map p228; ☑ 0361-335 1079; www.mrssippybali. com; Jl Taman Ganesha; cover 100,000Rp; ⊙10am-9pm) This Mediterranean-style beach club pretty much has it all – booze, international DJs, a saltwater swimming pool and three levels of diving platforms. It's not currently a late-night spot, but it offers the best daytime and early-evening parties in south Bali.

Mirror
CLUB

(Map p228; ☑ 0811 399 3010; www.mirror.id; Jl Petitenget 106; ⊙11pm-4am Wed-Sat) This club is big with south Bali expats, who may own those designer shops you were in a few hours before. The interior is sort of like a cathedral out of *Harry Potter*, albeit with an unholy amount of lighting effects. Mainstream electronica blares forth.

Warung Pantai
BAR

(Batu Belig Beach; ⊙8am-9pm) A bunch of drinking shacks line this inviting stretch of beach just north of the W Bali hotel including Pantai, which offers up cheap drinks, mismatched tables, splendid surf and sunset views, and loungers on the sand.

🛍 Shopping

You'll find boutiques interspersed with trendy restaurants on Jl Petitenget. Jl Raya Kerobokan, extending north from Jl Sunset, has interesting shops primarily selling decorator items and housewares. Wander Jl Raya Mertanadi for an ever-changing lineup of homewares shops, many of them more factory than showroom.

★ Victory Art
HOMEWARES

(☑ 0812 3681 67877; Jl Gunung Tangkuban Perahu; ⊙8am-5pm) As much spectacle as store, this corner place is jammed with intriguing works of new art. All manner of primitive faces gaze out from the array of merchandise that's inspired by indigenous cultures from across Indonesia.

Tulola
JEWELLERY

(Map p228; ☑ 0361-473 0261; www.shoptulola. com; Jl Petitenget; ⊙11am-7pm) This is the jewellery shop of noted Balinese-American designer Sri Luce Rusna. High-end items are created in Bali and displayed in this exquisite boutique.

My Basket Bali
HOMEWARES

(☑ 0361-994 3683; https://my-basket-bali. business.site; Jl Gunung Athena 39B; ⊙10am-5pm Mon-Fri) If it can be woven from fibre, it's at My Basket Bali. Baskets here look as good as they are practical.

Ayun Tailor
CLOTHING

(Map p228; ☑ 0821 8996 5056; Jl Batu Belig; ⊙10am-6pm) Ayun is an excellent tailor. Buy batik or other fabric at one of Bali's many textile emporiums and she'll turn it into an outfit for a man, woman or child.

ℹ Getting There & Away

Although the beach may seem tantalisingly close, few roads or *gang* actually reach the sand from the east. Note also that Jl Raya Kerobokan can come to a fume-filled stop for extended periods.

ℹ Getting Around

Bali Bike Rental (Map p228; ☑ 0855 7467 9030; www.balibikerental.com; Jl Raya Kerobokan 71; rental per day from US$10; ⊙8am-7pm) An alternative to the thousands of freelance motorbike renters in Bali. For the extra money, you get a motorbike in prime shape along with extras such as clean helmets, roadside assistance and more. Faster, more powerful motorcycles are also available.

CANGGU REGION

☑ 0361

The Canggu region, north and west of Kerobokan, is Bali's fastest-growing area. Much of the growth is centred along the coast, anchored by the endless swathe of beach, which, despite rampant development, remains fairly uncrowded. Kerobokan morphs into Umalas inland and Canggu to the west, while neighbouring Echo Beach is a big construction site.

Cloistered villas lure expats who whisk past the remaining rice farmers on motorbikes or in air-con comfort. Amid this maze of too-narrow lanes you'll find creative cafes, trendy restaurants and appealing shops. Follow the sounds of the surf to great beaches such as the one at Batu Bolong.

Canggu

📞 0361 / POP 7090

More a state of mind than a place, Canggu is the catch-all name given to the wildly popular stretch of land between Kerobokan and Pantai Batu Mejan. It's packed with an ever-changing and alluring collection of businesses, especially casual cafes. Four main strips have emerged, all running down to the beaches: two along meandering Jl Pantai Berawa as well as Jl Pantai Batu Bolong and Jl Pantai Batu Mejan.

◎ Sights

The beaches of the Canggu area continue the sweep of sand that starts in Kuta. Their personalities vary from hip hang-out to sparsely populated – the latter can often be found a mere 10-minute amble away from the crowded areas.

Very popular for surfing, the beaches draw a lot of locals and expat residents on weekends. Access to parking areas usually costs 5000Rp and there are cafes and warungs for those who work up an appetite in the water or watching others in the water.

★ Pantai Batu Bolong   BEACH

(parking motorbike/car 2000/5000Rp) The beach at Batu Bolong is the most popular in the Canggu area. There's almost always a good mix of locals, expats and visitors hanging out in the cafes, surfing the breaks or watching it all from the sand. There are rental loungers, umbrellas and beer vendors.

You can also rent surfboards (100,000Rp per day) and take lessons. Overlooking it all is the centuries-old Pura Batu Mejan complex.

Pantai Berawa   BEACH

(parking motorbike/car 2000/5000Rp) Greyish Berawa Beach ('Brawa Beach' on many signs) has a plethora of trendy and popular beach cafes and bars. The grey volcanic sand here slopes steeply into foaming water. Overlooking it all behind Finn's Beach Club is the vast estate of fashionista Paul Ropp.

Pantai Perancak   BEACH

A couple of drinks vendors and a large parking area are the major amenities at this beach, which is rarely crowded. The large temple is Pura Dalem Perancak. Thronged Pantai Berawa is an enjoyable 500m walk along the wave-tossed sands.

🛏 Sleeping

Canggu has all types of places to stay. Guesthouses self-billed as 'surf camps' have proliferated. For longer-term lodging, besides searching online, check the bulletin board at **Warung Varuna** (📞 0818 0551 8790; www. facebook.com/warungvaruna; Jl Pantai Batu Bolong 89A; mains 20,000-40,000Rp; ⊙ 8am-10.30pm).

Serenity Eco Guesthouse   GUESTHOUSE $

(📞 0361-846 9251; www.serenityecoguesthouse. com; Jl Nelayan; dm/r from 160,000/400,000Rp; ❋ 🛜 ☲) 🏄 This hotel is an oasis among the sterility of walled villas, run by inexperienced and lovable staff. Rooms range from singles with shared bathrooms to nice doubles with bathrooms (some fan-only). The grounds are eccentric; Pantai Nelayan is a five-minute walk. There are yoga classes (from 120,000Rp) and you can rent surfboards and bikes. This place makes an effort to minimise its carbon footprint.

Big Brother Surf Inn   GUESTHOUSE $

(📞 0812 3838 0385; www.big-brother-surf-inn-canggu.bali-tophotels.com/en; Jl Pantai Berawa 20; r US$40; ❋ 🛜 ☲) This sleek take on a traditional Balinese guesthouse has clean lines and plenty of minimalist white. The six rooms are airy and have outdoor sitting areas overlooking a garden with barbecue facilities and a pool. It's in a quiet location back off the road; despite the name, your high jinks are unlikely to end up on a reality TV show.

Widi Homestay   HOMESTAY $

(📞 0819 3626 0860; widihomestay@yahoo.co.id; Jl Pantai Berawa; r from 250,000Rp; ❋ 🛜) There's no faux-hipster vibe here with fake nihilist bromides, just a spotless, friendly, family-run homestay. The four rooms have hot water and air-con; the beach is barely 100m away.

Canggu Surf Hostel   HOSTEL $

(📞 0813 5303 1293; www.canggusurfhostels. com; Jl Raya Semat; dm 100,000-160,000Rp; r 400,000Rp; ❋ 🛜 ☲) This well-equipped hostel has a split personality: two locations, with the other just around the corner on Jl Pantai Berawa. There are eight-, six- and four-bed rooms plus private rooms. Enjoy multiple public spaces, pools, kitchens and lockable surfboard storage.

★ Sedasa   BOUTIQUE HOTEL $$

(📞 0361-844 6655; www.sedasa.com; Jl Pantai Berawa; r incl breakfast 700,000-890,000Rp; ❋ 🛜 ☲) Both intimate and stylish, Sedasa has an understated Balinese elegance. The

BALI CANGGU

Canggu

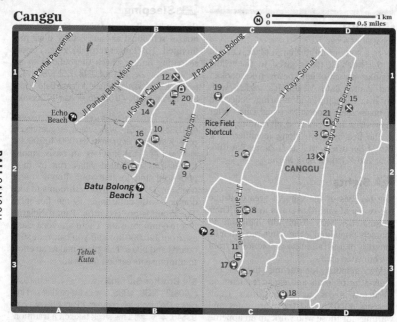

Canggu

◎ Top Sights
1 Batu Bolong Beach B2

◎ Sights
Berawa Beach .... (see 7)
2 Prancak Beach C3

▣ Sleeping
3 Big Brother Surf Inn D2
4 Calmtree Bungalows B1
5 Canggu Surf Hostel C2
6 Hotel Tugu Bali B2
7 Legong Keraton C3
8 Sedasa C2
9 Serenity Eco Guesthouse B2
10 Slow B2
11 Widi Homestay C3

✕ Eating
Betelnut Cafe .... (see 4)
12 Deus Ex Machina B1
13 Green Ginger D2
14 Mocca B1
15 Warung Goûthé D1
16 Warung Varuna B2

◉ Drinking & Nightlife
17 Finns Beach Club C3
18 La Laguna C3
19 Pretty Poison C1

◉ Shopping
20 Dylan Board Store B1
21 It Was All a Dream D1
Love Anchor .... (see 20)

---

10 large rooms overlook a small pool and have designer furniture. The beanbags on the rooftop make a good place to relax with a book. Downstairs there's an organic cafe. It's a five-minute walk to the beach, and there's free bike rental and a shuttle into Seminyak.

Calmtree Bungalows GUESTHOUSE **$$**
(☎0851 0074 7009; www.thecalmtreebungalows. com; Jl Pantai Batu Bolong; r from 640,000Rp; ⌘⌘) Right in the middle of the heart of Batu Bolong, this family-run compound

has 10 traditional-style units around a pool. Inside the thatched walls you'll find rustic style fused with a touch of modern. The bathrooms are open-air. There's no air-con but there are nets and fans – think of it as atmospheric. Great staff.

Legong Keraton HOTEL **$$**
(☎0361-473 0280; www.legongkeratonhotel.com; Jl Pantai Berawa; r 820,000-1,400,000Rp; ⌘@⌘⌘) The Canggu boom has caught up with this well-run 40-room beachfront resort. The grounds are shaded by palms and the pool

borders the beach. The best rooms are in bungalow units facing the surf. Long isolated, the hotel is now in the centre of the action.

★ Hotel Tugu Bali
HOTEL $$$

(📞0361-473 1701; www.tuguhotels.com; Jl Pantai Batu Bolong; r incl breakfast from US$400; ❇@🅿🛜🏊) Right at Batu Bolong Beach, this exquisite hotel blurs the boundaries between accommodation and a museum-gallery, especially the Walter Spies and Le Mayeur Pavilions, where memorabilia from the artists' lives decorates the rooms. There's a spa and a high-style beachfront bar, Ji. The stunning collection of antiques and artwork begins in the lobby and extends throughout the hotel.

Slow
BOUTIQUE HOTEL $$$

(📞0361-209 9000; http://theslow.id; Jl Pantai Batu 97; r from 2,400,000Rp; ❇🛜🏊) Raising the design bar in Canggu with its 'tropical brutalism' style, the Slow's aesthetic is defined by elegant spaces with clean lines, natural colour schemes, abundant hanging foliage and the owner's edgy personal art collection. Rooms are expansive, with every modern comfort.

✖ Eating

Canggu is where you'll find some of Bali's most innovative and affordable places to eat. Look along the main strips, as new cafes and restaurants seem to open daily.

Betelnut Cafe
CAFE $

(📞0821 4680 7233; Jl Pantai Batu Bolong 60; mains 45,000-60,000Rp; ❷8am-10pm; ❇🛜🎵) There's a hippy-chic vibe at this thatched cafe with a mellow open-air dining room upstairs. The menu leans towards healthy, including juices and lots of mains featuring veggies, but not too healthy – you can also get burgers and fries. It has tasty baked goods and nice shakes.

Green Ginger
ASIAN $

(📞0878 6211 2729; www.elephantbali.com/green-ginger; Jl Pantai Berawa; meals from 55,000Rp; ❷8am-9pm; 🛜🎵) An attractive little restaurant on the fast-changing strip in Canggu, Green Ginger specialises in fresh and tasty vegetarian and noodle dishes from across Asia.

★ Warung Goûthé
BISTRO $$

(📞0878 8947 0638; www.facebook.com/warung gouthe; Jl Pantai Berawa 7A; mains from 60,000Rp; ❷9am-5pm Mon-Sat) Superbly prepared and presented casual meals are the hallmark of

this open-front cafe. The very short menu changes each day depending on what's fresh. The French owners can take a simple chicken sandwich and elevate it to magnificent and memorable. The desserts alone should cause you to stop in whenever you are nearby.

★ Mocca
CAFE $$

(📞0361-907 4512; www.facebook.com/themocca; Gg Nyepi; mains 60,000-90,000Rp; ❷7am-10pm) Tucked away from the bustle of Jl Batu Bolong, this Canggu gem is equal parts charming cafe and boho concept store. Between the downstairs garden and upstairs open-air patio, both decked in potted palms and reclaimed wood furnishings, there isn't a bad seat in the house. Stellar service and a broad, multi-cuisine menu make it easy to linger for hours.

★ Deus Ex Machina
CAFE $$

(Temple of Enthusiasm; 📞0811 388 150; www.deuscustoms.com; Jl Batu Mejan 8; mains 60,000-170,000Rp; ❷7am-11pm; 🛜) This surreal venue amid Canggu's rice fields has many personas. If you're hungry, it's a restaurant-cafe-bar; for shoppers, it's a fashion label; if you're into culture, it's a contemporary-art gallery; for music lovers, it's a live-gig venue (Sunday afternoons) for local punk bands; for bikers, it's a custom-made motorcycle shop; if you want your beard trimmed, it's a barber...

🍷 Drinking & Nightlife

Grab a beer from a vendor on the beach or hit one of the beach clubs or eating venues nearby. The party doesn't go late yet; you'll still need to head south for that.

★ La Laguna
COCKTAIL BAR

(📞0812 3638 2272; www.lalagunabali.com; Jl Pantai Kayu Putih; ❷9am-midnight; 🛜) A sibling of Seminyak's La Favela (p231), La Laguna is one of Bali's most alluring bars. It combines a beatnik look with Moorish trappings and sparkling tiny lights. Explore the eclectic layout, and sit on a couch, sofa bed, a table inside or a picnic table in the garden. The drinks are good and the food is delicious (mains from 80,000Rp).

To arrive in style, walk along the beach and then take the footbridge right over the lagoon.

Pretty Poison
BAR

(📞0812 4622 9340; www.prettypoisonbar.com; Jl Subak Canggu; ❷4pm-midnight) Pretty Poison's

---

DON'T MISS

CANGGU BEACH WALK

You can usually walk the 4km of sand between Batu Belig Beach and Echo Beach in about one to two hours. It's a fascinating stroll and you'll see temples, tiny fishing encampments, crashing surf, lots of surfers, cool cafes and out-crops of upscale beach culture. The only catch is that after heavy rains some of the rivers may be too deep to cross, especially the one just northwest of Batu Belig. In any case, put your gear in waterproof bags in case you have to do some fording.

It's easy to find taxis at any of the larger beaches if you don't want to re-trace your steps.

---

bar overlooks an old-school '80s skate bowl, so a surfboard isn't the only board you to need to pack. Run by longtime Aussie expat and surfer Maree Suteja, it's a great place to hang out, with cheap beers and bands. Being Canggu, there's logo wear for sale. It's close to the chaotic comedy of the rice-field shortcut.

Finns Beach Club CLUB
(☑0361-844 6327; www.finnsbeachclub.com; Jl Pantai Berawa; ☺9am-11pm; 🕏) An enormous spectacle built from soaring bamboo, Finns overwhelms its beachfront. There are four huge pools, a vast 'VIP' area and a driving sound system. Hipster types fill seating areas and groups eyeing potential hook-ups cruise the scene. Day loungers require a pricey minimum spend of 500,000Rp; the price includes a towel. Pricey drinks flow; food spans the casual gamut.

🔒 Shopping

★**Love Anchor** MARKET
(☑0822 3660 4648; www.loveanchorcanggu.com; Jl Pantai Batu Bolong 56; ☺8am-midnight Mon-Fri, bazaar 9am-5pm Sat & Sun) Built in a traditional *joglo* style, this wood- and palm-tree-laden Canggu village is the trifecta of hipster retail, food and shopping. You can kick back with a Bintang or fuel up on everything from pizzas and burgers to smoothies and vegan-friendly fare before browsing boutiques and surf shops.

It Was All A Dream FASHION & ACCESSORIES
(☑0811 388 3322; Jl Pantai Berawa 14B; ☺10am-7pm) Great-quality leather bags, fun sunglasses, vintage jeans, jersey basics, embroidered kaftans and more. This hip boutique has original pieces at reasonable prices. It's run by a French-American pair of expat designers.

Dylan Board Store SPORTS & OUTDOORS
(☑0819 9982 5654; www.dylansurfboards.com; Jl Pantai Batu Bolong; ☺10am-8pm) Famed big-wave rider Dylan Longbottom runs this custom surfboard shop. A talented shaper, he creates boards for novices and pros alike. He also stocks plenty of his own designs that are ready to go.

ℹ Information

To stay current with the constant flurry of new openings, check out www.cangguguide.com.

MONEY

ATMs, basic shops and markets can be found on Canggu's main strip, Jl Pantai Berawa.

ℹ Getting There & Away

The airport taxi cartel charges 250,000Rp for a taxi.

You can reach the Canggu area by road from the south by taking Jl Batu Belig west in Kerobokan almost to the beach and then veering north past various huge villas and expat shops along a curved road. It's much longer to go up and around via the traffic-clogged Jl Raya Kerobokan.

Getting to the Canggu area can cost 150,000Rp or more by taxi from Kuta or Seminyak. Don't expect to find taxis cruising anywhere, although any business can call you one.

ℹ Getting Around

Bad, narrow and clogged roads will keep you stuck in traffic often during daylight. When possible, walk on the beach as a shortcut.

This is good motorbike country – many of the impromptu roads are barely wide enough for one car, let alone two. The narrow road called the 'rice-field shortcut' is a perfect example of the complete lack of adequate road planning and construction in the Canggu area. There are websites devoted to photos of vehicles that have plunged into the rice after they tried to treat it as a two-lane road.

Note that street names are ad hoc: 'Jl Pantai Berawa' comprises a tangle of seemingly separate roads.

SOUTH BALI & THE ISLANDS

You won't have seen Bali if you haven't fully explored south Bali. The island's capital, Denpasar, sprawls in all directions from the centre with traditional markets, busy malls, great eating and lashings of Balinese history and culture, even as it threatens to absorb Seminyak, Kuta and Sanur.

The Bukit Peninsula (the southern part of south Bali) has multiple personalities. In the east, Tanjung Benoa is a beach-fronted playground of package resorts while Nusa Dua attempts to bring order out of chaos with an insulated pasture of five-star hotels. The south coast sees posh cliff-side resorts, but the west side is where the real action is. Small coves and beaches dotted with edgy guesthouses and luxe eco-resorts enjoy a cool vibe and fab surfing.

To the east, Nusa Penida dominates the horizon, but in its lee you'll find Nusa Lembongan, the ultimate island escape from the island of Bali.

❶ Getting There & Away

In most of south Bali, you're never far from the airport. Other access depends on the often-jammed roads, although the toll road offers a quick trip between Sanur and Nusa Dua. Fast boats serve Nusa Lembongan and the islands.

Bukit Peninsula

✔ 0361

Hot and arid, the southern peninsula is known as Bukit (meaning 'hill' in Bahasa Indonesia). It's popular with visitors, from the cloistered climes of Nusa Dua to the sybaritic retreats along the south coast.

The booming west coast (often generically called Pecatu) with its string-of-pearls beaches is a real hotspot. Accommodation sits precariously on the sand at Balangan Beach, while the cliffs are dotted with idiosyncratic lodges at Bingin and elsewhere. New places sprout daily and most have views of the turbulent waters here, which have world-famous surf breaks all the way south to the important temple of Ulu Watu.

The south coast to the east and west of Ungasan is the site of some huge cliff-side resorts, with serene views of the limitless ocean, while Nusa Dua and Tanjung Benoa cater to more traditional package-holiday-makers seeking a homogenised experience.

❶ Getting There & Away

You'll need your own wheels – whether taxi, hire car or motorbike – to explore the Bukit. A one-way trip to the beaches along the west coast of the peninsula from Seminyak will take an hour driving, depending on traffic. The cost of a shared ride or taxi will cost from 150,000Rp. Expect to pay upwards of 5000Rp per vehicle to use the beach-access parking areas.

Jimbaran

✔ 0361 / POP 44,376

Teluk Jimbaran (Jimbaran Bay) is an appealing crescent of white-sand beach and blue sea fronted by a long string of seafood warungs (food stalls) and ending at the southern end in a bushy headland, home to the Four Seasons Jimbaran Bay. Despite increased popularity, Jimbaran remains a relaxed alternative to Kuta and Seminyak to the north (and as it's just south of the airport, you can't beat the access). Its markets offer a fascinating glimpse into local life.

◉ Sights

★ Jimbaran Beach
BEACH

One of Bali's best beaches, Jimbaran's 4km-long arc of sand is mostly clean and there is no shortage of places to get a snack, drink or seafood dinner, or to rent a sun lounge. The bay is protected by an unbroken coral reef, which keeps the surf more mellow than at popular Kuta further north, although you can still get breaks that are fun for bodysurfing.

★ Jimbaran Fish Market
MARKET

(Jimbaran Beach; ⊙ 6am-5pm) A popular morning stop on a Bukit peninsula amble, this fish market is smelly, lively and frenetic – watch where you step. Brightly painted boats bob along the shore while huge cases of everything from small sardines to fearsome langoustines are hawked. The action is fast and furious. Buy your seafood here and have one of the warungs cook it up or, for an even better price, buy direct from the boats between 6am and 7am.

❷ Drinking & Nightlife

Nightlife entirely revolves around the seafood restaurants. They tend to close by 10pm, so after that head north to the bright lights of Kuta and beyond.

Rock Bar
BAR

(✆ 0361-702222; www.ayanaresort.com/rockbar bali; Jl Karang Mas Sejahtera, Ayana Resort;

BALI BUKIT PENINSULA

DON'T MISS

JIMBARAN SEAFOOD RESTAURANTS

Jimbaran's seafood restaurants cook fresh, barbecued seafood every evening (most serve lunch as well), drawing tourists from across the south. The open-sided affairs are right by the beach and perfect for enjoying sea breezes and sunsets. Tables and chairs are set up on the sand almost to the water's edge. Arrive before sunset so you can get a good table and enjoy the show over a couple of beers before you dine.

Fixed prices for seafood platters in a plethora of varieties have become common and allow you to avoid the sport of choosing your fish and then paying for it by weight on scales that cause locals to break out in laughter. However, should you go this route, be sure to agree on costs first. Generally, you can enjoy a seafood feast, sides and a couple of beers for less than US$20 per person. Lobster (from US$30) will bump that figure up considerably, but you can keep the price low by purchasing your own lobster beforehand at the seafood market.

The best kitchens marinate the fish in garlic and lime, then douse it with chilli and oil while grilling it over coconut husks. Thick clouds of smoke from the coals are part of the atmosphere, as are roaming bands, who perform cheery cover tunes (think the *Macarena*). Almost all take credit cards.

Expect mixed seafood grills to cost 90,000Rp to 350,000Rp.

⊙ 4pm-midnight, to 1am Fri & Sat; 🐦) Star of a thousand glossy articles written about Bali, this bar perched 14m above the crashing Indian Ocean is very popular. In fact, at sunset the wait to ride the lift down to the bar can top one hour. There's a no-backpacks, no-singlets dress code. The food is Med-flavoured bar snacks.

❶ Getting There & Away

Plenty of taxis wait around the beachfront warungs in the evening to take diners home (about 150,000Rp to Seminyak in no traffic). Some of the seafood warungs provide free transport if you call first. Ask for a flat fee on your transport if you travel during high traffic times, from 4pm to 8pm. Sundays are remarkably traffic-free.

The Kura-Kura tourist bus (p216) has a route linking Jimbaran with its Kuta hub. Buses run every two hours and cost 50,000Rp.

Bingin

📞 0361

An ever-evolving scene, Bingin comprises scores of unconventionally stylish lodgings scattered across cliffs and on the strip of white-sand that is Bingin Beach below. Smooth Jl Pantai Bingin runs 1km off Jl Melasti (look for the thicket of accommodation signs) and then branches off into a tangle of lanes.

The scenery here is simply superb, with sylvan cliffs dropping down to surfer cafes and the foaming edge of the azure sea. The beach is a five-minute walk down fairly steep paths. The surf here is often savage but the boulder-strewn sands are serene and the roaring breakers mesmerising.

🛏 Sleeping

This is one of the Bukit's coolest places to stay. Numerous individual places are scattered along and near the cliffs, well off the main road. Basic accommodation is also available down the cliff at a string of bamboo-and-thatch surfer crash pads near the water.

Bingin Garden   GUESTHOUSE $
(📞 0816 472 2002; tommybarrell76@yahoo.com; off Jl Pantai Bingin; r with fan/air-con 320,000/460,000Rp; ❄ 🐦 ⧆) There's a relaxed hacienda feel to Bingin Garden, where eight bungalow-style rooms are set among an arid garden and a large pool. It's back off the cliffs and about 300m from the path down to the beach. It's run by gun local surfer Tommy Barrell and his lovely wife.

Mick's Place   BOUTIQUE HOTEL $$
(📞 0812 391 3337; www.micksplacebali.com; off Jl Pantai Bingin; r from US$100, villa from US$300; ❄ 🐦 ⧆) A hippie-chic playground where you rough it in style, Mick's never has more than 16 guests. Seven artful bungalows and one luxe villa are set in lush grounds. The turquoise water in the postage-stamp-sized infinity pool matches the turquoise sea below. By day there's a 180-degree view of the world-famous surf breaks.

Mu   GUESTHOUSE $$
(📞 0361-895 7442; www.mu-bali.com; off Jl Pantai Bingin; bungalows from US$90; ❄ 🐦 ⧆) 🌊 The

16 very individual bungalows with thatched roofs are scattered about a compound dominated by a cliff-side infinity pool. All have open-air living spaces and air-con bedrooms, some have hot tubs with a view. Some units have multiple bedrooms. There's an excellent cafe as well as a yoga studio.

★**Temple Lodge**　　　　BOUTIQUE HOTEL **$$**
(☑ 0857 3901 1572; www.thetemplelodge.com; off Jl Pantai Bingin; r from 1,200,000Rp; ❋ 🛜 🏊) 'Artsy and beautiful' just begins to describe this collection of huts and cottages made from thatch, driftwood and other natural materials. Each sits on a jutting shelf on the cliffs above the surf breaks, and there are superb views from the infinity pool and some of the nine units (some fan-only). There are morning yoga classes.

✖ Eating

All the places to stay have at least simple cafes. There are new ones popping up in the area all the time.

★**Cashew Tree**　　　　　　　CAFE **$**
(☑ 0813 5321 8157; www.facebook.com/the cashewtreebingin; Jl Pantai Bingin; meals from 55,000Rp; ☺ 8am-10pm; 🛜🍴) *The* place to hang out in Bingin. Surfers and beachgoers gather in this large garden for tasty vegetarian meals. Expect the likes of burritos, salads, sandwiches and smoothies – it's also a good spot for a drink. Thursday nights especially go off, with live bands attracting folk from up and down the coast.

ℹ Getting There & Away

A metered taxi from Kuta will cost about 250,000Rp and take at least an hour, depending on traffic. An elderly resident collects 3000/5000Rp for a motorbike/car at a T-junction near where you park for the trail down to the beach.

Padang Padang

☑ 0361

Padang Padang Beach and Impossibles Beach are the stuff tropical surf dreams are made of. The backdrop of rocky cliff faces gives them an isolated feel you won't get in Kuta or Seminyak. A very cool scene has developed, with groovy cafes, oddball sleeps and iconoclastic surf shops.

On Saturdays and full-moon nights there's a party on the beach at Padang Padang, with grilled seafood and tunes until dawn.

The namesake beach here is near Jl Labuan Sait and is fairly easily reached. Immediately east, Impossibles Beach is more of a challenge. Rocks and tide may prevent you from coming over from Padang Padang.

Labuan Sait Beach　　　　　BEACH
(Padang Padang Beach; adult/child 15,000/10,000Rp, parking per motorbike/car 5000/10,000Rp) Slight in size but not in perfection, this little cove is near the main Ulu Watu road where a stream flows into the sea. Parking is easy and it is a short walk to the beach, though you'll be hit up for parking and an entrance fee. Experienced surfers flock here for the tubes; on Saturday night everybody comes for the late-night beach party.

Impossibles Beach　　　　　BEACH
About 100m west of Jl Pantai Bingin on Jl Melasti, you'll see another turn towards the ocean. Follow this paved road for 700m and look for a scrawled sign on a wall reading Impossibles Beach. Follow the treacherous path and you'll soon understand the name. It's a tortuous trek but you'll be rewarded with an empty cove with splotches of creamy sand between boulders.

🏃 Activities

You can rent surfboards to hit the breaks right offshore, but be aware it can get very crowded in high season. Many surf competitions are held here.

★**Padang Padang**　　　　　SURFING
Padang for short, this super-shallow, left-hand reef break is off a very popular beach and just below some rickety accommodation joints where you can crash and watch the breaks. Check carefully before venturing out. It's a very demanding break that only works if it's over about 6ft from mid- to high tide. The best times for a good swell here are June to August.

Impossibles　　　　　　　SURFING
Just north of Padang Padang, this challenging outside reef break has three shifting peaks with fast left-hand tube sections that can join up if the conditions are perfect.

🛏 Sleeping

To get close to the waves, consider one of the cliff-side guesthouses that are reached by a steep path down from the bluff. The trail starts at the end of a twisting lane that runs for 200m from Jl Labuan Sait just west of **Om Burger** (☑0819 9905 5232; Jl Labuan Sait; mains from 55,000Rp, burgers from 75,000Rp; ☺7am-10pm; 🛜).

★ **Rock'n Reef**   BOUTIQUE HOTEL $$$
(☑0812 4636 4080; www.rock-n-reef.com; Jl Pemutih, off Jl Labuan Sait; r from 2,100,000Rp; ✳🛜) Seven individualistic bungalows are built into the rocks just above a low-tide patch of sand just east of Pantai Labuan Sait. All share the stunning views of the ocean directly in front and have a rustic, artful design with natural materials. There are private balconies and sunny decks. During peak surf season, staying here is a fantasy. It's 80 steps down from the clifftop.

PinkCoco Bali   HOTEL $$
(☑0361-895 7371; http://pnkhotels.com; Jl Labuan Sait; r US$75-135; ✳🛜🏊) One of the pools at this romantic hotel is suitably tiled pink. The 25 rooms have terraces and balconies. There is a lush Mexican motif throughout, with an appealing mix of white walls accented with bold, tropical colours. Surfers are catered to and you can rent bikes.

🍴 Eating

Padang Padang has a growing number of offbeat cafes that match the beachy vibe of the area. It's worth coming here for dinner, even if you're staying in Bingin or Ulu Watu.

★ **Bukit Cafe**   AUSTRALIAN $
(☑0822 3620 8392; www.bukitcafe.com; Jl Labuan Sait; mains 40,000-75,000Rp; ☺7am-10pm; 🍴) For heaping plates of Australian-style brunch composed of fresh, local ingredients, Bukit Cafe is unbeatable. Standout dishes include vegan pancakes, smoothie bowls and smashed avocado, and the open-air, convivial setting has loads of appeal.

Mango Tree Cafe   CAFE $$
(☑0878 6246 6763; www.themangotreecafe. com; Jl Labuan Sait 17; mains 40,000-120,000Rp; ☺7am-11pm) This two-level cafe has a long menu of healthy options. Sandwiches and the tasty burgers have amazing buns. The salads, soups, breakfast burritos and more are fresh and interesting. There are good juices and a decent drinks list. Try for a table under the namesake tree. On many nights there's live music.

ℹ️ Getting There & Away

A metered taxi from Kuta will cost about 200,000Rp and take at least an hour.

Ulu Watu
☑0361
Ulu Watu has become the generic name for the southwestern tip of the Bukit peninsula. It includes the much-revered temple and the fabled namesake surf breaks.

About 2km north of the temple there is a dramatic cliff with steps leading to the water and Suluban Beach. All manner of cafes and surf shops spill down the nearly sheer face to the water below. Views are stellar and it's quite the scene.

👁 Sights & Activities

★ **Pura Luhur Ulu Watu**   HINDU TEMPLE
(off Jl Ulu Watu; adult/child 50,000/30,000Rp, parking 2000Rp; ☺7am-7pm) This important temple is perched precipitously on the southwestern tip of the peninsula, atop sheer cliffs that drop straight into the ceaseless surf. Enter through an unusual arched gateway flanked by statues of Ganesha. Inside, the walls of coral bricks are covered with intricate carvings of Bali's mythological menagerie (note that there's also an earthbound menagerie of thieving monkeys). A popular Kecak dance (p244) is held in the temple grounds at sunset (arrive by 5pm).

Only Hindu worshippers can enter the small inner temple that is built on to the jutting tip of land. However, the views of the endless swells of the Indian Ocean from the cliffs are almost spiritual. At sunset, walk around the clifftop to the left (south) of the temple to lose some of the crowd.

Ulu Watu is one of several important temples to the spirits of the sea along the south coast of Bali. In the 11th century the Javanese priest Empu Kuturan first established a temple here. The complex was added to by Nirartha, another Javanese priest who is known for the seafront temples at Tanah Lot, Rambut Siwi and Pura Sakenan. Nirartha retreated to Ulu Watu for his final days when he attained *moksa* (freedom from earthly desires).

★ **Ulu Watu**   SURFING
On its day Ulu Watu is Bali's biggest and most powerful wave. It's the stuff of dreams and nightmares, and definitely not one for beginners! Since the early 1970s when it featured in the legendary surf flick *Morning of the Earth,* Ulu Watu has drawn surfers from around the world for left breaks that seem to go on forever.

Teluk Ulu Watu (Ulu Watu Bay) is a great set-up for surfers – locals will wax your

Ulu Watu

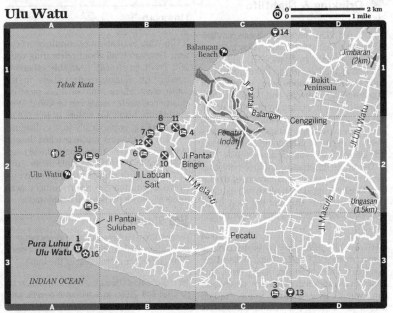

0 — 2 km
0 — 1 mile

Ulu Watu

board and get drinks for you. You'll have to carry your board down stairs through a cave to access the wave. There are seven different breaks and conditions change continuously.

🛏 Sleeping

The cliffs above the main Ulu Watu breaks are dotted with various accommodation options; since most people are here for the view, quality is not always assured.

★ Uluwatu Cottages   BUNGALOW $$
(☑ 0857 9268 1715; www.uluwatucottages.com; off Jl Labuan Sait; r from 1,200,000Rp; ❋ 🛜 ☒) Fourteen bungalows are spread across a large

site right on the cliff, just 400m east of the Ulu Watu cafes (about 200m off Jl Labuan Sait). The units are comfortable, have individual terraces and enjoy views that are simply stunning. The pool is large and a great place to lose a day.

Gong Accommodation   GUESTHOUSE $$
(☑ 0361-769976; Jl Pantai Suluban; r 450,000-550,000Rp; 🛜 ☒) The 20 tidy rooms here have good ventilation and hot water, and face a small compound with a lovely pool. Some 2nd-floor units have distant ocean views, TVs and air-con. It's about 1km south of the Ulu Watu cliff-side cafes; the host family is lovely.

🍷 Drinking & Nightlife

★ Omnia
CLUB

(📞 0361-848 2150; https://omniaclubs.com/bali; Jl Belimbing Sari; cover charge varies by day & event, check website for details; ⊙ 11am-10.30pm) Perched at the base of the Bukit peninsula, Bali's hottest day club is home to seekers of sunshine-fuelled revelry and house and hip-hop beats. The imposing architecture of the modern Cube bar is a stunning focal point, but a peek over its patio's glass barriers yields an eyeful of jagged cliffs, lush ocean-side canopy and hypnotic azure waves.

There's an impressive infinity pool that blends into a seamless panorama of the Indian Ocean, fringed with plush sun lounges. Cocktails are inventive and the food spans a broad range of cuisines and preparations.

★ Single Fin
CAFE $$

(📞 0878 6020 9038; www.singlefinbali.com; Jl Mamo; mains 70,000-170,000Rp; ⊙ 8am-11pm Mon-Thu, to midnight Fri-Sun; 📶🅿) From this triple-level cafe on its cliff-side perch, you can watch never-ending swells march across the Indian Ocean and the surfers carve it up when the waves are big. Drinks here aren't cheap, but the food (burgers, bowls, pasta, munchies) is tasty, the sunsets are killer and the Sunday night party is the best on the peninsula.

☆ Entertainment

★ Kecak Dance
DANCE

(Pura Luhur Ulu Watu, off Jl Ulu Watu; adult/child 100,000/50,000Rp; ⊙ sunset) Although the performance obviously caters for tourists, the gorgeous setting at Pura Luhur Ulu Watu (p242) in a small amphitheatre in a leafy part of the grounds makes it one of the more evocative on the island. The views out to sea are as inspiring as the dance. It's very popular in high season; expect crowds.

ℹ Getting There & Away

The best way to see the Ulu Watu region is with your own wheels. Note that the cops often set up checkpoints near Pecatu Indah for checks on motorcycle-riding Westerners. Be aware you may pay a fine for offences such as a 'loose' chin strap.

Coming to the Ulu Watu cliff-side cafes from the east on Jl Labuan Sait, you will first encounter an access road to parking near the cliffs. Continuing over a bridge, there is a side road that leads to another parking area, from where it is a pretty 200m walk north to the cliff-side cafes. A taxi ride out here will cost at least 200,000Rp from Kuta and takes more than an hour in traffic.

Ungasan

📞 0361 / POP 14,221

If Ulu Watu is all about celebrating surf culture, Ungasan is all about celebrating yourself. From crossroads near this otherwise nondescript village, roads radiate to the south coast where some of Bali's most exclusive oceanside resorts can be found. With the infinite turquoise waters of the Indian Ocean rolling hypnotically in the distance, it's hard not to think you've reached the end of the world, albeit a very comfortable one.

The scalloped cliff faces hide many a tiny cove beach with white sand. Some are now crowded with top-end resorts, others await discovery down perilous cliff-side stairs.

🛏 Sleeping

Several luxurious resorts have views out over the Indian Ocean from the high limestone cliffs on the southern coast of the Bukit.

★ Alila Villas Uluwatu
RESORT $$$

(📞 0361-848 2166; www.alilahotels.com/uluwatu; Jl Belimbing Sari; r incl breakfast from US$800; ❄@📶🏊) Visually stunning, this vast resort has an artful contemporary style that is at once light and airy while still conveying a sense of luxury. The 85-unit Alila offers gracious service in a setting where the blue of the ocean contrasts with the green of the surrounding (hotel-tended) rice fields. It's 2km off Jl Ulu Watu.

ℹ Getting There & Away

You'll be on your own for transport. Taxis from Seminyak run 200,000Rp and take an hour.

Nusa Dua

📞 0361

Nusa Dua translates literally as 'Two Islands' – although they are actually small raised headlands, each with a small temple. But Nusa Dua is much better known as Bali's gated compound of resort hotels. It's a vast and manicured place where you leave the chaos of the rest of the island behind as you pass the guards.

Built in the 1970s, Nusa Dua was designed to compete with international beach resorts the world over. Balinese 'culture', in the form of condensed cultural displays, is literally trucked in nightly in an effort to make it seem like less of a generic beach resort.

With more than 20 large resorts and thousands of hotel rooms, Nusa Dua can live up to some of its promise when full, but during slack times it's desolate.

◉ Sights

★ Pasifika Museum
MUSEUM

(📞0361-774935; www.museum-pasifika.com; Bali Collection shopping centre, block P; 100,000Rp; ⊙10am-6pm) When groups from nearby resorts aren't around, you'll probably have this large museum to yourself. A collection of art from Pacific Ocean cultures spans several centuries and includes more than 600 paintings (don't miss the tikis). The influential wave of European artists who thrived in Bali in the early 20th century is well represented. Look for works by Arie Smit, Adrien-Jean Le Mayeur de Merpres and Theo Meier. There are also works by Matisse and Gauguin.

⌷ Sleeping

Nusa Dua resorts are similar in several ways: they are big (some are huge) with most major international brands represented, and many are right on the placid beach.

Major international brands such as **Westin** (📞0361-771906; www.westin.com/bali; Jl Kw Nusa Dua Resort; r from US$200; ✲@🖥🛋) and **Hyatt** (📞0361-771234; www.hyatt.com; r from US$200; ✲@🖥🛋) have invested heavily, adding loads of amenities (such as elaborate pools and kids' day camps). Other hotels seem little changed from when they were built in the 1970s heyday of the Suharto era.

★ Sofitel Bali Nusa Dua Beach Resort
RESORT $$$

(📞0361-849 2888; www.sofitelbalinusadua.com; Jl Nusa Dua; r from US$200; ✲@🖥🛋) Making up part of the resort strip, the Sofitel has a vast pool that meanders past the 415 rooms, some of which have terraces with direct pool access. The room blocks are huge; many rooms have at least a glimpse of the water. The Sofitel's lavish Sunday brunch (11am to 3pm) is one of Bali's best; it costs from 400,000Rp.

✗ Eating

There are dozens of restaurants charging resort prices in the huge hotels. For nonguests, venture in if you want a bounteous Sunday brunch, such as the Sofitel's.

Good warungs cluster at the corner of Jl Srikandi and Jl Pantai Mengiat. Also along the latter street, just outside the central gate, open-air eateries offer an unpretentious dining alternative. None will win culinary awards, but most provide transport.

Warung Dobiel
BALINESE $

(📞0361-771633; Jl Srikandi 9; meals from 40,000Rp; ⊙9am-4pm) A bit of authentic food action amid the bland streets of Nusa, this is a good stop for *babi guling* (spit-roast pig). Pork soup is the perfect taste bud awakener, while the jackfruit is redolent with spices. Diners perch on stools and share tables. Watch out for 'foreigner' pricing.

❶ Getting There & Away

The Bali Mandara Toll Rd (motorbike/car 4000/11,000Rp) greatly speeds journeys between Nusa Dua and the airport and Sanur.

BUS

The Kura-Kura tourist bus (p216) has two routes linking Nusa Dua with its Kuta hub. Buses run every two hours and cost 50,000Rp.

Bali's Trans-Sarbagita bus system (p226) serves Nusa Dua on a route that follows the Jl Ngurah Rai Bypass up and around past Sanur to Batabulan.

SHUTTLE

Find out what shuttle-bus services your hotel provides before you start hailing taxis. A free **shuttle bus** (📞0361-771662; www.bali-collection.com/shuttle-bus; ⊙9am-10pm) connects all Nusa Dua and Tanjung Benoa resort hotels with the Bali Collection shopping centre about every hour.

TAXI

The taxi from the airport cartel is 150,000Rp; a metered taxi to the airport will be much less. Taxis to/from Seminyak average 150,000Rp for the 45-minute trip.

Tanjung Benoa
📞0361

The peninsula of Tanjung Benoa extends about 4km north from Nusa Dua to Benoa village. It's flat and lined with family-friendly resort hotels, most of midrange calibre. By day the waters buzz with the roar of dozens of motorised water-sports craft. Group tours arrive by the busload for a day's aquatic excitement.

Overall, Tanjung Benoa is a fairly sedate place, although the Bali Mandara Toll Rd speeds access to the nightlife diversions of Kuta and Seminyak.

➹ Courses

★ Bumbu Bali Cooking School
COOKING

(📞0361-774502; www.balifoods.com; Jl Pratama; course with/without market visit US$95/85; ⊙6am-3pm Mon, Wed & Fri) This much-lauded cooking school at the eponymous restaurant strives to get to the roots of Balinese cooking. Courses start with a 6am visit to Jimbaran's fish and morning markets, continue in the large kitchen and finish with lunch.

ⓘ Getting There & Away

Taxis from the airport cartel cost 200,000Rp. Occasional bemos (minibuses) shuttle up and down Jl Pratama (5000Rp) – although after about 3pm they become scarce.

A free **shuttle bus** (🌏 0361-771662; www. bali-collection.com/shuttle-bus; ⊙9am-10pm) connects Nusa Dua and Tanjung Benoa resort hotels with the Bali Collection shopping centre about every hour. Or stroll the Beach Promenade and enjoy the view in lieu of the bus. Many restaurants will provide transport from Nusa Dua and Tanjung Benoa hotels.

Sanur

🌏 0361 / POP 38,453

Many consider Sanur 'just right', as it lacks most of the hassles found towards Kuta while maintaining a good mix of restaurants and bars that aren't all owned by resorts.

The beach, while thin, is protected by a reef and breakwaters, so families appreciate the limpid waves. Sanur has a good range of places to stay and it's well placed for day trips. Really, it doesn't deserve its local moniker, 'Snore'.

Sanur stretches for about 5km along an east-facing coastline, with the lush and green landscaped grounds of resorts fronting right onto the sandy beach. West of the beachfront hotels is the busy main drag, Jl Danau Tamblingan, with hotel entrances and oodles of tourist shops, restaurants and cafes.

Noxious, traffic-choked Jl Ngurah Rai Bypass skirts the western side of the resort area, and is the main link to Kuta and the airport. Don't stay anyplace nearby.

⊙ Sights

Sanur's sights – views to Nusa Penida and of local life amid the tourism – are all readily apparent from its lovely beachfront walk.

★ **Museum Le Mayeur**   MUSEUM
(🌏 0361-286201; Jl Hang Tuah; adult/child 50,000/25,000Rp; ⊙8am-3.30pm Sat-Thu, 8.30am-12.30pm Fri) Artist Adrien-Jean Le Mayeur de Merpres (1880–1958) arrived in Bali in 1932, and married the beautiful Legong dancer Ni Polok three years later, when she was just 15. They lived in this compound

back when Sanur was still a quiet fishing village. After the artist's death, Ni Polok lived in the house until she died in 1985. Despite security (some of Le Mayeur's paintings have sold for US$150,000) and conservation problems, almost 90 of Le Mayeur's paintings are displayed.

Taman Festival Bali   RUINS
(Jalan Padang Galak 3) Taman Festival Bali is an abandoned theme park about a 20-minute drive north of Sanur. The 8-hectare park closed its doors in 2000 amidst the Asian economic crisis.

Sanur Beach   BEACH
Sanur Beach curves in a southwesterly direction and stretches for more than 5km. It is mostly clean and overall quite serene – much like the town itself. Offshore reefs mean that the surf is reduced to tiny waves lapping the shore. With a couple of unfortunate exceptions, the resorts along the sand are low-key, leaving the beach uncrowded.

🏃 Activities

Sanur's calm water and steady breeze make it a natural centre for wind- and kitesurfing.

Sanur's fickle breaks (tide conditions often don't produce waves) are offshore along the reef. The best area is called **Sanur Reef**, a right break in front of the Grand Bali Beach Hotel. Another good spot is known as the **Hyatt Reef**, in front of, you guessed it, the old Bali Hyatt.

You can get a boat out to the breaks from **Surya Water Sports** (🌏 0361-287956; www. balisuryadivecenter.com; Jl Duyung 10; ⊙8am-8pm; 👫).

★ **Rip Curl School of Surf**   KITESURFING
(🌏 0361-287749; www.ripcurlschoolofsurf.com; Beachfront Walk, Sanur Beach Hotel; kitesurfing lessons from 1,100,000Rp, rental per hour from 550,000Rp; ⊙8am-5pm) Sanur's reef-protected waters and regular offshore breezes make for good kitesurfing. The season runs from June to October. Rip Curl also rents boards for windsurfing and stand-up paddle boarding (including SUP yoga for 450,000Rp per hour) as well as kayaks.

Balinese Cooking Class   COOKING
(🌏 0361-288009; www.santrian.com; Puri Santrian, Beachfront Walk; 90min class from US$70; ⊙Wed & Fri) With a kitchen that's set on the beachfront, this is a memorable spot to learn to cook Balinese food. For a bit extra you can visit the market to source ingredients.

Sanur

Sanur

◎ **Top Sights**
1 Museum Le Mayeur B2

◎ **Sights**
2 Sanur Beach B6

◎ **Activities, Courses & Tours**
3 Balinese Cooking Class A7
4 Crystal Divers B5
5 Surya Water Sports B6

◎ **Sleeping**
6 Agung & Sue Watering Hole I A1
7 Maison Aurelia Sanur B5
8 Tandjung Sari B4
9 Yulia 1 Homestay A3

◎ **Eating**
10 Byrdhouse Beach Club B3
11 Char Ming A6
12 Nasi Bali Men Weti B3

◎ **Transport**
13 Fast Boat for Nusa Lembongan &
the Gili Islands B2
14 Perama A1
15 Public Boats B1
16 Rocky Fast Cruises B1
17 Scoot A1

Crystal Divers   DIVING
(☑ 0361-286737; www.crystal-divers.com; Jl Danau
Tamblingan 168; dives from 890,000Rp) This
slick diving operation has its own hotel (the
Santai) and a large diving pool. The shop
offers a long list of courses, including PADI
open-water (7,450,000Rp) and options for
beginners.

★**Power of Now Oasis**   YOGA
(☑ 0878 6153 4535; www.powerofnowoasis.com;
Beachfront Walk, Hotel Mercure; classes from
120,000Rp) Enjoy a yoga class in this atmospheric bamboo pavilion looking out to Sanur Beach. Several levels are offered. Sunrise
yoga is a popular choice.

🛏 Sleeping

Usually the best places to stay are right on
the beach; however, beware of properties
that have been coasting for decades. West of
Jl Danau Tamblingan there are budget guesthouses, oodles of midrange chains and villas.

Agung & Sue Watering Hole   GUESTHOUSE $
(☑ 0361-288289; www.wateringholesanurbali.com;
Jl Hang Tuah 35; r 280,000-450,000Rp; ❈ 🛜)
Ideally located for an early fast boat to Nusa
Lembongan, Nusa Penida or the Gilis, this

long-running guesthouse has a veteran conviviality. Rooms are standard, but the beer is indeed cold and Sanur Beach is a five-minute walk away.

Further south, Agung & Sue Watering Hole II is another lovely budget option, with a pool and rooms from 250,000Rp.

Yulia 1 Homestay
GUESTHOUSE $

(☑0361-288089; yulia1homestay@gmail.com; Jl Danau Tamblingan 38; r incl breakfast with fan/air-con from 250,000/350,000Rp; ✽🛜🛏) Run by a friendly family, this mellow guesthouse is set in a lovely bird-filled garden full of palms and flowers. Rooms vary in standards (some cold water, fan only), but all come with fridges. The plunge pool is a nice area for relaxing.

Maison Aurelia Sanur
HOTEL $$$

(☑0361-472 1111; http://preferencehotels.com/maison-aurelia; Jl Danau Tamblingan 140; r US$100-160; ✽🛜🛏) High-style on the far side from the beach, this four-storey hotel is a dramatic addition to Sanur's main drag. The 42 rooms are capacious, have balconies and boast a richly restful decor. Details are plush and comforts include fridges.

Gardenia
GUESTHOUSE $$

(☑0361-286301; www.gardeniaguesthouse bali.com; Jl Mertasari 2; r 650,000-755,000Rp; ✽🛜🛏) Like its many-petalled namesake, the Gardenia has many facets. The seven rooms are visions in white and sit well back from the road. Nice verandahs face a plunge pool in a pretty courtyard. Up front there is a good cafe.

★ Tandjung Sari
BOUTIQUE HOTEL $$$

(☑0361-288441; www.tandjungsarihotel.com; Jl Danau Tamblingan 41; bungalows 3,000,000Rp; ✽@🛜🛏) One of Bali's first boutique hotels, Tandjung Sari has flourished since it opened in 1967 and continues to be lauded for its relaxed style. The 29 traditional-style bungalows are beautifully decorated with crafts and antiques. The gracious staff are a delight. Local children practise Balinese dance by the pool at 3pm Friday and Sunday.

✗ Eating

Along the beach path, you can catch a meal, a drink or just some sea breeze in one of the traditional open-air pavilions or in a laid-back bar. And although there are plenty of uninspired places on Jl Danau Tamblingan, there are also some gems.

Nasi Bali Men Weti
BALINESE $

(Jl Segara Ayu; meals from 25,000Rp; ⊙7am-1pm) This simple stall prepares excellent *nasi campur*, the classic Balinese lunch plate of mixed dishes. Everything is very fresh and prepared while you wait in the inevitable queue. Enjoy your meal perched on a small stool.

Sari Bundo
INDONESIAN $

(☑0361-281389; Jl Danau Poso; mains from 20,000Rp; ⊙24hr) This spotless Padang-style shopfront is one of several at the south end of Sanur. Choose from an array of fresh and very spicy food. The curry chicken is a fiery treat that will have your tongue alternatively loving and hating you.

★ Char Ming
ASIAN $$

(☑0361-288029; www.charming-bali.com; Jl Danau Tamblingan N97; mains from 95,000Rp; ⊙5-11pm) Asian fusion with a French accent. A daily menu board lists the fresh seafood available for grilling. Look for regional dishes, many with modern flair. The highly stylised location features lush plantings and carved-wood details from vintage Javanese and Balinese structures.

Byrdhouse Beach Club
INTERNATIONAL $$

(☑0361-288407; www.facebook.com/byrdhouse beachclubbali; Segara Village, Sanur Beach; mains from 60,000Rp; ⊙6am-midnight; 🛜) With sun lounges, a swimming pool, a restaurant, bar and table tennis on-site, you could happily spend an entire day here by the beach. Check the club's Facebook page for upcoming events, including outdoor-cinema screenings and street-food stalls.

❶ Getting There & Away

BOAT

Fast boats (prices vary by destination) The myriad fast boats to Nusa Lembongan, Nusa Penida, Lombok and the Gilis depart from a strip of beach south of Jl Hang Tuah. None of these services use a dock – be prepared to wade to the boat. Most companies have shady waiting areas facing the beach.

Public boats (one way 150,000Rp) Regular boats to Nusa Lembongan and Nusa Penida depart from the beach at the end of Jl Hang Tuah three times daily (50,000Rp one way, 40 minutes).

Rocky Fast Cruises (☑0821 4404 0928, 0361-283624; www.rockyfastcruise.com; Jl Hang Tuah 41; return 500,000Rp; ⊙8am-10pm) Has an office for its services to Nusa Lembongan (500,000Rp return, 9am, 11am, 1pm and 4.30pm).

Scoot (☑0361-285522; www.scootcruise.
com; Jl Hang Tuah; return adult/child from
400,000/280,000Rp; ⊗8am-10pm) Has
an office for its network of services to Nusa
Lembongan, Lombok and the Gilis (adult/child
from 400,000/280,000Rp return). Boats to
Lembongan depart four times daily.

BUS

The Kura-Kura tourist bus (p216) has a route
linking Sanur with Kuta and Ubud. Buses run
every hour and cost 80,000Rp.

The **Perama office** (☑0361-751875; www.
peramatour.com; Jl Hang Tuah 39; ⊗7am-10pm)
is at Warung Pojok at the northern end of town.
Its destinations include Ubud (50,000Rp, one
hour), Padangbai (75,000Rp, two hours) and
Lovina (125,000Rp, three hours).

TAXI

A cartel of taxis at the airport has a set price of
250,000Rp to Sanur.

Denpasar

☑0361 / POP 970,000

Sprawling, hectic and ever-growing, Bali's
capital has been the focus of a lot of the island's growth and wealth over the last five
decades. It can seem a daunting and chaotic
place, but spend a little time on its tree-lined
streets in the relatively affluent government
and business district of Renon and you'll
discover a more genteel side.

Denpasar might not be a tropical paradise, but it's as much a part of 'the real Bali'
as the rice paddies and clifftop temples. This
is the hub of the island for nearly a million
locals and here you will find their shopping
malls and parks. Most enticing, however, are
the authentic restaurants and cafes aimed at
the burgeoning middle class.

BALI DENPASAR

VISITING BALI'S TRADITIONAL HEALERS

Bali's traditional healers, known as *balian*, play an important part in Bali's culture by
treating physical and mental illness, removing spells and channelling information from
the ancestors. Numbering about 8000, *balian* are the ultimate in community medicine,
making a commitment to serve their communities and turning no one away.

Lately, however, this system has come under stress in some areas due to the attention
brought by *Eat, Pray, Love* and other media coverage of Bali's healers. Curious tourists
are turning up in village compounds, taking the *balian's* time and attention from the ill.
However, that doesn't mean you shouldn't visit a *balian* if you're geniunely curious. Just
do so in a manner that befits the experience: gently.

Consider the following before a visit.

➡ Make an appointment before visiting a *balian*.

➡ Know that English is rarely spoken.

➡ Dress respectfully (long trousers and a shirt, better yet a sarong and sash).

➡ Women should not be menstruating.

➡ Never point your feet at the healer.

➡ Bring an offering into which you have tucked the consulting fee, which will average
about 250,000Rp per person.

➡ Understand what you're getting into: your treatment will be very public and probably
painful. It may include deep-tissue massage, being poked with sharp sticks or having
chewed herbs spat on you.

Finding a *balian* can take some work. Ask at your hotel, which can probably help with
making an appointment and providing a suitable offering for stashing your fee. Or consider getting a referral from **Made Surya** (www.balihealers.com; per hr/day US$35/200),
who is an authority on Bali's traditional healers and offers one- and two-day intensive
workshops on healing, magic, traditional systems and history, which include visits to
authentic *balian*. His website is an excellent resource on visiting healers in Bali and he
can also select an appropriate *balian* for you to visit and accompany you there as liaison
and translator.

Some Western medical professionals question whether serious medical issues can be
resolved by this type of healing, and patients should see a traditional healer in conjunction with a Western doctor if their ailment is serious.

Denpasar

Ubung Bus
& Bemo Terminal
(1.5km)

Jl Setiabudi

Jl Sutomo

Jl Kartini

Jl Nakula

Jl Werkudara

Jl Sahedawa

Jl Pattimura

Jl Kedondong

Jl Suli

Jl Belimbing

Jl Melati

Jl Kamboja

Jl Plawa

Jl Arjuna

Jl Karna

Jl Veteran

Jl Durian

Gunung Agung
Bemo Terminal
(200m)

Jl Gajah Mada

Jl Sumatra

Jl Surapati

Jl Surapati

Jl Imam Bonjol

Jl Thamrin

Jl Hasanudin

Jl Udayana

Jl Sugianyar

Jl Kapten Agung

Jl Diponegoro

Jl Udayana

Jl Nusakambangan

Jl Cok Agung Tresna

Jl Teuku Umar

RENON

Jl Jayagiri

SANGLAH

Damri
Office

Nasi Uduk
Kebon Kacang
(1.2km)

Letda Tantular

Jl Nias

Jl Diponegoro

Jl Pulau Kanrata

Jl Tukad Gangga

Jepun Bali (750m);
Benoa Harbour (6km)

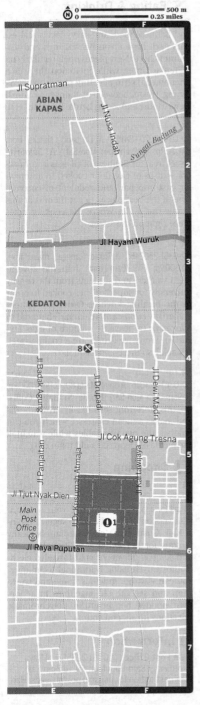

Denpasar

◎ Sights

Museum Negeri Propinsi Bali   MUSEUM
(☎0361-222680; Jl Mayor Wisnu; adult/child
50,000/25,000Rp; ⊗8am-5.30pm) Think of
this as the British Museum or the Smith-
sonian of Balinese culture. It's all here, but
unlike those world-class institutions, you
have to work at sorting it out – the museum
could use a dose of curatorial energy. Most
displays are labelled in English. The museum comprises several buildings and pavilions, including many examples of Balinese
architecture, housing prehistoric pieces, traditional artefacts, Barong (mythical lion-dog
creatures), ceremonial objects and rich displays of textiles. Ignore the 'guides'.

★ Bajra Sandhi Monument   MONUMENT
(Monument to the Struggle of the People of Bali;
☎0361-264517; Jl Raya Puputan, Renon; adult/
child 20,000/10,000Rp; ⊗9am-6pm) The centrepiece to a popular park, this huge monument is as big as its name. Inside the vaguely
Borobudur-like structure are dioramas trac-
ing Bali's history. Note that in the portrayal
of the 1906 battle with the Dutch, the King
of Badung is literally a sitting target. Take
the spiral stairs to the top for 360-degree
views.

Pura Jagatnatha   HINDU TEMPLE
(Jl Surapati) FREE The state temple, built in
1953, is dedicated to the supreme god, Sanghyang Widi. Part of its significance is its
statement of monotheism. Although the
Balinese recognise many gods, the belief in
one supreme god (who can have many man-
ifestations) brings Balinese Hinduism into

conformity with the first principle of Pancasila – the 'Belief in One God'.

Activities

Kube Dharma Bakti
MASSAGE

(☑ 0361-749 9440; Jl Serma Mendara 3; massage per hr 100,000Rp; ☺ 9am-10pm) Many Balinese wouldn't think of having a massage from anyone but a blind person. Government-sponsored schools offer lengthy courses to certify blind people in reflexology, shiatsu massage, anatomy and much more. In this airy building redolent with liniments you can choose from a range of therapies.

Festivals & Events

★ Bali Arts Festival
PERFORMING ARTS

(www.baliartsfestival.com; Taman Wedhi Budaya; ☺ mid-Jun–mid-Jul) This annual festival, based at Taman Wedhi Budaya arts centre, is an easy way to see a wide variety of traditional dance, music and crafts. The productions of the Ramayana and Mahabharata ballets are grand and the opening ceremony and parade in Denpasar are spectacles. Tickets are usually available before performances; schedules are online and at the Denpasar tourist office.

Sleeping

Denpasar has many new midpriced chain hotels, but it's hard to think of a compelling reason to stay here unless you want to revel in the city's bright lights. Most visitors stay in the tourist towns of the south and visit Denpasar as a day trip.

Nakula Familiar Inn
GUESTHOUSE $

(☑ 0361-226446; www.nakulafamiliarinn.com; Jl Nakula 4; r 200,000-300,000Rp; ❄ 🛜) The eight rooms at this sprightly urban family compound, a longtime traveller favourite, are clean and have small balconies. There is a nice courtyard and cafe in the middle. Tegal–Kereneng bemos go along Jl Nakula.

Inna Bali
HOTEL $$

(☑ 0361-225681; http://inna-bali-denpasar.denpasar area-hotels.com/en; Jl Veteran 3; r 400,000-1,000,000Rp; ❄ 🛜 🏊) The Inna Bali has simple gardens, a huge banyan tree and a certain nostalgic charm; it dates from 1927 and was once the main tourist hotel on the island. Room interiors are standard, but many have deeply shaded verandahs. Ongoing renovations have added an attractive colonial facade, including a decent sidewalk cafe.

Eating & Drinking

Denpasar has a good range of Indonesian and Balinese food, and savvy locals and expats each have favourite warungs and restaurants here. New places open regularly on Jl Teuku Umar, while in Renon there is a phenomenal strip of eating places on Jl Cok Agung Tresna between Jl Ramayana and Jl Dewi Madri and along Letda Tantular.

★ Men Gabrug
BALINESE $

(☑ 0361-7070 8415; Jl Drupadi; snacks from 10,000Rp; ☺ 9am-6pm Mon-Sat) A favourite sweet treat for Balinese of all ages is *jaje laklak* – disks of rice flour cooked in an open-air cast-iron pan and redolent of coconut. One of the best places to get them is at this family-run outlet where the cooking takes place right on the street.

★ Depot Cak Asmo
INDONESIAN $

(☑ 0361-256246; Jl Tukad Gangga; mains from 20,000Rp; ☺ 9.30am-11pm) Join the government workers and students from the nearby university for superb dishes cooked to order in the bustling kitchen. Order the buttery and crispy *cumi cumi* (calamari) battered in *telor asin* (a heavenly mixture of eggs and garlic). Fruity ice drinks are a cooling treat. It's halal, so there's no alcohol.

★ Bhineka Djaja
COFFEE

(☑ 0361-224016; Jl Gajah Mada 80; coffee 7000Rp; ☺ 9am-3pm Mon-Sat) Home to Bali's Coffee Co, this storefront sells locally grown beans and makes a mean espresso, which you can enjoy at the two tiny tables while watching the bustle of Denpasar's old main drag.

Shopping

★ Jepun Bali
TEXTILES

(☑ 0361-726526; Jl Raya Sesetan, Gang Ikan Mas 11; ☺ call for appointment) It's like your own private version of the Museum Negeri Propinsi Bali: Gusti Ayu Made Mardiani is locally famous for her *endek* (traditional sarong) and *songket* (silver- or gold-threaded cloth) clothes woven using traditional techniques. You can visit her gracious home and workshop and see the old machines in action, then ponder her beautiful polychromatic selections in silk and cotton.

Information

Main Post Office (☑ 0361-223565; Jl Raya Puptuan; ☺ 8am-9pm Mon-Fri, to 8pm Sat) Your best option for unusual postal needs. Has a photocopy centre and ATMs.

❶ Getting There & Away

Denpasar is the hub of public transport in Bali – you'll find buses and minibuses bound for all corners of the island.

BEMO & MINIBUS

The city has several bemo and bus terminals – if you're travelling by bemo around Bali you'll often have to go via Denpasar and transfer from one terminal to another by bemo (7000Rp).

Note that the bemo network is sputtering and fares are approximate and at times completely subjective. Drivers often try to charge nonlocals at least 25% more.

Ubung

Well north of the town, on the road to Gilimanuk, the **Ubung Bus & Bemo Terminal** (Jl HOS Cokroaminoto) is the hub for northern and western Bali. It also has long-distance buses in addition to the ones serving the terminal 12km northwest in Mengwi.

Destination	Fare
Gilimanuk (for the ferry to Java)	45,000Rp
Mengwi bus terminal	15,000Rp
Munduk	60,000Rp
Singaraja (via Pupuan or Bedugul)	70,000Rp

Batubulan

Located a very inconvenient 6km northeast of Denpasar on a road to Ubud, this terminal is for destinations in eastern and central Bali.

Destination	Fare
Amlapura	25,000Rp
Padangbai (for the Lombok ferry)	20,000Rp
Sanur	10,000Rp
Ubud	20,000Rp

Tegal

On the western side of town on Jl Iman Bonjol, **Tegal Bemo Terminal** (Jl Imam Bonjol) is the terminal for Kuta and the Bukit Peninsula.

Destination	Fare
Airport	15,000Rp
Jimbaran	20,000Rp
Kuta	15,000Rp

Kereneng

East of the town centre, **Kereneng Bemo Terminal** has bemos to Sanur (10,000Rp).

Wangaya

Near the centre of town, this small **terminal** (Jl Kartini) is the departure point for bemo services to northern Denpasar and the outlying Ubung bus terminal (8000Rp).

Gunung Agung

This **terminal** (Jl Gunung Agung), at the north-western corner of town (look for an orange sign), is on Jl Gunung Agung, and has bemos to Kerobokan and Canggu (15,000Rp).

BUS

Long-distance bus services use the Ubung Bus & Bemo Terminal, well north of town. Most long-distance services also stop at the Mengwi terminal (p215).

Damri office (☑ 0361-232793; Jl Diponegoro) Ticket office for long-distance buses.

Nusa Lembongan & Islands

☑ 0366

Look towards the open ocean southeast of Bali and the hazy bulk of Nusa Penida dominates the view. But for many visitors the real focus is Nusa Lembongan, which sits in the shadow of its vastly larger neighbour. Here, there's great surfing, amazing diving, languorous beaches and the kind of laid-back vibe travellers cherish.

Once ignored, Nusa Penida is now attracting visitors, but its dramatic vistas and unchanged village life are still yours to explore. Tiny Nusa Ceningan huddles between the larger islands. It's a quick and popular jaunt from Lembongan.

The islands have been a poor region for many years. Thin soils and a lack of fresh water do not permit the cultivation of rice, but other crops such as maize, cassava and beans are staples. The main cash crop has been seaweed, although the big harvest now comes on two legs.

Nusa Lembongan

☑ 0366 / POP 7529

Once the domain of shack-staying surfers, Nusa Lembongan has hit the big time. Yes, you can still get a simple room with a view of the surf breaks and the gorgeous sunsets, but now you can also stay in a boutique hotel and have a fabulous meal.

The new-found wealth is bringing changes, for instance, you'll see boys riding motorcycles 300m to school, temples being expensively renovated, multistorey hotels being built and time being marked by the arrival of tourist boats (which still lack any kind of dock). But even as Nusa Lembongan's popularity grows, it manages to keep a mellow vibe. You can still listen out for the crow of a rooster or the fall of a coconut, but you also need to be ready to get stuck in traffic.

◉ Sights

Pantai Tanjung Sanghyang
BEACH

(Mushroom Bay) This beautiful bay, unofficially named Mushroom Bay after the mushroom corals offshore, has a crescent of bright white beach. By day, the tranquillity can be disturbed by banana-boat riders or parasailers. Otherwise, this is a dream beach. The most interesting way to get here from Jungutbatu is to walk along the trail that starts from the southern end of the main beach and follows the coastline for a kilometre or so. Alternatively, take a boat or a motorbike from Jungutbatu.

Jungutbatu Beach
BEACH

The beach here, a mostly lovely arc of white sand with clear blue water, has views across to Gunung Agung in Bali. The pleasant **seawall walkway** is ideal for strolling, especially – as you'd guess – at sunset. Floating boats save the scene from being an idyllic cliché. The once redolent odour of drying farmed seaweed is fading away as all available land is turned over to tourism.

Pura Puseh
TEMPLE

At the north end of town where the island's main road passes, you can ascend a long stone staircase to Pura Puseh, the village temple. It has great views from its hilltop location.

🏃 Activities

Surfing

Surfing here is best in dry season (April to September), when the winds come from the southeast. It's not for beginners and can be dangerous even for experienced surfers.

There are three main breaks on the reef, all aptly named. From north to south are **Shipwrecks**, **Lacerations** and **Playgrounds**. Depending on where you are staying, you can paddle directly out to whichever of the three is closest (although at lowest tide you may have to do some walking so booties are essential); for others it's better to hire a boat. Prices are negotiable, from about 70,000Rp for a one-way trip – you tell the owner when to return. A fourth break – **Racecourses** – sometimes emerges south of Shipwreck.

The surf can be crowded here even when the island isn't – charter boats from Bali sometimes bring groups of surfers for day trips from the mainland for a minimum of 1,000,000Rp.

Thabu Surf Lessons
SURFING

(☑ 0812 4620 2766; http://thabusurflessons.webs.com; adult/child from 450,000/400,000Rp) Very professional surf instruction outfit that offers private and group lessons, with prices including gear and return boat transfer to Sanur's surf breaks. It also rents high-quality gear.

Diving

★ World Diving
DIVING

(☑ 0812 390 0686; www.world-diving.com; Jungutbatu Beach; intro dive 1,000,000Rp, open-water course 5,500,000Rp) World Diving, based at Pondok Baruna, is highly regarded. It offers a complete range of courses, plus diving trips to dive sites all around Nusa Lembongan and Nusa Penida. Equipment is first-rate.

Lembongan Dive Center
DIVING

(☑ 0821 4535 2666; www.lembongandivecenter.com; Jungubatu Beach; single dive from 550,000Rp, open-water course 4,950,000Rp) A recommended local dive centre.

Snorkelling

Good snorkelling can be had just off Tanjung Sanghyang, as well as in areas off the north coast of the island. You can charter a boat for about 200,000Rp per hour, depending on demand, distance and the number of passengers. A trip to the challenging waters of Nusa Penida costs from 300,000Rp for three hours; to the nearby mangroves also costs about 300,000Rp. Snorkelling gear can be rented for about 50,000Rp per day.

There's good drift snorkelling along the mangrove-filled channel west of Ceningan Point, between Lembongan and Ceningan.

🛏 Sleeping

Rooms and amenities generally become increasingly posh as you head south and west along the water to Mushroom Bay.

★ Pondok Baruna
GUESTHOUSE $

(☑ 0812 394 0992; www.pondokbaruna.com; Jungutbatu Beach; r from 400,000Rp; ❄ 🛜 ⛱) Associated with World Diving, a local dive operator, this place offers fantastic rooms with terraces facing the ocean. Six plusher rooms surround a dive pool behind

Nusa Lembongan

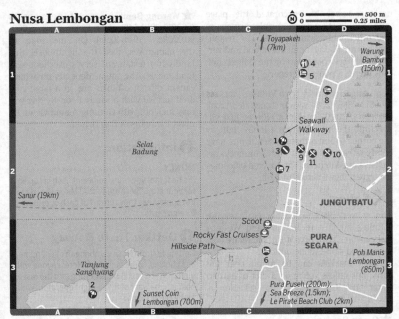

the beach. There are another eight rooms at sister site **Pondok Baruna Frangipani** (☑ 0823 3953 6271; www.pondokbaruna frangipani.com; Jungutbatu; r incl breakfast from 1,000,000Rp; ❋ 🖰 ☎) set back in the palm trees around a large pool.

Staff members, led by Putu, are charmers.

Poh Manis Lembongan   GUESTHOUSE **$**
(☑ 0821 4746 2726; r from US$43; ❋ 🖰 ☎) If Nusa Lembongan is a getaway, this is the getaway from Nusa Lembongan. Perched on a bluff on the southeast corner of the island, there are sweeping views of the other two Nusas. The pool area is lovely and the 10 rooms are light and airy with a woodsy charm.

★**Pemedal Beach**   GUESTHOUSE **$$**
(☑ 0822 4477 2888; www.pemedalbeach.com; Jungutbatu Beach; r from 975,000Rp; ❋ 🖰 ☎) A lovely affordable option if you want to be near a sandy beach; the 20 bungalows are set back a bit from the infinity pool.

Sunset Coin Lembongan   GUESTHOUSE **$$**
(☑ 0812 364 0799; www.sunsetcoinlembongan. com; Sunset Bay; r incl breakfast from 1,100,000Rp; ❋ 🖰 ☎) Run by an awesome family, this collection of 10 cottages is everything an island escape should be. It's near the sweet little spot of sand called Sunset Bay. The *lum-*

Nusa Lembongan

bung-style (thatched rice barn) units have terraces and fridges.

★**Indiana Kenanga**   BOUTIQUE HOTEL **$$$**
(☑ 0366-559 6371; www.indiana-kenanga-villas. com; Jungutbatu Beach; r US$240-400; ❋ 🖰 ☎) Two posh villas and 18 stylish suites shelter near a pool behind the beach at Lembongan's most upscale digs. The French

designer-owner has decorated the place with Buddhist statues, purple armchairs and other whimsical touches. The restaurant has an all-day menu of seafood and various surprises cooked up by the skilled chef, plus there's a poolside creperie!

Lembongan Island Beach Villas VILLA $$$
(📞 0813 3856 1208; www.lembonganresort.com; villa from 3,800,000Rp; ※ 🛜 🕿) Eleven luxe villas climb the hillside from a lobby right by the corner of Jungutbatu Beach. Units have comfy wicker loungers and hammocks as well as large kitchens. The covered balconies have great views across to Bali.

🍴 Eating

Almost every place to stay has a cafe serving – unless noted – Indonesian and Western dishes from about 50,000Rp. There are also many good stand-alone options.

Small markets can be found near the bank, but unless you're on a diet of bottled water and Ritz crackers, the selection is small.

★ Green Garden Lembongan INDONESIAN $
(📞 0813 374 1928; www.facebook.com/green gardenlembongan; Jungutbatu; mains 20,000-60,000Rp; ⏰ 7am-10pm; ※ 🛜 🐾) Tucked into a lovely garden on a side street off Jungutbatu Beach, this locally owned warung serves up tasty smoothie bowls and creative Indonesian dishes, many of which are vegetarian friendly (ie crumbed *tempe* with a mushroom-cream sauce). There are comfortable rooms in a garden (from 400,000Rp) and regular yoga classes.

Bali Eco Deli CAFE $
(📞 0812 3704 9234; www.baliecodeli.net; Jungutbatu; mains from 40,000Rp; ⏰ 7am-10pm) 🐾 This irresistible cafe has great green cred and is noted for giving back to the community. But what it gives customers is also good: fresh and creative breakfasts, healthy snacks, delicious baked goods, good coffees and juices plus an array of salads, all served in a garden setting.

Pondok Baruna Warung INDONESIAN $
(Jungutbatu; mains from 50,000Rp; ⏰ 8am-10pm) The dining part of the Baruna empire boasts some of the best food on the island. Look for excellent Balinese dishes as well as a range of fine curries. Many order not one but two chocolate brownies.

★ Warung Bambu SEAFOOD $$
(📞 0813 3867 5451; Jungutbatu; mains 35,000-90,000Rp; ⏰ 9am-10pm) On the road to the mangroves, past the lighthouse, this family-run restaurant serves excellent seafood meals. The menu depends on what's caught offshore. Tables are on a large covered terrace with a sandy floor. By day you may luck out with Gunung Agung views, by night the lights of Bali twinkle.

ℹ Information

MONEY
It's best that you bring sufficient cash in rupiah for your stay. There are four ATMs on the island but sometimes they run out of cash or refuse foreign cards.

ℹ Getting There & Away

Getting to/from Nusa Lembongan offers numerous choices, some quite fast. Note: anyone with money for a speedboat is getting into the fastboat act; be wary of fly-by-night operators with fly-by-night safety.

Boats anchor offshore, so be prepared to get your feet wet. And travel light – wheeled bags are comically inappropriate in the water and on the beach and dirt tracks. Porters will shoulder your steamer trunk for 20,000Rp (and don't be like some low-lifes we've seen who have stiffed them for their service). They'll also try to lead you to a particular hotel where they can collect a commission on your stay.

Public Fast Boats (📞 0823 3966 5478; one way 200,000Rp) leave almost hourly during daylight hours from Sanur Beach at Jl Hang Tuah, and take 40 minutes. They serve Jungutbatu and Pantai Tanjung Sanghyang.

Rocky Fast Cruises (📞 0361-448 2830; www. rockyfastcruise.com; Jungutbatu Beach) runs large boats daily from Bali's Serangan Harbour (one way/return 300,000/500,000Rp, 45 minutes).

Scoot (📞 0361-271030; www.scootcruise. com; Jungutbatu Beach) makes several trips daily from Sanur (one way from 280,000Rp, 35 minutes).

ℹ Getting Around

The island is fairly small and you can walk to most places. Cars, small motorcycles (60,000Rp per day) and bicycles (40,000Rp per day) are widely available for hire. One-way rides on motorcycles or trucks cost 15,000Rp and up. One unwelcome development is the SUV-sized golf carts that seem to be mostly rented by tourists who find a big cigar to be the perfect driving companion.

Nusa Ceningan

☑ 0361

Tiny Nusa Ceningan is connected to Nusa Lembongan by an atmospheric, narrow yellow **suspension bridge** crossing the lagoon, making it quite easy to explore the island. Besides the lagoon filled with frames for seaweed farming, you'll see several small agricultural plots and a fishing village. Nusa Ceningan is quite hilly and, if you're up for it, you can get glimpses of great scenery while wandering or cycling around. Key roads have been paved, which is opening up the island, although it is still very rural.

There's a **surf break**, named for its location at Ceningan Point, in the southwest; it's an exposed left-hander.

Tours

To really savour Nusa Ceningan, take an overnight tour of the island with JED (p214), a cultural organisation that gives people an in-depth look at village and cultural life. Trips include family accommodation in a village, local meals, a fascinating tour with seaweed workers and transport to/from mainland Bali.

🛏 Sleeping

Le Pirate Beach Club GUESTHOUSE **$$**

(☑ 0811 388 3701, reservations 0361-733493; https://lepirate.com/nusa-ceningan/; Jl Nusa Ceningan; r incl breakfast from 700,000Rp; ❉ 🐷 🛎) With a sprightly white and blue colour scheme, the theme here is retro-chic island kitsch. The accommodation consists of air-conditioned beach boxes, which range from bunk beds that sleep four to doubles. The popular restaurant looks over the small kidney-shaped pool and has broad views of the channel. Two-night minimum.

Secret Point Huts GUESTHOUSE **$$**

(☑ 0819 9937 0826; www.secretpointhuts.com; r from US$80; ❉ 🐷 🛎) In the southwest corner of the island overlooking the Ceningan Point surf break, this cute little resort has a tiny beach and clifftop bar. The rooms are in *lumbung* (rice barn) style bungalows with open-air bathrooms.

🍴 Eating

★ Sea Breeze INDONESIAN **$**

(☑ 0812 3956 7407; Jl Nusa Ceningan; mains 35,000-70,000Rp; ⊘ 8am-10pm) The charming Sea Breeze has a great location with views

of the channel and the seaweed harvest. An attractive open-air setting decorated with plants, bean bags and umbrellas overlooks an infinity pool with a swim-up bar. It offers an excellent seafood selection and does a tasty *nasi campur* – and the Bintang is always cold.

❶ Getting There & Away

To reach Nusa Ceningan you first travel to Nusa Lembongan, then walk or take a motorbike over the short bridge.

Nusa Penida

☑ 0366 / POP 37,581

Just beginning to appear on visitor itineraries, Nusa Penida still awaits proper discovery. It's an untrammelled place that answers the question: what would Bali be like if tourists never came? There are just a handful of formal activities and sights; instead, you go to Nusa Penida to explore and relax, to adapt to the slow rhythm of life here.

The population of around 37,000 is predominantly Hindu, although there is a Muslim community in Toyapakeh. It's an unforgiving area: Nusa Penida was once used as a place of banishment for criminals and other undesirables from the kingdom of Klungkung (now Semarapura), and still has a somewhat sinister reputation. Yet, it's also a centre of rebirth: the iconic Bali starling is being reintroduced here after being thought nearly extinct in the wild. And there's a growing visitor scene near Ped.

◉ Sights

★ Pura Dalem Penetaran Ped HINDU TEMPLE

FREE The important temple of Pura Dalem Penetaran Ped is near the beach at Ped, 3.5km east of Toyapakeh. It houses a shrine for the demon Jero Gede Macaling that is a source of power for practitioners of black magic, and a place of pilgrimage for those seeking protection from sickness and evil. The temple structure is sprawling and you will see people making offerings for safe sea voyages from Nusa Penida; you may wish to join them.

🏃 Activities

Quicksilver WATER SPORTS

(☑ 0361-721521; www.quicksilver-bali.com; adult/child US$110/55) Has day trips from Bali (that leave from Benoa Harbour). A large barge anchored off Toyapakeh is the base for all sorts of water sports. There are also village tours.

DIVING THE ISLANDS

There are great diving possibilities around the islands, from shallow and sheltered reefs, mainly on the northern side of Lembongan and Penida, to very demanding drift dives in the channel between Penida and the other two islands. Vigilant locals have protected their waters from dynamite bombing by renegade fishing boats, so the reefs are relatively intact. And a side result of tourism is that locals no longer rely so much on fishing. In 2012 the islands were designated the Nusa Penida Marine Protected Area, which encompasses more than 20,000 hectares of the surrounding waters.

If you arrange a dive trip from Padangbai or south Bali, stick with the most reputable operators as conditions here can be tricky and local knowledge is essential. Note that the open waters around Penida are challenging, even for experienced divers. Diving accidents regularly happen and people die diving in the waters around the islands every year.

Using one of the recommended operators on Nusa Lembongan puts you close to the action from the start. The large marine animals are a particular attraction, including turtles, sharks and manta rays. The large (3m fin-to-fin) and unusual *mola mola* (sunfish) is sometimes seen around the islands between mid-July and October, while manta rays are often seen south of Nusa Penida from June to October.

The best dive sites include **Blue Corner** and **Jackfish Point** off Nusa Lembongan and **Ceningan Point** at its tip. The channel between Ceningan and Penida is renowned for drift diving, but it is essential you have a good operator who can judge fast-changing currents and other conditions. Upswells can bring cold water from the open ocean to sites such as **Ceningan Wall**. This is one of the world's deepest natural channels and attracts all manner and sizes of fish.

Sites close to Nusa Penida include **Crystal Bay**, **SD**, **Pura Ped**, **Manta Point** and **Batu Aba**. Of these, Crystal Bay, SD and Pura Ped are suitable for novice divers and are good for snorkelling.

Octopus Dive　　　　　　　　　　DIVING
(☑ 0878 6268 0888, 0819 77677677; www.octopus diveindonesia.com; Bodong; 2-tank dives from 1,100,000Rp) A small and enthusiastic local dive operator.

🕝 Tours

★ Penida Tours　　　　　　　　　　TOUR
(☑ 0852 0587 1291; www.penidatours.com; Jl Raya Bodong; tours from 750,000Rp; ⊙ 9am-6pm) A great local operation that arranges cultural tours around Penida, covering anything from black magic to diving to camping trips. The office is located next door to Gallery cafe.

🛏 Sleeping

Full Moon Bungalows　　　　BUNGALOW $
(☑ 0852 0587 1291; www.fullmoon-bungalows.com; Jl Raya Ped, Ped; dm/r from 100,000/200,000Rp; ❄🛜) A well-run compound with 15 bungalows and dorms (some fan-only). Each is basic but comfortable with thatched walls. You're mere steps from Ped's small but delightful nightlife.

Ring Sameton Inn　　　　　　GUESTHOUSE $
(☑ 0813 798 5141; www.ringsameton-nusapenida. com; Bodong; r incl breakfast 400,000-500,000Rp;

❄🛜🛏) If you're seeking comfort, this is easily the best place to stay on Penida. As well as spiffy business-style rooms, there's a pool, an atmospheric restaurant and quick beach access.

🍴 Eating

★ Penida Colada　　　　　　　　CAFE $
(☑ 0821 4676 3627; www.facebook.com/penida colada; Bodong; mains 45,000-70,000Rp; ⊙ 9am-late; 🛜) The cocktails at this charming seaside-shack cafe, run by an Indo–Aussie couple, are a must. Fresh, creative concoctions include mojitos and daiquiris to go with a menu of grilled fish, BLTs and chips with aioli. There's often a seafood barbecue in the evenings. Enjoy the soothing sound of the ocean lapping at the narrow beach. *This* is Penida's nightlife.

ℹ Information

MONEY

The two ATMs are occasionally out of order or cash. Bring plenty of rupiah just in case.

TOURIST INFORMATION

Penida Tours is an excellent contact for island-wide info.

❶ Getting There & Away

The strait between Nusa Penida and southern Bali is deep and subject to heavy swells – if there is a strong tide, boats often have to wait. Charter boats to/from Kusamba are not recommended due to their small size and the potential for heavy seas.

FROM SANUR

Various speedboats leave from the same part of the beach as the fast boats to Nusa Lembongan and make the run in less than an hour.

Maruti Express (🖉 0361-465086, 0811 397 901; http://lembonganfastboats.com/ maruti_express.php; one way adult/child from 362,500/290,000Rp) One of several fast boats making the Penida run.

FROM NUSA LEMBONGAN

Nusa Penida public boats run between Lembongan town by the bridge and Toyapakeh (50,000Rp, 20 minutes). Boats depart from 6am, waiting for a crowd of at least six passengers. Chartering a boat costs a negotiable 300,000Rp to 400,000Rp each way.

FROM PADANGBAI

Fast boats run across the strait from Padangbai to Buyuk, 1km west of Sampalan on Nusa Penida (110,000Rp, 45 minutes, four daily). The boats run between 7am and noon.

A large public car ferry also operates daily (adult/child/motorbike/car) 31,000/26,000/52,000/380,000Rp) leaving at 11am each morning. It takes 40 minutes to two hours, depending on the sea.

❶ Getting Around

Bemos are rare after 10am. There are often people who can set you up with transport where boats arrive. Options for getting around.

Car & driver From 350,000Rp for a half day.

Motorcycle Easily hired for 80,000Rp per day.

Ojek Not common, but if you find a ride on the back of a motorcycle, expect to pay about 50,000Rp per hour.

UBUD REGION

Though Ubud will always claim the limelight in this region, there are some minor players well worthy of attention. A day spent visiting the temples of Tampaksiring, pausing en route to indulge in a photographic frenzy at the famed Ceking rice terraces, is time well spent, and the same can be said for a visit to the many traditional artisans' villages south of Ubud, which are deservedly famous for the quality of their craftmanship. Basing yourself in Ubud, which is replete with alluring sleeping and eating options, is a no-brainer, but so too is hopping on a motorcycle or organising a car and driver to see the rest that this part of Bali has to offer. There may be few top-drawer sights, but there are many scenic side roads that amply reward exploration.

Ubud

🖉 0361 / POP 10,870

Ubud is one of those places where a holiday of a few days can easily turn into a stay of weeks, months or even years. The size of the town's expat community attests to this, and so do the many novels and films that have been set here, creative responses to the seductive nature of this most cultured of all Balinese towns. This is a place where traditional Balinese culture imbues every waking moment, where colourful offerings adorn the streets and where the hypnotic strains of gamelan are an ever-present soundtrack to everyday life. It's also somewhere that is relentlessly on trend – a showcase of sustainable design, mindfulness, culinary inventiveness and the island's rich and alluring culture. Come here for relaxation, for rejuvenation and artistic appreciation.

⊙ Sights

Most sights in Ubud are easily reached on foot, all the better for exploring given the inherent interests and pleasures all around.

⭐ Agung Rai Museum of Art   GALLERY

(ARMA; Map p260; 🖉 0361-976659; www.arma bali.com/museum; Jl Raya Pengosekan; adult/child 100,000Rp/free; ⊙ 9am-6pm) If you only visit one museum in Ubud, make it this one. Founder Agung Rai built his fortune selling Balinese artwork to foreigners in the 1970s, and during his time as a dealer he also built one of Indonesia's most impressive private collections of art. This cultural compound opened in 1996 and displays his collection in two purpose-built gallery buildings – highlights include the wonderful 19th-century *Portrait of a Javanese Nobleman and his Wife* by Javanese artist Raden Saleh (1807–80).

⭐ Neka Art Museum   GALLERY

(Map p260; 🖉 0361-975074; www.museumneka. com; Jl Raya Sanggingan; adult/child 75,000Rp/ free; ⊙ 9am-5pm) Offering an excellent introduction to Balinese art, the top-notch

Ubud Area

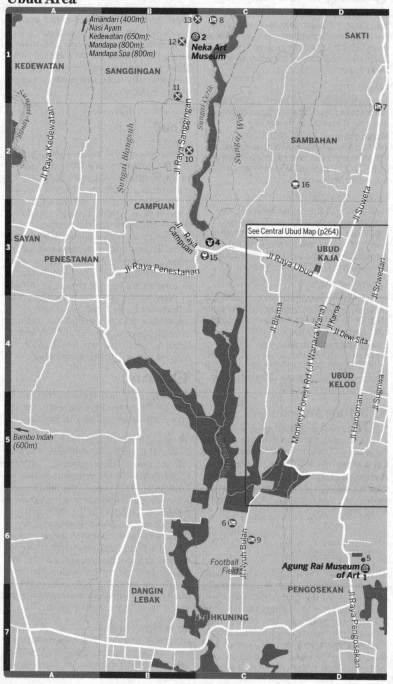

KEDEWATAN

SANGGINGAN

Amandari (400m);
Nasi Ayam
Kedewatan (650m);
Mandapa (800m);
Mandapa Spa (800m)

13 ⊗ ⦿ 8
12 ⊗   🏛 2
Neka Art Museum

SAKTI

11 ⊗

🏛 7

10 ⊗

SAMBAHAN

CAMPUAN

🍴 16

🌀 4
⦿ 15

See Central Ubud Map (p264)

UBUD KAJA

Jl Raya Ubud

Jl Raya Penestanan

PENESTANAN

SAYAN

Sungai Ayung

Jl Raya Kedewatan

Sungai Blangsuh

Jl Raya Sanggingan

Sungai Cerik

Sungai Wos

Jl Raya Campuan

Jl Srwedari

Jl Suweta

Jl Bisma

Jl Wanara Wana (Monkey Forest Rd)

Jl Kama

Jl Dewi Sita

UBUD KELOD

Jl Hanoman

Jl Sugriwa

Bambu Indah
(600m)

Sungai Tegal

6 ⦿
9 ⦿

Jl Nyuh Bulan

Football Field

DANGIN LEBAK

⦿ 5
Agung Rai Museum of Art 🏛 1

PENGOSEKAN

NYUHKUNING

Jl Raya Pengosekan

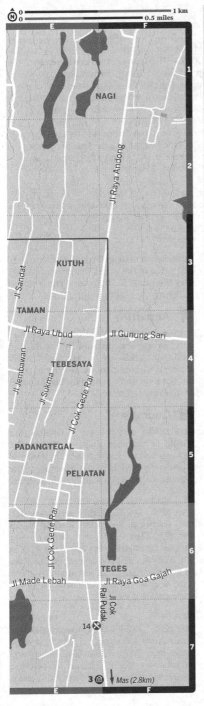

Ubud Area

◎ Top Sights
1 Agung Rai Museum of Art D6
2 Neka Art Museum B1

◎ Sights
3 Museum Rudana E7
4 Pura Gunung Lebah C3

✪ Activities, Courses & Tours
5 ARMA D6

🛏 Sleeping
6 Alam Indah C6
7 Bali Asli Lodge D2
8 Como Uma Ubud C1
9 Swasti Eco Cottages C6

✕ Eating
10 Dumbo B2
11 Mozaic B1
12 Room4Dessert B1
13 Uma Cucina B1
14 Warung Teges E7

🍷 Drinking & Nightlife
15 Bridges C3
16 Sweet Orange Warung D2

collection is displayed in a series of pavilions and halls. Don't miss the multiroom Balinese Painting Hall, which showcases *wayang* (puppet) style as well as the European-influenced Ubud and Batuan styles introduced in the 1920s and '30s. Also notable is the Lempad Pavilion, with works by the master I Gusti Nyoman Lempad (1862–1978), and the East-West Art Annexe, where works by Affandi (1907–90) and Widayat (1919–2002) impress. Good bookstore, too.

Pura Taman Saraswati HINDU TEMPLE
(Map p264; Jl Raya Ubud) FREE Waters from the temple at the rear of this site feed the pond in the front, which overflows with pretty lotus blossoms. There are carvings that honour Dewi Saraswati, the goddess of wisdom and the arts, who has clearly given her blessing to Ubud. Regular dance performances are staged here by night.

Museum Puri Lukisan MUSEUM
(Museum of Fine Arts; Map p264; ☎ 0361-975136; www.museumpurilukisan.com; off Jl Raya Ubud; adult/child 145,000Rp/free; ☺ 9am-5pm) It was in Ubud that the modern Balinese art movement started, when artists first began to abandon purely religious themes and court subjects for scenes of everyday life. This museum set in a lovely formal garden has four

DON'T MISS

UBUD MONKEY FOREST

One of Ubud's most famous sights (or should that be *infamous*) is the **monkey forest** (Mandala Wisata Wanara Wana; Map p264; ☑0361-971304; www.monkeyforestubud.com; Monkey Forest Rd; adult/child 80,000/60,000Rp; ☺8.30am-5.30pm). It's a cool and dense swath of jungle, which houses three holy temples. The sanctuary is inhabited by a band of over 600 grey-haired and greedy long-tailed Balinese macaques who are nothing like the innocent-looking doe-eyed monkeys on the brochures – they can bite, so be careful around them. Note that the temples are only open to worshippers.

Enter the monkey forest through one of three gates: the main one is at the southern end of Monkey Forest Rd. Useful brochures about the forest, macaques and temples are available at the ticket office. Free shuttles to get here and back drive a loop around central Ubud every 15 minutes, stopping on Jl Raya Ubud, Jl Hanoman and on Money Forest Rd – look for the lime-green buses.

Note that the monkeys keep a keen eye on passing tourists in hope of handouts. Irritating recorded warnings list all the ways monkeys can cause trouble: avoid eye contact and showing your teeth, including smiling, which is deemed a sign of aggression. Also, don't try to take bananas from the monkeys or feed them.

buildings displaying works from all schools and periods of Balinese art, with a focus on modern masters including I Gusti Nyoman Lempad (1862–1978), Ida Bagus Made (1915–99) and I Gusti Made Kwandji (1936–2013). All works are labelled in English.

Ubud Palace   PALACE
(Map p264; cnr Jl Raya Ubud & Jl Suweta; ☺9am-7pm) **FREE** This modest palace and its temple, **Puri Saren Agung** (Map p264; cnr Jl Raya Ubud & Jl Suweta) **FREE**, share a compound in the heart of Ubud. Most of its structures were built after the 1917 earthquake and the local royal family still lives here. You can wander around most of the compound and explore the many traditional, though not excessively ornate, buildings. The main pavilion often hosts evening dance performances.

Pura Gunung Lebah   HINDU TEMPLE
(Map p260; off Jl Raya Campuan) This old temple, which sits on a jutting rock at the confluence of two tributaries of Sungai Cerik (*campuan* means 'two rivers'), has recently benefited from a huge building campaign. The setting is magical; listen to the rushing waters while admiring the impressive *meru* (multi-tiered shrine) and a wealth of elaborate carvings.

Pura Penataran Sasih   HINDU TEMPLE
(Jl Raya Tampaksiring, Pejeng; 20,000Rp; ☺7am-5pm) This was once the state temple of the Pejeng kingdom. In the inner courtyard, high up in a pavilion and difficult to see, is the huge bronze drum known as the **Fallen Moon of Pejeng**. The hourglass-shaped

drum is 186cm long, the largest single-piece cast drum in the world. Estimates of its age vary from 1000 to 2000 years. The temple is in Pejeng, 5km east of central Ubud.

🏃 Activities

Yoga and meditation are popular activities here, as are spa sessions. Walks through local rice fields are popular and easily achieved without a guide. Cycling is possible, but local traffic conditions don't make it particularly enjoyable.

🎓 Courses

Ubud is the perfect place to develop your artistic or language skills, or learn about Balinese culture and cuisine. The range of courses offered could keep you busy for a year. With most classes you must book in advance.

⭐**Casa Luna Cooking School**   COOKING
(Map p264; ☑0361-973282; www.casalunabali. com; Honeymoon Guesthouse, Jl Bisma; classes from 400,000Rp) A different cooking class or food tour is offered every day of the week at this well-regarded cooking school associated with the Casa Luna restaurant. Half-day courses cover a range of dishes; some include a market visit.

⭐**ARMA**   CULTURAL TOUR
(Map p260; ☑0361-976659; www.armabali.com/ museum/cultural-workshops; Jl Raya Pengosekan; classes from US$25; ☺9am-6pm) A cultural powerhouse offering classes in painting, woodcarving, gamelan and batik. Other courses include Balinese dance and Hinduism.

☞ Tours

Specialised tours in Ubud include thematic walks and cultural adventures. Spending a few hours exploring the area with a local expert is a highlight for many.

Dhyana Putri Adventures   CULTURAL
(www.balispirit.com/tours/bali_tour_dhyana.html; half-/full-day tours US$120/185) Bicultural and trilingual, author and Balinese dance expert Rucina Ballinger offers custom tours, with an emphasis on Balinese performing arts and in-depth cultural experiences.

Ubud Tourist Information   CULTURAL
(Fabulous Ubud; Map p264; ✆ 0361-973285; www.fabulousubud.com; Jl Raya Ubud; tours 185,000-300,000Rp; ⊗ 8am-8pm) Owned and operated by members of Ubud's royal family, this travel and events agency runs interesting and affordable half- and full-day trips to a huge range of places, including Besakih and Kintamani.

Banyan Tree Cycling Tours   CYCLING
(✆ 0813 3879 8516; www.banyantreebiketours.com; tours adult/child from US$55/35) Enjoy day-long tours of remote villages in the hills north of Ubud. The tours are very popular, and emphasise interaction with villagers. Hiking and rafting trips are also available.

Bali Bird Walks   BIRDWATCHING
(✆ 0361-975009; www.balibirdwalk.com; tour incl lunch US$37; ⊗ 9am-12.30pm Tue, Fri, Sat & Sun) Started by Victor Mason more than three decades ago, this tour, ideal for keen birders, is still going strong. On a gentle morning's walk (from the long-closed Beggar's Bush Bar) you may see up to 30 of the 100-odd local species.

🎭 Festivals & Events

The Ubud area is one of the best places to see the many religious and cultural events celebrated in Bali each year. The Fabulous Ubud Tourist Information Centre (p272) is unmatched for its comprehensive information on local events.

★ Ubud Writers
& Readers Festival   LITERATURE
(www.ubudwritersfestival.com; 1-day pass 1,200,000Rp; ⊗ late Oct/early Nov) Southeast Asia's major literary event brings together writers and readers from around the world in a five-day celebration of writing – especially writing that touches on Bali.

BALI UBUD

SPAS & YOGA

Ubud brims with salons and spas where you can heal, pamper, rejuvenate or otherwise focus on your personal needs, physical and mental. Visiting a spa is at the top of many a traveller's itinerary and the business of spas, yoga and other treatments grows each year. Expect the latest trends from any of many practitioners and prepare to try some new therapies. You may also wish to seek out a *balian* (traditional healer).

Many spas also offer courses in therapies, treatments and activities such as yoga.

Yoga Barn (Map p264; ✆ 0361-971236; www.theyogabarn.com; off Jl Raya Pengosekan; classes from 130,000Rp; ⊗ 6am-9pm) The chakra for the yoga revolution in Ubud, the life force that is the Yoga Barn sits in its own lotus position amid trees near a river valley. The name exactly describes what you'll find: a huge space offering a similarly large range of classes in various yoga practices. There's also an on-site Ayurvedic spa and a garden cafe.

Mandapa Spa (✆ 0361-4792777; www.ritzcarlton.com/en/hotels/indonesia/mandapa/spa; Mandapa Resort, Kedewatan; massages 1,600,000-2,100,000Rp, facials 1,700,000-2,500,000Rp; ⊗ 9am-9pm) The sybaritic riverside spa and wellness centre at the Mandapa resort offers massage and beauty treatments, a yoga pavilion, a meditation temple, a vitality pool, a 24-hour fitness centre and saunas.

Radiantly Alive (Map p264; ✆ 0361-978055; www.radiantlyalive.com; Jl Jembawan 3; per class/3 classes/week 130,000/330,000/800,000Rp; ⊗ 7.30am-6pm) This school will appeal to those looking for an intimate space, and offers a mix of drop-in and long-term yoga classes in a number of disciplines.

Taksu Spa (Map p264; ✆ 0361-479 2525; www.taksuspa.com; Jl Goutama; massage from 450,000Rp; ⊗ 9am-10pm) One of Ubud's most popular spas, Taksu has a long and rather lavish menu of massages and beauty treatments, as well as a strong focus on yoga. There are private rooms for couples massages and a healthy garden cafe.

Central Ubud

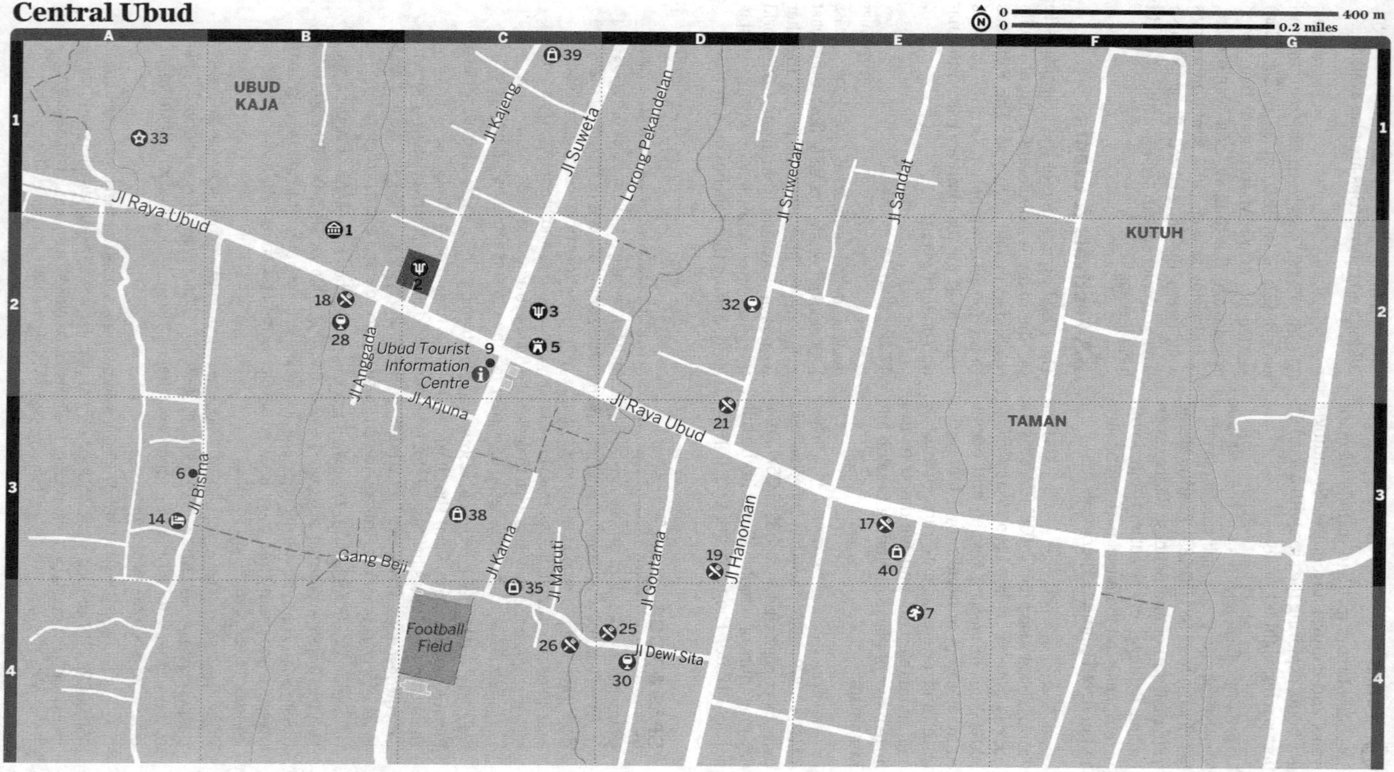

UBUD KAJA

KUTUH

TAMAN

Jl Raya Ubud

Jl Sandat

Jl Sriwedari

Jl Suweta

Jl Kajeng

Lorong Pekandelan

Jl Raya Ubud

Jl Hanoman

Jl Goutama

Jl Dewi Sita

Jl Maruti

Jl Karna

Jl Arjuna

Jl Anggada

Jl Bisma

Gang Beji

Ubud Tourist
Information
Centre

Football
Field

0   400 m
0   0.2 miles

1
33
39
2
3
5
9
32
21
19
25
30
26
35
17
40
7
38
18
28
6
14

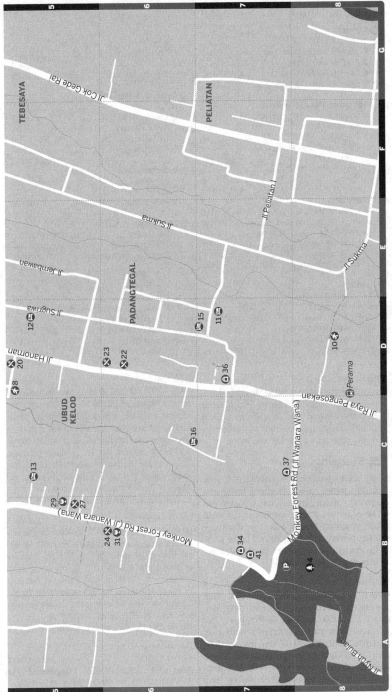

265

BALI UBUD

BALI UBUD

Central Ubud

◎ Sights
1 Museum Puri Lukisan B2
2 Pura Taman Saraswati C2
3 Puri Saren Agung................................. C2
4 Ubud Monkey Forest B8
5 Ubud Palace C2

◎ Activities, Courses & Tours
6 Casa Luna Cooking School A3
7 Radiantly Alive E4
8 Taksu Spa... D5
   Threads of Life Indonesian
   Textile Arts Center....................(see 39)
9 Ubud Tourist Information C2
10 Yoga Barn... D8

◎ Sleeping
11 Artotel Haniman Ubud D7
12 Batik Sekar Bali Guest House.............. D5
13 Komaneka at Monkey Forest............... C5
14 Ladera Villa Ubud................................. A3
15 Pande House D7
16 Three Win Homestay C6

◎ Eating
17 Bali Buda Shop E3
18 Casa Luna... B2
19 Clear.. D3
20 Earth Cafe & Market............................. D5
21 Hujan Locale.. D3
22 Kafe.. D6

◎ Sights (cont.)
23 Kebun D6
24 Liap Liap B6
25 Locavore D4
26 Pica C4
27 Watercress.. B5

◎ Drinking & Nightlife
28 Bar Luna.. B2
29 Laughing Buddha B5
30 Night Rooster D4
31 No Màs B6
32 Seniman Spirits D2

◎ Entertainment
   Paradiso ....(see 20)
33 Pura Dalem Ubud A1
   Pura Taman Saraswati................. (see 2)

◎ Shopping
   Balitaza..(see 26)
34 BaliZen B7
   Casa Luna Emporium ....(see 18)
35 Kou C4
36 Namaste.. D7
37 Pondok Bamboo Music Shop C7
38 Pusaka C3
39 Threads of Life Indonesian
   Textile Arts Center C1
40 Ubud Tea Room E3
41 Utama Spice B7

★ Bali Spirit Festival
DANCE, MUSIC

(www.balispiritfestival.com; ⊘ late Mar/early Apr) A popular yoga, dance and music festival from the people behind the Yoga Barn, a local yoga hub. There are hundreds of workshops and concerts, plus a market and more.

🛏 Sleeping

Ubud has a wonderful array of places to stay, including fabled resorts, boutique hotels and charming, simple homestays. Choices can be bewildering, so give some thought as to where you want to stay, especially if you are renting private accommodation via the web.

In general, Ubud offers good value for money at any price level.

★ Three Win Homestay
HOMESTAY $

(Map p264; ☑ 0812 3819 7835, 0819 9945 3319; www.threewinhomestay.com; Anila Ln, off Jl Hanoman; r 375,000-475,000Rp; 🌐🛜) Putu, her husband Sampo and her father Nyoman are understandably proud of the five modern guest rooms in their family compound. These have tile floors, comfortable beds and sparkling bathrooms; request one upstairs, for a spacious balcony overlooking the rooftops.

Bali Asli Lodge
HOMESTAY $

(Map p260; ☑ 0361-970537; www.baliaslilodge. com; Jl Suweta; r 250,000-300,000Rp; 🛜) Escape the central Ubud hubbub here. Made and Ketut are your friendly hosts, and their five rooms are in traditional Balinese stone-and-brick houses set in verdant gardens; interiors are clean and comfy. There are terraces where you can let the hours pass, and Made will cook meals on request. Town is a 15-minute walk away. Fabulous value.

Pande House
HOMESTAY $

(Map p264; ☑ 0361-970421; www.pandehomestay ubud.wordpress.com; Jl Sugriwa 59; r with fan/aircon from 250,000/400,000Rp; 🛜) Yet another one of Ubud's delightful family-compound homestays, old-fashioned Pande is but one of many clustered on this residential street. Each room has a terrace; the deluxe version has air-con. The frills are few and far between, but the welcome is warm.

Batik Sekar Bali Guest House
GUESTHOUSE $

(Map p264; ☑ 0361-975351; Jl Sugriwa 32; ⊘ r 250,000-350,000Rp; 🌐🛜) In a primo location, this family homestay offers the timeless

Ubud experience. Come and go past Made, Putu and their family as they make offerings and go about daily tasks. The four rooms have terraces and cold-water bathrooms.

★**Swasti Eco Cottages**   GUESTHOUSE **$$**
(Map p260; ☑ 0361-974079; www.baliswasti. com; JI Nyuh Bulan; r with fan/air-con from 600,000/900,000Rp; ❄@☎☲) ✐ A five-minute walk from the south entrance to the Monkey Forest, this compound has large grounds that feature an organic garden (produce is used in the cafe), a pool, spa and yoga shala. Some rooms are in simple two-storey blocks; others are in traditionally styled houses. Yoga and meditation classes are available.

Alam Indah   HOTEL **$$**
(Map p260; ☑ 0361-974629; www.alamindahbali. com; JI Nyuh Bulan; r 1,000,000-1,600,000Rp; ❄☎☲) Just south of the Monkey Forest, this spacious and tranquil resort has 16 rooms that are beautifully finished in natural materials to traditional designs. The Wos Valley views are entrancing, especially from the multilevel pool area. There's a free shuttle into central Ubud.

Artotel Haniman Ubud   HOTEL **$$**
(Map p264; ☑ 0361-9083470; www.artotel indonesia.com/haniman-ubud; JI Jatayu Ubud; r from 1,050,000Rp; P❄☎☲) The latest offering from Indonesia's hip Artotel chain, this place offers 22 good-size studios (20, 30 and 40 sq m) with amenities including a coffee machine. There's a small pool, a spa and a complimentary shuttle into central Ubud.

Ladera Villa Ubud   HOTEL **$$**
(Map p264; ☑ 0361-978127; JI Bisma 25; r from 950,000Rp, villa from 1,400,000Rp; ❄☎☲) Close to the central Ubud action but far enough removed to offer a tranquil retreat, this hotel offers an array of well-equipped rooms and more-luxurious villas; the villas have private pools and basic kitchens. Attentive service; excellent value.

★**Mandapa**   RESORT **$$$**
(☑ 0361-4792777; www.ritzcarlton.com; JI Kedewatan, Kedewatan; ste US$600-900, villa US$1000-5000Rp; P❄@☎☲) Set in a spectacular river valley enclosed by rice fields, this stunning Ritz Carlton resort is the size of a small village. It's replete with facilities – the luxe spa (p263) and Kubu (p269) restaurant are particularly impressive. Guests are offered a programme of 17 complimentary daily activities including yoga, aqua aerobics and a kids club. Suites and villas are large and gorgeous.

★**Komaneka at Monkey Forest**   BOUTIQUE HOTEL **$$$**
(Map p264; ☑ 361-4792518; www.komaneka.com; Monkey Forest Rd; ste 2,300,000-3,100,000Rp; villa 3,800,000-4,200,000Rp; P❄☎☲) It calls itself a resort, but this place has a boutique feel. The Monkey Forest Rd location may seem strange, but the hotel is hidden in lush gardens overlooking a rice field behind the Komaneka Art Gallery and is remarkably tranquil. Ultra-comfortable suites and villas have an elegant decor and abundant amenities; facilities include a restaurant (mains 79,000Rp to 129,000Rp) and spa.

Amandari   HOTEL **$$$**
(☑ 0361-975333; www.amanresorts.com; JI Raya Kedewatan; ste US$700-2400, villa US$4200-4500; P❄@☎☲) Luxurious Amandari does everything with the charm and grace of a classical Balinese dancer. Superb views over the green river valley – the 30m green-tiled swimming pool seems to drop right over the edge – are just some of the inducements. The 30 private pavilions (some with their own pools) are extremely comfortable and complimentary activities include yoga classes and afternoon tea.

★**Como Uma Ubud**   BOUTIQUE HOTEL **$$$**
(Map p260; ☑ 0361-972448; www.comohotels.com; JI Raya Sanggingan; r US$290-320, villa US$580-610; P❄☎☲) A celebration of contemporary Balinese style, this Australian-owned property is one of the few accommodation options in Ubud that can rightfully claim a boutique tag. The 46 rooms come in a variety of sizes but all are attractive and have good amenities; bathrooms are particularly nice. Facilities include an infinity pool, pool bar, spa, yoga pavilion and excellent Italian **restaurant** (pizzas 100,000-180,000Rp, mains 110,000-240,000Rp; ⊙noon-10.30pm Mon-Sat, from 11.30am Sun; ☎✐💷).

★**Bambu Indah**   RESORT **$$$**
(☑ 0361-977922; www.bambuindah.com; JI Banjar Baung; r US$95-495, 2-bedroom house US$645-695; P❄☎☲) ✐ A labour of love by expat entrepreneurs John and Cynthia Hardy, this eco-resort on a ridge near the Sungai Ayung (Ayung River) offers accommodation in 100-year-old Javanese wooden houses and new, quite extraordinary, structures made from natural materials. Some are simple,

BALI UBUD

others luxurious; all are super stylish. Facilities include tiers of natural swimming pools, an organic restaurant and massage pods.

✖ Eating

Ubud's cafes and restaurants are some of the best on Bali. Local and expat chefs produce a bounty of authentic Balinese dishes, plus inventive Asian and other international cuisines. Healthy menus abound. Cafes with good coffee seem as common as frangipani blossoms. Be sure to be seated by 9pm or your options will narrow rapidly. Book for dinner in high season.

★ Kafe   CAFE $

(Map p264; ✆0361-479 2078; www.kafe-bali. com; Jl Hanoman 44; sandwiches & wraps 65,000-89,000Rp, mains 39,000-97,000Rp; ⏰7am-11pm; 🛜🖉) 🍃 This is the type of place that Ubud does particularly well. Attractive decor, laid-back vibe, friendly staff and healthy food are the hallmarks, and together they form a tempting package. The huge organic menu has something for most tastes, with a huge range of vegan, veggie and raw offerings with Balinese, Indonesian, Indian and Mexican accents. Good value.

Nasi Ayam Kedewatan   BALINESE $

(✆0361-974795; Jl Raya Kedewatan, Kedewatan; mains 25,000-35,000Rp; ⏰8am-6pm) Few locals making the trek up the hill through Sayan pass this Bali version of a roadhouse without stopping. The star is *sate lilit*: chicken is minced, combined with a selection of spices including lemongrass, then moulded onto bamboo skewers and grilled. It's served as part of the *nasi ayam campur* (25,000Rp) or *nasi ayam pisah* (35,000Rp) set meals.

Liap Liap   INDONESIAN $

(Map p264; ✆0361-9080800; www.liapliap.com; Monkey Forest Rd; satays 35,000-65,000Rp; ⏰10am-11pm) The name references the sound that charcoal embers make as they heat up, paying tribute to the technique that chef Mandif Warokka uses when grilling the spicy Indonesian dishes that dominate the menu at this contemporary warung. Watch the grilling action in the front window while sipping a cocktail drawn from a long list of classics and house signatures.

Hujan Locale   INDONESIAN $$

(Map p264; ✆0813 3972 0306; www.hujanlocale. com; Jl Sriwedari 5; mains 120,000-200,000Rp; ⏰noon-10pm; 🛜🖉) Chef Will Meyrick is the culinary genius behind Mama San in

Seminyak, and his Ubud outpost is just as impressive. The menu delivers traditional Indonesian with modern, creative flair and the results are uniformly delicious. The setting within a chic colonial-style two-storey bungalow is casually stylish and cleverly flexible – enjoy cocktails and snacks in the downstairs lounge, lunch and dinner upstairs.

★ Dumbo   VEGETARIAN $$

(Map p260; ✆0812 3838 9993; www.dumbobali. com; Jl Raya Sanggingan; pizza 80,000-95,000Rp, small plates 55,000-80,000Rp, large plates 85,000-180,000Rp; ⏰9am-11pm; 🅿🛜) Music, mixology and Italian food are a particularly good trio, so you'd need to be a dumbo not to eat here, especially as pizzas cooked in a wood-fired oven are also on offer (after 4pm only). Trained bar staff and baristas ensure that the cocktails and coffee are as good as the food, and the DJ's playlist is a winner.

Clear   FUSION $$

(Map p264; ✆0878 6219 7585, 0361-889 4437; www.clearcafebali.com; Jl Hanoman 8; meals US$4-15; ⏰8am-10pm; 🛜🖉) Known for its theatrical decor and crowd-pleasing menu, Clear is one of Ubud's most popular eateries. The relentlessly healthy dishes feature local produce and have artful presentation; menu influences range from Japan (sushi) to Mexico (tacos, quesadillas), with loads of veggie and vegan options. No alcohol, but the huge choice of fruit smoothies, tonic, juices and milkshakes compensates. Cash only.

★ Watercress   CAFE $$

(Map p264; ✆0361-976127; www.watercressubud. com; Monkey Forest Rd; breakfast dishes 45,000-90,000Rp, sandwiches 65,000-75,000Rp, mains 90,000-290,000Rp; ⏰7.30am-11pm; 🛜) A young and fashionable crowd flocks to this Aussie-style contemporary cafe to nosh on all-day breakfasts, burgers, sourdough sandwiches, homemade cakes, gourmet salads and more. Drink good coffee during the day and cocktails at night (happy hour daily 5pm to 7pm, live music Friday).

Kebun   MEDITERRANEAN $$

(Map p264; ✆0361-972490; www.kebunbistro. com; Jl Hanoman 44; mains 65,000-155,000Rp; ⏰11am-11pm Mon-Fri, from 9am Sat & Sun; 🛜) Paris meets Ubud at this charming bistro and it's a good match. Your choice from the substantial cocktail and wine lists can be paired with French- and Italian-accented dishes large and small. Dine or sip a drink in the bar area, or claim a table on the terrace.

★**Pica** SOUTH AMERICAN $$$

(Map p264; ☑0361-971660; www.facebook.com/ PicaSouthAmericanKitchen; Jl Dewi Sita; mains 170,000-330,000Rp; ⊙6-10pm Tue-Sun; ⊛) Much-acclaimed, the contemporary South American cuisine served at this small restaurant is one of Ubud's culinary highlights. From the open kitchen, dishes making creative use of meat and fish issue forth – be sure to ask about daily specials. Ordering the delectable tre leche dessert should be mandatory. Bookings advisable.

Kubu MEDITERRANEAN $$$

(☑0361-4792777; www.ritzcarlton.com/en/hotels /indonesia/mandapa/dining; Mandapa Resort, Jl Kedewatan, Kedewatan; mains 280,000-500,000Rp, degustation menus 750,000-1,150,000Rp; ⊙6.30-11pm) Resembling a posh version of the Balinese bamboo hut that it is named for, Mandapa's premier restaurant offers a memorable and romantic dining experience. Reserve a table in the main dining area or opt for a private cabana overlooking the Sungai Ayung. Chef Maurizio Bombini's Mediterranean-European cuisine is as excellent as the surrounds and service. Book well in advance.

Mozaic FUSION $$$

(Map p260; ☑0361-975768; www.mozaic-bali. com; Jl Raya Sanggingan; lunch tasting menu 500,000-700,000Rp, dinner tasting menu 700,000-1,600,000Rp; ⊙6-9.45pm Mon-Wed, noon-2pm & 6-9.45pm Thu-Sun; ⊛☑) Chef Chris Salans oversees this much-lauded top-end restaurant. Fine French fusion cuisine features on a constantly changing seasonal menu that takes its influences from tropical Asia. Dine in an elegant garden twinkling with romantic lights or an ornate pavilion. Tasting menus are obligatory, unless you wish to limit yourself to tapas in the lounge (from 5pm). Lunch in high season only.

★**Room4Dessert** DESSERTS $$$

(R4D; Map p260; ☑0821 4429 3452; www.room4 dessert.asia; Jl Raya Sanggingan; tasting dessert & cocktail menu 1,000,000Rp; ⊙5-11pm Tue-Sun) Celebrity chef Will Goldfarb, who hails from the States and gained fame via Netflix's *Chef's Table*, runs what could be a nightclub but is in fact a dessert bar where patrons who book far enough in advance (you'll need to do so at least a month before your visit) can enjoy a decadent nine-course tasting menu matched with cocktails/mocktails/ wine.

🍸 **Drinking & Nightlife**

No one comes to Ubud for wild nightlife, although that may slowly be changing. A few bars get lively around sunset and later in the night; still, the venues don't aspire to the extremes of boozy debauchery and clubbing found in Kuta and Seminyak. Most bars close early in Ubud, often by 11pm.

The quality of the coffee served in Ubud's growing number of cafes is good, with many places roasting their own beans and employing expert baristas.

Bar Luna LOUNGE

(Map p264; ☑0361-977409; www.facebook.com/ barlunaubud; Jl Raya Ubud; ⊙3-11pm; ⊛) The basement bar at Casa Luna hosts a popular jazz club on Sunday evenings from 7.30pm – bookings recommended. On other days, the 5pm happy hour and tasty tapas menu are lures. It's a hive of activity and literary chatter during the Ubud Writers & Readers Festival.

★**Sweet Orange Warung** CAFE

(Map p260; ☑0813 3877 8689; www.sweetorange warung.com; Jl Subak Juwak; ⊙9am-9pm) An idyllic location in the midst of a rice field a short walk from the centre of town makes this a wonderful spot for a drink or simple meal. You'll be serenaded by water running through the farming channels, birds singing and local children playing. Drinks include French-press coffee, beer and fresh juice.

Laughing Buddha LOUNGE

(Map p264; ☑0361-970928; www.facebook.com/ laughingbuddhabali; Monkey Forest Rd; ⊙11am-1am; ⊛) Head to this popular bar between 8pm and 11pm, when musicians (rock, blues, latin, acoustic and more) entertain the crowd. The kitchen serves Asian bites.

★**Bridges** LOUNGE

(Map p260; ☑0361-970095; www.bridgesbali.com; Jl Raya Campuan, Bridges Bali; ⊙4-11.30pm daily, happy hour 4-6.30pm Sat-Thu) The namesake bridges are right outside the Divine Wine & Cocktail Bar on the lower level of this bar/ restaurant complex, which has sweeping views of the river gorge. You'll hear the rush of the water far below while you indulge in a top-end cocktail. There are gourmet bites for sharing and a long wine list for exploring.

No Màs BAR

(Map p264; ☑0361-9080800; www.nomasubud. com; Monkey Forest Rd; ⊙5pm-1am) DJs and Latin bands crank the volume up every

BALI UBUD

DON'T MISS

BALINESE DANCE

Dances performed for visitors are usually adapted and abbreviated to some extent to make them more enjoyable, but usually have appreciative locals in the audience (or peering around the screen!). It's also common to combine the features of more than one traditional dance in a single performance.

Fabulous Ubud Tourist Information Centre (p272) can supply a performance schedule and also sells tickets (usually between 75,000Rp and 100,000Rp). For performances outside Ubud, transport is often included in the price. Tickets are also sold at many hotels, at the venues and by street vendors – all charge the same price.

Kecak

Probably the best-known dance for its spellbinding, hair-raising atmosphere, the Kecak features a 'choir' of men and boys who sit in concentric circles and slip into a trance as they chant and sing 'chak-a-chak-a-chak', imitating a troupe of monkeys. Sometimes called the 'vocal gamelan', this is the only music to accompany the dance re-enactment from the Hindu epic Ramayana, the familiar love story about Prince Rama and his Princess Sita.

Barong & Rangda

The Barong is a good but mischievous and fun-loving shaggy dog-lion, with huge eyes and a mouth that clacks away to much dramatic effect. Because this character is the good protector of a village, the actors playing the Barong (who are utterly lost under layers of fur-clad costume) will emote a variety of winsome antics.

Meanwhile, the widow-witch Rangda is bad through and through. The Queen of Black Magic, the character's monstrous persona can include flames shooting out her ears, a tongue dripping fire, a mane of wild hair and large breasts.

The story features a duel between the Rangda and the Barong, whose supporters draw their kris (traditional daggers) and rush in to help. The long-tongued, sharp-fanged Rangda throws them into a trance, making them stab themselves. It's quite a spectacle. Thankfully, the Barong casts a spell that neutralises the power of the kris so it cannot harm them.

Legong

Characterised by flashing eyes and quivering hands, this most graceful of Balinese dances is performed by young girls. Their talent is so revered that in old age, a classic dancer will be remembered as a 'great Legong'.

Peliatan's famous dance troupe, Gunung Sari, is often seen in Ubud and is particularly noted for its Legong Keraton (Legong of the Palace). The very stylised and symbolic story involves two Legong girls dancing in mirror image. They are elaborately made up and dressed in gold brocade, relating a story about a king who takes a maiden captive and consequently starts a war, in which he dies.

night at this small bar on one of the town's main strips, and there are occasional theme nights too. It can get hot when the dancing starts, but the pool bar in the rear garden provides a welcome relief.

★ **Night Rooster** COCKTAIL BAR
(Map p264; ☑ 0361-977733; www.locavore.co.id/nightrooster; Jl Dewi Sita 10B; ⊗ 4pm-midnight Mon-Sat) From the same folks at **Locavore** (Map p264; ☑ 0361-977733; www.restaurantlocavore.com; Jl Dewi Sita; 5-course menu 675,000-775,000Rp, 7-course menu 775,000-875,000Rp; ⊗ 6.30-9pm Mon, noon-2pm & 6.30-9pm Tue-Sat; ⓟ❄️🛜), this neighbouring, 2nd-storey cocktail bar has a talented mixologist and

some fascinating flavour combos. Inventive cocktails include things such as jackfruit-infused dry gin, homemade bitters and flaming cassia bark. The selection of appetisers and cheese and charcuterie platters makes for satisfying pairings.

Seniman Spirits BAR
(Bar Seniman; Map p264; www.senimancoffee.com; Jl Sriwedari; ⊗ 6pm-midnight) The highly caffeinated masterminds behind the Seniman coffee brand recently opened this bar next to their coffee studio, and it has become one of Ubud's most fashionable drinking dens. Unsurprisingly, espresso martinis are the cocktail of choice.

☆ Entertainment

Few travel experiences are more magical than watching Balinese dance, especially in Ubud. It's the perfect base for nightly cultural entertainment and for events in surrounding villages. In Ubud you can see Kecak, Legong and Barong dances, Mahabharata and Ramayana ballets, *wayang kulit* (shadow-puppet plays) and gamelan (traditional Javanese and Balinese orchestras). There are eight or more performances each night.

★ Pura Dalem Ubud   DANCE

(Map p264; Jl Raya Ubud; adult/child under 10yr 80,000/40,000Rp; ☺ Mon-Sat) This open-air venue in a temple compound has a flame-lit, carved-stone backdrop and is an evocative place to see a dance performance. Different companies perform Legong (7.30pm Tuesday and Saturday), Jegog (7.30pm Wednesday), Barong (7pm Thursday) and the Kecak fire dance (7.30pm Monday and Friday).

★ Pura Taman Saraswati   DANCE

(Ubud Water Palace; Map p264; Jl Raya Ubud; tickets 80,000Rp; ☺ 7.30pm) The beauty of the setting may distract you from the dancers, although at night you can't see the lily pads and lotus flowers that are such an attraction by day. Janger dance is performed on Sunday and Monday, the Ramayana ballet on Wednesday and Legong on Saturday. On Tuesday and Thursday, women play the gamelan and children dance.

Paradiso   CINEMA

(Map p264; ☎ 0361-976546; www.paradisoubud. com; Jl Gautama Selatan; incl food or drinks 50,000Rp; ☺ films from 5pm) Sharing a building with the vegan **Earth Cafe & Market** (www.earthcafebali.com; mains 79,000-98,000Rp; ☺ 7am-10pm; 🛜🍴), this surprisingly plush 150-seat cinema screens two films daily. The price of admission is redeemable against items from the cafe menu – so a great deal. Mondays are half-price; on Tuesday and Thursday a community choir sings here. Check the website for a schedule.

🛍 Shopping

Ubud is home to art shops, boutiques and galleries. Many offer items that have been made locally. There's also an enormous number of craft galleries, studios and workshops in villages north and south.

The area's main shopping strip has moved to Jl Peliatan in Tebesaya and Peliatan. Here you'll find all the stores and shops that supply locals with their daily needs.

★ Threads of Life
Indonesian Textile Arts Center   TEXTILES

(Map p264; ☎ 0361-972187; www.threadsoflife. com; Jl Kajeng 24; ☺ 10am-7pm) This textile gallery and shop sponsors the production of naturally dyed, handmade ritual textiles from around Indonesia. It exists to help recover skills in danger of being lost to modern dyeing and weaving methods. Commissioned pieces are displayed in the gallery, which has good explanatory material, and other textiles are available for purchase. It also runs regular textile-appreciation **courses** (2hr class 200,000-400,000Rp).

BaliZen   TEXTILES

(Map p264; ☎ 0361-976022; www.tokobalizen.com; Monkey Forest Rd; ☺ 9am-8pm) Locally made cushions, bed and home linens, kimonos and kids clothing are sold at this stylish boutique, all made with fabrics featuring designs drawn from nature or utilising traditional Balinese motifs. It also sells natural bath products and traditional Balinese umbrellas.

★ Kou   COSMETICS

(Map p264; ☎ 0361-971905, 0821 4556 9663; www. facebook.com/koubali.naturalsoap; Jl Dewi Sita; ☺ 9am-8pm) Concocted from pure coconut oil, the handmade soaps sold here will bring the evocative scents of frangipani, tuberose, jasmine, orange and lemon tea-tree to your bathroom. The attractive packaging makes products suitable for gifts. It also operates Kou Cuisine.

Balitaza   SPICES

(Map p264; ☎ 0811 393 9499; www.balitaza.com; Jl Dewi Sita; ☺ 9.30am-9.30pm) Coconut sugar, traditional Balinese coffee, herbal teas and Indonesian herbs and spices make great gifts to take home, especially with their attractive packaging.

Utama Spice   COSMETICS

(Map p264; ☎ 0361-975051; www.utamaspice bali.com; Monkey Forest Rd; ☺ 9am-8.30pm) The scent of Utama's Balinese-made natural skincare products wafts out into the street, luring shoppers inside to investigate the pricey but nice essential oils, cosmetics and toiletries sold here. All are made without parabens, mineral oils, synthetic fragrances and artificial colourants.

BALI UBUD

UBUD'S BEST BUYS

You can spend days in and around Ubud shopping. Head to Monkey Forest Rd and Jl Dewi Sita – boutiques there are a cut above the Ubud average. Start with the sweetly-scented Kou (p271) and then add to your shopping bag at nearby homewares, clothing, jewellery and produce shops.

Arts and crafts and yoga goods are found everywhere and at every price point and quality.

Ubud is the best place in Bali for books. Selections are wide and varied, especially for tomes on Balinese art and culture.

Casa Luna Emporium
HOMEWARES
(Map p264; ☑0361-971605; www.casalunabali.com/the-emporium; Jl Raya Ubud 23; ⊗8.30am-10pm) Yet another enterprise started by local entrepreneur Janet DeNeefe, this shop sells its own brand of cotton bedlinen, cushion covers and napery, as well as handwoven textiles, batik, furniture and art made by Balinese artisans. It's accessed via a staircase next to the Casa Luna restaurant.

Namaste
GIFTS & SOUVENIRS
(Map p264; ☑0361-970528; www.facebook.com/namastethespiritualshop; Jl Hanoman 64; ⊗9am-7pm) Just the place to buy a crystal to get your spiritual house in order, Namaste stocks a top range of New Age supplies. Incense, yoga mats, moody instrumental music – it's all here.

Pondok Bamboo Music Shop
MUSICAL INSTRUMENTS
(Map p264; ☑0361-974807; Monkey Forest Rd; ⊗9am-8pm) Hear the music of a thousand bamboo wind chimes at this store owned by noted gamelan musician Nyoman Warsa, who also offers music lessons (per hour 150,000Rp to 200,000Rp).

Pusaka
CLOTHING
(Map p264; ☑0821 4649 8865; Monkey Forest Rd 71; 9am-9pm) Stylish Balinese-made clothing, toys, jewellery, textiles and shoes are sold at this branch of Denpasar's popular Ethnologi boutique.

Ubud Tea Room
FOOD & DRINKS
(Map p264; Jl Jembawan; ⊗7am-9pm) This hole-in-the-wall shop is lined with glass jars of teas grown in Bali, including fragrant herbal infusions. It shares premises with **Bali Buda** (☑0361-976324; www.balibuda.com; mains 38,000-67,000Rp, pizzas 63,000-81,000Rp; ⊗7am-10pm; ⌨).

ⓘ Information

Ubud Tourist Information Centre (Map p264; ☑0361-973285; www.fabulousubud.com; Jl Raya Ubud; ⊗8am-9pm; ☎) is operated by the Ubud royal family. It offers up-to-date details on events, ceremonies and traditional dances held in the area; dance tickets and tours are also sold here.

MONEY

Ubud has numerous banks and ATMs. Be aware that the skimming of cards at kiosk ATMs has been reported; try to use ATMs attached to banks as these have better security.

ⓘ Getting There & Away

SHUTTLE BUS

Perama (Map p264; ☑0361-973316; www.peramatour.com; Jl Raya Pengosekan; ⊗7am-9pm) has bus services to Sanur (50,000Rp, one hour), Kuta and the airport (60,000Rp, two hours) and Padangbai (75,000Rp, two hours). Its terminal is located in Padangtegal, south of the centre; to get to/from your destination in Ubud will cost another 15,000Rp.

Kura-Kura Bus (www.kura2bus.com; Jl Raya Ubud) runs a tourist shuttle bus (line 5) between Kuta, Sanur and Ubud (one way 80,000Rp, four daily). The main Ubud stop is in front of the Puri Lukisan Museum on Jl Raya Ubud.

ⓘ Getting Around

Many high-end spas, hotels and restaurants located outside the town centre offer free shuttles for guests and customers. Ask about this before booking accommodation.

TO/FROM THE AIRPORT

A taxi or hired car with driver from the airport to Ubud will cost 350,000Rp (400,000Rp between midnight and 6am). A hired car with driver to the airport will cost about the same.

CAR & MOTORCYCLE

With numerous attractions nearby and no public transport, renting a car or motorcycle is sensible. Ask at your accommodation or hire a car and driver.

Expect to pay around 50,000Rp per day for a late model motorbike in good condition, considerably more for a car.

Most drivers are very fair; a few – often from out of the area – not so much. If you find a driver you like, get their number and call to organise rides during your stay. From central Ubud to, say, Sangginggan should cost about 40,000Rp. A ride from the palace to the end of Jl Hanoman should cost about 20,000Rp.

It's easy to get a ride on an *ojek* (motorbike taxi); rates are half those of cars.

TAXI

There are no metered taxis based in Ubud – those that honk their horns at you have usually dropped off passengers from southern Bali and are hoping for a fare back. There are plenty of drivers with private vehicles on the streets hectoring passers-by, in contrast some quietly hold up 'transport' signs.

South of Ubud

The roads between Ubud and south Bali are lined with little shops making and selling handicrafts. Many visitors shop along the route as they head to and from Ubud – sometimes by the busload – but as much of the craftwork is done in small workshops and family compounds on quiet back roads, it's worth veering off the major roads. If you do this, you'll likely discover temples and atmospheric villages, too.

Bedulu

☑ 0361 / POP 10,300

Bedulu was once the capital of a great kingdom. The legendary Dalem Bedaulu ruled the Pejeng dynasty from here, and was the last Balinese king to withstand the onslaught of the powerful Majapahit from Java. He was defeated by Gajah Mada in 1343. The capital shifted several times after this, to Gelgel and then later to Klungkung (Semarapura). Today Bedulu is absorbed into the greater Ubud sprawl, and is worth visiting for its temples.

◉ Sights

Yeh Pulu   HISTORIC SITE

(adult/child 15,000/7500Rp; ☺8am-5.30pm) Set amid rice terraces, this 25m-long carved cliff face next to the Sungai Petanu is believed to be the remnants of a 14th-century hermitage. Even if your interest in carved Hindu art is minor, the site is attractive and you're likely to have it all to yourself. Apart from the figure of Ganesha, elephant-headed son of Shiva, most scenes depict scenes of everyday life. From the site entrance, a 300m walk on a gently inclined path goes to the carvings.

You can walk between Yeh Pulu and Goa Gajah, following small paths through the paddy fields, but you might need to pay a local to guide you. By car or bicycle, look for the signs to 'Relief Yeh Pulu' or 'Villa Yeh Pulu', east of Goa Gajah.

Goa Gajah   CAVE

(Elephant Cave; Jl Raya Goa Gajah; adult/child 50,000/25,00Rp, parking per car/motorcycle 5000/2000Rp; ☺7.30am-7pm) Visitors enter this rock-hewn cave through the cavernous mouth of a demon. Inside, there are fragmentary remains of a lingam, the phallic symbol of the Hindu god Shiva, and its female counterpart the yoni, as well as a statue of Shiva's son, the elephant-headed god Ganesha. Outside, two square bathing pools have waterspouts held by six female figures. Located 2km southeast of Ubud on the road to Bedulu, the compound has a sideshow atmosphere and is inevitably crammed with foreign tourists.

❶ Getting There & Away

The road from Ubud is reasonably flat, so coming to Bedulu by bicycle or on foot is an option.

Mas

☑ 0361 / POP 13,120

Mas means 'gold' in Bahasa Indonesia, but woodcarving is the principal craft in this artisans' village just south of Ubud. Stores and galleries line the main road, Jl Raya Mas, and workshops are located both here and in side streets.

◉ Sights

★ **Setia Darma House**
of Mask and Puppets   MUSEUM

(☑0361-898 7493; www.maskandpuppets.com; Jl Tegal Bingin; admission by donation; ☺8am-6pm) This is one of the best museums in the Ubud area, home to more than 7000 ceremonial masks and puppets from Bali, other parts of Indonesia, Asia and beyond. All are beautifully displayed in a series of renovated historic buildings. Among the many treasures, look for the amazing Barong Landung puppets and the Kamasan paintings. There's also a large collection of puppets from other countries. The museum is about 2km northeast of the main Mas crossroads.

Tonyraka Art Lounge   GALLERY

(☑0812 3600 8035; www.tonyrakaartgallery.com; Jl Raya Mas 86; ☺10am-5pm) One of the

BALI'S VILLAGE ARTISTS

In small villages throughout the Ubud region, from Sebatu to Mas and beyond across Bali, you'll see small signs for artists and craftspeople, often near the local temple. As one local told us, 'we are only as rich of a village as our art', so the people who create the ceremonial costumes, masks, *kris* (traditional dagger), musical instruments and all the other beautiful aspects of Balinese life and religion are accorded great honour. It's a symbiotic relationship, with the artist never charging the village for the work and the village in turn seeing to the welfare of the artist. Often there are many artists in residence because few events would bring more shame to a village than having to go to another village to procure a needed sacred object.

premier galleries in the Ubud area, showing top-notch Balinese tribal and contemporary art. Come to browse, buy and to enjoy lunch or a coffee at the chic cafe, which is one of the best in the Ubud area.

Museum Rudana　　　　　GALLERY
(Map p260; ☑0361-975779; www.museumrudana. com; Jl Raya Mas; 50,000Rp; ☉9.30am-5pm) This imposing museum overlooking rice fields is the creation of local politician and art lover Nyoman Rudana and his wife, Ni Wayan Olasthini. The three floors contain more than 400 traditional paintings, including a calendar dated to the 1840s, some Lempad drawings and more modern pieces. The museum is located next to the Rudana's commercial gallery.

🎓 Courses

Ida Bagus Anom　　　　　ART
(☑0812 380 1924, 0898 914 2606; www.balimask making.com; Jl Raya Mas; 4hr class 250,000Rp; ☉hours vary) Three generations of some of Bali's best mask carvers will show you their secrets in a family compound opposite the football field; a mask usually takes 10 days to make.

🍴 Eating

There are plenty of eateries – warungs (food stands), cafes and restaurants – on Jl Raya Mas.

Warung Teges　　　　　BALINESE $
(Map p260; ☑0361-975251; Jl Cok Rai Pudak; nasi campur 25,000Rp; ☉8am-6pm) This ultra-simple warung serves only one dish – *nasi campur* – and it's one of the better versions available in the Ubud area. The restaurant gets just about everything right, from the pork sausage to the chicken satay, the *babi guling* to the tempeh. The sambal is delicious: fresh and tangy, with a perfect amount of heat.

⭐**Art Lounge Cafe**　　　　　CAFE $$
(☑0361-908 2435; www.facebook.com/Tonyraka ArtLounge; Jl Raya Mas 86; panini 73,000-88,000Rp, mains 45,000-135,000Rp; ☉8am-10pm; 🛜🅿) An outpost of Bali chic on one of the main roads between Ubud and the coast, this fashionable cafe in the Tonyraka Art Lounge is an excellent lunch, dinner or coffee spot. Staff know how to make a good coffee, and the food is good – we particularly recommend the cakes.

Bebek Semar Warung　　　　　BALINESE $$
(☑0361-974677; Jl Raya Mas 165; mains 85,000-135,000Rp; ☉8am-9pm) It doesn't look promising from the street but step through to the breezy dining area and you'll be confronted with a green vista of rice fields stretching off to palm trees. The Balinese duck dishes that are the house specialty are unusual and delicious. Find it 1km south of where Jl Raya Mas meets Jl Raya Pengosekan.

ℹ️ Getting There & Away

South of Ubud, the roads are mostly flat so cyclists will be pleased, although the main roads can be busy. Otherwise you'll want your own wheels in this region. The back roads are great for cycling and walking.

Batubulan

☑0361 / POP 8450

Stone carving is the main craft of Batubulan, and the start of the main road to Ubud from south Bali is lined with outlets for stone sculptures. Workshops are found right along the road to Tegaltamu, with another batch further north around Silakarang. The village is also the source of the stunning temple-gate guardians seen all over Bali. The stone used for these sculptures is a porous grey volcanic rock called *paras,* which resembles pumice; it's soft and surprisingly light. It also ages quickly, so that 'ancient' work may be years rather than centuries old.

◉ Sights

Pura Puseh Desa Batubulan   HINDU TEMPLE
(Jl Raya Batuan; by donation; ⊙8am-noon) The temples around Batubulan are noted for their fine stonework. Just 200m to the east of the busy main road, Pura Puseh Desa Batubulan is worth a visit for its perfectly balanced overall composition. Statues draw on ancient Hindu and Buddhist iconography and Balinese mythology; however, they are not old – many are copied from books on archaeology.

Bali Bird Park   BIRD SANCTUARY
(📲0361-299352; www.balibirdpark.com; Jl Serma Cok Ngurah Gambir; adult/child 2-12yr 385,000/192,500Rp; ⊙9am-5.30pm; 🅿🚼) More than 1000 birds from 250 species and seven regions of the world flit about here, including rare cendrawasih (bird of paradise) from Papua and the all-but-vanished Bali starlings. Many are housed in special walk-through aviaries. Daily free-flight bird and bird of prey shows are staged, along with pelican and lory feedings. The park is popular with kids; allow at least two hours.

Bali Reptile Park   ANIMAL SANCTUARY
(Jl Serma Cok Ngurah Gambir; adult/child 2-12yr 100,000/50,000Rp; ⊙9am-5pm) This sanctuary claims to have the most complete collection of reptiles in Southeast Asia. There are snakes and lizards galore. Try to time your visit with the daily feedings of the park's huge prehistoric Komodo dragons (11am and 2.30pm).

❶ Getting There & Away

You'll need your own transport to explore here. The roads are mostly flat so good for cyclists, although the main roads can be busy.

North of Ubud

North of Ubud, Bali becomes cooler and more lush. Ancient sites and natural beauty abound. A popular route from Ubud northeast towards Gunung Batur passes through Tegallalang, home to the photogenic Ceking rice terraces, and then continues via Tampaksiring, passing Gunung Kawi Sebatu, Pura Gunung Kawi and Tirta Empul en route. The scenery on this route is green and extremely picturesque – you'll see farmers working in their fields, colourful flags fluttering in the wind and plenty of rice terraces and roadside shrines.

◉ Sights

Gunung Kawi Sebatu   HINDU TEMPLE
(Sebatu; adult/child 15,000/7500Rp, parking 5000Rp) The western approach to this water temple in Sebatu offers wonderful views down on to the complex – many visitors are content to admire these from the side of the road rather than entering the actual temple. Inside, spring-fed pools are set against a lush green backdrop. The temple is dedicated to Vishnu and is used locally for purification rituals.

❶ Getting There & Away

You'll need your own transport to explore this part of the island.

Tampaksiring
📲0361 / POP 10,480
Located in the Pakerisan Valley, 18km northeast of Ubud, Tampaksiring was the base of one of the major kingdoms during Bali's pre-colonial period. It's home to both Pura Tirta Empul, an ancient and important water temple, and Gunung Kawi, one of the most impressive ancient sites in Bali. The area is replete with terraced rice fields running down to the river and streams – wonderful subject matter for photographers.

◉ Sights

Gunung Kawi   MONUMENT
(adult/child 15,000/7500Rp, parking 2000Rp; ⊙7am-5pm) One of Bali's oldest and most important monuments, this river-valley complex consists of 10 huge *candi* (shrines) cut out of rock faces. Each is believed to be a memorial to a member of 11th-century Balinese royalty. Legends relate that the whole group was carved out of the rock in one hard-working night by the mighty fingernails of Kebo Iwa. You'll need to be fit to explore here, as access to the valley and shrines is via a steep 250-step staircase.

Pura Tirta Empul   HINDU TEMPLE
(Holy Spring Temple; Tampaksiring; adult/child 15,000/7500Rp, parking 5000Rp; ⊙7am-6pm) Discovered in AD 962 and believed to have magical powers, the holy springs at this water temple close to the ancient site of Gunung Kawi bubble up into a large pool and gush out through waterspouts into a *petirtaan* (bathing area) used for ritual purification. The water can be polluted, so bathing isn't recommended.

MARIUS DOBILAS/SHUTTERSTOCK ©

. **Barong dancer (p270)**
he Barong dance is a crowd-pleaser, starring
arong, the mischievous shaggy dog-lion.

. **Pura Luhur Ulu Watu (p242)**
he Hindu temple Ulu Watu is perched on the
outhwestern edge of the Bukit Peninsula.

. **Surfboards, Kuta (p217)**
urfboards can be hired right on Kuta Beach,
here surf lessons are also available.

. **Potato Head (p234), Kerobokan**
he highest-profile beach club in Bali has a
empting in-pool bar and multiple restaurants.

PHOTOGRAPHER253/SHUTTERSTOCK ©

EAST BALI

Exploring east Bali is one of the island's great pleasures. Rice terraces spill down hillsides, wild volcanic beaches are pounded by surf and traditional villages are barely touched by modernity. Watching over this region is Gunung Agung, the 3142m active volcano known as the 'Navel of the World' and 'Mother Mountain'.

Temples, palaces and whimsically designed water gardens are dotted throughout the landscape. Two of the temples – Pura Besakih and Pura Lempuyang – are among Bali's most important pilgrimage sites, and evocative reminders of the island's royal dynasties can be found in Klungkung (Semarapura), in Amlapura and at Tirta Gangga.

Up on the northeast coast, Amed and Tulamben are laid-back beach destinations for those keen to escape the crowds on the south coast. Diving, snorkelling, enjoying yoga and lazing by swimming pools are the priorities up here, and can be enjoyed by travellers on every budget.

ⓘ Getting There & Away

The coastal highway links most places of interest in east Bali. Otherwise you'll find hillside roads that weave through the lush, green countryside. Shuttle services run to/from south Bali, the port town of Padangbai and the tourist enclave of Candidasa. Additional shuttles head to the northeast coast by demand.

Bangli

⏺ 0366 / POP KAWAN 8390, CEMPAGA 7520

Halfway up the slope to Penelokan, Bangli, once the capital of a kingdom, is a humble market town noteworthy for its sprawling temple, Pura Kehen, which is on a beautiful jungle road that runs east past rice terraces and connects at Sekar with roads to Rendang and Sideman.

◎ Sights

★ Pura Kehen   HINDU TEMPLE

(Jl Sriwijaya, Cempaga; adult/child incl sarong 30,000Rp/free, parking 2000Rp; ⊗9am-5pm) The state temple of the Bangli kingdom, Pura Kehen is a miniature version of Pura Besakih, Bali's most important temple. It's terraced up the hillside, with a flight of steps leading to the beautifully decorated entrance. The first courtyard has a huge banyan tree with a *kulkul* (hollow tree-trunk drum used to sound warnings) entwined in its branches and the inner courtyard has an 11-roof *meru* (multitiered shrine). Other shrines have thrones for the Hindu trinity: Brahma, Shiva and Vishnu.

ⓘ Getting There & Away

Most people visit Bangli under their own steam or on organised tours to Pura Besakih.

Klungkung (Semarapura)

⏺ 0366 / POP 22,610

Officially called Semarapura but commonly known by its traditional name Klungkung, this district capital is home to the historically significant Puri Agung Semarapura (Klungkung Palace), a relic of the days of Klungkung's rajas, the Dewa Agungs. Once the centre of Bali's most important kingdom, the town retains the palace compound and a few temples from its royal past and has a busy market opposite the centrally located palace compound.

◎ Sights

★ Puri Agung Semarapura   PALACE

(Klungkung Palace; Jl Untung Surapati; adult/child 50,000/25,000Rp; ⊗8am-5pm) Built when the Dewa Agung dynasty moved here in 1710, this palace compound was laid out as a large square, believed to be in the form of a mandala, with courtyards, gardens, pavilions and moats. Most of the original palace and grounds were destroyed by the 1908 Dutch attacks; all that remain are the carved **Pemedal Agung**, the gateway on the south side of the square, the Kertha Gosa and the Bale Kambang.

The ticket office is on the opposite side of Jl Untung Surapati, next to the **Puputan Monument** (Jl Untung Surapati).

Bale Kambang   HISTORIC BUILDING

(Floating Pavilion; Jl Untung Surapati, Puri Agung Semarapura; admission incl in palace ticket; ⊗8am-6pm) Located within the palace compound, the ceiling of this beautiful floating *bale* (open-sided pavilion) showcases rows of paintings dealing with various subjects. The first row is based on the astrological calendar, the second on the folk tale of Pan and Men Brayut and their 18 children, and the upper rows on the adventures of the hero Sutasona.

East Bali

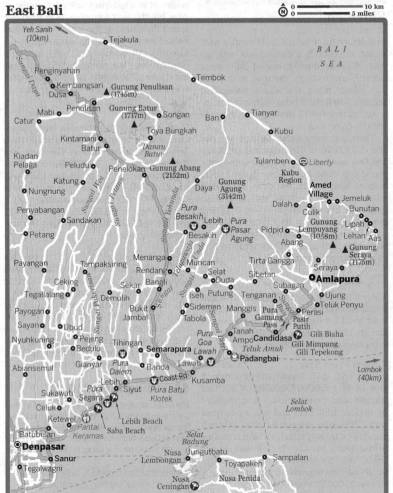

Kertha Gosa
HISTORIC BUILDING

(Hall of Justice; Jl Untung Surapati, Puri Agung Semarapura; admission incl in palace ticket; ⊙8am-6pm) This open-sided pavilion in the northeastern corner of Puri Agung Semarapura was effectively the supreme court of the Klungkung kingdom, where disputes and cases that could not be settled at village level were eventually brought. A superb example of Klungkung architecture, it features a ceiling covered with fine 20th-century paintings in Kamasan (aka Wayang) style. These replaced the original 19th-century cloth paintings, which had deteriorated over time, and depict the Garuda story among other scenes.

🛈 Getting There & Away

The best way to visit Klungkung is with your own transport and as part of a circuit taking in other sites up the mountains and along the coast.

This is one of the few towns in east Bali with a functioning *terminal bis* (bus station). Located south of the palace compound, just off Jl Puputan, it has bemo and bus services to/from Denpasar's Batubulan terminal (25,000Rp), Amlapura (20,000Rp), Padangbai (25,000Rp), Sideman (15,000Rp) and Gianyar (20,000Rp).

Sidemen

📞 0366 / POP 3780

In Sidemen (pronounced Si-da-men), a walk in any direction is a communion with nature. Winding through one of Bali's most beautiful river valleys, the road to this hilltop village offers marvellous paddy-field scenery, a delightful rural character and extraordinary views of Gunung Agung (when the clouds permit).

There are many **walks** through the rice and chilli fields in the multihued green valley. One involves a spectacular three-hour, round-trip climb up to **Pura Bukit Tageh**, a small temple with big views. No matter where you stay, you'll be able to arrange guides for in-depth hiking (about 75,000Rp per person for a two-hour hike) or just set out on your own exploration. Many of the resorts offer their guests guided walks as part of activities programmes, too.

🛏 Sleeping

There is a decent range of resorts, hotels and guesthouses at various budget levels in Sidemen; most are located on Jl Raya Tebola. It can get cool and misty at night, so pack an extra layer or two of clothing.

Khrisna Home Stay   HOMESTAY $$
(📞 0815 5832 1543; pinpinaryadi@yahoo.com; Jl Raya Tebola; r 350,000-700,000Rp; 🛜📶) This friendly nine-room homestay is surrounded by organic fruit trees and has a cute pool area. The rooms are comfortable, although the singles are very small; all have fans. One deluxe double has a lovely view over the rice fields. The little restaurant serves excellent breakfasts and vegetable-dominated dinners (mains 35,000Rp to 50,000Rp).

★ Alamdhari Resort & Spa   HOTEL
(📞 0812 3700 6290; www.alamdhari.com; Jl Raya Tebola; r from 800,000Rp; ✳🛜📶) This boutique choice is pleasing to both the eye and the wallet. The 14 rooms are light and airy, with comfortable beds, fans, excellent bathrooms and good-sized balconies. The view from the pool – best appreciated from one of the comfy sun lounges provided – is spectacular, and facilities include a modest restaurant and a small spa.

★ Darmada Eco Resort   RESORT $$
(📞 0853 3803 2100; www.darmadabali.com; Jl Raya Luah; r 500,000-700,000Rp, f 900,000-1,100,000Rp; 🛜📶) Rooms at this well-priced resort set in a lush river valley are simple affairs, but this isn't a problem as most guests spend their time in the lovely spring-water swimming pool or taking advantage of the extensive programme of paid activities (meditation, yoga, massage, trekking, cooking classes). The resort's riverside restaurant is excellent. Wi-fi in common areas only.

🍴 Eating

Most accommodation options have restaurants and there are warungs along Jl Raya Tebola. The restaurants at Darmada Eco Resort, **Samanvaya** (📞 0821 4710 3884; www.samanvaya-bali.com; Jl Raya Tebola; r US$90-142, ste US$124-170; 🅿🛜📶) and **Wapa di Ume** (📞 0366-543 7600; www.wapadiumesidemen.com; Jl Raya Tebola; r US$300-350, ste US$380-430, pool villa US$530-580.; 🅿✳@🛜📶) 🍴 welcome non-guests.

★ Dapur Kapulaga   BALINESE $
(📞 0852 3861 5775; Jl Raya Tebola; mains 32,000-50,000Rp; ⊙1-10pm; 🍴) 🍴 Serving a predominantly organic menu of Western and Balinese staples, this friendly and clean warung with its distinctive checkerboard-tiled floor is a great choice. You'll find it in front of the Alamdhari Resort & Spa. No alcohol, but the house-concocted Sidemen Cooler steps into the breach nicely.

ℹ Getting There & Away

The Sideman road can be a beautiful part of any day trip from south Bali or Ubud. It connects in the north with the Rendang–Amlapura road just west of Duda. Unfortunately the road is busy due to huge trucks hauling rocks for Bali's incessant construction.

A less-travelled route to Pura Besakih goes northeast from Klungkung (Semarapura), via Sideman and Iseh, to another scenic treat: the Rendang–Amlapura road.

Near the centre of Sideman, a small road heads west for 500m to a fork where signs will direct you to various guesthouses.

You'll need your own transport to access the Sideman area.

Gunung Agung

Bali's highest and most revered mountain, Gunung Agung is an imposing volcano that can be seen from most of south and east Bali when clear of cloud and mist. Most sources say it's 3142m high. The summit is an oval crater, about 700m across, with its highest point on the western edge above Pura Besakih.

As it's the spiritual centre of Bali, traditional houses are laid out on an axis in line with Agung and many locals always know where they are in relation to the peak, which is thought to house ancestral spirits. The volcano has been erupting sporadically since November 2017, and an official Level 3 (standby) alert is current, with an exclusion zone of 4km around the volcano's crater.

◉ Sights

★ Pura Besakih   HINDU TEMPLE
(60,000Rp, parking 5000Rp) Perched nearly 1000m up the side of Gunung Agung, this is Bali's most important Hindu temple. The site encompasses 23 separate but related temples, with the largest and most important being **Pura Penataran Agung**, built on six levels terraced up the slope. It has an imposing *candi bentar* (split gateway); note that tourists are not allowed inside. The Pura Besakih complex hosts frequent ceremonies, but the recent eruptions of the volcano have kept both worshipper and visitor numbers down.

The precise origins of the temple complex are not totally clear, but it almost certainly dates from prehistoric times. The stone bases of Pura Penataran Agung and several other temples resemble megalithic stepped pyramids and date back at least 2000 years. It was certainly used as a Hindu place of worship from 1284, when the first Javanese conquerors settled in Bali. By the 15th century Besakih had become a state temple of the Gelgel dynasty.

When you reach the site there are two parking areas: Parkir Bawa and Parking Atas. The former is the main parking area and the first you'll encounter coming from the south; all tourists must park here. There is a ticket office close by. Sarongs and sashes are available next to the office, and must be worn; rental is included in your ticket. Many visitors bring their own.

🏃 Activities

Climbing Gunung Agung takes you through verdant forest in the clouds and rewards with sweeping (dawn) views. It's best to climb during the dry season (April to September); July to September are the most reliable months. At other times the paths can be slippery and dangerous and the views are clouded over (especially true in January and February). Climbing is not permitted when major religious events are being held at Pura Besakih, which generally includes most of April.

AN UNHOLY EXPERIENCE?

Some visitors to Pura Besakih report being hassled by touts and scammed by locals; others have an enjoyable, hassle-free experience. What follows are some of the possible ploys you should be aware of before a visit:

➡ Unofficial and official guides hang around looking for visitors. They may emphatically tell you that guide services are compulsory, tell you that temples are 'closed for a ceremony' and quote a ridiculously high price for a short visit. None of this is true: you may always walk among the temples and no 'guide' can get you into a closed temple. Only hire a guide if you want one, and always agree on a fee before you start.

➡ Once inside the complex, you may receive offers to 'come pray with me'. Visitors who seize on this chance to gain entry to a forbidden temple can face demands of 100,000Rp or more.

➡ Never allow anyone to keep the ticket you are issued with. It's just an excuse for someone else to sell you another.

➡ Local women may try to give you offerings – if you accept them, they will then demand 10,000Rp or so. It is not necessary to make offerings in the temples.

➡ Sarong and sash hire is included in the ticket price – get one when you pay for your ticket. Alternatively, bring your own.

➡ A scooter ride up the hill from the ticket office is also included in the ticket price. Drivers will ask for a tip but this is at your discretion.

ⓘ TIPS FOR CLIMBING GUNUNG AGUNG

➡ Always check official warnings before planning or setting out on a climb.

➡ Use a guide.

➡ Respect your guide's pauses at shrines for prayers on the sacred mountain.

➡ Get to the top before 8am – the clouds that often obscure the view of Agung also obscure the view from Agung.

➡ Take a strong torch (flashlight), extra batteries, plenty of water (2L per person), snack food, waterproof clothing and a warm jumper (sweater).

➡ Wear strong shoes or boots and have manicured toes – the trail is very steep and the descent is especially hard on your feet.

➡ This is a hard climb, don't fool yourself.

➡ Take frequent rests and don't be afraid to ask your guide to slow down.

Guides

Trips with guides on either of the routes up Gunung Agung generally include breakfast and other meals as well as a place to stay, but be sure to confirm all details in advance. Guides are also able to arrange transport.

Most of the places to stay in the region, including those at Selat, along the Sidemen road and at Tirta Gangga, will recommend guides for Gunung Agung climbs.

Most guides charge between 600,000Rp and 900,000Rp per person for the climb from Pura Besikah and 450,000Rp to 600,000Rp per person from Pura Pasar Agung.

I Ketut Uriada　　　　　　　　HIKING

(☑ 0812 364 6426; ketut.uriada@gmail.com) This knowledgeable guide in Muncan can arrange treks throughout the region. He also operates a small guesthouse (rooms 125,000Rp to 160,000Rp) and can organise transport to/from the area.

Wayan Tegteg　　　　　　　　HIKING

(☑ 0813 3852 5677; www.facebook.com/wayan. tegteg.7) A recommended Gunung Agung guide who wins plaudits from hikers.

ⓘ Getting There & Away

Usually you'll make arrangements with your guide to get to the trailheads for a climb. There is no public transport.

Coast Road to Kusamba

☑ 0361

The coastal highway between Sanur and Kusamba runs alongside a swathe of black-sand beaches and past two of the island's best surf breaks (at Keramas and Ketewel).

There aren't many compelling reasons to pause on your journey, as most beaches are dirty and many aren't safe to swim at. The highway is lined with stores, factories and warungs (food stalls) used by truckers.

◉ Sights

Pantai Keramas　　　　　　　BEACH

(Keramas) There are some villa and hotel projects are sprouting here. The surf is consistent and world-class.

🛏 Sleeping

Hotels are slowly being constructed, but there are few tempting choices. The excellent Hotel Komune is an exception to this rule.

★ Hotel Komune　　　　　　RESORT $$$

(☑ 0361-301 8888; www.komuneresorts.com; Jl Pantai Keramas, Keramas; r from US$99, ste from US$130, villas from US$250; P ✱ 🛜 ☲) 🖉 A resort in the true sense of the word, Komune offers everything needed for an active and enjoyable holiday. The surf here is among Bali's best, although not suitable for beginners. Other activities include yoga, meditation and kids movie nights. Rooms are stylish and comfortable.

The beachfront **Beach Club** (www.komune resorts.com/keramasbali/beach-club; sandwiches & burgers 65,000-95,000Rp, mains 58,000-250,000Rp; ⊙ 6.30am-11pm; 🛜 🖉 🖶) 🖉 with a restaurant, bar and pool has a party vibe at every time of the day.

Light towers make it possible for surfers to take their boards out at night; board and wetsuit hire is available. The kids club has a trampoline, swing and skate park.

Padangbai

This little beach town is the port for public ferries connecting Bali with Lombok and Nusa Penida; there are also fast boats to Lombok and the Gilis. When not inundated by travellers in transit, it has a laid-back vibe and its accommodation, eating and drinking options are solidly geared towards the backpacker and diving markets. Though its location on a small bay with a curve of beach is attractive, the town itself is utilitarian.

🏃 Activities

The main activities are diving and snorkelling; there are a number of dive centres and shops on Jl Silayukti, opposite the main beach.

Diving & Snorkelling

There is good diving on the coral reefs around Padangbai, but the water can be a bit cold and visibility is not always ideal. The most popular local dives are **Blue Lagoon** and **Teluk Jepun** (Jepun Bay), both in Teluk Amuk, the bay just east of Padangbai. There's a good range of soft and hard corals and varied marine life, including sharks, turtles and wrasse, and a 23m wall at Blue Lagoon.

Many local outfits offer diving trips in the area, including to Gili Tepekong and Gili Biaha and on to Tulamben and Nusa Penida.

One of the best and most accessible walk-in snorkel sites is off **Blue Lagoon Beach**. Note that it is subject to strong currents when the tide is out. Other sites such as

Teluk Jepun can be reached by local boat (or check with the dive operators to see if they have any room on their boats; the cost will be around 130,000Rp). Snorkel-set hire costs around 50,000Rp per day.

The local dive shops can organise snorkelling trips for beginners and experienced snorkellers (450,000Rp to 750,000Rp per person) and will also hire snorkel gear by the half- or full day.

OK Divers
DIVING

(📱 0811 385 8830; www.okdiversbali.com; Jl Silayukti 6, OK Divers Resort; 2 dives 1,080,000Rp) Offers a range of PADI diving courses and diving safaris around the island, as well as local dives and snorkelling opportunities. The associated resort offers good accommodation.

Water Worxx
DIVING

(📱 0363-41220; www.waterworxbali.com; Jl Silayukti; 2 dives US$80-125) A well-regarded dive operator offering trips to surrounding areas, plus PADI and SSI courses. Can also arrange dives for travellers with disabilities.

Geko Dive
DIVING

(📱 0363-41516; www.gekodivebali.com; Jl Silayukti; dives from 650,000Rp) With a base just across from the beach, this long-established PADI-accredited operator offers equipment hire, dives and snorkelling trips.

🛌 Sleeping

Decent accommodation options are thin on the ground, with dark, dirty and depressing homestays and guesthouses well

---

BALI PADANGBAI

COAST ROAD BEACHES

As you head east on the coast road from Sanur, pretty much any road or lane heading south will end up at a beach.

The shoreline is striking, with beaches in volcanic shades of grey pounded by waves. The entire coast has great religious significance and there are oodles of temples scattered along it. At the many small coastal-village beaches, cremation formalities reach their conclusion when the ashes are consigned to the sea. Ritual purification ceremonies for temple artefacts are also held on these beaches. Some key points:

➤ Ketewel and Keramas are top spots for surfing.

➤ Swimming in the often pounding surf is dangerous.

➤ Most beaches have no shade.

➤ Many beaches have a food or drinks vendor or two.

➤ You'll need your own transport to reach these beaches.

➤ Locals will sometimes charge you an access fee – about 5000Rp.

➤ Rubbish is a depressing fact at most of the beaches.

Padangbai

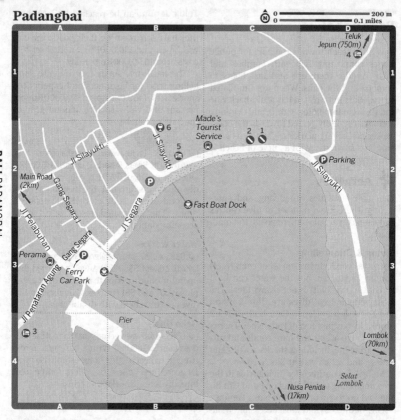

Padangbai

represented. Fortunately, there are a couple of decent hostels and at least two resorts worthy of the appellation. Most accommodation choices sit in the budget category.

Bamboo Paradise HOSTEL **$**
(☑ 0363-4381765, 0822 6630 4330; www.facebook.com/bambooparadisebali; Jl Penataran Agung; dm 135,000Rp; r 200,000-400,000Rp; ❄🛜) Padangbai's best budget accommodation is in a leafy street close to the port. It's had a full makeover but the laid-back vibe, bar, lounge, dorm accommodation and good breakfast continue. There is one six-bed mixed dorm with bathroom and air-con and six private rooms.

OK Divers Resort & Spa RESORT **$$**
(☑ 0811 385 8830; www.okdiversbali.com; Jl Silayukti 6; r from 990,000Rp; 🅿❄🛜🏊) 🍴 Facilities here are the best the town has to offer, with a spa, two pools, a well-regarded dive centre and a pavilion cafe. Rooms are well set up and the ferry pier is a short walk. Two-tank dive trips start at 1,000,000Rp; snorkelling trips cost 260,000Rp.

★ Bloo Lagoon Eco Village   RESORT $$$

(📞 0363-41211; www.bloolagoon.com; Jl Silayuk-ti; 1-/2-/3-bed bungalow from US$124/181/202; 🅿❄@🛜🐟) 🏊 Crowning a clifftop at the town's eastern edge, this place is notable for its sea-facing yoga deck (free classes daily), well-priced spa (massages 210,000Rp to 300,000Rp) and kid-friendly pool with water slide. The 25 guest bungalows come with one, two or three bedrooms. All overlook Blue Lagoon Beach and have large outdoor living terraces, kitchens and open-air bathrooms; some have air-con.

✖ Eating

Beach fare and backpacker staples dominate menus in Padangbai – lots of fresh seafood, Indonesian classics, pizza, burgers and, yes, banana pancakes. You can easily laze away a few hours soaking up the scene at the places along Jl Segara and Jl Silayukti, which have harbour views during the day and cool breezes in the evening.

★ Colonial Restaurant   CAFE $$

(📞 0811 397 8837; www.facebook.com/thecolonial padangbai; Jl Silayukti 6, OK Divers Resort & Spa; mains 50,000-150,000Rp; ⏰7am-11pm; 🛜🏊) The most stylish eatery in town, this pavilion cafe overlooking the pool at the OK Divers resort is a great place to while away a few hours. Food is much better than the Padangbai norm, with an eclectic range of both Western and Indonesian choices on offer. Drinks include fresh juices, milkshakes and Bintang on tap. Patrons can use the pool.

🍺 Drinking & Nightlife

Most of Padangbai's bars and cafes are clustered in the town centre, east of the port; many of the bars offer live music a few nights a week.

★ Omang Omang   BAR

(📞 0363-438 1251; www.facebook.com/Omang Omang999; Jl Silayukti 12) A loyal crew of Omangsters (regulars) joins a constant stream of blow-ins at this friendly eatery, bar and live-music venue. Nosh on toasties, tacos, burgers and Indonesian favourites, down an ice-cold Bintang or two and rock along with the house blues band on Monday nights.

ℹ Information

There are several ATMs around town, including one on Jl Pelabuhan near the port and another on Jl Segara opposite the main beach.

ℹ Getting There & Away

BOAT

Anyone who carries your luggage on or off the ferries or fast boats will expect to be paid, so agree on the price first or carry your own stuff.

Ignore touts who meet all arriving boats and departing passengers. Only buy public ferry tickets from the official window in the ferry building.

From Lombok & Gili Islands

You can travel to/from Lombok on fast boat or public ferry, and head to/from the Gilis by fast boat. Be sure to consider important safety information.

Fast Boats Several companies link Padangbai to the Gilis and Lombok; they have offices on the waterfront. Fares are negotiable and start at 250,000Rp one-way. Travel times will be more than the 90 minutes advertised.

Public Ferries (off Jl Segara) Car ferries travel between Padangbai and Lembar on Lombok (adult/child/motorbike/car 46,000/29,000/129,000/917,000Rp; four to six hours). Passenger tickets are sold at an office at the port. Boats supposedly run 24 hours and leave about every 90 minutes.

From Nusa Penida

Public ferries (adult/child/motorbike/car 31,000/26,000/50,000/295,000Rp) leave most days; the trip takes one hour. Large car ferries leave from the main wharf at the port; smaller passenger-only ferries usually leave from the jetty to the left of the main wharf. Passenger tickets for the car ferries are sold at an office at the port; buy tickets for the smaller ferries on board.

TOURIST BUSES

Perama (📞 0361-751875; www.peramatour. com; Jl Pelabuhan) shuttles connect Padangbai with other parts of Bali. Destinations include Kuta, Denpasar airport, Sanur and Ubud (all 75,000Rp, three daily); Amed and Tulamben (100,000Rp, one daily); Lovina (175,000Rp, one daily); Candidasa (35,000Rp, three daily) and Tirta Gangga (75,000Rp, one daily). Buses leave from outside the Perama office in Jl Pelabuhan, near the port.

Made's Tourist Service (📞 0877 0145 0700, 0363-41441; ⏰ vary) also sells tickets for shuttles. Among other destinations, it can organise for you to get to Ubud (75,000Rp), Sanur (75,000Rp), Kuta (75,000Rp) and Denpasar airport (75,000Rp).

TAXI

Local taxis charge 300,000Rp to travel to Ubud and Sanur; it costs 350,000Rp to Kuta, Legian, Seminyak, Jimbaran or Denpasar airport.

Candidasa

📍 0363 / POP 2190

Officially known as Segkidu Village but called Candidasa for tourism purposes, this east coast settlement is heavily developed with hotels. The beach here was pretty well destroyed in the 1970s, when its offshore reef was mined for lime to make cement and other construction materials, so those seeking to swim, snorkel or dive in the sea should steer clear. However, the hinterland is attractive, the picturesque lagoon in the centre of town is full of water lillies that bloom in the morning and many of the local hotels have gorgeous beachside infinity pools where guests can laze their days away.

👁 Sights

A little bend in the east coast called Jasri Bay, just south of Amlapura, has earned the nickname **Teluk Penyu**, or Turtle Bay. The shelled critters do indeed come here to nest and there have been some efforts made to protect them. If you see a turtle or nest, be sure to keep your distance; never attempt to touch or pick up a wild sea turtle.

The main road east of Candidasa curves up to **Pura Gamang Pass** (*gamang* means 'to get dizzy' – an overstatement), from where you'll find fine views down to the coast and lots of greedy-faced monkeys (who have become so prolific that they have stripped crops bare from here up the mountain to Tenganan).

Pantai Pasir Putih
BEACH

(Virgin Beach) The most popular 'secret' beach on Bali, Pantai Pasir Putih (White Sand Beach) lives up to its name. Once a mooring spot for local fishing boats, this long crescent of white sand backed by coconut palms is now a popular tourist attraction, with thatched beach warungs and cafes lining the sand and souvenir stalls clustered around the car park. Sun lounges await bikini-clad bottoms. The water is safe for swimming and you can rent snorkelling gear to explore the sparkling aquamarine water.

From JI Raya Perasi (the main highway), look for the large 'White Sand Beach' sign and then turn off the main road and follow a paved track for 1.2km to a large dirt parking area; other tracks are signed 'Virgin Beach'. Locals will collect an access fee (10,000Rp per person including parking). Cars and motorbikes are barred from driving close to the beach. There's a track down to the sand from the parking area.

🏃 Activities

There are a few options for diving and offshore snorkelling here, but you'll be much happier heading northeast to Amed to enjoy these activities. Instead, consider taking a hike in the attractive hinterland.

Traditional villages dot the pretty countryside inland from Candidasa. If you walk along the coastline from Candidasa towards Amlapura, a trail climbs up over the headland, with fine views over the rocky islets off the coast and a good swathe of the region. Beyond this headland there's a long sweep of wide, exposed black-sand beach.

⭐ Trekking Candidasa
WALKING

(📞 0878 6145 2001; www.trekkingcandidasa.com; treks 250,000-350,000Rp) The delightful Somat leads walks through the verdant rice fields and hills behind Candidasa. There are two routes: an easy trek through the rice fields to the village of Tenganan and a more difficult trek to a nearby waterfall. Prices include transport and drinks.

🛏 Sleeping

Candidasa's busy main drag is well supplied with seaside accommodation, with most options on the beach side of the highway. Tranquil pockets can be found east of the centre along Jl Pantai Indah and also at Mendira Beach, at the western entrance to the town. To get to the Mendira Beach hotels, turn off the main road at the school and huge banyan tree (there's also a sign listing places to stay here).

Sleepy Croc
HOSTEL $

(📞 0363-4381003, 0877 6256 3736; Jl Raya Candidasa; dm 100,000Rp, breakfast 50,000Rp; 🅿✳🛜) This small backpacker-style hostel offers two dorms (one mixed, one female only); each sleeps eight and fronts onto the pool. Most action unfolds in the bar/restaurant fronting the street (mains 50,000Rp to 110,000Rp), and live music is staged there every Friday and Saturday night. Dorms have bunk beds, under-bed lockers, air-con and a bathroom.

⭐ Candi Beach Resort and Spa
RESORT $$$

(📞 0363-41234; www.candibeachbali.com; Jl Raya Mendira, Mendira Beach; r $US100-170, ste US$300-340, villa US$350-405; 🅿✳🛜🏊) ✒

Candidasa

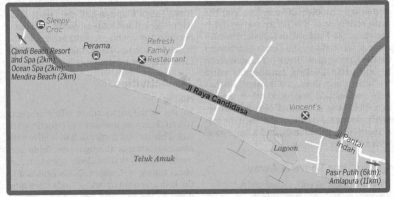

Stylish, environmentally conscious and lavishly endowed with facilities, this is undisputedly Candidasa's best accommodation option. Rooms come in six categories – luxury ocean view suites and villas are particularly swish, but all are impressive. There's a huge palm-fringed pool, a luxe **spa** (treatments 257,000-1,200,000Rp; ⊙by appointment) and two restaurants (one Asian and Western, the other Indonesian; mains 63,000Rp to 183,000Rp). The resort's private beach offers good snorkelling opportunities.

✕ Eating

Cafes and restaurants can be found on Jl Raya Candidasa. Though most suffer from traffic noise during the day, this usually abates after dark.

Refresh Family Restaurant　　HEALTH FOOD $
(☑ 0812 3751 6001; www.facebook.com/refresh
4family; Jl Raya Candidasa; breakfast dishes
25,000-50,000, mains 30,000-50,000; ⊙8am-
10pm; ☎☑⊞) Surfing the vegan, raw, organic and gluten-free culinary wave that
has deluged Bali in recent years, this simple
place has an exclusively vegetarian menu
that is chock-full of favourites such as laksa,
falafel, spicy wraps and nut curries. Breakfast choices include scrambled tofu, smoothie bowls and granola. The children's play
area is a popular feature.

★Vincent's　　INTERNATIONAL $$
(☑ 0363-41368; www.vincentsbali.com; Jl Raya
Candidasa; mains 75,000-295,000Rp; ⊙11am-
10pm; ☎☑) One of east Bali's better restaurants, Vincent's has several distinct open-air
rooms and a large rear garden. The comfy
front bar area hosts live jazz on both Monday (high season only) and Thursday (all year), kicking off around 7pm. The menu offers sandwiches, salads, Balinese staples and various Western dishes – the 'coconut texture' dessert is justly popular.

❶ Getting There & Away

Candidasa is on the main road between Amlapura and south Bali, but there is no regular public transport. **Perama** (☑ 0363-41114/5; Jl Raya Candidasa; ⊙7am-7pm) has an office on the main road and runs shuttle services to destinations including Kuta (75,000Rp, three hours, three daily) via Ubud (75,000Rp, two hours) and Sanur (75,000Rp, 2½ hours); Padangbai (35,000Rp, 30 minutes, three daily); Tirta Gangga (75,000Rp, 45 minutes, one daily); and Amed (100,000Rp, 75 minutes, one daily). A pick up from your hotel will cost an extra 15,000Rp.

Amlapura
☑ 0363 / POP 15.960

The capital of Karangasem is the smallest of Bali's district capitals and is notable for its multicultural population, with both Muslim and Chinese residents. This gives its night market a slightly different flavour to others on the island.

⊙ Sights

Amlapura's palaces – two in the town centre and one in Ujung, south of the city – are reminders of Karangasem's grand period as a kingdom supported by Dutch colonial power in the late 19th and early 20th centuries.

Puri Agung Karangasem
PALACE

(http://purikarangasem.com; Jl Teuku Umar; adult/child under 5yr 10,000/5000Rp; ⊙8am-5pm) The main residence in this palace compound is known as the Maskerdam (Amsterdam) because it was built by the Dutch as a reward for the Karangasem kingdom's acquiescence to Dutch rule. Looking considerably worse for wear these days (the Maskerdam has been uninhabited since 1966, when the last raja died), the compound also has an ornately decorated pavilion once used for royal tooth-filing ceremonies, and a large pond with a floating pavilion.

ⓘ Getting There & Away

The bus terminal recently closed, and public transport is pretty well non-existent.

Tirta Gangga

🗸 0363 / POP 7300

Tirta Gangga (Water of the Ganges) is the site of a *taman* (garden) built for the enjoyment of the last raja of Karangasem; it also has some of the best rice-terrace vistas in East Bali. Capping a sweep of green flowing down to the distant sea, it's an excellent place to overnight if you are heading to/from Pura Lempuyang. It's also a popular base for those wanting to hike the surrounding terraced countryside, which ripples with coursing water and is dotted with temples.

◉ Sights

★ Pura Lempuyang
HINDU TEMPLE

(Gunung Lempuyang; donation 10,000Rp, parking per car/scooter 2000Rp/free; ⊙24hr) One of the holiest temple complexes on the island (it and Pura Besakih are the most important in east Bali), this group of seven temples has a spectacular setting on the steep slope of Gunung Lempuyang, 10km northeast of Tirta Gangga.

From the car park, jeeps transport visitors up the steep road and to the security entrance for 20,000Rp per person; the same charge applies for the return trip.

★ Taman Tirta Gangga
GARDENS

(www.tirtagangga.nl; Jl Abang-Amlapura; adult/child 40,000/15,000Rp, swimming 20,000Rp, parking per car/scooter 5000/1000Rp; ⊙7am-7pm) This 1.2-hectare water palace serves as a fascinating reminder of the old Bali. Built for the last raja of Karangasem in 1946, it was almost fully destroyed by the eruption of

nearby Gunung Agung in 1963, but has subsequently been rebuilt. Admire the 11-tiered Nawa Sanga fountain and the ponds filled with huge koi and lotus blossoms, and jump between the round stepping stones in the water. It's also possible to take a swim in the huge stone spring-water pool.

🏃 Activities

Hiking

Hiking in the surrounding hills transports you far from your memories of frenetic south Bali. This far east corner of Bali is alive with coursing streams through rice fields and tropical forests that suddenly open to reveal vistas taking in Lombok, Nusa Penida and the lush green surrounding lands stretching down to the sea. The rice terraces around Tirta Gangga are some of the most beautiful in Bali. Back roads and walking paths take you to many picturesque traditional villages.

Sights that make a perfect excuse for a day trek are scattered in the surrounding hills. Among the possible treks is a six-hour loop to Tenganan village, plus shorter ones across the local hills, which include visits to remote temples and plenty of stunning vistas.

Guides for the more complex hikes are a good idea as they can help you plan routes and see things you simply would never find otherwise. Ask at any of the various accommodation options. Rates average about 100,000Rp per hour for one or two people.

Komang Gede Sutama
HIKING

(🗸0813 3877 0893; ⊙2/4/6hr guided hike for 2 people 150,000/350,000/550,000Rp) Local resident Komang Gede Sutama speaks basic English and has a good reputation as a guide to the countryside around Tirta Gangga and up to Gunung Agung.

🛏 Sleeping

There are a number of accommodation options in and around the water palace; the best are on the ridge in Ababi.

★ Pondok Batur Indah
HOMESTAY $

(🗸0812 398 9060, 0363-22342; pondokbaturindah@yahoo.com; Ababi; r 350,000-440,000Rp; 🛜) Jaw-dropping is the only word to use when describing the rice-terrace views enjoyed from the terrace of this homestay on the ridge above Tirta Gangga. The five rooms are simple but clean, with fans and basic bathrooms. There's an on-site restaurant serving home-style dishes (25,000Rp to

DON'T MISS

PURA LEMPUYANG

One of the eight temple complexes in the Pura Kahyangan Padma Bhuwana group, which mark the island's cardinal directions, Pura Lempuyang is perched on a hilltop on the side of 1058m Gunung Lempuyang, a twin of neighbouring 1175m Gunung Seraya. Together, the pair of mountains form the distinctive double peaks of basalt that loom over Amlapura to the south and Amed to the north. The complex, which comprises seven temples on the steep mountain slope, is one of the most important religious sites in east Bali.

The largest and most easily accessed temple here is Penataran Tempuyang, which has a wonderfully photogenic *candi bentar* (split temple gateway). The highest and most important temple is Pura Lempuyang Luhur, which also has a *candi bentar*. To visit all seven temples in the complex takes at least four hours and involves 2900 steps – only those who are fit should attempt it. Reaching Penataran Tempuyang is relatively easy, as it's only a five-minute uphill walk from the security entrance. Many visitors queue for hours to have their chance to be photographed in front of the *candi bentar* here.

From Penataran Tempuyang, the second temple is 2km uphill and after that the calf-punishing stair climb begins; it's 1700 steps from the second temple to Pura Lempuyang Luhur. Local guides congregate near the security check and charge 150,000/200,000/300,000/400,000Rp to the 1st/2nd/4th/top temple.

From the complex, the mottled green patchwork that is east Bali unfolds to the eye. The temple's significance means there are always faithful Balinese in meditative contemplation; be warned that temples sometimes close to visitors during ceremonies.

55,000Rp), and the water palace is a 10- to 15-minute walk away, down a steep set of steps.

Pondok Lembah Dukuh   GUESTHOUSE **$**
(☑ 0813 3829 5142; dukuhstay@gmail.com; Ababi; r 250,000-270,000Rp; q 350,000Rp; P☎) On the edge of a ridge commanding spectacular views over the rice fields, this guesthouse offers four charming bungalows with individual terraces. Rooms are small and basic, but a stay here is a good chance to get close to local life. The water palace is a 10- to 15-minute walk away, via a steep set of steps.

❶ Getting There & Away

You'll need your own transport to get here.

Amed & the Far East Coast

☑ 0363 / POP 3180

Stretching from Amed village to Bali's far eastern tip, this semi-arid coast draws visitors with its succession of small, scalloped, grey-sand beaches (some more rocks than sand), relaxed atmosphere and excellent diving and snorkelling.

'Amed' is actually a misnomer for the area, as the coast is a series of seaside *dusun* (small villages) that starts with Amed village in the north and then runs southeast to Aas. Amed village, Jemeluk, Lipah and Selang are popular destinations for scuba divers, freedivers and snorkellers, and the entire coastline is dotted with resorts boasting yoga shalas, infinity pools and pavilion restaurants.

🏃 Activities

Diving & Snorkelling

Snorkelling is excellent along the coast. Jemeluk is a protected area where you can admire live coral and plentiful fish within 100m of the beach. The coral gardens and colourful marine life at Selang are highlights. Snorkelling equipment rents for about 35,000Rp per day.

Diving is also good, with dive sites off Jemeluk, Lipah and Selang featuring coral slopes and drop-offs with soft and hard corals and abundant fish. Some are accessible from the beach, while others require a short boat ride. The *Liberty* wreck at Tulamben is only a 20-minute drive away.

Several dive operators have shown a commitment to the communities by organising regular beach clean-ups and educating locals on the need for conservation. All have similar prices for a long list of offerings (eg local two-dive packages start from around US$70).

Ocean Prana   DIVING
(☑ WhatsApp 061 435 441 414; www.oceanprana. com; Jl I Ketut Natih, Jemeluk; introductory course US$150, level 1-3 US$290-490) Courses at this

BALI ASLI

Located in the fertile green foothills of Gunung Agung, the farming village of Gelumpang may seem a strange place to find a world-class restaurant and cooking school. However, this is where much-travelled Australian chef Penelope Williams has established the renowned **Bali Asli** (📱 0822 3690 9215; www.baliasli.com.au; Jl Raya Gelumpang, Gelumpang; nasi campur 165,000-228,000Rp; ⊙10am-3pm; 🛜), which offers visitors to Bali a truly unique culinary experience. Asli is the Balinese term used for something that is created in the traditional way, and there is much that is traditional here – the Balinese menu changes daily, dictated by what is fresh at the local *pasar* (market) or has been harvested in the restaurant's own garden. Dishes are cooked on wood-fired, mud-brick stoves by local chefs – many female – and the results are enjoyed in a magnificent open-sided dining room overlooking rice terraces and the famous but often mist-shrouded volcano. The food is authentically village style – diners choose between an array of small dishes to make up a personalised and extremely flavoursome version of *nasi campur*.

The daily cooking classes include a hike into the surrounding countryside to visit locals farmers – maybe to see rice being planted or palm wine being made – or to a local market before heading back to the kitchen for a 2½-hour cooking class followed by lunch.

You'll need your own transport to get here. From the south coast, drive towards Amlapura via Jl Achmad Yani, turn right at the first traffic light and then left at the second traffic light onto the main road to Amed and Tirta Gangga. Soon you'll pass a football ground and big school on the left and should then turn right at the next traffic light. Follow this smaller road to the T-intersection then turn left and head up the hill, taking a sharp right turn to arrive at Bali Asli.

self-styled 'freediving village' are led by Yoram Zekri, a former world freediving vice-champion and French national multirecord holder. The village has its own practice pool, an organic cafe and excellent hostel-style accommodation. It also offers daily one-hour **yoga classes** at 6.30pm (100,000Rp).

Apneista   DIVING
(📱 0812 3826 7356; www.apneista.com; Green Leaf Cafe, Jl I Ketut Natih, Jemeluk; 2-day courses US$200; ⊙ 8.30am-10pm) Based at Jemeluk's laid-back **Green Leaf Cafe** (www.facebook.com/GreenLeafCafeAmed; breakfast dishes 36,000-60,000Rp, lunch mains 43,000-70,000Rp; ⊙8am-6pm; 🖉) 🍴, this outfit offers freediving classes, courses and workshops; its freediving technique uses tools from yoga and meditation.

Hiking

Before the Gunung Agung volcano started rumbling, visitors regularly trekked on a few trails heading inland from the coast, up the slopes of **Gunung Seraya** (1175m) and to some little-visited villages. The countryside is sparsely vegetated and most trails are well defined, so guides aren't usually required for shorter walks. Ask your hotel if it's safe to walk (staff are sure to be monitoring volcano

warnings) and if it's OK to set off, allow a good three hours to get to the top of Seraya, starting from the rocky ridge just east of Jemeluk Bay. Sunrises from here are spectacular but to enjoy one you'll need to climb in the dark; ask at your hotel about a guide to help you with this.

🛌 Sleeping

The Amed region offers overnight options at most price points and for many tastes and interests. There are dive resorts, health and meditation retreats and lots of hotels and guesthouses offering their guests bungalows, pools and restaurants. The only accommodation type lacking is the luxury resort – you'll need to head to Tulamben and the northeast coast to find these. Jemeluk and Amed village are the backpacker hubs.

⭐**Ocean Prana Hostel**   HOSTEL $
(📱 0363-430 1587, WhatsApp 61 435 441 414; www.oceanprana.com/hostel; Jl I Ketut Natih, Jemeluk; dm 150,000Rp; 🅿️❄️🛜🏊) Attached to the freediving school of the same name, this hostel has two thatched bungalows in a large compound. Each has four bunk beds downstairs, two single beds upstairs, power points, small lockers and an outdoor bath-

room with hot water. There's also a pool (often used for freediving training) and an organic cafe with table, beanbag and hammock seating. Breakfast costs 20,000Rp.

Galang Kangin Bungalows GUESTHOUSE $
(☑ 0363-23480; Jl Raya Amed, Jemeluk; r from 400,000Rp; P ❋ ☎) Basic choice that offers cheap-ish accommodation and a warung. Its biggest drawcard is the beachfront location.

★ Melasti Beach Bungalows HOMESTAY $$
(☑ 0877 6018 8093; www.melastibeachamed. com; Jl Melasti, Melasti Beach; r without bathroom 400,000Rp, ste 700,000-800,000Rp, bungalows 900,000-1,000,000Rp; P ❋ ☎) Located at Melasti Beach, west of Amed village, this stylish, good-value B&B is operated by American expat Missy, who is a genial and welcoming host. There are two bungalows, a luxurious suite and one room with an external bathroom on offer; the suite and bungalows have balconies with sea views. Breakfast is included, lunch and dinner can be arranged (mains 35,000Rp to 90,000Rp).

Meditasi RESORT $$
(☑ 0363-430 1793; www.facebook.com/meditasi bungalows; Aas; r 350,000-1,000,000Rp; P ❋ ☎) Get off the grid at this chilled-out hideaway. Meditation, healing and yoga classes help you relax and the rooms are well situated for good swimming and snorkelling. The best bet are the luxury rooms, complete with private gardens, air-con and sea-facing balconies; some standard rooms are limited to fans and cold-water bathrooms.

Anda Amed Resort HOTEL $$$
(☑ 0363-23498; www.andaamedresort.com; Jl Raya Lipah, Banutan; villa from 1,600,000Rp; P ❋ ☎ ☀) This whitewashed hillside hotel complex contrasts with its lushly green grounds. The infinity pool is an ahhh-inducing classic of the genre and has sweeping views of the sea from well above the road. Well-maintained one- or two-bedroom villas are set on a hillside terrace and have sea views.

Santai Hotel HOTEL $$$
(☑ 0363-23487; www.santaibali.com; Banutan Beach; bungalow 1,300,000-2,800,000Rp; P ❋ ☎ ☀) The name of this lovely clifftop option means 'relax', and its facilities make this easy, with a bougainvillea-fringed pool, plenty of sun lounges, a spa, beach bar and cafe. There's also a complimentary shuttle service to Lipah and Jemeluk beaches. Tra-

ditional thatched bungalows gathered from around the archipelago host 10 rooms with four-poster beds, open-air bathrooms and big balcony sofas.

✖ Eating

Almost every guesthouse and hotel has a restaurant or cafe, some are noteworthy. Amed village and Jemeluk are the restaurant and cafe hotspots. Gusto restaurant offers complimentary transport to/from hotels along the coast for its diners, and **Smiling Buddha Restaurant** (☑ 0828 372 2738; Meditasi Resort, Aas; mains 40,000-75,000Rp; ⊙ 8am-10pm; ☑) does the same for those who sign up for one of its cooking classes.

★ Warung Amsha BALINESE $
(☑ 0819 1650 6063; Amed Beach; mains 25,000-65,000Rp; ⊙ 11.30am-10pm; ☎) Tables at this popular beach warung are arranged on the sand and are hotly sought after – it's a good idea to make a booking or arrive early. The menu is resolutely local, featuring freshly caught fish (try the *pepes ikan* –spiced fish cooked in banana leaves) as well as chicken, veggies and spices grown and raised nearby. Juices, cocktails, lassies and beer are on offer.

Blue Earth Village Restaurant INDONESIAN $
(☑ 0821 4554 3699; www.blueearthvillage.com/ restaurant; Jemeluk Lookout; tapas 35,000-40,000Rp, mains 45,000-70,000Rp; ⊙ noon-10pm) Spectacular views and a wide array of menu choices lure diners away from the action in Jemeluk's main strip and up to this restaurant overlooking the blue waters of the bay. There are plenty of vegetarian and vegan options on offer, and the menu includes tapas, pasta, pizza, Thai noodles and Indonesian mains. It's an excellent spot for a sundowner.

★ Gusto INTERNATIONAL $$
(☑ 0813 3898 1394; www.facebook.com/Gusto -Amed-553633071346005; Jl Raya Amed, Bunutan; pizzas 70,000-85,000Rp, pastas 65,000-85,000Rp, mains 55,000-120,000Rp; ⊙ 2-10pm) Don't be put off by the unusual mix of cuisines on Gusto's menu (Indonesian, Italian and Hungarian) – the chefs have mastered them all. Serving the best pizzas on the east coast, homemade pasta dishes, schnitzels and Indonesian seafood dishes, it is a particularly good choice in daylight hours, when the sea view charms. It's small, so bookings are essential.

🔒 Shopping

★ Peduli Alam Bali   CONCEPT STORE

(☑ 0877 6156 2511; www.pedulialam.org; Jl Raya Lipah, Lipah; ☉ 9am-5pm Mon-Fri, to noon Sat) 🏃 A non-profit outfit encouraging recycling and raising eco-consciousness in Amed, Peduli Alam ('Protect Nature') collects 50 tonnes of rubbish from this part of the island each month, much of which is then used to make the bags and other items that are sold in this shop. The project gives employment to four truck drivers and 14 local women.

ℹ️ Getting There & Away

Most people drive here via the main highway from Amlapura and Culik. The spectacular road going all the way around the twin peaks from Aas to Ujung makes a good circle. You can arrange for a driver and car to/from south Bali and the airport for about 500,000Rp. No public transport.

Tulamben

📞 0363 / POP 8050

Tulamben's big attraction sunk over 60 years ago. The wreck of the US cargo ship *Liberty* is among the best and most popular dive sites in Bali and has transformed what was a tiny fishing village into an entire town based on diving. Even snorkellers can easily swim out and enjoy exploring the wreck and the coral reefs that are strung along the coastline. Swimming is a different story – the shore is made up of rather beautiful, large washed stones that are difficult to walk on, so visitors tend to swim in hotel pools.

For non-aquatic delights, check out the **morning market** in Tulamben village, 1.5km north of the dive site.

> ### THE WRECK OF THE LIBERTY
>
> In January 1942, the small US Navy cargo ship USAT *Liberty* was torpedoed by a Japanese submarine near Lombok. Taken in tow, it was beached at Tulamben so that its cargo of rubber and railway parts could be saved. The Japanese invasion prevented this and the ship sat on the beach until the 1963 eruption of Gunung Agung broke it in two and left it just off the shoreline, much to the delight of divers ever since. (And just for the record, it was *not* a Liberty-class WWII freighter.)

🏃 Activities

Diving & Snorkelling

The **shipwreck** USAT *Liberty* is about 50m directly offshore from Puri Madha Dive Resort; look for the schools of black snorkels. Swim straight out and you'll see the stern rearing up from the depths, heavily encrusted with coral and swarming with dozens of species of colourful fish – and with scuba divers most of the day. The ship is more than 100m long, but the hull is broken into sections and it's easy for divers to get inside. The bow is in quite good shape, the midship's region is badly mangled and the stern is almost intact – the best parts are between 15m and 30m deep. You will want at least two dives to really explore the wreck.

Many divers commute to Tulamben from Amed or Lovina, and in busy times it can get quite crowded between 11am and 4pm, with 50 or more divers at a time around the wreck. Stay the night in Tulamben to get an early start. Most hotels have their own dive centre and some offer good-value dive and accommodation packages for guests.

Puri Madha Dive Centre   DIVING

(☑ 0363-22921; www.purimadhadiveresort.com; ☉ 6am-6.30pm) Hires snorkelling gear (200,000Rp) and offers off-shore dives (one/two dives 700,000/1,200,000Rp) and PADI open water courses (two to three days 5,400,000Rp). It also offers dive and accommodation packages at its **resort** (r 550,000Rp, cottage 650,000Rp; ❄ 🛜 🏊).

Apnea Bali   DIVING

(☑ WhatsApp 0822 3739 8854, WhatsApp 0822 6612 5814; www.apneabali.com; Jl Kubu-Abang; courses from 800,000Rp) This polished operator on Tulamben's main strip specialises in freediving courses and trips for all skill levels, including down to the *Liberty* wreck. Choose from an introductory half-day course (800,000Rp), a 2-day course (3,200,000Rp) and a 3-day course (4,600,000Rp).

🛏️ Sleeping

Tulamben is a quiet place and is essentially built around the wreck – its hotels, all with a cafe or restaurant and most with dive centres, are spread along a 4km stretch either side of the main road. You can choose between roadside (cheaper) options or those by the water (nicer). At high tide even the rocky shore vanishes.

Siddhartha RESORT $$$
(☑ 0363-23034; www.siddhartha-bali.com; Kubu;
s €69-188, d €146-240, villas €210-370; P ❄ ☎)
The oceanside pool and yoga pavilion at
this swish German-owned resort are major
drawcards, as is the extensive range of fa-
cilities and amenities (restaurant, bar, dive
centre, gym, billiard and table-tennis tables,
TV room, spa). Well-spaced rooms and villas
are located in garden surrounds, and feature
comfortable beds and outdoor bathrooms;
villas have plunge pools.

❶ Getting There & Away

If you are driving to Lovina for the night, be sure
to leave by about 3pm so you'll still have a little
light when you get there.

The car park in front of the Puri Madha Dive
Resort is often full of vans dropping off organ-
ised groups of divers to the *Liberty* wreck, so you
may have trouble sourcing a park there. There is
paid parking near the Tauch Terminal Resort.

CENTRAL MOUNTAINS

Bali has a hot soul. The volcanoes stretching
along the island's spine are seemingly cones
of silence but their active spirits are just be-
low the surface, eager for expression.

Gunung Batur (1717m) is constantly
letting off steam; this place has an other-
worldly beauty that may overwhelm the at-
tendant hassles of a visit. At Danau Bratan
there are sacred Hindu temples, while the
village of Candikuning has an engrossing
botanic garden.

The old colonial village of Munduk, a hik-
ing centre, has views down the hills to the
coast of north Bali, which match the beauty
of the many nearby waterfalls, and the lakes
of Tamblingan and Buyan. In the shadow of
Gunung Batukau (2276m) you'll find one of
Bali's most mystic temples. And, just south,
the Unesco-listed ancient rice terraces
around Jatiluwih bedazzle.

Amid it all, little roads lead to untouched
villages. Start driving north from Antasari
for one surprise after another.

❶ Getting There & Away

To fully explore the mountains at the heart of
Bali, you will want your own vehicle. A car with
hired driver will keep you from getting lost on the
tangle of back roads, although that may be the
very point of your day out.

Danau Bratan Area

Approaching from south Bali, you gradually
leave the rice terraces behind and ascend
into the cool, often misty mountain country
around Danau Bratan. Candikuning is the
main village in the area, and has the impor-
tant and picturesque temple Pura Ulun Danu
Bratan. Munduk anchors the region with
fine trekking to waterfalls and cloud-cloaked
forests and nearby Danau Tamblingan.

❶ Getting There & Away

Danau Bratan is along the main north–south road
between south Bali and Singaraja. Bemos (mini-
buses) have largely gone the way of the dinosaur
and operate very infrequent services here, stop-
ping along the road in Bedugul and Candikuning
on runs between Denpasar's Ubung terminal and
Singaraja's Sangket terminal a couple of times
a week, at best, for around 100,000Rp. To get
around the scattered attractions of this region,
you'll want your own transport.

Candikuning

☑ 0368
Often misty, Candikuning is home to a good
botanic garden as well as one of Bali's most
photographed temples. There's also the sim-
ple beauty of Danau Bratan amid the bowl of
lushly forested mountains.

⊙ Sights

The broad green valley northwest of Danau
Bratan is actually the crater of an extinct
volcano. In the middle of the valley, on the
main road, Pancasari is a nontourist town
with a bustling market that happens every
three days.

Pura Ulun Danu Bratan HINDU TEMPLE
(off Jl Raya Denpasar-Singaraja; adult/child 50,000/
25,000Rp, parking 5000Rp; ⊙ 7am-4pm) An iconic
image of Bali, depicted on the 50,000Rp note,
this important Hindu-Buddhist temple was
founded in the 17th century. It is dedicated to
Dewi Danu, the goddess of the waters, and is
built on small islands. Pilgrimages and cere-
monies are held here to ensure that there is
a supply of water for farmers all over Bali as
part of the Unesco-recognised *subak* system.
Incredibly popular, you'll need to dodge selfie
sticks unless you set out early.

Bali Botanic Garden GARDENS
(☑ 0368-203 3211; www.krbali.lipi.go.id; Jl Kebun
Raya Eka Karya Bali; 20,000Rp, parking 6000Rp;

Danau Bratan Area

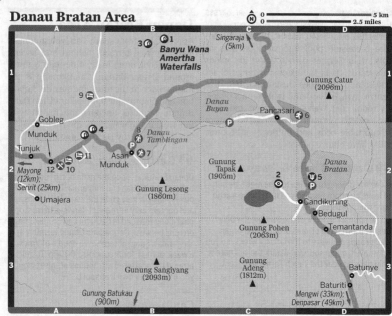

◔ 7am-6pm) This garden is a showplace. Established in 1959 as a branch of the national botanic gardens at Bogor, near Jakarta, it covers more than 154 hectares on the lower slopes of Gunung Pohen. Don't miss the **Panca Yadnya Garden** (Garden of Five Offerings), which preserves plants used in ancient Hindu ceremonies. For an extra 12,000Rp you can drive your own car (no motorbikes) about the gardens.

🏃 Activities

Handara Golf & Country Club Resort
GOLF

(📞0362-342 3048; www.handaragolfresort.com; greens fees from 1,000,000Rp; club rental from 450,000Rp) Just south of Pancasari, you will see the entrance to this well-situated, 18-hole golf course (compared with south Bali courses, there's plenty of water here). It also offers comfortable accommodation (rooms from US$100) in the sterile atmosphere of a 1970s resort (that could pass for Drax's lair in the Bond movie *Moonraker*).

The property's iconic gate draws more visitors to the area than the resort itself – pay 30,000Rp and get 10 minutes of selfie time in front of it.

Bali Treetop Adventure Park
OUTDOORS

(📞0361-934 0009; www.balitreetop.com; Jl Kebun Raya Eka Karya Bali, Bali Botanic Garden; adult/child from US$25/16; ◔9.30am-6pm) Within the

Bali Botanic Garden (p293), you can cavort like a bird or a squirrel at the Bali Treetop Adventure Park. Winches, ropes, nets and more let you explore the forest well above the ground. And it's not passive: you hoist, jump, balance and otherwise circumnavigate the park. Special programs are geared to different ages.

🛏 Sleeping

You'll find some simple guesthouses on the road to the botanic garden.

Kebun Raya Bali   GUESTHOUSE $$
(📞0368-2033211; www.kebunrayabali.com; Jl Kebun Raya Eka Karya Bali, Bali Botanic Garden; r incl breakfast from 450,000Rp) Wake up and smell the roses. The Bali Botanic Garden (p293) has 14 comfortable hotel-style rooms and a four-cottage guesthouse in the heart of the botanic gardens.

❶ Getting There & Away

Any minibus or bemo between south Bali and Singaraja will stop in Candikuning on request.

Danau Buyan & Danau Tamblingan

Northwest of Danau Bratan are two less-visited lakes, Danau Buyan and Danau Tamblingan, where some excellent guided hikes are on offer. The Munduk road on the hill above the lakes has sweeping views. There are several tiny villages and old temples along the shores of both lakes that reward those who take the time to explore. You'll leave crowded Bali behind and enjoy a tropical hike in nature, with few of the hassles so prevalent elsewhere.

🕴 Activities

⭐**Pramuwisata Amerta Jati**   HIKING
(📞0857 3715 4849; Munduk Rd; guided hikes 250,000-750,000Rp; ⊙8am-5pm) Located in a hut along the road above Danau Tamblingan, this group of excellent guides offers several different trips down and around the lakes. A popular two-hour trip includes ancient temples and a canoe trip on the lake (per person 250,000Rp). Trips can be as short as an hour or last all day.

⭐**Organisasi Pramuwisata Bangkit Bersama**   HIKING
(Guides Organization Standing Together; 📞0852 3867 8092; Danau Tamblingan, Asan Munduk; guid-

ed hikes from 200,000Rp; ⊙8.30am-4pm) This great group is based in a hut near the car park for Danau Tamblingan. Like the guiding group along the Munduk road, it offers a range of trips around the lakes, temples and mountains. You can ascend nearby Gunung Lesong for 600,000Rp.

❶ Getting There & Away

You will need your own wheels to explore the region around these two lakes. Danau Buyan has parking right at the lake, a pretty 1.5km drive off the main road. Danau Tamblingan has parking at the end of the road from the village of Asan Munduk.

Munduk
📞0362
The simple village of Munduk is one of Bali's most appealing mountain retreats. It has a cool misty ambience set among lush hillsides covered with jungle, rice fields, fruit trees and pretty much anything else that grows on the island. Waterfalls tumble off precipices by the dozen. There are hikes and treks galore and a number of really nice places to stay, from old Dutch colonial summer homes to retreats where you can plunge full-on into local culture. Many people come for a day and stay for a week.

◉ Sights

Heading to Munduk from Pancasari, the main road climbs steeply up the rim of the old volcanic crater. It's worth stopping to enjoy the views back over the valley and lakes – show a banana and the swarms of monkeys will get so excited they'll start spanking themselves with joy. Turning right (east) at the top will take you on a scenic descent to Singaraja. Taking a sharp left turn (west), you follow a ridgetop road with Danau Buyan on one side and a slope to the sea on the other.

At **Asan Munduk**, you'll find another T-junction. The left turn will take you down a road leading to Danau Tamblingan. Turning right takes you along beautiful winding roads to the main village of Munduk. Watch for superb panoramas of north Bali and the ocean.

⭐**Banyu Wana Amertha Waterfalls**   WATERFALL
(📞0857 3943 9299; www.facebook.com/banyu wanaamertha; Jl Bhuana Sari, Wanagiri; 20,000Rp, parking 2000Rp; ⊙8am-5pm) Developed as a tourist attraction in 2018, the falls here are among the best on Bali. It's about a

WORTH A TRIP

MUNDUK'S WATERFALLS

Munduk's many waterfalls include the following three, which you can visit on a hike of four to six hours (note that the myriad local maps given out by guesthouses and hotels can be vague on details and it's easy to take a wrong turn). Fortunately, even unplanned detours are scenic; but if you'd prefer more guidance, wonderful local expert guides like **Bayu Sunrise** (☑ 0877 6206 6287, WhatsApp 0877 6206 6063; bayusunrise9@gmail.com; waterfall excursions per car from Lovina/Ubud/south Bali 700,000/850,000/950,000Rp) can provide car pick up from anywhere on Bali and accompany you on the trails down to the falls. Clouds of mist from the water add to the already misty air; drips come off every leaf. There are a lot of often slippery and steep paths; rest up at tiny cafes perched above some of the falls.

Banyu Wana Amertha Waterfalls (p295) From the road running north along Danau Buyan, Jl Raya Wanagiri, head north on Jl Bhuana Sari for 1.8km and look for the signs for the parking area on the left. It's about a 500m walk from the car park to the path leading to the different falls.

Banyumala Twin Waterfalls Located in Wanagiri Village, the only thing giving these secluded falls away is the sign off the bumpy road. From Jl Raya Wanagiri, the road running north of Danau Buyan, follow the signs posted near the west end of the lake and take that road north 2.3km to the parking area. From there, the walk to the falls is about 20 minutes downhill.

Munduk Waterfall From the western edge of Danau Tamblingan, continue along the main road, Jl Munduk–Wanagiri, 4.6km to the Munduk Waterfall car park signs. From there, its a 700m walk to the falls.

20-minute walk from the car park; a 500m trail, which is paved only with concrete stones and logs, winds through a village and coffee plantation. You'll eventually arrive at a large sign, where the path diverges to four separate cascades. Touches like colourful shrubs, bamboo huts and bridges make them especially Insta-worthy. Get here before the crowds catch on.

Banyumala Twin Waterfalls   WATERFALL
(☑ 0819 1648 5556; Wanagiri Village; 20,000Rp, parking 2000Rp) In the secluded, picturesque highlands north of Munduk, a 15-minute hike down natural, bamboo-railed stairs leads to this powerful pair of cascades. Enjoy the view of them tumbling some 35m into the large natural pool that's warmed by the morning sun and is the perfect temperature for a swim.

Munduk Waterfall   WATERFALL
(Tanah Braak; 20,000Rp, parking 2000Rp) About 2km east of Munduk, look for signs for this waterfall (aka Tanah Braak) along the road. Though the signs say the trail is 700m long, it seems to be an underestimate. This is the easiest waterfall to access in the area without a map or guide – though in recent years, it's decreased in size.

🛏 Sleeping

Enjoy simple old Dutch houses in the village or more naturalistic places in the countryside. Most places have cafes, usually serving good local fare.

⭐**Puri Lumbung Cottages**   GUESTHOUSE $$
(☑ 0812 387 4042; www.purilumbung.com; cottage incl breakfast 900,000-1,800,000Rp; 🐾) 🌿 This lovely hotel has 46 bright two-storey thatched cottages and rooms set among rice fields. Enjoy intoxicating views (units 32 to 35 have the best) from the upstairs balconies. Dozens of hiking options and courses are offered.

Villa Dua Bintang   GUESTHOUSE $$
(☑ 0812 3700 5593, 0812 3709 3463; www.villa duabintang.com; Jl Batu Galih; r incl breakfast 800,000Rp; 🐾🍴) Hidden 500m down a tree-shaded lane that's off the main road, 1km east of Munduk. Eight gorgeous rooms are elaborately built amid fruit trees and forest (two rooms are family-size). The scent of cloves and nutmeg hangs in the air from the porch. There's a cafe.

⭐**Munduk Moding Plantation**   RESORT $$$
(☑ 0811 381 0123; www.mundukmodingplantation .com; Jl Raya Asah Gobleg; ste/villa from US$189/ $367; ❄🐾🍴) 🌿 Set among a coffee plantation, the modern Balinese-designed villas

and suites of this intimate eco-resort offer luxurious respite. But the real relaxation happens in the award-winning 18m infinity pool, where water blends seamlessly with sky; with such panoramic views of mountains and sea, which extend to Java on a clear day, it may very well be the best in all of Bali.

Munduk Moding Plantation's sustainability practices extend beyond environmental efforts. In addition to on-site water filtration, renewable energy production, a kitchen garden and ecological waste management initiatives, the coffee plantation provides social and economic development opportunities to support the local community.

Eating

There are a couple of cute warungs (food stalls) in the village and a few stores with very basic supplies (including insect spray). Guesthouses have cafes: the restaurant at Puri Lumbung Cottages is the best option for nonguests.

Don Biyu CAFE $
(☑ 0812 3709 3949; www.donbiyu.com; mains 22,000-87,000Rp; ☺ 7.30am-10pm; ☎) Catch up on your blog, enjoy good coffee or zone out before the sublime views, while choosing from a mix of Western and interesting Asian fare. Dishes are served in mellow open-air pavilions. It also has five double **rooms** (600,000Rp to 750,000Rp), all with balconies and views. It's on the main road leading into Munduk.

ℹ Getting There & Away

This is territory where you'll want your own vehicle or a car and driver. Driving to the north coast, the main road west of Munduk goes through a number of picturesque villages to Mayong (where you can head south to West Bali). The road then goes down to the sea at Seririt in North Bali.

Gunung Batukau Area

☑ 0361

Gunung Batukau is Bali's second-highest mountain (2276m), the third of Bali's three major mountains and the holy peak of the island's western end. It's often overlooked, which is probably a good thing given what the vendor hordes have done to Gunung Agung.

You can climb its slippery slopes from one of the island's holiest and most underrated temples, Pura Luhur Batukau, or just revel in the ancient rice-terrace greenery around Jatiluwih.

◎ Sights

★Pura Luhur Batukau HINDU TEMPLE
(Jl Penatahan-Wongayagede; adult/child 30,000/15,000Rp; ☺ 8am-6pm) On the slopes of Gunung Batukau, Pura Luhur Batukau was the state temple when Tabanan was an independent kingdom. It has a seven-roofed *meru* (multiroofed shrine) dedicated to Maha Dewa, the mountain's guardian spirit, as well as shrines for Bratan, Buyan and Tamblingan lakes. This is certainly the most spiritual temple you can easily visit in Bali.

The main *meru* in the inner courtyard have little doors shielding small ceremonial items. Outside the compound, the temple is surrounded by forest and the atmosphere is cool and misty; the chants of priests are backed by birds singing.

Facing the temple, take a short walk around to the left to see a small whitewater stream where the air resonates with tumbling water. Note the unusual fertility shrine.

There's a general lack of touts and other characters here – including hordes of tourists. Respect traditions and act appropriately while visiting temples. Sarong rental is included in the entrance price. Guides at the entrance offer worthwhile **two-hour jungle hikes** for 250,000Rp.

🏃 Activities

Gunung Batukau HIKING
At Pura Luhur Batukau you are fairly well up the side of Gunung Batukau. For the trek to the top of the 2276m peak, you'll need a guide, which can be arranged at the temple ticket booth. Expect to pay more than 1,000,000Rp for a muddy and arduous journey that will take at least seven hours in one direction. Be sure to negotiate.

The rewards are potentially amazing views (depending on mist) alternating with thick dripping jungle, and the knowledge that you've taken a trail that is much less travelled than the ones on the eastern peaks. You can get a taste of the adventure on a two-hour mini-jaunt (300,000Rp for two).

Staying the night up the mountain might be possible but the assumption is that you will go up and back the same day. Talk to the guides ahead of time to see if you can make special arrangements to camp on the mountain.

🛏 Sleeping

A couple of lodges are hidden away on the slopes of Gunung Batukau. You reach them via a spectacular small and twisting road that makes a long inverted V far up the mountain from Bajera and Pucuk on the main Tabanan–Gilimanuk road in west Bali.

★ Sarinbuana Eco Lodge   LODGE $$

(☑ 0361-743 5198; www.baliecolodge.com; Sarinbuana; bungalows 900,000-2,000,000Rp; 📶) 🌿
These beautiful two-level bungalows are built on the side of a hill just a 10-minute walk from a protected rainforest preserve. Notable amenities include fridges, marble bathrooms and handmade soap. Think rustic luxe – there's even a treehouse. The organic Balinese restaurant is excellent (mains 60,000Rp to 150,000Rp). There are cultural workshops, yoga classes and guided treks.

❶ Getting There & Away

The only realistic way to explore the Gunung Batukau area is with your own transport. There are two main approaches. The easiest is via Tabanan: take the Pura Luhur Batukau road north 9km to a fork in the road, then take the left-hand turn (towards the temple) and go a further 5km to a junction near a school in Wangayagede village. Here you can continue straight to the temple or turn right (east) for the rice fields of Jatiluwih.

The other way is to approach from the east. On the main Denpasar–Singaraja road, look for a small road to the west, just south of the Pacung Indah hotel. Here you follow a series of small paved roads west until you reach the Jatiluwih rice fields. You'll get lost, but locals will quickly set you right and the scenery is superb anyway.

Gunung Batur Area

☑ 0366

The Gunung Batur area is like a giant bowl, with its bottom half covered by water and a set of volcanic cones jutting out of the middle. Sound a bit spectacular? It is. On clear days – vital to appreciating the spectacle – the turquoise waters wrap around the newer volcanoes, which have paths of old lava flows snaking down their sides.

◉ Sights

In 2012 Unesco honoured the area by adding it to a list of more than 90 geologic wonders worldwide (www.globalgeopark. org) and naming it the **Batur Caldera Geopark** (www.baturglobalgeopark.com).

Some interesting signs detailing the unique geology of the area are posted along roads in the region; the **Batur Geopark Museum** (☑ 0366 - 91537, What'sApp 0818-0551-5504; www. baturglobalgeopark.com; Penelokan; ◷ 9am-4pm Mon, from 8am Tue-Fri, 8am-2pm Sat & Sun) FREE has full details.

The road around the southwestern rim of the Gunung Batur crater offers stunning vistas, though the villages around the crater rim have grown into one continuous, untidy strip. Kintamani is the main village, though the whole area is often referred to by that name. Coming from the south, the first village is Penelokan, where tour groups first stop to gasp at the view.

Day trippers should bring some sort of wrap in case the mist closes in and the temperature drops (it can get to 16°C).

Pura Puncak Penulisan   HINDU TEMPLE
(Penulisan) FREE Near the Penilusan road junction, several steep flights of steps lead to Bali's highest temple, Pura Puncak Penulisan (1745m). Inside the highest courtyard are rows of old statues and fragments of sculptures in the open *bale* (pavilion with steeply pitched thatch roof). Some of the sculptures date back to the 11th century. The temple views are superb: facing north, and weather permitting, you can see over the rice terraces clear to the Singaraja coast.

❶ Information

Services are limited in the Gunung Batur area, but there are a few ATMs along Jl Raya Penelokan.

DANGERS & ANNOYANCES

Be wary of touts on motorcycles, who will attempt to steer you to a tour or hotel of *their* choice as you descend into the Danau Batur area from the village of Penelokan. Very persistent, they offer no service of value and you should ignore them. Vendors in the area can be aggressive.

❶ Getting There & Away

The infrequent buses on the Denpasar–Singaraja route (via Batubulan, where you may need to change) will stop in Penelokan and Kintamani (about 40,000Rp). Better is to have your own transport. If you hire a car and driver, rebuff their buffet-lunch entreaties (these huge, mediocre restaurants give kickbacks).

If you arrive by private vehicle, you will be stopped at Penelokan or Kubupenelokan to buy an entry ticket (31,000Rp per person, beware of scams demanding even more) for the entire

Gunung Batur

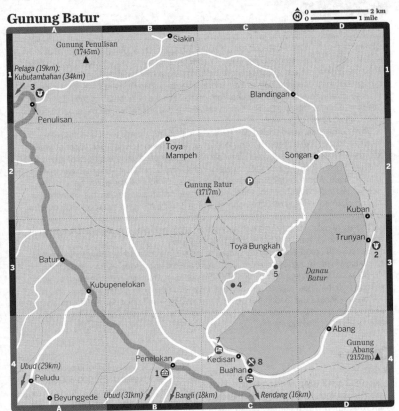

Gunung Batur area. You shouldn't be charged again – save your receipt.

ℹ️ Getting Around

It's best to arrange private transport to get around this area; bemos are rare and roads are small, winding and crowded.

Danau Batur

The little villages around Danau Batur have a crisp lakeside setting and views up to the surrounding peaks. There's a lot of fish farming, and the air is pungent with the smell of onions from the myriad tiny vegetable farms. Don't miss the trip along the east coast to Trunyan.

👁️ Sights

Pura Pancering Jagat   HINDU TEMPLE
(Trunyan) The village of Trunyan is known for the Pura Pancering Jagat, which is very impressive with its seven-roofed *meru*. Inside

Gunung Batur

the temple is a 4m-high statue of the village's guardian spirit, although tourists are not usually allowed in. Ignore the touts and guides lurking about and know that 5000Rp is the maximum you should pay to park here.

BALI GUNUNG BATUR AREA

JATILUWIH RICE FIELDS

The terraces of **Jatiluwih** (adult/child 40,000/30,000Rp, car 5000Rp) are part of Bali's emblematic – and Unesco-recognised – ancient rice-growing culture. You'll understand the nomination just viewing the panorama from the narrow, twisting 18km road, but getting out for a rice-field walk is even more rewarding, following the water as it runs through channels and bamboo pipes from one plot to the next. Much of the rice you'll see is traditional, rather than the hybrid versions grown elsewhere on the island. Look for heavy short husks of red rice.

Take some time, leave your driver behind and just find a place to sit and enjoy the views. It sounds like a cliché, but the longer you look the more you'll see. What at first seems like a vast palette of greens reveals itself to be rice at various stages of growth.

Note, however, that the terraces have become very popular and the road can be less than tranquil. Worse, tour companies now operate ATV tours through the heart of the rice fields. Under threat by Unesco to have the site's status rescinded, the government has proclaimed a freeze on development, which is not a moment too soon after developers announced plans to bulldoze terraces for hotels.

There are cafes for refreshments along the route, including a rather garish collection about mid-drive. Your best bet is to browse a couple.

Because the road is sharply curved, vehicles are forced to drive slowly, which makes the Jatiluwih route a good one for bikes. There are toll booths for visitors (adult/child 40,000/30,000Rp per person, plus 5000Rp per car), which does *not* seem to be going to road maintenance – it's rough. Still the drive won't take more than an hour.

You can access the road in the west off the road to Pura Luhur Batukau from Tabanan, and in the east off the main road to Bedugul near Pacung. Drivers all know this road well and locals offer directions.

👉 Tours

★ C.Bali
ADVENTURE

(📱 info 0813 5342 0541; www.c-bali.com; Hotel Segara, Kedisan; tours from 300,000Rp) Operated by an Australian-Dutch couple, C.Bali offers cultural bike tours around the region, canoe tours on Danau Batur and multiday trips. Prices include pick up across south Bali. Tours often fill up far in advance, so book ahead through the website.

🛌 Sleeping

A few guesthouses with lake views dot the shore.

Beware of the motorcycle touts, who will follow you down the hill from Penelokan trying to nab a hotel commission. Local hotels ask that you call ahead and reserve so that they have your name on record and thus can avoid paying the touts.

Baruna Cottages
GUESTHOUSE $

(📱 0813 5322 2896; www.barunacottage.com; Buahan; r/bungalow from 400,000/550,000Rp) The 10 rooms at this small and tidy compound vary greatly in design and size; the middle grade have the best views. It's right across the Trunyan road from the lake, and there's a cute cafe.

Hotel Segara
GUESTHOUSE $

(📱 0366-51136; www.segara-id.book.direct; Kedisan; r incl breakfast 250,000-600,000Rp; 🛜) The popular Segara has bungalows set around a cafe and courtyard. The cheaper of the 32 rooms have cold water; the best rooms have hot water and bathtubs – perfect for soaking after an early trek.

🍴 Eating

A couple of local cafes have decent meals; otherwise most guesthouses can supply food.

Kedisan Floating Hotel
BALINESE $

(📱 0366-51627, 0813 3775 5411; Kedisan; meals from 27,000Rp; ⊗ 8am-8pm; 🛜) This hotel on the shores of Danau Batur is hugely popular for its daily lunches. On weekends tourists vie with day-trippers from Denpasar for tables out on the piers over the lake. The Balinese food, which features fresh lake fish, is excellent. You can also stay here: the best rooms are cottages at the water's edge (from 500,000Rp).

ℹ️ Getting There & Away

Aside from hiking and trekking, you'll be happiest with your own wheels here.

Gunung Batur

Vulcanologists describe Gunung Batur as a 'double caldera', with one crater inside another. The outer crater is an oval about 14km long, with its western rim about 1500m above sea level. The inner is a classic volcano-shaped peak that reaches 1717m. Geological activity occurs regularly, and activity over the last decade has spawned several smaller cones on its western flank. There were major eruptions in 1917, 1926 and 1963.

One look at this other-worldly spectacle and you'll understand why people want to go through the many hassles and expenses of a trek. Note that the odds of clouds obscuring your reason for coming are greater from July to December, but at any time of year you should check conditions before committing to a trip, or even coming up the mountain.

🏃 Activities

Hiking

The cartel of local guides known as **PPPGB** (formerly HPPGB) has a monopoly on guided climbs up Gunung Batur. It requires all hiking agencies to hire at least one of its guides for trips up the mountain, and has a reputation for tough tactics in requiring climbers to use its guides and in negotiations for its services.

That said, many people use the services of PPPGB guides without incident, and some of the guides win plaudits from visitors due to their ideas for customising trips.

The following strategies should help you have a good climb:

➡ Be absolutely clear in your agreement with PPPGB about the terms you're agreeing to, such as whether fees are per person or per group, whether they include breakfast, and exactly where you will go.

➡ Deal with one of the hiking agencies as it will take care of all the arrangements.

PPPGB rates and times are posted at its main **Toya Bungkah office** (Mt Batur Tour Guides Association; ☑ 0366-52362; ⊙ 3am-9pm) and its second **access road office** (Mt Batur Tour Guides Association; ⊙ 3am-10am). Treks on offer include:

Mt Batur Sunrise A simple ascent and return; from 4am to 8am, 400,000Rp per person.

Mt Batur Main Crater Includes sunrise from the summit and time around the rim; from 4am to 9.30am, 500,000Rp per person.

Mt Batur Exploration Sunrise, caldera and some of the volcanic cones; from 4am to 10am, 650,000Rp per person.

If you're climbing before sunrise, take a flashlight or be sure that your guide provides you with one. You'll need good strong footwear, a hat, a sweater and drinking water.

BALI GUNUNG BATUR AREA

ℹ GUNUNG BATUR ROUTES

The climb to see the sunrise from Gunung Batur is still the most popular trek. In high season 100 or more people will arrive at the top for dawn. Guides will provide breakfast on the summit for a fee (50,000Rp), which often includes the novelty of cooking an egg or banana in the steaming holes at the top of the volcano. There are pricey refreshment stops along the way.

Most travellers use one of two trails that start near Toya Bungkah. The shorter one is straight up (three to four hours return), while a longer trek (five to six hours return) links the summit climb with the other craters. Climbers have reported that they have easily made this journey without a PPPGB guide, although it shouldn't be tried while it's dark because people have fallen to their deaths. The major obstacle is actually avoiding any hassle from the guides.

There are a few separate paths at first, but they all rejoin sooner or later and after about 30 minutes you'll be on a ridge with quite a well-defined track. It gets pretty steep towards the top and it can be hard walking over the loose volcanic sand – you'll climb up three steps only to slide back two. Allow about two hours to get to the top.

There's also a track that enables you to use private transport to within about 45 minutes' walk of the top. From Toya Bungkah, take the road northeast towards Songan and take the left fork after about 3.5km at Serongga, just before Songan. Follow this inner-rim road for another 1.7km to a well-signposted track on the left, which climbs another 1km or so to a car park. From here, the walking track is easy to follow to the top.

NORTH BALI

The land on the other side of the map, that's north Bali. Although one-sixth of the island's population lives here, this vast region is overlooked by many visitors who stay cocooned in the south Bali–Ubud axis.

The big draw here is the incredible diving and snorkelling at nearby Pulau Menjangan. Arcing around a nearby bay, booming Pemuteran may be Bali's best beach escape. To the east is Lovina, a sleepy beach strip with cheap hotels and even cheaper sunset beer specials. All along the north coast are interesting little boutique hotels, while inland you'll find quiet treks to waterfalls.

Getting to north Bali for once lives up to the cliché: it's half the fun.

ℹ️ Getting There & Away

Routes here follow the thinly populated coastlines east and west, or you can go up and over the mountains by any number of routes, marvelling at crater lakes and maybe stopping for a misty trek on the way.

Singaraja is the main hub for bus services. Buses from south Bali come here and there is service along the main coast roads east and west. Otherwise, note that heavy traffic can make journeys to the north from south Bali last three hours or more.

Lovina

📞 0362 / POP 20,550

'Relaxed' is how people most describe Lovina, and aside from the pushy touts, they're correct. This low-key, low-rise, low-priced beach resort town is a far cry from Seminyak. The waves are calm, the beach thin and over-amped attractions nil.

Lovina is sun-drenched, with patches of shade from palm trees. A highlight every afternoon at fishing villages such as Anturan is watching *prahu* (traditional outrigger canoes) being prepared for the night's fishing; as sunset reddens the sky, the lights of the fishing boats appear as bright dots across the horizon.

The Lovina tourist area stretches over 8km, and consists of a string of coastal villages – Kaliasem, Kalibukbuk, Anturan and Tukad Mungga – collectively known as Lovina. The main focus is Kalibukbuk, 10.5km west of Singaraja and the heart of Lovina. Daytime traffic on the main road is loud and fairly constant.

🏊 Activities

Dolphin Watching

Sunrise boat trips to see dolphins are Lovina's much-hyped tourist attraction, so much so that they have a monument in their honour.

Some days no dolphins are sighted, but most of the time at least a few surface.

Expect pressure from your hotel and touts selling dolphin trips. The price is fixed at 150,000/75,000Rp per adult/child by the boat-owners' cartel. Trips start at a nonholiday-like 5.30am and last about two hours. Note that the ocean can get pretty crowded with roaring powerboats.

There's great debate about what all this means to the dolphins. Do they like being chased by boats? If not, why do they keep coming back? Maybe it's the fish, of which there are plenty off Lovina.

Diving & Snorkelling

Diving on the local reef is better at lower depths and night diving is popular. Many people stay here and dive Pulau Menjangan, a 1½-hour drive west.

Generally, the water is clear and some parts of the reef are quite good for snorkelling, though the coral has been damaged by bleaching and, in places, by dynamite fishing. The best place is to the west, a few hundred metres offshore from Billibo Beach Cottages. A two-hour boat trip will cost about 450,000Rp per person, including equipment.

Spice Dive   DIVING
(📞 0813 3724 2221; www.balispicedive.com; off Jl Raya Lovina, Kalibukbuk; 2-tank dives from €80; ⊙ 8am-9pm) Spice Dive is a large operation. It offers snorkelling trips (€55) and night dives (€45), plus popular Pulau Menjangan trips (snorkel/dive €70/80). It's based at the west end of the beach path, with Spice Beach Club. It also has an office on Jl Bina Ria.

🍳 Courses

★ **Warung Bambu Pemaron**   COOKING
(📞 0362-31455; www.warung-bambu.mahanara. com; Pemaron; classes from 405,000Rp; ⊙ 8am-1pm) Start with a trip to a large Singaraja food market and then, in a breezy setting amid rice fields east of Lovina, learn to cook up to nine classic Balinese dishes. Levels range from beginner to advanced, and there are vegetarian options. The staff are

North Bali

10 km
5 miles

BALI SEA

Krabokan
Sinengdalem
Beratan
Silangsayang
Air Terjun Gitgit
Penarukan
Singaraja
Panci
Selat
Danau
Buyan
Gunung Adeng
Gunung
Tamblingan
Danau
Pantai Penimbangan
Anturan
Kalibukbuk
Munduk
Gunung Lesong
(1860m)
Gunung
Sangiyang
Gunung Batukau
(2276m)
Tukad Mungga
Lovina
Kaliasem
Dencarik
Air Panas
Banjar
Gbleg
Kayu
Putih
Pujungan
Seririt
Banjar Tega
Banjar
Pedewa
Ume
Anyar
Rangdu
Mayong
Pupuan
Batungsei
Kalisada
Cetukanbawang
Manggisari
Grokgak
Pemuteran
Banyupoh
Gondoi
Pura
Melanting
Gunung Musi
(1224m)
Gunung Patas
(1412m)
Banyuwedang
Gunung Merbuk
(1388m)
Bali Barat
National Park
Pulau
Menjangan
Gunung Prapat
Agung (310m)
Gunung Kelatakan
(698m)
Sumber
Kelompok
Gunung
Banyuwedang
(430m)
Labuan
Lalang
Kampung
Merah
Ketapang
(Java) (144m)
Pemaron
Pemuteran
Mendoyo
Gilimanuk
Cekik
Melaya
Negara
Kelatakan
Candikesuma

Lovina

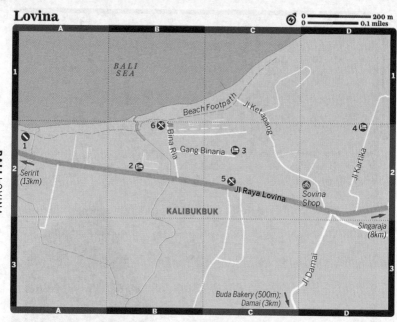

BALI LOVINA

Lovina

🟢 Activities, Courses & Tours
1 Spice Dive...A2

🛏 Sleeping
2 Funky Place B2
3 Harris Homestay C2
4 Villa Taman Ganesha.........................D2

❌ Eating
5 Global Village Kafe.............................C2
6 Sea Breeze Café B2

charming, and the fee includes transport within the area. When you're done, you get to feast on your labours.

🛏 Sleeping

Hotels are spread along Jl Raya Lovina and on the side roads going to the beach. Overall, choices tend to be more budget-focused; don't come here for a luxe experience. Be wary of hotels right on the main road due to traffic noise, or those near the late-night Kalibukbuk bars.

During slow periods, room prices are negotiable; beware of touts who'll lead you astray and quote prices that include a large kickback.

★ Funky Place
HOSTEL $

(☏ 0878 6325 3156; https://funky-place-lovina.business.site; Jl Seririt-Singaraja, Kalibukbuk; tent 135,000Rp, tree house 170,000Rp, dm 120,000-170,000Rp, r from 250,000Rp; 🛜) From the unicycle bar stools to the affordable tree house to the free foot massage, and with lots of reclaimed wood, clever signage and weird antiques scattered throughout, this compound is basically a backpacker's dream. There's a path directly to the beach, and it also holds BBQs, Balinese dancing events and beer-pong competitions. Live music happens every weekend.

Harris Homestay
HOMESTAY $

(☏ 0362-41152; Gang Binaria, Kalibukbuk; s/d incl breakfast from 130,000/150,000Rp; 🛜) Sprightly, tidy and white, Harris avoids the weary look of some neighbouring cheapies. The charming owner lives in the back; guests enjoy four bright, modern rooms up the front.

★ Villa Taman Ganesha
GUESTHOUSE $$

(☏ 0812 377 1381; www.taman-ganesha-lovina.com; Jl Kartika 45; r 550,000-700,000Rp; ❄🛜🏊) This lovely guesthouse is down a quiet lane lined with family compounds. The grounds are lush and fragrant with frangipani from around the world that have been collected by the owner, a landscape architect from

Germany. The three units are private and comfortable. The beach is 400m away and it's a 10-minute walk along the sand to Kalibukbuk.

Lovina BOUTIQUE HOTEL **$$$**
(☑ 0362-343 5800; www.thelovinabali.com; Jl Mas Lovina; ste from US$165; ✷ 🕸 🛏) Clean, modern lines are the hallmark of this luxe beach resort, which is walkably close to the centre of Kalibukbuk. The 66 rooms are large, all with sitting areas and terraces or balconies. The furnishings are all in light colours, which adds to the contemporary feel. The pool is huge; guests can use bikes, kayaks and more.

Eating

Just about every hotel has a cafe or restaurant. Walk along the beach footpath to choose from a selection of basic places with cold beer, standard food and sunsets.

Global Village Kafe CAFE **$**
(☑ 0362-41928; Jl Raya Lovina, Kalibukbuk; mains from 35,000Rp; ☺ 9am-10pm; 🕸) Che Guevara, Mikhail Gorbachev and Nelson Mandela are just some of the figures depicted in the paintings lining the walls of this artsy cafe. The baked goods, fruit drinks, pizzas, breakfasts, Indo classics and much more are excellent. There are free book and DVD exchanges, plus a selection of local handicrafts. Profits go to a foundation that funds local healthcare.

Sea Breeze Café INDONESIAN **$$**
(☑ 0362-41138; off Jl Bina Ria, Kalibukbuk; mains from 60,000Rp; ☺ 8am-10pm; 🕸) Right by the beach, this breezy cafe is the best – and most intimate – of the beachside choices. The Indonesian and Western dishes are well presented, as are the excellent breakfasts. The 'royal seafood platter' is like an entire fish market on a plate. The peanuts served with drinks are among Bali's best; they go great with sunset.

⭐ **Buda Bakery** BAKERY, CAFE **$$**
(☑ 0812 469 1779; off Jl Damai; mains 50,000-150,000Rp; ☺ 8am-9pm) North Bali's best bakery has a huge array of breads, cakes and other treats produced fresh daily. However, the real reason to make the 10-minute walk here from Jl Raya Lovina is for the upstairs cafe, which does simple yet superlative Indonesian and Western fare. Note that the baked goods often sell out fast.

⭐ **Damai** FUSION **$$$**
(☑ 0362-41008; www.thedamai.com; Jl Damai; 3-course meals from 485,000Rp; ☺ 7-11am, noon-4pm & 7-11pm; 🕸) Enjoy the renowned organic restaurant at this boutique hotel in the hills behind Lovina. Tables enjoy views across the north coast. The changing menu draws its fresh ingredients from the hotel's organic farm and the local fishing fleet. Dishes are artful and the wine list one of the best in Bali. Sunday brunch is popular. Call for pick up.

❶ Getting There & Away

BUS & BEMO
To reach Lovina from south Bali by public transport, take a bus from Denpasar's Ubung Bus & Bemo Terminal to the Sangket terminal in Singaraja. Once there take a bemo to Singaraja's Banyuasri terminal. Finally, get another bemo to the Lovina area. This will take much of a day.

Regular bemos go from Singaraja's Banyuasri terminal to Kalibukbuk (about 15,000Rp) – you can flag them down anywhere on the main road and may need to wait a while.

If you're coming by long-distance bus from the west, you can ask to be dropped off anywhere along the main road.

TOURIST SHUTTLE BUS
Perama (☑ 0362-41161; www.peramatour.com; Jl Raya Lovina, Anturan) buses stop in Anturan. Passengers are then ferried to other points on the Lovina strip (15,000Rp). There's a daily bus to/from the south, including Kuta, Sanur and Ubud (all 125,000Rp).

TOP BALI READS

Island of Bali (Miguel Covarrubias, 1937) The classic work about Bali and its civilisation.

Bali Soul Journals (Clare McAlaney, 2013) Written by a Bali expat and lavishly illustrated, it looks for Bali's soul today.

Bali Daze: Freefall Off the Tourist Trail (Cat Wheeler, 2011) Daily life in Ubud makes for an illuminating romp.

Secrets of Bali: Fresh Light on the Morning of the World (Jonathan Copeland and Ni Wayan Murni, 2010) A fun read about Bali and its people.

Eat, Pray, Love (Elizabeth Gilbert, 2007) This bestseller (and movie) lures believers to Bali every year.

ⓘ Getting Around

The Lovina strip is *very* spread out, but you can travel back and forth on bemos to Singaraja (10,000Rp). Note that these are often infrequent.

BICYCLE

Given its small size, Lovina is a nice town to see by bike. Hire one from **Sovina Shop** (☑ 0362-41402; Jl Mawar; ☉ 10am-10pm).

Pemuteran

☑ 0362 / POP 8620

This popular oasis in the northwestern corner of Bali has a number of artful resorts set on a little dog-bone-shaped bay that's incredibly calm, thanks to its location within an extinct volcano crater protected by flourishing coral reefs. The beach is decent, but most people come to view the undersea wonders just offshore and at nearby Pulau Menjangan.

The busy Singaraja–Gilimanuk road is the town's spine and ever more businesses aimed at visitors can be found along it. Despite its popularity, Pemuteran's community and tourism businesses have forged a sustainable vision for development that should be a model for the rest of Bali.

◉ Sights

Pemuteran Beach BEACH

The grey-brown sand is a little thin and definitely not powdery but you can't beat the setting. The blue waters and surrounding green hills make for a beautiful scene, especially when crimson and orange join the colour palette at sunset. Strolling the beach is popular, as you'd expect. The little fishing village is interesting; walk around to the eastern end of the dogbone to escape a lot of the development. Look for various traditional-style boats being built on the shore.

Proyek Penyu HATCHERY

(Project Turtle; ☑ 0362-93001; www.reefseen bali.com/turtle-hatchery; Reef Seen; adult/child 25,000Rp/free; ☉ 8am-5pm) 🌿 Pemuteran is home to the nonprofit Proyek Penyu, run by Reef Seen Divers' Resort. Turtle eggs and small turtles purchased from locals are looked after here until they're ready for ocean release. Thousands of turtles have been released since 1994. You can visit the small hatchery and make a donation to sponsor and release a tiny turtle. It's just off the main road, along the beach just east of Taman Selini Beach Bungalows.

🏊 Activities

Extensive coral reefs are about 3km offshore. Closer coral is being restored as part of the Bio Rocks project. **Diving** and **snorkelling** are universally popular and are offered by dive shops and hotels. You can rent snorkelling gear from 50,000Rp. The bay has a depth of less than 15m closer to the shore, so shore diving is popular, especially at night.

★**Reef Seen** DIVING

(☑ 0362-93001; www.reefseenbali.com; 2-tank dives from 1,755,000Rp) Right on the beach in a large compound, Reef Seen is a PADI dive centre and has a full complement of courses. It also offers pony rides on the beach for kids and some dive packages include accommodation at the dive complex (rooms from 525,000Rp). The company is active in local preservation efforts.

🛏 Sleeping

Pemuteran has one of the nicest selections of beachside hotels in Bali, plus a growing number of budget guesthouses. Many have a sense of style and all are low-key and relaxed, with easy access to the beach.

Some of the hotels are accessed directly off the main road, while others are off small roads that run either to the bay or south towards the mountains.

Pande Guest House GUESTHOUSE $

(☑ 0818 822 088; Jl Singaraja-Gilimanuk; r from 260,000Rp; ❋ 🛜) This guesthouse is well run and charming, with immaculate, comfy rooms featuring open-air bathrooms with lovely garden showers. It's one of the best budget options in town.

Double You Homestay GUESTHOUSE $

(☑ 0813 3842 7000; www.doubleyoupemuteran. com; off Jl Singaraja-Gilimanuk; r incl breakfast from 360,000Rp; ❋ 🛜) On a small lane south of the main road, this stylish guesthouse has nine immaculate units set in a flower-filled garden, with hot water and other comforts.

Kubuku Ecolodge GUESTHOUSE $$

(☑ 0362-343 7302; www.kubukubali.com; Jl Singaraja-Gilimanuk; r incl breakfast from 765,000Rp; ❋ 🛜) A slice of modern style in Pemuteran, Kubuku has a smallish pool with a bar and an inviting patch of lawn. The 17 comfortable rooms are decent value, and the

DON'T MISS

EXPLORING PULAU MENJANGAN

Bali's best-known underwater attraction, Pulau Menjangan is ringed by over a dozen superb dive sites. The experience is excellent – iconic tropical fish, soft corals, great visibility (usually), caves and spectacular drop-offs.

Lacy sea fans and various sponges provide both texture and hiding spots for small fish that together form a colour chart for the sea. Few can resist the silly charms of parrotfish and clownfish. Among larger creatures, you may see whales, whale sharks and manta rays.

Of the named sites here, most are close to shore and suitable for snorkellers or diving novices. But you can also venture out to where the depths turn black as the shallows drop off in dramatic cliffs, a magnet for experienced divers, who can choose from eight walls here.

This uninhabited island boasts what is thought to be Bali's oldest temple, **Pura Gili Kencana**, dating from the 14th century and about 300m from the pier. It has a huge Ganesha (elephant-headed Hindu deity) at the entrance. You can walk around the island in about an hour; unfortunately, the beaches often have garbage problems.

With its great selection of lodgings, Pemuteran is the ideal base for diving and snorkelling Pulau Menjangan. Dive shops and local hotels run snorkelling trips that cost US$65 to US$85; two-tank dive trips cost from US$95. Prices include the 250,000Rp park entrance fee (350,000Rp on Sundays and national holidays).

Some tours to Menjangan leave by boat right from Pemuteran Beach, which is the best option. Other trips involve a car ride and transfer at hassle-filled Banyuwedang, some 7km west of town.

restaurant serves tasty organic meals. The compound is down a lane on the mountain side of the main road.

★**Matahari Beach Resort** RESORT $$$
(☑0362-92312; www.matahari-beach-resort.com; Jl Singaraja-Gilimanuk; r from US$370; ❄🎧🏊) This lovely beachside resort, on the quieter east end of the bay, is set in spacious and verdant grounds. Widely spaced bungalows are works of traditional art. Common areas include a library and other luxuries. The spa is elegant and the beachside bar a good place for a pause as you explore the bay.

✖ Eating

Cafes and restaurants are found along the main drag. Otherwise the beachside hotels and resorts have good midrange restaurants. You can wander along the beach debating which one to choose.

★**Santai Warung** INDONESIAN $
(☑0852 3737 0220; https://santai-warung -pemuteran.business.site; Jl Hotel Taman Sari; mains from 35,000Rp; ⊙11am-9pm; 🖋) Follow the glowing lanterns off Pemuteran's main road to this adorable Indonesian restaurant, which serves up spicy, authentic dishes – in-

cluding lots of great vegetarian options – in a sweet garden setting that includes a traditional Javanese *joglo* house. Ask about cooking classes (from 300,000Rp).

Bali Balance Café & Bistro CAFE $
(☑0853 3745 5454; www.bali-balance.com; Jl Singaraja-Gilimanuk; mains from 30,000Rp; ⊙7.30am-7pm; 🎧) Excellent coffee, plus juices and tasty cakes, make this spotless cafe a good place for a pause any time. There's a short menu of sandwiches and salads, which can be enjoyed in the leafy back garden. It's on the hillside, roughly in the middle of the main strip.

La Casa Kita PIZZA $
(☑0852 3889 0253; Jl Gilimanuk-Seririk; mains 40,000-75,000Rp; ⊙10am-10pm) Grab a table and a cold Bintang on the outdoor lawn and choose from a menu with a classic holiday mix of thin-crust wood-fired pizzas plus Western and Indonesian dishes. It's on the main road across from Easy Divers.

ℹ Information

There are several ATMs on Pemuteran's main strip, which stretches along Jl Singaraja-Gilimanuk from the Matahari Beach Resort west to the lane down to the Taman Sari resort.

ℹ Getting There & Away

Pemuteran is served by buses on the Gilimanuk–Lovina–Singaraja run. To Pemuteran from Gilimanuk or Lovina, you should be able to negotiate a fare of around 20,000Rp. There's no stop, so just flag one down. It's a four-hour drive from South Bali, either over the hills or around the west coast. A private car and driver costs around 850,000Rp to either Ubud or Seminyak, among other destinations.

Singaraja

🖉 0362 / POP 120,000

Singaraja (which means 'lion king') is Bali's second-largest city and the capital of Buleleng Regency, which covers much of the north. With its tree-lined streets, surviving Dutch colonial buildings and charmingly sleepy waterfront area north of Jl Erlangga, it's worth exploring for a couple of hours. Most people stay in nearby Lovina.

Singaraja was the centre of Dutch power in Bali and remained the administrative centre for the Lesser Sunda Islands (Bali through to Timor) until 1953. It is one of the few places in Bali where there are visible traces of the Dutch period, as well as Chinese and Islamic influences. Today, Singaraja is a major educational and cultural centre, with several university campuses.

◉ Sights

At the old harbour and waterfront, you can get a whisper of when Singaraja was Bali's main port before WWII. At the north end of Jl Hasanudin, you'll find a modern **pier** out over the water with a couple of simple cafes and some vendors.

Across the parking lot, look for some **old Dutch warehouses**. Nearby are the conspicuous **Yudha Mandala Tama Monument** and the colourful Chinese temple, **Ling Gwan Kiong**. There are a few old canals here as well.

Walk up Jl Imam Bonjol and you'll see the art deco lines of late-colonial Dutch buildings. Just 2km west of the centre, **Pantai Penimbangan** is a popular beach area. The sand may be a narrow ribbon but there are dozens of seafood cafes that draw throngs of locals, especially on weekend evenings.

★ Sekumpul Waterfall WATERFALL
(Sekumpul Village; 20,000Rp, parking 2000Rp) Sitting 18km southeast of Singaraja, some six or seven separate waterfalls – all fed by upland streams – pour up to 80m over cliffs in a verdant bamboo-forested valley. From the car park, it's a hilly 45-minute, 1km walk through the tiny Sekumpul village, where trees of clove, cacao, jackfruit, mangosteen and more lead the way to steep stairs. Trails wind through the valley from one cascade to the other and its easy to while the day away in their splendor.

Given its remote location, hiring a driver to get you to Sekumpul is ideal. Bayu Sunrise (p296) goes the extra mile by providing transport from anywhere on Bali, in addition to accompanying you through the village and hiking to the falls.

From the car park, take a left and walk up the road. From here, it's 10 minutes to the official waterfall entrance. Beware of stalls marked 'Registration Station' in the area – they are not officially affiliated with the falls and have been known to trick tourists into paying up. When you see the 'Sekumpul Waterfall' sign, take another left and continue along the brick road past village residences and small shops – at the end of this path you'll find the official hut where you'll pay the admission fee. From here, continue down the trail to a steep hill where the stairs begin. You'll eventually make your way down to a stream (prepare to get your feet wet as you cross it); and the falls are shortly ahead.

✖ Eating

There are some good local options for meals in and around Singaraja.

Cozy Resto INDONESIAN $
(🖉 0362-28214; Jl Pantai Penimbangan; mains 25,000-90,000Rp; ⊗10am-10pm) One of the more established cafes at Pantai Penimbangan, Cozy has a long menu of Balinese, Indonesian and seafood dishes. Celebrating locals fill the open-air dining areas. Nearby, along the waterfront road, you'll find dozens more vendors and stalls with cheap and cheerful local fare.

Dapur Ibu INDONESIAN $
(🖉 0362-24474; Jl Jen Achmed Yani; mains 10,000-20,000Rp; ⊗8am-4pm) A nice local cafe with a small garden off the street. The nasi goreng (fried rice) is fresh and excellent; wash it down with a fresh juice or bubble tea.

Istana Cake & Bakery BAKERY $
(🖉 0362-21983; Jl Jen Achmed Yani; snacks from 3000Rp; ⊗8am-6pm) Fallen in love in Lovina? Get your wedding cake here. For lesser life

moments like the munchies, choose from an array of tasty baked goods. There is a freezer full of ice-cream cakes and treats.

❶ Information

Buleleng Tourism Office (Diparda; ☏ 0362-21342; Jl Kartini 6; ☺ 8am-3.30pm Mon-Fri) Has some OK maps and good information if you ask specifically about dance and other cultural events. It's 550m southeast of the Banyuasri bus station.

Singaraja Public Hospital (☏ 0362-22046, 0362-22573; Jl Ngurah Rai 30; ☺ 24hr) The largest hospital in northern Bali.

❶ Getting There & Away

Singaraja is the main transport hub for the northern coast, with three bemo/bus terminals. From the Sangket terminal, 10km south of town on the main road, minibuses go sporadically to Denpasar (Ubung terminal; 40,000Rp) via Bedugul/Pancasari.

The **Banyuasri terminal**, on the western side of town, has buses heading to Gilimanuk (60,000Rp, two hours) and bemos to Lovina (20,000Rp). For Java, several companies have services, which include the ferry trip across the Bali Strait.

The **Penarukan terminal** (off Jl Surapati), 2km east of town, has bemos to Yeh Sanih (20,000Rp) and Amlapura (about 30,000Rp, three hours) via the coastal road; and also minibuses to Denpasar (Batubulan terminal; 100,000Rp, three hours) via Kintamani.

Taman Nasional Bali Barat

☏ 0365

Most visitors to Bali's only national park, Bali Barat National Park (Taman Nasional Bali Barat), are struck by the mellifluous sounds emanating from the birds darting among the rustling trees.

The park covers 190 sq km of the western tip of Bali, including almost 70 sq km of coral reef and coastal waters. Together this represents a significant commitment to conservation on an island as densely populated as Bali.

It's a place where you can enjoy Bali's best diving at Pulau Menjangan, hike through forests and explore coastal mangroves.

🏃 Activities

By land, by boat or underwater, the park awaits exploration. You'll pay 250,000Rp to 350,000Rp to enter the park, depending on the day, plus another few thousand rupees for your activity within the park. You'll also need a guide and negotiating this fee can be confounding. Virtually all costs are variable. You can arrange things at the park offices in Cekik or Labuhan Lalang. **Iwan Melali** (☏ 0819 3167 5011; iwan.melali@gmail.com) is a knowledgeable, English-speaking guide who excels at tracking down wildlife.

Hiking

All hikers must be accompanied by an authorised guide. It's best to arrive the day before you want to hike and make arrangements at the park offices.

The set rates for guides in the park depend on the size of the group and the length of the hike – about 350,000Rp per hour for two people for up to two hours is the starting price. Transport costs and the price is negotiable. Early morning, say 6am, is the best time to start – it's cooler and you're more likely to see some wildlife.

If, once you're out, you have a good rapport with your guide, you might consider getting creative. Although you can try to customise your hike, the guides prefer to set itineraries, including some of the following sites.

From Sumber Kelompok, hikes head up **Gunung Kelatakan** (Mt Kelatakan; 698m), then down to the main road near Kelatakan village (six to seven hours). You may be able to get permission from park headquarters to stay overnight in the forest – if you don't have a tent, your guide can make a shelter from branches and leaves, which will be an adventure in itself. Clear streams abound in the dense woods.

A three- to four-hour hike will allow you to explore the **savannah** area along the coast northwest of Teluk Terima. You have a chance of seeing monitor lizards, barking deer and leaf monkeys – you may even spot a Bali starling, part of a release project in the park. The trek includes a ride to and from the trailhead.

From a trail west of Labuhan Lalang, a three-hour hike exploring **Teluk Terima** (Terima Bay) can begin at the mangroves. You then partially follow Sungai Terima (Terima River) into the hills and walk back down to the road. If you're lucky, you might see grey macaques, deer and leaf monkeys.

❶ Information

The **park headquarters** (☏ 0365-61060; Jl Raya Cekik; ☺ 6am-6pm) at Cekik displays a map of the park area, and has a little information about plants and wildlife. The **Labuhan Lalang Information Office** (Jl Singaraja-Gilimanuk; ⊙7am-7pm) is in a hut located in the parking area where boats leave for Pulau Menjangan.

You can arrange trekking guides and permits at either office; however, there are always a few characters hanging around, and determining who is an actual park official can be like spotting a Bali starling: difficult.

The main roads to Gilimanuk go through the national park, but you don't have to pay an entrance fee just to drive through. However, any activities in the park, such as hiking or diving Menjangan, require paying the 250,000Rp to 350,000Rp park fee plus any activity fees.

DANGERS & ANNOYANCES

People claiming to be guides hang around the park offices. Their legitimacy can be as hard to discern as their fees. Proffered plastic-laminated rate guides are often works of fiction. Negotiate hard. For hiking, the prices start at around 350,000Rp for two people for up to two hours. A boat ride through the mangroves starts at 700,000Rp for two people for up to three hours.

🛈 Getting There & Away

If you don't have transport, any Gilimanuk-bound bus or bemo from north or west Bali can drop you at park headquarters at Cekik (those from north Bali can drop you at Labuhan Lalang).

WEST BALI

Even as development from south Bali creeps ever further west (via hot spots such as Canggu), Bali's true west, which is off the busy main road from Tabanan to Gilimanuk, remains infrequently visited. It's easy to find serenity amid its wild beaches, jungle and rice fields.

On the coast, surfers hit the breaks at Balian and Medewi. Some of Bali's most sacred sites are here, from the ever-thronged Pura Tanah Lot to the lily-pad-dappled beauty of Pura Taman Ayun and on to the wonderful isolation of Pura Rambut Siwi.

The tidy town of Tabanan is at the hub of Bali's Unesco-listed *subak*, the system of irrigation that ensures everybody gets a fair share of the water. On narrow back roads you can cruise beside rushing streams with bamboo arching overhead and fruit piling up below.

🛈 Getting There & Away

The main road in west Bali links the port for Java ferries in Gilimanuk with Denpasar. Although portions of the route enjoy seaside vistas and rice-field views, most drivers will spend much of their time viewing the vehicle ahead; traffic is heavy and delays the norm. Buses run frequently on this route.

Pura Tanah Lot

Pura Tanah Lot (Beraban; adult/child 60,000/ 30,000Rp, parking cars/motorbikes 5000/2000Rp; ⊙7am-7pm) is a hugely popular tourist destination. It does have cultural significance to the Balinese, but this can be hard to discern amid the crowds, clamour and chaos – especially for the overhyped sunsets. It's the most visited and photographed temple in Bali; however, it has all the authenticity of a stage set – even the tower of rock that the temple sits upon is an artful reconstruction (the entire structure was crumbling) and more than one-third of the rock is artificial.

For the Balinese, Pura Tanah Lot is one of the most important and venerated sea temples. Like Pura Luhur Ulu Watu, at the tip of the southern Bukit Peninsula, and Pura Rambut Siwi to the west, it is closely associated with the Majapahit priest Nirartha. It's said that each of the sea temples was intended to be within sight of the next, so they formed a chain along Bali's southwestern coast – from Pura Tanah Lot you can usually see the clifftop site of Pura Ulu Watu far to the south, and the long sweep of sea shore west to Perancak, near Negara.

But at Tanah Lot itself you may just see from one vendor to the next. To reach the temple, take the walkways that run from the vast parking lots through a mind-boggling sideshow of tatty souvenir shops down to the sea. Clamorous announcements screech from loudspeakers.

You can walk over to the temple itself at low tide, but non-Balinese people are not allowed to enter.

You won't be able to miss the looming Pan Pacific Nirwana resort with its water-sucking golf course. It has been controversial since the day it was built, because many feel its greater height shows the temple disrespect.

If coming from south Bali, take the coastal road west from Kerobokan and follow the signs. From other parts of Bali, turn off the Denpasar–Gilimanuk road near Kediri

West Bali

20 km
10 miles

BALI SEA

Catur
Kladan
Pelaga
Penyabangan
Danau
Buyan
Gunung Catur (2096m)
Gitgit
Danau Bratan
Pacung
Batukau Reserve
Jatiluwih
Dukuh
Margarana
Jegu
Sembung
Wanasari
Pura Taman Ayun
Mengwi
Tabanan
Jl Bypass
Pejaten
Beraban
Seseh
Hot Springs
Sungai Yeh He
Selat
Gunung Sangiyang
Pura Luhur Batukau
Wangayagede
Pujungan
Blimbing
Byahan
Sanda
Pucuk
Kerambitan
Tibubiyu
Yeh Gangga
Pura Tanah Lot
Kayu Putih
Batungsel
Pupuan
Sungai Balian
Antosari
Lalang Linggah
Balian Beach
Kutuh
Lovina
Kalibukbuk
Mayong
Air Panas Banjur
Sungai Saba
Danau Tamblingan
Seririt
Manggissari
Bunut Bolong
Pulukan
BALI SEA
Air Satang
Pantai Medewi
Yeh Embang
Pura Rambut Siwi
Mendoyo
Gunung Patas (1412m)
Gunung Musi (1224m)
Gunung Mesehe (1344m)
Bali Barat National Park
Gunung Merbuk (1388m)
Jembrana
Negara
Loloan Timur
Perancak
Pura Gede Perancak
Pengambengan
Gunung Banyuwedang (430m)
Gunung Klatakan (698m)
Blimbingsari
Palasari
Candikesuma
Melaya
Selat Bali
Pura Pulaki
Pemuteran
Banyuwedang
Pulau Menjangan
Bali Barat National Park
Gilimanuk
Ketapang (Java) (4km)

DON'T MISS

PURA TAMAN AYUN

Don't miss one of the top temples on Bali, **Pura Taman Ayun** (Mengwi; adult/child 20,000/10,000Rp; ⊗8am-6.15pm), a serene place of enveloping calm. The huge royal water temple, surrounded by a wide, elegant moat, was the main temple of the Mengwi kingdom, which survived until 1891, when it was conquered by the neighbouring kingdoms of Tabanan and Badung. The temple was built in 1634 and extensively renovated in 1937. It's a spacious place to wander around, away from crowds.

The first courtyard is a large, open, grassy expanse and the inner courtyard has a multitude of *meru* (multitiered shrines). Lotus-blossoms fill the pools; the temple is part of the *subak* (complex rice-field irrigation system) sites recognised by Unesco in 2012. The market area immediately east of the temple has many good warungs for a simple lunch.

and follow the signs. During the pre- and post-sunset rush, traffic is awful with backups stretching for many kilometres.

Balian Beach

☑ 0361

Ever more popular, Balian Beach is a rolling area of dunes and knolls overlooking pounding surf. It attracts both surfers and those looking to escape the bustle of south Bali.

You can wander between cafes and join other travellers for a beer, to watch the sunset and to talk surf. There are simple places to rent boards along the black-sand beach, while nonsurfers can enjoy yoga or bodysurfing.

🛏 Sleeping

Much of the accommodation is fairly close together and near the beach, but there are also some comfortable homestays set back from the water.

Surya Homestay GUESTHOUSE $
(☑0813 3868 5643; https://suryahomestaybali.wordpress.com; Jl Pantai Balian 69; r 200,000-350,000Rp; ❀🛜) There are eight rooms in bungalow-style units at this sweet little family-run place (Wayan and Putu are charmers), which is about 200m along a

small lane from the main road. It's spotless, and rooms have cold water and fans or aircon. Ask about long-term rates.

Made's Homestay HOMESTAY $
(☑0812 396 3335; r 150,000-200,000Rp) Three basic bungalow-style units are surrounded by banana trees back from the beach. The rooms are basic, clean, large enough to hold numerous surfboards and they have cold-water showers.

★**Gajah Mina** BOUTIQUE HOTEL $$
(☑0812 381 1630; www.gajahminaresort.com; villa from 1,000,000Rp; ❀🛜🏊) Designed by the French architect-owner, this 11-unit boutique hotel is close to the ocean. The private, walled bungalows march out to a dramatic outcrop of stone surrounded by surf. The grounds are vast and there are little trails for wandering and pavilions for relaxing. The on-site seafood restaurant, **Naga** (mains from 70,000Rp), overlooks a picture-perfect private black-sand beach.

🍴 Eating

The larger places to stay have cafes open to one and all. It's a good place to wander and graze.

★**Sushi Surf** JAPANESE $$
(☑0812 3870 8446; Jl Pantai Balian; mains 30,000-120,000Rp; ⊗8am-10pm) *The* place for a sunset cocktail and bite of sushi. The surf action is arrayed out right in front of the quirky multilevel seating area. There are specials and a broad menu that goes beyond California rolls. It's run by the Pondok Pitaya people.

Tékor Bali INTERNATIONAL $
(☑0815 5832 3330; tekorbali@hotmail.com; off Jl Pantai Balian; mains from 30,000Rp; ⊗7.30am-10pm; 🛜) Down a small lane 100m back from the beach, this inviting restaurant with a grassy lawn feels a bit like you've come to a mate's backyard for a barbecue. The menu is broad, with all the usual local and surfer favourites, and the burgers are excellent. Cocktails are well made and there's cheap Bintang on tap.

ℹ Getting There & Away

Because the main west Bali road is usually jammed with traffic, Balian Beach is often at least a two-hour drive from Seminyak or the airport (55km). A car and driver will cost 900,000Rp or more for a day trip. You can also get a bus (60,000Rp) going to Gilimanuk from

Denpasar's Ubung terminal and be dropped off at the road entrance, which is 800m from the beach places.

Jembrana Coast

Jembrana, Bali's most sparsely populated district, offers beautiful scenery and little tourist development, with the exception of the surfing action at Medewi. The main road follows the south coast most of the way to Negara, and at Pulukan you can turn north to enjoy a remote and scenic drive to north Bali.

◉ Sights

Pura Rambut Siwi　　　　　　HINDU TEMPLE

Picturesquely situated on a clifftop overlooking a long, wide stretch of black-sand beach, this superb temple shaded by flowering frangipani trees is one of the important sea temples of west Bali. Like Pura Tanah Lot and Pura Luhur Ulu Watu, it was established in the 16th century by the priest Nirartha, who had a good eye for ocean scenery. Unlike Tanah Lot, it remains a peaceful and little-visited place: on non-ceremony days you'll just find a couple of lonely drink vendors.

Medewi

🕿 0365

This is the home of the surfing mecca of **Pantai Medewi** and its much-vaunted *long* left-hand wave. Rides of 200m to 400m are common.

The beach is a stretch of huge, smooth grey rocks interspersed among round black pebbles – think of it as free reflexology. Cattle and goats graze by the shore as spectators view the action out on the water. There are a few guesthouses plus a couple of surf shops (board rental from 100,000Rp per day).

Medewi proper is a classic market town with shops selling all the essentials of west Bali life.

🛏 Sleeping

Anara Surf Camp　　　　　　GUESTHOUSE $

(🕿 0817 0323 6684; www.facebook.com/anara surfcamp/; Medewi; r from 250,000Rp; 🕿) This surf camp and modern guesthouse is on the shores of Pantai Medewi, with the sea on one side and rice paddies on the other. There are different levels of accommodation, but all are newly constructed with attractive hardwoods, comfy four-poster beds and mosquito nets. A couple of bungalows near the water offer large glass windows and open-air bathrooms.

Surfboard rental costs just 70,000Rp per day, and instruction is also available. Be mindful of rip tides, as they're common in the stretch of ocean in front of the surf camp.

★ Puri Dajuma Cottages　　　　HOTEL $$

(🕿 0361-813230, 0811 388 709; www.dajuma.com; cottages from 1,600,000Rp; ❀ @ 🕿 ⛱) Coming from the east on the main road, you won't be able to miss this seaside resort, thanks to its prolific signage. Happily, the 35 rooms – either in suites, cottages or villas – actually live up to the billing. Each has private garden, hammock and walled outdoor bathroom; most have ocean views. The Medewi surf break is 2km west.

ℹ Getting There & Away

Medewi Beach is 75km from the airport. A car and driver will cost from 850,000Rp for a day trip. You can also get a bus (45,000Rp) going to Gilimanuk from Denpasar's Ubung terminal and be dropped off at the road entrance. On the main road, a large sign points down the short paved road (200m) to Pantai Medewi.

AT A GLANCE

POPULATION
9.7 million

TOP SURF SPOTS
Occy's Left (p414),
Supersuck (p357),
Tanjung Desert
(p321), T-Land
(p403)

BEST BEACH
Pantai Mawan (p331)

BEST WATERFALL
Air Terjun Sindang
Gila (p328)

BEST RESTAURANT
El Bazar (p333)

WHEN TO GO
Apr–Sep
The dry season
brings the best div-
ing visibility; travel-
lers flock to Komodo
and other locales.

May & Oct
Epic waves and thin
crowds in Rote and
Sumbawa.

Oct–Mar
Sumba's spectacular
Pasola festival, in
February, is reason
enough to visit in
wetter months.

Air Terjun Sindang Gila (p328)
TANARCH/SHUTTERSTOCK ©

Nusa Tenggara

I f you're seeking white sand, spectacular diving and surf, bubbling hot springs, majestic waterfalls and hidden traditional villages – away from Bali-esque crowds – then Nusa Tenggara is your wonderland. Spreading west from the Wallace Line dividing Asia from Australasia, this archipelago is jungle-green in the north and tending to drier savannah in the south and east. In between are limitless surf breaks and barrels, technicolor volcanic lakes, pink-sand beaches, swaggering dragons and underwater worlds filled with colour and creatures.

You'll also find a cultural diversity that's unmatched. Animist rituals and tribal traditions still thrive alongside minarets, convents and chapels. From a beach-forward, tourist-ready vacation to stepping outside your comfort zone for the sort of experiences that leave an indelible mark on your memory, you're exactly where you're supposed to be.

ℹ Getting There & Around

Overland travel is slow in mountainous Nusa Tenggara and it's foolish to rely on Google Map's estimated travel times with all those bends, potholes and road upgrades. Driving is time consuming, but beautiful. Busy Lombok, Sumbawa, Flores and Timor have decent, surfaced main roads and relatively comfortable bus services. Get off the highways and things slow down considerably, especially between December to March when rains wallop gravel and dirt roads. Ferry services are also victims of the wet season, with rough seas causing cancellations for days on end. During the rest of the year boats are consistent, but it's always wise to check ahead and allow extra days in your itinerary.

Several airlines cover inter-island routes, many of which start in Bali.

LOMBOK

POP 3.4 MILLION

Long overshadowed by its superstar neighbour across the Lombok Strait, Lombok has a steady hum about it that catches the ear of travellers looking for something different from Bali. Blessed with exquisite white-sand beaches, epic surf, a lush forested interior, and hiking trails through tobacco and rice fields, Lombok is fully loaded with equatorial allure. Oh, and you'll probably notice mighty Gunung Rinjani, Indonesia's second-highest volcano, its summit complete with hot springs and a dazzling crater lake.

And there's much more. Lombok's southern coastline is nature on a very grand scale: breathtaking turquoise bays, world-class surf breaks and massive headlands.

Transport options are good in Lombok and the mood could not be more laid-back. If you're planning to head further east in Nusa Tenggara, you can pass through Lombok overland to Sumbawa, or catch a boat to Flores.

ℹ Getting There & Away

AIR

Lombok is very accessible by air, with daily flights to/from major Indonesian destinations such as Jakarta and Denpasar, plenty more to lesser Indonesian hubs, and international connections with Singapore and Kuala Lumpur.

Lombok International Airport (p330), near Praya, is getting increasingly busy. There is good service to Bali and Java, with fewer services going east into Nusa Tenggara. Some routes to less-frequented Indonesian destinations require

transit through Denpasar, Jakarta and smaller domestic hubs such as Surabaya and Kupang. Daily flights also serve the international hubs of Singapore and Kuala Lumpur. You'll find travel agents for airline tickets in Kuta, Mataram and Senggigi.

BOAT

Public ferries connect Lembar on Lombok's west coast with Bali, and Labuhan Lombok on its east coast with Sumbawa. Fast-boat companies link Lombok with the Gili Islands and Bali. These are centred on Senggigi, Bangsal and Gili Gede.

PUBLIC BUS

Mandalika Terminal (p320) in Mataram is the departure point for major cities in Bali, Sumbawa, and Flores, via inter-island ferries. For long-distance services, book tickets a day or two ahead at the terminal, or from a travel agent.

If you get to the terminal before 8am without a reservation, there may indeed be a spare seat on a bus going in your direction, but don't count on it, especially during holidays.

There are direct buses from Denpasar on Bali that connect to the Padangbai–Lembar ferry and then continue on to the Mandalika Terminal in Mataram (225,000Rp). Buses also connect to Bima via the Lombok–Sumbawa ferry (225,000Rp).

TOURIST SHUTTLE BUS

There are tourist shuttle-bus services between the main tourist centres in Lombok (Senggigi and Kuta) and most tourist centres in south Bali and the Gilis. Typically these combine a minibus with public ferries. Tickets can be booked directly or with a travel agent.

ℹ Getting Around

Moving around Lombok is easy, with a good – though often traffic-clogged – road across the middle of the island between Mataram and Labuhan Lombok.

BOAT

Regular public and private water transport serves all the major offshore destinations in Lombok. Bear in mind that safety standards can be quite cavalier, and it's not uncommon to ride on crowded ferries in quite high seas. However, services will be cancelled when seas are too rough, a particular feature of the rainy season.

BUS & BEMO

Mandalika Terminal (p320) is 3km east of central Mataram; other regional terminals are in Praya, Anyar and Pancor (near Selong). You may have to go via one or more of these terminals to get from one part of Lombok to another, although you can flag bemos from the roadside.

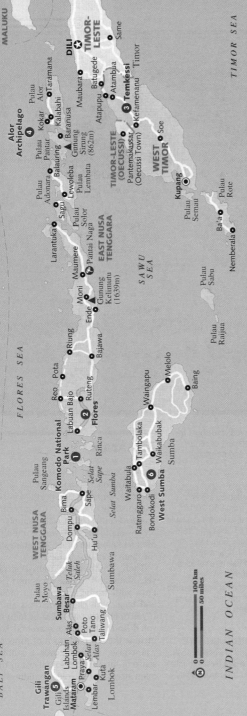

Nusa Tenggara Highlights

1 Komodo National Park (p366) Seeing dragons on land and then snorkelling or diving with underwater critters, big and small.

2 Flores (p368) Exploring a world of ancient cultures, volcanoes, lush rainforests and untrodden beaches.

3 Temkessi (p402) Discovering remote villages

characterised by beehive-shaped clan houses.

4 Alor Archipelago (p390) Diving this island chain that feels like one stop before the end of the world.

5 Gili Trawangan (p340) Plunging into watery pleasures by day and then choosing between many more at night.

6 West Sumba (p410) Bouncing between one sensational beach and the next before pausing at the ancient village of Ratenggaro and breathtaking Weekuri Lagoon.

Lombok

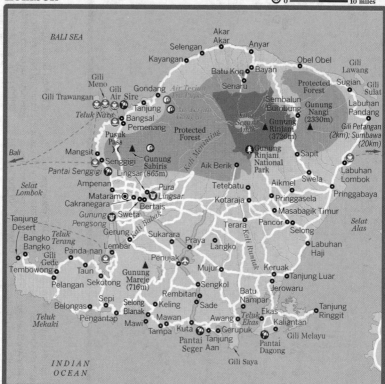

Fixed fares should be displayed, and short trips start at 5000Rp. Public transport becomes scarce in the late afternoon and normally ceases after dark.

CAR & MOTORBIKE

It's easy to hire a car in all the tourist areas (with/without driver per day from 600,000/350,000Rp). Motorbikes are also widely available from about 70,000Rp per day. Check your insurance arrangements carefully. Some agencies do not offer any coverage at all; others offer only basic coverage. Even insured Balinese vehicles are often not covered in Lombok.

There's little reason to bring a car or motorbike from Bali when you can avoid the ferry charges and easily rent your own wheels on Lombok.

TAXI

Reliable metered taxis operated by Blue Bird Lombok Taksi (p339) are found in west Lombok. Motorbike ride-hailing app **Go-Jek** (www.go-jek.com) is useful for cheap short trips around Mataram and west Lombok.

Mataram

📞 0370 / POP 420,000

Lombok's capital is a sprawling amalgam of several once-separate towns with fuzzy borders: Ampenan (the port), Mataram (the administrative centre), Cakranegara (the business centre, often called simply 'Cakra') and Sweta to the east, where you'll find the Mandalika bus terminal. Mataram stretches for 12km from east to west.

There aren't many tourist attractions, yet Mataram's broad tree-lined avenues buzz with traffic, thrum with motorbikes and teem with classic markets and malls. If you're hungry for a blast of Indo realism, you'll find it here. Sights around Mataram include the old port town of Ampenan – if you pause you'll discover a still-tangible sense of the Dutch colonial era in the leafy main street and the older buildings.

○ Sights

★ Pura Lingsar
TEMPLE

(off Jl Gora II; grounds free, temple entry by dona-tion; ⊙8am-6pm) Just 6km east of Mataram, in the village of Lingsar, this large temple compound is the holiest in Lombok. It was built in 1714 by King Anak Agung Ngurah and is nestled beautifully in lush rice fields. It is multi-denominational, with a temple for Balinese Hindus (Pura Gaduh) and one for followers of Lombok's mystical take on Islam, the Wektu Telu religion.

Islamic Center Nusa Tenggara Barat
MOSQUE

(☑0819 1732 5666; http://islamiccenter.ntbprov.go.id; cnr Jl Udayana & Jl Pejanggik; 5000Rp; ⊙casual visits 10am-5pm) Superficially dam-aged in the 2018 quakes, this towering green-and-gold mosque is the most striking building in Lombok, with fabulous views from the top of its tallest minaret (it rises 114m above Mataram). Foreigners in shorts will be provided with more modest clothing before entering.

Pura Meru
HINDU TEMPLE

(Jl Selaparang; ⊙8am-5pm) FREE Pura Meru is the largest and second-most important Hindu temple on Lombok. Built in 1720, it's dedicated to the Hindu trinity of Brah-ma, Vishnu and Shiva. The inner court has 33 small shrines and three thatched teak-wood *meru* (multi-tiered shrines). The cen-tral *meru*, with 11 tiers, is Shiva's house; the *meru* to the north, with nine tiers, is Vish-nu's; and the nine-tiered *meru* to the south is Brahma's.

🛏 Sleeping

Hotel Melati Viktor
GUESTHOUSE $

(☑0370-633830; Jl Abimanyu 1; r from 170,000Rp, with air-con 200,000Rp; ❄🛜) The high ceil-ings, 37 clean rooms and Balinese-style courtyards make this one of the most atmos-pheric and best-value places in a town filled with midrange chains. It's forever growing and is now spread across three buildings on either side of Jl Abimanyu.

Hotel Lombok Raya
HOTEL $$

(☑0370-632305; www.lombokrayahotel.com; Jl Panca Usaha 11; r incl breakfast 600,000-750,000Rp; 🅿❄🛜🏊) Lombok Raya is a well-located favourite of old-school business travellers, with 134 spacious, comfortable rooms with balconies. A glistening pool, well-equipped gym and bountiful breakfast buffet add to the appeal.

✕ Eating & Drinking

The streets around the faded Mataram Mall are lined with Western-style fast-food out-lets, Indonesian noodle bars and warungs (food shacks).

Taliwang Irama 3
INDONESIAN $

(☑0370-623163; Jl Ade Irma Suryani 53; mains 20,000-50,000Rp; ⊙11am-10pm) Excellent spicy Indonesian dishes lure diners day in, day out. Eat in the plant-shaded courtyard or inside. As testament to the popularity, there are vendors out front. The chicken here seems even more tender and spicy than the average bird on Lombok.

Mirasa
BAKERY $

(☑0370-633096; Jl AA Gde Ngurah 88; snacks from 4000Rp; ⊙6am-10pm) Cakra's middle-class families adore this modern bakery. It does doughnuts, cookies and cakes as well as local wonton stuffed with chicken.

★ Rollpin
INTERNATIONAL $$

(www.rollpin.id; Jl Ahmad Yani; mains 50,000-100,000Rp; ⊙noon-10pm Tue-Sun; 🛜) Fine dining, Mataram-style, in a leafy creekside setting northeast of the centre. Dig into grilled whole snapper, Lombok duck or steamed mahi-mahi and wash it down with creative mocktails like Pin Pure (mint, gin-ger, lime and honey). Excellent service and a lengthy kids menu add to the appeal.

Maktal Coffee Bar
COFFEE

(www.facebook.com/maktalcoffeebar; Jl Maktal; ⊙9am-11pm; 🛜) This hipstery little cof-fee bar does everything from cold drips to caramel lattes. The brews are local, strong, and you can buy the beans afterwards. Also does pancakes, dumplings and Indo staples (20,000Rp to 30,000Rp).

🛍 Shopping

★ Lombok Handicraft Centre
ARTS & CRAFTS

(Jl Kerajinan, off Jl Diponegoro; ⊙8am-6pm) At Sayang Sayang (2km north of Cakra), this centre offers a wide range of small shops; look for the arched sign over the narrow road that reads 'Handy Craft'. Browse crafts, including masks, textiles and ceramics from across Nusa Tenggara. This is a great place to stroll around.

★ **Pasar Mandalika** MARKET

(Bertais; ⊙ 6am-6pm) There are no tourists at this vast market near the Mandalika bus terminal in Bertais, but it has everything else: fruit and veggies, fish (fresh and dried), baskets full of colourful, aromatic spices and grains, freshly butchered beef, palm sugar, pungent bricks of shrimp paste and cheaper handicrafts than you will find anywhere else in west Lombok.

It's a great place to get localised after you've overdosed on the *bule* (slang for foreigner) circuit.

Lombok Epicentrum Mall MALL

(☑ 0370-617 2999; www.lombokepicentrum.com; Jl Sriwijaya 333; ⊙ 10am-10pm) With a cinema, food courts and the full spread of consumer pleasures, this four-floor mall is Lombok's biggest and fanciest.

❶ Information

ATM machines are ubiquitous near malls. Most banks are found on or around Jl Pejanggik.

Rumah Sakit Harapan Keluarga (☑ 0370-617 7009; www.harapankeluarga.co.id; Jl Ahmad Yani 9; ⊙ 24hr) The best private hospital on Lombok is just east of central Mataram and has English-speaking doctors.

Kantor Imigrasi (Immigration Office; ☑ 0370-632520; Jl Udayana 2; ⊙ 8am-noon & 1-4pm Mon-Fri) Government office for renewing your visa. The process takes three or four days.

❶ Getting There & Away

BOAT

Should you want to sail to a far-flung Indonesian island from Lombok, you can make schedule enquiries and purchase tickets at the local **Pelni Office** (☑ 0370-637212; www.pelni.co.id; Jl Industri 1; ⊙ 8am-noon & 1-3.30pm Mon-Thu & Sat, 8-11am Fri), the national shipping line.

BUS

The **Mandalika Terminal** (Jl Pasar Bertais B8, Sweta), 3km from the centre and surrounded by the city's main market, is Lombok's biggest bus and bemo hub. Use the official ticket office to avoid touts and take yellow bemos to the city centre (5000Rp).

Long-distance buses for Sumbawa and Flores depart from here twice daily at 9am and 3pm. If you're travelling to Labuan Bajo on Flores (375,000Rp, 24 hours), you'll have to overnight in Bima (225,000Rp, 12 hours) if you take the morning bus; the afternoon one is direct. Damri buses over to Maluk and the Sumbawa surf towns leave at 9am and 9pm (90,000Rp, six hours).

A direct shuttle bus to Kuta departs at 11am daily (1½ hours, 60,000Rp). Buses and bemos departing hourly from the Mandalika Terminal include the following:

Destination	Fare (Rp)	Duration
Airport (Damri Bus)	30,000	45min
Kuta (via Praya & Sengkol)	60,000	2-3hr
Labuhan Lombok	35,000	2½hr
Lembar	20,000	45min
Senggigi (via Ampenan)	15,000	1hr
Senggigi (direct Damri Bus)	40,000	45min

❶ Getting Around

For a reliable metered taxi, use Blue Bird Lombok Taksi (p339). Solo travellers should download **Go-Jek** (www.go-jek.com), an app for cheap and reliable *ojeks* (motorbike taxis).

Lembar

☑ 0370 / POP 44,500

Lembar is Lombok's main port for public ferries from Bali. The setting features azure inlets ringed by soaring green hills, but few folk stay longer than their ferry transit requires.

❶ Getting There & Away

Public ferries (adult/child/motorcycle/car 46,000/29,000/129,000/917,000Rp, five to six hours) travel between Lembar's large ferry port and Padangbai on Bali. Passenger tickets are sold near the pier. Boats supposedly run 24 hours and leave about every 1½ hours, but the service can be unreliable – boats have even caught fire and run aground.

Bemo and bus connections are abundant. Bemos run regularly to Mataram's Mandalika Bus Terminal (25,000Rp, one hour), from where there are many onward connections, so there's no reason to linger. Taxis cost around 100,000Rp to Mataram and 200,000Rp to Senggigi.

Southwestern Peninsula

The sweeping coastline that stretches west of Lembar is blessed with boutique sleeps on deserted beaches and tranquil offshore islands. You can while away weeks here among the famous surf breaks, salty old mosques, friendly locals and relatively pristine islands. In fact, the buzz has started,

SNORKELLING THE SOUTHWEST GILIS

With untouched corals and a wealth of marine life (including lionfish, scorpionfish, moray eels and large schools of fusiliers), snorkelling the shallow reefs around the Southwest Gilis is a highlight of any trip to Lombok.

The northwestern coast of Gili Gede provides the best shore snorkelling for those sleeping on the island, but you'll probably want to hire a boatman to take you to the southeastern coasts of **Gili Layar** and **Gili Rengit**, both of which have extremely healthy coral and massive schools of fish. You can also tack on tiny **Gili Goleng**, where seahorses amble around in the offshore seagrass. The entire trip should cost around 500,000Rp for the boat and gear.

Closer to Lembar are the smaller islands of the Gita Nada group (**Gili Nanggu**, **Gili Kedis**, **Gili Tangkong** and **Gili Sudak**), all of which are fantastic for snorkelling. Boatmen can take you here from Gili Gede for about 600,000Rp, or you can visit on a day trip from Kuta with Scuba Froggy (p332) or Mimpi Manis (p333).

and the beautiful offshore islands are now touted as 'the next Gilis'.

The only off-note on the landscape is the dull town of Sekotong, which you have to pass through on your way west. Otherwise, you follow the narrow coastal road along the contours of the peninsula, skirting white-sand beach after white-sand beach on your way to the village of Bangko Bangko and the legendary surf break, **Tanjung Desert** (Desert Point/Bangko Bangko; access per person/ vehicle 10,000/5000Rp).

Often called the world's best wave, this famous break draws skilled surfers from around the globe. Patience is a virtue as the conditions sometimes go calm for a time. But when the swells are coming in, you get very long, hollow waves that usually end in a barrel.

You'll discover a thin strip of white sand and a row of flimsy bamboo cafes where you can scarf down simple meals, quaff cold beer and gaze out at the break. Phone service is dodgy and the area gets very crowded during peak surfing season (May to October) so you may or may not find room at the very basic inns. **Desert Point Bungalows** (✆0878 6585 5310; nurbaya_sari@yahoo.com; Tanjung Desert; bungalow 200,000Rp) is the most 'upscale' place to stay (that's because there's a phone number you can try calling) with 10 rather shack-like bungalows. A generator provides power at certain times, and there's a two-level surf-viewing platform.

Infrequent bemos run between Lembar and Pelangan (30,000Rp, 1½ hours) via Sekotong and Tembowong. West of Pelangan transport is highly irregular. Although winding, the road is in good shape almost until the end, when suddenly it switches to deep-

ly rutted gravel and dirt. You can traverse it with a car or motorbike, but you'll have to drive at a walking pace. After 2km you'll reach a fork; turn right for the fishing village of Bangko Bangko. Turn left for another 1km of road misery that ends at the oceanic wonders of Tanjung Desert. There's an entrance fee of 10,000Rp per person and 5000Rp per vehicle.

Gili Gede & The Southwest Gilis

✆0370

Gili Gede (pronounced the way an Aussie might say g'day) is the largest and most developed of the Southwest Gilis with a few bungalows, some paved motorbike paths, friendly fishing villages and little else.

This chain of small sandy isles promises the peace and tranquility that were once hallmarks of those *other* Gili Islands to the north. On each island, soft white sands give way to turquoise waters and prismatic undersea realms that are ripe for exploration. To island hop these 'secret gilis' on a local fishing boat is to float back to a simpler time.

🛏 Sleeping & Eating

Gili Gede is the most natural base for exploring the Southwest Gilis with the largest selection of accommodation. Refreshingly, there is no real tourist ghetto here as small bungalow complexes are found on a variety of beaches across the island. You can also find more isolated accommodation on Gili Asahan and Gili Layar.

Most visitors eat where they sleep, through there are a few stand-alone restaurants on Gili Gede serving both Indonesian and European fare.

Via Vacare
BUNGALOW $

(📱 0812 3732 4565; www.viavacare.com; Gili Gede; all-inclusive dm 300,000Rp, s/d bungalow 500,000/750,000Rp) This all-inclusive resort for the backpacker set envisions itself as a place to practise the art of doing nothing. Rates include three daily meals, snorkelling gear, yoga (in high season) and transport to/ from the main harbour. The 'dorm' is just a mattress on an open-air platform, but the bungalows are spacious and have sea views. Expect cold bucket showers as there's no running water.

★ Hula Hoop
BUNGALOW $$

(www.hulagili.com; Gili Gede; r/bungalow 650,000/950,000Rp; 🛜) This fantastically bohemian getaway is tucked away on a quiet west-coast hill with four stylish *lumbung* (rice-barn) rooms and four bigger and better-appointed bungalows. All get a great breeze and offer spectacular sea and sunset views. There are also seaside hammocks and funky chill zones with hanging shell art.

★ Pearl Beach Resort
BUNGALOW $$

(📱 0819 0724 7696; www.pearlbeach-resort.com; Gili Asahan; cottage/bungalow from 790,000/ 1,190,000Rp; 🛜) One of the few places to sleep on Gili Asahan; cottages are simple, bamboo affairs with outdoor bathrooms and a hammock on the porch. The 10 bungalows are chic, with polished concrete floors, soaring ceilings, gorgeous outdoor bathrooms and fabulous daybed swings on the wooden porches. There's great diving, kayaks and more.

Kokomo Gili Gede
RESORT $$$

(📱 0819 0732 5135; http://kokomogiligede.com; Gili Gede; villas incl breakfast from 2,750,000Rp; ✳️🛜🌊) The poshest resort in the Southwest Gilis, Kokomo has 15 large villas in a beautiful position right by the ocean. Units have fridges and other kitchen appliances. The decor picks up the stark white beauty of the sand. A stay here will be a long study in white, backed by the blue of the water.

Tanjungan Bukit
INDONESIAN $$

(📱 0818 0529 0314; https://tanjungan-bukit-id. book.direct; Gili Gede; mains 40,000-90,000Rp) This is easily the island's most stylish bar and restaurant. Dine on fresh seafood and refined Sumatran fare at the bougainvillea-shaded tables, or down some cocktails (or wine by the glass!) on the beanbag-filled deck.

There are six beautifully designed bungalows surrounding a pool on the hill behind the restaurant (500,000Rp to 600,000Rp).

ℹ️ Getting There & Away

Taxi boats (per person from 25,000Rp) shuttle from Tembowong on the mainland to Gili Gede, Gili Asahan or Gili Layar. You'll see them near the old Pertamina gas station. There is no fixed price or schedule, but there are always boatmen waiting in the daylight hours. When you're done negotiating the price, they'll take you directly to your accommodation.

Gili Getaway (📱 0813 3707 4147; http://gili getaway.com; Kokomo Gili Gede) has daily fast boat services from Gili Gede to Gili T and Gili Air (450,000Rp), as well as Senggigi (250,000Rp) and Serangan Harbour on Bali (710,000Rp).

ℹ️ Getting Around

There are no cars or taxis on the island (though a few residents have motorbikes). Unless you hire a fisher to drop you at a distant beach, walking around the perimeter – or along interior paths – is the only way to get around.

Senggigi

📞 0370 / POP 52,000

Lombok's original tourist resort, Senggigi enjoys a fine location along a series of sweeping bays, with light-sand beaches below a backdrop of jungle-clad mountains and coconut palms. In the evening a setting blood-red sun sinks into the surf next to the giant triangular cone of Bali's Gunung Agung.

Far less trendy these days than the Gilis or Lombok's Kuta, Senggigi is a faded holiday town where the main attributes are its low prices and buzz-free vibe. The greater Senggigi area spans 10km of coastal road; the upscale neighbourhood of Mangsit is 3km north of central Senggigi, while just beyond lie the picturesque beaches of Malimbu and Nipah.

👁️ Sights

Pura Batu Bolong
HINDU TEMPLE

(off Jl Raya Senggigi; admission by donation; ⏰ 7am-7pm) It's not the grandest, but Pura Batu Bolong is Lombok's most appealing Hindu temple and is particularly lovely at sunset. Join ever-welcoming members of the Balinese community as they leave offerings at the 14 altars and pagodas that

Senggigi

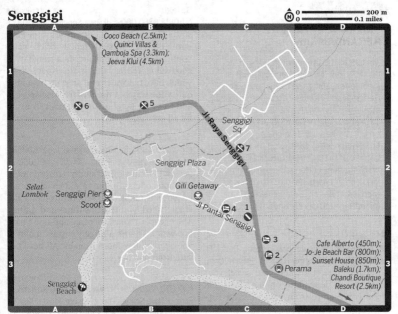

tumble down a rocky volcanic outcrop into the foaming sea about 2km south of central Senggigi. The rock underneath the temple has a natural hole, hence the name (*batu bolong* literally means 'rock with hole').

🏃 Activities

Snorkelling & Diving

There's reasonable snorkelling off the point in Senggigi, 3km north of the town. You can rent gear (per day 50,000Rp) from several spots on the beach. Diving trips from Senggigi usually visit the Gili Islands.

Blue Coral   DIVING
(☎0370-693441; bluecoral_diving@yahoo.com; Jl Raya Senggigi; 2 dives 850,000Rp, open-water course 4,950,000Rp; ⊙8am-6pm) This locally run dive shop in the heart of Senggigi offers no-decompression dives at between 18m and 22m deep in the waters off western Lombok and the Gili Islands. It also offers PADI certification courses and accommodation packages at the neat, modern guesthouse behind the shop.

Dream Divers   DIVING
(☎0812 3754 583; www.dreamdivers.com; Jl Raya Senggigi; intro dives from 910,000Rp) The Senggigi office of the Gili diving original.

Runs snorkelling trips out to the Gilis for 400,000Rp. It also runs dive courses and organises activities such as Rinjani treks.

Massages & Spas

Very determined local masseurs, armed with mats, oils and attitude, hunt for business on Senggigi's beaches. Expect to pay about 80,000Rp for one hour after bargaining. Most hotels can arrange a masseur to visit your room; rates start at about 100,000Rp. Be warned, some of the streetside 'salons' you'll find are fronts for more salacious services.

TAMAN WISATA ALAM KERANDANGAN

This pleasant, little-visited **nature reserve** (off Jl Wisata Alam; 5000Rp) is ideal for escaping the tourist bustle of Senggigi and indulging in a few hours of strolling in the rainforest. The Princess Twin and Swallow Cave waterfalls lie on the marked trail (which can get a little indistinct in parts) and there's the chance of seeing rare butterflies and black monkeys (alongside the common kind). To get here, head north of town to Mangsit, then take Jalan Wisata Alam inland through the Kerandangan Valley.

★**Qamboja Spa**   SPA

(☑0370-693800; www.quncivillas.com; Qunci Villas, Mangsit; massages from US$30; ⊙8am-10pm) Gorgeous hotel spa where you select your choice of oil depending on the effect and mood you require from your massage (up-lifting, harmony...); types available include Thai, Balinese and shiatsu. It also offers yoga classes at 8am daily.

🛏 Sleeping

Senggigi's accommodation is very spread out, but even if you're located a few kilometres away (say, in Mangsit), you won't be isolated as taxis are inexpensive. Travellers with a bigger budget will find an excellent spread of options; backpackers fewer.

Tempatku   GUESTHOUSE $

(☑0812 4612 9504; tempatkulombok@gmail.com; Jl Pantai Senggigi, Senggigi Plaza; r 200,000-250,000Rp; ❄🖥) A spotless, centrally located budget option above a tasty Indonesian restaurant of the same name. The large, tiled rooms have some nice local touches and share two common bathrooms with hot water. It's on the ocean side of the main drag.

BC Inn   GUESTHOUSE $

(☑0370-619 7880, 0876 595 0549; http://bcinnsenggigi.com; Jl Raya Senggigi; r from 200,000Rp; 🖥) Spick and span, comfortable and right in the heart of Senggigi, BC is named for the Blue Coral dive shop, which it sits behind. All rooms have satellite TV, wi-fi, decent beds, walk-in showers and wooden decor. Two people buying a dive package get a night free.

Baleku   GUESTHOUSE $

(☑0818 0360 0009; Jl Raya Senggigi; r 225,000-300,000Rp; ❄🖥🏊) Set 300m south of Pura Batu Bolong, this thatched brick compound is compact, but there's a range of 15 good-value rooms, the most expensive of which have hot water and air-con. It's a little out of the way but it offers free transport to and from Senggigi town. The pool seems to fill all available space.

Sendok Hotel   HOTEL $

(☑0813 3743 5453; Jl Raya Senggigi; dm 135,000Rp, r with fan/air-con from 200,000/400,000Rp; ❄🖥🏊) Fronted by a friendly bar-restaurant, this hotel offers 17 rooms amid lovingly tended gardens nibbled by sunburnt rabbits and embellished with Hindu shrines and statues. The cheaper rooms are basic and don't have hot water. There's a huge jump in quality if you spend a few more rupiahs. All have private front porches.

Sunset House   HOTEL $$

(☑0370-692020; www.sunsethouse-lombok.com; Jl Raya Senggigi 66; r incl breakfast 800,000-1,100,000Rp; ❄🖥🏊) Offers 20 rooms, all with a tasteful, well-equipped simplicity, in a quiet ocean-front location towards Pura Batu Bolong (p322). Rooms on the upper floors have sweeping ocean views towards Bali. Wi-fi is only available in public areas. Good pool area and deck.

★**Qunci Villas**   RESORT $$$

(☑0370-693800; www.quncivillas.com; Jl Raya Mangsit, Mangsit; r from 1,400,000Rp; ❄🖥🏊) A spectacular, lovingly imagined property that comes close to a luxe experience. Everything, from the food to the pool area to the spa, and especially the sea views (160m of beach-front), is magical. It has 78 rooms (including many villas) that, together with the other diversions here, give you little reason to leave. It's 1.2km north of Senggigi.

Chandi Boutique Resort   RESORT $$$

(☑0370-692198; www.the-chandi.com; Jl Raya Senggigi, Batu Layar; r from US$150; ❄🖥🏊) A stylish boutique hotel amid the palms about 1km south of Pura Batu Bolong (p322). Each of the 15 luxe bungalows has an outdoor living room and a hip modern interior with high ceilings and groovy outdoor bathrooms. The ample oceanfront perch is likely to absorb your daylight hours.

Jeeva Klui
RESORT $$$

(☑0370-693035; www.jeevaklui.com; Jl Raya Klui Beach; r from US$200, villas from US$265; ✳🛜☲) This is why you came to the tropics: a palm-shaded, shimmering infinity pool and a lovely, almost private beach, sheltered by a rocky outcrop. The 35 rooms and villas are evocatively thatched, and have bamboo columns and private porches. Villas are luxurious, private and have their own pools. It's one bay north of Mangsit.

🗙 Eating

Senggigi's dining scene ranges from fancy international eating to simple warungs. At sunset, locals head to hilltop lookouts alongside Jl Raya Senggigi where vendors sell grilled corn and fresh coconuts – a great experience for a sober sundowner. Many of the more tourist-oriented places offer free transport for evening diners – phone for a ride.

Warung Cak Poer
INDONESIAN $

(www.facebook.com/warungcakpoer; Jl Raya Senggigi; mains 20,000-30,000Rp; ⊙10am-11pm) This roadside warung south of town feeds the locals with hot-outta-the-wok Indo classics. Grab a plastic stool at a battered metal table, open a pack of *krupuk* (Indonesian crackers) and order the nasi goreng, made extra hot *(ekstra pedas)* and with extra garlic *(bawang putih ekstra)*. You'll be smiling (and sweating) through tears.

★Coco Beach
INDONESIAN $$

(☑0821 4468 3300; off Jl Raya Senggigi, Pantai Kerandangan; mains 55,000-80,000Rp; ⊙11am-9pm; 🅿) This wonderful beachside restaurant 2km north of Senggigi has a blissfully secluded setting off the main road, where dining takes place at individual thatch-covered tables. The nasi goreng and madras curry are locally renowned, and the seafood is the best in the area. There are also many choices for vegetarians. It has a full bar and blends its own authentic *jamu* tonics (herbal medicines).

★Cafe Alberto
ITALIAN $$

(☑0370-693039; www.cafealberto.com; Jl Raya Senggigi; mains 55,000-115,000Rp; ⊙8am-11pm; 🛜) This long-standing, beachside Italian kitchen serves a variety of pasta dishes, but is known for its pizza. It offers free transport to and from your hotel, as well as generous surprises (like nibbles or digestifs). Best bit:

wiggling your toes in the sand while sipping a cold one under the moonlight.

Square
INTERNATIONAL $$

(☑0370-693688; www.squarelombok.com; Jl Raya Senggigi; mains 100,000-200,000Rp; ⊙11am-11pm; 🛜) An upscale restaurant with beautifully crafted seating and a menu that features Western and Indonesian fusion fare. The cooking is a cut above the local norm in terms of ambition. Many newcomers to Indonesia have been introduced to the cuisine by the tourist-friendly tasting menu. Get a table away from the road noise.

Spice
INTERNATIONAL $$

(☑0370-619 7373; www.spice-lombok.com; Jl Raya Senggigi, Pasar Seni; mains 60,000-120,000Rp; ⊙noon-11pm) Spice has airy quarters in the back of the euphemistically named Art Market. Tables on the sand are perfect for sunset drinks chosen from the long list. There are upscale pub snacks. Later, the stylish upstairs dining room catches the breezes. The cuisine features global, island and beach flavours.

Asmara
INTERNATIONAL $$

(☑0370-693619; www.asmara-group.com; Jl Raya Senggigi; mains 45,000-150,000Rp; ⊙8am-11pm; 🛜👪) An ideal family choice, this place spans the culinary globe from tuna carpaccio to burgers to Lombok's own *Sate pusut* (minced-meat or fish sate). It also has a sizable kids menu. Service and presentation are smooth.

🍷 Drinking & Nightlife

Not too long ago, Senggigi's bar scene was pretty vanilla, with most cafes and restaurants doing double duty. However, like something out of a Pattaya fever dream, huge cinderblock buildings went up on the centre's outskirts in the 2010s, featuring karaoke joints and massage parlours.

Few miss the chance to enjoy a sunset beverage at one of the many low-key places along the beach.

Jo-Je Beach Bar
BAR

(☑0878-6388-1436; off Jl Raya Senggigi; ⊙8am-11pm) A classic beach bar with multicolour beanbags and happy-hour prices that coincide with the sunset. The cocktails are exceptionally strong and there's also OK Indonesian and Western food.

ⓘ Getting There & Away

BEMO

Regular bemos travel between Senggigi and Ampenan's Kebon Roek terminal (5000Rp, 30 minutes), where you can connect to Mataram (10,000Rp, 20 minutes). Wave them down on the main drag.

Bemos make the coast road run north towards Bangsal Harbour in the morning, less often later (20,000Rp, one hour). Note that you'll have to get off in Pemenang, from where it's a 1.2km walk to the harbour.

BOAT

Fast boats to Bali leave from the large **pier** right in the centre of the beach. Some companies sell tickets from an office out on the pier; others sell from the shore nearby.

Gili Getaway (☑ 0823 3918 8281; http://giligetaway.com; Jl Pantai Senggigi; ☻8am-4pm) Useful services to Gili T and Gili Air (both 200,000Rp) as well as to Gili Gede (250,000Rp).

Perama (☑ 0370-693008; www.peramatour.com; Jl Raya Senggigi; ☻7am-10pm) An economical shuttle-bus service that connects with the public ferry from Lembar to Padangbai in Bali (125,000Rp, 9am), from where there are onward shuttle-bus connections to Sanur, Kuta and Ubud (all 175,000Rp). These trips can take eight or more hours.

Scoot (☑ 0828 9701 5565; www.scootcruise.com; Senggigi Pier) Daily fast boats to Nusa Lembongan (675,000Rp) and Sanur (750,000Rp) on Bali. Look for large discounts on the published fares.

Kencana Adventure (☑ 0812 2206 6066; www.kencanaadventure.com; Jl Raya Senggigi, Senggigi; one-way from 2,250,000Rp; ☻9am-5pm Mon-Sat) For those going on adventures further into Nusa Tenggara, this operator has an office where you can get info about heading east to Labuan Bajo.

TAXI

A metered taxi to Lembar costs around 170,000Rp; to Praya around 200,000Rp; and to Bangsal Harbour, not served by public bemo, about 100,000Rp.

ⓘ Getting Around

Senggigi's central area is easy to negotiate on foot.

Motorcycles can be rented starting from 60,000Rp per day. Vehicle rental is competitive and ranges from 200,000Rp to 350,000Rp per day. A car and driver costs from 500,000Rp per day.

Sire

A hidden upmarket enclave, the Sire (or Sira) peninsula points out towards the three Gilis. It's blessed with gorgeous, broad white-sand beaches and good snorkelling offshore. Opulent resorts are now established here alongside a couple of fishing villages. Look out for the small **Hindu temple**, just beyond the Oberoi resort, which has shrines built into the coastal rocks and sublime ocean views.

Sire is a very short drive off the main road just north of Bangsal. The resorts can arrange any needed transport.

🛏 Sleeping

★ Rinjani Beach Eco Resort
BOUTIQUE HOTEL **$$**

(☑ 0819 3677 5960; www.rinjanibeach.com; Karang Atas; bungalows 350,000-1,350,000Rp; ❄ ✉) 🌿 This gem has bamboo bungalows, each with its own theme; hammocks on private porches; and access to a pool on the black-sand beach. Two cheaper, smaller cold-water bungalows cater to budget travellers. It also has a restaurant, plus sea kayaks and mountain bikes. Waste water is treated and used to water the lush grounds. It's just along the coast from Sire.

Tugu Lombok
RESORT **$$$**

(☑ 0370-612 0111; www.tuguhotels.com; bungalows/villas incl breakfast from US$220/330; ❄ 🛜 ✉) 🌿 An astonishing hotel, this larger-than-life amalgamation of luxury accommodation, eclectic design and spiritual Indonesian heritage sits on a wonderful white-sand beach. Room decor is a fantasy of Indonesian artistic heritage, while the exquisite spa is modelled on Java's Buddhist Borobudur. Smart green practices abound.

Northwest Coast

Market towns and glimpses of coast are the norm on the run around the northwest coast of Lombok. The green slopes of Gunung Rinjani increasingly dominate the inland view and traffic blissfully fades away.

Just northeast of Gondang village, which is on the main Bangsal–Bayan road, a 6km trail heads inland to **Air Terjun Tiu Pupas** (entry 30,000Rp), a 30m waterfall that's only worth seeing in the wet season. Trails continue from here to other wet-season waterfalls, including **Air Terjun Gangga**,

WEKTU TELU

Wektu Telu is a complex mixture of Hindu, Islamic and animist beliefs, though it's now officially classified as a sect of Islam. At its forefront is a physical concept of the Holy Trinity. The sun, moon and stars represent heaven, earth and water, while the head, body and limbs represent creativity, sensitivity and control.

As recently as 1965, the vast majority of Sasaks in northern Lombok were Wektu Telu, but under Suharto's 'New Order' government, indigenous religious beliefs were discouraged and enormous pressure was placed on Wektu Telu to become Wektu Lima (Muslims who pray five times a day). But in the Wektu Telu heartland around Bayan, locals have been able to maintain their unique beliefs by differentiating their cultural traditions (Wektu Telu) from religion (Islam). Most do not fast for the full month of Ramadan and only attend the mosque for special occasions, and there's also widespread consumption of *brem* (alcoholic rice wine).

the most beautiful of all. A guide (about 80,000Rp) is useful to navigate the confusing trails in these parts.

Wektu Telu, Lombok's animist-tinted form of Islam, was born in humble thatched mosques nestled in these Rinjani foothills. The best example is **Masjid Kuno Bayan Beleq**, next to the village of Beleq. Its low-slung roof, dirt floors and bamboo walls reportedly date from 1634, making this mosque the oldest on Lombok. Inside is a huge old drum that served as the call to prayer before PA systems.

❶ Getting There & Away

Public transport north from Bangsal is infrequent. Several bemos (minibuses) a day go from Mataram's Mandalika Terminal (p320) to Bayan, but you'll have to get connections in Pemenang and/or Anyar, which can be difficult to navigate. Simplify things and get your own wheels.

Senaru

The scenic villages that make up Senaru merge into one along a steep road with sweeping volcano and sea views. Most visitors here are Gunung Rinjani–bound, but beautiful walking trails and spectacular waterfalls beckon to those who aren't.

Senaru derives its name from *sinaru*, which means light. As you ascend the hill towards the sky and clouds, you'll see just why this makes sense.

Senaru was particularly hard hit by a string of high magnitude earthquakes that struck Lombok in 2018. The recuperation process is ongoing and returning tourists will be a vital part of it, putting trekking guides back to work and funnelling much

needed cash into the rebuilding of area homes.

◉ Sights

Gunung Rinjani   VOLCANO

Lording it over the northern half of Lombok, Gunung Rinjani (3726m) is Indonesia's second-tallest volcano. It's an astonishing peak, and sacred to Hindus and Sasaks who make pilgrimages to the summit and lake to leave offerings for the gods and spirits. To the Balinese, Rinjani is one of three sacred mountains, along with Bali's Agung and Java's Bromo. Sasaks ascend throughout the year around the full moon.

The mountain has climatic significance. Its peak attracts a steady stream of swirling rain clouds, while its ash emissions bring fertility to the island's rice fields and tobacco crops, feeding a tapestry of paddies, fields, and cashew and mango orchards.

Rinjani also attracts many trekkers who thrill to the otherworldly vistas. The volcano has become so popular that there were more than a thousand climbers on it during the first of the 2018 earthquakes, after which its slopes were evacuated. It remained closed for several months.

Inside Gunung Rinjani's immense caldera, sitting 600m below the rim, is the stunning, 6km-wide, turquoise crescent lake **Danau Segara Anak** (Child of the Sea). The Balinese toss gold and jewellery into the lake in a ceremony called *pekelan*, before they slog their way towards the sacred summit.

The mountain's newest cone, the minor peak of Gunung Baru (2351m), only emerged a couple of hundred years ago, its scarred, smouldering profile rising above the lake as an ominous reminder of the apocalyptic power of nature. This peak has been

A BIG SHAKE-UP ON RINJANI

An estimated 1090 trekkers, guides and support staff were on the slopes of Gunung Rinjani on 29 July 2018, when a shallow earthquake measuring 6.4 on the Richter scale struck the Sembalun Valley, triggering numerous landslides. Trapped on the volcano overnight, most tourists were rescued the following day in a large-scale evacuation operation that captured headlines around the world. Rinjani was subsequently closed to trekkers. Two additional earthquakes over the next three weeks, both measuring 6.9, further complicated plans for reopening Rinjani, as many area hotels and travel agencies were shaken to pieces.

Some local imams blamed the ballooning number of tourists climbing the sacred peak for causing the earthquakes, so there was some initial resistance to reopening it. However, the economic importance of the trekking industry in northern Lombok was hard to negate, and exploratory trips up Rinjani began in October to assess the viability of the original routes. The popular Senaru and Sembalun hiking trails had 14 landslide points apiece, with severe damage to many shelters, guard posts, park offices and water sources. Repair work is ongoing. The two-day, one-night Benang Stokel route to the crater rim from Aik Berik (about 30km east of Mataram on Rinjan's south side) was the only trek open at the time of research, as it did not have any landslide damage. However, there was a quota of only 150 people per day, and trekking down to the crater lake remained off limits. Trekking agencies in Senaru and the Sembalun Valley were operating alternative overnight treks up Gunung Nangi (2330m) and Bukit Pergasingan (1700m), as well as day trips to local waterfalls and villages, until paths up Rinjani reopened.

The following tour operators were up and running at the time of research and are your best sources for the latest information on routes and conditions:

John's Adventures (☑ 0817 578 8018; www.rinjanimaster.com)

Rudy Trekker (☑ 0812 3929 9896; www.rudytrekker.com)

Rinjani Information Centre (RIC; ☑ 0818 540 673; www.rinjaniinformationcentre.com; Sembalun Lawang; ⊘ 6am-6pm)

Senaru Trekking (☑ 0818 540 673; www.senarutrekking.com; Jl Pariwisata) ✎

erupting fitfully for the last decade, periodically belching plumes of smoke and ash over the entire Rinjani caldera. Also in the crater are natural hot springs known as Aiq Kalak. Locals suffering from skin diseases trek here with a satchel of medicinal herbs to bathe and scrub in the bubbling mineral water.

The official website of **Gunung Rinjani National Park** (Taman Nasional Gunung Rinjani; ☑ 0370-660 8874; www.rinjaninationalpark.com) has good maps, info and a useful section on reported scams by dodgy hiking operators.

Note that trekking independently up Gunung Rinjani is not allowed.

Air Terjun Sindang Gila   WATERFALL
(10,000Rp) This spectacular set of falls is a 20-minute walk from Senaru via a lovely forest and hillside trail. The hardy make for the creek, edge close and then get pounded by the hard, foaming cascade that explodes over black volcanic stone 40m above.

You do not need a guide to reach Air Terjun Sindang Gila; it is on a well-marked path.

Air Terjun Tiu Kelep   WATERFALL
A further 50 minutes or so uphill from the popular Air Terjun Sindang Gila is this waterfall with a swimming hole. The track is steep and guides are recommended (100,000Rp each; negotiable). Long-tailed macaques (locals call them *kera*) and the much rarer silvered leaf monkey sometimes appear.

🏃 Activities

The main reason that people come to Senaru is for the trek up Gunung Rinjani. But if you have extra time, or aren't heading up the volcano, there are other worthy hikes here.

Guided walks and community tourism activities can be arranged at most guesthouses – they include a **rice-terrace and waterfalls walk** (per person 200,000Rp), which takes in Air Terjun Sindang Gila, rice paddies and an old bamboo mosque, and the **Senaru Panorama Walk** (350,000Rp per person), which incorporates the former plus stunning views and insights into local traditions.

🛌 Sleeping

Senaru's accommodation options are strung along the 6.5km-long road that starts in Bayan and runs uphill via Batu Koq to the main Gunung Rinjani Park Office, which was severely damaged at the time of research. Most are simple mountain lodges; the cool altitude means you won't need air-con.

Rinjani Lodge GUESTHOUSE $$
(📞 0819 0738 4944; www.rinjanilodge.com; r from 1,100,000Rp; ❊ 🛜 ☲) The lodge has five bungalows, four family rooms, four triples and two pools (one exclusively for hotel guests, and one shared with restaurant visitors). The property has jaw-dropping views across north Lombok and is just down from the Air Terjun Sindang Gila entrance.

Rinjani Lighthouse GUESTHOUSE $$
(📞 0853 3707 6655; www.rinjanilighthouse.mm.st; Jl Pariwisata; r from 750,000Rp; 🛜) Set on a wide plateau just 200m from the Gunung Rinjani Park Office, this impressive guesthouse (with hot water) has six thatched-roof bungalows that sleep up to six. The owners are founts of Rinjani wisdom.

ℹ Getting There & Away

From Mataram's Mandalika Bus Terminal, catch a bus to Anyar (25,000Rp to 30,000Rp, 2½ hours). From there, you'll have to charter an *ojek* (per person from 30,000Rp, depending on your luggage, 20 minutes). Due to the hassle, most visitors arrive in private transport arranged by a trekking agency.

Sembalun Valley
📞 0376

High on the eastern side of Gunung Rinjani is what could be the mythical Shangri-La: the beautiful Sembalun Valley. This high plateau (about 1200m) is ringed by volcanoes and peaks. It's a rich farming region where the golden foothills turn vivid green in the wet season. When the high clouds part, Rinjani takes front stage.

The valley has two main settlements, Sembalun Lawang and Sembalun Bumbung, tranquil bread baskets primarily concerned with growing cabbage, potatoes, strawberries and, above all, garlic – though trekking tourism brings in a little income, too. Both villages were severely damaged in a series of high magnitude earthquakes in 2018.

🛌 Sleeping

Sembalun Lawang village is rustic; most guesthouses will heat *mandi* (bath) water for a fee. The Rinjani Information Centre (RIC) can direct you to small homestays where rooms cost between 150,000Rp and 500,000Rp.

Lembah Rinjani LODGE $
(📞 0852 3954 3279, 0818 0365 2511; www.facebook.com/lembahrinjani; Sembalun Lawang; r 350,000-450,000Rp) This property has 12 basic, clean, tiled rooms with private porches and breathtaking mountain and sunrise views. The cheaper rooms have cold-water showers.

ℹ Getting There & Away

From Mataram's Mandalika Terminal, take a bus to Aikmel (20,000Rp) and change there for a bemo to Sembalun Lawang (20,000Rp).

There's no public transport between Sembalun Lawang and Senaru, so you'll have to charter an *ojek* (motorcycle taxi), for a potentially uncomfortable ride costing about 200,000Rp.

Tetebatu
📞 0376

Laced with spring-fed streams emanating from the slopes of Rinjani and blessed with rich volcanic soil, Tetebatu is a Sasak breadbasket. The surrounding countryside is quilted with tobacco and rice fields, fruit orchards and cow pastures that fade into remnant monkey forest gushing with waterfalls. Tetebatu's sweet climate is ideal for long country walks (at 650m it's high enough to mute that hot, sticky coastal mercury). Dark nights come saturated with sound courtesy of a frog orchestra accompanied by countless gurgling brooks. Even insomniacs snore here.

👆 Tours

A typical walking tour of greater Tetebatu takes in the rice fields, spice shops, two **waterfalls** (entry by donation) and the **Taman Wisata Tetebatu** (Monkey Forest). Alternatively, you can take a cultural tour to visit nearby artisan towns, including the bamboo-basket village of **Loyok**, the potters village of **Masbagik Timur** and the weavers village of **Pringgasela**. Each has several shops, often with live demonstrations.

🛏 Sleeping & Eating

A mix of quality bungalows and guesthouses are nestled in the lush countryside. The places where you can stay also provide meals, though there are a few nice stand-alone restaurants, too.

⭐ Edriyan Bungalow
BUNGALOW $

(☎ 0853 3908 0120; http://edriyanbungalow tetebatu.blogspot.com; Jl Pariwisata Tetebatu; d from 400,000Rp, bungalow for 4 500,000Rp; 🛜 ❄) Three two-storey bamboo bungalows, each with intricate designs, offer astounding views over the glistening rice fields. Also on offer are an inviting pool, plant-filled gardens and Sasak cooking classes (200,000Rp, two hours) in the restaurant where you can learn how to make dishes such as jackfruit curry.

Pondok Indah Bungalows Tetebatu
BUNGALOW $

(☎ 0877 6172 2576; Jl Pariwisata Tetebatu; bungalow from 250,000Rp) Three bi-level thatched bungalows are set amid beautiful rice fields. Although appearing romantically rustic, conditions are not: each has a bathroom, hardwood floors, outdoor seating areas with fabulous views and more. The grounds are a floral mix of colours.

Hakiki Bungalows & Cafe
BUNGALOW $

(☎ 0818 0373 7407; www.hakiki-inn.com; Jl Kembang Kuning; r 175,000-450,000Rp; 🛜) A collection of seven bungalows in a blooming garden at the edge of the rice fields. You'll

---

CLIMBING GUNUNG RINJANI

Tetebatu makes a great alternative hiking base to Senaru and the Sembalun Valley for the climb up Gunung Rinjani, particularly for those short on time. You won't be able to dip into the lakes on the express two-day, one-night climbs from this side of the volcano with **Jaya Trekker** (☎ 0853 3792 0005; https:// jayatrekker.com; Jl Pariwisata Tetebatu) and other local agencies, but you're guaranteed to see less rubbish and a fraction of the tourists. Expect to pay about 1,750,000Rp for the trip, including a guide, porters, equipment, food and entrance to the park.

---

find it perched over the family rice plot about 600m from the intersection. There's even a honeymoon suite. Wi-fi is available in the cafe, which serves Indo classics, some nicely spicy.

Tetebatu Mountain Resort
BUNGALOW $$

(☎ 0853 3754 0777; www.mountainresort tetebatu.com; Jl Kembang Kuning; bungalows from 500,000Rp; 🛜 ❄) These Sasak bungalows with 23 rooms in total are some of the best digs in town. Four of them have separate bedrooms across two floors – perfect for travelling buddies – and a top-floor balcony with magical rice-field views.

Warung Monkey Forest
INDONESIAN $

(☎ 0853 3702 0691; Jl Pariwisata Tetebatu; mains 30,000-40,000Rp; ⊘ 8am-11pm) A fantastic little thatch-roofed restaurant with lots of veggie options, fresh fruit juices and helpful English-speaking owners. Find it on the way up to the Monkey Forest.

❶ Getting There & Away

All cross-island buses pass Pomotong (35,000Rp from Mandalika Terminal) on the main east–west highway. Get off here and you can hop an *ojek* (from 25,000Rp) to Tetebatu.

Most accommodation can arrange private transport from anywhere in Lombok. It's often easier and, if you have a group, just as cheap.

Praya
☎ 0370 / POP 55,040

Sprawling Praya's claim to fame is as the location for Lombok's airport. It's also the main town in the south, with tree-lined streets and the odd crumbling Dutch colonial relic.

❶ Getting There & Away

Surrounded by rice fields and 5km south of Praya proper is the modern **Lombok International Airport** (LOP; www.lombok-airport.co.id; Jl Bypass Bil Praya). The airport is not huge, but has a full range of services such as ATMs, convenience stores and coffee shops.

Thanks to multi-lane roads, the airport is less than a 45 minutes' drive from both Mataram and Kuta and is well linked to the rest of the island.

Damri operates regular tourist buses, timed to meet flights; buy tickets in the arrivals area. Destinations include Mataram's Mandalika Terminal (30,000Rp), Senggigi (40,000Rp) and east to Selong (35,000Rp).

Taxi counters outside arrivals offer fixed-price rides to destinations that include Kuta (150,000Rp, 30 minutes), Mataram (180,000Rp, 40 minutes), Senggigi (300,000Rp, 75 minutes) and Bangsal (350,000Rp, 1¾ hours), where you can access the Gili Islands.

Kuta

📞 0370 / POP 5000

Turquoise in the shallows and deep blue further out, Kuta's magnificent crescent bay remains beautiful from a distance. Up close, however, the reality is different. The slowly gestating, enormous Mandalika development has erased the once beloved yet shabby row of guesthouses, cafes and surfers bars here. Where bikini-clad travellers once shared the beach with goats, there are now gaudy concrete structures and virtually no sunbathers.

Kuta's once-funky scene has shifted inland, and its surfing and sandy pleasures are more focused on the stunning beaches to the west and, to a lesser extent, the east – although even here the land rush is evident as bulldozers carve up the hills.

Kuta's array of low-key cafes, shops and guesthouses is now centred on the intersection of Jl Raya Kuta and Jl Mawan, some 300m north of the beach.

👁 Sights

★ Pantai Mawan   BEACH

(parking car/motorbike 10,000/5000Rp) This beach is reason enough to venture down Kuta way. Some 8km west of Kuta and 600m off the main road, this half-moon cove is framed by soaring headlands with azure water and a swath of sand that's empty save for a fishing village of a few thatched houses. The beach is terrific for swimming. It has paved parking, some modest cafes and large trees for shade. Sun lounger rentals are 50,000Rp.

Tanjung Aan   BEACH

(car/motorbike 20,000/10,000Rp) Some 5km east of Kuta, Tanjung Aan (aka A'an, Ann) is a spectacular sight: a giant horseshoe bay with two sweeping arcs of fine sand with the ends punctuated by waves crashing on the rocks. Swimming is good here and there are trees and shelters for shade, plus safe parking (for a small charge). **Warung Turtle**, at the east end of the beach, has cheery service and cheap beer, while the western headland

---

SURFING THE SOUTH COAST

Stellar lefts and rights break on the reefs off Kuta Bay (Telek Kuta) and east of Tanjung Aan. Around 7km east of Kuta is the fishing village of Gerupuk (p334), where there's a series of reef breaks, both close to the shore and further out, but they require a boat, at a negotiable 200,000Rp per two-hour session.

Wise surfers buzz past Gerupuk and take the road to Ekas (p335), where crowds are thin and two breaks, Inside Ekas and Outside Ekas, keep wave hunters happy. These also require a boat for about 400,000Rp. West of Kuta, you'll find Mawan, a stunning swimming beach; **Mawi**, a popular surf paradise with world-class swells and a strong rip tide; and lastly, the long white sands of **Selong Blanak** (parking 10,000Rp), a great spot for beginners.

Bukit Merese is worth climbing for spectacular sunsets.

Pantai Areguling   BEACH

(car/motorbike 10,000/5000Rp) Look for a steep track off the main coast road 6km west of Kuta. A rough 2km ride brings you to this broad bay with a wide beach of beige sand. It's a little scruffy, but you can't beat the sense of space. Construction on the headland foreshadows changes to come.

Pantai Seger   BEACH

(car/motorbike 10,000/5000Rp) Pantai Seger, a lovely beach about 2km east of Kuta around the first headland, has unbelievably turquoise water, decent swimming (though no shade) and a break 200m offshore. There are two more beaches nearby, a decent cafe and vendors renting snorkelling gear.

🏃 Activities

There's a whole row of activity sales agents along Jl Pariwisata and the main road leading to the waterfront. They can set you up on anything from surf tours to snorkelling in obscure locations. Don't be afraid to haggle.

★ Mana Retreat Lombok   YOGA

(📞 0853 38628 659; http://manalombok.com; Jl Baturiti; class 100,000Rp; ⊗ 8am-6.30pm) An open thatched pavilion in a serene jungly setting with vinyasa, yin/yang, surfer

NUSA TENGGARA KUTA

BAU NYALE FESTIVAL

On the 19th day of the 10th month in the Sasak calendar (generally February or March), hundreds of Sasaks gather on Pantai Seger (p331) for a big **festival** (Pantai Seger; ⏾ Feb or Mar) involving stick fighting, live bands and the odd, worm-like *nyale*.

When night falls, fires are built and teens sit around competing in a Sasak poetry slam, where they spit rhyming couplets called *pantun* back and forth. At dawn the next day, the first of millions of *nyale* (which appear here annually) are caught, then teenage girls and boys take to the sea separately in decorated boats, and chase one another with lots of noise and laughter. The *nyale* are eaten raw or grilled, and are considered to be an aphrodisiac. A good catch is a sign that a bumper crop of rice is coming.

yoga and more. Yogis can also sleep on-site in rooms and bungalows (dm/d from 300,000/900,000Rp).

★ Scuba Froggy   DIVING
(☑ 0878 6454 1402; www.scubafroggy.com; Jl Mawan; single dive 600,000Rp, open-water course 5,500,000Rp; ⏾ 9am-7pm) Runs local trips to two-dozen dive sites, most no deeper than 18m. From June to November, staff also run trips to the spectacular and challenging ocean pinnacles in Belongas Bay, famous for schooling hammerheads and mobula rays. Snorkelling trips to the Southwest Gilis are 750,000Rp. It also rents out kayaks (80,000Rp per hour).

Whatsup? Lombok   WATER SPORTS
(☑ 0878 6597 8701; http://whatsuplombok.com; Jl Pariwisata; SUP/kayak/kitesurfing rentals per hr 200,000/150,000/400,000Rp; ⏾ 8am-8pm) South Kuta's bays are known for being excellent places for kitesurfing, stand-up paddleboarding (SUP) and kayaking. At this shop you can rent gear, take lessons and join tours.

Kimen Surf   SURFING
(☑ 0878 6590 0017; www.kuta-lombok.net; Jl Mawan; board rental per day 100,000Rp, lessons per person from 400,000Rp; ⏾ 8am-8pm) This well-regarded local surf shop provides swell forecasts, tips, kitesurfing, board rent-

al, repairs and lessons. It also runs guided excursions to breaks such as Gerupuk (700,000Rp) and has an on-site cafe with strong espresso coffees.

🛏 Sleeping

Kuta offers a fantastic spread of options for all budgets. Prices increase markedly in the high season through July and August. Beware of ageing, rundown hotels along Jl Pariwisata.

★ Livingroom Hostel   HOSTEL $
(☑ 0823 3942 1868; www.thelivingroomlombok. com; Jl Mawan; dm/r from 130,000/320,000Rp; ❄ 🎧 🏊) Centrally located Livingroom is everything you'd want in a hostel. It's got an eclectic bar with swings for seats, home-baked bread for breakfast, clean and well-equipped rooms and even a small pool. One of the Hungarian owners is a woodworker and this place is his Sistine Chapel.

★ Kuta Cabana Lodge   LODGE $
(www.facebook.com/kutacabanalodge; off Jl Sengkol; r incl breakfast from 400,000Rp; ❄ 🎧) This eclectic thatch-roofed lodge spills down a hill just east of town, offering sweeping views over the bay from each artfully designed room. Teachers from Ashtari run yoga classes in the top-floor *shala*, while the French-flavoured restaurant, The Other Place, draws big crowds for the tangerine sunsets (mains 50,000Rp to 80,000Rp).

★ Lara Homestay   GUESTHOUSE $
(☑ 0877 6310 0315; http://larahomestay.com; Jl Raya Kuta Pujut Lombok Tengah; r from 300,000Rp; ❄ 🎧) This excellent family-run guesthouse is on a quiet, tree-shaded back lane close to the heart of Kuta. Service could not be cheerier. Rooms in the multistorey main building are sparkling and great value. The breakfasts are tasty.

Bombora Bungalows   BUNGALOW $
(☑ 0370-650 2571; bomborabungalows@yahoo. com; Jl Raya Kuta; standard/superior r 425,000/575,000Rp; ❄ 🎧 🏊) One of the best places for a low-cost stay in Kuta, these eight bungalows (some fan-cooled, all with bathrooms) are built around a lovely pool area. Coconut palms shade loungers, pink-flamingo inflatables stand ready and the entire place feels like an escape from the hubbub of town. The staff understand the needs of surfers and pretty much everyone else.

Mimpi Manis B&B **$**

(☑ 081 836 9950; www.mimpimanis.com; Jl Raya Kuta; dm/d 100,000/150,000-250,000Rp; ✳🤍) Run by Made and Gemma, a friendly Balinese/British couple, 'Sweet Dreams' is an inviting B&B offering spotless dorm and private rooms, some with air-con and showers. Located 1km inland, it's more peaceful than central Kuta options, with plenty of good books to borrow. It also offers a free drop-off service to the beach and town, plus bike and motorbike rental.

Snorkelling trips to the Southwest Gilis are from 350,000Rp per person, and six-hour fishing trips are 600,000Rp (minimum two people). The owners will prepare a barbecue of your catch at no extra charge.

★ Yuli's Homestay HOMESTAY **$$**

(☑ 0819 1710 0983; www.yulishomestay.com; Jl Baturiti; r incl breakfast 425,000-700,000Rp; ✳🤍🏊) The 32 rooms at this ever-expanding place are immaculately clean, spacious and nicely furnished with huge beds and wardrobes. It also has big front terraces and cold-water bathrooms, not to mention a guest kitchen, a garden and three pools to enjoy.

Blue Monkey Villas BUNGALOW **$$**

(☑ 0853 3775 6416; bluemonkeyvilllas@gmail.com; Pantai Areguling; r 500,000-1,000,000Rp; 🤍🏊) Set on a knoll about Pantai Areguling, 8km west of Kuta, this collection of traditional-style bungalows has sweeping views of the bay. The beach is a 500m walk down the hill. A simple cafe serves meals, where the view will compete with your food for your attention.

Puri Rinjani Bungalows BUNGALOW **$$**

(☑ 0370-615 4849; Jl Pariwisata; r from 700,000Rp; ✳🤍🏊) A solid beachfront option that gets everything right: it's sparklingly clean, well-managed and has a lovely pool area, with statues decorating the grounds. The 19 rooms are bright and airy and have nice, firm beds.

 Eating

Kuta's dining scene is getting more creative each day. There's a wide variety of choices – all casual – at great prices.

★ Milk Espresso CAFE **$$**

(www.facebook.com/milkespresso; Jl Raya Kuta; mains 55,000-130,000Rp; ☺7am-midnight; 🤍) Hopping all day long, this trendy bi-level cafe breathlessly segues from bountiful breakfasts to midday nibbles, healthy dinners and classy evening cocktails. Oh, and the strong coffee is sure to rev your engine any time of day!

★ El Bazar MEDITERRANEAN **$$**

(☑ 0819 9911 3026; www.elbazarlombok.com; Jl Raya Kuta; mains 75,000-185,000Rp; ☺7.30am-11pm) Kuta's most popular restaurant lives up to its stellar reputation with authentic tastes from around the Mediterranean. Kick things off with a meze platter and then move on to excellent kebabs, falafels or Moroccan tagines.

Sea Salt SEAFOOD **$$**

(☑ 0813 8198 7104; Jl Pariwisata; mains 60,000-90,000Rp; ☺11am-10pm) That a Scottish-owned, vaguely Greek seafood restaurant is one of Kuta's best speaks volumes for where the dining scene is at. At this small, arched dining room, open to the beach and hung with bird cages and shrimp traps, let super-enthusiastic, barefoot staff fuss over you as you tuck into the day's catch.

Warung Bule SEAFOOD **$$**

(☑ 0370-615 8625; Jl Pariwisata; mains 60,000-85,000Rp; ☺10am-11pm; 🤍) Tucked away from the main thoroughfares, on a quiet stretch of Kuta Beach, this friendly, spotlessly tiled warung is one of the best in town. The grilled barracuda with Sasak spices is fantastic, while the trio of lobster, prawns and mahi-mahi (385,000Rp, expensive by local standards) is a full seafood fix. It can get very busy in high season.

Ashtari INTERNATIONAL **$$**

(☑ 0812 3608 0862; www.ashtarilombok.com; Jl Mawan; mains 40,000-100,000Rp; ☺8am-9pm) Perched on a mountaintop 2km west of town on the road to Mawan, this breezy, Mediterranean-themed lounge-restaurant has spectacular vistas of pristine bays and rocky peninsulas that take turns spilling further out to sea. It's a slick yoga-luxe sort of place with several options for vegans.

Well-trained teachers offer a variety of yoga classes (100,000Rp) in a peaceful spot below the restaurant from 7am to 6.30pm

🎙 **Drinking & Nightlife**

There are a couple of raucous beachfront bars where there are often well-advertised parties. Impromptu beer bashes set up on the sand right near the centre of town.

NUSA TENGGARA KUTA

★ The Bus   BAR

(☑ 0823 4089 7270; www.facebook.com/thebus lombok; Jl Raya Kuta; ⊙ 6pm-midnight) Great tunes, colourful graffiti art and fab pizzas make this a must-visit come nightfall. Sit on pallet furniture in a rocky patch of central Kuta and let the wizards inside the namesake 1974 VW bus craft you some of the cheapest, tastiest cocktails in town. DJs spin Wednesday and Saturday.

ℹ Information

MONEY

Kuta has a half-dozen ATMs and is a good place to stock up on rupiahs before travelling further afield in south Lombok.

DANGERS & ANNOYANCES

➡ If you decide to rent a bicycle or motorbike, take care with whom you deal – arrangements are informal and rental contracts are hardly ever exchanged. There are reports of some visitors having motorbikes stolen (often at late-night beach parties) and then having to pay substantial sums of money as compensation to the owner. Renting a motorbike from your guesthouse is the safest option.

➡ As you drive up the coastal road west and east of Kuta, keep an eye out – especially after dark. There have been rare reports of muggings in the area.

➡ The throngs of vendors, many of them children selling friendship bands, are relentless.

HEALTH

Blue Island Medical Clinic (☑ 0819 9970 5700; http://blueislandclinic.com; Jl Raya Kuta; ⊙ 24hr) Your best bet for minor issues in southern Lombok. For anything major, head to Mataram.

ℹ Getting There & Away

Outside the daily morning Damri bus to Kuta from Mataram's Mandalika Bus Terminal (1½ hours, 60,000Rp), there is no real public transport linking the two cities.

Simpler are the daily ride-share cars serving Mataram, plus Senggigi and Lembar (all 100,000Rp). Shared cars to the airport cost 60,000Rp, though a taxi may be simpler if you fly out at an odd hour (150,000Rp). Other ride-share destinations include Bangsal (110,000Rp) for Gili Islands public boats and Seminyak (Bali) via the public ferry (180,000Rp). All are advertised widely on sandwich boards across Kuta.

ℹ Getting Around

Guesthouses rent out motorbikes for about 70,000Rp per day. *Ojeks* (motorbike taxis) are less frequent here than elsewhere in Lombok (most visitors rent their own wheels) but can often be hailed from the junction in the centre of town. Good paved roads run east to the various beaches. It's a terrific motorbike ride. Your own wheels are essential for exploring the beaches in the west. Cyclists will need to be ready for hills and narrow, curving roads.

East of Kuta

A good paved road runs along the coast to the east and Ekas, passing a seemingly endless series of beautiful bays punctuated by head-lands. It's a terrific motorbike ride.

Gerupuk

☑ 0370

Just 1.6km past Tanjung Aan beach, Gerupuk is a fascinating little ramshackle coastal village where the thousand or so local souls earn their keep from fishing, seaweed harvesting and lobster exports. Oh, and guiding and ferrying surfers to the five exceptional surf breaks in its huge bay.

As you'll see from the nascent grand boulevards and vast earthworks between Tanjung Aan and Gerupuk, construction on the gigantic Mandalika resort complex is under way in fits and starts. Expect the area to change greatly in the next few years. Judging by the way the existing mangroves have been destroyed, concerns about environmental damage are well placed.

🏃 Activities

To surf in the bay you'll need to hire a boat to ferry you from the fishing harbour, skirting the netted lobster farms, to the break (200,000Rp). The boat operator will help you find the right wave and wait patiently. There are four waves inside and a left break outside on the point. All can get head high or bigger when the swell hits.

🛏 Sleeping & Eating

Surf Camp Lombok   RESORT $$

(☑ 0852 3744 5949; www.surfcampindonesia.com; 1 week from €690) Lodging at this fun surf resort at the eastern end of Gerupuk village is in a bamboo Borneo-style longhouse, albeit with lots of high-tech diversions. The beach setting feels lush and remote. All meals are included plus surf lessons, yoga and more. Rooms sleep five, except for three doubles. Recycling and other ecofriendly practices are embraced.

Inlight Lombok Resort   BOUTIQUE HOTEL **$$$**
(☑0853 3803 8280; www.inlightlombok.com; r from 1,400,000Rp; ✳🛜☷) Curvaceously designed by the Russian architect-owner, this stunning hotel on a secluded beach just south of Gerupuk was built for detoxing. Wi-fi is only available in common areas, there is no alcohol and the health-food restaurant has an energising pescetarian menu. The four rooms, while not quite as show-stopping as the grounds, are spacious and comfortable with astonishing views.

Fin   CAFE **$**
(☑0823 3956 4781; www.facebook.com/fin gerupuk; mains 45,000-60,000Rp; ☻7.30am-4.30pm) 🍴 This airy turquoise-and-white cafe with distressed wood furnishings and birdcages for light fixtures is the kind of place you might expect to find in Gili T, not Gerupuk. But it's a welcome addition, with espresso coffees, yoghurt bowls, wheatgrass shots and veggie sandwiches.

Ekas

☑0370

Ekas is an uncrowded find, where the breaks and soaring cliffs recall Bali's Ulu Watu – an almost deserted Ulu Watu.

Ekas itself is a sleepy little village, but head south into the peninsula and you'll soon make the sorts of jaw-dropping discoveries that will have you Instagramming like mad.

🛏 Sleeping

There are posh boutique resorts hidden on the beautiful coves south of Ekas. Also look out for new and simple guesthouses along the rural roads.

Ekas Breaks   GUESTHOUSE **$$**
(☑0822 3791 6767; www.ekasbreaks.com; r incl breakfast 600,000-900,000Rp; ✳🛜☷) Some 2km from Ekas' surf breaks and beaches amid rolling land is this sun-kissed compound. Some rooms are in a traditional *lumbung* style with thatched walls; others are in a modern style, with whitewashed walls and open bathrooms (we prefer those). The cafe makes a good mix of Western and Indo meals.

★Heaven on the Planet   BOUTIQUE HOTEL **$$$**
(☑0812 375 1103; www.heavenontheplanet.com; Ekas Bay; per person all-inclusive US$120-240; ✳🛜☷) The aptly named Heaven on the

BUMBANGKU

Gerupuk's beach is narrow; much nicer is the powdery sand across the bay at **Bumbangku**. Follow a narrow track off the main road for 2.5km and you'll find this idyllic and often deserted beach. The structures you see out in the bay are pearl farms. **Bumbangku Beach Cottages** (☑0821 4715 3876; www.bumbangkulombok.com; Jl Raya Awang, Bumbangku; r 250,000-750,000Rp; ✳) has 25 rooms here ranging from simple bamboo huts on stilts with outdoor bathrooms and cold water to much nicer concrete rooms with hot water and air-con.

Planet has units scattered along a cliff's edge, from where you'll have spectacular bird's-eye views of the sea. Others are down at the idyllic beach. Each is utterly different. Heaven is primarily a posh and idiosyncratic surf resort, but kitesurfing, scuba diving, yoga and snorkelling are also possible. Meals are bountiful and creative.

West of Kuta

West of Kuta is a series of awesome beaches and ideal surf breaks. Developers are nosing around here, and land has changed hands, but for now it remains almost pristine and the region has a raw beauty. In anticipation of future developments, the road has been much improved. It meanders inland, skirting tobacco, sweet potato and rice fields in between turn-offs to the sand and glimpses of the gorgeous coast.

Selong Blanak

☑0370

Just when you think you've seen the most beautiful sands Kuta has to offer, you reach this wide, sugar-white beach with water streaked a thousand shades of blue, ideal for swimming. You can rent surfboards (per day 50,000Rp) and arrange for a boat out to area breaks (from 100,000Rp). The car park is just 400m off the main drag on a good road, the turn is 18km west of Kuta. The beach is popular with locals, loungers rent for 50,000Rp per day and there are lots of bamboo warungs.

Selong Blanak gets stiff competition in the fabulous sweepstakes from nearby **Pantai Mawi**, a quiet cove for in-the-know surfers with legendary barrels. Watch out for the strong rip tide. There's parking and vendors; surfboard rental is 50,000Rp for two hours. The turn for the beach is 16km west of Kuta; it's then a 3km drive down a rough road to the beach.

🛏 Sleeping & Eating

Lodgings here skew upmarket, though you'll find the odd homestay or budget bungalow in the mix. Dining options from budget to top end can be found here, mostly near the beach in Selong Blanak.

Tiki Lodge
RESORT $$

(📞 0822 4744 7274; www.tikilombok.com; Jl Selong Belanak; r from 650,000Rp; 🛜🍴) Comfortable thatch-roofed villas with bamboo beds and luxurious outdoor bathrooms surround an emerald-green pool in these jungly grounds. Breakfast and afternoon tea are included in the rate.

Sempiak Villas
RESORT $$

(📞 0821 4430 3337; www.sempiakvillas.com; villas from 960,000Rp; 🅿🛜🍴) Tucked away on the cliffs, this fabulous boutique resort is one of the Kuta area's most upscale properties. Seven villas are built into the hillside above the beach and feature antique wood; some have covered decks with stupendous views. Another five cheaper villas lie down below. It has a beach club for daytime frolics and dinners on the sand.

Laut Biru Bar & Restaurant
SEAFOOD $$

(📞 0821 4430 3339; mains 45,000-90,000Rp; 🕗 8am-10pm; 🛜) This seaside cafe at Sempiak Villas keeps it simple with Indo classics for lunch and dinner, though the setting is anything but. You'll dine in a fancy whitewashed building with high ceilings, hanging shell art and remixed world music floating out toward the sandy patio.

Belongas

Save a big 'Wow!' for this curving double bay with a sinuous strand of white ribbon that provides a brilliant line between the blue water and green hills. Nearby Bali has nothing even remotely like this beach and it's still yours to explore, as development has barely touched this area.

There are two famed dive sites here: **Magnet** and **Cathedrals**. Spotting conditions peak in mid-September when you may see schooling mobula rays in addition to hammerheads, which school around the pinnacle (a towering rock that breaks the surface of the ocean and is the heart of the dive sites) from June to November. It's not an easy dive, so you must be experienced and prepared for strong currents.

Belongas Bay is a focus area for Senggigi based **Dive Zone** (📞 0819 0785 2073; www.dive-zone-lombok.com; 2 local boat dives 1,650,000Rp), which runs trips out of the **Belongas Bay Lodge** (📞 0370-645974; www.thelodge-lombok .com; bungalows 850,000-950,000Rp, meals 75,000Rp). This lodge offers spacious wooden bungalows with tiled roofs in a lovely coconut grove. It's fairly simple, which goes with the serene setting right on the water. Access is via a thin, severely rutted and challenging dirt road that's ill suited to novice motorbikers. Advanced bookings are essential.

East Lombok

📞 0376

All most travellers see of Lombok's east coast is Labuhan Lombok, the port for ferries to Sumbawa. But the road around the northeast coast is pretty good, with isolated black-sand beaches, particularly at Obel Obel – the route can be traversed if you're hoping to complete a circumnavigation. From Labuhan Pandan, or from further north at Sugian, you can charter a boat to Gili Sulat or Gili Pentangan. Both islands have lovely white beaches and good coral for snorkelling, but no facilities.

South of Labuhan Lombok, Selong, the capital of the east Lombok administrative district, has some dusty Dutch colonial buildings, while the fishing port of Tanjung Luar has stilted Bugis-style houses. In Keruak you'll see wooden boats being built, and in the traditional Sasak village of Sukaraja it's possible to buy woodcarvings. Just west of Keruak a road leads south via Jerowaru to Ekas and the spectacular southeastern peninsula.

Labuhan Lombok

📞 0376 / POP 38,519

Labuhan Lombok (also known as Labuhan Kayangan or Tanjung Kayangan) is the port for ferries and boats to Sumbawa. The town centre of Labuhan Lombok, 3km west of the ferry terminal, is a scruffy place, but it does have great views of Gunung Rinjani. Do check out the giant mahogany trees about 4km north of the harbour and consider a trip out to **Gili Kondo**, an idyllic islet just offshore that's great for camping and snorkelling.

ⓘ Getting There & Away

BUS & BEMO

Regular buses and bemos buzz between Mandalika Terminal in Mataram and Labuhan Lombok; the journey takes 2½ hours (35,000Rp). Some buses will only drop you off at the port entrance road, from where you can catch another bemo to the ferry terminal (5000Rp, 10 minutes). Don't walk – it's too far.

BOAT

Ferries run almost hourly, 24 hours a day, between Labuhan Lombok and Poto Tano on Sumbawa (passengers 17,000Rp, cars 431,000Rp, motorcycles 49,500Rp, 1½ hours). Through buses to points east from Bali and Lombok include the ferry fare.

Small fishing boats can take you to Gili Kondo for the day for about 750,000Rp, though many organise tours from Tetebatu or Senaru.

GILI ISLANDS

Floating in a turquoise sea and fringed by white sand and coconut palms, the Gilis are a tropical vision of delight. And they're booming right along with Bali – the once deserted coastal paths are now filling in with large resorts, hip guesthouses and sand-between-the-toes cafes.

The lure of big tourist dollars tugs against the traditionally laid-back culture of the islands, the alternative spirit imported by Western partygoers and a buoyant green sensibility. While the outcome is uncertain, for now the Gili Air and Meno retain their languorous charm (partly due to local efforts to exclude dogs and motorbikes from the islands) while Gili Trawangan (aka Gili T) continues its frenetic pursuit of pleasure.

Each island has its own unique appeal. Gili T is the most cosmopolitan, with a raucous party scene and plenty of upscale dining and accommodation. Gili Air has an appealing mix of buzz and bliss, while little Gili Meno has the strongest local character.

ⓘ Information

DANGERS & ANNOYANCES

➡ Although it's rare, some foreign women have experienced sexual harassment and even assault while on the Gilis – it's best not to walk home alone to the quieter parts of the islands.

➡ As tranquil as the seas appear, currents are strong in the channels between the islands. Do not try to swim between the Gili Islands as it can be deadly.

➡ Bike riders (almost entirely tourists) regularly plough into and injure people on Gili T's main drag. *Cidomo* (horse-drawn carts) hauling construction goods are almost as bad, and pack considerably more punch.

Theft

Immediately report thefts to the island *kepala desa* (village head), who will deal with the issue; staff at the dive schools will direct you to him.

While police used to only visit the Gilis sporadically, they set up shop on all three islands due to

Gili Islands

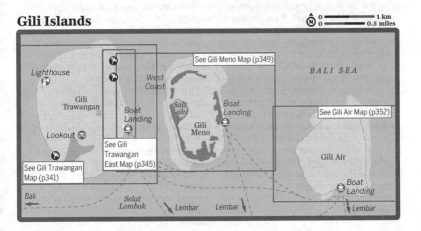

the looting that followed the 2018 earthquakes. Many predict that they are now here to stay.

Drugs & Alcohol

The drug trade remains endemic in Trawangan where you'll get offers of everything from meth to ecstasy and mushrooms. The last of these is openly advertised in cafes. Remember, Indonesia has a strong anti-drugs policy; those caught in possession of or taking drugs risk jail or worse.

Tourists have been poisoned by adulterated *arak* (colourless, distilled palm spirits) on the Gilis, as happens in Bali and Lombok. Skip it, and beware of cut-price cocktails.

❶ Getting There & Away

Most hotels and many guesthouses will help you sort out your transport options to and from the Gilis as part of your reservation. If you use an online booking website, contact the hotel directly afterwards. Some high-end resorts have their own boats for transporting guests.

FROM BALI

Fast boats advertise swift connections between Bali and Gili Trawangan (45 minutes to 2½ hours, depending on destination). They leave from several departure points in Bali, including Benoa Harbour, Sanur, Padangbai and Amed. Some go via Nusa Lembongan. Many dock at Teluk Nare/ Teluk Kade on Lombok north of Senggigi before continuing on to Air and Trawangan (you'll have to transfer for Meno in most cases).

The website **Gili Bookings** (www.gilibookings. com) presents a range of boat operators and prices in response to your booking request. It's useful for getting an idea of the services offered, but it is not comprehensive and you may get a better price by buying direct from the operator.

Other considerations:

➺ Fares are not fixed, especially in quiet times – you should be able to get discounts on published fares. That said, not all fast boats are created equal, and paying a higher fare for a more sturdy boat may just save you from a regurgitated breakfast.

➺ If you don't need transport to/from the boat, ask for a discount.

➺ The advertised times are illusionary. Boats are cancelled, unplanned stops are made or boats simply run very late. Give yourself a wide margin of error if planning onward connections (flights from Lombok or Bali, for instance).

➺ Book ahead in July and August.

➺ The sea between Bali and Lombok can get very rough (particularly during rainy season) and fast boats can be cancelled for days on end.

➺ The fast boats are unregulated, and operating and safety standards vary widely. There have been some major accidents, with boats sinking and passengers killed.

Operators include the following:

Blue Water Express (☑ 0813 3841 8988, 0361-895 1111; www.bluewater-express.com; one-way from 750,000Rp) Professionally run company with boats from Serangan and Padangbai (Bali), to Teluk Kade, Gili T and Gili Air.

Gili Getaway (☑ 0813 3707 4147, 0821 4489 9502; www.giligetaway.com; one-way Bali to Gilis adult/child 710,000/550,000Rp) Very

---

GILI STRONG: REBUILDING PARADISE

When a 6.4 magnitude earthquake rattled mainland Lombok on 29 July 2018, most on the Gili Islands simply shrugged their shoulders. Little did they know that it was a 'foreshock' for a larger 6.9 earthquake the following Sunday, August 5, that would topple resorts and restaurants across this mini-archipelago.

A tsunami warning prompted the majority of those staying on Trawangan to spend the night on the Gilis' lone hill. Many on the flatter islands of Air and Meno huddled together on interior fields. Thankfully, the tsunami waves never materialised, but the prolonged and chaotic rescue operation the following day captured global headlines.

There were widespread reports of looting on the Gili Islands in the immediate aftermath, forcing the police to set up posts on each island. Many businesses were shaken up beyond repair, particularly on the southeastern corner of Meno, in the main village of Trawangan and along Trawangan's western coastline. In general, businesses built of bamboo or wood fared far better than those made of concrete.

Residents rallied around the motto 'Gili Strong' in the weeks after the quake and used it as a marketing pitch to lure tourists back. By September, a few fast boats had resumed services from Bali, carrying intrepid visitors to these battered isles. Rebuilding was hampered slightly by a lack of workers (many were busy caring for families back on mainland Lombok). Yet the islands have shown incredible resilience and are well on their way to recovery.

professional; links Serangan on Bali with Gili T and Gili Air as well as Senggigi and Gili Gede.

Gili Gili Fast Boat (☑ 0818 0858 8777; www.giligilifastboat.com; 1-way from 690,000Rp) Links Padangbai (Bali) with Bangsal Harbour (Lombok), Gili T and Gili Air.

Perama (☑ 0361-750808; www.peramatour.com; per person 1-way 400,000Rp) Links Padangbai, the Gilis and Senggigi by a not-so-fast boat.

Scoot (☑ 0361-271030; www.scootcruise.com; one-way 750,000Rp) Boats link Sanur, Nusa Lembongan, Senggigi and the Gilis.

FROM LOMBOK

Coming from Lombok, you can travel by fast boat from Teluk Nare/Teluk Kade north of Senggigi. Many of these services are operated by hotels and dive outfits based in the Gilis (making pre-arranged diving/accommodation and transfer options appealing), but private charters with local owners are also possible. Most people still use the public boats that leave from Bangsal Harbour.

Boat tickets at Bangsal Harbour are sold at the port's large ticket office, which is where you can also charter a boat. Buy a ticket elsewhere and you're getting played.

Public boats to the Gilis run most frequently before noon; after that you shouldn't wait much more than an hour for boats to Gili T or Gili Air, while special boats depart for Gili Meno at 2pm and 5pm. With the exception of these afternoon transfers to Gili Meno, all boats leave, in both directions, only when full – about 45 people. If the seas are high and the boat (over)loaded, riding these battered outriggers can be a hair-raising experience. When no public boat is running to your Gili, you may have to charter a boat (350,000Rp to 500,000Rp, for up to 10 people), or decide this is the safer option in any case.

One-way public fares are 14,000Rp to Gili Air, 15,000Rp to Gili Meno (25,000Rp for the special afternoon boats) and 20,000Rp to Gili Trawangan. Boats often pull up on the beaches; be prepared to wade ashore.

Public fast boats now run almost hourly in daytime on a route linking Gili T, Gili Meno, Gili Air and Bangsal; they cost 85,000Rp.

Although Bangsal Harbour has had a bad reputation for years, hassles here are much reduced. One still-common rort is for shuttle buses to drop passengers just short of the harbour, where *cidomo* drivers, claiming there's some distance to go, ask 60,000Rp to complete the journey. Ignore them and walk the last 300m. Other touts may claim the public boats aren't running, or that you need to buy mosquito repellent and sunblock before getting to the Gilis. Ignore them too, but note that anyone who helps you with

LOMBOK FOREST TOUR

The food-themed **Lombok Forest Tour** (☑ 0823 4277 5358; www.facebook.com/myforestadventure; Bangsal harbour; half-day tour 400,000Rp) departs from Bangsal Harbour and is a great pre- or post-Gili Islands trip into Lombok's little-visited northwestern interior. Depending on the time of year, Ikbal and his team may have you climbing a palm tree to tap it for nectar, sampling the fruit of the cacao and coffee plants or foraging for all sorts of delectable surprises.

bags deserves a tip (10,000Rp per bag is appropriate). There are ATMs.

Coming by public transport via Mataram and Senggigi, catch a bus or bemo to Pemenang, from where it's a 1.2km walk to Bangsal Harbour – or 5000Rp by *ojek* (motorcycle taxi). A metered taxi to the port will take you to the harbour. From Senggigi, Perama (p326) offers a bus and boat connection to the Gilis for a reasonable 150,000Rp (two hours).

Arriving in Bangsal, you'll be offered rides in shared vehicles at the port. To Senggigi, 100,000Rp is a fair price. Otherwise, walk 500m down the access road past the huge tsunami shelter to the **Blue Bird Lombok Taksi stand** (☑ 0370-645000; www.bluebirdgroup.com), always the best taxi choice, for metered rides to Senggigi (around 100,000Rp), the airport (220,000Rp) and Kuta (250,000Rp).

❶ Getting Around

There's no motorised transport on the Gilis – one of their greatest charms. There are *cidomos* (horse-drawn carts), but due to animal welfare concerns, we can't recommend using them.

BOAT

Public fast boats run almost hourly in daytime on a route linking Gili T, Gili Meno, Gili Air and Bangsal; they cost 85,000Rp. This makes it easy to hop from one Gili to another.

There's also a slow island-hopping boat service that loops between all three islands (25,000Rp to 35,000Rp). There is typically a morning boat and an afternoon one, but it's best to check the latest timetable at the islands' docks. You can always charter boats between the islands (300,000Rp to 400,000Rp).

CIDOMO

We cannot recommend using *cidomo* (horse-drawn carts) due to the significant concerns about the treatment of the horses.

WALKING & CYCLING

The Gilis are flat and easy to get around by foot. Bicycles are available for hire on all three islands (40,000Rp to 60,000Rp per day). They are great for quickly getting around on the paved lanes inland, though much less fun on the perimeter paths along the water as there are long stretches of deep sand that mean you'll be shoving your bike along in the hot sun.

Gili Trawangan

📞 0370 / POP 1700

Gili Trawangan's heaving main drag, busy with bikes, *cidomos* and mobs of barely clad visitors, can surprise those expecting a languid island retreat. Instead, a bustling string of lounge bars, hip guesthouses, waterfront cafes, convenience stores and dive schools clamours for attention.

And yet behind this glitzy facade, a bohemian character endures, with rickety warungs and reggae joints surviving between the cocktail tables, and quiet retreats dotting the much-less-busy north coast. Even as massive 200-plus-room hotels begin to colonise the gentrifying west coast, you can head just inland to a village laced with sandy lanes roamed by free-range roosters, fussing *ibu* (mothers) and wild-haired kids playing hopscotch. Here the call of the muezzin, not happy hour, defines the time of day.

🏖 Beaches

Gili T is ringed by the sort of powdery white sand people expect to find on Bali, but don't. It can be crowded along the bar-lined main part of the strip, but walk just a bit north or south and west and you'll find some of Gili T's nicest swimming and snorkelling beaches. You can discover more solitude in parts of the west and north coasts, where it will be you and your towel on the sand – although water and Bintang vendors are never far away.

Note that at low tide large portions of the west and north coasts have rocks and coral near the surface, which makes trying to get off the shore deeply unpleasant.

Many people simply enjoy the sensational views of Lombok and Gunung Rinjani (from the east coast) as well as Bali and Gunung Agung (west).

🏃 Activities

Almost everything to do on Gili T will involve the water at some point, though yoga, spas and culinary classes all vie for attention.

Diving & Snorkelling

There's fun snorkelling off the beach 200m north of the boat landing – the coral isn't in the best shape here, but there are tons of fish and turtles. The reef is in slightly better shape off the northwest coast, but at low tide you'll have to scramble over some sharp dead coral (bring rubber booties) to access it. Snorkel-gear rental averages 50,000Rp per day.

Trawangan is a major diving hot spot, with two-dozen professional scuba and freediving schools. Most dive schools and shops have good accommodation for clients who want to book a package.

Safety standards are reasonably high, but with the proliferation of new dive schools on Gili T, several have formed the Gili Island Divers Association (GIDA). We highly recommend diving with GIDA-associated shops, which come together for monthly meetings on conservation and dive-impact issues. They all observe common standards relating to the safety and number of their divers. They carry oxygen on their boats, have working radios and dedicate time and resources to the preservation of the reefs, waters and shoreline. They also have a price agreement for fun dives, training and certification. Sample prices:

Introductory Dive 900,000Rp

Open Water Course 5,500,000Rp

Rescue Diver & EFR Course 7,000,000Rp

★ **Freedive Gili**   DIVING
(Map p345; 📞 0370-619 7180; www.freedive gili.com; Jl Raya Trawangan; level I/level II course 4,250,000/5,595,000Rp; ⏱ 8am-8pm) Freediving is a breath-holding technique that allows you to explore greater depths than snorkelling (to 30m and beyond). Owned by an expert diver who has touched 111m on a single breath, Freedive Gili offers two-day level I and three-day level II courses. After a two-day course many students are able to get down to 20m.

★ **Blue Marlin Dive**   DIVING
(Map p345; 📞 0370-613 2424; www.bluemarlin dive.com; Jl Raya Trawangan; introductory dive 950,000Rp) This is Gili T's original dive shop

Gili Trawangan

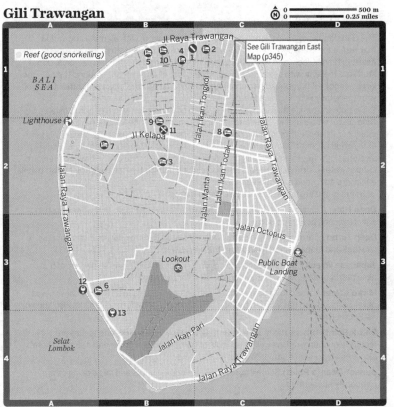

See Gili Trawangan East Map (p345)

Reef (good snorkelling)

BALI SEA

Lighthouse

Jl Raya Trawangan

Jl Kelapa

Jalan Ikan Tongkol

Jalan Manta

Jalan Ikan Todak

Jalan Raya Trawangan

Jalan Octopus

Lookout

Public Boat Landing

Selat Lombok

Jalan Ikan Pari

Jalan Raya Trawangan

and one of the best tech diving schools in the world. It's also home to one of Gili T's classic – and liveliest – bars.

Trawangan Dive   DIVING
(Map p345; ☏0370-614 9220; www.trawangan dive.com; Jl Raya Trawangan; 5 guided nitrox boat dives from 2,700,000Rp) 🏊 A top, long-running dive shop and GIDA member with a fun pool-party vibe. Ask how you can join the regular beach clean-ups with the Gili Eco Trust. Also runs Biorock coral gardening courses and a wide range of tech courses (including rebreather training).

Manta Dive   DIVING
(Map p345; ☏0878 6555 6914; www.manta-dive. com; Jl Raya Trawangan; open-water courses 5,500,000Rp) The biggest SSI dive school and one of the best on the island, Manta has a large compound that spans the main road. It has instructor training, tech programs and a pool.

Gili Trawangan

DIVING THE GILIS

The Gili Islands are an extremely popular dive destination, with plentiful and varied marine life to be encountered across about 25 closely packed sites. Turtles (green and hawksbill) and black- and white-tip reef sharks are common, and the macro life (small stuff) is excellent, with seahorses, pipefish and lots of crustaceans. Around the full moon, large schools of bumphead parrotfish appear to feast on coral spawn; at other times of year (generally February and March) manta rays cruise past dive sites.

Do note that while the Gilis have their share of virgin sites, years of bomb fishing, El Niño–induced bleaching, coral anchoring and poor tourist behaviour have damaged many corals above 18m, making deeper dives more visually appealing. Visibility is generally good (20m to 30m), temperatures range from 25°C to 30°C and usually calm stretches of water make the Gilis an excellent place to learn to dive. However, there are deeper waters, stronger currents and more challenging sites, too, catering to drift diving and more advanced practitioners.

Some of the best dive sites include the following:

Deep Halik A canyon-like site ideally suited to drift diving. Black- and white-tip sharks are often seen at 28m to 30m.

Deep Turbo At around 30m, this site is ideally suited to nitrox diving. It has impressive sea fans and leopard sharks hidden in the crevasses.

Japanese Wreck For experienced divers only (it lies at 45m), this shipwreck of a Japanese patrol boat (c WWII) is another site ideal for tech divers.

Mirko's Reef Named for a beloved dive instructor who passed away, this canyon was never bombed and has vibrant, pristine soft and table coral formations. It's also known as 'Secret Reef'.

Shark Point Perhaps the most exhilarating Gili dive: reef sharks and turtles are very regularly encountered, as well as schools of bumphead parrotfish and mantas. There's also a newly sunken tugboat to explore.

Sunset (Manta Point) Some impressive table coral; sharks and large pelagics are frequently encountered.

Lutwala Dive DIVING
(Map p341; ☑ 0877 6549 2615; www.lutwala. com; Jl Raya Trawangan; divemaster course 14,000,000Rp; ☺ 8am-6pm) A nitrox and five-star PADI centre, this dive shop is a member of GIDA (Gili Islands Divers Association) and rents top-quality snorkelling gear. There's accommodation on-site (rooms from 700,000Rp) plus a very nice garden cafe-bar to relax in post-plunge. Make sure you say hello to the parrots.

Surfing

Trawangan has a fast right reef break off its southern tip that is best surfed December to March or on a windless high-season day. The beach nearby is lined with vendors renting boards.

Walking & Cycling

Trawangan is perfect for exploring on foot or by bike. You can walk around the whole island in a couple of hours – if you finish at the hill on the southwestern corner (which

has the remains of an old Japanese gun placement circa WWII), you'll have terrific sunset views of Bali's Gunung Agung.

Bikes (per day from 40,000Rp to 70,000Rp; bargain hard) are a great way to get around. You'll find loads of rental outlets on the main strip, or your guesthouse can help you out. Beware the sandy, bike-unfriendly north coast and note that the paths across the interior of the island are usually in the best shape for cycling.

Sila CYCLING
(Map p345; ☑ 0878 6562 3015; Jl Raya Trawangan; bike rentals per day from 50,000Rp) Has a huge range of bikes for rent, including two-seaters. Also does boat trips.

Yoga & Wellness
Desha Spa MASSAGE
(Map p345; ☑ 0877 6510 5828; Jl Kelapa; ☺ 9am-9pm) Not as bare-bones as the massage parlours on the strip nor as posh and expensive as the hotel spas, this spot on the cross-

island road is your happy medium. In addition to the standard massage options, there are coconut scrubs, pedicures, facials or aloe vera sunburn treatments.

Gili Yoga
YOGA

(Map p345; ☑0370-619 7180; www.giliyoga.com; Jl Raya Trawangan; classes from 120,000Rp; ⏰7am-6pm) Runs vinyasa, fusion, yin and hatha classes. It's attached to Freedive Gili (p340).

Courses

Sweet & Spicy Cooking School
COOKING

(Map p345; ☑0878 6577 6429; www.facebook.com/gilicookingschool; Jl Raya Trawangan; classes from 385,000Rp) Learn how to transform chillis and myriad other seasonings into spicy and flavourful Indonesian dishes at these entertaining daily cooking classes. As always, you get to eat your work.

🛏 Sleeping

Gili T has reached a saturation point with hundreds of registered places to stay, ranging from thatched huts to sleek, air-conditioned villas with private pools. In peak season (July and August) the best places can book out, but with so much competition, prices have dropped considerably. You'll find steep low-season discounts.

★Gili Beach Bum Hotel
HOSTEL $

(Map p345; ☑0877 6526 7037; www.gilibeachbum.com; Jl Raya Trawangan; dm/r from 150,000/350,000Rp; ❄️🛜🏊) This co-ed dorm complex has 19 triple rooms, some under a thatched Torajan-style roof. The rooms have concrete floors, high ceilings, lockers and their own bathrooms. Out front is the Lava Bar (open until 1am and often heaving) and there are weekly pool parties.

Gili La Boheme Sister
HOSTEL $

(Map p345; ☑0853 3733 4339; Jl Ikan Duyung; dm with fan/air-con 130,000/150,000Rp; ❄️🛜) Exposed brick walls, repurposed wood, tiled floors and a rainbow of colours – that's the design formula at this quirky, eye-pleasing hostel. Some beds are located in funky hexagonal rooms and there are several chill common areas.

Gili Mansion
HOSTEL $

(Map p345; ☑0852 3836 3836; https://gilimansion.com; Jl Ikan Hiu; dm/d from 80,000/200,000Rp; ❄️🛜🏊) Though the gimmicky castle theme is a real island buzzkill, this always-booming hostel is nevertheless one of the best budget bets in town with clean three-bed dorms, super cheap (if soulless) private rooms and a non-stop party vibe centred around the pool.

Mango Tree Homestay
HOMESTAY $

(Map p345; ☑0823 5912 0421; Jl Karang Biru; d 300,000Rp) This friendly homestay in a quieter part of the village offers eight simple doubles facing each other across a shady, fern-filled courtyard. The young staff are relaxed but competent, ukelele music frequently sweetens the air and bikes can be hired for 40,000Rp per day.

Woodstock
BUNGALOW $

(Map p345; ☑0878 6433 7237; www.woodstockgili.com; Jl Karang Biru; r with fan/air-con from 350,000/600,000Rp; ❄️🛜🏊) Should the vibe surprise you, given the name? Commune with the spirit of the Dead, drop out with Baez and turn on with Hendrix in 12 good-value rooms with tribal accents, private porches and outdoor bathrooms, all surrounding a laid-back pool area.

★Blu d'aMare
BUNGALOW $$

(Map p345; ☑0858 8866 2490; Jl Raya Trawangan; r from 500,000Rp; ❄️🛜) At Blu d'aMare you can bed down in one of five lovely 1920s Javanese houses (joglo). Features include gorgeous old wood floors, queen beds, and freshwater showers in a sunken bathroom. It has a fine, Euro-accented cafe.

★Eden Cottages
COTTAGE $$

(Map p341; ☑0819 1799 6151; www.edencottages.com; Jl Lili Laut; cottages 600,000-900,000Rp; ❄️🛜🏊) Eden takes the form of six posh, upgraded bungalows wrapped around a pool, fringed by a garden and shaded by a coconut grove. Rooms have tasteful furnishings, stone bathrooms, TV-DVD and freshwater showers. The charming expat owner does all she can to ensure her guests' serenity. The veggie cafe-bar is a delight.

Gili Teak Resort
BOUTIQUE HOTEL $$

(Map p341; ☑0853 3383 6324; www.giliteak.com; Jl Raya Trawangan; r from 1,200,000Rp; ❄️🛜🏊) New Age bungalows have teak walls and a stylish, simple design that lets in lots of light. Terraces for each of the 11 units have plush loungers, plus there's a lovely seating area down by the ocean, all of which begs guests to settle back, relax and let the days drift by. The grounds on a quiet stretch of west coast are attractive.

Coconut Garden
BUNGALOW $$

(Map p341; ☑0819 0795 6926; www.coconut gardenresort.com; off Jl Kelapa; r incl breakfast from 750,000Rp; ❋ 🛜 ⏣) An atmospheric spot with six bright and airy glass-fronted Javanese-style houses with tiled roofs connected to outdoor terrazzo bathrooms. Expect plush linens, queen beds, a rolling lawn dotted with coco palms and a small pool. It's on its own in a quiet inland quarter of the island and can be hard to find. Call ahead.

Jali Resort
BOUTIQUE HOTEL $$

(Map p341; ☑0817 000 5254; www.jaliresort gilitrawangan.com; Jl Nautilius; r incl breakfast 1,350,000Rp; ❋ 🛜 ⏣) Sixteen turquoise-tiled rooms surround a frangipani-shaded pool in this exceedingly stylish and pleasantly compact boutique hotel.

Indigo Bungalows
GUESTHOUSE $$

(Map p345; ☑0818 0371 0909; www.facebook. com/indigogilit; Jl Penyu; r from 550,000Rp; ❋ 🛜 ⏣) In the crowded Gili T midrange market, Indigo stands out for its attention to detail. The six rooms have hot water, patios and views of the pool or gardens. It's got a nice, quiet compound feel.

Amora Villa
BUNGALOW $$

(Map p345; ☑0822 3521 5244; https://amoravilla gili.com; off Jl Kepiting; bungalow incl breakfast 500,000-1,500,000Rp; ❋ 🛜 ⏣) Thirteen *lumbung* (rice-barn) cottages, set deep in the village, tucked up against the hillside, surrounding a large pool. They're a great deal off season, but overpriced in peak times.

Alexyane Paradise
BUNGALOW $$

(Map p345; ☑0878 6599 9645; oceanepara-dise@hotmail.com; Jl Ikan Baronang; r 300,000-900,000Rp; ❋ 🛜) Five great-quality dark-wood cottages (one is family-sized) with high ceilings, bamboo beds and lovely light-flooded outdoor bathrooms.

Balé Sampan
HOTEL $$

(Map p345; www.balesampanbungalows.com; Jl Raya Trawangan; r incl breakfast garden/pool 910,000/1,000,000Rp; ❋ 🛜 ⏣) On a nice wide-open stretch of beach. The 13 fine modern-edge rooms have stone bathrooms and plush duvet covers. Other highlights include a freshwater pool and a proper English breakfast.

Alam Gili
HOTEL $$

(Map p341; ☑0370-613 0466; www.alamgili.com; Jl Raya Trawangan; r from US$75; ❋ 🛜 ⏣) A lush mature garden and a quiet beach location

are the main draws here. The nine rooms and villas in a small compound boast elegant lashings of old-school Balinese style. A small pool and a cafe are on the beach.

★ Gili Treehouses
VILLA $$$

(Map p341; ☑0819 1601 6634, WhatsApp +6428 408 2789; www.gilitreehouses.com; off Jl Kelapa; r from 2,800,000Rp; ❋ 🛜 ⏣) These five 'tree houses' (really stilted wooden villas) are a welcome change from the tried and true Gili T villa concept. Though tightly packed together, each feels remarkably secluded with cool chill spaces below the rooms that have kitchenettes, loungers and private pools. Perks include free bikes and portable wi-fi boxes.

★ Wilson's Retreat
RESORT $$$

(Map p341; ☑0878 6177 2111; www.wilsons-retreat.com; Jl Raya Trawangan; r/villa incl breakfast from 1,400,000/2,500,000Rp; ❋ 🛜 ⏣) Wilson's has 16 rooms plus four villas with private pools. The setting is expansive, stylish and classy, but it still manages some Gili languor. The excellent cafe overlooks a fine stretch of beach.

★ Gili Joglo
VILLA $$$

(Map p345; ☑0813 5678 4741; www.gilijoglo.com; Jl Ikan Hiu; villas from 1,500,000Rp; ❋ 🛜) You'll find three fabulous villas here. One is crafted out of an antique *joglo* (traditional Javanese house) with polished concrete floors, two bedrooms and a massive indoor/outdoor great room. Though slightly smaller, we prefer the one built from two 1950s *gladaks* (middle-class homes). Rooms come with butler service.

Pearl of Trawangan
RESORT $$$

(Map p345; ☑0813 3715 6999; www.pearlof trawangan.com; Jl Raya Trawangan; r incl breakfast from 1,600,000Rp; ❋ 🛜 ⏣) Sinuous bamboo and thatch architecture echo the snakelike curves of the pool at this upscale property at the south end of the strip. There are tidy bungalows with 91 rooms on the inland side of the beach walk. Terraces boast very comfortable loungers. On the actual beach, there's a plush beach club.

Gili Eco Villas
VILLA $$$

(Map p341; ☑0370-613 6057; www.giliecovillas. com; Jl Raya Trawangan; r/villa from US$120/250; ❋ 🛜 ⏣) 🌱 Nineteen classy rooms and villas, made from recycled teak salvaged from old Javanese colonial buildings, are set back from the beach on Trawangan's relaxed

Gili Trawangan East

N 0 ——— 200 m
0 ——— 0.1 miles

Trawangan Slope (15m)

BALI SEA

Jalan Raya Trawangan
Jalan Nautilius **21**
Jalan Ikan Kakatua **2**
Jl Kelapa
11
10
Jalan Ikan Duyung **13**
Jl Penyu **16**
19
Jalan Karang Biru **15** **7** *Mosque*
17 **14**
Jalan Octopus **6** **12**
24 **3**
9 **25**
Jalan Kepiting *Public Boat Landing*
Jalan Bintang Laut **4**
22
Jalan Gumi-Cumi **20**
1
26 **5**
Jalan Raya Trawangan
+ *Blue Island Medical Clinic*
18
23

Gili Trawangan East

Activities, Courses & Tours
1 Blue Marlin Dive Centre	A6
2 Desha Spa	A3
Freedive Gili	(see 3)
3 Gili Yoga	B5
4 Manta Dive	B5
5 Sila	A6
6 Sweet & Spicy Cooking School	B5
7 Trawangan Dive	B4

Sleeping
8 Alexyane Paradise	A6
9 Amora Villa	A5
10 Balé Sampan	A4
11 Blu d'aMare	A3
12 Gili Beach Bum Hotel	B5
13 Gili Joglo	A4
14 Gili La Boheme Sister	A4
15 Gili Mansion	A4
16 Indigo Bungalows	A4
17 Mango Tree Homestay	A4
18 Pearl of Trawangan	A7
19 Woodstock	A4

Eating
20 Fan	A6
21 Hellocapitano	A3
22 Kayu Café	B5
23 Pearl Beach Lounge	A7
24 Regina	A5
25 Warung Dewi	B5

Drinking & Nightlife
Blue Marlin	(see 1)
26 Tir na Nog	A6

Shopping
Abdi	(see 22)

north coast. Comfort and style are combined with solid green principles (water is recycled and there's an organic vegetable garden).

Kelapa Villas VILLA $$$
(Map p341; ☑ 0812 375 6003; www.kelapavillas. com; Jl Kelapa; villas from 1,500,000Rp; ❄ ☎ ⚌) Luxury development in an inland location with a selection of 18 commodious villas (all with private pools) that offer style and space in abundance. A tennis court and a gym are in the complex.

✕ Eating

Gili T now rivals Bali in its culinary prowess with slick coffee shops, creative Indo fusion eateries and plenty of vegan and health-food cafes. In the evenings, numerous places on the main strip display and grill delicious fresh seafood. Pick by what looks good (it should all be superfresh), and by whose grilling skills seem to be superior.

★ Jali Kitchen
ASIAN $

(Map p341; ☑ 0817 000 5254; www.facebook.com/Jali.Kitchen; Jl Nautilius, Jali Resort; mains 45,000-70,000Rp; ⊙ 7am-11pm; 🛜🍴) Distressed wood, gorgeous tiles and abundant foliage combine to give this eye-pleasing restaurant a chic and earthy vibe. The Asian-fusion dishes combine the familiar with the exotic in intriguing ways, and there are several options for vegetarians. Vietnamese noodles, the curries and the pad Thai are standouts.

★ Warung Dewi
INDONESIAN $

(Map p345; ☑ 0819 0763 3826; Jl Kardinal; mains 25,000-35,000Rp; ⊙ 7am-8pm) The best traditional warung on Gili T is just a few steps back from the high-priced bustle of the main strip. The *nasi campur* is fantastic (coconut sambal, jackfruit curry, fried chicken and several vegetable sides is a common combination) while vegetarians will like the *plecing kangkung* (a spicy Sasak water spinach dish).

Hellocapitano
CAFE $

(Map p345; ☑ 0853 3313 4110; www.hellocapitano.com; Jl Nautilius; mains 45,000-75,000Rp; ⊙ 7am-9pm) A whimsical little pastel shack where you can order delicious smoothie bowls, iced lattes, burgers or local bites (try the chicken rendang!). Sit upstairs for a breezy sea view and be sure to ask the owner about his land- and water-based island tours.

★ Pituq Waroeng
VEGAN $$

(Map p341; ☑ 0812 3677 5161; http://pituq.com; Jl Kelapa; small plates 20,000-30,000Rp; ⊙ 9am-10pm; 🍴) Enjoy classic Indonesian fare reinterpreted as exquisite vegan tapas at this back-lane haven. Gather a group of friends, sit together at one of the low-rise tables and order like there is no tomorrow as proceeds go to a variety of projects to improve local living conditions.

Fan
CHINESE $$

(Map p345; ☑ 0852 5331 9394; www.facebook.com/fanchinesefood; Jl Cumi Cumi; mains 50,000-85,000Rp; ⊙ 11.30am-9.30pm) Homemade dumplings, wontons and broad noodles are the stars of this tiny Chinese restaurant that feels like a secret hideaway. You'll dine at one long table under a tree and leave with new friends.

Pearl Beach Lounge
INTERNATIONAL $$

(Map p345; ☑ 0370-619 4884; www.pearlbeachlounge.com; Jl Raya Trawangan; mains 70,000-200,000Rp; ⊙ 7am-11pm; 🛜) The bamboo flows only a little less fluidly than the beer at this high-concept beachside lounge and restaurant. During the day, spending 100,000Rp on food and drink from the burger- and salad-filled menu gets you access to comfy beach loungers. At night the striking bamboo main pavilion comes alive, and more complex steak and seafood mains are on offer.

Regina
PIZZA $$

(Map p345; ☑ 0877 6506 6255; Jl Ikan Hiu; pizza 40,000-100,000Rp; ⊙ 5-11pm) The wood-fired oven rarely gets a break at this excellent Italian joint, just inland. At busy times there's a long line for takeaway pizzas, but a better option is to find a bamboo table in the garden and have some cold ones with the fine thin-crust pies. A sign announces: 'no pizza pineapple'. Ahh, the sound of authenticity...

Kayu Cafe
CAFE $$

(Map p345; ☑ 0819 1749 6698; www.facebook.com/kayucafe; Jl Raya Trawangan; mains 60,000-80,000Rp; ⊙ 7am-9pm; 🛜) Kayu has a lovely array of healthy baked goods, salads, sandwiches, rice bowls and the island's best juices. Savour it in air-con comfort or across the lane where the beachside tables have sweeping views of the boats zipping to and fro.

🍷 Drinking & Nightlife

Gili T has oodles of beachside drinking dens, ranging from sleek lounge bars to simple shacks. Parties are held several nights a week, shifting between mainstay bars such as Tir na Nog and various other upstarts. The strip south of the pier is the centre for raucous nightlife with places that were once bars now rapidly evolving into full-fledged clubs.

★ Casa Vintage Beach
CAFE $$

(Map p341; www.casavintagebeach.com; Jl Raya Trawangan; mains 70,000-120,000Rp; ⊙ 10am-11pm) Facing Bali's Gunung Agung (which sometimes appears through the haze) and some superb sunsets, Casa Vintage is the best place to enjoy a sundowner on Trawangan. A brochure-perfect beach is littered with cushions and loungers, trees shelter hammocks and trestles. The food is fresh and healthy, with juices, smoothies, wraps and other tasty fare.

Exile BAR

(Map p341; ☑0819 0772 1858; http://theexile gilit.com; Jl Raya Trawangan; ⊙8am-late) This locally owned beach bar has a party vibe at all hours. It's 20 minutes from the main strip on foot, or an easy bike ride. There is also a compound of 10 woven bamboo bungalows with rooms (from 350,000Rp), just in case home seems too far away.

Tir na Nog PUB

(Map p345; ☑0370-613 9463; www.tirnanogbar. com; Jl Raya Trawangan; ⊙7am-2am Thu-Tue, to 3am Wed; ☎) Known simply as 'the Irish', this hangar of hangovers has a sports-bar interior with big screens. Its shoreside open-air bar is probably the busiest meeting spot on the island. It serves bar chow such as fajitas and spicy wings (mains 50,000Rp to 100,000Rp). Jovial mayhem truly reigns on 'party night' every Wednesday. There's also live music Sunday nights.

Blue Marlin BAR

(Map p345; Jl Raya Trawangan; ⊙8am-late) Of all the party bars, this upper-level venue has the largest dance floor and the meanest sound system – it pumps trance and tribal beats on Mondays.

NUSA TENGGARA GILI TRAWANGAN

GREEN GILI

When you pay your hotel or diving bill on the Gilis you may be offered the chance to pay an 'Eco Donation' (50,000Rp per person). It's a voluntary donation, set up by the pioneering **Gili Eco Trust** (www.giliecotrust.com) to improve the islands' environment.

It's a worthy cause. The environmental pressure on the Gilis as their popularity has grown is enormous. Intensive development and rubbish plus offshore reef damage from fishers using cyanide and dynamite to harvest fish have been just some of the problems. Up to 10,000 visitors and workers arrive on the islands each day.

Gili Eco Trust has several initiatives to help:

➜ Selling reusable shopping bags to cut down on plastic-bag use, and encouraging restaurants to stop using plastic straws (we didn't see any when we visited!).

➜ An aggressive education campaign to get locals and business owners to recycle their rubbish. There are now over 1000 recycling bins on the islands.

➜ A long-term scheme to recycle virtually all the trash on the islands with a rubbish bank.

➜ Care of the islands' horses – vet clinics are offered and there are education programs in horse care for drivers.

➜ Biorock, an artificial reef-restoration program that now has over 150 installations around the islands.

➜ Installing more than 150 mooring buoys to stop coral anchoring.

There are many ways visitors to the Gilis can help, in addition to paying the Eco Tax:

Clean up the beach Gili Eco Trust organises regular beach clean-ups (typically on Fridays at 5pm). More hands are always needed and you'll be rewarded for your time with some free treats or a beer from the weekly sponsor.

Report horse mistreatment Anyone seeing a *cidomo* (horse-drawn cart) driver mistreating a horse can get the number of the cart and report it to the Eco Trust (0813 3960 0553), which will follow up with the driver. Unfortunately, many transport carts with their heavy loads of construction supplies and Bintang have no cart numbers for reporting.

Build a reef For 10,000,000Rp you'll get two dives a day for two weeks, the opportunity to help build a Biorock installation, and various specialist diving certifications. Gili Eco Trust has details.

Refill water bottles Help cut down on plastic waste by refilling your water bottle at designated stations all across the Gilis. Some places offer water refills for free; others for about 2000Rp or 3000Rp (way cheaper than buying a new bottle!). Download the app Refill Bali to find the closest tank.

Shopping

Abdi CLOTHING

(Map p345; Jl Raya Trawangan; ☺10am-8pm) Forgot your favourite frock? Shop for flouncy beachwear at this stylish shop.

Information

Gili T has abundant ATMs on the main strip and even on the west coast.

Blue Island Medical Clinic (Map p345; ☑0819 9970 5701; http://blueislandclinic.com; Jl Raya Trawangan; ☺24hr) Medical clinic among the shops immediately south of Hotel Vila Ombak. Also has clinics on Gili Air and Gili Meno.

Getting There & Away

You can buy tickets and catch public and island-hopping boats at the **public boat landing** (Map p341). While you wait for your ship to sail, note the amazing number of Bintang bottles arriving full and leaving empty. Several of the fast-boat companies have offices on Gili T. These fast boats anchor all along the beach on the east side.

Gili Meno

☑0370 / POP 750

Gili Meno is the smallest of the three Gili Islands and a good setting for your desert-island fantasy. Ringed by gorgeous beaches and teeming reefs, Meno is also the quietest and most traditional of the three, beloved more of honeymooners and mature travellers than the full-moon-party set.

Most accommodation is strung out along the east coast, near the most picturesque beach. Inland you'll find scattered homesteads, coconut plantations and a salty lake. The once-lonely west coast is seeing some high-profile development, including a soon-to-open enormous beachside condo project called Bask (www.baskgilimeno.com) that is slated to have over 85 villas. It's got some powerful Australian backers and a high-profile pitchman, ex-*Baywatch* star David Hasselhoff (aka 'The Hoff').

Beaches

Ringed by sand, Gili Meno has one of the best strips of beach in the Gilis at its southeast corner. The beach is wide and the sand powdery white; swimming and snorkelling are excellent. The west coast is rockier, with outcrops and coral near the surface at low tide. Meno's northeast also has nice sand, although erosion is a problem in parts.

Activities

Like the other Gilis, most of the fun here involves getting wet. Additionally, walking around the island is scenic and takes less than two hours.

Although you can rent bikes for 50,000Rp per day, you won't get far. The beach path from the southern tip right around up the west coast to the bottom of the salt lake is a shadeless dry sand path that may have you pushing your ride. You can go for a little jaunt to the northwest coast on the good path along the north side of the lake, but again, soft sand along the very north makes riding a chore.

Diving & Snorkelling

Snorkelling is good off the northeast coast, on the west coast towards the north, and also around the site of the vast new Bask hotel on the west coast, where you'll find the underwater sculpture Nest. Gear is available from 50,000Rp per day from guesthouses or dive shops (of which there are only a few on this island). **Meno Slope** and **Meno Wall** are two top dive sites.

★**Nest** SNORKELLING

Gili Meno's most photographed sight, Nest isn't even on the island itself, but rather just offshore from the BASK resort. BASK commissioned British artist Jason deCaires Taylor to create an underwater sculpture comprised of 48 life-sized human figures made from pH neutral, environmental grade concrete. Over time, the figures will provide a new home for soft corals and sponges, contributing to reef regeneration.

Nest is easily accessible from the shore in about 3m of water, though most of its visitors boat over from Gili T and Gili Air.

Gili Meno Divers DIVING

(☑0878 6409 5490; www.gilimenodivers.com; Kontiki Cottages; introductory dive from 900,000Rp; ☺9am-5pm) French and Indonesian owned, this well-respected dive shop offers a range of courses, including freediving and underwater photography.

Blue Ocean WATER SPORTS

(☑0813 3950 9859; Fantastic Cottages; boat tours per person 150,000Rp) The irrepressible Mr Dean offers snorkelling boat tours of the rich waters around the Gilis. Tours are two to three hours. He'll drop you at another

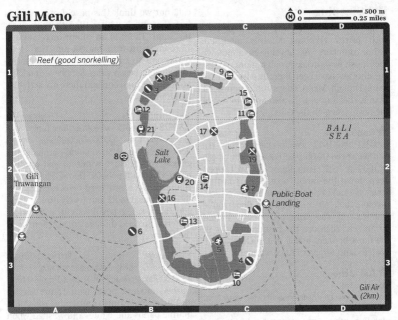

Gili Meno

Gili Meno

island, so you can check out underwater delights as you island-hop.

Divine Divers — DIVING

(☑ 0852 4057 0777; www.divinedivers.com; guided dives from 490,000Rp) This Meno-only dive shop is on a sweet slice of beach on the west coast. It has six rooms, a pool and good dive-and-stay packages.

Blue Marlin Dive — DIVING

(☑ 0370-639980; www.bluemarlindive.com; guided boat dives 490,000Rp) The Meno outlet of the Trawangan original, this is a well-respected mainstream dive shop.

Yoga
★ Mao Meno — YOGA

(☑ 0817 003 0777; www.mao-meno.com; classes from 120,000Rp) Offers two daily classes in styles that include hatha and vinyasa in a beautiful natural wood pavilion. It has cottages on its inland compound that range from simple to luxurious and rent from US$36 per night.

🛏 Sleeping

Meno now leads the way in Gili growth, with prices climbing sharply alongside visitor numbers. As developers announce their posh new projects, older, more modest guesthouses have been literally wiped off the map. Though Meno skews more upmarket than its neighbours, it's also home to two of the best hostels in the Gilis.

★ Rabbit Tree   HOSTEL $

(☑0812 9149 1843; www.therabbittree.com; dm with fan/air-con 110,000/135,000Rp, d with air-con 240,000Rp; ✳🛜) You know you've tripped deep down the rabbit hole when you find yourself sleeping on a dorm bed in a technicolour ball pit, or when the floor you're walking on suddenly becomes a netted hammock. Such are the befuddling joys of the most bonkers hostel in the Gilis, a true Wonderland for every Alice wannabe.

★ Gili Meno
Eco Hostel   HOSTEL $

(www.facebook.com/gilimenoecohostel; dm/r from 100,000/225,000Rp) 🏖 A fantasy in driftwood, bamboo and coconut-palm thatch, this is the place you dream about when you're stuck in the freezing cold at home waiting for a train. A shady lounge, tree houses, and a beach bar open onto the sand. There are trivia nights, pizza nights, music, bonfires and other social activities.

★ Meno Dream Resort   BUNGALOW $$

(☑0819 1596 1251; http://gilimenobungalows. com; bungalows incl breakfast from 500,000Rp; ✳🛜🍴) This intimate property has just five bungalows surrounding a central pool and tranquil garden. Each has a unique character with art on the walls, gorgeous sunken showers and covered verandas. Guests rave about the onsite restaurant, free bikes and friendly service from owners Made and Berni.

Biru Meno
Beach Bungalows   BUNGALOW $$

(☑0823 4143 4317; www.birumeno.com; d/f bungalow 1,000,000/1,500,000Rp; ✳🛜) Attractive bungalows in a tree-shaded compound are the headline feature in this unassuming but welcoming resort. The beach is just over the shore path. The cafe has a wood-burning pizza oven.

Seri Resort   RESORT $$

(☑0822 3759 6677; www.seriresortgilimeno.com; r 400,000-1,600,000Rp; ✳🛜🍴) It's a tough call, but we think this beachfront resort is just *that* much whiter than the surrounding sand. There is an interesting range of 75 rooms here, from budget huts that share bathrooms to suites in three-storey blocks, to luxurious beach villas. Service is good, the atmosphere high end and there are activities including yoga.

Ana Bungalows   BUNGALOW $$

(☑0878 6169 6315; www.anawarung.com; r with fan/air-con from 400,000/600,000Rp; ✳🛜) Four pitched-roof, thatch-and-bamboo bungalows with picture windows and outdoor bathrooms with pebbled floors. This family-run place has a cute used-book exchange on the beach next to its four lovely dining *berugas* (open-sided pavilions) lit with paper lanterns. Seafood dinners are excellent, as is the location.

Mahamaya   BOUTIQUE HOTEL $$$

(☑0811 390 5828; www.mahamaya.co; r from 2,150,000Rp; ✳🛜🍴) 🏖 A blindingly white-washed modern pearl with resort service and 19 rooms featuring attractive rough-cut marble patios and white- and washed-wood furnishings. The restaurant is good; have dinner at the water's edge at your own private table.

🍴 Eating

Meno's dining scene is not nearly as developed as that of neighbouring islands, but almost all of its restaurants have absorbing sea views (which is just as well as service can be painfully slow).

Breakfast at one of the cafes on Meno's east coast is a sublime experience of turquoise water and Gunung Rinjani views.

★ Warung Pak
Man Buati   INDONESIAN $

(mains 25,000Rp; ⊙7am-9pm) Chef Juno became something of a local hero after the 2018 earthquakes when he tirelessly fed the Meno community with all the food he could muster. His homestyle Indonesian cooking remains the stuff of island legends.

Sasak Cafe   INDONESIAN $

(☑0332-662379; mains 40,000-45,000Rp; ⊙kitchen 7am-9pm, bar to late) Set on Meno's quiet western shore, this island-casual resto does crispy fish and other yummy Sasak dishes. At sunset, enjoy cocktails and live music as the sky takes on a rosy glow.

Ya Ya Warung INDONESIAN $
(dishes 15,000-30,000Rp; ⊘8am-10pm) Defining ramshackle, this beach food stall serves up Indonesian faves, curries, pancakes and plenty of pasta, along with the views you came to Meno to enjoy.

Webe Café INDONESIAN $
(☑0852 3787 3339; mains 30,000-75,000Rp; ⊘8am-8pm) Webe Café is a wonderful location for a meal, with low tables sunk in the sand (and some under shade) and the turquoise water just a metre away. It scores well for Sasak and Indonesian food such as *kelak kuning* (snapper in yellow spice); staff fire up a seafood barbecue most nights, too. Service can be slow.

🍸 Drinking & Nightlife

Meno is the kind of island where you stroll along a white beach, then plop down under a bamboo thatched shack for a cold beer while sand tickles your toes.

★ Brother Hood BAR
(☑0819 0717 9286; ⊘workshops 9am-5pm, cafe 8am-midnight) 🌿 Part educational hub promoting a cleaner island through garbage pick-ups (each Sunday at 3.30pm) and part workshop where you can learn to make dreamcatchers, glass cups, bamboo straws and other upcycled art (workshops by donation). Come 5pm, however, it's a raging reggae bar with the coolest vibe in the Gilis. It's right on the small lake.

Diana Café BAR
(☑0819 3317 1943; ⊘8am-2pm & 5-10pm) If you find the pace of life on Meno too busy, head to this thoroughly chilled little tiki bar. Diana couldn't be simpler: a bamboo-and-thatch bar, a few tables, hammocks and huts on the sand, a whimsical coral garden and sweet reggae in the air. Happy hours are 5pm to 7pm and the food (mains 35,000Rp to 40,000Rp) is good.

🛍 Shopping

Art Shop Botol ARTS & CRAFTS
(⊘hours vary) Art Shop Botol is a large handicrafts stall just south of Kontiki Meno hotel. Choose from masks, Sasak water baskets, wood carvings and gourds. It's run by an elderly shopkeeper with 11 children and countless grandchildren.

ℹ Information

Meno has three ATMs.

ℹ Getting There & Away

The **public boat landing** is an increasingly busy place. None of the fast boats from Bali directly serve Meno, although some provide connections. Otherwise, you can go to Gili Trawangan or Gili Air and take the regular interisland fast boat. The beach landing is the choppiest of the three Gilis; sometimes a small lighter is required to get passengers out to the fast boats.

Gili Air
☑0370 / POP 1900

Closest to Lombok, Gili Air blends Gili T's buzz and bustle with Meno's minimalist vibe. The white-sand beaches here are arguably the best of the Gili bunch and there's just enough nightlife to keep the sociable happy. Snorkelling is good right from the main strip along the east coast – a lovely sandy lane dotted with bamboo bungalows and little restaurants where you can eat virtually on top of a turquoise sea.

Though tourism dominates Gili Air's economy, coconuts, fishing and manufacturing of the fake distressed fishing-boat wood vital to any stylish Gili guesthouse are important income streams. Buzzy little strips have developed along the beaches in the southeast and the west, although the lanes are still more sandy than paved.

🏖 Beaches

The entire east side of the island has great beaches with powdery white sand and a gentle slope into beautiful turquoise water, with a foot-friendly sandy bottom. There are also good, private spots the rest of the way around Gili Air, but low-tide rocks and coral are a problem. For drinks and sunset, head north.

🏃 Activities

Bikes can be rented for 40,000Rp to 70,000Rp a day, but large sections of the coastal path in the north and west are annoying to ride, as long slogs of deep sand swallow the trail at times and mud after rains can make it impassable. Inland lanes, however, are mostly concrete and very rideable. Some shops have fat bikes (bikes with huge tyres) that make sand a little more manageable.

Diving & Snorkelling

The entire east coast has an offshore reef teeming with colourful fish; there's a drop-off

NUSA TENGGARA GILI AIR

Gili Air

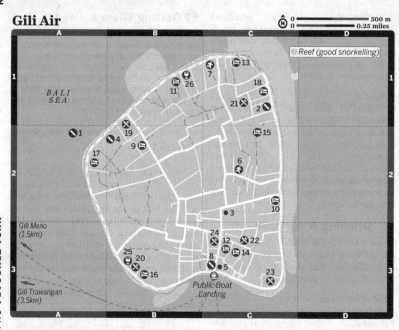

N   0 _____ 500 m
     0 _____ 0.25 miles

Reef (good snorkelling)

BALI SEA

Gili Meno
(1.5km)

Gili Trawangan
(3.5km)

Public Boat Landing

Gili Air

about 100m to 200m out. Snorkelling gear is easily hired from guesthouses and dive shops for about 50,000Rp per day. **Air Wall** is a beautiful soft-coral wall off the island's west, while off the north there's **Frogfish Point** and **Hans Reef**. Snorkelling spots can be reached from the eastern and northeastern beaches.

Gili Air has an excellent collection of dive shops, which charge the standard Gili rates.

★ Gili Air Divers
DIVING

(📞 0878 6536 7551; www.giliairdivers.com; Grand Sunset; guided diving boat trip from 500,000Rp; ⏰ 8am-8pm) 🌿 This French-Indo-owned dive shop on the west coast is long on charm and skill. Introductory freediving classes and SSI Level 1 and 2 courses are also available.

Blue Marine Dive Centre
DIVING

(📞 0853 3884 3596; www.bluemarinedive. com; night dive/5 dives 660,000/2,430,000Rp;

⊘ 7.30am-7.30pm) 🏄 Blue Marine has a nice location on the quiet northeastern corner of the island. As well as diving, it offers free-diving, stand-up paddleboarding and yoga (120,000Rp per class). The owner is active in reef preservation efforts.

Oceans 5   DIVING
(🔲 0813 3877 7144; www.oceans5dive.com; single dives from 490,000Rp) 🏄 Has a 25m training pool, an in-house marine biologist and nice hotel rooms. Also offers a program of yoga diving and emphasises sustainable diving practices to its guests.

Surfing
Directly off the southern tip of the island there's **Play Gili**, a short, peeling right-hand break that can get big at times. May to October brings the best conditions.

Yoga & Wellness
★ Flowers & Fire Yoga   YOGA
(http://flowersandfire.yoga; 1/3/5 classes 120,000/330,0000/500,000Rp; ⊘9am-6pm) A welcoming, spiritual and serene yoga garden for pre- and post-beach classes. It also has a great health-food cafe, popular curry and movie nights, and on-site accommodation ranging from a luxe dorm (think Egyptian cotton sheets, 300,000Rp) to well-designed bungalows (1,000,000Rp). Guests get discounts on classes.

H2O Yoga   YOGA
(🔲 0877 6103 8836; www.h2oyogaandmedit ation.com; 108 Buddha Way; class 120,000Rp) This wonderful yoga and meditation centre is found down a well-signposted lane leading inland from Gili Air's eastern shore. Top-quality classes are held in one of two lovely thatched *shalas*. H2O also offers a day spa, a pool (with aqua yoga classes), accommodation (rooms from 300,000Rp) and seven-day retreats (from US$625).

H2O's Good Earth Cafe sells restorative and healthy post-yoga treats from 7am to 4.30pm.

Harmony Spa   SPA
(🔲 0812 386 5883; www.facebook.com/harmony giliair; massages from 120,000Rp; ⊘9am-8pm) The beautiful north-coast location alone will make you feel renewed. Facials, body treatments and more are on offer. Call first.

🍴 Courses

Gili Cooking Classes   COOKING
(🔲 0877 6506 7210; www.gilicookingclasses.com; classes from 290,000Rp) This slick operation has a large kitchen for daily classes right on the strip. You have a range of options for what you'll learn to cook – choose wisely as you'll be eating your work.

🛏 Sleeping
Gili Air's dozens of places to stay are mostly located on the east coast, though you'll find more isolation in the west. Bungalows, in one shape or another, are the uniting theme.

Begadang   HOSTEL $
(begadangbackpackers@gmail.com; dm/d/tr from 200,000/250,000/350,000Rp; 🅱🛜🛁) This sprawling complex of basic bungalows in the northern interior of Gili Air is truly back-packer central, with a mushroom-shaped pool, heaps of inflatables, a hopping bar, a ping-pong table and even life-sized Connect Four. The cheaper doubles are little more than a mattress in a two-by-two-metre hut. The air-con triples are much nicer for small groups.

Hideout   HOSTEL $
(🔲 0812 3842 9728; www.giliairhostel.com; dm/r incl breakfast from 125,000/300,000Rp; ⊘recep-tion 7.30am-7pm; 🅱🛜) Refurbished rooms at this fun hostel have three beds and a bath-room apiece. The decor defines cheery and it has a cool bar, hot showers, free breakfast and a huge frangipani tree.

Bintang Beach 2   BUNGALOW $
(🔲 0819 742 3519; bungalow from 250,000Rp; 🅱🛜) On Gili Air's quiet northwest coast, this sandy but tidy compound has 25 basic bungalows (ranging from budget-friendly and fan-cooled to mildly snazzy) and an open-sided beach-bar/restaurant that's a delightful place to linger. This en-terprising clan has a few other guesthouses nearby. It also rents bikes and snorkelling gear, and can take care of your laundry.

★ Sejuk Cottages   BUNGALOW $$
(🔲 0813 3953 5387; d from 450,000Rp, f 1,350,000Rp; 🅱🛜🛁) Thirteen well-built, tastefully designed thatched *lumbung* (rice-barn) cottages, and pretty two- and three-storey cottages (some have rooftop liv-ing rooms) scattered around a fine tropical garden with a spring-fed pool. Some rooms are fan-only; others have rooftop hammocks.

★ Biba Beach Village
BUNGALOW $$

(☑ 0819 1727 4648; www.bibabeach.com; bungalow incl breakfast 800,000-1,600,000Rp; ❋ ⓦ) Biba offers nine lovely, spacious bungalows with large verandas, and grotto-like bathrooms that have walls inlaid with shells and coral. The gorgeous garden overlooks a great stretch of beach. Biba is also home to a good Italian restaurant (9am to 10pm). The best rooms have sea views.

Grand Sunset
BUNGALOW $$

(☑ 0819 3433 7000; www.grandsunsetgiliair.com; r 600,000-1,900,000Rp; ❋ ⓦ ⛱) These 25 sturdily built, bungalow-style rooms reflect the ethos of this modest resort: solid. Bathrooms are well designed and open-air, rooms have all the basic comforts, the pool is large and the beachside loungers have superb views. Plus there's the quietude that comes with the location on the sunset side of Air.

Rival Village
GUESTHOUSE $$

(☑ 0819 1749 8187; www.facebook.com/rival villagegiliair; r 300,000-600,000Rp; ❋ ⓦ) This modest four-room guesthouse just gets everything right. The French owners have created a sparklingly clean little compound amid family houses off one of the village's main paths. Rooms are large, the bathrooms are open-air, breakfast is delicious – everything works. *Très bon!*

Youpy Bungalows
BUNGALOW $$

(☑ 0852 5371 5405; rizkylily7@gmail.com; r 450,000-800,000Rp; ❋ ⓦ) Among the outcrop of driftwood-decorated beach cafes and guesthouses strung along the coast north of Blue Marine Dive Centre, Youpy has some of the best-quality bungalows. Bathrooms have beachy designs, the beds are big and the ceilings are high.

Pelangi Cottages
BUNGALOW $$

(☑ 0819 0703 7970, 0819 3316 8648; pelangi-cottages@yahoo.co.id; r incl breakfast 400,000-700,000Rp; ❋ ⓦ ⛱) Set on the scenic northern end of the island with coral reef out front, this place has 10 spacious but basic concrete and wood bungalows and great sunset views.

Vyaana Resort
RESORT $$$

(☑ 0877 6538 8515; www.vyaanagiliair.com; r incl breakfast 1,600,000Rp; ❋ ⓦ ⛱) The swath of beach on the sunset side of Gili Air is still fairly quiet, and this bungalow compound is a fine place to enjoy it. The eight (slightly overpriced) units are widely spaced for privacy, and cute little artistic touches abound.

Villa Casa Mio
BUNGALOW $$$

(☑ 0370-619 8437; www.giliair.com; cottages incl breakfast from 1,500,000Rp; ❋ ⓦ ⛱) Casa Mio has fine cottages with pretty garden bathrooms, as well as a riot of knick-knacks from the artistic to the kitsch. The floridly named rooms ('Ocean of Love', 'Tropical Smile') have fridges, stereos and nice sun decks with loungers. It's on a great beach, plus there's a shade-fringed pool.

✖ Eating

Most places on Gili Air are locally owned and offer an unbeatable setting for a meal, with tables overlooking the water. Some of the most interesting new restaurants are opening on the backstreets of the village.

Warung Bambu
INDONESIAN $

(☑ 0878 6405 0402; mains 20,000-30,000Rp; ⏱ 10am-10pm) A cheap, friendly and artfully decorated option for tasty local food (try the *tempe* curry!). It's two blocks in from the boat landing.

★ Pachamama
HEALTH FOOD $$

(☑ 0878 6415 2100; www.pachamamagiliair.com; mains 70,000-85,000Rp; ⏱ 10am-10pm Mon-Sat; ☑) This oh-so-hip health-food restaurant brews its own kombucha, crafts exotic smoothies and cold-brew coffee (or cocktails!) and has lots of flavourful veg, vegan and gluten-free options. It's a bit out of the way in the northern interior, but well worth the hike.

★ Ruby's Cafe
INDONESIAN $$

(☑ 0878 6575 6064; mains 45,000-90,000Rp; ⏱ noon-10pm) At this expanded back-lane eatery, one of the finest places to eat in the Gilis, candles flicker atop wooden tables. The menu is short with daily specials; the secret here is the namesake genius in the kitchen. The calamari is perfectly light and crispy, the green curry is flavourful and nuanced, the burgers are simply superb. Great desserts, too.

Mowie's
FUSION $$

(☑ 0878 6423 1384; www.mowiesbargiliair.com; mains 55,000-90,000Rp; ⏱ 8am-9pm) With a menu full of creative Indonesian and Western fusion fare, an ideal sunset location on the beach and chill EDM tunes after dark, Mowie's is the kind of place where you could show up for lunch and never leave.

Boogils Sunset Lounge SEAFOOD $$
(☑0819 3301 7727; mains 40,000-120,000Rp;
⊙9am-11pm) More ambitious than your usual
beachside bamboo hang-outs, Boogils offers
a nightly seafood barbecue and an ever-
changing line-up of fresh fare. Good pasta
shows what the Italians can do with *mie*
(noodles). Come for drinks, stay for sunset
and then have a moonlit meal. (On a bike,
buzz over via the paved interior lanes.)

Scallywags Beach Club INTERNATIONAL $$
(☑0819 1743 2086; www.scallywagsresort.com;
mains 50,000-150,000Rp; ⊙7am-11pm; 🛜)
Set on Gili Air's softest and widest beach,
Scallywags offers elegant decor, upscale
comfort food, great barbecue, homemade
gelato and superb cocktails here. But the
best feature is the alluring beach dotted
with loungers. The choice of sambals is
sublime.

🍷 Drinking & Nightlife

Gili Air is usually a mellow place, but there
are full-moon parties and things can rev up
at the sunset bars in high season. The largest concentration of bars is on the otherwise
tranquil northern coast.

Pura Vida LOUNGE
(www.facebook.com/puravidagiliair; ⊙11am-11pm)
A stylish bar with huge pillows and a rainbow of tables and chairs on the sand. Classy
jazz plays over the sound system and some
nights there's live reggae music. A wood-
fired oven produces great thin-crust pizzas
through the evening. Tops at sunset.

Coffee & Thyme CAFE
(☑0821 4499 3622; www.coffeeandthyme.co;
⊙7am-7pm) Right in the thick of things,
where boats to Gili Air disgorge their
sun-seeking seafarers, Coffee & Thyme is a
bustling, part-open-air cafe that makes some
of the best coffee in the Gilis. Also good if
you're craving a Western-style breakfast,
lunch wrap or muffin.

Lucky's Bar BAR
(⊙7am-late) A great beach bar: lounge back
on bamboo recliners and watch the sun set
behind Gili Meno. There are DJs on Sundays
and monthly full-moon parties with fire
dancing.

❶ Information

There are ATMs scattered around the island,
most notably in the south near the boat landing.

❶ Getting There & Away

The **public boat landing** is busy. Gili Air's commerce and popularity mean that public boats fill
rather quickly for the 15-minute ride to Bangsal.
The ticket office has a shady waiting area.

SUMBAWA

Elaborately contorted and sprawling into
the sea, Sumbawa is all volcanic ridges,
terraced rice fields, dry expanses and sheltered bays. Though well connected to Bali
and Lombok, it's a very different sort of
place – far less developed, mostly very dry,
much poorer, extremely conservative and
split between two distinct peoples. Those
who speak Sumbawanese probably reached
the west of the island from Lombok, while
Bimanese speakers dominate the Tambora
Peninsula and the east. Although Sumbawa
is an overwhelmingly Islamic island, in remote parts underground *adat* (traditional
law and lore) still thrives.

Mostly traffic-free and in great shape, the
Trans-Sumbawa Hwy is excellent for getting
quickly between Lombok and Flores. Transport connections off this trunk road are
infrequent and uncomfortable, and most
overland travellers don't even get off the
bus in Sumbawa as they float and roll from
Lombok to Flores. For now, it's the domain
of surfers, miners and mullahs.

Note that English is not as widely understood on Sumbawa as it is on neighbouring
islands. A translating app can help bridge
the language gap.

❶ Dangers & Annoyances

The island is more conservative in terms of
religion than neighbouring Lombok or Flores;
behave and dress modestly at all times.

❶ Getting There & Away

There are airports on either end of Sumbawa in
Bima and Sumbawa Besar, which receive domestic flights from nearby islands. Most visitors
arrive on ferries from either Lombok or Flores.

❶ Getting Around

Sumbawa's main highway runs from Taliwang
(near the west coast) through Sumbawa Besar,
Dompu and Bima to Sape (the ferry port on the
east coast). Fleets of long-distance buses, some
of them air-conditioned, run between the west
coast ferry port of Poto Tano and Sape, serving
all the major towns between.

Sumbawa

N 0 ——— 50 km
0 ——— 25 miles

You'll need private transport to navigate Sumbawa's outskirts effectively.

Car hire is possible through hotels: depending on your destination, the cost will be about 600,000Rp to 800,000Rp per day, including a driver and fuel. Motorbikes cost 50,000Rp to 80,000Rp a day.

West Sumbawa

✔ 0372

West Sumbawa is dry and rolling. Beaches are wide, sugar-white and framed with domed headlands. Bays are enormous and dynamic: they can be tranquil one hour and fold into overhead barrels the next. Sumbawa Besar, the largest city here, is a humble and devoutly Muslim place with a good morning market. Pulau Moyo, a lush jewel off the northern shore, has revered diving and snorkelling. Once solely the domain of the rich and famous, it now has options for travellers on any budget.

Poto Tano

✔ 0372 / POP 9330

Poto Tano, the main port for ferries to/from Lombok, is a ramshackle harbour, fringed by stilt-fishing villages with tremendous views of Gunung Rinjani. It's a pretty place, but there's no need to stay here.

Ferries (www.indonesiaferry.co.id) run almost hourly, 24 hours a day, between Labuhan Lombok and Poto Tano (passengers/motorbikes/cars 21,000/59,500/475,000Rp, 1½ hours). Through buses to Lombok include the ferry fare.

Buses meet the ferry and go to Sumbawa Besar (35,000Rp, 2½ hours) or Taliwang

(25,000Rp, one hour), where you can catch infrequent transport further south.

Jelenga

✔ 0372 / POP 200

Set along an enormous horseshoe bay, Jelenga is a humble country beach town with rice fields, goat farms and a world-class left break known as **Scar Reef**. It's one of the most serene beaches in Sumbawa and is the perfect base for low-key travellers to kick around in the sand for a few days. Find it by turning toward the coast in **Jereweh**, 11km south of the regional capital Taliwang.

🛏 Sleeping

A handful of quality lodges line the sand along Jelenga's shores. While most are aimed at surfers, non-surfers will feel more welcomed here than at any other surf town in West Sumbawa. All hotels along the beach in Jelenga have restaurants serving a combination of Western and Indonesian cuisine.

★ Scar Reef Lodge LODGE $$

(✆ 0812 3980 4885; www.scarreeflodge.com; r US$35-55, cabin for 6 from US$120; ❄ 🗢) A modern lodge for surfers. The five rooms (two of which are air-conditioned) have soaring ceilings, wood furnishings and a common beachside restaurant and lounge area. It also has a cabin for groups, plenty of beach pouffes and a yoga *shala* for DIY sun salutations. Surf, SUP and motorbike rentals are all available.

ℹ Information

The nearest ATMs are along the main road through Taliwang.

ⓘ Getting There & Away

The small, conservative town of Taliwang is the regional transport hub. Buses go from Taliwang to Poto Tano (25,000Rp, one hour) almost hourly, where you can hop on a bus to Mataram or Sumbawa Besar. Early morning and evening buses head to Maluk (30,000Rp, one hour).

The 45-minute *ojek* (motorcycle taxi) ride from Taliwang to Jelenga costs 50,000Rp. Most hotels in Jelenga can arrange private transfers from nearby destinations and will rent motorbikes for about 70,000Rp per day.

Maluk

📞 0372 / POP

South of Taliwang, the beaches and bays try to outdo one another. Your first stop is the working-class commercial district of Maluk, 30km south of Taliwang. Yes, the town is ugly, but the beach is superb. The sand is a blend of white and gold, and the bay is buffered by two headlands. There's good swimming in the shallows, and when the swell hits, the reef further out sculpts perfect barrels.

Directly south of Maluk, within walking distance of the beach (though it is a long walk), is **Supersuck**, consistently rated the best left in the world. Surfers descend regularly from Hawaii's North Shore to surf here – which should tell you something – and many lifelong surfers have proclaimed it the finest barrel of their lives. It really pumps in the dry season (May to October).

One of the world's largest copper mines, about 20km inland of Maluk, has driven a wave of development and attracted scores of employees from across Indonesia and abroad. The PT Amman Mineral Nusa Tenggara (AMNT) employs about 3000 workers, and has had a huge impact on the area (you'll see its vast port facilities along the coastal road). Most of the expat restaurant and bar traffic is in Townsite, a private company enclave complete with a golf course and other amenities. Casual visits are discouraged (except for the golf course, which is open to the general public).

🛏 Sleeping

Dreamtime
Sumbawa Homestay GUESTHOUSE $

(📞 0821 4523 9696; http://dreamtimesumbawa. com; Jl Pasir Putih; dm 55,000Rp, d with/without air-con 300,000/200,000Rp; ❄ 🛜) The ultimate surf-bum crash-pad with a curtained-off dorm and cosy patio-facing rooms.

Dreamtime is set a block back from the beach in the heart of the village, and staff are extremely knowledgeable about the nearby waves. Fast fibre-optic wi-fi is a plus.

★ Merdeka House GUESTHOUSE $$

(📞 0878 6350 4946; www.merdekahouse.com; Jl Raya Balas; r from 300,000Rp; 🛜) What a view you will have if you end a hard day in the waves at this hilltop guesthouse, whose communal lounge and kitchen overlook two stunning bays. The six rooms are spacious and spotless. Perks include an honesty bar, free snorkels, cheap board rentals (50,000Rp per day) and a helpful area guide typed up by the friendly Aussie owners.

ⓘ Information

Banks and ATMs, such as **BNI** (📞 0372-635146; Jl Raya Maluk; ⊘ 8am-4pm Mon-Fri, ATM 24hr), cluster most thickly along Jl Raya Maluk, the road through the centre of town.

ⓘ Getting There & Away

Buses leave Terminal Maluk, north of town across from the entrance to the PT AMNT mine (look for the big gates and massive parking area), for Sumbawa Besar (40,000Rp, four hours, two daily). Arrive well in advance to book a seat. From Lombok, purchase a through ticket with Damri from Mataram to Maluk (90,000Rp).

A car and driver to/from Poto Tano costs 400,000Rp (1½ hours).

Most people arrive here from Labuan Lombok (adult/child 160,000/110,000Rp, surfboards 25,000Rp, 1½ hours) on the fast ferry, **KSB Express** (📞 0823 4190 8689; https://ksb express.com). It docks in Benete Harbour, just north of Maluk.

Rantung Beach & Around

📞 0372 / POP 8180

Rantung Beach is a laid-back place with a classic surfer feel. Its secluded and majestic bay is framed by 100m-high headlands and most everything is within easy walking distance. It's part of the spread-out settlement of Sekongkang, which also includes two other superb beaches with a handful of surf breaks. The best range of accommodation and restaurants is to be found along the coast a few kilometres from the centre of town, especially at Rantung Beach.

The water is crystal clear and waves roll in year-round at **Yo Yo's**, a right break at the north end of the bay. **Hook**, which breaks at the edge of the northern bluff, is also a terrific right. The next bay down is where you'll find **Tropical**, another phenomenal beach (named for the nearby resort) and home to great left and right breaks that beginners will enjoy. Immediately south of Tropical is **Remo's Left**, a solid A-frame.

North of Rantung is **Pantai Lawar**, a tree-shaded stretch of white sand on a turquoise lagoon sheltered by volcanic bluffs draped in jungle. When the surf is flat, come here to swim and snorkel.

🛏️ Sleeping & Eating

Beachside guesthouses and bungalows cater to the surfing set and most guesthouses also feed their guests.

Santai Beach Bungalows   BUNGALOW $
(📱 0878 6393 5758; Rantung Beach; r without/with bathroom 150,000/200,000Rp, with air-con & breakfast 300,000Rp; ❈ 🛜) The choice budget spot in the area offers a collection of 12 spacious, well-tended tiled rooms. Those with private bathroom have sensational sea views, which anyone can enjoy from the thatched restaurant (dishes 30,000Rp to 60,000Rp), where there's also a pool table to gather around for post-surf beers. Book ahead: when that swell hits it's full for weeks.

Yo Yo's Hotel   RESORT $$
(📱 0878 6695 0576; yoyoshotel@yahoo.co.id; Rantung Beach; s/d from 200,000/350,000Rp; ❈ 🛜) A vast beachfront complex with a range of 15 rooms. Deluxe rooms are quite large and well appointed with wood furnishings. Standard rooms are smaller and a bit worn. Monkeys wander the grounds and a large two-storey bar (with cocktails!) and cafe (dishes 30,000Rp to 80,000Rp) overlooks the surf.

**Rantung Beach
Bar & Cottages**   BUNGALOW $$
(📱 0819 1700 7481; Rantung Beach; r from 200,000Rp, cottages from 400,000Rp; ❈ 🛜) The mining crowd has enjoyed more than a few sundowners at the vast and open beachside cafe here (dishes 40,000Rp to 60,000Rp); the food always delivers – we love the crunchy chips and huge burgers. Five refined, spacious cottages have queen beds and leafy private decks with sea views. Behind them is a row of cheaper rooms.

Lisa's Garden   INTERNATIONAL $
(📱 0822 3650 7340; Rantung Beach; mains 20,000-65,000Rp; ⊙7am-10pm; 🛜) Those craving things like French-press coffee, avocado toast, salads, granola or burritos – all excep-

tionally rare on Sumbawa – will love this cheap open-air eatery, which has an upstairs deck overlooking the waves.

ℹ️ Getting There & Away

The tourist-oriented minibuses of **Sekongkang Trans** (📱 0853 3324 1931; www.facebook. com/sekongkangtrans; Jl Raya Sekongkang) leave every day at 7am and 7pm for the six-hour journey to Mataram via the Poto Tano ferry (120,000Rp). The air-conditioned bus can pick up in Maluk and Jereweh (15 and 30 minutes after departing from Sekongkang) if contacted in advance. Departures from Mataram to Sekongkang are also at 7am and 7pm.

Sekongkang Trans is the only bus that travels all the way to Sekongkang. At all other times you'll need to charter an *ojek* (around 20,000Rp) to get here from Maluk, the nearest town on the public-bus network.

Sumbawa Besar
📱 0371 / POP 59,000

Sumbawa Besar, often shortened to 'Sumbawa', is the principal market town of the island's west. It's leafy, devoutly Muslim (oversupply of karaoke bars notwithstanding) and runs on the bushels of beans, rice and corn cultivated on the outskirts. It's a pleasant enough place for those transiting to Pulau Moyo, but there's not much to see here aside from the old palace and a lively morning market. Most travellers simply consider this town a respite while journeying along the Trans-Sumbawa Hwy.

👁️ Sights

Dalam Loka   PALACE
(Sultan's Palace; Jl Dalam Loka 1; ⊙8am-noon & 1-5pm Mon-Fri, 8-11am & 1.30-5pm Sat & Sun) FREE The Dalam Loka was built over 200 years ago for Sultan Mohammad Jalaluddin III and presently covers an entire city block. The remains of this once-imposing structure are in fair condition and are still used for political events. You can wander the grounds and scurry over the creaking floorboards inside to see old photos of the royal family, antique parasols and carriages.

🛏️ Sleeping & Eating

Samawa Transit Hotel   HOTEL $$
(📱 0371-21754; Jl Garuda 41; s/d from 400,000/ 420,000Rp; ❈ 🛜) Conveniently located across the main road and to the left as you emerge from the airport is this low-rise, caramel-toned compound. Its rooms are

spacious and spotless, with high ceilings, cheery bathroom tiles, flatscreen TVs, hot water and decent beds. VIP rooms are larger, quieter and have private balconies.

★**Cipta Sari Bakery** BAKERY $
(☑0371-21496; Jl Hasanuddin 47; snacks from 4000Rp; ⊗8am-7pm) Don't pass through town without a stop at this excellent bakery on a shady stretch of the main drag. Pause for coffee or a cold drink, and be sure to stock up for your journey: the various baked goods, pastries and savoury treats are the best you'll find between here and Bima.

Aneka Rasa Jaya CHINESE $
(☑0371-21291; Jl Hasanuddin 14; mains 25,000-50,000Rp; ⊗8am-3pm & 6-9.30pm) Clean and popular, this Chinese seafood house plates tender fish fillets, prawns, squid, crab and scallops in oyster, Szechuan or sweet-and-sour sauce. The *soto kepiting* (crab soup) is good, as is anything with noodles.

ℹ Information

There are numerous banks and ATMs all along Jl Hasanuddin.
Kantor Imigrasi (Immigration Office; Jl Garuda 41; ⊗8am-3pm Mon-Thu, to noon Fri) It'll take at least two days to extend your visa here.
Klinik Surya Medika Sumbawa (☑0371-262 0023; Jl Hasanuddin 20A; ⊗24hr) Hospital with 24-hour care.

ℹ Getting There & Away

AIR
Sultan Muhammad Kaharuddin III Airport is very close to the centre. Garuda and Wings Air fly to Lombok daily.

BUS
Sumbawa Besar's main long-distance bus station is **Terminal Sumur Payung** (Jl Lintas Sumbawa), 5.5km northwest of town on the highway. Destinations served include the following:
Bima 100,000Rp, seven hours, several daily
Mataram 90,000Rp (including ferry ticket), six hours, several daily
Poto Tano 35,000Rp, 2½ hours, hourly from 8am to midnight

ℹ Getting Around

It's easy to walk into town from the airport – just turn to your right as you exit the terminal; the walk is less than 1km. Alternatively, you can arrange transport with local guesthouses.
Bemos cost 5000Rp for trips anywhere around town.

Pulau Moyo

Moyo is a gently arcing crescent of jungled volcanic rock that floats atop the azure seas north of Sumbawa Besar. About half the size of Singapore, it's home to just 2000 people spread across six small villages. The largest, **Labuhan Aji**, is an authentic Sumbawanese town that has only recently opened up to tourism. It lies on a pebbly beach (better suited for snorkelling than swimming) and is the kind of throw-back island paradise where electricity only works in the evening and locals are still amused to see foreigners.

The majority of the island, and its rich reefs, form a nature reserve laced with trails, dripping with waterfalls and offering some of the best diving west of Komodo. Loggerhead and green turtles hatch on the beaches, long-tail macaques patrol the canopy, and wild pigs, barking deer and a diverse bird population all call Moyo home.

◉ Sights

Mata Jitu Waterfall WATERFALL
Pulau Moyo's most famous attraction is this fairytale waterfall, whose cascading pools of turquoise water have entranced at least one princess (locals call it Lady Diana Waterfall because she visited in 1993). A sign in Labuhan Aji says it's 7km away, but this is a marketing ploy to get you on an *ojek* (100,000Rp). It's actually a relatively easy 4km hike (bring your swimsuit!).

If you go on your own, you'll need to pay a 25,000Rp 'island tax' to your hotel in advance.

☆ Activities

Hiking and snorkelling are the big draws here. You can also charter local boats for trips to offshore dive sites or stunning beaches like **Tanjung Pasir** in the south of the island.

Maleo Moyo DIVING
(DJL Diving; ☑0812 8472 9535; http://scuba divemoyo.com; Labuhan Aji; shore/boat dive 400,000/600,000K, discover scuba 800,000Rp; ⊗8am-5pm) The only PADI dive shop in Labuhan Aji with two comfortable boats, one of which is often used to take snorkellers to offshore reefs like Takat Sagele and Sengalo. Sign up for daily leisure diving or multiday dive safaris.

Maleo Moyo also has a row of bright and airy bungalows (400,000Rp to 600,000Rp)

WORTH A TRIP

SNORKEL SPOTS

There is decent coral in the waters just off Labuhan Aji. A better spot that's also accessible from the shore and has larger schools of fish is **Crocodile Head**. To reach it, hike or bike 5km south of Labuhan Aji on the path toward the Amanwana Resort until you see a sign indicating the turn-off.

Just northeast of Pulau Moyo is small **Pulau Satonda**, which also has good beaches and tremendous snorkelling. Maleo Moyo (p359) can arrange the two-hour boat ride to visit (2,000,000Rp).

and a divers' crash pad with dorm beds (100,000Rp) and basic rooms (200,000Rp).

🛏 Sleeping

Labuhan Aji is the island's main village and the only place set up for tourism. You'll find basic homestays and midrange bungalows along its beach, while the island's long-running luxe resort lies in a secluded spot 7km to the south.

Most places only have electricity from 6pm to 6am.

Most accommodation along the beach have on-site restaurants, and there are three simple warungs hidden away along the laneways of Labuhan Aji.

Devi Homestay
HOMESTAY $

(☑ 0853 3993 2815; Labuhan Aji; r without bathroom 100,000Rp, with full board 200,000Rp) The nicest of the ultra-basic homestays in town, set just back from the pier. All rooms have mattresses on the floor and shared bathrooms, but if you ask for the ones in the front you'll also get a patio overlooking the sea.

★ Sunset Moyo Bungalows
BUNGALOW $$

(☑ 0852 0517 1191; http://sunsetmoyobungalows. com; Labuhan Aji; bungalow d/tr 650,000/ 750,000Rp) Everything is just so at this appropriately named getaway, whose terraced front deck is like a mini-amphitheatre for dreamy sunsets. The five bungalows are full of playful touches, like tree-trunk sinks and outdoor showers, while the overwater swing out front was surely built for Instagram travel porn. The friendly owners can arrange bikes, hikes, snorkelling and massages.

Maryan Moyo
BUNGALOW $$

(www.facebook.com/moyobungalows; Labuhan Aji; bungalow with/without air-con 600,000/ 500,000Rp; ❄) Sleep to the sounds of lapping waves in one of five stilted bungalows, each with a sturdy wooden frame, stone-tiled bathroom and covered deck facing the sea. Umbrellas and sun loungers on the beach out front add to the soporific vibe.

★ Amanwana Resort
RESORT $$$

(☑ 0371-22233; www.amanresorts.com; all-inclusive jungle/ocean-view tents from US$910/1090; ❄ @ 🖥) On Moyo's western side, 7km south of Labuhan Aji, Amanwana is the ultimate island hideaway. Guests stay in lavish permanent tents with antique wood furnishings, king-sized beds and air-con, but nature still rules here. The resort is built around diving, hiking and mountain biking. Guests arrive by private seaplane or helicopter from Bali, or from mainland Sumbawa on an Amanwana boat.

ⓘ Getting There & Away

Public boats depart daily at noon from Sumbawa Besar for the two-hour journey to Labuhan Aji (75,000Rp). The normal departure point is Muara Kali, but when tides are low they will leave from Pantai Goa on the other side of town. The return trip from Labuhan Aji is at 7am each morning.

The seas around Moyo get turbulent from December to March and boat captains understandably may refuse to risk a journey. They may also refuse to depart on the rare occasion when there are not enough passengers, in which case those in a rush may have to charter an entire boat for as much as 2,000,000Rp.

A popular alternative to the Sumbawa Besar route for those climbing Gunung Tambora is to arrange a boat over to the east side of the island, followed by a land transfer to Labuhan Aji. Rik Stoetman at Visit Tambora can make all the necessary arrangements.

East Sumbawa

☑ 0373

Twisted into a shape all its own, and linguistically and culturally distinct from the west, the eastern half of Sumbawa sees the most visitors thanks to accessible year-round surf near Hu'u village. Adventurous souls may also want to tackle majestic Gunung Tambora, a mountain that changed the world.

Gunung Tambora

☑ 0373

Looming over central Sumbawa is the 2722m volcano Gunung Tambora. Its peak was obliterated during the epic eruption of April 1815. Two hundred years later much of the mountain was declared a national park.

Today from the summit you'll have spectacular views of the 6km-wide caldera, which contains a two-coloured lake, and endless ocean vistas that stretch as far as Gunung Rinjani (Lombok). A basic climb to the crater rim takes at least two days; if you want to venture down into the spectacular crater – one of the world's deepest – add another three days.

The base for ascents is the remote village of **Pancasila** near the town of **Calabai** on the western slope; here you can organise climbs. Contacts to organise climbs include **Pak Saiful** (☑ 0859 3703 0848, 0823 4069 3138; Pancasila) and **Rik Stoetman** (Rik Stoetman; ☑ 0813 5337 0951; https://visittambora.com; near Pancasila). Both can rent rooms (from 150,000Rp to 300,000Rp) and handle transport and logistical issues.

A two-day guided trek up Gunung Tambora should cost about 2,000,000Rp per person for groups of three or more, including guides, porters, camping equipment, meals and accommodation in Pancasila on either end. Also included is the 150,000Rp park entrance fee.

ℹ Getting There & Away

The road along the peninsula from the Trans-Sumbawa Hwy to Calabai is much improved. You can hire a private taxi from Bima Airport for 1,300,000Rp, or hop on a very crowded bus from Bima's Terminal Dara (70,000Rp, five hours, 6am and 3pm daily) to Calabai. From Calabai take an *ojek* (30,000Rp, 20 minutes) to Pancasila.

Pantai Lakey

☑ 0373

Pantai Lakey, a gentle crescent of golden sand, is where Sumbawa's tourist pulse beats, thanks to seven world-class surf breaks that curl and crash in one massive bay, and a string of modest beach guesthouses, all linked by a sandy path studded with bars. While there's an agreeable beach-bum ambience, Lakey isn't as polished as surf towns on neighbouring islands to the west, and nonsurfers may find little to hold their attention.

Hu'u is a small, poor, and very friendly fishing village, 3km north of Lakey. Neat and shady, suffused with the scent of drying fish and blessed with breathtaking pink sunsets, it's the nearest public-transport node to Lakey.

The area is the centre of a push to increase tourism on Sumbawa. New roads mean you can now easily drive east from Hu'u, and north to Bima via Parado, enjoying some superb sea views along the way.

🏃 Activities

This is one of Indonesia's best surfing destinations, blessed with almost-guaranteed surf. **Lakey Peak** and **Lakey Pipe** are the best-known waves and are within paddling distance of the various hotels and guesthouses. You'll need to rent a motorbike or hire an *ojek* to get to **Nungas**, **Cobblestone** and **Nangadoro**. **Periscope** is 150m from

---

THE YEAR WITHOUT SUMMER

After a few days of tremors the top blew off Gunung Tambora on 10 April 1815 in what is the most powerful eruption in modern history. Tens of thousands of Sumbawans were killed, molten rock was sent more than 40km into the sky, and the explosion was heard 2000km away (by comparison, the 1873 eruption of Krakatoa was one-tenth the size).

In the months and years that followed, weather was affected worldwide as the cloud of ash blotted out the sun. In Europe 1816 came to be known as 'the year without summer'. Crops failed, temperatures plummeted, disease spread and tens of thousands died across the globe. Historical evidence is everywhere, including in the works of JMW Turner, whose paintings from the period feature shocking orange colours in the dim, ash-filled skies.

Two books vividly illustrate how Tambora's eruption changed the planet: *Tambora* by Gillen D'Arcy Wood and *Tambora: Travels to Sumbawa and the Mountain that Changed the World* by Derek Pugh.

the sand at the far north end of the bay near **Maci Point**, which is another good spot. When the swell gets really big, there's a beach break at Hu'u as well.

Most surfers share the cost of a boat (from 800,000Rp, maximum five people) to get to the breaks and back. Waves can be very good (and very big) year-round, but the most consistent swell arrives between June and August.

Inexperienced surfers should be cautious. Waves break over a shallow reef and serious accidents do happen, especially when the tide's out.

From August to October the wind gusts, which turns Pantai Lakey into Indonesia's best kitesurfing destination – it's regarded as one of the 10 best in the world. Kites descend on Lakey Pipe and Nungas when it's pumping.

Joey Barrel's Board Shop SURFING
(Jl Raya Hu'u; ⊘ 7am-6pm) Out on the main drag, this small shop offers ding repairs, board rental (per day from 50,000Rp), surfing supplies and board sales. It's open when the owner isn't at the breaks.

🛏 Sleeping

There are plenty of decent-value digs strung along Pantai Lakey. A paved path skirts the beach, linking guesthouses.

Any Lestari BUNGALOW $
(☑ 0813 3982 3018; Jl Rya Hu'u; r 300,000-650,000Rp; ⊛ 🗧) A 35-room bungalow complex that stretches back from the beach. All bungalows are spacious with tiled rooms and private patios, but some are in better shape than others. The most expensive rooms have Siberian air-con, hot water and satellite TV. The waterfront bar and restaurant, Blue Lagoon, draws a steady crowd.

★ Rock Pool
Home Stay HOMESTAY $$
(☑ 0813 3733 6856; http://rockpoolhomestay.com; Jl Pantai Nunggas Lakey; r 400,000-500,000Rp; ⊛ 🗧) Set amid tropical gardens, the six rooms at Rock Pool are some of the nicest on Pantai Lakey, with air-con, decent wi-fi and fabulous views across the breaks towards the rolling hills of Sumbawa. The open-sided restaurant Ali's Bar, a great place to enjoy offshore breezes and beers after a day's surfing, serves Indonesian and Western food from 7am to 10pm.

Vivi's Lakey Peak Homestay HOMESTAY $$
(☑ 0823 4049 9139; www.lakeypeakhomestay.com; Jl Pantai Lakey; s/d/tr 250,000/350,000/450,000Rp; ⊛ 🗧) Set along a little lane between the beach and the main road, this five-room compound offers the area's warmest welcome, with Vivian and her Sumbawanese-Australian family your generous hosts. Rooms are modern and large with nice furnishings, the yard is shaded by banana trees and there's a sociable, open-sided cafe. The cooking is excellent!

Fishing trips can also be organised.

★ Lakey Peak Haven HOTEL $$$
(☑ 0821 4413 6320; www.lakeypeakhaven.com; Jl Raya Hu'u; s/d from US$70/80; ⊛ 🗧🗧) Removed from the action on a hill above town, this highly manicured Bali-style 'haven' is easily the best accommodation option in town with two-storey surf 'shacks' overlooking a chequered pool deck and the distant breaks. Reserve in advance as it doesn't accept walk-ups.

🍴 Eating & Drinking

Most guesthouses have their own cafe-bars, and there are simple refreshment stalls and warungs along the beachfront path.

Mamat Warung INDONESIAN $
(Jl Raya Hu'u; mains 20,000-30,000Rp; ⊘ 7am-10pm) While it lacks a sea view, this simple warung out on the main road serves up Lakey's cheapest and most authentic Indonesian fare, including *sate*, gado gado (a peanut-sauced salad) and plenty of tempe dishes for vegetarians.

Wreck INTERNATIONAL $$
(Jl Raya Hu'u; mains 50,000-65,000Rp; ⊘ 8am-9pm) A beached Sumbawanese boat, its prow pointing to Lakey's famous breaks, has been turned into a breezy, open-sided restaurant that does surprisingly good 'Mexican' food, alongside Indonesian and Western standards. If the local interpretation of quesadillas, fajitas and burritos doesn't appeal, try the spicy fish in banana leaves, or simply sink a beer and some balls around the threadbare pool table.

Fatmah's INTERNATIONAL $$
(off Jl Raya Hu'u; mains 30,000-75,000Rp; ⊘ 7am-9pm; 🗧) Once humble, Fatmah's has taken a slight turn upmarket in recent years. Tables sit in a raised bleached-wood house overlooking the beach where you can watch the sun set or the kitesurfers swoop, as you tuck

into juices, *ayam lalapan* (fried chicken and sambal), or Western fare like pastas and Aussie meat pies ... all to the beat of EDM.

ⓘ Information

The nearest ATMs are 37km north in Dompu.

ⓘ Getting There & Away

Some buses run direct from Bima (55,000Rp to 60,000Rp) or you may have to change at Dompu on the Trans-Sumbawa Hwy. *Ojeks* to/from Dompu cost 80,000Rp.

Try doing this with a surfboard and you'll see why so many people take a taxi from Bima Airport (800,000Rp for up to four people).

ⓘ Getting Around

The *ojek* cartel is omnipresent in Lakey; rates to the breaks range from 30,000Rp to 80,000Rp. It's generally cheaper to rent your own motorbike from any shop on the main road (from 50,000Rp per day), all of which have special board racks.

Bima

🕿 0374 / POP 153,000

East Sumbawa's largest metropolitan centre is a conservative Islamic place. It has few sights, the streets can be traffic-choked, the architecture is charmless and crumbling, and the vibe is unappealing after dark. It's only worth overnighting here if it suits your flight or cross-Sumbawa driving plans. If you're heading to Pantai Lakey, there's no need to stop, and if you want a morning ferry to Flores, you're better off staying in Sape.

◉ Sights

Museum Asi Mbojo   MUSEUM

(Jl Sultan Ibrahim; 3000Rp; ⊙ 8am-4pm Mon-Sat) The old Sultan's Palace, former home of Bima's rulers, still reflects the colonial style of a 1927 renovation. Past the large verandas, the interior is home to a grab bag of dusty curios, including a royal crown, battle flags and weapons. A modest wooden building next to the palace has an evocative and traditional look. The weedy grounds are large; the area outside the northern fence is a favourite night-time spot for prostitutes.

🛏 Sleeping & Eating

Hotel Lila Graha   HOTEL $

(🕿 0374-42740; Jl Lombok 20; r with fan/air-con from 200,000/300,000Rp; ❄🛜) The dim, tiled Lila Graha is a decent, central option if you must overnight in Bima. Its four storeys hold a wide range of rooms. Ground-floor suite rooms are newest and nicest, but there's wi-fi in the lobby only.

★**Marina Hotel**   HOTEL $$

(🕿 0374-42072; www.marinabima.com; Jl Sultan Kaharuddin 4; r 420,000-890,000Rp; ❄🛜) Bima's best sleep is very central. The 52 rooms in this four-storey building (there's an elevator) are bright and airy, with large flat-screen TVs, glassed-in showers and plush bed linens. All rooms get plenty of light, though some have more windows than others. There are sweeping views from the common lounge.

Pasar Malam   MARKET $

(Night Market; Jl Sultan Ibrahim; ⊙ 6-11pm) Dine cheaply at the night market, located in and around the soccer field. There's fish and chicken *sate*, mie goreng (fried noodles) and nasi goreng (fried rice), *bakso* (meatball soup) and various deep-fried treats, including bananas aplenty.

☆ Entertainment

Pacuan Kuda   HORSE RACING

(Desa Panda) Horse racing is held at least four times a year, in April or May, July, August and December, at the Desa Panda horse stadium, 12km west of town on the Trans-Sumbawa Hwy. There's a large grandstand, a gaggle of warungs and plenty of cheering as horses, ridden by children between the ages of nine and 15, thunder around a dusty track.

ⓘ Information

There are plenty of banks and ATMs in Bima, especially along the town's main drag, Jl Sultan Hasanuddin.

ⓘ Getting There & Away

AIR

Bima's **Sultan Muhammad Salahudin Airport** (BMU; Jl Salahudin) is the main airport for travellers to Pantai Lakey. During peak season (June to August), when flights from Labuan Bajo (Flores) to Bali are often fully booked, you can make the 10-hour ferry and bus trip from Labuan Bajo to Bima, then find a seat on a less-packed Bima–Bali flight. Services include the following:

Bali (Denpasar) Nam Air, Wings Air; 1¼ hours; daily.

Lombok Wings Air, Nam Air, Garuda; one hour, daily.

Makassar (Sulawesi) Wings Air; 1¼ hours, daily.

The airport sits amid salt flats, 12km west of the centre, on the way to Dompu and the road to Pantai Lakey. You can walk out to the main road and catch a passing bus. Alternatively, taxis meet arrivals, charging 120,000Rp to Bima or 800,000Rp to Pantai Lakey.

BOAT

Pelni boats travel from Bima to Waingapu on Sumba (three times monthly), Ende on Flores (four times monthly), Kupang on West Timor (three times monthly), Benoa on Bali (seven times monthly) and Sulawesi (five times monthly). Book with the **Pelni office** (☑ 0374-42046; www.pelni.co.id; Jl Kesatria 2; ⊙ 8am-noon & 1-3.30pm Mon-Fri) in central Bima.

BUS

Buses leave from **Terminal Dara** (Jl Sultan Kaharuddin), a 10-minute walk south along Jl Sultan Kaharuddin from the centre of town. Routes include the following:

Dompu 25,000Rp, two hours, almost hourly from 7am to 4pm

Mataram 250,000Rp, 11 to 14 hours, two daily

Sape 30,000Rp, two hours, almost hourly from 7am to 4pm

Sumbawa Besar 80,000Rp, six hours, several daily (mostly before noon)

Sape

☑ 0374 / POP 53,000

Sape's got a tumbledown port-town vibe, perfumed with the conspicuous scent of drying cuttlefish. The outskirts are quilted in rice fields backed by jungled hills, while *benhur* (horse-drawn carts) and early morning commerce whirl past the colourful wooden stilt homes in town. If you're catching a morning ferry, consider staying at **Losmen Mutiara** (☑ 0374-71337; Jl Pelabuhan Sape; r 70,000-160,000Rp; 🖳🛜). Right next to the port gates and the last bus stop, it's a decent enough place with 20 rooms spread across two floors. Across the street is **Rumah Makan Citra Minang** (Jl Pelabuhan Sape; mains 30,000Rp; ⊙ 8am-9pm), whose smiling chefs bring the finest and spiciest Padang dishes to life.

🛈 Getting There & Away

BOAT

The ferry port is 4km east of Sape's diminutive centre. Regular breakdowns and rough seas disrupt ferry services – always double-check the latest schedules at www.indonesiaferry.co.id. Ferries from Sape include Labuan Bajo (Flores; 60,000Rp, six hours, daily) and Waikelo (Sumba;

69,000Rp, eight hours, three weekly) north of Tambolaka.

BUS

Express buses with service to Lombok (250,000Rp, 12 to 15 hours) meet arriving ferries. Buses leave almost every hour for Bima (30,000Rp, two hours), where you can catch buses to other Sumbawa destinations. Taxi drivers may claim that buses have stopped running and you must charter their vehicle to Bima (350,000Rp, 1½ hours); this is usually not true.

KOMODO & RINCA ISLANDS

Parked neatly between Sumbawa and Flores, the Unesco-recognised Komodo National Park (p366) is one of Indonesia's treasures and covers 1817 sq km. Its underwater world is legendary. Above the waters, Komodo and Rinca islands are home to the famous prehistoric Komodo dragons, or *ora,* the world's largest lizards.

Padar Island, conveniently positioned between Komodo and Rinca, is a highly prized photography perch, gifting those who climb the stairs an outlook of three perfect bays that transition from aquamarine to sapphire blue.

These isolated islands, with jagged hills, carpeted with savannah and fringed with mangroves, are surrounded by tempestuous waters. Warm and cold currents converge and breed nutritious thermal climes and rip tides that attract large schools of pelagics, including dolphins, sharks, manta rays and blue whales. The coral here is mostly pristine.

Komodo

POP 3,267

Spectacular Komodo, its steep hillsides jade in the short wet season (December to March) and frazzled by sun to a rusty tan that makes its crystal waters pop the rest of the year, is the largest island in Komodo National Park. A succession of peninsulas spread east, each providing a different perspective, with some fringed in pink sand due to red coral offshore.

On its south coast is the entrance to **Loh Liang** and the PHKA office, where boats dock and guided walks and treks start. The fishing village of **Kampung Komodo** is a 30-minute boat ride south of Loh Liang. It's

Komodo & Rinca Islands

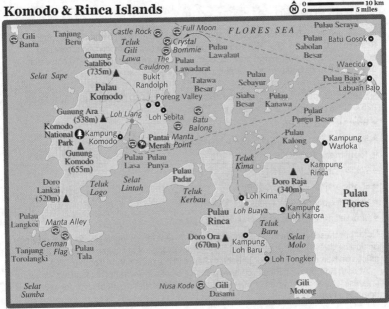

a friendly, stilted Bugis village filled with goats, chickens and children. The locals, said to be descendants of convicts exiled to the island by Sumbawanese Sultans in the 19th century, are used to seeing tourists. You can spend your time simply absorbing village life and gazing out over the water.

Activities

Walking & Trekking

The 150,000Rp entrance fee at Komodo includes a choice of three walks: the **short walk** (1.5km, 45 minutes), which includes a stop at an artificial waterhole that attracts diminutive local deer, wild boar and of course *ora*; the **medium walk** (2km, 1½ hours), which includes a hill with sweeping views and a chance to see colourful cockatoos; and the **long walk** (4km, two hours), which includes the features of the shorter hikes and gets you much further from the peak-season crowds.

You can also negotiate for adventure treks (from 500,000Rp for up to five people). These treks are up to 10km long and can last four or more hours, so bring plenty of water. There are two paths. One climbs the 538m-high **Gunung Ara**, with expansive views from the top. The other, **Poreng Valley**, has an out-in-the-wild feeling. Watch for wildlife on your way over **Bukit Randolph**,

which passes a memorial to 79-year-old Randolph Von Reding who disappeared on Komodo in 1974, then head to **Loh Sebita**. It's challenging, the sea views are spectacular and you'll likely see a dragon or two – as well as buffalo, deer, wild boar and Komodo's rich bird life. Organise your boat to pick you up in Loh Sebita so you don't have to retrace your steps.

Water Sports

Almost everybody who visits Komodo hires a boat in Labuan Bajo or visits as part of a liveaboard itinerary. Day trips always offer snorkelling (gear included) as part of the itinerary as well as a stop at an island beach. Many snorkel around the small island of **Pulau Lasa** near Kampung Komodo, and just off the pink sands of **Pantai Merah** (Red Beach; although it's usually referred to as the Pink Beach).

People who stay on Komodo can arrange for kayaking and sunrise dolphin tours.

Sleeping & Eating

In the village of Kampung Komodo, you'll find a few very basic homestays that give you a bed and some meals. Either turn up and let locals guide you to one (rooms cost from about 200,000Rp per night) or arrange your stay in advance with **Usman Ranger**

VISITING KOMODO NATIONAL PARK

Established in 1980 and declared a World Heritage Site and a Man and the Biosphere Reserve by Unesco in 1986, **Komodo National Park** (www.komodonationalpark.org) covers 1817 sq km. Within that area are Komodo, Rinca and Padar Islands; a constellation of smaller islands and an incomparably rich marine ecosystem.

Fees for visitors add up quickly:

➡ Landing fee per person for Komodo and Rinca islands: 150,000Rp (Monday to Friday); 225,000Rp (weekends and holidays)

➡ Boat fee: 100,000Rp

➡ Ranger-guided walk fee: 80,000Rp (maximum four people)

➡ Tourism tax: 100,000Rp

➡ Wildlife observation fee: 10,000Rp

➡ Hiking or trekking fee: 5,000Rp

➡ Diving fee per person per day: 25,000Rp

➡ Snorkelling fee per person per day: 15,000Rp

Note that these fees are often changing, with constant talk of increases. Tour operators (including dive shops) usually collect the fees in advance. If not, you pay them in the park offices on Komodo or Rinca, or at Labuan Bajo's PHKA Information Booth (p376).

At both Komodo and Rinca you have a choice of walks, from short to long, which you organise with a ranger when you arrive at the relevant island's park office. Longer walks demand a higher price.

(☑ 0812 3956 6140). English is often minimal, so get your ranger to work out the nitty-gritty before you bed down for the night.

Any place you stay will provide you with simple meals, but be sure to confirm this with your ranger. Memorising the Bahasa Indonesia word for eat and food, *makan*, can get you a long way.

Komodo Guesthouse　　　GUESTHOUSE $$
(☑ 0812 3956 6140; Loh Liang; r from 400,000Rp) Located on Komodo Island and just five-minutes' walk from the dock, this six-room guesthouse has a long, covered porch that's elevated and offers ocean views. Rooms are basic but have fans (there's electricity from 6pm to midnight) and you can organise meals through park rangers. Reserve when you arrive on the island or ahead by phone.

🛈 Getting There & Away

Competition for Komodo day trips from Labuan Bajo (p369) is fierce. Join one of the many tours hawked by operators in town, which cost from 500,000Rp per person, including a light lunch and stops for beach fun and snorkelling. As it takes 3½ hours to reach Komodo, day trips leave around 5.30am and return around 6pm. You can also charter a local boat from 2,000,000Rp and pick your itinerary, which is a great deal when split between four to six people. Just be sure to make the proper safety checks before committing. Overnight charters leave around 7am and start at 2,000,000Rp per person.

A speedboat costing from 1,500,000Rp per person will cover the distance to Komodo in under an hour and arrive at hot spots before the crowds. Charter your own from around 7,000,000Rp for a full day out, which can include stops at both Komodo and Rinca. The many liveaboard schemes almost always include a stop at Komodo at some point, as do the private boats making the run between Flores, Lombok and Bali.

Rinca

Rinca is slightly smaller than nearby Komodo, closer to Labuan Bajo and easily done in a day trip. It packs a lot into a small space and for many it's a more convenient but just as worthy destination as Komodo. The island combines mangroves, light forest, sun-drenched hills and – of course – Komodo dragons. Due to its smaller size and a tendency for *ora* to hang around Loh Buaya's camp kitchen, you're more likely to see the beasts on Rinca than Komodo.

🏃 Activities

From the boat dock it's a 10-minute walk across tidal flats, home to long-tail macaques and wild water buffalo, to the PHKA station camp at Loh Buaya. Three guided walks are included in the 80,000Rp admission fee: the **short walk** (500m, one hour) takes in mangroves and some *ora* nesting sites; the **medium walk** (1.5km, 90 minutes) is 'just right' as it includes the shady lowlands plus a trip up a hillside where the views across the arid landscape to achingly turquoise waters and pearly white specks of beach are spectacular; and the **long walk** (4km, three hours), which takes in all the island's attractions.

Besides dragons, you may see tiny Timor deer, snakes, monkeys, wild boar and an array of birds. There are supposedly no set dragon-feeding places on Rinca, but you're almost guaranteed to see the massive beasts near the camp kitchen at Loh Buaya, so you do the maths.

🛏 Sleeping & Eating

You can stay in a spare room in the ranger's dorm (from 300,000Rp), but there's little reason to as the site lacks charm and Labuan Bajo is nearby.

There is a simple daytime cafe at the ranger station where you can stock up on water, have a snack and enjoy a cold beer while watching grazing deer nervously eyeing *ora*.

❶ Getting There & Away

Day trips to Rinca start at 400,000Rp and the choices are many. Chartering a speedboat to Rinca costs around 5,000,000Rp from Labuan Bajo (p369) and takes less than an hour each way. Boats usually return via small island beaches and snorkelling spots.

At Rinca, boats dock at the sheltered lagoon at Loh Kima, which at busy times may have over two dozen wooden vessels tied together.

KOMODO DRAGONS

The *ora* (Komodo dragon) is a monitor lizard, albeit one on steroids. Growing up to 3m in length and weighing up to 150kg, they are an awesome sight and must-see during any visit to Komodo National Park. Standard day tours tend to arrive in the middle of the day, when *ora* lounge about lethargically. They're much more active at dawn and dusk, but even when resting, they can be as fearsome as their looks imply. Park rangers keep them from attacking tourists; random encounters are a bad idea. Some dragon details:

➡ They are omnivorous, and enjoy eating their young. Juvenile dragons live in trees to avoid becoming a meal for adults.

➡ *Ora* often rise up on their hind legs just before attacking, and the tail can deliver well-aimed blows that knock down their prey.

➡ Long thought to be a type of bacteria, venom (located in glands between the dragons' teeth) is their secret weapon. One bite from a dragon leads to septic infections that inevitably kill the victim. The venom is loaded with toxins that promote bleeding and the huge lizard lopes along after its victim waiting for it to die, usually within a week.

➡ Komodos can eat up to 80% of their body weight in a single sitting. They will then retire for up to a month to digest the massive meal.

➡ On Komodo, *ora* have been seen chasing deer into the ocean and then waiting on shore while the hapless mammal tries to return. Eventually the exhausted animal staggers onto the beach, where the dragon inflicts its ultimately deadly bite.

➡ There is no accepted reason why the dragons are only found in this small area of Indonesia, although it's thought that their ancestors came from Australia four million years ago.

➡ It's estimated that there are up to 5000 in the wild today, but there are concerns that only a few hundred or so are egg-laying females.

➡ In 2006, two female dragons kept isolated from other dragons their entire lives laid fertilised eggs, which hatched successfully. The process, parthenogenesis, is incredibly rare and occurs when an unfertilised egg develops into an embryo without being fertilised by a sperm.

Flores

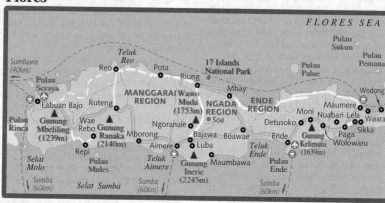

FLORES

Flores, the island given a pretty but incongruous Portuguese name by its 16th-century colonists, has grown greatly in popularity. The serpentine, 670km Trans-Flores Hwy runs the length of the island, skirting knife-edge ridges, brushing by paddy-fringed villages and opening up dozens of areas few tourists explore.

The island is a cacophony of smells, swinging between coffee roasting in the hills, clove cigarettes, exhaust fumes and the unmistakable scent of the ocean. In the west, Labuan Bajo is a booming tourist town combining tropical beauty with nearby attractions such as Komodo National Park, superb dive spots and white-sand islands.

The east is attracting an ever-greater number of travellers chasing smouldering volcanoes, emerald rice terraces, prehistoric riddles, exotic cultures, hot springs and hidden beaches. Away from the port towns most people are nominally Catholic. Many more are part of cultures dating back centuries, living in traditional villages seemingly unchanged in millennia.

ℹ Information

Foreign aid money has funded a string of useful tourist offices in key towns across Flores. Their enthusiastic assistance includes free town maps and several publications well worth their modest prices, a huge, detailed island map and books covering activities and culture.

ℹ Getting There & Away

AIR

Flights connect Flores with Bali, Lombok and Kupang (West Timor), among other destinations. Labuan Bajo is the main gateway, while Maumere and Ende are also serviced by daily flights. It's easy to fly into Labuan Bajo, tour the island, and fly out of Maumere. Be aware that flights are booked solid at peak times.

BOAT

Daily ferries (www.indonesiaferry.co.id) connect Labuan Bajo with Sape (Sumbawa), while weekly services go to Bira (Sulawesi) and Pulau Jampea (Sulawesi). From Larantuka (Flores), three ferries go each week to Kupang (West Timor). From Ende, weekly boats will take you to Waingapu (Sumba) and Kupang (West Timor).

ℹ Getting Around

The Trans-Flores Hwy, the spine of the island, twists and turns through beautiful countryside and skirts photogenic volcanoes, but don't make the mistake of taking Google Maps' estimated journey times as gospel.

The improving roads mean that more and more visitors are hiring motorcycles in Labuan Bajo and heading east. This can cost from 75,000Rp per day plus petrol. It's not for the faint of heart: riding can be hazardous and exhausting.

Regular buses run between Labuan Bajo and Maumere. They're cheap and cramped. Much more comfortable and only somewhat more expensive are public minibuses (often a Toyota Kijang), which link major towns in air-con comfort.

Many travellers hire a car and driver, which costs from 800,000Rp to 1,200,000Rp per day, depending on English-speaking and tour-guiding capabilities. If you have a group of six, this is a fair deal. Many drivers also work as guides and can arrange detailed, island-wide itineraries. Your accommodation will usually be able to recommend someone reliable, but stop for a bite or drink anywhere in Flores and you're likely to meet someone who will recommend a friend.

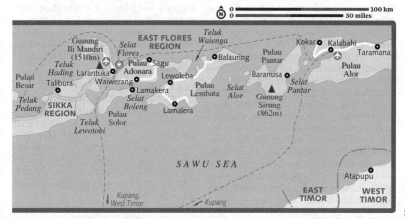

Based in Labuan Bajo, Andy Rona (p372) is an excellent driver and guide, who has a network of reliable colleagues.

Labuan Bajo

✆ 0385 / POP 6300

This dusty, busy harbour town is perpetually being upgraded to cope with more travellers. It's the jumping-off point to see famous dragons at Komodo National Park and to be awed by world-class diving, but those who stay a little longer fall in love with 'Bajo' (attested to by a healthy expat community).

Everything you need is located on one-way Jl Soekarno Hatta, which is crammed with Western restaurants, local *rumah makans* (eating houses) and plenty of accommodation, travel agents and dive shops. The waterfront bustles with daily life, and connections to other parts of Indonesia are effortless.

Atmospheric old corrugated tin shacks are being replaced by the glossy new marina and an expanding line-up of five-star resorts. Add in the town's role as the jumping-off point for trans-Flores adventures and expanded air service and you can see why the boom just keeps booming.

🏃 Activities

Labuan Bajo's pristine coastline is mostly occupied by hotels, making excursions to nearby islands essential day trips for snorkelling and lounging on palm-fringed beaches. **Pantai Waecicu** is on Bajo's mainland, where you can snorkel around the tiny islet of **Kukusan Kecil**. **Pulau Bidadari** (Angel Island) has crystalline water filled with fish and baby sharks. **Pulau Seraya** and **Pulau Kanawa** have postcard-perfect beaches and resorts taking advantage of them, while **Pulau Kalong** is home to thousands of flying fox bats, active from dusk. Travellers with more time won't regret staying on a liveaboard boat and island-hopping further out from Labuan Bajo.

Diving & Snorkelling

With impressive muck diving and coral sites within 1½ hours of Bajo, scuba opportunities abound well before Komodo National Park. But beneath the surface of Komodo lies one of the world's most biodiverse marine environments: vibrant reefs, mangroves, sand banks and drop-offs to teeming deep-water habitats supporting thousands of species of tropical fish, turtles, marine mammals, crustaceans and more.

Outstanding sites include: **Batu Bolong**, a tiny island surrounded by coral walls where you might see Napoleon wrasse and white-tip sharks; **Sebayur Kecil**, an almost current-free site where parrotfish, cuttlefish and blue spotted rays are common; **Karang Makassar** (Manta Point), which offers guaranteed sightings of graceful manta rays during rainy season from December to March (and often outside it); **Siaba Besar**, known as Turtle Town for its local residents; and **Crystal Rock**, where advanced divers navigate the soft coral-covered sea mount spotting sharks and larger fish.

An agreement between members of the Dive Operators Community of Komodo (DOCK) ensures similar prices: 1,650,000Rp for three dives on a day trip is a common rate, as is 5,500,000Rp for a three-day Open

Water Diver certification. Many shops also offer Divemaster and speciality courses.

Dive operators line Jl Soekarno Hatta. It's best to shop around, but not always possible to survey the equipment and boats before making a decision. Ask plenty of questions and request to see photographs – staff should produce answers and a good gut feeling, but bring anything you deem essential.

Snorkelling trips are also available (around 700,000Rp for three sites and a visit to the dragons). Your hotel will rent snorkelling gear or know who does. Local shops loan masks and fins for around 60,000Rp per day. July and August is peak season but in March, April and September visitor numbers thin and diving is magical.

Flores Diving Centre
DIVING

(☑ 0822 4791 8573, 0812 3880 1183; www.flores divingcentre.com; Jl Soekarno Hatta; day trip/eco-dive from 1,650,000/750,000Rp; ⏲ 8.30am-7.30pm) 🐾 Offers all of the usual daily dive trips, courses and liveaboard safaris (on an impressive steel boat), but with the addition of an eco-dive – a not-for-profit initiative where people participate in a clean-up dive before two fun dives outside the national park.

Divine Diving
DIVING

(☑ 0813 5305 2200; www.divinediving.com; Jl Soekarno Hatta; day trips from 1,350,000Rp; ⏲ 6.30am-8pm) 🐾 A proud supporter of numerous environmental and wildlife non-profit organisations, Divine Diving offers two- and three-dive day trips, PADI courses and liveaboard adventures capped at eight people.

Manta Rhei
DIVING

(☑ 0812 9025 0791, 0821 4440 1355; www.manta rhei.com; Jl Soekarno Hatta 16; day trips from 1,650,000Rp; ⏲ 9am-7.30pm Mon-Sat, 2-7.30pm Sun) The only dive centre promising Belgian waffles after a day in the water, Manta Rhei specialises in themed day trips (Crazy Shark Day, Manic Manta Day, etc.) and PADI courses. Nitrox dives and *pinisi* (Sulawesi schooner) liveaboard (from 4,500,000Rp per person, per night), complete with hot tub, also available.

Uber Scuba
DIVING

(☑ 0813 3961 9724; www.uberscubakomodo.com; Jl Soekarno Hatta; 3-dive fun dive 1,650,000Rp; ⏲ 8.30am-8pm) This dive shop is one of the best riding the wave of ever-increasing visitor numbers. Besides an extensive range of

fun dives and courses, it offers all-inclusive liveaboard diving packages (three nights, 10 dives for US$815). The company owns the liveaboard, day-trip boats and a speedboat that accompanies the day-trip boats as an extra safety measure.

Blue Marlin
DIVING

(☑ 0385-41789; www.bluemarlindivekomodo.com; Jl Soekarno Hatta; day trips from 1,400,000Rp; ⏲ 8am-8pm) Most dive schools in Bajo teach the basics in the ocean, but Blue Marlin makes a splash with the town's only purpose-built dive pool. Day-trip from a 15m-long custom fibreglass boat, or take *Toby* the speedboat and arrive at dive sites before the crowds.

There's a restaurant and bar onsite (mains 36,000Rp to 60,000Rp) and accommodation (dorms from 150,000Rp, doubles from 950,000Rp).

Wicked Diving
DIVING

(☑ 0812 3964 1143; www.wickeddiving.com; Jl Soekarno Hatta; 3-/6-night trips from US$685/1125; ⏲ 9am-7pm) Wicked offers popular multi-day liveaboard excursions on a *pinisi* (Sulawesan schooner). It also organises day trips through local operators.

Komodo Dive Center
DIVING

(☑ 0812 3630 3644, 0811 3897 007; www.komodo divecenter.com; Jl Soekarno Hatta; day trips from 1,350,000Rp, 4-day liveaboard from €750; ⏲ 7am-7pm) Offers a full range of day trips, multi-day tours and PADI courses. Promotes use of nitrox and extensive range of gear rentals. Do your due diligence from the beanbags on the wooden porch.

Massage & Spa

★ Yayasan Ayo Mandiri
SPA

(☑ 0385-41318; www.yam-flores.com; Jl Puncak Waringin; 60/90min massages 150,000/180,000Rp; ⏲ 9am-12.30pm & 3-8pm Mon-Sat) A not-for-profit foundation that trains locals with disabilities, ranging from vision to physical impairment, in massage therapy, providing employment to an otherwise marginalised community. The quality of treatments rivals other spas in town. Visit for acupressure, hot stone and reflexology massages; manicures and pedicures; facials and more. Look for the big red 'massage' sign.

👉 Tours

Alongside dedicated tour companies in Labuan Bajo, there are drivers that plan and lead trips. Budget between 800,000Rp to

Labuan Bajo

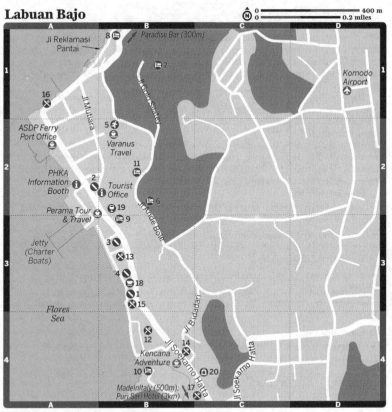

Labuan Bajo

BOAT TOURS BETWEEN LOMBOK & FLORES

Travelling by sea between Lombok and Labuan Bajo is a popular way to get to Flores and you'll glimpse more of the region's spectacular coastline and dodge the slog by bus across Sumbawa. Typical three- and four-day itineraries take in snorkelling at Pulau Satonda or Pulau Moyo off the coast of Sumbawa, and throw in a dragon-spotting walk on Komodo or Rinca.

These are no luxury cruises – a lot depends on the boat, the crew and your fellow travellers. Some operators have reneged on 'all-inclusive' deals en route, and others operate decrepit old tugs without life jackets or radio. Plus this crossing can be hazardous when seas are rough.

Most travellers enjoy the journey though, whether it involves bedding down on a mattress on deck (recommended) or in a tiny cabin. The cost for a three- to four-day itinerary ranges from about US$170 to US$400 per person and includes all meals, basic beverages and use of snorkelling gear.

Other considerations:

➜ Carefully vet your boat for safety (p798); check for safety equipment, locate exits and avoid overcrowded vessels.

➜ Understand what's included and not included in the price. For instance, if drinking water is included, how much is provided? If you need more, can you buy it on the boat or do you need to bring your own?

➜ Taking snacks is a good idea as food might only be available during meal times.

➜ If you are flexible, you can often save money by travelling west from Flores, as travelling eastwards is more popular. Look for deals at agents once you're in Labuan Bajo.

Providers include:

➜ Kencana Adventure (p377) Offers basic three-day/two-night boat trips between Lombok and Labuan Bajo.

➜ Perama Tour & Travel (p377) Runs basic boat trips between Lombok and Labuan Bajo with deck accommodation as well as small two-person cabins.

1,200,000Rp per day – the price rises with guide qualifications and English-speaking capability.

Andy Rona　　　　　　　　　　　　　TOURS
(☏ WhatsApp 0813 3798 0855; andyrona7@gmail. com) An excellent guide and driver with a network of reliable colleagues and a penchant for reggae. He will point you in the right direction if he's booked up. A five-day adventure across Flores costs 1,000,000Rp per day for one to four people.

Wicked Adventures　　　　　　　ADVENTURE
(☏ 0812 3607 9641; www.wickedadventures.com; Jl Soekarno Hatta; 1-day kayak trips from US$100; ⏰ 9am-7pm) 🏄 An offshoot of the recommended Wicked Diving (p370) and located beneath it, this group runs kayak trips with local guides in Komodo National Park. Other adventures include Wae Rebo hikes and trips to Wicked's turtle conservation camp on a south Flores beach. Ask about their

Wicked Good community and environment initiatives.

🛏 Sleeping

It seems every week there's a new place to stay in Labuan Bajo. Even so, during July and August travellers can outnumber beds, so book well ahead. Accommodation is concentrated around the centre of town. Don't settle for neglected hostels when spiffy new ones are the same price. Lush hotels are mostly outside the main drag, but if budget allows, nearby island resorts make for private paradises.

🛏 Central Area

⭐ **Ciao Hostel**　　　　　　　　　　HOSTEL $
(☏ 0852 2038 3641; www.ciaohostel.net; Jl Golo Silatey, off Jl Ande Bole; dm 160,000-230,000Rp; ❄ 🛜) Labuan Bajo's best hostel has spacious ocean-view dorms with four to 12 beds – the latter in the popular, open-air room with

panoramic vistas and mosquito nets. There's plenty to love: the free shuttle to town and the airport, the rooftop bar, Pida Loca Reso (mains 47,000Rp to 85,000Rp), voting for nightly movies and cheery staff.

One Tree Hill · HOSTEL $

(☑0812 4644 6414; onetreehill360@gmail.com; Jl Verhoeven, Pantai Klumpang, Desa Batu Cermin; dm with fan/air-con from 125,000/155,000Rp; ❄️🛜) This 56-bed hostel from Tree Top (p376) should really provide transfers into town, but it's a must-visit for anyone with wheels. With both sunset and sunrise views, colourful wooden rooms summit at the open-air, beanbag-filled **Tre360 Bar** (4pm to 8pm weekdays, to 10pm weekends). Breakfast isn't included but there's a common kitchen. Limited wi-fi at the bar.

The Palm · HOSTEL $

(☑0812 9655 2231; www.facebook.com/thepalm komodo; Jl Puncak Waringin; dm 200,000Rp; ❄️🏊) Peppered with quote decals ('Always remember, karma comes back') and adored for its pool and friendly staff, this five-room, 29-bed dorm nails the balance between backpacker fun and relaxation. There's a female-only room, individual power sockets and reading lights, air-con, pool parties and a restaurant (mains 50,000Rp to 150,000Rp, open 9.30am until 10pm). Speedboat day trips are competitively priced.

Green Hill Bed Station · HOSTEL $

(☑0813 7429 3693; https://green-hill-bed-station. business.site; Jl Soekarno Hatta; dm 175,000Rp; ❄️🛜) This central, 30-bed hostel from **Green Hill Boutique Hotel** (☑0813 3826 2247, 0385-41289; www.greenhillboutiquehotel. com; Jl Soekarno Hatta; r 500,000-700,000Rp; ❄️🛜) is perfect for travellers who want a hostel set-up without the rowdy crowd. Immaculate and comfortable with privacy curtains and individual power outlets, reading lights and large lockers, the shared hot-water bathrooms wouldn't be out of place in a design magazine. Free airport transfers.

Le Pirate Boatel · HOUSEBOAT $$

(☑0822 3724 4539; www.lepirate.com/boatel; Waecicu Bay; r 700,000Rp; 🛜) Halfway between staying in town and on a liveaboard, the charming, 10-room Boatel from Le Pirate (p376) is permanently docked a 10-minute, free boat shuttle from Bajo. Each room has a deck with a hammock and sun-bathing net over the water. Bathrooms are shared,

breakfast is included and there's a restaurant on board. Take advantage of happy hour and free snorkelling.

Escape Bajo · GUESTHOUSE $$

(☑0822 3532 6699, 0385-2440011; www.face book.com/escapebajo.brewbitebed; Jl Binongko; dm/d 175,000/585,000Rp; ❄️🛜) This swish, minimalist spot delivers on its tagline: brew (the trendy coffee shop opens 6am to 10pm), bite (there's a small menu of Indonesian and Western fare, 40,000Rp to 68,000Rp) and bed (six lush dorm beds boast individual power outlets, and two of the six ocean-view rooms are leased long term).

Join rooftop sunset yoga every Monday for 100,000Rp.

La Boheme Bajo · HOSTEL $$

(☑0385-244 0442, WhatsApp 0813 3828 9524; www.backpacking-indonesia.com; Jl Goron Talo; dm/r from 100,000/250,000Rp; ❄️🛜) Laid-back beach vibes abound at this large hostel, where free banana pancakes are available 24 hours. There's a restaurant (11am to 11pm; mains 35,000Rp to 70,000Rp), beanbags for chilling out, a cinema room, pool table, guest kitchen and strong wi-fi. It's about 1km from the centre of town, down a side street on the right heading south.

Palulu Garden Homestay · HOMESTAY $$

(☑0822 3658 4279; www.palulugarden.wordpress. com; Jl Ande Bole; dm 85,000Rp, r with fan/air-con 250,000/350,000Rp; ❄️) Long-time local guide Kornelis Gega runs this four-room family homestay above the town centre. The basic, ramshackle dorm has six beds (two people can share the largest for 120,000Rp total) and there are three clean private rooms. Kornelis can help with trip planning, transport arrangements and motorbike hire (75,000Rp per day). Say hi to Charlie Chaplin, the cat.

★Scuba Junkie
Komodo Beach Resort · DIVE RESORT $$$

(☑0822 3724 8059, 0812 3651 7973; www.scuba junkiekomodo.com; Warloka Flores; 3-night all-inclusive packages bale/d from 4,740,000/ 6,250,000Rp) 🤿 A world-away from the bustle, this fantastic dive resort is on an isolated bay about an hour south of Bajo by boat. Rinca Island is nearby as are oodles of dive sites, which you'll get to explore with dives included in the accommodation packages. Stay in breezy beach bales or sea-view rooms and relax on the picturesque jetty.

★**Villa Domanik** BUNGALOW **$$$**
(☑0852 3814 7795; www.villadomanik.com; Jl Belakang Pertamina, Pasar Baru, Desa Gorontalo; bungalows/2-bedroom villas from 1,100,000/2,300,000Rp; P ❄ ☎ ⛶) Villa Domanik is bliss. On a hilltop outside Bajo, it has manicured gardens and a view of the Flores Sea from the pool. The three bungalows have outdoor bathrooms and wooden finishes, while a second, self-contained, two-bedroom villa is on the way. Food is a highlight, as is the sunset. In high season there's a two-night minimum stay.

Bayview Gardens Hotel INN **$$$**
(☑0385-41549; www.bayview-gardens.com; Jl Ande Bole; r from 850,000Rp; ❄ ☎ ⛶) Each of these 16 rooms tucked into the hillside – but still close to town – has a harbour view, best enjoyed during a balcony breakfast. Harbor Master Suites have day beds and outdoor showers; wooden Seaview Suits were crafted by a boat builder. Wi-fi only in the restaurant and by the picture-postcard perfect pool. Prices jump in high season.

Puri Sari Hotel BOUTIQUE HOTEL **$$$**
(☑0385-244 3710; www.purisaribeachhotel.net; Jl Pantai Pede; r/villas from 950,000/3,000,000Rp; ❄ ☎ ⛶) A two-storey, ranch-style hotel owned by an Indonesian-Japanese couple. There's a shady garden, beachside pool, friendly management and worthy buffet breakfast. The 21 rooms have queen-sized wooden beds and wide private terraces. It offers free shuttles to and from the airport, and another to town every two hours. Prices jump in high season.

🛏 Island Hotels

Although close to Labuan Bajo, the surrounding island hotels and resorts feel like a world apart. All offer some form of boat transfer to/from town – in an hour or less you can escape to your own tropical paradise.

Flores XPirates Dive Camp HUT **$$**
(☑0811 3985 344; http://xpiratesdivecamp.com; Pulau Sebayur; dm/d/bungalow per person all-inclusive 400,000/450,000/600,000Rp; ☎) ✐ A solar-powered island dive camp with new huts, breezy bungalows and a six-bed dorm. There's a restaurant with wi-fi, dive centre and brilliant snorkelling near the 180m jetty and reef, where a coral propagation program is underway. Prices include buffet meals and

boat transfers. Full-board dive packages available from 3,700,000Rp per person.

Those who wish to day trip to the island can do so for 250,000Rp per person, including lunch.

★**Angel Island Resort** DIVE RESORT **$$$**
(☑0385-41443, WhatsApp 0812 3660 8475; www.angelisleflores.com; Pulau Bidadari; per night from 4,000,000Rp; ❄ ☎) ✐ Set on its own 15-hectare island linked to Labuan Bajo by private boat, this resort offers delightful garden-ensconced cottages behind one of three white-sand beaches. All meals are included and the food and service are casual and superb. Don't miss snorkelling at the protected reef, birdwatching and free kayaking. Minimum two-night stay.

Komodo Resort Diving Club RESORT **$$$**
(☑0385-42094, island number 0813 3761 6625, office 8am-5pm 0812 3810 3244; www.komodoresort.com; Pulau Sebayur; d/tr/f incl meals 2,820,000/9,548,000/10,936,800Rp; ❄ ☎) With 18 *lumbung* (rice barn) style bungalows and four family rooms spread along a white-sand beach, this is a truly beautiful island resort. Bungalows have wooden floors, king beds, plush linen, 24-hour electricity, tented marble bathrooms with hot water and more. Rates include three excellent meals, but diving is separate. There's also a spa and beach bar. Minimum three-night stay.

Sudamala Resort Seraya RESORT **$$$**
(☑0361 288555, 0821 4647 1362; www.sudamalaresorts.com/seraya; Pulau Seraya; d per person from USD$325-450; ❄ ☎ ⛶) Get-away-from-it-all bliss exists on Pulau Seraya. Stay in flawless, whitewashed wood-and-thatch-bungalows set on a white-sand beach with offshore snorkelling. There's a spa, restaurant and rugged hilltop where you can wonder at spectacular sunsets for days on end. It's only 20 minutes by boat from Bajo. Minimum three-night stay.

The pick-up point is at Bamboo Cafe (p376) on Bajo's main drag.

Eating

Bajo's popularity has seen an influx of Western restaurants, from enviable Italian to Instagram-worthy seaside smoothie bowls. Hit the Pasar Malam for seafood, and Padang restaurants at the southern end of Jl Soekarno Hatta to eat beside locals. Further south the street forks left into the Trans-

Flores Hwy, where street vendors sell *pisang goreng* (fried banana) and pancake-like *terang bulan*.

Pasar Malam
INDONESIAN $

(Night Market; off Jl Soekarno Hatta; mains 25,000-80,000Rp; ⊙6pm-midnight) Bajo town's most atmospheric dinner spot. Waterfront stalls with hand-painted names are fronted by tables of fresh seafood, with others specialising in more affordable nasi goreng, *mie goreng* and *bakso* (meatball noodle soup). Shop around before committing to a fish and BYO Bintang.

Blue Corner
INDONESIAN $

(☑0813 3762 0744; Jl Soekarno Hatta; mains 25,000-55,000Rp; ⊙10am-9pm) If you have a predilection for local food, seek out this family-run warung with pink and blue walls. There's no English menu, but pictures on posters help. Juices are half the price of the Pasar Malam and *sop buntut* (oxtail soup) is the speciality – try the fried version.

Rumah Makan Garuda
INDONESIAN $

(Garuda; ☑0853 3864 2021; Jl Soekarno Hatta; mains 30,000-55,000Rp; ⊙7am-10pm) There are plenty of Padang restaurants at the southern end of Jl Soekarno Hatta, but Garuda is our pick. Point-and-order from the stacked window display: beef *rendang*, jackfruit curry, fried chicken or fish, tempe, egg and – if you're game – offal. Load up with garlicky sambal from tabletop jars.

Happy Banana
JAPANESE $$

(☑0385-41467; happybananalb@gmail.com; Jl Soekarno Hatta; breakfast 46,000-120,000Rp, mains 84,000-105,000Rp; ⊙7am-11pm; ﹡ 🛜 🖉) This inviting spot has something for everyone, including vegans. Staff are trained in the art of sushi, with everything from udon noodles to gyoza made from scratch. The 'no rules' policy means you can start the day with a chia bowl and poached eggs or finish with fluffy gnocchi and tempura. Save room for vegan chocolate mousse.

★ MadeInItaly
ITALIAN $$

(☑0385-244 0222; www.miirestaurants.com; Jl Pantai Pede; main 85,000-170,000Rp; ⊙11am-11pm; ﹡🛜) Bajo's best Italian is known for superb thin-crust pizza and fresh pasta. Sit in a stylish, semi-open dining room or air-conditioned cellar with river-stone walls. Ingredients are imported from Italy and grown on restaurant-owned organic farms. For a luxury experience, enquire about the Culinary Journey island boat trip. There's also a bottle shop on-site.

La Cucina
ITALIAN $$

(☑0812 3851 2172; lacucinakomodo@gmail.com; Jl Soekarno Hatta 46; mains 52,000-90,000Rp; ⊙6.30am-10.30pm; 🛜) This small, beachy dining room with its blue colour palette, fishing-net decorations and rustic wooden tables is a crowd favourite. Homemade pasta and pizza are the menu picks, but expect to join the end of a queue in peak season.

CLIMBING, CANYONING & CAVING

Shake off your sea legs by heading east of Labuan Bajo and exploring on land. Local tour operators on Jl Soekarno Hatta organise both best-of and custom itineraries.

Climbing up the rainforested slopes of **Gunung Mbeliling** (1239m) is popular. Leaving from Roe Village, 27km east of Bajo, the trip usually takes two days and includes six to eight hours of hiking through a fraction of the 150 sq km. Bonuses are a sunrise at the summit and a stop-off at **Air Terjun Cunca Rami**, a cooling cascade with freshwater swimming holes. A guide is recommended.

If you like canyoning, you'll enjoy the **Cunca Wulang Cascades**, 30km southeast of Bajo. Local guides lead you from Wersawe Village through rice fields, candlenut and coffee plantations to a winding canyon studded with rock water slides, swimming holes and waterfalls. Trips generally last half a day.

There are two caves worth exploring in Labuan Bajo. You only need an hour to visit **Gua Batu Cermin** (20,000Rp entry per person, guides optional but unnecessary for 50,000Rp), the 'Stone Mirror Cave' about 7km out of the town centre. Highlights include donning a hard hat and squeezing through tight spaces to see a whole fossilised turtle and coral gardens. Bring a torch. **Gua Rangko** (entry 20,000Rp) is more popular, an oceanic cave famed for its sunlit turquoise water (visit in the afternoon for the best light), stalagmites and stalactites. Drive from Labuan Bajo to Rangko Village, then don't pay more than 250,000Rp for the boat to get there.

Bamboo Cafe
CAFE $$

(📞0812 3697 4461; Jl Soekarno Hatta; breakfast 25,000-65,000Rp, mains 45,000-75,000Rp; ⏰6am-9pm; 📶🍽️) Sit in white cane chairs and admire the hand-painted wall map while enjoying all-day breakfast made with vibrant ingredients from local farms. Booster juices and cold-brew coffee accompany smoothie bowls, eggs, toasties and wholefoods.

Tree Top
INTERNATIONAL $$

(📞0385-41561, 0812 3803 9888; Jl Soekarno Hatta 22; mains 35,000-200,000Rp; ⏰7am-11pm; 📶) This open-air, double-decker restaurant is a fantastic place to watch the sunset, especially if you nab the table that juts out to the harbour. While both Indonesian and Western food is better elsewhere, it's worth lingering for the view. There's a billiard table on the ground floor, shared with **Eco Tree O'tel** (double rooms from 680,000Rp).

Drinking & Nightlife

Bajo's popularity with backpackers, European diving instructors and music-loving locals translates to plenty of places to wet your whistle.

De'Flo Cafe & Ole-Ole
COFFEE

(📞0822 8888 9118; https://deflocafeoleole.business.site; Jl Soekarno Hatta 22; snacks 20,000-45,000Rp; ⏰7am-10pm; 📶) Owned and operated by enthusiastic university graduates from Jakarta, this tranquil coffee shop a level down from Tree Top is the best place in Bajo for a caffeine fix. De'Flo serves local Manggarai and limited-edition, single-origin coffee any way you like it, along with traditional cakes, snacks and ethical handicrafts, packaged for all your souvenir needs.

Le Pirate
BAR

(📞0361-733493, 0385-41962, 0822 3724 4539; www.lepirate.com/labuan-bajo; Jl Soekarno Hatta; ⏰7am-11pm; 📶) This colourful 1st-floor bar is a popular space for a drink after a day on the water. There's live music (8pm to 10pm Tuesday, Thursday and Saturday) and film nights (Monday and Wednesday). There's also a decent restaurant (mains 60,000Rp to 110,000Rp), rooftop bar and stylish but poky accommodation (private bunk from 500,000Rp, double from 650,000Rp).

Paradise Bar
BAR

(📞0812 1341 5306; Jl Binongko; ⏰5pm-midnight Mon-Fri & Sun, to 2am Sat; 📶) 'Come to Paradise' is a common phrase in Bajo, referring to the bar-slash-nightclub famed for sea and sunset views. It's a preposterously lovely place for a cocktail; come nightfall live music provides a party vibe. Saturdays see a 65,000Rp cover charge, including a drink.

Paradise is a 10-minute stroll uphill from central Labuan Bajo. *Ojeks* hang around to take you home after dark, though they charge a premium.

Cafe in Hit
CAFE

(📞0812 3642 4411; Jl Soekarno Hatta; coffee/light meals from 30,000/25,000Rp; ⏰7am-10pm; 📶) Labuan Bajo's answer to Starbucks, this casual coffee house serves ice-cold frappes alongside strong wi-fi. People-watch from above the street or browse shelves of local beans and second-hand books. Order from the giant blackboard.

Shopping

Magnolia Boutique Komodo
FASHION & ACCESSORIES

(📞0812 3912 7007; hesty.hapsari@gmail.com; Jl Soekarno Hatta; ⏰8am-9pm) At Labuan Bajo's best fashion store, all pieces are locally made, with some also designed in Flores. There's plenty for the ladies, from linen clothing to contemporary caps made with naturally dyed ikat (patterned cloth), as well as shirts and tees for the blokes and adorable children's clothing. There are plans to move to the marina complex.

ℹ️ Information

Banks and ATMs line Jl Soekarno Hatta.

PHKA Information Booth (📞0385-41005; off Jl Soekarno Hatta; ⏰7-11am & 2-4pm Mon-Sat, 7-10am Sun) On a small access road next to the entrance to the docks, this PHKA (Komodo National Park Authority) booth provides information and permits.

Tourist Office (📞0361-271145, WhatsApp 0812 3746 9880; www.florestourism.com; Jl Mutiara; ⏰8.30am-4pm Mon-Sat) Excellent office with details on activities, updated maps and books plus transport and ticket info. Plan your visit on the porch, then rent a mountain bike for the day (75,000Rp).

ℹ️ Getting There & Away

AIR

Labuan Bajo's **Komodo Airport** (Bandar Udara Komodo) has a sizeable terminal and lengthened runway, a hint at expected tourism growth.

Garuda, Nam Air, TransNusa, Wings Air and Batik Air serve destinations including Denpasar, Jakarta and Kupang, and have counters in the terminal. There are several daily flights to/from Bali, although these are booked solid at busy times. Don't expect to just turn up and go.

BOAT

The ASDP ferry from Labuan Bajo to Sape runs every morning at 9.30am. It costs 60,000Rp and takes six hours. Confirm all times carefully. Buy your tickets the day of departure at the **ferry port office** (www.indonesiaferry.co.id; Jl Soekarno Hatta; ◷ 8am-noon).

Agents for the boats running between Labuan Bajo and Lombok (p372) line Jl Soekarno Hatta. **Kencana Adventure** (✆ 0812 2206 6066; www.kencanaadventure.com; Jl Soekarno Hatta, Beta Bajo Hotel; one-way from 2,250,000Rp) and **Perama Tour & Travel** (✆ 0385-42016, 0385-42015; www.peramatour.com; Jl Soekarno Hatta; one-way per person deck/cabin from 2,200,000/3,300,000Rp; ◷ 7.30am-10pm) offer multiday boat trips between Lombok and Labuan Bajo.

Easily missed on a side street leading uphill from Jl Mutiara, **Varanus Travel** (Pelni Agent; ✆ 0385-41106; off Jl Mutiara; ◷ 9am-7pm Mon-Sat, 11am-6pm Sun) is the official Pelni agent and the place to get tickets for long-distance boat travel. Schedules posted in the windows outline services, including Makassar and the east coast of Sulawesi as well as Bima, Lembar and Benoa (Bali).

To get to Komodo, schedule in a day trip from Labuan Bajo. Join one of the many tours hawked by operators in town, which cost from 500,000Rp per person. Most leave around 5.30am and return around 6pm. Alternatively, charter a local boat or speedboat for a day or overnight.

BUS

The Labuan Bajo bus terminal is about 7km out of town; most people book their tickets through a hotel or agency. With an advance ticket, the bus will pick you up from your accommodation.

Ticket sellers for long-distance travel to Lombok and Bali via ferries and air-con buses work the ferry port office.

ℹ Getting Around

The airport is 1.5km from town. Some hotels offer free rides in and out. A private taxi to town and anywhere within town costs 50,000Rp.

Most places are walkable in Labuan Bajo. An *ojek* ride costs 5000Rp to 10,000Rp. Bemos do continual loops around the centre, following the one-way traffic, and cost 5000Rp per ride. The price may double if you have a sizeable bag.

Manggarai Country

✆ 0385

To compare gradations of beauty on Flores is as futile as it is fun. And if you do get into such a debate, know that if you've explored Manggarai's dense and lush rainforests, studded with towering stands of bamboo and elegant tree ferns, and climbed its mountains to isolated villages accessible only by trail, you may have the trump card.

Ruteng

✆ 0385 / POP 38,888

Surrounded by lush peaks and terraced rice fields, the staid and sprawling market city of Ruteng is the natural base for exploring Manggarai Regency. This predominantly Catholic town is a four-hour drive from Labuan Bajo. Should you take in a few sights, you'll be overnighting here. Fun fact: smaller streets here are named after animals, such as Jl Gajah (elephant), Jl Kelinci (rabbit) and Jl Kuda Belang (zebra).

◎ Sights

★ **Spider Web Rice Fields**   VIEWPOINT
(Lingko Fields; Cara Village, Cancar, off Trans-Flores Hwy) The greatest local site is actually 20km west of Ruteng near Cara *kampung*. The legendary Spider Web Rice Fields are vast creations shaped as implied, which is also the shape of Manggarai roofs that fairly divide property between families. For the best view, stop at the small pavilion, pay 25,000Rp and ascend a dirt path to the main viewing ridge.

BUSES FROM LABUAN BAJO

DESTINATION	TYPE	FARE (RP)	DURATION (HR)	FREQUENCY
Bajawa	bus	210,000	10	several daily
Denpasar (Bali)	bus & ferry	580,000	36	1 daily
Mataram (Lombok)	bus & ferry	370,000	24	1 daily
Ruteng	bus	100,000	4	every 2hr, 6am-6pm

Liang Bua
CAVE

(entry 30,000Rp) The limestone Liang Bua cave, where the remains of the Flores 'hobbit' were famously found in 2003, is about 14km north of Ruteng. Archaeologists believe that the lip along the entrance permitted sediment to build up as water flowed through the cave over the millennia, sealing in human and animal remains. Listen out for rumours of more recent, sacred sightings.

Local guides, whose service is included in your 30,000Rp entry fee, will meet you at the cave's entrance and explain why Liang Bua is considered sacred. The road to the cave is bumpy and can be impassable during rainy season. In the cave itself are remnants of excavations; a small, separate museum contains information in Indonesian, photographs, fossil casts and replica bones. To get here take an *ojek* (100,000Rp) from Ruteng.

🛏 Sleeping

Ruteng has a number of quiet, orderly homestays and some stale but reliable hotels. Remember it's somewhat elevated compared to Bajo and can get chilly at night.

Spring Hill Bungalows
BUNGALOW $$

(📱0813 3937 2345, 0385-22514; springhillbungalowsruteng@gmail.com; Jl Kasturi 8; r from 750,000Rp; 📶) Ruteng's nicest accommodation. Twelve deluxe bungalows set around a lily pond (with more on the way) have plush bedding and wooden feature walls inset with televisions. There's even a hairdryer in the bathroom, but the two-bedroom suite for four (1,750,000Rp) boasts a wooden deck with outdoor spa bath. The restaurant (mains 35,000Rp to 95,000Rp) has a snow ice machine.

D-Rima Homestay
HOMESTAY $$

(📱0813 7951 188; deddydarung@gmail.com; Jl Kelinci; s/d 150,000/250,000-300,000Rp; 📶) A cosy, three-room homestay run by a beautiful family brimming with information about the local area. The hot-water bathroom is shared between two rooms; the largest and most expensive has its own. Motorbike and car rental is available, as are home-cooked vegetarian dinners (45,000Rp per person).

Hobbit Hill Homestay
GUESTHOUSE $$

(📱0812 4648 7553; www.ruteng.id; Jl Liang Bua Golobila; d/bungalow from 250,000/480,000Rp) Two kilometres from the centre of town towards Gua Liang Bua and surrounded by rice terraces is this welcoming, three-bedroom guesthouse. Two rooms have private toilets (only one is an ensuite), while the separate bungalow accommodates four people. The view from the property is especially impressive at sunrise. Generous breakfast included and home-cooked meals from 30,000Rp.

✖ Eating & Drinking

Rumah Makan Cha Cha
INDONESIAN $

(📱0385-21489, 0812 3698 9009; ywidianita@hotmail.com; Jl Diponegoro 12; mains 15,000-50,000Rp; ⊗noon-9pm; 📶) Named after the owner's daughter, Ruteng's best restaurant is all wooden with framed Flores attractions on the walls and gingham table covers. The Indo standards are well prepared and it's a clean, relaxing place. *Nasi lontong opor* (chicken in coconut milk with rice) and *nasi soto ayam* (chicken soup with glass noodles, bean sprouts, egg, potato chips and rice) come recommended.

Kopi Mane Inspiration
CAFE

(📱0821 4733 4545, 0813 8008 2778; Jl Yos Sudarso 12; mains 20,000-35,000Rp; ⊗8am-2am; 📶) A solid spot for a Manggarai coffee to power your day. Buy a bag of ground and roasted beans to take home or order cheap-eat Indonesian fare from a blackboard menu. Tourist information available, along with motorbikes rented at 100,000Rp per day.

❶ Getting There & Away

The bus terminal for eastward destinations is 3.5km out of Ruteng; a bemo or *ojek* there costs from 5000Rp to 10,000Rp. Local buses heading west run from an unofficial, central terminal near the **pasar** (Market; Jl Bhayangkara; ⊗7am-5pm). Regular buses head to Bajawa and Labuan Bajo (110,000Rp, five and four hours respectively).

Wae Rebo

Wae Rebo is the best of Manggarai's traditional villages. Road improvements have opened up the area, but it's still remote.

A village visit involves a splendid but challenging 9km hike that takes three to four hours and winds past waterfalls and swimming holes, as well as spectacular views of the Savu Sea. A donation of 200,000Rp per person is expected for a visit, or 320,000Rp if you stay overnight in a *mbaru tembong* (traditional home). The next morning retrace your steps or hike another six hours over a pass to another trailhead; arrange for pick up here in advance.

Arrange for guides (400,000Rp) and porters (250,000Rp) at the local guesthouses. Don't expect to be automatically treated to indigenous music, dance and weaving demonstrations – these cost extra and are usually organised for larger tour groups. Be sure to start very early, to avoid the sweltering heat of midday. Bring water.

🛏 Sleeping

Given that early morning is the optimal time to start the trek to Wae Rebo, you'll want to stay near the trailhead as opposed to in Ruteng.

Wae Rebo Lodge GUESTHOUSE $
(📱0852 3934 4046, 0812 3712 1903, WhatsApp 085 339 021 145; martin_anggo@yahoo.com; Dintor; r per person 250,000Rp) A purpose-built lodge run by Martin, a local from Wae Rebo. It sits serenely amid rice fields with views of both sunrise and sunset and is some 9km from the trailhead. Meals are included in the rate and you can make all trekking arrangements here. Ten per cent of Martin's profits go towards supporting the community.

Wae Rebo Homestay HOMESTAY $
(📱0813 3935 0775; Denge; r per person 200,000Rp) Right at the trailhead, this is the original place to sleep for people making the Wae Rebo trek. Friendly owner Blasius is a Wae Rebo expert and operates the small visitor centre as well as the 15-room homestay. Ask him about village visits and transport. If the phone signal is patchy, send him an SMS.

❶ Getting There & Away

It's about a three-hour drive from Ruteng to the village trailhead in Denge. You'll need your own wheels for this.

Bajawa

📞0384 / POP 45,000

Framed by forested volcanoes and blessed with a cooler climate, Bajawa is a laid-back, predominantly Catholic hill town. Perched at 1100m above sea level, it's the de facto trading post of the local Ngada people and a great base from which to explore dozens of traditional villages or to stay put and mingle with locals. Gunung Inerie, a perfectly conical volcano at 2245m, looms to the south, where you'll also find active hot springs. **Wawo Muda** (Jl Wawo Muda) is another fa-

vourite thanks to its Kelimutu-esque lake, left behind after an eruption in 2001.

🏃 Activities

★**Gunung Inerie** HIKING
A breathtakingly beautiful volcano looming above Bajawa, Gunung Inerie (2245m), just 10km from town, beckons all would-be climbers. The journey is difficult, but this spectacularly jagged cone is worth sweating for. You can do it as an eight-hour round trip, but it's also possible to camp by the lake. We recommend starting around 3am to catch the sunrise.

With an English-speaking guide and transport from Bajawa, expect to pay about 800,000Rp for one and 1,000,000Rp for two people. Bring water.

Air Panas Soa HOT SPRINGS
(per person 14,000Rp; ⊙7am-6pm) The most serviced hot springs in the region, situated east of town on the rough road to Riung. There are two man-made pools (one is a scintillating 45°C; the other a more pedestrian 35°C to 40°C) and one natural pool (25°C to 30°C). It has modern buildings and can get busy. Air Panas Malanage (p381) is a more natural option.

🛏 Sleeping

Thanks to a growth spurt in Bajawa tourism, locals are opening homestays all over town. Friendly and informative, they're the best accommodation option as hotels can be tired or soulless.

Marselino's Homestay HOMESTAY $
(📱0852 3913 1331; www.floresholiday.wordpress. com; Jl Pipipodo; s/d from 150,000/160,000Rp; 🛜) A centrally located simple affair with three rooms and a living and dining room as common space. Enjoy a hot shower and a breakfast of nasi goreng and fruit. The best thing about this place is the owner, an established tour guide worth calling on for all your Flores needs (tours from 250,000Rp per person per day).

Madja Edelweis Homestay HOMESTAY $
(📱0812 3779 5490; austynobabtista@gmail.com; Jl Pipipodo; r 150,000-300,000Rp; 🛜) Not to be confused with the bland Edelweis Hotel on the main drag, this eight-room homestay has an assortment of comfortable and colourful rooms. The owner is exceedingly helpful, renting motorbikes for 80,000Rp a day and organising trips around Flores. The

wi-fi is fast, a generous breakfast is included and there's a guest kitchen.

★ **Manulalu**   BUNGALOW **$$$**

(✆ 0812 5182 0885; villamanulalu@gmail.com; Mangulewa; d/bungalows from 460,000/ 1,200,000Rp) Split into two nearby properties, Manulalu Hills and Manulalu Jungle are about 20km from Bajawa and 3km from Bena along a scenic, winding road. Hills has eight stylish rooms, but the seven Jungle bungalows, modelled on traditional houses, are something from a fairytale; think beautiful bathrooms and day beds on wooden decks perfect for admiring one of Flores' most spectacular outlooks.

✖ Eating

Rumah Makan Anugerah   INDONESIAN **$**

(✆ 0812 1694 7158; Jl Sudirman; mains 25,000-50,000Rp; ⊙ 8am-10.30pm) This small, spotless family-run *rumah makan* (eating house) is a great choice for a cheap lunch. Some menu items veer towards Chinese, while others such as *nasi babi rica rica* (spicy pork with rice) keep it in the archipelago. Save room for sweets from the cabinet.

❶ Information

Tourist Office (✆ 0852 3904 3771; www. welcome2flores.com; Jl Ahmad Yani 2; ⊙ 8am-6pm) Small but highly useful information centre covering guided trips, hikes, vehicle rental, transport tickets and more. Plenty of Ngada info. The owner is also a guide so the office sometimes closes when they are on the road.

BNI Bank (Jl Marta Dinata; ⊙ 8am-4pm Mon-Fri, 7.30am-4pm Sat) In the centre; has an ATM and exchanges US dollars.

❶ Getting There & Away

There are buses and bemos to various destinations. Buses don't necessarily leave on time – only when the bus is almost full. Kijangs, or share cars, also leave throughout the day from the **bemo terminal** (Jl Basoeki Rahmat). Rates are up to 30% more than bus fares. Bus services include the following:

Ende (70,000Rp, five hours, several times daily)

Labuan Bajo (150,000Rp, 10 hours, several times daily)

Ruteng (80,000Rp, five hours, frequent services from 8am to 11am)

❶ Getting Around

Bemos cruise town for 5000Rp a ride, but it is easy to walk almost everywhere except to the bus terminals.

Trucks serve remote routes; most leave traditional villages in the morning and return in the afternoon.

Motorcycles cost 100,000Rp a day. A private vehicle with a driver is 800,000Rp; expect to pay more the further out you explore. Most hotels can arrange rental.

Bajawa Turelelo Soa Airport is a small, domestic airport 25km from Bajawa and about 6km outside Soa. Wings Air and TransNusa both fly daily to Kupang in West Timor (one hour), while Wings also flies daily to Labuan Bajo (35 minutes).

Around Bajawa

Bajawa's big draw is the chance to explore villages in the gorgeous countryside. The fascinating architecture of the traditional houses features carved poles supporting conical thatched roofs. It's possible to visit the area alone, but you'll learn a lot more about the culture and customs with a guide. Some organise meals in their home villages, others suggest treks to seldom-visited villages accessible only by trail.

Locals and homestay owners can arrange day trips by car from 600,000Rp per person, or jump on the back of a motorbike with a guide for between 400,000Rp to 500,000Rp. A classic one-day itinerary would start in Bajawa and include Bena, Luba, Tololela and Air Panas Malanage hot springs. It's customary to make a donation to the head of traditional villages you visit. Make sure you do this directly, rather than through a guide, to ensure the money is received in full.

Bena

Resting on Inerie's flank, Bena is one of the most traditional Ngada villages. It's home to nine clans and its stone monuments are the region's best. Houses with high, thatched roofs line up in two rows on a ridge. They're interspersed with ancestral totems including megalithic tombs, *ngadhu* (thatched parasol-like structures) and *bhaga* (miniature thatched-roof houses). Most houses have male or female figurines on their roofs, while doorways are decorated with buffalo horns and jawbones – a sign of family prosperity.

Although the village is crowded when tour groups arrive during high season, and all villagers are now officially Catholic and attend a local missionary school, traditional beliefs and customs endure. Sacrifices are held three times each year, and village elders still talk about a rigidly enforced caste system that prevented 'mixed' relationships, with those defying the adat facing serious consequences.

Bena is the most visited Ngada village, and weavings and souvenir stalls line the front of houses. It's so popular that an entrance fee has replaced donations – a set 25,000Rp per person, and there are official opening hours (6am to 6pm). Some travellers might prefer the atmosphere at lesser-visited villages nearby. You can spend the night at Bena for 150,000Rp per person, which includes meals of boiled cassava and banana. Bena is reached by a good 12km road from Langa, a traditional town 7km from Bajawa. An *ojek* ride here costs 100,000Rp return.

The natural hot springs of **Air Panas Malanage** (entry 10,000Rp) are 6km from Bena and unofficially staffed by friendly locals. At the base of one of the many volcanoes, two streams – one hot, one cold – mix together in a temperate pool. Soak amid the scents of coconut, hazelnut, vanilla and clove. Basic change facilities onsite.

Luba

Tucked into the jungle like a beautiful secret at the foot of Gunung Inerie, this traditional village is only a few hundred metres from Bena and much more intimate. Four welcoming clans live here in a baker's dozen of homes. You'll see four *ngadhu* and *bhaga* and houses decorated with depictions of symbolic horses, buffalo and snakes. Photography is welcomed by most; leave a donation of at least 20,000Rp. Hire an *ojek* from Bajawa for 100,000Rp return, or walk from Bena.

Tololela

A mere 4km walk from Bena (about 90 minutes) brings you to this seldom-visited Ngada settlement which consists of three linked traditional villages. Residents love receiving visitors (donate at least 20,000Rp per person) and you can sip simple refreshments while everyone satisfies their mutual curiosity.

Wawo Muda

Wawo Muda (1753m) is the latest volcano to emerge in Flores, exploding in 2001 and leaving behind a mini-Kelimutu, complete with several small crater lakes coloured variously burnt orange, yellow and green. Pine trees charred by the eruption stand in isolated patches, and there are spectacular views

---

OFF THE BEATEN TRACK

PAULENI–BELARAGHI VILLAGE TREK

Most visitors to the Bajawa area rely on hired vehicles to whisk them between traditional villages. It's much more fulfilling to trek through the rainforest to villages such as **Belaraghi**, accessible only by trail. Your trek will begin in **Pauleni Village**, approximately 45km (90 minutes) from Bajawa by car. From there it's a steep 90-minute hike to a village of welcoming locals. There are more than a dozen traditional homes here. The hike can be done in a day trip, but you'll be tired by now, so you may as well stay the night. The *kepala kampung* (village head) offers a bed and meals for 250,000Rp per person. Ask a Bajawa area guide to help arrange the trip.

---

of Gunung Inerie. The area is best visited in the wet season from December to March, if the trails are not too muddy. The lakes usually evaporate in the dry season.

To reach Wawo Muda, take an ojek to the village of Ngoranale, near Menge (100,000Rp return), then walk an hour up an easy-to-follow trail. Some ojek drivers may offer to take you the whole way up, as the path is doable on a motorbike. A car and driver will cost 700,000Rp round trip. You can get a local guide to accompany you for around 250,000Rp.

Riung

☏ 0384 / POP 13,875

Riung is a charming and isolated little town, stilted with fishers' shacks and framed by coconut palms. Coming from Ende you'll drive along an arid coastline that skirts a spectacularly blasted volcano, before a burst of foliage swallows the road as it winds into town. The main attraction is Seventeen Islands Marine Park. Relatively challenging roads keep Riung from development.

⊙ Sights

Seventeen Islands
Marine Park   MARINE RESERVE
(Pulau Tujuh Belas) These uninhabited islands are as diverse as they are beautiful. The mangrove isle of Pulau Ontoloe hosts a massive colony of flying foxes and a few Komodo

TOURING THE SEVENTEEN ISLANDS

Guides can be organised at hotels and guesthouses, or at the waterfront. The standard is a day-long boat trip to Seventeen Islands Marine Park (p381), including lunch, snorkelling and four island stops, the first almost always being Pulau Ontoloe. We recommend Al Itchan, owner of Del Mar Cafe.

Before going to the islands you must sign in and pay 100,000Rp per person at a separate booth by the dock. Your captain or guide should pay the anchorage fees for your boat.

Tour options include the following:

➡ A boat-only day trip without a guide for four to six people costs 500,000Rp to 600,000Rp. Captains don't know the best spots to take the plunge, but you can follow other boats.

➡ A boat day trip with at least four snorkelling stops, a guide and a beach barbecue for four people is organised by Itchan for 1,600,000Rp.

➡ Overnight camping on Palau Rutong, organised by Itchan, costs 3,400,000Rp for two people and includes boat rides, snorkelling and meals.

dragons, while Pulau Rutong and Pulau Temba boast picture-perfect white sand and turquoise waters. There's great snorkelling near Pulau Tiga, Pulau Laingjawa and Pulau Bakau, but wherever you visit, you won't be disappointed.

🛏 Sleeping & Eating

Del Mar Cafe
GUESTHOUSE $$

(📱0813 8759 0964, 0812 4659 8232; d/tr 400,000/500,000Rp; ❄) Off the main road heading to the pier, these 12 air-conditioned rooms with timber furniture and private bathrooms are owned by the area's top guide, Al Itchan. There's a small warung on-site, strung with shells and fairy lights, that rumbles with rock and roll, and grills fish over smouldering coconut husks (mains from 30,000Rp; open 7am to 11pm).

Nirvana Bungalows
BUNGALOW $$

(📱0813 3710 6007; www.nirvanabungalows.doodle kit.com; d/tr/f 400,000/500,000/600,000Rp; ❄) Nine fun, detached hippy shacks with colourful walls, a smattering of inspirational sayings ('If life was easy where would all the adventures be?') and private patios where breakfast is served overlooking the tranquil garden. It's located near the port, and the engaging owner offers guided trips to the islands. Organise ahead for a grilled fish dinner.

Pato Resto
INDONESIAN $

(📱0812 4698 7688; mains 25,000-55,000Rp; ⊙8am-11pm; 🍴) One of Riung's best restaurants is also its most unassuming. This simple haunt with checkered tables and plastic chairs is the place to try local Indonesian food. Located on the main road, its succinct whiteboard menu (in English) changes with the seasons and daily catch. Seafood is a must, but there are plenty of veg dishes, too.

Rico Rico
INDONESIAN $

(📱0812 3019 8727, WhatsApp 0813 3890 5597; mains 30,000-45,000Rp; ⊙6am-10pm) One of the few eating options in Riung and right beside the pier, this is a convenient pre- or post-boat trip dining spot. Food is cheap and basic, but the grilled fish with fresh tomato sauce comes comes highly recommended. Visit at night for live music.

Rico Rico also organises snorkelling day trips (from 300,000Rp per person for a group), boats to Labuan Bajo (3,500,000Rp for two), camping on the beach (100,00Rp per person) and overnight island camping (2,000,000Rp for two, all-inclusive).

ℹ Information

There's a BRI ATM but no official currency exchange facilities in Riung. It's safest to bring ample rupiah.

There's no useful internet and 3G data is patchy.

ℹ Getting There & Away

Riung is 75km and about two hours over rough roads from the turn-off at Boawae on the Trans-Flores Hwy. There is a *much* worse 79km road to Riung from Bajawa that takes about four hours by a daily bus costing 35,000Rp. It's slightly quicker by car – a share taxi costs 60,000Rp per person while a private car is 700,000Rp total. Ende is also four hours by a daily bus at 70,000Rp per passenger.

If you can't bear the Trans-Flores Hwy for another second, consider chartering a boat from Riung all the way to Labuan Bajo from 3,000,000Rp, which takes seven to 10 hours. It's a bit pricey, but you'll enjoy a coastline most visitors never see, stopping in virgin coves and snorkelling along the way. Just bring headphones or earplugs. Those outboard motors are loud!

Ende

📞 0381 / POP 110,000

The most apparent merit of this muggy port town is its spectacular surrounds. The eye-catching cones of **Gunung Meja** (661m) and **Gunung Iya** (627m) loom over the city and the black-sand and cobblestone coastline. Views get even better just northeast of Ende as the road to Kelimutu rises along a ridge, overlooking a roaring river and cliffs that tumble with waterfalls in the wet season from December to March. Throw in coffee and clove drying on tarps on the side of the road, jade rice terraces, and women picking macadamia nuts from bamboo ladders, and you have some of Flores' most jaw-dropping scenery.

You don't need long to cover Ende's compact and atmospheric centre. Most treat it as a pit stop on the way to elsewhere, but there's some intrigue to its grittiness. The central airport is a useful hub for connections to Labuan Bajo, Kupang (West Timor) and Tambolaka (Sumba).

⊙ Sights

There's less to see and more to 'soak up' in Ende. The black-sand beach is a morbid reminder of Indonesia's litter problem, but the views are dramatic and there's always something interesting happening at the waterfront.

Ikat Market   MARKET

(cnr Jls Kathedral & Pasar; ⊘5am-5pm) The ikat market sells hand-woven tapestries from across Flores and Sumba. Bargaining is acceptable, but bear in mind you're expected to make good on any offer that's accepted. Shops can be closed during lunch.

Pasar   MARKET

(Market; Jl Pasar; ⊘7am-6pm) Meander through the aromatic market that stretches from the waterfront into the streets. Expect plastic tubs of vegetables, fruit and an astonishing selection of fish.

🛏 Sleeping

Accommodation is plentiful and spread around town, but lacklustre. Many people

Ende

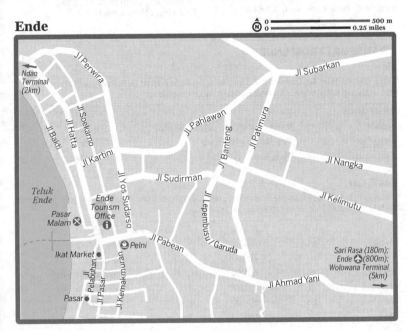

NUSA TENGGARA ENDE

blow through Ende on their way east to Moni, but an overnight stay will result in a good feed, a little atmosphere and a well-rested start onward to Moni in the morning.

Dasi Guest House
GUESTHOUSE $$

(☏0852 1863 8432, 0381-262 7049; yosdam@yahoo.co.id; Jl Durian Atas 2; dm/s/d from 100,000/200,000/250,000Rp; ❄️ 🛜) This friendly guesthouse (with a hostel vibe) fulfils its motto, 'feel like home', thanks to the helpful staff. There are 15 basic rooms and 11 private dorm beds, each in its own cubicle. The common room has views to the south. Free airport transfers.

🍴 Eating

⭐ Sari Rasa
INDONESIAN $

(☏0812 3925 3699; Jl Ahmad Yani; mains 25,000-45,000Rp; ⏰6.30-10pm) This sparkling-clean, bare-walled restaurant is filled with travellers out for a taste of local food, but who come back for Martin, the charismatic owner and self-appointed 'captain of the boat'. He'll colourfully explain the short, whiteboard-scrawled menu cooked by his wife as jazz plays in the background.

The *ayam goreng* (fried chicken) uses free-range village chickens, marinated, tenderised then fried. *Empal* is the Javanese answer to brisket – a hunk of tender, spiced fried beef. Both come with a mound of addictive *serundeng* (spiced, grated coconut) on top.

Pasar Malam
SEAFOOD $

(Night Market; Jl Bakti; mains from 15,000Rp; ⏰5pm-midnight) At sunset the smell of grilled fish wafts through the air at this beachside market. Browse the many stalls and feast on what looks best. Remember to shop around before settling; a bigger fish equals a bigger price.

ℹ️ Information

There are two tourist information centres in Ende, both with enthusiastic staff who dispense up-to-date information. **Flores Tourist Office** (☏0381-23141; www.florestourism.com; Jl Bhakti 1; ⏰8am-5pm Mon-Fri) is located near the beach; has Flores-wide information.

ATMs and banks dot the centre.

ℹ️ Getting There & Away

Air and ferry schedules in East Nusa Tenggara are historically fluid and it's best to confirm all times and carriers prior to planning your trip.

BOAT

Pelni (☏0381-21043; Jl Kathedral 2; ⏰8am-noon & 2-4pm Mon-Sat) has boats every two weeks to Waingapu, Bali and Surabaya, then east to Kupang and Sabu. ASDP ferries (www.indonesiaferry.co.id) serve Waingapu (82,000Rp, 13 hours, weekly).

TRANSPORT FROM ENDE

Air

Wings, Garuda, Nam Air, TransNusa and Susi Air serve **Ende Airport** (H Hasan Aroeboesman Airport; Jl Ahmad Yani), which is located almost in the centre of town.

DESTINATION	AIRLINE	FREQUENCY
Kupang	Nam Air, TransNusa, Wings Air, Garuda	daily
Labuan Bajo	Wings Air, Lion Air, Garuda	daily
Tambolaka	Wings Air	daily

Bus & Car

East-bound buses leave from the Roworeke terminal, 8km from town. Buses heading west leave from the Ndao terminal, 2km north of town on the beach road.

DESTINATION	TYPE	FARE (RP)	DURATION (HR)	FREQUENCY
Bajawa	bus	80,000	5	several daily
Labuan Bajo	bus	200,000	12-15	daily, 6am
Maumere	bus	80,000	5	regularly, 7am-4pm
Maumere	car	150,000	4½	regularly, 7am-4pm
Moni	bus	50,000	2	several daily
Moni	car	100,000	1½	hourly, 6am-4pm

ⓘ Getting Around

Airport taxis to most hotels cost around 50,000Rp per car. Bemos and *ojeks* run frequently to just about everywhere for a flat rate of 5000Rp.

Kelimutu

Kelimutu (1639m), a sacred and extinct volcano, is the centrepiece of the mountainous, jungle-clad **national park** (admission per person Mon-Sat 150,000Rp, Sun 225,000Rp, per motorbike/car 5000/10,000Rp; ☺ ticket office 5am-5pm) of the same name. There aren't many better reasons to wake up before dawn than to witness the sun cresting Kelimutu's western rim, filtering mist into the sky and revealing three deep, volcanic lakes – nicknamed the tri-coloured lakes because for years each one was a different striking shade. Less than 30 minutes by car from Moni, the park shelters endangered flora and fauna (including 19 rare avian species) and other peaks such as Mount Kelibara (1731m).

Alert local guides if you dream about the sacred lakes – apparently siren-like spirits have lured people to their demise, which can be avoided if the right prayers and offerings are made.

Kelimutu is sacred to the local Lio people, who believe the souls of the dead migrate here: young people's souls go to the warmth of Tiwu Koo Fai Nuwa Muri; old people's to the cold of Tiwu Ata Bupu; and those of the wicked to Tiwu Ata Polo. Pork, betel nuts, rice and other valuable offerings are left on ceremonial rocks beside the lakes, amid the dancing of the Lio's annual 'Feed the Spirit of the Forefathers' ceremony, on August 14.

Ever since locals led early Dutch settlers here, sightseers have made the sunrise trek. Most visitors glimpse the lakes at dawn, leaving nearby Moni at 4am for early morning views after the pre-dawn mist rises, and before clouds drift in. Afternoons are usually empty and peaceful at the top of Mt Kelimutu, and when the sun is high, the colours sparkle.

There's a staircase up to the highest lookout, Inspiration Point, from where all three lakes are visible. It's not advisable to scramble around the craters' loose scree. The footing's so bad and the drop so steep that a few careless hikers have perished here.

It's worth staying in Moni rather than attempting Kelimutu as a day trip, should bad weather obscure the view or close the road to the top. Remain flexible with onward travel plans, especially during wetter months.

🏃 Activities

For a beautiful walk through the lush local landscape, hire transport one-way to the lakes and then walk back to Moni. The stroll down the mountain, through the village, past rice fields and along cascading streams, takes about three hours and isn't too taxing. A *jalan potong* (shortcut) leaves the road back to Moni 3km south of the ticket office and goes through Manukako village, then meanders back to the main road 750m uphill from Moni. A second path diverges from the trail and goes through Tomo, Mboti, Topo Mboti, Kolorongo and Koposili villages, skirts a waterfall and returns to Moni without rejoining the highway. It's possible (although not essential) to hire a guide in Moni (350,000Rp) to show you the way.

ⓘ Getting There & Away

The ticket office is 8.5km up the paved access road, which connects to the Trans-Flores Hwy 2km west of Moni. The parking area for the lake is another 4km. From the car park it's a nice 20-minute walk up through the pines to Inspiration Point. To get here from Moni, hire an *ojek* (60,000/100,000Rp one way/return) or car (250,000/350,000Rp one way/return), maximum five people.

Moni

☑ 0361 / POP 7,604

People often skip Moni, making a beeline for Kelimutu and treating its volcanic lakes as a day trip. These people miss out. If you're not in a rush, a couple of nights in Moni – a lovely, picturesque hill town fringed by rice fields, lush volcanic peaks and hot springs – will bring you back down to earth. It's slow-paced and easy-going thanks to friendly locals and an unexpected Rasta community, who live to play music and invite travellers to join in at every turn. The Tuesday market, held on the soccer pitch, is a major local draw and good place to snare local ikat (patterned textiles).

🏃 Activities

Apart from the trek to/from Kelimutu, there are several other walks from Moni. About 750m along the Ende road from the centre of Moni, paths lead down to a 10m air terjun (waterfall), with a swimming hole and **air panas** (hot springs) near the falls. The trail branches to the left of **Rainbow Cafe** (☑0813 3947 7300; ana.rainbow@ovi.com; Jl Trans Flores; mains 30,000-80,000Rp; ⊗9am-9pm). A must-visit is the breathtaking hot spring in the middle of the rice fields at **Kolorongo** (3.5km from Moni) on the way to Kelimutu. Or walk south past the church to **Potu** and **Woloara** (about 2.5km from Moni).

🛏 Sleeping

It seems every local in Moni is building a homestay along the Trans-Flores Hwy. Most are budget to midrange, but prices will jump in the near future – already there's a discrepancy between accommodation of the same standard. Do your research so you don't get ripped off. Booking ahead from June to August is recommended, but locals should know someone with a bed if you get stuck.

Legend Guest House
GUESTHOUSE $

(☑0813 9831 3581; ino.alexander99@gmail.com; off Jl Trans Flores, behind market; r 200,000Rp) You'll feel like family at this budget, three-bedroom guesthouse. Rooms are simple, spotless and share a bathroom (with a pebbled shower). Ask owner Ino about booking day trips...and to hear him sing at Mopi's Place. The guesthouse is next to the market, which makes for a great atmosphere but not the best sleep-in.

Mahoni Guest House
GUESTHOUSE $$

(☑0813 7212 3313; Jl Trans Flores; r 350,000Rp) Look for a friendly group of Rastas sitting under a dried grass umbrella in front of a white house and you've found Mahoni. Owner Galank is welcoming to all who stay in the four sparkling rooms with hot showers. Banana pancakes and fresh fruit are included for breakfast; a taste of local life all day.

Bintang Lodge
GUESTHOUSE $$

(☑0812 3761 6940, WhatsApp 0823 4103 6979; www.bintang-lodge.com; Jl Trans Flores; r 300,000-600,000Rp) Bintang is one of the best guesthouses in town, offering five large, centrally located and renovated rooms. It has hot water and the cafe (mains 30,000Rp to 99,000Rp) has an open terrace with views over the green surrounds. Owner Tobias is a fount of local information.

★Kelimutu Crater Lakes Ecolodge
LODGE $$$

(☑0852 3324 8518, 0361-747 4205; www.ecolodgesindonesia.com; Jl Ende-Maumere Km54; r/villas from 800,000/1,000,000Rp; ❄) 🍃 Easily the nicest spot in Moni. Nestled by the riverside east of town are 21 rooms and villas, all with pebbled tiles, hot water, some solar power and outdoor sitting areas. Cross the bridge over a babbling stream and check out the rice terraces. The restaurant (mains from 40,000Rp to 65,000Rp) serves local specialities.

🍽 Eating

★Mopi's Place
CAFE $

(☑0812 3956 4019, 0813 3736 5682; Jl Trans Flores; mains 25,000-55,000Rp; ⊗8am-10pm; 🔊🍴) This open-sided Indo-Australian affair starts with local coffee, house-made soy milk and freshly baked bread; it progresses to exceptional Indonesian mains with plenty of veg options and – if the musically gifted locals are around – morphs into a dance floor as live reggae echoes off the mountains.

Order by noon and you can be sitting down to an evening *nasi bamboo* buffet of *tapa kolo* – coconut rice cooked over coals in a bamboo tube, with chicken (and/or fish), veggies and accompaniments (150,000Rp per person, for a minimum of two).

Good Moni
INDONESIAN $$

(☑0813 5377 5320; Jl Trans Flores; mains 40,000-80,000Rp; ⊗8am-9pm; 🔊) With a friendly chef-owner and misty view of the hills, this open-air restaurant at the top of town is worth a stop. Indonesian food is the speciality, but there's pasta available, too. Check out the blackboard for the daily special and be sure to try the Moni croquette. Perhaps the only place in Moni for wi-fi.

❶ Getting There & Away

It's always best to travel in the morning, when buses are often half empty; afternoon buses are usually overcrowded. Don't book through your homestay – hail the bus as it passes through town.

A private car from Ende airport to Moni costs 500,000Rp one way. Book via the stand near baggage collection.

Motorbikes (100,000Rp) and cars with a driver (800,000Rp) are available per day from Bintang Lodge.

Always organise drivers and transport through trusted locals, accommodation and homestays – avoid opportunists hawking transport on the street as there have been reports of scams. If you're unsure, ask Tobias at Bintang.

Paga

☑ 0382 / POP 14,500

Halfway between Moni and Maumere you'll find a string of beaches that is the stuff of Flores fantasy. The Trans-Flores Hwy swoops down to the shore at this rice-farming and fishing hamlet, where the wide rushing river meets the placid bay.

◉ Sights

The lush scenery lures you inland from beautiful beaches. You can hike to megalithic stone graves and amazing ocean views at the nearby village of **Nuabari**. Agustinus Naban (www.floresgids.com) of Restaurant Laryss will guide you for 500,000Rp per day.

Pantai Paga   BEACH
The Trans-Flores Hwy parallels this beautiful long stretch of white sand. The water is perfect for swimming and you can easily lounge away an afternoon.

★ Pantai Koka   BEACH
(entry per person/car 10,000/20,000Rp) About 5km west of Pantai Paga, look for a small, partially paved road that runs for 2km through a cocoa plantation to a stunning double bay. Facing a promontory are two perfect crescents of sand; one protected and another with views out to sea. Eat grilled fish (50,000Rp) at **Blasius Homestay**, or stay in the basic bamboo accommodation (rooms 200,000Rp).

🛏 Sleeping & Eating

Inna's Homestay   HOMESTAY $$
(☑ 0813 3833 4170; innanadoke@gmail.com; Jl Maumere-Ende, Pantai Paga; r 300,000-450,000Rp) An absolute beachfront, four-room homestay with a back porch and hammock for maximum ocean enjoyment.

Rooms are basic but spotless. One has an impressively renovated bathroom. Fan cooling assists the ocean breeze.

★ Restaurant Laryss   SEAFOOD $$
(☑ 0852 5334 2802; www.floresgids.com; Jl Raya Maumere-Ende; mains 30,000-35,000Rp, fish up to 150,000Rp; ⊙ kitchen 9am-10pm) Don't miss this beachside fish shack. Sit at a tree-shaded table on the sand and order the catch of the day or a soul-stirring *ikan kuah assam* (tamarind fish soup). The sambal here demands second helpings. Owner and guide Agustinus Naban's wife, Cecilia, rubs fish with turmeric and ginger, douses it with lime and then roasts it over coconut shells.

Two very basic rooms (200,000Rp) match the ad hoc architecture and open directly onto the sand.

ℹ Getting There & Away

Flag down passing buses, which run regularly during daylight hours. East to Maumere costs 15,000Rp; west to Moni costs 30,000Rp. A share taxi from Moni to Paga costs from 50,000Rp per person.

Maumere

☑ 0382 / POP 67,000

Blessed with a long, languid coastline backed by layered hills and fringed with islands, Maumere is a logical terminus to a trans-Flores tour. With good air connections to Bali and Timor, it's a gateway to Flores Timur (East Flores). Largely razed in the devastating earthquake of 1992, it's been thoroughly rebuilt and is now a busy, dusty urban hub.

Thankfully, you don't have to stay in the city, with the nicest accommodation options along the coast to the east. Divers will appreciate Maumere's 'sea gardens', destroyed in the quake but now recovered, as well as the diving hot spot accessible from Waiara (p389).

TRANSPORT FROM MONI

DESTINATION	TYPE	FARE (RP)	DURATION (HR)	FREQUENCY
Ende	bus	30,000	2	several daily
Ende	share taxi	50,000	1½	several daily
Maumere	bus	50,000	3	several daily
Maumere	share taxi	80,000	2½	several daily

🛏 Sleeping & Eating

★ Pantai Paris Homestay
HOMESTAY $

(☑ 0812 3895 8183; www.pantaiparishomestay. wordpress.com; Pantai Paris, Jl Larantuka-Maumere; dm/r from 135,000/350,000Rp; 🛜) 🌿 Run by an environmentally and socially conscious family, this tropical garden setting beside the sea is our pick for budget accommodation. There are four private rooms with bamboo furniture and mosquito nets and the spacious, nine-bed dorm shares a lovely, semi-outdoor bathroom. Join in a Sunday beach or snorkelling clean-up or support locals with disabilities by buying organic, homemade tea.

Charismatic owner, Susi, makes her own jam, chocolate and even dragonfruit wine. There's a small shop at the entrance selling accessories made from rubbish collected off the beach and the homestay works closely with an NGO to help educate people on waste management. Close to the airport and Terminal Lokaria.

Wailiti Hotel
HOTEL $$

(☑ 0382-23416, 0821 4717 5576; wailitihotel@ yahoo.co.id; Jl Da Silva; r/bungalow from 400,000/ 450,000Rp; ❄🛜🏊) Maumere's most pleasant accommodation offers tidy rooms and bungalows in spacious grounds on a narrow black-sand beach, complete with novelty animal paddle boats for hire. The simple restaurant serves acceptable seafood and Indonesian standards (mains 35,000Rp to 60,000Rp), and there's a dive shop on-site. It's 6.5km west of the centre; a taxi from the airport costs 100,000Rp.

Pasar Malam
INDONESIAN $

(Night Market; off Jl Slamet Riyadi; mains from 15,000Rp; ⏰5-11pm) As well as dirt-cheap Indonesian favourites like nasi goreng, Maumere's large night market, unsurprisingly, has plenty of stalls grilling fresh fish.

ℹ Information

Banks and ATMs dot the centre.

ℹ Getting There & Away

AIR

Maumere is connected to Bali and Kupang. Airline offices and travel agents are clustered in the centre on Jl Pasar Baru Timur.

Maumere's **Frans Seda Airport** (Wai Oti Airport) is 3km east of town, 800m off the Maumere-Larantuka road.

A taxi to/from town is a non-negotiable, flat fee of 60,000Rp.

BUS

There are two bus terminals. Buses and Kijang heading east to Larantuka leave from **Terminal Lokaria** (Jl Raja Centis), 3km east of town. **Terminal Madawat** (Jl Gajah Mada), 1km southwest of town, is the place for westbound departures. Schedules are rarely precise – be prepared to wait around until there are sufficient passengers, and watch out for buses that pick up passengers from the streets adjoining the terminals, without actually entering them.

ℹ Getting Around

Car rental, including driver and fuel, costs 800,000Rp to 1,000,000Rp per day, depending on your destination. You can organise vehicle and motorbike rental at hotels for 100,000Rp.

TRANSPORT FROM MAUMERE

Air

DESTINATION	AIRLINE	DURATION (HR)	FREQUENCY
Bali	Garuda, Wings Air	2	daily
Kupang	Nam Air, Wings Air	1	daily

Bus

DESTINATION	TYPE	PRICE (RP)	DURATION (HR)	FREQUENCY
Ende	bus	80,000	5	several daily
Ende	car	100,000	4½	several daily
Larantuka	bus	60,000	4	several daily
Larantuka	car	80,000	3	several daily
Moni	bus	50,000	2½	several daily
Moni	car	80,000	3	several daily

Waiara

Waiara is the departure point for the Maumere 'sea gardens', once regarded as one of Asia's finest dive destinations. The 1992 earthquake and tsunami destroyed the reefs around Pulau Penman, Pulau Besar and Pulau Babi but they've now recovered – with the exception of 'The Crack' near Pulau Babi, a consequence of the earthquake and now a diving hot spot where sea life flourishes.

🛏 Sleeping

Wiara is home to some of the region's nicer accommodation options, featuring beachside resorts.

Sea World Club   RESORT $$
(Pondok Dunia Laut; ☑ 0382-242 5089, 0821 47770 0188; www.flores-seaworldclub.com; Jl Nai Roa; d/tr cottages from 600,000/650,000Rp, beachfront bungalows from 1,100,000Rp; ※ 🛜) Just off the Larantuka road is this modest black-sand beach resort, established to provide local jobs and build tourism. There are simple, thatched cottages and more modern and comfortable air-conditioned bungalows. Expect to add up to an additional 200,000Rp per night to listed prices during busy months.

There's an adequate restaurant (mains 45,000Rp to 95,000Rp) and dive shop (1,000,000Rp for two dives including gear).

Coconut Garden
Beach Resort   RESORT $$
(☑ 0821 4426 0185; www.coconutgardenbeach resort.com; Jl Nasional Larantuka Km15; r from 750,000Rp; ※ 🛜) Set among coconut palms, this resort is so spotless it feels like someone's raking the sand as you walk. Eight bamboo bungalows have undulating roofs and gorgeous outdoor bathrooms, but you're paying mostly for the setting with the pricey budget rooms (shared bathroom). There's a restaurant (mains 33,000Rp to 77,000Rp) and water sports, but we love the little details most.

ℹ Getting There & Away

To get to Waiara, catch any Talibura- or Larantuka-bound bus from Maumere 12km to Waiara. It will cost 10,000Rp and take around 20 minutes. Resorts are signposted from the highway.

Wodong

The pod of beaches and resorts just east of Waiara centres on Wodong, 26km east of Maumere. The narrow, palm-dappled beaches here, which include Ahuwair, Wodong and Waiterang, are tranquil and beautiful.

There's an impressive variety of dive and snorkelling sites with plenty of marine life offshore around Pulau Babi, Pulau Besar and Pulau Pangabatang, a sunken Japanese WWII ship, and colourful microlife in the 'muck' (shallow mudflats). Damage to the reefs from a devastating tsunami in 1992 has largely been overcome by new coral growth. In November whale-watching trips are also offered, although you'll probably see migrating sperm whales spout from the beach.

🛏 Sleeping

Most accommodation options are basic but tasteful beach hideaways located down trails 10m to 500m from the road; they are signposted from the highway.

Sunset Cottages   BUNGALOW $
(☑ 0812 4602 3954, 0821 4768 7254; sunsetcottages@yahoo.com.uk; Jl Maumere-Larantuka Km28; d/f 250,000/350,000Rp) Nestled on a secluded black-sand beach with island views, Sunset Cottages is shaded by swaying coco palms. The thatched, coconut-wood-and-bamboo bungalows have Western toilets and *mandis* (ladle baths), with decks overlooking the sea. Snorkel gear is available for hire (25,000Rp per day) and there's a restaurant (mains 25,000Rp to 40,000Rp). Pop next door to **Sante Sante** (☑ 0813 3734 8453; www.santesante-homestay-flores.com; Wairterang Beach; r 200,000-350,000Rp, camping s/d 80,000/120,000Rp) for a sunset drink.

Lena House   BUNGALOW $
(☑ 0813 3940 7733; www.lenahouseflores.com; Jl Maumere-Larantuka Km28; r from 175,000Rp) Lena House has 10 clean bamboo bungalows spread across two properties (Lena 2 is reached by boat) on a spectacular bay framed by jungled mountains. The sweet family arranges snorkelling trips (100,000Rp per person) and treks up Gunung Egon (100,000Rp), although you may choose just to stretch out under the palms and let your mind drift.

★ Ankermi Happy Dive   BUNGALOW $$
(☑ text only 0821 4778 1036; www.ankermi-happy dive.com; Jl Larantuka-Maumere, Watumita; s/d

bungalow from 295,000/365,000Rp; ✴ ✖) Run by Claudia and Kermi, Balinese-influenced Ankermi has eight cute, tiled and thatched bungalows with private porches and stunning sea views (fan only) or garden views (with air-con). The dive shop is the best in the Maumere area (shore/night/boat dives from €25/35/35). Locally grown, organic rice and vegetables feature in the restaurant (mains 42,000Rp to 95,000Rp).

ℹ Getting There & Away

Wodong, the main village in the area, is on the Maumere–Larantuka road. Take any Talibura, Nangahale or Larantuka bemo or bus from the Lokaria (p388) terminal in Maumere for 5000Rp. A bemo from Wodong to Waiterang costs another 5000Rp. A car from Maumere is around 150,000Rp to 200,000Rp and an *ojek* 75,000Rp to 100,000Rp one way. Buses pass by throughout the day.

ALOR ARCHIPELAGO

The east end of the Lesser Sunda Islands – the chain stretching east of Java – is wild, volcanic and drop-dead gorgeous. There are crumbling red-clay roads, jagged peaks, white-sand beaches and crystal-clear bays offering remarkable diving.

Isolated from the outside world and one another by rugged terrain, the 212,000 inhabitants of this tiny archipelago are divided into 134 tribes speaking 18 languages and 52 dialects. Although the Dutch installed local rajas along the coastal regions after 1908, they had little influence, with people still taking heads into the 1950s. These days animist traditions have been mostly replaced by Muslim and Christian ones. In more populated areas mosques dot the coast beside eye-catching, pastel-tiled graves.

Though a network of simple roads now covers Pulau Alor, boats are still a common form of transport. The few visitors who land here tend to linger on nearby Pulau Kepa or dive these waters from liveaboards.

Kalabahi

☑ 0386 / POP 61,000

Kalabahi is the chief town on Pulau Alor, located at the end of a spectacular 15km-long, palm-fringed bay on the south coast. Travellers come here to explore its coasts and nearby islands, using the town as a base that pales in comparison to the beaches and promise of diving. Other than some impressive banyan trees that make great points of reference, there's not much to see in the town's dusty main drag, unless *you* happen to be passing by – expect locals to yell out and stop for a chat. Keep an eye out for school children and government officials wearing woven ikat vests over their uniforms on Thursdays to upkeep tradition.

◉ Sights & Activities

Pasar Kedelang   MARKET

(Kedelang; ⊙ 7.30am-7.30pm) Mingle with locals at Alor's most exciting fresh-produce market. Pyramids of vegetables are piled on

---

ALOR OFFSHORE

Alor's dive operators regularly visit upwards of 42 dive sites, sprinkled throughout the archipelago. There are wall dives, slopes, caves, pinnacles, reefs and impressive muck diving in the Alor bay. What makes Alor special are its completely unspoiled reefs with vibrant soft and hard coral intact. Dive sites are never crowded, the water is crystal clear and you may well see a thresher shark, pod of dolphins or, come November, migrating sperm whales. Just know that the current is frequently unpredictable and the water can be as low as 22°C. The cool temperature is what keeps the coral nourished, and spectacular. It's best to have 30 dives under your belt before venturing into these waters.

All divers must pay a marine park fee of 50,000Rp per day to fund the management of a 4000-sq-km marine park. The WWF works with the government to help manage and take care of this unique marine environment.

Sandwiched between Pulau Pantar and Alor is **Pulau Pura**, which has some of Alor's best dive sites. **Pulau Ternate**, not to be confused with the Maluku version, also has some magnificent dive and snorkel sites. **Uma Pura** is an interesting weaving village on Ternate, with a rather prominent wooden church. To get there, charter a boat from Alor Besar or Alor Kecil (150,000Rp), or take a motorbike to the Padang location of Alor Besar Village and pay 10,000Rp each way.

tables; betel nut, flower and leaves are arranged on tarps on the ground; and *kenari* (almond-like nut) is everywhere. Pick up nasi and accompaniments wrapped up for 5000Rp and bring your bargaining hat to purchase local ikat.

Pantai Maimol   BEACH
One of the best beaches near Kalabahi is this ribbon of white sand 10km out of town on the airport road. You can easily laze away a few hours here. When we last visited, hotel construction was about to commence across the road.

Museum Seribu Moko   MUSEUM
(Museum of 1000 Drums; ☑ 0852 3868 9169; Jl Diponegoro; entry 15,000Rp; ⊘ 8am-1pm Mon-Thu, to 11am Fri) Named for its collection of *moko* (bronze drums; the 1000 is purely figurative), this humble museum located just west of the market has some decent English booklets about the collection, which includes more than 700 cultural artefacts from Alor's 17 districts and, of course, drums. Some bear designs dating to Southeast Asia in 700 BC and another was supposedly uncovered after its location was revealed in a dream.

Alor Dive   DIVING
(☑ 0813 3964 8148, 0386-222 2663; www.alor-dive. com; Jl Suka Maju; 2-dive day trips from €79; ⊘ 8am-4pm) This dive shop run by a German expat organises all manner of diving trips, from half-day to a week or more. It has years of experience in the beautiful local waters.

🛏 Sleeping & Eating

Cantik Homestay   GUESTHOUSE $
(☑ 0821 4450 9941, 0386-21030; Jl Dahlia 12; s/d 150,000/200,000Rp; ❄) These 12 tiled rooms with private bathrooms and air-con are basic but quiet, located in a shady residential neighbourhood. Rent a motorbike for the day (75,000Rp) and stick around for communal meals (from 25,000Rp per person) as the co-owner is a wonderful cook. At breakfast, Jacob the caged bird will wish you good morning in both English and Indonesian.

Dinda Home Stay across the road is a good alternative (singles and doubles cost 200,000Rp and 250,000Rp).

Pulo Alor Hotel   HOTEL $$
(☑ 0386-21727, 0852 3380 0512; puloalorhotel@ gmail.com; Jl Eltari 12; r from 549,000Rp; ❄ 🛜 ☰) Although a little bland, this is the best option for travellers used to hotel accommodation. There are 30 rooms with televisions,

desks and bottled water, plus a terrace with a view of Alor Bay and the green hills beyond. Pool and restaurant on-site. Free airport pick up.

Rumah Makan Jember   INDONESIAN $
(☑ 0813 5392 9118; Jl Pamglima Polim 20; mains 15,000-30,000Rp; ⊘ 7am-7.30pm) Before you turn down Jl Suka Maju to reach Alor Dive, stop at this fantastic local haunt. Make a beeline for the counter, piled with *sayur* (vegetables), chicken *sate,* noodles, tempe and more. Make your decision and then pull up a chair in what feels like someone's tiled dining room, complete with garish green curtains.

Resto Mama   INDONESIAN $$
(☑ 0822 1320 2525; Jl Buton 15; mains 25,000-65,000Rp; ⊘ 10am-10pm Mon-Fri & Sun, to 11pm Sat; 🐾) This wood-and-bamboo dining room is perched over the bay on stilts, 50m west of Pasar Kedelang. There's plenty of seafood and Indo fare, but the house speciality is *ikan kuah assam mama,* a sweet-and-sour fish soup with a fiery, tamarind-inflected broth. Service can be painfully slow. Ask about using the karaoke room (50,000Rp for one hour).

ℹ Information

Bank BNI (Jl Sudirman; ⊘ 8am-4pm Mon-Fri) ATM available.

Hospital (☑ 0386-21008; Jl Dr Soetomo 8; ⊘ 24hr) Centrally located, 24-hour hospital.

ℹ Getting There & Away

Wings Air makes the 45-minute flight to Kupang. The tiny **airport** is comically disorganised, and 16km from Kalabahi. Check in early to avoid the mad scrum.

ADSP ferries serve Kupang and Larantuka. Ferries leave from the **ferry terminal** 1km southwest of the town centre; it's a 10-minute walk or a 3000Rp bemo ride. There are two weekly to Kupang (114,000Rp to 168,000Rp, 18 hours), and one to Larantuka (107,000Rp, 12 hours). Pelni ships leave from the **main pier** in the centre of town and visit Kupang, Sabu, Rote, Ende, Waingapu, Bima and more on a monthly schedule serviced by three ships. The **Pelni office** (☑ 0386-21195; www.pelni.co.id; Jl Cokroaminoto 5; ⊘ 8am-5pm) is near the pier.

Buses and bemos to Alor Kecil cost 5000Rp and take 30 minutes. To Alor Besar it's 7000Rp for the 40-minute journey. Both leave from the central Kalabahi Pasar Tabakar and Pasar Kedelang. You can also take a taxi from the airport from 150,000Rp to 200,000Rp.

❶ Getting Around

The airport is 16km from town. Taxis cost a fixed 100,000Rp, or 50,000Rp for one person.

Transport around town costs 3000Rp by bemo. To get out to the villages, look for blue bemos that cost between 5000Rp and 10,000Rp.

Rent a motorbike at Cantik Homestay (p391) for 75,000Rp per day, elsewhere they're 100,000Rp. *Ojeks* are easily hired for 150,000Rp per day.

Around Kalabahi

About 13km east of central Kalabahi is **Desa Takpala**, the majestically preserved, mountain-top village of the Abui people, Alor's largest ethnic group. It's one of the more accessible and tourist-friendly villages, with locals happy to show you their multi-level houses with pyramid-shaped grass roofs designed to store food. A 50,000Rp donation is appropriate when signing the guestbook.

If you happen to visit at the same time as a larger group, the experience can feel a little contrived; visitors dress up in traditional garb and take photographs and a small handicraft market suddenly appears. On the plus side, only larger groups generally organise traditional lego lego dancing demonstrations due to the cost, so you might be able to piggyback off bigger numbers and join in. Christian from Cantik Homestay (p391) can organise the performance from 1,500,000Rp.

You can also do a fascinating village tour of Alor's bird's head, the island's distinctively shaped northern peninsula. From Kalabahi head northeast to **Mombang**, up through the clove trees and coffee plots of **Kopidil** (where they make ceremonial clothes out of tree bark) to **Tulta**, and then to the stunning sweep of white sand that is **Batu Putih**. It's backed by granite bluffs and cornfields, and cradles a turquoise and emerald lagoon, 10km north of Mali. Hire a motorbike (100,000Rp per day) or charter an ojek (150,000Rp per day). Bring plenty of water, a boxed lunch, *pinang* (betel nut), smokes and the best Bahasa Indonesia you've got to share with your new friends.

For hikers or motorcyclists who like rugged backcountry, consider a longer trip; two or three days hiking along the verdant, mountainous spine of Central Alor. One route connects **Mainang** with **Kelaisi** and on to **Apui**. Another loop begins in **Ateng**, stops in **Melang** and ends in **Lakwati**. These are all very poor, purely traditional villages. The roads and trails are very bad, so are not easy journeys. You'll be sleeping in basic village accommodation (per person from 100,000Rp), and meals will be extremely basic, too. Not all villages have toilets, and you'll need to bring extra food and water. Be prepared.

🏖 Beaches

There are nice coral beaches in both **Alor Besar** and nearby **Alor Kecil**, with excellent snorkelling. The best is at **Sebanjar**, 3km north of Alor Kecil. The water here is wonderfully cool, with a stunning soft-coral garden offshore. Alor Kecil is also the jumping-off point for **Pulau Kepa**.

🏃 Activities

Lazy Turtle Dive   DIVING
(☑ 0813 3759 1497; www.lazyturtledive.com; Jl Raya, Alor Kecil, next to Dermaga Jetty; daily drive trips/4-night package from 1,200,000/6,000,000Rp; ⊙8am-6pm) This Australian-UK operation opposite Pulau Kepa runs a slick ship. Book in for daily dives or accommodation packages and then jump aboard *Naughty Nudi* to explore Alor's reefs and muck sites. Upon your return, enjoy an outdoor shower, make the most of the camera-charging station and chill out in the *lopo* (meeting house).

🛏 Sleeping & Eating

Beach Bungalow Resort   BUNGALOW $$
(Alor Beach Bungalows; ☑ 0823 4109 5312; Pantai Sebanjar; bungalows 250,000Rp) These nine, basic but large wooden bungalows might be dark and have bucket-flush toilets, but it's all about location. Positioned on Pantai Sebanjar, one of Alor's best snorkelling spots, where the coral beach blushes pink in the sun. Let the lovely ladies know what you're craving and they'll grill fish, chicken and big serves of fresh vegetables (from 25,000Rp).

★ La P'tite Kepa   DIVE RESORT $$
(☑ SMS/WhatsApp only 0813 3910 2403; www.la -petite-kepa.com; Pulau Kepa; bungalow with/without bathroom per person 550,000/425,000Rp) 🌿 Upon arriving at the airport, drivers shout, 'La P'tite Kepa?' – thus is the popularity of this French-owned, solar-powered dive resort. There are 11 bungalows, three of which are traditional Alor home replicas with shared bathrooms, relaxing open decks and beds in the roof. Fresh and memorable meals are eaten family-style, but bringing

PANTAR

The second-largest island of the Alor group is way off the beaten track. A daily ferry from Kalabahi (50,000Rp, from three hours depending on the weather) docks at **Baranusa** with a straggle of coconut palms, a **homestay** and a couple of kiosks.

Smouldering Gunung Sirung (862m) draws a few hearty climbers each year. From Baranusa, take a truck to Kakamauta and walk for two to three hours to Sirung's crater. Bring water from Baranusa and get permission from locals before hiking; they believe that climbing Gunung Sirung at certain times of year can cause it to erupt and destroy precious harvests.

Built and operated by a French-Slovenian couple on the island's eastern shore, **Alor Divers** (☑ 0813 1780 4133; www.alor-divers.com; 4-night dive packages from €740) 🏊 caters exclusively to divers and their plus-ones. Guests stay in smart, thatched bungalows and dive at least twice daily. Orcas, sperm and pilot whales migrate off the west coast in June and December.

cheese and chocolate is playfully encouraged by staff.

Most of the bungalows are standard thatched bamboo bungalows with attached outdoor bathrooms. All have sea and island views. There are three beaches, including an exquisite sliver of white sand on the west side with spectacular sunset views and good snorkelling offshore. Snorkelling equipment is available for 50,000Rp per day, and snorkellers can join the dive boat for 100,000Rp per day. In July and August divers get priority for bookings. Reserve your room well in advance.

The resort recycles, and conserves water and power. It costs 20,000Rp each way to get there by local fishing boat from the mainland.

★ Celyn Kafe   CAFE $
(☑ 0812 3909 4800; Pantai Mali; snacks 8,000-27,000Rp; ☯ 8am-9pm) Set on the sand, framed by mangroves and shaded by palm trees, this is Alor's best spot to while away an afternoon. Order from the blackboard menu: there's juice, tea and coffee a dozen ways – but don't leave without *ubi goreng sambal,* crunchy-fried fingers of cassava with mild chilli sauce; Alor's answer to wedges.

When we last visited two guesthouses were under construction.

🛍 Shopping

Sentra Tenun
Ikat Gunung Mako   TEXTILES
(Tenun Mako; ☑ 0813 3914 8116; Jl Sumur Tuti Panjaitan, Pantai Hula, Alor Besar) Ten metres off the road beneath some banana trees you'll find Mama Sariat Libana, mother of Alornese

ikat, holding court or playing cards. Originally from nearby Ternate Island, she not only supports local weavers by providing this basic showroom, but is responsible for uncovering 202 colours from natural materials, including several kinds of seaweed.

WEST TIMOR

It doesn't take much for West Timor to get under your skin. A smile in someone's direction will see their face erupt in one, too. It might reveal teeth stained red from chewing betel; one framed by wrinkles in the rugged countryside; or a yelp and wave from a music-thumping bemo in Kupang – the coastal capital and East Nusa Tenggara's metropolis.

Within its mountainous, *lontar* palm-studded land, animist traditions persist alongside tribal dialects and chiefs preserve *adat* (traditional law) in traditional beehive-hut villages. Hit up one of the many weekly markets and you'll not only get a feel for rural Timor life, but be the star attraction as you eavesdrop on one of 14 different languages spoken on the island. Although West Timor is a relatively undiscovered gem, you'll still be welcomed wherever you go.

History

The Tetun (or Tetum) of central Timor are one of the largest ethnic groups on the island and boast the dominant indigenous language. Before Portuguese and Dutch colonisation, they were fragmented into dozens of small states led by various chiefs. Conflict was common, and headhunting a popular pastime.

West Timor

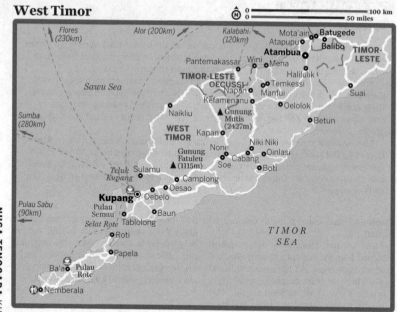

The first Europeans in Timor were the Portuguese, who prized its endemic *cendana* (sandalwood) trees. When the Dutch landed in Kupang in the mid-17th century, a prolonged battle for control of the sandalwood trade began, which the Dutch eventually won. The two colonial powers divvied the island in a series of treaties signed between 1859 and 1913. Portugal was awarded the eastern half plus the enclave of Oecussi, the island's first settlement.

Neither European power penetrated far into the interior until the 1920s, and the island's political structure was left largely intact. The colonisers spread Christianity and ruled through the native aristocracy, but some locals claim Europeans corrupted Timor's royal bloodlines by aligning with imported, and eventually triumphant, Rotenese kingdoms. When Indonesia won independence in 1949 the Dutch left West Timor, but the Portuguese still held East Timor. In 1975 East Timor declared itself independent from Portugal and shortly afterwards Indonesia invaded, setting the stage for the tragedy that continued until 2002 when East Timor's independence was officially recognised.

During August 1999, in a UN-sponsored referendum, the people of East Timor voted in favour of independence. Violence erupted when pro-Jakarta militias, backed by the Indonesian military, destroyed buildings and infrastructure across the East, leaving up to 1400 civilians dead before peacekeepers intervened. Back in West Timor, the militias were responsible for the lynching of three foreign UN workers in Atambua in 2000, making Indonesia an international pariah. After several turbulent years, relations normalised by 2006 and road and transport links were restored.

Kupang

📞 0380 / POP 370,000

Kupang is the capital of Nusa Tenggara Timur (NTT). Despite the city's scruffy waterfront, sprawling gnarl of traffic and the almost complete lack of endearing cultural or architectural elements, there is a certain ill-defined charm. Besides, there are atmospheric markets in the centre, spots to relax beside locals and a smattering of nearby natural wonders. The chaos can be contagious – it's a university town, after all – even if you're just popping in and out.

Kupang's a regional transport hub, but don't be surprised if between trips to the interior, Alor or Rote you discover that it grows on you. England's Captain Bligh had a similar epiphany when he spent 47 days here after that emasculating mutiny on the *Bounty* in 1789.

◉ Sights

The heart of old Kupang centres on the **old port area** and its surrounding cacophonous market. Look closely and you'll see a few traces of Dutch colonial times, when Kupang was considered a genteel tropical idyll.

On Kupang's west coast, south of the centre, lies a local haunt not often visited by international travellers: **Gua Kristal** (Crystal Cave; Bolok), the Crystal Cave, where locals swim and partake in photoshoots. If you take the coastal road to get to Gua Kristal, you'll pass **Gua Monyet**, the Monkey Cave. It's well signposted and you're likely to see monkeys on the side of the road. Unfortunately it seems that they're drawn to the area more by rubbish than by habitat.

Continue out of Kupang city on Jl Alfons Nisnoni for around 25km to arrive at **Pantai Tablolong** (Tablolong), which is about 13.5km southwest from the waterfall **Air Terjun Oenesu** (3000Rp). This lovely beach is a surprisingly pleasant stretch of sand free from Kupang's city grit.

Pantai Tedis   BEACH
(cnr Jl Soekarno & Siliwangi; snacks/smoothies from 7000/10,000Rp; ☺ from 5pm) Don't miss the atmosphere – or sunset – at this local hangout where Jl Soekarno intersects with the oceanfront. The sand vendors set up stalls and seating, while those in the know chow down on grilled corn and *pisang goreng* (fried plantain banana), the latter served with chocolate and grated *keju* (cheese). This is also the best place for smoothies, from mango and dragonfruit to avocado spiked with chocolate sauce.

Museum Nusa Tenggara Timur   MUSEUM
(☑ 0380-832471; Jl Frans Seda 64; by donation; ☺ 8am-3.30pm Mon-Fri) This regional museum has skulls, seashells, stone tools, swords, gourds and antique looms from across the province, plus an entire blue whale skeleton in a separate building. Displays (some in English), cover historical moments and cultural topics, including plants that create dyes for traditional fabrics.

☞ Tours

Kupang is a gateway to West Timor's fascinating and welcoming traditional villages. Bahasa Indonesia, let alone English, is often not spoken. The villages can also be a minefield – albeit a friendly minefield – of cultural dos and don'ts. A local guide is essential.

Oney Meda (☑ 0813 3940 4204; onymeda@ gmail.com; ½ day tour 300,000Rp) An English-speaking guide with nearly two decades of experience organising anthropological tours and treks throughout West Timor and Alor.

Edwin Lerrick (☑ 0812 377 0533; lavalonbar @gmail.com; per day from 400,000Rp) The irrepressible owner of Kupang's Lavalon Bar & Hostel (p396) is also a guide, with deep regional knowledge and connections throughout West Timor.

Willy Kadati (☑ 0812 5231 0678; willdk678@ gmail.com) Recommended by Lonely Planet in 1995, Willy took time off to do research for various organisations and universities; he is now back with more cultural, botanic and ikat knowledge than ever.

Aka Nahak (☑ 0813 3820 0634, 0852 346 3194; timorguide@gmail.com) Kefamenanu-based guide Aka has been touring Timor since 1988. He's enthusiastic with a sense of humour and will proudly show you his handwritten guestbooks.

🛏 Sleeping

Near the airport and the new commercial district there are several large and bland chain hotels, such as the Neo Aston and the Amaris. Properties on the waterfront are more atmospheric and come with ocean

---

THE TIMORESE SPIRIT

Throughout West Timor, but especially on the way to **Oelolok** from Kefamenanu (p401), you'll notice cloudy water bottles on rickety wooden shelves on the side of the road. Introducing *sopi*, the local alcohol made from palm juice. Every family distills theirs a little differently, using various herbs and plants like red wood, wild black pepper and types of mangroves. It takes about five hours to fill eight small water bottles. Many families use the income to send their kids to school, so it would be a shame not to support the cause: it's 25,000Rp or double for the good stuff. If you want to see the process, simply ask – the family will be surprised but delighted, so long as you buy a bottle or two on the way out.

Kupang

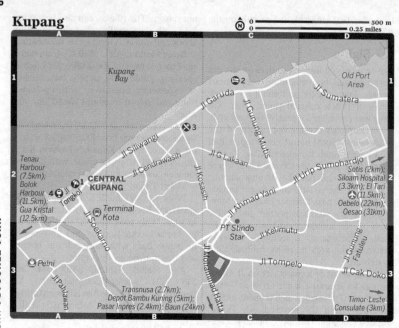

Map scale: 0 — 500 m / 0 — 0.25 miles

Kupang

◉ Sights
1 Pantai Tedis A2

🛏 Sleeping
2 Lavalon Bar & Hostel C1

✗ Eating
3 Pasar Malam B1

🍸 Drinking & Nightlife
4 999 Restaurant & Bar A2

breezes, views and sometimes pools. There are budget-friendly homestays, too.

★ Lavalon Cafe & Hostel   HOSTEL **$**
(📞 0812 377 0533; www.lavalontouristinfo.com; Jl Sumatera 44; dm from 70,000Rp, r 160,000-260,000Rp; ❄ 🛜) Run by living Nusa Tenggara encyclopedia and former Indonesian film star Edwin Lerrick (p395), Lavalon is Kupang's best-value accommodation. Rooms are worn but clean (some with Western bathrooms). Pay extra for the corner room with air-con, hot water and a window that opens to the sea. Edwin goes well out of his way to help anyone with information and bookings.

Also an avid cook, he has put together a small but tasty menu of speciality Indo-

nesian dishes and Western comfort food, which can be enjoyed in the small common area by the ocean. He arranges cars and drivers plus motorcycles (70,000Rp to 100,000Rp per day). Phone or WhatsApp ahead to guarantee a booking.

★ Sotis Hotel   HOTEL **$$**
(📞 0380-843 8000, 0380-843 8888; www.sotis hotels.com; Jl Timor Raya Km3; r from 650,000Rp; 🛜❄) One of Kupang's better accommodation options, the 88 newish rooms at this waterfront mid-rise are stylish with pops of colour. There are two pools, a spa, restaurant with live music, bar with pool tables and a cake shop. Ask for a sea view.

Hotel La Hasienda   HOTEL **$$**
(📞 0380-855 2717, SMS or WhatsApp 0812 3841 7459; www.hotellahasienda.com; Jl Adi Sucipto, Penfui; d from 395,000-500,000Rp; ❄🛜❄) You've got to feel for whoever covered this three-storey, family-run hotel in mosaic tiles. It adds to the Mexican vibe, with a rooftop terrace and bar, faded-ochre walls and cowboy paraphernalia. The 22 rooms are spotless with air-con and hot water and on-site restaurant (mains 25,000Rp to 85,000Rp). Note that it's closer to the airport than town.

Eating

As you'd expect, seafood is big in Kupang. Another local speciality is succulent *se'i babi* (pork smoked over kesambi wood and leaves); it's used as the base for various sauces and is served with noodles, rice and plenty of sambal.

★ Depot Bambu Kuning   INDONESIAN $
(☑ 0813 3336 8812, 0813 3910 9030; Jl Perintis Kemerdekaan 4; se'i babi portion/kg 20,000/170,000Rp; ☺ 10am-10pm) A popular place for authentic Kupang *se'i babi*. Choose from chopped up meat or ribs, both served with rice and a rich pork soup with red beans. *Sate* and a couple of veg dishes are also available. Check out the outdoor cooking area piled with *kesambi* leaves for smoking the meat.

Pasar Malam   MARKET $
(Night Market; Jl Kosasih; mains from 50,000Rp; ☺ 6pm-midnight) As tiny tailor shops finish up for the day, stallholders begin setting up this lamp-lit market. You're here for seafood, whether *ikan* (fish), *cumi* (squid), *kepiting* (crab) or *udang* (prawns), but you can also pick up Indo standards like grilled chicken, *bakso* (meatball noodle soup) and gado gado for a steal.

▼ Drinking & Nightlife

As the largest city in a predominantly Christian region, Kupang has decent drinking options. You'll find karaoke bars on Jl Sudirman and a few 'pubs' on Jl Timor Raya.

999 Restaurant & Bar   BAR
(☑ 0380-802 0999; www.999-kupang.com; Jl Tongkol 3; mains 38,000-140,000Rp; ☺ 10am-midnight; ☜) In the shadow of an old fort, this tropical outdoor bar has an expansive thatched roof, views of the shabby beach and the ever-present sound of rolling surf. There's a pool table, comfortable repurposed tyre seats, a full bar including plenty of cocktails and a decent menu, too. Regular live music and a full band on Sat nights.

🛍 Shopping

Sandalwood oil is trickier to find than it used to be, thanks to strict regulations that only allow harvest on one's own land. Some shops still sell it, and the purest oils are upwards of 300,000Rp for a small vial.

Ina Ndao   TEXTILES
(☑ 0380-821178, 0812 378 5620; ina_ndao@yahoo.com; Jl Kebun Raya II; ☺ 8am-7pm Mon-Sat, 7-11am Sun) It's worth seeking out this neighbourhood ikat shop. Textile lovers will be pleased with the wares sourced from across Nusa Tenggara, and you can take home a neat pair of ikat espadrilles. It offers naturally and chemically dyed varieties, and staff demonstrate the weaving process upon request. Accepts credit cards.

Pasar Inpres   MARKET
(off Jl Soeharto; ☺ 4am-7pm) The main market is the rambling Pasar Inpres, south of the city. It's mostly fruit and vegetables, but *ti'i langga* (*lontar*-leaf hats with a centre plume) from Rote make an authentic, but novel souvenir. For more variety, check out **Pasar Oeba** off Jl Ahmed Yani, in between Lavalon and Swiss-Belinn, about 1km from each and walking distance to the Pasar Ikan (fish market).

ℹ Information

Kupang has scores of banks and ATMs throughout town.

PT Stindo Star (☑ 0380-809 0583, 0380-809 0584; Jl Urip Sumohardjo 2; ☺ 9am-6pm) An efficient travel agency that sells airline tickets.

Siloam Hospital (☑ 1 500 911, 0380-853 0900; www.siloamhospitals.com; Jl R W Monginsidi, off Jl Eltari, Lippo Plaza; ☺ 24hr) An upscale hospital attached to the Lippo Plaza shopping mall.

ℹ Getting There & Away

AIR
Kupang is the most important hub for air travel in Nusa Tenggara, thanks to **El Tari Airport** (☑ 0380-882031; www.kupang-airport.com; Jl Adi Sucipto). There are frequent flights to Bali and a web of services across the region.

BOAT
Tenau Harbor, 7km west of the centre, is where the fast ferry to Rote docks. Bolok Harbour, 11km west of the centre, is where you get regular ASDP ferries (www.indonesiaferry.co.id) to Kalabahi, Rote and Waingapu. There are three sailings weekly for Larantuka (105,000Rp, 15 hours).

Pelni (☑ 0380-821944; www.pelni.co.id; Jl Pahlawan 7; ☺ 8am-4pm) serves Tenau Harbor on a twice-monthly loop that includes Larantuka and Maumere. Its office is near the waterfront.

BUS

Kupang's intercity bus terminal, **Terminal Oebobo** (Jl Frans Seda), is located around 7km from the airport, but people tend to use the shadow terminal in Oesapa, tour agencies or get picked up from hotels.

ⓘ Getting Around

TO/FROM THE AIRPORT

Kupang's El Tari Airport (p397) is 15km east of the town centre.

Taxis from the airport to town cost a fixed 70,000Rp. An *ojek* will cost 30,000Rp. For public transport, turn left out of the terminal and walk 1km to the junction with the main highway, from where bemos to town cost 3000Rp (possibly 5000Rp with a bag).

Going to the airport, take the Penfui or Baumata bemo to the junction and walk.

BEMO

A ride in one of Kupang's bass-thumping bemos (3000Rp, or 5000Rp with luggage) is one of the city's essential experiences (Kupang is too spread out to walk). Each bemo has an entertaining Western name, like Man Tap, Cold Play or City Car. Windscreens are festooned with soft toys, girlie silhouettes and Jesus. The low-rider paint job is of the *Fast & Furious* colourful variety, while banks of subwoofers will have your butt involuntarily shaking. Clap loudly when you want to stop.

Bemos stop running by 8pm. The bemo hub is the Terminal Kota terminal. Useful bemo routes:

1 & 2 Kuanino–Oepura; passing many popular hotels.

5 Oebobo–Airnona–Bakunase; passing the main post office.

6 Goes to the Flobamora shopping mall and the post office.

10 Kelapa Lima–Walikota; from Kota Kupang terminal to the tourist office, Oebobo bus terminal and Museum Nusa Tenggara Timur.

Bemos running outside Kupang use names instead of numbers. Tenau and Bolok Harbour bemos run to the docks; Penfui and Baumata bemos link to the airport.

TRANSPORT FROM KUPANG

Air

DESTINATION	AIRLINE	DURATION (HR)	FREQUENCY
Alor Island	Wings Air	¾	two daily
Bajawa	Wings Air, TransNusa	1	two daily
Denpasar	Garuda, Lion Air, Nam Air	1¾	several daily
Jakarta	Batik Air, Garuda, Citilink Indonesia	3	several daily
Labuan Bajo	Wings Air, Garuda, Nam Air	1½	several daily
Maumere	Nam Air, Wings Air, TransNusa	1	1-2 daily
Tambolaka	Nam Air, Wings Air, Garuda	1½	several daily
Waingapu	Nam Air, Wings Air	1	several daily

Boat

DESTINATION	TYPE	FARE (RP)	DURATION (HR)	FREQUENCY
Kalabahi	ferry	116,000	15	noon Tue & Sat
Larantuka	ferry	105,000	15	three weekly
Rote	ferry	55,000	5	6am daily
Rote	Bahari Express	138,000-168,000	2	9am daily
Waingapu	ferry	162,000	28	three weekly

Bus

DESTINATION	FARE (RP)	DURATION (HR)	FREQUENCY
Kefamenanu	50,000	5½	several times daily
Niki Niki	35,000	3½	hourly
Soe	30,000	3	hourly

CAR & MOTORCYCLE

It's possible to rent a car with a driver from 750,000Rp to 1,000,000Rp per day, depending on the destination. Motorcycles cost 75,000Rp a day at Lavalon Bar & Hostel (p396), but 100,000Rp or more elsewhere. Your accommodation will be able to organise it for you.

Around Kupang

Baun

Travel 25km from Kupang along a road with a single rough patch and you reach Baun, the heart of the Amarasi kingdom. In the 1970s its people began building roads without government assistance or machines, the deal being that if you worked on the road, you could build your house near it. Robert 'Robbi' Koroh, the 20th *raja* (king), still resides here in a former medical clinic. His palace, **Sonaf Baun** (⌨ 0812 3644 5787; Kelurahan Teunbaun), might not be flash, but he can organise weaving demonstrations, ikat trading and has an impressive fossil collection. Robbi doesn't speak English but is a wealth of information, so you'll need a guide to translate if you want to do more than look around.

Visit Baun on a Saturday morning to soak up the atmosphere of the weekly market. If you have a spare 30 million rupiah you can purchase one of Baun's famous *sapi* (cows). Don't leave town without trying the most authentic se'i babi smoked pork in West Timor at **Se'i Babi Om Ba'i** (500g/1kg pork 80,000/160,000Rp; ☺ 6-11am or til sold out), which cooks between 12 and 30 whole pigs daily.

❶ Getting There & Away

Jump on one of the open-backed utes en route to Baun from Kupang. It's similar to a bemo and leaves from Pasar Inpres (p397) for 10,000Rp. An *ojek* already heading in that direction starts around 50,000Rp, one way.

Oebelo & Oesao

Oebelo, a small salt-mining town 22km from Kupang on the Soe road, is notable for a unique Rotenese musical-instrument workshop, **Sasandu** (⌨ 0852 3948 7808; Jl Timor Raya; ☺ 9am-6pm), that makes and plays traditional 32-stringed harps.

Oesao is another 6km down the road and is a mandatory stop for one marvellous reason: **Inzana** (Jl Timor Raya; bag of treats 10,000Rp; ☺ 4am-10pm), a roadside sweet shop just east of the main market that serves a variety of traditional Timorese *kue* (cakes). Your driver will know the place.

Between the two lies an opportunity to get off the beaten track and see how palm sugar is made by locals. Don't leave without tasting the caramelised disks of golden sugar.

❶ Getting There & Away

The cheapest way to get here from Kupang is by bemo. Bemos with Kupang-Oesao on top of the vehicles go to both Oebelo (22km) and Oesao (30km) and cost 5000Rp and 10,000Rp respectively, one way. If you've hired a motorbike, it's an easy side trip from Kupang.

Soe

⌨ 0388 / POP 29,000

About 110km northeast of Kupang, the cool, leafy market town of Soe (800m) makes a decent base from which to explore West Timor's interior, even if there's not a lot to see in town. The traditional villages scattered throughout the interior are some of the most intriguing in all of Nusa Tenggara.

🛏 Sleeping & Eating

Hotel Bahagia I   GUESTHOUSE $

(⌨ 0853 3830 3809; Jl Diponegoro 22; s/d/VIP r 150,000/200,000/300,000Rp) Right in the centre of Soe, and not to be confused with Bahagia II on the outskirts, Bahagia I offers a range of rooms from small, dark cubbies to spacious suites. It's a compact courtyard building with a little breezy terrace, but don't expect air-con, hot water, wi-fi or English.

If you're in transit but not staying overnight, you can drop 125,000Rp on a room for two hours of rest. There's a bank across the road.

Dena Hotel   HOTEL $$

(⌨ 0812 3696 9222, 0388-21616; hotel_dena@yahoo.com; Jl Hayam Wuruk, Pasar Inpres; s/d from 200,000/225,000Rp; ❋) Although these beige rooms aren't about to win design awards, they're as clean and serviced as they come in Soe. Some have Indonesian toilets, so inspect before you decide. The most expensive have air-con (350,000Rp for a double). It's across the road from the market, ATM and a great little Padang restaurant.

★ **Depot Remaja**　　　INDONESIAN $
(Jl Gajah Mada; mains from 20,000Rp; ⊙10am-
10pm; 🍴) This modest and clean diner specialises in succulent *se'i babi*, the iconic
Kupang pork smoked over *kesambi* wood.
But the fun doesn't stop there; try the
warming pork soup – which is more of a
stew – and one of the many veg options, like
jantung pisang (banana flower salad).

Warung Putra Lamongan　　INDONESIAN $
(🍴0823 4096 4969; Jl El Tari; mains 15,000-
30,000Rp; ⊙10am-10pm) You'll smell this
place before you see it, thanks to the grill
charring *sate* out the front. Within the orange walls are a handful of large tables
populated by locals digging into grilled and
fried chicken, fish, tempe and *tongseng*, a
Javanese stew with goat or beef. The *sambal
terasi*, made with shrimp paste, is addictive.

🛍 Shopping

Timor Art Shop　　　ARTS & CRAFTS
(🍴0853 3783 5390; Jl Bill Nope 17; ⊙6am-8pm)
If you're interested in antiques and handicrafts, don't miss this shop that could double
as a museum. You'll find Timor's best selection of masks, sculpture, hand-spun fabrics
and carvings at unbelievable prices. There's
no sign, so call owner Alfred Maku first. He
speaks excellent English. Opening hours can
vary.

ℹ Information

There are ATMs and banks around town, including a full BNI branch.

Tourist Information Centre (🍴0368-21149;
Jl Diponegoro 39; ⊙7am-4pm Mon-Fri) Has
information on the surrounding area and is a
good place to arrange guides, should you catch
someone there who speaks English.

ℹ Getting There & Away

The Haumeni bus terminal is 4km west of town
and 3000Rp by bemo, but people tend to flag
down buses on the side of the road instead. Regular buses go from Soe to Kupang, taking three
hours and costing 30,000Rp. Knock off half an
hour for buses to Kefamenanu and Oinlasi, both
25,000Rp. Bemos cover Niki Niki for 10,000Rp.

TIMOR-LESTE VISA RUN

Crossing the border into Timor-Leste is not nearly as complicated or lengthy as it used
to be. You can still make the 12-hour, one-way journey to the considerably more expensive Dili for 225,000Rp, but it's no longer necessary to visit the Indonesia Consulate.

Instead, the easiest way to do the visa run is to cross the border at Napan, just over
20km north of Kefamenanu; Atapupu, which will only cost 50,000Rp by *ojek* from Atambua; or catch the bus to Batugade via Mota'ain. Once at the border, present your author-
isation letter, US$30 and proof of an onward journey, and continue with a free 90-day
visa. If you're short on time, you could conceivably catch the 45-minute morning Wings
Air flight from Kupang to Atambua, cross the border and then fly back to Kupang in time
for lunch. A one-way flight starts at around 350,000Rp.

But first you need to get an approved visa application letter. Apply at the **Timor-
Leste Consulate** (🍴0380-855 4552; Jl Frans Seda; ⊙8-11.30am & 1.30-3.30pm Mon-Thu,
to 3pm Fri) in Kupang with a valid passport, a photocopy of it, passport photos and either
proof or return tickets or a bank statement. You'll receive the letter and stamp within
one to three working days. If you attempt this a few days before Christmas, you're likely
to be out of luck as staff go on holiday. Also be aware that the consulate is closed on
weekends.

Note that since 2015, some European citizens who fall into the Schengen Agreement
can stay in Timor-Leste without a visa for up to 90 days, every 180 days.

Timor Tour & Travel (🍴0812 379 4199, 0380-881543; Jl Timor Raya Km8, Oesapa; one-way
225,000Rp) and **Paradise Tour & Travel** (🍴0813 3935 6679; Jl Pulau Indah, Oesapa) operate buses. Departures can be as early as 5am, so brace yourself. Call for a hotel pick up
or ask Edwin from Lavalon (p396) to lend a hand.

It's also worth checking the daily cost of the visa overstay fine – at the time of writing,
it's 300,000Rp per day, so it's worth weighing up cost and convenience (accommodation and a bus fare will be more expensive than paying a fine for a couple of days). Check
the current price of the fine to avoid being caught out; rumours are circulating that it
could jump significantly.

Around Soe

None

POP 238

None is one of the area's best attractions, despite fires destroying three *ume bubu* (traditional beehive huts) in as many years. A compact, gravel trail runs for 1km from where the bemo drops you on the main road; so you can walk or drive past corn, pumpkin and bean fields to the entrance. None is home to 56 families that have lived here for 10 generations. Parents still bury their placenta in their hut after childbirth, and the village is protected by a native rock fort that abuts a sheer cliff.

At the cliff's edge you'll find a 300-year-old banyan tree and a totem pole where shamans once met with warriors before they left on headhunting expeditions. The wise ones consulted chicken eggs and a wooden staff before predicting if the warriors would prevail. If there was a speck of blood in the egg, a sign of poor fortune, they'd delay their attack.

Villagers might break out their looms at the village *lopo* (meeting place) for weaving demonstrations upon request. It's so peaceful here that it's hard to believe they were taking heads just two generations ago, the last conflict in 1944. You can also arrange for traditional dances. Leave an offering of 50,000Rp for up to a few people.

ⓘ Getting There & Away

You can reach None, 18km east of Soe, on an *ojek* (30,000Rp to 50,000Rp, 45 minutes), or hop on a Soe–Niki Niki bemo for 5000Rp.

Oinlasi

We'll let others speculate about why local governments keep the road to the important market town of Oinlasi in such miserable condition. But the painful drive is worth it, especially on Tuesdays, when a **traditional market** spreads for more than 400m along a ridge overlooking two valleys. Villagers from the surrounding hills, many of whom wear traditional ikat, descend to barter, buy and sell weavings, carvings, masks and elaborately carved betel-nut containers, along with fruit, livestock, local sweets and some of the worst popular music ever recorded. The market starts early in the morning and continues until 2pm, but is at its best before 10am.

WORTH A TRIP

AIR TERJUN OEHALA

Look for a road going north off the main highway, drive 6km and turn east at a sign for 'Oehala'. After 3km is a parking area, from which it's a short walk down steep steps to the gushing water of **Air Terjun Oehala** diffusing over huge boulders in a silvery sheen. The jungle setting hasn't seen any maintenance for years, but on the plus side it makes the whole thing feel very *Jurassic Park*. Crowds leave rubbish behind on weekends.

ⓘ Getting There & Away

Regular buses from Soe cost 20,000Rp and make the 51km, 1½ to two-hour trip along the twisted, rutted mountain road to Oinlasi. Turn south off the main highway at Cabang, which is 5km east of the turn for None.

Kefamenanu

☏ 0388 / POP 42,840

A former Portuguese stronghold, Kefamenanu is a quiet hill town. Still, it remains devoutly Catholic and has a couple of impressive colonial churches. Most importantly it's the jumping-off point for Temkessi (p402), one of West Timor's 'can't miss' villages. Known locally as Kefa, the town lies at the heart of an important weaving region. Prepare to haggle! Note that the town mostly shuts up shop on Sundays.

🛏 Sleeping & Eating

Hotel Ariesta　　　　　　　　HOTEL $

(☏ 0388-31007; Jl Basuki Rahman 29; r standard/superior/ste 120,000/290,000/385,000Rp; ❊ 🛜) Set on a leafy backstreet, this long-time budget joint sprawls across 42 rooms in a modern annex and weathered original block. Economy rooms are best avoided, the all-suite annex boasts plenty of light and a private porch, and the midrange deluxe rooms with air-con and hot water have the Goldilocks effect – just right. BYO loo paper.

Rents motorbikes for 70,000Rp per day.

New Victory Hotel　　　　　　HOTEL $$

(Hotel Victory II; ☏ 0388-243 0090; Jl Kartini 199; r 350,000Rp; 🛜) This hotel has 23 clean rooms with questionably patterned wallpaper, air-conditioning, TV, hot water and breakfast included. Strangely, there is an

TRADITIONAL HOUSES

Central West Timor is dotted with *ume bubu* (beehive-shaped hut) villages that are home to local Dawan people. Without windows and only a 1m-high doorway, *ume bubu* can get cramped and smoky. Government authorities deemed them a health hazard and have subsidised cold, concrete boxes, which the Dawan themselves have deemed a health hazard. They've built new *ume bubu* – or rehabbed their old ones – behind the approved houses, and live there.

enormous gym and exercise hall here, with Zumba and aerobics. There are plans to double in size.

Rumah Makan Pondok Selera
INDONESIAN $

(Jl El Tari; mains 15,000-30,000Rp; ⏱10am-9pm Mon-Sat; 🛜🍴) A tiny, delicious menu served in a big, dining-room space. This *rumah makan* boasts some of the best tempe and tofu in Nusa Tengarra, a giant serve that comes with *lalapan* (raw veg nibbles) and sweet, chunky sambal made with fresh tomato. There's also gado gado and *ikan kua asam* (sour fish soup).

Rumah Makan Padang 2
INDONESIAN $

(☎0388-31841; Jl El Tari; mains 20,000-30,000Rp; ⏱9am-9pm) Motorbikes pull up outside this corner Padang restaurant and hint at its popularity. Specialities such as *ayam rica rica* (chicken fried in a sweet, spicy sauce), *rendang*, boiled cassava leaves and fish curry are piled onto plates in this green-walled establishment. Cool down with *sirsak* (soursop) juice.

ℹ️ Information

There are banks and foreign-card friendly ATMs scattered around town, often within walking distance of hotels.

The tourist office, **Dinas Pariwisata** (☎0388-21520; Jl Sudirman; ⏱7am-3pm Mon-Fri), is opposite the field north of the highway and can help locate a guide.

ℹ️ Getting There & Away

The bus terminal is in Kefamenanu's centre, 50m from the Jl El Tari market, which blooms most days. From here between about 6am and 4pm there are regular buses to Kupang

(50,000Rp, five hours) and Soe (25,000Rp, two hours); Atambua (20,000Rp) on the Timor-Leste border is only 20,000Rp and 1½ hours away.

Hotel Ariesta (p401) rents motorbikes for 70,000Rp per day. Rental cars in Kefa cost 650,000Rp per day with driver.

Timor Tour & Travel (☎0388-243 0624; Jl Ahmad Yani) You can join express minibuses running between Kupang (95,000Rp, five hours) and Dili in Timor-Leste (180,000Rp, 7½ hours). Tickets are sold at an office 4km east of the centre on the main highway; pick ups are made at hotels.

Around Kefamenanu

Maslete

Just 3.5km from Kefamenanu is this traditional village and *sonaf* (palace). Made from wood carved with mythical birds and an imposing grass roof with hanging dried corn, you'll find the king sitting on his sheltered porch. Although his eyes are cloudy blue from blindness and he doesn't speak English ('We are like the cow and buffalo talking,' he might observe) a guide will translate as you're quizzed by the Catholic animist about life in your part of the world.

Temkessi & Around

Accessible through a keyhole between jutting limestone cliffs, 50km northeast of Kefa, Temkessi is one of West Timor's most isolated and best-preserved villages. The drive across wind-swept ridges, with distant views out to sea, sets the otherworldly mood, but upon arrival you'll be met by giggling children and perhaps a puppy or piglet.

Back along the road from the main highway, 19km from Kefa, Maubesi is home to the Kefa Regency's best **textile market** (Maubesi; ⏱Thu). Market day is Thursday, when along with produce, animals and pottery, ikat is displayed beneath tamarind trees. If you're not passing by on a Thursday, **Maubesi Art Shop** (☎0852 8508 5867; ⏱hours vary) has a terrific selection of local ikat and handicrafts.

ℹ️ Getting There & Away

Regular buses run from Kefa to Manufui, about 8km from Temkessi. On market day in Manufui (Saturday), trucks or buses should run through to Temkessi. Otherwise, charter an *ojek*, or better, secure your own wheels.

ROTE

A slender, rain-starved limestone jewel with powdery white-sand beaches and epic surf, Rote floats southwest of West Timor, but has an identity of its own. For tourists it's all about the surf, which can be gentle enough for beginners and wild enough for experts.

Ba'a, Rote's commercial centre, is a sleepy port town on the west coast where fast ferry and flights land, but people don't tend to linger. Stunning Pantai Nemberala is home to the world-renowned T-Land break, and there are dozens of hidden beaches to the south and north. To find them you'll roll through villages, over natural limestone bridges and through undulating savannah that turns from green in the December to March wet season to gold in the dry season, which is also when offshore winds fold swells into barrels. Don't overlook the tiny offshore islands where you can find gorgeous ikat, turquoise bays and more surf.

ℹ Information

Internet access is sparse, but you can get 3G data in some places, including Nemberala.

There's a BRI ATM in Ba'a but it usually refuses foreign cards. Bring plenty of rupiah as exchanging cash is difficult.

ℹ Getting There & Away

AIR

Wings Air operates flights between Kupang and Ba'a twice daily. They take 30 minutes and the afternoon flight allows for a same-day connection from Bali, although transporting surfboards can complicate the transfer and add to the costs (Wings Air charges 200,000Rp per board).

BOAT

The swiftest and most comfortable way to reach Rote is via the Baharai Express (executive/VIP 138,000Rp/168,000Rp, two hours), a fast ferry that departs from Kupang at 9am daily (and sometimes at 2pm between Wednesday and Monday), docks at Ba'a and returns at 11am. Book your ticket in advance and arrive at the dock at least half an hour early. Be warned, this service is often cancelled due to rough seas.

There's also a daily slow ferry (55,000Rp, five hours) that docks at Pantai Baru, north of Ba'a, but by the time you charter transport to Nemberala, it will cost you more than the fast ferry.

ℹ Getting Around

Local touts will try to convince you that to get to Nemberala from the fast-boat port in Ba'a you'll have to charter a bemo (from 300,000Rp, two hours). This is only a good option if you are sharing with a group, but just outside the harbour gates you can easily flag down a public bemo (with/without surfboard 100,000/50,000Rp). You can also arrange with your hotel for a car to pick you up for about 400,000Rp.

Many of the resorts offer transfer packages from Kupang's airport via the fast ferry and on to the resort. These are undeniably seamless, but can cost US$100 or more.

Once you're in Nemberala, hire a motorbike (100,000Rp per day) through your hotel or guesthouse, and explore.

Nemberala

Nemberala is a chilled-out fishing village on an exquisite white-sand beach. It's sheltered by a reef that helps form the legendary 'left', T-Land. Don't expect an isolated vibe here as an influx of visitors, expats and vacation home owners have bought up large swatches of beachfront in the area. New businesses are opening to serve these devotees.

Still, Nemberala hasn't gone all flash: the local pigs, goats, cows, chickens and other critters still freely wander the beach and resorts, and you still need to avoid getting conked on the head by a falling coconut. Explore the surrounding lonely limestone coast by motorbike in order to absorb its majesty.

🏃 Activities

The **T-Land** wave gets big, especially between June and August, but it's not heavy, so the fear factor isn't ridiculous. Like other once-undiscovered waves in east Indo, the line-up gets busy in the high season. If you prefer a heavier, hollow wave, your first stop should be 3km north of Nemberala at **Suckie Mama's**.

Many resorts rent high-quality boards from about 100,000Rp per day.

🛏 Sleeping

The surf season peaks between June and September. Accommodation range and value are solid, but there aren't a lot of rooms – book ahead. While most of the lodges and guesthouses are all inclusive, some local warungs have appeared, so you have options to vary your vittles.

Ti Rosa BUNGALOW **$**
(📱 0823 3915 2620; per person incl meals from 250,000Rp) Run by sweet Ibu Martine and her son, this fine collection of eight lime-green,

concrete bungalows is super clean, shaded by palms and is the cheapest beach option available. Budget surfers love it so much that some book rooms for the whole season. Turn right at the first intersection in town and head north along the dirt road for 500m.

Anugerah Surf & Dive Resort   BUNGALOW $$
(☑ 0811 382 3441, 0813 5334 3993; www.surfdiverote.com; s/d incl meals from 565,000/904,000Rp; ❉) The 40 cute and compact *lontar*-palm bungalows range from newish to older, and come with a variety of patios and *mandis,* wooden furniture, outdoor bathrooms and more. It's right on the beach opposite T-Land. The restaurant, with ikat tablecloths, serves *ikan bakar* (grilled fish) amid a menu that changes daily. Reserve ahead during surf season.

Scuba diving is also offered; per person, all gear included is 1,470,000Rp for two dives.

★ Malole Surf House   SURF CAMP $$$
(☑ 0813 5317 7264, 0813 3776 7412; www.rotesurfhouse.com; s/d per person incl 3 meals from US$105/126; ❉ @ � 🛜) Built by surf legend Felipe Pomar, this lodge blends comfort, cuisine and style better than anywhere else in Rote. Four rooms are set in a large wooden house and guesthouse with day beds, ikat bedspreads, limitless laundry and more. You'll hit the right waves at the right time via three boats. Closed during wet season; mid-November to March.

Sublime international seafood is but one highlight of the kitchen, which carves fresh sashimi, bakes fresh bread and blends spectacular soups and curries. Mountain bikes, fishing trips and island excursions are also on offer. The level of comfort and elegance here feels effortless (it isn't) and belies its extremely remote location.

Villa Santai   BUNGALOW $$$
(☑ 0812 3941 4568; www.surfroteisland.com; per person s/d incl meals from 1,400,000/1,200,000Rp) Hugely popular for its highly personalised service, this small resort has four bungalows. The top one has sweeping views of powdery white sand and T-Land, to which unlimited surf transfers are free. The food is fresh, local and copious. There's a full bar and many end their day with a G&T sundowner, soaking up the surf action.

Of the four bungalows, one can accommodate up to four people and another has two bedrooms, a lounge, kitchen and outdoor living area.

Nemberala Beach Resort   RESORT $$$
(☑ 0813 3773 1851; www.nemberalabeachresort.com; surfers/nonsurfer per person from US$190/170; ❉ ❉) Right on the ocean, this relaxed four-star, all-inclusive spot has a total of eight rooms in four spacious slate-and-timber bungalows with outdoor baths and freshwater showers. There's a swimming pool, spa, volleyball court, pool table and a terrific beach bar. Join the daily yoga classes on the beachfront deck. It's closed from 1 December to 1 March.

There's a speedboat to whisk you out to nearby surf breaks, and excursions to limestone caves and tidal lagoons are also on offer. Fishing trips for dog-toothed tuna and mackerel can also be arranged.

Around Nemberala

If you rent a motorbike and drive the spectacularly rutted coastal road north or south, you'll notice that you're within reach of a half-dozen other desolate beaches and a few superb, uncharted surf breaks. Beginners take note: just north of the Nemberala fishing-boat harbour is a terrific novice break called **Squealers**.

The village of **Boni** lies about 15km from Nemberala, near the northern coast, and is one of the last villages on Rote where traditional religion is still followed. Market day is Thursday.

About 8km south of Nemberala, **Bo'a** has a spectacular white-sand beach and consistent off-season surf. Set on a notch in the headland that bisects this absurdly wide and beautiful bay, **Bo'a Hill Surf House** (☑ 0822 7771 7774, 0822 7771 7775; www.surfrote.com; per person incl meals from 800,000Rp) 🏄 has beautiful bungalows set on a three-hectare site with stunning views. The eco-cred is strong here. The owner grows fruit and herbs, raises pigs and ducks, collects honey, and is a superb guide to local delights on land and sea.

From Bo'a continue south over the dry rocky road – look out for monkeys – and after you traverse the natural limestone bridge, negotiate the descent and reach **Oeseli** village. Then make a right on the dirt road, which leads to another superb beach with some good waves, and a huge natural tidal lagoon that shelters local fishing boats and floods limestone bat caves. There's an ideal kitesurf launch here, too.

The southernmost island in Indonesia, **Pulau Ndana**, can be reached by local fishing boat from Nemberala. Although it's currently a military camp it can still be visited, but for years it was uninhabited. Legend has it that the entire population was murdered in a 17th-century revenge act, staining the island's small lake with the victims' blood. Today Ndana is known for its wildlife and superb snorkelling. Look out for wild deer and a wide variety of birds, as well as for nesting turtles on the beaches.

Pulau Ndao has more powdery white-sand beaches, limestone bluffs and a tidy, charming ikat-weaving, lontar-tapping (collecting *nirah* sap from lontar palm tree flowers) fishing village that's home to nearly 600 people who speak their own indigenous dialect, Bahasa Ndao. There are some fantastic swimming beaches up the west and east coasts, and good though inconsistent surf off the southern point.

Ndao is 10km west of Nemberala. To get here you'll have to charter a boat (800,000Rp to 1,000,000Rp, maximum five people). You could easily combine a visit here with nearby **Pulau Do'o**, a flat spit of pale golden sand with terrific though finicky surf. You can see Do'o from Pantai Nemberala.

SUMBA

0387

There's something truly enchanting about Sumba. With its rugged, undulating savannah and low limestone hills growing maize and rice, it's nothing like Indonesia's northern volcanic islands. Scattered throughout the countryside are hilltop villages with tall, symbolic grass roofs clustered around megalithic tombs, where nominally Protestant villagers still respect indigenous *marapu* (spiritual forces) with bloody sacrificial rites.

Encircling Sumba are white-sand beaches that are the stuff of dreams, as are the island's secret swimming spots and waterfalls further inland. Throw in some of Indonesia's most prized ikat (patterned textiles) and the annual Pasola festival (p26) and you have one of the most diverse islands in Indonesia where *adat* runs deep and small children with big smiles shout 'hello mister', irrespective of gender.

One of Indonesia's poorest islands, an influx of investment has seen villages swap thatched roofs for tin. Traditional dress is reserved for special occasions and remote villagers expect generous donations from visitors.

OFF THE BEATEN TRACK

AIR TERJUN TANGGEDU

Northwest of Waingapu is arguably Sumba's best **waterfall** (Tanggedu Waterfall). Expect to spend two hours or more making the 60-or-so-km journey along roads that leave a lot to be desired, followed by a 40-minute walk through savannah or grasslands, depending on the time of year. What awaits will blow you away: two rivers run between time-layered limestone cliffs and converge into waterfall terraces that feed into multiple pools.

ⓘ Getting There & Away

Sumba's links to greater Indonesia are ever-improving. Airports in Tambolaka and Waingapu have daily flights to Bali, Kupang (West Timor) and Ende (Flores). Ferries run to Flores, Kupang and Sape in Sumbawa. If you're going on a Sumba deep dive, consider flying into either Waingapu or Tambolaka and out of the other, to avoid long backtracks on the main trans-Sumba highway.

Waingapu

0387 / POP 52,000

Waingapu is a laid-back town with a split personality: there's the leafy, dusty centre interspersed with accommodation and small *toko* (stores), the old harbour that becomes redolent with the smell of grilled fish after sundown when the Pasar Malam (p407) kicks off, and villages in the middle of it all, where chickens bolt between *marapu* tomb stones adorned with carved crocodile and deer statues.

Waingapu also has some ikat stores and workshops, and traders lugging bundles of textiles and carvings hang around hotels touting for rupiah. It's a mostly walkable place, and you'll spot grazing buffalo and horses as you explore. Since becoming an administrative centre after the Dutch military 'pacified' the island in 1906, Waingapu remains Sumba's main trading post for textiles, prized Sumbanese horses, dyewoods and lumber.

🛏 Sleeping

Breakfast and free airport transfers (if you call in advance) are usually included in accommodation rates. There's a decent range of options and budgets, from rooms with a view to rooms in the village.

Sumba

Ñ 0 — 20 km
0 — 10 miles

Kupang; West Timor

Sabu Island

SAWU SEA

Ende; Flores

Aimere; Flores

Sape; Sumbawa

Selat Sumba

INDIAN OCEAN

KODI · **WEJEWA BARAT** · **WEJEWA TIMUR** · **LEMBOYA** · **LOLI** · **MEMBORO** · **WEST SUMBA** · **ANAKALANG** · **WANOKAKA** · **EAST SUMBA** · **MANGILI** · **WAIJELU**

Bukabari · Pantai Tosi · Kori · Perou · Ratenggaro · Wainyapu · Panenggoede · Bondokodi · Weha · Rara · Waikelo · Waitabula · Tambolaka · Airport · Tambolaka · Waimangura · Waibanca · Tanareu · Weeleo · Waimanura · Waikabubak · Gallu Bakul · Kabonduk · Pasunga · Maderi · Manuakalada · Manaca · Waiwarungu · Kahale · Gaura · Kadenga · Pantai Krewe · Pantai Marosi · Pantai Patiala · Gunung Wattumandeta (888m)

Tanjung Sasar · Wunga · Napu · Rambangaru · Mondu · Prai Liang · Pantai Kambera · Prai Liang · Maru · Lenang · Praikarambua · Kondamara · Lewa · Watumbelar · Tidas · Konda · Maloba · Air Terjun Tanggedu · Kanatang · Waingapu · Mauliru · Makamenggit · Praipaha · Praibakul · Lahara · Karita · Tarimbang · Prainghareha · Londolima · Pantai Londolima · Tanjung Laundi · Teluk Wainagapu Whuata · Tanjung Whuata · Kawangu · Maujawa · Wera Beach · Maubakat · Kataka · Lajuli · Kotakawau · Maubokul · Lumbung · Mahubokul · Melahar · Tanarara · Ramuk · Air Terjun Laputi · Wahang · Tawui · Lai Tunggi · Katundu · Nggongi · Aukakehok · Gunung Wanggameti (1225m) · Lepanjir · Kananggar · Kabenda · Langgai · Hambautang · Manukangga · Pulau Salura · Pulau Kotak · Pulau Mangudu

Petawang · Melolo · Praiyawang · Rende · Nusa · Tanjung Undu · Hanggaroro · Air Terjun Waimarang · Hanggaroru · Kabaaru · Mburukulu · Laiwita · Pamburu · Baing · Kalala · Tanjung Nginju · Maukabuni · Kamanghi

Teluk Mambong

See Enlargement

Enlargement:
0 — 2 km
0 — 1 mile

Taramanu · Praibakul · Praigoli · Waigalli · Waihura · Pantai Wonokaka · Rua · Pedede Watu · Watu · Watukarere · Nihi Sumba · Kadolu · Waihoii · Pantai Nihiwatu · Pantai Rua

Mr. R. Home Stay GUESTHOUSE $
([☑] 0853 3744 6164; Kandara Belankang SMP Kristen; r 200,000Rp; [❄]) A plain, clean guesthouse with an out-of-place dolphin water feature, overlooking a rice paddy with grazing buffalo. There are six rooms with air-con, TV and long pillows to hug should you get lonely. Food is ordered from nearby **Sacca Resto** ([☑] 0851 0270 7222, 0387-62677; saccacellular@gmail.com; Jl S Parman 88, Tandarotu Waingapu; r from 350,000Rp; [❄][☎]) and if you're lucky, the hot water will be working.

★ **Morinda Villa & Resto** CABIN $$
([☑] 0812 379 5355; freddy_ikat@yahoo.com; Bendungan Lambanapu; r from 650,000-750,000Rp) About 11km south of the airport and perched on a hill, Morinda Villa has five cabins with eye-popping views. Each has a traditional grass roof, huge windows and a balcony for a peek into local life on the river. There's hot water, a restaurant (mains 25,000Rp to 100,000Rp, open 11am until 9pm) and an ikat shop on-site.

★ **Praikamarru Guest House** BUNGALOW $$
([☑] 0813 3809 3459; www.prailiu.org; Jl Umbu Rara Meha 22; r/bungalow 250,000/275,000Rp) Run by an Australian who married a local king and now welcomes guests into village life. Stay in one of two spacious bamboo bungalows with *alang alang* grass roofs, comfortable beds with ikat throws and even a fridge; or in one of two basic rooms (shared squat toilet) in a traditional house with bamboo mats and a people-watching porch.

Enjoy freshly baked bread and fruit every morning and delicious local food with the family for 50,000Rp per meal. Ask owners Sarah and Umbu anything you like about local culture and the *marapu* religion – they're more than happy to share. Look for the tree adorned in animal skulls, remnants of sacrificial ceremonies. Motorbike rental for 75,000Rp per day.

Padadita Beach Hotel HOTEL $$
([☑] 0812 3899 5246; padaditabeachhotel@gmail.com; Jl Airlangga Padadita; r 465,000-675,000Rp; [❄][☎]) Some staff are more helpful than others and the grounds need greenery, but beyond that are 65 sparkling rooms with hot water and wooden furniture. Some rooms have ocean views. There's beach access, a restaurant serving buffet breakfast (mains 25,000Rp to 75,000Rp) and free airport transfers.

✖ Eating

★ **PC Corner** INDONESIAN $
([☑] 0387-256 0142, 0812 2317 1725, 0852 3702 8401; lusijowin@gmail.com; Jl Radamata 1; mains 25,000-50,000Rp; [☺] 8am-10pm Mon-Fri, 9am-11pm Sat, 4-10pm Sun; [☎]) Pause for a photo in front of the bohemian 'dream big, work hard, stay focus' mural before continuing up stairs to this open-air cafe with vintage furniture and dreamcatchers. Eat veg dishes like papaya flower with *kangkung* (water spinach) and free-range *kampung* chicken. There's a band from 7pm on Saturday, a killer view and charging points at every table.

★ **Pasar Malam** INDONESIAN $
(Night Market; off Jl Yos Sudarso; mains from 15,000Rp; [☺] 6-11pm) The best dinner options turn up at dusk: a couple of warungs and half a dozen gas-lit carts at the old wharf grill and fry seafood on the cheap. In the centre of town at the southern fork of Jl Ahmad Yani are more street eats, like *sate ayam* (chicken satay) and *bakso* (noodle soup), from 10,000Rp.

Mr Cafe INDONESIAN $
([☑] 0852 5341 0000, 0387-61605; sarmanse@ymail.com; Jl Umbu Tipuk Marisi 1; mains 15,000-45,000Rp; [☺] 8am-10pm) Join workers on comfy plastic chairs and order from a large selection of Indonesian dishes. Although locals recommend fried tofu and tempe, the *rawon* (a fragrant beef soup with a complex broth) is an experience worth having. An offshoot, Mr Bakery, is next door (baked goods 8000Rp to 15,000Rp). Don't miss *sirsak* (soursop) juice.

Leslie Cafe INDONESIAN $
([☑] 0821 4698 5678; Jl Lalamentik; mains 25,000-60,000Rp; [☺] 8am-9pm Mon-Sat) This small restaurant with a wooden bar, tables and some rattan lounge chairs is plastered in framed

NUSA TENGGARA WAINGAPU

SUMBA'S BEST WEBSITE
A true labour of love by German Matthias Jungk, www.sumba-information.com is a vast compendium for all things Sumba. You can buy a pdf version of the website for €5. Jungk has also created a superbly detailed *and* accurate map of Sumba, which you can use online or buy. Best of all, this invaluable resource is continually updated.

quotes that will make you laugh and cringe. A pizza and burger make a cameo on the small Indonesian menu and there's a laundry service available for 8000Rp per kg.

Shopping

There are a few 'art shops' selling Sumbanese ikat and artefacts. Vendors also squat patiently all day outside hotels. Prices are fair and there's more choice here than in the countryside. East Sumbanese is renowned across East Nusa Tengarra for having some of the most detailed ikat motifs – buy here before venturing west, where it can look more basic and modern.

Praikundu Ikat Centre TEXTILES

(☑ 0812 3758 4629; kornelis.ndapakamang@gmail.com; Jl S Parman, Kelurahan Lambanapu; ⊙ hrs vary) This small weaving centre is 2.5km off the main road, sticking to the left fork. Run by Kornelis Ndapakamang, it's hung with some of Sumba's most prized ikat, all naturally dyed with detailed motifs. Kornelis will happily chat in Bahasa Indonesia, explaining how his members are keeping Sumbanese traditions alive. Lengthier ikat workshops available upon request.

There are also three rooms available in the on-site homestay; two doubles and another with two single beds off a sweet communal living and dining space. The cost is 200,000Rp per night, per person. Rooms share a clean squat toilet and *mandi*. Kornelis' wife cooks traditional meals for 60,000Rp a pop.

Ama Tukang TEXTILES

(☑ 0812 3622 5231; Jl Hawan Waruk 53; ⊙ 24hr) A series of rooms and houses championing ikat and jewellery, where guests can see everything from motif design to colouring and weaving. The collection features *marapu*, animals and village scenes – all hung on display beside dried corn in the rafters. There's also decent accommodation from 250,000Rp per night.

There are currently four rooms with aircon available and another eight on the way, which will have hot water. Motorbike rental is available for 150,000Rp per day, as are cars from 600,000Rp to 800,000Rp. To get here, head south of the bridge on the southern side of Waingapu and turn right onto the street.

ℹ Information

There are several ATMs around town.

ℹ Getting There & Away

AIR

The airport is 6km south on the Melolo road. A taxi into town costs a standard 60,000Rp, but most hotels offer a free pick-up and drop-off service. It's 5000Rp for a bemo ride to any destination around town, and 10,000Rp to the western bus terminal, although there are fewer bemos than there used to be. An *ojek* around town is between 5000Rp to 10,000Rp.

TX Waingapu (☑ 0821 4509 5477, 0812 1718 1930, 0387-61534; www.txtravel.com; Jl Beringin 12; ⊙ 8.15am-5pm Sun-Fri, to 4pm Sat) is a travel agency that books airline tickets.

BOAT

Pelni ships leave from the newer Darmaga dock to the west of town but their **ticket office** (☑ 0387-61665; www.pelni.co.id; Jl Hasanuddin 1; ⊙ 7am-noon, 1.30-5pm) is at the old port. Schedules are subject to change: check with

TRANSPORT FROM WAINGAPU

Air

DESTINATION	AIRLINE	DURATION (HR)	FREQUENCY
Denpasar	Nam Air, Wings Air	1½	1-2 daily
Kupang	Nam Air, Wings Air, TransNusa	1	2-3 daily

Boat

DESTINATION	COMPANY	FARE (RP)	DURATION (HR)	FREQUENCY
Aimere (Flores)	ASDP	81,000	10	two weekly
Ende (Flores)	ASDP	83,000	13	weekly
Kupang (West Timor)	ASDP	176,000	28	three weekly
Sabu	ASDP	97,000	12	weekly

ASDP (☎ 0214-288 2233; www.indonesiaferry. co.id; Pelabuhan Waingapu) or see the timetables at the port.

BUS & BEMO

Bemos from Waingapu's Terminal Kota run to Londolima and Prailiu.

Three daily buses head northwest to Puru Kambera (15,000Rp to 20,000Rp, one hour). There are also several daily buses to Waikabubak (50,000Rp, five hours).

The terminal for eastbound buses is in the southern part of town, close to the market. The West Sumba terminal, aka Terminal Kota, is about 5km west of town.

ℹ Getting Around

Sumba has some of the highest car-rental rates in Nusa Tenggara. Even after bargaining, 800,000Rp is a good price per day, including driver and petrol. Expect to pay more if you want your driver to double as a guide – 1,200,000Rp is a good price. As is the case across Indonesia, bargaining is acceptable and multiday tours are great leverage. Virtually any hotel can arrange motorcycle rental but Praikamarru Guest House (p407) has the best rate at 75,000Rp per day; expect to pay around 100,000Rp elsewhere.

East Sumba

Southeast of Waingapu in dry, undulating savannah interspersed with cashew orchards are several traditional villages, some with striking ancestral tombs. This area produces some of Sumba's best ikat. Most villages are quite used to tourists, but it's hit and miss as to whether there are people around when you visit. Either way, it's appropriate to donate at least 20,000Rp. Be prepared for plenty of attention from handicraft vendors.

Praiyawang & Rende

Nestled in a shallow valley between grassy hills, **Praiyawang** is a traditional compound of Sumbanese houses and the ceremonial focus of the more modern village of **Rende**, located 7km south of Melolo. It has an imposing line-up of nine stone-slab tombs, the largest is that of a chief of this former kingdom. Shaped like a buffalo, it consists of four stone pillars 2m high, supporting a monstrous slab about 5m long, 2.5m wide and 1m thick. Two stone tablets stand atop the main slab, carved with figures. A massive Sumbanese house with concrete pillars

WERA BEACH RESORT

About 39km east of the airport, this French-run **resort** (☎ 0812 3758 1671; www.sumbaeastresort.com; Jl Melolo, Pantai Wera; bungalow/house from 750,000/1,500,000Rp) and a slice of heaven is a peaceful oasis with two houses. Interiors are pristine white, decked out in rattan furniture and have kitchens; they're available as one-or two-bedroom stays and the two bedder can sleep five. There's also a neat, bamboo bungalow on the beach. The open-air restaurant (mains 45,000Rp to 220,000Rp) serves French food while wind chimes tinkle in the breeze.

faces the tombs, along with a number of *rumah adat* (traditional houses).

Within the tombs, it's permitted to bury siblings together, and grandchildren and grandparents, but the deceased can't be buried alongside their parents. Crocodile statues represent the king, turtles are only seen on women's tombs and cockatoos and horses are symbols of democracy and ruling.

Air Terjun Waimarang is a waterfall south of Melolo and inland from Praiyawang, and so best visited at the same time as the village. You can hit up Praiyawang on the way back to Waingapu. It's a smooth road to get to this stunning Sumbanese waterfall, followed by around 8km of bumps before arriving at the car park. Pay a nominal fee for leaving your vehicle, before walking for around 20 minutes on challenging terrain to reach a startlingly blue pool in the middle of the jungle, surrounded by limestone walls. Bring your camera, avoid weekends and come early.

ℹ Getting There & Away

Several buses go from Waingapu to Rende (20,000Rp), starting around 7am. The last bus back to Waingapu leaves at 3pm.

Kalala

Kalala, 125km from Waingapu and 2km down a dirt road from the nearby village of **Baing**, is a special part of Sumba, seemingly only discovered by surfers. It's an absolutely stunning stretch of white-sand beach that arcs toward the coastal mountains, which tumble down to form East Sumba's southernmost point. Waves break 500m offshore.

Sumba Adventure Resort (☑ WhatsApp 0812 3999 2865, WhatsApp 0811 386 2905; www. sumbaadventureresort.com; Jl Biang, Wula Meca Suar, Wula Biang; camping/cabin per person from 150,000/400,000Rp; 🛜) is a secluded place 2km east of Kalala Beach on a wide strip of sand where pigs frolic and harvested seaweed dries in the sun. There are two, basic A-frame bamboo huts, an open-walled bungalow and spacious family option with mosquito nets and an outdoor shower. Fabulous food is 150,000Rp per day per person. Don't miss out on quad biking.

The team can organise surf, snorkel, fishing, cruising and hiking trips, but if you pay 850,000Rp per person they'll throw in all meals, surf and snorkel gear during your stay. There's a discount of 20% for the second person onwards. Transport from Waingapu airport is between 600,000Rp to 900,000Rp.

ⓘ Getting There & Away

Several buses go to Baing each day from Waingapu, taking four hours and costing 40,000Rp. The road is sealed all the way but is bumpy past Melolo. A dirt track with many branches runs from Baing to Kalala. Buses will sometimes drop you off at the beach, if you ask.

South Central Sumba

It's worth toughing out access issues to get to this part of the island, especially if you're a keen surfer. Although there are daily buses from Waingapu to Tarimbang and trucks to Praingkareha, getting around may require a 4WD, motorcycle and even some hiking.

If you're looking for deserted waves, check out **Pantai Tarimbang**, a life-altering crescent of white sand framed by a massive limestone bluff 95km southwest of Waingapu. The beach thumps with terrific surf, there's snorkelling nearby and beach-shack accommodation is available at **Marthen's Homestay** (☑ 0852 8116 5137; Jl Gereja Tarimbang; dm/s/d incl all meals 300,000/400,000/700,000Rp). The *kepala desa* had just started building a traditional village accommodation concept when we last visited, set to offer three, seven-room houses and a bungalow.

West Sumba
☑ 0387

If you're hungry for traditional Sumbanese culture, head west into the rice fields that crawl up blue mountains, carved by rivers and sprouting with bamboo and coconut palms. *Kampung* of high-roofed houses are still clustered on their hilltops, surrounding the imposing stone tombs of their ancestors. Rituals and ceremonies involve animal sacrifices and can take place at any time. Outsiders are welcome, but make a donation – your guide will know how much (usually 20,000Rp to 50,000Rp). Even though *kampung* seem accustomed to visiting foreigners, gifts of betel nut help warm the waters and are a sign of respect.

West Sumba is most easily traversed and experienced with a guide, especially if you don't speak Bahasa Indonesia. In the west, locals get around with giant knives called *parang* strapped to their waist, but it's mostly for show. Still, it is ill-advised to travel after dark in West Sumba.

Waikabubak
☑ 0387 / POP 29,000

A country market town, home to thatched clan houses and rows of concrete shops, administrative buildings and tin-roof homes sprouting satellite dishes, Waikabubak makes Waingapu feel like a metropolis. It's a welcoming place, surrounded by thick stands of mahogany and lush rice fields. At about 600m above sea level, it's cooler than the east and a good base for exploring the traditional villages of West Sumba.

The food market is on daily from 7am until 10pm. On your way here from Waingapu, about 15km out of town, look out for **Bukit Raksasa Tidur** (Sleeping Giant Hill) – no prizes for guessing what the landscape looks like, but it's a great photo opportunity.

◉ Sights & Tours

Within the town are some friendly and quite traditional *kampung* (villages) with stone-slab tombs and thatched houses. You can tell the wealthier families by the detail and intricacy – or otherwise – of the tombs. You don't need a guide here if you're just looking around. Locals are happy to show off their spacious homes lashed with old ironwood columns and beams. Some children mug for the camera, others giggle and disappear around corners. Old folks will offer betel

Waikabubak

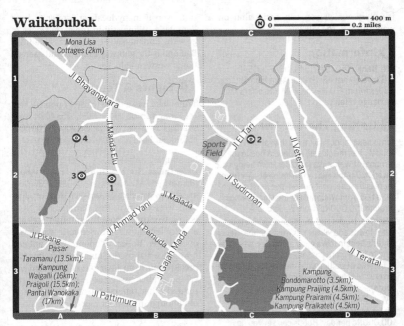

nut. Bring your own to share and offer a donation (minimum 20,000Rp to 50,000Rp).

Kampung Tambelar (off Jl Sudirman), just off Jl Sudirman, has very impressive *kubur batu* (stone graves), but the most interesting *kampung* are on the western edge of town. It's only a short stroll from most hotels to **Kampung Prai Klembung** (off Jl Manda Elu) and then up the hill that juts from the centre of town to **Kampung Tarung** (off Jl Manda Elu) and **Kampung Waitabar** (Jl Manda Elu).

Other interesting *kampung* occupying ridge or hilltop positions outside town include **Praijing**, with traditional huts set around some cool, primitive stone tombs and surrounded by coconut palm and bamboo groves. **Bondomarotto**, **Kampung Prairami** and **Kampung Praikateti** are also beautifully located on adjacent hilltops. You can take a bemo to the turn-off for Praijing (5000Rp).

🛏 Sleeping & Eating

Mona Lisa Cottages   GUESTHOUSE **$$**
(📞 0387-21364, 0813 3943 0825; Jl Adhyaska 30; s from 200,000Rp, d 300,000-750,000Rp; 🕸 🛜) The best night's sleep is 2km northwest of town opposite rice fields. It includes fan-cooled budget rooms, higher-end units and renovated cottages with peaked tin roofs, private patios and bamboo furnishings. Some have air-con.

Waikabubak

D'Sumba Ate   INTERNATIONAL **$$**
(📞 0812 3868 3588; Jl Ahmad Yani 148A; mains 30,000-80,000Rp; 🕙 10am-11pm; 🛜) This cool, bamboo restaurant serves up wood-fired pizzas, pasta and burgers alongside the usual Indo suspects.

If you know what's good for you, you'll eat *ayam betutu kampung dan urap*, a Balinese-spiced village chicken with plenty of condiments and coconut greens. Take the wooden bridge over the pond to **Kakitangan Spa**, a simple operation by the same folk with massages from 50,000Rp per hour.

🛍 Shopping

Traders gather at hotels with ikat from East Sumba, jewellery and various carvings. Kampung Tarung is known for beaded jewellery, which you can easily find on a walk through the village.

❶ Information

BNI Bank (☎ 0387-21549, 0387-321540; Jl Bhayangkara 48; ☉ 8am-4pm Mon-Thu, 7.30am-4pm Fri) Has an ATM and offers fair exchange rates.

❶ Getting There & Away

Tambolaka, about 45km northwest of Waikabubak, has the closest airport. A bus to the terminal at Waitabula (an older town being swallowed by Tambolaka) and a bemo or *ojek* from there is the cheapest option, but most people get a taxi from Waitabula or charter a bemo (around 150,000Rp) from Waikabubak.

Bemos, trucks and minibuses service most other towns and villages in West Sumba. Generally, it's best to leave early in the day, when they tend to have more passengers and depart quickly, instead of waiting until they're full. There are several daily buses to Waingapu (60,000Rp, five hours).

Waikabubak is the place to rent a motorcycle for exploring West Sumba. Expect to pay 100,000Rp per day. Hotels can set you up with motorbike or car rental. The latter costs 500,000Rp with a driver if you're sticking to town, otherwise it's from 800,000Rp to 1,000,000Rp.

Tambolaka

☎ 0387

Located 45km northwest of Waikabubak, this once-sleepy market town has become West Sumba's main transport hub – it's booming and the name of the airport, Tambolaka, has been transferred to the rest of town, including in tourism brochures and other government literature. We've followed suit, even if many locals still refer to it as Waitabula. While still in the early stages of growth, Tambolaka is easily accessible from Bali and is the gateway to the island's sensational western half.

◉ Sights & Tours

Tambolaka has a daily market opposite **Hotel Sinar Tambolaka** (☎ 0387-253 4088; www.sinartambolaka.com; Jl Tambolaka; r 200,000-450,000Rp, 1-bed villa 750,000Rp; ❇ 🛜 ❄).

Lembaga Studi & Pelestarian Budaya Sumba   MUSEUM
(Rumah Budaya Culture House; ☎ 0813 3936 2164; museum by donation; ☉ 8am-4pm Mon-Sat) Just 3km west of town, this Catholic-run NGO is in a working coconut plantation and has an excellent cultural museum. It was developed by Fr Robert Ramone, who noticed how, once baptised, Sumbanese frequently break clean from their old culture and develop negative associations with the *marapu* and other totems. There are displays of old photographs, money, pottery, ikat, stone carvings and more.

The complex also has 10 basic rooms for rent (300,000Rp to 600,000Rp). Sit on one of the private porches and let the quiet envelop you. It also has an ikat museum on-site.

Sumba Adventure Tours & Travel   TOURS
(☎ 0813 3710 7845; www.sumbaadventuretours.com; Jl Timotius Tako Geli 2; guide per day 300,000Rp, car & driver per day 800,000-1,000,000Rp; ☉ 8am-5pm) With an office close to the airport, experienced guide Philip Renggi and his team of guides lead trips into seldom-explored villages, including his na-

---

VISITING VILLAGES

Many Sumbanese villagers are now accustomed to tourists. If you're interested in their weavings or other artefacts, the villagers put you down as a potential trader. If all you want to do is chat and look around, use basic manners and ask first, or risk them being confused or offended. Often the tables turn, and you might feel under the microscope.

On Sumba, offering *pinang* (betel nut) is the traditional way of greeting guests or hosts. You can buy it at most markets in Sumba, and it's a respectful ice breaker. Offer it to the *kepala desa* (village head) or to whoever gives you their time.

Many villages keep a visitors book, which villagers will produce for you to sign, and you should donate between 2000Rp and 5000Rp per person, placed in the book when signing and handed back. Hiring a guide to isolated villages is a big help and offers some protection from falling into the wrong situation. Take the time to chat with the villagers to be seen as a guest, rather than a customer or visiting alien.

tive Manuakalada and Waiwarungu, where there are several sacred *marapu* houses that only shaman can enter. He can arrange itineraries, set you up for Pasola (p26), rent cars and more. Look for his office near Rumah Makan Richard.

🛏 Sleeping & Eating

New hotels are shooting up in Tambolaka, a contrast against more timeworn guesthouses. There are some pleasant, quiet – and in some cases more expensive – options 20 minutes outside of town.

Penginapan Melati GUESTHOUSE $
(☎0813 5396 6066; Jl Sapurata; r with fan/aircon 175,000/250,000Rp; ❄🛜) With 14 simple rooms that are much cleaner than the gloomy fish tank in reception, you can expect plenty of images of the host family, Virgin Mother and Il Papa to brighten things up. There are rain shower heads in the bathrooms and a Padang-style restaurant next door. Look for the green and orange stripes in lieu of signage.

★Oro Beach Houses & Restaurant BUNGALOW $$
(☎0813 3911 0068, WhatsApp 0813 3978 0610; www.oro-beachbungalows.com; Weepangali; villa/bungalow 735,000/850,000Rp) ⌖ On four wild beachfront hectares, you can nest in a circular thatched bungalow with canopied driftwood beds and outdoor bathrooms. Oro offers excellent meals, mountain bikes and snorkelling (each 50,000Rp) just off its stunning 200m-long beach.

★Maringi Eco Resort by Sumba Hospitality Foundation RESORT $$$
(☎0822 366 15505; www.sumbahospitality foundation.org; Jl Mananga Aba, Desa Karuni; pavilions/deluxe r 1,000,000/1,500,000Rp; ❄🛜🏊) ⌖ Where to start with this incredible complex: that it's a not-for-profit NGO where students from Sumba learn the art of hospitality before landing top hotel jobs in Indonesia? Or the brilliantly designed bamboo pavilions with giant glass oval doors and outdoor bathrooms? Maybe its sustainability, reusing water in the garden and harnessing solar. This is so much more than accommodation.

Mario Hotel & Cafe HOTEL $$$
(☎0813 3939 0337, 0823 1220 1571, 0812 3971 0000; www.mariohotel.net; Pantai Kita, Mananga Aba; r 850,000-950,000Rp; ❄@🏊) Drastic upgrades to the property accompanied the

WEEKURI LAGOON

Almost as far west as you can get on Sumba is one of the island's most magical spots, **Weekuri Lagoon** (Weekuri Lake). On one side, locals and tourists rent black rubber rings for 10,000Rp and float in the cool, crystal water; on the other, the Indian Ocean rages against rocks and bursts through cracks and blowholes, best viewed from the bisecting bridge. Allow at least half a day to enjoy it, a bargain at 20,000Rp per person. It's about 45km from Tambolaka.

There are more than half a dozen small, dirt roads leading off Jl Waitabula-Bondokodi that eventually get you to the aquamarine waters of this jaw-droppingly beautiful wonder. There are vendors selling cup noodles, coconuts and other snacks, but avoid purchasing bracelets illegally made from turtle shells.

arrival of electricity here in 2017. Twelve rooms face the beach, while two cheaper rooms in traditional houses with outdoor bathrooms have more space and character. The restaurant (mains from 40,000Rp, open 7am to 9pm) overlooks a pool with inbuilt lounges, surrounded by bougainvillea and frangipani.

Warungku INDONESIAN $
(☎0812 5250 5000; Jl Ranggaroko; mains 20,000-40,000Rp; ⊙8am-11pm) Set back from the main road in a walled compound, this open-air restaurant, complete with water feature and karaoke, has excellent versions of Indo classics. It's a pretty garden setting, and you can while away a few hours grazing and sipping *jus semangka* (watermelon juice).

Warung Gula Garam INTERNATIONAL $$
(☎0812 3672 4266; www.facebook.com/Warung GG; Jl Soeharto; mains 25,000-110,000Rp; ⊙10am-4pm; 🛜) Run by expat Frenchman Louis, this thatched open-air cafe near the airport plays funky-fresh R&B tunes and serves surprisingly good wood-fired pizza, plus other Western and Indo comfort fare.

Dishes include chicken cordon bleu and sausages with mash and veg. There's also locally approved beef rendang, and more than passable coffee and juices.

WEST SUMBA BEACHES

The beaches on West Sumba's south coast remain largely undiscovered, except by surfers in search of the perfect break and those with deep pockets staying in **Nihi Sumba** (☏0361-757149; www.nihi.com; bungalows & villas from US$845; ✲ 🗊 ≋). The world-class surf spot known as **Occy's Left**, featured in the film *The Green Iguana*, is on **Pantai Nihiwatu**, an achingly stunning stretch of sand buffered by a limestone headland.

From Pantai Nihiwatu, the magic starts at **Pantai Wanokaka**'s craggy palm-dotted cliffs, a bay bobbing with fishing boats and a beachfront Pasola site. Here most of the action gathers around the concrete public fishers house, where you can see the catch in the morning and watch fisherfolk mend nets come late afternoon. **Rua**, the next in a series of luscious south Sumba beaches, is 10km southwest of the Padede Weri junction, or continue along the road from Waeiwuang Village until you hit the coast. Expect more lovely pale golden sand, turquoise water and great waves when the swell hits between June and September.

Heading west again, the road passes through the village of Lamboya, with rice fields scalloped into the inland side of the rugged coastal mountains and a Pasola field set on rolling grassland that attracts thousands of people in February. From here there's yet another turn-off south to surf hot spot **Pantai Kerewe** and the glassy seas of **Pantai Tarakaha**. Here you'll find **Magic Mountain** if you know where to look – a coral-draped, underwater volcano that is Sumba's best dive site. Next is **Pantai Watubela** (Patiala Bawa, Waikabubak), another nearby beach with perfect sand and limestone caves. Further along the coast are the idyllic white sands of **Pantai Marosi**, about 35km from Waikabubak.

ℹ️ Information

BNI Bank (Jl Jenderal Sudirman; ⊙8am-4pm Mon-Thu, 7.30am-4pm Fri) Has an ATM and exchanges money.

ℹ️ Getting There & Away

AIR

Tambolaka Airport is shiny and modern. There are daily flights to Bali and Kupang in West Timor with Garuda, Nam Air and Wings Air. Note that on some airline and booking websites the destination is listed as 'Waikabubak'.

BOAT

Waikelo, a small and predominantly Muslim town north of Tambolaka, has a little, picturesque harbour that's the main port for West Sumba and offers a ferry service to Sape in Sumbawa (52,000Rp, three weekly). It takes nine hours, depending on the weather.

BUS

Buses leave throughout the day for Waikabubak, which takes an hour and costs between 15,000Rp to 20,000Rp, departing from the centre of town.

Wanokaka

☏ 0361 / POP 14,163

The Wanokaka district south of Waikabubak has stunning mountain scenery, coastline and several traditional *kampung*. It's a gorgeous drive from Waikabubak taking a sealed, narrow road that splits at Padede Weri junction, 6km from town. This is where white-headed eagles soar over mountains that tumble to the azure sea. Turn left at the junction and the road passes through the riverside settlement of **Taramanu**, 5km further on.

Downhill from Taramanu is **Kampung Waigalli** on a promontory above the sea, and beyond that a nearly 200-year-old Watu Kajiwa tomb in the deeply traditional village of **Praigoli**. About 5km onwards is **Waeiwuang**, featuring a stone tomb with a 2.5m-tall fleur-de-lis.

Take the right fork before Sumba Nautil and you'll reach **Litikaha**, where a gravel road leads to the panoramic villages of **Tokahale**, **Kahale** and **Malisu**. It's a 15-minute 4WD drive, or park on the road and walk to all three in about two hours.

ℹ️ Getting There & Away

A few buses run between Waikabubak and the many Wanokaka villages, but by far the best way to visit the area is by car or motorbike. Most roads are sealed and traffic is minimal. The hills south of Waikabubak are a taxing yet exhilarating ride for cyclists, but travelling by any vehicle in West Sumba at night is not recommended.

Pero

Pero is a small Muslim fishing village with a natural harbour inlet sheltered by a sandbar and mangroves. It tends to waft with racks of squid drying in the sun outside fisherman shacks, but the beach just north of town has blonde sand, a palm-and-scrubby-grass backdrop and a sneaky left-hand break just offshore, as well as ideal side shore wind for kitesurfers. From here to the west, you won't hit land again until Africa. To visit traditional *kampung*, go north or south along the coastline.

The long-running **Homestay Stori** (☑ 0813 3943 3906; per person incl all meals 150,000Rp) is owned by a hospitable family and has four rooms available in a frayed concrete home with peeling linoleum floors and shared slimy mandis out the back. But, hey, it's cheap. Around the corner (and run by the same family) is a nicer option: **Merzy Home Stay** (☑ 0813 3780 3613, 0813 3755 7272; hatijahstory@gmail.com; Kodi Pero; per person incl all meals 250,000Rp). There are eight rooms in a cacophony of patterns, but only one with a private toilet and mandi, the rest share three. From Tambolaka there are frequent bemos and trucks to Pero.

Ratenggaro

One of Sumba's best villages and most famous spots is close to Pero. Kampung Ratenggaro is known for its prime real estate position on a grassy bluff above a river with breathtaking views of the sea. Across the river you'll spot **Wainyapu** and on the way to Ratenggaro, the roadside tombs of **Kampung Ranggabaki** and **Kampung Paronambaroro** through the trees.

The remarkable village hasn't had much luck: in 1964 a fire burnt 57 traditional houses to the ground, while another in 2004 flattened 13 more. Government assistance helped to rebuild the 12 houses (and make them a tourist hot spot). They're supported by intricately carved columns, one for each cardinal point. Bapa Lucas is the man in charge, and he's all too happy to share his knowledge, translator permitting.

❶ Getting There & Away

Take the paved road from Bondokodi, or go off-road for about 3km along Pantai Radakapal – a sliver of white sand along a pasture – and you'll come to the *kampung* of Ratenggaro, framed by a low rock wall.

HARIZ ADIT/SHUTTERSTOCK ©

1. Borobudur Temple (p118)
The largest Buddhist temple in the world, the complex features 432 seated Buddha statues.

2. Diving, Pulau Weh (p547)
Some of the best diving and snorkelling spots in the Indian Ocean can be found off Pulau Weh.

3. Tengger crater, Gunung Bromo (p192)
The slopes of the volcano can be reached on a 40-minute hike from Cemoro Lawang.

4. Karimunjawa Islands (p165)
Only five of the 27 islands that make up the magical Karimunjawa Islands are inhabited.

AT A GLANCE

POPULATION
1.7 million

MOST HISTORIC FORTS
Benteng Belgica (p450), Benteng Duurstede (p444), Benteng Tahula (p430), Benteng Tolukko (p424)

BEST BIRD WATCHING
Manusela National Park (p446)

BEST FOR REGIONAL CUISINE
Kedai Mita (p427)

BEST HOTEL
Molana Island Resort (p445)

WHEN TO GO
Nov–Mar
Spectacular diving; the best time to visit.

Apr–May & Sep–Oct
Shoulder seasons; a good time for the Banda and Kei Islands.

Jun–Aug
Monsoons hit Ambon and nearby islands, but northern Maluku is normally dry.

Pantai Ngurtavur (p460)

Maluku

The idyllic islands of Maluku once played an unlikely but hugely important role in global geopolitics and economics. Between the 16th and 18th centuries, Maluku was the world's only source of nutmeg, cloves and mace, then vital and very valuable commodities. The search and subsequent fight for control of the Spice Islands helped kick-start European colonialism and, thanks to a series of wrong turns and one auspicious land swap, shaped the modern world.

Once the islands' spice monopoly was broken, Maluku returned to gentle obscurity. Today the region is a little-visited tropical paradise that seems almost too good to be true. Inter-island transport can prove infuriatingly inconvenient, but with flexibility and patience you can explore pristine reefs, stroll empty stretches of powdery white sand and climb perfectly formed volcanoes, while Maluku's complex web of cultures welcomes visitors with an effusive, gentle charm.

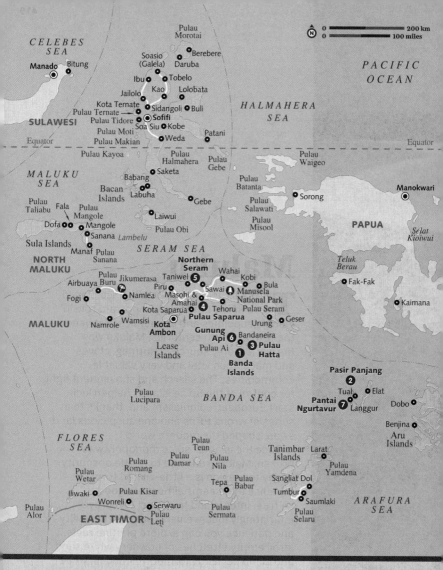

Maluku Highlights

1 Banda Islands (p447)
Snorkelling and diving some of the world's finest accessible coral gardens.

2 Pasir Panjang (p461)
Unwinding on this superb sweep of white sand in the Kei Islands.

3 Pulau Hatta (p455)
Lazing at a beachside homestay with beautiful coral on your doorstep.

4 Pulau Saparua (p444)
Using this laid-back island as a base to explore stunning offshore reefs and beaches.

5 Northern Seram (p447)
Getting away from it all at the gorgeous and isolated bay of Teluk Sawai.

6 Gunung Api (p454)
Climbing this pocket-sized Mt Fuji for peerless views over the Banda Islands.

7 Pantai Ngurtavur (p460)
Posing for selfies on this sublime sandbar, supposedly the longest in Indonesia.

ℹ️ Getting There & Away

AIR

Ambon, Ternate and, to a lesser extent, Langgur on the Kei Islands are the region's air hubs. All have daily flights to Jakarta, although only Ambon and Ternate have direct connections. Most flights go via Makassar and Manado in Sulawesi or Surabaya in Java. There are daily direct flights from Ambon to destinations in Papua.

SEA

From northern Maluku, Pelni liners depart Ternate four times a month for Ambon (18 hours), Makassar (58 hours) and Surabaya (92 hours). Once a month, one of those liners travels on from Ambon to various ports in Papua. Pelni ships bound for Papua also depart from northern Halmahera a couple of times a month.

From Ambon, Pelni liners run to Makassar (45 hours) and Surabaya (77 hours) four times a month. Pelni ships also travel from Ambon to the Banda (9 hours) and Kei Islands (21 hours) four times a month and on to Papua (40 hours) twice a month.

ℹ️ Getting Around

AIR

Garuda Indonesia (www.garuda-indonesia.com), Batik Air (www.batikair.com), Wings Air (www.lionair.co.id), Lion Air (www.lionair.co.id), Sriwijaya Air (www.sriwijayaair.co.id) and NAM Air (www.sriwijayaair.co.id) criss-cross the skies of Maluku. There are frequent daily flights between Ambon, Ternate and Langgur in the Kei Islands. At the time of research, there was no air link between Ambon and Bandaneira.

BOAT

The Pelni schedules change frequently but you can usually count on the routes that connect Ternate to Ambon and Ambon with the Banda Islands then onwards to the Kei Islands. Some medium-range hops are served by uncomfortable ASDP ferries or by wooden boats known as *kapal motor*. Perintis cargo boats are bigger but are not designed with passengers in mind (bring waterproof clothes). Speedboats link nearby islands and roadless villages.

Locals use very specific terms for boat types: if there isn't a *spid* (a covered multi-engine speedboat) to your destination, there might still be a *Johnson* (an outboard-powered longboat) or a *ketingting/lape-lape* (a smaller, short-hop motorised outrigger canoe).

Regular speedboats connect short and midrange destinations (eg Ternate–Tidore, Ternate–Halmahera, Ambon–Lease Islands, Ambon–Seram). There are fewer boats in the monsoon season, June-August, and they usually travel in the mornings when seas are calmest. If the weather is especially bad, boats won't run. Chartering is widely available.

The twice-weekly *Express Bahari 2B* from Ambon to Bandaneira is usually suspended during the rainy season of June to August, and doesn't always run at other times of the year either.

ROAD TRANSPORT

In mountainous Maluku, the asphalted roads on the big islands can be surprisingly good, but some areas have only dirt tracks or no roads at all. Shorter routes are generally operated by *bemo* (minibus), better known across Maluku as *mobil or auto*. On Halmahera and Seram, shared Kijangs (fancy seven-seat Toyotas) predominate. Taxis are available on the largest islands but are expensive. Renting an *ojek* (motorcycle taxi) is much cheaper and often the fastest way around the islands.

NORTH MALUKU

North Maluku's historically and politically most significant islands are the pyramid-like volcanic cones of Ternate and Tidore. Once the world's only source of cloves, the spice trade made these ancient Islamic island sultanates the most powerful territories in medieval Maluku.

Today, Tidore slumbers in obscurity but Ternate is still the main hub of North Maluku (Maluku Utara, or 'Malut'), although Sofifi on neighbouring Halmahera was named the province's official capital in 2007 and many government offices have relocated there. Few islands in North Maluku have any real history of tourism, so visits beyond Ternate will often prove to be something of an adventure. Vast Halmahera in particular offers white-sand beaches, tasty diving and a little-known national park, but much of its potential remains untapped.

History

Ternate and Tidore's wealth was founded on the islands being the only known source of cloves, which were enormously valued in medieval Europe as food preservatives and 'cures' for everything from toothache to halitosis and sexual dysfunction. Funded by the spice trade, the sultans of Ternate and Tidore became powerful, yet wasted much of their wealth fighting each other.

In 1511 the first Portuguese settlers arrived in Ternate. Tidore quickly responded by inviting in the Spaniards. Both islands

THE MALUKAN PALATE

Despite what you'll see in most restaurants, Maluku's traditional staple isn't rice but *kasbi* (boiled cassava) or *papeda* (sago congee, called *popeda* in Ternate), a thick, colourless, sodium-packed goo that you ladle into plates of *kuah ikan* (fish soup), then suck down as though trying to swallow a live jellyfish. Odd, but surprisingly good when accompanied with *sayur garu* (papaya flower), *kohu-kohu* (smoked fish with green beans and fresh coconut), *papari* (a unique mixed vegetable), *keladi*-root, and cassava leaf. For protein, fish and seafood are king, typically served with a chilli, shallot and citrus dip called *colo colo* or *dabu dabu*.

Originally unique to the Banda Islands, the spice-yielding kernel of nutmeg (*pala*) grows within a fruit that itself makes deliciously tart jams and distinctive sweet 'wine', available at Ambon's Sibu-Sibu (p440). Nutmeg grows best in the shade of magnificent *kenari* trees, which themselves yield an almond-like nut (used locally in confectionery and sauces) and timber (for *kora kora* canoes). *Kenari*-nut chunks also float atop *rarobang*, a distinctive spiced coffee.

found their hospitality rapidly exhausted as the Europeans tried to corner the spice market and preach Christianity. When Ternate's Muslim population – already offended by the Europeans' imported pigs and heavy-handed 'justice' – rebelled in 1570, Ternate's Sultan Hairun (Khairun) was executed and his head exhibited on a pike. The besieged Portuguese held out in their citadel until 1575 when the new Ternatean sultan – the same Babullah whose name graces Ternate's airport – took it over as his palace.

The Spaniards, and later the Dutch, made themselves equally unpopular. In a history that's as fascinating as it is complicated, they played Ternate off against Tidore and also confronted one another for control of an elusive clove monopoly. The Dutch prevailed eventually, though the sultanates survived, remaining well-respected institutions to this day.

❶ Getting There & Away

Ternate is the principal gateway to North Maluku.

AIR

Ternate's airport has daily direct connections to Jakarta, Makassar, Manado, Ambon and Buli in eastern Halmahera. Batik Air, Garuda, Sriwijaya Air, Wings Air and Lion Air serve the routes.

BOAT

Two Pelni liners head to Ambon each month from Ternate, while two Pelni ships a month travel from Ternate to Papua.

Daily speedboats link Ternate, Halmahera, Tidore and the other islands.

❶ Getting Around

Roads are pretty good on Ternate and Tidore, as well as in northern Halmahera. Elsewhere, they can be rough and in poor condition.

Bemos, Kijangs, *ojeks* and *bentor* (motorcycle-rickshaws) link towns and villages on the islands.

Pulau Ternate

☑ 0921

The dramatic volcanic cone of Gunung Api Gamalama (1721m) dominates Pulau Ternate. Settlements are sprinkled around its lower coastal slopes with villages on the east coast coalescing into North Maluku's biggest town, Kota Ternate. The city makes a useful transport gateway for the region and has fishing harbours bobbing with colourful boats and a few remaining stilt-house neighbourhoods.

Ternate is not big: you can drive around it on an *ojek* in a few hours. It's a worthwhile trip that takes in a few reasonable beaches, friendly villages and one crocodile-infested crater lake.

❍ Sights

Jikomalamo   BEACH

A couple of kilometres past Sulamadaha, a lane runs right off the highway down to the secluded stilted village of Jikomalamo. There are some small sandy coves here for swimming and snorkelling, although be careful of the current, and a couple of simple restaurants. It's a pleasant spot to kick back for a few hours.

Pulau Ternate

Danau Tolire Besar   LAKE
Beyond the village of Takome, a paved lane off the road climbs to the rim of Danau Tolire Besar. Startlingly sheer cliffs plummet down to the lugubriously green, crocodile-infested waters of this deep crater lake. Locals offer guide services should you want to descend (1½ hours return on foot).

Sulamadaha   BEACH
(motorbike/car parking 5000/10,000Rp) A slender black-sand beach with heavy swells and sadly ruined coral, Sulamadaha is a popular local hangout at weekends. There are fine views across to the offshore volcanic cone of Pulau Hiri, the last step of the Sultan of Ternate and his family's *Sound of Music*-style escape from Ternate during WWII.

Public longboats cross to Pulau Hiri (10,000Rp per person) from a cove 800m east of the beach.

Danau Laguna   LAKE
Danau Laguna is a pleasant, spring-fed bowl lake with a lushly forested perimeter. When viewed from above (take the steep lane to the west of the lagoon), there are great views across the straits to the conical islands of Tidore and Maitara, as featured on Indonesia's 1000Rp notes.

🛏 Sleeping

Almost all accommodation on Pulau Ternate can be found in Kota Ternate. There's a good mix of boutique and midrange hotels as well as homestays.

🍴 Eating

Most restaurants are located in Kota Ternate, where you'll find a spread of solid *rumah makan* (eating houses), as well as a handful of more upmarket seafood restaurants.

❶ Getting There & Away

Ternate's airport has daily connections to Jakarta, Sulawesi, Halmahera and Ambon.

Four Pelni ships call at Ternate each month, travelling on to South Maluku and Papua. Four Pelni ships a month travel from Ternate back to Sulawesi and Java.

Daily speedboats connect Pulau Ternate to the neighbouring islands of Tidore and Halmahera.

❶ Getting Around

Bemos (5000Rp to 10,000Rp) connect Kota Ternate to outlying villages, but none go all the way around the island. Travelling by *ojek* is the best way to circumnavigate the island (120,000Rp per day).

Kota Ternate

📞 0921 / POP 185,705

Ternate is gorgeous, swathed in jungle and wild clove trees. However, when you first land here, in the looming shadow of Gamalama, with several more volcanic islands dotting the deep blue channel beyond, you may be shocked by Kota Ternate's frenetic pace. The commercial and transport hub of North Maluku, Kota Ternate is booming as new investment floods in. Unsurprisingly, the locals are pleased and, in 2017, the city was voted the happiest in all Indonesia. With 16th-century forts to explore, superb seafood to enjoy and easy access to the rest of the island and its attractions, visitors will be smiling too.

◉ Sights

Benteng Tolukko   FORT

(Map p425; admission 10,000Rp donation) A tiny, beautifully situated fort surrounded by a vivid tropical garden, Benteng Tolukko was the first Portuguese stronghold on Ternate (dating back to 1512). It's better preserved than the town's two other *benteng*, inviting a stroll on the cramped battlements for yet

another stunning view across to Tidore and Halmahera. If it's locked, knock on the door of the family home next door; they have the key.

Keraton   MUSEUM

(Istana Kesultan; Map p425; 📞0921-312 1166; admission by donation; ⊙9am-5pm Mon-Fri, to 3pm Sat, to 1pm Sun) Built in 1834 and restored in semi-colonial style, the Sultan's Palace is technically a family home, although no one is in residence owing to a dispute over the succession between the sons of the last sultan, who passed away in 2015. There's a small but interesting collection of historic weaponry and memorabilia from the reigns of past sultans, whose lineage dates back to 1257. The Keraton is sometimes closed during advertised hours. No shorts or skirts above the knee allowed.

Majolica Ulama Indonesia   MOSQUE

(Masjid Al Munawwah; Map p426; Jl Sultan Djabir Sjah) It's hardly the Hagia Sophia, and the seaward minarets have been reclaimed by the sea (only the crumbled footings remain), but this concrete-and-tile mosque dominates the central foreshore of Kota Ternate, and has been listed amongst the most impressive mosques in all Indonesia. Its architectural highlight is the centralised dome, covered in the repeating name of Allah highlighted in Arabic calligraphy.

Non-Muslims can visit outside prayer times.

Benteng Oranye   FORT

(Map p426) Known to the Portuguese as Fort Malayo, the Dutch-built Benteng Oranye, which dates from the early 17th century, is a sprawling, largely ruinous complex inhabited by goats, rusted cannons and a few army families. Once home to the Dutch governor, it's now overgrown, neglected and (in parts) unsympathetically concreted. You can still wander some sections of cannon-topped bastion, accessed through a restored gateway arch. Sadly, there's little evidence the fort is being looked after.

Benteng Kalamata   FORT

The 1540 Benteng Kalamata is dramatically situated on the waterfront 1km southwest of Bastiong, staring down Ternate's old foe, Tidore. You can wander the unusual angular geometry of its outer walls, but may have to slip the grumpy caretaker 5000Rp.

🛏 Sleeping

Breakfast is normally included in the room price.

★Kurnia Homestay
HOMESTAY **$**

(Map p425; ☑ 0821 8888 7379; kurnia.homestay@ outlook.com; Block G, No.8 Maliaro; r 150,000-250,000Rp; ✲) Run by charming Aty, the Kurnia is a pleasant homestay in a quiet neighbourhood 1km from the town centre. There's no air-con but plenty of fans, comfortable beds, private bathrooms with Western toilets and a living room. Aty speaks great English and can arrange guides or rent you a motorbike (100,000Rp). Call ahead and she'll pick you up.

Tiara Inn
GUESTHOUSE **$**

(Map p426; ☑ 0921-311 1017; Jl Salim Fabanyo 1; s/d/superior r 200,000/220,000/250,000Rp; ✲ 🛜) The Tiara is a little tarnished these days – rooms are functional and bathrooms can smell a little – but it's clean and the air-con works well enough. No English spoken.

Emerald Hotel
HOTEL **$$**

(Map p426; ☑ 0921-312 8188, 0921-312 8288; emeraldternate@yahoo.com; Jl Branjang 28; r 490,000-690,000Rp; 🅿✲🛜) On a quieter side street off Jl Pattimura, the Emerald is one of the best mid-rangers in town. Standard rooms are compact, but the others are big and all are comfortable with good beds. There's a decent wi-fi connection, friendly staff and some gleaming equestrian statuary in the lobby.

Muara Hotel
HOTEL **$$**

(Map p426; ☑ 0921-312 5553; www.muarahotels. com; Jl Merdeka 19; r 650,000-790,000Rp; ✲🛜) Located above the shopping mall of the same name, the Muara's rooms are big and bright and the best come with balconies offering great views over Benteng Oranye towards the sea. The downside is that the bathrooms need an upgrade and the fittings are functional. The attached restaurant is OK.

Austine Hotel
HOTEL **$$**

(Map p426; ☑ 0921-311 0815; www.austinehotel. com; Jl Christina Martha Tiahahu; r 470,000-570,000Rp; ✲🛜) One of Ternate's new crop of midrange hotels, the Austine has comfortable, well-kept rooms. There are fine views of Gamalama from the most expensive ones, but the cheapest lack windows. Efficient staff and some English spoken.

Kota Ternate Ⓝ 0 ▬▬▬ 400 m
0 ▬▬▬ 0.2 miles

MALUKU PULAU TERNATE

Central Kota Ternate

N

0 — 200 m
0 — 0.1 miles

A **B** **C** **D**

Jl Salak

Jl Sultan Khairun

Jl Pahlawan Revolusi

Fish Market

1

🏛 1

Jl Pipit

12 🔒

📷 7

Jl Nuri (Jl Alfred Wallace)

Jl Ketilang

CENTRE

2

Jl Bangau

Jl Merdeka

Sidangoli (Pulau Halmahera)

Jl Cendrawasih

Jl Nukila

Jl Maleo

Jl Branjang

2 🚤

Jl Kakatua

11 ✕

5

Langang Buana
Travel & Tour

Jl Nasution

3

10 ✕ $

Jl Pattimura

Jl Mononutu

Jl Senang

4 📷

8 📷

Kie Raha Stadium

Jl Stadion

Jl Hassan Senen

BNI $

Sorong

4

9 ✕

Jl Mononutu

Jl Salim Fabanyo

Jl Pahlawan Revolusi

Jl Sali Effendi

Jl Nuku

6 📷

5

Jl Seruni

Jl Ahmad Yani

3 📷

Jl Hajar Dewantara
('School Road')

Jl Hasan Esa

Jl Mawar

Jl Anggrek

Pelni ⚓

Sofifi (Pulau Halmahera)

6

Jl Z A Syah

Jl Kyai Kyaya Kusuma

Jl Kamboja

Teluk Dodinga

KOTA BARU

7

Bastiong;
Main Island Road

Central Kota Ternate

Archie Menara   HOTEL $$
(Map p426; ☎0921-312 2100; menara_archie
@gmail.com; Jl Nuku 101; r/ste 425,000-
460,000/650,000Rp; ❄🛜) The newest and
best of the three Archies; the most expensive
rooms come with sea views. All are spacious,
comfortable, clean and reasonably modern.

Hotel Archie   HOTEL $$
(Map p426; ☎0921-311 0555; Jl Nuku 6; r 175,000-
380,000Rp; ❄🛜) Old-fashioned rooms at
the original of the Archie empire, but for
the price they are good enough and well-
maintained, if not very exciting.

★ Villa Ma'rasai   INN $$$
(☎0813 5490 8708; www.vilamarasai.com; Jl
Kampus II; r 725,000-1,300,000Rp; ❄🛜🏊) This
sweet boutique sleep has 19 rooms, which
book up fast, spread across two buildings.
Rooms are immaculate – light and spa-
cious with hardwood floors, high ceilings,
balconies and tasteful furnishings – but
none have TVs. Located on Gamalama's
lower slopes among clove trees and coco-
nut palms – 7km from the town centre –
most rooms have stunning sea views across
to Tidore.

Pleasant owner Hasrun speaks good Eng-
lish and can organise tours, hikes and dive
trips. There's a small swimming pool and
you can also rent a motorbike (150,000Rp
per day) here.

**★ Grand Dafam
Bela Ternate**   HOTEL $$$
(Map p425; ☎0921-312 1800; info@granddafam
-belaternate.com; Jl Jati Raya 500; r 850,000-
1,200,000, ste 2,500,000-10,000,000Rp; ❄🛜🏊)
Formerly the Bela International Hotel, the
Grand Dafam offers a four-star hotel experience at three-star prices. Rooms come
with all the trimmings, including balconies,
service is solicitous and there's a big pool,
as well as a spa, a restaurant and a bar that
serves (expensive) beer. The hotel is south of
the town centre.

🍴 Eating

Several shacks north of the bemo terminal
and around the market serve local specialities such as *ikan gohu* (raw tuna 'cooked' in
citrus) and *popeda* (sago congee).

At night, the waterfront comes alive with
open-air cafes and restaurants.

★ Kedai Mita   INDONESIAN $
(Map p425; mains 20,000-80,000Rp; ⊙9am-
midnight) Relocated to the waterfront, this
simple, partly open-air, family-run restaurant is one of the best in town for Malukan staples (alongside classic Indo fare). At
lunchtimes, try the *popeda* (sago congee)
spread. The *ikan gohu* (raw tuna 'cooked'
in *calamansi* juice with chillies, basil and
steamed cassava) is great at any time.

★ Royal's Restaurant   INDONESIAN $
(Map p426; Jl Branjang; mains 27,000-80,000Rp;
⊙10am-midnight) Swish by Ternate standards, Royal's is a popular spot thanks to its
wide-ranging Chinese-Indonesian menu,
which has a big focus on fish and seafood
but also covers chicken, beef and duck dishes. There are a few veggie options too. This
is the only restaurant we know of in Ternate
that serves (expensive) beer. It's not on the
menu: ask. Fish is priced by weight.

**Rumah Makan
Popeda Gamalama**   INDONESIAN $
(Map p425; mains 35,000Rp; ⊙5am-5pm) Buried
at the far end of the market, this is a great
spot to try *popeda*. An array of fish, stewed
greens, mushrooms, pumpkin and sambals
accompanies the mucilaginous sago-flour
glue that is *popeda*. Leave your textural food
fears at the door: the locals will be thrilled to
have you. Most *ojek* drivers know the place.

Bakso Lapangan Tembak Senayan

INDONESIAN $

(Map p426; ☑ 0921-326 028; Jl Mononutu; mains 21,000-48,000Rp; ⏱ 10am-10pm) This fan-cooled, brick-and-timber eating house specialises in *bakso* (meatballs) various ways, including fried or bobbing in clear soup. The other Indonesian staples – noodles, fried rice, flour-dusted squid and the like – can all be depended on.

Floridas

SEAFOOD $$

(☑ 0921-312 4430; Jl Raya Ngade; mains 40,000-80,000Rp; ⏱ 9am-10pm) Floridas is a locally famous seafood restaurant, thanks in part to its seafront balcony with peerless views to Tidore and Maitara. But it's also a good place to tuck into *ikan woku balanga*: fish steak roasted with *kenari* nut, chilli, lemongrass and other aromatics. Fish is priced by the weight and is a little more expensive than elsewhere in town.

K62

CAFE $$

(Map p426; Jl Pattimura 62; mains 33,000-93,000Rp; ⏱ 10am-11pm Mon-Fri, to midnight Sat-Sun) Smart two-storey cafe and restaurant that serves clean and reliable Indonesian staples and a few pan-Asian and Western dishes, as well as decent coffee, tea and juices. There's gentle live music in the evenings. Prices are high by local standards, but you're paying for the air-conditioned comfort.

🛍 Shopping

Jatiland Mall

MALL

(Map p426; Jl Sultan M Djabir Shah; ⏱ 10am-10pm) Bustling waterfront Jatiland Mall is not going to give Jakarta or Surabaya any mall envy. But you can find cafes with wi-fi, fast-food outlets and a basic food court, a pharmacy, mobile phone and camera shops and lots of clothes outlets. The mall is also home to the only cinema in North Maluku.

ℹ Information

BNI (Map p426; Jl Pahlawan Revolusi; ⏱ 8am-3pm Mon-Fri, to 1pm Sat) The only bank to change money: US dollars only, with a minimum US$100 exchange.

Langang Buana Travel & Tour (Map p426; ☑ 0921-312 3999; Jl Pattimura 62; ⏱ 8am-

TRANSPORT FROM PULAU TERNATE

Air

DESTINATION	AIRLINE	FREQUENCY
Ambon	Garuda, Sriwijaya, NAM	daily
Jakarta	Batik Air, Garuda, Lion Air, Sriwijaya	daily
Makassar	Garuda, Lion Air, Sriwijaya	daily
Manado	Garuda, NAM, Wings Air	daily
Surabaya	Sriwijaya	daily

Boat

DESTINATION	PORT	TYPE	FARE (RP)	DURATION	FREQUENCY
Ambon via Namlea	Ahmad Yani	Pelni	varies	18hr	2 monthly
Jailolo (Pulau Halmahera)	Dufa Dufa	*kapal motor*	40,000	1½hr	3 daily
Jailolo (Pulau Halmahera)	Dufa Dufa	speedboat	60,000	1hr	when full
Rum (Pulau Tidore)	Bastiong Ferry Port	car ferry	7,000	45min	7am, 1pm, 4pm, 6pm
Rum (Pulau Tidore)	Bastiong Ferry Port	speedboat	10,000, charters 100,000	20min	when full
Sidangoli (Pulau Halmahera)	Mesjid Raya	speedboat	60,000, charters 350,000	20min	when full
Sofifi (Pulau Halmahera)	Kota Baru	speedboat	50,000, charters 300,000	40min	when full
Sorong (Papua)	Ahmad Yani	Pelni	varies	17hr	2 monthly

11pm) Travel agent that changes US dollars at an acceptable rate.

Ternate City Tourist Office (Map p425; ☑ 0921-311 1211, 0813 222 7667; Jl Pattimura 160; ⊙8am-2.30pm Mon-Fri) Staff are knowledgeable and will do all they can to help. They can arrange guides for Gamalama hikes. Look for the office signed 'Dinas Pariwisata', opposite the police station.

ℹ Getting There & Away

There's a **Pelni office** (Map p426; ☑ 0921-312 1434; www.pelni.co.id; ⊙9am-4pm Mon-Sat) near the port. Frequent daily speedboats connect Kota Ternate to Tidore and Halmahera.

Batik Air, Garuda, Lion Air, NAM, Sriwijaya Air and Wings Air all fly in and out of Ternate. There are daily direct connections to Jakarta, Surabaya, Makassar and Manado on Sulawesi, and Ambon.

ℹ Getting Around

Taxis charge an exorbitant 150,000Rp for the 6km from Babullah Airport to central Ternate, although most can be bargained down to 100,000Rp. Ojeks will do this run for as little as 20,000Rp, however, and bemos (from outside Hairun University, a 10-minute walk south) cost only 5000Rp to the bemo terminal behind the central market. From the terminal, bemos run in all directions (5000-10,000Rp) but ojeks (from 5000Rp per ride) are generally more convenient and much faster.

Motorbikes can be rented at Villa Ma'rasai (p427) and Kurnia Homestay (p425).

Gunung Api Gamalama

The volcanic cone of **Gamalama** dominates Ternate, rising to 1721m. Major eruptions in 1775 and 1840 wreaked havoc on the island. Gamalama still spews out lava, ash and smoke periodically, but it is possible to climb the peak for stupendous views. It's an eight-hour round-trip and a tough ascent even if you are fit. Don't attempt it in the rain. You'll need a guide too, as the trail isn't marked and the locals don't want you trampling through their farms.

The tourist office in Kota Ternate can arrange a guide (100,000Rp).

ℹ Getting There & Away

Gamalama's lower slopes begin at the outskirts of Kota Ternate, a 10,000Rp ride on an ojek from the centre of town.

Pulau Tidore
☑ 0921

Less populous, less mercantile and less frenetic than Ternate, Tidore makes a refreshing escape from the bustle of its historical enemy. The sultanate – which endured from 1109 until the Sukarno era – was re-established in 1999. Today, the 36th sultan presides over a sublime volcanic island dotted with brightly painted wooden homes bordered by flower gardens, shaded by mango trees and coconut palms, and scented by sheets of cloves and nutmeg sun-drying in the street. Hire an *ojek* and you can spin all the way around the island in a few hours.

◉ Sights

Pulau Maitara   ISLAND
A three-minute speedboat hop from Rum, Pulau Maitara's clear waters are fine for snorkelling and swimming but watch out for the numerous sea urchins.

Pulau Mare   ISLAND
This small island south of Pulau Tidore is famed for its attractive, simple pottery. Speedboats to Pulau Mare can be chartered in Seli (100,000Rp).

Pulau Tidore Ⓝ 0 ____ 4 km
                      0 ____ 2 miles

MALUKU PULAU TIDORE

TIDORE DIALECT

In Tidorean dialect *sukur dofu* means 'thank you', *saki* means 'delicious' and *sterek (lau)* means '(very) good'.

Pantai Kajoli
BEACH

Down on Tidore's southern coast, slender and small Pantai Kajoli is the island's best strip of white sand.

Getting There & Away

Daily speedboats link Tidore with Ternate and Halmahera.

Getting Around

Frequent bemos run from Rum to Soasio (15,000Rp) and to Goto (20,000Rp) using the south-coast road.

Ojeks circumnavigate the island for negotiable rates (from 100,000Rp).

Bentor (motorcycle-rickshaws) run around Soasio and Goto (5000Rp).

Soasio

0921 / POP 7500

Drowsy Soasio feels more like an overgrown village than an island capital. It has fewer shops than nearby port town Goto, but a monopoly on Tidore's cultural and historical sights. Soasio is also where you'll find the best spread of accommodation on the island.

Sights

Benteng Tahula
FORT

(JI Lain) FREE A legacy of Spain's short-lived presence in Tidore, this early 17th-century fort is well preserved, with orderly market gardens within and spectacular views to Halmahera from the battlements. It's a steep climb to the top. The fort is always open.

Benteng Torre
FORT

FREE No less spectacular than its nearby twin, Benteng Tahula, Torre was built by the Spanish in the early 17th century. Broken lava flows, vivid tropical foliage and commanding views of southern approaches to the island make this a worthy, picturesque traipse up the hill from the centre of Soasio.

Sonyine Malige
MUSEUM

(Sultan's Memorial Museum; JI Lain; ⊙9am-2pm Mon-Fri) Around 200m north of Benteng Tahula, the Sonyine Malige Sultan's Memorial Museum displays the sultan's throne and giant spittoons, plus the royal crown topped with cassowary feathers (considered as magical as Ternate's own *mahkota*, or royal crown).

To enter the museum, you'll have to first find the curator, Umar Muhammad, who works at the DIKNAS office in the Dinas Pendidikan dan Kebudayan building, 2km north. Umar has been known to demand hefty entry fees of up to 100,000Rp.

Sleeping & Eating

Penginapan Tidore Puri
HOMESTAY $$

(☑0813 4057 1599; JI Sultan Syaifuddin 48; r 200,000-300,000Rp; ❈ ◉) The cheapest rooms aren't big, but all the rooms at this homestay in old Soasio are clean, well-kept and set around an attractive terrace used for breakfast. They all come with air-con.

Penginapan Seroja
HOMESTAY $$

(☑0921-316 1456, 0813 8512 3408; JI Sultan Syaifuddin; r 275,000Rp; ❈ ◉) Blessed with tropical blooms in the garden and stunning views of Halmahera, this waterside homestay lies 100m north of the stairway to Benteng Tahula and is run by a charming *ibu* (auntie) who can really cook. The rooms themselves, though, are basic and old with primitive bathrooms, although they do have

BOATS FROM PULAU TIDORE

DESTINATION	PORT	TYPE	FARE (RP)	DURATION (MIN)	FREQUENCY
Bastiong	Rum	ferry	7000	45	3 daily
Bastiong	Rum	speedboat	10,000	20	when full
Sofifi (Pulau Halmahera)	Goto	speedboat	50,000	40	when full 7-9am
Pulau Maitara	Rum	speedboat	5000	3	when full
Pulau Mare	Seli	speedboat	100,000	15	charter

Western-style toilets. Wi-fi is 5000Rp per day extra.

Rumah Makan Taman Siswa   INDONESIAN $
(Jl Taman Siswa; mains 15,000-35,000Rp; ⊗8am-10pm) No frills here, but they do a very solid *ayam lalapan* (fried chicken, rice and veggies with a spicy sauce), as well as *bakso* (meatballs) and rice dishes.

ℹ Information

BNI (Jl Taman Siswa; ⊗8am-3pm Mon-Fri, to 1pm Sat) The BNI branch in Soasio. It has an ATM.

ℹ Getting There & Away

Frequent bemos connect Soasio with Rum (15,000Rp) and Goto (5000Rp).

Pulau Halmahera

Maluku's biggest island is comprised of four mountainous peninsulas, several volcanic cones and dozens of offshore islands. As it's sparsely populated and hard to get around, Halmahera's potential for diving, birdwatching and beach-bumming remains almost entirely untapped.

Not even making Sofifi the provincial capital of Maluku has done much to stimulate tourism on Halmahera. While the north of the island is reasonably developed, and parts of the east are seeing some mining investment, much of the south remains way off the beaten track with roads ending past the town of Mafa. The interior of eastern Halmahera with its national park and rare bird species is equally little-visited. Don't expect to hear much English, but intrepid travellers with plenty of time have some fascinating possibilities for exploration here.

Gunung Dukono   VOLCANO
Despite being an active volcano that continues to belch ash and smoke, it's possible to climb the almost 1400m-high Dukono in six sweaty hours if you are fit. If you don't want to hike back the same day, you could camp out overnight. The tourist office in Tobelo can arrange a guide and transport for 1,500,000Rp.

Pantai Kupa Kupa   BEACH
(Kupa Kupa) This attractive, part-shaded white-sand beach – popular on weekends with the locals – is good for swimming and there's reasonable snorkelling just offshore. There's an oil terminal at the far southern end of the beach, but walk north and there's plenty of photogenic views.

Pantai Luari   BEACH
(Luari) This pretty, horseshoe-shaped bay about 13km north of Tobelo has a shady white-sand beach that's fine for swimming. There's decent snorkelling and diving off the cape here.

★**Pantai Kupa**
Kupa Cottages   BUNGALOW $$
(📲0812 4477 6773; kupakupacottages@gmail.com; Kupa Kupa; r/bungalow/family cottage 300,000/400,000/600,000Rp; ❄🛜) Deliciously laidback Kupa Kupa Cottages offers plenty of reasons to stay a few nights at its well-kept bungalows decorated with Papuan handicrafts. Surrounded by a lush garden and with the beach out front, there's a fabulous cafe for meals and bay views, and owner Ona is lovely. Cheaper rooms in the main house share bathrooms.

ℹ Getting There & Away

There are flights to Galela and Kao in northern Halmahera from Manado in Sulawesi. A direct daily flight from Ternate connects to Buli in eastern Halmahera.

One or two Pelni liners loop around Halmahera each month from Ternate and/or Bitung (Sulawesi).

By far the most popular way to access the island is by speedboats from Ternate that leave when they are full. For the northwestern coast head for Jailolo (60,000Rp, one hour). For Tobelo, Galela and the east, cross initially to Sofifi (50,000Rp, 40 minutes) or Sidangoli (60,000Rp, 30 minutes). You can also charter a boat to Sofifi for 300,000Rp, or to Sidangoli for 350,000Rp.

ℹ Getting Around

Shared Kijang taxis link Jailolo, Sofifi and Sidangoli with Tobelo via a long, languid coastline, alternating between white- and black-sand beaches and lush coconut groves. Infrequent bemos move between villages in northern Halmahera.

Ojeks and *bentor* (motorcycle-rickshaws) can be found in the towns.

Sofifi

📲0921 / POP 36,197
Sofifi isn't the most remarkable of towns, despite being anointed as the capital of North Maluku in 2007. A spread-out place connected by wide roads and interspersed with

Pulau Halmahera

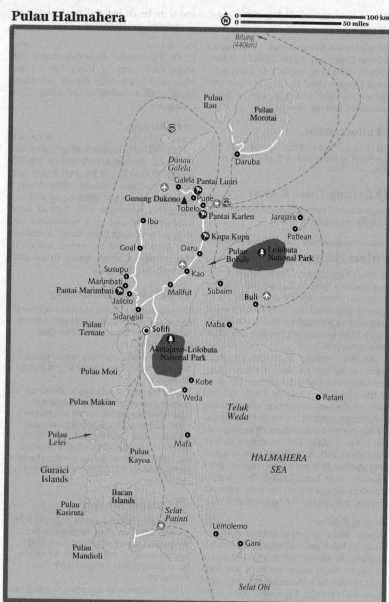

0   100 km
0   50 miles

forlorn-looking government buildings, Sofifi serves travellers mainly as a junction on the route to Tobelo. While the seaside setting is attractive, overlooking mangroves and with Ternate in the far distance, there's no reason to stay here and most people move on swiftly.

🛏 Sleeping & Eating

Bolote Hotel HOTEL $

(☏ 0812 4491 2011; Jl Gosale Punjak; deluxe/superior 250,000/300,000Rp; ❄ ☏) The best of Sofifi's limited selection of hotels, the Bolote is up a hill on the road that leads to Tobelo. Rooms are decent-sized and most come with balconies, but they're a little beaten up and the Western-style bathrooms have cold water only. Beds are OK.

Rumah Makan Nasbag   INDONESIAN $

(Jl Trans Halmahera; mains 15,000-35,000Rp; ⊙8am-10pm) This seafront place ticks over with a steady stream of locals. You can pick and choose from the chicken and veggies on display or go for fresh fish, grilled or fried. It also serves rice and noodle dishes.

❶ Getting There & Away

Sofifi–Ternate speedboats (50,000Rp, 40 minutes) leave when full, which is fairly frequently.

Kijangs (shared taxis) bound for Tobelo (130,000Rp, 3½ hours) and Weda (100,000Rp, 2½ hours) wait by the dock until early afternoon. You can hire your own taxi to Tobelo (800,000Rp) as well.

Jailolo

📞 0922 / POP 27,541

Famed for its fragrant durians, the little port of Jailolo steams gently away at the base of a lush volcanic cone, among the mangroves. Before being incorporated by Ternate, Jailolo was an independent sultanate. Today, not even a stone remains of Jailolo's former *keraton* (palace), abandoned in the 1730s. However, the sultan was reinstated in 2003 and now lives in a modest beachfront villa in nearby Marimbati.

Few foreigners pass through Jailolo. Those who do are normally on their way north, or overnighting before a boat ride the next day.

🛏 Sleeping & Eating

Penginapan Camar   GUESTHOUSE $

(📞 0813 4033 0000; Jl Gufasa; r with fan/air-con 92,500/175,000-230,000Rp; ❄) Only a few doors from the central market, Penginapan Camar has a mix of rudimentary rooms, The best offer a bit of space, a basic *mandi* (ladle bath) bathroom and air-con. The cheapest are windowless, bathroom-less cells. But all rooms could do with new beds.

Sabua Gaba   HOTEL $$

(📞 0822 726 0763; Jl Raya Guemadu; s/d 250,000/500,000Rp; ❄🛜) Right by the waterfront, a 10-minute walk west of the speedboat jetty, the most expensive rooms here are swish by Jailolo standards: spacious, modern and well-kept with decent bath-

rooms. The cheaper singles are set around a sheltered communal area and are clean but small with *mandi* (ladle bath) bathroom.

D'Hoek Hotel   HOTEL $$

(📞 0922-222 1200; Jl Soekarno; r 220,000-580,000Rp; ❄🛜) The more you pay at this friendly, if not very clean, place, the bigger the room. All rooms have Western toilets and air-con, but are otherwise bland and undistinguished. It's on the outskirts of town, a 10,000Rp *bentor* ride from the port. Breakfast is included.

Rumah Makan Rahma   INDONESIAN $

(Jl Puaen; soup 25,000Rp; ⊙9am-10pm) Just southeast of the town's main mosque, this place only serves *coto makassar*, a season-yourself lemongrass-based soup served with stewed beef, sticky pucks of coconut rice, hard-boiled eggs, deep-fried shallots, sambal and lime wedges. What it lacks in variety it more than makes up for in quality.

❶ Information

At the time of research, ATMs in Jailolo were not accepting international cards. Bring cash.

❶ Getting There & Away

Large speedboats to Dufa Dufa (Ternate, 60,000Rp, one hour) leave throughout the day when full. You can also hop on a slower, wooden *kapal motor* (40,000Rp, two hours, three daily).

A couple of shared Kijang taxis depart for Tobelo (150,000Rp, four to five hours) and points north each morning. Ask your accommodation to arrange a pick up.

MALUKU PULAU HALMAHERA

> **WORTH A TRIP**
>
> ## MARIMBATI
>
> A pleasant *ojek* excursion from Jailolo takes you to Marimbati and its long, black-sand beach. You'll likely have it all to yourself. En route, the road passes through a mix of Christian and Muslim villages, where you'll see many of the thatched, traditional houses known as *rumah adat*. Reached by an entirely different road via Akelamo, **Susupu** is a picturesque, volcano-backed village at the far-northern end of Marimbati Beach.
>
> Marimbati is 12km north of Jailolo, which is a 30-minute ride away by ojek (30,000Rp).

ⓘ Getting Around

Bentor (motorcycle-rickshaws) cruise around town (5000Rp to 10,000Rp).

Tobelo

☑ 0924 / POP 29,377

Tobelo sits close to the still-active volcano of Dukono, but that hasn't stopped it becoming the most bustling town in Halmahera. However, it remains relaxed and low-key by any standards, a sprawling and predominantly Christian place with a bay fronted by a pretty jigsaw of atolls, all ringed with pale, sandy beaches. Some of Halmahera's finest strips of sand can be found north and south of Tobelo, and are easily accessible on day trips, while there's sound snorkelling and a fair few dive sites within easy reach.

🏃 Activities

Firman Dive Guide   DIVING
(☑ 0812 4215 1172, 0856 363 432; itang_hui@ yahoo.com) Firman is the number-one dive guide in northern Halmahera. He speaks good English and can advise on the best dive sights and local diving conditions.

🛌 Sleeping

Greenland Hotel   HOTEL $$
(☑ 0812 440 9313; Jl Samping; r/cottage 350,000-450,000/600,000Rp; ❋ ⓢ) A few hundred metres back from a black-sand beach – you can snorkel at the atolls 400m offshore – the serene Greenland has neat, clean and modern rooms with comfy beds. The wood-framed cottages are small but well kept.

Elizabeth Inn   HOTEL $$
(☑ 0924-262 1885; elizabethhotel@gmail.com; Jl Kemakmuran; r 350,000-500,000Rp; ❋ ⓢ) Behind the beige tiles of the Elizabeth's lobby you'll find clean rooms with comfortable beds, TVs and air-con. Bathrooms are compact but they do have hot water. The only difference between the cheapest and most expensive rooms is their size. Breakfast is included.

Bianda Hotel   HOTEL $$
(☑ 0924-262 2123; Jl Kemakmuran; r 260,000-450,000Rp; ❋ ⓢ) Looking a little worn now, the Bianda remains a popular choice. Rooms are reasonably spacious and modern, although the standards are a tight squeeze and lack hot water. Only the deluxe rooms come with double beds. A little English is spoken.

🍴 Eating

★ My Home Cafe   INDONESIAN $
(Jl Bhayangkara; mains 30,000-70,000Rp; ⓣ 10am-10pm) The most atmospheric place to eat in Tobelo – a courtyard garden with a small ornamental pond, packed with plants and lit by lanterns – this cute place also does decent *ikan bakar* (grilled fish), as well as the usual Indonesian staples. It's good for a coffee break too.

Podo Moro   INDONESIAN $
(Jl Kemakmuran; mains 35,000-60,000Rp; ⓣ noon-midnight) Fish and more fish (although, inevitably, chicken is also on the menu) grilled delightfully in front of you at this popular place that stays open later than most restaurants in Tobelo. Fish is priced by weight but is very reasonable, unless you're going for crab.

Waroeng Family   INDONESIAN $
(☑ 0924-262 1238; Jl Kemakmuran; mains 40,000-60,000Rp; ⓣ 10am-10pm) Locals push through the carved wooden doors, hunker down under pastel walls adorned with patterned fans, and scratch their heads over the choice: either *ikan bakar* (grilled fish) or *ayam goreng* (fried chicken). Both come with sambal, steamed cassava and garlic-sautéed water spinach, and both are delicious.

🛍 Shopping

Tondano Indah   ALCOHOL
(Jl Kemakmuran; ⓣ 8am-11pm) Minimart that sells beer, as well as whisky and gin.

ⓘ Information

There are ATMs dotted around the centre of town (at the Jl Kemakmuran/Pelabuhan junction).

Kantor Pariwisata Halmahera Utara (Jl Bhayangkara, Kantor Bupati, 2nd fl; ⓣ 8am-noon & 1-4pm Mon-Fri) An essential depository of information on Halmahera Utara, including diving sites and guides, natural attractions – they can organise a guide to climb Gunung Dukono – and WWII relics. The charming staff speak English well and have some maps and tourist literature to give away.

ⓘ Getting There & Away

The nearest airport, in Galela, has four flights a week to Manado in Sulawesi, but none to Ternate.

Daily Kijangs to Sofifi (130,000Rp, 3½ hours) and Jailolo (150,000Rp, four hours) leave from the **bemo terminal** (Jl Trans Halut, Wosia) in

PULAU MOROTAI

Sitting in beautiful turquoise waters, Morotai was once part of the sultanate of Ternate. The island remained obscure until World War II, when its minor Japanese base was captured by the Allies and used to bomb Manila to bits. Among the Japanese defenders who retreated to Morotai's mountain hinterland was Private Teruo Nakamura: only in 1973 did he discover that the war was over.

Morotai has been designated for development by Indonesia's Ministry of Tourism. Investment in new infrastructure is expected, along with resorts and hotels. For now, though, Morotai sees little tourist traffic, its coastal villages linked by a road that gets progressively worse the further north you travel from Daruba, the island's main settlement. There are some attractive beaches, potential surf in the far north, as well as a few WWII relics, but the best beaches and prime snorkel and dive spots are offshore on the nearby islands.

Wings Air operates a daily flight from Morotai to Ternate.

Speedboats leave Tobelo (Halmahera) for Morotai (105,000Rp, 1½ hours) when full from 8am but they become far scarcer in the afternoon. There's sometimes a *kapal motor* from Tobelo at 1pm (50,000Rp, three hours).

Wosia on the southern outskirts of Tobelo, or will pick you up from your hotel until around 1pm. There are far more Kijangs to Sofifi than to Jailolo.

Infrequent bemos run to Kao (25,000Rp, 1½ hours) and Daru (15,000Rp, one hour).

Hiring an *ojek* for the day (100,000Rp) is the best way to get to the outlying beaches.

BOATS FROM TOBELO

Speedboats to Morotai (105,000Rp, 1½ hours) depart between 8am and 6pm.

❶ Getting Around

Ojeks and *bentor* (motorcycle-rickshaws) zip around town (5000Rp to 10,000Rp).

Eastern Halmahera

Way off the tourism radar, eastern Halmahera appeals to travellers who fancy plunging into the remote Aketajawe-Lolobata National Park, or being an area's first foreigner in a generation. Deep in the riverine hinterland, at least a two-day trek from Subaim, Jarajara or Patlean, live the nomadic Togutil people. The fine sandy beach and coral reef at Jarajara offer swimming and diving possibilities.

Aketajawe-Lolobata
National Park   NATIONAL PARK

Established in 2004, this national park is especially interesting for birdwatchers, who can spot rare kingfishers, goshawks and crows, as well as many other species. The park is also home to the 2000-odd semi-nomadic Togutil people. Covered in thick rainforest, the park is threatened by illegal logging and mining. At the time of research, it was unclear whether there was access to the area.

❶ Getting There & Away

There's a daily flight from Ternate to Buli.

Boats from Tobelo in northern Halmahera run to Subaim (Tuesday and Thursday), Patlean (Sunday), Jarajara (some Tuesdays) and Maba (three weekly). If you book in advance through a tourist agency, you can arrange longboat transfers that allow hop-offs at intermediate villages en route.

PULAU AMBON

Maluku's most prominent and populous island is lush and gently mountainous, indented with two great hoops of bay. Around the busy capital Kota Ambon, villages merge into a long, green, suburban ribbon. West of the airport, this gives way to a string of charming coastal villages where, if you take the time to explore, you'll discover Ambon is not just an unavoidable step on the road to the lovely Lease, Banda and Kei Islands. The bay is known for excellent muck-diving, while the southern coast has clear waters and intact coral.

The more developed southern part of Ambon is called Leitimur. It's joined to the northern Leihitu area by a narrow neck of land at Passo and a bridge further west.

Pulau Ambon

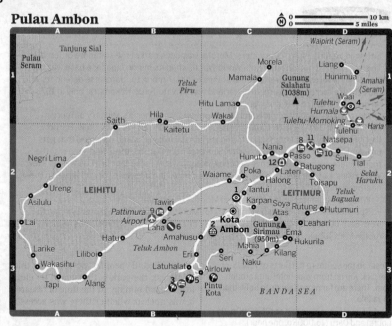

Pulau Ambon

◎ Sights
1	Commonwealth War Cemetery	C2
2	Museum Siwalima	C3
3	Namalatu Beach	B3
4	Sacred Eels of Waai	D1
5	Santai Beach	B3

◎ Activities, Courses & Tours
6	Blue Rose Divers	B3
	Dive Bluemotion	(see 6)
	Dive into Ambon	(see 10)

◎ Sleeping
7	Collin Beach Hotel	B3
8	Maluku Resort & Spa	D2
9	Mornoa Michael Guesthouse	B2
10	The Natsepa	D2

◎ Eating
11	Gaba Gaba	D2

◎ Shopping
12	Ambon City Center	C2

History

Until 1512 Ambon was ruled by Ternate. The sultans brought the civilising force of Islam to the island's north coast and developed Hitu Lama as a major spice-trading port.

When the Portuguese displaced the Ternateans, they found Ambon's less-developed, non-Islamicised south more receptive to Christianity, and built the fortress around which Kota Ambon would eventually evolve. The Portuguese were easily displaced by the Dutch in the early 17th century. Ambon briefly served the VOC (Dutch East India Company) as its pre-Jakarta capital, and the island became the world's largest producer of cloves.

During WWII, when Kota Ambon was a Japanese military headquarters, Allied bombing destroyed most of its once-attractive colonial architecture. In 1950, the island was briefly the centre of the southern Malukan independence movement, extinguished within a few months by the Indonesian military.

From 1999 until mid-2002, Ambon was ripped apart by Christian–Muslim intercommunal violence, leaving Kota Ambon looking like 1980s Beirut. Sectarian violence flared again in 2011 and 2012 but, thankfully, on a much smaller scale.

ⓘ Information

There are many banks in Kota Ambon, as well as ATMs spread around the island.

Kota Ambon

📞 0911 / POP 331,254

By the region's dreamy tropical standards, Maluku's capital is a sprawling metropolis. Sights are minimal and the architecture is mostly undistinguished, but there is a strong cafe culture, decent accommodation and some good restaurants. Divers can use the city as a convenient base for nearby offshore fun, while the beaches of Pulau Ambon are an easy commute from Kota Ambon. Alternatively, just chill out while you plan your onward travel to the Banda and Kei Islands, the real highlights of the region.

⊙ Sights

Commonwealth War Cemetery   CEMETERY

(Map p436; Tantui) Known to locals as the Australian Cemetery, this neatly manicured cemetery was designed by a British landscape architect in honour of Allied servicemen who died in Maluku and Sulawesi in WWII. To add to its poignancy, it's built on the site of a former POW camp.

Museum Siwalima   MUSEUM

(Map p436; 📞0911-341652; Jl Dr Malaiholio; 10,000Rp; ⊙8am-4pm Mon-Fri, 10am-3pm Sat & Sun) This modest museum is ten minutes south of Kota Ambon, set in sloping landscaped gardens adorned with Japanese and Dutch cannons and a scowling statue of Pattimura, *parang* (machete) aloft. The collection is dedicated to Malukan material culture, including fish traps, stone tools, model longboats, an elongated *tifa* drum crafted from bamboo and ancient bone, and brass jewellery. It makes a worthy diversion from Ambon's hustle. You might have to hunt down the caretaker to open the museum.

Traditional Indonesian wedding costumes from across the archipelago's many regions are exhibited in the topmost gallery. Bemos bound for Latuhalat pass the entrance (5000Rp). An *ojek* to the door is 15,000Rp.

Benteng Victoria   FORTRESS

(Map p440) Undramatic Benteng Victoria (out of bounds due to army use) is a Dutch-era fortress. The site of Indonesian national hero Pattimura's hanging, it's fronted by a gilded statue of Slamet Riyadi, an Indonesian commander who died retaking the place in 1950.

Masjid Raya al-Fatah   MOSQUE

(Map p440; Jl Sultan Babullah) The town's biggest mosque, Masjid Raya al-Fatah is a modern concrete affair, its gold-and-brown onion dome visible across much of central Ambon. Non-Muslims can visit outside of prayer times.

Francis Xavier Cathedral   CHURCH

(Map p440; Jl Pattimura) `FREE` Named for the Basque missionary who visited Maluku in the 16th century, Francis Xavier Cathedral has a facade crusted with statues of saints and glimmering steeples.

🏋 Activities

Nakamura   SPA

(Map p440; 📞0911-345557; Jl Phillips Latumahina SK 5/7; treatments 100,000-270,000Rp; ⊙10am-10pm) This Japanese-style spa, replete with gurgling fountains, trilling birdsong and rice

---

DIVING AMBON

Ambon's wide urban bay – as deep as 500m in some places – and abundance of underwater life make it a celebrated muck-diving location. There are as many as 30 dive sites within the bay alone, plus many more sites around the coast and nearby **Tiga Islands**.

Highlights include coral-crusted volcanic pinnacles off **Mahia**, the blue hole at **Hukurila**, a huge underwater arch at **Pintu Kota**, and the **Duke of Sparta shipwreck**, which was allegedly sunk by the CIA in 1958. Also, during action-packed drift dives between the Tiga Islands you'll meet bumphead parrotfish, Napoleons, dogtooth tuna, vast schools of fusiliers, dolphins, sharks and turtles. You can also glimpse the big stuff at **Tanjung Sial Timur** (Bad Corner), where strong currents attract pelagic fish off the southern tip of Seram.

But as special as those sites can be, it's the muck that draws the crowds for such oddities as the psychedelic frogfish, 15 varieties of rhinopia, manta shrimp, zebra crabs, banded pipefish, pygmy squid and seahorses. Plan your trip between October and April: most local dive outfits close down between May and September.

paper-walled cubicles, is the ideal antidote to the bustle of Ambon. Choose from a variety of massage treatments.

🛏 Sleeping

Penginapan Asri
GUESTHOUSE $

(Map p440; ☎ 0911-311217; Jl Baru 33; r with fan 125,000Rp, with air-con 175,000-190,000Rp; ❈ 🛜) Located down a side street in the heart of downtown, the Asri is a long-standing Ambon budget crash pad with a variety of room options. The cheapest share bathrooms, many lack windows and all are no-frills, but if you're catching a Pelni the next day, or lost your wallet, it's only five-minute walk from the port.

Penginapan the Royal
GUESTHOUSE $

(Map p440; ☎ 0911-348077; Jl Anthony Rhebok 1D; s/d 220,000/248,000Rp; ❈ 🛜) Some rooms here are a little musty and/or smell of stale smoke while many are windowless, but they are clean enough and the beds are better than the price suggests. The central location is a bonus.

The City Hotel
HOTEL $$

(☎ 0911-382 9990; www.cityhotelambon.com; Jl Tulukabessy 39; tw & d incl breakfast 550,000-700,000Rp; ❈ 🛜) Standing out from the mid-range crowd thanks to its solicitous staff, rooftop restaurant and distinctive design – all stripped pine and artwork – the City offers a less anonymous experience than other options in the same price band. Discounts of 10% are sometimes on offer.

Orchid Hotel
HOTEL $$

(Map p440; ☎ 0911-346363; Jl Pattimura 5; d 400,000-440,000Rp; ❈ 🛜) One of Ambon's crop of modern midrange sleeps, the Orchid offers large rooms with high ceilings, wood

TRANSPORT FROM PULAU AMBON

Air

Ambon's airport, Bandara Pattimura (p441), is near the village of Laha and is serviced by Batik Air, Citilink, Garuda (p441), NAM Air and Sriwijaya Air (p441).

At the time of research, there were no flights between Ambon and Bandaneira.

DESTINATION	AIRLINE	FREQUENCY
Jakarta	Batik Air, Citilink, Lion, Garuda	10 direct daily
Langgur	Garuda, Lion, Wings Air	6 direct daily
Makassar	Batik Air, Citilink, Lion, Garuda	10 direct daily
Sorong	Batik Air, Garuda, Wings Air	1 direct daily
Ternate	Batik Air, Garuda, Sriwijaya, NAM Air	1 direct daily

Boat

Tulehu-Hurnala (Map p436; Jl Propinsi) Main port for large speedboats (ferries) to outer islands.

Tulehu-Momoking (Map p436; Jl Propinsi) Port for small boats to outlying islands.

DESTINATION	PORT	TYPE	FARE (RP)	DURATION (HR)	FREQUENCY
Amahai (Pulau Seram)	Tulehu-Hurnala	Bahari Express	economy/VIP 115,000/260,000	2½	9am & 4pm daily
Bandaneira	Tulehu-Hurnala	Bahari Express	economy/VIP 410,000/650,000	6	Tue & Sat 9am
Haria (Pulau Saparua)	Tulehu-Hurnala	Bahari Express	economy/VIP 65,000/150,000	1	9am daily
Haria (Pulau Saparua)	Tulehu-Momoking	speedboat	50,000	1	when full
Papus	Kota Ambon	Pelni	varies	40	2-3 monthly
Bandaneira & Tual	Kota Ambon	Pelni	varies	9-12	2-5 monthly
Waipirit (Pulau Seram)	Hunimua	car ferry	varies	2-3	3 daily

furnishings and decent beds. Some cheaper rooms only have windows overlooking the corridors. Staff are helpful and breakfast is good.

Hero Hotel Ambon
HOTEL **$$**

(Map p440; ☑ 0911-342898; herohotelambon2@gmail.com; Jl Wim Reawaru 7B; s/d incl breakfast from 445,000/475,000Rp; 💥🛜) Rooms are immaculate and good value at this contemporary hotel with a decent downstairs cafe-restaurant and a reasonably quiet but central side-street location. Deluxe rooms are smaller than the executive ones, but otherwise you get the same slick styling and facilities such as satellite TV and hot water.

Biz@ Hotel
HOTEL **$$**

(Map p440; ☑ 0911-382 1988; BiZahotel@yahoo.com; Jl Said Perintah 37; d 388,000-645,000Rp; 💥🛜) Generic, functional rooms with small bathrooms, but everything is spotless, beds are comfortable and fixtures are modern. The downstairs **Cafe Biz** (Map p440; coffee from 12,000Rp; ⊙ 9am-1am) is very popular with the locals.

Hotel Mutiara
HOTEL **$$**

(Map p440; ☑ 0911-353075; Jl Pattimura 12; d 300,000-700,000Rp; 💥🛜) Rooms are old-fashioned here, but both they and the bathrooms are bigger than can be found at many other places in Ambon. All come with windows and are well-maintained. The attached restaurant is pretty good and staff are pleasant.

Swiss-Belhotel
HOTEL **$$$**

(Map p440; ☑ 0911-322888; www.swiss-belhotel.com; Jl Benteng Kapaha; deluxe 1,000,000-1,100,000, ste 1,700,000-4,300,000Rp; 💥🛜) Kota Ambon's swishest hotel has sizeable and comfortable rooms that come with all mod cons, although the bathrooms are less impressive than you'd expect. The efficient staff speak good English. There's a gym, a restaurant and a bar, but the swimming pool remains a work in progress. Discounts of 30% are sometimes available.

🍴 Eating

Ambon Manise is well named: the variety of traditional cakes sold in every *rumah kopi* betrays the local sweet tooth. Cheap *rumah makan* abound, especially around Mardika Market and ports, and evening warungs appear on Jl Sultan Babullah, AY Patti and Pantai Mardika.

Rumah Makan Puti Bungsu
INDONESIAN **$**

(Map p440; Jl Said Perintah; meals 25,000-60,000Rp; ⊙ 8am-10pm) Excellent and justifiably popular pick-and-mix place with a good selection of fish, beef and chicken cooked in a variety of ways, as well as veggies, potato-and-omelette slices and sambals to spice it all up.

Rumah Makan Nifia
INDONESIAN **$**

(Map p440; Jl AM Sangaji; meals 20,000-50,000Rp; ⊙ 7am-10pm) A pick-and-mix warung with alarming lime-and-orange decor and a devoted following. Dishes are fresh, rotate frequently, and include several varieties of roasted and baked fish, fried chicken and tempeh, curried and stir-fried vegetables, beef *rendang* (cooked in spicy coconut milk), and a tasty *soto ayam* (chicken soup) that's ideal for monsoon season.

Sarinda
BAKERY **$**

(Map p440; ☑ 0911-355109; Jl Sultan Hairun 11; pastries from 8000Rp; ⊙ 8am-10pm; 🛜) With its lovely Dutch-colonial windows, outside terrace seating and central location, this bakery is a good place to start the day with fresh bread, pastries and decent coffee. There's a second branch on Jl Sam Ratulangi.

⭐ Bayview Restaurant
INTERNATIONAL **$$**

(Jl Tulukabessy 39; mains 50,000-180,000Rp; ⊙ 7am-midnight; 💥🛜) Some of the best dining views of Ambon's bay and harbour are from the terrace of this relaxed restaurant atop the City Hotel. The menu specialises in Western comfort food – pasta, grilled fish, steaks, burgers and salads – plus a few Indonesian favourites. There's a selection of beers to choose from (including Guinness), as well as decent coffee. Occasional live music.

Sari Gurih
SEAFOOD **$$**

(Map p440; ☑ 0911-341888; Jl Anthony Rhebok; mains 30,000-125,000Rp, set menus 60,000-80,000Rp; ⊙ 9am-11pm) Sari Gurih is a great place to eat Malukan seafood. Fish is priced by weight: choose from what's on display and it'll be slapped on the grill. The sound of karaoke emerges from its private rooms on busy nights.

Ratu Gurih
SEAFOOD **$$**

(Map p440; ☑ 0911-341202; Jl Diponegoro 26; mains from 30,000Rp, fish priced by weight; ⊙ 9am-10pm; 💥) The *ikan bakar* (grilled fish) – perfectly chargrilled by the coal-stoking chef,

Kota Ambon

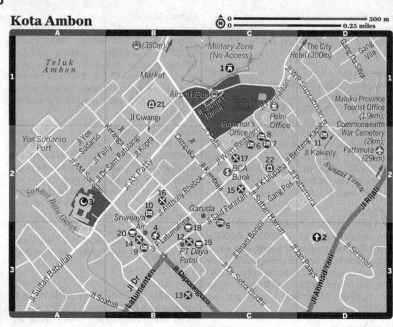

Kota Ambon

smothered in chilli and served alongside three tasty sambals – is fall-off-the-bone fresh. If you're tired of Indonesian staples, it offers Chinese choices too and there's an air-con dining area. Usually closes for a few hours in the afternoon.

🍷 Drinking & Nightlife

★ Sibu-Sibu
CAFE

(Map p440; ☑ 0911-312525; Jl Said Perintah 47A; coffee 10,000-15,000Rp, snacks 3000-25,000Rp; ⊗ 7am-11pm; 🛜) Local heroes and stars of screen and song deck the walls of this ever-popular coffee shop and bar, which plays live Malukan and Hawaiian music while serving snacks such as *koyabu* (cassava cake) and *lopis pulut* (sticky rice with palm jaggery). Order a cold Bintang beer, or go for the signature strong ginger coffee mixed with spices and nuts.

Kopi Tradisi Joas
CAFE

(Map p440; ☑ 0911-341518; Jl Said Perintah; coffee 12,000-19,000Rp; ⊗ 8am-8pm Mon-Sat) With old-school wooden tables, a tiled floor and ancient posters on the walls, this local institution attracts Ambon's movers and shakers. They while away the hours over rich mocha-style 'secret-recipe' coffees and slices of deep-fried breadfruit (*sukun goreng*, 2000Rp). Get a table out back under the avocado tree.

The Pension Cafe
CAFE

(Map p440; Jl AM Sangaji; coffee, juices & snacks 10,000-25,000Rp; ☺10am-11pm; ☞) More of a hipster hangout than downtown's other cafes, but friendly and welcoming too. Perch on the cushions that line the walls or grab a table. There's gentle live music most evenings and a selection of Indonesian staple dishes.

🛍 Shopping

Plaza Ambon
MALL

(Map p440; Jl Sam Ratulangi; ☺9am-10pm) Plaza Ambon is the city's cross between a proper shopping mall and an old-school market. In addition to byzantine market stalls, it has the requisite fast-food choices, a Matahari store and a big Foodmart grocer for self-caterers.

Ambon City Center
MALL

(Map p436; ☑0911-362957; Jl Wolter Monginsidi; ☺8am-10pm) Ambon City Center is actually in Passo, some way out of town. It's the biggest mall in Maluku, and the place to reconnect with your favourite brands or stock up on groceries at its enormous Hypermart.

Ud Inti
ALCOHOL

(Map p440; Jl K Ulupaha; ☺1pm-11.30pm) This hole-in-the-wall Chinese-run minimart is one of the few shops in town where you can buy beer, as well as whisky, gin and rum.

❶ Information

International ATMs are sprinkled throughout Ambon's city centre. Change or withdraw enough money in Ambon for trips to outlying islands where there are no exchange facilities and ATMs sometimes don't work.

BCA Bank (Bank Central Asia; Map p440; Jl Sultan Hairun 24; ☺8am-3pm Mon-Fri) Exchanges euros and Australian and US dollars, and has a battalion of ATMs.

Maluku Province Tourist Office (Dinas Parawisata; ☑0911-312300; Jl Jenderal Sudirman; ☺8am-4pm Mon-Fri) A handy source of info

(some of it in English) on Ambon, the Bandas, Seram and other neighbouring islands.

PT Daya Patal (Map p440; ☑0911-353344; spicetr@gmail.com; Jl Said Perintah 53A; ☺9am-7pm Mon-Sat, from noon Sun) Ever-obliging agency with helpful English-speaking staff who are the best source of up-to-date travel information. Sells airline tickets, as well as speedboat and Pelni tickets, for a small commission.

❶ Getting There & Away

AIR

Pattimura Airport is 37km round the bay from central Kota Ambon.

Airlines include Batik Air, Citilink, **Garuda** (Map p440; www.garuda-indonesia.com; Jl Pardeis Tengah; ☺9am-5pm), NAM and **Sriwijaya Air** (Map p440; ☑0911-354498; Jl AM Sangaji 79; ☺9am-6pm).

BOAT

Pelni liners arrive and depart at Yos Sudarso Port close to the centre of town.

All other boats depart from Tulehu (15,000Rp, one hour)

❶ Getting Around

TO/FROM THE AIRPORT

Ambon's **Pattimura Airport** (Map p436; Jl Propinsi) is located near the village of Laha.

The Damri **airport bus** (Map p440; Jl Slamet Riyadi; per person 35,000Rp) leaves from the landward side of the Peace Gong four times daily (4.30am, 5am, 10am and 1pm – timed for airline departures). It departs from the airport for the city centre after inbound flights land (at approximately 7am, 8am, 1pm and 4pm).

Hatu- and Laha-bound bemos pass by the airport gates (10,000Rp, one hour).

A taxi between Kota Ambon and the airport costs 150,000Rp.

BEMO

Green bemos circulate within the city centre and blue bemos head out of town. Traffic jams near Mardika Market (the terminus) can be bad – consider getting off 200m away.

Ultra-frequent Lin III bemos (*mobils*) head southwest down Jl Pantai Mardika and either Jl Dr Sam Ratulangi or Jl AY Patty, swinging around the Trikora monument on to Jl Dr Latumenten. After 2km they loop back via Jl Sultan Babullah and Jl Yos Sudarso.

Tantui bemos run northeast from Mardika, passing the Commonwealth War Cemetery, then looping back past the tourist office.

Ojeks can be found all over town (from 5000Rp).

Southern Leitimur

Latuhalat, the southern tip of Leitimur, straddles a low pass culminating in Santai and Namalatu, a pair of well-shaded beaches that are popular with locals at weekends. Neither offers great swimming but divers and snorkellers will find plenty of reef action offshore. You can walk between the two beaches in 15 minutes. This is a much more tranquil part of the island than busy Kota Ambon, but you're still only a 40-minute bemo ride from the city.

Namalatu Beach   BEACH

(Map p436; Namalatu; 3000Rp) Close to Leitimur's far southern tip, this shady south coast beach isn't great for swimming, but it's a popular hangout for the locals at the weekend.

Santai Beach   BEACH

(Map p436; 3000Rp) This modest, partly rocky beach comes alive at the weekends when the locals arrive in force.

Collin Beach Hotel   HOTEL $$

(Map p436; ☑ 0911-323125; collinbeachhotel@ yahoo.com; Jl Amalanite 1; d 240,000-360,000Rp; ✳ ☎) Sandwiched between the popular beaches of Santai and Namalatu, this laid-back resort is set around a large garden. Rooms are big and comfortable, without being very exciting, and this is an ideal spot to escape the hustle of Kota Ambon. There's an on-site restaurant and motorbikes can be hired (75,000Rp per day).

ⓘ Getting There & Away

Latuhalat bemos (their signs are abbreviated to 'Lt Halat') from Kota Ambon (5000Rp, 40 minutes) run to Namalatu along a pretty waterside road through Eri.

Eastern Leihitu

Most people head to this part of Ambon to catch a ferry from Tulehu to the outlying islands, but nearby Teluk Baguala and Natsepa beach are two of eastern Leihitu's beauty spots, popular with locals for weekend swims and roadside *rujak* (fruit salad in a spicy chilli, tamarind and shrimp-paste dressing). In the village of Waai, beyond Tulehu, you'll find tame moray eels at one of Ambon's more unusual tourist attractions.

⊙ Sights & Activities

Sacred Eels of Waai   POND

(Air Waiselaka; Map p436; 10,000Rp; ⊘ 8am-5pm) Waai is famous for its 'lucky' *belut* (moray eels). For 10,000Rp, a 'guide' tempts the eels from dark recesses in a concrete-sided pond by feeding them raw eggs. The eels are so tame you can pet them, a rather slimy sensation. The pond, known as Air Waiselaka, is two blocks inland from Jl Propinsi near the beginning of Waai Village.

Dive into Ambon   DIVING

(Map p436; ☑ 0812 4436 7169; www.diveinto ambon.com; Jl Propinsi, Maluku Resort & Spa; 3 dives US$160; ⊘ Sep-May) Based at the Maluku Resort & Spa, Dive into Ambon has more direct access to the coral sites of the island's southern coast than Ambon's other operators. It's an efficient, well-established outfit, but pricier than other local dive shops.

⌂ Sleeping & Eating

Maluku Resort
& Spa   RESORT $$$

(Map p436; ☑ 0911-361970; www.malukuresort. com; Jl Propinsi; deluxe/cottage 880,000/ 1,375,000Rp; ✳ ☎ ☲) Formerly the Baguala Bay Resort, this family-friendly place is set around a swimming pool in a lovely waterfront palm garden with fine bay views, especially enchanting at night. The cottages, with white stone walls and rain showers, are sizeable and inviting, but all the rooms are well maintained. There's an on-site spa and restaurant, as well as Dive into Ambon.

The Natsepa   RESORT $$$

(Map p436; ☑ 0911-362555; www.thenatsepa. com; Jl Raya Natsepa 36; r 990,000-1,700,000, ste 2,400,000-2,900,000Rp; ✳ ☎ ☲) Big and modern rooms, if a touch plain, at a sprawling complex set around carefully tended lawns and with a scenic bay location. Some rooms have private pools – at extra cost – and, along with the decent service, a gym and a restaurant help to make this Ambon's top hotel. Nonetheless, the four-star polish has worn off in places.

Gaba Gaba   INDONESIAN $$

(Map p436; Jl Propinsi; mains 30,000-75,000Rp; ⊘ 11am-11pm; ☎) The setting is great, with stunning views of Natsepa bay and a scattering of wooden cabanas shaded by coconut palms to eat in. The menu of grilled fish and rice and noodle dishes is less spectacular, but the food is solid enough. There's a kids' play area and wi-fi, so everyone should be happy.

ℹ Getting There & Away

Bemos from Mardika (Kota Ambon) run frequently to Waai and Tulehu, via Natsepa (5000Rp to 15,000Rp).

Northern & Western Leihitu

For most travellers Western Leihitu is the location of the airport. But this lightly populated region is also home to some of Ambon's most picturesque and archetypal coastal villages, where you'll find ancient forts, churches and mosques. Laha, close to the airport, is Ambon's muck-diving centre with a couple of dive operators located in the village.

◉ Sights & Activities

Mesjid Wapaue   MOSQUE
(Kaitetu) Kaitetu's pretty little wood and thatch-roofed Mesjid Wapaue was originally built in 1414 on nearby Gunung Wawane. The mosque was supposedly transferred to the present site in 1664 by 'supernatural powers'. It's reputedly the oldest mosque on Pulau Ambon still in use. Non-Muslims can visit outside prayer times.

Gereja Tua Hila   CHURCH
(Hila) This photogenic wooden, thatched-roofed Catholic church was built by the Portuguese. It's closed to the public.

Benteng Amsterdam   FORTRESS
(Hila; 20,000Rp; ⊙8am-6pm) In Hila, the 1649 Benteng Amsterdam is an impressive, old, walled fort. Though the walls are obviously rebuilt with concrete, the inner tower, with its brick floors and thick walls, is fluttering with resident swallows. Gates were open when we visited but you may have to seek out the keyholder in town.

Blue Rose Divers   DIVING
(Map p436; ☑0821 3229 0547; www.bluerose divers.com; Laha; 1 dive/gear rental 350,000/150,000Rp; ⊙Sep-Apr) Blue Rose is located in Laha on Ambon Bay, although it will still take groups to visit the coral south of Leitimur, weather and fuel surcharge permitting. It's a local operation, the cheapest way to dive Ambon's bay, as well as Pulau Tiga and the WWII wreck off Waiame.

Critter Junkies   DIVING
(Map p436; ☑0812 3871 9813; https://critter junkies.com; Laha; 1 dive incl equipment 450,000Rp; ⊙Sep-May) With perhaps the Bay's best dive site on its doorstep, this established operator (formerly Dive Bluemotion) couldn't be closer to the action. Rates include equipment and the more you dive, the less you pay.

🛏 Sleeping

Momoa Michael Guesthouse   HOMESTAY $
(Map p436; ☑0813 4302 8872; erenst_michael@ yahoo.co.id; Jl Propinsi, Laha; r incl breakfast 150,000Rp; ❄🛜) Just off the main road opposite the eastern end of the airport runway and run by the supremely helpful Michael, this cosy homestay offers three plain rooms with comfortable beds (one with air-con). All share a clean bathroom but there's no hot water. If you're arriving by plane, they'll pick you up.

Penginapan Patra   GUESTHOUSE $
(☑0813 4323 0559; Laha; r 150,000-300,000Rp; ⊙closed May-Aug; ❄) Hidden in quaint Laha village, the Patra has a pleasant little rear sitting area on stilts, overlooking a boat-and-mangrove-filled inlet. Rooms are old-fashioned but clean enough and the cheapest share bathrooms. They close between May and August: the diving low season.

ℹ Getting There & Away

Bemos (7000Rp) leave from Hunut to Hila and from Kota Ambon to Liliboi. To close the loop, charter an ojek from near the airport. If you're just heading to Laha, then take any Laha or Hatu-bound bemo (10,000Rp).

LEASE ISLANDS

☑0921

Pronounced 'leh-a-say', these easily accessible yet delightfully laid-back islands have a scattering of old-world villages, lovely bays, and the odd great-value beach retreat. There's also decent diving and snorkelling off Pulau Molana and Nusa Laut, two of the smaller islands of the group. Despite being only an hour by boat from Ambon, the Lease Islands feel remote and outside of the main island of Pulau Saparua, foreign tourists are rare and little English is spoken.

Lease Islands

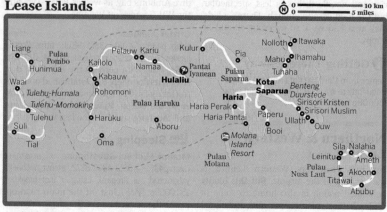

ⓘ Getting There & Away

There's a daily speedboat from Tuhelu (Ambon) to Haria, the main port on Pulau Saparua, at 9am (65,000Rp, one hour). It returns to Ambon at 7am.

Small speedboats travel between Haria and Tuhelu in Ambon throughout the day, leaving when they have six passengers (50,000Rp per person, one hour). Or you can charter the whole boat for 300,000Rp.

Pulau Saparua

The most developed of the Lease Islands, Pulau Saparua is also the only island of the group with tourist infrastructure. Blessed with good coral- and muck-diving just offshore, significant historical remains, white-sand beaches and dense forests, Saparua is only an hour by boat from Ambon.

🏃 Activities

Mahu Lodge can organise dive and snorkelling trips to spots around Pulau Saparua and the nearby islands.

Ullath in Saparua's southeast has a reasonable beach, while nearby **Ouw** has a good one and boasts a small tumbledown fort. Ouw is also famous for its elegantly simple pottery (*sempe*). None is obviously on show but any local can lead you to a workshop, where 10,000Rp to 20,000Rp is a reasonable donation to watch *ibu* throw pots in back-porch studios, serenaded by the surf. Their clay comes from Saparua's mountain, it's spun on a wheel, sculpted with a thick chunk of green papaya, and tamped at the rim with a bamboo rod.

ⓘ Getting Around

Bemos meet the speedboat when it arrives in Haria. There are fairly frequent bemos between Haria and Kota Saparua (5000Rp, 10 minutes); far less frequent bemos travel to and from Mahu (10,000Rp, 30 minutes).

Motorbikes (100,000Rp per day) can be hired at Mahu Lodge.

Kota Saparua

☏ 0931 / POP 5000

Suffused with durian musk, the jungle-island town of Kota Saparua is Pulau Saparua's 'capital'. It's a friendly place with a ramshackle charm. Jl Muka Pasar is the main drag, where you'll find guesthouses, a few *rumah makan* and the **market** (Jl Muka Pasar; ⊗ 6am-3pm).

◉ Sights

Benteng Duurstede   FORTRESS

FREE The low-walled 1676 Benteng Duurstede, famously besieged by Pattimura in 1817, has been refaced with mouldering grey concrete, but the (locked) gateway is original and the cannon-studded ramparts survey a gorgeous sweep of turquoise bay.

🛏 Sleeping

Penginapan Perdana   GUESTHOUSE $

(☏ 0931-21069; Jl Muka Pasar; r 110,000-192,500Rp; ❄) Incorporating the former Penginapan Lease Indah, the Perdana is the best choice in Kota Saparua. The more expensive rooms are clean with reasonable beds and *mandi* bathrooms. The fan-cooled cheapies out back around the garden are far less attractive. Prices include breakfast.

Penginapan Mandiri

GUESTHOUSE $

(📞 0931-21063; Jl Muka Pasar; r with fan 110,000-132,000Rp, with air-con 165,000Rp; ❄) Adjacent to the market, the Mandiri has sleepy staff and small, basic rooms with *mandi* (ladle bath) bathrooms and Disney-themed cabinets. Its greatest asset is the terrace overlooking the fort and the bay beyond.

❶ Getting There & Away

Kota Saparua's access port is Haria. From Kota Saparua, *ojek* fares include Haria (7000Rp, 10 minutes), Itawaka (20,000Rp, 30 minutes), Mahu (15,000Rp, 20 minutes), Ouw (20,000Rp, 30 minutes) and Kulur (35,000Rp, 40 minutes). Infrequent bemos run around the island from the small **terminal** (Jl Belakang) in Kota Saparua (5000Rp to 10,000Rp).

Mahu

Super-relaxed Mahu in the north of Pulau Saparua is a fine place to kick back for a few days. There's good muck-diving off the average beach here, but you're just a short boat ride from some far better stretches of sand and a number of excellent dive and snorkel spots.

Mahu Lodge

LODGE $$

(📞 0811 977 232; mahu_lodge@yahoo.com; Mahu; r with breakfast and dinner 250,000Rp; ❄ ❄) The 20-room Mahu Lodge offers sizeable, old-fashioned and clean rooms set around a fine garden with a swimming pool and hammocks to laze in while gazing out at the placid bay beyond. Genial owner Paul speaks good English and runs his own dive operation from September to April, specialising in trips to Itawaka, Nusa Laut and Pulau Molana.

❶ Getting There & Away

Infrequent bemos run to Mahu from Kota Saparua (10,000Rp, 30 minutes). An *ojek* will cost 15,000Rp.

Motorbikes (100,000Rp per day) can be hired at Mahu Lodge.

Pulau Molana

Uninhabited, roadless Pulau Molana has several great diving spots, especially at the north and south of the island. There's great swimming off soft white sand at the island's northernmost tip, while directly west a coral wall offers excellent snorkelling. There's a single resort here, but most people visit on day trips from Pulau Saparua.

★ Molana Island Resort

BUNGALOW $$$

(📞 0817 762 833; www.molanaisland.net; Pulau Molana; r 850,000-1,100,000Rp, minimum stay 3 days) This blissful island hideaway, with 11 rooms in three bungalows that only open in the dry season when guests are expected, is ideal for a small group of friends. The resort can arrange everything: meals, transfers from Haria or Ambon, boats to dive sites, while fishing trips, jungle treks and beachside barbecues are all enticing possibilities.

❶ Getting There & Away

If you're staying at the Molana Island Resort, they will pick you up at the airport in Ambon. Otherwise, access is via day trips from Pulau Saparua or Ambon. Or you can hire your own speedboat at Haria (600,000Rp return).

PULAU SERAM

📞 0914

Some Malukans call Seram 'Nusa Ina' (Mother Island), believing that all life sprang from 'Nunusaku', a mythical peak ambiguously located in the island's western mountains. Seram's mountains rise over 3000m and the wild, thickly forested and little-accessed interior of the island is home to a number of minority tribes such as the Nua-ulu (Upper River) or Alifuro people, who sport red bandanas and were headhunters as recently as the 1940s. Visiting them usually requires a serious trek into remote Manusela National Park, for which you'll need guides and

PATTIMURA

In 1817, the Dutch faced a small but emotionally charged uprising led by Thomas Matulessy, who briefly managed to gain control of Saparua's Benteng Duurstede. He killed all the fortress defenders but spared a six-year-old Dutch boy. For this 'mercy' Matulessy was popularly dubbed Pattimura ('big-hearted'). The rebels were rapidly defeated and dispatched to the gallows but have since been immortalised as symbols of anticolonial resistance. Today, their statues dot the whole of Maluku, and Pattimura even features on Indonesia's 1000Rp banknotes.

MALUKU PULAU SERAM

Pulau Seram

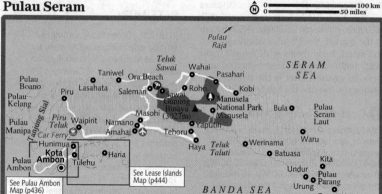

permits. Far more accessible is the beautiful and dramatic bay of Teluk Sawai on the northern coast, where white-sand beaches and decent snorkelling awaits.

Manusela National Park NATIONAL PARK
Established in 1997, this remote national park mostly attracts birdwatchers drawn by the chance to see rare parrots. Home to four villages and a number of minority peoples, the park is mountainous and covered in thick jungle. Hiking is arduous here. A guide and permits are needed to visit, which can be arranged at the tourist office in Seram's capital Masohi.

ℹ Getting There & Away
Daily speedboats connect Tulehu (Ambon) with Amahai, Seram's main port (economy/VIP 115,000/260,000Rp, 2½ hours), departing at 9am and 4pm. On Sundays, there's an extra departure at 11am. Boats return to Tulehu at 7am and 2pm.

ℹ Getting Around
Ojeks (20,000Rp) and bemos (10,000Rp) connect Amahai with Seram's capital Masohi.

From Masohi, shared Kijang taxis make the run to Sawai (100,000Rp per person, 800,000Rp charter, three to four hours) on a poor road that winds through Seram's stunning mountainous interior.

Masohi, Namano & Amahai

Masohi, the purpose-built capital of Central Maluku, is only useful to travellers as a transport interchange. The market, ATMs

and restaurants are all scattered along the main street, Jl Soulissa, which becomes Jl Martha Tiahahu as it continues 6km through Namano to Amahai.

🍴 Sleeping & Eating
Numerous cheap eateries and evening warung tents are dotted along Jl Soulissa, Masohi's main drag, especially within a block or two of the market.

Hotel Isabela HOTEL $$
(☑0914-21541; Jl Manusela 17; r with fan 165,000Rp, with air-con 250,000-350,000Rp; ❄🛜🏊) The cheapest rooms here are windowless cells, but the others are big and comfortable enough, if old-fashioned, with reasonable beds. A sizeable swimming pool, open to non-guests, is plonked in the car park. It's about 100m up a lane off the main road.

Penginapan Irene GUESTHOUSE $$
(☑0914-21238; Jl MC Tiahahu; r with fan 165,000Rp, with air-con 220,000-385,000Rp; ❄🛜) The Irene (pronounced 'ee-reh-neh') is friendly with rooms placed around a courtyard that's set back from the road. It's worth spending extra for the better rooms here: the cheaper ones come with *mandi* (ladle bath) bathrooms and bad beds. No English spoken.

ℹ Information
Central Maluku Tourist Office (Dinas Kebudayan & Parawisata; ☑0914-22429; Jl Imam Bonjol; ⊗8am-2pm Mon-Sat) The staff are friendly, but there's little information on offer in either spoken or written English. This is the

place to begin the three-stage application for permits to visit Manusela National Park.

🛈 Getting There & Away

Frequent bemos from the **Bemo Terminal** (Jl Soulissa) next to the market run to Amahai. An *ojek* is 20,000Rp.

Shared Kijang taxis for Sawai depart from Jl Soulissa, 400m north of the market on the other side of the road. You'll see the cars and drivers waiting.

Northern Seram

Seram's most accessible scenic highlight is **Teluk Sawai**, a beautiful wide bay backed by soaring cliffs and rugged, forested peaks on Seram's northern coast. Hidden from the best views by a headland, the photogenic stilt-house village of **Sawai** is a superbly relaxed place and especially magical at night when you can contemplate the moonlit sea. From Sawai, boat or kayak trips take you to offshore coral gardens, or to the nearby white-sand beach at **Ora**.

🏃 Activities

Potential snorkelling excursions include an expensive speedboat ride (2,500,000Rp, four hours) to the awesome dive and snorkel sites of **Pulau Raja** off Papua, or to Sawai's spectacular western side, where dramatic cliffs rise up above the picturesque village of **Saleman**. It's famed for flocks of bat-like Lusiala birds, which emerge at dusk.

🛏 Sleeping & Eating

There are no formal restaurants in Sawai, although a few soup and noodle stands appear in the late afternoon. Eat where you stay.

Penginapan Lisar Bahari   HOMESTAY **$$**
(📲 0821 1118 1137; Sawai; r incl meals per person 330,000Rp) Perched above the sea and linked by wooden walkways, this long-standing traveller favourite juts out over Teluk Sawai. It offers large and simple wooden rooms with OK beds and basic bathrooms. Not much English is spoken, but the staff cook great meals, offer free kayaks and can organise boat and snorkelling trips (from 350,000Rp per day).

★ Ora Beach Resort   BUNGALOW **$$$**
(📲 0812 4889 6616; www.exoticorabeach.com; Ora Beach; rooms/cottages/house 850,000/1,350,000/3,500,000Rp, meals per day 363,000Rp)

Romantically rustic cottages are stilted over the sea and enjoy fabulous bay views, but all the accommodation here shares a lovely white-sand beach backed by jungly forest. Activities include snorkelling tours to offshore islands and trips up the Salawai River into the exotic and remote Manusela National Park. Rooms can be booked through Maluku Resort & Spa (p442) in Ambon.

🛈 Getting There & Away

Shared Kijang taxis (100,000Rp per person, 800,000Rp charter, three to four hours) connect Sawai to Masohi, departing daily between 8am and 9am from the side of Sawai's mosque.

BANDA ISLANDS

🗐 0910 / POP 18,500

Combining natural beauty, a warm local heart, and a palpable and fascinating history, this remote cluster of 10 picturesque islands isn't just Maluku's choice travel destination, it's one of the best in Indonesia. Particularly impressive undersea drop-offs are vibrantly plastered with multicoloured coral gardens offering superlative snorkelling and diving. The central islands – Pulau Neira and Pulau Banda Besar (the great nutmeg island) – curl in picturesque crescents around a pocket-sized tropical Mt Fuji (Gunung Api, 656m).

Outlying Hatta, Ai and Neilaka each have undeveloped picture-postcard beaches. And Run, a gnarled limestone island sprouting with nutmeg and cloves, is one drop-dead gorgeous historical footnote. Getting to the islands takes time but with a fast-boat service from Ambon (in the dry season anyway) and talk of a new airport, Banda is becoming more accessible and seems set to see more visitors in the near future. So get here now, before everyone else does.

History

Nutmeg, once produced almost exclusively in the Banda Islands, was one of the medieval world's most expensive commodities. Its cultivation takes knowledge but minimal effort, so the drudgery of manual labour was virtually unknown in the Bandas. Food, cloth and all the necessities of life could be easily traded for spices with eager Arab, Chinese, Javanese and Bugis merchants, who queued up to do business. Things started to go wrong when the Europeans arrived;

Banda Islands

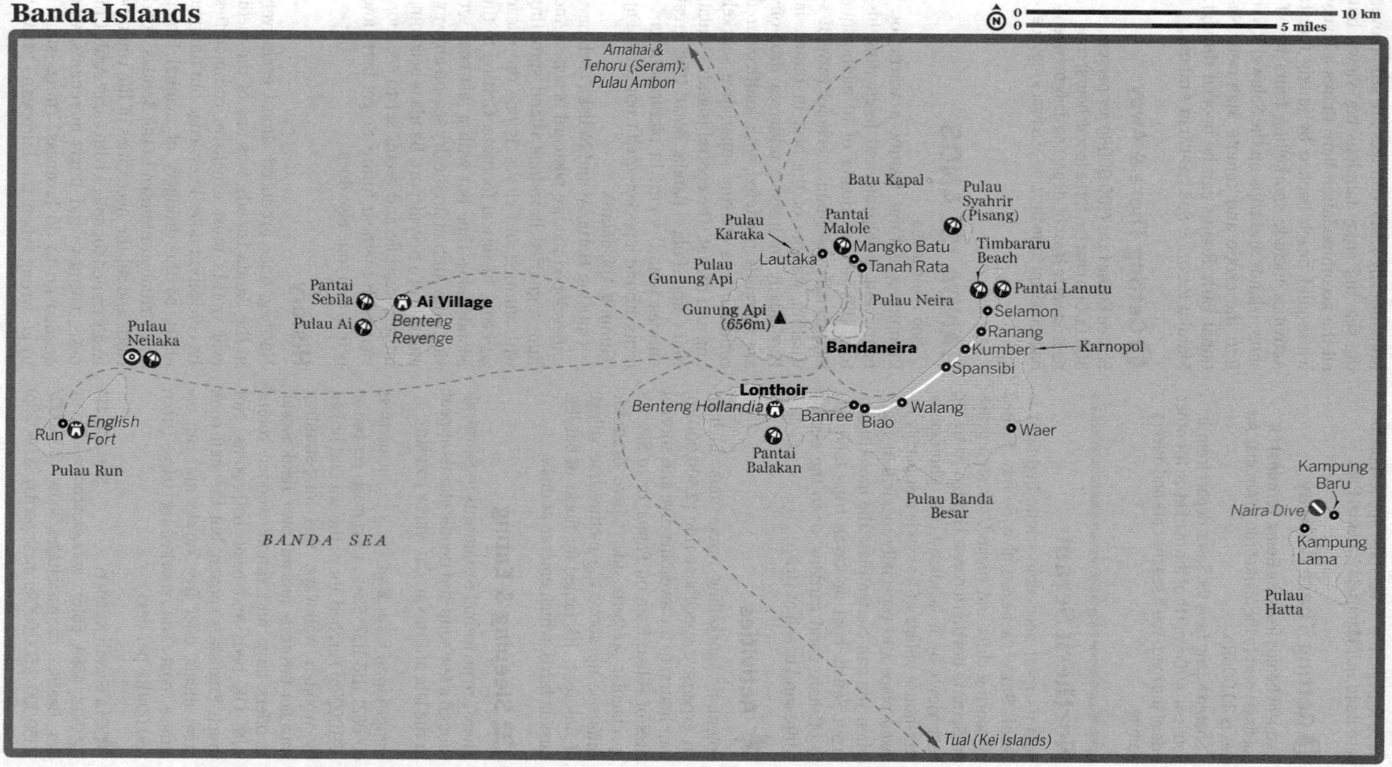

○ 0 ──── 10 km
○ 0 ──── 5 miles

Kampung Baru
Kampung Lama
Naira Dive
Pulau Hatta

Karnopol
Painai Lanutu
Selamon
Ranang
Kumber
Spansibi
Waer

Timbararu Beach
Pulau Syahrir (Pisang)
Batu Kapal
Mangko Batu
Painai Malole
Tanah Rata
Bandaneira
Pulau Neira

Walang
Pulau Banda Besar

Lautaka
Pulau Karaka
Pulau Gunung Api
Gunung Api (656m)▲

Banree Biao
Lonthoir
Painai Balakan
Benteng Hollandia

Tual (Kei Islands)

Amahal & Tehoru (Seram); Pulau Ambon

BANDA SEA

Painai Sebila
Pulau Ai
Ai Village
Benteng Revenge

English Fort
Pulau Neilaka
Run
Pulau Run

the Portuguese in 1512, then (especially) the Dutch from 1599.

These strange barbarians had no foodstuffs to trade, just knives, impractical woollens and useless trinkets of mere novelty value. So when the Dutch demanded a trade monopoly, the notion was laughable. However, since they were dangerously armed, some *orang kaya* (elders) signed a 'contract' to keep them quiet. Nobody took it at all seriously. The Dutch sailed away and were promptly forgotten. But a few years later they were back, furious to find the English merrily trading nutmeg on Pulau Run and Pulau Ai. Entrenching themselves by force, the dominant Dutch played cat and mouse with the deliberately provocative English, while trying unsuccessfully to enforce their mythical monopoly on the locals. In 1621, Jan Pieterszoon Coen, the new governor general of the VOC (Dutch East India Company), ordered the virtual genocide of the Bandanese. Just a few hundred survivors escaped to the Kei Islands.

Coen's VOC thereupon provided slaves and land grants to oddball Dutch applicants in return for a promise that they'd settle permanently in the Bandas and produce fixed-price spices exclusively for the company. These folk, known as *perkeniers* (from the Dutch word *perk,* meaning 'ground' or 'garden'), established nearly 70 plantations, mostly on Banda Besar and Ai.

This system survived for almost 200 years but corruption and mismanagement meant that the monopoly was never as profitable as it might have been. By the 1930s, the Bandas were a place of genteel exile for better-behaved anti-Dutch dissidents, including Mohammed Hatta (future Indonesian vice president) and Sutan Syahrir (later prime minister). The small school they organised while in Bandaneira inspired a whole generation of anticolonial youth.

In the 1998–99 troubles, churches were burnt and at least five people were killed at Walang including the 'last *perkenier'*, Wim van den Broeke. Most of the Christian minority fled to Seram or Ambon, but the islands rapidly returned to their delightful calm.

Sleeping

There are a steadily increasing number of guesthouses and homestays in the Banda Islands; most places are basic and functional. The vast majority are located on Ban-

SNORKELLING & DIVING

Crystal-clear seas, shallow-water drop-offs and coral gardens teeming with multicoloured reef life offer magnificently pristine diving and snorkelling off Hatta, Banda Besar and Ai. Some Bandaneira homestays rent fins and snorkels to guests (from 45,000Rp per day).

Liveaboards descend on the Bandas en route from Komodo Island to the Raja Ampat Islands. In addition to visiting all the popular dive sites around Run, Hatta, Ai and the lava flow off the coast of Pulau Gunung Api, they muck-dive the channel between Bandaneira, Api and Banda Besar.

daneira and Hatta, with far fewer options on Ai, Run and Banda Besar.

Eating

Bandaneira has a few simple restaurants and cafes. Elsewhere, you'll be eating where you stay.

Getting There & Away

AIR

At the time of research, no planes were flying into the Banda Islands. When they do, the flight takes 40 minutes. Planes book up fast and won't fly in bad weather.

SEA

The *Express Bahari 2B* fast boat leaves Tulehu (economy/VIP 410,000/650,000Rp, six to seven hours) in Ambon for Bandaneira at 9am on Tuesday and Saturday, returning at the same time on Wednesday and Sunday. The boat doesn't usually run in the rainy season, from June to August, and is prone to cancellation at other times of the year if seas are rough.

Up to four Pelni ships a month make the nine-hour journey from Ambon to Bandaneira, some travelling on to the Kei Islands and Papua.

Bandaneira

☏ 0910 / POP 9000

Bandaneira, on Pulau Neira, is the Bandas' main town and port with an engaging colonial village vibe and liveaboard dive boats moored in the harbour. In the Dutch era the *perkeniers* (spice producers) virtually bankrupted themselves maintaining a European lifestyle, even after the end of the nutmeg

Bandaneira

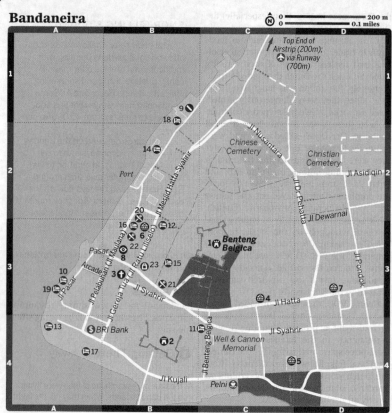

monopoly made that untenable. Today a fair amount of colonial-era architecture still lines Bandaneira's narrow, flower-filled streets. It's a charming place to wander aimlessly, admire tumbledown Dutch villas, ponder mouldering ruins and watch glorious cloudscapes over neighbouring island volcano Gunung Api.

◉ Sights

Several Dutch-era buildings have been restored. If you manage to gain access (knock and hope!), much of the fun is hearing the fascinating life stories of the septuagenarian caretakers, assuming your Bahasa Indonesia is up to the task. Donations (10,000Rp to 20,000Rp per person) are appropriate.

★ Benteng Belgica   FORTRESS
(entry by donation) A classic star fort, the Unesco-nominated Benteng Belgica was built on the hill above Benteng Nassau in 1611, when it became apparent the lower bastion

was an inadequate defence. The five massive sharp-pointed bastions were expensively crafted to deflect the cannon fire of a potential English naval bombardment. The fort is open sporadically, but guesthouses can track down the key-keeper.

Schelling House   HISTORIC BUILDING
(Jl Hatta; ⊙ by appointment) This massive columned house, owned by the daughter of the last Banda king, has a leafy courtyard, high ceilings and, in the the master bathroom, a stone tub resting against an exposed coral wall. Make sure to wander up to the special shuttered loft in the rear courtyard. The house is sometimes open for community events and exhibitions. Otherwise, look for the key-holder.

Rumah Budaya   MUSEUM
(Jl Gereja Tua; 20,000Rp; ⊙ 9am-5pm by appointment) Bandaneira's little museum displays colonial artefacts including coins, silver-

Bandaneira

ware, crockery, pipes, swords and flintlock pistols and muskets. There's also a smattering of Bandanese stuff, including the *parang* (machete) and *kapsete* (helmet) used in the *Cakalele* (the warrior dance once performed by up to 50 young males that went underground following the 1621 massacre). The caretaker Iqbal or his wife Ibu Feni have the key. They live 200m north of the museum on the same side of the street.

Hatta's House   HISTORIC BUILDING
(Jl Hatta; entry by donation) Of three early-20th-century 'exile houses' in Banda, Mohammed Hatta's house is the most appealing. It's partly furnished and photos of the dissident, his typewriter, distinctive spectacles and neatly folded suit are all on display. In the courtyard, where there are vintage clay cisterns and an old brick well sprouting with bromeliads, you'll also find a schoolhouse that Hatta founded during his exile. Ask at your guesthouse to find the key-holder.

Dutch Church   CHURCH
(Jl Gereja Tua) This restored 1852 Dutch church with a portico of four chubby columns is open for services. Inside are a decorative bell-clock and wooden pews, as well as ancient flagstones marking the deaths of former Dutch governors of the island.

Benteng Nassau   FORTRESS
Quietly crumbling among tropical foliage, Nassau was the scene of the Banda Massacre, the greatest obscenity in the violent history of Dutch Banda. The fort was built in 1609, against the wishes of the *orang kaya* (local leaders) by Dutch Admiral Verhoeff, on foundations abandoned by the Portuguese 80 years earlier.

Istana Mini   HISTORIC BUILDING
(Jl Kujali) This grand, atmospheric yet empty 1820s mansion gives a sense of the scale of the Dutch enterprise in the Banda Islands. Once the residence of the colonial governors, it's now largely neglected. You can find 19th-century plaques and a bust of Willem III in the shady courtyard. The doors at the back of the building are sometimes open, revealing a tiled floor and a sole chandelier inside.

Sun Tien Kong Chinese Temple   TEMPLE
(Jl Pelabuhan; ☺ by appointment) There are still a few Chinese families living on Bandaneira and the 300-year-old Sun Tien Kong Temple is testament to the ancient Chinese involvement in the Banda spice trade. Ask for the key at the Chinese-run grocery store almost opposite. Otherwise, the temple is open at Chinese New Year.

🏃 Activities

Dive Bluemotion   DIVING
(☑ 0812 4714 3922; www.dive-bluemotion.com; Jl Pelabuhan, Baba Lagoon Hotel; dives 550,000Rp; equipment per day 200,000Rp; snorkelling 150,000Rp; ☺ Feb-May & Sep-Dec) One of only three land-based dive operations in the Bandas, Bluemotion has well-maintained gear, two boats and fair prices (cheaper the more dives you do). Marine park fees for Ai and Hatta (50,000Rp per person) apply, and

SPOTTING MANDARIN FISH

A notable marine attraction is to spot populations of mandarin fish that emerge at dusk from rubble piles within Neira harbour. Snorkellers can find them near Vita Guesthouse, and divers can find deeper-water populations just off the Hotel Maulana, where most of the muck-diving happens. Bring underwater torches.

trips include lunch. It's closed during the unsettled months of January and from June to August.

The Nutmeg Tree   DIVING
(☑0823 9919 7798; www.divebanda.info; Jl Pelabuhan; single dive 550,000Rp, gear rental 200,000Rp; ☺Mar-Jun & Sep-Dec) This dive centre is attached to the guesthouse of the same name. All-inclusive dive and accommodation packages start at 10,600Rp for five days and equipment and boats are well-maintained.

🛏 Sleeping

Vita Guesthouse   GUESTHOUSE $
(☑0910-21332, 0812 4706 7099; Jl Pasar; d incl breakfast with fan 220,000Rp, with air-con 275,000-350,000Rp; ❀🛜) Budget-friendly Vita offers a great bayside location with seven simple but sizeable rooms set in a colonnaded L-shape around a waterfront palm garden (ideal for an evening drink, contemplating Gunung Api). The beds are adequate, and bathrooms have Western toilets and cold showers. Staff are pleasant and boat trips can be arranged.

Bintang Laut   GUESTHOUSE $
(☑0822 4830 7056; Jl Pantai Serua; r 220,000-275,000Rp; ❀🛜) The more expensive rooms have views over the harbour towards Gunung Api, but all are clean and comfortable for the price. Bathrooms are very cramped. There's a pleasant terrace for breakfast and snorkelling trips can be arranged.

Pantai Nassau Guesthouse   GUESTHOUSE $
(☑0813 4326 6771; Jl Kujali; r with fan/air-con 200,000/250,000Rp; ❀🛜) Perched on a small black-sand beach with harbour views towards Banda Besar, the four rooms at this quiet guesthouse are reasonably-sized, bright and clean. Breakfast is included in the price, but no other meals are available.

★**Cilu Bintang Estate**   BOUTIQUE HOTEL $$
(☑0813 3034 3377, 0910-21604; www.cilubintang.com; Jl Benteng Belgica; d 350,000-850,000Rp; ❀🛜) For comfort, service and value, Cilu Bintang remains head and shoulders above any other accommodation in the Banda Islands – an immaculate Dutch-colonial reproduction offering stylish, sizeable rooms with shared terraces, enticing four-poster beds and decent bathrooms. The location is convenient but serene, the on-site restaurant is the best around, and boat trips and tours can be arranged.

★**The Nutmeg Tree**   HOTEL $$
(☑8239 919 7798; www.thenutmegtree.co; Jl Pelabuhan; r 720,000Rp; ❀🛜) A rustic boutique hotel in an 1859 Dutch colonial-era house; characterful if slightly overpriced rooms come with rain showers, solid wood furniture and rugs covering the stone-flagged floors. There's a big garden with shady spots running down to the waterfront, an in-house dive operation and owner Reza is friendly.

Mutiara Guesthouse   GUESTHOUSE $$
(☑0813 3034 3377, 0910-21344; www.cilubintang.com; s/d 250,000/300,000Rp; ❀🛜) A guesthouse with a colonial homestay feel, Mutiara is owned by the same team who run the more upmarket Cilu Bintang. There's no hot water but rooms are cosy, the vibe is friendly and the front garden is a wonderful spot for an afternoon siesta, or to watch the resident cuscus, a tree-dwelling marsupial, raiding the cinnamon tree at night.

Delfika   GUESTHOUSE $$
(☑0910-21027; delfika1@yahoo.com; Jl Gereja Tua; r with fan/air-con 300,000/350,000Rp; ❀🛜) Set around a pleasant, plant-filled courtyard, the charming Delfika has a range of mostly well-renovated and large rooms, although beds can be a little creaky and bathrooms are basic. There's a bric-a-brac-stuffed sitting room and the attached cafe is one of Banda's best.

New Selecta Hotel   HOTEL $$
(☑0910-21029, 0812 4702 0529; Jl Pelabuhan; r 450,000Rp; ❀🛜) New Selecta's name is reminiscent of a bad DJ and it's an oddity in untouristy Bandaneira, offering a chain hotel-like experience with little atmosphere and generic rooms. But they are comfortable and well kept, if compact, and come with

proper showers. Rooms on the higher floors have bay views.

Delfika 2
GUESTHOUSE $$

(📱0910-21127; r 250,000-350,000Rp; ❄️🖤🛜) A guesthouse of two halves (and floors); the more modern and expensive upstairs rooms offer splendid bay and volcano views. Downstairs rooms are old-fashioned and not worth the money. It's located on a twisting alley between the market and the sea.

Hotel Maulana
HOTEL $$

(📱0910-21022; Jl Pelabuhan; r 375,000-650,000Rp, f 450,000Rp plus 10% service charge; ❄️🛜) You're paying for the prime location on the waterfront – with great views from the garden and the huge communal terrace on the upper floor – at this long-standing hotel in a dilapidated but still impressive Dutch colonial building crying out for a makeover. The rooms need updating, while the 10% service charge is cheeky given the lackadaisical staff.

🍴 Eating

At night, street vendors set up, offering pre-smoked fish on a stick, chicken *sate*, sticky rice, dried nutmeg-fruit slices and delicious *halua-kenari* (almond brittle). Most guesthouses will serve lunch and/or dinner (from 50,000Rp per person per meal) if notified in advance.

Nutmeg Cafe
INDONESIAN $

(Jl Hatta; mains 15,000-70,000Rp; ☺8am-10pm) Bolted on to a family home, sleepy and shuttered Nutmeg Cafe is a charmer. It serves noodles, juices, fish and rice, a good *soto ayam* and thick pancakes to slather with house-jarred nutmeg jam.

Rumah Makan Nusantara
INDONESIAN $

(Jl Pelabuhan; mains 25,000-35,000Rp; ☺8am-10pm) A friendly main street spot for *ikan bakar* (grilled fish), *soto ayam* (chicken soup), and rice and noodle dishes. Decent juice, coffee and cold Bintang (50,000Rp) are on offer too, making this a popular meeting place.

★ Cilu Bintang Estate
INDONESIAN $$

(📱0910-21604, 0813 3034 3377; www.cilubin-tang.com; Jl Benteng Belgica; mains 40,000-80,000Rp, buffet 100,000Rp; ☺7-9pm; 🛜) The best place to stay in Bandaneira is also a good place to eat. During high season, or when there are enough guests, there's an excellent evening buffet of spanking-fresh baked fish, soups liberally spiced with Banda nutmeg and cinnamon, curries, fritters, salads and more. But you can also order off a menu of mostly Indonesian classics.

Delfika Cafe
INDONESIAN $$

(Jl Gereja Tua; mains 25,000-75,000Rp; ☺10am-10pm; 🛜) Attached to the penginapan of the same name, Delfika serves seasonal fruit juices, delicious nutmeg-jam pancakes, *soto ayam* (chicken soup), *nasi ikan* (rice and fish) and a variety of fried noodle and vegetable dishes. Look out for local favourites such as fish in nutmeg sauce and aubergine with *kenari*-almond sauce. No alcohol.

Namasawar
INDONESIAN $$

(📱0910-21136; Jl Pelabuhan; mains 25,000-80,000Rp; ☺7am-10pm) Opening on to the courtyard of the owner's house, this reliable *rumah makan* (eating house) offers ice cream and some Western dishes, alongside well-executed Indonesian staples.

🔒 Shopping

Minimart
ALCOHOL

(Jl Gereja Tua; ☺9am-1am) Hole-in-the-wall, no-name minimart that sells beer and stays open later than most other shops in Bandaneira.

❶ Information

There's no tourist office in Bandaneira, but several guesthouses have helpful English-speaking owners and they are generally the best source of local information. Most guesthouses can arrange charter boats for snorkelling trips.

BRI Bank (Jl Kujali; ☺Mon-Fri 8am-3pm, Sat to 1pm) Has a 24-hour ATM (which only accepts MasterCard), but you can't change money here.

❶ Getting There & Away

Despite having a small airport, which is reportedly set for a major upgrade, and a fast-boat link to Ambon, getting to Bandaneira still often involves a long and uncomfortable ride on a Pelni ship.

AIR

Small propeller planes are supposed to link Bandaneira and Ambon, with the airline operating the route changing each year, but at the time of research the route wasn't being flown by any airline. When planes do fly, it's wise to book tickets well in advance. Cancellations are likely in bad weather.

BOAT

A twice-weekly fast ferry has made reaching the Bandas much easier in dry season (the service is generally suspended between June and August). But the speedboat is also sometimes out of action at other times of the year too. When operating, the *Express Bahari 2B* leaves Tulehu on Ambon for Bandaneira at 9am on Tuesday and Saturday, returning at the same time on Wednesday and Sunday (regular/VIP 410,000/650,000Rp, six hours).

You can normally count on four **Pelni** (☑ 0910-21196; www.pelni.co.id; Jl Kujali; ⊙ 8.30am-1pm & 4-6pm Mon-Sat) ships a month travelling between Ambon and Banda, a nine-hour journey in calm seas, before journeying on to the Kei and Aru islands and then Papua. Economy adult tickets are 115,000Rp. Pelni timetables (available online) change monthly. The ships are always packed and normally dirty. Beware of pickpockets at any Pelni embarkation or disembarkation.

❶ Getting Around

The island is small and walkable but *ojeks* save sweat at 3000Rp for a short trip, 10,000Rp to the airport or 15,000Rp to Pantai Malole. Cilu Bintang (p452) rents old pushbikes (50,000Rp per day). Several guesthouses offer free airport pick ups.

Typical boat-charter rates for full-day trips include snorkelling stops on Ai (500,000Rp), Hatta (600,000Rp), Karnopol and Pisang (400,000Rp), or Run (700,000Rp). Run trips normally include a stop on Ai and Neilaka as well.

Pulau Gunung Api

This impish little 656m volcano has always been a threat to Bandaneira, Banda Besar and anyone attempting to farm its fertile slopes. Its last eruption in 1988 killed three people, destroyed more than 300 houses and filled the sky with ash for days. Historically, Gunung Api's eruptions have often proven to be spookily accurate omens of approaching European invaders or traders.

The waters around Gunung Api are home to lurid purple-and-orange sea squirts, remarkably fast-growing table corals, leatherback turtles and concentrations of (mostly harmless) sea snakes. The submerged north-coast lava flows ('New Lava') are especially good for snorkelling and shallow dives.

★ Gunung Api   VOLCANO

The 656m-high still-active volcano of Gunung Api can be climbed for awesome views (especially at sunrise) in two to three hours if you are fit, but the unrelenting slope is arduous and the loose scree is dangerous on descent. Take lots of water and don't climb if it is wet. Guides (from 100,000Rp) are prepared to accompany hikers but the path up is fairly obvious. Your boatman will drop you at the start of the trail.

Allan's Bungalows   BUNGALOW $$

(☑ 0812 4706 7099; allandarman@gmail.com; Pulau Gunung Api; bungalows 250,000-350,000Rp; 🛜) Allan's has five bungalows, all jutting out over the bay and sharing a terrace. The largest and most expensive is well-suited to a family. Rooms come with comfy four-poster beds, OK bathrooms and are fan-only. It's super peaceful at night as you gaze across the bay at the lights of Bandaneira. Kayaks (50,000Rp) and snorkelling gear (45,000Rp) can be rented.

❶ Getting There & Away

No scheduled boat service connects Gunung Api and Bandaneira. Your guesthouse will act as your taxi service across the bay, or hail any passing local in a boat (5,000Rp).

BOATS FROM BANDANEIRA

DESTINATION	TYPE	FARE (RP)	DURATION (HR)	FREQUENCY
Amahai (Pulau Seram)	*kapal malolo* (cargo)	40,000	9	varies
Pulau Ai	public longboat	25,000	1	11am, 1pm daily
Pulau Ambon	Pelni	varies	9	four per month
Pulau Ambon	*kapal malolo* (cargo)	40,000	15	varies
Pulau Banda Besar	public longboat	5000	15min	when full
Pulau Run	public longboat	30,000	2	1pm daily
Tehoru (Pulau Seram)	longboat	6,000,000	4	charter
Pulau Hatta	public longboat	50,000	1½	11am

Pulau Banda Besar

The largest island of the group, hilly Banda Besar makes a great day trip and offers the chance to wander through the **Kelly Plantation**, where centuries-old, buttressed *kenari* trees tower protectively over a nutmeg grove. Banda Besar is also home to the Van den Broeke Plantation, known as the last Dutch-owned plantation in the Banda Islands until its owner was killed in the 1998–99 sectarian violence.

Most boats from Bandaneira arrive at Walang. A 25-minute walk west of Walang is Lonthoir, the largest village on the island. A long stairway from behind the Masjid Al Taqwa mosque in Lonthoir leads to the Kelly Plantation and Benteng Hollandia. In the northwest of Banda Besar, the secluded white-sand beach of Timbararu, a short walk from the village of Selamon, offers great snorkelling. There is also fine snorkelling off the east coast, although you'll need a boat to visit.

Benteng Hollandia   FORT

(Lonthoir) One of Banda's best views is from the chunky, overgrown ruins of Benteng Hollandia. Built in 1624, this was once one of the biggest Dutch fortresses in the East Indies until it was shattered by a devastating 1743 earthquake. Set high above the village of Lonthoir, make the 15-minute climb to enjoy perfect palm-framed views of Gunung Api with a magical foreground of sapphire shallows.

ℹ️ Information

Cilu Bintang (p452) on Bandaneira offers informative tours of the Kelly and Van den Broeke plantations (per person 200,000Rp, minimum four people).

ℹ️ Getting There & Around

Boats shuttle regularly from Bandaneira to several Banda Besar jetties, most frequently to Walang (per person/boat 5000/50,000Rp, 15 minutes).

Ojeks from the jetty at Walang run to Lonthoir (5000Rp) and Selamon (15,000Rp).

Pulau Hatta

A stunning flying-saucer-shaped island of jungle-swathed limestone trimmed with white sand, Pulau Hatta, once known as Rozengain, has no nutmeg. Thus its only historical relevance was a comical episode where eccentric English Captain Courthope raised a flag merely to enrage the Dutch.

These days Hatta is one of the most popular destinations in the Banda Islands, thanks to its crystal-clear waters and reefs rich with marine life. Just off the fine beach at Kampung Lama, where the island's accommodation is clustered, a natural underwater 'bridge' creates a beautiful blue hole over part of Hatta's stunning vertical drop-off. Forests of delicate soft coral alongside huge table and fern corals, clouds of reef fish and superb visibility make this Banda's top snorkelling spot. Leatherback turtles, reef sharks, trigger fish and a seemingly endless roll-call of species can easily be encountered.

🏊 Activities

Bring your own snorkelling gear if possible, as only a few places rent fins and masks.

Naira Dive   DIVING

(☑ 0813 4347 0279; www.nairadive.com; Kampung Lama; ⊙ 7am-6pm; diving Feb-May & Aug-Dec) A long-standing Banda dive shop, Naira Dive is the only dive operator based on Hatta. It leads trips to dive sites off Pulau Gunung Api and Bandaneira too. Various multiday packages are available.

🛏️ Sleeping

There's an ever-growing number of homestays on Hatta, virtually all stationed in a line on the beach at Kampung Lama. Many have just one or two rooms and almost all offer similar, basic accommodation: plain fan-only rooms with a bed and mosquito net, plus a rudimentary bathroom. Meals are included in the price.

Rozengain Vitalia
Guesthouse   GUESTHOUSE $$

(☑ 0822 4803 3199; Kampung Lama; r/bungalow incl meals 250,000/300,000Rp) The biggest guesthouse on Hatta, with seven concrete rooms, two wooden ones and a big bungalow set back from the beach, this place attracts people here for the long haul. Rooms are decent-sized, although the bathrooms are still basic. Owner Sofian speaks some English.

Homestay Sara   HOMESTAY $$

(☑ 0813 4472 3338; Kampung Lama; r incl meals 250,000Rp) Sara doesn't speak English, but she is friendly and offers big wooden rooms with attached Western toilets and *mandi* (ladle bath) bathrooms. All share a terrace looking out on the beach.

ℹ Getting There & Away

There's a 7am boat from Hatta to Bandaneira (50,000Rp, 1½ hours), which returns to Hatta at 11am.

You'll need to charter a boat (600,000Rp) for a day trip from Bandaneira.

Pulau Ai

Ai's greatest attraction is snorkelling or diving the remarkably accessible, brilliantly pristine coral drop-offs just a flipper-flap away. There's a lot to see directly in front of the village, especially in October when groups of Napoleon fish appear along with migrating dolphins and whales. Sea life is likewise impressive off Pantai Sebila, the island's best beach (a 15-minute walk west of the village), where an exceptionally stark wall, crusted with coral and laced with sea anemones, juts straight down.

Ai is essentially just an extended village interspersed with plantations. The island blipped on the global map in the 17th century, when English agents armed the locals against a 1615 Dutch attack. The islanders inflicted some 200 casualties on the astonished Dutch. Their reward was to be abandoned by the British and then massacred by the returning Dutch. Ai was subsequently repopulated with slaves and prisoners.

Benteng Revenge   FORT

Ai's four-pointed star fortress sits in the centre of the village, its walls still intact. The fort has been known as Benteng Revenge ever since the locals were slaughtered by the Dutch after siding with the British for control of the spice trade.

Ardhy Guesthouse   GUESTHOUSE $

(☑0812 4862 2559; Jl Patalima; r incl meals 150,000Rp) Simple fan-only rooms with *mandi* (ladle bath) bathrooms in a biggish house a five-minute walk east of the jetty. Look for the sign. The helpful owner speaks a little English.

★ CDS Bungalow   BUNGALOW $$

(☑0813 8198 4414; Pulau Ai; r per person/2 people incl meals 300,000/500,000Rp) To find the class crashpad on Ai, walk up from the jetty, right at the T-intersection, past the fort, then

500m further past a school and pineapple plantations. Once there, you'll find three wooden bungalows with decent beds and bathrooms and a wide veranda stilted over a secluded beach that's fine for snorkelling. Good food too. Some English spoken.

Green Coconut   GUESTHOUSE $$

(☑0812 4241 0667; ayem_nasrun@yahoo.com; Jl Patalima; r incl meals 250,000Rp) The Green Coconut has a pleasant seafront location in the village (walk east from the jetty), with a common dining room and wonderful sea views from the shared balcony (if you're lucky you'll spot Napoleon fish). Rooms are decent-sized and come with some furniture, although the beds can be lumpy.

ℹ Getting There & Away

Two or three passenger boats (25,000Rp, one hour) leave Ai for Bandaneira when full between 7am and 8am, returning between 11am and 1pm.

To make day trips from Bandaneira you'll have to charter a boat (500,000Rp). A combined charter to Ai, Run and Neilaka is 700,000Rp.

Pulau Run

Run, for all its historical gravitas, is simply a remote chunk of limestone, swathed in jungle and surrounded by deep blue sea. The village is an appealing little network of steps and concrete paths backed by vine-draped limestone cliffs, with attractive views between the tamarind trees from the top end of Jl Eldorado.

Run's main attraction is diving the wall that lies 70m to 150m off the island's northwestern coast (accessible by boat), known as **Depan Kampung** (next to the village). Visibility is magnificent.

Pulau Neilaka   ISLAND

Off the northern tip of Run are the postcard-perfect, powdery white sands of Pulau Neilaka, an islet so small you can explore it in 10 minutes, drinking in dazzlingly photogenic views of Gunung Api.

English Fort   FORT

The old English Fort (once held by Captain Courthope) perpetuated the Spice Wars and resulted in the great trade of Run for Manhattan. From the pier, walk to the main lower path, turn right, and follow the stairs up, up and up to the rough track leading to the vague, overgrown ruins.

ℹ Getting There & Away

A morning boat (30,000Rp, two hours) leaves Run at 7am for Bandaneira, returning around 1pm.

Chartering (700,000Rp return from Bandaneira) is the only way to do a day trip. You'll need a boat anyway to reach Neilaka and the offshore drop-offs, plus you can stop by Pulau Ai on your way home.

KEI ISLANDS

☑ 0916 / POP 172,100

The trump cards for the Kei Islands are kilometres of stunning white-sand beaches and a deeply hospitable population. Beneath the majority Christian facade, Kei culture is fascinatingly distinctive with three castes, holy trees, bride prices paid in *lela* (antique table cannons) and a strong belief in *sasi* (a prohibition spell). In Kei language *bokbok* means 'good', *hanarun (li)* means '(very) beautiful' and *enbal* (cassava) is a local food staple.

The driest season is September to December. While the islands are all reef-fringed, illegal fishing has affected the coral in some places.

ℹ Getting There & Away

AIR

All flights in or out of Langgur's small airport go via Ambon, Makassar or Manado. There are daily connections to Jakarta.

BOAT

Four Pelni ships a month call at the Kei Islands en route from Ambon, before travelling on to the Aru Islands and Papua.

ℹ Getting Around

A daily speedboat connects Kei Kecil and Kei Besar. To reach the other islands, you are reliant on expensive boat charters.

Tual & Langgur

Bridging the two central islands of Kei Kecil and Kei Dullah, these twin towns form the Kei Islands' commercial centre and transport gateway. Christian Langgur is marginally more relaxed, strung along broad avenues. Tual, predominantly Muslim, is home to the main port in the Kei Islands. It's a jumble of different cultures, including the

---

GO ON, TAKE NEW YORK!

After the 1616 Dutch ravaging of Ai, English forces retreated to their trading post on Run. Increasingly besieged, the same eccentric Captain Courthope who had taunted the Dutch on Hatta (formerly Rozengain), put honour above survival in a preposterously futile last stand, refusing even the most reasonable offers to leave. Somehow British sovereignty was maintained, even after the 1621 Dutch atrocities during which all of Run's nutmeg trees were systematically destroyed. The Dutch eventually took Run, so the English agreed, in 1674, to swap it for a (then equally useless) North American island. That island was Manhattan. Not a bad deal, as it turned out.

---

descendants of Arabs who migrated from the Middle East 250 years ago.

🛏 Sleeping & Eating

Langgur offers the best accommodation options for a range of budgets, although most visitors wisely head straight for the beach.

★ Grand Vilia Hotel   HOTEL $$

(Map p458; ☑ 0916-252 0035; www.grandvilia hotel.com; Jl Telaver 1; r 600,000-850,000Rp; ❄✳☎☲) By far the best hotel in Langgur, the Grand Vilia has spacious, comfortable and modern rooms with excellent beds, decent bathrooms and safety boxes. There's also a small pool and staff are efficient.

Hotel Dragon   HOTEL $$

(Map p460; ☑ 0916-22082; Jl Jenderal Sudirman 154; r 130,000-330,000Rp; ℙ✳☎) There's a languid, siesta-at-any-time-of-the-day feel to the Dragon, but that's not out of keeping with Langgur generally. There are a variety of room options at this sprawling place, ranging from clean budget singles that share squat toilets and *mandi* (ladle bath) bathrooms, to big, comfortable-enough room with hot water and Western toilets.

Hotel Suita   HOT

(Map p460; ☑ 0916-24007; suitahotel_lang ymail.com; Jl Jenderal Sudirman 99; r 35 600,000Rp; ✳☎) Behind the tiled where there's a useful travel agent a local Garuda desk, the Suita is rat' ed. Bathrooms especially are plai

Tual & Langgur

MALUKU PULAU KEI KECIL

namesake town; the trip costs 150,000Rp in a taxi or 50,000Rp by *ojek*.

All flights in and out of Langgur go via Ambon, Makassar or Manado. If you're flying to Ambon, aim for a southern window for gorgeous views of Tayando and the Bandas en route. There are daily connections to Jakarta.

BEMO (MOBIL) & OJEK

Mobil for Debut (5000Rp, one hour) and infrequent ones to Ohoidertawun, Ohoililir, and Ngur Bloat (all 5000Rp, one hour) depart from the **bemo terminal** (Map p458; Pasar Langgur) in the south of town beside Pasar Langgur. Or you can take an *ojek* (30,000Rp, 30 minutes) or taxi (150,000Rp, 20 minutes).

BOAT

Up to four **Pelni** (Map p458; ☑ 0916-22520; www.pelni.co.id; Jl Pattimura; ⊙ 8am-2pm) liners call monthly, bound for Bandaneira (12 hours), Ambon (22 hours) or east to the Aru Islands (eight hours), Kaimana (22 hours) and Fak Fak (36 hours) in Papua.

Pelni ships dock in Tual, just across the bridge from Langgur on neighbouring Pulau Dullah. An ojek from Tual to Langgur is 10,000Rp, or 40,000Rp to Pasir Panjang or Ohoidertawun.

Watdek Ferry Terminal (Off Jl Jenderal Sudirman) The daily speedboat to Pulau Kei Besar (50,000Rp, 1¼ hours) departs from here at 9am.

ⓘ Getting Around

Bemos (from 3000Rp) are common along Jl Jenderal Sudirman, mostly continuing to Tual's big Pasar Masrun market. Southbound from Tual, 'Langgur' bemos pass Hotel Vilia and terminate at Pasar Langgur.

Ojeks start at 5000Rp per ride. Savana Cottages (p461) in Ohoidertawun offers motorbike rental (semi-auto/auto 50,000/75,000Rp per day plus fuel).

Pulau Kei Kecil

Separated from neighbouring Pulau Dullah by a narrow strip of water, Kei Kecil is the most developed of the Kei Islands, with bustling Langgur as its commercial and transport hub. Kecil is also home to many of the best beaches in the island group, including Pasir Panjang and the wonderful bay of Ohoidertawun. The northwest of the island is the most touristed strip, although relatively few foreigners make it here, but new roads mean that getting to the far south and east coast – almost virgin territory for travellers – is much easier than it was.

Little English is spoken here, but the locals are overwhelmingly friendly and pleased to see visitors to their island.

★ Pantai Ngurtavur   BEACH
(Pulau Waha) The most popular Instagram and selfie destination in the Kei Islands for domestic tourists, Pantai Ngurtavur is a stunning and slender strip of sand – supposedly the longest sandbar in Indonesia – emerging out of the Banda Sea just off Pulau Waha at low tide. It's only accessible by charter boat (700,000Rp, 1½ hours), from the port of Debut on Kei Kecil's west coast.

Remember, the beach is only visible at low tide, so arrange your trip accordingly.

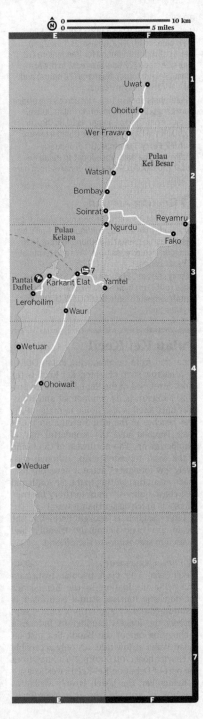

Kei Islands

reasonably sized rooms are light and the beds are OK.

Warung Saraba SEAFOOD $
(Map p460; beside Watdek Bridge; mains 20,000-40,000Rp, fish by weight; ☺11am-2am) This local institution is a no-frills wooden hut perched above the water. The service isn't great, but you can't go wrong with the grilled or fried fish. Choose from the fresh catch (prices by weight). Look for the ramshackle green building by the bridge that connects Langgur to Tual.

🛍 Shopping

Gota DEPARTMENT STORE
(Map p460; Jl Jenderal Sudirman; ☺9am-10pm) The biggest supermarket and department store (second floor) in Langgur. Stock up on packaged food, fruit, cheap clothes and phone accessories.

ℹ Information

BNI Bank (Bank Negara Indonesia; Map p458; Jl Dr Laimena; ☺8am-3pm Mon-Fri, to 1pm Sat) Has the only official currency exchange (poor rates) and an ATM. Also has ATMs (Jl Jenderal Sudirman) in Langgur.

Tourist Office (Dinas Parawisata; Map p458; ☎0813 4331 2704; Jl Hotel Langgur; ☺8am-2.30pm Mon-Sat) The helpful staff will track down their boss Vicky, who speaks good English and is a great source of local information.

ℹ Getting There & Away

AIR

The only airport in the Kei Islands is called 'Langgur' and is a 30-minute drive south of its

MALUKU TUAL & LANGGUR

Kei Islands

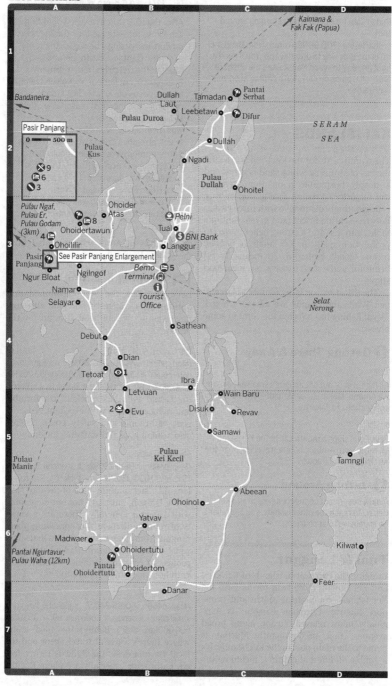

Kaimana &
Fak Fak (Papua)

Bandaneira

Pasir Panjang

0 — 500 m

9
6
3

Pulau
Kus

Dullah
Laut
Tamadan
Pantai
Serbat
Leebetawi
Difur
Pulau Duroa
Dullah
SERAM
SEA
Ngadi
Pulau
Dullah
Ohoitel

Pulau Ngaf,
Pulau Er,
Pulau Godam
(3km)
Ohoider
Atas
Pelni
7
8
Ohoidertawun
Tual
4
BNI Bank
Ohoililir
Langgur
Pasir
Panjang
See Pasir Panjang Enlargement
Ngilngof
Bemo
Terminal
5
Ngur Bloat
Namar
Tourist
Office
Selayar
Selat
Nerong
Sathean

Debut
Dian

Tetoat
1
Ibra
Letvuan
Wain Baru
2
Evu
Disuk
Revav
Samawi
Pulau
Kei Kecil
Tamngil
Pulau
Manir
Abeean
Ohoinol
Yatvav
Madwaer
Kilwat
Ohoidertutu
Pantai Ngurtavur;
Pulau Waha (12km)
Pantai
Ohoidertutu
Ohoidertom
Feer
Danar

❶ Getting There & Away

A morning boat (30,000Rp, two hours) leaves Run at 7am for Bandaneira, returning around 1pm.

Chartering (700,000Rp return from Bandaneira) is the only way to do a day trip. You'll need a boat anyway to reach Neilaka and the offshore drop-offs, plus you can stop by Pulau Ai on your way home.

KEI ISLANDS

☑ 0916 / POP 172,100

The trump cards for the Kei Islands are kilometres of stunning white-sand beaches and a deeply hospitable population. Beneath the majority Christian facade, Kei culture is fascinatingly distinctive with three castes, holy trees, bride prices paid in *lela* (antique table cannons) and a strong belief in *sasi* (a prohibition spell). In Kei language *bokbok* means 'good', *hanarun (li)* means '(very) beautiful' and *enbal* (cassava) is a local food staple.

The driest season is September to December. While the islands are all reef-fringed, illegal fishing has affected the coral in some places.

❶ Getting There & Away

AIR

All flights in or out of Langgur's small airport go via Ambon, Makassar or Manado. There are daily connections to Jakarta.

BOAT

Four Pelni ships a month call at the Kei Islands en route from Ambon, before travelling on to the Aru Islands and Papua.

❶ Getting Around

A daily speedboat connects Kei Kecil and Kei Besar. To reach the other islands, you are reliant on expensive boat charters.

Tual & Langgur

Bridging the two central islands of Kei Kecil and Kei Dullah, these twin towns form the Kei Islands' commercial centre and transport gateway. Christian Langgur is marginally more relaxed, strung along broad avenues. Tual, predominantly Muslim, is home to the main port in the Kei Islands. It's a jumble of different cultures, including the

---

GO ON, TAKE NEW YORK!

After the 1616 Dutch ravaging of Ai, English forces retreated to their trading post on Run. Increasingly besieged, the same eccentric Captain Courthope who had taunted the Dutch on Hatta (formerly Rozengain), put honour above survival in a preposterously futile last stand, refusing even the most reasonable offers to leave. Somehow British sovereignty was maintained, even after the 1621 Dutch atrocities during which all of Run's nutmeg trees were systematically destroyed. The Dutch eventually took Run, so the English agreed, in 1674, to swap it for a (then equally useless) North American island. That island was Manhattan. Not a bad deal, as it turned out.

---

descendants of Arabs who migrated from the Middle East 250 years ago.

🛏 Sleeping & Eating

Langgur offers the best accommodation options for a range of budgets, although most visitors wisely head straight for the beach.

★**Grand Vilia Hotel**　　　　　HOTEL $$
(Map p458; ☑ 0916-252 0035; www.grandvilia hotel.com; Jl Telaver 1; r 600,000-850,000Rp; ❄ ❋ 🛜 ☁) By far the best hotel in Langgur, the Grand Vilia has spacious, comfortable and modern rooms with excellent beds, decent bathrooms and safety boxes. There's also a small pool and staff are efficient.

Hotel Dragon　　　　　　　HOTEL $$
(Map p460; ☑ 0916-22082; Jl Jenderal Sudirman 154; r 130,000-330,000Rp; P ❋ 🛜) There's a languid, siesta-at-any-time-of-the-day feel to the Dragon, but that's not out of keeping with Langgur generally. There are a variety of room options at this sprawling place, ranging from clean budget singles that share squat toilets and *mandi* (ladle bath) bathrooms, to big, comfortable-enough rooms with hot water and Western toilets.

Hotel Suita　　　　　　　　HOTEL $$
(Map p460; ☑ 0916-24007; suitahotel_langgur@ ymail.com; Jl Jenderal Sudirman 99; r 355,000-600,000Rp; ❋ 🛜) Behind the tiled lobby, where there's a useful travel agent and the local Garuda desk, the Suita is rather faded. Bathrooms especially are plain. But the

Enterprising locals on Pulau Waha may try and charge you a 200,000Rp 'tax' for your presence on their sand.

Meti Kei Festival CULTURAL
(Pasir Panjang, Pulau Kei Cecil; ☉ Oct) Held every October, Meti Kei festival celebrates a natural phenomenon where the tide recedes way off Kei Kecil for a few weeks a year, sometimes up to 5km or more offshore. The locals celebrate on Pasir Panjang and other beaches with an orgy of fishing, using spears or traditional 'nets' made of coconut palm leaves to sweep in the fish.

Getting Around

Infrequent bemos (from 5000Rp) run from Langgur's bemo terminal to points around Kei Kecil. *Ojeks* are the easiest way to get around and cost 150,000Rp per day to hire.

Ohoidertawun

The charming village of Ohoidertawun sits by a lovely bay that at low tide becomes a vast, white-sand tidal flat where craftspeople sit in the palm shade carving out canoes. A **holy tree** on the waterfront beside Savana Cottages is believed to enforce peace or bind relationships. A footpath and stairway leads north to **Ohoider Atas** village. At low tide you can splash across the sand flats past small caves cut in the limestone cliffs (some contain human bones). After around 25 minutes you'll begin to notice the mysterious red-and-orange petroglyphs painted on the cliff faces.

Activities

Guesthouses can organise snorkelling trips to the nearby, coral-rich reefs of Pulau Ngaf, Pulau Er and Pulau Godam (700,000Rp per day).

Snorkelling gear can be rented (50,000Rp per day) and motorbikes can be hired (semi-auto/auto 50,000/75,000Rp per day).

Sleeping

Savana Cottages BUNGALOW $
(Map p458; ☑ 0813 4308 3856; Ohoidertawun; r 225,000Rp, meals 170,000Rp) For pure soporific serenity, few budget guesthouses in Indonesia can beat Savana Cottages. Watch the swooping curlews and the tide retreating in the moonlight, while sipping an ice-cold beer or swinging from the hammock between sighing casuarina. Four simple, compact, fan-only, bamboo-and-wood rooms

share *mandi* (ladle bath) bathrooms. Owners Lucy and Gerson are charming and helpful. Dinner is excellent.

Getting There & Away

Infrequent bemos run from the village to Langgur (5000Rp).

An *ojek* to/from Langgur should cost 30,000Rp (30 minutes). An *ojek* to Pasir Panjang is 15,000Rp.

Pasir Panjang

The Kei Islands' most famous tourist draw is Pasir Panjang, 3km of highly photogenic white sand so powdery it feels like flour, fringed with swaying coconut palms. Despite its beauty, the beach is often quiet, except on local holidays and weekends when karaoke outfits crank up the volume near the beach's access points: Ngur Bloat (south) and Ohoililir (north).

Like many beaches on Kei Kecil, Pasir Panjang is very shallow. At low tide, the water recedes a long way. Snorkellers will find more joy at the reefs of the nearby islands.

Activities

The nearby islands of Pulau Ngaf, Pulau Er and Pulau Godam offer fine snorkelling and

SASI SAVVY

Call it 'magic' or 'earth knowledge', Maluku experiences many hidden undercurrents of almost voodoo-esque beliefs, beautifully described in Lyall Watson's book *Gifts of Unexpected Things*. One such belief still widely prevalent is *sasi*, a kind of 'prohibition spell' used to protect property and prevent trespass. Physically the only barrier is a *janur* palm frond. But few would dare to break a *sasi* for fear of unknown 'effects'. For countless generations *sasi* have prevented the theft of coconuts and ensured that fish aren't caught during the breeding season. However, in 2003 some cunning Kei Islanders put a *sasi* on the Tual–Langgur bridge. With the bridge off limits the boatmen made hay, until the authorities finally stumped up the cash for a *sasi*-removal ceremony. Other jokers made a *sasi* across the access route to Tual's government offices so employees couldn't get to work.

MALUKU PULAU KEI KECIL

PULAU TANIMBAR KEI

A series of outlying islands with lovely beaches and turquoise waters surrounds Kei Kecil, the most intriguing of which is Pulau Tanimbar Kei, southwest of Ohoidertutu. The island is famed for its traditional village, powdery sand and magnificent snorkelling. There's no tourist infrastructure but the locals here are friendly and welcoming.

Upon arrival, visit the *kepala desa* (village head) to arrange a homestay. Expect to pay 200,000Rp or more for full board.

The only way to get to Tanimbar Kei is by chartering your own speedboat from Langgur or Debut (2,000,000Rp round trip, two hours), or with local villagers who come to Langgur to shop. Their powered canoes are the cheaper (50,000Rp, three hours) option. However, you may have to wait a few days for a ride back.

diving. Guesthouses can arrange charter boats (700,000Rp per day), but bring your own gear.

Kei Pirate Divers
DIVING

(Map p458; ☑ 0813 3951 7790; www.kei-pirate-divers.com; Ngur Bloat; 2 dives inc equipment rental 1,450,000Rp; ⊙ 7am-5pm) The only dive operator based in the Kei Islands, Kei Pirate Divers is German-run and gets good feedback, taking small groups to dive sites around Kei Kecil and Kei Besar. They're open year-round.

🛏 Sleeping & Eating

A growing number of guesthouses can be found at the Ngur Bloat end of the beach. Most are simple, fan-only places but almost all have wi-fi (there's no phone signal at Pasir Panjang).

Johanna Cottage
GUESTHOUSE $$

(Map p458; ☑ 0822 382 4447; Ngur Bloat; r 250,000Rp, meals 50,000Rp; 🛜) Friendly and sweet Johanna offers two simple but spotless rooms with fans, OK beds and reasonable bathrooms, both with terraces directly overlooking the far southern end of the beach. Her cottage is popular, so call ahead.

Coaster Cottages
GUESTHOUSE $$

(Map p458; ☑ 0813 4347 2978; bob.ayz@yahoo.co.id; Ohoililir; old/new r 165,000/250,000Rp, cottage/villa 350,000/800,000Rp, meals per day 125,000Rp) At the beach's reputedly haunted and much quieter northern end, 700m beyond Ohoililir village, Coaster Cottages is a wi-fi–less retreat with a variety of rooms. All are spacious with high ceilings, if plain and sometimes a little musty. The cottage and villa make sense for groups. Affable owner Bob speaks good English and can arrange boat trips.

Evalin
INDONESIAN $$

(Map p458; Ngur Bloat; mains 35,000-100,000Rp; ⊙ 8am-10pm; 🛜) Pasir Panjang's only genuine restaurant is set back from the Ngur Bloat end of the beach. Unpretentious Evalin specialises in fish, grilled or fried, as well as chicken, rice and noodle dishes and breakfast. There's outdoor seating and they serve beer too. Get here earlyish, as they have been known to run out of food at busy times.

ⓘ Getting There & Away

Infrequent bemos (5000Rp) run to the bemo terminal (p460) in Langgur.

An *ojek* to/from Langgur costs 30,000Rp (30 minutes).

Southern Kei Kecil

Despite its relative proximity to Langgur, you may be surprised by just how remote the far south of Kei Kecil feels. The only way down here is by *ojek* or rented motorbike, but if you make the journey there are caves, freshwater springs and stunning beaches to enjoy, as well as villages that hardly see foreigners. Folks will be joyfully surprised at your presence.

◉ Sights & Activities

Pantai Ohoidertutu
BEACH

(Map p458) Down at the island's cape, you'll discover an absolutely magnificent sweep of powdery white sand known as Pantai Ohoidertutu. You'll likely have it all to yourself, unless it is a holiday or weekend.

Goa Hawang Caves
CAVE

(Map p458; 10,000Rp; ⊙ 8am-6pm) Off the road to Letvuan are these striking limestone grottoes with luminous blue water that's great to swim in, plus resident bats and big spiders. The caves can get crowded at weekends.

Evu Freshwater Pool SWIMMING
(Map p458; Evu; 20,000Rp; ☺6am-6pm) This outdoor swimming pool is filled with clean, cool water from mountain springs that also supply water to Langgur. It's a popular spot at weekends.

🛏 Sleeping

There are no hotels or guesthouses in southern Kei Kecil, but it's an easy day trip from Langgur or Pasir Panjang. If you are stuck overnight, ask the local village chief if he can arrange a homestay.

❶ Getting There & Away

The only way to travel to the far south of Kei Kecil is by ojek (150,000Rp round trip) or rented motorbike. Roads have improved but can be rough in places.

Pulau Kei Besar

Scenic Kei Besar is a long ridge of lush, steep, forested hills edged with remote, traditional villages and a few white-sand beaches (better for taking photos than for swimming). Roads are very poor – no more than dirt trails in places – and outside of a handful of places in the main village of Elat there are no guesthouses or restaurants. Expect intense curiosity from locals and take your best *kamus* (dictionary) as nobody speaks English.

◎ Sights & Activities

Easy *ojek* excursions from Elat include picturesque Yamtel village (4km east), Waur (4km south), or the charming west-coast villages of Ngurdu (3km), Soinrat (4km), Bombay (7km) and Watsin (8km), all with bay views, stone stairways and rocky terraces.

The east coast has attractive tidal rock pools but no beaches. Villages are comparatively isolated, steeped in superstitious traditions, and locals tend to speak the local Kei language rather than Bahasa Indonesia. Banda Ely is the extreme northeast in a settlement founded by Bandanese refugees from Dutch atrocities. Its predominantly Muslim people preserve their Bandanese culture.

There are lots of big fish to be seen diving off Kei Besar's far southern tip but strong currents mean the area is for experienced divers only. Kei Pirate Divers on Kei Kecil can organise day trips.

Pantai Daftel BEACH
(Map p458) Southwest of Elat, a lane through palm fronds and bougainvillea leads 6km to Pantai Daftel, 1.8km of shallow and slender white-sand beach that stretches all the way to the village of Lerohoilim. An *ojek* from Elat to Pantai Daftel costs 20,000Rp.

🛏 Sleeping

Penginapan Sanohi GUESTHOUSE $
(Map p458; Elat; r 150,000Rp) There's one fan-only room with a shared bathroom at this no-sign place on the road from the jetty and just before the mosque in Elat. Look for the downstairs restaurant (which serves tasty chicken).

❶ Getting There & Away

A daily speedboat leaves Elat at 2pm for Waldek in Langgur (50,000Rp, 1¼ hours), returning to Elat at 9am. En route notice the *bagang* (fishing platforms) sitting above the sea like giant wooden spiders.

Ojeks meet the speedboat at Elat.

AT A GLANCE

POPULATION
3.37 million

HIGHEST PEAKS
Carstensz Pyramid
(p496), Gunung
Trikora (p496)

BEST DIVE SITE
Sauwandarek Jetty
(p475)

BEST BEACHES
Padaido Islands
(p495)

**BEST FOR
SEAFOOD**
Resto & Cafe Rumah
Laut (p487)

WHEN TO GO
Apr–Dec
Generally benign
weather in the
Baliem Valley.

Aug
With the Baliem
Valley Festival comes
feasting and fun (and
inflated prices).

Oct–Mar
Ideal conditions for
marvelling at the
aquatic wonders
of the Raja Ampat
Islands.

Dani tribesperson (p501), Baliem Valley
GUDKOV ANDREY/SHUTTERSTOCK ©

Papua

Even a country as full of adventure as Indonesia has its final frontier. And here it is: Papua (formerly Irian Jaya), half of the world's second-biggest island, New Guinea. It may be the youngest part of Indonesia, but Papua's rich tribal traditions span thousands of years. This is a place where some people still hunt their food with bows and arrows. A place where roads are so scarce, that to travel between towns you often have to take to the air or the water. So unlike any other part of Indonesia, the province can feel like a different country – which is what many Papuans, who are Melanesian and ethnically distinct from other Indonesians, would prefer it to be.

Travel here is a challenge, and it's not cheap. But those who do so are awed by the charm of Papua's peoples, the resilience of its cultures and the grandeur of its dramatic landscapes and idyllic seascapes.

Papua Highlights

1 Baliem Valley (p497) Hiking among the thatched-hut villages, tribal culture and mountain grandeur.

2 Raja Ampat Islands (p473) Diving and snorkelling in the real-life tropical aquarium.

3 Korowai (p509) Hiking through steamy lowland jungle to visit the world's most accomplished tree house architects.

4 Nabire (p495) Swimming and scuba diving with whale sharks.

5 Pegunungan Arfak (p484) Hiking into the mountains in search of birds of paradise and other exotic wildlife.

6 Pulau Biak (p492) Checking out WWII sites and enjoying island life among friendly folk.

7 Wasur National Park (p507) Searching out the indigenous lowland culture and Australia-like flora and fauna.

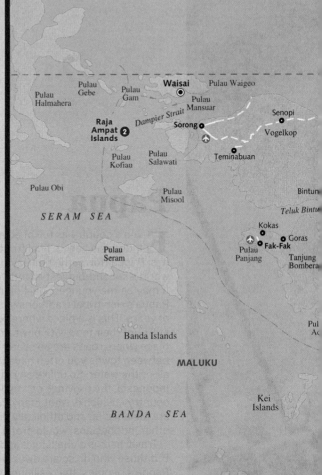

PACIFIC OCEAN

0 — 250 km
0 — 150 miles

Equator

Pulau Supiori
Yenggarbun
Pulau Numfor
Sorendiweri
Wardo
anokwari
Yemburwo
Minyambou
6 Pulau Biak
Pegunungan
Kota Biak
5 Arfak
Ransiki
Pulau Yapen
ggi
Wooi
es
Manawi
Mumi
Pulau Rumberpon
Serui
Mioswaar
Sarmi
Pulau Roon
Cenderawasih
Bay National Park
Pegunungan Cyclop
Jayapura
Wasior
Moor Islands
Danau Sentani
Sentani
Vanimo
Teluk Cenderawasih
Kali
Kali Tariku
Mamberamo
Pegunungan Foja
Arso
Sengge
Uska
Kaimana
Lobo
4 Nabire
Carstensz Pyramid
(Puncak Jaya)
(4884m)
Mulia
Taritatu
riton
Bay
Teluk
riton)
Enarotali
Ilaga
Kali
Balim
1 Baliem Valley
Kosarek
Danau Paniai
Wamena
Tembagapura
Pegunungan
Angguruk
Puncak Mandala
(4700m)
Timika
Lorentz National Park
Gunung Trikora
(4750m)
Jayawijaya
Sumo
Nalca
Langda
Dekai
Amamapare
3 Korowai
Mabul
Ewer
Asmat Region
Yanirumah
Kali Eilanden
Agats
Atsy
Senggo
Tanahmerah
Ocenep
PAPUA NEW GUINEA
Aru Islands
ARU SEA
Kepi
Kali Digul
Selat Muli
Bada
Muting
ARAFURA SEA
Pulau Yos Sudarso
Kimaam
Kali Bian
Wasur National Park
7 Sota
Merauke
Rawa Biru
Pulau Komoran

History

It's estimated that Papua has been inhabited for 30,000 or 40,000 years, but contact with the outside world was minimal until the mid-20th century. Three colonial powers agreed to divide the island of New Guinea between them in the late 19th century: Holland got the western half, and Britain and Germany got the southeastern and northeastern quarters respectively (together these two parts now comprise the country of Papua New Guinea). Dutch involvement with Papua was minimal up until WWII when Japan seized most of New Guinea in 1942. Japan was then driven out in 1944 by Allied forces under US general Douglas MacArthur.

Indonesia Takes Over

When the Netherlands withdrew from the rest of the Dutch East Indies (which became Indonesia) in 1949, it hung on to its half of New Guinea, and then began to prepare it for independence with a target date of 1970. Indonesia's President Sukarno had other ideas and in 1962 Indonesian troops began infiltrating the territory in preparation for an invasion. Under pressure from the US, which didn't want to risk a damaging defeat for its Dutch ally by the Soviet-backed Sukarno regime, the Netherlands signed the New York Agreement of 15 August 1962. Under this agreement, Papua became an Indonesian province in 1963. The Papuan people were to confirm or reject Indonesian sovereignty in a UN-supervised vote within six years. In 1969, against a background of Papuan revolt and military counter-operations that killed thousands, Indonesia decided that the sovereignty vote would involve just over 1000 selected 'representatives' of the Papuan people. Subjected to threats, the chosen few voted for integration with Indonesia in what was officially named the Act of Free Choice.

The following decades saw a steady influx of Indonesian settlers into Papua – not just officially sponsored transmigrants but also 'spontaneous' migrants in search of economic opportunity. Intermittent revolts and sporadic actions by the small, primitively armed Organisasi Papua Merdeka (Free Papua Organisation; OPM) guerrilla movement were usually followed by drastic Indonesian retaliation, which at times included bombing and strafing of Papuan villages. In the early years, Indonesia invested little in Papuans' economic or educational development, while the administration, security forces and business interests extracted resources such as oil, minerals and timber.

Papua in the 21st Century

Following the fall of the Suharto regime in 1998, the *reformasi* (reform) period in Indonesian politics led many Papuans to hope that Papuan independence might be on the cards. In June 2000 the Papua People's Congress (more than 2500 Papuan delegates meeting in Jayapura) declared that Papua no longer recognised Indonesian rule and delegated a smaller body, the Papua Council Presidium, to seek a UN-sponsored referendum on Papuan independence. But the 'Papuan Spring' was short lived. The second half of 2000 saw a big security force build up in Papua, and attacks on pro-independence demonstrators. In 2001, the Papua Council Presidium's leader Theys Eluay was murdered by Indonesian soldiers.

The year 2001 also saw the passing of a Special Autonomy charter for Papua – Jakarta's response to Papuan grievances. The major provision was to give Papua a bigger share (70% to 80%) of the tax take from its own resources, plus more money to develop education and health. But many Papuans argue that Special Autonomy has not benefited them significantly, complaining that too much of the money disappears into the hands of the bureaucracy. They also complain that non-Papuans control Papua's economy and government in their own interests, and are exploiting Papua's natural resources with minimal benefit for the native people. The Grasberg Mine, part-owned by US mining company Freeport-McMoRan and the Indonesian government, is digging the world's biggest recoverable lodes of gold and copper out of the mountains north of Timika, and using the Indonesian police and army as part of its security force, is often considered a classic symbol. Its troubled relationship with local communities has seen violence on numerous occasions, and its installations and workers have been targets of attacks usually attributed to the OPM.

Pro-independence activism and OPM activity continued in Papua in in the early 2000s, with killings, torture, rape and disappearances carried out by the Indonesian security forces reported by human-rights bodies. Papuans received jail sentences of 10 years or more for simply raising the Morning Star flag, the symbol of Papuan independence. A meeting of the Papua People's Congress in 2011 reaffirmed its independence declaration but was broken up by troops, with six people reported killed.

More recently, living standards in many of Papua's villages have risen, with the Indonesian government investing in new roads, infrastructure, schools and tourism projects to employ native Papuans. Government handouts of cash and (sometimes) rice have quieted some voices of opposition, as has hiring some former dissenters to local police forces. Still, a staggering number of Papuans express hopes to be free of Indonesian rule. Their chances of achieving it in the near future seem slim, as by some estimates, half of Papua's four million people are non-Papuans.

Culture

Papua is a land of hundreds of cultures – those of the 200-plus indigenous peoples and those of all the immigrants from other parts of Indonesia, who dominate in the cities and now make up about half of Papua's population. Relations between native Papuans and immigrants can be good on a person-to-person level but poor when it comes to group dynamics. The immigrants are predominantly Muslim, while Papuans are mostly Christian with an undercoat of traditional animism.

Indigenous Papuan culture is much more apparent in the villages than the towns. It has altered a lot under the influence of Christian missionaries and Indonesian government.

---

❶ PAPUA TRAVEL PERMIT

In the fairly recent past, visiting Papua meant filling out reams of forms and obtaining a special travel permit known as a *surat keterangan jalan* (commonly called a *surat jalan*). Recently, though, permit restrictions have been eased for many areas (though this could just as easily be reversed). At the time of research, exactly where a *surat jalan* was required seemed to depend on whom you asked. The police in Jayapura insisted one was required for almost every town and area in Papua, but the reality was that in all but the remotest areas you now very rarely get asked to produce a *surat jalan*. To be on the safe side, however, if you're heading to the Baliem Valley, Yali country, Agats and the Korowai region it's better to get one.

A *surat jalan* is usually easily obtained from the police in the capitals of Papua's 30-odd *kabupaten* (regencies). The relevant police departments are typically open from about 8am to 2pm Monday to Saturday; times and days vary, and some departments can attend to you outside their official hours. Take your passport, two passport photos, and photocopies of your passport's personal details page and your Indonesian visa. The procedure normally takes about an hour and no payment should be requested. The duration of the permit depends on how long you request and the expiry date of your visa.

Some police stations will only issue a *surat jalan* for their own regencies or limited other destinations. The best place to obtain a wide-ranging *surat jalan* is the polresta (p488) or polda (p488) in Jayapura, where you can present a list of almost every place that you intend to visit, the exception being places considered West Papua. Take care not to omit any obscure, small, off-the-beaten-track places, and you can ideally get everything included on one *surat jalan*. You might have similar luck in other relatively large cities such as Biak or Manokwari.

Once you have your *surat jalan*, make several photocopies of it. In remoter areas your hotel should report your arrival to the police and they will likely need photocopies of your passport and/or *surat jalan* to do so. In a few places you may need to report to the police yourself. Carry your *surat jalan* on out-of-town trips.

Some parts of Papua are sometimes off limits to tourists, usually because of Organisasi Papua Merdeka (Free Papua Organisation; OPM) activity. When you apply for a *surat jalan*, the police will tell you if anywhere on your itinerary is off limits.

Note: some Indonesian embassies may tell you that in order to visit Papua you must obtain a special permit from the Indonesian immigration authorities and/or the police department in Jakarta – some have even reportedly refused visas to applicants who said they planned to visit Papua. This is not true. In practice, as long as you have an Indonesian visa then you're free to travel to and around Papua (and don't worry, airlines never ask to see a *surat jalan*).

Tribal warfare, headhunting and cannibalism, practised by some tribes well into the second half of the 20th century, have all but disappeared. But reverence for ancestors and pride in cultural traditions such as dances, dress and woodcarving persist. Papuan woodcarving is prized throughout Indonesia and beyond: the Asmat and Kamoro peoples produce the most striking work.

Tribal culture varies from area to area starting with languages, of which Papua has approximately 280. Traditional housing varies with the environment – people who live close to the water often live in stilt houses, the Dani of the Baliem Valley inhabit snug, round, wood-and-thatch huts known as *honai,* and the Korowai of the southern jungles once built their homes high in trees (but have since descended to safer abodes). Gender roles remain traditional. Polygamy is still practised by some men, and women do most of the carrying as well as domestic tasks.

Wildlife

Thanks to Papua's former existence as part of the Australian continent (it was still joined to Australia 10,000 years ago), its wildlife has big differences from the rest of Indonesia. Marsupials such as tree kangaroos, wallabies, bandicoots and cuscuses dwell here, as well as echidnas, which, along with Australia's duck-billed platypuses, are the world's only egg-laying mammals.

Papua is still three-quarters covered in forest. Its diverse ecosystems range from savannahs and mangroves to rainforest, montane forest and the glaciers around 4884m Carstensz Pyramid (Puncak Jaya), the highest peak in Oceania. It's home to more than half the animal and plant species in Indonesia, including more than 190 mammals, 550 breeding birds, 2650 fish and more than 2000 types of orchid.

The megastars of the feathered tribe are the birds of paradise, whose fantastically coloured males perform weird and wonderful mating dances. Also here are large, ground-dwelling cassowaries, colourful parrots and lorikeets, unique types of kookaburra, crowned pigeons, cockatoos, hornbills, and the curious bowerbirds, whose males elaborately decorate ground-level dens in an effort to find mates.

Marine life is even more fantastic and varied, especially around the Vogelkop peninsula, where the still-being-explored seas of the Raja Ampat Islands have earned a reputation for some of the world's best scuba diving.

New species continue to be found in the sea and on land. New discoveries on and around the Vogelkop peninsula have in recent years included two new types of crayfish, at least seven new variations of fish, four new orchids and even a new bird of paradise. The bird is particularly exciting because scientists previously believed that there was just one variety of the superb bird of paradise, which puts on one of the world's most captivating – if slightly creepy – mating dances. (It spreads a black cape and hypnotically semi-circles the female.) The new species, dubbed the Vogelkop superb bird of paradise, sings slightly different songs than its cousin, and when dancing it shuffles its feet and glides rather than bending at the knee and bouncing. Over in the Misool Private Marine Reserve, a new sand perch was unearthed in 2018, and it's likely that many more creatures await discovery throughout New Guinea.

Economic developments threaten Papua's wildlife. Forests are under assault from logging (much of it illegal, with the timber smuggled out to Asia), road construction, mining, transmigration settlements and burgeoning oil-palm plantations. Bird-of-paradise feathers have long been used in Papuan traditional dress, and they became so popular as European fashion accessories before WWI that the birds came close to extinction. Trade in the feathers has been illegal in Indonesia since 1990, but birds of paradise continue to be smuggled out of Papua.

👉 Tours & Guides

While travel in Papua is, in many cases, no more challenging than anywhere else in Indonesia, there are certain areas where the logistical difficulties of travel mean that it makes sense to take a guided tour. This is particularly true of the Asmat and Korowai regions, and the little-explored Mamberamo basin in the north. Guided tours are essential (given the bureaucracy involved) for mountaineers wanting to climb Papua's high peaks such as Carstensz Pyramid (Puncak Jaya) or Gunung Trikora.

Some guides and agencies offer trips in specific regions, while others bring visitors to a range of Papua destinations.

Adventure Indonesia (www.adventure indonesia.com) Top Indonesian adventure-tourism firm that does Asmat, Carstensz

Pyramid (Puncak Jaya), Korowai and Baliem Valley trips.

Antoni Sitepu (📱0812 4770 8187; www.papua jayatours.com) Based in Jayapura, Antoni has been guiding trips around Papua and beyond since 1993. He speaks excellent English and is well-versed in the ways of the local tribes in the Baliem Valley, Korowai and Yali country. Very nice guy.

PT.Ekowisata Papua Tours & Travel (📱0812 4036 4457, 0852 4494 0860; www. discoverpapua.com; ⊗8am-4pm) An efficient, well-established Biak-based agency that can set up just about any trip you want throughout Papua.

Papua Expeditions (www.papuaexpeditions. com) This ecotourism-minded, Sorong-based company specialises in birding in all the best Papuan destinations. Its website is a great resource.

❶ Getting There & Around

Although the controversial Trans-Papua Hwy is under construction, intercity roads are still a thing of the future for Papua. Boats are an option for travelling to Papua and between its coastal towns if you have enough time, or along its rivers if you have enough money. Flying is the most common way to reach Papua and to travel between its cities and towns.

AIR

To fly to Papua you must first get to Jakarta, Makassar, Denpasar, Surabaya, Manado or Ambon, then take a domestic flight. For the Baliem Valley, fly first to Jayapura and take an onward flight to Wamena from there. Jayapura is served by multiple airlines from Jakarta and Makassar, and by Garuda from Denpasar (via Timika). Jakarta–Jayapura fares start at around 1,500,000Rp one-way. For the Raja Ampat Islands, fly to nearby Sorong from Jakarta, Makassar or Manado.

Most commercial flights within Papua cost around 600,000Rp to 1,200,000Rp, plus or minus a hundred thousand or two.

Missionary airlines such as the Roman Catholic Associated Mission Aviation (AMA) do a lot of flying between small, remote airstrips. They will sometimes carry tourists if they have spare seats. Chartering a small plane for seven to 12 people is another option for routes not served by scheduled flights. Airlines servicing Papua include Batik Air (www.batikair.com), Citilink (www.citilink.co.id), Garuda Indonesia (www. garuda-indonesia.com), Lion Air (www.lionair. co.id), NAM Air (www.sriwijayaair.co.id), Sriwijaya Air (www.sriwijayaair.co.id), Susi Air (www. susiair.com; flies small planes on local routes

❶ PAPUA TRAVEL WARNING

Outbreaks of civil unrest often involve the Organisasi Papua Merdeka (Free Papua Organisation; OPM) or the Indonesian army or the police. Many of these incidents occur in remote parts of the highlands (the Carstensz Pyramid area was particularly unstable at the time of research) or around the Freeport mine near Timika, although the Baliem Valley and the Jayapura areas also see some violence.

Although foreigners are rarely targets or victims of violence in Papua, you should stay abreast of current events and ask the police if you have concerns about particular places.

within Papua), Trigana Air (www.trigana-air.com) and Wings Air (www.lionair.co.id).

BOAT

Every two weeks, five Pelni liners sail into Sorong from Maluku, Sulawesi, Kalimantan or Java, continue to Jayapura via various intermediate ports along Papua's north coast, then head back out again. There are also a few sailings connecting Agats and Merauke on Papua's south coast with Sorong and ports in Maluku. Note that these ferries are incredibly slow and often populated with shady figures and pickpockets.

Various smaller, less-comfortable passenger boats serve minor ports, offshore islands and routes on a few rivers; some have more or less fixed schedules, others don't. On routes without any public service, you can charter a boat, which might be a fast, powerful speedboat, or a *longbot* (large motorised canoe) or a *ketinting* (smaller motorised canoe; long-tail boat). Charter costs are negotiable and depend on the boat, its fuel consumption, the distance and the petrol price. Expect to pay a considerable sum, though.

WEST PAPUA

The province of West Papua chiefly comprises two large peninsulas – the Vogelkop (also known as Bird's Head, Kepala Burung and Semdoberai) and the more southerly Bomberai Peninsula – and several hundred offshore islands. The attractions here are primarily natural – above all the world-class diving and gorgeous island scenery of the Raja Ampat Islands. Sorong and Manokwari are well-provided urban bases from which to launch your explorations.

Sorong

📞 0951 / POP 219,960

Papua's second-biggest city, Sorong sits at the northwestern tip of the Bird's Head Peninsula (Kepala Burung or, in Dutch, Vogelkop). It's a busy port and base for oil and logging operations in the region and an air hub for West Papua, but few travellers hang around longer than it takes to get on a boat to the Raja Ampat Islands.

🛏 Sleeping

Waigo Splash Sorong
HOTEL $$

(📞 0951-333500, 0951-331991; Jl Yos Sudarso; d incl breakfast 485,000-600,000Rp; ❄️ 🛜) In the thick of the action facing the Tembok Berlin waterfront, Waigo offers fair-value, large and bright rooms, which have a few nice touches such as art and masks on the walls. The in-house restaurant Kuskus (mains 25,000Rp to 65,000Rp) is good value but there are other dining options nearby.

JE Meridien Hotel
HOTEL $$

(📞 0951-327999; jemeridien.sorong@yahoo.com; Jl Basuki Rahmat Km7.5; r 534,000-836,500Rp, ste from 1,009,000Rp, all incl breakfast; ❄️ 🛜) Handily located opposite the airport, the Meridien offers nicely aged, slightly old-fashioned rooms of generous proportions. Rooms come with TV and tea and coffee makers, plus you can get a free ride to the airport or the Raja Ampat ferry. The buzzing lobby has a good coffee shop and restaurant.

★ Swiss-Belhotel Sorong
BUSINESS HOTEL $$$

(📞 0951-321199; www.swiss-belhotel.com; Jl Jendral Sudirman; d incl breakfast from 800,500Rp; ❄️ 🛜 🏊) Opened in 2014, the Swiss-Belhotel is one of the swankier options in town – though if it were in Jakarta it mightn't earn its four-star status. The staff are exceptionally helpful, there's a pool and a good in-house restaurant with a spectacular buffet breakfast.

Favehotel
DESIGN HOTEL $$

(📞 0951-317 3888; www.favehotels.com; Jl Basuki Rahmat; d incl breakfast from 630,000Rp; ❄️ 🛜) Staying close to the airport isn't a bad idea in Sorong as it's still within easy reach of downtown or the harbour. This six-storey boutique hotel offers a comfortable contemporary stay with splashes of pink throughout its posh lobby, meeting rooms and 75 stylish units. A cheerful, artsy hotel restaurant, Lime Cafe, serves tasty Indonesian and international dishes.

🍴 Eating

Sorong restaurants are some of the only places to purchase alcoholic drinks in Papua, where it's generally illegal to sell or consume booze. There are a few nice restaurants on and around the waterfront Tembok Berlin (Jl Sudarso), as well as dozens of seafood stalls that set up there in the evenings.

🛍 Shopping

Misool Filling Station
CAFE $$

(📞 0813-5406 0519; Jl Basuki Rahmat; ⏰ 7am-7pm; ❄️ 🛜) Directly opposite the airport entrance, this two-storey cafe and boutique is a great place to drop in for coffee, smoothies and snacks but also to browse for last-minute Raja Ampat purchases such as dive equipment, guidebooks or flip-flops. A small percentage of the revenue goes towards protecting the surrounding coral reefs. Free wifi and tourist info, too.

FLIGHTS FROM SORONG

DESTINATION	AIRLINE	FREQUENCY
Ambon	Wings Air, Garuda, Lion Air, Sriwijaya Air, Nam Air	daily
Fak-Fak	Wings Air	3 weekly
Jakarta	Sriwijaya Air, Batik, Garuda	daily
Jayapura	Garuda, Lion Air, Sriwijaya Air, Nam Air	daily
Kaimana	Wings Air	3 weekly
Makassar	Garuda, Sriwijaya Air, Batik	daily
Manado	Garuda, Lion Air, Nam Air	daily
Manokwari	Garuda, Sriwijaya Air, Wings Air, Batik	daily
Timika	Garuda, Sriwijaya Air, Nam Air	daily

ℹ Information

There are plenty of ATMs scattered around town.

Hotels usually offer wi-fi, as does the Misool Filling Station across from the entrance to the airport.

Polresta Sorong (☑ 0951-321929, 0811 487 2016; Jl Yani I) Head to this police station, 1km west of the airport, for a *surat jalan* (travel permit). It's unlikely you'll be asked to show it in Sorong or anywhere in Raja Ampat, though.

ℹ Getting There & Away

AIR

All airlines have ticket counters at the airport.

BOAT

Pelni (☑ 0852 5500 0497; Jl Yani 13), near the western end of Jl Yani, has several ships sailing every two weeks east to Jayapura (via assorted intermediate ports, including Manokwari, Biak and Nabire) and west to ports in Maluku, Sulawesi and Java. Another ferry heads down to Agats and Merauke on Papua's south coast about every two weeks.

Boats for the Raja Ampat Islands depart regularly from **Pelabuhan Feri** (Pelabuhan Rakyat; Jl Feri, off Jl Sudirman).

ℹ Getting Around

Official airport taxis charge 100,000Rp to hotels at the western end of town; on the street outside you can charter a public *taksi* for half that or less. Catch a yellow public *taksi* (minibus; 5000Rp) going west outside the airport to Terminal Remu (600m), then change there to another for Jl Yos Sudarso. Short *ojek* (motorcycle) rides of 2km to 3km cost 15,000Rp; between the western end of town and the airport expect to pay 35,000Rp.

Raja Ampat Islands

The sparsely populated Raja Ampat Islands comprise more than 1500 islands just off Sorong. With their sublime scenery of steep, jungle-covered islands, fine white-sand beaches, hidden lagoons, spooky caves, weird mushroom-shaped islets and pellucid turquoise waters, Raja Ampat is without question one of the most beautiful island chains in the world.

Unadulterated beauty isn't the only thing drawing people here, though. Raja Ampat also has abundant wildlife, with a couple of species of birds of paradise dancing in the trees and a diversity of marine life and coral reef systems that are a diver's dream come true (and fantastic for snorkellers and kayakers, too).

So great is the quantity and variety of marine life here that scientists have described Raja Ampat as a biological hot spot and believe that the reef systems here restock reefs throughout the South Pacific and Indian Oceans.

🏃 Activities

Diving

You can get up close to huge manta rays and giant clams, gape at schools of barracuda, fusiliers or parrotfish, peer at tiny pygmy seahorses or multicoloured nudibranchs, and, with luck, encounter wobbegong and epaulette (walking) sharks. The reefs have hundreds of brilliantly coloured soft and hard corals, and the marine topography varies from vertical walls and pinnacles to reef flats and underwater ridges. To generalise, Raja Ampat is better suited to advanced divers; it's not exactly a learn-to-dive hot spot. There are, however, some dive spots and courses suitable for relative novices.

Most dives are drift dives. Beware: the currents that whip you along the edge of the reefs can be very strong. You can dive year-round, although the usually smooth seas can get rough from July to September (the Raja Ampat/Sorong area gets its heavier rain from May to October). The dive resorts generally offer packages of a week or more and focus on spots within about 10km of their resort. Some will take nonguests diving if they have places available, for around 550,000Rp per dive, plus extra for equipment rentals. Valid insurance and dive cards are required at reputable dive operators.

Many of the ever-growing number of homestays on Arborek, Pulau Kri and Pulau Gam also offer diving services, but only highly experienced divers should consider these options – the guides can be short on professional training and the equipment is sometimes subpar. We've heard numerous stories of people who've signed up to dive with a homestay and run into problems, including sickness due to poor air quality in tanks, severe cases of the bends and having to be rescued by boats from the top-end dive resorts. If you do dive with a homestay, ask to see its certification. There's a decompression chamber in Waisai, but the quality of the facility is unreliable; the nearest decent chamber is far away in Manado, in north Sulawesi.

Raja Ampat Islands

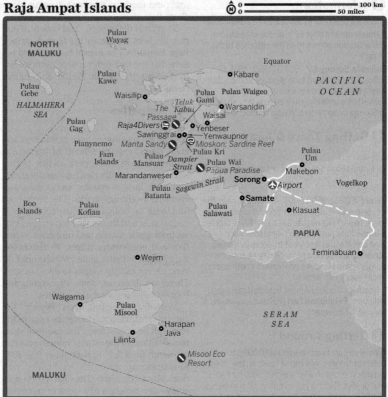

★ Wayag

ISLAND

These small, uninhabited and incredibly picturesque islands, 30km beyond Waigeo, feature heavily in Raja Ampat promotional material. It's mainly liveaboards that dive here, but Wayag also attracts nondivers for its scenery, snorkelling and the challenge of scaling its highest peak, Pindito, also known as Wayag I. A second, slightly lower peak (referred to as Wayag II) offers equally breathtaking views.

The most popular dive site in Wayag is Eagle Rock, an advanced endeavor with considerable current and frequent sightings of wobbegong sharks, sweetlips, barracudas, reef sharks and manta rays. Wayag's Gate, a less challenging site with little to no current, features awe-inspiring coral and the occasional manta ray.

An all-day speedboat round-trip from Waisai for six to 10 people usually costs between 15,000,000Rp and 20,000,000Rp.

Pianynemo

ISLAND

(Fam Islands) Often referred to as Little Wayag, this scenic overlook offers the famous striking views of the jagged Fam Islands poking out of calm, turquoise waters. Getting here is relatively cheap, fast and simple compared to Wayag, as many of the region's accommodation is within an hour or two of the site by speedboat. Also, the hike is a breeze thanks to stairs and a viewing platform. Nearby, a second, slightly more challenging climb offers views of the lovely Star Lagoon.

The hikes are just a few minutes from some top-notch undersea experiences, so visitors often dive, snorkel and scale Pianynemo all in one trip. There are also some local residents selling coconut water and oil, along with coconut crabs, which are thought to be endangered. Do not buy the crabs.

★**Sauwandarek Jetty** DIVE SITE
(Sauwandarek Village) An absolutely stunning dive and snorkel site, with water clear as quartz and an abundance of marine creatures rarely spotted elsewhere, as well as a coral restoration project. Historically, this has been a popular feeding area, and for that reason, hundreds (if not thousands) of fish congregate in and around the multi-coloured hard and soft corals, along with octopuses, massive turtles and giant clams.

At the time of research, a homestay was opening near the jetty, and it's likely to become a favourite among snorkellers.

Blue Magic DIVE SITE
The runaway favourite among local dive professionals who have seen it all, this submerged seamount teems with life, including tassled wobbegong sharks, schools of barracuda and jacks, massive manta rays and plenty of corals and smaller creatures such as pygmy seahorses. Best to dive here with stronger current and an advanced certification.

Fam Islands DIVING
Calm waters, stunning coral and masses of fish, notably at the Melissa's Garden dive site. Fam Channel, Anita's Garden and Rufus (a lovely wall dive) are also popular and teeming with undersea creatures large and small.

Mike's Point DIVE SITE
A popular and advanced dive site, just off Pulau Kerupiar. The island was mistaken for a Japanese ship during WWII and subsequently bombed, and while the damage is still visible above the water, the undersea life has burgeoned beneath. There's lots of hard and soft coral and big schools of sweet lips,

jacks and barracuda. There's also a famous overhang and a gorgonian fan garden.

Careful planning and an experienced dive masters are essential, as there can be dangerous down currents here.

Manta Sandy DIVE SITE
At this famous site between Mansuar and Arborek islands, numbers of huge manta rays, some with wingspans over 5m, wait above large coral heads to be cleaned by small wrasses. Best visited from October to April.

In recent years, the dive site has been bombarded with visitors who are not always respectful of the manta rays. As a result, visitation is now capped at 20 divers per day, and must be booked in advance. Your dive operator will handle this.

Cape Kri DIVE SITE
The fish numbers and variety at the eastern point of Pulau Kri have to be seen to be believed. A world-record 374 fish species in one dive was counted in 2012. Schools of barracuda, jacks, batfish and snapper coexist with small reef fish, rays, sharks, turtles and grouper. Beautiful coral too. Currents can be strong, so you'll need a minimum of 50 logged dives.

Sardine Reef DIVE SITE
Sardine, 4km northeast of Kri, slopes down to 33m, and has so many fish that it can get quite dark. The fish-and-coral combination is great for photographers. Currents can be strong.

Pulau Misool DIVING
This remote southern island – especially the small islands off its southeastern corner – has stunning coral. The pristine reefs attract pygmy seahorses, epaulette sharks,

---

DIVE OPERATOR CHECKLIST

Before choosing a dive operation in Raja Ampat, check that it meets the following recommended requirements.

➡ The shop employs certified dive masters and/or instructors.

➡ The condition of the rental equipment and storage facility meet your standards.

➡ The boats are in good condition and are not overloaded on dive trips.

➡ The dive shop has oxygen and first aid kits, along with staff trained in responding to emergencies.

➡ The dive shop either requires or strongly recommends that individuals carry dive insurance.

➡ The dive shop responds promptly and professionally to questions.

manta rays and a vast range of schooling fish. Liveaboards visit the region, but the easiest way to dive around Misool is to stay on the island.

A regular fast ferry run by Marina Express now services Misool, and several new homestays have opened up in the area, prompting an increase in visitors.

The Passage   DIVING
This 20m-wide channel between Waigeo and Gam is effectively a saltwater river. Its dive sites are heaven for advanced macro-enthusiasts for the nudibranchs, sponges and tunicates ('sea squirts'). Sharks, archerfish, turtles, rays and schools of bumphead parrotfish are seen here, too. Beware of crocodiles.

Teluk Kabui   DIVING
The bay between Waigeo and Gam is packed with picturesque jungle-topped limestone islets. The Batu Lima dive spot in the bay's entrance has a great variety of fish and beautiful soft corals. Schools of barracuda and wobbegong sharks tend to hang around here also.

Snorkelling
There are strong currents in some areas of the Raja Ampat Islands, but snorkellers can enjoy top dive locations including Cape

---

> ## VOLUNTEERING
>
> **Barefoot Conservation** (🚇 in the UK +44 333577 0067; www.barefootconser vation.org; Pulau Arborek; 3-week package all meals incl w/without dive certification £1595/1395) is a marine conservation volunteer program based on Pulau Arborek, involving basic accommodation and meals as well as an education in monitoring local coral reefs, with built-in scuba training and certification. Additionally, the nonprofit runs a manta ray identification program, several community development projects and a liveaboard dive boat (Ratu Laut) that takes volunteers to remote and beloved islands such as Wayag.
>
> Rooms are private or dorm-style and constructed of wood and thatch, all with shared bathrooms. Volunteering requires a minimum of three-week commitment if you are not yet scuba-certified.

Kri, Manta Sandy (although the manta rays are often a bit deep to see properly), the Fam Islands, Pulau Wai and Mioskon (10km northeast of Kri). Trips cost around 200,000Rp per person.

You can also see wonderful coral and marine life just by stepping off the beach or plopping in off the jetty in many places. The Arborkek, Yenbuba and Sauwandarek jetties are particularly rewarding. Most accommodation, including homestays, can rent or loan snorkelling gear.

Be sure to ask about potential hazards before setting out; some areas are known for their populations of large saltwater crocodiles. Also, keep in mind that as the pace of development increases around the islands, crocs may begin turning up in less expected places.

Birdwatching
The many exotic birds on the islands include two fantastically coloured endemic birds of paradise, the red and the Wilson's. The red male has a spectacular courtship dance in which he spreads his wings and shakes like a big butterfly. Village guides in Waisai and Pulau Gam provide a relatively easy way to see this, charging around 300,000Rp per person for early-morning walks to nearby display spots. More experienced birders seeking a guide with deep knowledge will want to go with Charles Roring (p485), who charges 500,000Rp per day and brings a spotting scope, field guide and sound player. Sorong-based Papua Expeditions (www.papuaexpeditions.com) also offers specialised Raja Ampat birding trips.

Island Climbing
The two most gorgeous overlooks in Raja Ampat are at Wayag (p474), and Pianynemo (p474). At both attractions, the authorities will ask to see your Raja Ampat tourist tag.

Kayaking
⭐ **Kayak4Conservation**   KAYAKING
(K4C; 🚇 0811 483 4617, 0811 485 7905; www.kayak 4conservation.com; Pulau Kri; 8-day packages per person from €1270) 🌿 Established by the forward-thinking folk at Papua Diving and the Raja Ampat Research & Conservation Centre (RARCC) on Pulau Kri, Kayak4Conservation organises exciting multi-day expeditions around the Raja Ampat Islands by kayak, staying at locally owned guesthouses and guided by a community member. There

are weekly excursions – see the website for tour dates.

🛌 Sleeping

Accommodation options in Raja Ampat are growing fast (some people worry that it's too fast and lacking regulation) and can be divided into three options: high-quality dedicated dive lodges, homestays and liveaboard dive boats. Land-based accommodation is for the most part spread across the islands of Waigeo, Kri, Arborek, Gam, Batanta, Mansuar and Misool. Kri is the most centrally located.

Upmarket dive lodges typically include stylish bungalows with private bathrooms, excellent restaurants and professional dive instruction, and they are often booked up weeks or even months in advance. They typically offer packages including 'unlimited' diving (up to four boat dives per day within about 10km, plus house-reef dives), accommodation, meals and Sorong transfers on fixed days of the week. Transfers from Waisai are also possible. More distant dives, equipment rental and transfers on nonstandard days cost extra. Most dive resorts offer cheaper rates for nondivers.

A growing number of much less expensive 'homestays' are opening up on several islands – the majority on Kri, Gam and Arborek. Few of them are actual homestays but groups of purposely built palm-thatch huts close to or even over the water. Several now have private bathrooms but most just have shared *mandi* (ladle bath).

They all offer snorkelling, birdwatching and other outings. Three (mainly fish-based) meals a day are usually part of the deal. Homestays will normally pick you up in Waisai if you contact them a day or two ahead (best by phone, SMS or WhatsApp), typically for 1,000,000Rp per boat return-trip to Kri, Gam, Arborek and increasingly more distant places. Boat outings can cost anything from 400,000Rp to 1,500,000Rp, or even more, depending how far you go.

The Waisai Tourist Information Centre (p481) connect you with homestays, or visit www.stayrajaampat.com, which lists all homestays and includes contact details, rates and reviews. A warning: tourism is a relatively new industry here, and operators often have little experience or training. Many are poor stewards of the environment, failing to manage waste sustainably and illegally hunting lobster and coconut crab to serve at mealtimes.

🛌 Pulau Kri

⭐ Yenkoranu Homestay   HOMESTAY $$
(✐Whatsapp 0821 9797 8897; https://yenkoranu.com; Pulau Kri; s/d incl meals from 500,000/800,000Rp, sea-view cottage s/d 650,000/950,000Rp) This well-run beachfront Kri homestay is halfway to being a resort, with a professional dive shop and a superb house reef burgeoning right off the jetty. A range of simple cottages all have en suite bathrooms, along with an overwater restaurant featuring cold Bintang. The operators also run a budget-friendly, Papua-owned liveaboard (p480).

Speedboat transfers to and from Waisai are 800,000Rp each way, with the cost shared among passengers.

Mangkur Kodon Homestay   HOMESTAY $$
(✐0852 4335 9154; Pulau Kri; s/d incl meals 500,000/850,000Rp) Occupying a glorious beach at the western tip of Kri, with shallow waters stretching out to Pulau Mansuar, Mangkur Kodon comprises 10 simple palm-thatch bungalows, six of them on stilts over the water. There's top-class snorkelling right out front and a couple more hut operations nearby, making this an isolated but sociable retreat.

It's on the far southwestern edge of the island, and a short walk (or wade at high tide) from the other accommodation options.

Koranu Fyak Bungalows   HOMESTAY $$
(✐0823 9740 1047; s/d incl meals 400,000/700,000Rp) This expat-managed Kri homestay understands the needs of backpackers and serves them up simple thatched huts with separate shared bathrooms lined up along a sparkly white beach. If you don't like dogs, steer clear; there are loads of them hanging around here. English and Spanish spoken.

⭐ Kri Eco Resort   RESORT $$$
(✐0811 483 4614; www.papua-diving.com; Pulau Kri; s/d 7 nights €1100/1780, with unlimited diving package from €1880/3330; ☏) 🐟 Kri Eco is the original Raja Ampat dive lodge. It's a professional operation with a gorgeous setting; baby black-tip reef sharks are frequently seen swimming in the shallows below the restaurant. Most rooms are on stilts at the edge of the crystal-clear water with onland, shared bathrooms (with *mandis* and

hot-water showers) but there are two deluxe en suite cottages.

The owner is a prominent conservationist and the resort donates 10% of the profits to local communities and sustainability initiatives. Naturally all meals are included and you can choose from unlimited diving package or paying for dives (€53) as you go.

Sorido Bay Resort
RESORT $$$

(☑0811 483 4614; www.papua-diving.com; Pulau Kri; 7-night unlimited diving package €2793-3883; ✳️🛜) 🚤 Sorido offers top diving standards along with Western-style comforts, such as air-con, camera workstations and hot showers in spacious, well-equipped beachfront bungalows. The tucked-away location fronting a divine beach is superb, and the operators are good stewards of the environment.

Owner Max Ammer pioneered diving in Raja Ampat after he stumbled upon the potential while searching the area for crashed WWII aircraft. From that you will probably quite rightly deduce that he's a real character who'll add much to your stay.

At research time he was looking to purchase the resort's first solar-powered dive boat (and later, a whole fleet of these). He was also negotiating with village elders on Kri to lease more land and keep it pristine, preventing more homestays from popping up.

🛏 Pulau Gam

Kordiris Homestay & Diving
GUESTHOUSE $$

(☑0852 4412 4338; kordirisrajaampat@gmail.com; Pulau Gam; r incl meals per person 400,000Rp) This well-organised homestay, which sits in a secluded, dreamy bay dotted with tiny coral islands, is one of the best on Pulau Gam. Rooms are made of palm thatch, and while some are in the cool shade of trees, others sit over the crystal-clear water or on the salty white sand. There's a dive centre on-site (500,000Rp per dive), but no certification program.

Mambefor Homestay
HOMESTAY $$

(☑0812 4880 9542, 0852 5453 2631; Sawinggrai Village, Pulau Gam; r incl meals per person 350,000Rp) A basic little over-water homestay right on the jetty in Sawinggrai village, with a view of surfacing marine creatures and a short walk to prime red-bird-of-paradise-watching territory. There are six rooms

with floor mattresses and shared bathrooms (squat toilet and bucket showers) 50m away. As such, a stay here is more about cultural interaction than beach lounging.

Don't expect much privacy – or much beach.

★ Raja Ampat Biodiversity
LODGE $$$

(☑0821 8922 2577; www.rajaampatbiodiversity. com; Pantai Yenanas, Pulau Gam; 7-night incl meals & 14 dives s/d from €1557/2877) Two kilometres east of Yenbeser village on Gam, Biodiversity is one of the overall best-value places to stay on the islands. Accommodations include nine spacious, comfortable cabins featuring private, beachfront pergolas with sunbeds. Good Indonesian and international food is served, and the new bar offers cocktails, wine and beer.

The dive operation is of a high standard, and PADI and SSI diving courses are offered too. During research, a massage and yoga centre were under construction. Packages shorter than a week are available, and transfers from Waisai cost €40 per person each way.

Papua Explorers Resort
RESORT $$$

(☑0822 4814 8888; www.papuaexplorers.com; 7-night dive package incl meals s/d €2865/4700, incl 3 boat dives daily & unlimited house-reef dives; ✳️🛜) One of the flashiest and biggest of the dive resorts, Papua Explorers is set in a large, pretty bay and has 15 palatial over-water bungalows. It's all very polished – maybe too much for some – and food has left some guests unimpressed. All bungalows have elegant furnishings and tribal decoration, hot-water bathrooms, terraces with easy sea access and in-room wi-fi.

Raja4Divers
RESORT $$$

(☑0811 485 7711; www.raja4divers.com; Pulau Pef; 7-night unlimited diving package s/d €3350/5200; @🛜) A classy small resort on an idyllic island beach with a reef out front, Raja4Divers sits off western Gam, giving better access to some superb dives that are beyond the normal reach of Dampier Strait resorts. The large, airy water's-edge bungalows are decked with intriguing artefacts and are as refined as they come.

There's no extra charge for distant dives here, but you do have to pay (€250 per person return) for the scheduled Sorong transfers. Rental equipment and the marine park fee aren't included either.

PROTECTING THE MARINE EPICENTRE

••••••••••••••••••••

Marine biologists consider eastern Indonesia to be the world's epicentre of marine life, and Raja Ampat – dubbed a 'species factory' by conservationists – harbours the greatest diversity of all. This includes more than 1400 reef-fish species and more than 600 hard corals (more than 75% of the world total). Ocean currents carry coral larvae from here to the Indian and Pacific Oceans to replenish other reefs.

Seven marine protected areas, covering 9000 sq km, were established in 2007 to protect Raja Ampat's reefs from threats such as cyanide and dynamite fishing, large-scale commercial fishing and the effects of mining. In 2010, the entire 50,000-sq-km Raja Ampat area was declared a shark sanctuary. This was a significant move against the practice of shark finning, which threatens numerous shark species with extinction, mainly to satisfy demand (primarily in China) for shark-fin soup. In 2014 the Indonesian government went one step further with the establishment of a nationwide ray and shark sanctuary, which means it's now illegal to hunt for rays or sharks anywhere in Indonesian waters. Most recently, turtles, Napoleon wrasse and lobsters (dependent on size) were added to the list. The problem, of course, is that Indonesia is a very watery country, hence difficult to patrol.

Responsible tourism can also play a part in the conservation effort, providing sustainable income sources for local people and funds for conservation initiatives. Foreign visitors must pay 1,000,000Rp for a tourist tag (pin/badge) to visit the islands (Indonesians pay 500,000Rp): you can get one at Waisai's Tourist Information Centre (p481). Most dive resorts and liveaboards include the tourist tag in their package rates. The money goes to conservation, community development and the Raja Ampat Tourism Department, in roughly equal shares.

Note that in recent years, many homestays have sprung up and allowed guests to slide by without paying the park fee, leading to a considerable shortfall in conservation funding. There is an ongoing discussion about enforcing steep penalties should this continue; be sure to pay the fee in Waisai and keep the tourist tag on you at all times. Also, when selecting a homestay, ask if the property uses sustainable practices in the disposal of its waste, and whether lobster or coconut crab is (illegally) served at mealtime. If you don't like the answers, continue your search.

🛏 Pulau Misool

★ Nut Tonton Homestay   HOMESTAY $$

(☑ 0852 3465 3800; nuttonton@gmail.com; Misool; r incl meals from 600,000Rp) This newer homestay in the vicinity of Pulau Misool is an absolute dream for the secluded location and setting, with six overwater bungalows backed by enormous rock formations, mere steps from the white-sand beach and coral gardens. Standard rooms have floor mattresses, mosquito nets, outdoor showers and squat toilets; deluxe rooms are larger and have flush toilets.

The homestay also offers a jetty and a long boat to whisk you around Misool's enchanting islands. The boat transfer from Misool's ferry dock to the homestay costs 350,000Rp per person each way.

Harafat Jaya Homestay   HOMESTAY $$

(☑ 0813 4435 3030; Harapan Jaya Village, Pulau Yapen; r incl meals per person 450,000Rp) This homestay was the first on the large, remote Pulau Misool (actually it's on a small offshore island, next to the village of Harapan Jaya). Other Misool homestays have since opened and eclipsed Harafat Jaya, but it's still a decent base for exploring Misool's breathtaking islands, beaches, caves and waterfalls.

Getting there either involves charting an expensive speedboat or taking scheduled, five-hour ferry rides to and from Sorong.

Misool   RESORT $$$

(www.misoolecoresort.com; Pulau Batbitim, South Raja Ampat; 7-night package with/without unlimited diving from US$2825/1045; ⊘ closed from early June to late Sept; ❋ 🛜) ✎ On a beautiful private island off southeastern Misool, this comfortable dive resort has a strong conservation and community ethos and superb dive sites within a few minutes' boat ride. Guests choose from overwater cottages in splashing distance from the reef, and secluded, beachfront villas; all with open-air

LIVEABOARDS

The ultimate Raja Ampat experience could be cruising around on a Bugis-style schooner specially kitted out for divers. Some 40-plus Indonesian- and foreign-owned liveaboards do regular one- to two-week dive cruises, usually starting and ending in Sorong. Some itineraries combine Raja Ampat with Maluku, Teluk Cenderawasih or Triton Bay (Teluk Triton) south of Kaimana. Most boats carry 12 to 16 passengers and some are luxurious, with air-conditioned cabins and en-suite bathrooms. Most cruises run between November and April, when Raja Ampat seas are calmest. It typically costs between US$300 and US$500 per person per day. A few recommended operators include:

Grand Komodo (www.grandkomodo.com) A long-running Indonesian operation, which has multiple liveaboards operating year-round and is among the least expensive.

Seven Seas (www.thesevenseas.net) The Seven Seas is probably the last word in Raja Ampat liveaboard luxury.

Shakti (www.shakti-raja-ampat.com) Well-established, quality operator.

Pindito (www.pindito.com) Beautiful boat, cruising in a beautiful place.

Ambai (www.indocruises.com) Excellent operator around Raja Ampat and elsewhere.

Samambaia (www.facebook.com/samambaialiveaboard) A magnificent *pinisi* ship with modern trappings; accommodates 14 passengers.

Those intent on spending less should look into budget liveaboard **KLM Insos Raja Ampat** (✆0813 5400 1932; 7-day cruise & dive package per person from €1500), which takes up to nine passengers (and no fewer than eight) on multiday diving trips to highly desirable, far-flung sites and islands. Barefoot Conservation (p476) also operates a lower-cost liveaboard for volunteers.

See www.cruisingindonesia.com or www.diverajaampat.org for lists of high-quality operators.

bathrooms. The resort recently celebrated its 10-year anniversary, and is wildly popular.

The place has quite an interesting backstory, as it was constructed on the site of a former shark finning camp. The owners now protect a 1220-sq-km private marine reserve in collaboration with a sister NGO organisation, Misool Foundation (www.misool foundation.org), together spearheading sustainable employment options, community education initiatives and conservation projects such as a recycling program.

Speedboat transfers from Sorong are US$335 per person.

📛 Other Islands

★ Cove Eco Resort
RESORT $$$

(✆0821 1000 8548; www.coveecoresort.com; Pulau Yeben; 7-day all-incl without/with diving package from US$1859/2483; 🛜) Centrally located from many of Raja Ampat's finest diving spots and land-based excursions, this year-old, intimate private-island resort simply has it all. Dreamy oceanfront villas? Check. Best meals in Raja Ampat? Check. Spectacular, knowledgeable staff. Check. And the ac-

tual cheque? Very reasonable, considering that boat transport and an excursion to Pianynemo and the Fam Islands are included.

Excursions to other areas such as Wayag have an additional cost, but it is divided among attending guests.

The island's perks also include private beaches and snorkelling spots, along with a hiking trail through the forest and over the top of the island. Translucent kayaks and paddleboards are free for guests, and an ideal way to visit dozens of baby sharks that live around the mangrove nursery fronting the resort. There's also a recreation area with ping pong and a pool table.

Agusta Eco Resort
RESORT $$$

(✆0821 9922-6357; www.agustaresort.com; Pulau Agusta; 7-night incl meals s/d €2180/3300; ❄🛜🏊) Tucked away on a dreamy private island, Agusta excels for its stylish beachfront villas, top-notch Italian restaurant and exceptional hospitality. The swimming pool (a rarity in Raja Ampat) comes in handy for scuba training with the resort's excellent dive operation, which zips guests around the islands to most of the area's top undersea attractions.

Unique offerings include a lovely hike to a lighthouse and night dives on a thriving reef discovered by one of the dive masters.

Dive packages begin at €550 for 11 dives (one night dive is included). Equipment rental and private divemasters cost extra. Snorkelling packages and excursions are also on offer.

Papua Paradise
RESORT $$$

(www.papuaparadise.com; Pulau Birie; 7-night unlimited diving package s/d €2282/3836; 🛜) With large, elegant over-water bungalows on a gorgeous, pristine, small island off northern Batanta, and masses of good diving nearby, this resort is among the best in Raja Ampat. It's also a good base for birdwatching (including the red and Wilson's birds of paradise) and offers PADI courses. Bonus points for the dreamy spa.

Raja Ampat Dive Lodge
RESORT $$$

(📱0812 3872 672; www.grandkomodo.com/raja-ampat-dive-lodge; Pulau Mansuar; 7-night all-incl diving package US$2,546; ⚒🛜) A recommended resort that also runs six liveaboard vessels and a resort in Komodo, all under the umbrella of Grand Komodo (www.grandkomodo.com). The beachfront lodge is beloved for its secluded locale, highly professional dive operation and wood-panelled beach villas, each with a relaxing porch overlooking the Dampier Strait.

ⓘ Getting There & Around

Waisai has an airport, but at the time of writing there were only limited-seat Susi Air flights on Monday and Friday between Sorong and Waisai.

Fast Bahari Express passenger boats (economy/VIP 100,000/215,000Rp, two hours) depart at 9am and 2pm daily for Waisai from Sorong's Pelabuhan Feri (p473). The boats head back from Waisai at 9am and 2pm as well. PT Fajar has a ferry offering the same routes at the same times.

Marina Express runs a boat service between Sorong and Misool three times a week, for 250,000Rp each way. It leaves from Sorong's Pelabuhan Feri (p473) Monday, Wednesday and Friday at noon and returns from Misool at 8am on Tuesday, Thursday and Saturday. The journey takes about five hours.

An overnight Fajar Indah boat to Waigama and Lilinta on Misool leaves at midnight on Tuesday (economy/VIP 200,000/300,000Rp) arriving in Misool on Wednesday around 9am. The boat returns Friday morning at 9am, arriving in Sorong around 5pm.

Ojeks to Pelabuhan Feri cost around 20,000Rp from the western end of Sorong or outside the airport; a taxi is around 50,000Rp. *Ojeks* between port and town in Waisai (2km) are 20,000Rp.

Other passenger boats to and around the islands are irregular. To arrange transport around the islands once there, your best bet is to ask at your accommodation or the **Waisai Tourist Information Centre** (Waisai; ⊘11am-4pm). Prices depend on boat, distance and petrol prices and are usually negotiable.

Manokwari

📞 0986 / POP 164,586

Capital of Papua Barat (West Papua) province, Manokwari sits on Teluk Cenderawasih near the northeastern corner of the Vogelkop. It merits a visit mainly for the natural attractions in the surrounding area, notably the Pegunungan Arfak. Most travellers' facilities are in the area called Kota, on the eastern side of the Teluk Sawaisu inlet. Local transport terminals and the airport (7km from town) are to the west and southwest.

◉ Sights & Activities

Pulau Mansinam
ISLAND

Two German missionaries settled on Mansinam Island off Manokwari in 1855 and became the first to spread Christianity in Papua. The picturesque, rainforest-covered island is home to a small village, a none-too-subtle church, and a wannabe Rio de Janeiro statue of Christ. There's also a pleasant beach along its western and southern shores. The coral reef off the southern end offers good snorkelling.

Outrigger **boats** (10,000Rp one way) sail to Mansinam from Kwawi, 2.5km southeast of central Manokwari, when they have enough passengers.

Pantai Pasir Putih
BEACH

About 5km southeast of town, this 600m curve of clean white sand and clear water is good for swimming, and snorkelling if you have your own gear. It's generally quiet – except on the weekends when half of Manokwari invades.

Taman Gunung Meja
WALKING

(Table Mountain Park) The protected forest makes an enjoyable walk if you start early enough to catch the birdlife and morning cool. A 1km walk up from Jl Brawijaya brings you to the white entrance gate, from

Manokwari

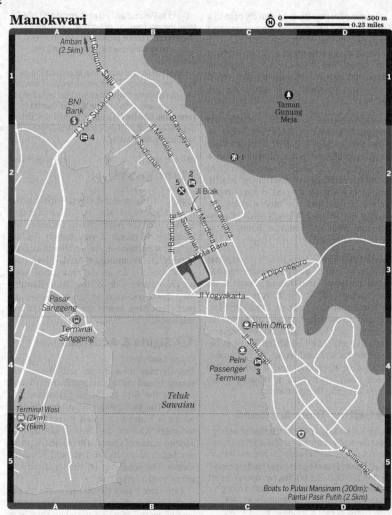

where a fairly level 3km track, mostly paved, runs north through the forest.

After 800m the **Tugu Jepang**, a Japanese WWII monument, stands 100m to the left along a branch track. From the far end of the forest track, follow the paved road 600m past houses, then go left at a T-junction. This brings you in 400m to the Manokwari–Amban road, where you can catch a *taksi* or *ojek* back to town.

🛏 Sleeping

Hotel Mangga
HOTEL $
(📞 0629-8621 1693; www.mangga-hotel.com; Jl Siliwangi 1; r from 250,000Rp; ❄) The paint

may be peeling and the furniture may hail from decades forgotten, but this old, yellow-walled hotel will suit budget back-packers just fine. The owner speaks English, the beds are comfy and rooms come with air-con and (sometimes) hot water.

The location is also a plus, as the hotel is close to the ferry terminal and is flanked by a laundry business, an internet cafe, a couple of ATMs and some seriously tasty warungs.

★ Mansinam Beach Hotel
HOTEL $$
(📞 0986-213585; www.hotelmansinambeach.com; Jl Pasir Putih 7; r incl breakfast 450,000-780,000Rp;

Manokwari

❇🛜) About 5km southeast of the city centre, this beach hotel offers the best value in town, with affordable third-storey rooms offering views of Mansinam Island. Some lower-level rooms smell a bit funky, so ask to see a few before committing. The breezy waterfront **restaurant** (Mansinam Beach Hotel; mains 75,000Rp-250,000Rp) is tops for spicy seafood.

Billy Jaya Hotel HOTEL $$
(📞0811 480 8567, 0986-215432; hotelbillyjaya@yahoo.com.sg; Jl Merdeka 57; r incl breakfast 250,000-900,000Rp; ❇🛜) The older, cheaper rooms (up to 350,000Rp) range from small and dark to large, windowed and acceptable. The newer section is much better, with shiny tiled floors and nice white bedding. The old Vespa with sidecar in the hotel lobby is an unusual talking point. The hotel offers free airport drop-offs (though, sadly, not in the Vespa).

Swiss-Belhotel BUSINESS HOTEL $$$
(📞0821 9768 2825, 0986-212999; www.swiss-belhotel.com; Jl Yos Sudarso 8; r incl breakfast from 900,000Rp; ❇🛜❄) The best hotel in town has comfy but surprisingly tired rooms, and the restaurant (mains 72,000Rp to 300,000Rp) provides a wide range of Asian dishes, plus steaks. It's not deserving of its four stars.

🍴 Eating

⭐ **Billy Cafe & Tuna House** SEAFOOD $
(📞0986-211036; Jl Merdeka 57; mains 30,000-60,000Rp; ⊙8am-9pm) Visitors enter this Disney-esque seafood spot through the toothy mouth of a giant shark replica, and the dining room is adorned in big fake trees and real aquariums populated with a diverse array of aquatic life. It's unclear if any of those fish are on the menu, but there are definitely some tasty seafood dishes. Kids will adore the place.

Rumah Makan Salam Manis INDONESIAN $
(Jl Merdeka; mains 20,000-40,000Rp; ⊙9am-10pm) Renowned far and wide for its *nasi ayam panggang lalapan* (grilled chicken with green vegetables and rice), this two-storey place is an excellent choice for a communal meal while sat cross-legged at low tables surrounded by pot plants on the second floor. Very popular with locals.

ℹ Information

BNI Bank (Jl Yos Sudarso) With ATM.
Police Station (Jl Bhayangkhara; ⊙9am-5pm) You can get your *surat jalan* here, but it's not usually necessary in the region. It's 1km southeast of the port.

ℹ Getting There & Away

Tickets for the small planes of Susi Air (www.susiair.com) are only sold at the airport, 6km southwest of town. The office is open 9am-5pm.

Every two weeks **Pelni** (📞0986-215167; Jl Siliwangi 24) has several sailings from its **passenger terminal** to Jayapura, Sorong, Makassar and Nabire, with less frequent departures for Biak, Ternate, Ambon and Banda. Once a week, ASDP Indonesia Ferry also offers sailings to Biak and Nabire (via Wasior).

FLIGHTS FROM MANOKWARI

DESTINATION	AIRLINE	FREQUENCY
Ambon	Wings Air, Garuda	3 weekly
Biak	Garuda, Susi Air, Sriwijaya Air	daily
Jakarta	Garuda, Sriwijaya Air	daily
Jayapura	Garuda, Sriwijaya Air	daily
Kaimana	Wings Air	3 weekly
Makassar	Garuda (not direct), Sriwijaya Air	daily
Sorong	Sriwijaya Air, Garuda	daily

OFF THE BEATEN TRACK

TRITON BAY

A few years back, word got out that the undersea ecosystems of Triton Bay (Teluk Triton) might be more impressive than those of Raja Ampat. That's still up for debate, but certainly the wealth of marine life here is extraordinary.

Of the many highlights are pygmy seahorses, Nursalim flasher wrasse, Triton Bay walking sharks, wobbegong sharks, big pods of dolphins, marlin, groupers, sweetlips, large schools of fusiliers and surgeonfish and arguably the most spectacular soft corals in the world. And if all that weren't enough, there's also the big daddy of them all, whale sharks, which are attracted to the fishing *bagang* (platform).

There are now more than 30 identified dive sites ranging from pinnacles to shallow soft-coral gardens and drift and wall dives. The one downside is that average visibility ranges from 8m to 10m, though it can be up to 25m or as little as 5m.

Very few people have had the opportunity to dive here, and only the occasional liveaboard boat comes through. But with the 2015 opening of **Triton Bay Divers** (www.tritonbaydivers.com; Aiduma Island; 7-nights full board incl 15 dives €2090 per person; ⊙ closed Jun–mid-Sep), the first resort in the area, the reefs became easier to access. The resort is set on Aiduma Island, with just six elegant wooden cottages on a beautiful white sand beach. A full board of Asian and international meals is provided to guests.

Access to Triton Bay is via Kaimana. Wings Air (www.lionair.co.id) connects Kaimana with Sorong, and Garuda flies there from Ambon six days a week.

Upon arrival in Kaimana, Triton Bay Divers retrieves guests in a speedboat and transfers them to the island resort. The ride takes around two hours and is free on Saturdays. Otherwise it costs €165 per boat (with a maximum of five people).

❶ Getting Around

Airport taxis to town cost 100,000Rp. Some public *taksi* (5000Rp) pass the airport, bound for **Terminal Wosi** (Jl Pasir), halfway to the centre. At Wosi you might find another *taksi* direct to Kota (5000Rp); otherwise get one to **Terminal Sanggeng**, then another (or walk) to Kota. Terminal Sanggeng is the starting point for very frequent public *taksi* running through Kota and out to Kwawi and Pantai Pasir Putih.

Traveling by *ojek* in town costs 10,000Rp per ride. From the city to the airport it's around 20,000Rp.

Around Manokwari

Several interesting places around Manokwari are best visited on multiday trips.

Pegunungan Arfak

The thickly forested Arfak Mountains, rising to more than 2800m south of Manokwari, are a region of beautiful tropical scenery, exotic wildlife (especially birds) and a mostly indigenous Papuan population referred to as the Hatam-Moley, who once occupied traditional 'thousand-leg' stilt houses. The first and one of the biggest Papuan revolts against Indonesian rule happened here from 1965 to 1968.

The best-known birdwatching base is the Mokwam region, a collection of three small villages called Syobri, Kwau and Mokwam, all perched a few kilometres down a side road about 50km from Manokwari. In February and March, visitors may also observe spectacular, iridescent birdwing butterflies with wingspans of up to 25cm.

☞ Tours

Fees for birdwatching tours range from 700,000Rp to 800,000Rp per day, with additional fees if you stay in a guesthouse or make use of hides, firewood, porters or cooks.

Hans Mandacan   BIRDWATCHING
(📱 081 344 214965; 700,000Rp per day) Hans is an excellent local guide, with intimate knowledge of the mountain and its birdlife. He's also very skilled at setting up a campsite and maintaining his hides, from which visitors can watch several species of birds of paradise feeding on forest fruit. These include the superb bird of paradise, the magnificent bird of paradise, the black sicklebill and the Western parotia.

Hans can also take you on treks to bowerbird nests and a mountaintop overlook.

Zeth Wonggor BIRDWATCHING
(☑0852 5405 3754; guiding fee 800,000Rp per day) In Syobri ask for Zeth Wonggor, a highly experienced guide who has worked here with, among others, Sir David Attenborough. He has forest hides for viewing the magnificent bird of paradise, Western parotia and Arfak astrapia (also birds of paradise), the Vogelkop bowerbird and other exotic feathery species.

Arfak Paradigalla Tours BIRDWATCHING, HIKING
(☑0812 4809 2764; yoris_tours@yahoo.com) This effusive one-man, English- and Dutch-speaking outfit offers city tours as well as Arfak trips. Yoris Wanggai is very knowledgeable about the area's birds, plants and insects. He charges around 800,000Rp per day for overnight trips, not including transport, accommodation or food.

🛏 Sleeping & Eating

There are basic guesthouses in two of the villages: Syobri and Mokwam, and also a more isolated, mountainside guesthouse surrounded by flowers, off the main road.

Simple meals are available in the villages but are pricey (you'll be charged for both the cooks and the food). It's wise to bring your own food from Manokwari.

**Papuan Lorikeet
Guesthouse** GUESTHOUSE $
(☑081 344 214965; 150,000Rp per person) Owned and operated by Hans Mandacan, this mountainside retreat offers a couple of lovely hardwood guesthouses on stilts, surrounded by flowers and gorgeous butterflies. The only downfall is that the beds don't have real mattresses and aren't comfortable.

ⓘ Getting There & Away

You can get a 4WD double-cabin pickup to Mokwam (150,000Rp, 2 hours) from around 7am, 100m along the street past Manokwari's Terminal Wosi. Talk to drivers the day before or get to the stop in good time if you don't want to end up chartering a whole vehicle for 1,300,000Rp (one way).

Getting back to Manokwari is easier. You can wait at the **main intersection** on the road to the Mokwam villages, and jump in any 4WD vehicle headed for Manokwari (100,000Rp).

Tambrauw

To the west of Manokwari, the mountains and coastline of the little-explored Tambrauw Regency are brimming with natural

> ### SENOPI & AIWATAR HILL
>
> The Senopi area, though closed to visitors at the time of research due to tribal conflict over land rights, will someday again be ripe for exploring. The main draw to Senopi is a day's walk through the forest at Aiwatar hill, a salt water spring surrounded by coastal vegetation (40km from the sea). Each morning, thousands of birds pop in for a drink.

splendor and adventure. The tree-shrouded peaks are home to birds of paradise and other exotic species, the offshore islands are ringed with coral reefs and the secluded white-sand shoreline is a nesting site for leatherback, Olive Ridley and green turtles.

Fledgling ecotourism projects are emerging around the region, driven mainly by the need to employ locals with something other than logging, mining and poaching wildlife. Village activities within these projects can be fascinating, but also frustrating, as some locals have continued shooting birds of paradise and other wildlife out of the trees.

The education must begin somewhere, though. At the moment, it's difficult to visit the area without the assistance of guide **Charles Roring** (☑0813 3224 5180; www.manokwaripapua.blogspot.com), who is closely linked with the projects and funnels visitors through them.

Charles offers hiking, camping, birding, nature and snorkelling trips all over the Vogelkop peninsula and as far as Triton Bay (Teluk Triton), south of Kaimana. His guiding fee is usually between 350,000Rp and 500,000Rp per day, depending on group size and destination.

NORTHERN PAPUA

Papua provincial capital, Jayapura, and its airport town Sentani, are hubs of Papuan travel, and there's a small selection of appealing things to see and do in and around these towns. Further west, Biak is a relaxed offshore island that's good for beach lazing, snorkelling and diving, and has evocative land-based and underwater WWII sites to investigate. Nabire is the starting point for trips to snorkel and scuba dive with whale sharks.

Jayapura

📞 0967 / POP 315,870

Downtown Jayapura is hot and buzzing with traffic, but it is perched beautifully between steep, forested hills opening onto Teluk Imbi, and has an appealing tropical air.

A small settlement named Hollandia was established here by the Dutch in 1910. In 1944, 80,000 Allied troops landed here to dislodge the Japanese in the largest amphibious operation of WWII in the southwestern Pacific. After WWII, Hollandia became capital of Dutch New Guinea. Following the Indonesian takeover in 1963, it was renamed Jayapura ('Victory City') in 1968. A public consultation exercise in 2010 favoured changing the name to Port Numbay, a name popular with indigenous Papuans, but this has yet to be officially ratified.

The city stretches 6km northeast from its centre, and its conurbation includes the formerly separate towns of Argapura, Hamadi, Entrop, Abepura and Waena. Cenderawasih University at Abepura is a hotbed of Papuan nationalism.

🅞 Sights

Museum Loka Budaya
MUSEUM

(📞 0852 4438 0693; Jl Abepura, Abepura; 25,000Rp; ⏰ 9am-4pm Mon-Fri) Cenderawasih University's cultural museum contains a fascinating range of Papuan artefacts including the best collection of Asmat carvings and 'devil-dance' costumes outside Agats, most of which was selected by Michael Rockefeller and his team in the 1950s for exhibition in New York City's Metropolitan Museum of Art. The art remained in Papua after Rockefeller's canoe capsized near the Asmat region and he disappeared, presumed drowned or eaten by cannibals.

The museum also contains fine crafts from several other areas, historical photos and musical instruments. Additionally, there's a collection of stuffed Papuan fauna, which includes a monitor lizard, a cuscus and some birds of paradise. The museum is next to the large Auditorium Universitas Cenderawasih on the main road in Abepura.

Pantai Base G
BEACH

Base G beach is nearly 3km long, sandy, clean and lined with wooden picnic platforms. The best beach easily accessible from Jayapura, it is usually near-empty, except on Sunday when locals come in droves to bathe, walk and pray. Beware the many rocks in the water. Base G was the American forces' administrative HQ in 1944.

Frequent 'Base G' *taksi* (5000Rp) start from Jl Sam Ratulangi for the 5km trip; the beach is a 10-minute walk downhill from the last stop.

🛏 Sleeping

Amabel Hotel
HOTEL $$

(📞 0967-522102; amabelhotel@yahoo.com; Jl Apo Tugu 100; s/tw/d incl breakfast 297,000/363,000/418,000Rp; ❄️🛜) Jayapura's best budget option and often full, the Amabel has neat little rooms with windows and an inexpensive restaurant. It's up a small, leafy side street, a block southwest of the landmark Mal Jayapura shopping mall.

Hotel Grand View
HOTEL $$

(📞 0967-550646; Jl Pasifik Permai 5; d incl breakfast 550,000-650,000Rp; ❄️🛜) Grand View is an ageing place with plain but bright, no-frills rooms, half of which peer directly out over the waters of the bay. There's a downstairs cafe-restaurant and it's a short walk to the waterfront fish restaurants.

⭐ Favehotel
BOUTIQUE HOTEL $$

(📞 0967-5161888; www.favehotels.com; Jl Ahmad Yani 12; r incl breakfast from 588,000Rp; ❄️🛜) The fancy hotels in Jayapura are mostly tame when it comes to design. Not the case with Favehotel. Sleek and modern with magenta accents at every turn, this boutique property stands tall and exuberant at the city centre, and its Lime Restaurant features indoor and terrace dining, with a stellar Indonesian menu. Amenities include a spa, executive lounge and ballroom.

Events are frequent, so don't be surprised if you're sharing the hotel with a wedding or two.

Hotel Yasmin
HOTEL $$$

(📞 0811 482 7174, 0967-533222; www.yasminjayapura.co.id; Jl Percetakan 8; s 600,000-1,600,000Rp, d 680,000-1,600,000Rp; ❄️🛜) A quite classy place with well-equipped but small rooms, and a 24-hour restaurant. Some of the cheapest rooms lack windows and are dark, but head up a price band and you get smart, spacious and great-value rooms.

Swiss-Belhotel
BUSINESS HOTEL $$$

(📞 0967-551888; www.swiss-belhotel.com; Jl Pasifik Permai; r incl breakfast from 1,735,000Rp;

Jayapura

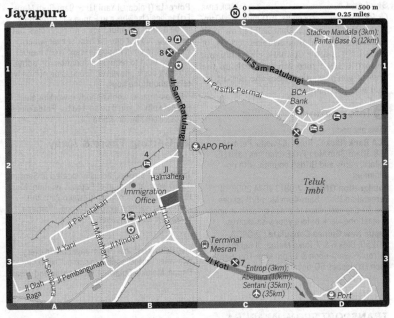

⊛ ⚆ ⊠) There's nothing very Papuan about it, but the Swiss-Bel provides high-quality, European-style comfort in a harbourside location and it has a good open-air pool. Check the website for discounts, especially at weekends.

✗ Eating & Drinking

Unlike much of the rest of Papua, most restaurants in Jayapura serve Bintang, and hotel bars even sell cocktails. Entrop offers a few bars and nightclubs but they're often empty, particularly of tourists.

Waroeng Pojok   INDONESIAN $
(Mal Jayapura; mains 35,000-40,000Rp; ☺10am-9pm) Part of a small national chain of cool, comfy restaurants serving classic Javanese cuisine and frothy milkshakes and juices. It makes a delicious change from the endless oily nasi goreng of small-town Papua or the sweet potatoes of the mountains. It's on the 2nd floor of the Mal Jayapura shopping mall.

★Resto &
Cafe Rumah Laut   SEAFOOD $$
(☑0967-537673; Jl Koti; mains 40,000-150,000Rp; ☺10am-10pm) This stylish upmarket place, built on stilts above the waters of Jayapura bay and filled with Papuan tribal art, is where locals come when they want to im-

Jayapura

⊜ Sleeping
1	Amabel Hotel	B1
2	Favehotel	B3
3	Hotel Grand View	D2
4	Hotel Yasmin	B2
5	Swiss-Belhotel	D2

⊗ Eating
6	Duta Cafe	D2
7	Resto & Cafe Rumah Laut	C3
8	Waroeng Pojok	B1

⊜ Shopping
9	Mal Jayapura	B1

press. The wide-ranging menu takes in Indonesian and Chinese, but is mostly about seafood priced by weight. If you're not eating, at least come for a drink on the deck.

Duta Cafe   SEAFOOD $$
(☑0812 4011 8494; off Jl Pasifik Permai; mains from 40,000Rp, whole fish from 100,000Rp; ☺9am-11pm) Open-air and harbourfront, Duta Cafe serves up excellent *ikan bakar* (grilled fish, priced by weighht) and offers a lively scene in the evenings. It's at one end of a string of similar overwater fish restaurants just west of Swiss-Bel Hotel.

Sky Land JUICE BAR
(Jl Raya Abepura; coconuts 15,000Rp; ⊙10am-5.30pm Mon-Sat, noon-5.30pm Sun) Sip on fresh coconut water at this scenic overlook of Teluk Imbi and the dramatic cliffs plunging toward it. It's a nice way to break up the drive if you're coming from the airport on your way to Argapura.

ⓘ Information

ATMs abound.

BCA Bank (Blok C, Ruko, Jl Pasifik Permai; ⊙8.30am-3pm Mon-Fri) Exchanges cash US dollars, euros and British pounds, with no minimum.

Immigration Office (☏ 0813 7074 2956; Jl Percetakan 15; ⊙8am-4pm Mon-Fri) Issues one 30-day extension to a visa on arrival; apply at least one week before your visa expires.

Papua New Guinea Consulate (☏ 0967-531250; Blok 6 & 7, Ruko Matoa, Jl Kelapa Dua, Entrop; ⊙9am-noon & 1-2pm Mon-Thu, 9am-noon Fri) Issues 60-day tourist visas.

Polresta (Polda; Jl Yani 11; ⊙9am-3pm Mon-Fri) Police elsewhere in Papua will often only issue a *surat jalan* for their own regencies, but here you can get one for almost everywhere you want to go in Papua (except West Papua). They do tend to request a donation for 'administrative costs', however. Processing normally takes about one hour.

In some cases when nobody is working the Polresta office, you'll be sent to the **Polda** office across from Mal Jayapura.

ⓘ Getting There & Away

AIR

Jayapura's airport, actually located at Sentani, 42km west, is the hub of Papuan aviation. Most flights arrive and depart between 7am and 2pm. Destinations include Sorong, Wamena, Makassar and Denpasar.

BOAT

Five Pelni liners leave from Jayapura in every two-week period, sailing to some 20 ports in Papua, Maluku, Sulawesi, Kalimantan and Java.

TRANSPORT FROM JAYAPURA

Air

DESTINATION	AIRLINE	FREQUENCY
Biak	Garuda, Sriwijaya Air	daily
Dekai	Trigana, Lion Air, Wings Air	daily
Denpasar	Garuda (via Timika)	daily
Jakarta	Garuda, Lion Air, Batik Air, Citilink	daily
Kaimana	Wings Air (via Nabire)	daily
Makassar	Garuda, Batik Air, Lion Air, Sriwijaya Air, Citilink	daily
Manado	Lion Air (via Sorong), Nam Air (via Sorong), Garuda (via Sorong)	daily
Manokwari	Garuda, Sriwijaya	daily
Merauke	Garuda, Lion Air, Sriwijaya	daily
Nabire	Wings Air, Garuda, Nam Air	daily
Sorong	Garuda, Lion Air, Nam Air	daily
Wamena	Trigana, Wings Air, Lion Air	daily

Boat

DESTINATION	FARE (RP; ECONOMY CLASS)	DURATION	FREQUENCY (PER 2 WEEKS)
Ambon	420,000	2½-4 days	1
Biak	632,500	17-25hr	1
Makassar	763,000	4-5 days	4
Manokwari	271,000	1-2 days	4
Nabire	256,000	15-32hr	2
Sorong	370,000	1½-2½ days	5

ⓘ **GETTING TO PNG: JAYAPURA TO VANIMO**

There is one land border crossing between Papua and Papua New Guinea that is open to foreigners. It's at Skouw (opposite Wutung, PNG), 55km east of Jayapura and 40km west of Vanimo, PNG. This border suffers occasional temporary closures, usually due to political tensions.

Getting to the border To cross the land border into PNG, you need a visa beforehand. The PNG consulate at Jayapura issues (free) 60-day tourist visas. You'll need to apply a week in advance, as securing the visa can take up to five business days. It usually takes around three, but there are no guarantees. An application must include: a typed cover letter stating where you want to go in PNG and why; proof of funds in the form of a recent bank statement; a photocopy of a confirmed onward air ticket; a photocopy of your passport and visa (be sure this is clearly visible); and two colour photos (4cm by 6cm), with your signature on the back. Regulations and practices at the consulate vary from time to time and you might also be asked to supply a sponsor's or invitation letter from PNG (if this is impossible, explain why in your letter of request).

To get to the border from Jayapura or Sentani, you usually need to charter a *taksi* for 600,000Rp to 800,000Rp, or take the 7am bus for 100,000Rp per person. The trip takes about two hours.

At the border Exit stamps for Indonesia are now obtained at the border and are free of charge, as is entering Papua New Guinea. The border is open from 8am-4pm.

Moving on Buses and vans link the border to Vanimo's market area for around K20.

The **port** (Jl Koti) is accessible by any *taksi* heading to Hamadi or Entrop. Pelni tickets are available there or at travel agencies.

Perintis boats also head along the coast to places like Manokwari, Sorong and even Agats, putting in at smaller ports en route and even heading to villages up rivers such as the Mamberamo. They normally leave from the **APO port** (Jl Sam Ratulangi) and typically take a week to arrive in a destination. Finding out about schedules will be a challenge. Bring food and drinks.

ⓘ Getting Around

Official airport taxis from the airport at Sentani to central Jayapura cost 250,000Rp. If you organise a taxi yourself without going through the taxi booths, they will quote you the same fare but with bargaining will drop to 200,000Rp.

Going by public *taksi* from Sentani to Jayapura involves three changes and takes about 1½ hours if the traffic is on your side. Fortunately, each change is just a hop into another vehicle waiting at the same stop. Start with one from Sentani (outside the airport gate or heading to the right along the main road 400m straight ahead) to Waena (10,000Rp, 20 to 30 minutes). Then it's Waena to Abepura (5000Rp, 10 to 15 minutes), Abepura to Entrop (5000Rp, 20 minutes) and Entrop to Jayapura (5000Rp, 20 minutes). Heading back from Jayapura, go through the same routine in reverse. You can pick up Entrop-bound *taksi* on Jl Percetakan or at **Terminal Mesran** (Jl Koti).

Sentani

☑ 0967 / POP 44,779

Sentani, the growing airport town 36km west of Jayapura, sits between the forested Pegunungan Cyclop and beautiful Danau Sentani, which hosts a lovely festival in June and features island fishing villages accessible by boat.

🎉 Festivals & Events

Festival Danau Sentani   CULTURAL
(☉ mid-Jun) The Lake Sentani Festival, inaugurated in 2008, features spectacular traditional dances and chanting as well as boat events, music, crafts and hair braiding. It's very popular with locals and lately has taken place at Kalkhote, on the lakeside 8km east of Sentani town.

🛏 Sleeping

Rasen Hotel   HOTEL **$$**
(☑ 0967-594455;   rasenhotel_papua@yahoo. com; Jl Penerangan; incl breakfast s 300,000Rp, d 420,000-480,000Rp; ⊛ ⊚) The best budget choice near the airport, the Rasen has small, clean rooms with hot showers and TV, plus a decent restaurant and free airport drop-offs. Unsurprisingly it fills up, so try to call ahead. Some staff speak English.

Sentani

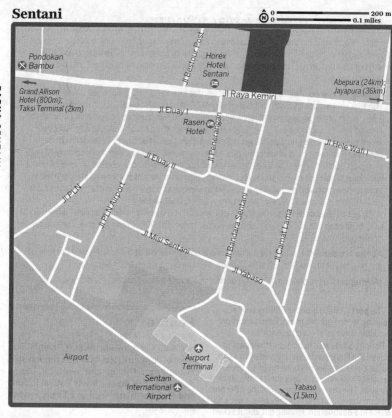

★ **Horex Hotel**
Sentani   BUSINESS HOTEL **$$**
(☐ 0967-519 1999; www.myhorison.com; Jl Raya Kemiri 79; d incl breakfast 670,000-800,000Rp; ❋ 🛜) Horex Hotel is a business hotel but no worse for that and weary tourists will find it an ideal spot to clean up and spoil themselves. Rooms are large and immaculate, with super comfy king beds and 24-hour room service. Staff are exceptionally well trained and the breakfast buffet is spectacular. Walking distance from the airport.

Grand Allison Hotel   BUSINESS HOTEL **$$$**
(☐ 0967-592210; www.grandallisonsentani.com; Jl Raya Kemiri 282; r incl breakfast from 999,000Rp; ❋ 🛜 🏊) Quite possibly the fanciest hotel in Papua, the Grand Allison is business slick with international-standard rooms, facilities and unprecedented service. A highlight is the lovely swimming pool complex. Book online for discounts. The hotel restaurant,

Pepito, offers an international menu, a fine cocktail list and a grand piano.

🍴 Eating

Pondokan Bambu   INDONESIAN **$**
(☐ 0811 481 2484; Jl Raya Kemiri; mains 20,000-45,000Rp; ⊙ 6am-6pm Mon-Sat) Follow the reggae music into this funky warung bedecked in jungle wall murals on Sentani's main drag. You'll be wowed by the spicy, tender BBQ chicken and refreshing smoothies (yes to the jackfruit!), and an attached cafe also serves Vietnamese-style and syphon coffee using beans from all over Papua.

★ **Yougwa Restaurant**   INDONESIAN **$$**
(☐ 0822 3952 7778; Jl Raya Sentani 122; mains 30,000-100,000Rp; ⊙ 10am-7pm Mon-Sat, 11am-5pm Sun) Sentani's most charming afternoon dining is on Yougwa's breezy wooden terraces set over the lake, 13km east of town. Try *ikan gabus* (snakeskin fish), a tasty lake

fish, or the spicy *mujair* fish. Locals also love the sago, a gooey (and frankly kind of tasteless) dish made from the boiled heart of the sago palm.

❶ Information

The Polresta (p488) in Jayapura, 35km west of Sentani, takes about an hour to issue a *surat jalan*. An *ojek* from Sentani is 100,000Rp one-way. The Polda (p488) can also issue the *surat jalan*.

❶ Getting There & Around

Taxis at the **airport** ask an unbelievable 100,000Rp to take you the few hundred metres to most hotels, and even *ojeks* want 25,000Rp. Outside the airport gate, *ojeks* are 10,000Rp.

Public *taksi* (5000Rp) marked 'Trm Sentani-Hawai' shuttle up and down Jl Raya Kemiri between the *taksi* terminal at the western end of town and the Hawai area in the east.

Around Sentani

Several interesting places around Sentani can be easily visited on day trips.

Danau Sentani

You get a bird's-eye view of 96.5-sq-km Danau Sentani, snaking its way between picturesque green hills, as you fly in or out of Sentani. This beautiful lake has 19 islands and numerous fascinating Papuan fishing villages of wooden stilt houses along its shores.

◉ Sights

Pulau Asei   ISLAND

Asei is the main centre for Sentani bark paintings. Originally done only on bark clothing for women of the chiefs' families, bark paintings are now a Sentani art form. To reach Asei, take a *taksi* (5000Rp) to Kampung Harapan, then an *ojek* 2km south to the lake (10,000Rp), then a boat to and from the island (300,000Rp round trip).

Tugu MacArthur   MONUMENT

FREE For breathtaking views of Danau Sentani, head up to the MacArthur monument on Gunung Ifar. This was where General Douglas MacArthur set up his headquarters after his US forces took Jayapura (then called Hollandia) in April 1944. Today the site is occupied by a small monument and a room with displays on the American and Japanese participation in the fighting.

Situs Megalitik
Tutari   ARCHAEOLOGICAL SITE

(Tutari Megalithic Site) On the right as you enter the village of Doyo Lama, 6km west of Sentani, you'll see the entrance to Situs Megalitik Tutari. This mysterious hillside site comprises various arrangements of rocks and stones, and dozens of rock paintings of fish, turtles, crocodiles and lizards. They are of uncertain age but still considered sacred by the villagers. The paintings are in six different fenced areas, all reached by a 1km concrete path. The lake views are also worthwhile.

PAPUA AROUND SENTANI

Around Jayapura & Sentani

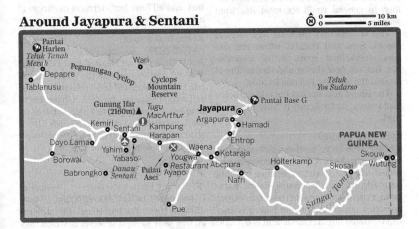

Pulau Biak

Biak (1898 sq km) is one of Papua's biggest offshore islands. It's a relaxed and friendly place with good snorkelling and diving. It was once a popular destination with foreign travellers to Papua but today has been rather eclipsed by the Raja Ampat Islands.

Biak saw fierce fighting in WWII, with about 10,000 Japanese and nearly 500 Americans reported killed in the month-long Battle of Biak (1944). There are several historic sties worth visiting, including a cave that the US dropped a bomb on, killing 3000 Japanese soldiers, and a sunken US seaplane that's now home to lots of fish and coral.

❶ Getting Around

Public *taksi* and a few buses reach most places of interest around the island. You can make things easier by chartering a car or *ojek*, or by taking a trip with PT.Ekowisata Papua Tours & Travel (p471). Away from the south coast, most villages are little more than a handful of huts, with no accommodation or food for travellers.

Kota Biak

📞 0981 / POP 41,250

This main town is your obvious, and only real, base on Pulau Biak. The airport is 3km east of the centre, along Jl Yani, which becomes Jl Prof M Yamin.

🏃 Activities

Though Biak is not in the same league as the Raja Ampat Islands as a scuba destination, there is still some good diving and snorkelling. In general you'll see most fish from May to July.

East of Kota Biak there are wall dives at Marau, Saba and Wadibu, which are also good snorkelling spots, as is Anggaduber. But the best diving and snorkelling is around the offshore Padaido Islands.

The island also attracts the odd hardcore exploratory surfer between November and April.

Byak Divers Papua
DIVING
(📞0852 4496 0506; biakdivers.ulis@yahoo.co.id; 5-day/4-night dive package 6,500,000Rp) A seasoned divemaster with experience working on a Raja Ampat liveaboard, Yulius Kapitarau runs this reputable, boutique diving operation out of his home in Biak. His English is limited but his enthusiasm is not, and

Yulius knows all the best spots. He offers dive packages in conjunction with stays at the Hotel Mapia Biak.

At the time of research, Yulius had plans to open an office in town.

★ Catalina Wreck
DIVE SITE
The same amphibious American aircraft used to fight the Japanese during World War II is now a lovely abode for sea creatures 30m below the surface just off the island. In place of the bombs and torpedoes it once carried, the craft is now equipped with hard and soft corals and a multitude of angelfish, squirrelfish and damselfish that reside within the guts on the plane. Divers will also spot starfish and nudibranch in nearby coral.

No record of the seaplane, or what brought it down, has ever surfaced.

🛏 Sleeping

Intsia Beach Hotel
HOTEL $
(📞0981-21891; Jl Monginsidi 7; r incl meals 250,000Rp; ❄🐱) The best value hotel in Biak isn't anything fancy, but rooms are adequate, beds are decent and included meals are tasty (though the coffee and white bread breakfast leaves something to be desired). The hotel isn't actually on a beach, but the sea view is pretty and dive operators can scoop you up from here with a boat.

★ Padaido Hotel
HOTEL $$
(hotpadaido@hotmail.com; Jl Monginsidi 16; r incl breakfast 400,000Rp; ❄) A hidden delight with just five immaculate, cheery marine-themed rooms. They're full of thoughtful touches such as lights you can switch on/off from bed, and all have leafy terraces overlooking a small and pretty harbour.

Asana Biak Papua
HOTEL $$$
(📞0981-21139; www.aerowisatahotels.com; Jl Prof M Yamin 4; r incl breakfast from 795,000Rp; ❄🐱🏊) Almost opposite the airport terminal, this rambling old hotel received a major renovation that has brought it bang up to date but still managed to retain some of its 1953 colonial-era ambience. There's also a spacious Indonesian restaurant and a lovely oceanfront swimming pool.

🍴 Eating

★ Warung Makan Barokah
SEAFOOD $$
(Jl Ahmat Yani; mains 25,000-90,000Rp; ⊙4pm-midnight) If you like barbecued fish or chicken in a tasty sauce (the secret of which they

Pulau Biak

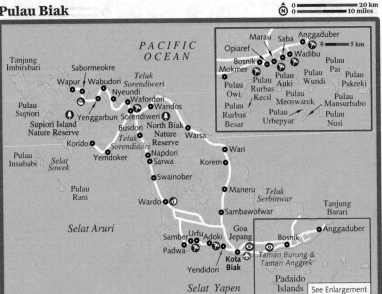

do not want to give away) and served with green veg, rice and sambal, then this eternally popular place is for you. It's cheap, simple and frankly brilliant.

Afterwards pop over the road to the market to grab some fruit for a takeaway dessert.

Furama Restaurant INDONESIAN, CHINESE $$
(☑ 0981-22022; Jl Ahmad Yani 22; mains 40,000-80,000Rp; ⊘ 9am-10pm Mon-Sat; 🅱) Offers cold Guinness and Bintang as well as plenty of good-quality Chinese and Indonesian dishes, including braised frog and stirred papaya flowers. It's one of the few places in town that actually feels like a proper restaurant.

❶ Information

Bank Mandiri (cnr Jl Imam Bonjol & Jl Yani; ⊘ 8am-3pm Mon-Fri) Exchanges cash US dollars and has Visa and Plus ATMs.

PT.Ekowisata Papua Tours & Travel (p471) A well-established agency that can set up just about any trip you want, not only around Biak but throughout Papua and beyond. The experienced, capable manager, Benny Lesomar, speaks excellent English. Call and he'll meet you in town.

Police Station (Jl Diponegoro 3; ⊘ 8am-3pm Mon-Fri) *Surat jalan* are issued in an hour or so

here. For Biak, you normally only need one if you stay on an offshore island.

❶ Getting There & Away

AIR

Tickets for **Garuda** (Jl Sudirman 3; ⊘ 8am-3.30pm Mon-Fri, 9am-3pm Sat & Sun), **NAM Air** (☑ 0981-26577; www.sriwijayaair.co.id; Jl Prof M Yamin 1) and **Sriwijaya Air** (☑ 0981-26577; www.sriwijayaair.co.id; Jl Prof M Yamin 1) are sold at travel agencies as well as their offices. Tickets for the small planes of **Susi Air** (☑ 0811 211 3090, 0811 211 3080; www.susiair.com; airport; ⊘ 6am-3pm) are sold only at the airport. Between them, Garuda, NAM Air and Sriwijaya Air fly at least once a day to Jayapura and Jakarta. Garuda also flies daily to Nabire and Makassar. NAM Air also flies to Meruake three times weekly. Susi Air heads to Manokwari three times weekly and to Nabire daily.

BOAT

ASDP Indonesia Ferry (☑ 0981-22577; Jl Suci 21) Has weekly boats on for Manokwari and Nabire, sailing from Mokmer (6km east of Kota Biak).

Pelni (☑ 0981-23255; Jl Sudirman 37) Every two weeks, Pelni has three liners heading east to Jayapura and west to Sorong and beyond. Some Sorong-bound sailings also call at Nabire and Manokwari.

Kota Biak

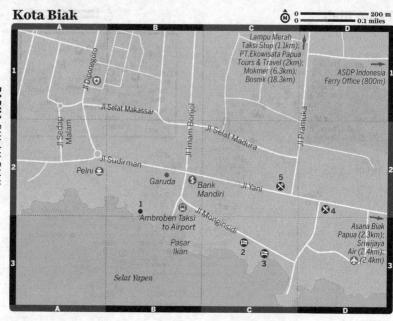

Kota Biak

🏃 Activities, Courses & Tours
1 Byak Divers Papua B2

🛏 Sleeping
2 Intsia Beach Hotel.............................. C3
3 Padaido Hotel C3

🍴 Eating
4 Furama Restaurant............................. D2
5 Warung Makan Barokah..................... C2

TAKSI
Blue *taksi* to Bosnik (10,000Rp, 30 to 40 minutes), passing Mokmer and Taman Burung, run every few minutes; you can catch them at the 'Lampu Merah' (Traffic Lights) stop on Jl Bosnik Raya in the northeast of town. The main terminal for other *taksi* is Terminal Darfuar, about 5km northwest of downtown. On most routes, service winds down in the afternoon.

ℹ Getting Around
Yellow public *taksi* (5000Rp) going to the right (west) outside the airport terminal head into town. Returning, take one marked '**Ambroben**' from the corner of Jl Imam Bonjol and Jl Monginsidi or heading east along Jl Yani. A taxi from the airport to a downtown hotel is around 100,000Rp.

Around Kota Biak

👁 Sights

Goa Jepang   CAVE
(📱0812 9388 2131; Jl Goa Jepang; 50,000Rp; ⊙7am-5.30pm) The Japanese Cave, 4km northeast of Kota Biak, was used as a base and hideout in WWII by thousands of Japanese soldiers. A tunnel from it is said to lead 3km to the coast at Parai, but an earthquake made it impassable. In 1944, an estimated 3000 Japanese died when US forces bombed a hole in the cave roof, dropped petrol drums into it and then bombarded it from above.

Taman Burung & Taman Anggrek   GARDENS
(Jl Bosnik Raya Km12; 20,000Rp; ⊙8am-6pm) At Ibdi, 12km east of Kota Biak on the Bosnik road, the Bird & Orchid Garden contains a sizeable collection of (caged) Papuan birds, including strikingly coloured lories, hornbills, cockatoos and three sad-looking cassowaries in cages that are far too small for such birds. Mixing it up with the birds are dozens of types of orchid.

Bosnik & Around

Bosnik, 18km from Kota Biak, is a laid-back village strung along the coast for 2km. Its daily morning **market** (⊘8am-3pm Tue, Thu & Sat) is bustling on Tuesday, Thursday and Saturday, when Padaido islanders come in large numbers. The beaches are far from the best in Indonesia, but there's one attractive stretch of sand at the eastern end of town, **Pantai Segara Indah** (10,000Rp parking fee), that is lively on weekends and tranquil during the week. Continue a bit further east and you'll come to a less-frequented beach, **Pantai Anggopi**, and a fresh water lagoon just beside the sea.

The thing to do is grab some snacks at the market and bring them to Pantai Segara Indah, then rent a gazebo and feast. There is one tiny restaurant with no name, located across from the market.

Bosnik-route *taksi* from Kota Biak usually go as far as Opiaref, where the coast road turns inland. You can continue on foot 6km through Opiaref to Marau, Saba and Wadibu, where a road heads 500m inland to join the Anggaduber road.

Padaido Islands

This lovely cluster of 36 islands and islets (only 13 of them inhabited) makes for a great day trip from Kota Biak or Bosnik, and you can stay overnight on some islands. Virtually all have jungle-backed, white-sand beaches with crystal-clear waters, coral reefs and plenty of marine life.

Biak Padaido Divers (⊘0813 4436 6385, 0822 3904 0283; biakpadaidodivers@yahoo.co.id; 2-tank dive 900,000-3,000,000Rp, full equipment rental 300,000Rp, full-day snorkelling trip 1,500,000Rp) offers diving trips and snorkelling trips all around the islands. Alternatively, you could come out here on a day trip from Kota Biak with Byak Divers Papua (p492).

Top sites include the western end of Pulau Owi, with good coral and big fish; Pulau Rurbas Besar for coral, sharks, turtles and more big fish; and Pulau Wundi, with a cave, a long wall and good coral.

More recently discovered spots include Pulau Pakreki, where white tip and grey reef sharks, batfish and Napoleon wrasse are frequently spotted. A new wall dive off Pulau Mansur Babo is great for schools of barracuda, a variety of reef sharks and lots of coral.

The best snorkelling spots include Pulau Wundi, which has good coral and many fish near the surface, Pulau Rurbas Kecil and Pulau Meoswarek.

You can normally find accommodation for 100,000Rp per person in an island house or by asking the local church-keeper. There is also a four-room guesthouse run by Biak Padaido Divers owner Erick Farwas on Pulau Wundi.

Nabire
☑0984 / POP 45,000

For travellers the main attraction of this relatively prosperous town is swimming with whale sharks. Growing over 10m long, whale sharks feed mainly on plankton but also on small fish and for this reason they hang around fishing platforms called *bagan* in the southwest of Teluk Cenderawasih, 1½ hours from Nabire by boat. Close encounters with at least a few of these harmless giants are almost guaranteed any day of the year. Don't touch or interfere with the whale sharks, and try to discourage locals from doing so as well.

◎ Sights

★**Taman Nasional
Teluk Cenderawasih**   NATIONAL PARK
(entrance fee 150,000Rp) After fishermen set out wooden platforms to lure fish in the '90s, some unexpectedly large ones began showing up. Whale sharks! In 2002, this special habitat became Indonesia's largest marine park, a whopping 1,453,500 hectares off the Vogelkop peninsula. Since then, 160 different whale sharks have been spotted and a few have been tagged with satellite technology. The trackers have shown that some of these creatures live in the bay – and can be visited by tourists – year-round.

Swimming with a whale shark (or five) is an undeniably epic experience, but there are some important rules. Visitors must be accompanied by a guide, and only six snorkellers or divers can partake at a time. Touching a whale shark is forbidden, and guests must stay at least 3m from the tails and 2m from the heads, or else they may get inadvertently whacked by the shark.

There are additional, daily fees for snorkelling (15,000Rp), scuba diving (35,000Rp) and underwater photography (250,000Rp). The money goes toward protection not only of whale sharks, but also more than 150 coral species and many marine creatures threatened with extinction. The park is currently under consideration for World Heritage site status.

PAPUA'S HIGHEST PEAKS

Papua contains the tallest mountains in Oceania including the granddaddy of them all, the 4884m **Carstensz Pyramid** (Puncak Jaya) and the 4750m **Gunung Trikora**, which comes in at number three. Carstensz Pyramid has several rapidly retreating glaciers and both mountains are frequently dusted in snow.

Climbing Gunung Trikora is possible, but requires several nights camping at high, cold altitudes, along with a stash of permits and the services of a recognised Indonesian tour company. At research time, climbing Carstensz Pyramid had become a challenge due to political instability and violence nearby. The only safe way to reach the summit was to helicopter in, bypassing the troubled regions normally navigated on foot. Beyond that, a high level of fitness, lots of preparation and solid mountaineering skills are required for Carstensz Pyramid. Note that altitude sickness can be a danger here.

Adventure Indonesia (www.adventureindonesia.com) is one reliable operator offering trekking up Gunung Trikora and helicopter expeditions to Carstensz Pyramid.

🛏 Sleeping

Hotel Nusantara
HOTEL **$$**

(☑ 0984-22442; Jl Pemuda; r incl breakfast 308,000-528,000Rp; ✴🐕🛜) The best deal in Nabire is this charming hotel, though guests in the less expensive rooms go without hot water or sinks. The staff couldn't be more welcoming, though, and there's some lovely landscaping in a large, central courtyard.

★ Kamusioh Guesthouse
GUESTHOUSE **$$**

(☑ 0984-23124; Jl Nylur 5; r 350,000-450,000Rp; ✴🛜) Down a quaint side street, this bright-yellow, nine-room guesthouse is homely and welcoming, with a garden full of tropical foliage, an elegant dining area and a full kitchen available to guests. Hot water, air-con and one day of wi-fi are included; additional usage of wi-fi costs 10,000Rp per day. Breakfast, tuna pasta, beer and soft drinks are also available for an additional cost.

Kali Lemon Dive Resort
RESORT **$$$**

(☑ 0812 4891 651; www.kalilemon.com; r all-inclusive 5,000,000Rp per person; 🛜) An intimate and castaway-cool beach resort, snugly ensconced between the jungle and the sea just a couple of minutes from the whale shark platforms. There are six bungalows, adeptly constructed from local hardwoods, and one dreamy treehouse that juts out over the sea. Everything is included in the price: accommodation, meals, diving, snorkelling, birds-of-paradise-watching and all transport.

Rooms are fan-cooled and there is no hot water. Also, the dive gear is barely adequate and the local 'dive masters' need further training. For professional service and better equipment, contact Yulius Kapitarau of Byak Divers Papua (p492), who accompanies groups to the resort. In addition to scuba diving with the whale sharks, there are several nearby dive sites where divers can check out coral reefs, giant clams, pygmy seahorses and a large variety of sharks. Spotty wi-fi is available for 15,000Rp per hour.

🍴 Eating

Rumah Makan Selera
CHINESE **$**

(☑ 0812 4055 4500; Jl Pemuda; mains 50,000-70,000Rp; ⏰ 9am-10pm) It looks like a run-of-the-mill Chinese and seafood joint, but when the heaping plate of *ayam masak Lombok* (a spicy duck dish) arrives, you might just fall out of your chair. Not only do you get basically an entire duck for 60,000Rp, but it's crunchy on the outside, tender on the inside, and bathed in a delicious amalgam of sweet and spicy sauces.

The menu is enormous, and does not include English translations. Also the staff speaks no English. Just get the duck.

🛍 Shopping

Wisata Hati
ARTS & CRAFTS

(☑ 0823 9806 6696; Jl Jend Sudirman; ⏰ 8am-8pm Mon-Sat) Local handicrafts from the Mee tribe are available at this tidy little shop in central Nabire. Prized items include bags woven from orchid bark, and various souvenirs made with imitation cassowary and birds-of-paradise feathers.

ℹ Getting There & Away

Wings Air flies to Ambon four times each week, while Garuda Airlines, Wings Air and Trigana fly daily to Jayapura. Garuda and Susi Air fly daily to Biak.

Pelni sails three times every two weeks to Jayapura (once via Biak), and three times to Manokwari, Sorong and beyond.

ⓘ Getting Around

There are two options for getting to the whale sharks from Nabire.

The first involves chartering a 4WD vehicle and driver for 800,000Rp for a 1.5-hour drive west to **Wagi Beach**, then a 40-minute boat ride (around 1,500,000Rp round trip). The drive back will again cost around 800,000Rp, unless you can bargain it down.

A more direct (but costlier) option is to charter a boat **directly from Nabire**, for a cool 5,000,000Rp. When seas are calm the trip takes 1.5 hours each way. When rough, 2 hours.

BALIEM VALLEY

The legendary Baliem Valley is the most popular and most accessible destination in Papua's interior. The Dani people who live here were still dependent on tools of stone, bone and wood when a natural-history expedition led by American Richard Archbold chanced upon the valley in 1938. Dani life has since changed enormously with stone axes being replaced by mobile phones and age-old belief systems with Christianity, but even so the changes are often skin-deep and the valley and surrounding highlands remain one of the world's last fascinatingly traditional areas. Visiting the Baliem Valley and trekking through high mountain scenery, past neat and orderly Dani villages, takes you to a world far removed from Jakarta and is an honour and an experience to be savoured. For most people it is the highlight of Papua.

Wamena

☏ 0969 / POP 31,720

The obligatory base for travels around the Baliem Valley, Wamena is a sprawling Indonesian creation peppered with attractions such as farmers markets and surrounded by Dani villages, some of which display their 200-year-old mummified ancestors.

Baliem Valley

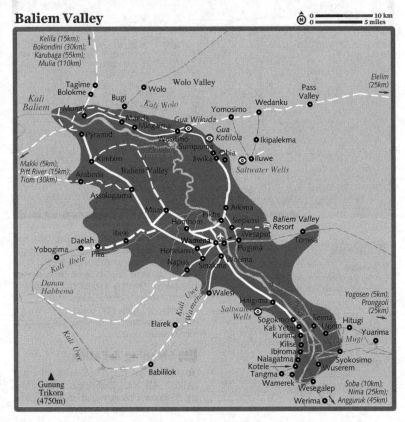

Wamena

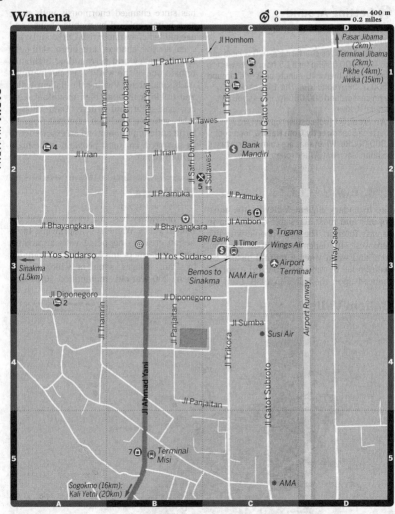

Wamena

🛏 Sleeping
1 Baliem Pilamo Hotel C1
2 Hogorasuok Guesthouse A3
3 Mas Budi C1
4 Putri Dani Hotel A2

✕ Eating
5 Cafe Pilamo B2

🛍 Shopping
6 Oi-Tourism C2
7 Pasar Misi B5

The population is a mix of Papuans and non-Papuans, and the latter run most of the businesses. Penis gourds worn by the Dani tribesmen were once banned here, during Indonesia's 'Operasi Koteka' (an attempt to force the men to wear clothes) in the 1970s. But some old men who come into town for supplies or to hawk their wares are regularly seen wearing them.

🍴 Sleeping & Eating

★ **Hogorasuok Guesthouse** GUESTHOUSE $$
(☎0852 5431 2442, 0969-32382; www.wamena. org; Jl Pangeran Diponegoro; s/d incl breakfast from

300,000/400,000Rp; 📶) On a quiet block just a short walk from the airport, this quaint guesthouse is the best backpacker option in town. There are just six rooms that are smallish but very tidy, surrounding a verdant courtyard. Note that the place is likely to book up in advance, particularly in August.

★ Baliem Pilamo Hotel
HOTEL $$

(📱 0813 4409 0719; baliempilamohotel@yahoo. co.id; Jl Trikora 114; r incl breakfast from 456,000Rp; 📶) The hotel of choice for most visitors. The more expensive rooms are tasteful, contemporary, brown-and-white affairs in the newer section at the rear. Of the cheaper ones, the standards are smallish and plain but acceptable, and the superiors have a semi-luxurious feel and quirky garden-style bathrooms. It's 20,000Rp for three hours of barely functioning wi-fi.

Mas Budi
HOTEL $$

(📱 0969-31214, 0811 4814 003; Jl Patimura; r incl breakfast from 420,000Rp) Run by the same owners as the Baliem Pilamo, this newer hotel offers 16 adequate rooms, all with hot water. The attached restaurant serves up some delicious local specialities such as fried shrimp, goldfish, deer meat, and the unbeatable tamarillo juice. Be warned, though, the kitchen can take up to two hours to prepare your food.

Putri Dani Hotel
HOTEL $$

(📱 0969-31223; Jl Irian 40; r incl breakfast from 650,000Rp; 📶) This small family-run place offers 15 spotless, comfortable rooms with hot showers and endless tea and coffee. The back rooms surround a Japanese garden complete with a fish-filled water feature.

Cafe Pilamo
INDONESIAN $$

(Jl Safri Darwin 2; mains 35,000-90,000Rp; ⊘9am-10pm, to 5pm Sun) Cafe Pilamo is clean and pleasant, and even has three pool tables upstairs, but beware the karaoke, which may start up at any time. It has a long menu of Indonesian dishes, passable burgers and fantastic juices as well as espresso coffees.

🛍 Shopping

The Dani are experts in the art of body adornment. Handicrafts include necklaces, pectorals, armbands and nose piercings, made from pig tusks, cowrie shells, bone, carved stone or feathers, as well as grass skirts, carved spears and arrows, *noken* (women's bark-string bags), and assorted head decorations, made of cassowary or bird-of-paradise (or chicken) feathers and topped off with pig tusks.

Generally, it's cheaper to buy in the villages, but it's also worth checking out Wamena's main market, **Pasar Jibama** (Pasar Baru; Jl JB Wenas; ⊘8am-6pm), 2km north of town, which is full of neat piles of fruit and veggies, pigs off to slaughter and slippery fish from the coast. It's a sight in its own right. Also, check out the NGO-run **Oi-Tourism** (Jl Gatot Subroto; ⊘7am-5pm Mon-Sat), or the handful of craft shops on Jl Trikora north of Jl Ambon. Asmat, Korowai and PNG artefacts are also available in the souvenir shops. Avoid buying items made from bird-of-paradise or cassowary feathers and any other products made from wild animals. Not only is it pushing these creatures closer to extinction, but trade in such items is illegal and airport customs will confiscate them and perhaps fine you.

Of course, the most popular souvenir is the penis gourd. These cost from about 20,000Rp to 100,000Rp, depending on size, materials and negotiation. Changing rooms in which to try them on aren't provided!

BALIEM VALLEY FESTIVAL

To coincide with the busiest tourism season, a three-day **festival** (⊘Aug) is held in the Baliem Valley during the second week of August. The highlight is mock tribal fighting, where village men dress up in full regalia and enact an old-fashioned tribal battle and accompanying rituals.

The festival also features pig feasts, traditional costumes and Dani music on instruments such as the *pikon* (a kind of mouth harp). Other goings-on include pig races, tourist-only spear-throwing and archery contests.

The spectacle can be interesting, but feels a bit phoney and even exploitative at times, with tourists chasing after tribesmen for photographs. Visiting the tribes in their villages is a far more authentic and rewarding experience.

Wamena's three main markets, all functioning daily, are colourful places where you can pick up bundles of veggies for your trek. As well as Pasar Jibama, there's also **Pasar Misi** (Jl Ahmad Yani; ⊗8am-6pm), in the south of town, and Pasar Sinakma, 2km west.

ⓘ Dangers & Annoyances

Local guides may approach you as you step off the plane at Wamena airport. If you haven't made prior arrangements for one to meet you, treat any guide who approaches you with caution and firmness. If you accept any help at all, they may try to interpret this as an agreement to hire them, and can be hard to shake. Guides are useful for many tasks, from trekking to arranging pig feasts, but you might not want to choose the one who's trying to choose you, and the best guides don't usually need to tout for business at the airport.

ⓘ Information

No banks exchange travellers cheques. They'll change some foreign currencies to rupiah but the rate is bad.

Bank Mandiri (Jl Trikora 92; ⊗8.30am-3pm) ATM accepts Visa, Visa Electron and Plus cards.

BRI Bank (Bank Rakyat Indonesia; cnr Jl Yos Sudarso & Jl Trikora; ⊗8am-3pm) ATM accepts MasterCard and Cirrus.

Papua.com (☑0822 2624 1111; fuj0627@ yahoo.co.jp; Jl Ahmad Yani 49; per hour 12,000Rp; ⊗8am-6.30pm Mon-Sat) This efficient internet cafe has fax and scanning services. Its owner is a highly experienced Papua traveller and a willing mine of information. He sometimes runs trips up the mountain to search for wild dogs.

Police Station (☑0969-31072, 0969-110; Jl Safri Darwin 1; ⊗8am-2pm Mon-Sat) Come here to obtain a *surat jalan*.

ⓘ Getting There & Away

AIR

Flights can be heavily booked, especially in August. The carriers between Jayapura (Sentani) and Wamena are **Wings Air** (☑0811 420 757, 0804 177 8899; www.lionair.co.id; Bandar Udara Airport; ⊗5am-3pm), **NAM Air** (☑0967-5189788; Bandar Udara Airport) and **Trigana** (☑0967-34590; www.trigana-air. com; Bandar Udara Airport; ⊗6am-3pm), and all operate out of Wamena's **airport terminal** (Jl Gatot Subroto). There are numerous flights each day, and all cost around 650,000Rp. Wings flies twice daily in either direction. **Susi Air** (☑0811 211 3080; www.susiair.com; Jl Gatot Subroto; ⊗6am-3pm) operates small planes to remote airfields such as Dekai, Elelim, Kenyan and others. You can charter a plane with them to fly to Angguruk in Yali country.

Mission airline **AMA** (Associated Mission Aviation; ☑0967-591009; www.amapapua.com; Jl Gatot Subroto; ⊗6am-3pm Mon-Sat) flies small planes to many small highland airstrips. They may carry tourists if spare seats are available. There is a better chance of getting a seat flying back to Wamena than for outbound flights. A seat from Angguruk to Wamena, for example, costs about 700,000Rp if you are lucky enough to get one. AMA also allows tourists to charter a flight to Angguruk for 14,250,000Rp. Another missionary airline, MAF, once carried tourists but no longer does.

PUBLIC BEMO

Overcrowded bemos head out along the main roads from several starting points around Wamena. Most just leave when they are full. The main terminals – **Terminal Jibama** (Jl JB Wenas), **Terminal Misi** (Jl Kurima) and **Sinakma** (Jl Timor) – are at Wamena's three markets. Bemos get scarce after 3pm and don't run on

BEMOS FROM WAMENA

DESTINATION	DEPARTURE POINT	FARE (RP)	DURATION
Aikima	Jibama	20,000	15min
Ibele	Sinakma	25,000	30min
Jiwika	junction 600m past Jibama	25,000	40min
Kali Yetni	Misi	25,000	1hr
Kimbim	Jibama	30,000	1¾min
Makki	Sinakma	100,000	3hr
Meagaima	Jibama	20,000	1hr
Sogokmo	Misi	25,000	35min
Tagime	Jibama	30,000	1¾hr
Tiom	Sinakma	200,000	4hr
Wosilimo	Jibama	25,000	40min

THE DANI

Dani is an umbrella name for around 30 clans in the main Baliem Valley and its side-valleys and some Mamberamo tributary valleys to the north. The total population is thought to exceed 200,000 people.

Most Dani speak Bahasa Indonesia but appreciate a greeting in their own language. Around Wamena, the general greeting is *la'uk* to one person, and *la'uk nyak* to more than one – except that men say *nayak* to one other man and *nayak lak* to more than one man. *Wa, wa* is another common greeting expressing respect or offering thanks.

Many older Dani men still wear a penis sheath (*horim* in Dani, *koteka* in Bahasa Indonesia) made from a cultivated gourd, and little else apart from a few neck, head or arm adornments. Others now prefer T-shirts and trousers or shorts. In the past women used to go bare-breasted, but it is less common to see that nowadays, though some still sport grass skirts. Women often still carry string bags called *noken* on their backs, strapped over the head and heavily laden with vegetables, babies or pigs. *Noken* are made from shredded tree bark, rolled into thread. Some Dani wear pig fat in their hair and cover their bodies in pig fat and soot for warmth.

After Christian missionaries arrived in 1954 and most Dani converted, their traditional pastime of village warfare went out the window. Villages used to go to war over land disputes, wife stealing or even pig stealing, with combat happening in brief, semi-ritualised clashes (with a few woundings and deaths nevertheless). Today such quarrels are normally settled by other, usually legalistic, means.

A Dutch government post was established in Wamena in 1956, and since the 1960s, Indonesia has added its own brand of colonialism, bringing immigrants, government schools, police, soldiers, shops, motor vehicles and *becak* (bicycle-rickshaws) to the valley. Big changes have been wrought in Dani life, but their identity and culture have proved resilient. Tensions between Dani and the security forces and Indonesian immigrants periodically erupt into violence, most notably during a large-scale uprising in 1977 and again in 2000, when clashes led to a temporary exodus of non-Papuans.

Today, villages remain composed of extended-family compounds, each containing a few *honai* (circular thatched huts). The men sleep in a dedicated men's hut, visiting the women's huts only for sex. *Honai* interiors have a lower level with a fire for warmth and sometimes cooking, and an upper platform for sleeping.

After a birth, sex is taboo for the mother for two to five years, apparently to give the child exclusive use of her milk. Some Dani are still polygamous: the standard bride price is five pigs, and a man's status is measured mainly by how many wives and pigs he has. One of the more unusual (and now prohibited) Dani customs is to amputate one or two joints of a finger when a spouse or child dies. This was most frequently done by battering the finger with a rock, and many older Dani have the ends of fingers missing.

One thing that hasn't changed, and probably never will, is the Dani's love for the sweet potato, grown on extensive plots and terraces all over the valley. The Dani don't mess about with fancy sauces or curries to go with their potatoes. They like them plain and steamed for each and every meal. If you spend long enough in the villages, you may get very tired of them!

Sunday. Few villages or attractions are signposted, so ask the conductor to tell you where to get off.

CHARTERED BEMO & CAR

For more comfort than the public *bemos*, consider chartering a vehicle for out-of-town trips. A bemo costs around 400,000Rp one-way to Kali Yetni (a common trek starting point), or 800,000Rp for a return trip of about two hours to Jiwika. Cars (parked opposite the airport) cost 800,000Rp a day (possibly 1,000,000Rp

in August) for a full-day trip around the northern ends of the valley.

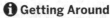

ⓘ Getting Around

For trips within town, *ojeks* and *becaks* charge around 10,000Rp. Bemos marked 'A2' (5000Rp) run up Jl Trikora to Terminal Jibama. An *ojek* or *becak* to Terminal Jibama is 15,000Rp. During the Baliem Valley Festival all prices skyrocket.

Northeastern Baliem Valley

A couple of intersesting villages along the northeastern Baliem Valley are within day-trip reach of Wamena, and some side valleys offer good hiking.

Sights

Werapak Elosak Mummy　　HISTORIC SITE
(100,000Rp) About 8km from Wamena, non-descript Aikima is famous for its Werapak Elosak mummy, the (supposedly) 300-year-old corpse of a great chief, which was preserved (by smoking) to retain some of his power for the village. You'll probably be asked to pay 100,000Rp per person for a viewing, but you can bargain.

Wimontok Mabel Mummy　　HISTORIC SITE
(130,000Rp) The celebrated mummy is kept at the tiny settlement of Sumpaima, 300m north of Jiwika along the main road from the main village entrance (look for the black 'Mummy' sign). Wimontok Mabel was a powerful 18th-century chief here and his blackened corpse is the best preserved and most accessible of its kind near Wamena.

You will likely be asked for around 130,000Rp per person for a viewing. You can try bargaining but don't expect much of a reduction.

Air Garam　　AREA
At Iluwe, 1½ hours up a steep path from Jiwika, is Air Garam, a group of saltwater wells. Villagers soak sections of banana trunk in the water, then dry and burn them and use the resulting ashes as salt. Village boys will show you the way for around 50,000Rp, but to see the process at work, try to find a woman who will accompany you (100,000Rp per person). To avoid climbing in the midday heat, start from Jiwika before 10am.

HIKING & TREKKING THE BALIEM VALLEY

Beyond the reach of roads in the Baliem Valley, you come closer to traditional Dani life. In one day you may climb narrow rainforest trails, stroll well-graded paths past terraces of purple-leafed sweet-potato plants, wend through villages of grass-roofed *honai* (circular thatched huts), cross rivers on wobbly hanging footbridges, and traverse hillsides where the only sounds are birds, wind and water far below.

The classic trekking area, offering up to a week of walking, is in the south of the valley (beyond Kali Yetni), along with branch valleys to the east and west. Dani life here is still relatively traditional, the scenery gorgeous and the walking varied. It can rain here at any time of year, but from April to December most days are fine and warm and the evenings cool. From January to March, mud and rain can make trekking hard work.

Accommodation is available in nearly all villages. Some have dedicated guest houses (sometimes in *honai*-style huts); elsewhere you can often stay in a teacher's house, the school or other houses. Either way you'll usually be asked a standard 150,000Rp per person (guides and porters excluded). You sleep on the floor, but it may be softened with dried grass (so not very soft at all!) and you may get a mat. It gets surprisingly cold at night. It's a good idea to bring a decent sleeping bag and some thermals and fleeces. Other items worth bringing along include a torch, a solar-powered charger or spare batteries for your devices (there's little or no electricity in the villages), a book (evenings can be long) and a water bottle and purifying pills (you'll be refilling from streams a lot of the time). Good hiking boots are essential and walking poles are a good idea. Sunscreen, sunglasses, a sunhat and wet-weather gear (including gaiters or waterproof trousers) are also essential.

Larger villages have kiosks selling basics such as biscuits, noodles and rice (the final reliable supplies are at Manda and Kimbim in the north and Kurima in the south) and you can obtain sweet potatoes, other vegetables or fruit here and there. To be on the safe side, take enough food with you from Wamena. Villages can normally supply firewood for cooking for 20,000Rp per load.

Guides & Porters

In the more frequented trekking areas it's technically possible to head off alone and ask the way as you go, or pick up a local porter-slash-guide for 250,000Rp a day if you need one. However, you would need to have excellent Bahasa Indonesia language abilities and, ideally,

Gua Wikuda

CAVE

(30,000Rp) In Wosilimo, a 45-minute drive northwest from Wamena, Gua Wikuda is said to be several kilometres long, with an underground river that reaches Danau Anegerak. It's possible to visit the first hundred metres of the cave which has a few stalagmites and stalactites. Ask for the lights to be turned on.

It'll cost you about 35,000Rp to get there on a bemo from Wamena.

Gua Kotilola

CAVE

(50,000Rp; ☺8am-4pm) The road north from Jiwika is flanked by rocky hills with several caves. Gua Kotilola is a sizeable cavern up a short, pretty path behind a Dani compound, about 5km north of Jiwika. It contains the bones of past tribal-war victims – though they don't show these to outsiders. It's difficult to justify the high entry fee.

🛏 Sleeping

★ **Baliem Valley Resort**   RESORT $$$

(✆0812 4802 3489, Germany +49 6051 61388; www.baliem-valley-resort.de;   s/d incl breakfast €110/126) This stunning hotel occupies a gorgeous hillside position 21km east of Wamena, with large, rustic-style but comfortable guest cottages in picturesque grounds. A superb collection of Papuan (especially Asmat) art adorns the semi-open-air dining hall. The German owner has a wealth of Papua expertise and offers a variety of excursions and expeditions.

❶ Getting There & Away

Baliem Valley Resort can arrange private 4WD transport for a fee. Bemos for Jiwika and Wosilimo leave from Terminal Jibama in Wamena and cost little. Visitors can also travel by ojek (150,000Rp one way) or private taxi (around 1,000,000Rp round trip). The villages are within 45 minutes of Wamena.

a grasp of the local Dani language to really pull this off. Trails are unmarked and often faint and confusing and there's frequently nobody around to point out the correct route. It would be very easy for a foreign trekker walking alone to get very lost. To summarise: get a guide!

Finding a good, reliable guide can be a challenge. You should allow at least one day to find a guide you're happy with and make trek preparations. Tricks played by unscrupulous guides may include pocketing some of the money you've given them to get supplies (go with them or get the supplies yourself); sending a junior replacement at the last minute; asking for more money mid-trek and refusing to continue without it; or disappearing and leaving you in the hands of a porter.

A good source of recommendations for reliable guides in Wamena is Papua.com (p500). It's worth seeking out one of the Baliem Valley's 15 or so officially licensed guides. These are not the only good guides around, but they usually speak reasonable English, and have a professional reputation to look after.

There are no fixed prices in the Baliem trekking world. Hard bargaining is the norm. Don't be put off by glum faces and do insist on clarifying any grey areas. No decent guide will agree to anything he's unhappy about. Official licensed guides request 500,000Rp per day (and more for harder treks to, for example, the Yali or Korowai areas), but some decent, English-speaking guides will work for less. You'll find a number of dependable agencies and individual guides in Wamena. There are also excellent trekking guides based elsewhere in Papua who will always be happy to act as a guide in the Baliem Valley; try Antoni Sitepu (p471).

In addition to a guide, porters are a good idea and cost 150,000Rp each per day, depending partly on the toughness of the trek. A cook costs 300,000Rp per day, but guides or porters can cook if you're looking to cut costs. You'll have to provide enough food for the whole team (for two trekkers, a guide and two porters doing a one-week trek this is likely to cost around 3,000,000Rp to 3,500,000Rp in total) and probably cigarettes for them and your village hosts. It's a good idea to have the whole agreement written down and signed by your guide before you start, and it's normal to pay some money up front (70% is usual) and the rest at the end. Do not pay the entire cost of the trip up front! A 10% tip at the end is also expected for the guide, and 100,000Rp is acceptable for other members of the team.

Northwestern Baliem Valley

The western side of the Baliem Valley is less scenic than the eastern, but there are a few worthwhile attractions in the region. **Kimbim** is a pleasant administrative centre with a few shops and the main market outside Wamena, it's busiest on Monday and Saturday.

Sights

Danau Habbema

LAKE

This lovely lake, 30km west of Wamena as the crow flies, sits amid alpine grasslands at 3400m altitude, with dramatic, snow-capped mountains in view (4750m Gunung Trikora rises to the south). The fascinating ecosystem and its flora are draws for nature lovers. The ideal way to visit Habbema is to drive there and trek back through rainforest

---

HIKING THE SOUTHERN BALIEM VALLEY

South of Wamena, the Baliem Valley narrows and Kali Baliem (Baliem River) becomes a ferocious torrent. For the small number of hikers who come to Papua the southern Baliem Valley is easily the most popular hiking destination. The scenery is spectacular, the walking exhilarating and the village life fascinating.

From Kurima, the first village most trekkers reach, you can access a network of trails linking villages on the west side of the Baliem. Five- or six-day treks can begin on either the east or the west side of the river, as a couple of bridges link the sides with one another to form a circular route.

Walking times are based on an average 'tourist pace', including rest stops.

Day One

The paved road from Wamena passes through Sogokmo village after 16km (you may have to change vehicle here) and ends at the small but turbulent river, Kali Yetni. This is where you start walking. The only way across the Yetni is on precarious logs for which you need a helping hand from a guide. It's a 45-minute walk from the Yetni to Kurima, a largish village with a police station (show your *surat jalan* here).

If you don't have someone to help you over the Yetni, start walking from Sogokmo, from where it's a 20-minute walk down to a metal hanging bridge over the Baliem. A path then leads down the east bank to neat Seima (1½ hours), from where you can descend to Kurima in 30 minutes, recrossing the Baliem by another hanging bridge.

One hour south (uphill) from Kurima you reach Kilise, a *honai* (circular thatched hut) village with glorious views. Total walk time: two hours.

Day Two

From Kilise follow the gently rising and falling trail for an hour or two to the pretty village of Ibiroma, which offers splendid views up the imposing-looking Mugi Valley on the other side of the river. After a further hour of walking, the trail descends very steeply to Nalagatma with its attractive wooden church on a grassy plain. From here the trail narrows and disappears in and out of thick vegetation as it descends all the way to the Kali Baliem.

Continue 50 minutes further on and you reach the *honai* of tiny Kotele where the trail bends and provides the first views of the massive mountains to the south through which you will pass in a few days. It's now just a 40-minute walk very steeply downwards along a trail that is treacherously slippery after rain to a stream, small bridge and delightful Wamerek. Total walk time: four to five hours.

Day Three

Today is a long, hard slog, but by the end of it you will be high in the mountains. One hour of walking from Wamerek will bring you to a rickety wooden bridge over the angry Kali Baliem. One look at this bridge, with its missing wooden planks and gentle sway in the breeze, might be enough to make some people decide they don't like hiking after all. Assuming you make it over the river, it's about a three-hour unrelentingly steep uphill slog to almost the very top of the mountain (look out for the high waterfall near the top where you can take an

and villages (three to four days). To do this you will need a guide; find one in Wamena.

The usual route starting from the lake is via Yobogima (a forest clearing) and then through a spectacular gorge to Daela village and on to Pilia and Ibele.

It's also possible to visit Habbema as a day trip from Wamena – the drive is around two hours each way. The road is paved for about half the way, and passes through a military checkpoint at Napua, 7km from Wamena. You can get a 4WD taxi in Wamena for around 2,000,000Rp round trip.

Alongga Huby Mummy HISTORIC SITE
(Araboda; 80,000Rp) The 280-year-old Alongga Huby mummy can be viewed in Araboda; viewings cost around 80,000Rp (plus another 50,000Rp to the holder).

Pyramid VILLAGE
Pyramid is a graceful mission village named after the shape of a nearby hill.

exhilarating shower). After reaching a bit of level ground, it's another 20 minutes uphill to a small hamlet of perfectly formed huts which are often half-hidden under a cold mist. The path continues up through the mist-soaked mountains to Wesagalep village which is situated on a small, cold ridge with remarkable mountain vistas. Overnight in the village school/hall. Total walk time: five to six hours.

Day Four
Day four starts rudely with a steep, breathless 20-minute climb to a low pass. Don't follow the obvious trail straight ahead (this just leads to gardens), but instead turn right along the fainter trail. After 45 minutes of steep climbing through muddy, muggy jungle the reward is a narrow, grassy ridge with endless views in all directions. The path skips along a spur before plummeting downwards for about three hours to the Kali Lubuk where you can reward yourself with a refreshing (read: bloody freezing) dip.

The path then climbs up another ridge dipping in and out of often very boggy forest before reaching a final ridge and dropping down to Userem village where accommodation is available in a teacher's house for the usual 150,000Rp per person. Total walk time: five to six hours.

Day Five
This is a fairly short and gentle day, though the temperature and humidity rise fast as you descend. From Wuserem work your way along a spur for half an hour, from where there are memorable views to the north up towards Wamena. By now the track is fairly wide and well maintained and more and more villages start appearing. Descend gently and turn to the east into the Mugi Valley. From this point it's just 45 minutes to an hour down to riverside Syokosimo, which has a basic wooden hut, teacher's home and schoolhouse to stay in. You can have a dip in the river and enjoy an afternoon of rest. Total walk time: three to four hours.

Day Six
From Syokosimo follow the trail along the river heading further up the Mugi Valley. After 20 minutes you'll come to Yuarima and a small bridge, built only of vines and tree branches, that crosses the river. From the other side a gentle climb takes you through beautiful meadows and past little farmsteads. Soon you'll be out of the Mugi Valley and back into the Baliem Valley proper and the village of Hitugi (1½ hours after setting off). The path wends downhill for just over an hour to Ugem village. Both villages have accommodation.

Continue onwards; nearly five hours after setting out that morning you reach Seima. On the opposite bank of the Kali Baliem you'll be able to see where you started trekking several days ago. You could stop in Seima for the night but most people choose to press on for a further 1½ hours. From Seima continue along the track heading north. It wends in and out of forest and farmland before dropping down to the river, which you eventually cross on a scary yellow hanging bridge, built of metal and sticks (some of which are missing). After a 10-minute uphill walk you'll reach the tarmac road, the village of Sogokmo and transport back to Wamena. Total walk time: six to seven hours.

ℹ Getting There & Away

You'll need to charter a car to reach this area. From Wamena the going rate is around 1,000,000Rp return.

Yali Country

Over the eastern walls of the Baliem Valley, amid scenery that is often just as stunning, lies the home of the Yali people. Only contacted in the 1960s and rumoured to have cannibalised a missionary or two, the Yali are one of the more traditional highland peoples. Although many villagers have in the last 15 years taken to shorts and T-shirts, the older men may still be seen in 'skirts' of rattan hoops, with penis gourds protruding from underneath. Missionaries provide much of the infrastructure here, such as schools and transport.

Yali country is a great destination for more adventurous trekkers with time to explore. From here, you can trek southeastwards into the territory of the Mek people, who are similarly small in stature to the Yali (their main village is Nalca), and even cross Papua's north–south watershed to Langda, the main village of the Una people (considered pygmies).

The most popular trekking route to Yali runs from Sogokmo or Kurima to Ugem, then up the Mugi Valley, over 3500m-plus Gunung Elit with at least one night (but often two) camping, then down to Abiyangge, Piliam and Pronggoli in Yali country. There are sections of long, steep ascent, and the upper reaches over Gunung Elit involve

---

PIG FEASTS & WARRIOR DANCES

Anemangi, just behind Sumpaima, and Obia (Isinapma) to the south of Jiwika, are among villages where traditional Dani pig feasts and colourful warrior dances based on ritual warfare can be staged for tourists, if requested a day or two ahead. A typical price for a warrior dance alone is about 1,500,000Rp depending on the number of dancers, and there may also be a demonstration for how to make fire with all natural materials. For the pig feast you'll pay at least 2,000,000Rp and more if you're a large group, plus you buy the pig (a small one costs about 2,000,000Rp).

---

climbing up and down several rustic wooden ladders. From Pronggoli to Angguruk, the biggest Yali village (with a large market twice a week), takes another one or two days.

An easier but longer option, about eight days from Sugokmo to Angguruk and still with plenty of up and down, is the southern loop via Wesagalep, Werima, Soba and Ninia.

Whichever route you take, you should have an experienced guide. You should be able to organise one in Wamena. Antoni Sitepu (p471) is particularly knowledgeable about the area, having led multiple treks to some of the farther-flung and more traditional villages, including Una and Kosarek.

Village stays are basic and cost 150,000Rp per person per night. Angguruk is the most developed of the villages and as such offers a good guest house. Other villages put travellers up in *honai*, school houses and other suitable structures.

Your guide will employ a chef and pack food for the entire trip. In villages, you may be able to supplement this with packaged noodles, sweet potatoes, taro and incredibly sugary coffee.

ℹ Getting There & Away

Villages with airstrips include Angguruk, Pronggoli, Kosarek and Welarek.

Susi Air (p500) operates charter planes to Angguruk, and Catholic missionary air service AMA (p500) flies small planes to many small highland airstrips. They may carry tourists if spare seats are available. There is a better chance of getting a seat flying back to Wamena than for outbound flights. A seat from Angguruk to Wamena, for example, costs about 700,000Rp if you are lucky enough to get one. AMA also allows tourists to charter a flight to Angguruk for 14,250,000Rp.

From Wamena, you need about a week to walk here (the Yali themselves can do it, barefoot, in two days).

SOUTHERN PAPUA

Few travellers make it to the low-lying, river-strewn south, but Wasur National Park, accessed from Merauke, is one of Papua's best wildlife destinations (for a few months a year), while the Asmat region provides a fascinating taste of life along jungle rivers with a headhunting past and marvellous woodcarving artisanry. Korowai is home to the world's most skilled tree house architects.

RIVER SURFING KEPALA ARUS

Only one group of international wave chasers has ever attempted to surf Kepala Arus, a strong tidal bore where the Digul and Mappi rivers merge in Papua's seldom-visited southern interior. But Merauke-based guide Bony Kondahon swears that any relatively confident surfer or stand-up paddleboarder can take it on, and we believe him.

Quite a lot of planning goes into the trip, as the 2m wave only appears for four or five days at a time, usually breaking just before the full and new moons and largely depending on tidal intensity. Also, be sure to come between May and October, or you'll have to surf this thing in the dark.

You bring the surfboard (or SUP and paddle), and the local team of experienced boat drivers in Bade will bring you to the wave. The ride is 'gutsy' according to the professionals, and lasts a few minutes (up to half a kilometre), starting very far downriver near Isyaman village and travelling to another village called Mam (both in Asmat territory). A spot in between called Muara Kalamati apparently offers the biggest thrills. There are crocs nearby but they rarely turn up during the day.

Staying in Bade is an experience of its own, and spectators may also find the journey (which involves chartering a plane for 59,000,000Rp or taking a combination of boats and 4WD taxis for a negotiable 8,500,000Rp) worthwhile. In Bade, there's one basic hotel and a restaurant serving deer and some strange-looking river fish. Well before dawn, prayers begin emanating from the local mosque.

Merauke

📞 0971 / POP 87,600

Merauke is a reasonably prosperous and orderly town of wide, straight streets, renowned as the most southeasterly settlement in Indonesia. The best reason to visit is nearby Wasur National Park, which is like a small slice of Australian bush in Indonesia, wallabies and all.

It's 6km from the airport at the southeast end of town to the port on Sungai Maro at the northwest end. The main street, running almost the whole way, is Jl Raya Mandala.

🛏 Sleeping & Eating

Marina Hotel HOTEL $
(📞 0971-326240; Jl Raya Mandala 23; s/d 165,000/220,000Rp) Best deal in town with acceptable, clean rooms and cold showers. Also rents motorbikes for 50,000Rp per day.

Hotel Megaria HOTEL $$
(📞 0971-321932; www.megariahotel.com; Jl Raya Mandala 166; r incl breakfast from 390,000Rp; ❄) The Megaria has a selection of 42 large, well-furnished rooms that wouldn't win awards for being at the cutting edge of style but are otherwise OK. Get one as far away from the road as possible.

Swiss-Belhotel BUSINESS HOTEL $$$
(📞 0971-326333; www.swiss-belhotel.com; Jl Raya Mandala 53; r incl breakfast from 1,005,000Rp;

❄ 🛜 🏊) The most stylish and luxurious option in town, the Swiss-Belhotel offers all the business-class frills. There are some niggles, though, like uneven water pressure in the showers and overly inquisitive staff members.

❶ Getting There & Away

Garuda, Lion Air and Sriwijaya Air fly daily to Jayapura. Batik Air offers a flight to Jakarta with a stopover in Makassar. Airport taxis cost 100,000Rp into town. Yellow public *taksi* (4000Rp) from the airport parking area, or the road just outside, run along Jl Raya Mandala.

About every two weeks, a Pelni ferry sails from Merauke to Agats and Sorong. Another sails to Agats then through southern and central Maluku to Sulawesi, every four weeks. Smaller boats run up and down the coast to Agats and as far inland as Tanahmerah.

Wasur National Park

The 4130-sq-km **Wasur National Park** (📞 0971-324532; 150,000Rp per day), stretching between Merauke and the PNG border, will fascinate anyone with an interest in birds and marsupials. But come in the later part of the dry season (mid-July to early November), otherwise most tracks will be impassable.

Bony Kondahon (📞 0813 4458 3646; bonykondahon@rocketmail.com), an excellent Merauke-based guide, can help with

---

HARVESTING SAGO

Perhaps the most impressive endeavor of the Korowai (other than tree house building, of course) is that of sago harvesting. The laborious process begins with tribe members chopping down a large palm tree with a stone axe, then splitting open the core and beating it to a pulp with stone tools while entertaining themselves with traditional songs. Next, they send the material with river water through a natural filtration system (constructed entirely of palm tree parts), which separates a nutritious starch that can feed a family for weeks. The endeavor takes the better part of a day and is often undertaken mainly by women.

---

arrangements and show you the park. He charges 700,000Rp per day for guiding and cooking and maintains a nice campsite (with one hut on stilts) in the park's northwest.

Part of the Trans-Fly biome straddling the Indonesia–PNG border, Wasur is a low-lying area of savannahs, swamps, forests and slow-moving rivers that inundate much of the land during the wet season. Wasur's marsupials include wallabies and small kangaroos, though illegal hunting means numbers have fallen. There are also nocturnal cuscuses and sugar gliders and towering termite mounds. Among the 350-plus birds are cassowaries, kookaburras, cockatoos, brolgas, magpie geese and three types of bird of paradise.

The southern part of the park is the best for wildlife-spotting as it has more open grasslands and coastal areas. At **Rawa Biru**, an indigenous village 45km east of Merauke (300,000Rp one way by *ojek*, or 2,500,000Rp to 4,000,000Rp round trip in a rented 4WD vehicle with driver), you can stay in local houses for 150,000Rp per person (bring food and mosquito nets). From Rawa Biru it's a two- to three-hour walk to **Prem**, with a small savannah surrounded by water, and a good chance of seeing wallabies and various waterbirds. Also within reach (20km) is **Yakiu**, where chances are high of seeing the greater, king and red birds of paradise in the early morning and late afternoon. In the south part of the park, you may also be asked for a 300,000Rp 'land owner fee' (this ostensibly incentivises locals to protect rather than hunt wildlife).

Asmat Region

The Asmat region is a massive, remote, low-lying area of muddy, snaking rivers, mangrove forests and tidal swamps, where many villages, including their streets, are built entirely on stilts. The Asmat people, formerly feared for their headhunting and cannibalism, are now most celebrated for their woodcarvings – the most spectacular of Papuan arts. It's a fascinating area to explore but it requires time, money and patience.

Most visitors who do make it here spend time boating along the jungle-lined rivers to different villages, seeing and buying Asmat artefacts, and maybe seeing a traditional dance or ceremony.

Villages to visit for their carving and ceremonial canoe welcomings and races include Atsy, Ambisu, Jow and Amborep, all of which are south of Agats, or Sawa Erma to the north. These traditional celebrations are costly, but the price per person drops as group size increases.

Agats

📞 0902 / POP 1400

Capital of the Asmat Region is the overgrown village of Agats, on the Aswet estuary. Due to the extraordinary tides and location, its streets are raised boardwalks. It's a curious and charming place to wander around, with markets, shops, mosques, churches and unsightly monuments on a bustling waterfront.

👁 Sights

Museum Kebudayaan dan Kemajuan Asmat MUSEUM
(Asmat Museum of Culture & Progress; 📞 0821 4742 3651, caretaker John Ohoiwirin 0813 9478 8993; http://asmatmuseum.com; Jl Missi; admission by donation; ⏲ 8.30-10.30am & 11am-2pm Mon-Sat) This museum has a fantastic collection of Asmat art and artefacts, from *bis* poles and skulls to full-body dance outfits. The collection is split between this location (which still keeps regular hours), and a newer one on Jalan Yos Sudarso at the southern end of town that has struggled for nearly three years to officially open its doors.

The collection, which belongs to a German art-collecting couple and the previous Bishop of Agats, includes feast masks, carvings, woven art, tools, bows, arrows and more.

Impressive carvings created for the annual competition during Pesta Budaya Asmat, a culture festival are displayed in the old location. Guests can sometimes visit the new one by contacting caretaker John Ohoiwirin, who does his best to get people in. At the time of research, though, the boardwalk leading to the entrance of the new structure was severely damaged.

🎭 Festivals & Events

Memorable and incredibly odd celebrations referred to as Asmat Feasts often begin when the chief of an Asmat village has a dream, during which his ancestors give instructions to prepare a feast. The chief will then discuss the plan with other area chiefs and recruit villagers to start gathering sago worms, bananas and other forest foods. Villagers also craft masks and other costume items, sometimes over a period of months, before everything is deemed ready.

During the feast, villagers perform what's referred to as a 'satanic dance', although it has nothing to do with the devil. Rather, it is a way of summoning tribal ancestors.

Pesta Budaya Asmat CULTURAL
(⊙ Oct) Over five days, Agats comes alive with this exhibition of the region's craftsmanship and culture. Festivities include carving contests, canoe races and tribal ceremonies.

🛏 Sleeping

Hotel Assedu HOTEL **$$**
(☑ 0813 4302 4240; Jl Pemda 1; s/d incl breakfast 440,000/495,000Rp, s/d with air-con 522,500/605,000Rp; ❄) This government-run hotel has clean rooms with comfy beds and almost-tasteful plastic flowers. Due to an earthquake, the floors slant considerably.

🛍 Shopping

★ Asmat Queen Art Shop GIFTS & SOUVENIRS
(☑ 0813 4006 3500; Jl Sudarso; ⊙ 8am-8pm) A longstanding tribal art emporium offering up some of Asmat's finest pieces, including shields, spears, totem poles, costumes, wood carvings, drums and even crocodile skulls. Expect to spend upwards of 700,000Rp (and possibly much, much more). Items are much cheaper if you buy them in the villages, but usually of lower quality.

❶ Getting There & Away

Agats has an airport (Ewer), with a few regular flights and frequent charters connecting it to Jayapura, Merauke and Timika. Visitors also arrive and depart by longboat (which is very expensive and time-consuming) or ferry (which is cheap but even more time-consuming).

Korowai

Far inland, in the region of the Dairam and upper Sirets rivers, live the Korowai people, semi-nomads and architects of towering tree houses that historically protected them against animals, enemies, floods, mosquitoes and (apparently) evil spirits. The Korowai were not contacted by missionaries until the 1970s, and though many have since settled in new villages of ground-level houses, a select few still live their traditional way of life, wearing little clothing and employing stone and bone tools.

Most Papua-based tour companies offer tours to this area (an organised tour is, for all intents and purposes, the only feasible way of currently visiting). Depending on group size, you're looking at €1500 to €2000 per person for a 10-day trip, with perhaps half that time actually in Korowai territory.

Top guides for Korowai are Antoni Sitepu (p471) and Bony Kondahon (p507).

Two Korowai villages that feature tall tree houses and often host tourists are Ngguari and Haiganop. These villages will demonstrate traditional activities, including sago harvesting, trap building, fish poisoning and sago worm (beetle grub) gathering. Although grubs are often eaten raw, the women also cook them over an open fire.

Bold travellers are welcomed to climb into the highest tree houses and pitch tents inside them. (Note that at least one visitor has died from the impact of a fall from a precarious ladder, as have a great many tribespeoples.) Most of the villages also offer lower tree house options and huts on stilts.

Prized dog-tooth necklaces are often available for purchase and cost around 1,000,000Rp. Grass skirts, bows and arrows and tools may also be for sale.

❶ Getting There & Away

Tours typically fly from Jayapura or Wamena to Dekai, then boat down Kali Brazza and up Kali Pulau to the first Korowai village, Mabul. You then spend some days walking along muddy, slippery trails through hot, humid jungles.

AT A GLANCE

POPULATION
51 million

MOST ACTIVE VOLCANOES
Gunung Sinabung (p527), Gunung Merapi (p572), Gunung Kerinci (p583)

BEST BEACH
Pulau Bintan (p591)

BEST SEAFOOD
Rapi Seafood (p538)

BEST COLONIAL ARCHITECTURE
Medan (p515)

WHEN TO GO
Apr–Oct
Hit the waves on the Mentawais and Pulau Nias.

May–Sep
Travelling during dry season maximises wildlife sightings in the jungle.

Nov–Mar
Monsoon season, but there are significant accommodation discounts.

Banyak Islands (p553)
GONZALO JARA/SHUTTERSTOCK ©

Sumatra

Few isles tempt the imagination with the lure of adventure quite like the wild land of Sumatra. An island of extraordinary beauty, it bubbles with life and vibrates under the power of nature. Eruptions, earthquakes and tsunamis are Sumatran headline-grabbers. Steaming volcanoes brew and bluster while standing guard over lakes that sleepily lap the edges of craters. Orang-utan-filled jungles host not only our red-haired cousins, but also tigers, rhinos and elephants. And down at sea level, idyllic deserted beaches are bombarded by clear barrels of surf.

As varied as the land, the people of Sumatra are a spicy broth of mixed cultures, from the devout Muslims in Aceh to the hedonistic Batak Christians around Danau Toba and the matrilineal Minangkabau of Padang. All are unified by a fear, respect and love of the wild and wondrous land of Sumatra.

Sumatra Highlights

1 Danau Toba (p529) Delving into the fascinating Batak culture on the shores of Southeast Asia's largest lake.

2 Bukit Lawang (p521) Trekking through the jungle in search of orang-utans.

3 Banyak Islands (p553) Finding your desert-island paradise and snorkelling Sumatra's best reefs.

4 Pulau Weh (p547) Swimming with sharks and turtles in the coral garden off this tiny island.

5 Kerinci Seblat National Park (p582) Searching for tigers and pristine lakes and hiking up volcanoes.

6 Bukittinggi (p572) Exploring the heartland of the Minangkabau.

7 Ketambe (p556) Getting into the jungle experience at the heart of the Gunung Leuser National Park.

8 Mentawai Islands (p565) Living the surfer dream and visiting pristine beaches and hunter-gatherer tribes.

9 Bengkulu (p585) Trekking to villages in the countryside around Sumatra's most pleasant city.

10 Berastagi (p525) Hiking to a steaming volcanic peak near this hill town.

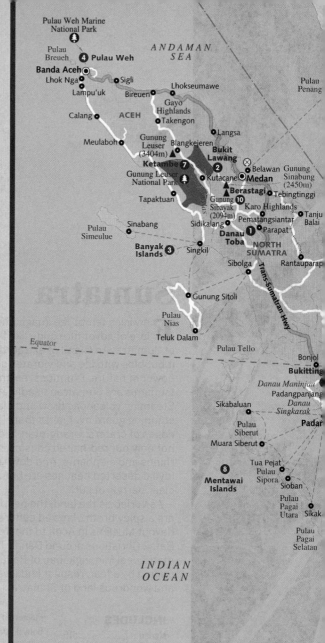

History

Pre-Islamic history is often more myth than fact, but archaeological evidence suggests that Sumatra was the gateway for migrating tribes from mainland Southeast Asia.

The Strait of Melaka, an important trade route between China and India, exposed the east coast of Sumatra to the region's superpowers and cultural influences such as Islam. The kingdom of Sriwijaya emerged as a local player at the end of the 7th century, with its capital presumably based near the modern city of Palembang. After Sriwijaya's influence waned, Aceh, at the northern tip of Sumatra, assumed control of trade through the strait. The era of Aceh's sultanate prevailed until the beginning of the 17th century, when Dutch traders claimed a piece of the spice trade.

The most influential port of the day, Samudra, near Lhokseumawe, eventually became the name that traders used to refer to the entire island. It was Marco Polo who corrupted the name to 'Sumatra' in his 1292 report on the area.

Throughout the colonial era, Sumatra saw many foreign powers stake a claim in its resources: the Dutch based themselves in the west Sumatran port of Padang, the British ruled in Bencoolen (now Bengkulu), American traders monopolised pepper exports from Aceh, and the Chinese exploited the reserves on the islands of Bangka and Belitung, east of Palembang.

In the early 19th century, the Dutch attempted to assert military control over all of Sumatra, a move met with resistance by its disparate tribes. In 1863 the Dutch finally established authority over Pulau Nias. Treaties and alliances brought other areas of Sumatra under Dutch rule.

The Dutch were never welcomed in Sumatra, which contributed several key figures to the independence struggle. Yet Sumatra was dissatisfied with Jakarta's rule. Between 1958 and 1961, rebel groups based in Bukittinggi and the mountains of South Sumatra resisted centralisation, which led to clashes with the Indonesian military. Fiercely independent Aceh proved to be Jakarta's most troublesome region. Aceh's separatist movement started in the late 1970s and continued until 2006.

No human conflict could compare to the destruction that occurred on Boxing Day in 2004, when a 9.0-plus-magnitude earthquake off the northwestern coast of Sumatra triggered a region-wide tsunami, killing over 170,000 people, mainly in Aceh. The one silver lining to the disaster was that the rescue and reconstruction efforts have brought peace to the region, and it has largely held to date.

🛈 Getting There & Away

AIR

Medan is Sumatra's primary international hub, with frequent flights from its new airport to mainland Southeast Asian cities such as Singapore, Kuala Lumpur, Penang and Bangkok. In West Sumatra, Padang receives flights from Kuala Lumpur. Banda Aceh, Palembang, Pulau Batam and Pekanbaru also receive international flights from mainland Southeast Asia.

You can catch a plane from Jakarta to every major Sumatran city with **Garuda** (www.garuda-indonesia.com), **Citilink** (www.citilink.co.id), **Lion Air** (www.lionair.co.id) or **Sriwijaya Air** (www.sriwijayaair.co.id), among others. Flights from Sumatra to other parts of Indonesia typically connect through Jakarta.

A warning: when oil-palm plantations on Sumatra's east coast are burnt (annually, usually during dry season), the smoke frequently results in the closure of Pekanbaru and Jambi airports.

BOAT

Budget airlines have signalled the end of some international ferries, such as the Penang–Medan route. However, on Sumatra's east coast, ferries run from both Dumai and the Riau Islands (namely Pulau Batam and Pulau Bintan) to both Malaysia and Singapore.

For Malaysia, there are regular services to Melaka, Port Dickson and Klang (for Kuala Lumpur) from Dumai. To Singapore, ferries make the quick hop from Pulau Batam and Pulau Bintan, the primary islands in the Riau archipelago. From Batam and Bintan, boats set sail for Dumai and Tanjung Buton, from where there are buses to Pekanbaru on Sumatra's mainland.

Ferries cross the narrow Sunda Strait, which links the southeastern tip of Sumatra at Bakauheni to Java's westernmost point of Merak. The sea crossing is a brief dip in a day-long voyage that requires several hours' worth of bus transport between both ports and Jakarta and, on the Sumatra side, Bandar Lampung.

🛈 Getting Around

AIR

Short plane journeys can be an attractive alternative to spending an eternity on packed buses. Competition between domestic carriers means internal flights are inexpensive and largely reliable, with the exception of Susi Air and its small planes, which are particularly susceptible to bad weather. Dry-season smog affects planes along the east coast.

Useful air hops include those from Medan to Pulau Weh, Banda Aceh and Padang, Palembang to Jambi, and Pulau Batam to Padang and Bengkulu.

BOAT

Most boat travel within Sumatra connects the main island with the many satellite islands lining the coast. The most commonly used routes link Banda Aceh with Pulau Weh; Padang with the Mentawai Islands; and Singkil with the Banyak Islands or Pulau Nias. Most long-distance ferries have several classes, ranging from dilapidated and crowded to air-conditioned and less crowded, though still dilapidated. The Mentawai Islands are now served by a comfortable large speedboat.

BUS

Bus is the most common mode of transport around Sumatra, and in some cases it's the only option for intercity travel. But it is far from efficient or comfortable, since all types of buses – from economy sardine cans to modern air-con coaches – are subject to the same traffic snarls along Sumatra's single carriageways, as well as the potholes and endless stops to pick up or drop off passengers. At the top of the class structure are superexecutive or VIP buses with reclining seats, deep-freeze air-con, toilets and an all-night serenade of karaoke. Smart passengers come prepared with a jacket and earplugs.

In some towns, you can go straight to the bus terminal to buy tickets and board buses, while other towns rely on bus-company offices outside the terminals. Ticket prices vary greatly depending on the quality of the bus and the perceived gullibility of the traveller; ask at your guesthouse how much a ticket is supposed to cost.

Minibus

For midrange and shorter journeys, many locals and travellers use minibus and shared-car services. They are not necessarily faster or more comfortable, but can be more convenient than hustling out to bus terminals as they run intercity and door-to-door.

LOCAL TRANSPORT

The best means of getting around for locals and travellers alike are online taxis such as **Grab** (www.grab.com/id/en) and **Go-Jek** (www.go-jek.com), which are booked through smartphone apps. These offer much cheaper and faster alternatives not only to regular taxis and *ojeks* (motorcycle taxis), but other forms of local transport as well.

Otherwise the usual Indonesian forms of transport – *labi-labi* or *angkot* (small minibus), *ojek*, *becak* (motorcycle-rickshaw or bicycle-rickshaw) and *bendi* (two-person horse-drawn cart) – are available in Sumatran towns and cities. Establish a price for a becak ride before

climbing aboard. For an *angkot,* you pay after you disembark.

TRAIN

The only three useful train services in Sumatra run from Medan's new airport to the centre of Medan, and from Bandar Lampung to Palembang and Lahat (for the Pasemah Highlands).

NORTH SUMATRA

For many visitors, the northern part of Sumatra bordering Aceh is their primary focus. With good air connections to Medan, from here you can trek in search of orang-utans in Bukit Lawang, climb volcanoes from Berastagi, laze away on the shores of Danau Toba, skim the waves off the Banyaks and Nias, and easily venture further north to Pulau Weh or south to Padang and the Mentawais.

North Sumatra stretches from the Indian Ocean to the Strait of Melaka. From sea to shining sea, it is anything but homogeneous. The rolling landscape varies from sweaty plains to cool highlands, while the houses of worship switch between the metal domes of mosques to the arrow-straight steeples of Christian churches. In the highlands around Danau Toba are the delightful Batak, and then there's the megalithic culture of Pulau Nias.

Medan

🎵 061 / POP 2.2 MILLION

Sumatra's major metropolis, and Indonesia's third-largest city, Medan is the first (or final) port of call for many visitors to the island. Given it's not on the coast, and there's no mountain backdrop or even a grand river, Medan is much maligned among many travellers as a soulless industrialised city, a necessary evil to reach more exciting destinations. While it does have issues with traffic and pollution, it's a city with real Indonesian urban character. If you can get over the culture shock and give Medan a bit of time, you'll discover there's more than a hint of fascinating, crumbling Dutch-colonial-era charm, plus some worthwhile sightseeing and shopping, contemporary nightlife and restaurants, and old-school backstreet food stalls.

👁 Sights

Ghosts of Medan's colonial-era mercantile past are still visible along Jl Ahmad Yani from Jl Palang Merah north to Lapangan Merdeka, a former parade ground

Medan

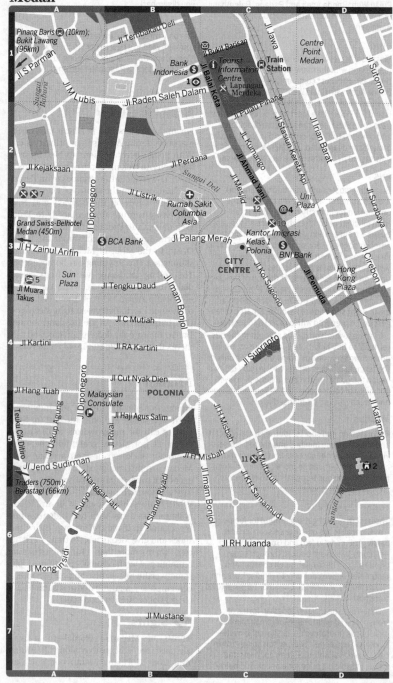

Pinang Baris (10km); Bukit Lawang (96km)

Jl Tembakau Deli

Jl S Parman

Jl M Lubis

Sungai Babura

Bukit Barisan

Bank Indonesia

Tourist Information Centre

Jl Balai Kota

Train Station

Centre Point Medan

Jl Jawa

Jl Sutomo

Jl Raden Saleh Dalam

Lapangan Merdeka

Jl Pulau Pinang

Jl Kurnango

Jl Kejaksaan

Jl Perdana

Sungai Deli

Jl Ahmad Yani

Jl Stasiun Kereta Api

Jl Irian Barat

9 ✕ ✕ 7

Jl Diponegoro

Jl Listrik

Rumah Sakit Columbia Asia

Jl Mesjid

12

Uni Plaza

🏛 4

Jl Surabaya

Grand Swiss-Belhotel Medan (450m)

Jl H Zainul Arifin

BCA Bank

Jl Palang Merah

Kantor Imigrasi Kelas 1 Polonia

CITY CENTRE

10

BNI Bank

Jl Cirebon

Jl Muara Takus

5

Sun Plaza

Jl Tengku Daud

Jl Imam Bonjol

Jl Kol Sugiono

Jl Pemuda

Hong Kong Plaza

Jl Kartini

Jl C Mutiah

Jl RA Kartini

Jl Hang Tuah

Teuku Cik Ditiro

Jl Cut Nyak Dien

POLONIA

Jl Diponegoro

Malaysian Consulate

Jl Haji Agus Salim

Jl Rivai

Jl Suprapto

Jl Katamso

Jl Uskup Agung

Jl Jend Sudirman

Traders (750m); Berastagi (66km)

Jl H Misbah

Jl H Misbah

11 ✕

Jl Imam Bonjol

Jl Multatuli

Jl H Samanhudi

Jl KH Samanhudi

🏯 2

Jl Nanggar Jati

Jl Suryo

Jl Slamet Riyadi

Sungai Deli

Jl RH Juanda

Jl Mong Insidi

Jl Mustang

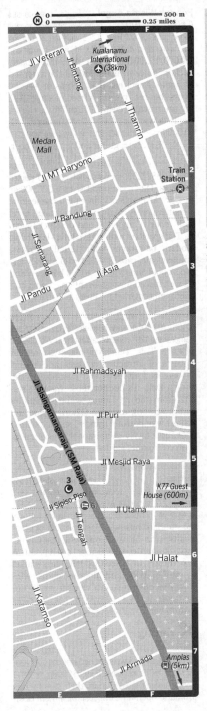

Medan

◎ Sights

◎ Sleeping

◎ Eating

surrounded by handsome colonial-era buildings, such as Bank Indonesia (p519), **Balai Kota** (Town Hall; Jl Balai Kota) and the main post office (p519).

★ **Museum of North Sumatra**　MUSEUM

(Museum Negeri Provinsi Sumatera Utara; Jl HM Joni 51; 10,000Rp; ◎9am-4pm Mon-Thu, to 3.15pm Fri-Sun) Housed in a striking traditional building, this museum has a well-presented collection ranging from early North Sumatran civilisations and Hindu, Buddhist and Islamic periods to Dutch colonial-era and military history. Highlights include fine stone carvings and extravagantly carved wooden dragon coffins from Nias, Batak scrolls for fending off misfortune, fine textiles and a *keris* (ornamental dagger) collection. It's a short way southeast of the city centre.

Istana Maimoon　PALACE

(Jl Katamso; 5000Rp; ◎8am-6pm) The grand, 30-room Maimoon Palace was built by the Sultan of Deli in 1888 and features Malay, Mughal and Italian influences. Only the main room, which features the lavish inauguration throne, is open to the public. Here you can check out a modest *keris* (ornamental dagger) collection and dress up in traditional Malay costume for a photo (20,000Rp).

Mesjid Raya　MOSQUE

(cnr Jl Mesjid Raya & SM Raja; entry by donation; ◎9am-5pm, except during prayer times) The impressive Grand Mosque was commissioned by the Sultan of Deli in 1906. The Moroccan-style building has a grand entrance, towering ceilings, ornate carvings, Italian marble and stained glass from China.

Tjong A Fie Mansion
HISTORIC BUILDING

(www.tjongafiemansion.org; Jl Ahmad Yani 105; 35,000Rp; ⊙9am-5pm) The home of a famous Chinese merchant who died in 1921 – formerly the wealthiest resident of Medan – mixes opulent Victorian and Chinese styles. The original hand-painted ceilings, Tjong's huge bedroom, imported dark-wood furniture inlaid with marble and mother-of-pearl, interesting art pieces, an upstairs ballroom and Taoist temples help to make it one of the most impressive historic buildings in town.

Graha Maria Annai Velangkanni
CHURCH

(www.velangkanni.com; Jl Sakura II; ⊙24hr) One for advocates of religious diversity and quirky architecture, this surreal Catholic church combines Hindu and Islamic architecture styles with a curved walking bridge leading up to its entrance. It's 8km southwest of the city centre (around 60,000Rp with a Grab taxi).

ᗘ Tours

Tri Jaya Tour & Travel
TOURS

(☑061-703 2967; www.trijaya-travel.com; Hotel Deli River, Jl Raya Namorambe 129; 2-person tour US$70) Superb historical city tours as well as themed multiday tours of Sumatra. You can also pick up the book *Tours Through Historic Medan and Its Surroundings,* written by the company's owner.

🛏 Sleeping

K77 Guest House
GUESTHOUSE $

(☑061-736 7087, 0813 9653 8897; www.k77guesthousemedan.blogspot.com; Jl Seto 6B; dm/r/f from 100,000/200,000/320,000Rp; ❇🛜) The best backpackers in Medan is this homestay in a quiet residential street east of the centre. Spotlessly clean rooms, comfy beds and friendly, helpful hosts Johan and Lola add up to all the things a budget guesthouse should be. The dorm has four single beds; all rooms share bathrooms and have air-con.

Dazhong Backpackers Hostel
HOSTEL $

(☑0822 7309 3888; www.dazhongx.com; Jl Muara Takus 28; s/d from 75,000/100,000Rp; 🛜) One of Medan's few budget options is this centrally located hostel that gets rave reviews from backpackers. Proud owner Mr Yauw certainly isn't lacking in confidence, and he strives to ensure his guests are looked after and is a good source of info. Rooms that share bathrooms are a bit cramped and grotty, but the price is right.

Pondok Wisata Angel
GUESTHOUSE $

(☑061-732 0702; pondokwisataangelangel@yahoo.com; Jl SM Raja 70; s with fan 80,000Rp, dm with air-con 80,000Rp, d with fan/air-con 130,000/150,000Rp; ❇🛜) A central backpacker choice near the Mesjid Raya (Grand Mosque), Angel has poky rooms on wooden floors that are in serious need of some TLC, but are passably clean. A highlight is the sociable downstairs **Angel Cafe** (mains 10,000-50,000Rp; ⊙7am-midnight; 🛜), where you can use wi-fi, strum a guitar and get a cold beer.

Ibis Styles Medan Patimura
HOTEL $$

(☑061-8881 2300; www.accorhotels.com; Jl Kapten Pattimura 442; r incl breakfast from 500,000Rp; ❇🛜❄) An excellent choice for those seeking a contemporary, well-priced, midrange hotel with modern amenities and designer touches. The spacious rooms have king-sized beds, modern bathrooms with rainfall showers, minibar, safe, cable TV, fast wi-fi and icy air-con. A pool and gym are added bonuses, and it's well placed for restaurants, a cinema and handy supermarket for beers and snacks.

Hotel Deli River
HOTEL $$

(☑061-703 2964; www.hotel-deliriver.com; Jl Raya Namorambe 129; r incl breakfast from 720,000Rp; ❇🛜❄) This Dutch-colonial-style retreat consists of attractive cottages and rooms shaded by fruit trees and overlooking the Sungai Deli. It's one for those wanting respite from the city smog while remaining within striking distance (12km) of Medan. It has a wonderfully tranquil setting, with a pool and a lovely restaurant that uses spices sourced from its garden.

Grand Swiss-Belhotel Medan
BUSINESS HOTEL $$$

(☑061-457 6999; www.swiss-belhotel.com; Jl S Parman 217; d incl breakfast 868,000-1,300,000Rp; ❇@🛜❄) This huge, five-star hotel follows the standard business-class formula of great facilities, an array of different restaurants and a guaranteed good night's sleep. But it also throws in a see-through, glass-walled swimming pool and floor-to-ceiling windows that offer great city views from the upper floors. It has a classy lobby bar as well as rooftop bar **The View** (⊙6pm-1am).

🍴 Eating

Sibolang Durian
STREET FOOD $

(☑061-456 8496; www.sibolangdurian.com; Jl Iskandar Muda 75C-D; per piece from 35,000Rp; ⊙24hr) If you haven't tried durian, then stop by this 'aromatic' open-air eating establishment dedicated to the world's smelliest fruit. It's not just some random street vendor, this is a brightly lit neon 24-hour temple to durian, with picnic tables full of locals eagerly scooping out the flesh of this gooey local treat.

Medan Vegetarian　　INDONESIAN, VEGETARIAN $
(☑061-415 5570; Jl Airlangga 23A-25; per dish 7000Rp; ☉8am-9pm; 🐵🍴) No more food envy from vegetarians who miss out on those famous Padang dishes – here you'll get the full array of delicious mock beef *rendang*, satay chicken and coconut curries, and they nail the taste and texture. As with typical Padang food there's no menu, so point to the dishes you're after (no English is spoken).

Socrates Vegan (☑061-456 8950; Jl Airlangga 14; mains 25,000-50,000Rp; ☉10am-10pm Wed-Mon; 🍴) is another vegetarian restaurant a few buildings up that's more contemporary in style.

Soto Kesawan　　INDONESIAN $
(Jl Ahmad Yani; dishes 27,000Rp; ☉8am-4.30pm) A local institution that's been around for some 60 years, this hole-in-the-wall joint is always busy with folk digging into *soto kesawan* (coconut milk with prawns, chicken, potato and beef offal), a Medan specialty.

Tip Top Restaurant　　INTERNATIONAL $
(☑061-451 4442; Jl Ahmad Yani 92; mains 26,000-73,000Rp; ☉8am-11pm; 🐵🍴) One for nostalgia buffs, here at this colonial-era relic only the prices have changed. Medan's oldest restaurant dates to 1934 and is great for a taste of bygone imperialism, with its regal white-uniformed waiters serving an array of Padang, Chinese and international dishes (though it's the old-school ice cream and desserts that are most worth trying).

A cold beer on its streetside terrace is another reason to drop by. The big negative here, however, is that shark-fin soup is featured on the menu. Eating shark fin is not recommended, as preparing the dish involves cutting the fin off the shark and then throwing the shark back into the water for it to die a painful and lingering death.

Merdeka Walk　　SOUTHEAST ASIAN $
(Lapangan Merdeka, Jl Balai Kota; dishes 10,000-45,000Rp; ☉11am-11pm; 🍴) Inspired by Singapore's alfresco dining, this contemporary collection of outdoor eating establishments in Lapangan Merdeka offers everything from doughnut stalls and fast-food chains to breezy sit-down restaurants serving grilled seafood and Malaysian-style noodles. Hours vary but it's liveliest after 5pm – come for the atmosphere rather than low prices.

The Thirty Six　　CAFE $$
(☑061-453 0970; Jl Multatuli 36; mains 38,000-120,000Rp; ☉11am-midnight; 🐵🍴) With its polished concrete floors, low-hanging light bulbs and vertical garden this is one of Medan's more stylish hang-outs. It does the likes of white truffle fries, seafood mac 'n' cheese, buttermilk waffles and pulled roast-beef sandwiches, but, its juicy Big R Burger is the standout. All-day breakfasts are another reason to come, as are the cold beers and specialty coffees.

🍸 Drinking & Nightlife

Level 02　　ROOFTOP BAR
(☑061-4556 6492; Jl Iskandar Muda; ☉4pm-midnight Sun-Thu, to 1am Fri & Sat) Channelling a hip Jakarta rooftop bar is this vibrant open-air space that's a great spot for a balmy evening with Balinese craft beers, wine and well-priced cocktails. The food's a highlight, with the likes of crab bao, lobster rolls, pub classics and the weekend brunch. There's an indoors area if you want air-con, plus an on-site wine store.

Traders　　COCKTAIL BAR
(Jl Kapten Pattimura 423; ☉noon-1am) With its long and glamorous list of cocktails (135,000Rp) and equally glamorous people, swanky Traders is the place to be seen in Medan. There are cold beers on tap, along with a semi-decent wine list.

ℹ️ Information

MEDICAL SERVICES
Rumah Sakit Columbia Asia (☑061-456 6368, 0811 617 1333; www.columbiaasia.com; Jl Listrik 2A; ☉24hr) The best hospital in the city, with a 24-hour walk-in clinic and pharmacy, as well as English-speaking doctors and specialists. For an ambulance, dial 118.

MONEY
Medan has branches of just about every bank operating in Indonesia, including **Bank Indonesia** (Jl Balai Kota; ☉8am-4pm Mon-Fri), **BCA Bank** (cnr Jl Diponegoro & Jl H Zainal Arifin; ☉8am-4pm Mon-Fri) and **BNI Bank** (Jl Pemuda; ☉24hr). Most bank headquarters sit along the junction of Jl Diponegoro and Jl H Zainal Arifin.

POST
Main Post Office (Jl Bukit Barisan; ☉8am-6pm) In an old Dutch building opposite Lapangan Merdeka.

TOURIST INFORMATION

Tourist Information Centre (Jl Balai Kota, Merdeka Walk; ⊙9am-9pm) Opposite the main post office at the edge of Merdeka Walk is this tiny tourist information booth, which is worth a visit for its city booklet on colonial architecture.

VISA

A 30-day visa on arrival is available at Medan's airport for most nationalities, but double-check the latest situation before departing.

Kantor Imigrasi Kelas 1 Polonia (☑0811 606 9973; http://polonia.imigrasi.go.id; Jl Mangkubumi 2; ⊙8am-4pm Mon-Fri) processes visa extensions. These cost 355,000Rp, and technically take three to four working days, and

cannot be processed until a few days before your current visa expires. Bring photocopies of your passport and Indonesian visa, as well as your onward ticket.

🚈 Getting There & Away

AIR

Kualanamu International Airport (☑061-8888 0300; www.kualanamu-airport.co.id) is 39km from the city centre and connected to central Medan by frequent trains and buses.

BUS

There are two major bus terminals in Medan. Purchase tickets from ticket offices outside the terminals.

TRANSPORT FROM MEDAN

Air

DESTINATION	AIRLINE	FREQUENCY
Banda Aceh	Lion Air, Citilink	4 daily
Bandung	Citilink, Lion Air	3 daily
Bangkok	AirAsia	1 daily
Gunung Sitoli	Garuda, Wings Air	6 daily
Jakarta	Batik Air, Citilink, Garuda, Lion Air, Sriwijaya Air	42 daily
Jambi	Wings Air	1 daily
Kuala Lumpur	Batik Air, AirAsia, Lion Air, Malaysia Airlines, Malindo Air	4-11 daily
Padang	Lion Air, Sriwijaya Air	3 daily
Palembang	AirAsia, Garuda, Lion Air	2 daily
Pekanbaru	Citilink, Lion Air	4 daily
Penang	AirAsia, Lion Air, Sriwijaya Air	8 daily
Pulau Batam	Citilink, Lion Air	6 daily
Pulau Simeulue	Wings Air	1 daily
Sibolga	Garuda, Wings Air	3-4 daily
Silangit	Batik Air, Wings Air	2 daily
Singapore	AirAsia, Jetstar, Silk Air, Singapore Airlines	6-7 daily
Surabaya	Lion Air	1 daily
Yogyakarta	AirAsia, Citilink	2 daily

Bus

DESTINATION	FARE (RP)	DURATION (HR)	FREQUENCY
Banda Aceh	150,000-330,000	12	several daily
Berastagi	13,000	3-4	numerous daily
Bukit Lawang	30,000	4-5	several daily
Bukittinggi	180,000-290,000	16-20	several daily
Kutacane (for Ketambe)	80,000	7	1 daily
Parapat (for Danau Toba)	42,000	5-6	several daily
Sibolga	120,000-150,000	11	several daily
Singkil	130,000	9	several daily

The **Amplas Bus Terminal** (Jl SM Raja), which serves Parapat (for Danau Toba) and other southern destinations, is 6.5km south of the city centre. Almost any *angkot* heading south on Jl SM Raja will get you to Amplas (5000Rp); Grab (p515) or Go-Jek (p515) taxis are better options, however.

The **Pinang Baris Bus Terminal** (Jl Pinang Baris), 10km west of the city centre, serves Bukit Lawang, Berastagi and Banda Aceh. However, to avoid aggresive touts at Pinang Baris, travellers are now taking the buses leaving 900m further north at the stop outside Mawar Bakery in Kampung Lalang – so ask to be dropped off there.

Minivans to Singkil and Kutacane (for Ketambe) leave from **Padang Bulan Terminal** (Jl Jamin Ginting) south of the city centre.

Most lodgings and numerous travel agencies along Jl Katamso can arrange a space for you on a shared door-to-door taxi to popular destinations such as Bukit Lawang (from 120,000Rp), Berastagi (from 120,000Rp), Danau Toba (90,000Rp) and Kutacane (130,000Rp); it's pricier than a bus but faster and slightly more comfortable.

ⓘ Getting Around

Grab (p515) and Go-Jek (p515) online taxis and *ojeks* are by far the cheapest and fastest ways of getting around town.

Otherwise, hundreds of *angkot* zip around Medan's streets and charge 5000Rp to 15,000Rp per ride. A few helpful routes include the white Mr X from Jl SM Raja to Kesawan Sq, Lapangan Merdeka and the train station, and the yellow 64 from Maimoon Palace to Sun Plaza. Becak journeys across the city centre cost between 20,000Rp and 30,000Rp.

TO & FROM THE AIRPORT

The cheapest way to get from the airport to the city is with the frequent **Damri shuttle buses** (Jl Gatot Subroto 30) departing from in front of the terminal. There are buses to central Medan (20,000Rp), Amplas (15,000Rp) and Binjai (40,000Rp). To the airport, the Damri shuttle departs from the Carrefour at Medan Fair Plaza (20,000Rp) every 15 minutes.

The fastest and most comfortable way to reach central Medan from the airport is by air-conditioned **Railink train** (☑ 061-456 1331; www.railink.co.id; 100,000Rp, 45 minutes, 4.40am to 11.40pm). From Medan city centre, trains run between 3.30am and 9.10pm. Trains depart roughly every hour.

Taxis from the airport charge a basic fare of 10,000Rp, with an additional 3500Rp per kilometre. A journey to the city centre will cost around 200,000Rp and take an hour depending on traffic.

To the airport with Grab (p515) expect to pay around 100,000Rp from the city centre for a taxi, though only drop-offs are allowed.

Paradep Shuttle (☑ 0811 621 2407) has airport buses to Sianta (one way 55,000Rp).

Bukit Lawang

☑ 061 / POP 2000

Bukit Lawang, 96km northwest of Medan, is a sprawling tourist village laced along the fast-flowing Sungai Bohorok and bordered by the dense vertical-rising jungle of Gunung Leuser National Park. Its legend is built around the orang-utan rehabilitation centre set up here in 1973 and, although the feeding platform has closed, this is still the best place in Sumatra to spot habituated orang-utans on a trek.

Trekking aside, it's a very traveller-friendly place, where you can while away the days lounging in hammocks, splashing or tubing in the river and enjoying some of the best-value jungle resorts in Sumatra.

⊙ Sights

The vast Gunung Leuser National Park, one of the richest tropical-forest ecosystems in the world, is home to eight species of primates plus tigers, rhinos, elephants and leopards. However, aside from orang-utans, gibbons, various macaque species and the curious Thomas's leaf monkey, you'll be very lucky to see any other large mammals here, as oil-palm plantations extend close to the edge of the village. At weekends, when foreign tourists are joined by masses of domestic visitors, Bukit Lawang can feel rather overrun, so try to arrive on a weekday.

🏃 Activities

Hiking

Treks into the Gunung Leuser National Park require a permit and guide and can last anywhere from three hours to several days. Most people opt for two days so they can spend the night in the jungle, which increases their likelihood of seeing orang-utans and other wildlife. It's best to hike in the smallest group possible and to set off early.

The best way to book guides is through your guesthouse. Green Hill (p522), On the Rocks (p523) and Rainforest Guesthouse (p523) in particular are good places to ensure you'll get a responsible, knowledgeable guide.

Orang-utan sightings are highly likely, but not guaranteed. When you do come across them, always remain quiet, don't use flash photography, keep a safe distance and do not attempt to feed or touch the animals. Not only are orang-utans susceptible to many human illnesses, but those in pursuit of that perfect selfie risk having their backpacks or phones snatched away or even getting attacked. Don't forget that these are wild, immensely strong animals that can crack your head like a coconut if they wish to: keep your distance.

That said, a sighting of these comical red hairy creatures, swinging freely through the trees, is nothing short of magical, and visitors are often surprised at how close they do come.

Take your time in choosing a guide, as jungle practices are not as regulated as they should be. Talk to returning hikers and decide how much jungle time you really need. People who trek with guides from the village have mainly positive feedback, with the greatest kudos going to the nightly meals and campfire socials. Common complaints include guides who don't know much about the flora and fauna, the bunching together of trekking groups and the feeding of orangutans. If you see any guides feeding orangutans, it's imperative you report them to the authorities at the Bukit Lawang Visitors Centre (p524).

'Rafting' (an extra 165,000Rp per person) back to town, which actually involves sitting on rubber tubes tied together, is a popular option that allows you to trek deeper into the jungle and makes for a fun and relaxing way to finish your trek. Prices include basic meals, guide fees, camping equipment and the park permit. Camping involves a tarpaulin sheet thrown over bamboo poles, with everyone sleeping in the same tent.

JUNGLE HIKING FEES

Guide rates are fixed by the Sumatra Guide Association and are quoted in euros (though payable in rupiah). Prices are based on a three-person minimum; if there are fewer than three people, then the cost based on three people must be paid in full by the couple or the solo traveller.

DURATION	COST PER PERSON
Half-day	€35
1 day	€45
2 days	€80
3 days	€110
4 days	€155
5 days	€190

Hiking in the jungle is no stroll in the park. You'll encounter steep, slippery ascents and precipitous drops amid intense humidity, so a good level of fitness is essential. The trails can be well-worn paths or barely visible breaks in the underbrush. Pack at least two bottles of water per day and wear sturdy footwear.

Tubing & Rafting

Giant inflated truck inner tubes can be rented (15,000Rp per day) at several places along the river; carry your tube upstream and ride the Sungai Bohorok rapids back. On weekends the river near the bridge resembles a water theme park, but don't underestimate the river. Currents are extremely strong, and when the water is high, tubing is officially off limits, though few will tell you this. Avoid the very last section as you approach the village centre.

Guides can also organise full-day rafting trips on the Sungai Wampu for €65 per person.

🛏 Sleeping

Guesthouses along the river offer plenty of rustic charm, and cater more to a backpacker crowd, though there are a few more up-market options too. The further upriver you go, the more likely you are to spot wildlife from your porch hammock. Across the river are some more laid-back options. Only a few guesthouses have hot water; some provide fans.

★ Green Hill
GUESTHOUSE $

(☑ 0813 7034 9124; www.greenhillbukitlawang.com; d with shared bathroom 100,000Rp, d/tr/q with private bathroom 200,000/250,000/300,000Rp,; 🐦) 🍃 Run by an English conservation scientist and her Sumatran husband, Green Hill has lovely stilt-high rooms ideal for couples and families, with cool en suite bamboo-shoot showers that afford stunning jungle views while you wash. There's also a budget room. They also run Kuta Langis Base Camp, a tranquil jungle retreat.

Junia Guesthouse
GUESTHOUSE $

(☑ 0813 9677 2807; www.juniaguesthouse-bukitlawang.com; r incl breakfast 155,000-570,000Rp) On the other side of the river from Bukit Lawang's main settlement is this friendly, mellow guesthouse, which has put some effort into making things sprightly, and features unique bathrooms carved into the rock face. Its choice of nine rooms range from basic fan options to air-con bungalows, and its large restaurant/bar is a cool place to hang out in the evenings.

Ida Guesthouse
GUESTHOUSE $

(☑ 0813 7660 0684; r 80,000-200,000Rp; 🛜) One of the first guesthouses you'll encounter along the river access path is this excellent-value, friendly guesthouse, with spotless rooms painted in lime green and with Western bathrooms. Upstairs has outdoor terrace seating overlooking the jungle, and there's a restaurant by the river for evening beers.

Rainforest Guesthouse
GUESTHOUSE $

(☑ 0813 6219 9018, 0813 6207 0656; www.rainforestguesthouse.com; d with shared bathroom 50,000Rp, with private bathroom 75,000-200,000Rp, family r 500,000Rp; 🛜) One of Bukit Lawang's most popular backpacker places for many a year, Rainforest has a cluster of rooms set close to the gurgling river. The cheaper ones have shared bathrooms, but pricier rooms come with bathrooms and fans. There's a little restaurant with good local and Western food and river views, and it's a super place to meet other budget travellers.

The place is still known locally as Nora's. Nora sadly passed away in 2014, and these days her fun-loving sister Nella, a great source of local info, has taken over.

★ On the Rocks
BUNGALOW $$

(☑ 0812 6303 1119; www.ontherocksbl.com; r 200,000-500,000Rp, villa 1,000,000Rp; 🛜) More on the hill than on the rocks, the nine 'tribal' huts here verge on being luxurious in a rustic way. Each hut has a verandah and sunken bathroom, and all are shrouded in peace and beautiful jungle views. It's across the river and a fair hike from Bukit Lawang's main strip, so it's a good thing the restaurant serves decent meals.

It's very kid-friendly, and has easy access to the jungle for treks. It's run by a German-Indonesian couple and their friendly team of staff.

★ Back to Nature
GUESTHOUSE $$

(☑ 0821 7055 6999, 0813 7540 0921; www.backtonaturebukitlawang.com; camping 50,000Rp, d 300,000-750,000Rp; 🛜) 🌿 Living up to its name, this lodge is on a gorgeous bend in the river a 45-minute walk from civilisation. Aca, the eco-minded owner, has preserved a giant patch of jungle that was otherwise destined to become an oil-palm plantation, and has built comfortable wooden rooms raised off the ground on stilts, plus private cottages

overlooking the jungle, which are perfect for couples.

Luxury rooms feature outdoor bathtubs with essential oils sourced from medicinal plants in the jungle. Camping is also a good option for budget travellers, and tents can be provided. Treks and pick-ups from Bukit Lawang are also offered.

EcoTravel Cottages
LODGE $$

(☑ 0822 7609 2633; www.sumatra-ecotravel.com; r 290,000-640,000Rp; ❄🛜) With huge four-poster beds, immense rooms, hammocks on porches and immaculate hot-water bathrooms, this riverfront lodge combines the ultimate in creature comforts with professionally run tours by Sumatra Ecotravel. Its deck chairs overlooking the river and jungle are great for kicking back. There are only five rooms, so reservations are a good idea.

Kuta Langis Base Camp
GUESTHOUSE $$

(☑ 0813 7034 9124; Bohorok; per person incl meals & transport 1,500,000Rp, minimum 2-night stay) On a beautiful tract of fertile land that edges directly onto Gunung Leuser National Park, this rustic hideaway is the place to escape Bukit Lawang's tourist centre. Set up by the folk from Green Hill, this former oil-palm plantation was built with trekkers in mind, but is also a wonderful place to chill out among nature. It's about 15km north of town.

Its two rooms are no frills (there's no wi-fi, TV or modern comforts), which is part of the appeal. The creek at the foot of the property is great for cooling off, and is a launching point for treks into the national park.

🍴 Eating & Drinking

Most guesthouses have their own restaurant offering a menu of both Western and Indonesian dishes. Otherwise there are some decent eating places along the river.

Lawang Inn
INDONESIAN $

(www.lawanginn.com; mains around 40,000Rp; ☉ 7am-10pm; 🛜🍴) Lawang Inn is located in the heart of the Bukit Lawang village, with a menu that comprises large portions of curries and sambal dishes, including good tempe and tofu options for vegetarians. They bake their own bread and do burgers, as well as barbecues if you pre-order. There's an impressive bar upstairs.

Waterstones
INDONESIAN $$

(www.waterstoneguesthouse.com; mains 75,000Rp; ☉ 9am-9pm; 🛜) This stylish restaurant sits directly on a dramatic bend of the river and features a mishmash of designer furniture and industrial light fittings. While its prices are high for what is fairly standard Indonesian fare, it makes a good spot for a late-afternoon beer and has a tasty rendition of guacamole and chips. There's live music Tuesday and Friday.

Cafeteria Gua Lawang
COFFEE

(☺4pm-midnight) For something different, check out this cafe that's built within a natural grotto, with murals on the walls and strong Gayo Aceh coffee and cheap beers. It also does local and international food if you're peckish.

ℹ Information

The nearby village of Gotong Royong is where most facilities can be found. If you arrive by public bus it's about a 1km walk north to the area where Bukit Lawang's accommodation begins.

Bukit Lawang Visitors Centre (☺7am-3pm) It's worth dropping in before trekking to see interesting displays of the flora and fauna found in Gunung Leuser National Park.

DANGERS & ANNOYANCES

There's a proliferation of guides in Bukit Lawang, and if you haven't prebooked a tour before your arrival in town, some pesky guides may be keen to escort you to a guesthouse and sign you up for a jungle hike the minute you arrive. Be polite and feel no obligation to book anything unless you want to.

There's also little reason to sign up for cut-price trekking tours organised by Medan's budget hotels; everything can be organised within moments of arriving in Bukit Lawang.

MONEY

At the time of research the closest ATMs were in Bohorok, 15km from Bukit Lawang, but given there's now a convenience store in Bukit Lawang, there's a good chance it'll get its own ATM soon.

You'll find money changers along the strip in the nearby village of Gotong Royong.

ℹ Getting There & Away

Direct public buses depart Medan for Bukit Lawang (30,000Rp, four hours) between 6am and 5pm, terminating at Gotong Royong, from where it's a becak ride (around 10,000Rp) to the main centre. From Medan, avoid the Pinang Baris bus terminal (notorious for its touts) and instead head 900m north to find the Mawar Bakery in Kampung Lampung, from where orange buses leave every 30 minutes.

From Medan airport you can also take the ALS bus to Binjai (40,000Rp, two hours, every 45 minutes); from Binjai, buses either leave from the Supermall, or you will need to take a becak (20,000Rp) to the Bukit Lawang bus stop, where the orange PB Semesta minibus (30,000Rp to 50,000Rp, two hours) continues to Gotong Royong terminal.

The most hassle-free way to get to Bukit Lawang from Medan is with the tourist minibuses (120,000Rp, three hours, departure around 10am). These offer a door-to-door pick-up service. From Bukit Lawang they leave at around 8am. Tourist minibuses also go to Medan's Kualanamu International Airport (190,000Rp, around four hours), departing Bukit Lawang daily at 8am.

Tourist minibuses depart for Berastagi (170,000Rp, four to five hours) and Parapat (for Danau Toba; 230,000Rp, six hours), both daily at 8.30am. There's also a bus to Banda Aceh (350,000Rp, 15½ hours) departing at 2.30pm.

Bukit Lawang is also a handy jumping-off point for day trips or onward travel to Tangkahan. Chartering a private vehicle (one way/return 600,000/750,000Rp) is by far the best way, otherwise you'll have to head to Binjai, from where you can get a connecting bus to Tangkahan (25,000Rp), which will take a full day.

By private car expect to pay around 600,000Rp to Medan, 800,000Rp to Berastagi and 1,200,000Rp to Danau Toba.

Tangkahan

A low-key alternative to the Bukit Lawang tourist scene, tiny, remote Tangkahan sits on the edge of Gunung Leuser National Park, and offers wonderful opportunities for jungle trekking, river tubing and spotting orang-utan during fruit season. However, it's developed a reputation as a place for elephant interaction, with some 10 elephants kept as part of a post-logging conservation program.

Tangkahan is not so much a village as a bus stop, a park entrance and a handful of basic riverside bungalows on the wild banks of the Sungai Kualsa Buluh.

🏃 Activities

A popular activity with both locals and visitors is renting a rubber tube (10,000Rp) and floating down the shallow river below Jungle Lodge and Dreamland Resort. Longer tubing adventures (180,000Rp, including lunch and transport) can be arranged at the CTO Visitor Centre.

Jungle Hikes
HIKING

The CTO Visitor Centre can arrange a guide to take you hiking in the Gunung Leuser National Park. A 2½-hour 'taster' is 694,400Rp for two people, while the full-day option is 1,452,000Rp for three people, which includes park permits. Good footwear is a must; prepare to get very muddy.

Elephant Interaction WILDLIFE

(elephant bathing 250,000Rp; ⊘elephant bathing 8.30am & 3.30pm Sat-Thu, elephant grazing 8.30am & 1.30pm) For most travellers, the elephants are the main draw in Tangkahan. While elephant rides are available, they're considered by many animal-welfare groups to be harmful to the animals, so opt for other activities such as giving them their daily bath. On Fridays and public holidays there are no elephant-based activities. Book directly through the CTO Visitor Centre.

There are also 'Exploring with Elephants' tours (per person 750,000Rp), where you walk alongside them in the jungle and watch them graze, as well as bathe them.

Note that elephants (even 'domesticated' ones) kill hundreds of people every year and you should exercise extreme caution in their vicinity.

🛏 Sleeping

Dreamland Resort BUNGALOW $

(☑0812 6963 1400; r incl breakfast 250,000Rp; ❄) Run by two friendly young brothers who speak good English, Dreamland has three appealing A-frame cottages with private bathrooms sitting partially hidden amid lush greenery. Its boutique cafe gives you a spectacular bird's-eye view of the river, with a full bar and board games available. It's accessed via the suspension bridge, on the right side of Mega Inn, through the fruit plantation.

Jungle Lodge GUESTHOUSE $

(☑0813 7633 4787; www.junglelodge.de; r 150,000-200,000Rp, family r 300,000Rp; 🛜) This German-Indonesian-run resort is the pick of Tangkahan's riverfront accommodation, with modern bungalows in sprawling clifftop gardens – the best have balconies with great views of the river below. The large, thatched restaurant overlooking the bubbling river is a fine place to hang out. The nearby stairs lead directly down to the river and hot spring for swimming.

❶ Information

CTO Visitor Centre (☑0852 7560 5865; www.tangkahanecotourism.com; ⊘8am-5pm) Near the bus stop in the centre of the village, the visitor centre organises everything from elephant bathing to jungle treks, tubing and caving; pay your fees here.

The closest ATM is 12km south of Tangkahan in an isolated location set up for palm-oil workers.

❶ Getting There & Away

Tangkahan is not particularly easy to get to; it's accessed by terrible, unsealed roads for the most part. Five direct morning buses go from Medan's Pinang Baris terminal (50,000Rp including baggage, four hours).

From Bukit Lawang you could take a bus to Binjai, then connect to one of the twice-daily buses directly to Tangkahan (50,000RP, four hours). If you're travelling solo, get a guide to take you directly from Bukit Lawang on a motorbike (one way/return 250,000/300,000Rp, two hours) – but be warned that the road is unpaved and it's an uncomfortable ride. Alternatively, team up with other travellers to hire a 4WD (600,000Rp to 700,000Rp, 2½ hours) from either Medan or Bukit Lawang.

Berastagi & Around

☑ 0628 / POP 44,800

At an altitude of 1300m, Berastagi is a cool mountain retreat and market town, established by colonial Dutch traders escaping the heat of sea-level Medan.

Since it's only two hours out of Medan, it's a popular retreat on weekends, when main-street traffic almost comes to a standstill. For travellers the main attraction is climbing active volcano Gunung Sibayak and exploring the surrounding Karo Highlands and villages, where vestiges of indigenous Karo Batak culture remain in the shape of the immense wooden houses with soaring thatched roofs and cattle-horn adornments.

On a clear day you can see both Gunung Sinabung to the west and the smoking Gunung Sibayak to the north. Sinabung erupted without much warning in the summer of 2015, causing the evacuation of thousands of people residing on its foothills. It still erupts intermittently and is indefinitely off limits to hikers.

⊙ Sights

⊙ Berastagi

St Francis of Assisi
Catholic Church CHURCH

(Jl Sakti Giri; ⊘24hr) Definitely not your everyday church, St Francis of Assisi is built

Berastagi

St Francis of Assisi
Catholic Church
(400m);
Gundaling Hill (3.5km);
Gunung Sibayak
Trail Base (4km);
Medan (66km);
Bukit Lawang (136km)

Gunung
Sinabung
(12 km)

Pasar Buah

Jl Gundaling

Jl Perwira

Museum
Pusaka Karo

Jl Veteran

Kopi Ta
Kopikaro

Rumah
Makan
Eropah

Jl Trimurti

Sibayak
Trans Tour
& Travel

Losmen
Sibayak
Guesthouse

Sibayak
Cafe

Jl Masjid

Jl Veteran

Jl Perniagaan

Jl Pasar

BPK Rumah
Gerga (750m);
Nachelle
Homestay
(1.4km);
Kabanjahe
(12 km);
Dokan (28 km);
Parapat (111km)

Wisma
Sibayak

Jl Udara

Lingga (11km);
Gunung Sinabung;
Ketambe (173km)

in a monumental Karo Batak style, with a traditional multitiered pointed-roof design topped with buffalo horns. The interior features stained-glass windows and an impressive soaring ceiling. Sunday mass (8am to 11am) has a gospel-style service. Also on the grounds is a traditional Karo house relocated from Dokan, which features some interesting photography and cultural relics.

Museum Pusaka Karo   MUSEUM

(Jl Perwira 3; adult/child 5000/1000Rp; ☉9am-12.30pm & 1.30-4.30pm Mon-Fri, 8.30am-1pm Sat) Set up inside the old Catholic church (c 1956) is this central museum, across from the tourist information centre, with beautifully presented displays on Karo culture and crafts, including weaponry, costumes, instruments such as gongs and traditional *padung padung* (earrings). Check out the scale model of the traditional Karo house. All captions are in English.

⊙ Around Berastagi

★ Gunung Sibayak   VOLCANO

(10,000Rp) Gunung Sibayak (2094m) is one of Indonesia's most accessible volcanoes. A guide is only really essential if you're taking the route through the jungle, but if you're trekking alone it's still a very good idea as the weather can change quickly; a German tourist got lost and perished here in 2017. The hike can be done in five hours return, and you should set out as early as possible.

Getting to the summit for sunrise is a popular time to go, but you'll have to take private transport at that hour, or you'll need to camp overnight.

If you're walking from Berastagi, guides can be booked at the tourist office and guesthouses for 200,000Rp (for up to three people, three hours walk one way). Otherwise, you can charter a vehicle part of the way for around 500,000Rp (for five people), from where it's a one-hour walk from the carpark – this is by far the best option for sunrise. Solo travellers can request they join an existing group to keep costs down.

The easiest way is to take the track that starts to the northwest of Berastagi, a 10-minute walk past the Sibayak Multinational Resthouse. Take the left-hand path beside the hut where you pay the entrance fee. From here, it's a 7km route (about three hours) to the top and fairly easy to follow, mostly along a road.

Rather than trekking from Berastagi, you can catch one of the green Kama minibuses (4000Rp) to the base of the volcano, from where it's a two-hour climb to the summit. The first bus is at 7am. There are steps part of the way, but this track is narrower and in poorer condition than the one from Berastagi.

The longest option, which should be done with a guide, is to trek through the jungle from Air Terjun Panorama; this waterfall is on the Medan road, about 5km north of Berastagi. Allow at least five hours for the walk from here.

Trails on Gunung Sibayak are neither clearly marked nor well maintained, and it is easy to get lost. During wet season, paths can be extremely slippery or even washed out. Be prepared for abrupt weather changes and bring supplies including food, drinks, warm clothing, rain gear and a torch, in case you get caught out after dark. Before setting out, pick up a map from any of the guesthouses in Berastagi and peruse their guestbooks for comments and warnings about the hike. Don't forget to pack your swimmers and a towel so you can enjoy the hot springs on the way down.

Gunung Sinabung VOLCANO
While today it's one of the most active volcanoes on the planet, remarkably Gunung Sinabung lay dormant for over 400 years until its dramatic eruption in 2010. At the time of research it remained strictly off limits for tourists, as well as for the thousands of locals who remain unable to return to their homes (turning the abandoned villages into ghost towns). Since 2010 it has remained extremely volatile, erupting periodically each year, with 23 people being killed in that time.

While the 5km exclusion zone prohibits anyone from getting close (although almost all tour operators arrange trips to the abandoned villages), you will be able to get good views of the volcano from Berastagi, particularly if it's erupting, when you'll be able to witness its lava flow.

Lingga VILLAGE
(⊙8am-5pm) The most visited of the villages around Berastagi, Lingga, a few kilometres northwest of Kabanjahe, has just a couple of traditional houses with characteristic soaring thatched roofs topped with cattle horns. There's a 5000Rp fee if you want to go inside the houses. To get here, take a yellow KT minibus from Berastagi (7000Rp, 45 minutes). Some only go as far as Kabanjahe, so check first if you'll have to change.

Museum Karolingga MUSEUM
(off Jl Kiras Bangun, Lingga; entry by donation; ⊙7am-8pm) On the road leading into the village of Lingga is this interesting little museum inside a traditional building with displays on Karo culture and artefacts. If the weather's clear, you'll get a good photo op with Gunung Sinabung looming in the background. Across the road is a fascinating church, also built in a traditional Karo design.

Air Terjun Sipiso-Piso WATERFALL
(adult/child 4000/2000Rp; ⊙8am-6pm) These narrow but impressive falls cascade 120m down to the northern end of Danau Toba, 24km from Kabanjahe and about 300m from the main road. It's worth a photo stop en route between Berastagi and Toba, or as part of a tour, but not necessarily as a trip in its own right. There's a panoramic viewpoint

at the car park, otherwise it's a 45-minute-return walk down the stairs for a closer look.

Take the Bintang Karo bus from Berastagi (8000Rp, one hour).

Dokan VILLAGE
The charming village of Dokan is around 16km south of Kabanjahe. Some half a dozen traditional houses can be found here and they're all occupied, which makes the place more interesting than any of the museum-like traditional buildings you might have seen elsewhere. However, as they remain family homes you're unlikely to be invited inside to look around. You can get here by the occasional direct minibus from Kabanjahe (7000Rp).

Rumah Bolon PALACE
(Pematang Purba; 3000Rp; ⊙9am-5pm) Located between Berastagi and Danau Toba, this impressive, well-tended palace complex sits on the edge of the village of Pematang Purba. It was the home of the Simalungan Batak chiefs until the last one died in 1947. It's a peaceful site to explore and you can go inside a number of the magnificent traditional buildings. Most people visit as part of a tour from Berastagi, but otherwise you can take an *angkot* to Kabanjahe (5000Rp), from where there are connections to Rumah Bolon (10,000Rp).

Taman Alam Lumbini BUDDHIST TEMPLE
(www.tamanalamlumbini.org; off Jl Barusjahe; ⊙9am-5pm) Located 6km east of Berastagi, this gleaming golden Buddhist temple is a replica of the famous Shwedagon Pagoda in Yangon, Myanmar. You'll need to arrange a taxi or *ojek* to get here.

◎ Semangat Gunung

On the descent from Gunung Sibayak, you can stop off at the various hot springs in **Semangat Gunung**, on the road towards Berastagi. You'll be disappointed if you're expecting natural springs; instead, you'll find a complex of small concrete pools – but the forested outlooks are lovely. Have a look at a few to decide on which is the nicest; **Mitra Sibayak** (5000Rp) is probably the most scenic and is open 24 hours.

They are best visited on the weekend; on weekdays public transport stops at around 3pm or 4pm and you may face a long walk to the main road. To get here you can take the yellow KT minibus from Berastagi (6000Rp, 30 minutes).

🛏 Sleeping

★ Nachelle Homestay
GUESTHOUSE $

(☎ 0813 6242 9977, 0821 6275 7658; www.nachelle
homestay.wordpress.com; Jl Veteran; r with shared
bathroom 190,000-220,000Rp, with private bathroom 280,000-400,000Rp; 📶) By far the most
traveller-friendly place in Berastagi, Nachelle Homestay is run by Mery and Abdy,
who speak excellent English and will issue
you with a map. Rooms are modern, super-
clean and comfortable, and there's a rooftop
terrace with views of Sinabung. It has an
unconventional location set back from the
main road with no sign; call for directions.

The tours with Abdy, who has an excellent
knowledge of the region and Karo culture,
are worth doing.

Wisma Sibayak
GUESTHOUSE $

(☎ 0628-91104; Jl Udara 1; r with shared bathroom 60,000-80,000Rp, with private bathroom
150,000Rp; @📶) This centrally located guesthouse has a prim, old-school feel – there's a
10pm curfew and extra cost for hot showers
– but the cheapest rooms really are cheap,
and the better ones are clean and spacious.
There's also an inviting little restaurant with
cold beers and a menu catering to backpackers, making this one of the best choices for
independent travellers.

Losmen Sibayak Guesthouse
GUESTHOUSE $

(☎ 0628-91122; dicksonpelawi@yahoo.com; Jl
Veteran 119; r with shared/private bathroom from
75,000/100,000Rp; @📶) Behind Sibayak
Trans Tour & Travel, this longstanding
cheapie has rooms that have a lot of Indonesian personality, making the place feel more
like a homestay. The best rooms come with
hot water (150,000Rp). Wi-fi is in the lobby.

🍴 Eating & Drinking

BPK Rumah Gerga
INDONESIAN $

(Jl Veteran; meals 20,000Rp; ⏰10am-6.30pm)
A good place to sample local Karo cuisine
is this shack restaurant with wood-crate-
panelled walls decorated in murals. The speciality here is BPK (babi panggang Karo).

Try to get here before 5pm as they sometimes sell out of food. It's close to Nachelle
Homestay, otherwise it's a 15-minute walk
from the giant cabbage monument.

Rumah Makan Eropah
CHINESE $

(Jl Veteran 20; mains 20,000-60,000Rp; ⏰8am-
8pm; 📶) Feast on pork-belly soup, pork with
green chilli, sweet and sour fish, fresh vegetables or a host of noodle and rice dishes
at this welcoming Chinese place. Cold beer
is available.

Sibayak Cafe
INTERNATIONAL $$

(☎ 0821 6301 8989; Jl Veteran 121; mains 20,000-
85,000Rp; ⏰8am-10pm; 📶) Next to Losmen
Sibayak Guesthouse, this bright, modern,
open-fronted place is where a youthful
crowd meets for pizza and smoothies or ice-
cold Bintangs. It also does jaffles, sandwiches
and mie goreng (fried noodles) and the like.

Kopi Ta Kopikaro
COFFEE

(Jl Veteran; ⏰7.30am-6pm) This cool little cafe
plays local indie music and serves excellent
coffee using beans sourced locally (and from
across Indonesia), made by friendly baristas
who know their stuff. It also does simple lo-
cal meals.

ℹ Information

Some recommended places for onward travel
advice as well as local tours are **Sibayak Trans
Tour & Travel** (☎ 0628-91122; dicksonpelawi@
yahoo.com; Jl Veteran 119; ⏰7am-10pm), Na-
chelle Homestay and the **tourist information
centre** (☎ 0628-91084, 0852 9752 4725; Jl
Gundaling 1; ⏰7.30am-6pm).

There are ATMs and banks halfway between
the giant cabbage landmark and the war monu-
ment on Jl Veteran.

ℹ Getting There & Away

The **bus terminal** (Jl Veteran) is conveniently
located in the town centre. Long-distance buses
pass through Berastagi en route to Kabanjahe,
the local hub. You can catch buses to Medan's
Padang Bulan (13,000Rp, three to four hours)

LOCAL SPECIALITIES

Rich volcanic soils in the surrounding
countryside supply produce to North
Sumatra, which passes through Berast-
agi's markets. Local specialities include
passionfruit and marquisa Bandung
(large, sweet, yellow-skinned fruit), plus
marquisa asam manis (purple-skinned
fruit), which make delicious drinks.

Berastagi is a largely Christian com-
munity, so you can get babi (pork) here,
including the Karo dish babi panggang
Karo (BPK; barbecued pork and rice,
served with banana flower or cassava
leaves, green chilli sauce, soup and pig
blood).

Another local favourite is pisang
goreng (fried banana).

anywhere along the main street between 6am and 8pm. There's also an Almasar bus that goes to Medan's airport (40,000Rp) departing every two hours.

The cheapest way to reach Danau Toba is to catch an *angkot* to Kabanjahe (5000Rp, 20 minutes), change to a bus for Pematangsiantar (20,000Rp, 2½ hours), then connect with a Parapat-bound bus (15,000Rp, 1½ hours). There are no direct buses for Bukit Lawang, so take a bus to Medan's Pinang Baris (the stop at Mawar Bakery; 13,000Rp, two to four hours) and change for Bukit Lawang (30,000Rp, five hours). Berastagi is the southern approach for visits to Gunung Leuser National Park; catch a bus to Kutacane (50,000Rp) from where it's a 20,000Rp bus ride to Ketambe. Otherwise a shared taxi departs Berastagi at 2pm for Ketambe (250,000Rp).

Several private companies run a shared minibus or car service, connecting Berastagi to Medan's Padang Bulan (100,000Rp, 2½ hours) and Medan's Kualanamu International Airport (150,000Rp, three hours); Bukit Lawang (150,000Rp, three to four hours) at 8am and 2pm; and Danau Toba (to Parapat; 150,000Rp, 3½ to four hours) at 1pm.

❶ Getting Around

Angkot to the surrounding villages leave from the bus terminal. They run every few minutes between Berastagi and Kabanjahe (5000Rp), the major population and transport centre of the highlands. You can wave them down anywhere along the main road.

Parapat

☑ 0625 / POP 5500

The mainland departure point for Danau Toba, Parapat is a lakeside town with a handful of hotels, restaurants and travel agents. Unless you arrive too late to catch a boat to Tuk Tuk, there's no reason to overnight here.

The commercial sector of this cramped town is clumped along the Trans-Sumatran Hwy (Jl SM Raja) and has banks, ATMs and plenty of basic eating places. Most buses and minibuses pick up and drop off passengers at ticket agents along the highway or at the pier.

🛏 Sleeping & Eating

The highway strip (Jl SM Raja) is well equipped to feed the passing traveller, and there are a handful of restaurants near the boat dock.

Melissa Palace   HOTEL $
(☑ 0813 9223 6383; Jl Nelson Purba 28; r incl breakfast 200,000-265,000Rp; ❀) A welcom-

ing cheapie with spacious, comfortable rooms (but temperamental plumbing) and a rooftop hang-out: watch out for monkeys. It's ideal for catching the morning ferry if you get in too late to catch the last boat to Tuk Tuk.

❶ Getting There & Around

BUS

The **bus terminal** (Jl SM Raja) is about 2km east of town, but it's infrequently used by travellers. From here you could, however, make your way by public bus to Berastagi (48,000Rp, five hours, via Pematang Siantar and then Kabanjahe), Medan (42,000Rp, five to six hours) and Sibolga (70,000Rp, seven hours).

PT Bagus Holidays (☑ 0813 6113 5704, 0813 9638 0170) is one of several operators next to the ferry pier that arranges tourist minibuses and car transfers to the most popular destinations. Don't think these are quick trips though – the long-distance journeys are longer and more cramped than equivalent bus journeys. Tourist minibuses go to Medan (90,000Rp, five hours), Berastagi (140,000Rp, 3½ hours), Bukittinggi (190,000Rp to 290,000Rp, 19 hours), Bukit Lawang (180,000Rp, seven hours), Padang (180,000Rp to 280,000Rp, 18 hours) and Sibolga (150,000Rp, six hours).

A car to Medan is about 600,000Rp.

Angkot run constantly between the ferry dock and the bus terminal (3000Rp).

Danau Toba

☑ 0625 / POP 131,000

Danau Toba has been part of traveller folklore for decades. This grand ocean-blue lake, found up among Sumatra's volcanic peaks, is where the amiable Christian Batak people reside. The secret of this almost mythical place was opened up by intrepid travellers years ago. While these days Tuk Tuk – the knobby village on the lake's inner island – is on the beaten Sumatran overland path, it's still one of the undisputed highlights of central Sumatra.

Danau Toba is the largest lake in Southeast Asia, covering a massive 1707 sq km. In the middle of this huge expanse is Pulau Samosir, a wedge-shaped island almost as big as Singapore that was created by an eruption between 30,000 and 75,000 years ago. In fact, Samosir isn't actually an island at all. It's linked to the mainland by a narrow isthmus at the town of Pangururan – and then cut again by a canal.

Danau Toba

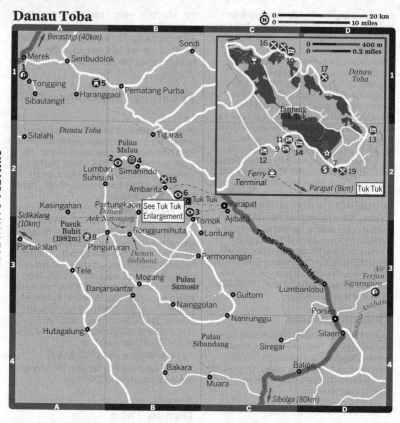

◉ Sights

King Sidabutar's Grave
HISTORIC SITE

(Tomok; entry by donation; ◷ dawn-dusk) Located 5km southeast of Tuk Tuk, near the Tomok

ferry terminal, is a complex of royal Batak tombs. At the entrance you'll pass sarcophagi of royal members and family, but to find the tomb of King Sidabutar you'll need to go

500m past the souvenir stalls and look for the sign. Close by are some well-preserved traditional Batak houses and the Museum Tomok, which has interesting displays of Batak artefacts.

Batak Graves   HISTORIC SITE
Amid the fertile rice fields between Simanindo and Pangururan are these large multistorey graves decorated with the distinctive miniature Batak-style house and a simple white cross. Batak graves reflect the animistic attitudes of sheltering the dead (who are dug out 10 to 15 years after their original internment and reburied after the polishing of the bones).

Museum Huta Bolon Simanindo   MUSEUM
(Simanindo; 10,000Rp; ⊗8am-4pm) At Samosir's northern tip, in the village of Simanindo, 15km north of Tuk Tuk, there's a beautifully restored traditional house that now functions as a museum. It was formerly the home of Rajah Simalungun, a Batak king, and his 14 wives. The roof was originally decorated with 10 buffalo horns, representing the 10 generations of the dynasty. There's also a complex of traditional houses, where traditional Batak dances are performed at 10.30am and 11.45am Monday to Saturday and 11.45am Sunday.

Stone Chairs   HISTORIC SITE
(Ambarita; 10,000Rp, guide 50,000Rp; ⊗7am-6pm) In the village of Ambarita, 5km north of Tuk Tuk, is a group of 300-year-old stone chairs, where important matters were discussed among village elders. Here wrongdoers were tried and led to a further group of stone furnishings where they were bound, blindfolded, sliced, rubbed with garlic and chilli, and then beheaded. Rumours abound that this story is the product of an overactive imagination and that the chairs are just 60 years old. There are also eight Batak houses here.

🏃 Activities

Cycling & Motorcycling
Pulau Samosir's sleepy roads make the island perfect for exploring by motorbike or bicycle. Zipping through the scenic countryside enclosed by lush volcanic mountains and stunning Danau Toba is the highlight for many who visit. The rice paddies and friendly villages are cultivated around sober Protestant-style churches and tombs merging traditional Batak architecture and Christian crosses.

For panoramic views of the entire lake, head up the winding road to **Pusuk Buhit**

(Holy Mountain), just to the west of Pulau Samosir.

Swimming
Danau Toba reaches a depth of 450m in places and is refreshingly cool. The best swimming on the south coast is said to be at Carolina Cottages, and many cottages on the north coast maintain weed-free swimming. There are also a couple of attractive beaches on Samosir's north coast. Unfortunately jet skis and jet boats are a bit of a blight on the otherwise tranquil scenery.

Hiking
There are several worthwhile hikes on Pulau Samosir and around Danau Toba. The trails aren't well marked and can be difficult to find, so check with your guesthouse about which ones are doable and ask for a map. In wet season (December to March) the steep inclines are very muddy and slippery.

The central highlands of Samosir are about 700m above the lake and on a clear day afford stunning views of mist-cloaked mountains. The top of the escarpment forms a large plateau and at its heart is a small lake, Danau Sidihoni. Much of the plateau is covered with cinnamon, clove and coffee plantations, interspersed with pine forest and the odd waterfall.

Guides aren't essential but they are a good idea if you're alone, as visitors have gotten lost in the past. The going rate is around 200,000Rp; Liberta Homestay (p532) can help arrange one. Otherwise Tabo Cottages offers more specialised trekking tours.

👉 Tours & Courses

Tabo Cottages Tours   CULTURAL
(📱0625-451318; www.tabocottages.com; Jl Lingkar Tuktuk, Tuk Tuk; 2-person tours 600,000-1,200,000Rp) Tabo Cottages (p533) runs specialty tours with themes that include Batik culture, cycling, food and coffee. They are also developing signed hiking trails across Pulau Samosir. Prices are for two people and include lunch. Spaces are limited and guests staying at the cottages are given priority.

Juwita Cafe   COOKING
(📱0625-451217; Jl Lingkar Tuktuk, Tuk Tuk; 1/2/3/4 dishes 250,000/325,000/350,000/375,000Rp) Friendly matriarch and owner Heddy hosts cooking courses during which you'll learn a few Batak-inspired Indonesian recipes using a choice of vegetarian, chicken or fish ingredients. Courses last around 2½ hours

THE BATAKS

British traveller William Marsden astonished the 'civilised' world in 1783 when he returned to London with an account of a cannibalistic kingdom in the interior of Sumatra that, nevertheless, had a highly developed culture and a system of writing. The Bataks have been a subject of fascination ever since.

The Bataks are a Proto-Malay people descended from neolithic mountain tribes from northern Thailand and Myanmar (Burma) who were driven out by migrating Mongolian and Siamese tribes. When the Bataks arrived in Sumatra they trekked inland, making their first settlements around Danau Toba, where the surrounding mountains provided a natural protective barrier. They lived in virtual isolation for centuries.

The Bataks were among the most warlike peoples in Sumatra, and villages were constantly feuding. They were so mistrustful that they did not build or maintain natural paths between villages, or construct bridges. The practice of ritual cannibalism, which involved eating the flesh of a slain enemy or a person found guilty of a serious breach of *adat* (traditional law), survived among the Toba Bataks until 1816.

Today there are more than six million Bataks, divided into six main linguistic groups, and their lands extend 200km north and 300km south of Danau Toba. Technically they are only supposed to marry other Bataks (if outside their own clan), but over the years several foreigners have married in; they had to be 'adopted' by a Batak clan first.

The Bataks have long been squeezed between the Islamic strongholds of Aceh and West Sumatra, and despite several Acehnese attempts to conquer and convert, it was the European missionaries who finally quelled them with Christianity.

The majority of today's Bataks are Protestant Christians, although many still practise elements of traditional animist belief and ritual, particularly when it comes to honouring dead ancestors, who are buried in elaborate tombs and dug up after 10 to 15 years so that their bones can be cleaned, polished and reburied. The Bataks also believe the banyan to be the tree of life; they tell a legend of their omnipotent god Ompung, who created all living creatures by dislodging decayed branches of a huge banyan into the sea.

Music is a great part of Batak culture and a Batak man is never far from his guitar. The Bataks are also famous for their powerful and emotive hymn singing. Most of their musical instruments are similar to those found elsewhere in Indonesia – cloth-covered copper gongs in varying sizes struck with wooden hammers; a small two-stringed violin, which makes a pure but harsh sound; and a kind of reedy clarinet.

and you'll get to eat whatever you've cooked. Book a day in advance.

✯ Festivals & Events

Danau Toba Festival CULTURAL
This week-long festival features Batak cultural performances, with canoe races being the highlight. The month it's held varies year to year, so check ahead.

🛏 Sleeping

★ Liberta Homestay GUESTHOUSE $
(☑ 0625-451035; liberta_homestay@yahoo.co.id; Jl Lingkar Tuktuk, Tuk Tuk; r with shared bathroom 44,000Rp, with private bathroom 66,000-88,000Rp; 🛜) This backpacker fave close to the ferry dock has limited lake views, but a chill universe is created by a lush garden and arty versions of traditional Batak houses. Crawling around the garden paths, balconies and shortened doors of the rooms is cool, there's a good

cafe, and the popular Mr Moon and Freddy are great sources of travel information.

Romlan Guesthouse GUESTHOUSE $
(☑ 0822 7685 5722, 0625-451386; www.romlantuk.com; Tuk Tuk; r with shared bathroom 50,000-135,000Rp, with private bathroom 160,000Rp; 🌐🛜) Run by a German-Indonesian family, this waterfront guesthouse is one of the original places to stay in Tuk Tuk and it's still going strong. Choose between a Western-style room with hot shower and verandah, one of two traditional Batak houses, or save your pennies in the budget room.

There's no sign, so look out for Hotel Sumber Pulo Mas, which it shares a driveway with, or better yet ask the ferry to drop you directly at its doorstep.

Bagus Bay Homestay GUESTHOUSE $
(☑ 0823 6822 9003, 0625-451287; www.bagusbay.com; Jl Lingkar Tuktuk, Tuk Tuk; s with shared

bathroom from 50,000Rp, d 100,000-300,000Rp; @🛜) Rooms in traditional Batak houses overlook avocado trees, a children's playground and a grassy badminton court at this excellent budget resort. The more expensive rooms come with hot water and lake views, and pot plants add a nice green touch. At night its restaurant, which has Batak dance at 8.15pm on Wednesday and Saturday, is a lively spot for travellers to congregate.

It has a well-stocked bar, pool table and motorbikes for rent (per day 70,000Rp).

Merlyn Guesthouse GUESTHOUSE $
(📋0813 6116 9130; merlynguesthouse@mail.com; Jl Lingkar Tuktuk, Tuk Tuk; r 100,000-150,000Rp; 🛜) On the lakeshore is this old-school Danau Toba–style guesthouse run by an Indonesian-German couple. The cheaper rooms are in traditional, character-filled wooden Batak houses with dwarf-sized doors and shared bathrooms, otherwise there are modern rooms in sunny colours with hot-water bathrooms. All look out to the lake and well-maintained garden.

Harriara Guesthouse GUESTHOUSE $
(📋0813 7539 7765, 0625-451183; harriaraguesthouse88@gmail.com; Jl Lingkar Tuktuk, Tuk Tuk; r 200,000-300,000Rp; 🛜) This guesthouse has a top-notch lakeside setting, riotous tropical flower gardens and sparkling rooms with mosquito nets and porches overlooking the water. There's good swimming from the front lawn. If there's nobody at the reception ask at the restaurants across the road.

⭐Tabo Cottages RESORT $$
(📋0625-451318; www.tabocottages.com; Jl Lingkar Tuktuk, Tuk Tuk; r incl breakfast 390,000-490,000Rp, cottage 680,000-750,000Rp; ✳@🛜🏊) The most stylish accommodation on Pulau Samosir is this sprawling German-run lakeside place that has the feel and professionalism of a laid-back resort. Rooms are inside blocks of beautiful Batak-style buildings, with huge bathrooms and hammocks, and there's a superb lakefront pool. Owner Annette is a treasure trove of information on Batak culture.

The homemade bread and cakes at the attached German bakery are worth a stop. It also roasts its own coffee beans, which are grown on the island. Its tours (p531) are another highlight.

⭐Horas Family Home COTTAGE $$$
(📋0813 6105 1419, 0813 6206 0838; www.holidaysumatra.com; Jl Lingkar Tuktuk, Tuk Tuk; family cottages 700,000-1,000,000Rp; ✳🛜🏊) Horas Family Home is perfect for those wanting a homely space with cooking facilities, and is a unique option for those seeking something different. Best is its gorgeous, renovated traditional Batak house, with original furnishings and self-contained modern facilities. Dutch-Indonesian hosts Berend and Mian are exceptionally helpful and knowledgable about Batak culture.

The superb food options include fresh fish, freshwater prawns, wild pork and forest snake, and there's a fish pond from where you can catch your dinner for free. Organic vegetables are grown in the garden, and you're free to pick them yourself.

A swimming pool and kayaks round out the experience. Also be sure to admire Berend's impressive collection of orchids. Transfers and tours can be organised on request.

🍴 Eating

Lots of resorts and guesthouses in Tuk Tuk have their own restaurants, but there are some very good independent places as well, many serving the Batak specialty of barbecued carp (most from fish farms), along with Indonesian and Western fare.

Poppy's Restaurant INDONESIAN $
(📋0813 6123 9828; Jl Lingkar Tuktuk, Tuk Tuk; mains 30,000-55,000Rp; ⊙7am-10pm) An old-school traveller hang-out, Poppy's has fantastic lake views that make it the perfect place to enjoy a cold beer. It has a classic Toba menu of Indonesian mains, grilled fish and pizza, along with friendly staff, a book exchange and very cheap rooms (100,000Rp) looking out to the water.

Borobudur House VEGAN, ICE CREAM $
(Martoba, Samosir; mains 35,000-55,000Rp; ⊙10am-6pm; 🌱) The Buddhist shrines

---

MAGIC MUSHROOMS

Magic or 'special' omelettes used to be common on restaurant menus but these days their availability is more discreet. We probably don't need to tell you that the mushrooms contained in these are not of the sort that you can buy at your local supermarket, and should be treated with caution or avoided completely. Though you will see signs advertising them on the street in Tuk Tuk, it is important to understand they are technically illegal.

scattered about set the mood at this waterfront cafe that specialises in vegan cuisine. Expect the likes of potato *rendang*, tofu steaks, and guacamole dips with homemade chips. However, it's most famous for its delicious homemade sorbet (25,000Rp) in flavours including durian, dragon fruit and pineapple.

Today's Cafe INTERNATIONAL **$**

(Jl Lingkar Tuktuk 30, Tuk Tuk; mains 20,000-65,000Rp; ⊗9am-10pm; 🛜🥄) This little wooden shack has a laid-back vibe that's in keeping with Tuk Tuk life. It's run by a couple of friendly ladies who whip up some fabulous and eclectic dishes such as *saksang* (chopped pork with brown coconut sauce, cream and a wealth of spices), aubergine curry and chapatis with guacamole. Homemade yoghurt is a hit for breakfast. Also does beers and spirits.

⭐ **Jenny's Restaurant** INTERNATIONAL **$$**

(Jl Lingkar Tuktuk, Tuk Tuk; mains 44,000-80,000Rp; ⊗8am-10pm) Jenny's has long been a standout on the northern edge of Tuk Tuk, with all kinds of breakfasts, noodles, curries and rice dishes. But the one dish that really shines is the lake fish grilled on charcoal right in front of you and served with chips and salad – available from 6pm. Follow it up with the generously portioned fruit pancake.

Cold beer and *arak* cocktails are on the menu.

⭐ **Maruba** INDONESIAN **$$**

(Jl Lingkar Tuktuk, Tuk Tuk; mains 35,000-95,000Rp; ⊗7.30am-10pm) Tucked away between the Amartoba Hotel and Rodeo guesthouse, Maruba is well worth seeking out for its peerless Batak dishes cooked by the talented proprietor. Freshwater lobster, *na neura*

(raw fish marinated with candlenut, lime juice and spices) and *saksang* are real local treats. A range of burgers and sandwiches feature homemade bread and baguettes.

 Drinking & Nightlife

Brando's Blues Bar BAR

(📞0852 3822 0226, 0625-451084; Jl Lingkar Tuktuk, Tuk Tuk; ⊗noon-late) One of a handful of genuine bars in Tuk Tuk, with pool tables and occasional live bands, that gets particularly lively on weekends. Happy hour is a civilised 6pm to 10pm and you can take to the small dance floor during the reggae and house sets.

Roy's Pub LIVE MUSIC

(📞0812 6456 6363, 0821 7417 4576; Jl Lingkar Tuktuk, Tuk Tuk; ⊗9pm-2am Tue, Thu & Sat; 🛜) The best nights out on Pulau Samosir are the Tuesday, Thursday and Saturday live-music nights (normally with local rock bands) at Roy's, a graffiti-splattered building with a dancing vibe. Great, alcohol-fuelled fun.

 Shopping

In Tuk Tuk's many souvenir shops, look for local Gayo embroidery made into a range of bags, cushion covers and place mats.

Around Tuk Tuk, woodcarvers sell figures, masks, boxes and *porhalaan* (traditional Batak calendars made of wood and buffalo bone). You'll also find traditional musical instruments and elaborately carved totem poles that untwist into several sections for easier transport.

 Information

There are ATMs in **Ambarita** (⊗24hr), **Tomok** (Jl Pulau Samosir) and Pangururan, with the **Mandiri Bank ATM** (Jl Lingkar Tuktuk) in Tuk Tuk the most convenient for tourists.

BATAK PUPPET DANCE

A purely Batak tradition is the Sigalegale puppet dance, once performed at funerals but now more often a part of wedding ceremonies. The life-sized puppet, carved from the wood of a banyan tree, is dressed in the traditional costume of red turban, loose shirt and blue sarong. The Sigalegale stand up on long, wooden boxes where the operator makes them dance to gamelan (percussion orchestra) music accompanied by flute and drums.

One story of the origin of the Sigalegale puppet concerns a widow who lived on Samosir. Bereft and lonely after the death of her husband, she made a wooden image of him and whenever she felt lonely hired a *dalang* (puppeteer and storyteller) to make the puppet dance and a *dukun* (mystic) to communicate with the soul of her husband.

Whatever its origins, the Sigalegale soon became part of Batak culture and were used at funeral ceremonies to revive the souls of the dead and to communicate with them. Personal possessions of the deceased were used to decorate the puppet, and the *dukun* would invite the deceased's soul to enter the wooden puppet as it danced on top of the grave.

SUMATRA DANAU TOBA

Foreign-exchange rates at the island's hotels and money changers are pretty awful.

Getting There & Away

AIR

Silangit International Airport (www.silangit-airport.co.id/en), located 77km south of Parapat, receives daily flights from Medan (30 minutes) and Jakarta (two hours). If flying from Medan, keep in mind that given it's a further two-hour taxi drive to Parapat (around 400,000Rp), you'll only really be saving a couple of hours. Direct flights from Singapore are planned in the future.

DESTINATION	AIRLINE	FREQUENCY
Medan	Wings Air	daily
Jakarta	Batik Air, Citilink, Sriwijaya Air	4 daily

BOAT

Ferries between Parapat and Tuk Tuk (15,000Rp, 11 daily) operate about every hour from 8.30am to 7pm. **Ferries** stop at Bagus Bay (35 minutes), then continue north, stopping on request.

The first and last ferries from Tuk Tuk leave at 7am and 5.30pm respectively; check exact times with your lodgings.

When leaving for Parapat, stand on your hotel jetty and wave a ferry down.

Fourteen ferries a day shuttle motorbikes and people between Parapat and Tomok (10,000Rp), from 7am to 7pm. From Tomok there's also a car ferry with four or five services a day.

LAND

For direct buses to Medan, Bukit Lawang and Berastagi you'll need to get to Parapat. A private car to Medan will cost about 600,000Rp. Otherwise to get to Berastagi from Samosir you'll need to take a string of public buses. Catch a bus from Tomok to Pangururan (20,000Rp, one hour), then take another bus to Berastagi (60,000Rp, three hours), which also continues on to Medan. This bus goes via Sidikalang (40,000Rp), which is also a transfer point to Kutacane and Singkil. Most guesthouses and travel agencies can prebook the pricier, direct shared-minibus tickets from Parapat for you.

Getting to Singkil involves several connecting public buses and shared cars along a Tomok–Pangururan–Sidikalang–Singkil route (200,000Rp, nine to 12 hours), which will likely involve a night in Sidikalang; for more info enquire at Liberta Homestay (p532), or Banyak Island Travel (p552) in Singkil. Otherwise a private car will cost 1,200,000Rp to 1,600,000Rp.

Getting Around

Local buses serve the whole of Samosir except Tuk Tuk. Minibuses run between Tomok and

Ambarita (5000Rp), continuing to Simanindo (10,000Rp) and Pangururan (20,000Rp); flag them down on the main road. Services dry up after 5pm. The peaceful, generally well-maintained (yet narrow) island roads are good for travelling by motorbike (70,000Rp to 100,000Rp per day) or bicycle (30,000Rp to 40,000Rp per day), both easily rented from guesthouses and tourist shops around Tuk Tuk.

Sibolga

0631 / POP 86,500

Sibolga is one of two jump-off points for boats to Pulau Nias (the other being Singkil), with daily departures to the island. It's not a particularly pleasant port town and is renowned for its touts. Dragging around surf gear can invite inflated prices: bargain hard or accept a degree of extra 'service'. Arrive as early in the day as possible to ensure a place on a boat departing that evening.

There are numerous ATMs. **BNI Bank** (Jl Katamso) is a good bet.

Sleeping

Hotel Wisata Indah   RESORT $$
(*0631-23688; Jl Katamso 51; r incl breakfast 450,000-600,000Rp; ❄ ☎ ✉) If you absolutely must stay overnight in Sibolga, Hotel Wisata Indah is the pick of a pretty uninspiring lot. Its dated, shabby rooms offer sea views, and the staff are helpful but speak little English. Its only saving grace is its pool and outdoor restaurant serving beer.

Getting There & Away

AIR

Sibolga is linked to Medan by three to four daily flights with Wings Air and Garuda, and to Jakarta by a daily Garuda flight.

BOAT

Boats to Pulau Nias leave from the **ferry terminal** (Jl Horas) at the end of Jl Horas. **ASDP** (*0811 626 5229; www.indonesiaferry.co.id) runs three services a week (Tuesday, Thursday and Saturday) to Gunung Sitoli at 7pm (economy/VIP 65,000/120,000Rp, 10 to 13 hours). Ferries to Teluk Dalam leave only on Monday at 6pm (economy/VIP 78,000/140,000Rp, 11 to 14 hours). A car/motorbike costs 1,178,000/118,000Rp.

Buy tickets from the harbour. VIP class is air-conditioned; if travelling economy, get there early to claim your seat. Ferries generally leave one to two hours late. If you arrive in Sibolga and are told you have just missed the boat it is often worth going to the harbour yourself to verify this. Surfboards sometimes incur extra charges.

BUSES FROM SIBOLGA

DESTINATION	FARE (RP)	DURATION (HR)	FREQUENCY
Bukittinggi	150,000-250,000	13-14	several daily
Medan	120,000-150,000	8-14	several daily
Padang	150,000-250,000	16	several daily
Parapat	100,000-120,000	6-7	1 daily
Singkil	120,000-140,000	6	several daily

SUMATRA PULAU NIAS

BUS

The **bus terminal** (Jl SM Raja) is on Jl SM Raja, 2km from the harbour. You can ask the bus driver to drop you off at the harbour. A becak between the two should be around 8000Rp.

PULAU NIAS

☑ 0639

The Indian Ocean roars its way to Indonesia, arriving in one of the world's most spectacular surf breaks here on remote Pulau Nias: a sizeable but solitary rock off the northern Sumatran coast. Surfers have been coming here for decades for the waves on superb Teluk Sorake, which has deservedly kept this far-flung island on the international surfing circuit. Away from the waves, the fascinating traditional villages, architecture and ancient megalithic monuments have great appeal for non-surfers.

Chloroquine-resistant malaria has been reported on Nias, so be sure to take appropriate precautions.

Visit Nias Island (www.visitniasisland. com) offers an excellent overview of things to do on the island.

History

Local legend has it that Niassans are the descendants of six gods who came to earth and settled in the central highlands. Anthropologists link them to just about everyone: the Bataks of Sumatra, the Naga of Assam in India, the aborigines of Taiwan and various Dayak groups in Kalimantan.

Nias' history is the stuff of campfire tales, with prominent themes of headhunting, dark magic and human sacrifice; but this isn't ancient history – the first Aussie surfers to ride Sorake's waves in the 1970s were stalked by a rogue shaman bent on collecting a human head.

Traditionally, Niassan villages were presided over by a village chief, who headed a council of elders. Beneath the aristocratic upper caste were the common people, and below them the slaves, who were often traded. Until the first years of the 19th century, Nias' only connection with the outside world was through the slave trade.

Sometimes villages would band together to form federations, who often fought each other. Prior to the Dutch conquest and the arrival of missionaries, intervillage warfare was fast and furious, spurred on by the desire for revenge, slaves or human heads. Heads were needed for stately burials, wedding dowries and the construction of new villages.

When the people weren't warring, they were farming, a tradition that continues today. They cultivated yams, rice, maize and taro, despite the thick jungle, and raised pigs as a source of food and a symbol of wealth and prestige; the more pigs you had, the higher your status in the village. Gold and copper work, as well as woodcarving, were important industries.

The indigenous religion was thought to have been a combination of animism and ancestor worship, with some Hindu influences. Today the dominant religions on Nias are Christianity and Islam, overlaid with traditional beliefs.

The island did not come under full Dutch control until 1914. Today's population of about 656,000 is spread through more than 650 villages, some inaccessible by road.

❶ Getting There & Away

These days most travellers fly to Nias, but the slow ferry is still an option.

AIR

Binaka Airport (p538), around 20km south of Gunung Sitoli, is served by Wings Air and Garuda flights from Medan (one hour, six daily) and Padang (one hour, one daily). Extra charges generally apply to surfboards.

BOAT

Ferries link Nias with the mainland towns of Sibolga and Singkil. Twice-weekly ferries from

Pulau Nias

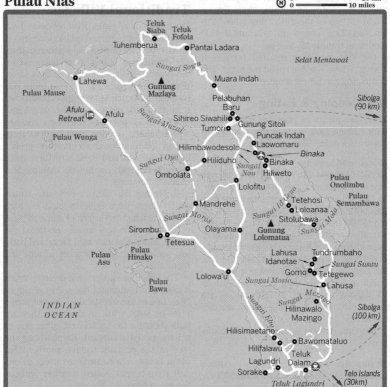

Singkil (economy 52,000Rp, six hours) arrive on Monday and Thursday mornings and depart those same days at around 9pm.

ASDP ferries (p535) from Sibolga to Gunung Sitoli leave on Tuesday, Thursday and Saturday at 7pm (economy/VIP 65,000/120,000Rp, 10 to 13 hours), and a weekly ferry to Teluk Dam leaves on Monday at 6pm (economy/VIP 78,000/140,000Rp, 11 to 14 hours). ASDP ferries also connect Teluk Dalam with the Telo Islands to the south (41,000Rp to 80,000Rp, six hours) on Tuesday, Thursday and Friday.

Pelni (📞 162) has a boat that sails to Padang twice a month.

Gunung Sitoli

POP 130,000

Gunung Sitoli, on the northeastern coast of Pulau Nias, is the island's main town. It has the feel of any other big, sprawling city on Sumatra's mainland. Rebuilt after the 2005 tsunami, it serves as the main entry and exit point to Nias, and for the most part is of little interest to tourists. The one exception is its excellent museum, which is a must for those interested in indigenous culture.

There are ATMs at Binaka Airport, as well as several in the city that accept both Mastercard and Visa.

⊙ Sights

★ **Museum Pusaka Nias**   MUSEUM
(📞 0639-21920; www.museum-nias.org; Jl Yos Sudarso 134A; 20,000Rp; ⊗ 8am-5pm Mon-Sat, 12.30-5.30pm Sun) This superb museum, housed inside several traditional-style buildings, offers an in-depth introduction to the indigenous culture of Nias. The displays run the gamut from jewellery worn by noblemen, weapons, crocodile-hide battle armour and traditional fishing and hunting equipment to headhunting sculptures and paraphernalia, wood carvings used in ancestor worship, ceremonial drums, *nifolasara*

(boat-like) coffins with dragon heads, and microliths (anthropomorphic stone figures found on top of megaliths throughout Pulau Nias). One room features beautiful scale models of traditional houses.

Outside are some restored traditional houses, where you can spend the night. The depressing zoo is best avoided.

🛏 Sleeping & Eating

There are plenty of places to eat in town, with Padang food, seafood restaurants and a few cafes doing Western dishes.

Museum Nias Lodges   GUESTHOUSE $
(📞 0812 6490 4744, 0812 6246 3919; www.museum
-nias.org; Museum Pusaka Nias, Jl Yos Sudarso 134; s/d incl breakfast with shared bathroom
100,000/200,000Rp, r with private bathroom & air-
con 450,000Rp; ❋ 🖤) A fairly unique choice,
not only because you get to spend a night at
the museum, but because it's inside a traditional Nias house. Purpose built for tourists,
the pick are the Bawöganöwö and Ulunoyo
buildings, equipped with mod cons such as
TV, air-con and wi-fi. Budgets rooms are
in a more ordinary double-storey wooden
building.

Museum entry is free for those who stay here.

★ Rapi Seafood   SEAFOOD $
(📞 0639-22247; Jl Kelapa 15; mains from 35,000Rp;
⊘ 6-10pm) This nondescript place in central
Gunung Sitoli is responsible for some of the
best and freshest seafood we've ever had in
Sumatra. Choose your dinner, then have it
grilled, with sweet and spicy sauce if you
like. The squid also comes with different
sauces and the monster-sized grilled prawns
are sheer perfection. Speaking some Bahasa
Indonesia is a definite boon.

❶ Getting There & Away

Gunung Sitoli's **Binaka Airport**, 20km south of
town, is where most tourists arrive via flights
from Medan or Padang. Susi Air occasionally
offers flights to the Telo Islands.

By boat there are several services during
the week to both Sibolga and Singkil on the
mainland.

Public transport is relatively infrequent, but
there are buses to Teluk Dalam (90,000Rp,
three hours), which sometimes continue on
to Sorake. Otherwise count on paying around
500,000Rp for a private vehicle to Sorake (2½
hours). A bus from the airport to Gunung Sitoli is
around 60,000Rp, or 80,000Rp for a becak.

Traditional Villages

For hundreds of years, Nias residents built elaborate villages around cobblestone streets lined with rows of ship-like wooden houses. The traditional homes were balanced on tall wooden pylons and topped by a steep, thatched roof. Some say the boat motif was inspired by Dutch spice ships. Constructed from local teak and held together with hand-hewn wooden pegs, the houses are adorned with symbolic wooden carvings. The technology of traditional architecture proved quite absorbent and these structures fared better in the 2005 earthquake than modern concrete buildings.

Reflecting the island's defensive strate-gies, villages were typically built on high ground reached by dozens of stone steps. A protective stone wall usually encircled the village. Stone was also used for carved bath-ing pools, staircases, benches, chairs and memorials.

The island has geographic diversity when it comes to traditional houses. In northern Nias, homes are freestanding, oblong struc-tures on stilts, while in the south they are built shoulder to shoulder on either side of a long, paved courtyard. Emphasising the roof as the primary feature, southern Ni-assan houses are constructed using pylons and cross-beams slotted together without the use of bindings or nails.

Gomo & Around

The villages around Gomo, in the central highlands, contain some of the island's best examples of stone carvings and *menhirs* (single standing stones), some thought to be 3000 years old. Such examples can be found in the village of **Tundrumbaho**, 5km from Gomo; **Lahusa Idanotae**, halfway between Gomo and Tundrumbaho; and at **Tetegewo**, 7km south of Gomo. Getting to this area is a bit of a challenge, since the roads are in poor condition.

Hilinawalo Mazingo

Omo Hada   ARCHITECTURE
(Chieftain's House) One of only five such sur-viving buildings on Pulau Nias, the Omo Hada is situated in the prestigious 'up-stream' direction of the remote Hilinawalo Mazingo village, garnering the first rays of morning light. It still serves its traditional purpose as a meeting hall for seven neigh-

WEST COAST

Adventurous surfers are heading to Pulau Nias' west coast in search of empty waves and as-yet-undiscovered spots, given Sorake's consistent (and sometimes overwhelming) popularity.

Much of the west coast is still a DIY adventure; some surfers stay in losmen (basic accommodation) around the village of Afulu and hire local boats to take them up and down the coast.

Further afield are the islands of Asu and Bawa. More exposed than Nias itself, these islands see bigger and more consistent waves. With a left-hander at Asu and a strong right-hander at Bawa, good surf is almost guaranteed regardless of wind direction. The risk of malaria is high on these islands, however, particularly on Bawa, which has a large swamp in its interior.

Afulu Retreat (Darus Surfcamp; ☑ 0823 0416 2558; per person incl meals 250,000Rp; ✳) On Walo Beach, just north of Afulu, these bungalows are the best of Pulau Nias' west-coast surfing lodgings. Choose between the three breezy bungalows with their own out-door bathroom or bunk with fellow surfers in a basic shared room. The owners cook up mega platters of fish, and have an excellent knowledge of everything surfing in Nias.

Ina Silvi Cottage (☑ 0821 6099 3580, 0822 7734 2628; www.inasilvicottage.com; Pulau Asu; r 300,000Rp; 🛜) On the east coast of Pulau Asu are these idyllic bungalows, run by Mama Silvi (who speaks perfect English) and her family, that sit directly on the white sandy beach. It's a popular choice for both surfers and non-surfers alike, and a 1km walk to the nearest break. There's good food, cold beer and wi-fi.

Asu Surf Camp (☑ 0852 8561 0931; www.asucamp.com; Pulau Asu; per person per night AU$220; ✳🛜) A spot purely for surfers, this luxury camp gets rave reviews for its un-crowded waves, excellent food and relaxed vibe. The price includes speedboat transfers to top surfing spots.

Getting There & Away

Sirombu on Nias' west coast is the jumping-off point for the islands of Asu and Bawa. Ask around to see if any public buses will be heading there; otherwise you can charter a car for about 700,000Rp to Sirombu from Gunung Sitoli.

From Sirombu there's a daily boat to Asu at 2pm (50,000Rp, four to five hours); it returns at 6.30am. Otherwise you can charter a boat (700,000Rp, maximum 10 people) from local fishermen at Sirombu, or even from Teluk Dalam (1,500,000Rp) to save yourself the hassle of getting to Sirombu first.

bouring villages. You'll need a local guide and sturdy motorbike to negotiate the bad roads to get here.

In order to repair damage from age and climate, villagers have been trained in traditional carpentry skills, preserving crafts that were nearing extinction.

Bawomataluo

Perched on a hill about 400m above sea level, Bawomataluo (Sun Hill) is the most famous, and the most accessible, of the southern villages on Pulau Nias. It is also the setting for *lompat batu* (stone jumping). The final approach is up 88 steep stone steps flanked by stone dragons, and houses are arranged along two main stone-paved avenues. Bawo-

mataluo is well worth exploring, but be prepared for eager knick-knack sellers.

Stone jumping was once a form of war training; the jumpers had to leap over a 1.8m-high stone wall, traditionally topped with pointed sticks. These days the sticks are left off – and the motivation is financial (200,000Rp per jump outside ceremonial occasions). There are also cultural displays of war dances, traditionally performed by young, single males.

From Bawomataluo, you can see the rooftops of nearby Orihili. A stone staircase and a trail lead downhill to the village.

Bawomataluo is 15km from Teluk Dalam and is accessible by public transport (9000Rp) or an *ojek* (30,000Rp) to Sorake; guesthouses in Sorake can also arrange transfers.

OFF THE BEATEN TRACK

TELO ISLANDS

If Nias was the original surfers' paradise and the Mentawai Islands are currently in vogue, then tomorrow's slice of surfing paradise could be the Telo Islands. This group of islands sits to the north of the main Mentawain island of Siberut and until recently it was almost completely unknown to the outside world.

Today, liveaboard surf-charter boats have started adding the islands to their more ambitious itineraries, though the islands' relative remoteness still means uncrowded waves. Non-surfing travellers are very rare visitors to the Telo Islands, but if you have patience and a sense of adventure, they offer enormous potential for beach lounging, village living and snorkelling.

Telo Island Surf House (☏ 0813 6364 4963, 0853 6264 1331; www.teloislandsurfhouse. com; Pulau Sibaranun; r incl meals from 300,000Rp) A great budget option is this relaxed two-storey wooden house overlooking the surf on Pulau Sibaranun. It's pretty old-school with limited electricity, but will give you a taste of what things were like before the luxury villas moved in. It's run by local surfer Andreas and his family, and they have a boat to access (from 350,000Rp) wherever the surf's pumping.

To get here take the ferry (400,000Rp) from Teluk Dalam in South Nias to the harbour at Pulau Tello, from where Andreas can pick you up by boat.

Resort Latitude Zero (www.resortlatitudezero.com; Pulau Sifauruasi; per person incl meals & transport 7/10 days AUD$4360/5740; ❊ ⑤ ⊠) A luxurious surfing resort sitting on its own private island, this place has excellent access to Telo's 18 breaks, sea views from its sumptuous rooms and verandahs, an infinity pool and a family-friendly beach. There are stand-up paddleboards (SUPs), kayaks, snorkelling gear and also a gym for non-surfers. Liveaboard charters are available for exploring the surrounding surf spots. Seven-, 10- and 14-day packages available.

Getting There & Away

Ferries travel from Teluk Dalam in Nias every other day to Pulau Tello (40,000Rp), the main administrative island, and irregular boats sail between the Telo Islands and Padang. If staying in one of the resorts, the boat transfer from Padang is usually included in the rates.

Chief's House
ARCHITECTURE

Bawomataluo's two streets meet opposite the impressive chief's house, which is thought to be both the oldest and the largest on Nias. You can poke around its heavy wooden-beamed interior and admire the drum that signals the beginning and end of meetings, as well as the original wooden carvings and rows of pigs' jawbones. Outside is the chief's stone throne, next to a large stone phallus and stone tables where the deceased were once left to decay.

Hilisimaetano

There are more than 100 traditional houses in the large village of Hilisimaetano, 16km northwest of Teluk Dalam. Stone jumping and traditional dancing are performed here during special events.

Hilisimaetano is 10km north of Sorake. It can be reached by infrequent public transport from Teluk Dalam (7000Rp), otherwise you'll need to arrange private transport.

Botohili & Hilimaeta

Botohili, a small village on the hillside above the peninsula of Pantai Lagundri, has two rows of traditional houses, with a number of new houses breaking up the skyline. The remains of the original entrance, stone chairs and paving can still be seen. It's about a 10-minute walk here from Pantai Sorake.

A 2km walk or ride from Lagundri along a steep, partially paved road, the traditional village of **Hilimaetaniha** is one of the quietest on Pulau Nias. Friendly locals sit by their traditional houses, some of them brightly tiled or painted, and children fly kites along the only street. The *lompat batu* (stone jumping) pylon can still be seen here and there are a number of stone monuments, including a 2m-high stone penis. A long pathway of stone steps leads uphill to the village.

It's about a 25-minute walk here from Pantai Sorake; otherwise an *ojek* will cost around 15,000Rp.

Pantai Sorake & Teluk Lagundri

A fish-hook piece of land creates the perfect horseshoe bay of Teluk Lagundri and the Point surf break at Pantai Sorake, which is generally regarded as one of the best right-handers in the world. The main surfing season is June to October, with a peak in July and August when the waves can be very solid. Folks refer to this area interchangeably as Sorake or Lagundri.

The waves discovered here in 1975 by Aussie surfers Kevin Lovett and John Giesel have become shallower and more perfectly shaped and powerful following the 2004 earthquake and tsunami. With a couple of exceptions, all accommodation sits cheek by jowl along Pantai Sorake, which is considered to be more protected from possible future disasters.

🛌 Sleeping & Eating

The western part of the bay, known as Pantai Sorake, is the primary location for lodgings, and you'll likely get a view straight out to the surf. A lot of surfers come here on multiday packages, which include airport transfers and all meals, but it's always possible to rent a room by the night. Check out www.visitniasisland.com for listings.

Most of the guesthouses have attached restaurants doing Indonesian dishes, barbecue fish and burgers, chips and the like.

Harus Damai Inn   GUESTHOUSE $
(☑ 0813 7706 3712; Pantai Lagundri; r 200,000-350,000Rp; ❄) Right on Pantai Lagundri, this is the place for non-surfers, with a mellow little beach with no (or little) waves. Even though it's directly on the beach, none of its nine rooms have views; the pick are on the ground floor, while those in the two-storey block are fairly grim. It has a breezy seafront restaurant doing grilled fish, curries and cold beer.

They have boards to rent.

★ Key Hole Surf Camp   SURF CAMP $$
(☑ 0813 7469 2530, 0822 7644 9999; www.niaskeyholesurfcamp.com; Pantai Sorake; r from 300,000Rp; ❄ 🛜) Run by local surfer Timmy and his friendly family, the old favourite Key Hole Surf Camp is right in the thick of things. It has eight comfortable, air-conditioned rooms and its restaurant serves anything from pizza to lobster. Their 10-day packages (US$500) are also worth considering; these include meals, airport pick-ups, motorcycle rental and island excursions.

Surf lessons are also available on Pantai Lagundri. There's also a boat for liveaboard surf trips to Telo and other outlying waves.

Hash & Family Surf Camp   GUESTHOUSE $$$
(☑ 0852 9704 9557; www.surfhousenias.com; Pantai Sorake; dm/s/d incl meals US$50/100/150; ❄ 🛜) Things don't get much better for surfers than having unencumbered views of one of the world's most famous right-handers from their window. All looking out to the Point, rooms are large and comfortable and come with air-con, wi-fi and hot water, while the attractive restaurant and bar are the best in Sorake.

ℹ Getting There & Away

Pantai Sorake is located 100km south of Pulau Nias' airport. Transport is inclusive for many guesthouse prebookings, otherwise it's around 500,000Rp (2½ hours) by taxi. It's about 130,000Rp by bus, but you'll have to transfer at Teluk Dalam.

Teluk Dalam

POP 76,750

Teluk Dalam is the capital of South Nias regency, and Pulau Nias' second city. It's a squat little port town that's as loud and chaotic as much larger cities. You'll need to pass through Teluk Dalam for transit connections to/from Pantai Sorake, to pick up provisions or to access ATMs.

A public bus from Gunung Sitoli to Teluk Dalam is around 90,000Rp for the three-hour drive. To Sorake it's around 25,000Rp by *ojek*, or 50,000Rp by becak.

From the harbour here you can get ferries to Pulau Tello, and Sibolga on the mainland.

🍽 Eating

Mari Rasa   INDONESIAN $
(Jl Pelita; mains 25,000Rp; ⏱10am-6pm) About half a block from the main road in Teluk Dalam, Mari Rasa is locally famous for its *babi panggang* (grilled pork) and *lomok-lomok* (pork belly) served with rice, local greens, dark chilli sauce and a bowlful of flavourful, spicy broth. It's a great place to hit if you're waiting for a night boat or a pick-up.

ACEH

Sumatra's northernmost province, Aceh is both a fiercely proud and prosperous region. It's blessed with rainforests that feature incredible biodiversity, as well as pristine

Aceh

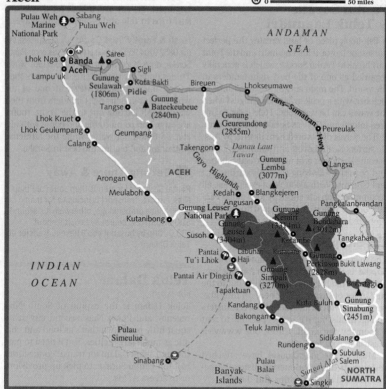

islands popular with beachgoers, divers and surfers alike. However, over the years, this western tip of the Indonesian archipelago has grabbed headlines for all the wrong reasons. Earthquakes, tsunamis, civil war and sharia law are the main associations people have with Sumatra's northernmost state. With the reconstruction from the 2004 Boxing Day tsunami long completed, post-tsunami Aceh is slowly healing the social wounds incurred by the natural disaster and the previous civil war. Still, while the guns have been laid down and a degree of autonomy has been granted to the province, there are occasional blips on the road to peace, and a prevailing belief in the rest of Sumatra that the people of Aceh are keen to spread their conservative Islamic ways across the whole country.

History

In the days of sailing ships, Aceh's important strategic position along the spice-trade route was a crucial factor in contributing to its wealth and importance, bringing an influx of both traders and immigrants. Aceh was also Islam's entry to the archipelago, while the capital, Banda Aceh, was a centre of Islamic learning and a gateway for Mecca-bound pilgrims.

Though Aceh's power began to decline towards the end of the 17th century, the province remained independent of the Dutch until war was declared in 1871. It was 35 years before the fighting stopped and the last of the sultans, Tuanku Muhamat Dawot, surrendered.

In 1951 the Indonesian government incorporated Aceh's territory into the province of North Sumatra. The prominent Islamic Party was angered at being lumped together with the Christian Bataks, and proclaimed Aceh an independent Islamic Republic in September 1953. Prolonged conflict ensued, and in 1959 the government was forced to give Aceh 'special district' status, granting a high degree of autonomy in religious, cultural and educational matters.

The formation of Gerakan Aceh Merdeka (GAM; Free Aceh Movement) in December 1976 and the subsequent struggle with the Indonesian military led to nearly 30 years of deaths, torture, and disappearances occurring on an almost daily basis, perpetuated by both sides against the civilian population, with thousands displaced.

At the turn of the millennium there was a brief ceasefire and Aceh was granted the right to implement sharia law, followed by an escalation of conflict, the imposition of martial law and a full-scale military assault on the separatists, which was brought to an abrupt end by the 2004 tsunami. The province remains largely peaceful, in spite of occasional bouts of unrest courtesy of a GAM rebel splinter group that remains disaffected with former colleagues who now run the province.

Banda Aceh

☑ 0651 / POP 223,500

Banda Aceh is a surprisingly relaxed and charming provincial capital that more than deserves a day or two en route to Pulau Weh.

Given that Banda Aceh bore the brunt of the 2004 tsunami, with 61,000 killed here, and that much of the city had to be rebuilt, it's little wonder that it looks well maintained and affluent, with broad streets, pavements and parks. The magnificent central mosque – Indonesia's best – still stands as the city's crowning glory, along with the poignant Tsunami Museum.

Banda Aceh is still a fiercely religious city and its ornate mosques are at the centre of daily life. Respectfully dressed visitors shouldn't face any hassles and most travellers find the Acehnese to be friendly and extremely hospitable.

◉ Sights

★ **Mesjid Raya Baiturrahman**   MOSQUE

(entry by donation; ⊘5am-10pm) With its brilliant white walls, ebony-black domes and towering minaret, this 19th-century mosque is a dazzling sight. The best time to visit is during Friday-afternoon prayers, when the entire building and courtyard are filled with people. A recent addition to the tiled courtyard is a series of retractable shades, offering all-weather protection for worshippers. A headscarf is required for women.

The first section of the mosque was built by the Dutch in 1879 as a conciliatory gesture towards the Acehnese after the original one burnt down. Two more domes – one on either side of the first – were added by the Dutch in 1936, and another two by the Indonesian government in 1957. The mosque survived intact after the 2004 earthquake and tsunami, a sign interpreted by many residents as direct intervention by the Divine. During this time the mosque served as an unofficial crisis centre for survivors, and bodies awaiting identification were laid on the public square in front of the mosque.

Gunongan   HISTORIC BUILDING

(Jl Teuku Umar; ⊘8am-6pm) FREE All that remains of Aceh's powerful sultanates today is on view at Gunongan. Built by Sultan Iskandar Muda (1607–36) as a gift for his Malay princess wife, it was intended as a private playground and bathing place. The building consists of an intriguing series of blinding white peaks with narrow stairways and a walkway leading to ridges, which represent the hills of the princess' native land. Ask around for someone to unlock the gate for you.

Museum Negeri Banda Aceh   MUSEUM

(☑ 0651-23144; www.museum.acehprov.go.id; Jl Alauddin Mahmudsyah 12; 5000Rp; ⊘8am-noon & 2-4.15pm Tue-Sun) This state museum displays Acehnese weaponry, household furnishings, ceremonial costumes, everyday clothing, gold jewellery, calligraphy and some magnificently carved *recong* (Acehnese daggers) and swords. It also covers the history of Islam in Aceh, Dutch history and local freedom fighters, and there's even a section on coffee.

In the same complex is the **Rumah Aceh** (⊘9am-4pm Tue-Thu, Sat & Sun, 9am-noon & 2-4pm Fri) FREE, a fine example of traditional Acehnese architecture, built without nails and held together with cord and pegs.

Kherkhof   CEMETERY

(Dutch Cemetery; Jl Teuku Umar; ⊘8am-6pm) FREE The Kherkhof is the last resting place of more than 2000 Dutch and Indonesian soldiers who died fighting the Acehnese. The entrance is around 50m west of the Tsunami Museum. Tablets set into the walls by the entrance gate are inscribed with the names of the dead soldiers and the plain white crosses in the eastern part of the cemetery were replacements for the gravestones destroyed by the 2004 tsunami.

SUMATRA BANDA ACEH

Banda Aceh

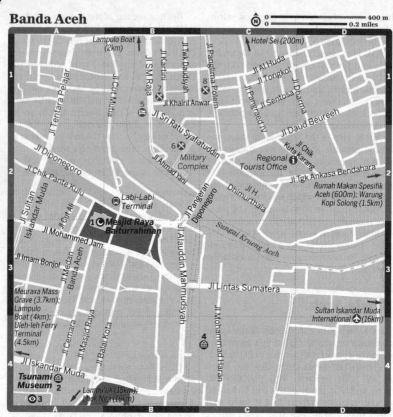

0   400 m
0   0.2 miles

Banda Aceh

Sleeping

There's not much in the way of budget accommodation in Banda, but there are some very reasonable and central midrange places in the market area around Jl Khairil Anwar.

★ Linda's Homestay   HOMESTAY $$

(☎ 0823 6436 4130; www.lindas-homestay.blogspot.com; Jl Mata Lorong Rahmat 3, Lambneu Barat; r incl breakfast 350,000-600,000Rp; ❄ 🛜) Staying in the home of hospitable Linda, 4km out of town, is a good way to experience local life in a family home and to learn about Acehnese culture. Many travellers rave about the hospitality and the home cooking (classes available); the Gayo filter coffee is also top notch. The house is spotless and decorated in traditional Islamic motifs and ornate furniture.

Hotel Sei   HOTEL $$

(☎ 0651-21866; Jl Tanoh Abe 71, Kampung Mulia; d incl breakfast 425,000-900,000Rp; ste 1,050,000Rp; 🅿 ❄ 🛜) This lemon-yellow hotel down a quiet side street north of the centre is one of Banda Aceh's swankier, but overpriced, options. Expect compact rooms with reliable wi-fi, the arctic chill of air-con, a pleasant respite from the outdoors, as well as friendly service and a seemingly deserted but actually decent restaurant.

Hotel Medan   HOTEL $$
(☑ 0651-21501; www.hotel-medan.com; Jl Ahmad Yani 17; r incl breakfast 300,000-560,000Rp; ❄@🛜) One of Banda Aceh's most established midrange options, Hotel Medan has a good central location in the happening market area north of the river. Rooms are clean and comfortable, though quite dated, with a retro Soviet feel.

Padé Hotel   HOTEL $$$
(☑ 0651-49999; www.thepade.com; Jl Soekarno-Hatta 1; r/ste incl breakfast from 800,000/1,500,000Rp; ❄🛜⛱) Banda Aceh's most luxurious sleeping option is this classy hotel that features a sumptuous traditional Islamic design and date palms that channel the Middle East. It's essentially a business hotel, however, with quality rooms, professional staff and an attractive infinity pool surrounded by frangipani trees.

🍴 Eating & Drinking

Because of sharia law, alcohol is not openly available, with the exception of a few restaurants and hotels catering to Westerners, which discreetly serve beer and wine.

Rumah Makan Spesifik Aceh   INDONESIAN $
(☑ 0852 7777 5812; Jl T Hasan Dek; meals around 35,000Rp; ⊙11am-10pm Sat-Thu, 8.30am-noon & 2-10pm Fri) An excellent introduction to Acehnese cuisine, with such delights as *asam keeng* (hot and sour soup), *udang goreng kunyit* (turmeric shrimp) and curried fish.

Mie Razali   NOODLES $
(Jl Panglima Polem; mains 10,000-30,000Rp; ⊙11am-11am) The best place in Banda Aceh to sample *mie aceh,* Acehnese spicy noodles

SUMATRA BANDA ACEH

REMEMBERING THE 2004 TSUNAMI

Few people in Aceh will ever forget 26 December 2004. An immense tsunami swept inland, killing 170,000 people and altering the physical and emotional landscape of the province forever. In spite of the extensive rebuilding that has removed most signs of physical damage, stark reminders of the devastation remain in the form of many memorials that both honour those killed and allow visitors to comprehend the full horror of what transpired. For many residents of the province the tsunami is a sensitive subject, as many lost loved ones. However, if interest is expressed in a delicate manner, no offence is taken.

Tsunami Museum (www.museumtsunami.blogspot.com; Jl Iskandar Muda 3; ⊙9am-4pm Sat-Thu, 9am-noon & 2-4pm Fri) FREE A visit to this beautifully designed, hard-hitting museum commences with a walk through a dark, dripping tunnel that symbolises the tsunami waves. This is followed by a powerful set of images of the devastation projected from tombstone-like receptacles, and a circular chamber engraved with the names of the lost. Upstairs a very graphic short film is shown, along with photographs of loss, displacement, rebuilding, hopefulness and reunited families. Other displays explain how earthquakes and tsunamis are created and how Aceh's landscape was altered by the disaster (look out for the 'before' and 'after' scale models of the city).

Lampulo Boat (off Jl Matahari) The most famous of the tsunami sights is the fishing boat resting on the house in Lampulo village, about 2km north of the city and 1km from where it was docked. It's said that 59 villagers survived the tsunami by climbing into the stuck boat.

PLTD Apung I (Jl Harapan; ⊙9am-noon & 2-5.30pm Sat-Thu, 2-5pm Fri) FREE This 2500-tonne power-generator vessel was carried almost 5km inland by the tsunami wave. It's now preserved as a memorial about 2km southwest of the city centre.

Mass Graves There are four mass graves around Banda Aceh where the dead were buried post-tsunami. The largest site is **Siron Tsunami Memorial Park**, located on the road to the airport, where 46,000 unidentified bodies were buried. Near Uleh-leh port, **Meuraxa mass grave** (Jl Sultan Iskandar Muda) is the most visited site. Other grave sites include those at the **Lhok Nga Tsunami Monument** and **Darusalam**. Families who wish to mourn their unlocated loved ones choose one of the mass graves based on geographic proximity; they have no other evidence of where to offer their prayers.

served with chicken or seafood. Razali gets busy in the evenings so you may have to wait for a table.

Ice Cream Gunung Salju
ICE CREAM $

(Jl Kartini; ice cream from 8000Rp; ⊙noon-10pm Sat-Thu, 2-10pm Fri) This downtown place is a local institution notable for its delicious homemade ice cream. It has a heap of flavours, including local offerings such as avocado, durian and jackfruit, as well as all the usual suspects. It's a pretty local set-up with no English, and it also sells Indonesia dishes.

Country Steakhouse
INTERNATIONAL $$

(☑0651-24213; off Jl Sri Ratu Safiatuddin 45B; mains 25,000-120,000Rp; ⊙5-10pm; ❄🐦) Well hidden down an alley out of view is this cosy, wood-panelled restaurant that has a speakeasy feel, and specialises in Western food and cold beers. New Zealand steaks and lamb chops are the specialities, as well as fish and chips, burgers, sandwiches, pastas and Indonesian standards. They can procure pricey Australian red wine with a day's notice. Credit cards accepted.

Warung Kopi Solong
CAFE

(Jl Teuku Iskandar 13-14; ⊙6am-11.30pm; 🐦) Banda Aceh's most famous coffee house has been doing business since 1974. It's an excellent place to try *kopi sanger* (coffee with condensed milk) – strained through a sock! You can buy 250g and 500g bags of finely ground, locally grown arabica coffee. *Mie aceh* (Acehnese noodles) and other dishes and snacks are available. It's 2.5km east of the centre; take a becak.

ℹ️ Information

MONEY
There are lots of ATMs around town, mainly on Jl Panglima Polem and Jl Sri Ratu Safiatuddin.

OPENING HOURS
If you're in town on a Friday be aware that all museums, restaurants, cafes and shops close from noon to 2pm for prayer time.

TOURIST INFORMATION
Regional Tourist Office (Dinas Parawisata; ☑0821 6644 1925; www.acehtourism.travel; Jl Chik Kuta Karang 3; ⊙8am-5pm Mon-Fri) On the 1st floor of a government building; the staff here led by Rahmadani (Danny) are exceptionally friendly and sometimes have free copies of an excellent guidebook to the province.

Otherwise the Banda Aceh tourism website (www.bandaacehtourism.com) has good info.

ℹ️ Getting There & Away

AIR
Sultan Iskandar Muda International Airport (www.sultaniskandarmuda-airport.co.id) is 16km southeast of the centre. A 30-day visa on arrival is available for most nationalities.

BOAT
Express boats and car ferries serving Pulau Weh depart at least twice daily from the port at Uleh-leh, 5km west of Banda Aceh's city centre. Express boats depart at 10am and 4pm daily, with an additional 8am service from Friday to Sunday. Car ferries depart at 11am and 4pm Saturday, Sunday and Wednesday, and at 2pm Monday, Tuesday, Thursday and Friday.

TRANSPORT FROM BANDA ACEH

Air

DESTINATION	AIRLINE	FREQUENCY
Jakarta	Batik Air, Garuda	6 daily
Kuala Lumpur (Malaysia)	AirAsia	1-2 daily
Kutacane	Susi Air	2 weekly
Medan	Citilink, Lion Air	4 daily
Penang (Malaysia)	Firefly	4 weekly

Bus

DESTINATION	FARE (RP)	DURATION (HR)	FREQUENCY
Bukit Lawang	350,000	16	daily
Ketambe/Kutacane	250,000	15-18	daily
Medan	150,000-330,000	12	hourly, around 9am-10pm
Singkil	220,000	14	9pm

BUS

Terminal Bus Bathoh (Jl Mohammed Hasan) is 4km south of the city centre. Large buses to Medan depart from here.

ⓘ Getting Around

Taxis from the airport charge 100,000Rp to the city centre and 140,000Rp to Uleh-leh port.

Online taxi companies Grab (p515) and Go-Jek (p515) both operate in Banda Aceh, and are the cheapest way to get around.

Labi-labi are the local minibuses and cost 2500Rp for trips around town, though sights in the central area can easily be covered on foot or by becak. The most useful services are the blue *labi-labi* for Uleh-leh (10,000Rp, 35 minutes) and the white one to Lhok Nga and Lampu'uk (16,000Rp). The **labi-labi terminal** (Jl Diponegoro; ⊙7am-5pm) is just north of the Mesjid Raya Baiturrahman.

From the bus terminal, a becak into town will cost around 30,000Rp. A becak around town should cost between 15,000Rp and 30,000Rp, depending on your destination. A becak to Uleh-leh from the city centre is 40,000Rp and a taxi 70,000Rp.

For a reliable ride or a city tour aboard a deluxe, wi-fi-enabled becak, call English-speaking **Little John** (☑0813 6023 1339).

Pulau Weh

☑0652 / POP 32,300

Tiny Pulau Weh (also known as Sabang) has been drawing travellers – mostly divers and in-the-know backpackers – for at least a couple of decades now but its charm hasn't faded: it's too remote for that. Ferrying out to this tiny island is an adventure, and exploring its beaches, jungle and clear waters, or just chilling in a hammock at your budget bungalow, are the rewards for travellers who've journeyed up through the turbulent greater mainland below. Snorkellers and divers bubble through the great walls of swaying sea fans, deep canyons and rock pinnacles, ogling the dazzling kaleidoscope of marine life, including manta rays and whale sharks. Both figuratively and geographically, Pulau Weh is the cherry on top for many visitors to Sumatra.

🏃 Activities

Most travellers come to Pulau Weh for the diving and snorkelling, which is considered some of the best in the Indian Ocean. On an average day, you're likely to spot morays, lionfish, schools of tuna, barracuda, jacks and giant trevally, along with eagle rays, manta and stingrays. During plankton blooms, whale sharks come to graze. Unlike at other dive sites, the coral fields take a back seat to the sea life and landscapes. The macro diving is also impressive, and there's a WWII wreck for experienced divers. There are close to 20 dive sites around the island, mostly in and around Iboih and Gapang, which is where dive operators are based. To respect the local religious customs there's no diving from sunset on Thursday to 2pm Friday.

Snorkelling is also a big highlight, and you will see an impressive diversity of colourful fish, and often turtles as well. Gear can be hired almost anywhere for around 30,000Rp per day.

ⓘ Getting There & Away

AIR

The small **Maimun Saleh Airport**, 2km south of Sabang, has connections to Medan with Garuda Indonesia and Wings four times a week. Cancellations do occur, so factor this into your travel plans if you have a connecting flight to catch.

BOAT

Slow car ferries and express passenger ferries ply the route between Uleh-leh, 5km northwest of Banda Aceh on the mainland, and Balohan port, around 8km south of Sabang on Pulau Weh. You should get to the port at least 45 minutes before departure to get a ticket. Ferry service is weather dependent.

The 'slow ferry' (economy/air-con 27,000/45,000Rp, two hours) leaves Pulau Weh daily at 8am and 2.30pm, returning from Uleh-leh on the mainland at 8am and 2pm, and sometimes 11am. On Wednesday, Saturday and Sunday, there's an additional service from Pulau Weh at 1.30pm.

The **Express Ferry** (☑0651-43791, 0652-332 4800; economy/business 80,000/100,000Rp) runs from Pulau Weh to Uleh-leh at 8am and 2.30pm daily (45 minutes to one hour), with an additional service at 4pm Friday to Sunday in season (usually July through August). Services from the mainland to Pulau Weh depart at 10am and 4pm, with an additional weekend service at 10am.

ⓘ Getting Around

There is no regular public bus service on the island, but from the Balohan port, a handful of *labi-labi* (minibuses) meet the boats and head to Sabang (25,000Rp, 15 minutes), and Gapang/Iboih (60,000Rp, 40 minutes). Becaks charge around 80,000Rp from the port to Gapang, 100,000Rp to Iboih and 50,000Rp to Sumur Tiga, near Sabang.

Many lodgings rent out motorbikes for around 100,000Rp per day.

ISLAND TOUR BY MOTORBIKE

Pulau Weh is a delight to explore on a rented scooter thanks to its relatively compact size, light traffic and picturesque scenery.

If you start from Ipoih and follow the road 8km north through the forest reserve, you'll reach **Kilometer Nol**, where a fairly tacky, run-down 44m-high globe-shaped monument marks the northernmost tip of Indonesia. If you want a more natural outlook, walk down the hill to the boardwalk for peaceful ocean views. Head back south until you almost reach Gapang; the westbound turnoff leads 1km to **Llong Angen**, a rocky beach ideal for sunset watching, then a further 2km to **Gua Sarang** (Swallow Cave; 5000Rp), a picturesque cove for swimming and snorkelling.

Head back and go southeast past Gapang for 8km; just before you reach the village of Pria Laot, a road leads 1km towards **Pria Lot Falls**. It's a five-minute scramble over rocks to reach the beautiful swimming hole at the falls. East past Pria Laot, you hit a T-junction; take the southbound branch and pass between **Gunung Kulan**, the island's highest volcano, on your right, and **Gunung Merapi** (Berapi; Jaboi), a semi-active volcano, with its steaming sulphurous fumaroles puffing steam from its rocky landscape.

Head east along the coast. You'll pass some mediocre **hot springs** near Keuneukai village, which also has a nice **beach** – however, it's a conservative village so women will need to cover up if swimming. Carry on to Balohan port and take the less frequented road north across the island, towards Sabang, passing **Danau Anak Laut**, a serene freshwater lake that supplies the island with its drinking water. Near Sabang, it's worth seeking out the old **Merbabu cemetery**, where there are Dutch, French, Javanese, Acehnese and Japanese laid to rest. Further south is a **Japanese WWII bunker**, one of several remnants from the occupation of Pulau Weh from 1942 to 1945.

If you don't want to motorbike around the island alone, you can arrange a becak for a day-long tour for about 350,000Rp.

A taxi from Sumur Tiga to the airport is 100,000Rp; from Gapang/Iboih it's around 150,000Rp.

Sabang

Pulau Weh's main township (signposted Kota or Kota Sabang) is a mix of traditional fishing village, big-town bustle and old colonial-era villas. During Dutch rule, Sabang was a major coal and water depot for steamships. The town enjoyed a brief revival in the 1970s as a duty-free port, but these days it's a bit more relaxed, and its inhabitants generally fish or make rattan furniture. The main lures for travellers are the nearby beaches, which are the best on Pulau Weh.

🛏 Sleeping

⭐ **Freddies**   LODGE **$$**
(☎ 0813 602 55001; www.santai-sabang.com; Pantai Sumur Tiga; r 375,000-470,000Rp; ❄ 🌐) This delightful cluster of breezy rooms sits above Pulau Weh's nicest stretch of white-sand beach, which has a small coral reef. It's perfect for those content with snorkelling off the strategically placed pontoon and swinging in a hammock. Freddie, the South African owner, is responsible both for the delicious, varied

buffet dinners (65,000Rp) and for the genuine feeling of camaraderie among the guests.

Its restaurant is also a highlight, with pizza, seafood barbecues, Indonesian dishes and daily buffet (65,000Rp). There's also a good range of alcohol (beer, spirits, wine), which you're likely to get served in a coffee mug, speakeasy-style!

⭐ **Casa Nemo**   BUNGALOW **$$**
(☎ 0813 6299 9942; www.casanemo.com; Pantai Sumur Tiga; r with shared bathroom 150,000Rp, bungalow 390,000-500,000Rp, 2-bedroom apt from 700,000Rp; ❄ 🌐) There's a fabulous range of rooms and cottages cascading down the cliff side at this Mediterranean-feeling resort. Although it caters to all travellers (the 'backpacker' rooms are a bargain), there's a feeling of upmarket exclusivity, from the beautiful waterfront deck restaurant to the day spa. Great for a splurge.

Its waterside restaurant and bar (open 10am to 11pm) is equally luxurious and has a great selection of dishes, from pizzas to Acehnese fish curry (50,000Rp).

ℹ Information

BRI Bank (Jl Perdagangan) Has an ATM, as do a couple of other banks here.

❶ Getting There & Away

Pantai Sumur Tiga is a short drive from Sabang city, in the northeast corner of Pulau Weh. From Balohan Port it's a 20-minute becak (60,000Rp) or taxi ride (100,000Rp), and similar prices to the airport. To Gapang it's around 100,000Rp by becak.

Gapang

Occupying a sandy cove, with a great reef for snorkelling just offshore, Gapang is an appealing stretch of beach lined with shack restaurants, simple guesthouses and Pulau Weh's best dive outfits. Although quieter than Iboih, there's a developing scene here with the quality dive outfits drawing plenty of travellers.

🏃 Activities

Lumba Lumba Diving Centre   DIVING
(📞0811 682 787; www.lumbalumba.com; Gapang Beach; discover dive 685,000Rp, open-water course 4,500,000Rp; ⊗dive shop 8am-8pm) This long-established and professional Dutch-run diving centre has been introducing divers to Pulau Weh's underwater world for decades now. Owners Ton and Marjan Egbers maintain a helpful website with detailed descriptions of dives and need-to-know information. Highly recommended.

Monster Divers   DIVING
(📞0813 1453 2827, 0812 6960 6857; www.monster divers.com; Gapang Beach; discover scuba dive 650,000Rp, 1/2 dives 390,000/780,000Rp) A popular, professional diving outfit with Spanish owners and local instructors, with a big range of boat and shore dives, PADI courses and night dives. Accommodation is on the way, and they've just opened up their Catalonian-influenced Monster restaurant next door.

Bubble Addict   DIVING
(📞0852 9690 4984; www.bubble-addict.com; Gapang Beach) This French-owned dive operator, located at the far end of Gapang Beach, has an enthusiastic team of local and foreign instructors. They offer Discover dives (590,000Rp), open-water courses (3,950,000Rp), shore dives (180,000Rp) and fun dives (from 370,000Rp), as well night dives and specialty courses. They have lodgings out the back (per night diver/non-diver 350,000/400,000Rp), with more on the way.

Flying Elephant Yoga   YOGA
(📞0852 9690 4984; www.flyingelephantyoga.com; Gapang Beach; ⊗6.30pm Mon-Sat) Run by enthusiastic yogi Tomomi, Flying Elephant's

yoga space is upstairs from the dive school Bubble Addict, with evening one-hour Vinyasa sessions held on a pay-what-you-want arrangement (or free if you're diving here). There are also private one-hour lessons (150,000Rp) and day packages, such as its blissful combos of diving, yoga, meditation and massage (500,000Rp per day).

Blue Addiction Freedive Weh   DIVING
(📞0813 5628 1527; www.facebook.com/BAFree diveWeh; Gapang Beach) At this French-run dive outfit you can learn the art of free diving, enabling you to plunge the ocean depths without the burden of heavy diving apparatus.

🛌 Sleeping

★Lumba Lumba   RESORT $$
(📞0811 682 787; www.lumbalumba.com; Gapang Beach; d with shared/private bathroom 200,000/300,000Rp, bungalow 500,000Rp; ❋🛜) Behind the diving centre of the same name, Lumba Lumba offers some of the best-quality accommodation in Gapang. Wood-decked cottages have tiled rooms, fans and Western toilets, while simpler budget rooms have shared bathrooms. Accommodation is mostly for divers, but Lumba Lumba will happily rent out any spare rooms.

🍴 Eating

Monster   SPANISH $
(Gapang Beach; mains 35,000-55,000Rp; ⊗8am-5pm) A part of the Spanish-run Monster Divers dive shop, this relaxed beachside cafe does Catalonian-influenced dishes such as yellowfin-tuna burgers with *brava* sauce (spicy aioli), *escalivada* (smoky grilled vegetables) and *creama catalana* (egg custard pudding), along with salads and other international mains. Look out for their themed nights, when they cook up anything from paella to pizzas.

Tipsy Toby Cafe   CAFE $
(Gapang Beach; mains from 30,000Rp; ⊗8.30am-6pm) Sharing space with Bubble Addict is this lively hang-out in Gapang Beach where divers gather in the evenings to socialise over cold beers, bagel burgers, naan pizza, coffee and smoothies. There are weekly barbecues as well. It stays open later on Wednesday and Saturday evenings. Upstairs is Flying Elephant Yoga.

Barracuda   INDONESIAN $
(Gapang Beach; mains 15,000-60,000Rp; ⊗8am-9pm; 🛜) The lime-green furniture and

decking will draw your eye to this breezy alfresco restaurant in the middle of Gapang Beach, but it's the Acehnese seafood curries, fresh food (such as burgers and wraps), smoothies and apple pie that keep people coming back.

ℹ Getting There & Away

The turnoff for Gapang is 2km before Iboih; it's 80,000Rp by becak from the harbour, or around 180,000Rp by taxi. Sometimes *labi-labi* (minibuses) meet the boats, which cost 60,000Rp to Gapang.

Iboih

Iboih (*ee*-boh) is Pulau Weh's backpacker central: old-school budget bungalows are draped along a rocky headland plunging down to iridescent waters that seem too good to be true. A jungle path leads past the village well and up and over a small hill to the bungalow strip. The village itself is lined with shops and snorkel-hire places, but this is still a conservative area, so change out of swimwear when going beyond the bungalow strip.

🏃 Activities

Rubiah Tirta Divers   DIVING
(☑ 0823 6000 2100, 0652-332 4555; www.rubiah divers.com; Iboih Beach; 1/3/5 dives with equipment 320,000/900,000/1,400,000Rp) This local-run PADI outfit in Iboih village is the longest-running dive operation on Pulau Weh and gets consistently good feedback from travellers. It also offers open-water courses and Discover Scuba (500,000Rp) and shore dives.

🛏 Sleeping

⭐ **Olala**   HUT $
(☑ 0852 6060 7311, 0852 332 4199; eka.enk@ gmail.com; r with shared bathroom 100,000Rp, with private bathroom 200,000-250,000Rp; 🛜) Offering cheap and cheerful huts on stilts, Olala caters both to shoestringers (with basic huts with shared bathrooms) and those who want their own bathroom and fan. The best huts are over the water. The restaurant is a popular traveller hang-out and one of the best on the jungle strip. There's good snorkelling straight out front.

Yulia's   BUNGALOW $$
(☑ 0821 6856 4383; r with shared bathroom 100,000-150,000Rp, with private bathroom 200,000-650,000Rp; ❄🛜) One of the last resorts at the end of the bungalow strip, Yulia's has grown and blossomed into Iboih's most upmarket accommodation. Like tropical Swiss chalets, the quality, spacious timber bungalows are scattered along the hillside and down to the water's edge. The best have air-con, hot water, sea views and breakfast included. The overwater restaurant is a charm.

Iboih Inn   BUNGALOW $$
(☑ 0812 699 1659, 0811 841 570; www.iboihinn. com; Iboih Beach; r incl breakfast from 325,000Rp, with air-con 475,000-675,000Rp; ❄🛜) The top huts at this relatively upmarket option come with hot-water showers, air-con and fab sea views, and there are cheaper wooden shacks back up the hill. The loungey overwater restaurant with floating jetty is a great place to while away an afternoon, and is a good launching point for snorkelling.

🍴 Eating

⭐ **Bixio Cafe**   ITALIAN $
(☑ 0821 6430 1071, 0821 6616 7091; www.bixio wehbungalows.com; Long Beach; pasta 45,000Rp; ⊙ noon-9pm Wed-Mon; 🛜) Who would have thought Sumatra's best Italian food was hiding in a remote corner of Pulau Weh? Sit by the lapping waves and dig into Luca and Eva's wonderful, authentic and freshly made pastas and gnocchi with fresh traditional sauces – but leave room for the divine tiramisu.

It's in Long Beach, about 3km northwest from Iboih.

There are also three appealing bungalows (300,000Rp) here for rent if you wish to linger longer.

Dee Dee's Kitchen   INTERNATIONAL $
(mains 25,000-50,000Rp; ⊙ 8am-9pm; 🛜🍴) On the same strip of beach as Rubiah Tirta Divers, Dee Dee cooks up an eclectic selection of dishes, from excellent homemade chapati with guacamole to pasta dishes, crispy *tempe* tortilla wraps, tofu burgers and *mie aceh* (Acehnese noodles).

Nasaka Coffee   CAFE $
(Iboih Beach; mains 25,000-55,000Rp; ⊙ 8.30am-midnight; 🛜) Bringing a taste of contemporary cafe style to the beach is this classy waterfront joint that does the best coffee on Pulau Weh. Choose from manual brews served in a beaker, traditional Aceh-style *kopi sanger* or a long black with coconut milk. The food's good too, including the charcoal-bun fish burger with lime mayo

that you can enjoy looking out to the turquoise sea.

❶ Information

There are a few ATMs here for cash withdrawals.

❶ Getting There & Away

A becak here from the harbour or the airport is around 100,000Rp.

Aceh's West Coast

Rounding the northwestern tip of Sumatra's finger of land is a string of little villages and endless beaches backed by densely forested hills. Most of the houses along the coast are identical in design, having been rebuilt after the 2004 tsunami. For the time being, the appealing west coast attracts the more intrepid travellers heading overland between Singkil and Banda Aceh, as well as surfers and kitesurfers in search of wind and waves.

Lhok Nga & Lampu'uk

Comprehensively rebuilt after the 2004 tsunami, the coastal weekend spots in Lampu'uk are beginning to attract more surfers and kitesurfers as the word spreads. Surfing season is from October to April, though there are also waves at the beach in front of the cement factory the rest of the year, which is also when there are favourable winds for kitesurfing.

Lhok Nga has decent waves too, and it's becoming particularly popular with kitesurfers. Given it's only 14km from Banda Aceh it's an easy day trip as well.

🛏 Sleeping

Eddie's Homestay   HOMESTAY $
(☑0813 6031 9126; www.eddieshomestay. com; Lhok Nga; s with shared bathroom & fan 100,000Rp, d with shared bathroom & air-con 200,000Rp, r with private bathroom & air-con 300,000-500,000Rp, deluxe r 2,000,000Rp; ❇🛜) Eddie's gets consistently good feedback from the surfing crowd both for its laid-back vibe and its comfy rooms (the cheaper ones share facilities). There's also a new fancy option, a deluxe room that has a jacuzzi and large TV.

Joel's Bungalows   BUNGALOW $
(☑0813 7528 7765; Lampu'uk; r 150,000-500,000Rp) Joel's Bungalows is the area's leg-endary surfer hang-out. It's a bit rundown these days, however, and in need of maintenance, but its bungalows and rooms (which come in an array of sizes and styles) all overlook the beach. Its on-site restaurant does wood-fired pizza and cold beers.

Though the waves right here are not suitable for surfing (and can be dangerous for swimming), there is easy access to two left-hand breaks and one right-hander. Further south along the main beach at Lampu'uk, Joel's Bungalows 2 is ideal for kitesurfers.

🍷 Drinking & Nightlife

Saho Coffee   COFFEE
(Lhok Nga; ⊙8am-10pm) This cool little coffee roaster by the beach serves A-grade Acehnese brews along with simple food items. It rents out surfboards too (per half-day 70,000Rp).

❶ Getting There & Away

Take *labi-labi* number '04' (15,000Rp, 20 minutes) from the terminal (p547) just north of Mesjid Raya Baiturrahman in Banda Aceh for both Lhok Nga and Lampu'uk. A becak costs 50,000Rp to 80,000Rp and a taxi is around 100,000Rp to 150,000Rp; a taxi with Grab (p515) is about 60,000Rp.

Singkil

☑0658 / POP 46,800

Singkil is a remote, sleepy port town with welcoming locals at the mouth of Sungai Alas. It's the departure point for island adventures to the Banyaks, Pulau Nias and Pulau Simeulue, but it's worth lingering here for a day or two to explore the swampy surroundings, which are home to crocodiles, wild orang-utans and more.

Unusually for Indonesia, Singkil is very spread out and has no real centre.

🏃 Activities

Swamp Tours   BOATING
(per boat from 700,000Rp) A rewarding day trip from Singkil involves taking a single-engine canoe up the Sungai Gedang, past two friendly waterfront villages and deeper into the great morass in search of wild orang-utans, monkeys, crocs and plenty of birdlife. Start out as early as possible to maximise your chances of seeing riverside wildlife. Book via Mr Darmawan at Banyak Island Travel.

OFF THE BEATEN TRACK

PULAU SIMEULUE

The isolated island of Simeulue, about 150km west of Tapaktuan, is a rocky volcanic outcrop blanketed in rainforest and fringed with clove and coconut plantations. An increasing number of surfers make it out here (although wave quality is generally not considered to be as high as on some other offshore Sumatran islands – particularly since the 2004 tsunami), but non-surfing travellers are a rare breed indeed. This is a pity because the island holds decent potential for genuine, off-the-beaten-track adventure, and is relatively easy to get around, with the ring road around the island mostly accessible by local minibuses. It's a fairly conservative Muslim society, so tourists need to dress moderately, ie wearing a shirt in villages, and swimwear other than bikinis if swimming on beaches outside the resorts.

There are ATMs but it's advisable to bring lots of cash as they're not to be relied upon.

Frazha Homestay (☑ 0813 6015 2738; Alus Alus; per person incl meals & transport 350,000Rp) Run by Akil and his family, Frazha is a good choice for those looking to keep it local. Its two bungalows are in a coconut grove by a beach that's good for swimming, making it a good choice for non-surfers. Motorbike rental is inclusive in the rates, and Dylan's Right reef break is only a 15-minute drive away. They have a boat, too, for outlying waves.

Simeulue Surf Lodges (☑ 0627-149553; www.simeulue-surflodges.com; per person incl meals from US$65; ☒) Centrally located in front of Dylan's Right surf break is this Dutch-owned place with well-maintained thatched beach huts, a lovely natural plunge pool and sun deck overlooking the ocean. Rates include daily use of a motorcycle for exploring the island and nearby waves.

Moon Beach Resort (☑ 0812 8868 4000; www.simeulue-resort.com; r incl meals & transport from AUD$120; ❈❧) Set up by an Aussie builder who helped construct local villages following the 2004 tsnuami, these modernised bungalows are located halfway between the Peak and Dylan's Right surf breaks. Rooms all have air-con, wi-fi and cable TV with live sport, making it a good choice for those seeking a bit of comfort in between catching waves. There's a nice beach for non-surfers too.

Getting There & Away

Wings Air has a daily flight from Medan (one hour, from 850,000Rp) to Simeulue's airport, which is located on the southwest of the island, a short drive from the surf camps. Be aware the baggage limit is only 10kg.

A ferry from Simeulue's port town of Sinabang to Singkil (71,000Rp to 120,000Rp, 12 hours) leaves twice a week on Wednesday and Sunday at 7pm.

🛏 Sleeping & Eating

★ **Sapo Belen Lodge** LODGE $
(☑ 0813 6196 0997; Jl Bahari 55; d incl breakfast 150,000Rp) An unexpected find in the gritty port town of Singkil is this attractive traditional house featuring a polished-wood interior, antiques and plenty of books. It's by far the nicest place to stay here, with well-priced rooms that have mosquito nets, bathrooms and Achenese coffee cakes for breakfast. It's just off the main street, and a good place to meet fellow travellers to share boat costs.

ⓘ Information

Mr Darmawan from **Banyak Island Travel** (☑ 0821 6645 7040, 0813 7721 9667, 0813 6017 0808; dmawan_skl76@yahoo.com) is Singkil's definitive source of local info.

There's a BRI Bank with an ATM, however, it's always best to bring extra cash in case it's not working.

ⓘ Getting There & Away

AIR

At the time of research there were no flights to Singkil's airport, but check with Susi Air (www.susiair.com) to see if it has resumed flights between Singkil and Medan on its 12-seater planes.

BOAT

From the port off the main street, overnight ferries depart on Wednesday and Sunday for Gunung Sitoli (52,000Rp, six hours) on Pulau Nias at 11pm. If you want a private cabin it's possible to rent one from the crew for around 250,000Rp.

Ferries also head to Sinabang on Pulau Simeulue (71,000Rp to 120,000Rp, 12 hours) at 5pm on Monday and Thursday. Get to the port an hour before departure to secure a seat.

Local boats to Pulau Balai in the Banyaks depart from the jetty at the end of the main street.

BUS & CAR

There are daily minibuses from Singkil to various destinations. You can also charter a car to any destination; this is particularly worthwhile if you're heading for Tuk Tuk on Danau Toba (1,200,000Rp, seven hours) since getting there by public transport requires three bus changes and takes at least 12 hours. Private cars to Medan cost 750,000Rp. Mr Darmawan at Banyak Island Travel has great info on bus schedules and car bookings.

Banyak Islands

If you've ever dreamt about having a tropical island entirely to yourself, complete with palm trees, powdery white beaches and crystal-clear waters, the Banyak Islands is a great place to fulfil your Robinson Crusoe fantasy. A cluster of 99 mostly uninhabited islands, the Banyak (Many) Islands are situated about 30km west of Singkil. Remote they might be, but they are now very much on the radar of paradise-seeking travellers and surfers. As well as having arguably the finest beaches in Sumatra and a handful of quality surf spots, the Banyaks feature Sumatra's best snorkelling, with beautiful underwater forests of colourful coral (at least where there has been no past dynamite fishing).

Only two of the islands are properly inhabited: the town of Balai on Pulau Balai is the main entry point to the islands; low-key Haloban on Pulau Tuangku is the other main village.

◉ Sights

Pulau Sikandang   ISLAND
This largish island with pristine beaches takes a couple of hours to walk around. It's one of the most popular places to stay with several guesthouses set up here. Snorkelling is possible but there's a steep drop-off near the shore off the main beach.

Pulau Bangkaru   ISLAND
The second-largest of the Banyak Islands, Pulau Bangkaru is home to a turtle conservation project, so visits are strictly controlled and you're only allowed on the island with a certified guide. At the time of research the conservation project is up in the air due to the demise of the previous management body; check what's happening with Mr Darmawan at Banyak Island Travel.

Pulau Bangkaru has pristine beaches, excellent surfing off the south coast and plenty of scope for jungle trekking.

Pulau Tuangku   ISLAND
Covered in dense jungle, Pulau Tuangku is the largest of the Banyak Islands. Surfers head to Ujung Lolok, the headland at the south of the island, complete with several world-class breaks. In the northern part of the island is Haloban, a friendly village; Suka Makmur, a Christian village, is further south. With a guide it's possible to summit Gunung Tiusa (313m), for an epic view of the surrounding islands (five hours return), and visit a cave full of stalagmites.

Pulau Palambak Besar   ISLAND
Rather out of the way, this medium-sized island is covered in coconut trees, and has a couple of jungle paths you can walk and a gorgeous stretch of beach, though the snorkelling is not great. Here you'll find the lovely Palambak Island Resort (p555).

Pulau Tailana   ISLAND
The small island of Pulau Tailana is renowned for reefs that are waves of colour. The island has a popular guesthouse.

BUSES FROM SINGKIL

DESTINATION	FARE (RP)	DURATION (HR)	FREQUENCY
Banda Aceh	220,000–280,000	15	daily at 2pm & 4pm
Kutacane (for Ketambe)	180,000	10	daily at 6pm
Medan	130,000	10	nightly at 8pm
Sibolga	120,000	6	daily at 8am

Pulau Laman
ISLAND

There's good snorkelling between Pulau Laman and Pulau Laureh, with some remarkable growths of vivid blue coral.

Pulau Asok
ISLAND

A crescent-shaped, uninhabited island with pristine beaches on either side as well as excellent snorkelling.

Pulau Ragu-Ragu
ISLAND

Offers some excellent snorkelling. Dugongs are sometimes sighted in the mornings off the island's north shore.

Pulau Balai
ISLAND

One of two inhabited islands in the Banyaks, connected to the mainland by frequent public boats. It has no attractions of its own, but has a mellow atmosphere, friendly locals, cheap losmen and restaurants, and is useful as a transfer point.

Pulau Lambodong
ISLAND

Uninhabited small island with white sandy beach, popular with day trippers from neighbouring Banyak islands.

Activities

Kayaking

Kayaking the calm, crystal-clear waters between dozens of idyllic islands is a great way to explore the Banyaks. With **Rega and Anhar** (☑ 0821 6199 7974, 0852 7771 1108; kayak hire per day 150,000Rp), you can arrange anything from beginner routes to multi-day challenges for experienced kayakers (around 350,000Rp per person per day for the latter).

Snorkelling & Diving

The reefs in the Banyaks teem with colourful fish and corals and there are fabulous snorkelling possibilities off almost any island. The visibility is excellent and most lodgings rent snorkelling masks. Standout islands for snorkelling include Pulau Asok and Pulau Pabisi.

Surfing

Many visitors to the Banyaks are surfers, and there are some world-class surf spots here off Pulau Tuangku and Pulau Bangkaru, as well as some more average waves. However, the line-up can get rather crowded, particularly around Ujung Lolok, with up to 30 surfers regularly fighting over one peak.

It's mostly surfers who flock to Pulau Tuangku's southernmost tip, **Ujung Lolok**. Many come on liveaboard surfing charter boats, while others rent a local fishing boat and live on it. However, there's plenty of other accommodation available these days.

Banyak Islands

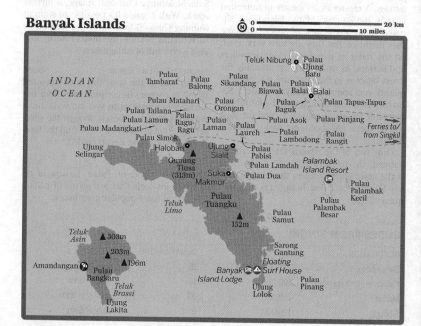

🛏 Sleeping & Eating

You can live out your castaway fantasies by camping wild on one of the numerous uninhabited islands. Tents can be arranged through Mr Darmawan at Banyak Island Travel (p552); bring all your food and water with you – stock up in Singkil or Balai, or catch your own dinner!

Most bungalows have meals as part of their package stays, and normally include locally caught fish and other Indonesian staples.

🛏 Pulai Balai

Homestay Lae Kombih   GUESTHOUSE $
(☑0852 9689 5929; Jl Iskandar Muda, Pulau Balai; r with shared/private bathroom & fan from 50,000/75,000Rp, with private bathroom & air-con 150,000Rp; ❄) This guesthouse overlooks the water and has hot and stuffy rooms, but what do you expect at these prices? It also has passable air-con rooms. The owner is very friendly and speaks English. Opposite is his sister's restaurant, Rumah Makan Lae Kombih, which does tasty local dishes; go for the fish curry.

🛏 Pulau Palambak Basar

Palambak Island Resort   BUNGALOW $
(☑0812 608 1916, 0852 7501 7309; www.palambak islandresort.com; Pulau Palambak Besar; per person incl meals 250,000Rp) The only accommodation on Pulau Palambak Besar is in these 10 lovely bungalows with shared bathrooms fronting a stunning beach. There's a nice restaurant doing good food, plus plenty of books, board games and beers in the fridge. Jungle trekking in the island interior is possible, as well as snorkelling and kayaking. They can arrange transfers and speedboat pick-up from Singkil (1,600,000Rp).

🛏 Pulau Tailana

Pondok Tailana   BUNGALOW $
(☑0822 7449 9207; www.tailana.webs.com; Pulau Tailana; r incl meals 250,000Rp) Just the place for those wanting to keep things blissfully simple, Pondok Tailana is also a launching point for island-hopping, snorkelling and jungle trekking. Lodgings consist of seven basic beach huts with shared bathrooms and hammocks by the water. However, there are some maintenance issues and the food can be a mixed bag.

🛏 Pulau Sikandang

★**Nina's Bungalows**   BUNGALOW $
(☑0852 7086 8591; www.banyak-island-bungalow. com; Pulau Sikandang; r 200,000Rp, house 800,000Rp; ❄@) The Banyak hot spot for backpackers at the time of research, Nina's comprises five spacious, thatched bungalows with hammocks swinging on shady porches. The beach is pristine and the water gin-clear. Helpful manager Rius takes good care of guests, and the food gets positive reviews. There's also beer available.

Nina's also has a fabulous beach house right on the water, full of rustic charm and with two bedrooms, small kitchen, solar power and Western bathroom.

🛏 Pulau Tuangku

The southern tip of the island attracts almost exclusively a surfing crowd.

The main village of Haloban has one basic losmen (100,000Rp per person); what the locals lack in English-speaking skills they more than make up for with enthusiasm and friendliness.

Banyak Island Lodge   LODGE $$$
(☑in USA +1 904-669-3286; www.banyaksurfbun galows.com; Pulau Tuangku; per person incl meals & transport for 7 days US$1050; ☎) The only land-based accommodation on Pulau Tuangku is this surf lodge situated in the so-called Bay of Plenty. Rates include transfers and full board. There are five fan-cooled bungalows with twin beds and mozzie nets overlooking Gunters and Camel Back waves out front. The lounge serves local and Western dishes to the accompaniment of surf chat.

Floating Surf House   SURF CAMP $$$
(☑0822 7214 4450; www.floatingsurfhouse.com; Pulau Tuangku; 10-night stay with fan/air-con US$1699/1899; ❄☎) Sitting in the calm waters of the Bay of Plenty, near Ujung Lolok and within easy reach of Dindos, Gunters and Lolok Point waves, this surf-camp-on-a-raft provides unique accommodation for those chasing the waves. Owned by local surfer Erwin, it has two basic, three-bed rooms for solo guests, two doubles and a stilt house.

ℹ Getting There & Away

There are two ferries a week from Singkil to Balai (Tuesday 10am and Friday 2pm, 30,000Rp, 3½ to four hours), returning on Wednesday and Sunday at 2pm. Local boats depart Singkil for Balai

(50,000Rp, three to five hours) and Haloban (75,000Rp, five to six hours) daily between 8am and noon (depending on the tides), returning in the afternoon. During the worst of the rough seas in October and November, boats may not run for days.

By far the most convenient – but expensive – way to reach the islands is to charter a speedboat. Destinations (and one-way costs) from Singkil: Balai (1,500,000Rp); Sikandang (1,600,000Rp); Palambak (1,600,000Rp); Tailana (1,800,000Rp); Ujung Lolok (2,100,000Rp).

However, if you can get the wooden boat to Balai or Haloban it'll be much cheaper to arrange a speedboat onward to the islands; most lodgings can arrange speedboat pick-up.

Enquire in Balai about hiring a fishing boat (600,000Rp to 2,500,000Rp per day, depending on boat size, with all the rice and fish you can eat). Mr Darmawan at Banyak Island Travel (p552) can also assist.

Gunung Leuser National Park

📞 0642

The Aceh section of Gunung Leuser National Park has slipped under the tourist radar for years, seeing only a trickle of visitors while the masses head to the more hyped Bukit Lawang. Its jungle is basically the same, minus the well-worn paths and tourists clambering about trying to spot semi-wild orang-utans. This is the place for a *real* jungle experience.

Unesco-listed Gunung Leuser National Park is one of the world's most important and biologically diverse conservation areas. It is often described as a complete ecosystem laboratory because of the range of forest and species types.

Within the park's boundaries live some of the planet's most endangered and exotic species: tigers, rhinoceroses, elephants and orang-utans. Although the likelihood of seeing most of these celebrity animals is remote, you have a good chance of seeing orang-utans, and you can be sure of encountering plenty of other primates.

Gunung Leuser National Park's habitats range from the swamp forests of the west coast to the dense lowland rainforests of the interior. Much of the area around Ketambe is virgin forest. Above 1500m, the permanent mist has created moss forests rich in epiphytes and orchids. Rare flora includes two members of the rafflesia family, *Rafflesia acehensis* and *Rafflesia zippelnii*, which are found along Sungai Alas.

More than 300 bird species have been recorded in the park, including the bizarre rhinoceros hornbill, the helmeted hornbill and woodpeckers.

The national park faces a great number of challenges. Poachers have virtually wiped out the crocodile population and have severely reduced the number of tigers and rhinoceroses. According to the Indonesian Forum for the Environment, over a fifth of the park has been adversely affected by illegal logging and road construction. A highly controversial road project called Ladia Galaska runs through the park, linking the east and west coasts of the province. Furthermore, during the civil conflict in Aceh, the jungle was a stronghold of GAM militants, and the national park saw fighting between GAM and Indonesian troops.

The park receives a lot of rain throughout the year, but rain showers tend to lessen in frequency and duration between December and March.

ℹ️ Getting There & Away

While Bukit Lawang and Tangkahan are most accessible in terms of their proximity to Medan, Ketambe and Kedah are easily reachable if you're travelling through North Sumatra or Aceh. Most visitors arrive via Kutacane by bus, a one-hour drive south of Ketambe, from where you can take a bus or *ojek*.

You can also fly to Kutacane from Banda Aceh, but this is on a tiny aircraft (and with only 10kg luggage allowed) and is not for the faint hearted. There are also flights to Blangkejeren, which is 30-minute drive from Kedah.

Otherwise there are long-distance buses from Banda Aceh that pass through the Gayo Highlands via Takengon and the interior of the national park. Kedah is located a two-hour drive from Ketambe, or 30 minutes from Blangkejeren.

Ketambe

One of the best places in Asia to spot orang-utans in the wild, Ketambe is in the heart of the Alas Valley, and is the main tourist centre of Gunung Leuser National Park. A handful of guesthouses are spread along the road through Ketambe, hemmed in between the river and the jungle. It's one of the most chilled-out places in the north of Sumatra, and a few lazy days relaxing beside the river and partaking in some jungle hiking is likely to be a highlight of your Sumatran adventures.

Ketambe is one of the main access points to the park. Directly across the river is Ketambe Research Station, a world-renowned conservation research facility, which is off limits to tourists. Ketambe has a few basic shops and restaurants, but Kutacane, 43km away, is the closest town of any note and is the place to go for transport and ATMs.

🏃 Activities

Permits to Gunung Leuser National Park (150,000Rp per day) can be arranged at guesthouses in Ketambe. Guides can also be hired from any guesthouse in Ketambe; ask other travellers for recommendations.

Rafting & Tubing

Rafting (half/full day around 800,000/ 1,000,000Rp) is a fun way to see the forest and keep cool at the same time. Most guesthouses can help organise this. Tubing can also be arranged for around 100,000Rp.

Hiking

For serious trekkers and jungle enthusiasts, the trekking around Ketambe (half day/full day/overnight 250,000/400,000/900,000Rp) offers a much more authentic experience than that near Bukit Lawang. Be prepared for extreme terrain, leeches and mosquitoes, and bring plenty of water. Guides can tailor a trip to specific requests. One of the more popular hikes is a three-day walk to some hot springs deep in the forest.

Gunung Kemiri HIKING
At 3314m, this is the second-highest peak in Gunung Leuser National Park. The return trek takes five to six days, starting from the village of Gumpang, north of Ketambe. It takes in some of the park's richest primate habitat, of orang-utans, macaques, siamangs and gibbons, and passes through tiger habitat as well.

Gunung Leuser HIKING
The park's highest peak is, of course, Gunung Leuser (3404m). Only the physically fit should attempt the 12-day return trek to the summit (seven days up, five days down). The walk starts from the village of Angusan, northwest of Blangkejeren.

Bukit Lawang HIKING
Starting one hour south of Kutacane, this five- to six-day trek through tough terrain passes over 20 river crossings; in the wet season it can take up to 10 days and can be a real slog. You have a good chance of seeing orang-utans and gibbons, and the trek passes through areas that elephants are known to inhabit.

You can arrange to have your luggage delivered to Bukit Lawang separately.

🛏 Sleeping

⭐ **Thousand Hills Guest House** BUNGALOW $
(📱0812 6417 6752; www.thousandhillsketambe. net; s/d/tr 100,000/150,000/200,000Rp) The first Ketambe guesthouse you'll come across if approaching from the south and the most charming of its accommodation options, this place consists of cute thatched bungalows hiding in beautiful garden and forest surrounds. The indomitable Joseph is full of advice and can organise jungle guides.

⭐ **Friendship Guesthouse** GUESTHOUSE $
(📱0852 9688 3624; www.ketambe.com; Jl Blangkejeren Km32; r 50,000-100,000Rp; 🖥) This well-priced guesthouse has a beautiful riverside location and charming, colourful wooden bungalows equipped with Western toilets. The cheapest rooms are very basic. The main hang-out area is decked out with photos of travellers engaging in jungle stuff. Led by Ahmad, the staff are friendly, and it's a good place to arrange guides. Its website is an excellent resource for local info.

Leuser Ketambe Guesthouse GUESTHOUSE $
(📱0853 6062 6329; www.ketambetour.com; r 100,000-200,000Rp) Ketambe's most unique choice is this dated guesthouse that's the only accommodation inside Gunung Leuser National Park. It has the eerie ambience of an old country manor lost to the jungle, and its large, run-down rooms (with carpet) are in two large wooden houses. There's also a restaurant here overlooking the river. Take care walking along the mossy paths – they're slippery!

Wisma Cinta Alam BUNGALOW $
(📱0852 7086 4580; johanketambe@gmail.com; Jl Blangkejeren, Km32; s 50,000Rp, d 80,000-150,000Rp) Run by veteran guide and rafter Johan, these well-established bungalows are set on lovingly maintained grounds. The cheaper rooms sit in a row in a barrack-like construction, while the pricier ones are little bungalows in their own right; both come with showers and real beds. Excellent, knowledgable guides can be organised here. It's also a good choice for those keen on rafting.

Wisma Sadar Wisata GUESTHOUSE $
(📱0852 7615 5741; www.ketambe.net; Jl Blangkejeren, Km32; r 50,000-80,000Rp; 🖥) Here you'll find a range of good-value Karo-style

bungalows, some of which back onto nature and overlook the river – Room 5 is the pick. Ayuni and her daughter Mira are entertaining hosts, there's good food and jungle guides can be easily arranged.

ℹ️ Information

There are no ATMs in Ketambe; the closest town to get money is Kutacane.

ℹ️ Getting There & Away

There are two weekly flights between Kutacane and Banda Aceh with Susi Air (www.susiair.com) on Monday and Wednesday. Book directly at their office at the airport.

From Kutacane there are countless *labi-labi* to Ketambe (25,000Rp including luggage, one hour), but they stop running around 6pm; arrange pick-up with your guesthouse if arriving later. A private car is around 100,000Rp.

All north-bound buses from Kutacane pass through Ketambe. If you want to arrive in Takengon during daylight hours, catch a minibus to Blangkejeren around 8am by standing ready on the main road; with later ones, you miss the 11am connection and will be stuck in Blangkejeren until 4pm or 5pm, when a minibus leaves for Banda Aceh via Takengon.

If travelling south to Danau Toba, catch a Sidikalang-bound bus from Kutacane, then another to Pangururan, and then one to Samosir Island. For Berastagi, there's a direct minibus from Kutacane.

A shared taxi from Medan to Kutacane (seven hours) is around 130,000Rp.

A private car to Medan is around 1,000,000Rp; to Berastagi 800,000Rp, Danau Toba 1,300,000Rp, Singkil 1,500,000Rp and Bukit Lawang 1,500,000Rp.

Kedah

Located 15km west of the scrappy town of Blangkejeren, the small village of Kedah has seen very few visitors since the conflict in Aceh, making it ripe for off-the-beaten-track

travel. At the northern edge of Gunung Leuser National Park, Kedah is a magnificent starting point for treks into the jungle, which is home to orang-utans, gibbons and other exotic wildlife, birds and plants.

🍴 Sleeping & Eating

Simple, local meals are available at Rainforest Lodge. It's a good idea to stock up on extras in Blangkejeren, especially if you're off trekking. Blangkejeren has basic restaurants.

⭐ **Rainforest Lodge**   LODGE $
(📱 0813 6229 1844; www.gunung-leuser-trek.net; r 150,000Rp) Rainforest Lodge has simple but pleasant bungalows along a river in beautiful jungle surrounds, with plenty of opportunities for wildlife-spotting. Let Mr Jally here know in advance that you're coming. It's a 50-minute walk from Kedah village and is literally in the middle of nowhere. Rooms are basic; some have attached bathrooms. Bring your own towel and toiletries.

Mr Jally can organise jungle treks for around 500,000Rp per day, including food and guide; these are serious adventures, from the three-day summit of Gunung Angkosan to a six-day expedition to an immense waterfall in the upper Alas Valley. Shorter treks can also be arranged, including night treks. Park permit fees are collected intermittently and the cost is not included.

ℹ️ Getting There & Away

Susi Air has two weekly flights to Blangkejeren from both Medan and Banda Aceh (around 370,000Rp, one hour) on its tiny planes, but take note of the 10kg luggage limit.

There are also buses to Blangkejeren from Banda Aceh (220,000Rp) and Kutacane (70,000Rp).

From Blangkejeren you can take an *ojek* (50,000Rp to 60,000Rp, 20 minutes) to Kedah. Mr Jally from Rainforest Lodge can assist.

BUSES FROM KUTACANE & KETAMBE

DESTINATION	FARE (RP)	DURATION (HR)	FREQUENCY
Banda Aceh (via Takengon)	250,000	16	daily
Berastagi	60,000	6	daily
Blangkejeren (for Kedah)	60,000	4	7 daily
Medan	80,000	7	several daily
Sidikalang	70,000	3½	daily
Singkil	180,000	10	daily

WEST SUMATRA

In Sumatra Barat (West Sumatra), fertile uplands ring jungle-clad volcanoes, waterfalls cascade into deep ravines and nature takes a breath in deep, still lakes. Rainforest still clings to the steepest slopes, while rice, tapioca, cinnamon and coffee bring in the wealth.

This is the heartland of the matriarchal Minangkabau, an intelligent, culturally rich and politically savvy people who have successfully exported their culture, language, cuisine and beliefs throughout Indonesia and whose soaring architecture dominates the cities and villages.

Coastal Padang is a transport hub and popular pit stop for surfers, trekkers and indigenous-culture enthusiasts bound for the Mentawai Islands. Scenic traveller-friendly Bukittinggi is surrounded by picturesque villages where traditional artisans still ply their trades, while the gorgeous Danau Maninjau, the secluded Harau Valley and Kerinci Seblat

National Park provide plenty of scope for outdoor adventure.

History

Little is known about the area's history before the arrival of Islam in the 14th century. However, the abundance of megalithic remains around the towns of Batu Sangkar and Payakumbuh, near Bukittinggi, suggest that the central highlands supported a sizeable community some 2000 years ago.

After the arrival of Islam, the region was split into small Muslim states ruled by sultans. It remained this way until the beginning of the 19th century, when war erupted between followers of the Islamic fundamentalist Padri movement and supporters of the local chiefs, adherents to the Minangkabau *adat* (traditional laws and regulations). The Padris were so named because their leaders were haji, pilgrims who had made their way to Mecca via the Achenese port of Pedir. They returned from the haj determined to

SUMATRA WEST SUMATRA

West Sumatra

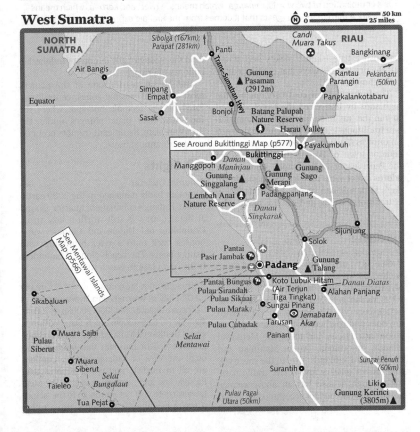

N 0 ————— 50 km
   0 ————— 25 miles

NORTH SUMATRA

Sibolga (167km); Parapat (281km)

Panti

Candi Muara Takus **RIAU**

Bangkinang

Air Bangis

Trans-Sumatran Hwy

Gunung Pasaman (2912m)

Rantau Parangin Pekanbaru (50km)

Simpang Empat

Equator

Sasak

Bonjol

Pangkalankotabaru

Batang Palupah Nature Reserve

Harau Valley

See Around Bukittinggi Map (p577)

Payakumbuh

Manggopoh

Danau Maninjau

Bukittinggi

Gunung Singgalang

Gunung Merapi

Gunung Sago

Lembah Anai Nature Reserve

Padangpanjang

Danau Singkarak

Sijunjung

Pantai Pasir Jambak

Solok

Gunung Talang

Padang

See Mentawai Islands Map (p566)

Pantai Bungus (Air Terjun Tiga Tingkat)

Koto Lubuk Hitam

Danau Diatas

Alahan Panjang

Pulau Sirandah

Pulau Sikuai

Sungai Pinang

Sikabaluan

Pulau Marak

Pulau Cubadak

Tarusan

Jemabatan Akar

Painan

Muara Sajbi

Pulau Siberut

Selat Mentawai

Muara Siberut

Selat Bungalaut

Surantih

Sungai Penuh (60km)

Taieleo

Liki

Gunung Kerinci (3805m)

Tua Pejat

Pulau Pagai Utara (50km)

THE MINANGKABAU

Legend has it that the Minangkabau are descended from the wandering Macedonian conqueror Alexander the Great. According to the story, the ancestors of the Minangkabau arrived in Sumatra under the leadership of King Maharjo Dirajo, the youngest son of Alexander.

Anthropologists, however, suggest that the Minangkabau arrived in West Sumatra from the Malay Peninsula some time between 1000 and 2000 BC, probably by following Sungai Batang Hari upstream from the Strait of Melaka to the highlands of the Bukit Barisan mountains.

Even if they don't have Alexander's bloodline, the Minangkabau reflect his wanderlust and love of battle, albeit in the milder form of buffalo fighting. Their success in buffalo fighting is believed to have bestowed the people with their tribal name, and the horns of the beast are the focus of their architecture and traditional costumes.

The legend of how the Minangkabau named themselves begins with an imminent attack by a Javanese king. Rather than pit two armies against each other, the Minangkabau proposed a fight between two bulls. When the time came, the West Sumatrans dispatched a tiny calf to fight the enormous Javanese bull, but the half-starved calf was outfitted with sharp metal spears to its horns. Believing the Javanese bull to be its mother, the calf rushed to suckle and ripped the bull's belly to shreds. When the bull finally dropped dead, the people of West Sumatra shouted '*Minangkabau, minangkabau!*', which literally means, 'The buffalo wins, the buffalo wins!'

Linguistic sticklers, though, prefer the far more prosaic explanation that Minangkabau is a combination of two words: *minanga*, which means 'a river', and *kerbau*, which means 'buffalo'. A third theory suggests that it comes from the archaic expression *pinang kabhu*, which means 'original home' – Minangkabau being the cradle of Malay civilisation.

establish a true Islamic society and stamp out the pre-Islamic ways that dominated the ruling houses.

The Padris had won control of much of the highlands by 1821 when the Dutch decided to join the fray in support of the Minangkabau traditional leaders. The fighting dragged on until 1837, when the Dutch overcame the equator town of Bonjol, the stronghold of the Padri leader Imam Bonjol, whose name adorns street signs all over Indonesia. In today's Minangkabau society, a curious fusion of traditional beliefs and Islam is practised.

Padang

📞 0751 / POP 1 MILLION

Padang is an urban-Indonesian sprawl sandwiched between the Indian Ocean and the Minangkabau hills. It is to West Sumatra what Medan is to North Sumatra (but with better scenery) – a handy transport hub with air, boat and road connections to major regional attractions, including the Mentawai Islands, Bukittinggi, Danau Maninjau and the Kerinci Highlands. Due to the sheer volume of backpacker and surfer traffic passing through, it also has an above-average amount of good budget accommodation and an excellent dining scene, with its regional

food the most globally famous of Indonesian culinary offerings.

Padang sits astride one of the planet's most powerful seismic zones, centrally located on the tectonic hot spot where the Indo-Australian plate plunges under the Eurasian plate. Significant tremors occur on an almost annual basis.

👁 Sights

Colonial Quarter AREA

Although badly damaged in the 2009 earthquake, Padang's colonial-era quarter around Jl Batang Arau is still worth a lazy stroll. Crumbling old Dutch and Chinese warehouses back onto a river brimming with fishing boats. The beach along Jl Samudera is the best place to watch sunsets.

Adityawarman Museum MUSEUM

(📞 0751-31523; www.museumadityawarman.org; Jl Diponegoro 10; adult/child 3000/2000Rp; ⊙ 7.30am-4pm Tue-Fri, 8am-4.30pm Sat & Sun) Within a grand traditional Minangkabau-style building is this excellent museum that offers a thorough overview of Padang culture. Captions are all in English, and cover Minangkabau lifestyle and architecture, as well as the Mentawais; try to visit before you go to the islands if you're heading there. There's also a rather sobering display on the natural disasters that have impacted Padang over the years.

Tours

Regina Adventures
TOURS, SURFING

(☑ 0812 6774 5464, 0751-781 0835; www.regina adventures.com; Jl Pampangan 54; 8-day Mentawai surf packages per person from US$515) Local operator Elvis offers trekking and surfing on the Mentawai Islands, boat charters, trips to Danau Maninjau and Bukittinggi, and ascents of Gunung Merapi and Gunung Kerinci. Check the website for the good-value surf trips to Mentawai and Krui further south.

⚒ Festivals & Events

Dragon Boat Festival
SPORTS

(www.facebook.com/padanginternationaldragon boatindonesia; ☉ Jul/Aug) This festival involves boat-racing competitions between international teams. Check details on Facebook.

🛏 Sleeping

★ Bat & Arrow
GUESTHOUSE $

(☑ 0751-893552; Jl Batang Arau 25; r incl breakfast with shared bathroom 150,000-250,000Rp, with private bathroom 300,000-450,000Rp; ❋ 🛜) With a great location in the atmospheric old quarter along the river, this unique choice is upstairs from its popular eponymous bar (p563). It's more of an art hotel than guesthouse, with rooms featuring creative touches mixed with the creature comforts of cable TV, air-con and wi-fi. While the common areas are a bit dark it's enlivened by the contemporary installations throughout.

★ New House Padang
GUESTHOUSE $

(☑ 0751-25982; www.newhousepadang.com; Jl HOS Cokroaminoto 104; dm/d with shared bathroom from 100,000/250,000Rp, d with private bathroom 330,000Rp; ❋ 🛜) Popular with surfers and backpackers alike, this friendly and relaxed six-room guesthouse is the perfect mix of budget and style. A compact Zen garden combines with colourful rooms (some with terrace), contemporary artwork and a vast common area. Shared bathrooms are spotless and have hot water. The French owner is on hand to advise about surfing and onward travel.

Riverside Hostel
HOSTEL $

(☑ 0751-895 6623; http://riverside-hostel-padang. business.site; Jl Batang Arau 66C; dm 125,000-145,000Rp, d incl breakfast 270,000Rp; ❋ 🛜) Within a converted old house, this rather refined hostel has polished hardwood floors, exposed brick walls and antique decorations. Boutique rooms and dorms (with curtains for privacy) are spacious, and there's a huge country-style kitchen and a comfy lounge, making the Riverside Hostel a cut above most backpacker places. It's down a lane near the boat dock.

Yani's Homestay
HOMESTAY $

(☑ 0852 6380 1686; www.yanihomestaypadang. wordpress.com; Jl Nipah 1; dm 80,000Rp, r 120,000-200,000Rp; ❋ 🛜) Run by a friendly young owner who's an excellent source of info, this central homestay provides bona fide backpacker digs in the form of an air-con dorm with lockers and rooms with colourful bedspreads. The best rooms have private bathrooms. There are also motorbikes for rent (for 60,000Rp a day).

Brigitte's House
HOSTEL $

(☑ 0813 7425 7162; www.brigitteshousepadang. com; Jl Kampung Sebalah 1/14; dm/s/d from 95,000/120,000/250,000Rp, d with air-con 250,000-350,000Rp; ❋ 🛜) Down a backstreet just off Jl Nipah, Brigitte's is a great backpacker pad with a relaxed ambience and chilled lounge and kitchen areas. The singles are poky but the dorms and doubles are spacious, while the air-con rooms are in a separate apartment building a block away. Brigitte is a treasure trove of information on buses, ferries and Mentawai adventures.

Savali Hotel
HOTEL $$$

(☑ 0751-27660; www.savalihotel.com; Jl Hayam Wuruk 31; r incl breakfast 700,000-900,000Rp; ❋ 🛜 ⊞) The centrally located Savali is just a short stroll from the beach and good restaurants. The hotel's 23 rooms are set around a Zen-style garden, the plunge pool is welcome on sultry equatorial afternoons and there's an on-site wine bar and good **coffee shop** (☑ 0751-30051; www.elscoffee.com; ☉ 10am-11pm Sun-Thu, to 1am Fri & Sat; 🛜) next door.

🍴 Eating

★ Sari Raso
INDONESIAN $

(☑ 0751-33498; Jl Karya 3; meals around 30,000Rp; ☉ 8am-7pm) Pick from a multitude of spicy dishes at this classic Padang chain, housed within a classy art deco colonial building. Do not miss the beef *rendang;* it's as good as we've ever had.

Pondok Indah Jaya
INDONESIAN $

(☑ 0751-25128; Jl Niaga 138; meals around 30,000Rp; ☉ 7am-9pm; ❋) This warung is an excellent intro to Padang cuisine. The staff will talk you through the selection of dishes, including spicy tofu, beef *rendang, ayam* sambal and

Padang

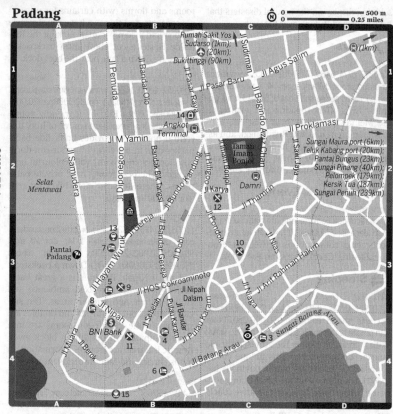

Padang

◎ Sights
1 Adityawarman Museum	B2
2 Colonial Quarter	C4

◎ Sleeping
3 Bat & Arrow	C4
4 Brigitte's House	B4
5 New House Padang	B3
6 Riverside Hostel	B4
7 Savali Hotel	B3
8 Yani's Homestay	A3

◎ Eating
9 Ikan Bakar Pak Tri's	B3
10 Pondok Indah Jaya	C3

11 Safari Garden	B4
12 Sari Raso	C2

◎ Drinking & Nightlife
Bat & Arrow	(see 3)
El's Coffee	(see 7)
13 Teebox	B3

◎ Shopping
14 Pasar Raya	B1

◎ Transport
Mentawai Fast	(see 15)
15 Sungari Muara Ferry Dock	B4

tempe. Cool the fire in your mouth with some *sirsak* (soursop), cucumber or mango juice.

Safari Garden STEAK $$
(☏ 0751-36055; www.safarigarden.net; Jl Nipah 21; mains 45,000-315,000Rp; ◎10am-midnight Mon-Fri, to 1am Sat & Sun; ❀ 🛜) This stylish,

convivial steakhouse with exposed-brick walls and rustic log-lined booths is a fine place for a splurge, or just some good coffee. The specialty is Wagyu beef steaks (from 200,000Rp), but there's a menu of pizzas (including a *rendang* version), Balinese *nasi campur*, Japanese and Korean, seafood and homemade gelato. There's cold beer and a good selection of fresh juice too.

Ikan Bakar Pak Tri's SEAFOOD $$
(Jl HOS Cokroaminoto 91; meals from 50,000Rp; ☺10am-9pm) Here the fish and squid are sold by weight or portion and flame-grilled to perfection with a sweet, spicy sambal sauce. The selection includes shoals of different fish and squid, with a supporting cast of *kangkung* (water spinach) and aubergine dishes. Grab a spot at the shared tables and tuck in for a quintessential Padang experience.

🍸 Drinking & Nightlife

★ **Bat & Arrow** PUB
(Jl Batang Arau 25; ☺2pm-midnight; 🛜) Overlooking the river in the colonial quarter, this sprawling, atmospheric 'ruin pub' feels a bit like a bombed-out building, but instead is Padang's top traveller hang-out. The beer garden fills up nightly with surfers, backpackers and locals. Beer, pizza and pub food (mains 20,000Rp to 100,000Rp) are on the menu, and there are pool tables and live music.

Teebox BAR
(Jl Diponegoro 25; ☺10am-2am) Teebox is a fairly tacky entertainment complex with a bar, DJs, bands, karaoke, pool tables and restaurants, but it's an option if you're looking to kick on.

🛍 Shopping

Pasar Raya MARKET
(Jl Pasar Raya; ☺8am-8pm) Translating as 'big market', Pasar Raya lives up to its name: this massive, sprawling site is the centre of Padang's shopping universe. Here you'll be able to find anything from fresh fruit, clothing and accessories to bootleg goods. It's a good spot for taking photos, but watch out for pickpockets. It's next to a large new mall.

ℹ Information

There are banks and ATMs all over town, including a **BNI Bank** (Jl Nipah) close to guesthouses.
Padang Imigrasi Office (📞 0751-705 5113; www.imigrasipadang.com; Jl Khatib Sulaiman 50; ☺9am-4pm Mon-Fri) Thirty-day visa extensions can be obtained for 350,000Rp here; allow three to four working days for processing. It's about 5km north of the centre.

ℹ Getting There & Away

AIR
Padang's airport, **Bandara Internasional Minangkabau** (Jl Adinegoro), is 20km north of town.

BOAT
Padang has regular connections to the Mentawai Islands (p570) by boat. The **Sungari Muara Ferry Dock** is the dock used by the fast-boat service.

BUS
Tranex buses (📞 0751-705 8577) depart for Bukittinggi (30,000Rp) from the city's northern fringes, outside the Wisma Indah building. They're half the price of door-to-door minibuses but you have to catch any white *angkot* (3000Rp) heading north on Jl Permuda (ask for 'Tranex' or 'Wisma Indah'), and then find transport from the Bukittinggi bus terminal, which is miles from the centre. In reality you save very little money this way.

PADANG CUISINE

With *nasi Padang* (Padang cuisine), you sit down and the whole kit and caboodle gets laid out in front of you. You decide which items look tasty and push the others aside, only paying for what you eat.

The most famous Padang dish is *rendang*, chunks of beef or buffalo simmered slowly in coconut milk until the sauce is reduced to a rich paste and the meat becomes dark and dried. Other popular dishes include *telor balado* (egg dusted with red chilli), *ayam bakar* (charcoal-grilled chicken marinated in coconut sauce), *ikan panggang* (fish baked in coconut and chilli) and *gulai merah kambing* (red mutton curry).

Most groups of two people pick one or two meat dishes and a vegetable, usually *kangkung* (water spinach), and load up with a plate or two of rice. Carbs are manna in Padang cuisine. Vegetarians should ask for tempe or *tahu* (tofu), which comes in a spicy sambal, as well as *gulai nangka* (jackfruit curry).

Before digging into the meal with your right hand, wash up in the provided bowl of water. Food and sauces should be spooned onto your plate of rice, then mixed together with the fingers. The rice will be easier to handle if it is a little wet. Use your fingers to scoop up the food, and your thumb to push it into your mouth. It's messy even for the locals.

Minibuses to Bukittinggi (50,000Rp) and other destinations depart from a variety of offices scattered around the city and offer a door-to-door service. **AWR Travel** (☑ 0751-37337) is a reliable company offering hotel pick-up, otherwise ask your lodgings to arrange a pick-up.

Most minibuses offer pick-up services or depart from Jl Jhoni Anwar. **Safa Marwa** (☑ 0852 6355 8899) has regular departures to Sungai Penuh (for Kerinci Seblat National Park). **Putra Mandau** (☑ 0812 8130 3039; Jl Jhoni Anwar) links Padang to Dumai (180,000Rp, 12 hours) if you're travelling to/from Sumatra by sea from Malaysia or Singapore. To get to Jl Jhoni Anwar, catch an *angkot* (3000Rp) north along Jl Permuda and Jl S Parman, get off at the white mosque around 5km north of central Padang, and turn right into Jl Jhoni Anwar.

❶ Getting Around

Grab (p515) and Go-Jek (p515) online taxis both operate in Padang, and are by far the easiest and cheapest ways to travel around town.

Otherwise there are numerous *angkot* (3000Rp) around town, operating out of the **angkot terminal** (Jl M Yamin). Padang has no becaks but there are plenty of *ojeks* – if you're walking around town they'll often beep to get your attention.

TO & FROM THE AIRPORT

Taxis charge around 150,000Rp to/from the airport. If you're travelling light, step outside the airport boundaries and hail an *ojek* (motorcycle that takes passengers) to central Padang. Online ride services are much cheaper (car/motorbike around 80,000/40,000Rp, 45 minutes), but are only allowed to drop off.

The recently opened **Minangkabau Airport Rail Link** has five trains a day to the airport (10,000Rp, 40 minutes), departing every two hours from 6.15am until 4.20pm; from the airport the first train is at 7.40am and the last is at 5.55pm.

White airport buses with **Damri** (☑ 0751-780 6335; 23,500Rp, one hour) are the cheapest option, running roughly hourly between 6.15am and 5.15pm. Tell the conductor your accommodation and street and they'll drop you at the right stop.

Pantai Bungus & Sungai Pinang

If Padang's traffic is frying your brains, or you're waiting for a boat, kick back on one of the nearby beaches: there's a heap of islands to explore, and they're exactly the kind of places you'll end up staying longer than you expected.

Pantai Bungus, 23km south of Padang, is conveniently close to the ferry port of Teluk Kabung, but still sufficiently relaxed to unkink the most frazzled traveller. Further south along the coast is **Sungai Pinang**, with its somnolent fishing-village vibe.

TRANSPORT FROM PADANG

Air

DESTINATION	AIRLINE	FREQUENCY
Bengkulu	Wings Air	1 daily
Gunung Sitoli	Wings Air	1 daily
Jakarta	Batik Air, Citilink, Lion Air, Garuda, Sriwijaya Air	25-30 daily
Jambi	Wings Air	1 daily
Kuala Lumpur	AirAsia	3 daily
Medan	Lion Air, Sriwijaya Air	3 daily
Palembang	Wings Air	1 daily
Pekanbaru	Wings Air	1 daily
Pulau Batam	Citilink, Lion Air	4 daily

Bus

DESTINATION	FARE (RP)	DURATION (HR)	FREQUENCY
Bukittinggi	50,000	3	hourly 6am-6pm
Jambi	120,000-240,000	12	2 daily
Kerinci (for Sungai Penuh & Kersik Tua)	100,000-125,000	7-9	10am daily
Parapat (for Danau Toba)	180,000-280,000	18	1pm daily

🛏 Sleeping

⭐ Rimba Ecolodge
BUNGALOW **$$**

(☑0821 7082 6361; www.rimba-ecoproject.com; r incl meals with shared/private bathroom from 200,000/300,000Rp; 🛜) 🐾 Rimba Ecolodge is an intimate French-Indonesian-run place reachable by boat. Monkeys (both silvered leaf and red leaf species) come to explore the beach where the breeze-cooled bungalows are situated and there's a timeless, tranquil air to the place. The pricier rooms (350,000Rp) have hot water, while wi-fi is an additional 10,000Rp per day.

The food served here features plenty of fresh fish and seafood, and there's a social vibe with communal dinners, cold beer and *arak* cocktails. Other perks include use of a traditional canoe, good snorkelling, beach volleyball, jungle trekking, plenty of hammocks and a waterfront treehouse for sunset views.

Staff work closely with local fishing communities in coral reef and wildlife rehabilitation; some proceeds go to their NGO fund.

Keep an eye out for Bilbo, the resident owl, who comes and goes. It costs about 400,000Rp to get here by boat, or 200,000Rp from Sungai Pinang village.

Ricky's Beach House
GUESTHOUSE **$$**

(☑0813 6381 1786; www.authenticsumatra.com/rickys-beach-house; Sungai Pinang; r incl meals per person 300,000-400,000Rp; ❄🛜) Ricky's Beach House is the kind of place where backpackers extend their stay indefinitely. And why would you want to leave the Rasta-coloured beach house, the little beach bungalows or the hammock-hung bar where someone is always ready to break out the guitar and the bongos? Call ahead for transport.

Great snorkelling, beach volleyball, surf lessons and village tours will keep you busy. The food is tasty and there's cold beer. The website has good info on the area, as well as details on getting here by public transport; otherwise expect to pay 350,000Rp for a taxi-boat trip out from Padang.

Cubadak Paradiso Village
RESORT **$$$**

(☑0812 663 7609, 0812 660 3766; www.cubadak -paradisovillage.com; Pulau Cubadak; r incl full board US$120-190, minimum 2 nights) Cubadak Paradiso Village is found on tranquil Pulau Cubadak, where 12 bungalows perch above the teal waters. You can snorkel off your front porch or go diving or canoeing. Pick-up from Padang and boat transport are included.

ℹ Getting There & Away

To reach Pantai Bungus from Padang, take a blue *angkot* labelled 'Kabung Bungus' (15,000Rp, one hour), or a Go-Jek (p515; 30,000Rp), Grab (p515; 80,000Rp) or regular taxi (120,000Rp). There's no public transport to Sungai Pinang; it's an hour's drive along a very rough road from Bungus, so arrange transport from Padang.

While previously you had to take a boat to reach the guesthouses, a new road means that many can, for the most part, be accessed by car and a shorter boat ride, keeping costs down.

Mentawai Islands

While surfers have long flocked to the Mentawai Islands for its legendary waves, it's a destination that will also have a far-flung appeal to independent travellers, in particular for those wanting to meet the island's tattooed hunter-gatherer tribes. The islands' pristine beaches are also magnificent and as idyllic as any you'll find anywhere in Sumatra.

Though only 150km from the mainland, the Mentawai Islands and its people were kept isolated until the 19th century by strong winds, unpredictable currents and razor-sharp reefs. It's thought that the archipelago separated from Sumatra some 500,000 years ago, resulting in unique flora and fauna that sees Mentawai ranked alongside Madagascar in terms of endemic primate population. Of particular interest is *siamang kerdil*, a rare species of black-and-yellow monkey, named *simpai Mentawai* by the locals.

Orientation

The largest of the Mentawai Islands, Siberut, is home to the majority of the Mentawai population and is the most studied and protected island in the archipelago. About 60% of Siberut is still covered with tropical rainforest, which shelters a rich biological community that has earned it a designation as a Unesco biosphere reserve. The western half of the island is protected as the Siberut National Park.

Pulau Sipora is home to Tua Pejat, the seat of regional government and a surfer drop-off point. With only 10% of the original rainforest remaining, it's also the most developed of the Mentawai Islands.

Further south are the Pulau Pagai islands – Utara (North) and Selatan (South) – which rarely see independent travellers.

Mentawai Islands

| 0 | 20 km |
| 0 | 10 miles |

Kagologo
Sawunduken
Muara Sigep
Sikabaluan
Seripuguna

Siberut National Park

Boats to Padang

Muara Simatalu
Saoppu
Sagaragara
Muara Saibi

Pulau Siberut

Interisland Ferry

Sabagalet

Rokdok

Selat Mentawai

Muara Siberut
Katorai
Boats to Padang
Sikirorau

Pulau Masalot

Pulau Masokut

Pulau Mainuk

Selat Bungalaut

Pulau Karangmajat

Pulau Awera

Pulau Simakakang

Siberimanua
Tua Pejat
Boats to Padang
Sigoisooinan

Maileppet
Sioban

Pulau Sipora

Boats to Padang

Beriolou

Pulau Siduamata

Katiet

Selat Sipura

Pasar Puat

Pulau Silabusabeu

Pulau Pagai Utara

Boats to Padang

Taikaguru
Sikakap

Simakalo

Pulau Pagai Selatan

Bubuget

Pulau Taitaitanopo

INDIAN OCEAN

Pulau Sanding

Activities

Hiking

The river scene from the film *Apocalypse Now* might flash into your mind as you head upstream in a longboat and watch the people and villages growing wilder by the minute. Soon you're out of the canoe and following a wild-eyed *sikerei* (shaman) covered in tattoos and a loincloth through the mud for the next few hours, passing waterfalls, balancing on slippery tree branches and swimming across rivers until you reach his humble abode on poles in the middle of nowhere.

There's been fervent discussion about the authenticity of these trips, and what actually constitutes a traditional lifestyle. There is scope for both off-the-beaten-track adventure, where you turn up in remote villages and witness Mentawai life as it really is, and more organised ventures where villagers get paid by your guide to dress up in traditional gear, show you how to fish and hunt and engage you in their daily activities.

Mainland tour agencies tend to offer multiday treks, ranging from six to 10 days, but it's entirely possible to find your own guide, do an independent trip and decide for yourself how long you wish to go for. That said, longer hikes allow you to penetrate deeper into the island and stay in more remote villages, whereas if you opt for just a couple of nights with the Mentawai people, you're more likely to end up in a village not far removed from Muara Siberut where the villagers expect to be paid to have their photos taken.

Many hotels and guesthouses in and around Padang can offer treks or recommend guides. Blogs, forums and other travellers can be invaluable sources of info as well. If you have plenty of time, you can just turn up in the Mentawais and ask around at the jetty cafes in Maileppet and Muara Siberut, though a good, recommended guide that you make advance arrangements with can be invaluable. Prices are around 3,500,000Rp for three days/two nights, which include local transport, food, accommodation, a guide and permits, but excludes the ferry from Padang. When talking to a prospective guide, clarify exactly what is and isn't included, and try to get a detailed breakdown of prices (guide fee per day, food, accommodation and boat), bearing in mind that accommodation prices will be the least of your expenses.

Mentawai Ecotourism is a popular operator, while guides can also be arranged at the guesthouses in Padang.

★**Mentawai Ecotourism** TREKKING
(☎ 0823 8573 0254; www.mentawaiecotourism.com; per person 2/3/4/6 nights 3,390,000/3,785,500/4,237,500/5,085,000Rp) 🏄 Set up to empower local Mentawai people and foster responsible tourism, this tour operator runs treks into the jungle to visit local tribes. Based in Siberut, guides can take you on trips lasting anywhere from two to six nights, and these include a number of boat rides, jungle trekking and staying overnight with indigenous communities.

Its pricing system is broken down on the website so you know where your money is going.

Optional add-on activities can include anything from getting inked with a traditional Mentawai tattoo to ceremonial dance performances, hunting and fishing, and making loincloths.

Prices are all inclusive, but you'll need to get yourself to Siberut from Padang; the more people on the trip, the less the cost. You'll be given a rubbish bag at the start to clear out all waste you take in.

The company is affiliated with the Suku Mentawai Cultural & Environmental Education Program (www.sukumentawai.org), an Australian NGO that assists Mentawai villages; 10% of trekking fees go here. It was set up by filmmaker Rob Henry, who spent eight years living with indigenous communities and produced the documentary *As Worlds Divide* (2017), which focuses on the issues these communities face today.

Surfing

The Mentawai Islands have consistent surf year-round at dozens of legendary breaks. Mentawai waves are not for beginners; most breaks are reef breaks, some of them very shallow. The season peaks between April and October, with off-season waves kinder on intermediate surfers. Choose between staying at land-based losmen, surf camps

HIKING ESSENTIALS

➡ Dress for mud wrestling. Most of your gear will get trashed, so leave behind your finest garments and bear in mind you may need to swim across the odd river.

➡ Double-bag everything in plastic bags (or carry your gear in a dry bag) and keep one set of clothes dry for the evenings.

➡ Don't walk in flip-flops (thongs) – step into deep bog and you'll never see them again. Trainers or trekking boots are a must. Keep flip-flops handy for downtime in the villages.

➡ Travel light. Large packs are a hindrance and anything tied to the outside is a goner.

➡ Prepare for poor water sanitation. The local rivers serve all purposes, so water purification (tablets or Steripen) is recommended, as is a water pump to filter out impurities. Alternatively, you can carry your weight in bottled water.

➡ Take precautions against chloroquine-resistant malaria, which still exists on Siberut, though SurfAid (www.surfaidinternational.org) has been actively working to limit its spread. DDT-strength insect repellent is advisable, as are mosquito nets if you're travelling independently (tour agencies tend to provide them).

➡ Don't expect electricity in the evenings. A torch is your best friend, especially when it comes to negotiating your way to the local privy at night.

➡ Prepare for rain. May is generally the driest month, while October and November are the wettest – but it can rain at any time. The easiest thing is to just accept that you're going to get wet.

➡ Don't go to the toilet in the river. Instead use the forest; dig and fill a hole, and dispose of toilet paper by burning it.

➡ Buy essential supplies in Padang, where there is greater choice (and cheaper prices) than in Siberut.

➡ Buy items for bartering and as gifts. If heading to remote communities, remember that everything tends to be shared, so bring plenty of food. While tobacco is popular, a more positive contribution can be practical items such as machete blades, chisels, scissors, sewing kits and beads for jewellery. Buying a pig (around 500,000Rp) for dinner will also get you in the good books. All can be arranged for purchase in Muara Siberut.

ⓘ SURF TAX

In 2016 the Mentawai government introduced a 'retribution' tax on visiting surfers, with the proceeds to be directed to local communities. Surfers now pay 1,000,000Rp for up to 15 days, or 100,000Rp per day for short stays. Most surf-tour companies can arrange payment, otherwise you'll have to pay on arrival. Note that payment is in rupiah only.

and resorts, or liveaboard boat charters, which head further afield.

With patience, attitude and a handful of contacts it's possible to put together your own independent surfing safari for a fraction of the cost of a package tour. Budget accommodation is on the increase throughout the Mentawais and chartering a longboat is relatively easy.

The most consistent cluster of waves is in the **Playground** area, but things can get rather crowded during peak season. The most unpeopled waves are off the practically uninhabited **Pulau Pagai Selatan**; due to their remoteness, they're the domain of charter-boat surfers.

Check some of the more popular surfing blogs, such as GlobalSurfers (www.global surfers.com) and WannaSurf (www.wanna surf.com) for the latest intel.

🛌 Sleeping

Most visitors to the Mentawais arrive on prebooked packages that cover accommodation, meals and boat transfers. However, if you're prepared to chance your luck in finding a boat ride, most lodges will accept walk-in guests

There's a plethora of surf resorts in the Playground and Tua Pejat areas, a couple in Katiet and Pulau Pagai Utara and Pulau Pagai Selatan. Niang Niang Island has the best choice for budget travellers.

There are a couple of basic hotels in both Muara Siberut and Tua Pejat if you get stuck waiting for a ferry.

Trekking guides will organise family homestays for around 100,000Rp per night.

🛌 Playground

Ebay Surfcamp
LODGE $
(Mentawai Ebay Playground Surfcamp; ☑ 0821 704 8373; www.mentawaiebayplaygroundsurf.camp;

Pulau Masokut; per person incl meals 300,000Rp) Probably the best of the Mentawai budget options is this relaxed guesthouse on a grassy property 50m from an idyllic beach that's perfect for swimming. Rooms are bare bones, and share bathrooms. Staff are friendly, the food is excellent, the beer is cold and the coconuts are free. The manager Emmanuel speaks good English, but isn't always around.

Beng Bengs Surf Camp
LODGE $$$
(☑ 0812 8811 0432; www.bengbengssurfcamp mentawai.com; Pulau Masokut; per person incl meals & transport US$120; ❇ 🛜) Run by Italian surfer Massimo, this popular surf camp has a dream location overlooking a white sandy beach and surf breaks. Rooms are a mix of shared spaces and a double, and are set inside a traditional Mentawai house with contemporary hot-water bathrooms, vibrant Euro decor and beanbags. Its beach bar is the place to be along this stretch of Nyang Nyang.

Staff are friendly and knowledgable about surf spots, and there's homemade pasta and pizza available.

★ Mentawai Surf Retreat
SURF CAMP $$$
(☑ 0812 6157 0187, 0751-36345; www.mentawaisurf ingretreat.com; Pulau Masokut; per person incl food per night US$200, minimum 7 nights; ☉ Feb-Nov; 🛜) With Pitstops breaking right in front of its three breezy Mentawai-style cottages, this intimate surf retreat has an enviable location on Pulau Masokut. It's popular for its comforts (king-sized beds, large open bathrooms), immediate proximity to several good waves, delicious food and fully stocked bar overlooking the surf (you can BYO also). It's professionally run and a good source of local info.

★ Botik Resort
RESORT $$$
(☑ 0812 8824 6151; www.botikresort.com; Pulau Bocek; per person incl meals & boat trips US$210; ❇🛜) Boasting one of Mentawai's most stunning white sandy beaches, crystal-clear waters and coconut trees, this Spanish-owned resort truly is your clichéd version of paradise. It's well located near a heap of surf breaks, while its beach, snorkelling and yoga space make it a good choice for non-surfers too. The three huge, air-conditioned bungalows are atmospheric and comfortable, and the food is excellent.

Kandui Villas
RESORT $$$
(☑ 0812 6636 841, 0812 6621 077; www.kandui villas.com; Pulau Karangmajat; 7 nights for surfers/non-surfers US$1855/1225; ❇🛜❄) Located on

Pulau Karangmajat, American-owned Kandui Villas is a short paddle from Kandui Left, not far from the legendary Rifles. It offers unlimited speedboat transfers to the waves, making this the pro-surfer digs of choice. Guests are lodged in 12 luxurious, breezy *umas* (Mentawai-style cottages) with king-sized beds. For non-surfers there's an infinity pool, stand-up paddleboarding, kayaking and yoga.

Wavepark Resort RESORT **$$$**
(☏ 0812 663 5551; www.wavepark.com; Pulau Siaimu; 10-night package incl meals & transfers US$2950; ❄️ @ 🛜) Located on a private island,

THE MENTAWAIANS

The untouched, the unbaptised and the unphotographed have long drawn Westerners to distant corners of the globe. And the Mentawaians have seen every sort of self-anointed discoverer: the colonial entrepreneurs hoping to harness the land for profit, missionaries trading medicine for souls and modern-day tourists eager to experience life before the machine.

Very little is known about the origins of the Mentawaians, but it is assumed that they emigrated from Sumatra to Nias and made their way to Siberut from there.

At the time of contact with missionaries, the Mentawaians had their own language, *adat* (traditional laws and regulations) and religion, and were skilled boatbuilders. They lived a hunter-gatherer existence.

Traditional clothing was a loincloth made from the bark of the breadfruit tree for men and a bark skirt for women. Mentawaians wore bands of red-coloured rattan, beads and imported brass rings. They filed their teeth into points and decorated their bodies with tattoos.

After independence, the Indonesian government banned many of the Mentawaians' customs, such as tattoos, sharpened teeth and long hair. Although the ban has not been enforced, many villagers have adopted modern fashions.

Traditional villages are built along riverbanks and consist of one or more *uma* (communal houses) surrounded by *lalep* (single-storey family houses). Several families live in the same building. Bachelors and widows have their own quarters, known as *rusuk*, identical to the family longhouse except they have no altar.

Although essentially patriarchal, society is organised on egalitarian principles. There are no inherited titles or positions and no subordinate roles. It is the *uma*, not the village itself, which is pivotal to society. It is here that discussions affecting the community take place.

The native Sibulungan religion is a form of animism, involving the worship of nature spirits and a belief in the existence of ghosts, as well as the soul. The chief nature spirits are those of the sky, the sea, the jungle and the earth. The sky spirits are considered the most influential. There are also two river spirits: Ina Oinan (Mother of Rivers) is beneficent, while Kameinan (Father's Sister) is regarded as evil.

German missionary August Lett was the first to attempt to convert the local people, but he was not entirely successful: eight years after his arrival Lett was murdered by the locals. Somehow the mission managed to survive, however, and 11 baptisms had been recorded by 1916. There are now more than 80 Protestant churches throughout the islands.

More than 50 years after the Protestants, Catholic missionaries moved in to vie for converts. They opened a mission – a combined church, school and clinic – and free medicines and clothes were given to any islander who converted.

Islam was introduced when government officials were appointed from Padang during the Dutch era. Today more than half the population claims to be Protestant, 16% Catholic and 13% Muslim, though the number of Muslims is growing due to government efforts at Islamisation.

Change continues to come quickly here. Tourism, logging, *transmigrasi* (a government-sponsored scheme enabling settlers to move from overcrowded regions to sparsely populated ones) and other government-backed attempts to mainstream the culture have separated the people from the jungle. And if the rumoured development of the Mentawai Bay Project – a theme-park resort with direct flights from Singapore – ever gets off the ground, then things could change even faster.

An interesting documentary that explores the issues facing the Mentawaians today is *As Worlds Divide* (2017), made by Australian filmmaker Rob Henry, who spent eight years living among the islands' indigenous communities.

Wavepark has a front-row view of Hideaways from its lookout tower, and large, comfortable, breezy bungalows (with the best bathrooms in the Mentawais). Non-surfing activities (sea kayaking, snorkelling) make it a favourite with surfing or non-surfing returning couples, and the excellent bar-restaurant screens surfing photos of the day.

Surfers can also get a drone sent up to take footage of their sessions.

Shadow Mentawai Surf Camp SURF CAMP **$$$**
(☑ 0812 7788 6064; www.theshadowmentawai.com; Pulau Buasak; surfers/non-surfers per day incl meals & boat trips from US$120/75; 🛜) On tiny, lush Pulau Buasak on the outskirts of Playground, Shadow is run by friendly local surfer brothers Ade (along with his Spanish wife) and Dodi and their crew. Solo surfers lodge in cosy two-person bunk rooms with air-con, while couples are more likely to end up in the thatched cottage with a simple outdoor Indonesian bathroom.

It has an appealing traveller vibe not found at Mentawai's other surf resorts. For non-surfers there are stand-up paddleboards (SUPs), traditional canoes and snorkelling.

🛏 Pulau Sipora/Tua Pejat

Oinan Surf Lodge GUESTHOUSE **$$**
(☑ 0821 7086 6999, 0821 7433 8168; www.oinanlodge.com; Jl Mappadejat, Km4, Pulau Sipora; s incl breakfast with shared/private bathroom 350,000/400,000Rp; d 450,000-600,000Rp; 🌬🛜) Not actually by the sea, the hilly Oinan Surf Lodge, around 4km from Tua Pejat (*ojek*/taxi ride 20,000/100,000Rp), has amazing terrace views of the iconic Telescopes wave. Rooms are stylish and chic (one with shared bathroom), and the lodge has its own boat (around 500,000Rp for five people) for easy transport to other good breaks.

★ Aloita Resort & Spa RESORT **$$$**
(☑ 0813 2097 1810; www.aloitaresort.com; Pulau Silabok; s/d/tr incl meals US$200/300/420; 🌬🛜) 🍃 Ten bungalows in a garden setting occupy a private beach here within easy reach of the breaks Telescopes and Iceland, and there's a beginner's surf break a short walk away. Italian-run Aloita offers diving and paddleboarding, and its spa and yoga terrace make it a good option for surfers planning on bringing partners or family.

Aloita contributes to the local community by employing local staff and funding a school.

★ Togat Nusa RESORT **$$$**
(☑ 0812 6728 7537; www.togatnusaretreat.com; Pulau Pitojat; 9 nights incl meals US$2600; 🌬🛜) On the private 12-hectare island of Pitojat, Togat Nusa has four bungalows catering to only eight guests at a time. The funky and stylish accommodation is crafted using recycled driftwood and stained glass, and snorkelling and romantic beach dinners make it a good option for surfing or non-surfing couples. The excellent bar is haunted by a guest-loving langur.

🛏 Katiet

Hollow Tree's Surf Resort SURF RESORT **$$$**
(☑ 0812 4636 2664; www.htsresort.com; Katiet, South Sipora; per person incl meals & boat trips US$200; 🌬🛜🏊) With an enviable location in front of the legendary HT's right-hander and just a short hop from Lance's Left, Bintangs, Cobra's and even a couple of beach breaks, Hollow Tree's is all about the creature comforts (hot showers, air-con), combined with killer views. Downtime fun includes paddleboarding, snorkelling, fishing and snoozing under palm trees.

ⓘ Information

There's an ATM in Tua Pejat, but don't rely on it.

ⓘ Getting There & Away

AIR

There are no scheduled flights to Rokot Airport on Pulau Sipora. It could be worth checking if Susi Air (www.susiair.com) has resumed flights from Padang; however, in the past flights were unreliable, with weather delays and last-minute cancellations.

BOAT

The Mentawai Islands have become considerably easier to reach with the introduction of **Mentawai Fast** (☑ 0751-893489; www.mentawaifast.com; one way from 295,000Rp, plus surfboard 230,000-690,000Rp), a 200-seat speedboat. There are also three ferries that make the overnight journey from the Sumatran mainland to the islands. The trip on the ferries takes around 10 to 12 hours, depending on sea conditions. In Padang, ferries can be booked through most surfer-friendly homestays, as well as tour agencies.

ⓘ Getting Around

If you're travelling independently, transport between the Mentawai Islands or surfing spots is an easy way to drift into insolvency. You have three options: charter a speedboat, catch one of the three inter-island ferries, whose schedules are prone to delays and changes, or ask around to see if you can share a boat with another group.

Single-engine longboats can be hired from the main villages; if you want to hire a more comfortable two-engine speedboat with a roof, expect to pay considerably more. Sample charter routes (for up to five passengers) include Muara Siberut to Ebay (1,500,000Rp, 1½ hours), Ebay to Playgrounds (1,000,000Rp, 30 minutes),

Playgrounds to Tua Pejat (3,500,000Rp, 2½ hours), and Sioban to Katiet (1,500,000Rp, two hours). As petrol prices keep increasing, expect the charter prices to rise.

If you have more time than money, you can island-hop all the way from Siberut to Sao (near Katiet) using the three inter-island ferries, *KM Beriloga*, *KM Simasini* and *KM Simatalu*; ticket prices start from 25,000Rp. That's right: a tiny fraction of speedboat costs, thanks to

FERRIES FROM THE MENTAWAI ISLANDS

Mentawai Fast conveniently runs from the dock in central Padang; note that when it stops at Sikabaluan en route to Siberut from Padang, the total journey time to Siberut is six hours. Get to the dock at least 30 minutes before departure. Pre-booking is a good idea during peak season.

DAY	ROUTE	DEPARTURE TIME
Monday	Padang–Tua Pejat	6am
Monday	Tua Pejat–Padang	3pm
Tuesday	Padang–Sikabaluan–Siberut	7am
Tuesday	Siberut–Padang	3pm
Wednesday	Padang–Tua Pejat	7am
Wednesday	Tua Pejat–Padang	3pm
Thursday	Padang–Siberut	7am
Thursday	Siberut–Padang	3pm
Friday	Padang–Tua Pejat	7am
Friday	Tua Pejat–Padang	3pm
Saturday	Padang–Sikabaluan-Siberut	7am
Saturday	Siberut–Padang	3pm
Sunday	Padang–Tua Pejat	7am
Sunday	Tua Pejat–Padang	3pm

Ambu Ambu & Gambolo (☏ 0751-27153) are the biggest ferries connecting Padang and the Mentawai Islands. Options include air-conditioned VIP seats (123,000Rp), more basic economy seats (92,000Rp) and wooden berths you can lie down on (50,000Rp). Of the two, the *Gambolo* is more comfortable, though both tend to be very crowded. Both ferries leave from the Teluk Kabung port at Bungus, around 20km south of Padang; which is something for budget travellers to keep in mind given it's about 75,000Rp with Grab taxi (p515; 100,000Rp by normal taxi) to get there.

DAY	ROUTE	DEPARTURE TIME	VESSEL NAME
Monday	Tua Pejat–Padang	8pm	*Gambolo*
Tuesday	Bungus–Sikakap	5pm	*Ambu Ambu*
Wednesday	Bungus–Siberut	7pm	*Gambolo*
Wednesday	Sikakap–Padang	5pm	*Ambu Ambu*
Thursday	Bungus–Tua Pejat	8pm	*Ambu Ambu*
Thursday	Siberut–Padang	8pm	*Gambolo*
Friday	Bungus–Siberut	7pm	*Gambolo*
Friday	Tua Pejat–Padang	8pm	*Ambu Ambu*
Saturday	Bungus–Sikakap	5pm	*Ambu Ambu*
Saturday	Siberut–Padang	8pm	*Gambolo*
Sunday	Bungus–Tua Pejat	8pm	*Gambolo*
Sunday	Sikakap–Padang	5pm	*Ambu Ambu*

INTERISLAND FERRY CONNECTIONS

DEPARTURE	DESTINATION	VESSEL NAME	FREQUENCY
Maileppet	Tua Pejat	KM Beriloga, KM Simatalu	Monday, Thursday, Friday, Sunday
Sao (Katiet)	Sioban, Tua Pejat	KM Simatalu	Tuesday
Sikakap	Tua Pejat	KM Simasini	Wednesday, Sunday
Tua Pejat	Maileppet	KM Beriloga, KM Simasini	Tuesday, Wednesday, Thursday, Sunday
Tua Pejat	Sikakap	KM Simasini	Monday, Saturday

government subsidies. Check the latest timings with your fixer or your surf camp.

Bukittinggi

📞 0752 / POP 117,000

The market town of Bukittinggi sits high above the valley mists as three sentinels – fire-breathing Merapi, benign Singgalang and distant Sago – all look on impassively. As well as being a handy base to explore Danau Maninjau and the surrounding countryside, the town itself is an interesting spot for a night or two. There are some worthwhile historical sights, including a Dutch fort and Japanese WWII tunnels, as well as attractive local landmarks. At an elevation of 930m it has a refreshingly temperate climate all year round.

It's a popular stopover for those heading between Padang and Danau Toba.

◉ Sights

Gua Jepang CAVE

(Japanese Caves; 20,000Rp; ⏰ 6.30am-7pm) This extensive network of underground WWII Japanese bunkers built into a cliff face stretches for nearly 1.5km. It was built by local forced labour in 1942, and exploring its tunnels (used as living quarters, prison and torture area, and for storing ammunition and launching offensives) can be a rather spooky experience. English-speaking guides (30,000Rp) are available at the entrance across from Taman Panorama, about 1km from the centre of Bukittinggi.

Benteng de Kock VIEWPOINT

(Benteng Fort; Jl Benteng; 20,000Rp; ⏰ 8am-6pm) Benteng de Kock was built by the Dutch during the Padri Wars. Other than a few cannons and ramparts, there's not much to it now apart from the nice gardens and fine views over town. The entrance is down a fairly discreet side street running off Jl Teuku Umar. Connecting it with a depressing zoo

(we don't recommend visiting it) is the attractive Minangkabau-style Limpapeh bridge, stretching 90m above the road. This prominent city landmark was erected in 1992.

Jam Gadang LANDMARK

(Big Clock Tower; btwn Jl Istana & Jl Sudirman) Built in the 1920s to house a clock that was a gift from the Dutch queen, Jam Gadang is Bukittinggi's town emblem and focal point. Independence in 1945 saw the unique retrofit of a Minangkabau roof. In the evenings it's illuminated with neon lights and makes for an atmospheric place to stroll among local families.

◉ Around Bukittinggi

Gunung Merapi VOLCANO

(20,000Rp) The smouldering summit of Gunung Merapi (2891m), one of Sumatra's most active volcanoes, looms large over Bukittinggi around 16km to the east. If Merapi is benign, then visitors typically hike overnight to view sunrise from the summit from the village of Koto Baru; it's a 12-hour round trip. You'll need good walking boots, warm clothing, a torch, food and drink and a guide. Travel agencies in Bukittinggi do guided trips to Merapi for around 400,000Rp per person (minimum two people).

Batang Palupuh Nature Reserve NATURE RESERVE

This reserve, 16km north of Bukittinggi, is home to many orchid species, as well as the massive *Rafflesia arnoldii* and *Amorphophallus titanum*, the largest flowers on the planet – the latter endemic to Sumatra. The rafflesia blooms throughout the year, if briefly, whereas you have to be incredibly lucky to catch the *Amorphophallus titanum* in bloom at all. Both flowers reek like roadkill. Local buses to Palupuh cost 10,000Rp, a taxi is 10,000Rp and a Grab online taxi 40,000Rp.

The blossom of the parasitic rafflesia measures nearly a metre across and can

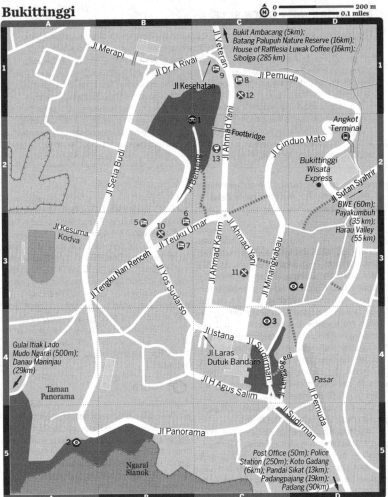

Bukittinggi

MINANGKABAU WOMEN RULE

Though Minangkabau society is Islamic, it's still matrilineal. According to Minangkabau *adat* (traditional laws and regulations), property and wealth are passed down through the female line. Every Minangkabau belongs to his or her mother's clan. At the basic level of the clan is the *sapariouk*, those matri-related kin, who eat together. These include the mother, the grandchildren and the son-in-law. The name comes from the word *periouk* (rice pot). The eldest living female is the matriarch. The most important male member of the household is the mother's eldest brother, who replaces the father in being responsible for the children's education, upbringing and marriage prospects. But consensus is at the core of the Minangkabau ruling philosophy and the division of power between the sexes is regarded as complementary – like the skin and the nail act together to form the fingertip, according to a local expression.

weigh up to 11kg, while the inflorescence of *Amorphophallus titanum* can extend to over 3m in circumference.

House of Rafflesia Luwak Coffee
PLANTATION

(☑ 0819 3353 8136, 0813 7417 8971; www.rafflesia luwakcoffee.org; Desa Batang Palupuh) At this plantation in Batang Palupuh, friendly owner Umul Khairi is happy to explain the process of harvesting, drying and roasting *kopi luwak* – a smooth, earthy brew produced from coffee beans ingested and excreted by civets (cat-like mammals). While the *luwak* coffee industry has come under fire for 'farming' civets to meet demand for the brew, the House of Rafflesia still operates in the traditional way, collecting wild civet 'poo' off the jungle floor.

You can also taste (20,000Rp) and purchase (from 200,000Rp) the beans.

Minangkabau cooking classes (per person 350,000Rp) are also on offer. The multicourse menu includes beef *rendang* and chicken curry, and Umul will even run the course for solo travellers. Book via the website or phone to confirm at least one day before you visit.

Gunung Singgalang
VOLCANO

(10,000Rp) Climbing dormant Gunung Singgalang (2877m) is a more adventurous undertaking than Gunung Merapi. Highly recommended English-speaking guide Dedi (0813 7425 1312), based in Pandai Sikat – the best starting point for the climb – charges 350,000Rp, and the climb is an eight- to nine-hour roundtrip. Otherwise you can arrange trips through Hello Guesthouse for 400,000Rp (minimum two people) including guide, transport and food. There are campsites by the beautiful crater lake, Telago Dewi.

PT Studio Songket Palantaloom
ARTS CENTRE

(☑ 0823 8936 8875, 0752-783 4253; www.palan taloom.com; Jorong Panca, SMKN1, Batu Taba; ⊙ 8.30am-noon & 1-4pm Mon-Sat) Handicraft and textile fans should not miss this place near Simpang Bukit Batabuah, 7km southeast of Bukittinggi. Dedicated to revitalising the traditional Minangkabau art of weaving *songket* (silver- or gold-threaded cloth), the studio has trained young weavers (aged 18 to 28) in the art of producing Sumatra's finest. Phone ahead, and catch a yellow *opelet* from the Aur Kuning bus terminal to Batu Taba (4500Rp), getting off at the SMKN1 (high school).

Tours

Roni's Tours
ADVENTURE

(☑ 0812 675 0688; www.ronistours.com; Orchid Hotel, Jl Teuku Umar 11) Based at the Orchid Hotel, Roni's can arrange everything from local tours to Danau Maninjau and the Harau Valley, to trips to further-afield locations such as the Mentawai Islands and Kerinci Seblat National Park.

Armando
DRIVING

(☑ 0812 674 1852; arisna_sejati@yahoo.co.id; day tour from 300,000Rp) Armando is a helpful and knowledgable English-speaking guide who is happy to give you cultural tours of the Bukittinggi area on the back of his motorcycle. He also rents motorbikes (75,000Rp).

Festivals & Events

Oxen Racing
SPORTS

(50,000Rp; ⊙ noon-4pm Sat) Local farmer-jockeys race twin oxen through a muddy paddy field, balancing precariously on the wooden runners. This spectacle, which animal-welfare experts claim uses inhumane tactics to make the beasts run, takes place most Saturdays near Simasur market in Batu Sangkar, 41km southeast of Bukittinggi.

🛏 Sleeping

★ Hello Guesthouse
GUESTHOUSE $

(☑ 0752-21542; www.helloguesthouse.net; Jl Teuku Umar 6B; dm/s/d/f incl breakfast from 75,000/150 ,000/175,000/350,000Rp; ☎) This bright and modern guesthouse is run by thoughtful owner Ling, who understands the needs of budget travellers. She is happy to provide maps of town, has displays on town attractions, and has fitted the rooms with super-comfy mattresses and hot-water showers. There are also newly installed futuristic capsules, complete with flashing sci-fi gadgetry.

Earplugs (10,000Rp) are available to counter noise from the nearby mosque. It's often full so book ahead.

Orchid Hotel
HOTEL $

(☑ 0752-32634; roni_orchid@hotmail.com; Jl Teuku Umar 11; r incl breakfast 150,000-180,000Rp; ☎) This popular budget inn has a good travel desk, helpful staff and a sociable downstairs space. Rooms on three levels are pretty basic, but all have attached bath and the more expensive ones come with hot water. Wi-fi is in the lobby only.

Rajawali Homestay
HOMESTAY $

(☑ 0752-31095; ulrich.rudolph@web.de; Jl Ahmad Yani 152; r from 90,000Rp) The seven rooms at this friendly but very basic homestay come with Indonesian bathrooms and creaky beds. Owner Yanna is good for a chat.

Treeli Hotel
BOUTIQUE HOTEL $$

(☑ 0752-625350; treeliboutiquehotel@gmail. com; Jl Kesehatan 36A; r incl breakfast 475,000-790,000Rp; ❄☎) An excellent addition to Bukittinggi's rather tired midrange sleeping options, contemporary Treeli gets a lot of things right. Rooms are compact and quiet, with modern bathrooms and all sorts of mod cons. An excellent breakfast is served on the breezy roof terrace and the restaurant specialises in Chinese-style seafood dishes.

Grand Rocky Hotel
HOTEL $$$

(☑ 0752-627000; www.rockyhotelsgroup.com; Jl Yos Sudarso; r incl breakfast from 880,000Rp; ❄☎≈) Adding a touch of kitschy Vegas glamour to Bukittinggi's top-end range, the Grand Rocky stands sentinel above town, its lobby bustling with bow-tied staff. Rooms are spacious and modern, views stretch to the Sianok Canyon, and it's just a short downhill stroll to the brightish lights of central Bukittinggi. Check online for good discounts if you're keen for a mini splurge.

🍴 Eating & Drinking

RM Selamat
INDONESIAN $

(Jl Ahmad Yani; rendang 21,000Rp; ⏰ 6.30am-9.30pm) Padang food in West Sumatra rarely disappoints, and this cafeteria-style restaurant is famous for its authentic smoky beef *rendang*, among its assortment of delicious dishes to choose from.

De Kock Cafe
PUB FOOD $

(☑ 0821 7492 9888; Jl Teuku Umar 18; mains from 25,000Rp; ⏰ 7am-1am; ☎) De Kock (which translates to 'cannon', in case you're wondering) has a smoky salon atmosphere that's popular with both locals and tourists who come here for beers and a mixture of Western pub food (pizzas, steak sandwiches) and Indonesian dishes. It has surprisingly good breakfast options too. There's live music on Saturday.

Gulai Itiak Lado Mudo Ngarai
INDONESIAN $

(Jl Binuang 41; mains 30,000Rp; ⏰ 7am-4pm) This simple restaurant is a good place to sample delicious *itiak lado mudo* (duck in green chilli), a regional specialty. It's in a valley area near to the river a couple of kilometres west of Bukittinggi on the road to Danau Maninjau.

Turret Cafe
CAFE $

(Jl Ahmad Yani 140-142; mains 25,000-60,000Rp; ⏰ 11am-10pm; ☎) This old-school Bukittinggi traveller haunt offers a smattering of Western dishes with the odd inclusion of *mie goreng* (fried noodles), beef *rendang*, green curry, cold beer and the best guacamole in town.

Bedudal Cafe
BAR

(Jl Ahmad Yani 105; ⏰ 9am-midnight; ☎) Grab a beer (small/large 30,000/45,000Rp) and make yourself comfortable amid the wooden carvings and pop-culture posters and chat to the friendly youthful staff. There's a menu of Indonesian dishes (20,000Rp to 35,000Rp) along with bar snacks. Guitars are on hand for occasional jam sessions.

Taruko Caferesto
CAFE

(Jl Raya Lembah Maninjau; ⏰ 8am-6pm) Around 4km west of Bukittinggi is this tranquil cafe set in an attractive thatched building overlooking ridiculously picturesque countryside – complete with bubbling brook. It's a perfect spot to while away a few hours, or grab a coffee en route to Danau Maninjau. Indonesian dishes, pancakes and omelettes are on the menu, but it's more about the view than the food here.

🛍 Shopping

Jl Minangkabau is good for shopping for woven bags and batik shirts, while upper Jl Ahmad Yani has traditional crafts and antiques.

Beautiful red and gold Minangkabau embroidery can be found at **Pasar Atas** (Jl Minangkabau; ⊙8am-8pm) and around town.

ℹ Information

Banks and ATMs are scattered along Jl Ahmad Yani and Jl A Karim.

ℹ Getting There & Away

The chaos of the main bus terminal, Aur Kuning, 3km south of town, can be reached by *angkot* (3000Rp) or *ojek* (10,000Rp to 15,000Rp); ask for 'terminal'. Heading to central Bukittinggi on arrival ask for 'Kampung Cina'.

The main bus terminal is useful for some bus departures but not all. Minibuses to Sibolga (200,000Rp, 12 hours) depart from offices on Jl Veteran, as do minibuses to Parapat (350,000Rp, 18 hours); scheduled door-to-door transfers to Padang (50,000Rp, three hours) are more convenient than waiting for a bus at the terminal. Most lodgings can point you in the right direction and assist with booking passage.

For Harau Valley catch a minibus to Tanjung Pati from the Simpang Raya restaurant close to the terminal; from Tanjung Pati you'll then need to take a becak (20,000Rp).

The best way to get to Dumai – for ferries to Melaka and Kuala Lumpur in Malaysia – is with the travel agency **Bukittinggi Wisata Express** (BWE; ☎0752-625139, 0752-625140; Jl Pemuda 81). Minibuses leave Bukittinggi nightly at 8pm (120,000Rp, nine hours), to link with the ferry from Dumai to Batam (350,000Rp, 6am) and Melaka (335,000Rp, 9.30am). Prebooking is required. BWE can also book the ferry; you'll need to drop in the day before departure with your passport.

ℹ Getting Around

Angkot (Jl Pemuda) around town cost 3000Rp. *Bendi* rides are around 50,000Rp. An *ojek* from the bus terminal to the city centre costs 10,000Rp to 15,000Rp, while a taxi costs 50,000Rp but can take up to 30 minutes in heavy traffic.

Transfers to Padang's airport can be arranged from any travel agent for around 50,000Rp. A private taxi to the airport is 250,000Rp to 300,000Rp.

Some guesthouses rent out mopeds for 75,000Rp per day, or contact Roni's Tours (p574) at the Orchid Hotel.

South of Bukittinggi

The rich volcanic soil of the hilly countryside around Bukittinggi oozes fertility. Stop by the roadside and you can spot cinnamon, betel-nut, avocado, coffee, mango and papaya trees. Rice, tapioca and potatoes grow in terraces, while bamboo waterwheels feed irrigation ditches and drive wooden grinding mills. You may see a wedding parade. The bride and groom, dressed in full traditional regalia, are accompanied by musicians, family members and half the village. The Minangkabau tribal flags (red, black and yellow) typically mark the site of the festivities.

The sights in this area can be combined into a scenic day tour, either by renting a motorbike, taking a motorbike tour (300,000Rp) or hiring a car and driver (600,000Rp).

◉ Sights

Grand Palace of Pagaruyuang　　PALACE
(Istano Basa Pagaruyuang; Jl Sutan Alam Bagagarsyah, Silinduang Bulan; 25,000Rp; ⊙7am-7pm) In the village of Silinduang Bulan, 5km north of Batu Sangkar, the heartland of the red Tanah Datar clan of Minangkabau, is this epic palace, a replica of the former home of

BUSES FROM BUKITTINGGI

DESTINATION	FARE (RP)	DURATION (HR)	FREQUENCY
Bengkulu	180,000-230,000	18	2-3 daily
Danau Maninjau	20,000	1½	3 daily
Dumai	125,000-240,000	10	10am, 5pm, 7pm daily
Medan	180,000-290,000	20	several daily
Padang	20,000-30,000	3-4	frequent
Parapat (for Danau Toba)	185,000-205,000	16	several daily
Pekanbaru	80,000-120,000	7	6 daily
Sibolga (for Pulau Nias)	150,000-260,000	12	several daily

Around Bukittinggi

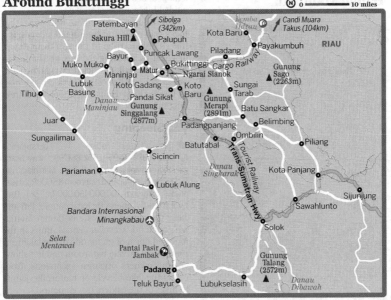

the rulers of the ancient Minangkabau kingdom of Payaruyung. It's equally impressive within, with soaring pillars and ceilings, and walls covered in brightly coloured ceremonial banners. There's a museum inside (no English captions), and three levels you can clamber up for views of the surrounding village and countryside.

A fire razed it to the ground in 2007, but it has been reconstructed. Batu Sangkar can be reached via public bus (22,000Rp, 1½ hours) from Bukittinggi, where you can continue by *ojek* (8000Rp) to Silinduang Bulan. Try to visit during the week, as weekends can get busy.

Istano Silinduang Bulan   PALACE
(Queen's Palace; Jl Sutan Alam Bagagarsyah, Silinduang Bulan; 5000Rp; ⊙9am-5.30pm) Near the Grand Palace in Silinduang Bulan is the much smaller and lower-key, but equally ornate, Istano Silinduang Bulan. It's still used for important clan meetings today. It was damaged by lightning in 2011, but has been rebuilt since.

Belimbing   VILLAGE
Belimbing, a village southeast of Batu Sangkar, is comprised of one of the largest surviving collections of traditional architecture in the highlands. Many of the homes are 300 years old and in various states of decay, including one that's set aside as a heritage site

(entry by donation). Most owners have built modern homes nearby and use the relics for ceremonial purposes.

Danau Maninjau

The first glimpse of this perfectly formed volcanic lake sucks your breath away as you lurch over the caldera lip and hurtle towards the first of the 44 (numbered) hairpin bends down to the lakeshore. Monkeys watch your progress from the crash barriers as the road takes you down from the lush rainforest of the highlands to the ever-expanding farms and paddies of the lowlands.

When the traveller tide receded from Bukittinggi, Danau Maninjau was left high and dry. The locals looked to more sustainable sources of income and aquaculture to fill the void. Fish farms now dot the lake foreshore, outnumbering tourists.

The lake is 460m above sea level and encircled by a 60km road. Most places of interest spread out north from Maninjau village to Bayur (3.5km away) and beyond. If coming by bus, tell the conductor where you're staying and you'll be dropped off at the right spot.

◉ Sights & Activities

Swimming and canoeing in the lake (warmed by subterranean springs) are the main

Danau Maninjau

Danau Maninjau

drawcards here, but there are plenty of other options.

If you're not up for hiking, it takes roughly three hours to circumnavigate the lake on a moped. Beach Guest House organises both guided hikes and motorbike tours.

The caldera, covered in rainforest that hides waterfalls and traditional villages, is a hiker's dream. Hike to the rim from Bayur, or cheat by catching the bus up the hill to Matur, then walking back down via the lookout at **Puncak Lawang**. Check out the map at Beach Guest House for more good trekking information.

🛏 Sleeping

⭐ Beach Guest House   GUESTHOUSE $
(📞0813 6379 7005, 0752-861799; www.beach guesthousemaninjau.com; Jl Raya Maninjau; dm 50,000Rp, d with shared bathroom 85,000Rp, d with private bathroom 100,000-150,000Rp; 🛜) Run by a friendly, energetic local couple, Fifi and Jack, this hostel and cafe is Danau Maninjau's bona fide traveller central. Bunk in the four-bed dorm or go for one of the lakefront rooms with private bathroom and hot shower. The owners organise excursions, from round-the-lake bicycle or motorbike jaunts to hikes of the caldera (seven hours).

Muaro Beach Bungalows   BUNGALOW $
(📞0813 3924 0042; neni967@yahoo.com; Jl Muaro Pisang 53, Maninjau; r 150,000-200,000Rp; 🛜) Down a maze of footpaths about 300m northwest of the main intersection, these beachfront bungalows are a good deal in central Maninjau. The small beach area is (almost) free of aquaculture, and there's a charming lakeside restaurant. They hire out stand-up paddleboards (SUPs; per hour 30,000Rp) and motorbikes (per day 80,000Rp), and have tours of the surrounding area (300,000Rp) and Harau Valley (500,00Rp).

House of Annisa   HISTORIC HOTEL $$
(📞0822 6891 2625; Jl H Udin Rahmani; r incl breakfast 400,000Rp) More like a museum than a guesthouse, this wonderful Dutch heritage villa has been lovingly restored by the great-grandchildren of the original owners. There are three romantic rooms, one with a brass four-poster bed festooned with mirrors; bathrooms are shared. Unique touches include elegant Arabic calligraphy carved into the outside walls and a gorgeous balcony with antique benches and chairs. Call in advance.

🍴 Eating

Bagoes Cafe   CAFE $
(Jl Raya Maninjau, Maninjau; mains 15,000-50,000Rp; ⊗8am-9pm; 🛜🅿) At the traveller

HARAU VALLEY

Heading east from Bukittinggi takes you through the tapioca-growing area of **Piladang**, famous for *keropok* (tapioca crackers), and the sprawling agricultural centre of **Paya-kumbuh**. Of Minangkabau's three clans, this is the territory of the 50 Kota (50 Villages) yellow branch. Rice paddies with wallowing buffalo flank the narrow road that leads to the tiny village of Harau, the volcanoes looming behind them. Venture another 3km and spectacular, vertical 100m cliffs, seemingly made of painted rock, rise up to enclose the claustrophobic Harau Valley, 15km northeast of Payakumbuh and 55km from Bukittinggi.

The most direct ways to reach Harau from Bukittinggi are by private car (250,000Rp), renting a motorbike (60,000Rp to 75,000Rp) or taking an *ojek* (200,000Rp, two hours). Alternatively, take a Po Sarah Group minibus from the bus terminal to Tanjung Pati (20,000Rp to 25,000Rp), and then a becak to Harau (20,000Rp).

Lemba Harau (5000Rp) Lemba Harau and other waterfalls in the Harau Valley attract day trippers from Bukittinggi, particularly during the rainy season; if the weather's been dry, the falls are reduced to mere trickles.

Ikbal (☑ 0852 6378 1842) An excellent local rock-climbing contact is Ikbal at the Abdi Homestay, who offers guided climbing excursions for 300,000Rp.

Abdi Homestay (☑ 0852 6378 1842; ikbalharau@yahoo.com; Kab 50 Kota; per person incl breakfast 150,000Rp) Run by young and energetic owners Ikbal and Noni, Abdi Homestay is the loveliest place to stay in the Harau Valley. Eight adorable thatched bungalows (with mosquito nets and bamboo showers) sit on the edge of verdant rice paddies and lotus ponds, with sheer cliffs forming a dramatic backrop. Ikbal leads day hikes (200,000Rp per person) to the top of the cliffs and surrounding countryside.

Meals include one of the best chicken *rendang* you'll ever have (though you'll need to pre-order). Cooking classes (150,000Rp) include a visit to the market.

Harau Resort (Lembah Echo; ☑ 0812 6619 1501, 0822 7271 7448; www.harau-resort.com; Tara-tang Lb Limpato; r incl breakfast from 400,000Rp) Sitting right under the cliffs in the narrow-est part of the Harau Valley is Harau Resort (aka Lembah Echo), with its beautiful grounds encroached on by a jungle full of monkeys. It has Minangkabau-style cottages and classy (if dark) rooms with hardwood furniture and hot showers. Little English is spoken.

favourite Beach Guest House in Maninjau village, Bagoes combines backpacker staples with local dishes such as vegetable gado gado, *mie goreng* and lake fish. The lakeside deck is a fine place for a large, ice-cold Bintang (40,000Rp), and movie nights are occasionally held.

★**Waterfront Zalino**   INDONESIAN **$$**
(☑ 0752-61740, 0815 3454 6280; mains 32,000-65,000Rp; ⊙8am-9pm; 🛜) This place with a great lakeside location showcases some local seafood specialties, such as *udang* (freshwater lake shrimp), freshwater lobster and grilled catfish. As well as cold beer it also serves a delicious soursop fruit wine (both non-alcoholic and alcoholic varietals). It's around 1km north of Maninjau's main intersection.

Zal – AKA 'Mr Porcupine' – can organise all manner of tours, including fishing and trekking.

ℹ Information

BRI Bank (Jl Maninjau) Has an ATM, but it only dispenses small amounts. Stock up on rupiah in Bukittinggi.

ℹ Getting There & Away

Your best bet to get here from Bukittinggi is by minivans (30,000Rp) that offer pick-up service; try **Koga Travel** (☑ 0823 8222 8699) or get in touch with the guesthouses to arrange these. Otherwise there are infrequent **buses** (Jl Maninjau) between Maninjau and Bukittinggi (20,000Rp, 1¾ hours, three daily).

ℹ Getting Around

Rent mountain bikes (per day 45,000Rp), motorcycles (per day from 80,000Rp) and canoes (per day 40,000Rp) from Beach Guest House, Muaro Beach Bungalows or Waterfront Zalino.

Minibuses (5000Rp) travel the lake road during daylight hours. An *ojek* from the intersection to Bayur will cost around 5000Rp.

Kerinci Valley

Kerinci is a stunning mountain valley tucked away high in the Bukit Barisan on Jambi's western border. Many of the cool, lush forests are protected as the Kerinci Seblat National Park, one of the last strongholds of the Sumatran tiger. The valley's many lakes and jungle-shrouded mountains and volcanoes make it a big draw for hikers in search of off-the-beaten-track adventure. To the south is picturesque Danau Kerinci and a patchwork of rich farmland. Tea and cinnamon account for much of the valley's wealth, with the former ringing the higher villages and the latter forming a buffer between the farmland and rainforest.

Minangkabau and native Kerincinese make up most of the population, with a sprinkling of Batak and Javanese who are drawn by the rich soil. Kerinci is in Jambi province but has a close geographic proximity to Padang.

❶ Getting There & Away

Kerinci has an airport 10km east of Sungai Penuh, which has a daily Wings Air flight to Jambi.

Getting here by bus or shared taxi is also possible, with services from Kerinci heading south to Bengkulu, eastwards to Jambi and north to Padang and Bukittinggi.

Sungai Penuh

📞 0748 / POP 96,000

Sungai Penuh ('Full River') is the regional administrative centre and transport hub for the valley. There is a lively market, and the town makes an excellent central base for venturing into the wilds of Kerinci Seblat National Park and the surrounding villages. All up it's a pleasant little town with friendly locals, excellent cafes, reliable internet and some spectacular viewpoints looking out to the valley.

◉ Sights

Bukit Khayangan   VIEWPOINT
For fantastic, sweeping panoramas of Kerinci Valley head up to this hilltop lookout, especially popular with locals for sunrise and sunset. To get here take the road that winds around the outskirts of town; by *ojek* expect to pay around 50,000Rp return, otherwise it's a three-hour walk up and down.

Mesjid Agung Pondok Tinggi   MOSQUE
(Jl Soekarno Hatta; entry by donation) Head west up Jl Sudirman (past the post office) and turn left, where you'll find this old wooden mosque with a pagoda-style roof. Built in 1874 without a single nail, the interior contains elaborately carved beams and old Dutch tiles. Ask the caretaker for permission to enter, and dress appropriately to visit.

☞ Tours

★ **Wild Sumatra Adventures**   CULTURAL
(📞 0812 6017 3651; www.wildsumatra.com/kerinci) Based in Sungai Penuh, enthusiastic expat Luke Mackin is a passionate and knowledgable source of information on the surrounding area, especially the Kerinci Seblat National Park. He has numerous alliances with local trekking guides and villages, and can organise guides and transport to various attractions. See the website for the many possibilities, from the popular Five Lakes hike to night safaris and multiday jungle treks.

🛏 Sleeping

Sungai Penuh's choice of budget accommodation is uninspiring, though there are some OK midrange options that are worth spending a bit extra for. If you're looking for greater cultural immersion, Wild Sumatra Adventures can help you organise homestays in villages surrounding Sungai Penuh. Expect to pay around 50,000Rp per night to stay with a local family.

Hotel Jaya Wisata   HOTEL $
(📞 0748-21221; www.hoteljayawisata.com; Jl Martadinata 7; r incl breakfast with fan/air-con from 160,000/400,000Rp; ❉ 🛜) Your options here range from rather depressing cold-water rooms downstairs that could seriously use a coat of paint, to more spacious and stylish rooms upstairs. The location is great – near the cheap eats of the night market. Otherwise there's also Jaya Wisata 2, a more relaxed option with a garden setting in Sungai Penuh's outlying surrounds.

Hotel Mahkota   HOTEL $
(📞 0821 8146 3344, 0748-21640; Jl Depati Parbo; r incl breakfast 150,000-365,000Rp; ❉ 🛜 ⌘) One of Sungai Penuh's better hotels, Mahkota is fronted by a rather grand reception building, and though rooms are fairly generic, they're comfortable enough and livened up with some flashy motifs. The highlight is its large swimming pool; however, beware it gets packed with local kids on weekends. It's located 2km from the city centre along the main road heading out of town.

✖ Eating & Drinking

★ Korintji Heritage
INDONESIAN $

(www.korintji.com; Jl Prof Dr Yakub Isman 1C; mains 15,000-65,000Rp; ⊗10am-11pm; 🖘) Set up as a social enterprise to empower locals, this fantastic new cafe in Sungai Penuh is set inside an atmospheric bamboo building overlooking the town and valley. As well as tasty Indonesian dishes, highlights include Danau Kerinci lobster (from 50,000Rp) and steaks (from 150,000Rp). It does excellent local, single-origin filter coffee, and has an on-site shop selling local delicacies.

Rumah Makan Dendeng Batokok
INDONESIAN $

(Jl Muradi; dishes 20,000Rp; ⊗8am-8pm) Carnivores shouldn't leave town without trying the regional specialty *dendeng batokok* (thinly sliced beef strips barbecued on charcoal), which is grilled street-side at this centrally located warung across from Hotel Yani.

Pasar Malam
MARKET $

(off Jl Muradi; meals from 20,000Rp; ⊗5-10pm) The centrally located *pasar malam* (night market) is a terrific place to try local specialties, such as *martabak* (sweet pancake filled with coconut or banana), *martabak mesir* (square pancake filled with meat and vegetables), *mie bakso* (noodle soup with meatballs), and *sate* with a red gravy rather than peanut sauce.

Wiyuka Coffee
COFFEE

(Jl Ahmad Yani; ⊗11am-10pm; 🖘) This excellent coffee shop gives Sungai Penuh a cool, urban touch. Here you can sample quality beans from all over Sumatra and beyond, and there's local dishes (mains from 16,000Rp) and free wi-fi.

🛍 Shopping

Avail
SPORTS & OUTDOORS

(Jl Muradi 7; ⊗8am-11pm) This outdoor adventure store is handy if you're climbing Gunung Kerinci or going on a multiday trek into the jungle. It has a good selection of camping goods, including waterproof gear, hiking boots and cooking equipment.

ℹ Information

Kantor Taman Nasional Kerinci Seblat
(Kerinci Seblat National Park Office; ☑0748-22250; Jl Basuki Rahmat 11; ⊗8am-4pm) This park headquarters sells permits; they never seem to answer the phone, so just turn up. If it's closed, you can get permits from Wild Sumatra Adventures or guesthouses in Lempur Tengah or Kersik Tua.

There are several ATMs in town. **BNI Bank** (Jl Ahmad Yani) is a centrally located option.

ℹ Getting There & Away

Safa Marwa (☑0852 6312 7199, 0748-22376; Jl Yos Sudarso 20) has minibuses between Sungai Penuh and destinations such as Padang, Bukittinggi, Bengkulu and Jambi.

Lempur Tengah

☑0748 / POP 4800

In the southern end of the Kerinci Valley, Lempur Tengah is a small, scrappy rural town, with its verdant, mountainous surrounds making it one of Kerinci's more relaxed and picturesque bases. It offers a handy launching point for walks to Danau Kaco, as well as for the Five Lakes trek, Renah Kemumu and Gunung Kunyit.

Cinnamon is one of its main industries, and you'll see stacks of it drying in many locals' front yards. Lempur is also known for its historic centuries-old wooden mosque featuring a pagoda-style roof and decorative wood carving.

Local tour operator **Explore Kerinci** (☑0813 6631 9255; www.explorekerinci.com) is based in town and covers all outdoor adventures.

🛏 Sleeping

Zacky's Homestay
GUESTHOUSE $

(☑0813 6631 9255; r with shared bathroom incl breakfast 150,000Rp; 🖘) This place is run by local guide Zacky, who set up Explore Kerinci. The rooms are upstairs in a sizeable house with a wraparound balcony to kick back and take things slow. Along with his other guesthouse (p582), this relaxed lodge is the best

---

BUSES FROM SUNGAI PENUH

DESTINATION	FARE (RP)	DURATION (HR)	FREQUENCY
Bengkulu	125,000	10	daily (9am)
Bukittinggi	120,000	10	daily (7.30pm)
Jambi	130,000-150,000	10	2 daily (10am, 7pm)
Padang	100,000-125,000	9	2 daily (9.15am, 7pm)

place to stay in town. Its Cinnamon Cafe restaurant does a good *ayam penyet* (flattened Javanese-style grilled chicken; 18,000Rp).

Cinnamon Guesthouse GUESTHOUSE $
(☑0813 6631 9255; dm/r 50,000/250,000Rp; 🛜) Zacky's other lodge is located 2km south of town and it looks to be the pick of places to stay around Lempur Tengah. Its setting is superb, looking out to idyllic countryside, and its choices of cheap dorms or en suite rooms will keep folks happy.

ℹ️ Information

There's a BRI Bank ATM to the north of town.

ℹ️ Getting There & Away

Three buses to Sungai Penuh (20,000Rp, 1½ hours) leave in the morning at 7am, 7.30am and 8am. Coming from Sungai Penuh they depart in the afternoon at noon, 1pm and 2pm. Otherwise an *ojek* will cost around 70,000Rp.

Kersik Tua

At 1500m, surrounded by tea plantations and dominated by the massive cone of Gunung Kerinci (3805m), Kersik Tua makes a pleasant base for scaling the imposing volcano.

The town sprawls along one side of the main road, with tea plantations and the mountain on the other. The Kerinci Seblat National Park turn-off is indicated by a *harimau* (Sumatran tiger) statue.

Trekking gear, supplies, guides and transport can all be arranged here. The town has a market on Saturday and a couple of ATMs.

🛏️ Sleeping & Eating

There are several basic homestays spread out along the main road, most of which look out to Gunung Kerinci.

While none of the restaurants here sell beer, one of the grocery stores has a stash of ice-cold beer for takeaway. **Shelter Coffee** (Jl Muara Labuh-Sungai Penuh; ⊙10am-10pm) is a cool little coffee shop if you're in need of caffeine.

Subandi Homestay HOMESTAY $
(☑0812 7411 4273; subandi.homestay@gmail.com; Jl Muara Labuh-Sungai Penuh; r with shared/private bathroom from 150,000/200,000Rp) Just south of the statue on the main road is the best base camp in Kersik Tua. Subandi is the only English-speaking homestay; owner Pak is a fount of local knowledge and can organise mountain, jungle and wildlife treks of vary-

ing difficulty and duration. Subandi was undergoing renovations at the time of research to add rooms, some with private bathrooms.

ℹ️ Getting There & Away

The village is 52km north of Sungai Penuh on the road to Padang and can be reached by any Padang–Kerinci bus. Minibuses (15,000Rp, 1½ hours) trundle north from Sungai Penuh to Kersik Tua between 8am and 5pm, and north from Kersik Tua to Pelompek (6000Rp), 8km away.

Pelompek

The small, gritty village of Pelompek, 8km north of Kersik Tua, makes a good base for a night or two if you're looking to climb Gunung Tajuh. The homestays in town can arrange guides and permits for Gunungs Kerinci and Tajuh. Monday is market day and is the most interesting time to visit.

🛏️ Sleeping

Kerinci View Homestay GUESTHOUSE $
(☑0812 7111 7133; www.kerincimountain.com; tr 250,000Rp) Just outside Pelompek among pastoral surrounds is this homestay that lives up to its name, with the volcano on full show. The rooms here are brightly decorated and have hot-water showers. It's the best option for trekkers looking for a guide to Gunung Tujuh (400,000Rp), or for booking a tour of the region; owner Mr Rapani is an experienced and well-regarded guide.

ℹ️ Getting There & Away

Buses pass along the main street fairly regularly to Kersik Tua (6000Rp, 30 minutes) and Sungai Penuh (20,000Rp, two hours).

Kerinci Seblat National Park

The largest national park in Sumatra, Kerinci Seblat National Park (Taman Nasional Kerinci Seblat; TNKS) covers a 350km swathe of the Bukit Barisan range and protects 13,791 sq km of prime equatorial rainforest spread over four provinces, with almost 40% of the park falling within Jambi's boundaries.

Most of the protected area is dense rainforest, and its inaccessibility is the very reason the park is one of the last strongholds of the endangered *harimau* (Sumatran tiger). Kerinci Seblat National Park is known as having the highest population and occurrence of tigers anywhere in Sumatra, with 80% of the park showing signs of the species. Kerinci's climate is temperate, and

ORANG PENDEK

Every culture that has lived among trees tells stories about elusive creatures that straddle myth and reality. Tales about leprechauns, fairies and even Sasquatch have existed for so long that it is impossible to determine which came first: the spotting or the story. The Indonesian version of these myths is the *orang pendek*, which has been occasionally spotted but more frequently talked about in the Kerinci forests for generations.

Villagers who claim to have seen *orang pendek* describe the creature as being about 1m tall, more ape than human, but walking upright on the ground. The creature's reclusive habits made it a celebrity in local mythology. Common folk stories say that the *orang pendek* has feet that face backwards so that it can't be tracked through the forest, or that it belongs to the supernatural, not the world of flesh and blood. Others say that the first-hand accounts were only spottings of sun bears.

Scientists have joined the conversation by tramping through the forest hoping to document the existence of *orang pendek*. British researchers succeeded in making a plaster cast of an animal footprint that fits the *orang pendek* description and doesn't match any other known primate. Hair samples with no other documented matches have also led researchers to believe that there is merit to the local lore. Two members of Fauna & Flora International, a British-based research team, even reported separate sightings, but were unable to collect conclusive evidence. Researchers sponsored by the National Geographic Society have resumed the search by placing motion-sensitive cameras in strategic spots in the jungle. So little is known about this region and so many areas are so remote that researchers are hopeful that the *orang pendek* will eventually wander into the frame.

If nothing else, the *orang pendek* helps illuminate aspects of Sumatrans' linguistic and cultural relationship with the jungle. Bahasa Indonesia makes little distinction between man and ape; for example, 'orang-utan' (forest man) or 'orang rimba' ('people of the forest', the preferred term for the Kubu tribe) may reflect a perceived blood tie between forest dwellers. This imprecision is often used for comic effect. A common joke is that the *orang pendek* (which means 'short man') does indeed exist, followed by the punchline that the shortest person in the room is the missing link.

---

downright cold as you gain altitude. Bring warm clothes and rain gear.

◉ Sights

The volcanic legacy of the Kerinci Valley is evident in its many hot springs. These range from the semi-grotty **Air Panas** near the village of Semurup (11km north of Sungai Penuh), which is hugely popular with locals, to **Air Panas Situs 2** across the valley, in a more natural setting, and **Grao Sakti**, more impressive still, located near the forest village of Renah Kemumu.

★ Gunung Kerinci   VOLCANO

Dominating the northern end of Kerinci Seblat National Park is Gunung Kerinci (3805m), Southeast Asia's tallest volcano and one of Sumatra's most active. On clear days the summit offers fantastic views of Danau Gunung Tujuh and the surrounding valleys and mountains.

Summit treks usually start from the national park entrance, 5km from Kersik Tua, and tackle the mountain over two days, camping overnight. A fully guided trip with food, permits, transport and all gear costs anywhere from 900,000Rp to 1,500,000Rp per person.

The highest campsite, at 3400m, is normally reached after six hours. The following morning, allow an hour to reach the summit by sunrise. The path is very steep and eroded, and above the treeline the scree is extremely slippery. A guide is mandatory and you'll need full camping gear, warm and waterproof clothes, and a head torch (all of which can be hired in Kersik Tua). Nights are freezing. Do not attempt the climb in wet weather. Fully self-sufficient parties needing a guide will only pay around 700,000Rp per person.

Botanists and twitchers from around the world come for the rare flora and fauna, such as Javanese edelweiss, Schneider's pitta and the crested wood partridge. Nepenthes (pitcher plants), squirrels, geckos and long-tailed macaques can be found in the lower forest, and troops of yellow-handed mitered langurs are also seen.

Goa Kasah   CAVE

Considered to be the largest cave system in the Kerinci Valley, and not yet fully explored,

KERINCI SEBLAT NATIONAL PARK'S FLORA & FAUNA

As with many of Sumatra's protected areas, encroachment by farmers, illegal logging and poaching are all serious issues for Kerinci. The park wardens are a passionate and dedicated lot, and they do stop a lot of the poaching, but greater numbers and more funds are desperately needed. The plight of the Sumatran tiger has been highlighted by Sir David Attenborough as part of Fauna & Flora International's Tiger Project (www.fauna -flora.org), aimed at saving the Sumatran tiger from extinction.

While the park does have a significant tiger population, spying one in the wild is very rare, and sightings are usually restricted to paw prints and droppings. In previous centuries, local Kerinci people were thought to be weretigers (a shape-shifting synthesis of man and beast), and the tiger is still important in local mysticism and mythology.

Because of the great elevation range within the park, Kerinci has a unique diversity of flora and fauna. Edelweiss and other high-altitude flowers grow in the forest. Lower altitudes bring pitcher plants, orchids, rafflesia and the giant *Amorphophallus*.

The park sees relatively few visitors, and its minimal tourist infrastructure is limited to the north around the dual attractions of Gunung Kerinci and Gunung Tujuh. While the park's northern region is more visited, the southern area features elephants – absent in the north – and also has interesting forest-edge communities living within the park's boundaries, plus excellent trekking through pristine forests.

Contact Wild Sumatra Adventures (p580) or Explore Kerinci (p581) if you're keen to explore the park's southern reaches with organised guides and treks. There are buffer areas for local cultivation and agriculture at the northern and southern edges of the park.

Goa Kasah makes for a good day trek (around 2½ hours one way) from the village of Sungai Sampun. The hike isn't very strenuous, and runs largely through picturesque rice fields before ascending some forested foothills.

Danau Kaco
LAKE

(Glass Lake) A two- to three-hour ramble through the jungle along a largely flat (and muddy) path, Danau Kaco will stop you dead in your tracks because you just won't believe the sight of this small, sapphire-coloured swimming hole, with incredible visibility into its 20m depths. The trail here starts near the village of Lempur Tengah (p581), an hour's drive from Sungai Penuh.

Danau Gunung Tujuh
LAKE

(Seven Mountain Lake) At 1996m, the beautiful caldera of Danau Gunung Tujuh is the highest in Southeast Asia and makes for a pleasant day ascent or part of a multiday trek. It takes 3½ hours to climb to the lake from the park entrance, which is 2km from Pelompek village. Camp near the lake if staying overnight. An *ojek* to the trailhead costs around 15,000Rp. Homestays in Kersik Tua and Pelompek can organise two- or three-day treks (from 300,000Rp per day), including a canoe crossing.

Wildlife in this area includes tapirs and Siamang gibbons, and one of the signature sounds of the Kerinci forests is the hooting and howling call of the gibbon.

Danau Kerinci
LAKE

Danau Kerinci, 20km south of Sungai Penuh, is a sizeable lake nestled between Gunung Raya (2535m) and rice paddies. Stone carvings around the lake suggest that the area supported a large population in megalithic times. **Batu Gong** (Gong Stone), in the village of Muak, 25km from Sungai Penuh, is thought to have been carved 2000 years ago. To reach the lake, catch a public bus from Sungai Penuh to Sanggaran Agung (15,000Rp). The last return bus leaves around 5pm.

Air Terjun Telun Berasap
WATERFALL

Impressive waterfalls dot the whole Kerinci Valley. The easiest to find are the Air Terjun Telun Berasap in the 'Letter W' village 4km north of Pelompek. Look for the 'Air Terjun Telun Berasap' sign then walk 300m to a deep, fern-lined ravine where a thunderous torrent of water crashes onto rocks below.

Other impressive falls include the 75m-tall **Pancuran Rayo**, reachable via a half-hour drive south and then a three-hour hike from Sungai Penuh.

Activities

★ Night Safari
SAFARI

Easily doable from Sungai Penuh, a night safari involves driving a stretch of the winding southbound road that passes through the Kerinci Seblat National Park after dark, looking for wildlife in the trees and undergrowth with torches. If you're lucky, you'll spot slow loris, civets, flying squirrels, owls and even the odd tiger. Walking is not advisable, lest you become a cat's dinner.

Renah Kemumu HIKING

This is an excellent jungle trek to the remote village of Renah Kemumu that sits in the jungle within the boundaries of the Kerinci Seblat National Park. From Lempur Tengah it takes around 12 to 15 hours one way; you'll be accompanied by Siamang gibbon calls, with plenty of bird and potential large mammal sightings en route.

🛏 Sleeping

Sungai Penuh (p580), Kersik Tua (p580) and Lempur Tengah (p581) are the main towns that travellers use as bases for jaunts into the national park. It's also possible to camp inside the park, but you'll need to take a permit and a guide, best arranged through Wild Sumatra Adventures (p580) or Explore Kerinci (p581).

ⓘ Information

Permits and guides are required to enter Kerinci Seblat National Park. Both can be arranged at the Kantor Taman Nasional Kerinci Seblat (park office; p581) in Sungai Penuh or through your losmen. There's a park office at the entrance to Danau Gunung Tujuh, but it's rarely staffed.

Permits cost 150,000Rp, English-speaking-guide rates are around 300,000Rp per day, and porters can be hired for 250,000Rp per day. Be sure to clarify exactly what the rates entail, as camping gear, food and transport may be considered additional costs.

ⓘ Getting There & Away

While some sights within the national park are accessed by hiking directly out of town, for others you'll need to arrange a car or ojek to reach the trailhead to begin your trek.

BENGKULU

☏ 0736 / POP 351,000

The quiet provincial capital of Bengkulu is a real hidden gem and quite possibly the nicest city in Sumatra. Its pedestrian-friendly streets are not desperately traffic-clogged, the beach is kept clean by locals, and there's a decent eating scene to boot. The city itself is quite light on attractions, beyond a few interesting reminders of the colonial era and an expansive beach. But travellers are be-

ginning to discover the multiple natural attractions beyond the city limits, which make Bengkulu an excellent destination in its own right, rather than just a handy stopover between Padang and Bukittinggi to the north and Krui and Bandar Lampung to the south.

History

Little is known of Bengkulu before it came under the influence of the Majapahits from Java at the end of the 13th century. Until then it appears to have existed in almost total isolation, divided between a number of small kingdoms such as Sungai Lebong in the Curup area. It even developed its own cuneiform script, ka-ga-nga.

In 1685, after having been kicked out of Banten in Java, the British moved into Bengkulu (Bencoolen, as they called it) in search of pepper. The venture was not exactly a roaring success. Isolation, boredom and constant rain sapped the British will, and malaria ravaged their numbers.

The colony was still not a likely prospect in 1818 when Sir Stamford Raffles arrived as its British-appointed ruler. In the short time he was there, Raffles made the pepper market profitable and planted cash crops of coffee, nutmeg and sugar cane. In 1824 Bengkulu was traded for the Dutch outpost of Melaka as a guarantee not to interfere with British interests in Singapore.

From 1938 to 1941 Bengkulu was a home-in-domestic-exile for Indonesia's first president, Sukarno; his house today is a **museum** (Rumah Pengasingan Bung Karno; Jl Soekarno Hatta; 3000Rp; ☉ 8am-6pm).

⊙ Sights

★ Fort Marlborough FORT

(Benteng Marlborough; Jl Benteng; 5000Rp; ☉ 7.30am-6.30pm) Set on a hill overlooking the Indian Ocean, the star-shaped Benteng Marlborough, a former British fort, became the seat of British power in Bengkulu after 1719, when it replaced nearby Fort York. Despite its sturdy defences the fort was attacked and overrun twice – once by a local rebellion just after its completion in 1719, and then by the French in 1760. It was also used by the Dutch, Japanese and Indonesian military.

Today the complex comprises museums in the original fort building, along with historic cannons and gravestones. There are a few interesting old engravings and copies of official correspondence from the time of British rule, and you can also see where the

HIKING & TREKKING

The Bengkulu region has a huge wealth of attractions that are only beginning to be explored by travellers. These range from multiday volcano and jungle treks, and exploring hot springs, lakes and rivers, to participating in elephant conservation and interacting with locals in remote villages. Most of these trips are arranged through the highly recommended Wild Sumatra Tours, which is on hand to advise and organise, guided by your specific interests. Prices are based on two participants: the more participants, the cheaper it is.

Beringin Tiga & Curug Embun This is a straightforward hike through coffee and palm-sugar plantations, finishing at a campsite near a beautiful natural hot spring. From here you can take short hikes to visit the Beringin Tiga falls and the remarkable Curug Embun falls, which comprises two falls: one cold and the other fed by hot springs, with great swimming where the two meet. Safety ropes assist descents to Curug Embun. It's 33km south of Curup, which is an 84km drive northeast of Bengkulu.

Bukit Daun Famous for its seven multicoloured boiling pools, the whitest allegedly home to the Kawah Putri spirit who'll come if you call her, Bukit Daun makes for a challenging three-day adventure. It involves trekking through tobacco and coffee plantations and dense jungle, two nights camping in the jungle and a pit stop to wash in a small waterfall.

Bukit Kaba (permit 100,000Rp) This active volcano with three craters makes for a relatively straightforward ascent with two trail options: an easier gravel path or a tougher trail through dense jungle. Both take around three hours. From the top there are spectacular views of the surrounding countryside and a whiff of sulphur from the single active crater. Camping near the summit so you can explore the craters is highly recommended. It's around 30km from Curup.

Seblat Elephant Conservation Centre (☑ 0811 731 1003; www.wildsumatratours.com/seblat-elephant-conservation-center; 2 days/1 night for 2 people US$500) This is a conservation project set up to manage human-elephant conflict, as well as to protect the forests and wildlife. Here you can assist mahouts on elephant treks, on anything from two-day trips to 10-day jungle patrols on the lookout for wild elephants and tigers. While the centre is one of only a handful of legitimate elephant conservation centres in Indonesia, note that elephant rides present various animal-welfare issues, so you might want to reconsider taking part. It's very much a grassroots initiative and is not designed with tourists in mind, so the camping and jungle conditions can make it rough going. It's located near Mukomuko, en route between Bengkulu and Sungai Penuh, so it's a good stopover for those heading to Kerinci. Funds generated by visitors contribute to the care of elephants in residence, the protection of wild elephants in the region, and jungle patrols to prevent poaching.

Dutch incarcerated Indonesia's President Sukarno during his internal exile. You can walk up along the fortress walls for views of the coast and the surrounding town.

British Cemetery   CEMETERY
(Jl Rejamat; ⊙ 6am-6.30pm) **FREE** A fascinating remnant from the British rule in Bengkulu is this historical cemetery featuring gravestones of the English dating back to 1770. It's a well-maintained site at the rear of the church.

Pantai Panjang   BEACH
Bengkulu's main beach, Pantai Panjang, is 7km of clean white sand. Strong surf and currents make it unsafe for swimming, but there are decent surf breaks towards the northern and southern ends of the beach. Unusually for Sumatra, there's also a jogging track that stretches the length of the beach, shaded by pine trees.

State Museum of Bengkulu Province   MUSEUM
(Museum Negeri Provinsi Bengkulu; ☑ 0736-22098; Jl Pembangunan 8; 3000Rp; ⊙ 8am-3pm Mon-Fri, to noon Sat & Sun) Like every provincial capital in Sumatra, Bengkulu has a museum covering the local traditional culture, with exhibits including Arabic-influenced lettered Besurek batik, traditional architecture, cooking utensils, weaponry, manuscripts and displays on British rule. There are no English captions.

☞ Tours

★ **Wild Sumatra Tours**   ADVENTURE
(☑ 0811 731 1003; www.wildsumatratours.com) The indefatigable Josh and his team have

done wonders in terms of opening up the Bengkulu region to adventurous travellers. Whether you're into trekking, jungle adventure, volcano climbing, caving, river tubing or swimming in pristine, remote waterfalls or hot springs, these guys can help you organise your adventure. They also run Bengkulu city tours.

🛏 Sleeping

Tropicana Guesthouse GUESTHOUSE $
(📱 0736-732 5328; http://tropicanaguesthouse.busi ness.site; Jl Muhammad Hasan 48; r incl breakfast with shared/private bathroom 150,000/220,000Rp, ste 320,000Rp; 🌀 🛜) Well located within walking distance of most places of interest, the laid-back Tropicana makes for an excellent budget choice. Painted in mauve, rooms are a tad garish, but they're well priced and comfortable, with air-con and wi-fi. There's a small communal kitchen with fridge, nasi goreng for breakfast, and the owner speaks English.

Pring Gading Surf Camp GUESTHOUSE $
(📱 0852 3330 9595, 0812 7330 9595; yadi.pring gading@gmail.com; Jl Jenggalu; r incl breakfast with fan/air-con 100,000/200,000Rp; 🌀 🛜) At the southern end of the city, and not far from the beach, Yadi's place is the heart and soul of the local surfer community, with boards as well as motorbikes (both 50,000Rp) for rent. It's all a bit ramshackle, but that's part of the appeal, and the rooms themselves are spotless. Yadi and Vivi also run a good cafe. You'll get to sample their pastries for breakfast.

Splash Hotel BOUTIQUE HOTEL $$
(📱 0736-23333; www.hotel-splash.com; Jl Sudirman 48; r incl breakfast from 495,000Rp; 🌀 🛜) Bengkulu's first stab at a designer hotel is a goodie and features a colourful designer lobby and well-appointed rooms with modern bathrooms. There's an on-site cafe and restaurant, and the location on one of the city's top food streets, lined with myriad stalls in the evenings, is a boon for the hungry.

🍴 Eating & Drinking

Bencoolen Coffee House BISTRO $
(Jl BRI; mains 18,000-60,000Rp; ⊙3-11pm Tue-Sun) Just across from the British Cemetery is this German-owned cafe that's the go-to place if you're hankering for Western comfort food. Decide between stone-oven pizza, bratwurst or burgers, while being sure to leave room for the homemade ice cream or red velvet cake. It's a lovely garden space that's also perfect for a cold beer or coffee.

★ Marola SEAFOOD $$
(Jl Pariwisata; mains around 70,000Rp; ⊙8am-8.30pm Tue-Sun, to 4pm Mon) At this classic, locally famous seafood joint by the beach, near central Bengkulu, you can choose from ultra-fresh giant prawns, squid and fish, then pay by weight, and pick from an array of sauces you'd like your seafood cooked in. Wash it down with a cold beer, and kick back to enjoy the balmy evening.

Aloha INTERNATIONAL $$
(📱 0812 7846 6691; www.aloharesto.com; Jl Pariwisata; mains from 35,000Rp; ⊙10am-11.30pm; 🛜 📱) Just across from the beach is this Australian-owned place that does primarily Western pub food, along with seafood dishes and Indonesian staples. They serve beer, but it's pricey and not always cold.

Edu Coffee CAFE
(📱 0736-22626; Jl Suprapto 1-2; ⊙9am-11pm; 🛜) One for coffee aficionados, Edu Coffee is a microroastery that sources arabica beans locally as well as from across the archipelago. It has all the tools of the trade to prepare the perfect cup – AeroPress, V60, siphon, espresso machine and *tubruk* (unfiltered coffee); ask if owner Andy is around to see what seasonal concoctions he's brewing. They also do food and cold beers.

ⓘ Information

Bengkulu has no shortage of ATMs accepting foreign cards.

BUSES FROM BENGKULU

DESTINATION	FARE (RP)	DURATION (HR)	FREQUENCY
Bandar Lampung	150,000-350,000	8	several daily
Bukittinggi	150,000-200,000	17	several daily
Jakarta	340,000-400,000	22-30	numerous daily
Krui	250,000	10	several daily
Padang	235,000	15	several daily
Sungai Penuh	130,000	10-12	2 daily

CANDI MUARA TAKUS

Hidden away in a jungle clearing halfway between Bukittinggi and Pekanbaru are these low-key Buddhist **temple ruins** (Kampar; 8000Rp; ⊘8am-6pm), believed to date to the 11th century. A part of the Sriwijaya kingdom, the complex (which was restored in 1980) is compact in size, with only four brick-and-stone stupas, however it's an incredibly peaceful and evocative site. Most notable are the towering 14m-tall lotus-shaped Candi Mahugai, and Candi Tua, which resembles a UFO that's landed on a platform.

It's 90km north of Harau Valley, around a two-hour drive. To get here you can rent a motorbike from Abdi Homestay (75,000Rp; p579), or take an *ojek* (175,000Rp) or private car (500,000Rp).

ⓘ Getting There & Away

AIR

Bengkulu's **Fatmawati Soekarno Airport** (Jl Bandara Fatmawati Soekarno) is 10km southeast of town and has 10 daily flights to Jakarta with Citilink, Lion Air, Garuda, Sriwijaya Air and Batik Air. Garuda and Wings Air have daily flights to Palembang, Padang and Pulau Batam.

BUS

The bus-company offices in Tanah Patah along Jl Parman or Jl MT Haryono are your best bet. Ask around and you'll quickly be steered to the most appropriate company for your destination. Jakarta is served by large buses, while other destinations are served by minibuses.

ⓘ Getting Around

From Bengkulu's airport, taxis charge around 50,000Rp.

Download the apps for Grab (p515) and Go-Jek (p515) for the quickest and cheapest ways to get around. Otherwise there are the usual *angkot*, *ojek* and taxi options.

RIAU

The landscape and character of Riau province is distinct from northern and western Sumatra. Rather than being shaped by mountains and volcanoes, Riau's character was carved by rivers and narrow ocean passages. Trading towns sprang up along the important navigation route of the Strait of Melaka, across which Riau claims cultural cousins.

For the port towns, such as Pekanbaru, and the Riau Islands, proximity to Singapore and Kuala Lumpur has ensured greater access to the outside world than the towns of the interior Sumatran jungle. The discovery of oil and gas reserves has also built an educated and middle-class population in Pekanbaru.

The interior of the province more closely resembles Sumatra as a whole: sparse population, dense jungle, Buddhist temple ruins, surviving pockets of nomadic peoples (including the Sakai, Kubu and Jambisal) and endangered species, such as the Sumatran rhinoceros and tiger.

History

Riau's position at the southern entrance to the Strait of Melaka, the gateway for trade between India and China, was strategically significant. From the 16th century, the Riau Islands were ruled by a variety of Malay kingdoms, which had to fight off constant attacks by pirates and the Portuguese, Dutch and English. The Dutch eventually won control over the Strait of Melaka, and mainland Riau (then known as Siak) became their colony when the Sultan of Johor surrendered in 1745. However, Dutch interest lay in international trade, and it made little effort to develop the province.

Oil was discovered around Pekanbaru by US engineers before WWII, and the country around Pekanbaru is criss-crossed by pipelines that connect the oil wells to refineries at Dumai.

Pekanbaru

🖉 0761 / POP 1.1 MILLION

Purely one for lovers of big cities, Pekanbaru is possibly worth a night, with an interesting museum, some good spots to eat and a cool rooftop bar. However, in reality, pretty much the only reason why you'd briefly pass through Pekanbaru is if you're en route to the Riau Islands or Singapore via Dumai, or arriving from or heading west to Bukittinggi.

Indonesia's oil capital comes with all the hustle and bustle of a modern city, with the added plague of smoke from the burning oil-palm plantations periodically shutting down the city's airport during the dry season.

⊙ Sights

Museum Sang Nila Utama MUSEUM
(Jl Sudirman 194; ⊙8am-3pm Mon-Thu, to 1pm
Sat & Sun) FREE This museum does an excellent job in detailing Riau culture, with
interesting displays on ceremonial clothing,
architecture, traditional artefacts, batik and
natural history, plus a display on the Candi
Muara Takus Buddhist site. Upstairs there's
an eclectic collection of objects and coverage
of the local mining industry.

🛏 Sleeping

Red Planet Pekanbaru DESIGN HOTEL $
(☑0761-851008; www.redplanethotels.com; Jl
Tengku Zainal Abidin 23; r from 222,000Rp; ❄🤶)
This centrally located, reliable chain is just
a couple of blocks from the main road of Jl
Sudirman. Red Planet's snug rooms are all
blonde wood, with plenty of light and contemporary furnishings.

✗ Eating & Drinking

RM Kota Buana INDONESIAN $
(Jl H Cokroaminoto 16; meals around 30,000Rp;
⊙6.30am-8.30pm) In a city known for its quality Padang food, this longstanding, humble
restaurant is a standout in Pekanbaru. The
beef *rendang* and *ayam goreng* (fried chick-
en) are winning choices.

★Sky Garden & Lounge ROOFTOP BAR
(☑0761-861122; www.facebook.com/skygarden
pekanbaru; Jl Ahmad Yani; ⊙2-10pm Sun-Thu, to
midnight Fri & Sat) Escape Pekanbaru's grind
and head up to the top of Sumatra's tallest
building to enjoy a cold beer or cocktail with
360-degree city views. Its outdoor bar has a
luxurious feel with contemporary furniture
and palm trees, and there's an indoor cafe
with tempting cakes, charcoal bun burgers,
bar snacks and Indonesian dishes.

ⓘ Getting There & Away

AIR
Pekanbaru's airport, **Sultan Syarif Kasim II
Airport** (www.sultansyarifkasim2-airport.co.id),

is 10km south of the city. There are daily flights
to major towns across Sumatra and Java, as well
to Singapore and Malaysia.

BUS
Most buses depart from Pekanbaru's main bus
terminal, **Terminal AKAP** (Jl Tuanku Tambusai),
5km west of the city centre. However, it's best
to confirm with your hotel where your preferred
choice is departing from, as some companies bypass the terminal altogether. **Karya Maju Travel**
(☑0761-47133) runs a handy express minibus
(economy/executive 120,000/250,000Rp) to
Dumai, for ferries to Malaysia.

ⓘ Getting Around

Airport taxis and taxis from the bus terminal
charge around 100,000Rp to town. However, as
with all big Indonesian cities, Grab (p515) and
Go-Jek (p515) online taxis are the best means of
getting around. The city's Trans Metro (rapid bus
transit) service runs along Jl Sudirman to the
bus terminal (4000Rp).

Dumai

☑0765 / POP 316,700
Riau's second-largest city, Dumai is a gritty
port town that's only of note as a transport
hub for those catching the ferry to Malaysia or Pulau Batam. If you time it right, it's
relatively straighforward to link to or from
Bukittinggi without overnighting here.

If you need a bed for the night then it's best
to head to JL Sudirman, which has a string
of reliable three-star hotels. There's not too
many recommendable budget options.

ⓘ Getting There & Away

AIR
Wings Air operates daily flights from Pekanbaru
to Dumai (30 minutes, 420,000Rp).

BOAT
To Malaysia
If you're fresh from Malaysia, the port area will
seem like a bit of a scrum.

From Dumai several ferry companies operate
services to three different ports in Malaysia:

BUSES FROM PEKANBARU

DESTINATION	FARE (RP)	DURATION (HR)	FREQUENCY
Bengkulu	250,000	15	5pm daily
Bukittinggi	80,000-120,000	8	numerous daily
Dumai	80,000	5	hourly 7am to around 6pm
Jambi	180,000	12	2 daily

Melaka, Port Klang and Port Dickson. Note you'll need to pay an 50,000Rp departure tax in Dumai, while those arriving at Port Klang will need to pay the RM23 arrival tax.

You can buy tickets through **Indomal Express** (☑ 0853 7567 0000; www.facebook.com/indomaldumai; Jl Sudirman 425) for the following destinations:

Melaka (adult/child 320,000/160,000Rp, 2½ hours) Daily departures at 9.30am.

Port Klang (adult/child 350,000/175,000Rp, four hours) Three boats a week departing at noon on Monday, Wednesday and Friday.

Port Dickson (adult/child 330,000/125,000Rp, three hours) Leaving at 11am on Monday, Tuesday, Friday and Saturday.

To Pulau Batam

Dumai Express (☑ 0813 7882 2999) has a daily boat to Sekupang port on Pulau Batam (400,000Rp, seven hours), departing at 6am.

BUS

Buses connect Dumai to Bukittinggi (125,000Rp to 240,000Rp, 10 hours).There are regular buses from Dumai to Pekanbaru (80,000Rp, five hours), or more convenient express minibuses with **Karya Maju Travel** (☑ 0765-35239; from 120,000Rp).

If you're travelling from Bukittinggi, Bukittinggi Wisata Express (p576) has a nightly minibus (nine hours) linking with morning ferry departures from Dumai.

Pulau Batam

☑ 0778

Batam's golf resorts and casinos attract a weekender contingent from Singapore and mainland China. For travellers, Batam is no more than a transport hub with connections to many different parts of the country. With its multitude of massage parlours and bars there's a seedy aspect to it, so if you're winding up your stay in Indonesia before crossing the strait to Singapore, you're better off spending the night in Bintan.

On Batam, Singapore dollars are as easy to spend as Indonesian rupiah. There are plenty of ATMs at the airport and around Nagoya, Batam Centre and Sekupang.

Useful tourist websites include Enjoy Batam (www.enjoybatam.com) and Welcome to Batam (www.welcometobatam.com).

Getting There & Away

AIR

The **Hang Nadim Airport** is located on the eastern side of Pulau Batam. There are many daily flights to Jakarta, Medan and other major cities in Sumatra and Java.

BOAT
To Mainland Sumatra

From Batam's Sekupang port, **Dumai Express** (PT Lestari Indoma Bahari; ☑ 0765-31820; Sekupang Domestic Terminal) runs mainland Sumatra ferries daily to both Tanjung Buton (240,000Rp, four to five hours) and Dumai (400,000Rp, seven hours); a minibus links to Pekanbaru (around three hours).

Batam Jet (☑ 0778-427666; Sekupang Domestic Terminal) has a boat at 7pm from Sekupang to Dumai (400,000Rp, eight hours). You'll also need to pay 10,000Rp for a boarding pass.

To Malaysia

Passenger ferries (255,000Rp, two hours) run between Johor Bahru's Stulang Laut port and Batam Centre (15 per day) and Harbour Bay (four per day).

To Singapore

For Singapore, Batam's three main ports are Batam Centre, Harbour Bay (near Nagoya) and Sekupang on the northwest coast. In Singapore they arrive mainly at HarbourFront, as well as Tanah Merah.

The main ferry operators include **Batam Fast** (☑ 0778-321120; www.batamfast.com), **Majestic Ferry** (☑ Batam Centre 0778-479999, Sekupang 0778-323377; www.majesticfastferry.com) and **Sindo Ferry** (☑ Batam Centre 0778-465555, Harbour Bay 0778-381059, Sekupang 0778-321691; www.sindoferry.com.sg).

Getting Around

Trans Batam BRT (bus rapid transit) is the local public transport, with links to the port towns of Sekupang, Nagoya and Batam Centre.

Metered taxis and Grab (p515) online taxis are the primary ways to get around Pulau Batam. A taxi from the airport to Nagoya is around 130,000Rp. From Sekupang to Nagoya count on around 70,000Rp, or half this with Grab.

Nagoya

This original boom town shows a lot more skin than you'll find in the rest of Sumatra. The heart of town is the Nagoya Entertainment District, dotted with beer bars, shopping malls and massage parlours. It ain't pretty, but Nagoya is ultimately functional, and a good place for dining out and an overnight stay if you're travelling to or from Singapore by boat.

Sleeping & Eating

New Hotel Sinar Bulan　　　　　　HOTEL $
(☑ 0778-456757; Jl Pembangunan; r 220,000-300,000Rp; ❄ ☎) A friendly hotel just a couple of blocks from the Nagoya Hill Mall and

various eating establishments. While rooms are stock standard, the fact that they're clean and air-conditioned means this place is a win – especially if the helpful English-speaking staff are working. Across the road is the old hotel (rooms from 150,000Rp), which has a restaurant downstairs.

Indo Rasa INDONESIAN $
(Jl Imam Bonjol; dishes from 20,000Rp; ⏰8am-10pm) This lively food precinct in a building on the main thoroughfare across from Nagoya Hill is a good spot for local hawker-style food. There's a bunch of different stalls cooking up anything from *ayam penyet* (East Javanese fried chicken) to barbecue fish and Chinese dim sum. Cold beers are on hand to wash it down.

❶ Getting There & Away

Harbour Bay is the closest port to Nagoya, which has regular boats to Singapore. Nagoya is located around 16km west of Hang Nadim Airport, which is around 130,000Rp by taxi or 70,000Rp by Grab (p515). It's 24km to the harbour for boats to Tanjung Pinang.

Nagoya is linked by public transport to Sekupang and Batam Centre via the Trans Batam bus system.

Pulau Bintan

Just across the water from Singapore, Pulau Bintan has some of the nicest white-sand beaches in Sumatra. While it markets itself as a high-end playground for well-heeled visitors from Singapore and beyond, there is some affordable accommodation too.

Top-end resorts huddle around the Lagoi area on the island's north coast, in close proximity to Singapore. However, less exclusive options along the east coast around Pantai Trikora are equally nice.

Skip the pricey, all-inclusive Lagoi resorts and instead explore Bintan's cultural heart in the area around the island's largest town, Tanjung Pinang. A world away from ultra-clean Singapore, the noisy, dusty streets and mishmash of building styles exude a rustic charm.

Small boats run locals and visitors to Senggarang, where you'll find a Chinese village on stilts, and Penyenget, a small island with royal tombs, palaces, a mosque and a wonderfully rural atmosphere.

❶ Information

The Tourist Information Office (p593) in Trikora has a good website, although it's in Bahasa Indonesia; use Google Translate.

DANGERS & ANNOYANCES
The incredibly itchy bite of Bintan's tiny sand flies can be an irritant for beach goers. Bring along insect repellent containing DEET and remember to reapply it after swimming. Also pack calamine lotion to treat itchy bites; this is important as they can easily become infected.

❶ Getting There & Away

AIR
Raja Haji Fisabilillah Airport (☏0771-442434; www.rajahajifisabilillah-airport.co.id; Jl Adi Sucipto, Km12) is located in the southeast of Pulau Bintan. There are daily flights to Jakarta with Garuda, Lion Air and Sriwijaya Air. There are also direct flights to Pekanbaru.

BOAT
Pulau Bintan has two main ferry terminals, with destinations including Pulau Batam, Singapore, Malaysia and other islands in the Riau archipelago. Tanjung Pinang, on the western side of the island, is the busiest harbour and the best option for those heading to Pulau Batam or Pantai Trikora. If you're bound for the resort area of Lagoi, the Bandar Bentan Telani (BBT) ferry

SUMATRA PULAU BINTAN

BOATS FROM BATAM TO SINGAPORE

DEPARTURE/ARRIVAL	FERRY	PRICE (RP)	FREQUENCY
Batam Centre/HarbourFront	Batam Fast	103,000	12 daily
Harbour Bay/Tanah Merah & HarbourFront	Batam Fast	103,000	4 daily
Sekupang/HarbourFront	Batam Fast	260,000	10 daily
Batam Centre/HarbourFront	Majestic Ferry	195,000	14 daily
Batam Centre/Tanah Merah	Majestic Ferry	195,000	4 daily
Sekupang/HarbourFront	Majestic Ferry	195,000	9 daily
Batam Centre/HarbourFront	Sindo Ferry	103,000	12 daily
Harbour Bay/HarbourFront	Sindo Ferry	260,000	3 daily
Sekupang/HarbourFront	Sindo Ferry	103,000	8 daily

terminal is more convenient. Tandjunguban port on the west coast is another option for those heading to Batam.

To Singapore

Ferries from Tanjung Pinang and the Bandar Bentan Telani (BBT) ferry terminal depart to Singapore's Tanah Merah ferry terminal daily.

Ferry companies include Bintan Resort Ferries (p594), Majestic Fast Ferry and Sindo Ferry.

To Malaysia

From Tanjung Pinang ferry teminal there are boats to Johor Bahru's Berjaya Waterfront ferry terminal.

To Pulau Batam

Fast ferries (47,000Rp) depart from Tanjung Pinang's ferry terminal for Telaga Punggur on Batam every 30 minutes from 7.20am to 6.30pm daily; there are also two daily RORO (roll-on, roll-off) car ferries. Boats also depart from Tandjunguban port on the west coast, handy if you're coming from Trikora or Lagoi.

To Elsewhere in Indonesia

Daily ferries depart from Tanjung Pinang's ferry terminal to other islands in the Riau chain, such as Pulau Karimun, Pulau Kundur and Pulau Lingga.

❶ Getting Around

Bintan is one place in Indonesia where renting a car is a viable option, given the roads are relatively quiet and in good condition.

Supra (☑ 0859 7788 0090) is a reliable and friendly English-speaking taxi driver. Expect to pay around 300,000Rp from Tanjung Pinang to Trikora. He can hire out motorbikes too.

Tanjung Pinang

☑ 0771 / POP 225,000

Bintan's capital Tanjung Pinang is a historic port town and trade centre with a still-thriving market culture and plenty of hustle and bustle. Touts swarm as you get off the ferry, but the town is easy to navigate without their persistent 'assistance'. Few travellers linger long here, but there are a couple of worthwhile attractions that make it an interesting spot to spend a night.

◉ Sights

★ **Pulau Penyenget**   ISLAND
Pulau Penyenget, reached by frequent boats (7000Rp) from the Tanjung Pinang pier, was once the capital of the Riau rajahs. The ruins of the old palace of Rajah Ali and the tombs and graveyards of Rajah Jaafar and Rajah Ali are signposted inland. The most impres-

sive site is the sulphur-coloured mosque, with its many domes and minarets.

🛌 Sleeping & Eating

Hotel Panorama   HOTEL $
(☑ 0811 700 0432, 0771-22920; www.bintanpanorama.com; Jl Haji Agus Salim 21; d incl breakfast from 242,000Rp; ❄@☎) Hotel Panorama, a 10-minute walk from the Tanjung Pinang ferry terminal, has a stuffy English B&B feel to it, and features clean and spacious rooms. Hot-water showers, air-con, fast wi-fi, cable TV and room service ensure a comfortable stay. Rates includes a buffet breakfast in its downstairs restaurant, and there's a rooftop bar.

Melayu Square   INDONESIAN $
(Jl Hang Tuah; dishes around 20,000Rp; ☺5-10pm) Come sunset, stroll to this lively strip of food stalls that cook up fresh seafood, noodles and all kinds of streetside snacks.

❶ Information

Tourist Information Office (☑ 0771-318223; Jl Merdeka 5; ☺9am-5pm Mon-Fri) Outside the police station near the port is this small office that can assist with arranging tours and transport around the island.

❶ Getting There & Away

Tanjung Pinang is easily reached by boat from Singapore, Malaysia, Pulau Batam and other islands in the Riau Island chain.

Raja Haji Fisabilillah Airport (p591) is located 10km east of Tanjung Pinang and is easily reached by taxi. There are daily flights to Jakarta with Garuda, Lion Air and Sriwijaya Air.

Majestic Fast Ferry (☑ 0771-450 0199; www.majesticfastferry.com.sg; Sri Bintan Pura Ferry Terminal) and **Sindo Ferry** (☑ 0771-316886, in Singapore +65 6331 4122; www.sindoferry.com.sg; Sri Bintan Pura Ferry Terminal) sail around four times a day each from Tanjung Pinang to Singapore's Tanah Merah ferry terminal. To Malaysia, boats to Stulang Laut (310,000Rp, three hours) depart daily at 7am, 12.30pm and 3pm. Note there's a 60,000Rp departure tax.

Dumai Express (☑ 0852 6557 3188, 0813 7882 2999, 0771-25888; dumex_dumai@yahoo.com) has a daily ferry at 6am to Dumai (430,000Rp, nine hours) on mainland Sumatra.

Fast ferries to Pulau Batam (47,000Rp) depart every 30 minutes.

Senggarang

This predominantly Chinese village, on the other side of the bay from Tanjung Pinang on Pulau Bintan, is easily reached by a 25km taxi ride, or a 10-minute boat ride. The main attractions of this area are the floating stilt Chinese village and several Buddhist temples, including one that has been basically swallowed by a banyan tree.

Sights

Banyan Tree Temple   BUDDHIST TEMPLE

This particularly unusual temple is housed in a building dating from the early 19th century. Originally owned by a wealthy Chinese man, believed to be buried here, the building has, over the years, been swallowed up by the roots of a large banyan tree. It's only in recent decades that the site has become a shrine, as locals and devotees from further afield began to come here to give offerings and ask for blessings.

You can get back to the jetty from here without returning to the Vihara Dharma Sasana temple complex; just take the first left on your way back.

Vihara Dharma Sasana   BUDDHIST TEMPLE

This well-maintained temple complex, looking out to sea, is accessed through a beautifully decorative Chinese archway and contains three main temples. The oldest two, and the first ones you approach after walking through the archway, are thought to be between 200 and 300 years old, although they have been repainted and repaired many times. Their roof carvings are particularly ornate. Behind them is a more modern temple and two huge and very colourful Buddha statues.

Trikora & Around

Pulau Bintan's east coast is a more authentic and laid-back alternative to the manicured resorts of Lagoi, while still also lined with attractive white-sand beaches. The most established is Pantai Trikora, though Mutiara Beach further north along the coast is fast gaining in popularity. The small islands off Pantai Trikora are also worth visiting and have snorkelling outside the monsoon season. The Museum Bahari Bintan is a must-visit for those interested in Bintan's fascinating culture and history.

Sights

★ **Museum Bahari Bintan**   MUSEUM

(Jl Trikora, Km36; ⊙ 8.30am-4pm) FREE This fascinating maritime museum is a surprising find along this sleepy coastal road. Housed within a building shaped like a ship, it has an unlikely setting in the middle of an Is-

lamic study centre, which doubles as a **tourist information office** (www.bintantourism. com; ⊙ 8am-3.15pm Mon-Fri). It has beautifully presented exhibits that cover local curiosities such as the *kelong* (floating fishing buildings) you'll see out to sea and detailed model ships, and it provides interesting background on the lifestyle of the nomadic Orang Laut sea tribes.

Berakit   VILLAGE

(Panglong) On Pulau Bintan's far northeast tip, Berakit is a small, curious fishing village populated with Orang Laut (which translates to 'people of the sea'), a nomadic ethnic group known traditionally to reside in boats out at sea across the Malay region. Here they have a permanent settlement in stilt houses built over the water. Also in the village are two large igloo-shaped kilns that were used to produce charcoal, as well as a small church.

Sleeping

★ **Mutiara Beach Guesthouse**   GUESTHOUSE $$

(☑ 0821 7121 1988; www.mutiarabintan.com; Jl Trikora, Km 55; campsite incl breakfast 90,000Rp, d 500,000-1,100,000Rp; ❀ 🛜) At this Swiss-run hideaway, gorgeous thatched bungalows with spacious verandahs sit amid unruly vegetation right by a pristine beach; its shallow waters are good for swimming. Its restaurant serves local and Western dishes, and by the water it has a small beach club with deck lounges, satellite TV, bar and library. There's also its rustic **Aroma River Spa** (treatments from 280,000Rp; ⊙ 10am-6pm), perfect for relaxing close to nature.

There are also stand-up paddleboards (SUPs), kayaks, bicycles and snorkelling gear for hire.

★ **Trikora Beach Club**   RESORT $$$

(☑ 0811 7700 898; www.trikorabeachclub.com; Jl Pemukiman; d incl breakfast US$125-165; ❀ 🏊) Rustic whitewashed beach huts and a white sandy beach make this chillaxed resort popular with visitors from neighbouring Singapore looking for a quick, cheap getaway. The gorgeous blue-tiled pool is perfect for a cooling dip, as is the clear ocean, where you can try snorkelling and numerous water sports. The restaurant serves decent food.

Getting There & Away

Expect to pay around 300,000Rp for a taxi from Bandar Bentan Telani (BBT) ferry terminal in Lagoi to Trikora, and a similar price for a taxi from Tanjung Pinang. Supra (p592) is a recommended driver.

From both ferry terminals an *ojek* is around 150,000Rp.

Lagoi

Pulau Bintan's gated resort area stretches along the northern coastline of the island at Pasir Lagoi. The beaches are sandy and swimmable, the resorts have polished four- and five-star service, and there are water-sports and entertainment options for all ages. Weekday discounts can be as generous as 50% off.

🛏 Sleeping

★ Banyan Tree Bintan   RESORT $$$
(☑ 0770-693100; www.banyantree.com; Jl Teluk Berembang; d incl breakfast from 6,250,000Rp; ❇ 🖥 🛌) The private and privileged Banyan Tree has famed spa facilities and is a high-powered retreat deep in the jungle. The hotel shares a 900m-long beach with Angsana Resort & Spa Bintan.

Mayang Sari Beach Resort   RESORT $$$
(☑ 0770-692505; http://mayang.nirwanagardens. com; Jl Panglima Pantar; d incl breakfast from 2,350,000Rp; ❇ 🖥) This good-value, lower-end resort features 50 thatched-roof, Balinese-style chalets, each with its own verandah and choice of a garden or sea view. The property sits on a blissful white-sand beach, and features land and water sports as well a spa.

❶ Getting There & Around

If you're bound for the resort area of Lagoi, the Bandar Bentan Telani (BBT) ferry terminal is the most convenient ferry point on Pulau Bintan. **Bintan Resort Ferries** (☑ 0770-691935, in Singapore +65 6542 4372; www.brf.com.sg; Bandar Bentan Telani Ferry Terminal) connects with Singapore's Tanah Merah ferry terminal.

Shuttle services between the BBT ferry terminal and Lagoi resorts are usually part of their package prices.

JAMBI

☑ 0741 / POP 583,500

The capital of Jambi province is a busy river port about 155km from the mouth of the Sungai Batang Hari. The main reason to visit is for its large temple complex at Muara Jambi, 26km downstream from Jambi – the single biggest attraction on Sumatra's east coast.

Jambi also has a pleasantly low-key and friendly vibe, especially around the riverfront food stalls that kick off at dusk and look out at the city's abstract pedestrian bridge.

Jambi's ATMs cluster around Jl Dr Sutomo.

History

The province of Jambi was the heartland of the ancient kingdom of Malayu, which first rose to prominence in the 7th century. Much of Malayu's history is closely and confusingly entwined with that of its main regional rival, the Palembang-based kingdom of Sriwijaya.

It is assumed that the temple ruins at Muara Jambi mark the site of Malayu's former capital, the ancient city of Jambi (known to the Chinese as Chan Pi). The Malayu sent their first delegation to China in 644 and the Chinese scholar I Tsing spent a month in Malayu in 672. When he returned 20 years later he found that Malayu had been conquered by Sriwijaya. The Sriwijayans appear to have remained in control until the sudden collapse of their empire at the beginning of the 11th century.

Following Sriwijaya's demise, Malayu re-emerged as an independent kingdom and stayed that way until it became a dependency of Java's Majapahit empire, which ruled from 1278 until 1520. It then came under the sway of the Minangkabau people of West Sumatra before 1616, when it came under the control of the Dutch East India Company, which maintained a trade monopoly here until 1901 before moving its headquarters to Palembang.

◉ Sights

★ Muara Jambi   RUINS
(5000Rp; ⊙ 7am-6pm) This scattering of ruined and partially restored temples is the most important Hindu-Buddhist site in Sumatra. The temples are believed to mark the location of the ancient city of Jambi, capital of the kingdom of Malayu 1000 years ago. Most of the *candi* (temples) date from the 9th to the 13th centuries, when Jambi's power was at its peak. Grab a bicycle (per day 10,000Rp) at the entrance to explore the immensely peaceful forested site, marvelling at the temple stonework

The forested site covers 12 sq km along the northern bank of the Batang Hari. The entrance is through an ornate archway in the village of Muara Jambi and most places of interest are within a few minutes' walk. While you can wander to most of the tem-

ORANG RIMBA

Jambi's nomadic hunter-gatherers are known by many names: outsiders refer to the diverse tribes collectively as Kubu, an unflattering term, while they refer to themselves as Orang Rimba (People of the Forest) or Anak Dalam (Children of the Forest). Descended from the first wave of Malays to migrate to Sumatra, they once lived in highly mobile groups throughout Jambi's lowland forests.

As fixed communities began to dominate the province, the Orang Rimba retained their nomadic lifestyle and animistic beliefs, regarding their neighbours' adoption of Islam and agriculture as disrespectful towards the forest. Traditionally the Orang Rimba avoided contact with the outsiders, preferring to barter and trade by leaving goods on the fringes of the forest or relying on trusted intermediaries.

In the 1960s, the Indonesian government's social affairs and religion departments campaigned to assimilate the Orang Rimba into permanent camps and convert them to a monotheistic religion. Meanwhile the jungles were being transformed into rubber and oil-palm plantations during large-scale *transmigrasi* (government-sponsored schemes to encourage settlers to move from overcrowded regions to sparsely populated ones) from Java and Bali.

Some Orang Rimba assimilated and are now economically marginalised within the plantations, while others live off government funds and then return to the forests. Just over 2000 Orang Rimba retain their traditional lifestyles within the shrinking forest. The groups were given special settlement rights within Bukit Duabelas and Bukit Tigapuluh National Parks, but the protected forests are as vulnerable to illegal logging and poaching as other Sumatran parks.

According to the NGO groups that work with the Orang Rimba, it isn't a question of if the tribes will lose their jungle traditions but when. In the spirit of practical idealism, the organisation WARSI (www.warsi.or.id) established its alternative educational outreach. Rather than forcing educational institutions on the Orang Rimba, teachers join those that will accept an outsider and teach the children how to read, write and count – the equivalent of knowing how to hunt and forage in the settled communities.

Some of the issues that continue to face Orang Rimba communities living in a concession area are decrepit government housing, a lack of cultivable land in place of the jungle that's gone, and the inability to eat certain animals because members of Orang Rimba have been encouraged to embrace Islam.

ples on foot, to get to some of the more outlying western ruins it's best to get a bike. Much of the site still needs excavating and there is some debate as to whether visitors should be allowed to clamber all over the ruins and the restored temples.

Eight temples have been identified so far, each at the centre of its own low-walled compound. Some are accompanied by *perwara candi* (smaller side temples) and three have been restored to something close to their original form. The site is dotted with numerous *menapo* (smaller brick mounds), thought to be the ruins of other buildings – possibly dwellings for priests and other high officials.

The restored temple **Candi Gumpung**, straight ahead from the donation office, has a fiendish *makara* (demon head) guarding its steps. Excavation work here has yielded some important finds, including a *peripih* (stone box) containing sheets of gold inscribed with old Javanese characters, dating the temple back to the 9th century. A statue of Prajnyaparamita found here, and other stone carvings and ceramics, are among the highlights at the small **site museum** nearby. However, the best artefacts have been taken to Jakarta.

Candi Tinggi, 200m southeast of Candi Gumpung, is the finest of the temples uncovered so far. It dates from the 9th century but is built around another, older temple. A path leads east from Candi Tinggi to **Candi Astano**, 1.5km away, passing the attractive **Candi Kembar Batu**, surrounded by palm trees, and lots of *menapo* along the way.

The temples on the western side of the site are yet to be restored. They remain pretty much as they were found – minus the jungle, which was cleared in the 1980s. The western sites are signposted from Candi Gumpung. First stop, after 900m, is **Candi Gedong I**, followed 150m further on by

Candi Gedong II. They are independent temples despite what their names may suggest. The path continues west for another 1.5km to **Candi Kedaton**, the largest of the temples, which, apart from a staircase guarded by deity statuettes, comprises just the base foundation; it's a peaceful and evocative site. A further 900m northwest is **Candi Koto Mahligai**.

For centuries the site lay abandoned and overgrown in the jungle on the banks of the Batang Hari. It was 'rediscovered' in 1920 by a British army expedition sent to explore the region. The dwellings of the ordinary Malayu people have been replaced by contemporary stilt houses of the Muara Jambi village residents. According to Chinese records, Malayu people once lived along the river in stilted houses or in raft huts moored to the bank.

There is no public transport from Jambi (26km away) to Muara Jambi. You can charter a speedboat (400,000Rp) from Jambi's river pier to the site. A Grab taxi will cost around 120,000Rp one way, or you can hire an *ojek* (50,000Rp).

Museum Siginjai   MUSEUM
(www.museumsiginjei.blogspot.com; Jl Jenderal Urip Sumoharjo; adult/child 2000/1000Rp; ⊙8am-4pm Sun-Fri) This province museum covers all aspects of Jambi's cultural heritage, and is definitely worth a visit. Exhibits in English take in Buddhist temples in Muara Jambi, the Orang Rimba ethnic group, wildlife, and traditional architecture and everyday objects. It's 4km southwest from the city centre.

☞ Tours

★ **Padmasana Foundation**   TOURS
(☑0813 6619 7841, 0852 6600 8969, 0852 6609 1459; http://padmasanafoundation.blogspot.com; tours per person from 1,250,000Rp) The Padmasana Foundation is a nonprofit organisation dedicated to the preservation and excavation of the Muara Jambi ruins, and its members work together with the local community in the village next to the ruins. Staff can provide information and arrange both tours of the site and homestays in the village.

Guntur   TOURS
(☑0813 6833 0882; tours per person from 1,250,000Rp) For tours of Muara Jambi, highly knowledgable, enthusiastic and English-speaking Guntur is the best tour guide you can find in Jambi. Rates drop substantially if you're travelling in a group. He has an in-depth knowledge of the Kerinci Valley also.

🛏 Sleeping

Hotel Fortuna   HOTEL $
(☑0741-23161; Jl Gatot Subroto 84; r 185,000Rp; ❄🛜) A reasonable budget choice, Fortuna has simple and sparsely furnished rooms, but its main advantage is the central location, concealed in a quiet retail plaza across from the Abadi Hotel. There are Chinese noodle shops nearby for a quick breakfast. Staff won't win any congeniality prizes, though. Wi-fi is in the lobby only, and it's BYO toilet paper.

Hotel Duta   BOUTIQUE HOTEL $$
(☑0741-755918; hotelduta@yahoo.com; Jl Sam Ratulangi 65-68; r incl breakfast from 380,000Rp; ❄🛜) The Duta features compact rooms with modern decor and snazzy bathrooms. Flat-screen TVs – with plenty of English-language content – and a wildly ostentatious reception area are other cosmopolitan surprises in sleepy Jambi. The hotel could do with a refurb, however. It's a short stroll to alfresco street-food treats down on the riverbank.

✖ Eating & Drinking

Kopi Tiam Oey Jambi   INDONESIAN $
(Jl Sultan Agung; mains 18,000-60,000Rp; ⊙7am-10pm; ❄🛜) Opposite Jambi's magnificent mosque is this reliable cafe that ticks all the boxes for excellent single-origin coffee, air-conditioning and wi-fi. It also does an interesting selection of Indonesian dishes from across the archipelago that you don't often see on a menu. Its decor features a weird mishmash of Chinese and British bric-a-brac.

Taman Tanggo Rajo   INDONESIAN $
(Jl Raden Pamuk; snacks from 10,000Rp; ⊙5-11pm) This is Jambi's essential evening destination for promenading along the attractive, curved pedestrian bridge across the river that lights up at night. Stalls sell local favourites, such as *nanas goreng* (fried pineapples), *jagung bakar* (roasted corn slathered with coconut milk and chilli) and different kinds of *sate*.

Sky Lounge   BAR
(12th fl, Aston Jambi Hotel, Jl Sultan Agung 99; ⊙4pm-midnight Mon-Sat; 🛜) Jambi's finest

spot for a drink is this rooftop bar atop the **Aston Jambi Hotel** (☑ 0741-33777; www. astonhotelsinternational.com). Enjoy fantastic city views while sipping on cocktails, beer or wine, or come for a meal served on the outdoor terrace or indoor lounge. It attracts an affluent crowd and has regular bands and DJs.

❶ Getting There & Away

AIR

The **Sultan Thaha Airport** (www.sultanthaha -airport.co.id) is 6km east of Jambi's centre.

BUS

Bus-ticketing offices occupy two areas of Jambi: Simpang Rimbo, 8km west of town, and Simpang Kawat, 3.5km southwest of town on Jl M Yamin.

There are frequent economy buses to Palembang. Several minibus companies, including **Ratu Intan Permata** (☑ 0741-20784; Simpang Kawat, Jl M Yamin 26), offer comfortable door-to-door minibus services to Pekanbaru, Bengkulu, Palembang and Padang. **Safa Marwa** (☑ 0741-65756; Jl Pattimura 7) runs a similar service to Sungai Penuh in the Kerinci Valley. Buses depart from the companies' offices and can also pick up passengers around town.

❶ Getting Around

Grab (p515) and Go-Jek (p515) taxis both operate in Jambi and are the best means of getting around, both in terms of cost and efficiency. Expect to pay around 30,000Rp to the airport (compared to 50,000Rp in a standard taxi).

Otherwise, *ojeks* and taxis hang around next to shopping malls. An *ojek* to the bus offices in Simpang Rimbo is around 25,000Rp. For Simpang Kawat, count on 15,000Rp.

There is no public transport to Muara Jambi. You can charter a speedboat (400,000Rp) from Jambi's river pier to the site. A Grab taxi will cost around 120,000Rp one way, or you can hire an *ojek* (50,000Rp).

SOUTH SUMATRA

The eastern portion of South Sumatra shares a common Malay ancestry and influence with Riau and Jambi provinces due to its proximity to the shipping lane of the Strait of Melaka. Rivers define the character of the eastern lowlands, while the western high peaks of the Bukit Barisan form the province's rugged underbelly. The provincial capital of Palembang was formerly the central seat of the Buddhist Sriwijaya empire, whose control once reached all the way up the Malay Peninsula.

TRANSPORT FROM JAMBI

Air

DESTINATION	AIRLINE	FREQUENCY
Bandar Lampung	Wings Air	daily
Jakarta	Batik Air, Citilink, Garuda, Lion Air, Sriwijaya Air	14 daily
Medan	Wings Air	daily
Padang	Wings Air	daily
Palembang	Garuda, Wings Air	2 daily
Pekanbaru	Wings Air	daily
Pulau Batam	Lion Air, Sriwijaya Air	1-2 daily
Sungai Penuh (Kerinci)	Wings Air	daily

Bus

DESTINATION	FARE (RP)	DURATION (HR)	FREQUENCY
Bengkulu	180,000	10	several daily
Padang	120,000-190,000	11	2 daily
Palembang	120,000	7	several daily
Pekanbaru	150,000-190,000	12	daily
Sungai Penuh	150,000	8	10 daily

Despite the province's illustrious past, it's rather light on attractions, except for the hospitality that occurs in places where bilingual Indonesians don't get a lot of opportunity to practise their English, as well as the stunning scenery of the Pasemah Highlands.

Palembang

☑ 0711 / POP 1.7 MILLION

Sumatra's second-largest city is a major port that sits astride the Sungai Musi, the two halves of the city linked by the giant Jembatan Ampera (Ampera Bridge). While these days it's just another regular large Indonesian city, blighted by traffic jams and pollution, it does have a fascinating history as one of Southeast Asia's oldest cities. A thousand years ago Palembang was the capital of the highly developed Sriwijaya civilisation that ruled a huge slab of Southeast Asia, covering most of Sumatra, the Malay Peninsula, southern Thailand and Cambodia. Few relics from the period now remain outside the city museum.

While it's far from being an essential stop, if you're passing overland through the Pasemah Highlands or Jambi, Palembang is enough off the tourist radar to give it some appeal. Food is another reason to visit, with the city's spicy fare the subject of much debate (positive and negative) in Sumatra.

◉ Sights

Balaputra Dewa Museum   MUSEUM
(Museum Negeri Balaputra Dewa; ☑ 0711-412636; Jl Sriwijaya 1, Km5.5; 2000Rp; ⊗ 8.30am-3.30pm Tue-Fri, to 2pm Sat & Sun) This excellent museum showcases finds from Sriwijayan times, as well as megalithic carvings from the Pasemah Highlands, including the famous *batu gajah* (elephant stone). Other worthwhile displays include a rich collection of finely woven *songkets,* and coverage from more recent periods of rule including the Palembang sultanate, Dutch colonisation and Japanese WWII occupation. Behind the museum is a magnificent original *rumah limas* (traditional house) dating from 1830, which is featured on the 10,000Rp banknote.

**Sultan Mahmud
Badaruddin II Museum**   MUSEUM
(Jl Sultan Mahmud Badarudin 19; 5000Rp; ⊗ 8am-4pm Mon-Fri, 9am-3pm Sat & Sun) Along the banks of the Sungai Musi is this museum inside an attractive 19th-century building that incorporates a mix of European and local architectural styles. It was built in 1825 on the site of the palace of Sultan Mahmud Badaruddin, which was destroyed by the Dutch (who in doing so put an end to the Palembang Sultanate). The museum covers the city's packed history, from the Sriwijayan dynasty through to the sultanate period, and traditional South Sumatran artefacts.

🎇 Festivals & Events

Bidar Race   SPORTS
(⊗ 16 Jun & 17 Aug) *Bidar* (canoe) races are held on the Sungai Musi in the middle of town every 16 June (Palembang's birthday) and 17 August (Independence Day). A *bidar* is about 25m long and 1m wide and is powered by up to 60 rowers.

TRANSPORT FROM PALEMBANG

Bus

DESTINATION	FARE (RP)	DURATION (HR)	FREQUENCY
Bandar Lampung	200,000-230,000	10	2 daily
Bengkulu	220,000	8	several daily
Jakarta	250,000	15	1 daily
Jambi	70,000-150,000	6	several daily
Lahat	100,000	4-5	hourly

Train

DESTINATION	FARE (RP)	DURATION (HR)	FREQUENCY
Bandar Lampung	32,000-200,000	9-10	8.30pm & 9pm daily
Lahat	32,000-200,000	4	9.30am & 8pm daily
Lubuklinggau	32,000-200,000	7	9.30am & 8pm daily

🛏 Sleeping

MaxOne Hotels@
Vivo Palembang
DESIGN HOTEL **$$**

(📞 0711-817788; www.maxonepalembang.com; Jl R Soekamto RT 17; r from 289,000Rp; ❄ 🛜) Decorated in pop-art motifs and equipped with all your modern needs, this contemporary design hotel is a steal. Its attractive rooms are spacious and have comfy, large beds laden with pillows, along with cable TV. The lobby cafe is a bit soulless, but there's a massive shopping mall next door for food and more.

🍴 Eating & Drinking

Pempek Mei Hwa Cinde
INDONESIAN **$**

(http://pempek-mei-hua.business.site; Jl Letnan Jaimas 722; mains 20,000Rp; ⏲ 7.30am-5pm) Sneakily hidden away down a narrow side street, next to the lively produce market, is this pastel-pink warung that's always busy with locals stocking up on takeway *pempek* (fishcake made using tapioca). It's a good place to sample this Palembang specialty, with a range of *pempek* dishes including *pempek Lenggang*, which is filled with fried egg.

Rumah Makan Pindang
Musi Rawas
INDONESIAN **$**

(Jl Angkatan 45 18; mains from 40,000Rp; ⏲ 9am-9pm) A short ride northwest of the centre, this nondescript-looking restaurant is locally famous for its *pindang patin*, a spicy, sour, clear soup with patin fish. Other dishes are also sound ambassadors of southern Sumatran cuisine. A numbered system is used for queuing when the place gets busy.

Black Bulls
PUB

(www.black-bulls.business.site; Jl Abusamah 22; ⏲ 4pm-2am) One of Palembang's few options for a drink is this fairly uninspired Hard Rock Cafe–style bar in the north of town. It has a stage for live music and long tables for beers (small/large 30,000/67,000Rp), pricey cocktails (115,000Rp) and pub food.

❶ Getting There & Away

AIR
Sultan Badaruddin II Airport is 12km north of town. There are frequent daily flights to major towns in Sumatra and Java, as well as to Singapore and Malaysia.

BUS
The Karyajaya Bus Terminal is 12km from the town centre, but most companies have ticket offices on Jl Kol Atmo. Here you'll also find door-to-door minibus agents' offices.

EATING THE PALEMBANG WAY

Palembang fare is distinguished by its use of the infamously smelly durian that sends some folks running. The best-known dishes are *ikan brengkes* (fish served with a spicy durian-based sauce) and *pindang* (a spicy, clear fish soup). Another Palembang specialty is *pempek*, a mixture of sago, fish, tapioca and seasoning that is formed into balls and deep-fried or grilled. Served with a spicy sauce, *pempek* is widely available from street stalls and warungs.

Palembang food is normally served with a range of accompaniments. The main one is *sambal tempoyak*, a combination of fermented durian, *sambal terasi* (shrimp paste), lime juice and chilli that is mixed up and added to the rice. *Sambal buah* (fruit-based sambal), made with pineapple or sliced green mangoes, is also popular.

TRAIN
Stasiun Kertapati train station is 8km from the city centre on the southern side of the river.

❶ Getting Around
Grab (p515) and Go-Jek (p515) online taxis both operate in the city, and are the best option to get around if you have a smartphone.

Otherwise *angkot* trips around town cost a standard 3500Rp. They leave from around the huge roundabout at the junction of Jl Sudirman and Jl Merdeka. Any *angkot* marked 'Karyajaya' (5500Rp) will get you to the bus terminal. Any *angkot* marked 'Kertapati' (5500Rp) will get you to the train station. A taxi from the station to the town centre should cost around 80,000Rp.

Taxis to the airport cost around 120,000Rp.

LAMPUNG

At the very tip of this bow-shaped landmass is Sumatra's southernmost province, which was not given provincial status by Jakarta until 1964. Although the Lampungese have had a long history as a distinct culture, Jakarta's gravitational force has been altering Lampung's independent streak – largely in the form of the *transmigrasi* policies, designed to off-load excess population and turn a profit in the wilds of Sumatra.

Outside the provincial capital of Bandar Lampung, the province's robust coffee

PASEMAH HIGHLANDS

The Pasemah Highlands, tucked away in the Bukit Barisan west of Lahat, are famous for the mysterious megalithic monuments that dot the landscape. The stones have been dated back about 3000 years, but little else is known about them or the civilisation that carved them. While the museums of Palembang and Jakarta now house the pick of the stones, there are still plenty left in situ. Many are tricky to find, and you'll need your own transport (a guide isn't a bad idea either), but a large part of the appeal is being out in the beautiful countryside with Gunung Dempo looming in the background.

The main town of the highlands is Pagaralam, a fairly gritty city located 68km (two hours by bus) southwest of the Trans-Sumatran Hwy town of Lahat. Here you'll find ATMs, lodgings, restaurants, tour guides and general supplies.

If you're looking for a guide, get in touch with **Yayan Andriawan** (☏ 0822 7921 5310; yayanbaru131@yahoo.com), a Pagaralam-based guide specialising in trips to Dempo (one day/one night 500,000Rp) and surrounding megalithic sites (one day 300,000Rp). Motorbike hire is additional (around 60,000Rp if you bargain hard).

Batu Gajah (Elephant Stone) Just 3km south of Pagaralam, by the village of Berlumai, are these stone carvings scattered among an idyllic countryside of rice paddies and coffee plantations, with Gunung Dempo rising in the background. There's a remarkable collection of stone carvings among the paddies near Tanjung Aru. Look out for the one of a man fighting a giant serpent.

Batu Beribu In Tegurwangi, about 8km from Pagaralam on the road to Tanjung Sakti, Batu Beribu is the home of a cluster of four squat statues that sit under a small shelter by a stream. The site guardian will wander over and lead you to some nearby dolmen-style stone tombs. You can still make out a painting of three women and a dragon in one of them.

Tinggi Hari Tinggi Hari, 20km from Lahat, west of the small river town of Pulau Pinang, is a site featuring the best examples of early prehistoric stone sculpture in Indonesia. The Pasemah carvings fall into two distinct styles. The early style dates from around 3000 years ago and features fairly crude figures squatting with hands on knees or arms folded over chests. The later style, incorporating expressive facial features, dates from about 2000 years ago and is far more elaborate.

Gunung Dempo Gunung Dempo is a semi-active volcano and the highest (3159m) of the peaks surrounding the Pasemah Highlands that dominate Pagaralam. Allow two full days to complete a climb of the the volcano. A guide, such as Yayan Andriawan, is strongly recommended as trails can be difficult to find. The lower slopes are used as a tea-growing area, and there are *angkot* from Pagaralam to a tea factory.

Hotel Mirasa (☏ 0852 678 4684, 0730-621266; Jl Muhammad Nuh 80; r incl breakfast 130,000-200,000Rp; 🖥) Along the main Pagaralam thoroughfare is this run-down roadside motel with a range of rather musty rooms to choose from. You'll need to bring your own toilet paper and towel. The English-speaking manager can organise transport or guides to climb Gunung Dempo. The hotel is on the edge of town, about 2km from the bus terminal, and has a good view of the volcano.

Getting There & Away

Pagaralam's airport is 25km east of town, with direct flights from Palembang with Wings Air. A taxi from the airport is around 50,000Rp.

Every bus travelling along the Trans-Sumatran Hwy calls in at Lahat, nine hours northwest of Bandar Lampung and 12 hours southeast of Padang. There are regular buses to Lahat from Palembang (70,000Rp to 150,000Rp, four to five hours), and the town is a stop on the train line from Palembang to Lubuklinggau.

There are frequent small buses between Lahat and Pagaralam (30,000Rp, two hours). There are *opelet* (minibuses) to the villages near Pagaralam from the town centre's *stasiun taksi* (taxi station); all local services cost 3000Rp.

plantations dominate the economy and the unclaimed forests, closely followed by timber, pepper, rubber and the ever-increasing territory of oil-palm plantations.

Today many Jakarta weekenders hop over to tour the Krakatau volcano or visit the elephants of Way Kambas National Park. The rugged western seaboard is ostensibly protected as the Bukit Barisan Selatan National Park. On this west coast are some of Sumatra's best waves, luring surfers from around the world.

History

Long before Jakarta became the helm of this island chain, there's evidence that Lampung was part of the Palembang-based Sriwijayan empire until the 11th century, when the Jambi-based Malayu kingdom became the dominant regional power.

Megalithic remains at Pugungraharjo, on the plains to the east of Bandar Lampung, are thought to date back more than 1000 years and point to a combination of Hindu and Buddhist influences. The site is believed to have been occupied until the 16th century.

Lampung has long been famous for its prized pepper crop, which attracted the West Javanese sultanate of Banten to the area at the beginning of the 16th century and the Dutch East India Company in the late 17th century.

The Dutch finally took control of Lampung in 1856 and launched the first of the *transmigrasi* schemes that sought to ease the chronic overcrowding in Java and Bali.

Tanjung Setia & Krui

✎ 0728

Offering some of Sumatra's best and most accessible waves, the shores north and south of Krui's meandering coastline are dotted with surf breaks that are gaining more international recognition by the year. The surf season generally runs from April to October.

Most of the action is focused on the village of Tanjung Setia, 25km south of Krui. While surfers still make up 99% of the tourist traffic, the area's laconic and laid-back buzz is also perfect if you're overlanding to Java down Sumatra's south coast. Nonsurfers can try the sandy beaches along the coastline just south of Krui, which also has some beginner beach breaks.

Around midway between Bengkulu and Bandar Lampung, Tanjung Setia is a good

spot to relax and recharge after one too many long Sumatran bus journeys. It can also be used as a base to explore Bukit Barisan Selatan National Park.

🏃 Activities

Hello Mister ADVENTURE SPORTS
(✎ 0813 7365 8927, 0852 6928 7811; kruimotorent@gmail.com) Get in touch with the wisecracking Albert at Hello Mister in Tanjung Setia for everything from bus transport to Krui or Bandar Lampung and motorbike rental (60,000Rp per day) to jungle tours and surf lessons (200,000Rp per day) on more forgiving beach breaks towards Krui village. He can also arrange longer day trips south to the Bukit Barisan Selatan National Park.

🛏 Sleeping & Eating

Rumah Radja Losmen BUNGALOW $
(✎ 0813 6757 3778; earthcraft40@gmail.com; Tanjung Setia; r incl breakfast 200,000Rp; ❋ 🤶) This tranquil place, past Damai Bungalows, is run by friendly Aussie surfer Murray. Lodgings consist of a couple of comfy bungalows that catch the breeze. Breakfast is the only meal available but there's the bonus of a guest kitchen for those who want to surf rather than be tied to a feeding schedule.

★ Damai Bungalows BUNGALOW $$
(✎ 0822 7992 4449; www.damaibungalows.com; Jl Pantai Wisata, Tanjung Setia; r incl meals 350,000Rp; ❋ 🤶 🏊) Leafy gardens, fan-cooled bungalows with private outdoorsy bathrooms, the best surfer-lodge food and friendly underfoot dogs are the defining features of this chilled-out place. There's excellent service from the Aussie-Indonesian owners, and the bar – with quite possibly Sumatra's coldest beer – provides front-row views of the iconic Karang Nyimbor left-hander. Damai is often booked by groups, but individual guests are welcome.

★ Lovina Krui Surf BUNGALOW $$
(✎ 0821 8605 3980, 0853 7780 2212; www.lovinakruisurf.com; Jl Pantai Wisata, Tanjung Setia; r incl meals with fan/air-con 385,000/450,000Rp; ❋ @ 🤶 🏊) Run by laid-back husband-and-wife team Yoris and Fransiska, this original, lovingly designed spot has rooms inside a number of traditional Sumatran-style buildings. It has modern air-con rooms too, with hot water and cable TV. It's a casual hang-out with wi-fi, good travel advice, and a great bar with a pool table and seriously cold beer pulled from a freezer.

Amy's Place
RESORT $$

(www.amys-sumatra.com; Jl Pantai Wisata, Krui; per person incl meals US$65; 🛜🏊) Set up by expat American surfer gal and host Amy, this purpose-built surf resort on a garden property overlooks the waves. She goes to great lengths to keep rooms immaculate and comfortable, plus there's a pool, beachside deck for beers and a bohemian dining space for communal meals. It's located 3km south of Krui, with a heap of surf spots within close range.

Lani's Resto
INTERNATIONAL $$

(Jl Pantai Wisata, Tanjung Setia; mains from 60,000Rp; ⏲11am-7pm Mon-Sat Mar-Oct) The foil to Tanjung Setia's warungs, this stylish joint is run by a Hawaiian-Californian expat who serves all the comfort food you've been craving after a day out on the waves: tacos, burgers, pizza and cold beer. A lot of the food is proudly made from scratch, including the ice cream.

The views from its upstairs accommodation, **Lani's** (📱0821 1176 5964; r 450,000Rp; ❄@🛜), is impressive.

ℹ️ Information

Wi-fi is prevalent in the guesthouses in Tanjung Setia.

There are ATMs in Krui, but not in Tanjung Setia.

ℹ️ Getting There & Away

Buses between Bengkulu (250,000Rp, 10 hours, several daily) and Bandar Lampung (65,000Rp to 200,000Rp, seven to eight hours, several daily) will stop on request at Tanjung Setia. A private transfer to/from Bandar Lampung's airport is around 900,000Rp.

Bandar Lampung

📱0721 / POP 1,250,000

Perched on the hills overlooking Teluk Lampung, Bandar Lampung is Lampung's largest city and its administrative capital. Though it's a pretty scrappy and congested town, its surrounds are picturesque and it has some interesting sights, friendly locals, and contemporary cafes and pubs to while away a few hours. It's also a good launching point for trips to Way Kambas National Park or Krakatau; however, most travellers visit en route to/from Java.

👁️ Sights

Lampung Provincial Museum
MUSEUM

(Jl Pagar Alam 64; adult/child 4000/500Rp; ⏲8am-2pm Sat-Thu, to 10.30am Fri) Housed in an imposing building that incorporates a traditional design, the Lampung Provincial Museum is a bit of a mixed bag. It covers everything from neolithic relics to stuffed animals, with standout pieces from the Sriwijayan-empire era. It's 5km north of central Bandar Lampung; take a grey *angkot* (4000Rp) or Go-Jek (around 3000Rp).

Vihara Thay Hin Bio
BUDDHIST TEMPLE

(Jl Ikan Kakap 35; ⏲6am-5pm) Standing as a prominent landmark with its ornate, red-tiled Chinese gate is this attractive Buddhist temple that dates to the late 19th century. Inside it's equally atmospheric, with burning incense, candles and lanterns scattered among the ornamental pillars, Buddhist statues and intricate wood panels.

Krakatau Monument
MONUMENT

(Jl Veteran) The Krakatau monument is a lasting memorial to the force of the 1883 eruption and resulting tidal wave. Almost half of the 36,000 victims died in the 40m-high wave that funnelled up Teluk Lampung and devastated Telukbetung. The 19th-century huge steel maritime buoy that now comprises the monument was washed out of Teluk Lampung and deposited on this hillside.

🧭 Tours

Arie Tour & Travel
TRAVEL AGENCY

(📱0721-474675; www.arietour.com; Jl W Monginsidi 143; ⏲8am-9pm Mon-Fri, 9am-4pm Sat & Sun) A helpful travel agency located outside the city centre. Trips to Gunung Krakatau, Way Kambas and Bukit Barisan Selatan National Parks can be booked here, though it's fairly pricey.

🛏️ Sleeping

⭐ Flip Flop Hostel
HOSTEL $

(📱0813 6924 0888; Jl Pulau Sebuku 9; dm 98,000Rp; r 189,000-200,000Rp; ❄🛜) One of south Sumatra's best hostels, Flip Flop is an immaculate multilevel space that's lovingly decorated with vibrant furnishings, murals and pot plants. Private rooms have homely touches, while air-conditioned dorms are spotless and have their own bathrooms. The staff are lovely, and the lobby cafe does specialty coffees and Indonesian dishes. Upstairs there's terrace seating and a rooftop hang-out.

POP! Hotel Tanjung Karang
DESIGN HOTEL $$

(📱0721-241742; www.pophotels.com; Jl W Monginsidi 56; r without/with breakfast 298,000/318,000Rp; ♿❄@🛜) POP! is as subtle as the

Bandar Lampung

giant exclamation mark decorating the side
of the building. The decor is Google meets
pop art, the staff are young and helpful and
the strange airplane-like bathroom cubicles
feature powerful showers.

Emersia Hotel & Resort RESORT **$$$**
(☏0721-258258; www.emersiahotel.com; Jl W
Monginsidi 70; r/ste incl breakfast from 645,000/
1,645,000Rp; ❋ ⚹ ⚹) If you're completing
your Sumatran odyssey and wish to wash the
dust of the island off your feet, one of Bandar
Lampung's most luxurious hotels may be just
the place for it. Its elevated location means
that the best rooms and suites feature sea
views. There's a spa for pampering, a swimming
pool and a decent restaurant and cafe.

✗ Eating & Drinking

Pempek 123 SEAFOOD **$**
(Jl Ikan Belanak 15; per piece 5000Rp; ⊘8.30am-
6pm) Tucked down a residential side street
on the ground floor of an apartment build-
ing, this local haunt is a favourite for *pempek*
(deep-fried fish cake made using tapioca).
There's an array of choices, all accompanied
with soy sauce and sambal, but for some-
thing with more varied flavour go for the
tekwan (*pempek* mixed with noodles, soup
and greens).

Its shelves are lined with dried fish
snacks, condiments and local coffee beans
for purchase. It's a short walk from the
Krakatau Monument.

Kopi Oey INTERNATIONAL **$**
(www.kopioey.com; Jl W Monginsidi 56; mains
from 30,000Rp; ⊘8am-midnight; ⚹) With its
birdcage lights, outdoor terrace and Shang-
hai glamour posters, this offshoot of the
Jakarta-based empire conjures up an old-
world vibe. The menu runs the gamut from
fusion (spicy tuna spaghetti) to Javanese
classics (sweet-and-spicy lamb *tongseng*)
and *cap cai* (mixed vegetables) rice. It does
good breakfasts, filtered coffees and a more

eclectic range of beverages (egg coffee, iced grass jelly, hot turmeric).

Nudi
PUB

(☎ 0721-482738; www.nudieatdrinkleisure.com; Jl Gatot Subroto 16; ⊙ 9am-midnight; ☎) In a town where a beer isn't always easy to find, this spot is a bit of an oasis, opening up to a smart, leafy decor where you can prop up a stool at the bar and order a pint from its frosty taps. Otherwise grab a booth and a cocktail, or head to the rear dining area for pub food and Indonesian mains.

Flambojan
COFFEE

(Jl Flamboyan; ⊙ 8am-10pm; ☎) Comprising no more than a couple of chairs, a turntable and a cassette deck, this hipster coffee shop specialises in beans from across Sumatra. Get a takeaway or grab a seat out front to enjoy its pour-over filter brews, cold drip or a latte.

🛍 Shopping

Lampung produces weavings known as ship cloths (most feature ships), which use rich reds and blues to create primitive-looking geometric designs. Another type is *kain tapis*, a ceremonial cloth elaborately embroidered with gold thread.

ℹ Information

ATMs dot central Bandar Lampung.

ℹ Getting There & Away

AIR

Raden Inten II Airport (☎ 0721-769 7114) is 24km north of the city. There are numerous daily flights to Jakarta and Yogyakarta, as well Sumatra's major cities, but no direct flights to Medan.

BUS

Bandar Lampung's **Rajabasa Bus Terminal** is 10km north of town and serves long-distance destinations.

Damri (☎ 0751-780 6335, 0813 7929 0146) has bus-boat combination tickets that are the most convenient option for heading to Jakarta (160,000Rp to 235,000Rp, eight to 10 hours). Its buses leave from outside Bandar Lampung's train station at 8am, 9am, 10am, 8pm, 9pm and 10pm, shuttling passengers to the Bakauheni pier and then picking them up at Java's Merak pier for the final transfer to Jakarta's train station.

TRAIN

Tanjung Karang is the main station in the town centre; it's at the northern mouth of Jl Raden Intan. There are morning and overnight departures to Palembang (economy/business/executive 32,000/160,000/215,000Rp; nine to 10 hours) leaving at 8.30am and 9pm. It's also possible to take a train to Lahat for the Pasemah Highlands, but this involves an inconvenient change at Prabumulih.

ℹ Getting Around

From Bandar Lampung's airport, taxis charge around 130,000Rp for the ride into town. Go-Jek (p515) and Grab (p515) online taxis are the cheapest and fastest way to get around town. Otherwise all *angkot* pass through Jl Raden Intan and the standard fare around town is 5000Rp.

Way Kambas National Park

Way Kambas National Park (foreigner entrance fee 150,000Rp, ranger fee 300,000Rp) is one of the oldest reserves in Indonesia. It occupies 1300 sq km of coastal lowland forest around Sungai Way Kambas on the east coast of Lampung. What little remains of the heavily logged forests is home to endangered species of elephants, rhinos and tigers.

It is believed that around 180 wild Sumatran elephants (*Elephas maximus sumatrensis*) live in the park, but reliable

BUSES FROM BANDAR LAMPUNG

DESTINATION	FARE (RP)	DURATION (HR)	FREQUENCY
Bengkulu	150,000-350,000	18	several daily
Bukittinggi	350,000-450,000	24-30	daily
Jakarta	145,000-175,000	8-10	several daily
Kota Agung	25,000-30,000	3	several daily
Krui	65,000-200,000	7-8	several daily
Padang	350,000-450,000	21	daily
Palembang	150,000-250,000	12	2 daily
Way Kambas	40,000	4-5	several daily

estimates are uncertain and poaching and development pressures are constant. Another rare but endemic creature in Way Kambas is the Sumatran rhino, the only two-horned rhino of the Asian species; its hide is red in colour with a hairy coat. However sightings of it are *extremely* rare, as is spotting the Sumatran tiger, the other celebrity animal in the park.

Tourist facilities within the park are limited. About 13km from its entrance, on the main road, is the township, where there are lodgings and simple food options.

🏃 Activities

Satwa Elephant Ecolodge is the main tour operator to arrange trips into Way Kambas National Park. Their offerings include half-day safaris in open-air African-style jeeps (300,000Rp), night walks, boat trips on Sungai Way Kanan and surrounding waterways, and overnight camping trips.

Wildlife Watching

While short visits can be a wonderful way to experience the habitat of Way Kambas National Park, don't expect to see more than primates, deer and birdlife. For those serious about wildlife-watching you will need to allow at least three days to explore the park properly and to gain a full appreciation for its biodiversity. Be aware that on weekends the park is popular with domestic tourists taking a break from the concrete confines of Jakarta.

Herds of Sumatran elephant (a subspecies of the Asian elephant and found only in Sumatra and Kalimantan) are seen in the national park from time to time, but sightings of the Sumatran rhino and tiger are extremely rare, and only possible if you spend time deep inside the park. The most commonly spotted animals on a tour include the siamang, agile gibbon, white-handed gibbon, civet, sambar and barking deer. The park is also home to the tapir, dhole, sun bear, clouded leopard, tarsier, slow loris, porcupine, flying squirrel and gharial.

The park contains the Sumatran Rhino Sanctuary (www.rhinos.org), where seven rhinos formerly held in captivity have been introduced to wild surroundings in the hope of successful breeding, with each assigned a team of keepers to look after their health and nutritional needs. The Sumatran rhino is a solitary animal and its habitat in the wild is so fractured that conservationists fear the species will die out without intervention. Breeding centres for rhinos are a controversial component of species-protection campaigns as they are expensive to maintain and have reported few successful births. For more information, visit the website of the International Rhino Foundation (www.rhinos-irf.org), one of the lead organisations involved with the centre and wtih antipoaching patrols in the park. It's estimated that fewer than 30 wild Sumatran rhinos still survive within Way Kambas.

The area around Way Kanan, a subdistrict of the park, is frequently visited by birdwatchers, and has more than 400-plus species, with the white-winged duck, Storm's stork and hornbill being particularly sought after by twitchers.

While the Elephant Conversation Centre inside the park provides an important role in supporting orphaned and conflict elephants, it's not advised to ride them or participate in any hands-on activities.

🛏 Sleeping

By far the best place to stay is Satwa Elephant Ecolodge, just outside the park's entrance. There are also local homestay options in Plangijo village.

Camping on overnight safaris inside the park can be arranged through Satwa Elephant Ecolodge.

Satwa Elephant Ecolodge COTTAGE $$
(☐0725-764 5290, 0812 399 5212; www.ecolodges indonesia.com; Jl Taman Nasional Way Kambas, Plangijo; s/d incl breakfast US$55/60; 🐾) 🌿 This delightful, accredited ecolodge is located in Plangijo village 500m from Way Kambas National Park's entrance. Its spacious cottages are scattered through the lodge's leafy orchard of tropical fruit trees, and activities include jeep safaris, nature walks and river trips through the forest. The lodge is also popular with birdwatchers.

It caters to short-term visitors as well as offering a range of packages aimed at those more serious about wildlife spotting, which involves more time. Cash only.

ℹ Getting There & Away

The entrance to Way Kambas is 110km from Bandar Lampung. Take the bus from Bandar Lampung's Rajabasa Bus Terminal to Jepara and get off at Pasar Tridatu (50,000Rp, two hours), from where you'll need to take an *ojek* (20,000Rp) the rest of the way.

A day trip to Way Kambas costs around US$155 per person (minimum two people) and can be arranged through Arie Tour & Travel (p602) in Bandar Lampung or with tour operators in Jakarta.

Gunung Krakatau

The stuff of legends, Krakatau remains one of the world's most well-known volcanoes due to its infamous 19th-century eruption. When it blew its top in 1883 it may have come closer to destroying the planet than any other volcano in recent history. Tens of thousands were killed, either by the resulting tidal wave or by the pyroclastic flows that crossed 40km of ocean to incinerate Sumatran coastal villages. Its explosion was so violent it's still regarded as the loudest noise *ever* recorded; it was heard as far away as Perth, Australia. Afterwards all that was left was a smouldering caldera where a cluster of uninhabited islands had once been. Perhaps peace had come, thought local villagers. But Krakatau, like all scrappy villains, re-awoke in 1927 and resulting eruptions created a new volcanic cone, since christened Anak Krakatau (Child of Krakatau). On 22 December 2018 disaster struck again, with its eruption causing some 430 deaths from an ensuing tsunami devastating the coastal villages facing the Sunda Strait in both Sumatra and Java.

It's estimated that Anak Krakatau is growing by around 7m every year.

◉ Sights

Krakatau (often mispelt as Krakatoa) these days comprises a chain of four islands, of which the main attraction is Anak Krakatau – an active (and often very volatile) volcano. Boats disembark here, allowing you to scramble up its outer cone, but be aware that when the volcano is rumbling, ascents to the crater are forbidden. Try to check independently whether Krakatau is off limits by asking locals, checking news reports or visiting www.volcanodiscovery.com for up-to-date seismic activity. You'll also get to visit several of the nearby volcanic islands, including Rakata (Greater Krakatau), a fragment from the 1883 explosion, but now dormant. There's also some good snorkelling.

Most tourists visit Krakatau as a day trip, taking around three to four hours one way from Canti. Inclement weather can bring cancellations, and since seas can often be rough, it's best to arrange a lifejacket (which is often in the form of an inflatable tyre!).

🍴 Sleeping & Eating

Overnight trips to Krakatau involve camping on the island, but if you're day tripping there are sleeping options in the harbour town of Canti or nearby Kalianda. If you're OK with an early rise then Bandar Lampung is also possible. There are also basic losmen on nearby Pulau Sebesi, which is accessible by public boat.

For the volcano trip you'll need to bring your own food and water. At the harbour there are rows of simple shack restaurants doing basic *mie goreng* and nasi goreng options. Nearby Munca Indah also serves meals.

Hotel Beringin GUESTHOUSE **$**
(☑ 0857 6980 0079, 0727-322008; Jl Kusuma Bangsa 76, Kalianda; r 150,000-230,000Rp; ❋ 🛜) Located in the laid-back, attractive town of Kalianda, Beringin offers a handy base for those heading to Krakatau. It's in an appealing Dutch colonial villa, with a rather refined dining area, and air-conditioned rooms that are tidy, spacious and feature vibrant wallpaper, TVs and local-style toilets. Wi-fi is only in the common area. From here it's a 30-minute drive to the harbour in Canti.

Very limited English is spoken here.

Munca Indah VILLA **$$**
(☑ 0853 7927 0711; Jl Pesisir Raya, Canti; r 300,000-350,000Rp) This fairly scrappy property is one of the few options for staying in Canti, with overpriced villa-style rooms that cater more to the needs of local tourists. There's a restaurant (mains from 11,000Rp), and a viewing deck looking out to Krakatau's islands in the distance. They can arrange camping trips on an island near the volcano for 2,500,000Rp.

❶ Information

The closest ATM to Canti is in Kalianda, 7km away.

❶ Getting There & Away

Trips to Krakatau launch from West Java (p87) or from Canti on the Sumatran coast. Organised day trips with Arie Tour & Travel (p602) in Bandar Lampung cost around US$400 per person (based on two people).

For solo travellers, the best way to visit Krakatau is to join one of the existing tours that set out from the fishing village of Canti, located outside of Kalianda; weekends are your best bet.

Otherwise you'll have to charter your own boat (around 1,500,000Rp return), or you can take a public boat to Pulau Sebesi (20,000Rp, 2½ hours), from where boat charters will be even cheaper for the remaining two-hour trip. Canti was badly damaged by the tsunami in late 2018, including its main pier.

Kalianda is reachable with the frequent local buses from Bandar Lampung's Rajabasa Bus Terminal (27,000Rp, 2½ hours). Then you'll have to take an *ojek* to Canti (15,000Rp, 35 minutes) or an infrequent *angkot*.

Bukit Barisan Selatan National Park

At the southern tip of Sumatra, Bukit Barisan Selatan National Park comprises one of the island's last stands of lowland forests. For this reason the World Wildlife Fund has ranked it as one of the planet's most biologically outstanding habitats and is working to conserve the park's remaining Sumatran rhinos and tigers; it is also identified as the most important forest area for tiger conservation in the world. The park is also famous for many endemic bird species that prefer foothill climates, and several species of sea turtle that nest along the park's coastal zone.

Of the 3560 sq km originally designated as protected, less than 3240 sq km remain untouched. The usual suspects are responsible: illegal logging, illegal encroachment of coffee, pepper and other plantations, and poachers.

Tourist infrastructure in the park is very limited, bordering on nonexistent. An organised tour is your best bet; these can be arranged in Kota Agung or Krui.

Kantor Taman Nasional Bukit Barisan Selatan (☑0813 1011 1423, 0812 6036 3409; Jl Juanda 19; ☺8.30am-4pm Mon-Fri) sells permits for the park (weekdays/weekends 155,000/257,000Rp including insurance) and can arrange guides (150,000Rp per day) and provide trekking information; ask for Latief, who speaks excellent English. Note that permits here are only available Monday to Friday; on weekends you'll have to head to the Sedaya park office, which is open 8am to noon.

There are several basic guesthouses in Kota Agung and along the coast. Staying in Krui is also a possibility, from where you can visit the park on a day trip. There's a basic guesthouse (150,000Rp to 200,000Rp) in the actual park too, which you can book through the Kantor Taman Nasional Bukit Barisan Selatan office in Kota Agung.

❶ Getting There & Away

The main access point into Bukit Barisan Selatan National Park is through the town of Kota Agung, 80km west of Bandar Lampung.

There are frequent buses from Bandar Lampung to Kota Agung (25,000Rp to 30,000Rp, three hours).

From Bandar Lampung, Arie Tour & Travel (p602) can arrange tours for US$155 per person (for a group of two people). In Krui, Hello Mister (p601) offers a more affordable option by motorbike (around 400,000Rp). From Kota Agung expect to pay around 750,000Rp to rent a car and driver to explore the national park; this can be arranged through the park office, Kantor Taman Nasional Bukit Barisan Selatan.

Floating markets (p635), Banjarmasin
AZHAR ASKARI/SHUTTERSTOCK ©

Kalimantan

Kalimantan – the expansive Indonesian part of Borneo – is an adventure in every sense of the word. Remote jungle, snaking rivers and interior mountains serve up endless opportunities for epic rainforest exploration, while its cities are low-key and little visited by Indonesian standards. You can travel here for weeks without meeting another foreigner.

Kalimantan's natural resources have made it a prime target for exploitation and its once-abundant wildlife and rich traditional cultures are under threat. Protected areas mean this is still the best place in the world to see the noble orang-utan sharing the remaining jungle canopy with acrobatic gibbons and proboscis monkeys. The indigenous Dayak people have long lived in concert with this rich, challenging landscape and their longhouses can still be found near Kalimantan's many waterways, creating a sense of community unmatched elsewhere in the country.

Kalimantan Highlights

1 Cross-Borneo Trek (p613) Completing the landmark hike and river journeys – if you can.

2 Tanjung Puting National Park (p625) Meeting orang-utans and sailing Sungai Sekonyer.

3 Derawan Archipelago (p657) Diving into Kalimantan's best underwater and island life.

4 Sungai Mahakam (p648) Taking the slow boat.

5 Balikpapan (p640) Living it up with live music, shopping and fine dining.

6 Merabu (p656) Delving into Kalimantan's near and distant past.

7 Loksado (p639) Bamboo river rafting and settling into mountain village life.

8 Sukadana (p623) Taking the speedboat from Pontianak then spotting wild orang-utans in Gunung Palung National Park.

9 Banjarmasin (p635) Rising early for the floating markets.

10 Putussibau (p621) Visiting Dayak longhouses and remote national parks.

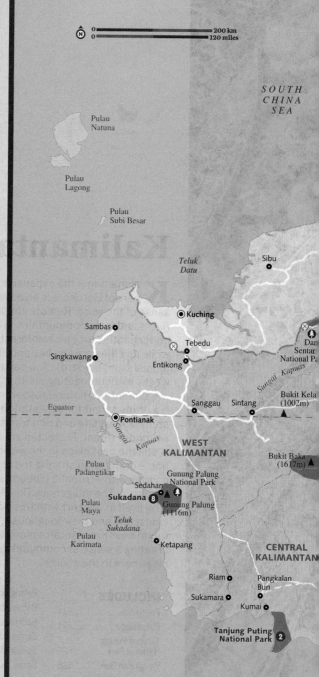

SOUTH
CHINA
SEA

Pulau
Natuna

Pulau
Lagong

Pulau
Subi Besar

*Teluk
Datu*

Sibu

⊙ Kuching

Sambas ⊙

Tebedu

Singkawang ⊙

Entikong

Dan
Sentar
National Pa

Sungai Kapuas

Bukit Kela
(1002m)

Sanggau   Sintang

Equator

⊙ Pontianak

Sungai Kapuas

WEST
KALIMANTAN

Bukit Baka
(1617m)

Pulau
Padangtikar

Gunung Palung
National Park

Sedahan

Sukadana **8**

Pulau
Maya

Gunung Palung
(1116m)

*Teluk
Sukadana*

Pulau
Karimata

Ketapang

CENTRAL
KALIMANTAN

Riam ⊙

Sukamara ⊙

Pangkalan
Bun

Kumai ⊙

Tanjung Puting
National Park **2**

JAVA SEA

History

Separated from Southeast Asia's mainland 10,000 years ago by rising seas, Kalimantan was originally populated by the Dayak, who still define its public image. The culture of these diverse forest tribes once included headhunting, extensive tattooing, stretched earlobes, blowguns and longhouses – horizontal apartment buildings big enough to house an entire village. That culture has been slowly dismantled by the modern world, so that some elements, such as headhunting, no longer exist, while others are slowly disappearing. Tribal identity persists, but many Dayak have either abandoned their traditional folk religion, Kaharingan, or combined it with Christianity (or Islam).

In addition to the Dayak, Kalimantan contains two other large ethnic groups: the Chinese and the Malay. The Chinese are the region's most successful merchants, having traded in Kalimantan since at least 300 BC. They're responsible for the bright red Confucian and Buddhist temples found in many port towns, and for a profusion of Chinese restaurants that offer some of Kalimantan's best dining. The Malays are predominantly Muslim, a religion that arrived with the Melaka empire in the 15th century. The most obvious signs of their presence are the grand mosques in major cities and towns, along with the call to prayer. Several palaces of Muslim sultanates, some still occupied by royal descendants, can be visited.

Since colonial times Kalimantan has been a destination for *transmigrasi*, the government-sponsored relocation of people from more densely populated areas of the archipelago. This and an influx of jobseekers from throughout Indonesia has led to some conflict, most notably a year-long struggle between Dayak and Madurese people (from the island of Madura) in 2001, which killed 500 people, and a smaller conflict in 2010 between Dayak and Bugis in Tarakan.

Most of the struggle in Kalimantan, however, has taken place over its bountiful natural resources, and involved foreign powers. Oil, rubber, spices, timber, coal, diamonds and gold have all been pawns on the board, causing many years of intrigue, starting with British and Dutch colonial interests. During WWII oil and other resources made Borneo (the island that is home to Kalimantan) an early target for Japan, leading to a brutal occupation in which some 21,000 people were murdered in West Kalimantan alone. In 1963 Indonesian President Sukarno led a failed attempt to take over all of Borneo by staging attacks on the Malaysian north.

Today the struggle for Kalimantan's resources is more insidious. As one watches the endless series of enormous coal barges proceeding down rivers lined with tin-roofed shacks, there is the constant sense of an ongoing plunder from which the local people benefit little. Meanwhile, as palm-oil plantations spread across the landscape, the great Bornean jungle recedes, never to return. Numerous conservation groups are struggling to halt the social and environmental damage, and to save some remarkable wildlife. Best to visit soon.

Wildlife

Kalimantan's flora and fauna are among the most diverse in the world. You can find more tree species in a single hectare of its rainforest than in all of the US and Canada combined. There are more than 220 species of mammals and over 420 species of birds found on Borneo, many of them endemic to the island. The region is best known for its orang-utans, Asia's only great ape and a rare but thrilling sight outside of Kalimantan's many rescue and rehabilitation centres. River cruising commonly reveals proboscis monkeys (unique to Borneo), macaques, gibbons, crocodiles (including gharials), monitor lizards and pythons. Hornbills are commonly seen flying overhead, and are a

---

ⓘ NATIONAL PARK COSTS

Kalimantan has some of the most pristine, remote and untouristed national parks in Indonesia, but accessing them comes at a cost. The standard entry fee (permit) for all parks is 150,000/225,000Rp weekdays/weekends per person per day. Guides (from 150,000Rp to 300,000Rp per day) are also compulsory in most parks and forest reserves. When you combine this with the high cost of transport to remote locations – often by motorboat or 4WD – plus accommodation and food, the expense of visiting a park really adds up, especially for solo travellers. Choose your park carefully and look for other travellers to share costs, or consider going through a tour company rather than going it alone.

CROSS-BORNEO TREK

Borneo offers one of the world's greatest adventure-travel routes. East and West Kalimantan are divided by the Muller mountain range, which also serves as the headwaters for Indonesia's two longest rivers (sungai). Sungai Kapuas snakes 1143km to the west coast near Pontianak, while Sungai Mahakam flows 930km to the east coast, by Samarinda. Thus by travelling up one river, hiking over the Muller Range and travelling down the other, it is possible to cross the world's third-largest island. Be forewarned, however: this journey holds significant hazards, from deadly rapids to remote and brutal hiking where the smallest misstep could have life-changing consequences. This should not be your first rainforest trek.

Like all good epics, this one comes in a trilogy.

Sungai Mahakam One of Kalimantan's last great river journeys, travelling the Mahakam can easily fill several days in a succession of boats, making side trips into lakes and marshes, spotting wildlife and visiting small river towns. The trek itself begins (or ends) at Tiong Ohang, up two boat-crushing sets of rapids from Long Bagun.

The Muller Mountains You do this jungle trek for the same reason you climb Mt Everest: because it's there. Noted for its river fording, hordes of leeches and treacherous slopes, the route requires the knowledge of a professional guiding company. If you walk a taxing eight hours a day, you can make it across in five days, but seven is more comfortable and safer. Budget for 10.

Sungai Kapuas The hulu (headwater) region of the Kapuas is home to many of Kalimantan's best and most accessible longhouses. However public-boat travel below Putussibau is nonexistent, meaning most trekkers fly or bus between Pontianak and Putussibau.

Debate rages as to which direction is preferable. The consensus seems to be that east-to-west is logistically simpler, while west-to-east is physically less brutal. Either way, success is a noteworthy achievement you'll remember for the rest of your life.

Recommended tour operators include Kompakh (p621) in Putussibau (if travelling west to east) and De'Gigant Tours (p645) in Samarinda (east to west).

spiritual symbol for many Dayak. Forests harbour the rare clouded leopards, sun bears, giant moths, tarantulas and more bizarre species of ants and spiders than you could ever conjure out of your wildest imagination. For divers the Derawan Archipelago is renowned for its turtles, manta rays and pelagics.

ⓘ Getting Around

Kalimantan is both immense and relatively undeveloped. River travel is as common as road travel, and transport options can form a complex picture. To assess the ever-changing transport options it is often easiest to visit a local travel agency.

Air Regional flights operated by Garuda, Lion Air/Wings, Swirijaya and Citilink, among others, are an efficient (and reasonably cheap) means of getting from one hub to another, while smaller prop planes may be your only option for some remote locations. Domestic flights between distant major centres such as Pontianak and Pangkalan Bun or Balikpapan may

be routed through Jakarta but most internal flights are short hops of under an hour.

Road Highways between major cities are improving rapidly, and range from excellent to pockmarked and unsealed. Buses are fairly ubiquitous, except in East and North Kalimantan. Most major routes offer air-con for an extra cost. A Kijang (4WD minivan) or 'travel' (shared taxi) often operates between towns and cities and can be chartered for five times the single-seat fare. Intracity travel usually involves a minibus known as an angkot or opelet that charges a flat fee per trip. To really go native, take an ojek (motorcycle taxi). Ride-sharing apps such as Gojek and Grab are increasingly popular in cities and are often the cheapest and most efficient way to get around – leading to the ongoing demise of becaks (bicycle taxis) and even angkots.

River A variety of craft ply the rivers, including the kapal biasa (large two-storey ferry), the klotok (smaller boat with covered deck space or cabins), speedboats and motorised canoes, including the ces (the local long-tail). Bring your earplugs.

WEST KALIMANTAN

Known locally as Kalbar – short for Kalimantan Bara – West Kalimantan is a sizeable province bordering Malaysian Sarawak to the north and the Java Sea to the west. Its capital, Pontianak, is a transport hub for flights and as a start or end point for the Cross-Borneo Trek (p613), while travellers with a passion for remote national parks and river journeys will find Kalimantan's longest river, Sungai Kapuas, and some very isolated pockets of near-pristine jungle wilderness, but overall the province is largely off the traveller radar.

Pontianak

📞 0561 / POP 574,000

Sprawling just south of the equator and split by the lower reaches of the Sungai Kapuas (the Kapuas River), Pontianak is urban Kalimantan in all its tin-roof, two-wheeled, traffic-jam glory. The main attraction here is the river itself – stroll along the boardwalks or cross by canoe taxi to get a feel for Indonesia's longest waterway.

Pontianak is also the main transport hub of West Kalimantan by air, boat and long-distance bus. From here you can head south by speedboat to Sukadana, north to Sinkawang (or cross-border to Kuching) or east to the Dayak longhouses and national parks of Kapuas Hulu.

◎ Sights

The best place to start an exploration of the city's river is from **Taman Alun Kapuas**, a small riverside park from where ferries and canoe taxis ply the waters. On the other side, where the river branches, **Kampung Beting** is a redeveloped district with a couple of sights and a new riverside promenade. Another good viewpoint is the **Kapuas Bridge** on Jl Sultan Hamid.

★ St Joseph's Cathedral   CATHEDRAL

(Jl Pattimura 195) Pontianak's dramatic domed cathedral was opened in 2015, replacing the earlier 1908 church deemed not large enough to accommodate the city's Catholic congregation. While obviously European in design, with its St Peter's–inspired dome, Corinthian columns and fine stained-glass windows, the architecture also incorporates Dayak influences, totems and motifs.

Taman Arboretum Sylva   FOREST

(Jl Ahmad Yani; ⊙24hr) FREE This small patch of Borneo jungle is a welcome relief from the urban jungle outside. It's a community project with an orchid garden and a boardwalk through the mini-forest. It's just off the large roundabout 3km southeast of the centre.

Mesjid Abdurrahman   MOSQUE

The wooden Mesjid Abdurrahman stands north of the river where a cannonball reportedly landed after Pontianak's first sultan fired it at a *pontianak* (the ghost of a woman who died during childbirth).

Istana Kadriah   MUSEUM

(admission by donation; ⊙10am-5pm) For an outing that will show you a bit of town, visit the wooden palace of Pontianak's first sultan on the east bank of the Kapuas; in a refurbishment project in 2017 it was painted lemon yellow but the interior retains its original charm. Explore the surrounding village on stilts for a glimpse into the city's past. Get there by canoe taxi (p619; regular/charter 2000/10,000Rp) from the foot of Jl Mahakam.

Tugu Khatulistiwa   MONUMENT

(Equator Monument; Jl Khatulistiwa; ⊙7.30am-4.30pm) If you want to stand on two hemispheres, you can formally do so here – though continental drift has moved the monument 117m south of the actual equator. The gift shop nearby has a colourful collection of T-shirts, sarongs and equator lamps. Cross the river by ferry and take an *opelet* 3km northwest on Jl Khatulistiwa.

Museum Provinsi
Kalimantan Barat   MUSEUM

(West Kalimantan Provincial Museum; Jl Ahmad Yani; Indonesian/foreigner 2000/10,000Rp; ⊙8am-2.30pm Tue-Thu, 8-11am & 1-2.30pm Fri, 8am-2pm Sat & Sun) In an imposing building this well-maintained collection of artefacts provides an informative English-language overview of local Dayak, Malay and Chinese cultures.

☞ Tours

Canopy Indonesia   ECOTOUR

(📞0812 5809 2228, 0811 574 2228; www.canopy indonesia.co.id; Jl Purnama II 20) ✐ Energetic couple Deny and Venie are passionate about sustainable tourism through community engagement. They reinvest much of the proceeds from their signature Danau Sentarum

National Park trips into developing new ecotourism programs throughout West Kalimantan. Their excellent coffee shop (p616) acts as a de facto tourist info centre.

Times Tours & Travel CULTURAL
(☑0819 560 1920; timestravell@yahoo.com; Jl Komyos Sudarso Blok H6) Specialising in cultural tours around Pontianak and Kalbar since 1995, English-speaking owner Iwan is super responsive and efficient. Call before visiting.

✦ Festivals & Events

Gawai Dayak Festival CULTURAL
(☉May) The Dayak harvest festival takes place in Pontianak at the end of May, but many villages hold their own sometime between April and June. These generally loud, chaotic and festive week-long affairs have plenty of dancing and food.

🛏 Sleeping

A decent range of budget and midrange hotels is concentrated in the commercial district south of the river, many on or just off Jl Gajah Mada.

★ Canopy Center Hostel HOSTEL $
(☑0811 574 2228; info.canopyindonesia@gmail.com; Jl Purnama II 20; dm/d/tr 75,000/150,000/200,000Rp; ❄🛜) Pontianak's only traveller hostel, Canopy is a great place to hang out and meet other travellers. Downstairs is an architecturally designed coffee shop, while upstairs are two spotless 14-bed dorms (male and female) and two en-suite rooms. It's in a quiet neighbourhood 6km south of the centre, which is both a blessing and a hindrance, though there's a motorbike for rent (50,000Rp).

★ My Home Hotel HOTEL $
(☑0565-202 2195; http://hotelsmyhome.com; Jl WR Supratman 33A; s/d 155,000/238,000Rp, executive from 300,000Rp; ❄🛜) This new budget-boutique hotel is an absolute steal, with midrange cleanliness and service, spring beds, spotless amenities, hot-water showers and good wi-fi. The cheaper rooms are pretty compact – for a bit extra you get more space and a city-view window.

Green Leaf Inn HOTEL $
(☑0561-769622; Jl Gajah Mada 65; s/d from 160,000/190,000Rp, superior from 248,000Rp; ❄🛜) Four-storey Green Leaf is a rare budget find among the hotels along Gajah Mada. Large superior rooms are spacious enough with clean tile floors, while the single rooms barely have space for a bed. All have air-con, cold water and contortionist showers. Breakfast for one is included; windows are not.

Aston Pontianak HOTEL $$
(☑0561-761118; www.astonhotelsinternational.com; Jl Gajah Mada 21; r incl breakfast 490,000-610,000Rp, ste from 1,250,000Rp; ❄🛜⊜) This central oasis of old-school luxury and sophisticated decor is a good deal at regularly discounted and weekend rates. Superiors are spacious, while the executive rooms add a bath and sofa. The 2nd-floor RiverX entertainment complex offers live music and DJs, and the substantial breakfast buffet will fuel you throughout the day.

Garuda Hotel HOTEL $$
(☑0561-736890; www.garudahotelpontianak.com; Jl Pahlawan 40; r incl breakfast 258,000-383,000Rp, ste from 417,000Rp; ❄🛜) Garuda is a solid, no-frills midranger away from the Jl Gajah Mada hustle but still close to the city-centre action. Rooms are simple and clean with hot showers, minibar and TV. The cheapest ones lack windows – head to the 3rd floor for city views.

Gardenia Resort & Spa HOTEL $$
(☑0561-672 6446; www.gardeniaresortandspa.com; Jl Ahmad Yani II; r/ste from 375,000/495,000Rp; ❄🛜⊜) The closest thing to a resort in Pontianak, the Gardenia is near the airport, making it a great option for those uninterested in the city itself. Spacious private villas connected by boardwalks to the spa and an alfresco restaurant – all built with Balinese notions – provide welcome respite from the chaos of urban Kalimantan.

🍴 Eating

At night Jl Gajah Mada becomes crowded with cafe culture, while seafood tents take over the Jl Diponegoro–Agus Salim median and Jl Setia Budi.

★ Chai Kue Siam A-Hin DUMPLINGS $
(Jl Siam; 10 dumplings from 20,000Rp; ☉10am-10pm) Pork or veggies, steamed or fried – whichever you desire, you'll be waiting your turn among the mob of locals jockeying for a table or takeaway. Other Chinese dishes on offer.

Pontianak

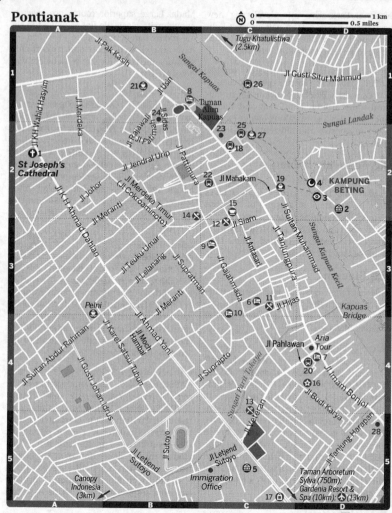

Canopy Center Cafe
CAFE **$**

(Jl Purnama II 20; mains 15,000-25,000Rp; ⊙8.30am-11pm Mon-Fri, to midnight Sat; ⊛) This bright, architect-designed cafe and work space combines great single-origin coffee with Indonesian and Western snacks from French fries to Balinese chicken. With a hostel (p615) upstairs, it's a great place to open (or close) your laptop and meet other travellers.

D'Grill
BARBECUE **$**

(☎0561-817 2576; Jl Veteran 9; mains 15,000-40,000Rp; ⊙9am-10pm; ⊛) D'Grill is a cosy little Korean-barbecue-style place with in-

viting alfresco cabanas at the side. Choose from beef, chicken, fish or shrimp and barbecue with a variety of spices, or try the regular menu of rice, noodles and *udang goreng* (fried prawns).

Mie Tiau Polo
INDONESIAN **$**

(Jl Pattimura; mains from 28,000Rp; ⊙10am-9pm) Not to be confused with Apollo to the left, the sign on which proudly states, 'Since 1968. Never moved.' Polo's sign retorts simply, 'Moved from next door'. The dispute is as legendary as the noodles they serve. Draw your own conclusions about which is the best...or oldest.

Pontianak

★ Abang Kepiting   SEAFOOD $$
(Jl Hijas; prices vary by weight; ⊙5-10pm) Buckets of iced fish, stingray, squid and prawns out front are begging to be steamed, fried or grilled to your liking. Treat yourself to an experience and dive into a pile of smoked crabs: a full-body, all-evening affair. Come early as it's extremely popular. Prices (by weight) vary enormously depending on the type of fish and the day's catch.

Kapuas Riverside
Restaurant   INDONESIAN $$
(Grand Kartika, Jl Rahadi Usman 2; mains 40,000-150,000Rp; ⊙7am-11pm; ⊛) The overwater restaurant at the **Grand Kartika** (⊠0561-734401; Jl Rahadi Usman 2; r incl breakfast 270,000-515,000Rp; ⊛⊛) has one of the best outlooks in the city. Watch the ferries cross Sungai Kapuas over a cold beer, or explore the reasonably priced menu of Western and Indonesian dishes, including crab and salted-fish fried rice, local river carp and spaghetti bolognese.

Drinking & Nightlife

Pontianak locals love their coffee and *warung kopi* (coffee shops) come alive along Jl Gajah Mada in the evening. Most of the fancy hotels serve cold beer, or you could try one of the karaoke clubs.

Warung Kopi Asiang   COFFEE
(Jl Merpati; ⊙6am-6pm) The most famous, and crowded, coffee house in the city, where Mr Asiang prepares a perfect brew to an adoring bunch of locals.

Café Tisya   LIVE MUSIC
(Jl Budi Karya; ⊙7pm-2am) Warm Bintang (with ice) is served discreetly, and loud live music of the keyboard-and-singing variety emanates from the stage. Depending on the night it may be a good place to meet locals and check out the entertainment scene.

Shopping

For general souvenirs, visit the craft shops lining Jl Pattimura.

Ayani Mega Mall   MALL
(Jl Ahmad Yani; ⊙10am-10pm) West Kalimantan's biggest shopping mall features a Hypermart, food court, Starbucks and a six-screen **cinema** (⊠0561-671 3897; Jl Ahmad Yani; tickets 45,000-60,000Rp; ⊙10am-10pm).

❶ Information

Immigration Office (⊠0561-765576; Jl Letjend Sutoyo; ⊙8am-4pm Mon-Fri)
Aria Tour (⊠0561-577868; Jl Tanjungpura 36; ⊙8am-5pm Mon-Sat, 9-11am Sun) Good for airline tickets and SJS buses to Kuching.

ⓘ Getting There & Away

AIR

There are regular international and domestic flights from Pontianak's **Supadio International Airport** (http://supadio-airport.co.id), 17km southeast of the centre. Airlines with office in Pontianak include the following:

Garuda (☎0561-734986; Jl Rahadi Usman 8A)

Lion Air (☎0561-742064; Mahkota Hotel, Jl Sidas)

Sriwijaya Air (Nam Air; ☎0561-768777; www. sriwijayaair.co.id; Jl Imam Bonjol No 26A)

Wings Air (Supadio International Airport)

Xpress Air (☎airport 0823 5791 9555, call centre 1 500 890; Supadio International Airport)

TRANSPORT FROM PONTIANAK

Air

DESTINATION	AIRLINE	FARE (RP)	DURATION	FREQUENCY
Balikpapan	Lion Air	470,000	1½hr	Mon, Wed, Fri, Sun
Bandung	Lion Air	770,000	1¼hr	1 daily
Batam	Lion Air, Citilink	420,000	1¼hr	1 daily
Jakarta	Garuda, Lion Air, Sriwijaya Air, Citilink	370,000	1½hr	25 daily
Ketapang	Nam, Wings Air, Garuda	320,000	30min	9 daily
Kuala Lumpur	AirAsia	470,000	2hr	1 daily
Kuching	AirAsia, Wings Air	250,000	45min	1-2 daily
Palangka Raya	Garuda	1,100,000	1¾hr	1 daily
Putussibau	Garuda, NAM, Wings Air	480,000	1hr	3 daily
Semarang	Lion Air	660,000	1½hr	2 daily
Sintang	NAM, Wings Air, Garuda	380,000	45min	3 daily
Surabaya	Lion Air, Citilink	450,000	1¼hr	4 daily
Yogyakarta	Nam, Xpress Air	650,000	1½hr	4 daily

Boat

DESTINATION	COMPANY	FARE (RP)	DURATION (HR)	FREQUENCY
Jakarta	Pelni	275,000	36	weekly
Natuna Islands	Pelni	184,000	28	weekly
Semarang	Pelni, Dharma Lautan Utama	270,000-290,000	40	Mon, Wed, Sat & Sun
Sukadana (longboat)	multiple operators	230,000	5	daily
Surabaya	Pelni	320,000	44	weekly

Bus

DESTINATION	COMPANY	FARE (RP)	DURATION (HR)	FREQUENCY
Brunei	ATS, Damri, SJS	750,000	26	daily
Kuching	ATS, Bintang Jaya, Bus Asia, Damri, Eva	230,000	9	daily
Pangkalan Bun	Damri	400,000	20	daily
Putussibau	Bis Sentosa, Perinti	200,000	12-14	daily
Singkawang	local minibus	50,000	3	daily
Sintang	ATS, Damri, Bis Sentosa, Perinti	160,000-200,000	8	daily

BOAT

Ships bound for Java leave from the main harbour on Jl Pak Kasih, north of the Grand Hotel Kartika. Jetboats to Ketapang were suspended at the time of research.

Dharma Lautan Utama (☑ 0561-765021; Jl Pak Kasih 42F)

Pelni (☑ 0561-748124; Jl Sultan Abdur Rahman 12)

Speedboats (☑ 0852 4572 0720, 0821 4850 7629) Boats to Sukadana (five hours) leave from behind the Kapuas Indah Building.

Canoe taxis to Istana Kadriah (per person 2000Rp)

There are no scheduled passenger boats upriver to Putussibau. However, if both your time and Bahasa Indonesia are abundant, negotiate a ride on a combination houseboat, freighter and general store that can take several days to a month to make the epic 900km journey.

BUS

International Malaysia and Brunei arrivals and departures take place at the massive **ALBN (Ambawang) Terminal** (Jl Trans Kalimantan), 10km east of the city. The taxi cartel has fixed the rates into town at 150,000Rp, but Go-Jek will get you there for 30,000Rp. Buy international tickets from **ATS** (☑ 0561-706 8670; Jl Pahlawan 58), **Damri** (☑ 0561-744859; Jl Pahlawan 226), or one of several companies along Jl Sisingamangaraja, such as **Eva** (Jl Sisingamangaraja) and **SJS** (Jl Sisingamangaraja).

Domestic Improved roads and newer fleets make bus travel within Kalimantan faster and leagues more comfortable than in the past. Regional buses still depart from within the city, with **Bis Sentosa** (☑ 0856 502 1219; Jl Kopten Marsan B5) and **Perintis** (☑ 0561-575693; Jl Koten Marsan) serving Putussibau, and Damri going to Pangkalan Bun. Minibuses for Sambas and Singkawang pick up on their way past the **Siantan ferry terminal**.

TAXI

Surya Express (p620) and Palapa Taxi (p620) run shared taxis to Sinkawang from Pontianak (120,000Rp) and direct from the airport (160,000Rp). Private taxi charters start at 700,000Rp per day.

❶ Getting Around

Judging by the number of motorbikes on Pontianak's streets, everyone has one – which means public transport is a struggling service. The cheapest and most efficient way to get around Pontianak is to download one of the ride-sharing apps (preferably Go-Jek, but also Grab) and use it to summon a motorbike or car.

---

❶ GETTING TO MALAYSIA: PONTIANAK TO KUCHING

Getting to the border A number of bus companies ply the route between Pontianak's ALBN Terminal and Kuching (230,000Rp, nine hours), passing through the Entikong–Tebedu crossing, 245km northeast of Pontianak.

At the border Citizens of the US, Canada, Australia, most Commonwealth countries and most of Western Europe receive a three-month visa on arrival at the road crossing between Entikong (Indonesia) and Tebedu (Malaysia).

Moving on Kuching is a transport hub with links to other parts of Sarawak and Peninsular Malaysia.

Airport taxis cost 120,000Rp to town (17km), but you can get to the airport with Go-Jek for around 50,000Rp.

Opelet (3000Rp) routes converge around Jl Sisingamangaraja and at the Siantan terminal on the north side of the river, but they're of limited use. Likewise, taxis are unmetered and scarce.

You may see a *becak* (bicycle rickshaw) around; for old times' sake you can take a short ride for 20,000Rp.

Singkawang

☑ 0562 / POP 193,000

Singkawang's vibrant Asian energy is unique in Kalimantan. The largely Hakka Chinese city has some classic shop houses, ancient ceramic kilns, the impressive night market of **Pasar Malam Hongkong** and nearly 1000 Chinese temples. The city swells beyond its streets during the **Cap Goh Meh** celebration on the 15th day of the lunar new year, when dragons and lions dance among Chinese and Dayak *tatungs* (holy men possessed by spirits who perform acts of self-mutilation and animal sacrifice). A *luar biasa* (extraordinary) spectacle.

The extensive beaches south of Singkawang offer everything from near-deserted getaways to garish 'resorts' that fill up on weekends. Most main beaches charge a 20,000Rp entry fee. It would be a stretch to call this coast idyllic, but on a sunny day it's worth a trip.

🛏️ Sleeping & Eating

Chinese food is the strong point here and the night market has a good range of cheap warungs and food stalls. Midrange hotels and the **Singkawang Grand Mall** (☑️0562-630 0000; ⏰10am-10pm) also offer decent dining.

Hotel Khatulistiwa   HOTEL **$**
(☑️0562-632854; Jl Diponegoro; r 140,000-270,000Rp; ❄️🛜) If you want to stay in the thick of the city action and close to Pasar Malam Hongkong (night market), this old-timer is among the best of the budget options. Rooms are a little frayed but comfortable.

⭐ **Villa Bukit Mas**   HOTEL **$$**
(☑️0851 0033 5666, 0562-420 0055; villabukit-mas@yahoo.co.id; Jl A Yani, Gg Batu Mas 6; d/tr/f/villa from 390,000/480,000/600,000/2,500,000R p; ❄️🛜🏊) The most satisfying stay in Singkawang is at this sophisticated hillside hotel with wooden floors, private porches and a refined seclusion. The best rooms follow a path up the hillside with views over town. The restaurant has grand open-air seating ringed by plumeria trees and overlooking the pool; it specialises in shabu-shabu (75,000Rp for two).

ℹ️ Getting There & Away

Minibuses (50,000Rp, three hours) operate erratically in the morning between Singkawang's bus terminal and Siantan ferry terminal in Pontianak.

SUNGAI KAPUAS

Indonesia's longest river, Sungai Kapuas, begins in the foothills of the Muller Mountains and snakes 1143km west to the sea. Along the way, the Kapuas Hulu (Upper Kapuas) features some of Kalimantan's oldest, friendliest and most vibrant longhouse communities, the photographer's paradise of Danau Sentarum and – waaay off in the distance – Bukit Raya, the tallest peak in Kalimantan. Unlike the Mahakam there is no *kapal biasa* (local boat) service, making river travel impractical, but improving roads between Pontianak and Putussibau make bus trips manageable, and regular flights from Pontianak to Sintang and Putussibau make the region easy to access.

Surya Express (☑️0858 2277 6969, 0812 5468 1818; Singkawang Grand Mall) and **Palapa Taxi** (☑️0851 0133 9999; Jl Niaga 25) have shared taxis leaving every hour or so direct to/from Pontianak (120,000Rp, three hours) and the airport (160,000Rp, four hours). Call for a pickup from your hotel.

Sintang
☑️0565 / POP 59,400

Sintang, at the confluence of Sungai Kapuas and Sungai Melawi, is a surprisingly large and vibrant town for this remote location. For travellers it's a break on the long overland journey between Pontianak and Putussibau, a jumping-off point for Danau Sentarum National Park (from the south) and a chance to climb Bukit Kelam, a 1000m-high granite outcrop looming in the distance.

Sintang is also the starting point for serious trips to **Bukit Baka–Bukit Raya National Park** and the seven-day expedition to climb Kalimantan's tallest mountain. Register (mandatory) at the park office, where they'll explain transport options.

👁️ Sights & Activities

Jasa Menenun Mandiri   GALLERY
(Rumah Betang Kobus; ☑️0565-21098; koperasi jmm@ymail.com; Jl Kelam 8; ⏰8am-4pm Mon-Fri, to noon Sat) This organisation actively works to preserve and reinvigorate the practice of traditional weaving. The excellent gallery, in a replica longhouse known locally as Rumah Betang Kobus, has the most extensive collection of reasonably priced ikat you'll find in Kalimantan.

Museum Kapuas Raya   MUSEUM
(Jl Sintang-Putussibau Km14, Tanjung Puri; ⏰8am-3pm Mon-Fri, 9am-3pm Sat & Sun) **FREE** This Dutch-sponsored local museum, about 12km east of Sintang on the road to Putussibau, is housed in enormous twin wooden buildings with three display areas covering local history, cultural heritage and ikat weaving.

Bukit Kelam   HIKING
This granite outcrop, 25km east of Sintang, can be seen from miles around, rising just over 1000m from the otherwise flat plain. It can be climbed in around four hours (seven hours return) if you're fit – steel ladders are in place for the final summit. Local guides charge 250,000Rp per person for an overnight trek, including camping, food and transport.

BETUNG KERIHUN NATIONAL PARK

One of Kalbar's most remote national parks, Betung Kerihun covers 8000 sq km in the northeast corner, where major watersheds drain the border with Malaysia. This expanse of mountains and old-growth forests offers a lifetime of exploration for trekkers and boaters. Although organised activities such as rafting and caving are available through Pontianak operators, park facilities are few and necessary river travel is expensive. This is raw adventure of a kind increasingly hard to find in Kalimantan.

Contact the **Betung Kerihun National Park office** (☑0567-21935; tn_betung kerihun@yahoo.com; Jl Banin 6; ☺8am-5pm Mon-Fri) in Putussibau. Here you can obtain brochures, talk to park staff and pay the permits (150,000/225,000Rp per person per day weekdays/weekends).

Kompakh in Putussibau can tailor guided tours to the park or help with transport arrangements.

🛏 Sleeping

Bagoes Guesthouse   HOTEL $

(☑0565-23733; Jl Dharma Putra 16; s/d/deluxe 180,000/250,000/350,000Rp) This tidy, two-level guesthouse is in a quiet area a couple of kilometres south of town. The 28 bright, clean rooms flank a relaxing common area with gnarled wood furniture. Breakfast is 50,000Rp. Head 350m southwest of the five-way intersection *(simpang lima)*.

My Home   HOTEL $$

(☑0565-202 2195; http://hotelsmyhome.com; Jl Lintas Melawi, Komplek Golden Square; d & tw incl breakfast 240,000-466,000Rp; ste from 888,000Rp; ❉🛜) The top midrange choice in Sintang has modern and tidy rooms with quality beds and hot showers – the smallest are pretty compact but are bargain priced. It's in an excellent location near the main river bridge and opposite the town's best coffee shops.

🍴 Eating & Drinking

★Kece Cafe   CAFE

(off Jl Lintas Melawi; ☺3pm-2am) One of a line of open-fronted cafes opposte My Home hotel, Kece is also one of the only places in Sintang where you can legally get a cold beer. There's open-mic-style live music on Wednesday and Saturday from 7pm. A large Bintang is 50,000Rp and there's a coffee and snack menu.

❶ Getting There & Away

Sintang's new **Tebelian Airport** opened in 2018, replacing Susilo Airport. Garuda, Nam Air, Wings Air and Lion Air have daily flights to Pontianak.

Bus services run daily to/from Pontianak (160,000Rp, seven to eight hours) from Terminal Sungai Durian. Putussibau-bound buses (140,000Rp, seven hours) also stop at the Jl Deponegoro/Jl PKP Mujahidin roundabout, where you'll find the **Damri** (Jl PKP Mujahidin) depot. For trips to Danau Sentarum go straight to the park office in Semitau on a minibus from Pasar Inpres (200,000Rp, five hours), or take a Putussibau-bound bus to Simpang Pala Kota (100,000Rp, 3½ hours) and wait for any vehicle to Semitau.

Putussibau

☑0567 / POP 12,500

Split by the broad upper Kapuas, Putussibau is the last stop for airlines and long-distance buses, as well as the last chance for an ATM, before launching into the wilderness. This small but lively market town is the jumping-off point for boats to Betung Kerihun National Park, Tanjung Lokan (for the Cross-Borneo Trek) and the northern access point for Danau Sentarum National Park.

Even if you're not making those trips, Putussibau is a good base for visiting some of the best-preserved traditional longhouses still in use in Kalimanatan.

☞ Tours

Kompakh   ADVENTURE

(☑0813 5260 1248, 0852 4545 0852; http://kompakhadventure.com; Jl Kenanga Komp Ruko Pemda 3D; ☺8am-4pm Mon-Sat, to noon Sun) The team at this WWF-supported ecotourism initiative knows everything about Kapuas Hulu, and offer tours ranging from Danau Sentarum National Park to longhouse visits, river cruising and jungle treks, including the Cross-Borneo Trek (p613).

LONGHOUSES AROUND PUTUSSIBAU

Some of Kalimantan's largest and most accessible *betang* (traditional Dayak longhouses) remain occupied and in use around Putussibau. A few can be easily visited by motorbike, taxi or chartered longboat without prior permission, while others further afield are best visited with a guide and advance notice (up to one week), particularly if you wish to stay overnight or see a dance performance. In any case, unless you speak Bahasa Indonesia, it pays to go with a guide or translator.

Some of these traditional Dayak dwellings house 30 families or more. Stand at one end of the communal front porch, and the other end disappears into converging lines interrupted occasionally by sleeping dogs or playing children. *Betang* range from historic and ornate affairs elevated on ironwood pillars to almost nondescript row houses with rusting corrugated-iron roofs resembling company barracks. Tragically the oldest longhouse in the region (if not Kalimantan), Betang Uluk Palin, burned down in 2014.

Many, but not all, *betang* welcome casual visitors, with overnight stays often possible. Ask permission before entering or taking photographs. Expect to be introduced to the headman or cultural liaison, who will invariably insist you join them for a cup of overly sweet coffee or tea, the modern equivalent of a welcoming ceremony. Seek out a local guide in Putussibau, or contact Kompakh (p621) for information.

Longhouses close to Putussibau include the following:

Ariung Mandalam Authentic and welcoming longhouse about 8km east of Putussibau. Follow Jl Mupa north of town, cross the bridge, turn left at Nanga Sambus village and look out for the sign. It's across the river via a swing bridge.

Betang Sauwes Tunggan (Jl Lintas Timur) About 7km southeast of Putussibau, Sauwes Tunggan is home to 30 families.

Melapi 1 The first of five *betang* along the Kapuas upriver of Putussibau. Head 10km southeast of town on Jl Lintas Timur, turn left at the church and hail a canoe taxi across the river. Or charter a boat from Putussibau dock. A homestay may be negotiable.

Further afield:

Betang Banua Tengah Built in 1864, this *betang* is home to Tamambaloh Apalin Dayak. Take the Badau bus or a taxi 50km northwest of Putussibau, then it's 4km southwest on a gravel road. A visit is best arranged in advance.

Betang Sadap One of the most welcoming longhouse communities, thanks to an ecotourism effort, this *betang* is 93km northwest of Putussibau.

🛏 Sleeping

Aman Sentosa Hotel
MOTEL **$**

(☑ 0567-21691; Jl Diponegoro 14; r 110,000-352,000Rp; 🕸 🛜) Although well worn, this line-up of cleanish concrete rooms orbiting a large central courtyard is a popular go-to choice in Putussibau for the handy market location and motorbike rental (100,000Rp per day). The cheapest rooms are fan-cooled hot boxes with cold-water *mandi* (Indonesian ladle bath), while the most expensive come with hot showers.

Rindu Kapuas
HOTEL **$**

(Mess Pemda; ☑ 0567-21010; Jl Merdeka 11; r 220,000-275,000Rp; 🕸 🛜) Known locally as Mess Pemda, this small, single-level government guesthouse is close to the river bridge and park. All rooms have air-con and

TV, arrayed around the central living area. A few motorbikes are available to rent for 150,000Rp per day.

Hotel Sanjaya
HOTEL **$$**

(☑ 0567 22157; Jl Yos Sudarso 129; d 275,000-385,000Rp, with shared bathroom 110,000-165,000Rp; 🕸 🛜) Next to the Damri office at the northern end of town, Sanjaya is reasonably well kept and friendly. Although there are a few budget rooms with shared bathroom, this is better treated as a midrange hotel.

🍴 Eating

Rumah Makan Dua Putri
INDONESIAN **$**

(Jl Merdeka 11; dishes 10,000-25,000Rp; ⊙ 7am-11pm) Specialising in Melayu dishes (similar to *nasi Padang*) where you choose from an array of prepared dishes, unassuming Dua Putri, just below the bridge, is the best in town. Excellent fresh juices, too.

Cafe Amanda
CAFE **$**

(Taman Alun; mains 10,000-25,000Rp; ⊙8am-11pm) This alfresco cafe occupies the riverside park near the bridge, making it a uniquely popular place to hang out with crowds of locals in the evenings. The menu is Indonesian staples such as nasi goreng, along with juices, shakes and coffee.

ⓘ Getting There & Away

Nam Air (airport) flies daily to/from Pontianak.

Bus services leave from **Bis Sentosa** (☑0567-22628; Jl Rahadi Usman) and **Perintis** (☑0567-21237; Jl Yos Sudarso 71) offices for Sintang (140,000Rp, seven hours, two daily) and Pontianak (200,000Rp, 12 hours, six daily 10am to 1.30pm). For Badau (80,000Rp, three hours) and Lanjak (130,000Rp, five hours, 8am) head to the bus terminal north of the market.

Damri (☑0812 5747 1896; Jl Yos Sudarso 132A) has an air-con bus to Kuching (360,000Rp, nine hours, 8am), with a change of bus at the border, as well as two daily buses to Lanjak (80,000Rp) and Badau (130,000Rp).

The boat pier is on Sungai Kapuas, east of the bridge.

For Cross-Borneo trekkers, the cost of the seven-hour downriver trip from Tanjung Lokan to Putussibau has been set at 1,500,000Rp per seat and up to 8,000,000Rp per boat. Upstream takes longer due to the current, and will cost more depending on conditions and water levels.

ⓘ Getting Around

A taxi from the airport to town costs 50,000Rp.

The only way to get around Putussibau is to walk, hire a motorbike from Aman Sentosa Hotel for 100,000Rp per day, or organise a car and driver (from 800,000Rp per day).

Sukadana

☑0534 / POP 21,400

Sukadana, gateway to Gunung Palung National Park, is a most welcome surprise, all the more so because few people seem to know about it. Half the fun is getting here, commonly via a scenic five-hour speedboat ride from Pontianak through tributaries, estuaries and the mangrove wonderland near Batu Ampar.

Sukadana is hidden in a fold of coastline betrayed by its major landmarks, the bone-white seafront mosque and the Mahkota

Kayong Hotel. South of town an attractive beach, surrounded by rolling rainforested hills where gibbons usher in the dawn with melodic duets, helps make this an excellent getaway.

Tourism is in its infancy, but ecotourism initiatives in the nearby village of Sedahan, and an increasing focus on the Karimata Islands to the west, are putting this little-known coastal town solidly on the radar.

⊙ Sights

For golden sunset views back across the bay, head out to the old harbour jetty, about 3km southwest of town. Also here is a new **mangrove boardwalk** that takes you deep into this otherwise impenetrable coastal forest ecosystem.

Pulau Datok Beach, 3km south of the centre, looks out on some alluring islands and has basic warungs and juice stalls.

Sedahan
VILLAGE

(☑English speaker Yayat 0857 5036 0155, Village head Pak Nazar 0896 3411 1189) Known for its high-quality rice, this verdant farming village at the foot of Gunung Palung, 10km northeast of Sukadana, has a unique attitude and aesthetic due to the Balinese migrants, whose culture blends with the local flavour. A nascent ecotourism initiative, including community homestays (175,000Rp per person with meals), has opened new opportunities and made Sedahan the natural base for visiting Gunung Palung National Park (p624). Local guides can arrange trips from here to Lubuk Baji in the park.

🛏 Sleeping & Eating

Penginapan Family
GUESTHOUSE **$**

(Jl Tanjungpura; r with fan 75,000Rp, s/d with air-con 200,000/220,000Rp; ❈ 🛜) The pick of the local losmen, though there's little English spoken. Larger air-con rooms are the best choice, but all have cold-water *mandi* and squat toilet. Economy rooms are a bit dreary and hot. The bonus here is bicycle/motorbike/car rental (30,000/75,000/300,000Rp per day) available.

Mahkota Kayong Hotel
HOTEL **$$**

(☑0534-303 1322; mahkotakayong.hotel@gmail.com; Jl Irama Laut; incl breakfast r 450,000-500,000Rp, ste 900,000Rp; ❈ 🛜) Built on piles over the water, this grand anomaly dwarfs everything in town except the adjacent mosque. It's often empty outside of weekends and occasional government conventions, which seems to make some staff forget why they are there. The more expensive sea-facing rooms have balconies with sunset views (only the suites have hot water). There's a restaurant, but no bar.

Rumah Makan Bang Adit SEAFOOD $
(Jl Kota Karang; mains 12,000-40,000Rp; ⊗8am-10pm) A good place to try local seafood, this busy restautrant near the mosque serves up grilled catfish, *udang goreng* (fried prawns) and squid, as well as 'village chicken'.

❶ Getting There & Away

Speedboats (☑ Jamal 0853 8672 6908) to Pontianak depart Sukadana harbour at 8.30am daily. The trip takes five hours with a brief stop midway at Kubu village. There may also be an afternoon boat – check the day before.

Public buses are erratic or nonexistent. For Ketapang, ask your hotel to arrange a *travel* (share taxi; 70,000Rp, 1½ hours) or try calling 0853 9116 4274. A charter taxi will cost 450,000Rp. Ketapang has onward bus connections and an airport that connects to Pontianak and Pangkalan Bun (for Tanjung Puting).

Gunung Palung National Park

Gunung Palung's mountain landscape, wildlife diversity and accessibility make it one of the premier rainforest trekking locations in Kalimantan, and thankfully after years of mismanagement and monopolisation, the park is, at least in part, open to visitors once more.

It's an exciting prospect: with a large population of wild orang-utans (thought to number almost 2000), hundreds of acrobatic gibbons, sun bears, clouded leopards and old-growth trees so large four people can't reach around them, the park is one of the last great pockets of primary rainforest on Borneo island.

Through the national park service and hard-working NGOs, Gunung Palung has made laudable progress toward both curbing illegal logging and opening the tourism market to local communities. However, official park zoning makes the primary forests at Cabang Panti research camp explicitly off-limits to tourism.

☞ Tours

From Sedahan a trip to the park begins with an *ojek* ride to the park entrance, then a two-hour hike up into the hills to the camp at Lubuk Baji, consisting of a basic shelter over a raised platform. From here local village guides will take you on forest walks in search of wildlife and waterfalls.

On top of the park entry fee, guides cost a fixed 150,000Rp per person per day, plus 100,000Rp for food (which the guides will prepare). Since only a small area of the park is accessible, most visitors find that one night is enough.

Canopy Indonesia (p614) also offers trips here from Pontianak.

❶ Information

Gunung Palung National Park Office (Jl Bhayangkara, Sukadana; ⊗7am-4pm Mon-Fri) Pay your park permits (150,000/225,000Rp per person per day weekdays/weekends) here.

❶ Getting There & Away

The main gateway town is Sukadana. From here it's 10km to Sedahan village by *ojek* (50,000Rp), then another 8km to the park entrance.

ASRI

Conservation organisation, **ASRI** (Alam Sehat Lestari; ☑0853 4963 3000; www.alamsehat lestari.org; Jl Sungai Mengkuang; ⊗8am-4pm Mon-Fri), applies a unique lever against the historical logging in Gunung Palung. It runs a medical clinic where communities who opt to conserve the forest and report illegal logging – acting as 'forest guardians' – receive incentives such as discounts on health, dental care and education. Patients are offered payment plans and allowed to barter using compost, handicrafts and seedlings for the reforestation sites.

Among the innovative community programs run by ASRI are Goats for Widows and a chainsaw buyback scheme encouraging loggers to switch professions.

If you're interested in helping out, six-week volunteer opportunities are available for medical and dental professionals, conservationists, engineers and other skilled tradespeople. Visitors are also welcome to call into the clinic and conservation centre to see the great work being done.

DANAU SENTARUM NATIONAL PARK

This superb seasonal wetland is a haven for photographers and one of West Kalimantan's most popular national parks. Some 4m to 6m of rainfall each year causes water levels to fluctuate by up to 12m – higher than a three-storey building. As the water recedes, the lake's 240 fish species are funnelled into narrowing channels, where they must contend with 800km of gill net, 20,000 traps and 500,000 hooks placed by fishers occupying 20 villages, who haul out as much as 13,000 tonnes of fish a year. Meanwhile 237 bird and 143 mammal species inhabit the 1320 sq km of peat swamp, lowland forest and seasonal grassland that's so compelling you'll be thankful you packed that extra memory card for your camera.

Access to the lakes, swamp forest and villages is by longboat.

Accommodation is either in a longhouse (120,000Rp per room) in the village of Pelaik, or at the national park 'resort' – basic rooms (150,000Rp) alongside the ranger station.

Arrange a tour through Canopy Indonesia (p614) in Pontianak (entering the park from the south), or Kompakh (p621) in Putussibau (entering from the north). Getting here takes some time and effort, which makes a tour a smart option.

Getting There & Away

Enter the park's network of lakes, creeks and channels from Lanjak in the north near Putussibau, or Semitau in the south near Sintang. Guides can help you register with the park office at either town (150,000/225,000Rp per person per weekday/weekend). Guides charge 150,000Rp per day.

Longboats into the park from Semitau cost around 250,000Rp and speedboats, 400,000Rp. From Lanjak longboats cost 800,000Rp and speedboats up to 2,400,000Rp depending on water levels.

CENTRAL KALIMANTAN

Central Kalimantan (Kalmantan Tengara, or KalTeng) is renowned primarily for the orang-utans of Tanjung Puting National Park, though provincial capital Palangka Raya and nearby Sebangau National Park also warrant stops on the long trip eastwards.

Created in 1957 to give the local Dayaks more autonomy from Banjarmasin, this is the only province in Kalimantan with a predominantly Dayak population.

Tanjung Puting National Park

Tanjung Puting is the most popular tourist destination in Kalimantan, and for good reason. A near guarantee that you'll see free-roaming orang-utans, combined with a storybook journey up a winding jungle river, gives this adventure world-class appeal. And though remote, the park is easily reached via direct flights from Jakarta and Surabaya.

The park is best seen from a *klotok*, a ramshackle, multistorey liveaboard boat that travels up Sungai Sekonyer from Ku-

mai to the legendary rehabilitation centre at Camp Leakey. During the day you can lounge on deck surveying the jungle for wildlife with binoculars as the boat chugs along its narrowing channel, stopping to convene with semiwild orang-utans at the three main feeding stations.

Despite an increase in visitor numbers and boats in recent years, the trip is still a fine introduction to the rainforest, and one of the most memorable experiences you'll have in Kalimantan.

⊙ Sights & Activities

The journey begins at the port town of Kumai, where *klotok* and speedboats gather to take you the short distance across to the mouth of Sungai Sekonyer. It is largely muddy due to upstream mining operations, although it eventually forks into a naturally tea-coloured tributary, typical of peatswamp waterways. The upriver journey contains several noteworthy stops – you won't necessarily see everything, nor will it be in this order.

Tanjung Harapan Orang-utan feeding station with refurbished interpretation centre; feedings at 3pm daily.

ORANG-UTANS 101

Four great ape species belong to the *Hominidae* family: orang-utans, chimpanzees, gorillas and humans. Although our auburn-haired cousins branched off from the family tree long ago, spend any time observing these *orang hutan* (Bahasa Indonesia for forest person, a name likely bestowed by the Dutch) and you'll notice similarities between us that are as striking as the differences.

The bond between a mother and her young is among the strongest in the animal kingdom. For the first two years infants are entirely dependent and carried everywhere. For up to seven years mothers continue to teach them how to thrive in the rainforest, including how to climb through the canopy and build a nest at night, the medicinal qualities of plants, what foods are poisonous, which critters they should avoid and how to locate reliable feeding trees.

The territorial males are entirely absent from child rearing, living mostly solitary lives punctuated by sometimes violent battles for alpha status. Once a young male secures a territory, he rapidly undergoes physical changes, growing impressive cheek pads and throat pouches. He advertises his dominion by issuing booming long calls that echo through the forest for kilometres. The call both induces stress in younger males – suppressing their sexual development – and attracts females ready for breeding. It is one of dozens of vocalisations orang-utans use to interact with each other and their surroundings.

For more information on orang-utan conservation efforts and volunteer opportunities in Kalimantan, check out the following.

Friends of the National Parks Foundation (www.fnpf.org) Funds forest restoration at Pasalat.

Orangutan Foundation International (www.orangutan.org) Founded by Biruté Galdikas; runs Tanjung Puting's feeding stations.

Orangutan Foundation UK (www.orangutan.org.uk) UK organisation focused on saving orang-utan habitats.

Orangutan Land Trust (www.forests4orangutans.org) Influences policy and supports a wide range of organisations dedicated to the long-term survival of orang-utans.

Sekonyer Village A small village that arose around Tanjung Harapan, but has since been relocated across the river, where most residents work in the palm-oil industry. There are a couple of lodgings here.

Pasalat A reforestation camp where Pak Ledan plants saplings and maintains the medicinal plant garden.

Pondok Tanggui Orang-utan feeding station; feedings at 9am daily.

Pondok Ambung Research station, popular for spotting tarantulas and glowing mushrooms on ranger-guided night hikes.

Camp Leakey The final stop. The original and still-active research station with an informative visitor centre. Feedings occur at 2pm daily at a platform a 30-minute walk from the visitor centre.

Klotok call at three stations where rangers stack piles of bananas and buckets of soy milk to feed the resident population of ex-captive and semi-wild orang-utans. There are no fences or cages, but you'll be kept at a distance by ropes – a boundary ignored by the animals themselves, who often wander nonchalantly through the shutter-snapping crowd on their way to lunch.

 Tours

Guides are mandated for all visitors to Tanjung Puting. You have the choice of hiring both a *klotok* and a guide yourself, or having a tour operator do it for you. The former is moderately cheaper, the latter leagues easier. Beware: some companies advertise under multiple websites (which never list who's behind them), and others are just resellers that double the price.

The ideal journey length is three days and two nights, giving you ample time to see everything. If you only have one day, you could charter a speedboat from Kumai to Camp Leakey (3,000,000Rp, two hours) for the 9am and 2pm feeding then return. Two days and one night is a good compromise on cost and time aboard a *klotok*, but you may have to skip one of the feeding stations.

There are now more than 100 *klotok* running nearly nonstop during the busy dry season (June through September), though at other times of the year the majority remain docked at Kumai while freelance guides patiently await their next trip. Toilets flush directly into the creek, a questionable practice anywhere, but even more concerning given the high traffic. Some *klotok* are now outfitted with freshwater tanks, which they fill in town for showers and dishwashing. In a move towards forest and river conservation, larger boats may be restricted from entering the final 8km to Camp Leakey.

DIY Tours

The cost of hiring a *klotok* varies with its size. They range from small (two to four passengers, from 800,000Rp per day) to large (eight to 10 passengers, from 1,500,000Rp per day), including captain and mate. Cooks are an additional 100,000Rp per day, with food on top of that. When you factor in a guide (150,000Rp to 300,000Rp per day), permits (150,000/225,000Rp per person per weekday/weekend) and boat parking fees (100,000Rp per boat per day), the total cost for a three-day, two-night guided trip for two people easily tops 5,000,000Rp, even if you painstakingly haggle every step of the way. In high season, when most of the boats are in use, prices can be 30% higher.

Considering these prices, the hassle, transport to/from the airport, and all the other moving parts, the additional cost you may pay going through a reasonably priced company suddenly feels more affordable.

Organised Tours

★ **Liesa Borneo Wild Orangutan** WILDLIFE
(☑ 0812 507 2343, 0852 4859 0487; www.liesa tanjungputing.com; Jl HM Idris 600) Based at Majid Hotel (p630), Liesa and Majid are widely regarded as the go-to people in Kumai when it comes to organising budget river tours. They own numerous *klotok* and can help solo travellers join with others to reduce costs.

Jenie Subaru ADVENTURE
(☑ 0857 6422 0991; jeniesubaru@gmail.com) 🏵 Reliable, long-running guide who can put together boats and guides trained in sus-

tainable tourism. Proceeds from his trips go towards buying land along the park's border to protect orang-utan habitat.

Borneo Hiju Travel WILDLIFE
(☑ 0852 4930 9250; www.orangutantravel.com; Jl Kawitan 1) Run by the excellent Ahmad Yani, the first official guide in the area.

Orangutan Green Tours ADVENTURE
(☑ 0812 508 6105, 0532-203 1736; www.orangu tangreentours.com; Jl Utama Pasir Panjang, Pangkalan Bun) Long-established operator with distinctive green boats. Excellent at logistics for large groups. Guiding pioneer Herman Herry Roustaman is also your point of contact if you're coming to Kumai aboard a yacht.

Orangutan House Boat Tours WILDLIFE
(☑ 0857 5134 9756; www.orangutanhouseboattour.com) Kumai-born Fardi is hard working and passionate about both his homeland and orang-utans. Travellers give consistently good feedback on his trips.

🛏 Sleeping

Nights are spent on your boat, or there are a couple of rustic resorts at Sekonyer village. The closest budget accommodation is at Kumai.

KLOTOK TRAVEL

One of the joys of Tanjung Puting National Park is travelling up the Sungai Sekonyer (Sekonyer River) by *klotok*, a covered, open-sided houseboat with a water-pump motor that makes the distinctive 'tok-tok-tok' noise. There are almost 100 *klotok* parked at Kumai dock, most of them built and operated locally. They range from small boats with just enough space on deck for one of two mattresses, a dining table and a viewing deck at the front, to lavish double-decker boats with private aircon cabins, expansive upper decks and hot showers.

Whether you go budget or luxury, expect superb meals prepared below deck, a helpful guide who can spot wildlife in the surrounding trees, and a peaceful nights' sleep moored on the riverbank listening to the sounds of the forest.

★ Rimba Lodge
HOTEL $$$

(☎0361-722775; www.ecolodgesinindonesia.com; Sekonyer village; incl breakfast s US$60-170, d US$78-180; ✿ 🖥) The only upmarket jungle resort near the park, Rimba is still pretty rustic for the price but manages to hit most of the ecoresort notes, with comfortable air-con rooms in three categories (Amethyst, Emerald and Diamond), solar power and an immersive jungle experience of forest walks and resident wildlife. It's just north of Sekonyer village, accessed by private jetty.

ℹ Information

Independent travellers must register at **Pangkalan Bun police station** upon arrival. Bring two photocopies of your passport and visa and 20,000Rp. Airport taxi drivers know the steps, but they charge 250,000Rp for the trip from the airport to the police station and then to Kumai. If you're with a tour or arrange a guide in advance, this process will be done for you.

ℹ Getting There & Away

Tanjung Puting is typically reached via a flight to Pangkalan Bun's Iskandar Airport, then taxi to Kumai (160,000Rp, 20 minutes). Buses also make the long trip from Pontianak or Palangka Raya.

Speedboats from Kumai cost 700,000Rp per day, and take about two hours to reach Camp Leakey, but this is pure transport, not wildlife spotting.

For the cheapest route to Sekonyer village, take a ferry from Kumai across the bay (5000Rp), then an *ojek* (25,000Rp, 30 minutes) to the village.

Pangkalan Bun

☎0532 / POP 200,000

Pangkalan Bun is largely a transit city for travellers heading to Tanjung Puting National Park, but it offers a few hidden surprises and is not a bad place to overnight. Unlike many Kalimantan towns, the residents have embraced the river instead of turning their backs on it, making a stroll along the boardwalk a colourful and engaging experience. Pangkalan Bun has the best range of accommodation close to Tanjung Puting, but with the airport some way south of town many travellers skip it and head straight to the national park.

◉ Sights & Activities

Wander downriver along the Sungai Arut boardwalk to experience local village life before concrete and asphalt. Brightly painted *ces* (long-tail canoes) are parked between equally rainbow-hued stilt houses fronted by floating outhouses and fish farms. If you tire of walking, wave to almost any boat to take you back (price negotiable, roughly 50,000Rp per hour).

Istana Kuning
PALACE

(Yellow Palace; 10,000Rp; ⊙9am-4pm) The mostly empty wooden hilltop palace overlooking Pangkalan Bun Park celebrates three architectural traditions of the sultans' assorted wives: Chinese, Dayak and Malay. Built in 1806 (and rebuilt in 1990 after it was burned to the ground), it is not yellow, but was traditionally draped in yellow fabric.

Istana Pangeran Mangkubumi
PALACE

(⊙gardens 8am-6pm) Built to house a sultan's seven daughters, this original, rambling wooden compound fights against gravity among well-kept gardens.

🛏 Sleeping

Hotel Tiara
HOTEL $

(☎0532-22717; Jl P Antasari 16; d with fan/air-con 150,000/200,000Rp, deluxe 225,000-350,000, all incl breakfast; ✿🖥) With its high-ceilinged, well-maintained rooms near the river, Hotel Tiara offers plain but good-value budget rooms in the original hotel and spacious, clean deluxe rooms in the newer adjacent wing with TV and hot water.

Arsela Hotel
BOUTIQUE HOTEL $$

(☎0532-28808; www.arselahotels.com; Jl Iskandar 15, Pangkalan Bun; d incl breakfast 435,000-495,000Rp; ✿🖥) This architecturally compelling building houses a main-street boutique hotel with lots of class. Rooms feature supercomfortable beds, wood accents, rattan furniture and a luxurious rain shower in the well-trimmed bathroom.

Attached Quizes Cafe offers decent food and there's a pleasant garden out the back.

Hotel Avilla
HOTEL $$

(☎0532-27709; Jl Diponegoro 81; r incl breakfast 440,000-730,000Rp; ✿🖥) Avilla is a decent midranger on the main road through the city. Rooms are simple but comfortable for the price and there's a pool out back, ac-

Pangkalan Bun

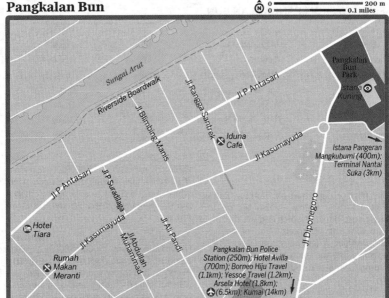

cessed via the rear underground car park. Walk-in promo rates can make this a real bargain.

Eating & Drinking

Midrange and top-end hotels have their own restaurants and there are a few decent family restaurants along Jl Iskander. There's a Hypermart and food court at **Citi Mall** (Jl Iskandar 89; ⊙10am-10pm).

Iduna Cafe CAFE **$**
(☑0532-21031; Jl Rangga Santrek 42; mains 15,000-60,000Rp; ⊙9am-9pm; ❉) This modern, air-conditioned cafe is the best place around for espresso coffee, milkshakes and bakery items, but it also does a shortlist of burgers, pasta and nasi goreng.

Rumah Makan Meranti INDONESIAN **$$**
(☑0532-27487; Jl DAH Hamza, Pangkalan Bun; mains 30,000-80,000Rp; ⊙9am-9pm) Solid furnishings and a welcoming but staid atmosphere greet diners at this popular local restaurant that's a cut above your average warung. Apart from the usual Indonesian fare, there are Western standards such as steak and pasta and local dishes such as fried pigeon, duck and river fish.

ⓘ Getting There & Away

AIR
Pangkalan Bun's **Iskandar Airport** (☑0532-27399) is about 6km southeast of the centre and 10km northwest of Kumai waterfront. Trigana, Wings Air and NAM Air fly to Jakarta, Surabaya and Semarang, while Trans Nusa makes the short hop to Palangka Raya. Flights to Banjarmasin and Balikpapan go via Palangka Raya or Jakarta.

BUS
The **Damri** (☑0812 5186 3651; Terminal Nantai Suka) bus service to Pontianak (400,000Rp, 13 hours, daily 7am) as well as all **Logos** (☑0532-24954; Terminal Nantai Suka) buses depart from **Terminal Nantai Suka** (Jl Jend A Yani), located about 4km northeast of the centre. **Yessoe Travel** (☑0532-21276; http://yessoetravel.com; Jl Kawitan 68) services depart from its own office and depot close to the city centre. Logos and Yessoe destinations include Palangka Raya (125,000Rp to 200,000Rp, 12 hours) and Banjarmasin (225,000Rp to 300,000Rp, 16 hours).

ⓘ Getting Around

Taxis from the airport (8km) cost 90,000Rp to Pangkalan Bun and 160,000Rp to Kumai. *Opelet* run on limited routes in Pangkalan Bun's riverside area. Taxis to Kumai cost 150,000Rp.

FLIGHTS FROM PANGKALAN BUN

DESTINATION	COMPANY	DURATION	FREQUENCY
Jakarta	Trigana, NAM Air	1¼hr	2 daily
Ketapang	Garuda	40min	Wed, Fri, Sun
Palangka Raya	Wings Air (via Sampit)	1¾hr	1 daily
Pontianak	Garuda (via Ketapang)	2hr	Wed, Fri, Sun
Sampit	Wings Air	30min	1 daily
Semarang	NAM, Trigana, Wings Air	1hr	3 daily
Surabaya	Trigana, NAM	1¼hr	2 daily

Kumai

☏ 0532 / POP 26,500

The port of departure for Tanjung Puting National Park, Kumai is also big on the bird's-nest industry, which endows the town with towering warehouses full of screeching swiftlets. A few guesthouses and basic warungs line the main street, Jl HM Idris, running parallel to Sungai Kumai (Kumai River).

Many travellers make a beeline to Kumai from the airport or Pangkalan Bun bus terminal, and backpackers sometimes meet at the national-park dock on the northern edge of town to hook up with a guide and share the price of a *klotok* (traditional houseboat).

🛏 Sleeping & Eating

Losmen Permata Hijau GUESTHOUSE $
(☏ 0532-61325; Jl HM Idris; r with fan/air-con 100,000/200,000Rp; ❄) These basic rooms are clean and the place is well kept, though the budget rooms share a bathroom and little English is spoken. It's easy to find on the main street near the **BNI ATM** (Jl HM Idris).

★ Majid Hotel HOTEL $
(☏ 0852 4859 0487, 0532-61740; reservation hoteltour@gmail.com; Jl HM Idris, Kumai; d incl breakfast 200,000-300,000Rp; ❄ 🛜) Across from the boat dock in Kumai, Majid Hotel has six small but very clean air-con rooms; the more expensive ones have hot water. Helpful English-speaking owners Majid and Liesa have several *klotok*, so can arrange good-value trips to Tanjung Puting National Park – if you book a trip you stay at the hotel for free.

At the time of writing Majid was also building a cafe, restaurant and homestay on the mangrove-lined riverfront across from Kumai town.

Rizky Akbar INDONESIAN $
(Jl HM Idris; mains 15,000-25,000Rp; ⊗ 7am-10pm; 🛜) This simple warung on the main street whips up excellent *soto ayam* (chicken soup), nasi goreng, fried fish and fresh fruit juices.

Acil Laila INDONESIAN $
(Jl Gerilya 5; mains 15,000-45,000Rp; ⊗ 9am-10pm) Don't let the displays of offal (hearts, livers, brains) throw you off: this place does a mean grilled chicken and a divine *nasi bakar* (seasoned rice wrapped in a banana leaf and charred to perfection).

❶ Getting There & Away

Get to Kumai from Pangkalan Bun on an *ojek* (50,000Rp) or by taxi – taxis from Pangkalan Bun's Iskandar Airport to Kumai cost a flat 160,000Rp, maximum three people.

Ferries run by **Pelni** (☏ 0532-24420) and **Dharma Lautan Utama** (☏ 0532-61205; https://tiket.dlu.co.id; Jl Bahari 561) connect Kumai with Semarang (200,000Rp, 28 hours) once or twice weekly, and Surabaya (230,000Rp, 28 hours) almost daily.

Anggun Jaya Travel (☏ 0532-61096, 0812 5366 2967; Jl Gerilya) sells boat, plane and Yessoe (p629) bus tickets.

Boats for Tanjing Puting National Park leave from a **dock** at the northern edge of town.

Rent a motorbike from Majid Hotel for 100,000Rp per day.

Palangka Raya

☏ 0536 / POP 377,000

Construction on Palangka Raya, originally envisioned by President Sukarno as a new capital city for Indonesia – and even for a pan-Asian state – began in 1957. It shows in the refreshingly ordered streets and wide boulevards. While Sukarno's dream died, the city remains progressive, with a youthful nightlife that transcends karaoke, some quality restaurants and upmarket river cruising. The market and old town are east, while government buildings and sprawl are west.

Sights & Activities

Bukit Raya Guesthouse can arrange mountain-biking trips with GPS tracks to the Tankiling Hills, 35km north pf Palangka Raya. Bike hire is 45,000/75,000Rp for a half/full day, plus transfers.

Museum Balanga   MUSEUM
(Jl Cilik Riwut Km2.5; 15,000Rp; ☉7.30am-3pm Mon-Fri, 8am-2pm Sat & Sun) An excellent museum on two levels introducing just enough Dayak ritual, custom and livelihood to inspire you to head into the forest in search of the real thing. There are some fine scale-model Dayak houses upstairs.

Tours

★ Wow Borneo   BOATING
(☏0536-322 2099; www.wowborneo.com; Jl Barito 11) Wow Borneo specialises in luxury river cruises aboard its fleet of five converted riverboats or custom-built boats that come with air-conditioned en-suite cabins and rattan sofas on the split-level decks. Cruise options include visiting Dayak villages and spotting orang-utans along the Sungai Rungan, Sungai Katingan in Sebangau National Park and Sungai Sekonyer in Tanjung Puting National Park.

It's all run by charming, professional staff with a wealth of area knowledge.

Be Borneo   ADVENTURE
(☏0852 5150 1009; http://beborneo.com; Jl Sepakat 9A No1) This small outfit headed by Indra Setiawan gets good reports for its adventure and wildlife tours in the local area and throughout Kalimantan.

Blue Betang   ADVENTURE
(☏0813 4965 5021; blubetang_eventorganizer@yahoo.co.id; 9916 Jl Beliang 29) Honest and earnest guide Dodi specialises in hands-on, immersive, affordable, go-anywhere travel deep into Dayak country. Also provides day trips in the immediate vicinity of Palangka Raya.

Sleeping

Hotel Mahkota   HOTEL $
(☏0536-3221672; Jl Nias 5; d 200,000-250,000Rp, VIP/deluxe 300,000/475,000Rp; ❋🛜) Borderline budget, this standard hotel offers a range of ageing, basic, clean rooms in a good location for exploring the market, river and old town. Hot-water showers start with the VIP rooms.

Hotel Dian Wisata   HOTEL $
(☏0536-322 1241; Jl Ahmad Yani 68; r with fan/aircon incl breakfast from 150,000/200,000Rp; ❋🛜) The odd design of this hotel, with its central, well-lit atrium and colourful stairwell leading down to subterranean rooms, separates it from the dull concrete boxes that define its competition.

★ Bukit Raya Guesthouse   GUESTHOUSE $$
(☏0811 528 400, 0811 521 525; www.bukit-raya.com; Jl Batu Suli 5D, Gang Bersama 2; d incl breakfast 440,000-800,000Rp; ❋🛜🏊) A gorgeous palm- and tree-filled garden, spotless timber cabins with lofts and a rough-hewn treehouse make this one of Kalimantan's most inviting and relaxing guesthouses. A labour of love for Swiss owners and long-time Borneo residents Thomas and Beatrice, Bukit Raya has lovely touches such as a natural swimming pool, rooftop garden, kitchen and library-lounge, all in a natural environment.

Scooters and mountain bikes are available for rent and the owners can arrange day trips to Tankiling Hills, boat trips or tours further afield.

Aquarius Boutique Hotel   HOTEL $$$
(☏0536-324 2121; www.aquariusboutiquehotels.com; Jl Imam Bonjol 5; d incl breakfast 735,000-1,000,000Rp, ste from 2,150,000Rp; ❋🛜🏊) A rooftop pool with a view. A 2nd-floor restaurant with a waterfall. A three-storey lounge, dance club and karaoke complex. This central four-star hotel has all the trimmings, even if it lacks of upkeep and charm. All room classes are the same size (except the suites), but have increasingly plush details. Avoid floors five and six due to noise.

Eating

Palangka Raya has some excellent restaurants. At night, seafood and nasi goreng stalls sprout along Jl Yos Sudarso near the *bundaran besar* (large roundabout).

Kampung Lauk   INDONESIAN $
(Jl Kapten Piere Tendean; mains 10,000-40,000Rp; ☉8am-9pm) This sprawling riverside place is like a mini-village of individual thatched *pondoks* linked by boardwalks, along which waiters scurry with trays of seafood and rice dishes. The speciality is local river fish and

KALIMANTAN PALANGKA RAYA

Palangka Raya

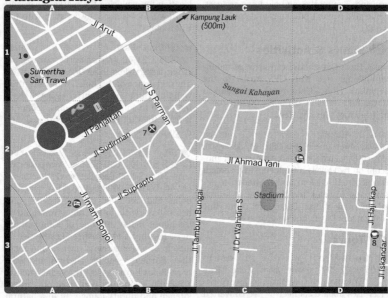

there's a rustic jungle feel despite being just across the Kayahan Bridge from the city centre. The set meals (from 115,000Rp for four people) are good value.

Al Mu'Minun INDONESIAN $
(📞 0536-322 8659; Jl Darmosugondo 5; mains 20,000-35,000Rp; ⏰ 7am-8pm) Meaty chunks of fish are grilled and barbecued streetside at this local favourite.

Family CHINESE $
(📞 0536-322 9560; Jl Bawean 8; mains 25,000-75,000Rp; ⏰ 9am-10pm; ❄️) Some of the best Chinese food in the city, served in air-conditioned comfort. It's known for its *ikan jelawat* (from 75,000Rp for two people), a river fish cooked many ways, but it also does a range of crab, prawn, squid and chicken dishes.

⭐ **Rumah Tjilik Riwut** INDONESIAN $$
(📞 0536-225430; Jl Sudirman 1; mains 15,000-60,000Rp; ⏰ 10am-10pm; 📶) This lovely garden restaurant-gallery in a traditional house specialises in local Dayak cuisine such as *juhu umbut ikan baung* (fish cooked in coconut milk and young rattan shoots), as well as having a broad menu of Indonesian fish and vegetable dishes. The garden is a pleasant place for coffee and a plate of roti or waffles after browsing the adjoining gallery.

🍷 Drinking & Nightlife

Palangka Raya has a small but sociable local bar scene. Even more unusual for this part of the world is the presence of liquour stores where you can buy cold beer or local fortified wine.

Coffee Garage CAFE
(Jl Haji Ikap 22; ⏰ 5.30pm-midnight; 📶) This neighbourhood cafe comes alive at night, serving all manner of coffee drinks in a colourfully painted house. It offers free wi-fi, basic food (spaghetti, desserts), outdoor seating and occasional live music.

⭐ Entertainment

The entertainment complex at the Aquarius Boutique Hotel offers three venues: **Blu Music Hall** (Jl Imam Bonjol 5; ⏰ 8pm-1am), a small but atmospheric blues bar; the **Vino Club** (Jl Imam Bonjol 5; ⏰ 10pm-3am), a cosy DJ club that doubles as the city's major performance venue; and **Luna Karaoke** (Jl Imam Bonjol 5; ⏰ 7pm-3am), which provides more traditional local entertainment. This is where the city's style-conscious young professionals come to hang out.

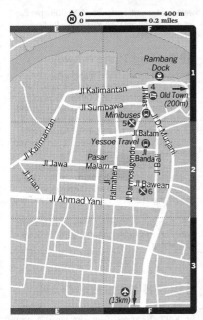

Palangka Raya

🏃 Activities, Courses & Tours
1 Wow Borneo.................................A1

🛏 Sleeping
2 Aquarius Boutique Hotel...................A3
3 Hotel Dian Wisata...........................D2
4 Hotel Mahkota..............................F1

🍴 Eating
5 Al Mu'Minun................................F2
6 Family.....................................F2
7 Rumah Tjilik Riwut.........................B2

🍷 Drinking & Nightlife
8 Coffee Garage..............................D3
Vino Club...............................(see 2)

🎭 Entertainment
Blu Music Hall.........................(see 2)
Luna Karaoke...........................(see 2)

Logos (Jl RTA Milono) has its own depot on Jl RTA Milono, with luxury buses to Pangkalan Bun (via Sampit, 150,000Rp to 175,000Rp) at 4pm, and Banjarmasin (85,000Rp to 100,000Rp) at 3am.

ℹ️ Information

Sumertha Sari Travel (📞 0812 5369 8549; Jl Tjilik Riwut Km0.5; ⏰ 8am-5pm) Kijang transport and charter.

ℹ️ Getting There & Away

AIR
Palangka Raya's **Tjilik Riwut Airport** is only about 3km east of the city centre as the crow flies, but 12km by road.

Between them Garuda, Lion/WIngs and Citilink fly daily to Balikpapan, Jakarta, Pontianak and Surabaya. There's one daily flight to Pangkalan Bun via Sampit.

BUS
Most long-haul buses deposit passengers at the AKAP terminal 10km south of town, which annoyingly has no public-transport options to the city. If you're coming from Banjarmasin, have the bus drop you at the Bangkirai four-way intersection 1.5km east of the terminal, and wait for an *angkot* heading north. Otherwise, an *ojek* will cost 50,000Rp. Coming from Pangkalan Bun, you can ask to be dropped in the city.

Yessoe Travel (📞 0536-322 1436, 0852 4679 8939; Jl Banda 7) has buses to Pangkalan Bun (125,000Rp to 175,000Rp, 10 hours) at 8am and 3.30pm and Banjarmasin (90,000Rp, six hours) at 2am.

ℹ️ Getting Around

Airport taxi service (12km, 20 minutes) costs 80,000Rp.

Orange **minibuses** (Jl Dr Murjani; *angkot* or 'taxis', 5000Rp) ply major thoroughfares, converging at Jl Darmosugondo near the market.

Hire a boat at **Rambang dock** (Dermaga Rambang) to tour around (150,000Rp per hour) or head further upriver.

Sebangau National Park

Spared the destruction of the Mega Rice Project (p634), this area of peat-swamp forest just south of Palangka Raya was gazetted as Sebangau National Park in 2004. Although it has seen its share of degradation, Sebangau is still home to more than 6000 wild orang-utans, and the forest itself is a fascinating draw.

Peat forms over thousands of years as organic material accumulates in seasonally flooded regions. The semi-decayed material can extend as deep as 20m below the surface, and contains more carbon than the forest growing above. Due to habitat loss, nearly half of the mammals and one-third of the bird species found in peat swamps are endangered or threatened.

Boat trips aside, hiking through a peat forest ranges from delightfully challenging to extremely adventurous. During the dry season the uneven spongy trail will occasionally give way as your foot plunges into a pocket of wet peat. During the rainy season, you may spend significant stretches submerged to your knees or chest as you hunt for hornbills, red leaf and proboscis monkeys and sun bears. Travelling by boat between ranger posts and dry hills makes for an extraordinary adventure through the true wilds of Borneo. Boats and guides can be hired at the Sebangau National Park Post in Bankirai village, south of Palangka Raya.

Sleeping

There are a number of basic 'resorts', or ranger posts, within the park where you can stay at considerable cost (2,500,000Rp). These include Sebangau Hulu in the north, Mangkok in the east and the WWF camp at Punggualas Lake in the west.

Information

The **national park post** (⊙8am-4pm) is in Bankirai village, south of Palangka Raya, while the main **national park office** (Jl Mahir Mahar; ⊙8am-4pm Mon-Fri) is on the main highway about 5km south of the city centre. Expenses include 150,000/225,000Rp per weekday/weekend for park entrance, 150,000Rp per day for a guide and 500,000Rp per day for boat rental plus fuel.

🛈 Getting There & Away

The closest access from Palangka Raya is Sungai Koran, on the north edge of the park. Take a regular *angkot* No 4 (10,000Rp, 40 minutes) or taxi south to Dermaga Kereng Bangkirai and talk to the rangers at the national park post. If nobody is around, try calling Pak Ian (☑0852 2191 9160). From here motorboats can take you into the park.

The west edge of the park is less degraded and is accessible via a two-hour drive to Baun Bango, where you can check in with the park rangers and arrange a boat to the WWF outpost on Punggualas Lake.

Wow Borneo (p631) offers two- or three-night luxury cruises to the park on board the *Spirit of Kailmantan*.

SOUTH KALIMANTAN

South Kalimantan (Kalimantan Selatan, or KalSel) ranges from lowland swamps to some of Kalimantan's most accessible mountain country. Most travellers visit the atmospheric capital, Banjarmasin, with a detour for hill trekking and bamboo rafting in elevated Loksado.

MEGA RICE DISASTER

On the drive between Palangka Raya and Banjarmasin you might notice a conspicuous lack of two things: forests and rice fields. The former is alarming since this area was once a densely treed home to orang-utans. The latter is tragic because the promise of rice destroyed the forest, leading to one of Indonesia's largest environmental disasters.

In the 1990s President Suharto decided to boost Indonesia's food production by converting one million hectares of 'unproductive' peat forest into verdant rice fields. After the trees were cleared and 4600km of canals dug to drain the swamps, 60,000 transmigrants were relocated from Java to discover one small but important detail Suharto overlooked: nothing grows on the acidic soils of drained peat.

As peat dries it collapses and oxidises, releasing sulphuric acid into the water and carbon dioxide into the atmosphere. Further, when it rains, compacted peat floods. Catastrophically. When it stops raining, dried peat burns. Unstoppably. During the powerful El Niño drought of 1997, mega fires released over one billion tonnes of carbon dioxide into the environment.

Today the area remains a wasteland. Some transmigrant communities have turned to illegal logging to try to make a living. Oil-palm companies eye the land for planting. Local NGOs try to block the drainage channels in a noble attempt to right the horrific wrong. Meanwhile Indonesia continues to import over one million metric tonnes of rice every year.

FLOATING MARKETS

Banjarmasin's most enduring attraction is a predawn boat ride to the floating markets, where goods and farm produce are bought and sold on the river. It starts before 5am with a prearranged boat and guide, either from a pickup point or where boats gather near Jembatan Merdeka (Merdeka Bridge). The journey follows canals or the main river, lined with ramshackle homes, where the day is just beginning with a bath and tooth-brushing in the murky, trash-strewn water.

There are two main markets. **Pasar Terapung Kuin** (Sungai Kuin), on the Kuin canal west of the centre towards Sungai Barito, is closer and consequently more touristy. **Pasar Terapung Lok Baintan** (Sungai Martapura), a good hour northeast of the centre by boat on the Sungai Martapura, is more traditional and authentic. Arrive early (make a 4.30am start) and you'll witness the first sales between the canoe vendors and the city traders who come to stock up their urban market stalls. As the sun rises and the early deals are done, women paddle canoes in search of more buyers among the tourist boats bristling with selfie sticks. If it all sounds a bit bizarre, that's because it is, but it's also profoundly educational, astoundingly beautiful and supremely photogenic.

Along with the produce, there are boats selling drinks, *sate* sticks and other snacks. If you're still hungry, ask your guide to pull in at one of the riverside *soto Banjar* restaurants.

A trip to Kuin can also be combined with a stop at **Pulau Kembang** (tours from 100,000Rp), where macaques walk the boardwalk, or at Masjid Sultan Suriansyah, site of the first (but not oldest) mosque in Kalimantan.

Arrange a guide who will secure a boat in advance. Tours including a guide cost about 200,000Rp to Kuin and 300,000Rp to Lok Baintan, and run from 4.30am or 5.30am to around 9.30am. Get to the dock early if you want to bargain with the boatmen. Any hotel can organise this trip and if your hotel is near the river, it will arrange a pickup.

Banjarmasin

📞 0511 / POP 830,000

Banjarmasin capitalises on its waterways and river life – its early-morning floating markets are among the most photogenic city sights in all of Kalimantan. But as more locals board up their back porches to bathe without fear of prying eyes and snapping cameras, and as the government buys up waterfront property for parks and mixed commerce, the riverfront dynamic is slowly changing, perhaps for the best. The rest of the city is a sprawling beast, with the chaotic commerce of the city centre turning eerily quiet at night, save for the night market holding out against the megamalls sprouting up in the suburbs.

If you're travelling overland around Kalimantan, Banjarmasin is an essential stopover and a good base for visiting the trekking region of Loksado.

⊙ Sights

Masjid Sultan Suriansyah　　MOSQUE

Though it marks the first Islamic place of worship in Borneo, the beautiful angular wooden building was reconstructed in 1746, leaving the oldest physical mosque accolade to Banua Lawas from the Tabalong Regency (1625). Take a Kuin *angkot* to the end of the line.

Mesjid Raya
Sabilal Muhtadin　　MOSQUE

(Jl Sudirman) This large, flat-domed mosque looks like something off a *Star Wars* set. During Ramadan, the famous **Pasar Wadai** (Cake Fair) runs along the adjacent riverfront.

Soetji Nurani Temple　　BUDDHIST TEMPLE

(Jl Niaga Timur 45) Step into this 1898 temple, and the hobbit-sized candles and incense coils that smoulder for days will transport you 3000km north to China.

⏱ Tours

Tailah　　TOURS

(📞 0858 2103 5791; tailahguide@yahoo.com; Jl Simpang Hasanuddin) Tailah is a experienced local guide specialising in treks to the Meratus Mountains and floating market trips. He has a small office in town.

Central Banjarmasin

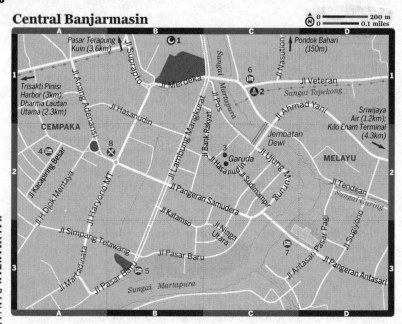

Central Banjarmasin

◎ Sights
1	Mesjid Raya Sabilal Muhtadin	B1
2	Soetji Nurani Temple	C1

✪ Activities, Courses & Tours
3	Tailah	C2

🛏 Sleeping
4	Hotel SAS	A2
5	Hotel Victoria River View	B3
6	Summer B&B	C1
7	Swiss-Belhotel Borneo	C3

✪ Eating
8	Cendrawasih Sarahai	B2

🍸 Drinking & Nightlife
	People's Place	(see 6)

Muhammad Yusuf TOURS
(☑ 0813 4732 5958; yusuf_guidekalimantan@yahoo.co.id) The energetic secretary of the thriving South Kalimantan Guiding Association can also help you find other guides in a pinch.

Mulyadi Yasin TOURS
(☑ 0813 5193 6200; yadi_yasin@yahoo.co.id) Professional and responsive.

Sarkani Gambi TOURS
(☑ 0813 5187 7858; kani286@yahoo.com) Friendly and informative Sarkani runs tours for large foreign groups as well as customised trips for individuals.

🛏 Sleeping

★ Hotel SAS HOTEL $
(☑ 0511-335 3054; Jl Kacapiring Besar 2; r incl breakfast 190,000-279,000Rp; 🏢🀫) A delightful find off a quiet side street, this hotel is built around an imposing Banjar home with towering roof and central stairs. The 13 *mandiangin* (architecture from the Mandiangin region) rooms are renovated to good effect – the best are at the front with verandas overlooking the street. Avoid the cheaper rooms at the rear.

Hotel Victoria River View HOTEL $$
(☑ 0511-336 0244; www.victoriabanjarmasin.com; Jl Lambung Mangkuat 48; r 340,000-650,000Rp, ste 900,000Rp; 🏢🀫) The riverside location is the trump card at this popular midranger. You only really get a river view in the 'Classic' rooms and above – as well as over breakfast at the Syphon Cafe – but all rooms are spacious and well equipped with minibar, hot showers and cable TV.

Summer B&B BOUTIQUE HOTEL **$$**
([☏] 0511-327 7007; summerbnb@gmail.com; Jl Veteran 3; r incl breakfast 300,000-400,000, ste 650,000Rp) Retro styling is a nice feature of this multistorey hotel, where each room is spotless and individually themed. The rooftop cafe and bar and close-to-riverside location clinch the deal.

Swiss-Belhotel Borneo HOTEL **$$**
([☏] 0511-327 1111; www.swiss-belhotel.com; Jl Pangeran Antasari 86A; r/ste incl breakfast 750,000/1,300,0000Rp; ❋ 🛜 🏊) This traditional, boutique-style hotel with warm wooden accents enjoys a fine central riverside location. The gardens and pool area are delightful and the amenities all live up to the four-star tag. Free floating-market trip included.

 Eating

Seek out the local speciality: *soto Banjar*, a delicious soup found across the city. The Kawasan Wisata Kuliner (tourist food region), riverside between the Merdeka and Dewi bridges, has many good, but not great, options.

Pondok Bahari INDONESIAN **$**
([☏] 0511-325 3688; Jl Simpang Pierre Tendean 108; mains 20,000-70,000Rp; ⊙ 24hr) Pull up some floor space near the fountain and sink your teeth into some *ketupat* (sticky rice cooked in woven banana-leaf packets). Locals recommend the *rowon daging* soup, a Banjar take on an east Java favourite. More atmospheric than most Kalimantan restaurants, and it's always open.

Cendrawasih Sarahai SEAFOOD **$**
(Jl Pangeran Samudera; mains 20,000-45,000Rp; ⊙ 9am-10pm) Delve deeper into Banjar cuisine at this renowned seafood spot where the catch is displayed in the window. Choose fish, seafood – massive prawns – or chicken grilled to order.

Soto Banjar
Bang Amat INDONESIAN **$**
(Jl Banua Anyar; mains 15,000-35,000Rp; ⊙ 7am-4pm) This is the best known *soto Banjar* place in town and is consequently a bit touristy. It's a simple-enough place, with plastic chairs and open sides, but the location on Sungai Martapura is fine and the food, including *soto* and *sate*, is authentic and tasty. It can be visited on the return trip from Lok Baintan market.

🍸 **Drinking & Nightlife**

Banjarmasin's nightlife is contained to karaoke clubs, and bars and nightclubs attached to hotels – some of which are pretty good.

★ **People's Place** PUB
([☏] 0511-327 7007; Jl Veteran 3; ⊙ 10am-11pm; 🛜) With 270 degrees of floor-to-ceiling windows and an open-air porch overlooking the river and mosque, this is *the* best hang-out in town. Cold beer, Western snacks and live acoustic music draw a youthful crowd. The lychee beer is super refreshing.

ℹ️ **Getting There & Away**

AIR

Syamsuddin Noor Airport is 26km from the city centre. Banjarmasin is reasonably well serviced by flights, though there's no longer a direct flight to Pangkalan Bun – the quickest route is with a change in Jakarta. Airlines with offices in Banjarmasin include the following:

Garuda ([☏] 0511-336 6747; Jl Hasanudin 31)

Lion Air ([☏] 0811 162 9873; Jl Ahmad Yani Km6; ⊙ 9.30am-7.30pm)

Sriwijaya Air ([☏] 0511-327 2377; Jl Ahmad Yani Km3.5; ⊙ 9am-5pm)

BOAT

Ocean ferries depart from Trisakti Pinisi Harbour, 3km west of the city on Jl Soetoyo. **Dharma Lautan Utama** ([☏] 0511-441 0555; www.

KALIMANTAN BANJARMASIN

FLIGHTS FROM BANJARMASIN

DESTINATION	AIRLINE	DURATION	FREQUENCY
Balikpapan	Lion Air, Sriwijaya Air, Wings Air, Garuda	1hr	6 daily
Jakarta	Citilink, Garuda, Lion Air	1¾hr	17 daily
Makassar	Sriwijaya Air, Lion Air	1¼hr	2 daily
Palangka Raya	Wings Air	45min	1 daily
Surabaya	Citilink, Lion Air	1hr	9 daily
Yogyakarta	Lion Air	1¼hr	1 daily

dluonline.co.id; Jl Yos Sudarso 4C) services Surabaya (275,000Rp, 22 hours, daily).

BUS

All buses leave from the Kilo Enam terminal at Jl Ahmad Yani Km6, southeast of the city centre and accessible by *angkot*.

Long-distance services include Balikpapan (150,000Rp to 205,000Rp, 12 hours), Samarinda (175,000Rp to 235,000Rp, 15 hours), Palangka Raya (85,000Rp to 100,000Rp, five hours) and Pangkalan Bun (215,000Rp to 260,000Rp, 12 hours). Regular buses to Kandangan (50,000Rp, four hours) also leave from here.

ℹ Getting Around

Angkot (5000Rp) routes are labelled by their destination, and fan out from terminals at Jl Pangeran Samudera circle, in the city core, and at Antasari Centre to the east. Becak and *ojeks* for hire gather around market areas. Ride-sharing app Go-Jek works well here.

Taxis to/from Syamsuddin Noor Airport cost 120,000Rp.

Kandangan

☑ 0517 / POP 43,700

A local transport hub on the road between Banjarmasin and Balikpapan, Kandangan is a fairly attractive town worth exploring as an overnight stop on the way to Loksado. Tidy and well planned, it has decent budget hotels, a bustling market and numerous restaurants. It's also the gateway to the buffalo herds of Negara.

🍴 Sleeping & Eating

★ Wisma Duta   HOTEL $

(☑ 0571-21073; Jl Permuda 9; r with fan/air-con incl breakfast 130,000/225,000Rp; ❄ 🕸) This converted country home is a rare and welcome find. Rattan walls in the entry lounge are a nice touch, even when adorned with assorted glass armaments. Head down the mural-covered alley northeast from the bus terminal and turn left.

Medina Guesthouse Syariah   HOTEL $$

(☑ 0517-21219; Jl M Johansyah 26; r incl breakfast 350,000-400,000Rp; ❄ 🕸) The fanciest of the central hotels, this guesthouse-style place offers a few extra comforts, including reliable hot showers. Just up the block from the bus terminal.

Warung Ketupat
Kandangan   INDONESIAN $

(Jl Ahmad Yani; mains 15,000-30,000Rp; ⊙ 6am-5pm) This open-fronted roadside warung is a great place to try the local speciality, *ketupat Kandangan* (sticky rice cakes served with coconut milk and broiled river fish). It's about 2km north of the centre – local drivers know it.

Sate Abadi   INDONESIAN $

(Jl Soeprapto; sate 2500Rp, mains 12,500-15,000Rp; ⊙ 9am-10pm) Chicken *sate* is the thing here, with skewers smoking away on the brazier, but the gado gado and *soto ayam* (chicken soup) are also winners.

WORTH A TRIP

CEMPAKA DIAMOND FIELDS

The **Cempaka diamond fields** (Desa Pumpung; ⊙ 8am-5pm Sat-Thu), about 40km southeast of Banjarmasin and 7km south of Banjarbaru, are the largest in Indonesia, yet traditional mining methods are still employed here. Wooden sluices filter muck from pits where men stand chest deep blasting away at the sediment with water cannons. This is mining at its most basic, cheap, picturesque and – for the bold – participatory. From the Banjarbaru roundabout take a green passenger truck southbound to Desa Pumpung (6000Rp, 15 minutes, 7km), then walk 700m south from the main road.

To see some of the fruits of all this labour, visit **Penggosokkan Intan** (Diamond Polishing & Information Center; ⊙ 9am-4pm Sat-Thu) in Banjarbaru. Lots of shops polish diamonds, but this is regarded as the official place for tourists to watch the process and to see how they test diamond purity. Ultimately it's still a diamond shop, though.

A trip to the diamond fields and shop can be combined with a stop at **Museum Lambung Mangkurat** (☑ 051 1477 2453; Jl Ahmad Yani 36; 5000Rp; ⊙ 8.30am-4pm Mon-Thu, Sat & Sun, to 11am Fri), an above-average museum of local arts and history. *Angkots* stop right outside the museum, or a half-day tour by taxi costs around 500,000Rp.

SWAMP BUFFALO COWBOYS

The flat floodplains and lowland swamp north of Kandangan make traditional farming all but impossible. Instead the region is home to a vast wetland ranch, where herds of swamp water buffalo are corralled in elevated pens by night and let out to swim to their waterlogged grazing areas by day.

Swamp cowboys in canoes herd the paddling bovine to pasture or to their favourite mudholes before leading them back to their corrals around dusk. It's an intriguing and photogenic sight best seen early in the morning or late afternoon. The best way to see it is to take a taxi (100,000Rp) or *ojek* (50,000Rp) to the riverside town of Negara, 30km northeast of Kandangan. From here charter a boat (250,000Rp) at the dock near the market. It takes just under an hour to reach herds.

The trip to Negara is itself memorable, along an elevated road through seasonally flooded wetlands lined with communities on stilts. There's no accommodation at Negara, but an alternative base for visiting the herds is Amuntai, 55km north of Kandangan, where you'll find a few hotels.

ℹ Getting There & Away

Minibuses run frequently to/from Banjarmasin's Kilo Enam terminal (50,000Rp, four hours) until mid-afternoon. Buses for Balikpapan (150,000Rp to 205,000Rp) and Samarinda (175,000Rp to 235,000Rp) pass through town on their way from Banjarmasin, but stop on the highway, not at the Kandangan terminal. Book ahead through Pulau Indah Jaya (p644) in Balikpapan.

Ojek (motorbike taxis) are abundant and Kandangan is one of the few places in Kalimantan where you'll find two-seater motorcycle *becaks* – they charge twice the price of an *ojek*.

Pickup trucks for Loksado (30,000Rp, 1½ hours) leave from a stop on Jl Hasan Basry, about 800m east of the bus terminal, at around 11am (check times locally), leaving when full. You can charter a vehicle for 250,000Rp.

Loksado

Pretty Loksado is the great escape from Banjarmasin. Nestled at the end of the road in the foothills of the Meratus Mountains, this is as close to an earthly Elysium as you'll find in Kalimantan. The main village sits inside a large bend in a clear chattering stream where bamboo rafts are corralled ready for the next adventure.

This is trekking country, with numerous trails fanning out. With a local guide you can base yourself here for treks to mountain peaks, waterfalls, remote Dayak villages and hard-to-find primary forest. Or do none of the above and just enjoy carefree mountain-town life, Kalimantan style. A lack of

wi-fi or even reliable 4G adds to the sense of isolation.

🏃 Activities

Mountain Hiking

Hiking trails in the Meratus combine forest, villages, rivers, suspension bridges and *balai adat* (community house) visits. One-day walks from Loksado reach a seemingly endless number of waterfalls, and range from moderate to billy-goating up the side of impossible slopes. A long history of shifting cultivation means it is a good five-hour walk to primary forest, but there's still plenty of picture-worthy scenery closer to town. For all but the closest destinations, a local guide is highly recommended. A popular multiday trek includes summiting 1901m **Gunung Besar** (aka Halau Halau, three to four days), the tallest mountain in the Meratus range and one of the few Kalimantan peaks with a view.

Be prepared for your particular route, read up on jungle hiking and don't be afraid to rein in your guide if the pace or terrain is beyond your skill level.

Bamboo Rafting

Being poled downriver on a narrow, hand-tied bamboo raft is the favourite activity in Loksado – guides and raft captains will seek you out on arrival and all accommodation places offer it. The standard trip is around two hours (300,000Rp for one or two people) from Loksado to the exit point, from where you return by *ojek* (15 minutes). There's a tea and snack stop halfway along the route, so take enough rupiah for a plate of *pisang goreng* (fried banana).

The experience ranges from relaxing to spirited, depending on water levels. After heavy rain the river swells and things can get risky, but the rafts will usually only go out in the right conditions.

👉 Tours

Although guided treks are commonly arranged in Banjarmasin, hiring a local guide (400,000Rp per day, plus food) can offer a more in-depth perspective and assist the local economy. An English-speaking guide makes sense for more involved trips, but day treks can be a world of fun with a dictionary, sign language and an enthusiastic villager.

Pak Amat TOURS
(☑0813 4876 6573) A personable, English-speaking Dayak and longstanding Loksado resident, with complete knowledge of the area.

🛏 Sleeping & Eating

Wisma Alya GUESTHOUSE $
(☑0821 5330 8276; r 150,000Rp) This two-storey guesthouse has just five bare wooden rooms and a fine balcony hanging over the rushing Sungai Amandit. Expect little more than a bed, a fan and a shared bathroom, but it's a great village hang-out run by a friendly family.

Mountain Meratus Resort LODGE $$
(☑0811 2269 920; r/villa 440,000/1,500,000Rp) Located 800m downriver from town, Mountain Meratus is Loksado's best accommodation, with a collection of well-crafted timber rooms with open-air stone bathrooms and hot water (in theory), comfy beds and verandas. The location on the river is fabulous and, although there's no restaurant, the large deck is a great place to relax.

ℹ Getting There & Away

Pickup trucks leave for Loksado from Kandangan (30,000Rp, 1½ hours) at around 11am. They leave Loksado for Kandangan at 6am. In either direction you can charter the vehicle for 250,000Rp.

Enquire at Wisma Alya for an *ojek* to trailheads or to hire a motorbike (75,000Rp per day).

EAST & NORTH KALIMANTAN

East Kalimantan (Kal Timur) holds many of those exotic notions you've been harbouring about Borneo: riding the *kapal biasa* (public boat) up the Sungai Mahakam in search of the heart of Borneo, diving with manta rays and whale sharks off the Derawan Archipelago and getting lost in Dayak culture and thick jungle around Merabu or Kutai National Park. But this region also has two of Kalimantan's biggest cities in Balikpapan and Samarinda, where nightlife, karaoke, shopping malls and the various trappings of modern life come into play.

North Kalimantan is more remote again and little visited, except by travellers making the crossing to or from Sabah in Malaysian Borneo. Note that East Kalimantan is on Central Indonesian Standard Time, one hour ahead of Jakarta and West Kalimantan.

Balikpapan
☑ 0542 / POP 701,000

Although not as populous as the capital Samarinda, Balikpapan is Kalimantan's only truly cosmopolitan metropolis thanks to a long history of oil money and foreign workers, and that makes it worth a look in its own right. It's still seen largely as a stepping stone to Samarinda, Derawan or Banjarmasin, but a night in Balikpapan's club scene will give you a whole new perspective on Borneo.

◉ Sights

Kemala Beach BEACH
(Jl Sudirman) A cleanish beach lined with a few cafes and restaurants, and a laid-back vibe. If you need a break from the jungle (urban or natural), this is your best local option. Although it gets hot at midday, you probably won't want to swim in the polluted waters with oil tankers sitting offshore.

Masjid Agung At-Taqwa MOSQUE
(Jl Sudirman) FREE An impressive sight, this mosque is adorned with a complex sheath of Islamic geometrical patterns, and is lit up in multicoloured splendour at night.

👉 Tours

Rimba Borneo Kalimantan TOURS
(☑0542-738569, 0812 5331 2333; www.borneo kalimantan.com; Jl Mayjend Sutoyo 33A) Pak Rus-

ATTRACTIONS AROUND BALIKPAPAN

Some interesting wildlife and conservation attractions are an easy day trip from Balikpapan, or can be visited on the trip between Balikpapan and Samarinda.

Samboja Lestari (☑ 0821 4941 8353; www.orangutan.or.id; Jl Balikpapan-Handil Km44; adult/child 500,000/250,000Rp; ☺ guided tours 8am-noon & 1-5pm) Samboja Lestari houses more than 150 orang-utans on a series of islands, along with a separate sun bear sanctuary. Half-day morning and afternoon tours include lunch or dinner (reserve ahead) and show off the centre's residents and accomplishments. For a more immersive experience, stay overnight at the stunning eco lodge. Samboja Lestari is part of the **Borneo Orangutan Survival Foundation** (☑ 0811 5200 0366; www.orangutan.or.id; Jl Cilik Riwut Km28, Nyaru Menteng Arboretum; admission by donation; ☺ 9am-3pm Sat & Sun).

KWPLH Sun Bear Conservation Center (☑ 0542-710 8304; www.beruangmadu.org; Jl Soekarno-Hatta Km23; ☺ 8am-5pm, feedings 9am & 3pm) This informative sun bear conservation centre is surprisingly straight to the point about the heartbreaking plight of all of Kalimantan's animals. Seven resident bears reside in the 1.3-hectare walled enclosure; walk the outer boardwalk or wait until feeding time when you can observe them near the clinic. Take *angkot* 8 to the large gate at Km23 (7000Rp), then walk or hitch 1.7km south. A taxi from Balikpapan should cost around 200,000Rp, including waiting time.

Bukit Bangkirai (☑ 0542-736066; canopy bridge 75,000Rp; ☺ sunrise-sunset) Standing 30m up on the canopy bridge among old-growth dipterocarp trees offers an impressive view and an adrenaline shot, but it's hard not to feel sad about the countless other trees no longer standing nearby – clear-cut by the very company preserving these relics. Take *angkot* 8 to Km38 (15,000Rp), then an *ojek* 20km west.

Sungai Wain Protection Forest (☑ 0812 580 6329; agusdin_wain@yahoo.co.id; guides 100,000Rp; ☺ 6am-6pm) In the mid-'90s, 82 orang-utans were released in this protected primary lowland forest, but fires and illegal logging have taken their toll. Get a 6am start to maximise wildlife viewing. Guides (compulsory) can be arranged at the park entrance. Take *angkot* 8 to Km15 (6000Rp), and an *ojek* 6km west.

Samboja Lodge (☑ 0821 5133 3773; www.sambojalodge.com; Balikpapan-Handil Km44; r/ste incl breakfast 1,550,000/2,225,000Rp; ❈ ⊛) This stunning jungle lodge at the Samboja Lestari orang-utan reserve offers an immersive experience. The lodge is designed and built using local material and with eco principles, mod cons and large windows for jungle viewing. Rates include guided tours and transport.

dy has been guiding throughout the island for 20 years and knows the land well.

🛏 Sleeping

Balikpapan is not a budget city but strong competition among midrange hotels means you can get some excellent deals, particularly online. This is a place to splurge a little.

My Home　　　　　　　　　GUESTHOUSE **$**
(☑ 0542-720 3999; www.myhomeguesthouse.com; Jl Sudirman; s 220,000Rp; d 250,000-280,000Rp; ❈ ⊛) Optimistically billing itself as a boutique guesthouse, My Home has a good location near the Ruko Bandar restaurant strip. Rooms – like the guesthouse itself – are compact but clean (though mostly windowless) and well equipped with cable TV, spring mattresses, air-con and hot-water showers.

Hotel Gajah Mada　　　　　　　HOTEL **$**
(☑ 0542-734634; Jl Sudirman 328; s/d 185,000/205,000Rp, with air-con from 270,000/290,000Rp, all incl breakfast; ❈ ⊛) Sneaking into the budget category thanks to its good-value fan rooms, Gajah Mada is a dated but popular and very central cheapie right in the thick of the action near Balikpapan Plaza. A breezy rear deck overlooks the ocean and a tatty beach.

Wisma Polda Kaltim　　　　　　HOTEL **$**
(☑ 0812 5490 2392, 0542-421260; Jl Sudirman 6; d 250,000-400,000Rp; ❈) The main reason to stay in this former police residence is the location backing onto Kemala Beach. The 12 rooms are reasonable value for Balikpapan, but don't come expecting luxury (there is no hot water) and it can feel very forlorn

Balikpapan

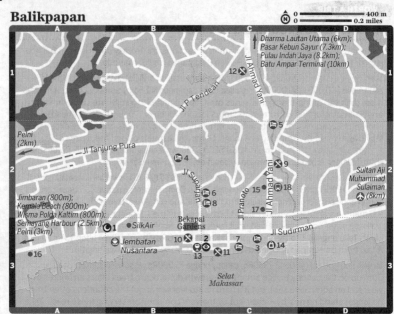

and quiet when there are no other guests around.

★ Hotel Ibis Balikpapan HOTEL $$

(📞 0542-820821; https://ibis.accorhotels.com; Jl Suparjan 2; d & tw 440,000Rp; ❈@🛜🏊) One of Balikpapan's great bargains when you consider that you can use the considerable amenities (pool, gym) of the adjoining five-star Novotel. The cosy, design-conscious rooms are all identical: stylish and sophisticated, with space-station bathrooms. The buffet breakfast costs an extra 90,000Rp if you book the lowest rate online.

Hotel Pacific HOTEL $$

(📞 0823 5225 8599, 0542-750888; www.hotel pacificbalikpapan.co.id; Jl Ahmad Yani 33; d incl breakfast 365,000-550,000Rp, ste from 750,000Rp; ❈🛜) An excellent, classic old-world Asian hotel with very accommodating staff and a convenient location for dining options. The wooden floor and dark trim are dated, but manage to be warming and plush rather than foreboding. Spotless bathrooms all come with bathtubs.

Novotel Balikpapan HOTEL $$

(📞 0542-820820; https://novotel.accorhotels.com; Jl Suparjan 2; r incl breakfast 700,000-860,000Rp; ❈🛜🏊) A family-friendly hotel, with an uber-modern interior and all amenities, in-

cluding a patisserie, cafe, gym and 2nd-floor outdoor pool. Online rates keep this in the midrange price with top-end service and facilities.

★ Hotel Gran Senyiur HOTEL $$$

(📞 0542-820211; http://senyiurhotels.com; Jl ARS Muhammad 7; r incl breakfast US$120-148, ste from US$155; ❈🛜🏊) Unique in Kalimantan, this luxury hotel proves to the younger generic business hotels that experience and wisdom count. Fine woodwork warms spaces throughout, and rooms are priced well for their five-star status. The world-class rooftop Sky Bar (p644) is worth a visit even if you're not staying.

🍴 Eating

Balikpapan has an excellent range of restaurants by Kalimantan city standards. For the best outlook head to the waterfront **Ruko Bandar** (Jl Sudirman) complex or Kemala Beach. In the evening a string of *coto Makassar* (traditional Sulawesi soup) stalls sets up on the waterfront just west of Ruko Bandar.

★ Warung Soto Kuin Abduh INDONESIAN $

(Jl Ahmad Yani; soto Banjar 16,000Rp; ⏰ 11am-11pm) *Soto Banjar* (chicken soup seasoned with a delicate blend of spices, including

Balikpapan

cinnamon) is naturally the dish of choice at this popular little warung, but you can also try *sate* chicken and *nasi sop* (soup with rice). You may have to wait for a seat or share a table. It's about 1km north of Jl Jenderal Sudirman.

Holland Bakery   BAKERY $
(www.hollandbakery.co.id; baked goods from 8000Rp; ☺7am-11pm) It's hard to miss this landmark corner bakery with the neon windmill on the roof. Excellent fresh bread, pastries and cakes.

Bondy   INTERNATIONAL $$
(☑0542-423646; Jl Ahmad Yani 1; mains 30,000-145,000Rp; ☺10am-9pm) Dine among sculpted bonsai trees and thriving flowers in a tranquil tiered courtyard at this eclectic eatery in the heart of the city. Popular with locals and expats, partly for its Western delights (burgers and hot dogs, Aussie steaks from 100,000Rp) and seafood but mostly for its extensive homemade ice-cream menu.

★Ocean's Resto   SEAFOOD $$
(☑0542-739439; Ruko Bandar; mains 60,000-320,000Rp; ☺10am-2am; 🐾) Fresh fish and crustaceans (the menu is a book in itself) are the standout here, but there's also steaks, burgers, pizzas, Indian and Indonesian dishes, all served in a fine open-air or indoor waterfront space. Ocean's anchors a row of cafes along the waterfront and is (deservedly) the most popular.

Most fish and seafood is priced by weight. If the dining area is full, pull up a stool at the bar.

Open House   INTERNATIONAL $$$
(☑0542-744823; Jl Puncak Markoni Atas 88; mains 75,000-300,000Rp; ☺11am-11pm) Balikpapan's most romantic place to blow your last rupiah on a date is defined by architecturally dizzying spaces atop a prominent hill. Reserve your *puncak* (summit) table for two at the top of the spiral staircase. The above-average food blends Mediterranean, international and Indian menus, from Australian lamb chops to chicken biryani; bring your own wine.

🍷 Drinking & Nightlife

Balikpapan's expat community has fuelled a more relaxed attitude towards alcohol and nightlife than is found in other parts of Kalimantan. Upper-end hotels have bars and nightclubs serving wine and spirits. To get the pulse of the local scene, the waterfront Ruko Bandar complex should be your first stop.

RPM Bar   BAR
(☑0857 6478 0888; ☺4pm-2am) Our favourite Ruko Bandar music bar, intimate RPM (Retro People of Music) has live music most nights on the ground-floor stage and DJs on the 3rd floor. It's a fine place to sit with a drink and mix with a young local crowd.

Seventh Street   IRISH PUB
(☑0821 5496 8203; Jl J Sudirman 7, Aston Balikpapan; ☺5pm-1am Mon-Sat) We're pretty sure this is Kalimantan's only Irish pub and it works hard at authenticity with snug booths, pool tables and beer taps – no Guinness on tap though (bottles only). Mingle with locals and expats, down a Jagermeister shot and listen

to live music in a space that will soon make you forget you're in Borneo.

Sky Bar
ROOFTOP BAR

(Hotel Gran Senyiur, Jl ARS Muhammad; ⊙ noon-midnight) Take the elevator to the 8th floor of the Hotel Gran Senyiur (p642) for awesome rooftop views from the Sky Bar. Drink prices aren't completely stratospheric (until they add the taxes) and there's a sophisticated grill restaurant.

🛍 Shopping

Pasar Kebun Sayur
GIFTS & SOUVENIRS

(⊙ 9am-6pm) An eclectic market for local handicrafts, gemstones and souvenirs. North of the city centre on yellow *angkot* 5.

Balikpapan Plaza
MALL

(http://plaza-balikpapan.com; cnr Jls Sudirman & Ahmad Yani; ⊙ 9am-10pm) Balikpapan Plaza shopping mall anchors the town centre with a Hypermart, Time Zone and food court.

ℹ Information

IMMIGRATION

Kantorimigrasi Kelas (☎ 0542-443186; http://balikpapan.imigrasi.go.id; Jl Mulawarman 94, Sepinggan)

TRAVEL AGENCIES

Aero Travel (☎ 0542-443350; Jl Ahmad Yani 19) Airline tickets.

New Sedayu Wisata (NSW; ☎ 0542-420601; Jl Sudirman 2B) Best source for all things ferry.

Totogasono Tours & Travel (☎ 0542-421539; www.totogasono.com; Jl Ahmad Yani 40; ⊙ 8am-5pm Mon-Sat) Efficient English-speaking agent for airline bookings. Has contracts with Rimba Borneo Kalimantan (p640) for trips up the Mahakam and beyond.

ℹ Getting There & Away

AIR

Sultan Aji Muhammad Sulaiman Airport (☎ 0542-757 7000; Jl Marsma Iswahyudi) is 9km east of the city centre. Airlines with offices in Balikpapan include the following:

Citilink (☎ 0542-764362; airport)

Garuda (☎ 0542-766844; airport)

Lion Air (☎ 0542-703 3761; airport)

SilkAir (☎ 0542-730800; Jl Sudirman 37, BRI Tower 6th fl; ⊙ 9am-4pm Mon-Fri, to 3pm Sat)

Sriwijaya Air (☎ 0542-749777; www.sriwijaya air.co.id; airport)

BOAT

Semayang Harbour, at the entrance to the gulf, is the main cargo and passenger port. Ferry operators:

Dharma Lautan Utama (☎ 0542-442222; Jl Soekarno-Hatta, Km0.5)

Jembatan Nusantara (☎ 0542-428888; Jl Sudirman 138; ⊙ 8am-8pm)

Pelni (☎ 0542-422110; www.pelni.co.id; Jl Yos Sudarso, near Pelabuhan Semayang)

Services include Makassar (213,000Rp, 24 hours), Pare Pare (197,000Rp, 18 hours), Surabaya (424,000Rp, 40 hours) and Tarakan-Nunukan (278,000Rp, 12 hours, three weekly).

BUS

Local buses to Samarinda (35,000Rp, three hours, departing every 15 minutes 5.30am to 8pm) and minibuses to other points north leave from Batu Ampar Terminal on *angkot* route 3 (light blue).

Kangaroo Premier (☎ 0812 555 1199; http:// kangaroo.id; Jl Ahmad Yani 34, Hotel Budiman Balikpapan; ⊙ 5am-11pm) Comfortable air-con minibuses depart every 10 minutes between Balikpapan (airport and Hotel Budiman) and Samarinda.

Pulau Indah Jaya (☎ 0542-423688; www. pulauindahjaya.com; Jl Soekarno-Hatta, Km2.5

FLIGHTS FROM BALIKPAPAN

DESTINATION	COMPANY	DURATION	FREQUENCY
Banjarmasin	Garuda, Lion Air, Wings Air, Sriwijaya Air	50min	6 daily
Berau	Garuda, Sriwijaya Air, Wings Air	50min	8 daily
Denpasar	Citilink	1½hr	Mon, Fri, Sun
Jakarta	Cililink, Garuda, Lion Air, Sriwijaya Air, Batik Air	2hr	18 daily
Makassar	Citilink, Garuda, Lion Air, Sriwijaya Air	1¼hr	7 daily
Singapore	SilkAir	2¼hr	Mon, Wed, Fri
Surabaya	Citilink, Lion Air, Sriwijaya Air	1½hr	15 daily
Tarakan	Garuda, Lion Air, Sriwijaya Air, Batik Air	1hr	6 daily
Yogyakarta	Citilink, Garuda, Lion Air	1¾hr	6 daily

No 58) The best of several companies for Banjarmasin (175,000Rp to 235,000Rp, 15 hours, eight times daily noon to 8pm).

ℹ️ Getting Around

Sultan Aji Muhammad Sulaiman Airport is 9km east of the city centre. A taxi to the city centre costs 70,000Rp. Alternatively, walk 150m to the road and hail a green-and-white *angkot* 7 heading west (5000Rp). From Batu Ampar bus terminal take blue *angkot* 6.

City *angkot* (per ride 5000Rp) run regular routes converging at Balikpapan Plaza. Useful routes include blue 6 north to Batu Ampar, blue 3 west to the port and green 7 to the airport.

Gojek and Grab ride services also operate in Balikpapan.

Samarinda

☑ 0541 / POP 843,000

With its position at the end of the mighty Sungai Mahakam, Samarinda feels like it should be exotic. But other than the spectacular new Islamic Center, Kalimantan's most impressive mosque, the city lacks much in the way of genuine charm. Sprawling on both sides of the river – though the city centre is a relatively compact area of the north bank – Samarinda's land has been opened for coal mining, resulting in numerous health and environmental effects, and causing hotels to advertise their 'flood-free event halls'. Meanwhile, a proliferation of monster malls has been gutting the city centre, leaving some streets eerily vacant; take a taxi after dark.

Samarinda has a decent range of accommodation and services, so most travellers spend a day or two here preparing for their river adventure or jungle treks to the north.

◎ Sights

★**Islamic Center**　MOSQUE
(Masjid Baitul Muttaqien; Jl Slamet Riyadi; mosque/tower free/10,000Rp; ☉ tower 10am-noon & 1.30-5.30pm) The western skyline of Samarinda is dominated by this must-see complex containing an ornate and colourful mosque with adjacent observation tower. The latter is the highest point in the city, offering panoramic views up and down a great bend in the Mahakam. The muezzin's sunset call is a captivating moment.

👣 Tours

De'Gigant Tours　TREKKING
(☑ 0812 584 6578; www.borneotourgigant.com; Jl Martadinata Raudah 21) De'Gigant specialises in trips in East Kalimantan, including houseboat tours up the Sungai Mahakam, and has safely shepherded dozens of clients through the renowned Cross-Borneo Trek (p613), which is a 17-day tour.

Abdullah　TOURS
(☑ 0821 5772 0171, 0813 4727 2817; doe1L@yahoo.com) Friendly, resourceful and realistic, Abdullah speaks excellent English and understands backpackers. Also a Dayak antiques agent.

Rustam　TOURS
(☑ 0812 585 4915; rustam_kalimantan@yahoo.co.id) Rustam universally gets good reviews.

🛏️ Sleeping

★**Kost Samarinda**　HOTEL $
(Samarinda Guesthouse; ☑ 0541-734337; www.kostsamarinda.com; Jl Pangeran Hidayatullah, Gang Batu 6; s/d 100,000/120,000Rp; ❈ 🐕) You can't beat the price at this excessively accommodating family guesthouse: a clean, cheap, friendly, no-frills place strategically located close to the central action. Rooms share three clean common bathrooms with cold-water shower. The icing on the cake, if you're comfortable in Samarinda traffic: motorbikes for rent (50,000Rp per day). It's down a small lane signposted off Jl Pangeran Hidayatullah.

Akasia 8 Guesthouse　GUESTHOUSE $
(☑ 0541-701 9590; Jl Yos Sudarso 34; s/d incl breakfast 145,000/180,000Rp, d with shared bathroom 160,000Rp) The overly small *mandi* (bathroom) at this clean and bare dockside losmen will torment your inner claustrophobe; spring for the en-suite option to buy some wiggle room. Handy riverfront location.

★**Aston Samarinda**　HOTEL $$
(☑ 0541-732600; www.astonsamarinda.com; Jl Pangeran Hidayatullah; r/ste incl breakfast from 700,000/850,000Rp; ❈ 🐕 🛉) Samarinda's best city-centre hotel is where you come for pampered luxury. The colonnaded pool with its two-storey waterfall may be ostentatious, but the rooms have just the right amount of style and comfort. Some superiors have grand river views, while others have no windows but extra space. Fine dining, superb

Samarinda

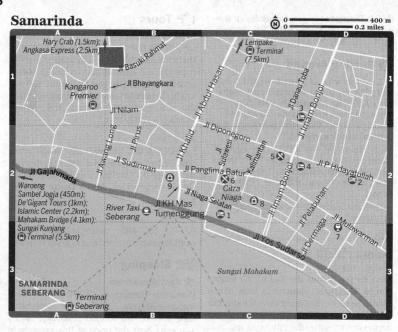

Samarinda

😴 Sleeping

🍴 Eating

🍷 Drinking & Nightlife

🛍 Shopping

buffet breakfast and an in-house spa round out the scene nicely.

Horison Samarinda HOTEL **$$**
(☎0541-727 2900; www.myhorison.com; Jl Imam Bonjol 9; r/ste incl breakfast 560,000/990,000Rp; ❄🛜🏊) This chain hotel adds a touch of class to the otherwise standard business-hotel market. The fresh rooms all have work desks, flat-screen TVs and bone-chilling central air-con. The top-floor indoor pool has expansive views, while the bottom-floor lobby has batik demonstrations.

🍴 Eating & Drinking

Rumah Makan Amado INDONESIAN **$**
(☎0813 5166 1119; Jl Pangeran Hidayatullah; mains 15,000-25,000Rp; ⊘8am-11pm) Widely regarded as serving the best *soto Banjar* in town,

Amado is always busy. Cheap, cheerful and speedy service.

⭐ Waroeng Sambel Jogja INDONESIAN **$$**
(☎0541-743913; Jl Gajah Mada 1; mains 22,000-75,000Rp; ⊘10am-11pm) Serving eight very different varieties of sambal (salsa) designed to knock your socks off, this large complex opposite the riverfront is packed on weekends. The house speciality, the oniony *sambel bawang Jogja,* and the sambel tempe are worth the trip.

Hary Crab SEAFOOD **$$**
(Jl Pahlawan 41; crab 80,000Rp; ⊘6-10pm) A unique local institution, these streetside outdoor benches set up in the evening and are generally packed with people who believe dinner should be a fully immersive affair.

Wear your bib and check prices, which are generally by weight, in advance.

Sari Pacific Restaurant · INTERNATIONAL $$

(Jl Panglima Batur; mains 35,000-135,000Rp; ⊙9am-10pm) Features a selection of New Zealand steaks (from 110,000Rp) as well as burgers, chicken, fish and Japanese dishes. The house favourite, *ikan patin bakar* (grilled fish), is pure greasy deliciousness. Bonus: fried ice cream!

Muse · CLUB

(Jl Mulawarman; ⊙5pm-3am) Muse is the most sophisticated nightlife venue in central Samarinda, with several floors of karaoke, DJs and live bands, as well as a chilled rooftop lounge-bar called the Beer House.

 Shopping

Citra Niaga · MARKET

This daily market contains several souvenir shops offering batik sarongs and Dayak carvings. Food stalls serve *amplang* (crunchy fishy puffs) and standard Indonesian fare.

Pasar Pagi · MARKET

(Morning Market; Jl Sudirman) A wonderfully chaotic morning market.

❶ Getting There & Away

AIR

Samarinda's new international APT Pranoto Airport (https://aptpranotoairport.com) officially opened in 2018, replacing the relatively tiny Termindung Airport. At the time of writing only Xpress Air and Susi Air were using the airport for flights to Melak, Berau and Balikpapan, but several airlines, including Garuda and Lion Air, have planned additional routes when the new airport is fully operational.

Angkasa Express (☑0541-200280; Plaza Lembuswana D3; ⊙8am-8pm Mon-Fri, to 1pm Sat) Air tickets.

BOAT

Mahakam public ferries *(kapal biasa)* leave at 7am from **Sungai Kunjang ferry terminal**, opposite the bus terminal, 6km upriver on green *angkot* A (5000Rp). Arrive early and pay on board. Pelni ferries no longer serve Samarinda.

BUS

Samarinda has three main bus terminals:

Sungai Kunjang bus terminal (Jl KH Mas Mansyur) Serves Mahakam river destinations (as far as Melak) and Balikpapan. It's 6km west of the city on green *angkot* A.

Lempake bus terminal Serves all points north, including an irregular morning bus to Berau. *Taksi gelap* (unlicensed taxis) for Berau troll the terminal, effectively killing the public bus market. It's 8km north of the city on red *angkot* B.

Terminal Seberang Serves Banjarmasin. It's across the river via water taxi.

Minibuses for Tenggarong leave from the east side of the Mahakam Bridge. Cross it on *angkot* G and head south 500m where buses gather opposite the PLTD electric station.

Kangaroo Premier (☑0812 555 1199; www. kangaroo.id; Jl WR Supratman 7A) sends minibuses to Balikpapan airport every 10 minutes (150,000Rp).

❶ Getting Around

Samarinda's new airport is in Sungai Siring, around 25km northeast of the city centre. Allow an hour by taxi.

Angkot (5000Rp) converge at Pasar Pagi market.

Cross-Mahakam **ferries** (Jl Gajah Mada) to Samarinda Seberang (5000Rp, or 20,000Rp to charter) leave from the boat dock on Jl Gajahmada.

KALIMANTAN SAMARINDA

BUSES FROM SAMARINDA

DESTINATION	TERMINAL	FARE (RP)	DURATION (HR)	FREQUENCY
Balikpapan	Sungai Kunjang	35,000	2	every 10min, 6am-8pm
Banjarmasin	Samarinda Seberang	175,000-235,000	16	25 daily 7am-5.45pm
Berau	Lempake	200,000	15	one daily
Bontang	Lempake	35,000	3	every 25min, 7am-7pm
Kota Bangun	Sungai Kunjang	35,000	3½	6 daily, 7am-3pm
Melak	Sungai Kunjang	110,000	9	2 daily
Sangatta	Lampake	45,000	4	every 25min, 6am-5pm
Tenggarong	roadside across bridge	25,000	1	regular when full

WORTH A TRIP

PAMPANG DAYAK CEREMONIES

Every Sunday at 2pm, the Kenyah Dayak village of Pampang (relocated here from the highlands in the 1970s) puts on a show (25,000Rp) of traditional dances aimed squarely at camera-toting tourists. Enjoy it for what it is: an engaging, staged performance that allows a long-marginalised group to benefit economically from its rich heritage. It is also one of the last places to see women with traditional long earlobes (photos 25,000Rp). Take a public minibus (15,000Rp, one hour) from Lempake bus terminal to the intersection 25km north of Samarinda (ask for Desa Budaya Pampang). A taxi for a return day trip should cost around 250,000Rp.

Sungai Mahakam

The mighty Mahakam, the second-longest river in Indonesia (after Kapuas), is a microcosm of Kalimantan. As you float upriver in search of the heart of Borneo, you'll pass countless barges hauling it downriver to sell to the highest bidder. You'll see centuries-old villages just around the bend from coal mines and logging camps, and impossibly tall trees looming next to oil-palm plantations. You'll pass imposing government offices with flash SUVs parked out front on your way to haggle over the price of a hand-carved *mandau* (machete) with a man who's barely keeping his family fed. This is Kalimantan in all of its conflicting, powerful, confusing and compelling beauty. And there is no better way to see it than on a trip up the Mahakam, a journey you'll remember for a lifetime.

◉ Sights & Activities

Travelling up this major artery of Kalimantan is a journey in the fullest sense of the word. As you head away from the industrial centre of Samarinda you slip deeper into the interior, and into Borneo's past. You won't be alone (there is a daily public boat, after all), but you won't see many other foreigners – if any.

Opportunities for exploration abound from towns and longhouses, to huge lakes, wetlands and tributary creeks. Wildlife is abundant, but elusive. Heading up the main river gets you into the interior, but taking any tributary will open up a whole new world of adventures and experiences.

Stages of Travel

The Mahakam stretches from Samarinda to the highlands through several distinct regions:

Lower Mahakam: Samarinda to Kota Bangun Many travellers opt to cover this fairly developed stretch by land. Otherwise it is an eight-hour journey from Samarinda by *kapal biasa,* which depart Samarinda every morning at 7am. Notable stops include the former Kutai sultanate in Tenggarong city.

The Lake District: Kota Bangun to Melak This diverse section of rivers, lakes and marshes is full of wildlife and dotted with villages, each completely unique in its own way. Base yourself in Muara Muntai for day trips to Lake Jempang, or take creative side passages upriver to Muara Pahu.

Middle Mahakam: Melak to Long Bagun The upper reach of the *kapal biasa* begins to feel like the wild Kalimantan you've dreamed about.

Upper Mahakam: Long Bagun to Tiong Ohang The most exhilarating and most dangerous part of the river includes two major sets of rapids that claim multiple lives each year.

Note that *kapal biasa* reach Long Bagun when water levels permit. Otherwise they stop in Tering or Long Iram, at which point speedboats will surround your boat looking for passengers for Long Bagun.

Guides

As you head further upriver, the need for Bahasa skills becomes more obvious, as English is almost nonexistent. You can get by with rudimentary phrases and travel safely without a guide, but if you're interested in visiting and staying in Dayak villages or learning more about the local wildlife and ecology, a good guide becomes extremely useful.

Most guides prefer package trips with pre-set costs, though some may agree to a more flexible itinerary for a daily fee, with you covering their food, lodging and transport as well. Independent guiding fees range widely, from 150,000Rp to 350,000Rp per day depending on experience, skill and demand. The best guides will look out for their client's financial interests, negotiating on your behalf and making savings that may defray their fee.

Take the time to find a suitable guide in Samarinda or Balikpapan, where they are relatively plentiful. A meeting is essential to confirm language skills and identify personality (in)compatibilities that can make or break a long trip together.

❶ Getting There & Away

Samarinda is the usual starting point for the Mahakam river trip, though some travellers get on at Tenggarong or Kota Bangun. The only airport along the river is at Melak.

Tenggarong

☑ 0541 / POP 75,000

Once the capital of the mighty Kutai sultanate, Tenggarong has been attempting to re-create its past glory, with mixed results. Flush with mining profits, the government has invested heavily in infrastructure – good. However, development largely focused on turning Kumala Island from a local wildlife haven into a gaudy tourist attraction, plagued by a corruption scandal – bad. In 2011 the 10-year-old bridge across the Mahakam, dubbed 'Indonesia's Golden Gate', suddenly collapsed into the river, killing 36 people. It has since been replaced.

◉ Sights

Mulawarman Museum　　　　MUSEUM
(Jl Diponegoro; 15,000Rp; ⊘8.30am-4pm Mon-Thu, to 11.30am Fri, to 4.30pm Sat & Sun) The former sultan's palace, built by the Dutch in 1937, is now a decent museum chronicling the culture, natural history and in-

dustry of Indonesia's oldest kingdom – as evidenced by 5th-century Sanskrit engravings (the originals are in Jakarta). The ornate Yuan and Ming Dynasty ceramics are compelling, while the wedding headwear from around Indonesia is entertaining. The architecturally incongruous building is itself an attraction, with strong parallel lines reminiscent of Frank Lloyd Wright's work.

★ Festivals & Events

Erau International
Folk & Art Festival　　　　　CULTURAL
(EIFAF; www.facebook.com/EIFAF) Originally held in celebration of a sultan's coronation, the Erau (from the Kutai word *eroh*, meaning joyful, boisterous crowd) became a bi-annual, then annual, gathering to celebrate local Dayak culture and custom. It's usually held in August, occasionally in June, and the main venue is the former royal palace. Book accommodation in advance.

🛏 Sleeping & Eating

Hotel Karya Tapin　　　　　HOTEL $
(☑0541-661258; Jl Maduningrat 29; r incl breakfast 250,000Rp; ❄️ ☎) Spotless lavender-striped rooms at this small hotel include high ceilings, TVs, showers and homely touches. Head west on Jl Kartini along the south bank of the creek beside the *keraton* (walled palace) to Jl Maduningrat. If it's full, Hotel Karya Tapin 2 is further south on Jl Patin.

Grand Elty Singgasana Hotel　HOTEL $$
(☑0541-664703; Jl Pahlawan 1; r incl breakfast 490,000-600,000Rp; ❄️ ☎ ≋) Tenggarong's best hotel is perched on a hillside south of town with views over the Mahakam. The stately wood-trimmed rooms are fading, and

---

THE LAST IRRAWADDY DOLPHINS

Once common along the Mahakam, the population of the critically endangered freshwater Irrawaddy dolphin *(pesut)* has declined precipitously in recent years. Today there are fewer than 70 left, and they must dodge gill nets and ship rotors in an increasingly murky river polluted with coal-mine and oil-palm-plantation run-off. The playful, round-faced survivors can often be seen in the Pela/Lake Semayang area and downriver between Muara Muntai and Kota Bangun.

YK-RASI (Rare Aquatic Species of Indonesia; ☑0541-744874; yk.rasi@gmail.com; Jl Kadrie Oening) is a Samarinda-based conservation NGO engaged in protecting the Mahakam ecosystem, especially the Irrawaddy dolphin. If you're interested in volunteering or learning more about local conservation issues, contact Danielle or Budiono. They can also recommend local guides for Sungai Mahakam trips.

staff seem surprised to discover someone is actually staying here, but there's a a lot to like about the light-filled restaurant, garden and outdoor pool with a view. There's even a nightclub here.

Etam Fried Chicken
INDONESIAN $

(☑ 0541-665701; Jl Muchsin Timbau; mains 15,000-30,000Rp; ⊙ 11am-10pm) The local recommendation for tasty fried (and more) chicken, 2km south of the museum.

ⓘ Getting There & Away

The *kapal biasa* dock (Pelabuhan Mangkurawang) is 2.5km north of town, with *angkot* (5000Rp) service to the centre. Boats pass heading downriver to Samarinda (25,000Rp, two hours) around 7am daily and upriver for Kota Bangun (50,000Rp, six hours) at 9am daily.

Timbau bus terminal (Jl Belida) is 400m south of the bridge and about 4km south of the museum area, with *angkot* service to the centre (5000Rp). Buses depart hourly from 9am to 4pm for Samarinda (25,000Rp), but you'll need to hail passing Kota Bangun–bound buses (30,000Rp) or Kijang buses (150,000Rp) on the street.

Kota Bangun

This small town is where many Mahakam journeys begin, since it's easily accessed by road from Samarinda. From here, take the *kapal biasa* direct to Muara Muntai on the river, or hire a *ces* to get there via the northern scenic route through Lakes Semayang and Melintang. You'll twist and turn through narrow channels, cross endless marshes and pass through forests of silver-barked trees, pausing to see the odd monkey or some of the last Irrawaddy dolphins (p649).

🛏 Sleeping

Penginapan Mukjizat
GUESTHOUSE $

(☑ 0541-666 3586; Jl A Yani 5; s/d 50,000/100,000Rp) The chill rear balcony above the river is a plus. Its proximity to the megaphonic mosque, not so much. The unsigned green wooden building is 150m downriver from the *kapal biasa* dock.

Penginapan Barokah
GUESTHOUSE $

(Jl HM Aini H 35; r with fan/air-con 60,000/130,000Rp; ✲) If you enjoyed visiting your grandmother's house, you'll enjoy staying at this friendly upstairs guesthouse. Enjoy the

---

CHARIOTS OF THE MAHAKAM

Several types of boat ply the waters of the Mahakam, each with their own appealing character.

Kapal biasa These bilevel riverboats are the long-haul workhorses of the Mahakam. Two boats depart daily from Samarinda, one bound for Long Bagun, the other for Melak. The open lower deck holds short-distance passengers sharing floor space with the cargo, motorbikes and fuel cans. Aft is a simple kitchen (meals 20,000Rp) and simpler toilets (visualise a hole in the deck). Long-distance passengers occupy the enclosed upper deck on a first-come, first-served basis, where 60 people or so bed down, side by side, on thin mattresses (provided). If you're making an overnight journey, head directly upstairs to stake a claim near an electrical plug, fan and window. The secret treasure is the foredeck balcony directly over the captain's chair, which provides the perfect elevated viewing platform. As the boat chugs deeper into the heart of Borneo, you can sit there serenely for hours in shaded comfort, munching on strange fruit from the last stop.

Longboats Also called *spid* (pronounced speed), these long motorboats with canvas tops and rows of seats are armed with racks of off-board horsepower, necessary for handling the rapids in the upper river. Epic front-seat views are paid for in spine-compressing bounces.

Ces Narrow wooden canoes powered by a lawnmower engine attached to a propeller via a long stalk – the same longtails seen elsewhere in Asia. These stylish crafts with their upturned snouts, raked sterns, cushioned seating and colourful paint jobs provide access to the narrow byways and shallow marshlands. There is *nothing* like exploring the jungle on a beautiful day in one of these: a private journey fit for a sultan (just bring earplugs).

foot-massaging floors in the clean shared *mandi*. It's 100m upriver of the *kapal biasa* dock.

❶ Getting There & Away

Kapal biasa pass in the afternoon (after 3pm) heading upriver, and in the predawn heading downriver. Buses to Samarinda (35,000Rp, four hours) leave at least three times daily between 7am and 2pm. Regular *ces* service runs to Muara Pela (30,000Rp), Semayang (50,000Rp) and Melintang (65,000Rp). Charter a private *ces* for dolphin watching, for the back-channel journey to Muara Muntai (400,000Rp) or for a day of sightseeing (750,000Rp).

Muara Muntai

Considering the price of ironwood these days, the streets of Muara Muntai might as well be paved with gold. This riverside town's nearly 20km network of richly weathered boardwalks clack loudly with passing motorbikes, adding to the rich Mahakam soundscape and giving the impression of a floating village. The sound of money has also caught the attention of unscrupulous traders who offer to replace the boardwalks at cost, then sell the 'reclaimed' lumber to builders in Bali, circumventing restrictions on the trade of new ironwood. Sadly a stretch of boardwalk in the village centre has been replaced with concrete.

Muara Muntai is an interesting place to wander and the best base for day trips to Lakes Jempang or Melintang.

🛏 Sleeping & Eating

Penginapan Sri Muntai   GUESTHOUSE $
(☑0812 5336 5605; Jl Surdiman; s/d 50,000/100,000Rp) Bright-green Sri Muntai, above a ground-level shop on the main (concreted) village strip, wins the award for best front porch: a breezy hang-out above the street. Small fan rooms line a central common area with shared *mandi* and showers at the rear. It's not much but it's the best budget place in the village.

Penginapan Abadi   GUESTHOUSE $$
(☑0853 4603 2899; Jl Kartini; s/d 200,000/ 350,000Rp; ❄) If you need air-conditioning, Abadi is a decent choice, tucked down a small lane near the village gate. The nine clean rooms all have air-con and TV, but share bathrooms and a front porch.

**Warung Makan
Yoyok Bakso**   INDONESIAN $
(Jl Kartini; mains 10,000-15,000Rp; ⊙9am-10pm) Reliable warung serving excellent *bakso* (meatball soup), along with nasi goreng, *mie goreng* and cold drinks.

❶ Getting There & Away

Kapal biasa pass in the afternoon (between 5pm and 6pm) heading upriver, and around midnight heading down.

A *ces* to/from Kota Bangun (the nearest bus stop) costs 200,000Rp for the two-hour journey.

Charter a *ces* (around 500,000Rp) to Lake Jempang country, to visit villages and longhouses, with the impeccably cheerful **Udin Ban** (☑0813 3241 2089). If he's not around, other local boatmen will find you.

Lake Jempang

Located south of the Mahakam, seasonally flooded Jempang is the largest of the three major wetlands in the lake region. This bird-watcher's paradise is home to more than 57 species of waterbirds, 12 birds of prey and six kingfishers. The fishing village of Jantur occupies the main outlet (sometimes inlet) on the east end, while the Dayak villages of Tanjung Isuy and Mancong (p652) are tucked away on the southwest end. During high water, *ces* can cut back to the main river at Muara Pahu from the west edge of the lake.

JANTUR

Jantur sits at the eastern side of Jempang and, during the wet season, it appears to be floating in the middle of the lake. It is built entirely on stilts in the marshy wetlands, which disappear under 6m of water in the rainy season. During the dry season, floating mats of water hyacinth can choke the channel through town, creating a transport nightmare.

TANJUNG ISUY

Tranquil and tiny Tanjung Isuy is the first Dayak village many people visit on their Mahakam journey. A fire took out the waterfront in 2015, giving the new mosque skyline supremacy; the resulting rebuild is more shanty town than traditional village, but the historical longhouse, Louu Taman Jamrud (p652), still stands as a sort of museum/craft shop/losmen and there are other traditional longhouses worthy of a visit nearby.

Few lamin (the local word for longhouse) around here are occupied outside of community ceremonies, but **Lamin Batu Bura** `FREE`, a Benuaq Dayak house, is an exception – you may find resident women sitting on the split bamboo floor weaving naturally dyed fibres of the doyo leaf into beautiful decorative cloth called *ulap doyo*. Walk or take an *ojek* 1.5km south of Tanjung Isuy dock, staying left at the fork.

Vacated in the 1970s and refurbished as a tourist hostel by the provincial government, **Louu Taman Jamrud** (Jl Indonesia Australia; r 110,000Rp) is a stately longhouse guarded by an impressive array of carved totems. Basic rooms have shared *mandi* (bathroom). If you just want to look around, ask at the shop across the road. The ladies there will happily also show you various carvings and jewellery for sale.

MANCONG

The small Dayak village of Mancong is worth a visit for its superb (but uninhabited) longhouse. For optimum jungle drama Mancong is best reached by boat on the Ohong creek from Lake Jempang. You'll meander past monitor lizards, sapphire-hued kingfishers, bulb-nosed proboscis monkeys, banded kraits and marauding macaques. They'll see you, but whether or not you see them is unknown. The journey beneath towering banyan trees is as much a part of the experience as your arrival.

The exquisitely restored 1930s **Mancong Longhouse** is flanked by intricately carved totems. Those with chickens represent a healing ceremony. The souvenir shop across the car park can rustle up blankets and mosquito nets if you absolutely must sleep in the otherwise vacant building (75,000Rp).

You can reach Mancong from Tanjung Isuy by boat or vehicle on an unpaved road. If water levels are high enough, charter a *ces* (return 500,000Rp, three hours). Alternatively ask in Tanjung Isuy about a Kijang (200,000Rp, 10km, 25 minutes).

Muara Pahu

Lining one side of a big curve in the Mahakam, Muara Pahu district is a collection of villages and the upriver exit point from Lake Jempang when the water is high enough. There's not much to do here – you can stroll the boardwalk, or sit and watch the tugboats haul coal downriver while waiting for the evening *kapal biasa*.

Melak

Melak, the last settlement of any size before you hit the upper Mahakam, is surprisingly modern and developed – at least once you leave the harbour area. Sendawar, the regency seat next door, is trying to out-develop itself, with each new government building more massive than the last. It is all very disorienting, and somewhat alarming considering this is likely a preview of what's to come upriver.

Centuries of culture, however, can't be erased with a few years of coal money. Spend any time here and you are as likely to find yourself invited to a Dayak funeral as to stumble across a cock fight. Start your wandering with the still-occupied longhouse at Eheng or the orchid preserve of **Kersik Luway** (⊙8am-4pm) `FREE`.

◉ Sights

Eheng   HISTORIC BUILDING
This rough wood-and-rattan Benauq Dayak longhouse is sparsely occupied during the day, but welcomes visitors – especially those interested in purchasing woven handicrafts, bracelets or an ornately carved *mandau* (machete). You may be able to negotiate a homestay, but be prepared with your own bedding. It's 30km southwest of Melak.

🛏 Sleeping & Eating

Hotel Flamboyan   HOTEL $
(☑0545-41033; Jl A Yani; r 150,000Rp; ☀) The only real attraction to this place is that it's opposite the boat dock – a welcome sight when you stumble off the *kapal biasa* at 1am. Tiny rooms lining a common hall have dilapidated private *mandi*, some with Western toilets, all with air-con. Marginally clean, but definitely not flamboyant.

Hotel Monita   HOTEL $$
(☑0545-41798; Jl Dr Sutoemo 76; r incl breakfast 240,000-420,000Rp; ☀🖤) Easily Melak's most comfortable hotel close to the river, but still about 1km uphill from the *kapal biasa* dock. It's popular with mining clients, but the 38 rooms, all with air-con and TV and most with hot showers, are rarely full. The restaurant can do dinner with a bit of notice.

ℹ Information

There are a number of international ATMs in Melak, including a BRI ATM about 50m from the boat dock.

Getting There & Away

Air Xpress Air flies to Samarinda on Monday, Wednesday and Friday and to Balikpapan Monday, Wednesday, Friday and Sunday. Susi Air services Samarinda via Data Dawai on Tuesday, Thursday and Saturday.

Boat *Kapal biasa* leave for Samarinda daily between 6pm and 7pm and pass heading upriver at 1am. Charter a *ces* for around 700,000Rp per day. Speedboats gather near the dock to take passengers downriver as far as Kota Bangun, but not upriver to Tering.

Bus Two buses for Samarinda depart in the morning (110,000Rp, nine hours).

Kijang Shared taxis run to Samarinda (250,000Rp, eight hours) and Balikpapan (300,000Rp, 12 hours). For Tering you'll need to charter a taxi (300,000Rp, one hour).

Tering

A planned community deep in gold-mining country, Tering is sometimes the last stop for *kapal biasa,* depending on the water level. It is really two settlements straddling the river: **Tering Baru**, a Malay village where the *kapal biasa* docks, and **Tering Lama**, a Bahau Dayak village on the northern bank, where a magnificent wooden church with intricate painted pillars has a bell tower supported by totem poles.

Kapal biasa arrive around 9am. Even during low water, they sometimes continue to Long Iram, an hour further upriver. Downriver *kapal biasa* leave around noon. A speedboat to Long Bagun is 300,000Rp for the four-hour journey. Kijang depart from the dock for Samarinda (300,000Rp) and Melak (charter 150,000Rp).

Long Bagun

The misty mountain village of Long Bagun is the end of the *kapal biasa* route at high water and is a fine terminus for your Mahakam adventure. Somewhere in the village, a local entrepreneur is bent over a grinder, polishing a semi-precious stone into a pendant, a Chinese shopkeeper is sweating over a forge, melting gold from nearby mines to sell in Samarinda, and a group of women is tying intricate beadwork for their children's next traditional dance performance. Only travellers determined to cover the whole Mahakam get this far, which is reward enough.

Boats pause at Ujoh Bilang, 3km downriver from Long Bagun, where you'll be required to register with the tourism office on the dock.

Speedboats heading up and downriver troll for passengers along the waterfront in the morning.

TIONG OHANG

Divided by the Mahakam, Tiong Ohang is united by its creaking suspension bridge, which offers scenic views of the surrounding hills. This is the last stop before starting, or ending, the second stage of the Cross-Borneo Trek (p613): the Muller Mountains. This is where local guides and porters assemble, but these services are best arranged in advance by a tour company.

A longboat from Long Bagun costs 1,000,000Rp and takes around four hours via numerous sets of rapids. The trailhead for the Muller Mountains is a further two hours upriver by *ces* (1,000,000Rp).

Muller Mountains

The demanding middle stage of the Cross-Borneo Trek (p613), the journey across the Muller Mountains is a very different experience from what precedes it. This is neither a cultural tour nor a wildlife-spotting expedition. In fact, views of any kind are scarce. This is a purpose-driven rainforest trek, and a difficult one.

Most people do the crossing in seven or more long, wet days. The trek follows a narrow path – if that – through a green maze with uncertain footing and near-constant creek crossings, some chest high. Campsites are a tarpaulin, and cooking is done over an open fire. There will be blood – from leeches, if nothing else. They are harmless, but their bites easily become infected in the damp environment.

All things considered, the experience hasn't changed much since George Muller first crossed his namesake range in 1825. While that first trek ended with the locals cutting off Muller's head (likely at the behest of the Sultan of Kutai), the primary risk today is breaking a leg or merely twisting an ankle so far from outside help. To that end, heed all the precautions and choose an experienced tour company or guide who has considered the concept of risk management.

The Muller trek is a horizontal Everest. You tackle it for the same reasons you climb. And when you succeed, it is both a lifetime memory and a noteworthy achievement.

Kutai National Park

Kutai National Park has seen its share of troubles. All but abandoned in the late '90s as a conservation failure ransacked by logging and fires, new studies are showing all is not lost. The wild orang-utan population has recovered to as many as 2000 individuals, and pockets of forest are still relatively intact. The Prevab station near Sangatta offers one of Kalimantan's best chances to see truly wild orang-utans, and numerous guides and tour companies from Samarinda and Balikpapan know the park well.

From the ranger station, several kilometres of trails fan out through decent secondary forest, where large buttressed trees still provide plenty of hiding spots for orangutans. The rangers are experts at moving slowly and listening for the telltale rustle of the canopy that betrays a critter's location. Bring mosquito repellent.

Call the lead ranger, Pak Supiani (0813 4634 8803), before visiting so he can organise your permit and a boat. Park permits are 150,000Rp per day (225,000Rp on weekends). Guides (required) cost 120,000Rp per two-hour trek.

Regular buses run from Samarinda to Sangatta (45,000Rp, four hours). Take a taxi from there to Kabo Jaya, where a park boat will ferry you to the ranger station (300,000Rp return, 15 minutes).

Berau

📋 0554 / POP TANJUNG REDEB 63,000

Berau is a sprawling East Kalimantan town that serves as a transit point for the Derawan Archipelago to the east and the karst wonderland of Merabu to the south. The main commercial centre on the river is called Tanjung Redeb, which is also used to refer to the town itself. An influx of mine workers and the odd tourist has boosted the amenities, but few travellers hang around here long. Berau is not easily reached by road from the south – most Derawan-bound travellers fly in and arrange transport out.

👁 Sights

Museum Batiwakkal
MUSEUM
(Jl Kuran, Gunung Tabur Keraton; admission by donation; ⏰8am-3pm Tue-Thu & Sun, to 1pm Sat) Located at the site of Berau's original *keraton* (royal palace), this 1981 building houses an eclectic collection of sultan-obilia starting from the 17th century. Get here by canoe taxi (5000Rp) from Jl Ahmad Yani.

Keraton Sambaliung
MUSEUM
(Jl ST Amuniddan, Sambaliung; ⏰9am-1pm Tue-Thu, Sat & Sun) **FREE** This 215-year-old *keraton* was built after descendants of brothers from other mothers (same father: the 9th sultan) got tired of alternating rule at Gunung Tabor and split the sultanate. The colossal stuffed crocodile outside is an impressive, if somewhat random, addition.

🛏 Sleeping

★Rumah Kedaung
GUESTHOUSE $$
(📋0821 5326 6291; rumahkedaung@yahoo.com; Jl Kedaung, Borneo IV, Sei Bedungun; r incl breakfast 385,000Rp; ✳🔋) Located in a quiet neighbourhood between the airport and Tanjung Redeb, this rustic guesthouse in a palm-filled garden is easily the most pleasant stay in Berau. The common areas are decked out with Dayak art, and the rough wood duplex bungalows have a creaky charm. The cafe serves up solid local fare – a plus since there is not much nearby.

Hotel Mitra
HOTEL $$
(📋0812 5315 0715; Jl Gajah Mada 531A; s/d incl breakfast 255,000/285,000Rp; ✳🔋) Clean, with friendly staff, Mitra is Berau's best budget choice with the feel of a large guesthouse. Staff are accustomed to dealing with foreigners, though there's still not much English spoken. All rooms have air-con and cold water only. Motorbikes are available for rent (100,000Rp a day).

Palmy Hotel
BOUTIQUE HOTEL $$
(📋0554-202 0333; palmyhotel@yahoo.com; Jl Pangeran Antasari 26; r incl breakfast 450,000-750,000Rp; ✳🔋) The original of three Palmy hotels in town, this boutique offering is compact and contemporary with a gym and an inviting ground-level cafe. Free airport transfers.

🍴 Eating & Drinking

★De Bunda Cafe
INDONESIAN $
(📋0812 5176 6811; Jl Pangeran Antasari 5; mains 15,000-50,000Rp; ⏰7am-5pm; 🔋) This fab

Berau

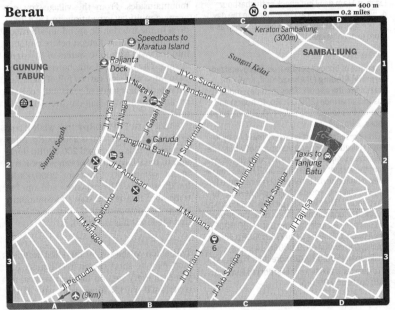

little cafe-bakery serves Indonesian staples such as *soto ayam* and nasi goreng along with unusual dishes such as roast duck and ribs. Good juices and cakes. Owner Ibu Ayu is well travelled and speaks English, though she's not often around.

Seafood Warungs SEAFOOD $
(Jl Pangeran Antasari; mains 20,000-70,000Rp) As night falls, basic seafood tents with bright banners set up opposite the Palmy Hotel in Tanjung Redeb. Depending on the day's catch you should be able to enjoy fresh fish, prawns, crab and squid – or fall back on grilled chicken.

Sky Lounge 360 ROOFTOP BAR
(Palmy Exclusive, Jl Pangeran Antasari; ⊙5pm-1am) The stylish, partially open-air rooftop bar at Palmy Exclusive is the place to come for a panoramic city view, live music on weekends and a range of beers and ciders.

⊕ Getting There & Away

AIR

There are seven direct flights daily from Berau to Balikpapan (one hour), with connections to other Indonesian cities. Xpress Air flies to Tarakan and Samarinda four times a week. Susi Air flies to Maratua on Thursday, continuing on to Tarakan. Airlines include the following:

Berau

◉ Sights
1 Museum Batiwakkal...............................A1

◉ Sleeping
2 Hotel Mitra B1
3 Palmy Hotel..B2

◉ Eating
4 De Bunda Cafe...B2
5 Seafood Warungs....................................A2

◉ Drinking & Nightlife
6 Sky Lounge...C3

Garuda (☑0554-202 0285; Jl Panglima Batur 396, Hotel Derawan Indah; ⊙8am-4.30pm Mon-Fri, 9am-3pm Sat & Sun)
Sriwijaya Air (☑0554-202 8777; airport)
Susi Air (☑0822 5541 9164; www.susiair.com; airport)
Wings Air (☑0811 162 9882; www.lionair.co.id; airport)
Xpress Air (☑0852 5514 5344; http://xpress air.co.id; airport)

BOAT

For the Maratua atoll it's still possible (and quicker) to take a public speedboat directly from Berau jetty in Tanjung Redeb via Sungai Berau (250,000Rp, three hours). These theoretically leave at 11am daily but check at the harbour or with your Maratua accommodation the day before. Maratua resorts also offer this trip as a more expensive charter.

BUS & TAXI

A handful of buses operate from the oversized **Terminal Rinding** (Jl Ahmad Yani, Km5), on the road to the airport. They include a morning bus to Samarinda (200,000Rp, 15 hours) and a Damri bus to Tanjung Selor (50,000Rp, three hours, 9am).

Otherwise transport is largely handled by Kijang (shared taxi) operators, many of whom are unlicensed. Kijang gather in the morning across from the former bus terminal on Jl H Isa I and require a minimum of three passengers (more for bigger vehicles); you can buy multiple seats to leave earlier. They will also pick up around town, so ask at your accommodation or at the airport. Destinations include Tanjung Batu (100,000Rp, three hours), Tanjung Selor (150,000Rp, three hours), Samarinda (400,000Rp, 14 hours) and Balikpapan (500,000Rp, more than 20 hours).

To charter a taxi from the airport to Tanjung Batu costs 650,000Rp.

Merabu

Isolated between a small river and a fortress of karst pinnacles, the Dayak Lebo villagers of Merabu never worried much about politics or the outside world. So they were understandably shocked the day in 2012 when they found bulldozers clearing nearby forests for an oil-palm plantation, and confused to learn their gardens were soon to become a coal mine.

Rather than be bought off, however, they waged a long (and occasionally ugly) battle for their homeland. Finally in 2014 they became the first village in Berau District to gain official recognition of their village forest, an important step towards securing the rights of indigenous communities. As part of their new forest management plan, Merabu has also opened its doors to ecotourism – an activity the village is particularly well positioned to provide.

It takes a bit of work to get here, but once you do, you may never want to leave.

Sights & Activities

The jagged limestone forest in the village's backyard is one of Kalimantan's least-explored and least-accessible regions, meaning its wildlife has largely been spared from overhunting. Orang-utans dwell in the lowlands, while clouded leopards prowl the mountainsides. From the village you can arrange multiday expeditions to Lake Tebo, deep in the interior, or spend an afternoon climbing to Puncak Ketepu before plunging into the vivid turquoise waters of **Nyadeng spring**. The drawcard site, however, is **Goa Beloyot**, a cliff-side cavern full of stencilled handprints thousands of years old, accessed by an adventurous half-day trek (bring a torch).

Guides cost 100,000Rp a trip, while a boat to Nyadeng and Ketepu is 230,000Rp. Additionally there is a required 200,000Rp donation to the village, and you can adopt a tree in the community forest for 2000Rp for three years. The expenses add up, but remember this is one way the community visionaries demonstrate to their neighbours that the forest has value as it is.

Puncak Ketepu   HIKING

This climb to the rim of the karst wonderland may be short (about two hours), but you earn every step on the near-vertical ascent. You'll quickly forget your pain as the fortress of pinnacles and ridges unfolds before you, begging you to continue into the great unknown. Do not even consider this hike in the rain, as the trail turns to grease.

Sleeping & Eating

Homestays cost a fixed 250,000Rp per night per room and will be allocated to you, or the more modern Lodge Merabu is available at 500,000Rp.

Meals are provided at your homestay for 25,000Rp each

Information

Before visiting contact the village head, **Franly Oley** (📱 0878 1030 3330; franlyoley@gmail.com), who speaks passable English and can arrange homestay, guide and transport. A village donation of 200,000Rp is requested.

Getting There & Away

The best transport option is to come from Berau to the north. Charter a Kijang (1,500,000Rp) for the four- to six-hour dirt-road journey through Lesan village. Driver Pak Asri (0853 4135 9088) is familiar with the route, or contact Franly Oley in advance.

Coming from the south, it's about seven hours (2,000,000Rp) from Sangatta. From Muara Wahau the route gets a little tricky, with a 4WD or a motorbike required for the sketchy road. Head 55km north to the Merapun gate (Garpu Dayak Merapun), then turn east into the oil-palm plantation. At the first major fork (15km) head left to Merapun to hire a boat to Merabu (price negotiable, 1½ hours) or turn right to continue 40km over land (impassable when wet) to the Lesan road, where you'll make a hard right. Just under 4km beyond, you'll arrive at the river. Merabu is opposite.

Once you arrive at the end of the road, shout across the river for a *ketinting* (canoe ferry; 25,000Rp).

Derawan Archipelago

The classic tropical islands of the Derawan Archipelago are where you go to trade jungle trekking and orang-utans for beachcombing and manta rays. Of the 31 named islands found here, the most accessible to visitors are tiny but increasingly busy Pulau Derawan and the peaceful paradise of the Maratua atoll, while the uninhabited Sangalaki and Kakaban islands are on every diving itinerary.

The scuba diving and snorkelling here rank among the best in Indonesia, offering an assortment of reef and pelagic species, including barracuda, sharks, mantas and turtles. Travel to and between the islands can be expensive, so plan your trip carefully and find friends to share costs with. Seas are rough in January and February, limiting diving and increasing travel risks.

Diving & Snorkelling

Most people come to Derawan for the superb diving and snorkelling. Apart from the many dive sites around Derawan, Maratua, Sangalaki and Kakaban, there are locations where manta rays, whale sharks and sea turtles are regularly sighted.The best time for diving is May to July. Note that currents can be strong, particularly around the Maratua atoll.

There are five main dive operators on Derawan and upmarket dive resorts on Maratua and Sangalaki. Expect to pay around US$100 for two boat dives and US$350 for a PADI open-water course. All of the lodges and resorts offer various dive and accommodation packages.

A full-day snorkelling trip costs between 1,500,000Rp and 2,000,000Rp depending on how far you go and the size of the boat. It is four hours of spine-compressing travel from Derawan to the popular snorkelling areas around Kakaban and Sangalaki and back. Count on six to seven hours if you include Maratua dive sites.

Pulau Derawan

POP 1800

The closest island to shore and the main diving and accommodation base, Derawan is just a speck in the Celebes Sea, barely (but just) visible from the mainland. Once a quiet fishing village, the western edge is now tightly packed with homestays, bungalows and timber jetties that seem to get longer each year, reaching out into the sea like tentacles. As a result it can get crowded (by Kalimantan standards) on weekends in high season and litter can be a problem, but the locals still maintain a friendly attitude, there's decent snorkelling off the stilted boardwalks and you can easily arrange transport to other islands from here.

🏃 Activities

Scuba Junkie Sangalaki   DIVING
(📞0813 3702 4553; www.sangalakidiveresort. com; snorkelling 450,000Rp, 2-/3-dive package with equipment 1,850,000/2,000,000Rp) Scuba Junkie brings its Sipadan experience to Derawan with professional staff, decent boats, an overwater lodge with dorms and bungalows, and an ecofriendly ethos.

Dive-accommodation packages and transfers from Berau or tarakan available.

Derawan Dive Resort   DIVING
(📞0811 542 4121; www.divederawan.com; jetty/ discover dive 550,000/650,000Rp, 3-dive package 1,500,000Rp) Dive from the private jetty or take a three-dive package to surrounding islands at Derawan's largest dive resort. Also does boat charters and accommodation.

Tasik Divers   DIVING
(📞0821 8960 7492; www.derawandivelodge.com; 3 dives US$165, with own equipment US$135) Established outfit at Derawan Dive Lodge (p658) with modern boats, small-group dive trips and PADI courses.

Borneo Diving   DIVING
(📞0811 536 363; www.borneo-diving.com; single dive 500,000Rp) Based at La Pauta at the main jetty, Borneo Dive has three boats and knowledgeable dive guides.

🛏 Sleeping

Overwater bungalows on stilt boardwalks are becoming the norm rather than the exception on Derawan, with more being built each year. Expect to pay a minimum 300,000Rp. There are lots of village homestays (look for signs) back from the shore charging around 200,000Rp for a room with fan and cold water.

Penginapan 88
GUESTHOUSE $$

(☑ 0813 4660 3944; d 500,000-700,000Rp; ✳) Roughly halfway along the village strip, this waterfront place has 10 overwater aircon rooms and a couple of 'penthouse' rooms way out on the end of the pier with unobstructed water views.

La Pauta
COTTAGE $$

(☑ 0813 1944 7742; www.lapautaderawanresort .com; d incl breakfast 300,000-900,000Rp; ✳) Beside the main jetty and with a relatively clean private beach, this is one of Derawan's best-value resorts, with well-designed timber rooms and cottages. The cheapest rooms share a bathroom but all have air-con. There's a dive shop but it doesn't feel like an exclusive dive resort. The overwater restaurant is one of the best on the island.

Reza Guesthouse
BUNGALOW $$

(☑ 0813 4795 5950; darjohnturtle@gmail.com; r 350,000-500,000Rp; ✳) These compact overwater bungalows are clean and well placed – the more expensive ones have air-con and hot water.

Derawan Dive Resort
RESORT $$

(☑ 0811 542 4121; www.divederawan.com; d/tr/ste incl breakfast from 525,000/585,000/1,430,000Rp; ✳) The largest dive resort on Derawan, this well-run place has 27 cottages scattered around a private beach, along with a snaking jetty and overwater restaurant. The timber Kalimantan-style cottages all have air-con and range from comfortable standard ones back from the beach, to deluxe 'floating' bungalows and suites on stilts with hot water and TV.

Derawan Beach Cafe & Cottages
GUESTHOUSE $$

(☑ 0853 4679 7578; d incl breakfast 550,000-880,000Rp; ✳) Towards the south end of the village strip, this group of waterfront cottages, including two premium overwater bungalows, boasts one of the longest jetties on the island and a small private beach. The best rooms have air-con and hot water.

Sari Cottages
GUESTHOUSE $$

(☑ 0813 4653 8448; r 400,000Rp; ✳) Centrally located Sari has 22 compact rooms, strung along two parallel piers connected by a footbridge. All have air-con, cold-water showers and private back verandas with at least partial water views. Turn off the street at the sign for 'Pinades', and keep walking the plank.

Miranda Homestay
HOMESTAY $$

(☑ 0813 4662 3550; r incl breakfast 300,000Rp; ✳) The eight clean waterside rooms are good value, all with air-con and bathroom. Ask about hiring Pak Marudi's *klotok* for snorkelling excursions (1,000,000Rp per day).

Derawan Dive Lodge
LODGE $$$

(☑ 0431-824445; www.derawandivelodge.com; s/d incl breakfast US$60/80; ✳) A small enclave of 10 comfortable, individually designed rooms, with a cosy outdoor cafe and private beach, at the western end of the island. If you want to combine a dive holiday with some intimate island life, this is one of the better choices on Derawan. All rooms are air-conditioned with hot showers. Add an extra US$20 for full board.

✕ Eating

There are just a handful of warungs on the main village strip, but they open on a whim or when the supplies come in from the mainland. Fresh seafood is the local speciality.

Rumah Makan Nur
INDONESIAN $

(☑ 0853 4689 7827; mains 25,000-80,000Rp) Nur's serves up tasty Indonesian favourites with creative twists such as shrimp and coconut aubergine with rice, or fried tempe with green beans.

Restaurant La Pauta
SEAFOOD $$

(mains 15,000-120,000Rp; ⊘ 7am-1pm & 5-10pm) The overwater restaurant at La Pauta is one of Derawan's best. Sit inside, or out on the breezy veranda overlooking the main dock. The speciality is local seafood, but all the Indonesian staples are on the menu and there's beer in the fridge.

ℹ Information

There are no ATMs or money-exchange facilities on the island. Bring plenty of cash.

There's no wi-fi on the island, but phone reception and 4G is reliable.

ℹ Getting There & Away

From the port of Tanjung Batu, 110km east of Berau, a regular morning boat takes passengers to Pulau Derawan (100,000Rp per person, 30 minutes). If you arrive later in the day you may have to charter a speedboat (300,000Rp, seats four) or ask around about sharing. Boats return from Derawan between 7am and 8am.

On Friday there's a direct speedboat from Tarakan to Pulau Derawan (300,000Rp, three hours, 10am), returning on Saturday at 10am.

ℹ️ Getting Around

Derawan is tiny: you can walk the main village strip from end to end in 15 minutes. Several places rent bicycles (50,000Rp per day), which are handy for making a circuit of the island.

Maratua Atoll

If you're willing to go a little further out than Derawan, Maratua is a slice of little-known heaven. This large (relative to the rest of the archipelago) U-shaped atoll is gradually developing, with a number of high-priced luxury resorts, but it's still very low key and independent travellers are a rare sight.

Four tiny fishing villages are evenly spaced along the narrow strip of land. Central to the island, the village of Tanjung Harapan offers several homestays, motorbike rental and access to the island's only upscale lodging options. Bohe Silian, at the southern end of the road and the island, also has a few homestays, pleasant sea views and Sembat cave – the coolest swimming hole on the island.

🛏️ Sleeping

Maratua has a handful of village homestays (from 250,000Rp for a room) and a clutch of reasonably flashy dive resorts. Accommodation here is overall much pricier than on Derawan. At the edge of the Maratua atoll and accessed by private boat transfers are three luxury dive resorts – Nunukan Island, Nabucco Island and Virgin Cocoa, owned by German company Extra Divers.

Maratua Guesthouse   GUESTHOUSE **$$$**
(www.maratuaguesthouse.com; Maratua Atoll; d & tw cabins incl meals US$113-133; ⊛) Nestled in a forest between the island's prettiest beach and an inland tidal pond, and with a house reef out front, this rustic place offers a commanding view of the Celebes Sea from its simple open-air restaurant and shady private cabins. Newer cabins back in the jungle are cheaper but all have attached bathroom, air-conditioning and soft beds.

★Nabucco Island Resort   RESORT **$$$**
(📞0812 540 6636; www.extradivers-worldwide.com; s/d/tr incl full board €136/208/282; ⊛ 🛜)
🏊 At the edge of the Maratua lagoon, this compact island dive resort packs plenty into a tiny manicured space. Surrounding a central common area, the varnished duplex bungalows each share an ocean-view porch with access to mangroves, a white-sand beach, or a slice of house reef. Dive packages start at €420 for 10 dives.

Virgin Cocoa   RESORT **$$$**
(📞0811 592 3450; http://virgincocoa.com; s/d with half board €239/318; ⊛ 🛜 🍴) Linked to Nunukan Island by a 1km-long boardwalk, Virgin Cocoa is Maratua's latest luxury offering. More a luxurious retreat than a dive resort, it has 18 cosy bungalows scattered among the palms, a pool, yoga centre, spa treatments and a sense of isolation. There's a house reef just off the beach for snorkelling.

Green Nirvana   RESORT **$$$**
(📞0812 5003 2622; www.greennirvanaresort.com; Jl Bayur, Payung-Payung; d incl breakfast from 1,500,000-2,300,000Rp, 3-bedroom house 7,600,000Rp; ⊛ 🍴) Mainland Maratua's flashest dive resort is a stylish collection of villas orbiting a pool and deck overlooking a gorgeous stretch of coast and a long pier. The resort is set a little back from the beach, but it's beautifully designed in concert with the surrounding environment. Multiday packages include transfers from the mainland.

Maratua Paradise Resort   RESORT **$$$**
(📞+60 088 224918; www.maratua.com; beach bungalow/water villa US$92/127; ⊛) Just south of the main village and jetty, Maratua Paradise is a popular choice for its beachfront and overwater villas – the only ones on the main island. The bungalows are looking a little tired for this price, but overall the resort ticks most boxes with its overwater restaurant, dive shop and opportunities for snorkelling off the beach.

Nunukan Island Resort   RESORT **$$$**
(📞0812 340 3451; www.nunukan-island.com; s/d/tr incl full board €136/208/282; ⊛ 🛜) From the long jetty welcoming you across the 4km house reef, to the common areas hovering over razor-sharp limestone, there is nothing typical – and everything exotic – about this island resort. The 22 luxurious beachfront bungalows have spacious porches with sofa

beds begging you to soak in the serenity. House-reef dive packages start at €360 for 10 dives.

❶ Getting There & Away

Maratua's airstrip has been open since 2016, but currently has only one scheduled weekly Susi Air flight on Wednesday from Tarakan and Berau. A weekly (Saturday) Garuda charter flight from Balikpapan can be booked through Nunukan Island Resort.

A chartered speedboat to Maratua from Tanjung Batu is 1,500,000Rp for the 1½-hour journey, or 1,000,000Rp for the one-hour trip from Derawan.

A daily public speedboat direct from Berau jetty in Tanjung Redeb via the Sungai Berau (250,000Rp, three hours) theoretically leaves at 11am, returning from Maratua's main jetty at 9am. Check schedules with your Maratua accommodation. Island resorts also offer this trip as a more expensive charter.

Pulau Kakaban & Pulau Sangalaki

Kakaban and Sangalaki, two undeveloped islands 40 minutes southwest of Maratua and an hour southeast of Derawan by boat, are on every diving or snorkelling day-trip itinerary, and for good reason.

Pulau Kakaban is famous for its inland lake (admission by donation) where bizarre stingless jellyfish have evolved. It's a 10-minute walk through the jungle along a boardwalk to reach the lake jetty, from where you can snorkel (don't use fins) in shallow waters amid an ethereal swarm

---

TURTLE CONSERVATION

Sea turtles are a common sight swimming beneath the boardwalks of Pulau Derawan or on diving and snorkelling trips, but the green and hawksbill turtles of Derawan archipelago are constantly under threat from poaching.

A long-running turtle conservation project on Pulau Sangalaki, currently administered by BKSDA Kaltim (bksda-kaltim.menlhk.go.id), seeks to protect the nesting sites on Sangalaki, monitor turtle numbers and habitat and clear the beaches to minimise disturbance. Ranger-guided trips to see turtle nesting sites can be arranged on Pulau Derawan or through Sangalaki Resort.

---

of jellyfish, some as tiny as your fingertip. If tides permit, snorkel through Kakaban's tidal-cave tunnel to a hidden outcrop of protected pristine coral.

Pulau Sangalaki is a real castaway island with decent diving and a small resort, but is known primarily for its consistent manta ray spotting. Trips to Manta Corner will usually result in numerous sightings.

🛏 Sleeping

Sangalaki Resort RESORT $$$
(☑ 0813 2011 8833; http://sangalakiresort.net; Pulau Sangalaki; s/d from US$200/250) Reopened in 2017, this resort is a surprising find on an otherwise pristine marine-park island. It's still fairly low key with 14 standalone cottages (raised on stilts so as not to hinder turtle movement). The bar and restaurant provides a focal point and there's an on-site dive shop and private boat, but nothing else on the island.

❶ Getting There & Away

Divers and snorkellers visit Sangalaki as part of a longer trip. If you're staying here the one-hour speedboat trip from Tanjung Batu costs around 1,000,000Rp; contact the resort to arrange a charter.

North Kalimantan

Because of its isolation, North Kalimantan contains some of the most pristine forests on Borneo, making it one of the last, and best, frontiers for hardcore jungle trekking. For the same reason, this is one of the most challenging and inaccessible parts of the island.

◉ Sights & Activities

The 13,600-sq-km **Kayan Mentarang National Park** represents a significant chunk of the heart of Borneo, and contains a dizzying diversity of life, with new species still being discovered. When it comes to travelling here, the rewards are returned in direct proportion to the level of difficulty.

The two best places from which to access the park are **Long Bawan** to the north, and **Long Punjungan** to the south. Many of the ecotourism initiatives developed by WWF (www.borneo-ecotourism.com) have been left fallow, but the information they provide is a great orientation to the area.

In Long Bawan contact English-speaking Alex Balang (☑ 0852 4705 7469, alexbalang

@hotmail.com) to get the lay of the land and to arrange treks further afield.

To the south the path is even more untrodden, and Bahasa Indonesia is essential. Start your journey at **Tanjung Selor**, where sizeable longboats powered by multiple outboard engines load wares for the long haul upstream to Long Punjungan. Pak Muming (☑ 0812 540 4256) at Hotel Asoy and Pak Heri (☑ 0822 5053 8995) both regularly make the trip.

ℹ Getting There & Away

The Tawah border crossing is a reasonably well-travelled route between Malaysia (Sabah) and Indonesia (Kalimantan). From Tawah there are numerous options for moving on by boat, while Nunukan and Tarakan have reasonably good transport connections, though navigating deeper into North Kalimantan can be difficult.

AIR

Tarakan is the main air hub, while Nunukan has a small airport.

There are flights from Tarakan to Berau (400,000Rp, 30 minutes), Balikpapan (400,000Rp, one hour), Nunukan (360,000Rp, 25 minutes), Jakarta, 1,400,000Rp, three hours), Long Bawan (450,000Rp, one hour) and Makassar (1,300,00Rp, 1¾ hours). Coming from Malaysia, there are three weekly flights between Tawau and Tarakan (RM280, 40 minutes).

BOAT

A variety of speedboats and ferries can get you between Malaysian and Indonesian Borneo. Services include Tawau (Sabah) to Nunukan (RM80, 1½ hours, two daily) and Tarakan (RM130, four hours, 10am Tuesday, Thursday and Saturday),

---

ℹ GETTING TO MALAYSIA: TARAKAN TO TAWAU

Getting to the border Travelling overland to the border with Sabah (Malaysia) involves a short ferry ride from Tarakan (400,000Rp, four hours, Monday, Wednesday and Friday) or Nunukan (200,000Rp, 1½ hours, two daily except Sunday). Tarakan can be reached directly by air from Berau and Balikpapan, or by a combination of bus and boat from Berau via Tanjung Selor.

At the border Citizens of the US, Canada, Australia, most Commonwealth countries and most of Western Europe receive a three-month visa on arrival (US$35) at the border between Nunukan (Indonesia) and Tawau (Malaysia).

Moving on Tawau has good air and bus connections with the rest of Sabah, including Kota Kinabalu and Sandakan.

Nunukan to Tarakan (240,000Rp, 2½ hours, five daily), Tarakan to Derawan (300,000Rp, three hours, 10am Friday) and Tarakan to Tanjung Selor (120,000Rp, one hour, daily).

BUS & TAXI

An air-con Damri bus departs from Tanjung Selor at 11am for Berau's Terminal Rinding (50,000Rp, three hours). Kinjang (shared taxis) also go to Berau (120,000Rp), leaving when full and dropping passengers in Tanjung Redeb.

There's also a Damri bus from Tanjung Selor's Pasar Induk to Malinau (130,000Rp, five hours).

AT A GLANCE

POPULATION
18.8 million

LARGEST LAKE
Danau Poso (p696)

**BEST FOR ADVEN-
TURE SPORTS**
Minahasa (p718)

**BEST REGIONAL
CUISINE**
Coto Nusantara
(p669)

BEST GUESTHOUSE
Sulawesi Castle
(p685)

**WHEN TO GO
Apr–Oct**
It's peak season
for scuba diving,
with calm seas and
incredible visibility.

Nov–Mar
Lembeh Strait
critters tend to come
out of the muck more
in the wet season.

Jun–Aug
The best months
to experience Tana
Toraja's biggest
funeral ceremonies.

Sulawesi

T he contents of Sulawesi are as beguiling as its shape. Just as this splay-limbed tropical island was formed by the complex and sometimes violent mashup of tectonic plates, its fascinating social fabric is the result of the complex and sometimes violent mashup of ethnic groups, religions and ecosystems.

Flanked by teeming waters and reefs, Sulawesi's interior is mountainous and cloaked in dense jungle. Here rare species such as nocturnal tarsiers and flamboyant maleo birds survive – as do proud cultures, long isolated by impenetrable topography from the onslaughts of modernity.

Meet the Toraja highlanders, with their elaborate funeral ceremonies; the Minahasans in the north, who offer spicy dishes made of everything from fish to stewed forest rat; and the lowland and coastal Bugis, Indonesia's most (in)famous seafarers.

It all combines – the land and the people – to make Sulawesi one of the most compelling islands in Indonesia.

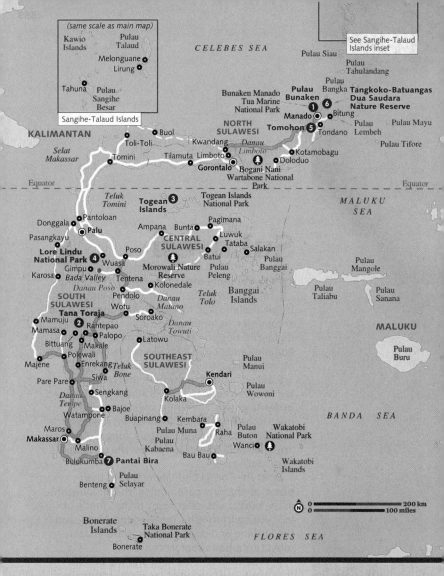

Sulawesi Highlights

❶ Pulau Bunaken (p713)
Snorkelling or diving along unbelievably rich coral drop-offs – some of Asia's best.

❷ Tana Toraja (p679)
Witnessing the ritual and tradition of an elaborate funeral ceremony.

❸ Togean Islands (p702)
Finding barefoot bliss in these off-grid, paradisaical islands.

❹ Lore Lindu National Park (p697) Staring into the stony faces of ancient megaliths.

❺ Tomohon (p717) Hiking, cycling and birdwatching in this stunning volcanic region.

❻ Tangkoko-Batuangas Dua Saudara Nature Reserve (p720) Spotting sprightly tarsiers, black macaques and a bevy of birds.

❼ Pantai Bira (p673)
Walking the beaches, diving the waters and exploring the diverse countryside.

History

The interior of Sulawesi provided a refuge for some of Indonesia's earliest inhabitants, some of whom preserved elements of their rich cultures well into the 20th century. The Makassarese and Bugis of the southwestern peninsula and the Christian Minahasans of the far north are the dominant groups in Sulawesi. The unique traditions, architecture and ceremonies of the Toraja people make the interior of South Sulawesi a deservedly popular destination.

Other minorities, particularly Bajau sea nomads, have played an integral role in the island's history. The rise of the kingdom of Gowa – Sulawesi's first major power – from the mid-16th century was partly due to its trading alliance with the Bajau. The Bajau supplied valuable sea produce, especially the Chinese delicacy trepang (sea cucumber), tortoiseshell, birds' nests and pearls, which attracted international traders to Gowa's capital, Makassar.

Makassar quickly became known as a cosmopolitan, tolerant and secure entrepôt that allowed traders to bypass the Dutch monopoly over the spice trade in the east – a considerable concern to the Dutch. In 1660 the Dutch sunk six Portuguese ships in Makassar harbour, captured the fort and in 1667 forced Gowa's ruler, Sultan Hasanuddin, into an alliance. Eventually, the Dutch managed to exclude all other foreign traders from Makassar, effectively shutting down the port.

Indonesia won its independence from the Dutch in 1945, but ongoing civil strife hampered Sulawesi's attempts at post-WWII reconstruction until well into the 1960s. A period of uninterrupted peace delivered unprecedented and accelerating development, particularly evident in the ever-growing Makassar metropolis.

Tragically, the Poso region in Central Sulawesi fell into a cycle of intercommunal violence in 1998, though things have calmed down considerably since. Since 2013 the development of the Trans-Sulawesi highway and the upgrading of several regional airports have improved the island's transport connections, boosting trade and tourism.

In 2018, Central Sulawesi was hit with a 7.4 magnitude earthquake, causing a tsunami that devastated the city of Palu and nearby Donggala. Over 1200 people lost their lives and many iconic buildings and hotels were destroyed. Despite the damage, the airport, immigration offices, and other key tourist services reopened mere days after the event. While effects of the damage will be noticeable for years to come, Palu is still a usable tourist hub for travel to other parts of Central Sulawesi.

ⓘ Getting There & Away

AIR
Domestic

The two main transport hubs are Makassar and Manado. Palu is the third most important airport and remains so even after the 2018 tsunami. In recent years Gorontalo, Luwuk, Poso and Kendari have all seen an increase in air traffic; minor airports at towns such as Ampana, Selayar and Naha (Sangihe-Talaud Islands) also provide useful links for travellers.

There are direct flights to Java, Bali, Kalimantan, Maluku and Papua.

International

Silk Air flies between Manado and Singapore four days a week (from around US$170, 3¾ hours). Air Asia flies from Makassar to Kuala Lumpur, Malaysia (from US$70, 3¼ hours).

BOAT

Sulawesi is well connected by sea, with around half the Pelni ferry fleet calling at Makassar, Bitung (the seaport for Manado), Pare Pare and Toli-Toli, as well as a few other minor towns.

ⓘ Getting Around

AIR

Wings Air and Garuda Indonesia are the main links within Sulawesi, with some flights by Sriwijaya Air.

BOAT

With the proliferation of affordable flights around Sulawesi, very few travellers now use Pelni ferries. But the *Tilongkabila* ferry still sails every two weeks from Makassar to Bau Bau, Raha and Kendari, up to Kolonedale, Luwuk, Gorontalo and Bitung and returns the same way to Makassar.

Elsewhere along the coast creaky old ferries and wooden boats run to destinations including the Togean Islands. Speedboats are occasionally available for charter. Around the southeastern peninsula, the *kapal cepat* (fast boats) and the 'superjet' are the way to go.

BUS, BEMO & KIJIANG

Excellent air-conditioned buses connect Rantepao with Makassar. Elsewhere you're looking at pretty clapped-out local buses that stop every few minutes. There are some decent long-distance bemo (minibus) services, particularly on the road across Central Sulawesi connecting Luwuk and Palu.

Shared Kijang or Avanza (names of vehicle types) have replaced buses entirely on some routes; these are quicker and cost a bit more, but aren't necessarily more comfortable.

In towns minibuses called *mikrolet* or *pete-pete* are the main mode of transport for locals. The ride-hailing app Grab (and to a lesser extent Go-Jek) is online in the major cities, evening the playing field when it comes to haggling (there is none).

SOUTH SULAWESI

South Sulawesi is huge. The sprawling capital and bustling port city of Makassar in the far south is tumultuous yet friendly, and likely where your journey will start or end. While you're there, feast on some of the best seafood on the island and explore the stunning karst landscapes just outside of town. If you have a little longer, the southeast corner of the peninsula is home to sleepy Pantai Bira with its world-class diving and fine sandy beaches.

South Sulawesi's drawcard site, however, is Tana Toraja – a spectacular highlands that should not be missed. There, you'll find a dizzying blend of mountains carved with rice paddies, outlandish funeral ceremonies, and some of the most fantastical traditional architecture in Asia. You could easily spend weeks trekking through the verdant hills, visiting hidden villages, and discovering forgotten waterfalls.

GUA LEANG LEANG

The **Gua Leang Leang** (Indonesian/foreigner 5000/20,000Rp; ⊘ dawn-dusk) caves are noted for their ancient paintings and handprints. Recent studies of nearby caves have placed the art at over 35,000 years old, making them the oldest pictographs in the world. There are 60 or so known caves in the Maros district; the limestone karst here has more holes than a Swiss cheese.

Catch a *pete-pete* from Maros to the Taman Purbakala Leang-Leang turn-off on the road to Bantimurung, and walk the last couple of kilometres.

History

The dominant powers in the south were long the Makassarese kingdom of Gowa (around the port of Makassar) and the Bugis kingdom of Bone. By the mid-16th century, Gowa had established itself at the head of a major trading bloc in eastern Indonesia. The king of Gowa adopted Islam in 1605 and Bone was soon subdued, spreading Islam to the whole Bugis–Makassarese area.

The Dutch United East India Company found Gowa a considerable hindrance to its plans to monopolise the spice trade until a deal was struck with the exiled Bugis prince Arung Palakka. The Dutch sponsored Palakka's return to Bone in 1666, prompting Bone to rise against the Makassarese. A year of fighting ensued and Sultan Hasanuddin of Gowa was forced to sign the Treaty of Bungaya in 1667, which severely reduced Gowa's power. Bone, under Palakka, then became the supreme state of South Sulawesi.

Rivalry between Bone and the other Bugis states continually reshaped the political landscape. After their brief absence during the Napoleonic Wars, the Dutch returned to a Bugis revolt led by the queen of Bone. This was suppressed, but rebellions continued until Makassarese and Bugis resistance was finally broken in the early years of the 20th century. Unrest lingered on until the early 1930s, and revolts against the central Indonesian government occurred again in the 1950s.

The Makassarese and Bugis are staunchly Islamic and independently minded. Makassar and Pare Pare are still the first to protest when the political or economic situation is uncertain.

Today a period of prosperity has brought stability, however, and Makassar's importance continues to grow as eastern Indonesia's foremost city.

Makassar

☑ 0411 / POP 1.5 MILLION

The gritty but energetic metropolis of Makassar is one of Indonesia's primary ports, and one of Indonesia's more engaging capitals north of Jakarta. It's a seething maelstrom of commerce and shipping, with a polyglot population of Makassarese, Bugis and Chinese residents. Although there are few major sights, the redeveloped Pantai Losari waterfront and the ambitious reclaimed 'Centre Point of Indonesia' project, with its globe structure and stunning 99-domed mosque, showcase new-found economic growth and city pride.

Makassar was the gateway to eastern Indonesia for centuries, and it was from here that the Dutch controlled much of the trade that passed between the West and the East. You can investigate the city's historical core – which retains some colonial charm – around Fort Rotterdam, which includes the remains of an ancient Gowanese fort and some striking Dutch buildings.

Note that the one-time name for Makassar, Ujung Pandang, is still in common use. Look for both names when arranging flights and other transport.

◎ Sights

Fort Rotterdam FORT

(Benteng Rotterdam; Jl Ujung Pandang; ☺8am-6pm) FREE One of the best-preserved examples of Dutch military architecture in Indonesia, Fort Rotterdam was built on the site of a Gowanese fort, itself built to repel the Dutch East India Company. Having failed to keep out the *orang belanda* (Dutch people), it was reconstructed by the new masters of Makassar after their 1667 conquest, and includes many fine, well-restored colonial structures. You can walk the enclave's stout ramparts, see sections of the original walls and, inside, visit the Museum Negeri La Galigo.

Pulau Samalona ISLAND

Just far enough away from Makassar to shed most (but not all) of the rubbish, the white sands of Pulau Samalona are popular with day trippers, particularly on weekends. There are patches of (degraded) coral offshore, some reef fish, and snorkelling gear for hire. Compared to Makassar harbour, the water's pretty clear. Cold drinks (including beer) and fresh fish are available, but bring your own water. It takes a full two minutes to walk around the entire island.

Boat charters for up to eight people (return 400,000Rp, 25 minutes one-way) can be found at the various peers along the Makassar waterfront.

Beteng Somba Opu RUINS

(Gowa; 2000Rp; ☺grounds dawn-dusk, museum 8am-5pm) Once the most formidable fortress in the archipelago, Somba Opu was decimated by the Dutch in 1669, then consumed by the Jeneberang River delta. One massive wall was excavated in the '80s and

'90s as part of a brief interest of historical preservation that also saw construction of several traditional houses and a small museum. Today, however, the park largely feels abandoned.

Pelabuhan Paotere PORT

(Paotere Harbour; 10,000Rp) Pelabuhan Paotere, 4km north of the city centre, is a large port where Bugis sailing ships berth. It's a working port, with requisite bustle and grime, but the ships are photogenic, and people generally friendly. The port and the nearby fish market are atmospheric places from dawn until mid-morning, when giant tuna and every sea creature imaginable are traded.

Museum Negeri La Galigo MUSEUM

(Fort Rotterdam, Jl Ujung Pandang; admission 10,000Rp; ☺8am-4.30pm) Spread across two buildings inside Fort Rotterdam, Museum Negeri La Galigo has an assortment of exhibits, including palaeolithic artefacts, rice bowls from Tana Toraja, Polynesian and Buddhist statues, musical instruments and traditional costumes – most accompanied by blocks of poorly translated English text. It's a modest collection, but worth the admission and half an hour's attention.

🛏 Sleeping

★ Dodo's Homestay HOMESTAY $

(☎0812 412 9913; http://dodopenman.blogspot. com; Jl Abdul Kadir, Komplek Hartaco Indah Blok 1Y/25; s/d 100,000/120,000Rp; 🌣🅿) An excellent homestay owned by Dodo, a super-friendly local who's been assisting travellers and collecting pens for more than 20 years. His spacious, air-conditioned house is in a quiet neighbourhood 7km south of the centre; one room has an en suite, and there's free tea and coffee. Dodo

Makassar

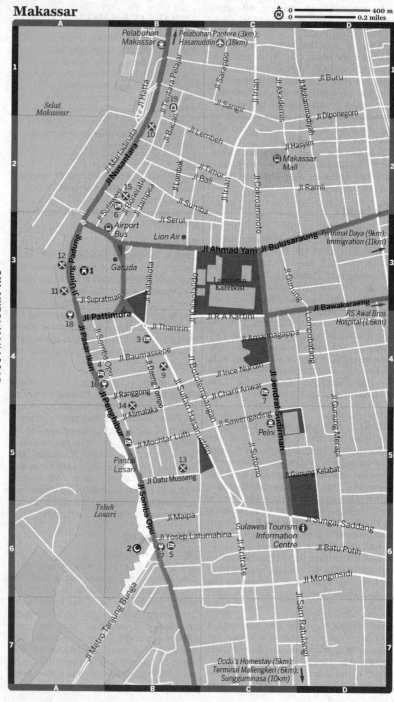

Makassar

arranges transport (including motorbike and car rental) and tours around Sulawesi.

Legenda Beril Hostel   HOSTEL $
(☏ 0411-894 1236; rinajun@yahoo.com; Jl Serui 2-4; r from 175,000Rp; ❋ 🛜) The basic ooms are kept clean and simple at this Chinatown place catering to budget travellers – many of whom congregate on the sunny front porch swapping tales from the road. Rina, the friendly English-speaking manager has excellent information about the area's attractions and transport options and can fast-track visa extensions for a fee.

Pod House   HOSTEL $
(☏ 0411-894 1760; info@podhousehotel.com; Jl Penghibur 58-59; capsule/r 150,000/230,000Rp; ❋ 🛜) Reviving the funky backpacker hostel concept, Pod House has an excellent location opposite Pantai Losari, friendly staff, clean rooms, and banks of budget curtained 'capsule' beds with private lockers and shared Western-style bathrooms. There's a ground-floor coffee shop and a rooftop terrace overlooking the waterfront with fine views of Asmaul Husnah mosque.

★ Ge JacMart   HOMESTAY $$
(☏ 0411-859421, 0811 721 625; www.ge-jacmart-homestay.blogspot.com; Jl Rambutan 3; d 250,000Rp; ⊜ ❋ 🛜) This sparkling white homestay down a quiet lane near the seafront is run by the hospitable Marlah Pongrekun and George Biuw. The breezy, immaculately clean home is splashed with art and has nine very comfortable rooms – each with private bathroom and hot water. Additional touches like bicycle rental (25,000Rp) make this Makassar's go-to lodging. Breakfast available.

Expressia   BOUTIQUE HOTEL $$
(☏ 0411-361 1123; www.expressiahotels.com; Jl Penghibur 6-7; d incl breakfast 330,000-420,000Rp; ❋ 🛜) This solid attempt at a boutique hotel delivers small but comfortable rooms with artistic accents and grey-tiled bathrooms with the ever-popular voyeur-glass between the shower and bedroom (with shade). The waterfront location near the action is ace, with views across to the 99-dome mosque.

Novotel Makassar Grand Shayla   HOTEL $$
(☏ 0411-361 9444; https://novotel.accorhotels.com; Jl Charil Anwar 28; r incl breakfast from 630,000Rp; ❋ 🛜 ❄) This sleek, contemporary hotel is the most luxurious base in the city, offering guests a 25m rooftop pool, a gym, a spa and children's game corner. The well-equipped modern rooms have artistic touches, fast wi-fi and luxury bedding. It's located about a 10-minute walk from the waterfront.

Aston Makassar   HOTEL $$
(☏ 0411-362 3222; www.astonhotelsinternational.com; Jl Sultan Hasanuddin 10; r incl breakfast from 730,000Rp; ❋ @ 🛜 ❄) Within walking distance of the seafront and Fort Rotterdam, this long-time stalwart has spacious and clean, if ageing, rooms with only a hint of stale cigarette musk. On the top two floors you'll find a 30m indoor pool, a gym, a spa and the sky bar-restaurant with commanding 180-degree views and some of the more affordable spirits in town.

✖ Eating

★ Coto Nusantara   SOUP $
(☏ 0822 5132 2220; Jl Nusantara 142; coto Makassar 25,000Rp; ⊙ 7am-6pm) Don't miss sampling the rich local beef soup of *coto Makassar* at this city-wide famous hole-in-the-wall near

the dockyards. The tiny bowl fills out to a meal once you help yourself to a few *ketupat* (rice steamed in palm leaves; 5000Rp), and attendant staff will bring you more *kua* (broth) at a moment's notice.

Rumah Makan Pate'ne
INDONESIAN $

(☑ 0411-361 5874; Jl Sulawesi 48; mains 30,000-40,000Rp; ☺ 8am-10pm; ✲) Serving up Makassarese and Indonesian classics, this simple backstreet place offers fine-value, authentic flavours. The *lele goreng* (deep-fried catfish) and *rujak manis* (tropical-fruit salad with a spicy-sweet palm sugar, tamarind and shrimp-paste dressing) are delicious, especially washed down with fresh melon, mango, apple or avocado juice.

Kampoeng Popsa
INTERNATIONAL $

(Jl Ujung Panjang; mains from 25,000Rp; ☺ 10am-midnight; ✲) This large, open-sided food court facing the harbour has sea breezes, a hip young clientele, a gregarious vibe, space for kids to run around, and lots of choices, from *mei titi* (crispy noodles with gravy, chicken and shrimp) and sushi, to noodle dishes and ice cream. Beers are served, and there's often live music at night.

Fish Warungs
HAWKER $

(Jl Ujung Pandang; per fish around 25,000Rp; ☺ 5-10.30pm) A string of makeshift fish warungs set up every night on the foreshore opposite Fort Rotterdam and south along the waterfront, serving some of the tastiest, cheapest seafood in town. Roaming buskers provide table-side entertainment.

RM Nelayan
SEAFOOD $$

(☑ 0411-361 0523; Jl Alimalaka 25; mains 40,000-80,000Rp; ☺ 10am-10pm; ✲) It's tough to resist the aromas emanating from this highly popular restaurant's fish barbecue. Step inside and receive a selection of six condiments placed on your table. Fish and shrimp are offered in a variety of styles, including North Sulawesi favourites of *rica-rica* (chilli pepper sauce) and *woku* (coconut, ginger and onion). Cold Bintangs are available.

Lae Lae
SEAFOOD $$

(☑ 0411-363 4326; Jl Datu Musseng 8; fish from 60,000Rp; ☺ 10am-midnight) A locally famous seafood restaurant, Lae Lae is a no-frills, no-fuss magnet for lovers of grilled fish. Enter past a smoking streetside barbecue, choose your piscine pleasure from deep tubs of fresh iced fish, and eat at long, battered metal tables, rubbing shoulders with the locals. Three sambals, rice and squeaky-fresh raw vegetables are the standard accompaniments.

Bistropolis
INTERNATIONAL $$

(☑ 0411-363 6988; www.bistropolis.net; Jl Sultan Hasanuddin 18; mains 50,000-100,000Rp; ☺ 10am-11pm Mon-Fri, to 1am Sat, to midnight Sun; ✲ 🔊) A stylish, atmospheric, air-conditioned bistro serving international standards that lean heavily toward pasta and pizza. It wouldn't survive long outside of Indonesia, but here it's a welcome break from rice and fish. Come for the delectable gelato (try the Bailey's flavour) and espresso that hits the spot. Watch for added taxes.

Drinking & Nightlife

The Level
BAR

(☑ 0411-831400; Jl Somba Opu 277C; ☺ 10am-3am; 🔊) Across from the floating mosque Masjid Amirul Mukminin (Jl Penghibur, near Pantai Losari), the Level actually has three levels: a chill coffee bar on the ground floor, a passable restaurant on the 2nd floor, and a thumping club up top. It's the last that attracts Makassar's young things, and hosts DJs and live bands. Dress sharp (no sandals or flip-flops).

Kafe Kareba
BEER GARDEN

(Jl Penghibur; ☺ 4pm-2am) This long-running beer garden and music stage masquerading as a seafood restaurant on the seafront is popular with locals and visitors downing Bintang and Guinness to the strains of karoako. To be fair, it does have a pretty extensive food menu if you need sustenance.

Zona Cafe
CLUB

(☑ 0411-362 3451; www.facebook.com/zonacafe makassar; Jl Ujung Pandang 2; entry 40,000-100,000Rp; ☺ noon-2am) This popular club draws a loyal young crowd with its DJs and bands from Jakarta and its regular drink promotions. Things start to kick off after 1am on weekends.

Shopping

Pasar Cina
MARKET

(Pasar Bacan; Jl Bacan; ☺ 6am-1pm) Thriving morning market in the heart of Chinatown with plenty of vegetables, herbs and animal parts.

Ratu Indah Mall
MALL

(www.malratuindah.co.id; Jl Sam Ratulangi; 8am-10pm) The best central mall, with (official) Apple and Samsung retailers, a Body Shop, a Matahari department store, adventure sports retailers, cafes and restaurants.

ℹ Information

IMMIGRATION

Immigration Office (Kantor Imigrasi Kelas I; ☑ 0411-584559; http://makassar.imigrasi. go.id; Jl Perintis Kemerdekaan 13; ☺ 8am-4pm Mon-Fri) Located 14km from the city centre on the road to the airport. Fairly efficient Visa on Arrival extensions.

MEDICAL SERVICES

RS Awal Bros Hospital (☑ 0411-454567; www.awalbros.com; Jl Jendral Urip Sumoharjo 43; ☺ 24hr) The most convenient and well-equipped hospital in Makassar. Some staff speak English. It's out near the toll road.

MONEY

Banks and ATMs are dotted all over the centre of the city. You'll also find ATMs and moneychangers at the airport.

TOURIST INFORMATION

South Sulawesi Tourism (☑ 0411-872336; www.visitsulawesi.id; Jl Jendral Sudirman 23, Gedung Mulo; ☺ 8am-5pm Mon-Fri) There's some printed English-language information available here, and the staff are helpful and friendly. Perhaps most useful is the compiled list of current bus companies servicing Tana Toraja they keep on hand.

TRAVEL AGENCIES

Makassar has many travel agencies offering flight bookings and tours, including trips to Tana Toraja. Don't make a hefty payment upfront; some travellers have reported making payments to seemingly professional 'tour organisers' whose tours never materialise.

He's not a conventional travel agent, but freelancer **Dodo Mursalim** (☑ 0812 412 9913; www. facebook.com/dodo.mursalim) helps hundreds of travellers each year with transport and tours, and has been doing so for decades. He's reliable, trustworthy and his rates are very reasonable.

ℹ Getting There & Away

AIR

Makassar's **Sultan Hasanuddin Airport** (www. hasanuddin-airport.co.id; Jl Raya Airport No 1) is well connected with other cities in Sulawesi as well as the rest of Indonesia, including Java, Bali Kalimantan and Maluku. International flights include Air Asia to Kuala Lumpur (four weekly) and Silk Air to Singapore (three weekly).

Note that many airline websites still use Makassar's former name, Ujung Pandang, for bookings.

Garuda (☑ 0811 441 4747; www.garuda-indo nesia.com; Jl Slamet Riyadi 6; ☺ 8am-5pm) Also operates Citilink.

Lion Air (☑ 0411-368 0777; www.lionair. co.id; Jl Ahmad Yani Blok 22-24, behind KFC; ☺ 8.30am-4.30pm Mon-Fri, to 2pm Sat, 10am-2pm Sun) Also operates Wings.

Sriwijaya Air (☑ 0411-424700; www.sriwijaya air.co.id; Jl Boulevard Raya 6-7; ☺ 8am-4.30pm Mon-Sat)

BOAT

Much of the Pelni ferry fleet stops in Makassar ready to whisk you (slowly) to just about anywhere in the country. Direct stops include Pare Pare and Bau Bau on Sulawesi, Surabaya on Java, and Labuan Bajo on Flores. Further destinations include Gorontalo and Bitung (Sulawesi), Tarakan and Balikpapan (East Kalimantan), Benoa (Bali), Teluk Priok (Jakarta, Java), Ambon (Maluku) and Sorong (Papua).

Pelni (☑ 0411-331401; www.pelni.co.id; Jl Jendral Sudirman 14; ☺ 8am-2pm Mon-Sat) tickets are available at the main office near Hotel Novotel, and agencies near the chaotic ferry port, **Pelabuhan Makassar** (off Jl Nusantara), in the city centre.

BUS & KIJANG

Makassar has numerous terminals for getting out of town, but the following three are most useful; you can reach them on separate *pete-pete* routes which converge at **Makassar Mall** (Jl Wahid Hasyim).

Terminal Daya (off Jl Perintis Kemerdekaan, behind Daya Grand Square Mall) Long-haul buses and Kijangs depart to all points north including Rantepao. Catch any *pete-pete* (5000Rp, 30 minutes) marked 'Daya' from Makassar Mall to the eastern suburbs.

Terminal Mallengkeri (Jl Mallengkeri) Mostly Kijangs and a few buses head southeast of Makassar including to Pantai Bira. Take a red *pete-pete* marked 'S Minasa' from Makassar Mall or from along Jl Jendral Sudirman.

Terminal Sungguminasa (east of Pasar Sungguminasa) It's easier to catch the regular *pete-pete* for Malino along Jl Malino near the terminal; to get here take a *pete-pete* marked 'S Minasa' from Makassar Mall or from along Jl Jendral Sudirman.

ℹ Getting Around

TO & FROM THE AIRPORT

Sultan Hasanuddin Airport (www.hasanuddin -airport.co.id; Jl Raya Airport No 1) is 22km northwest of Makassar city centre. At peak times, using the toll road can slash travel times in half.

Airport buses (Jl Riburani; 27,000Rp; ☺ 7am-5pm) with Damri run every hour between 7am and 5pm daily from the basement level of the airport to Jl Ahmad Yani in central Makassar, passing by Daya bus terminal.

Prepaid taxis are available in the arrivals area of the airport and cost from 110,000Rp to 150,000Rp not including the toll road (10,000Rp).

LOCAL TRANSPORT
Becak

Becak (bicycle rickshaw) drivers like to kerb-crawl, hoping you'll succumb to their badgering and/or the heat. Rates start from 10,000Rp.

Pete-Pete

The main *pete-pete* terminal is at the site of the old Makassar Mall (p671). Blue *pete-pete*

generally service destinations around town (5000Rp) while red ones go further afield (from 10,000Rp).

Taxi

Air-conditioned taxis have meters; a 2km ride costs about 18,000Rp. **Bluebird Taxis** (☑ 0411-441234; www.bluebirdgroup.com) are reliable, comfortable and operate 24 hours.

Grab

Ride hailing app Grab (www.grab.com/id) brings an *ojek* or car to your door within minutes with transparent pricing. Bahasa Indonesia is not required, but some drivers do like to call to confirm pick up points.

TRANSPORT FROM MAKASSAR
Flights within Sulawesi

DESTINATION	AIRLINE	FARE (RP)	DURATION (HR)	FREQUENCY
Bau Bau	Garuda, Wings Air	570,000	1¼	5 daily
Benteng (Selayar)	Garuda, Wings Air, TransNusa	330,000	50min	2-3 daily
Gorontalo	Garuda, Lion Air, Sriwijaya Air, Batik Air	530,000	1½	6 daily
Kendari	Garuda, Lion Air, Sriwijaya Air, Batik Air	320,000	1	7 daily
Luwuk	Garuda, Wings Air, Sriwijaya Air	675,000	1¾	3-4 daily
Manado	Garuda, Lion Air	580,000	1¾	5 daily
Palopo	Garuda, Wings Air	520,000	1	1-2 daily
Palu	Garuda, Lion Air, Sriwijaya Air, Batik Air	1,000,000	1¼	7-8 daily
Poso	Wings Air	1,560,000	1½	1 daily

Bus & Kijang

DESTINATION (TYPE)	TERMINAL	FARE (RP)	DURATION (HR)	FREQUENCY
Bulukumba (car)	Mallengkeri	60,000	4	on demand
Malino (*pete-pete*)	Sungguminasa	16,000	1½	frequent (mostly morning)
Morano (*pete-pete*)	Daya	10,000	40min	frequent
Palu	Daya	280,000	24	5pm daily
Pantai Bira (car)	Mallengkeri	80,000	5	on demand
Pare Pare	Damri (near Term. Daya)	40,000	3	4 daily
Rantepao	Daya	130,000-220,000	8	9am & 9pm
Selayar	Mallengkeri	150,000	8	3 daily
Sengkang (car)	Daya	100,000	4	on demand

The bus to Selayar can also drop you in Bulukumba or Pantai Bira, but most travellers opt for the cars that leave more frequently.

Malino

📞 0417 / POP 22,000

Malino is a pleasantly green and chilly hill-top town surrounded by waterfalls and rice terraces. It's famous as the meeting place of Kalimantan and east Indonesian leaders who endorsed the Netherlands' ill-fated plans for a federation. More recently, peace agreements have been struck for Maluku and Poso here. There are many scenic walks in the area, and a nascent mountain-bike scene.

Air Terjun Takapala WATERFALL

(3000Rp) A seasonally spectacular 100m-tall waterfall set amid rice fields 4km south of the town of Malino. It's easiest to get there via *ojek* (from 10,000Rp).

Grand Bukit Indah Resort LODGE $$

(📞 0417-21277; hotel.bukitindah@yahoo.com; Jl Endang 2; r incl breakfast 250,000-350,000Rp) It's not a 'grand resort' but the spacious tiled rooms with three beds, private man-dis, flat-screen TVs and front porches are kept tidy.

ⓘ Getting There & Away

Pete-pete services to Malino (16,000Rp, 2½ hours) congregate in the morning along Jl Malino near Terminal Sungguminasa (p671) in Makassar.

Pantai Bira

📞 0413

Goats outnumber vehicles in the isolated coastal village and dive centre of Pantai Bira – at least until the delightfully chaotic weekend warriors come in by the busload from Makassar. Most budget accommodation is found in the scruffy village of Pantai Bira, while quieter Pantai Bara, 3km away, offers more refined but siloed resorts. To truly get away from the crowds, head across to a homestay on Liukang Loe Island, a short boat ride away.

All of these beaches are very broad at low tide and there's decent snorkelling a short swim from the shore. You can explore more remote bays and neighbouring islands by boat, and there's plenty of interesting stops on the mainland accessible by bike or motorbike.

The diving here is dramatic, on a par with anywhere in Indonesia for 'big stuff': lots of sharks (including hammerheads), rays and pelagic fish.

◉ Sights

Pantai Bara BEACH

Around 3km northwest of Bira village, this quieter crescent of white sand is fringed by low cliffs and palms. You can stroll here in 30 minutes from Bira along the coast with the sand between your toes (low tide only) and marvel at the turquoise water and tropical vegetation. At high tide, use the newly paved-but-crumbling road behind the beach, which cuts through woodland that's home to monkeys and large monitor lizards.

Pantai Panrang Luhu BEACH

(Pantai Timur) Pantai Panrang Luhu is a coconut-fringed affair north of the ferry pier in Bira village. *Pinisi* ship builders operate under the cliffs on the north end, while a few guesthouses in the middle have liberated a 100m section of white sand beach from under the alarming piles of rubbish that plague this side of the cape.

Pantai Bira BEACH

Bira's main beach, just west of the village centre, is a glimmering crescent of white sand that is usually pleasant on the week-days but gets packed with day trippers on weekends. Beware of speedboats pulling inflatable bananas carrying local tourists if you decide to swim or snorkel here.

🏊 Activities

Bira is rightly renowned for its spectacular scuba diving (p675). Snorkelling is also impressive. Full-day boat trips to Pulau Liukang Loe and Pulau Kambing will cost about 400,000Rp per day for a boat seating eight to 10 people. Snorkelling on both sides of the cape is quite good, but due to the strong tides it's only possible for a few hours a day. Also, currents can be surprisingly strong and people have drowned. Equipment (mask and fins) can be rented

---

BIRA BEACHES

The Bira region is blessed with sweeping stretches of glistening white sand. Bear in mind that locals are fairly conservative and women typically wear long sleeves and pants. A bikini is acceptable (on beaches only) but you will get leered at, and Makassar day trippers will invariably ask for a photo with you. A polite *'jangan'* (never) usually ends inappropriate touching.

Pantai Bira & Around

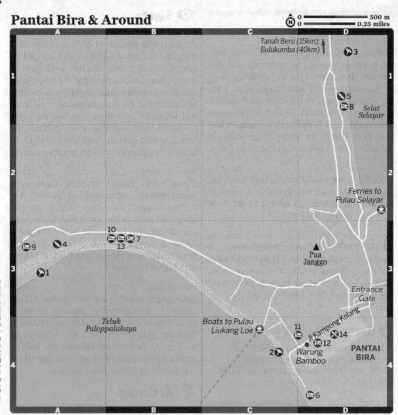

0   500 m
0   0.25 miles

Tanah Beru (15km);
Bulukumba (40km)

Selat
Selayar

Ferries to
Pulau Selayar

Pua
Janggo

Entrance
Gate

Teluk
Paloppalakaya

Boats to Pulau
Liukang Loe

Jl Kampong Kolang

Warung
Bamboo

PANTAI
BIRA

for about 50,000Rp per day from several hotels, and kiosks on the beach.

Sulawesi Dive Adventure   DIVING
(☑ 0821 9000 0221; www.sulawesidiveadventure.com; Pantai Panrang Luhu; dives US$35) This is a European-owned dive centre with good equipment, and excellent local dive instructors and guides who have decades of experience between them. Their operation is located on the east side of the cape, north of the ferry port at Pantai Panrang Luhu.

Bira Dive Camp   DIVING
(☑ 0823 4234 7304; www.biradivecamp.com; Pantai Bara; dives 490,000Rp, PADI Open Water course 490,000Rp) Under management by a young American pair, this chill operation has upped its professionalism considerably. They're geared toward backpackers and younger travellers, accommodating singles and accepting outside divers. The affiliated shared dorms and bungalows are extremely basic and cheap – hence the 'camp'.

South Sulawesi Divers DIVING
(☑0812 4443 6626; www.south-sulawesi-diver.
com; Jl Poros Bara, Pantai Bara; dives €40) A
well-managed, if somewhat lethargic, dive
centre started by Elvis, a serious German
diver who's long been operating in the region. Based out of Mangga Lodge (p676).

🛏 Sleeping

★ Salassa Guest House GUESTHOUSE $
(☑0812 426 5672; salassaguesthouse@yahoo.
com; Jl Kampong Kolang, Bira; r/bungalow incl
breakfast 150,000/350,000Rp) This family-run
institution has six cheap rooms with shared
mandi upstairs, and four sparkling bungalows with outdoor showers out back. However, the highlight is the exceedingly helpful
owners who are fluent in English and understand backpackers; unfortunately, they were
keen on selling when we last visited. Until
they do, at least hit up the restaurant (p676)
– the best in town.

Nini's Beach Bungalows BUNGALOW $$
(☑0821 9093 1175; www.facebook.com/ninis
beachbungalows; Pantai Bara; cottages incl
breakfast 650,000 & 700,000Rp; ❄🛜) You'll
get plenty of peace and quiet at this two-
cottage guesthouse perched on a prominent cliff above the beach. The view is excellent, the owners accommodating, and

the well-appointed rooms with outdoor
hot-water showers are welcoming. The only
thing that misses is the landscaping, which
feels a bit like an afterthought.

Cosmos Bungalows BUNGALOW $$
(☑0822 9260 8820; www.cosmosbungalows.com;
Pantai Bara; bungalows incl breakfast 350,000-
450,000Rp; 🛜) A long row of rustic-chic, beautifully built bungalows (some with outdoor
showers) descend down a narrow strip of
land to the coastal cliffs where you'll find the
tiny but welcoming restaurant clinging to the
rocks above the low-tide beach. Expect good
vibes all round and great local information.

Kaluku Cottages COTTAGE $$
(www.kalukucottages.com; Pantai Panrang Luhu;
bungalow/cottage from 350,000/1,250,000Rp; ❄)
OK, so the east side of the cape gets a lot
of rubbish washing in – appalling amounts.
That being said, the staff patrols the 50m of
white sand in front of the cottages several
times daily, keeping it blissfully pristine.
The rattan-walled rooms are also sparkling
clean, making this quiet place 3km from the
chaos of Bira beach a fine escape.

Patma Bira HOTEL $$
(☑0821 9030 1649; www.patmabirahotel.com; Pantai Bira; r from 400,000Rp) Smack in the middle
of the activity around Pantai Bira village,

SULAWESI PANTAI BIRA

BIRA'S TOP DIVE SITES

Famous as one of the 'sharkiest' spots in Indonesia, Bira offers truly spectacular scuba
diving. The islands off Bira lie at the tip of southern Sulawesi where oceanic currents
converge, bringing upswells of cool water from the depths and lots of pelagic life.

The seas can be rough off Pantai Bira and it's not always possible to reach islands
such as Kambing, around 7km south, which has several dive sites. But there are more
sheltered sites closer to shore, where you can spot macro life including nudibranchs,
seahorses and prolific reef fish. Pulau Kambing ranks among the region's highlights.

Favourite local dive sites:

Great Wall of Goat Kambing means 'goat' in Indonesian, and the unpopulated island's
eastern side has a remarkable vertical wall teeming with reef life. Sharks (including
hammerheads and threshers) and rays (including mantas and devil rays) are typically
encountered.

Cap Bira This impressive site off the extreme tip of the mainland has a lovely swim-
through; white-tip sharks, shrimps and pipefish are common.

Shark Point This is an easier dive with a sloped profile on the eastern side of Pulau
Liukang Loe. Expect beautiful coral, turtles, sea snakes and, of course, lots of sharks,
including 2m white-tips, black-tips and occasionally bull sharks.

Fish Market For experienced divers, this underwater sea mount teems with sea life,
including huge groupers, jacks and Napoleon wrasse. It's a simply astonishing dive.

Mola-Mola Point On the western side of Pulau Kambing, giant mola-mola are encountered
at this site that's suitable for advanced divers. August and September are the best months.

this venerable place is holding up well and maintains a relaxed and peaceful vibe, due in large part to the verdant gardens that front the large, immaculate tiled rooms. The staff is exceedingly friendly, location convenient, and prices discounted regularly.

★ Tevana House Reef
BUNGALOW $$$

(☑0812 4561 1678; www.facebook.com/Tevana HouseReef; Pantai Bara; bungalow from 850,000Rp; ☎) Elevating the area's offerings to a higher plane, Tevana's attention to detail is palpable in everything from their exquisitely landscaped cliffside grounds, to the four ironwood and coral bungalows with outdoor showers, to the rooftop sundeck above the excellent vegetarian restaurant.

Mangga Lodge
HOTEL $$$

(☑0413-270 0756; www.mangga-lodge.com; Pantai Bara; r incl breakfast from 950,000Rp; ❄☎) Set back a bit from Pantai Bara, this rambling white stone resort is a maze of archways, ponds, staircases and towers. The staff are exceedingly friendly, and the rooms are nicely apportioned, if a little musty – possibly due to a lack of use. It's a good choice for divers (as South Sulawesi Divers (p675) is based here) and there are numerous organised outings on offer.

Amatoa Beach Resort
RESORT $$$

(☑0812 4296 5500; www.amatoaresort.com; Jl Pasir Putih 6, Pantai Bira; r incl breakfast 1,700,000-3,000,000Rp; ❄☎✦) Tucked away from the rest of the world and perched on the rocks overlooking the ocean, this luxurious and intimate resort has a lush Mediterranean feel due to exposed stonework, billowing drapes, and whitewashed bungalows. Unfortunately the pretension is more polished than the service, but you'll likely have the place – and its narrow swimming pool – to yourself.

✕ Eating

RM Claudya
INDONESIAN $

(☑0823 4366 2323; Jl Kampong Kolang, Bira; 20,000-30,000Rp; ☉10am-10pm; ☎) Offering solid and affordable takes on Indonesian staples, this breezy *rumah makan* 500m inland from the busy beach is elevated enough above the road to give it a relaxed vibe.

Salassa
INDONESIAN $

(Jl Kampong Kolang, Bira; mains 30,000-45,000Rp; ☉7am-10pm) This open-sided restaurant in front of Salassa Guest House (p675) offers delicious homestyle cooking (try the fish 'à la Salassa' with peppers and spices), chicken,

rice and noodles dishes. If they're out of cold beer, Riswan's next door has bottles to go.

ℹ Information

Access to both Pantai Bira and Bara costs 40,000Rp per foreign visitor (one time payment) levied at the toll booth when you first enter.

ℹ Getting There & Away

BOAT

Pelabuhan Bira has twice-daily boats to **Pulau Selayar** (adult/child 24,000/11,000Rp, two hours, 10am and 4pm). There is also a direct boat to Labuan Bajo in Flores (120,000Rp, 30 hours) on Sunday at 11pm and Tuesday at 10am.

Departure times change frequently and ferries are regularly cancelled during high seas, sometimes for several days.

BUS, BEMO & KIJANG

From Makassar's Terminal Mallengkeri (p671), Kijangs go directly to Pantai Bira (80,000Rp, five to six hours). Alternatively, catch a Kijang to Bulukumba (60,000Rp), and another to Pantai Bira (20,000Rp). Two buses bound for Selayer leave at 9am and 1am from Makassar, and can drop you in Bira (120,000Rp).

Direct Kijangs returning from Pantai Bira to Makassar leave in the morning. Book via your lodging the day before and you'll be picked up. Alternatively, take a *pete-pete* from the ferry dock to Bulukumba and then a Kijang or bus to your next destination from there.

ℹ Getting Around

There is no public transport to speak of, though some locals will provide *ojek* service. Several places, including **Warung Bamboo** (Jl Kampong Kolang, Bira; scooter per day 80,000Rp; ☉7am-10pm), rent motorbikes in Bira. Bira is a 30- to 45-minute walk from Bara.

Pulau Liukang Loe

This small island with two tiny fishing villages is a popular destination for snorkelling trips. Weavers at **Ta'Buntuleng** village on the north coast make heavy, colourful cloth on hand looms under their houses. On the pretty beach west of the village there is an interesting old **graveyard**, and off the beach there are acres of sea grass and coral, but mind the currents.

Ocean Holiday
GUESTHOUSE $$

(☑0811 421 1418; Pulau Liukang Loe; r incl breakfast 250,000Rp; ❄) A modest guesthouse run by friendly village head, Jafar, has basic, but clean, rooms that come with your own beach (popular with snorkellers during the day) and your own pair of sleepy fishing villages separated by a 1km track.

❶ Getting There & Away

Snorkelling charters to Pulau Liukang Loe and the nearby, uninhabited Pulau Kambing cost around 400,000Rp per **boat** from Pantai Bira; most guesthouses and hotels can arrange trips. A one-way crossing is around 50,000Rp – cheaper if you play the waiting game.

Pulau Selayar

This long, narrow island lies off the south-western peninsula of Sulawesi and is inhab-ited by the Bugis, the Makassarese and the Konjo. Most reside along the infertile west coast and in **Benteng**, the main town. Sela-yar's long coastline is a repository of flotsam from nearby shipping lines, perhaps ac-counting for the presence of a 2000-year-old Vietnamese Dongson drum, kept in an an-nexe near the former **Benteng Bontoban-gun** (Bontobangun Fort), a few kilometres south of Benteng.

Selayar is a DIY adventurer's playground. Main attractions are its sandy beaches and coral reefs. Snorkelling around Pulau Pasi, opposite Benteng, is good, but you will have to charter a boat.

Selayar Eco Resort   BUNGALOW $$
(☑ 081 337 834 888; www.selayar-eco-resort.sitew. fr; bungalow with half/full board €60/70) This new outfit on the east coast embraces the fickle nature of Pulau Selayar: when seas get rough (May to November), they pack up and head to the west coast, creating custom packages that cater to your level of adventure: from camping on white-sand beaches to staying in partner resorts with daily snorkelling, div-ing, trekking or beachcombing expeditions.

Selayar Dive Resort   RESORT $$$
(www.selayar-dive-resort.com; s/d with fan €85/ 135, with air-con €135/160; ☺ Oct-Apr; ❄) A well-run German-owned place with eight thatched-roofed, sea-facing wooden bun-galows on a sandy beach on the southeast corner of the island. It's very much geared to divers, and there are experienced dive-masters to guide you around the fringing reefs and wall dives close by. Rates include all meals; minimum stay of one week. Two dives cost €90.

❶ Getting There & Away

Two daily ferries (24,000Rp, two hours) depart at 10am and 4pm from Bira heading to Pamatata on Pulau Selayar. Direct buses from Makassar (150,000Rp, eight hours, three daily) include the ferry toll.

Wings, Garuda, and TransNusa offer direct flights between **Aroeppala Airport** and Makass-ar (from 330,000Rp, daily).

Taka Bonerate Islands

Southeast of Pulau Selayar and north of Pu-lau Bonerate is the 2200-sq-km Taka Boner-ate, the world's third-largest atoll with some 500 sq km of coral reefs. The largest coral at-oll, Kwajalein in the Marshall Islands, is just 20% bigger. Some of the islands and exten-sive reefs in the region are now part of **Taka Bonerate National Park** (Taman Nasional Taka Bonerate), a marine reserve with a rich variety of sea and bird life.

Those who don't visit the atoll aboard their own liveboard will be corralled into a package visit that includes lodging, food and snorkelling or diving centred around Pulau Tinabo – which you'll likely share only with sea turtles and baby sharks milling off the white-sand beach.

❶ Getting There & Away

It's about eight hours by slow boat to Pulau Tinabo; the **park office** (Balai Taman Nasional; ☑ 0414-21565; www.tntakabonerate.com; Jl S Parman 40, Benteng, Pulau Selayar; ☺ 8am-4pm) in Selayar can help arrange a charter. Public boats to populated Pulau Bonerate leave irregularly from Selayar.

Watampone

☑ 0481 / POP 100,000
Watampone is the capital of the Bone (bone-eh) Regency, a former kingdom and the centre of Bugis political power. Bone was re-nowned for its fierce presence on the battle-field, and the kingdom long held out against Gowa's conquests of the peninsula. During colonial occupation, Bone was initially an ally of the Dutch, but later became a deadly thorn in their side for nearly a century until the Dutch quashed the rebellion in 1906.

Today, Watampone is a small, peaceful town that supplies the nearby farming com-munities. The only reason most foreigners come here is to go to/from Kolaka in South-east Sulawesi from the nearby port of Bajoe, or to break up a trip to Tana Toraja.

Museum Lapawawoi
MUSEUM
(Jl Thamrin; ⊙8am-4pm) FREE This small former palace houses one of Indonesia's more
interesting regional collections, including
an odd array of court memorabilia. You may
have to ask around for the curator to open it.

Wisma Amrach
GUESTHOUSE $
(☑0823 4512 3700; Jl A Yani 2A; r 100,000-
150,000Rp; ❄) This rambling home owned
by a local government official has several
tidy rooms clustered around common seating areas with actual attempts at decor
like statues and wall hangings (mostly certificates, but it's something). The place is
super-convenient to everything, including
transport out to the ferry pier.

❶ Getting There & Away

BOAT

Bajoe (bah-joy) port (Jl Yos Sudarso), 8km
east of Watampone has ferries to Kolaka (deck/
business class 75,000/116,000Rp, eight hours)
leaving around 5pm, 8pm and 11pm.

From Watampone, bemos go to Bajoe every
few minutes from a stop behind the market.
From the bus terminal at the end of the incredibly long causeway in Bajoe, buses and
cars troll for passengers just after the ferry
arrives.

BUS & BEMO

Terminal Petta Pongawai (Jl MT Haryono) is 4km west of town, so take an ojek
or bemo. Kijangs and buses travel to Pare
Pare (90,000Rp, four hours) and Makassar
(80,000Rp, four hours). Head to Bulukumba
(75,000Rp, 3½ hours) for connection to
Bira (25,000Rp, one hour). Buses leave for
Kendari (150,000Rp, 12 hours) at 4pm to
catch the 5pm ferry.

Panthers to Sengkang (40,000Rp, two hours)
leave from **Jl Veteran**, 2½km north of town.

Sengkang
☑0485 / POP 53,000
Sengkang is a small yet traffic-clogged town
with a nearby scenic lake, a traditional
hand-woven silk industry, and a large mosque
that's strangely mesmerising at night. It's
a convenient place to break the journey between Rantepao and Pantai Bira, but most
visitors are content with a single night. Catch
the sunrise on Danau Tempe then shop for all
your silk sari needs before moving on.

Silk Weaving
VILLAGE
Sengkang is known for its *sutera* (silk)
weaving, and hundreds of workshops in
surrounding villages can be great places to
watch the process and purchase direct. Nearby, Kampoeng BNI Sutra is the fruit of Bank
Negara Indonesia's Corporate Social Responsibility program, which provides low-interest
loans to foster business development. A variety of small shops offer sublime hand- and
factory-woven fabrics. The silkworm farms
are about 15km from Sengkang.

Danau Tempe
LAKE
(entrance 5000Rp) This large, shallow lake is
fringed by wetlands, with floating houses

SULAWESI SEAFARERS

The Bugis are Indonesia's best-known sailors, and carry and trade goods on their magnificent wooden schooners throughout Indonesia.

The Bugis' influence expanded rapidly after the fall of Makassar, which resulted in a
diaspora from South Sulawesi in the 17th and 18th centuries. They established strategic
trading posts at Kutai (Kalimantan), Johor (north of Singapore) and Selangor (near
Kuala Lumpur), and traded freely throughout the region. Bugis and Makassarese *pinisi*
(schooners) are still built along the south coasts of Sulawesi and Kalimantan, using centuries-old designs and techniques. You can see boats being built at Marumasa and Tanah
Beru, both near Bira.

The Bajau, Bugis, Butonese and Makassarese seafarers of Sulawesi have a 500-year
history of trading and cultural links with Indigenous Australians, and their ships are featured in pre-European Aboriginal cave art in northern Australia. British explorer Matthew
Flinders encountered 60 Indonesian schooners at Melville Bay in 1803; today many
more still make the risky (and illegal) journey to fish reefs in the cyclone belt off the
northern coast of Australia. Many Minahasans of North Sulawesi, relative newcomers to
sailing folklore, work on international shipping lines across the world. As with their Filipi-
no neighbours, the Minahasans' outward-looking culture, plus their language and sailing
skills, make them the first choice of many captains.

and magnificent birdlife. Geologists believe it was once a gulf between southern Toraja and the rest of South Sulawesi. As the lands merged, the gulf disappeared – and the lake will likely disappear as well. Hotels can charter you a boat (200,000Rp for two hours), allowing you to speed along Sungai Walanae, visit Salotangah floating village, cross to Batu Batu village on the other side, and return within two hours.

★**Amira Guesthouse**   GUESTHOUSE **$$**
(✆0852 9834 3824; anton.mandela@gmail.com; Jl A Malingkaan 3; r incl breakfast from 250,000Rp; ❉☎) These basic but clean rooms occupying the sprawling upstairs of a housing complex come with Anton, the helpful English-speaking owner who can arrange tours and even has his own lake boat. The guesthouse sits above a decent restaurant and is near the bus station and all the downtown chaos you can handle.

★**Bakso Pahlawan**   SOUP **$**
(Jl Pahlawan; bakso 18,000Rp; ◷11am-11pm) There's *bakso*, and then there's *bakso* stuffed with cheese, or with spicy chillies, or with a whole boiled egg. Gorge yourself for under 20,000Rp at our favourite meatball soup joint on the island.

Lesehan Jetpur   SEAFOOD **$**
(✆0813 5475 4111; Jl Bangau 1; mains 15,000-30,000Rp; ◷10am-10pm) A large, brightly lit and bustling place that's very popular with locals, Lesehan Jetpur offers authentic, inexpensive local food, including spicy chicken and plenty of fish on ice you can select yourself. It's 1km south of the large mosque, down a side road.

Losari Silk   FABRIC
(✆0485-22419; h.bajilosarisilk@gmail.com; Jl A Baso 4, Pasar Sempange; ◷7am-5pm) Snap photos in the crowded, clacking silk-weaving factory downstairs before dropping a bundle on high-end silk shirts and sarongs upstairs.

❶ Getting There & Away

All ground transport departs from **Terminal Callaccu** (Jl Andi Ninnong) just north of downtown. To get to/from Rantepao (six hours), take a bemo to Lawawoi (35,000Rp, 1½ hours) and catch a bus from there (50,000Rp, five hours); alternatively you can go via Palopo (60,000Rp, five hours). There are regular Avanza to/from Terminal Daya in Makassar (from 75,000Rp, five hours), but Kijangs (70,000Rp, four hours) are faster.

Pare Pare
✆0421 / POP 130,000
Pare Pare is a hilly city with plenty of greenery. It's sometimes used as a stopover between Tana Toraja and Makassar, though mostly you'll find yourself here after a long boat ride from Kalimantan.

Gazzaz   HOTEL **$$**
(✆0421-2733; Jl Daeng Parani 7; r 280,000-420,000Rp; ❉☎) Clean, modern, soulless hotel in prime position for the Pelni ferry.

Restoran Asia   CHINESE **$$**
(✆0421-21415; Jl Patompo 25; mains 35,000-70,000Rp; ◷8am-10pm; ❉) This well-run, clean, air-conditioned place has a particularly good seafood selection, great Chinese omelettes and cheap veggies.

❶ Getting There & Away

BOAT
Pare Pare has good boat connections to East Kalimantan. Pelni runs weekly to Balikpapan, and every one or two days passenger boats travel to Samarinda (22 hours) or Balikpapan (two nights), but these companies tend to have sketchier safety records than the Pelni ships. Schedules and bookings are available from agencies near the **port** (Pelabuhan Nusantara; Jl Andicammi).

BUS
Services to Makassar (three hours) include **Damri buses** (Jl Agus Salim; 42,000Rp) and **shared cars** (Jl Agus Salim; 40,000Rp). Catch transport to Sengkang (two hours) and Lawawoi (for transfer to Rantepao, 64,000Rp, five hours) from in front of the main mosque east of town centre. Cars for Polewali (two hours) leave from the Soreang Pertamina station 4km north of the city. Most long-haul buses pause at Terminal Induk, several kilometres south of the city, but it's often easier to hop on as they fly through town.

Tana Toraja
Home to some of Sulawesi's most stunning landscapes and one of Indonesia's most compelling traditional cultures, it's no wonder Tana Toraja is high on many bucket lists. The visual allure is immediate, with villages clustered around elaborately carved and painted houses with boat-shaped roofs, and towering terraces of emerald green rice paddies, all overseen by a protective necklace of jagged jungle-clad hills.

While most people consider attending a funeral here to be a highlight of their visit,

Tana Toraja

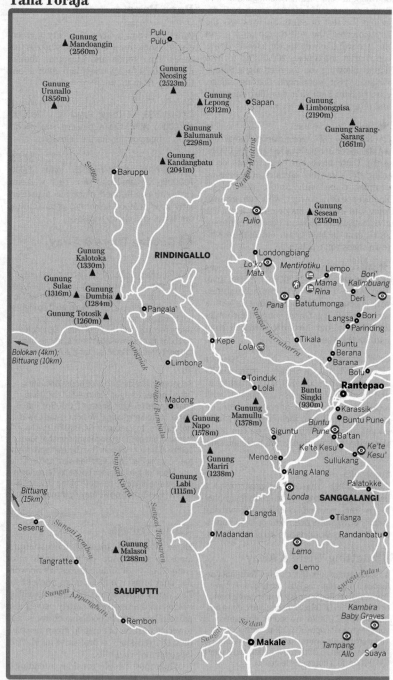

Gunung Mandoangin (2560m)

Pulu Pulu

Gunung Uranallo (1856m)

Gunung Neosing (2523m)

Gunung Lepong (2312m)

Sapan

Gunung Limbongpisa (2190m)

Gunung Balumanuk (2298m)

Gunung Sarang-Sarang (1661m)

Sungai

Gunung Kandangbatu (2041m)

Baruppu

Sungai Malino

Pulio

Gunung Sesean (2150m)

RINDINGALLO

Londongbiang

Lo'ko Mata

Mentirotiku

Lempo

Bori' Kalimbuang

Gunung Kalotoka (1330m)

Gunung Sulae (1316m)

Gunung Dumbia (1284m)

Pangala'

Mama Rina

Deri

Pana'

Batutumonga

Gunung Totosik (1260m)

Langsa

Bori

Parinding

Bolokan (4km); Bittuang (10km)

Kepe

Lolai

Sungai Barrubarra

Tikala

Buntu Berana

Barana

Sungai Sa'pak

Limbong

Bolu

Toinduk

Lolai

Rantepao

Madong

Sungai Bumbun

Gunung Napo (1578m)

Gunung Mamullu (1378m)

Buntu Singki (930m)

Karassik

Buntu Pune

Buntu Pune

Ba'tan

Siguntu

Ke'te Kesu'

Ke'te Kesu'

Bittuang (15km)

Gunung Mariri (1238m)

Mendoe

Sullukang

Gunung Labi (1115m)

Alang Alang

Palatokke

Seseng

Sungai Kurra

Sungai Talpparan

Londa

SANGGALANGI

Langda

Tilanga

Tangratte

Sungai Rembon

Gunung Malasoi (1288m)

Madandan

Randanbatu

Lemo

Lemo

Sungai Palau

Sungai Appanghatu

SALUPUTTI

Sa'dan

Kambira Baby Graves

Rembon

Sungai

Makale

Tampang Allo

Suaya

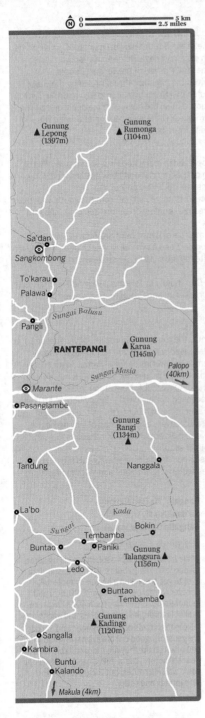

Tana Toraja also offers some great DIY trekking, cycling and motorbiking through its evergreen landscape of spellbinding beauty.

🏃 Activities

Trekking is the best way to reach isolated areas and to really get a feel for Torajan countryside and its people. Historically settlements have revolved around houses rather than 'villages', meaning civilisation is dispersed and you're never very far away from the next family group. Grab a good map, pick two points, and you'll likely find a path between them. However, note that with the rapid pace of development, many of the 'classic' backcountry treks now follow paved roads – and the asphalt tentacles grow daily. It's highly advisable to take a good map, such as the detailed Tana Toraja (1:85,000) map, published by Periplus. If you're taking advantage of Torajan hospitality, be sure to pay your way.

Routes are limited only by your imagination, but a few of our favourite treks include the following:

Batutumonga–Lo'ko' Mata–Pulio–Sapan–Pulu Pulu–Baruppu–Pangala' Three days; superb scenery, timeless villages and burning legs. Batutumonga to Pulio is freshly paved while the rest is more serious uphill stone or mud pathways.

Sa'dan–Sapan–Pulu Pulu–Baruppu–Pangala' Three-to-five days; tough and mountainous – an adventurous highlands trek in the truest sense.

Pangala'–Bolokan–Bittuang Two days; a well-marked route through pristine villages and coffee plantations.

Bittuang–Karaka–Ulusalu–Orobua–Mamasa Three to four days; tackle the steep forested ridge dividing Toraja and Mamasa. You'll want a guide for the as-of-yet undeveloped section between Ulusalu and Orobua.

ℹ️ Information

Independent guides are mostly based in Rantepao and hover around guesthouses or popular restaurants. Agencies can also arrange tours (including trekking and cultural tours), vehicles and guides.

ℹ️ Getting There & Away

Practically every traveller arriving in Tana Toraja disembarks in Rantepao. There are good bus

THE TORAJA

The Toraja inhabit the vast, rugged landscape of the South Sulawesi highlands. Their name is derived from the Bugis word *toriaja*, which once had negative connotations similar to 'hillbilly' or 'bumpkin'. Tana Toraja refers to the land (*tanah*) of the Torajan people.

For centuries Torajan life and culture survived the constant threat posed by the Bugis from the southwest. However, in 1905 the Dutch began a bloody campaign to bring Central Sulawesi under their control. Missionaries moved in on the heels of the troops, and by the time of WWII many of the great Torajan ceremonies (with the exception of the *tomate* – funeral celebrations) were rapidly disappearing from local culture.

Beliefs

Before the arrival of Christianity, the Toraja believed in many gods but worshipped Puang Matua as the special god of their family, clan or tribe. Christianity has undermined some traditional Torajan beliefs, but the ceremonies are still a vital part of life.

Torajan mythology suggests that their ancestors came by boat from the south, sailed up Sungai Sa'dan (Sa'dan River) and dwelt in the Enrekang region before being pushed into the mountains by the arrival of other groups.

Buffalo are a status symbol for the Toraja and are of paramount importance in various religious ceremonies. The buffalo has traditionally been a symbol of wealth and power; even land could be bought with buffalo. Sought-after albino buffalo can change hands for more than US$8000.

Despite the strength of traditional beliefs, Christianity in Toraja is a very active force. One of the first questions asked of you will be your religion, and Protestants are given immediate approval.

Funerals

Of all Torajan ceremonies, the most important is the *tomate* (funeral; literally 'deceased'). Without proper funeral rites the soul of the deceased will cause misfortune to its family.

The Toraja generally have two funeral ceremonies: one immediately after death and an elaborate second funeral after preparations have been made. The bigger funerals are usually scheduled during the dry months of July and August, but there are funerals year-round.

Until the time of the second funeral, the deceased remains in the family house. An invitation to visit the deceased is an honour. If you accept, remember to thank the deceased and ask permission of the deceased when you wish to leave – as you would of a living host.

The second funeral can be spread over several days and involve hundreds of guests, traditional dancing, lots of food, and ritual animal sacrifice.

The Toraja believe that the souls of animals should follow their masters to the next life, hence the importance of animal sacrifices. Festivities often include a form of bullfighting,

connections to Makassar as well as Tentena/Poso. Currently the fastest way here is via air from Makassar to Palopo then overland to Rantepao (1½ hours).

ⓘ Getting Around

BEMO & KIJANG

Local public transport leaves from stops around central Rantepao, as well as from the scruffy and muddy Terminal Bolu north of Rantepao and the town of Makale; there are regular bemos and Kijangs to all main villages. Some of the more useful services head to the following destinations from Rantepao and Makale:

Bittuang For treks to Mamasa; departs Makale only.

Lempo For hiking up to Batutumonga.

Pangala' Via Batutumonga.

Sa'dan Usually from Bolu.

Sangalla Departs Makale only.

MOTORBIKE & BICYCLE

While fresh ribbons of asphalt are killing some favourite trekking routes, it's now easier than ever to get around on a bicycle or motorbike. Scooter (rental per day from 75,000Rp) and mountain bikes (per day from 40,000Rp) are available through several hotels and agencies.

Note that roads out of Rantepao and Makale are generally good but always narrow and windy, and often steep; they are more suitable for experienced motorcyclists. Bikes can be used along some walking routes, but the trails are often very muddy and rocky.

usually held on the third day, using water buffalo that are eventually killed. The number of buffalo to be sacrificed is carefully negotiated, and depends on status and means. The meat is divided among the community as a one-off redistribution of wealth.

Some may find the water buffalo fights disturbing and the sacrifices very bloody and traumatic.

Visitors attending a funeral should wear black or dark-coloured clothing and bring shareable gifts like sweets or cigarettes for the family of the deceased.

Graves & Tau Tau

The Toraja believe that you can take possessions with you into the afterlife, and the dead generally go well equipped to their graves. Since this historically led to grave plundering, the Toraja started to hide their dead in caves.

These caves are hollowed out by specialist cave builders. Coffins are taken deep inside the caves, and *tau tau* (carved wooden figures) are placed on balconies in the rock face in front of the caves.

The *tau tau* symbolise the continuation of the person's life after death, and it is forbidden to touch one outside of certain ceremonies. Unfortunately, this has not prevented looters from stealing *tau tau* – which can be wildly expensive depending on the artist and type of wood – so many families now keep them in their homes.

That being said, you'll still see plenty of these statues at Lemo and most other grave sites.

Traditional Houses

One of the most noticeable aspects about Tana Toraja is the size and grandeur of the *tongkonan* (traditional Torajan house). It is the place for family gatherings and may not be bought or sold.

The towering roof, which rears up at either end, is the most striking aspect of a *tongkonan*. Some believe the roof represents the horns of a buffalo; others suggest it represents the bow and stern of a boat. Typically houses are oriented facing northeast toward the land of the living, with their backs facing southwest, or the land of the dead, thus some see the roof as bridge between the two worlds, grounded by the *a'riri posi'* (naval post), the centre pillar of the house.

The horns of buffalo and skulls of other animals sacrificed at funerals are mounted out front; the taller the stack, the older the household and the higher its status. Status is also indicated by how ornately the *tongkonan* is carved and painted, as lower classes were long forbidden to decorate their family houses.

SULAWESI TANA TORAJA

Rantepao

☑ 0423 / POP 26,500

Rantepao owes its existence to the Dutch who tried (with moderate success) to bring the family-centred rule of the Toraja highlands under centralised administration, creating two new seats of government: Rantepao and Makale. While that control shifted back and forth – or dissolved completely at times – Rantepao did grow into a small centre of trade and commerce for the northern Torajan communities.

Still something of an overgrown village, Rantepao is an easy-to-manage town that lies within striking distance of the region's major sites and offers a good range of accommodation and restaurants. The centre is a tad scruffy, but traffic isn't too heavy and the streets quickly merge with farmers' fields on Rantepao's outskirts; you're never far from the crow of a rooster. Nights can be cool and there is rain throughout the year, even in the dry season.

◎ Sights

Pasar Bolu MARKET

(☺ Tue & Sat) Heralded as the world's largest water buffalo market, this dusty, chaotic scene pops off every Tuesday and Saturday when stately beasts imported from around the world are put on display. Some of these animals cost more than a small car. Most are destined for slaughter at funeral ceremonies.

Rantepao

Jl Tengko Situru

Sungai Tikala

Sungai Sa'dan

Jl W Monginsidi

Cars to Pangala'

Terminal Bolu; Pasar Bolu (1.5km); Sa'dan (12km)

10

9

Jl Tappang

Jl Abdul Gani

Jl Pembangunan

Jl Taruna

Lebonna Tourist Service

Jl Emmy Saelan

11

Jl Niaga

Town Sq

Jl Sawerigading

Jl Andi Mapanyukki

3

12

7

Jl Landorundun

Jl Diponegoro

Terminal Bolu; Pasar Bolu (2km)

Jl Olah Raga

Jl Mangadil

Lapangan Bakti

8

13

Jl Merdeka

Jl Budi Utomo

Jl Pacuan Kuda

Jl Sam Ratulangi

Jl Kartika

Jl Ahmad Yani

Jl Pantekesu

Jl Taman Bahagia

Jl Pertanian

Government Tourist Office

Jl Kartika

2

4

Jl Kasuari

5

6

Jl Kete Kesu

Rosalina Homestay (200m)

1

SULAWESI TANA TORAJA

Rantepao

There's also a swift trade in pigs and roosters, and the more traditional market nearby is a social feast for the senses. Mornings are the best time to visit.

🏃 Activities

Hotels that have **swimming pools** allow nonguests to swim for a fee (from 15,000Rp).

Toraja One Stop Adventure   ADVENTURE SPORTS
(📞 0812 1458 7515; www.torajaonestopadventure.com; Jl Abdul Gani 14) Definitely the most professional outfit in town, this endeavour by Indonesian outdoor clothing store, Consina, has the kind of updated equipment and well-trained staff you want on your team when tackling whitewater adventures or extended mountain-biking trips. One day rafting from US$75, two day Sa'dan River expedition is US$250.

🛌 Sleeping

Prices in Rantepao rise in the peak tourist season (June to August), when some private homes also accept guests. Air-conditioning is rare (and largely not needed).

★ Pia's Poppies Hotel   GUESTHOUSE $
(📞 0423-21121, 0813 4242 8063; www.pias poppies.com; Jl Pongtiku, Lorong Merpati 4; s/d 220,000/240,000Rp; 🛜) This well-organised backpacker lodge with very helpful staff is in a tranquil location, 10 minutes' walk from the centre. Rooms face a quiet field and have quirky details such as boulders in the bathrooms. The cafe (p686) serves excellent local food, including Torajan *pa'piong,* and cold beer. Breakfast is available for an extra cost.

Rosalina Homestay   HOMESTAY $
(📞 0852 5572 5432; http://rosalinahomestay rantepao.blogspot.com; Jl Pongitiku Karassik; d with breakfast 200,000Rp; 🛜) Owned and operated by Enos, an experienced Torajan guide who understands customer service, Rosalina fea-

tures very clean upstairs rooms and a terrace overlooking rice paddies. The location is blissfully just south of town with rural views, but that means a 20-minute walk to the best restaurants; Enos rents motorbikes to guests or will lend you one for a quick trip.

Hotel Pison   HOTEL $
(📞 0423-21344; Jl Pongtiku Gang II 8; r from 220,000-300,000Rp; ❄🛜) At the southern end of town, family-run and fair-value Pison has midrange hotel styling at a budget rate with 32 ageing rooms in several price categories. Aircon and TV are standard and all but the very cheapest have hot water. There's a good restaurant; breakfast is not included.

★ Sulawesi Castle   GUESTHOUSE $$
(📞 0811 399 986; www.facebook.com/sulawesi castletoraja; Jl Kasuari 18; r incl breakfast 400,000-500,000Rp) Modern, comfortable rooms with splashes of colour and thoughtful touches make this sparkling new towering orange guesthouse a winner; the exceedingly helpful and gracious owner (who bakes bread) catapults it into a league of its own.

Luta Resort Toraja   HOTEL $$
(📞 0423-21060; Jl Ratulangi 26; r incl breakfast 550,000-895,000Rp; ❄🛜🏊) The only 'luxury' hotel in the centre does OK with its spacious but dated rooms trimmed with dark wood accents overlooking either the lush garden courtyard or river at the rear. Someone had a vision when they built this

---

> ### ℹ SITE ENTRANCE FEES
>
> Most of the tourist sites around Tana Toraja have an entry fee of 20,000Rp to 30,000Rp. There is usually a ticket booth at each place, complete with the odd souvenir stall...or 10 or more in the case of Lemo and Londa.

CHOOSING A GUIDE

Many guides in Tana Toraja hold a government-approved licence, obtained by undertaking a course in culture, language and etiquette, and being fluent in the local language. There are also competent guides with no certificate (and incompetent licensed guides). The best way to choose a guide is to sit down and talk through a trip before committing. If you feel you are being pressured (or hit on), this is probably a good sign to go and find a different guide.

Guides will approach you in guesthouses and cafes. Freelance guides charge 400,000Rp or so for an all-day circuit by motorbike, including a funeral if there's one on. You can also hire a guide with a car (for up to four people) for around 500,000Rp per day, but much of the Toraja region is only accessible on foot or by motorbike so this can be a limiting option. For trekking, guides charge about 500,000Rp per day. All these rates are slightly negotiable but the 100 or so guides in the area try to keep their rates equal and fixed. Larger tour agencies usually charge more than the rates quoted.

Hiring a guide can be useful to help you get your bearings, learn about the culture and cover a lot of ground quickly, but there's no reason why you can't explore the area without one if you have a decent map and a few relevant phrases of Bahasa Indonesia.

Torajan-inspired post-modern block, but the follow-through lacks enthusiasm. Staff are friendly. Wi-fi spotty.

Wisma Monika GUESTHOUSE $$
(☑ 0423-21216; Jl Ratulangi 36; r without/with air-con 350,000/450,000Rp; ❇ 🐾 🛜) A grandiose-looking cream villa close to plenty of eating options, with a choice of plain but well-maintained and clean rooms, all with bedside reading lights. The staff prepare a good breakfast, including pancakes, nasi goreng and fresh fruit juices. Prices drop with only rudimentary haggling.

Toraja Heritage Hotel RESORT $$$
(☑ 0423-21192; http://toraja-heritage.com; Jl Kete Kesu, above Karassik; r incl breakfast 1,100,000-1,400,000Rp; ❇ 🛜 🐾) The Heritage styles itself as a four-star resort, offering accommodation in huge *tongkonan*-style houses and a more conventional hotel block (which is fine, but not as atmospheric). Gardens are lush, the lagoon-like pool is great and there's a separate kids pool. Overall, it's a solid choice, but the hotel is in dire need of a thorough renovation.

🍴 Eating

Ayam Penyet Ria INDONESIAN $
(☑ 0423-25188; Jl Ahmad Yani 81; mains 20,000-31,000Rp; ⏱ 10am-10pm; 🛜) With a wide picture-book menu you're sure to find something to please at this large showroom-like institution on the main street. Most come for the *ayam penyet* (smashed chicken, a tender spicy deliciousness), though Indo-

nesian favourites such as gado-gado are available.

Sop Ubi Ma'Uni SOUP $
(☑ 0852 4296 5985; Jl Emmy Saelan; soup 12,000-15,000Rp; ⏱ 9am-8pm) You may think you know how delicious fried *ubi* (cassava) soup could be, but you ain't tried Ma'Uni's *sop ubi* yet. Come here when you're ready to dive bravely back into the local hole-in-the-wall food game. Score.

Rumah Makan Saruran INDONESIAN, CHINESE $
(☑ 0423-21079; Jl Andi Mappanyuki 119; mains 30,000-45,000Rp; ⏱ 8am-10pm) Oodles of fried noodles and reliable, freshly prepared Indonesian-style Chinese food is served at this hopping restaurant on the main drag. The bright and sociable dining room is an appropriate setting for some of Rantepao's best eating.

Pia's INTERNATIONAL $
(☑ 0423-21121; Jl Pongtiku 22; mains 35,000-50,000Rp; ⏱ 7-10am & 6-10pm; 🛜) The dining room at Pia's Poppies Hotel (p685) has great local food including *pa'piong* (80,000Rp), plus decent pizza. All food is cooked to request, so it's essential to order well ahead (at least two hours) or be prepared to wait (and wait). Bintangs cost just 35,000Rp. It's a 10-minute walk south of the centre. Closed for lunch.

Rimiko Restoran INDONESIAN $
(☑ 0423-23366; Jl Andi Mappanyukki 115; mains 25,000-55,000Rp; ⏱ 8am-10pm) A long-running, very friendly place that serves au-

thentic local food, including Torajan specialities such as buffalo, pork and eel in black
sauce, alongside Indo staples such as gado
gado. Book ahead for the *pa'piong* – pork or
chicken slow-cooked with wild local herbs in
bamboo over a fire.

Shopping

Rantepao is great for woodcarving, weaving
and basketry – the main crafts of Tana Toraja. Look for specialities from the region's
villages, such as Mamasan boxes (used
to store magic, salt and betel nuts), huge
horn necklaces and wooden figurines, and
high-quality woodcarvings by Ke'te Kesu'
and Londa carvers, such as trays, panels and
clocks, evocative of decorations on traditional houses.

Aryanion Store   CLOTHING
(Kaos Toraja; aryanion@yahoo.co.id; Jl Ratulangi
15; T-shirts 90,000Rp; ☺10am-9pm) This store
specialises in cool T-shirts (for both guys 'n'
gals) made from quality cotton. Check out
its Toraja motifs and stylish designs.

Todi   ARTS & CRAFTS
(☑0812 360 64922; www.todi.co.id; Jl Ahmad
Yani 63; ☺9am-6.40pm, from 1pm Sun) Sells
high-quality ikat, wood carvings and Torajan crafts. Prices are quite high, but some
bargaining is possible.

ℹ Information

Government Tourist Office (☑0423-21277;
www.halotorajautara.com; Jl Ahmad Yani;
☺9am-4pm Mon-Sat) The friendly, helpful
staff here can recommend guides and provide
accurate, independent information about local
sites, ceremonies and festivals.

> **BALOK**
>
> The local alcoholic drink, *balok* (palm
> wine; also known as *tuak* and tod-
> dy) is sold in jugs or bamboo tubes
> around town and comes in a variety of
> strengths, colours (from clear to dark
> red, achieved by adding bark) and fla-
> vours (from sweet to bitter). The mar-
> kets held at Rantepao and Makale have
> whole sections devoted to the sale of it.
> It doesn't get better with age; consume
> within 12 hours.

ℹ Getting There & Away

AIR

There were no flights to Rantepao at time of
research. Daily flights from Makassar to Palopo
(Wings and Garuda, 600,000Rp, one hour, one
to two times daily) with onward ground transport (40,000Rp, 1½ hours) are the best bet for
those in a hurry to get here.

BUS & BEMO

Most long-distance buses leave from the bus
company offices along Jl Andi Mappanyukki.
Prices vary according to speed and the level of
comfort. Try to book your ticket a day in advance.

From **Terminal Pasar Bolu**, 2km north of
Rantepao, there are regular vehicles to Palopo
(40,000Rp, 1½ hours), Sa'dan (10,000Rp,
45min), Batutumonga (25,000Rp, 45 minutes),
and Pulio (30,000Rp, 1½ hours). Your odds of
leaving in a timely manner increase with how
early you try. You can also get a bemo to Makale
(8000Rp, 30 minutes), but it's often easier to
catch transport at the corner of Jl Landorundun
and Jl Andi Mappanyukki.

Cars for Pangala' (40,000Rp, two hours) leave
from the **junction** just before the bridge at the
north end of town.

SULAWESI TANA TORAJA

LONG-DISTANCE BUSES FROM RANTEPAO

DESTINATION	FARE (RP)	DURATION (HR)	DEPARTS
Kendari	280,000	24	3 per week am
Makassar	150,000-370,000	8-9	many daily pm
Mamasa (car from Makale)	150,000	8-10	1 daily am
Palopo (car from Bolu)	40,000	1½	on demand
Palu	250,000	20	2-3 daily am
Pare Pare	80,000	5	2-3 daily am
Pendolo	150,000	8	2-3 daily am
Poso	200,000	12	2-3 daily am
Tentena	170,000	10	2-3 daily am

ⓘ Getting Around

Rantepao is small and easy to walk around. A motorcycle becak should cost around 5000Rp in town. Scooters cost from 80,000Rp per day to hire from guesthouses and agencies near Lapangan Bakti. **Lebonna** (☑ 0423-292 0926; Jl W Monginsidi 102) rents larger trail bikes for more remote excursions.

Batutumonga

One of the easiest places to stay overnight in Tana Toraja is, conveniently, one of the more beautiful. Batutumonga at Sesean Suloara' occupies a broad slope on the side of Gunung Sesean overlooking, well, just about everything. From here you will have panoramic views of Rantepao and the Sa'dan Valley, and stunning sunrises.

It's located about 20km north of Rantepao and if you're doing it right, getting here is half the fun. A winding trek through traditional villages and up pathways snaking between rice terraces is the best way to earn your reward, but for those pressed for time, you can also day-trip here for some hiking and a local lunch.

Mentirotiku GUESTHOUSE **$**
(☑ 0813 4206 6620; Batutumonga; r 150,000-400,000Rp) With commanding views and landscaped grounds, this place offers traditional *tongkonan* crash pads – inside are thin mattresses squashed together in compact wood-panelled spaces – or less-interesting, modern rooms with private

bathrooms. The huge restaurant (geared for tour groups) serves decent, Indo-Toraja food (mains 35,000Rp to 50,000Rp), although the view outperforms the kitchen.

Mama Rina GUESTHOUSE **$**
(☑ 0813 4159 4704; Batutumonga; r incl 2 meals for 1 person/2 or more people 150,000/350,000Rp) Mattresses on the floors of these two original, traditional tumbledown *tongkonan* provide as close to a rustic Torajan experience as you can get without actually staying in someone's house. Price includes dinner and breakfast at the elevated restaurant with just a sliver of a view.

ⓘ Getting There & Away

Bemo (12,000Rp, one hour) buzz up to Batutumonga from Terminal Bolu in Rantepao. Sometimes your ride may only go as far as Lempo – a steep, but pleasant 2km walk away.

North Highlands

With dramatic bowls of cascading rice terraces, small *tongkonan* villages and lots of harder-to-reach sights that don't make it on every tour-bus itinerary, the north is the most scenic region of Tana Toraja.

There's great trekking to be had here, but note you'll either be heading up or down.

Pana' TOMB
(Suloara; 30,000Rp) Whether its claim to be the oldest known baby grave in Toraja is accurate or not, this site is definitely one of

---

COFFEE IN TORAJA

Famous for its earthy, full-bodied taste (spicy, smoky and caramel notes, low acidity and a crisp finish), Toraja is one of Indonesia's most highly regarded regional coffees. Tana Toraja is one of the few areas where the Arabica bean (which is harder to cultivate and less disease resistant than other kinds) dominates, accounting for 96% of local cultivation. Due to the mountainous terrain, the crop is mostly grown on smallholdings, with low annual yields.

Coffee was introduced to Toraja in the mid-19th century by the Dutch, who controlled production. In 1890, as its value increased exponentially, a 'coffee war' erupted between Bugis and Toraja over trade routes.

Today most Torajan coffee is certified organic and produced by indigenous farmers: the volcanic soil, relatively cool climate and altitude (1400m to 1900m) is perfect for premium Arabica production. Coffee from the cooperative Petani Kopi Organik Toraja has fair-trade certification and is available in North America and Europe.

Torajan coffee is particularly sought after in Japan, where it's branded as Toarco Toraja. In the Toraja Utara district alone, 7000 small-scale farmers sell coffee beans to Toarco, accounting for an average of 50% of their income; this is way more than rice, for example.

Torajans are proud of their coffee notoriety and many restaurants serve the local brew.

EXPLORING TANA TORAJA'S COUNTRYSIDE

To really experience all that Tana Toraja has to offer, you'll need to spend a few days exploring the spectacular countryside. Stunning scenery, cascading rice fields, precipitous cliff graves, other-worldly *tau tau* (carved wooden figures), hanging graves, soaring *tongkonan* (traditional Torajan houses) and colourful ceremonies: this is the wild world of Tana Toraja.

Many places can be reached on day trips from Rantepao, and longer trips are possible by staying overnight in villages or camping out. The roads to major towns, such as Makale, Palopo, Sa'dan, Sesean Suloara' (Batutumonga), Madandan and Bittuang, are paved, but many other roads around Tana Toraja are constructed out of compacted boulders; vehicles won't get stuck, but your joints get rattled loose.

A few areas such as Londa, Lemo and Ke'te Kesu' are pretty touristy (complete with low-pressure hawkers selling trinkets and souvenirs) but for good reason: they're exceptionally beautiful. Beyond these places, most of the sights are more subdued – and there are plenty of undiscovered gems you might be lucky enough to stumble across.

Dare to take off on foot and stumble into your own private corner of awesome; pretty much every village is connected to the next via pathways wandering between rice paddies. If you're exploring the region on your own, note that signposts are few and far between, so take a paper map.

Torajan funeral ceremonies are best visited with a guide, who will be able to explain cultural etiquette; for instance, you should always have a gift for the deceased's family and it's customary to wear black or dark clothes.

the more compelling. The minimal development and quiet setting gives it a palpably sacred feel.

Lo'ko' Mata
TOMB

(admission 30,000Rp) High on the mountainside, this collection of rock tombs is unique for its location: bored into the sides of a giant round boulder about 3km northwest of Batutumonga. Look for the huge buffalo head carved under one and the intricate wood doors on others.

Lolai
VIEWPOINT

Billed as the 'Country Above the Clouds', the long north–south ridge line looming to the west of Rantepao certainly has spectacular views – especially at sunrise when the valley below is often filled with fog leaving just the tips of the highest karst peaks showing through. There are multiple official viewpoints mobbed by carloads of tourists; of them, **Tongkonan Lempe** is our favourite with its view across impressive rice terraces to Batutumonga ridge.

Pulio
VILLAGE

Perched on a hilltop above boulder-strewn rice terraces, this small village with anachronistic street lights makes an excellent jumping off point for treks farther afield – or a long walk down to Rantepao.

Gunung Sesean
HIKING

(Batutumonga) A 3.5km hike up the south ridge of Gunung Sesean takes you to stunning 360-degree views at 2150m. If your legs and lungs won't get you all the way, there are pretty nice lookouts along the way. Leaves from Batutumonga village.

North Lowlands

For lush river valley scenery and good shopping, head to the weaving villages in Sa'dan, where local women set up a market to sell their woven cloth. It's all handmade on simple looms, though not all is produced in the village.

Bori' Kalimbuang
RELIGIOUS SITE

(Bori; 30,000Rp) There are lots of places to see standing stones, but this is one of the nicer ones. With 102 stones – each representing a different funeral conducted at the site – this pleasantly arranged and well manicured collection of particularly large menhirs is attractive and peaceful. Nearby tombs as well as a tree bearing baby graves add to the sacred ambience.

Sangkombong
WORKSHOP

(Sa'dan) Rows of *tongkonan* also house several workshops of traditional weavers who are happy to demonstrate their handicraft. A variety of fabrics are on display from

DAY HIKES IN TANA TORAJA

West of Rantepao

The 3km walk from Siguntu to the Rantepao–Makale road at **Alang Alang** is also pleasant. Stop on the way at the traditional village of **Mendoe**. From Alang Alang, where a covered bridge crosses the river, head a few hundred metres to **Londa**, back to Rantepao, or remain on the western side of the river and continue walking south to the villages of **Langda** and **Madandan**.

Northeast Lowlands

The traditional *tongkonan* village of **Palawa'** is attractive and not often visited by tour groups. In the dry season you can walk southwest, fording a river and walking through rice fields to **Pangli**, which has *tau tau* and house graves, and then to Bori' Kalimbuang (p689), the site of an impressive *rante* (ceremonial ground) and some towering menhirs. Alternately, head over the hill between Palawa' and Bori' cutting the distance considerably. About 1km south of Bori' on the paved road, **Parinding** also has *tongkonan*, rice barns and 700-year-old cave graves. From here you can walk back to Rantepao or on to **Tikala**. This can also be a nice bicycle route starting and finishing in Rantepao.

Northwest Highlands

From **Pangala'**, a rambling market village northwest of Rantepao, follow the rarely travelled 15km track high above the river canyon to the valley of **Baruppu** and its network of pristine villages. Pangala' itself has a few streets, a little *ayam goreng* (fried chicken) stall, and is famous for being the hometown of Pongtiku, a fearless warrior who fought against the Dutch.

Pangala' is 30km from Rantepao (40,000Rp by Kijang).

---

antique blankets with traditional motifs to cheap scarves with Toraja-inspired scenes, all of which could be yours – for the right price.

East of Rantepao

This region is often visited on day tours while heading between north and south Tana Toraja. It's flatter than the north and beautiful, with plenty of rice fields, sleepy traditional villages and grazing buffalo. It's an excellent place to get lost on a motorbike.

Marante

VILLAGE

A thriving traditional village bursting with *tongkonan* (many new) just 5km northeast of Rantepao makes for a fine, relatively flat, excursion from town. Near Marante there are stone and hanging graves with several *tau tau*, skulls on the coffins and a cave with scattered bones. From the village, you can strike out cross-country, winding through rice paddies on your way back to Rantepao.

South of Rantepao

There are many popular cultural sights in this region and most are accessible by car. It's not a great region for walking, but it is suitable for a motorbike day tour. Tour buses love this area for the easy access but also because the sights are simply stunning.

★ Ke'te Kesu'

VILLAGE

(Jl Ke'te Kesu'; admission 30,000Rp; ⊙ 6am-6pm) The four stately *tongkonan* and many granaries that make up Ke'te Kesu' were moved to this picturesque site in 1927 when the savvy family head noticed the Dutch government largely ignored anyone too far from their administrative centres. Later, to share their heritage with the world while demonstrating the value of preserving traditions, Kesu'ers got their village designated as the first official *obyek wisata* (tourism site) in Toraja, and lobbied hard (with some success) for Unesco World Heritage attention.

On the cliff face behind the village there are cave graves and very old hanging graves – some reportedly 500 years old or more. Deteriorating coffins are suspended on wooden beams under an overhang, while others have fallen into jumbles below full of bones and skulls.

Shops near the car park sell intricate wood carvings – one way the locals hope to share Toraja with outsiders.

The village is 4km southeast of Rantepao and gets busy with tour groups in high season.

Lemo
TOMB

(admission 20,000Rp; ⊙7am-dusk) A veritable village of *tau tau* stare down with unblinking eyes and outstretched arms from this impressive burial cliff riddled with tombs. The sheer rock face has a whole series of balconies for statues of the deceased who feel as much a part of the community as their living relatives. The site is located at the head of a terraced valley making the whole scene hauntingly beautiful, especially in the early morning.

Londa
TOMB

(30,000Rp; ⊙7am-dusk) Live out your Indiana Jones fantasies at this extensive (and very popular) burial cave below a massive cliff face. Its entrance is guarded by a balcony of *tau tau,* while inside piles of coffins – many of them rotted away – and bones lie haphazardly on almost every ledge. Members of the upper class are placed in hanging caskets on the cliff face, some at dizzying heights, while commoners are placed in the caves, often without caskets at all.

A local myth says that the people buried here are the descendants of Tangdilinoq, chief of the Toraja; English-speaking guides with lanterns (50,000Rp) are eager to tell you all about it and more as you explore the depths of the caves. If you're thin, and don't suffer from claustrophobia, squeeze through the tunnel that connects the two main caves, passing some interesting stalactites and stalagmites.

Rantepao–Makale bemo will drop you off at the turn-off 5km south of Rantepao. From there it's a 2km walk (or *ojek*) from the cave.

Buntu Pune
VILLAGE

(Jl Ke'te Kesu') Buntu Pune village has two fine *tongkonan* houses and four rice barns some with ancient roofs covered in vegetation. According to local legend, one of the houses was built by Pong Maramba, an early-20th-century nobleman. During Dutch rule he was appointed head of the local district, but planned to rebel and was subsequently exiled to Ambon (Maluku), where he died. His body was returned to Tana Toraja and buried at the hill to the north of Buntu Pune.

Karassik
HISTORIC SITE

(Rantepao) On the outskirts of Rantepao, just off the road to Makale, Karassik holds an interesting array of obelisks moved here by the Dutch from Lantangin in 1906 – conditions demanded of them by local leader Pong Maramba if they wished to garrison their soldiers on his land.

Makale
☏0423 / POP 34,000

Makale is the administrative capital of Tana Toraja but there's little reason to stick around, other than to switch buses or visit the market. Built around an artificial lake, the town is ringed by cloud-shrouded hills.

The market, held every six days, is a blur of noise and colour. You'll see pigs strapped down with bamboo strips for buyers' close inspection, buckets of live eels, piles of fresh and dried fish, and a corner of the market reserved just for *balok* (palm spirit) sales.

GETTING TO THE TOGEAN ISLANDS FROM TANA TORAJA

Many visitors want to get from Tana Toraja to the Togean Islands. Here are your options:

Longest but most rewarding Bus to Tentena; two nights in Tentena with trip to Bada Valley; car to Ampana; overnight in Ampana; ferry to Togean Islands. Total time: three-plus days.

Quicker but tough going Bus to Poso; minibus from Poso to Ampana; ferry to Togeans. Total time: two days.

Most comfortable but most expensive Early car to Palopo; flight to Palu; overnight in Palu; flight to Ampana; afternoon speed to Togeans. Total time: 1½ days.

There are numerous other possibilities, including backtracking to Makassar and flying to Poso or Luwuk and then travelling overland to Ampana.

The price for a private air-conditioned car to drive from Rantepao to Ampana, with an overnight break in Tentena, starts at about 2,300,000Rp. Sharing a car can be a great option, allowing you to stop as you wish for photographs and meals.

TREKKING AROUND MAMASA

If you're heading into the hills, know that homestays can usually be negotiated in any village for anywhere between 50,000Rp to 150,000Rp per person, which will generally include a simple breakfast and dinner. For lunch, ask around; someone will surely offer to make you a meal for around 25,000Rp. Bring plenty of water and/or a water filter and warm clothes.

Your best route-finder is an offline satellite image on your phone (bring a backup charger) second only to the professional-quality hand-drawn maps created by the owner of Ramayana Inn in Mamasa.

Our favourite routes:

Mamasa–Orobua–Ulusalu–Karaka'–Bittuang Three to four days; a new take on an old classic, this Mamasa–Toraja trek gets you off the road and into the forest. You may want a guide between Orobua and Ulusalu.

Taupe–Ulumambi–Rantelemo–Mambi Three days; as if the scenery above Mamasa wasn't perfect enough, this route takes in Sambabo, a super-tall waterfall.

❶ Getting There & Away

Kijang connect Rantepao and Makale (8000Rp, 20 minutes) between dawn and dusk. Most of the bus companies based in Rantepao also have offices around the block southeast of the lake along Jls Merdeka, Pelita and Ichwan. The only transport between Tana Toraja and Mamasa is with private cars (150,000Rp, 10 hours) departing daily at around 8am from **Terminal Makale**.

East of Makale

This area is pretty far away from the tourist heartland, which means less crowds, and there are several intriguing sights.

★**Tampang Allo**   TOMB
(Sangalla; 20,000Rp) With its *tau tau*, cave site and peaceful rice paddy setting squeezed between a maze of cliffs, this is one of the more evocative sites in Tana Toraja. The graves reportedly belong to the chiefs of Sangalla, descendants of the mythical divine being Tamborolangiq who introduced the caste system and death rituals into Torajan society. Their skulls all look the same as any commoner's, however.

Take a Kijang from Makale to Sangalla; get off at Suaya, and walk the concrete path to Tampang Allo.

Kambira Baby Graves   CEMETERY
(Sangalla; 20,000Rp) Torajans traditionally inter deceased babies, who have not yet teethed, in trees, believing that these infants are more pure than adults, and that their bodies and spirits will be absorbed into the tree and continue to grow with it. This is one of the bigger arboreal graves in the region, holding around 20 deceased infants, though

the tree itself is now deceased as well. The site is a shady, tranquil spot and there's a superbly ornate *tongkonan* nearby.

Kambira is near Sangalla, which is served by Kijang from Makale, 9km to the west.

MAMASA VALLEY

An area of outstanding natural beauty in Sulawesi, the Mamasa Valley offers wonderful highland scenery and deep tribal traditions. Its history of difficult access has kept it off the beaten tourist trail, but road improvements are changing that.

Culturally there are both similarities and differences with neighbouring Toraja country. Torajan-style ceremonies survive in the Mamasa Valley, but these are generally far less ostentatious affairs. Like Torajan traditional houses, Mamasan *tongkonan* have long extended roof overhangs and their exteriors are carved with animal and human motifs.

Mamasans have embraced Christianity with unfettered enthusiasm: choir groups regularly meet up and down the valley. *Sambu* weaving is a craft that still thrives: these long strips of heavy woven material are stitched together to make blankets, which provide ideal insulation against the cold mountain nights, and are sold by many villagers.

❍ Sights

Taupe   VILLAGE
Getting to this traditional village with jungle walks and panoramic views has just enough ups and downs to make it an excellent bicycle

destination for those who don't mind a little sweat. It's about 5km northwest of Mamasa.

Ballapeu' VILLAGE

High in the Balla district, Ballapeu' has a fine collection of over 100 traditional houses. Women here are experts in traditional weaving.

Rante Buda HISTORIC BUILDING

(Rambuseratu; entry by donation) An impressive 25m-long *tongkonan* building known locally as a Banua Layuk (high house) is a historic chief's place with colourful motifs. This is one of the oldest and best preserved in the valley, built about 300 years ago for the chief of Rambusaratu, one of five local leaders. To visit, a donation of 10,000Rp to 15,000Rp is expected.

Osango VILLAGE

Osango is the site of *tedong-tedong* (tiny structures over graves that look like houses), which are supposedly up to 200 years old. There are lots of paths and the village is very spread out, so you may find that you'll need to ask for directions along the way.

Rantesepang VILLAGE

A couple of stores sell traditional fabrics in this roadside village that bills itself as the centre of Mamasa weaving. The path up the hill from the craft shop leads to a few workshops, where women craft long strips of heavy cloth for Mamasa's distinctive, colourful blankets.

Tedong Tedong Minanga TOMB

(Buntu Balla) A collection of wooden coffins shaped like boats and buffalo. Further up the road at Buntu Balla, traditional weavers can often be found working.

❶ Getting There & Away

Shared Kijang (p694) connect Mamasa Valley with Rantepao to the east in Toraja and Polewali to the south along the coast.

Mamasa

📱 0428 / POP 22,500

Mamasa is the only real town in the valley. The air is cool and clean and the folk are hospitable, but rampant construction gives it a bit of a frenetic feel. Market day is Monday, when hill people trade their produce and the streets are filled with colour and bustle.

Nusantara Hot Springs HOT SPRINGS

(📱 0821 8894 3331; Jl Poros Polewali; per person regular/VIP 5000/15,000Rp) This developed hot springs site on the edge of the river is

Mamasa

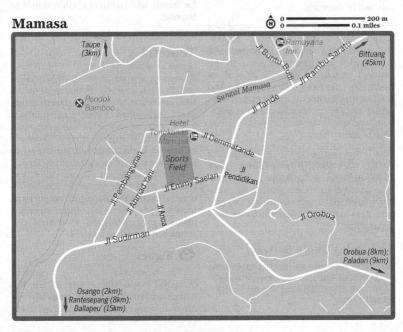

clean and relaxing. The VIP pool is a worthy upgrade if the regular pool is crowded. Once the attached hotel finishes its new rooms, this might make for a good base of operations.

Hotel Tongkonan Mamasa GUESTHOUSE $
(☑ 0813 1919 5535; Jl Demmatande; r incl breakfast 150,000-250,000Rp) One of best places in town, Hotel Tongkonan Mamasa's spacious rooms in this family house have en-suite bathrooms, and there's a distinct welcome feel thanks to the china cups on the table waiting for tea.

Ramayana Inn GUESTHOUSE $
(☑ 0852 9953 6811, 0854 204 0478; just off Jl Buntu Budi; r from 150,000Rp) This venerable place has been hosting travellers for years, and it shows. The two floors of spacious rooms are holding up OK, but the star attraction is the owner who makes professional-quality maps of the area in his spare time. Although he's frequently gone, you may be able convince his kids to make a copy for you.

Anoa Hotel HOTEL $$
(☑ 0428-284 1079; nic.sirina115@gmail.com; Jl Poros Polewali 158; r from 350,000Rp; ☎) Sparkling new, white-tiled rooms are clean and comfortable, and popular with tour buses. Note that some don't have windows – criminal in this part of the world.

Pondok Bamboo INDONESIAN $
(☑ 0853 9756 7706; mains 25,000-55,000Rp; ☻ 10am-10pm; ☎) An array of bamboo *pondok* (shaded platforms often found in rice paddies) arranged around aquaculture ponds give this place a relaxed feel. The food is filling and the juice is excellent, just don't expect it in a hurry. Located in a quiet neighbourhood across the river on the northwest edge of town.

Dian Satria Restaurant INDONESIAN $
(☑ 0813 4229 8849; Jl Poros Polewali; mains 20,000-30,000Rp; ☻ 7am-9.30pm) A welcoming, atmospheric place serving generous portions of noodle and rice dishes, and cold beer. Also has basic but decent rooms from 250,000Rp.

❶ Getting There & Away

Kijang from Polewali make the climb to Mamasa (90,000Rp, six hours) on demand (or when full). Try to score a front seat if you have any history of carsickness.

Kijang leave for Makale and Rantepao (150,000Rp, eight hours) daily in the morning. It's a rough, bumpy, impressively steep road over the pass that is not yet paved the entire way, making it a spicy ride during rainy season. Coming to Mamasa, secure your seat in the morning at the Makale terminal.

CENTRAL SULAWESI

Almost abandoned by tourism due to a period of religious violence, Central Sulawesi is now back on the map for travellers moving between the Togean Islands and Tana Toraja.

Settlements on the shores of Danau Poso are an ideal place to break up a long bus ride. Tranquil Tentena is the easiest place to arrange treks into the Lore Lindu National Park, which is filled with mysterious megaliths and has a wildlife-rich jungle. Those with the time and a nose for anthropology should head to Morowali Nature Reserve to seek out the Wana people, while beach bums can laze around on the white sands of Tanjung Karang near Palu.

In September 2018, a violent earthquake hit this region, sending a devastating tsunami into Palu Bay. Though the recovery of the city and immediately affected regions is ongoing, the area can still be used by tourists for transit, and conditions will continue to improve.

Tentena
☑ 0458 / POP 11,230
Tentena is a town of white picket fences and churches, cool breezes that come off the lake, and lots of wonderfully strange things to eat. Surrounded by clove-covered hills, it has an interesting market and some natural treasures to explore nearby. There are no beaches in the town itself, but it's easy to hire a motorbike or an *ojek* to get to some.

Not only is Tentena a convenient and peaceful place to break up the journey between Ampana and Rantepao, but its proximity to Bada Valley's mysterious megaliths makes it a mandatory stop for anyone with an interest in ancient cultures.

◉ Sights
Air Terjun Saluopa WATERFALL
(20,000Rp) If you have wheels you can visit this impressive, powerful waterfall that drops in stages through rainforest, 15km

THE 2018 SULAWESI EARTHQUAKE & TSUNAMI

On 28 September 2018, at approximately 6pm local time, a severe 7.4 magnitude earthquake hit the Donggala Regency in the 'neck' of the Minahasa Peninsula. Shortly afterwards, a tsunami barrelled down the Makassar Strait. Funnelled into Palu's bay, it reached 6m high in places as it swept over the city, displacing more than 60,000 people and killing over 1200 in Palu alone. A lack of infrastructure, a delayed response by officials, and the fear of additional tremors compounded the problems. Donggala was also hit, with water sending boats into houses, collapsing buildings, and causing great loss of life and suffering. Many buildings were totally demolished and many more were uninhabitable.

As a tourist, one of the ways you can help the region is by visiting. Most of Central Sulawesi was unaffected by the earthquake and tsunami, yet an economic aftershock has hit businesses in the surrounding region, as tourists have veered away even from areas totally untouched by the disaster. While damage in Palu and Donggala was catastrophic and repairs will be ongoing for many years, there's no need to avoid the whole of Central Sulawesi. Even Palu remains useful as a tourist entry and transit area, with basic services operational and some tourist-worthy hotels open.

west of Tentena. The falls are a spectacular place for a swim, and you can hike through the jungle and alongside a plunging river for a few kilometres – keep an eye out for monkeys and hornbills. Guides are available to take you on full day treks deeper into the rainforest.

Eel Traps
AREA

Tentena's pretty covered 210m bridge marks where Danau Poso (Lake Poso) ends and Sungai Poso (Poso River) begins its journey to the coast. V-shaped eel traps north of the bridge snare the 2m monsters for which Tentena is famous. Live specimens are available for inspection and consumption in local warungs.

Chartering a boat to explore the lake can be surprisingly difficult; the asking rate is 120,000Rp for two hours.

Siuri Beach
BEACH

Around 20km southwest of Tentena, this golden beach by the lake has great swimming with a water temperature of around 26°C year-round. There's a restaurant for lunch and drinks, and several lodging options.

✦ Festivals & Events

Festival Danau Poso
CULTURAL

(www.facebook.com/FestivalDanauPoso; ⊙ late Sep) Tentena is the host of the annual Festival Danau Poso, the undisputed highlight of Central Sulawesi's social calendar, in late September. Villagers from far afield gather for a colourful celebration of culture, with dancing, songs and traditional sports.

🛏 Sleeping & Eating

Victory Hotel
GUESTHOUSE $

(☏ 0458-21392; www.victorytentena.com; Jl Diponegoro 18; standard/deluxe r 150,000/250,000Rp; ☏) A very friendly family-run place with a wide choice of (ageing) rooms, from cell-like cheapies to spacious options with hot water. Most travellers happily end up here, thanks to the excellent info (maps are provided) and social areas. The owners can also sort out motorbikes, recommend good guides and do laundry. Wi-fi only really works in the public area.

★ Dolidi Ndano Towale
BUNGALOW $$

(☏ 0812 4523 9357; www.dolidi-ndano-towale.com; s/d incl breakfast 375,000/460,000Rp; ☏) This

BUSES FROM TENTENA

DESTINATION	FARE (RP)	DURATION (HR)	FREQUENCY	DEPARTURE
Ampana	800,000	4	charter	
Palu	130,000	8	2-3 daily	6pm
Pendolo	40,000	2	many	morning when full
Poso	40,000	2	many	morning when full
Rantepao	130,000	10	2-3 daily	3pm

DANAU POSO

Indonesia's third-largest lake, Danau Poso, covers an area of 323 sq km and reaches an average depth of 450m. The lake is 495m above sea level, so evenings there are pleasantly cool without being too cold. With mountains on all sides and mist hovering over the calm waters in the early morning, it's a captivating spot.

beautifully designed place has lovely lakeside cottages in a wonderful location on a sandy beach. There's a jetty for waterside drinks and a fine restaurant with sweeping views, and the manager is extremely informative and helpful. Tours of the lake and national parks can be arranged. It's 6km south of Tentena, down a bumpy access road hugging the lake.

Danau Poso Resort　　　　　RESORT $$
(☑ 0458-222 1771; danauposoresort@gmail.com; Jl Banua Mpogombo 1; r/ste 400,000/750,000Rp; ✳🅟✳) A new, modern, colourful hotel with breezy dining area and pool next to the lake. The large comfortable rooms climb the slope away from the water. Staff are trying hard to make sure this one develops a good reputation.

Siuri Cottages　　　　　　COTTAGE $$
(☑ 0852 4105 8225; cottages incl breakfast 270,000-370,000Rp) Twenty kilometers southwest of Tentena, this isolated place is something of a time warp; its spacious, comfortable timber cottages are complete with original 1980s decor, and there's no wi-fi. However, its location on a lovely, unspoiled lakeside beach more than compensates for the lack of modernity. The staff is eager to please and the hotel's restaurant is adequate.

Call ahead and the owners will pick you up for free from Tentena; if you stay a couple of nights, they'll drop you back there, too.

Ongga Bale　　　　　　　SEAFOOD $
(☑ 0813 5596 8368; Jl Setia Budi; fish per kg 80,000Rp; ⊙ 10am-11pm; 🅟) A large, well-organised restaurant on the main strip with tables on the riverbank. Pick a fish from the pools, choose a sauce, order a beer, and you're set. A large *ikan bakar* (grilled fish) will set you back around 45,000Rp.

❶ Getting There & Away

All manner of cars pass through Tentena on their way somewhere. Hanging out by the side of the road and flagging down an Avanza is perfectly acceptable. Buses can be booked at the **terminal** or your guesthouse may have contact info.

Ojek (10,000Rp) typically meet buses when they pull into town, but prepare yourself for the 3km walk if your arrival is delayed till the wee hours of the morn.

❶ Getting Around

The best way to get to the beaches and waterfalls is to rent a motorbike (per day 70,000Rp; ask at your hotel) or hire an *ojek* (per day around 130,000Rp).

Poso

☑ 0452 / POP 49,300

Poso is the main town, port and terminal for road transport on the northern coast of Central Sulawesi. For years, violence between Muslims and Christians made it a no-go zone, but tensions have eased. However, there's still no reason to visit other than to change buses, or break up a trip to/from Ampana and the Togean Islands.

Armada Losmen　　　　　GUESTHOUSE $
(☑ 0452-23070; Jl Pulau Sumatera 17; r with shared/private bathroom 90,000/220,000Rp; ✳)

BUSES FROM POSO

DESTINATION	TYPE	FARE (RP)	DURATION (HR)	FREQUENCY
Ampana	bus/car	70,000/100,000	4	9.30am & 5pm
Kolonodale	bus	120,000	8	8am
Makassar	bus	310,000	24	4 weekly
Manado	bus	320,000	30	daily
Palu	bus/minibus	80,000/110,000	6	9am
Tentena	car	50,000	2	9am & 2pm
Rantepao	bus	250,000	12	2pm (from Palu)

Right on the main drag, this losmen has a wide selection of bland but acceptably clean rooms tended by indifferent staff.

RM Raja Mujair   SEAFOOD $
(Jl Pulau Sumatera 27; fish 30,000-35,000Rp; ⊙10am-10pm) If it's *mujair* you want (it is), look no further. Choose your live tala-pia to be grilled, fried, or boiled in a bowl of vegetables. Chicken and prawns are also available – but those are already dead. The coconutty *sambal dabu dabu* (condiment of tomatoes, shallots and fresh chilli) here is second to none.

❶ Getting There & Away

AIR
Poso's **Kasiguncu airport**, 15km west of town, has one daily Wings Air flight to Makassar (from 1,000,000Rp).

BUS & MINIBUS
The **bus terminal** (Jl Diponegoro 4) is about 3km south of town. There are plenty of *ojek* and bemos that will buzz you into central Poso for 5000Rp.

For Palu and Ampana, you can also catch the minibuses from offices along Jl Pulau Sumatera. For Rantepao (Toraja) book in advance with an agent to ensure your seat.

Bemos to nearby villages and beaches leave from a terminal next to the market.

Lore Lindu National Park

As if having a lush jungle filled with impres-sive hornbills, pygmy buffalo *(anoa)*, and shy tarsiers wasn't enough, Lore Lindu is also fa-mous for its megaliths – giant freestanding stones carved into different characters or shapes by unknown people for mysterious purposes.

Covering an area of 2500 sq km, this re-mote national park, which is a Unesco Bio-sphere Reserve, has been barely touched by tourism. It's a perfect place to seek out an off-the-beaten-path adventure. Guides are mandatory for visiting the park, and highly recommended for touring the megalith are-as outside the park – especially if you actual-ly want to find them.

◎ Sights

★ Bada Valley   ARCHAEOLOGICAL SITE
Seemingly scattered haphazardly around the hills near Lore Lindu National Park are some 400 ancient stone megaliths of un-

---

GUIDED TOURS

Guides in Tentena can organise treks to Bada Valley and Lore Lindu National Park as well as **Morowali Nature Reserve**, the rarely visited home of the formerly nomadic Wana people. Dolidi Ndano Towale (p695) and Victory Hotel (p695) provide good recommendations.

A full day trip to see the megaliths in Bada will run to 1,500,000Rp including car and driver/guide.

---

known origin that might be over 5000 years old. A fine assortment of these can be found – with a guide – in Bada Valley, 60km west of Tentena, including the 4m tall, anatomically correct, leaning Palindo.

While you can see many of the statues in one long day from Tentena, several villages do have homestays or guesthouses including Bomba, Gintu and Tuare.

Behoa Valley   ARCHAEOLOGICAL SITE
(Besoa) The valley around Bariri village is littered with megalithic objects, including statues of human forms as well as massive *kalamba* (stone pots) and *tutu'na* (stone lids). The region is alternately called Behoa or Besoa. Trekking from here to Bada Valley (or vice versa) is popular.

Napu Valley   AREA
Several homestays in Napu Valley make it a good base of operation for exploring the eastern side of Lore Lindu. A handful of megaliths in nearby villages are accessible by paved road.

Danau Tambing   LAKE
Get away from it all at this pleasant and peace-ful mountain lake on the edge of Lore Lindu National Park – at least until it's mobbed on the weekend. It's a popular destination for birdwatchers, with over 200 known species in the vicinity, and is the departure point for hiking Gunung Rorekatimbu. You can pitch a tent on the well-manicured grounds and enjoy just being here.

Tickets for park entry are sold at the small field post next to the car park.

☞ Tours

Kamarora Village   OUTDOORS
Near Kamarora village are hot springs, waterfalls, and decent forest trekking. Pak

SULAWESI LORE LINDU NATIONAL PARK

GUIDES

For long-distance trekking, a guide is compulsory, and also necessary if you're intent on finding the megaliths. An organised one-day visit from Tentena with a guide and vehicle (for up to four people) costs about 2,200,000Rp, and prices go up from there. The guides from Tentena generally speak English.

If travelling independently, arrange a guide at Wuasa, Bomba, Badu or at the tourist office or national park office in Palu. Guides start at 250,000Rp for day trips, more for trekking; few speak much English.

Reimon (0813 5456 8722), the official park contact in this village, has long worked with tarsier researchers and is passionate about their protection and conservation. He monitors several pairs every morning, and knows their habits well. Call in advance to arrange a homestay and guided trips.

🛌 Sleeping

Penginapan Nasional　　　GUESTHOUSE $
(☑ 0813 4109 4094; Wuasa; r from 150,000Rp) New, clean, spacious rooms with ample common sitting areas make this a fine addition to the Wuasa lodging scene. The owner's daughter (who runs the place) speaks excellent English, and is actively seeking ways to enhance tourism in the area.

RM & Penginapan Sendy　　HOMESTAY $
(☑ 0813 4106 5109; Jl Pemuka 3, Wuasa; s/d 150,000/250,000Rp) This attractive homestay has tidy rooms with screened windows, and a very helpful owner, Ibu Sendy. At the time of research, the attached restaurant was about a metre shorter after an earthquake knocked it off its stilts, but it still serves filling meals (from 20,000Rp to 40,000Rp). Book in advance.

ⓘ Information

If you're headed to the east side of the park, buy national-park entry permits (per person per day 150,000Rp) at the small field office at Danau Tambing (p697). For excursions to the west side, purchase your tickets in advance at the Balai Taman Nasional Lore Lindu Office in Palu.

ⓘ Getting There & Away

There are three main approaches to the park: one from Tentena and two from Palu. From Palu, Kijang run all the way to Wuasa (105km, four hours) and Doda (132km, five hours) twice a day from Terminal Petobo (p700) along a paved road.

From Tentena, there is a daily bus to Bomba (66km, four hours); you can also charter cars, but these run according to demand and road conditions. Motorbikes and *ojek* are readily available in Wuasa, Gimpu, Doda and Bomba.

Palu

☑ 0451 / POP 351,000

Palu, the capital of Central Sulawesi, was hit by a major earthquake and tsunami in September 2018, which decimated the town and surrounding area. At the time of writing, Palu was still recovering. Nevertheless, it's a good place to do errands if you're heading to/from Kalimantan or Lore Lindu National Park. Nearby is the rarely visited yet architecturally interesting village of Dongalla and the beach area of Tanjung Karang.

Situated in a rain shadow for most of the year, Palu is one of the driest places in Indonesia. The city straddles the mighty Palu River, home to a healthy population of crocodiles which we've been assured never eat people.

Museum Sulawesi Tengah　　MUSEUM
(☑ 0451-22290; Jl Kemiri 23; 10,000Rp; ⊙ 8am-4pm Mon-Fri) This exceptionally good museum has cultural artefacts from the area's indigenous peoples. Unfortunately only half the signs are in English, but there are extremely informative English-speaking attendants who will happily show you around.

Rama Garden Hotel　　HOTEL $$
(☑ 0451-429500; www.hotelramagarden.com; Jl Tanjung Santigi 26; r incl breakfast 300,000-500,000Rp; ❈ @ 🛜 ☲) This labyrinthine hotel can be confusing, though fortunately lots of plants, green spaces, a pool and a terrace dining area all help you relax as you hunt for your room. Older options are toeing the line for value, but seeing active renovation. A new addition promises to be top-notch.

Hotel Sentral　　HOTEL $$
(☑ 0451-422789; Jl Monginsidi 71-73; r incl breakfast 300,000-750,000Rp; ❈ 🛜) Dependable but tired options in this venerable downtown location have seating in front of your room

and some attempts at greenery. Restaurants and a large supermarket are close by.

★ Maestro Pizza
PIZZA **$$**

(📞0451-421841; Jl MT Haryono 6; pizza from 85,000Rp; ⏰10am-10pm; 📶) Contemporary and clean, this is the place to come when you can't eat another grilled fish. The decor is more polished than the pizza, but we've yet to go home disappointed.

Kaledo Stereo
INDONESIAN **$$**

(📞0812 2443 7799; Jl Diponegoro 40; kaledo without/with the leg 30,000/60,000Rp; ⏰8am-9pm; 📶) This is perhaps the city's most famous *kaledo* restaurant, a bustling place where its spicy beef soup – a festival of cholesterol – is served in a bowl with a giant Fred Flintstone–style bone to chew on.

❶ Information

Balai Taman Nasional Lore Lindu Office
(📞0451-457623; www.lorelindu.info; Jl Prof Mohammad Yamin 53; ⏰8am-4pm Mon-Fri) Little English is spoken but the staff here do their best to help. They can set you up with guides for hiking and trekking in Lore Lindu National Park.

Immigration
(📞081 341 016969, 0451-421433; Tanjung Dako 19; ⏰8am-4pm Mon-Fri) Painless visa extensions in one or two days. Located next to Kantor Berita Antara news office.

❶ Getting There & Away

AIR

Palu's **Mutiara Sis Aljufri Airport** has direct flights to and from Jakarta, Surabaya and Balikpapan, and is well-connected to Northern Sulawesi destinations – except Manado, which currently requires a transit.

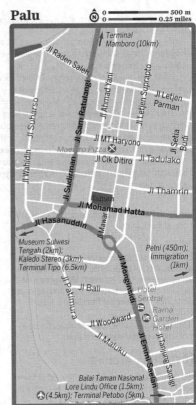

Palu

BOAT

Pelni ferries connect to East Kalimantan and Sulawesi ports, including boats to Balikpapan and Bitung. Ferries dock at Pantoloan, 22km north of Palu, which is accessible by *angkot* from Terminal Mamboro (p700), or by metered taxi (100,000Rp). The **Pelni office** (📞0451-421696; Jl Kartini; ⏰7.30am-noon & 1-4pm Mon-Fri,

BUSES FROM PALU

DESTINATION	TERMINAL	FARE (RP)	DURATION (HR)	FREQUENCY
Ampana		150,000	8	frequent
Behoa (Besoa; Lore Lindu)	Petobo	130,000	4	when full
Donggala (Tanjung Karang)	Tipo	25,000	1	when full
Makassar	Tipo	280,000	24	many daily
Manado	Mamboro	300,000	24	10am
Polewali	Tipo	220,000	18	many daily
Poso		110,000	6	frequent
Rantepao	Mamboro	250,000	20	7am
Wuasa (Lore Lindu)	Petobo	100,000	2½	when full

NATURAL DISASTER PRECAUTIONS

While you can't prevent natural disasters from occurring during your visit (though we hope they never will!), there are a few ways you can protect yourself while traveling in earthquake-prone areas.

Be aware of your surroundings. This includes not just checking your sleeping quarters for possible hazards (a large bookcase near your bed, for example) but also finding fire escapes and even the location of your hotel in relation to natural surroundings. Are you in a tsunami zone? Are you near a spot where a landslide might occur? Ask what natural disasters have occurred in this region previously if you're unsure.

Keep bottled water and your cellphone within reach in case of an emergency. You may be able to call for help, and, if trapped, extra water can be crucial for survival. Make sure friends or family know your location and itinerary. While it may be extreme, it never hurts to alert your country's consulate that you're travelling in the area in case of a major natural disaster.

8am-noon Sat) in Palu is efficient; there's another one at Pantoloan.

BUS & KIJANG

Long-haul buses to Makassar leave from **Terminal Tipo**, west of town, while buses to Poso and Rantepao leave from **Terminal Mamboro** east of town. For Lore Lindu National Park and regional points, head to **Terminal Petobo** in a suburb south of town.

Minibuses bound for Poso and Ampana leave from small companies around town.

ⓘ Getting Around

Palu's Mutiara airport is 6km southeast of town; it costs around 50,000Rp to/from the centre in a metered taxi or car.

Donggala & Tanjung Karang

Donggala city is a sleepy port full of colourful historic houses, flowering gardens and lots of interesting local characters. From here it's a short *ojek* (motorcycle) ride to Tanjung Karang's slice of white sand, studded with rickety beach bungalows, roaming buffalo and a decent dive centre.

In September 2018, an earthquake and tsunami caused severe damage to many parts of the coastline. Though the Donggala regency, a vast area that covers both sides of the Makassar Strait, was mostly okay, the city of Donggala suffered severe damage. The tourist areas listed here were lucky and escaped with only minor damage.

Harmoni   BUNGALOW $$
(📱0822 7109 8112; Tanjung Karang; bungalows 300,000Rp) You have your choice of places offering bare wooden and bamboo bungalows

with a mattress on the floor – lots of choices – but Harmoni stands out in one respect: it's sand all the way to water. And pretty trash-free sand at that.

Prince John Dive Resort   RESORT $$$
(📱0457-71710; www.prince-john-dive-resort.com; Tanjung Karang; bungalows for 2 people incl 2 meals 1,200,000-1,800,000Rp; ❄🛜) This long-loved resort is reason enough to come to Tanjung Karang. Three classes of rustic-chic wood-and-stone bungalows enjoy partial sea views (but not beach access), and are well-managed with German efficiency. The restaurant's food is delicious, and the communal sandy beach is a fine place to relax after a day of diving. Wi-fi is confined to reception and lounge areas.

ⓘ Getting There & Away

Kijangs to Donggala (25,000Rp) leave when full from Terminal Tipo, about 5km outside Palu. From Donggala you can catch an *ojek* the 5km to Tanjung Karang (8000Rp). A taxi/*ojek* from Palu costs around 120,000/55,000Rp.

Luwuk

📱0461 / POP 38,000

Set around a mountainous natural harbour, Luwuk is the biggest town on Sulawesi's remote eastern peninsula. Long isolated from the rest of the action, Luwuk now sees a trickle of travellers, thanks to improved air links. It's a possible stepping stone to the Togean Islands, and the jumping off point to the forgotten Banggai Islands.

There's decent diving to be had a few hours' drive to the east of Luwuk at the end of the peninsula. To the west, protected areas house healthy (for now) populations of maleo birds.

Air Terjun Piala & Laumarang
WATERFALL

Two impressive waterfalls up the canyon northwest of Luwuk make a fine afternoon excursion. Piala requires ducking under a fence at the aqueduct which may not appeal to some, but the government is actively improving the muddy road to Laumarang, which they hope to develop into a tourism destination. It's a steep 3km hike from the edge of town.

Grand Soho
HOTEL $$

(☑0461-325999; grandy.soho1@gmail.com; Jl Sungai Limboto 5; r from 330,000Rp; ❄️🛜) Sporting a breezy rooftop terrace overlooking the city, this new(ish) business hotel keeps it simple but clean. Alarmingly it is showing a little more wear than one would expect, but for now it's a solid, but not grand, midrange bet.

Tompotika Dive Lodge
BUNGALOW $$$

(☑0812 4494 2028; www.divingsulawesi-tompotika.com; Balantak; bungalow with full board per person €77-94; ❄️🛜) The tightly built, polished wood bungalows on the beach at this all-inclusive top-notch dive resort are spacious and relaxing. The staff bend over backward to accommodate their guests, who are mostly here for the superb diving. Some proceeds from the resort go toward community development and conservation of maleo birds, sea turtles, and other peninsula wildlife.

❶ Getting There & Away

Luwuk **airport** has direct connections to Palu (500,000Rp, one hour, three daily), Manado (1,200,000Rp, 1½ hours, one daily) and Makassar (600,000Rp, 1½ hours, four daily).

Both wooden and speed boats leave daily for Salakan Island in the Banggai Islands (100,000 Rp) at 1pm and 9pm, though schedules change frequently.

Private cars are currently your only option for transport to Ampana (150,000Rp, five hours).

Ampana

☑0464 / POP 18,385

The main reason for travellers to come to Ampana is to catch a boat to/from the Togean Islands. It's a laid-back, pleasant coastal town with a vibrant market and makes a good stopover while you recover from, or prepare for, an assault on the Togeans.

Tanjung Api
NATURAL FEATURE

The 42-sq-km Tanjung Api (Fire Cape) is home to *anoa* (pygmy buffalo), *babi rusa* (wild deer-like pigs), crocodiles, snakes and maleo birds, but most people come to see the burning coral cliff fuelled by a leak of natural gas. A visit to the park is more interesting at dusk. To get here you need to charter a boat 24km east around the rocky peninsula from Ampana.

Marina Cottages
COTTAGE $

(☑0822 9181 7019, 0464-21280; marina.cottages@yahoo.com; Jl Tanjung Api 33, Labuan; cottage with fan 180,000Rp, with air-con 300,000-550,000Rp; ❄️🛜) About 3km northeast of central Ampana, these very well-maintained wooden cottages occupy a smooth pebble beach. Bumping up from a standard gives a significant upgrade in quality; the shellacked deluxe cottages are on the beach. The open-sided restaurant has great views making it an ideal place for breakfast, beer or a meal.

Nebula Cottages
BUNGALOW $

(☑0822 5944 5457; www.nebulacottages.weebly.com; Jl Tanjung Api 5; bungalows incl breakfast with fan/air-con 200,000/350,000Rp; ❄️🛜) Tasteful, spacious wooden bungalows sit pretty in a coconut grove, close to the sea. The staff is eager to help and can arrange motorbike hire. Breakfast is excellent, with lots of fresh fruit and good tea and coffee. Located 2km northeast of the centre.

★ Lawaka Hotel
BOUTIQUE HOTEL $$

(☑0464-21690, mobile 0823 4343 5609; www.lawakahotel.com; Jl Tanjung Lawaka 10; r incl breakfast 300,000-750,000Rp; ❄️🛜) An unexpected find in deeply provincial Ampana, Lawaka feels like a hip hostel with its zany decor, cool cafe and urban art-enriched rooms that face a central garden. It was made for travellers, and the beer garden out back is a chill place to meet a few of them. It's about 1km east of the centre, just steps from the coast.

Warung Pangkep
SEAFOOD $

(Daeng Iwan; ☑0813 4116 1536; Jl A Yani; fish from 40,000Rp; ⊙8am-midnight; 🛜) We've repeatedly been told this place serves the best fish in town. We've repeatedly tried to find fault with that claim – but failed. Repeatedly. Fish are cooked to perfection on the grill in front of this airy favourite that has some of the spiciest sambal around. They also do a decent *soto Makassar* (spicy beef soup). It's 1km east of the centre.

ℹ️ Getting There & Away

AIR

At the time of research, the only direct flight to Ampana was on Wings from Palu (550,000Rp, 50 minutes, one daily), arriving and departing mid-morning.

The **Tanjung Api airport** is 6km east of the ferry dock; to or from the airport, the taxi bidding war starts at 50,000Rp and should end closer to 20,000Rp.

BOAT

Boats to Wakai and beyond leave from the **main boat dock** (Pelabuhan Ampana; Jl Yos Sudarso) at the end of Jl Yos Sudarso, in the centre of Ampana. Slow boats to Bomba leave from a **jetty** in Labuan village. Both Wakai and Bomba are on Pulau Batu Daka, in the Togean Islands.

BUS & MINIBUS

Minibuses travel each day to Luwuk (150,000Rp, six hours), Poso (100,000Rp, four hours) and Palu (150,000Rp, 10 hours). You can reserve them at different agencies in town, or mill about at the **Terminal Kota Ampana** (Jl Pulau Taupan) in the morning.

Togean Islands

It takes determination to get to the Togean Islands – but it takes far more determination to leave. You'll hop from one forested golden-beach island to the next, where hammocks are plentiful, worries scarce and the welcome genuine. Most islands have only a few family-run guesthouses, while popular Kadidiri has a small but lively beach scene with night-time bonfires and cold beers all around.

The rich diversity of marine life and astonishing coral formations are a magnet for divers and snorkellers; there are several professional scuba schools for training, courses and recreational dives. For truly spectacular diving, Una Una fits the bill perfectly.

> ### ℹ️ GETTING IN TOUCH WITH THE TOGEAN ISLANDS
>
> There's no internet on the Togean Islands and mobile phone reception is patchy at best. While many guesthouses have an email address and phone number, you may have to wait a few days or more before anyone writes back or returns your call.

On land, there's a surprising variety of wildlife to look for in the undisturbed and wild jungles, as well as other remote beaches to find. Around seven ethnic groups share this region, but all are happy to see visitors and are exceptionally hospitable.

🏃 Activities

The Togeans are the only place in Indonesia where you can find all three major reef environments – atoll, barrier and fringing reefs – in one location. Two atolls and their deep lagoons lie to the northwest of Pulau Batu Daka. Barrier reefs surround many islands at the 200m-depth contour (5km to 15km offshore), and fringing reefs surround all of the coasts, merging with sea grass and mangroves. There is also a well-preserved sunken WWII B-24 bomber plane (at a depth of between 14m and 22m).

The mix of coral and marine life is spectacular and unusually diverse. Dynamite and cyanide fishing has damaged some reefs in the past but recovery is well under way and many others remain untouched.

Highlights include spectacular open-water topography, with coral canyons, plunging drop-offs and some truly giant gorgonia corals. Reefs teem with hundreds of species of tropical fish, and macro life including seahorses, painted frogfishes and leaf scorpionfishes. Most sites in the Togeans rarely invite 'big stuff' but passing pelagics, including hammerhead sharks, are sometimes seen and schooling barracuda are regularly encountered. Colonies of dugong are also present.

Prices start from 450,000Rp per dive and PADI courses are available. Dive conditions (most of the year) are perfect for the inexperienced, with water temperatures at 28°C to 29°C, fine visibility and gentle currents. Pulau Kadidiri is the best place to organise activities.

Trips to Danau Mariona, where you can swim with stinger-free jellyfish (one of the few places in the world where this is possible), cost from 80,000Rp per person. Consider trekking around volcanic Pulau Una Una for land-based adventures, while several islands have jungle hikes to isolated beaches.

ℹ️ Information

Bring plenty of cash as there are no banks on the islands. If your hotel or guesthouse has a faint mobile signal it is sometimes possible to pay by card – but don't count on it.

Togean Islands

0 ————— 20 km
0 ————— 10 miles

Gunung Colo (506m)
Pulau Una Una
🏠 Sanctum

Teluk Tomini

Kadidiri Paradise Resort; Black Marlin Dive Resort
Pulau Taipi
Pulau Kadidiri
Pulau Kota
Katupat 🏠
Jellyfish Lake
🏠 Sunset Beach
Pulau Pohondongo
Wakai

Sera Beach Cottages; Sandy Bay Resort
Fadhila Cottages
Bolilanga Cottages
Malenge
Pulau Malenge
Lestari Cottages
Pulau Taoleh
Pulau Tongkabu
Kalia
Benteng
Pulau Talata Koh
Pulau Togean

Lia Beach
Popolii
Kanari
Dolong
Pulau Walea Kodi
Paotu

Gorontalo (110km)
Biga
Pulau Walea Bahi
Liang

Poya Lisa Cottages
Pulau Batu Daka
Palada
🏠 Poki Poki
Bomba
Ampana (40km)
Ampana (40km)

Selat Walea

❶ Getting There & Away

Yes, it's complicated. Getting to the Togeans is time-consuming and it's essential to factor in some wiggle room when travelling, as breakdowns and bad weather can affect ferry sailings, particularly in the rainy season (roughly from November to early April).

Your two gateway cities are Ampana (p701) to the south and Gorontalo (p708) much further away to the north.

You'll hit Ampana if you're coming overland from Tana Toraja, Palu, Poso or Luwuk. For those in a hurry, daily flights from Palu to Ampana (450,000Rp, 50 minutes) arrive at 10.10am – plenty of time to catch the afternoon speedboat to Bomba and Wakai.

Gorontolo makes sense for those working their way overland across North Sulawesi, but the boat from there only runs twice a week, and takes significantly longer.

Representatives from many of the resorts will meet ferries at arrival points in the Togeans to shuttle you to your accommodation, sometimes free of charge; arrange in advance.

Note: all of the information here is likely to change at a moment's notice; consult the website www.infotogian.weebly.com for generally up-to-date information.

FROM AMPANA

There are two daily speedboats to Wakai via Bomba (130,000Rp, 1½ hours) that leave at 9am and 12.30pm. Return trips leave Wakai at the same times. Book ahead, especially in peak periods.

The express boat to all major ports (Wakai–Katupat–Malenge–Dolong) leaves at 9.30am on Sunday, Tuesday and Wednesday. The old stalwart slow ferry follows the same route on the same days, but leaves at 10am. (Note, these boats do not stop at Bomba.)

Near-daily slow cargo boats to Bomba (35,000Rp, three hours) leave from a pier next to Marina Cottages (p701) at 9am.

Finally, there is an overnight ferry to Dolong that leaves at 9pm on Tuesday and Friday, returning from Dolong at 4pm on Thursday and Sunday – to arrive in Ampana at less-than-ideal 2am.

FROM GORONTALO

From Gorontalo the KM *Tuna Tomini* sails directly to Wakai (economy/business class 63,000/89,0000Rp, 13 hours) at 5pm on Tuesday and Friday. It arrives at 6am, giving you time to stretch your legs before catching a northbound boat if necessary.

Tickets go on sale at the dock four hours before departure. Once on board, the ferry crew will often sell foreigners their four-bunk cabins for a more private night – prices are extremely negotiable. Air-con is only available in business class.

Heading to Gorontalo, the ferry departs Wakai on Monday and Thursday at 4pm arriving at 5am.

Alternatively, you could go to Bumbulan port (a three-hour taxi or four-hour bus ride from Gorontalo) and catch the KM *Cengkih Afo* to Dolong on Pulau Walea Kodi (economy class 56,000Rp, five hours) on Sunday and Thursday at 9am. It returns Wednesday and Saturday at 8am.

❶ Getting Around

Use the Ampana–Dolong (p704) ferries to island-hop, or charter local boats.

Public boats also connect Wakai to Una Una (50,000Rp, three hours) leaving Wakai at 8am on Sunday, Tuesday and Friday and returning from Una Una at 7am on Monday, Wednesday and Saturday.

Finding a charter is relatively easy in Wakai, Bomba and Kadidiri, but it's more difficult to arrange in smaller settlements. Rates are fairly standard among the cartel of local operators (around 500,000Rp from Wakai or Kadidiri to Bomba). Ask at your accommodation.

Pulau Batu Daka

The largest and most accessible island of the Togeans is Pulau Batu Daka, which is home to the two main villages, Bomba and Wakai.

Bomba is a tiny outpost at the southwestern end of the island, which most travellers sail past on the way to and from Wakai. It's an appealing alternative to social Pulau Kadidiri, as it has some of the Togeans' best beaches, good snorkelling and is social in a very mellow way. It's a pleasant walk to the **bat caves** in the hills behind Bomba village, but you'll need a guide and a torch.

The largest settlement in the Togeans, **Wakai** is a small port that's mainly used as the departure point for boats to Pulau Kadidiri, but there are several well-stocked general stores and a lively market. A small **waterfall**, a few kilometres inland from Wakai, is a pleasant hike; ask for directions in the village.

Poya Lisa Cottages BUNGALOW $
(☏0823 4995 1833; www.poyalisa-bomba.com; Bomba; cottage per person incl meals 150,000-250,000Rp) On its own narrow private island, this little paradise has two perfect beaches, some interesting cliffs, and a dozen or so big, simple wooden bungalows. Service gets mixed reviews, but the meals here are among the best in the Togeans. They offer free snorkelling nearby, and affordable tours to distant reefs (from 300,000Rp). Diving is arranged with a neighbouring resort.

Poki Poki BUNGALOW $$
(www.pokipoki.land; bungalow per person incl meals from 250,000Rp) On a slim sandy beach on the island's southwestern coast, these simple, attractive wood-and-bamboo bungalows have decent bedding and private bathrooms. Snorkelling tours can be arranged. Single occupancy is twice the rate listed. Kids aged five to 12 can stay in their parents' room (per child 150,000Rp).

Pulau Kadidiri

Beautiful, thickly wooded Kadidiri, a 30-minute boat trip from Wakai, is definitely the island to go to if you're feeling social. Its popular lodging options are all close together, so you can stroll along a fine strip of sand

SULAWESI TOGEAN ISLANDS

AMPANA–DOLONG BOAT SCHEDULE

NORTH BOUND	EXPRESS		REGULAR	
	Departs (Sun, Tue, Wed)	Fare (Rp)	Departs (Sun, Tue, Wed)	Fare (Rp)
Ampana–Wakai	9.30am	90,000	10am	65,000
Wakai–Katupat	12.30pm	100,000	3pm	70,000
Katupat–Malenge	1pm	110,000	4.15pm	75,000
Malenge–Popolii*	1.30pm	120,000	5.30pm	80,000
Popolii–Dolong	2.15pm	120,000	7.45pm	80,000
(arrives Dolong)	(2.30pm)		(8.30pm)	

SOUTH BOUND	EXPRESS		REGULAR	
	Departs	Days	Departs	Days
Dolong–Popolii	6.30am	Mon, Wed, Fri	10pm	Tue, Thu, Sat
Popolii–Malenge*	6.45am	Mon, Wed, Fri	11pm**	Tue, Thu, Sat
Malenge–Katupat	7.30am	Mon, Wed, Fri	5.30am	Sun, Wed, Fri
Katupat–Wakai	8am	Mon, Wed, Fri	6.45am	Sun, Wed, Fri
Wakai–Ampana	9.30am	Mon, Wed, Fri	10am	Sun, Wed, Fri
(arrives Ampana)	(11.30am)		(2pm)	

*Express stops at Pulau Papan between Malenge and Popolii.

**Regular ferry overnights in Malenge; you can sleep on board.

for a drink elsewhere if your place has run out of beer. It's a 15-minute walk from the action through coconut groves to a lovely sandy cove, **Barracuda Beach.**

Pulau Kadidiri is the easiest place to organise the range of activities available in the Togean Islands. There's good snorkelling and swimming only metres from the shore and superb diving beyond. Boats to neighbouring islands for treks or swims are readily available.

🏃 Activities

In addition to diving equipment, snorkelling gear is available; in some places it's free for guests, in others you'll typically be charged 30,000Rp per day. Black Marlin Dive Resort and Kadidiri Paradise Resort are the island's main dive centres.

Black Marlin Dive Resort has kayaks for hire, which you can use to explore the sheltered lagoon behind Kadidiri Paradise Resort or the offshore islets. You can also hike island trails.

🛏 Sleeping

Black Marlin Dive Resort   RESORT $$
(☎0812 3830 7077; www.blackmarlindiving. com; bungalows per person incl meals 250,000-400,000Rp) A well-designed whitewashed resort that has a good vibe thanks to its lounging areas and attractive restaurant, which are ideal for socialising. Bungalows are smallish but stylish, and all have sea views from their front terraces, but are suffering from lack of maintenance. Diving is the thing here (500,000Rp for a day dive), and you'll be charged 10% extra if you don't do it.

★ Kadidiri Paradise Resort   RESORT $$
(☎Whatsapp 0821 4071 5684; www.kadidiriparadise.com; s/d incl meals from 360,000/600,000Rp, sea villa 780,000/1,300,000Rp) Kadidiri Paradise basks in a stunning location fronted by a small beach and a long private jetty that's perfect for snorkelling. The timber bungalows vary from ageing garden cottages to better sea-view rooms, all with attached bathroom, mosquito nets and generous front decks. Staff are sociable and it has the Togeans' only real bar with cocktail happy hour every evening at sunset.

The well-run dive centre offers single dives (500,000Rp), open-water certification (5,500,000Rp) and discounts of up to 10% on multiple dives.

> **ⓘ NATIONAL PARK ENTRANCE FEE**
>
> A renewed interest in the tourism potential and conservation needs of Togean Islands National Park lead to the implementation of a one-time entry fee (domestic/foreigner 5000/150,000Rp). This fee is collected in Ampana before the boat leaves, or at Wakai or Dolong if arriving from the north.

Pulau Una Una

Pulau Una Una, which consists mostly of active **Gunung Colo** (506m), was torn apart in 1983 when the volcano exploded. Ash covered 90% of the island, destroying all its houses and crops. Residents were safely evacuated, and many have since returned.

The offshore reefs here offer the best diving in the Togeans with schooling barracudas, Napoleon wrasse, packs of jacks and large rays. It's possible to climb the volcano in three hours, if conditions are favourable (it's highly active) and admire the awesome lava landscapes.

Sanctum   BUNGALOW $$
(☎0812 8532 5669; www.sanctumdiveindonesia. com; per person incl meals 450,000-900,000Rp) Comfortable little rooms (all with porches, some with shared bathrooms) on a slim black-sand beach, with reasonable rates and world-class diving on tap. Expect great international and local food, served family-style. The scuba shop here has a good reputation, and snorkellers can rent gear.

Pulau Togean

Pulau Togean is a large, forested island, fringed by mangroves. The ferry calls at the small fishing village of Katupat, which is good for supplies, and lies just a short boat ride away from two private island resorts. (The one resort on Togean itself is best accessed from Wakai.) Some of the best diving at the islands can be found off Togean's northern coast.

Danau Mariona   LAKE
(Jellyfish Lake) FREE Fascinating freaks of evolution, the jellyfish that have long floated in this lake without predators have gradually

lost their ability to sting, making for a truly surreal swimming experience.

Fadhila Cottages
BUNGALOW $$

(☑ 0852 4100 3685; www.fadhilacottage.com; Pulau Pangempang; r per person incl meals standard/superior 250,000/350,000Rp) Eighteen clean, wooden bungalows with terraces and hammocks line a palm-shaded beach facing either Katupat village or the ocean. There's a good PADI dive centre here and a breezy restaurant. Take a free canoe to find snorkelling spots around the island or join excursions further afield.

Bolilanga Cottages
GUESTHOUSE $$

(☑ 0852 4100 3685; www.bolilangaresort.com; Pulau Bolilanga; bungalows per person incl meals 200,000-450,000Rp) On a tiny speck of a white-sand-beach isle facing Katupat village, this family-run place is a slice of true tranquillity. Wooden bungalows (from basic to posh) with fresh-water bathrooms and mosquito nets all face the turquoise sea.

Pulau Malenge

Malenge is remote and secluded, with wonderful snorkelling around the island; head to Reef 5 for the best coral and sealife.

Some locals, with the aid of NGOs, have established excellent walking trails around the mangroves and jungles to help spot the particularly diverse fauna, including macaques, tarsiers, hornbills, cuscuses and salamanders.

The main village of **Malenge** is also fascinating to explore; it's a traditional Bajau settlement of timber houses and has a famous kilometre-long rickety 'bridge' (actually more of a gangplank), which allows you to (almost) walk on water.

★ Bahia Tomini
BUNGALOW $$

(☑ 0812 3880 2777, Ampana office 0852 4032 9259; www.bahiatomini.com; Pulau Malenge; bungalow per person incl meals 600,000-800,000Rp) Facing a secluded Malenge beach, this wonderful castaway location features four beautifully created seafacing wooden bungalows. The whole tiny operation is full of life, and incredibly welcoming. The three-night minimum may not be enough.

Sandy Bay Resort
BUNGALOW $$

(☑ 0823 4995 1833; www.sandybay-resort. com; per person incl meals 350,000-400,000Rp) Brought to you by the same fine folk behind Marina (p701) in Ampana, this well-placed

---

CONSERVATION OF THE TOGEAN ISLANDS

Home to more than 500 types of coral, 600 reef-fish species and an estimated 500 varieties of mollusc, Teluk Tomini around the Togean Islands is one of the richest reef areas in all of Indonesia.

The Togeans' shaky ecological record really started when cyanide and dynamite fishing were introduced to the islands in the early 1990s. While initially boosting the local catch, this also caused untold damage to fragile reef ecosystems. By the early 2000s, locals (often with help from local NGOs and dive centres) began to understand the destructiveness of these practices and many returned to traditional fishing techniques. Some villages even began creating their own protected areas and helped patrol reefs against illegal fishing.

Despite this, the Togeans are relatively poor islands and the fishing isn't what it used to be. The taking of valuable Napoleon wrasse (for foreign Chinese restaurants) has all but wiped out such fish from these waters, and resulted in a catastrophic increase in the number of crown-of-thorns starfish, which destroy coral at an alarming rate.

In 2004 the Indonesian Ministry of Forestry signed a bill that turned 3620 sq km of this fragile area into a national park; this was great news to conservation groups, but some local NGOs claim national-park status restricts local livelihoods and leaves the region open to other types of exploitation. In response to widespread dissent, little action was taken, and it stayed a park in name only for several years.

However, in 2017, Togean Islands National Park was declared a tourism area of national significance, and the government began plans to increase visitation, including better flights and new boat routes.

At the same time, the park sprang to life, cracking down on illegal logging, bringing in boats for patrols and increasing restoration activities. They also began levying a one-time entrance fee of 150,000Rp per foreigner – hopefully to support protection.

collection of wood bungalows with picture windows benefits from a long palm-fringed sandy beach that matches what you imagine a tropical paradise should look like.

Sera Beach Cottages
BUNGALOW $$

(☑0823 4995 1833; www.seramalengesulawesi. com; r per person incl meals 200,000-250,000Rp) On the north side of the island, situated on a lovely white-sand beach held in place by a seawall, Sera's provides well-built thatched bungalows (some in better shape than others) and a warm vibe.

Lestari Cottages
GUESTHOUSE $$

(☑0852 4100 3685; www.lestari-cottages. com; bungalows per person incl meals 200,000-350,000Rp) The setting here is spectacular, with jungle behind and a view in front of Malenge village, one of the prettiest stilt fishing villages in the archipelago. Long-running Lestari offers 10 sea-facing, rustic wooden bungalows, each with a verandah. When you're not snorkelling, you can try forest hikes and canoe excursions.

Pulau Walea Kodi

The busy fishing village of **Dolong** is the end of the ferry line from Ampana and your point of arrival in the Togeans if you're coming from Bumbulan. A pair of resorts occupy the northern coast of the hammerhead-shaped island, which is dotted with white-sand beaches and forested hills.

Lia Beach
COTTAGE $$

(Lia Beach Bamboo Resort; www.pae-lia-beach. com; r incl meals from 400,000Rp) Good for truly getting away from it all, the artistically presented, but not pretentious, gorgeous bamboo bungalows have everything you need to take a break – including exquisite isolation. When you're bored with just being, staff can arrange tours and diving with nearby operations.

NORTH SULAWESI

North Sulawesi has lots to offer in a relatively condensed space. You can dive some of the world's best coral reefs at Pulau Bunaken one day, explore volcanic scenery near Tomohon the next, and visit the lowland Tangkoko-Batuangas Dua Saudara Nature Reserve and its wildlife the day after. The Bitung area's world-class muck diving

THE BAJAU SEA GYPSIES

Nomadic Bajau 'sea gypsies' still dive for trepang (sea cucumber), pearls and other commercially important marine produce, as they have done for hundreds, perhaps thousands, of years. The Bajau are hunter-gatherers who spend much of their lives on boats, travelling as families wherever they go.

There are several permanent Bajau settlements around the Togean Islands, and even some stilt villages on offshore reefs, but the itinerant character of Bajau culture survives. Newlyweds are put in a canoe and pushed out to sea to make their place in the world. When they have children, fathers dive with their three-day-old babies to introduce them to life on the sea.

(including very quirky macro life) is another huge draw.

Economic prosperity from tourism and agriculture (mostly cloves and coconuts) means that North Sulawesi is the most developed province on the island. The two largest distinct groups in the region are the Minahasans and the Sangirese, but there are many more subgroups. Dutch influence is stronger here than anywhere else in the country: the Dutch language is still spoken among the older generation, and well-to-do families often send their children to study in the Netherlands.

History

A group of independent states was established at a meeting of the linguistically diverse Minahasan peoples around AD 670 at a stone now known as Watu Pinabetengan (near Kawangkoan).

In 1677 the Dutch occupied Pulau Sangir (now Pulau Sangihe) and, two years later, a treaty with the Minahasan chiefs saw the start of Dutch domination for the next 300 years. Although relations with the Dutch were often less than cordial, and the region did not actually come under direct Dutch rule until 1870, the Dutch and Minahasans eventually became so close that the north was often referred to as the 12th province of the Netherlands.

Christianity became a force in the early 1820s, and the wholesale conversion of the Minahasans was almost complete by 1860.

BOGANI NANI WARTABONE NATIONAL PARK

About 50km west of Kotamobagu, this very rarely visited 2871-sq-km national park has the highest conservation value in North Sulawesi, but it's pretty inaccessible. The park (formerly known as Dumoga-Bone) is at the headwaters of Sungai Dumoga (Dumoga River) and is a haven for rare flora and fauna. The maleo bird, a large megapode, is found in large numbers here (more than 3000 were released into the park in 2012). Other wildlife include the *yaki* (black-crested macaque) and a species of giant fruit bat only discovered in the 1990s.

Beyond the flora and fauna, there are several poorly understood archaeological sites near Toraut consisting of multiple large rooms carved into the sides of cliffs, presumably for burials. These sites are no longer used and are still hidden in the forest, lending your trek here a profound sense of adventure and discovery.

The area around Toraut has several trails, which take from one to nine hours to hike, and there are options for overnight jaunts through the jungle if you have camping equipment.

Tombun is known for its maleo bird population, and there are usually a few on hand at the nesting site. There are also a few established treks into the forest nearby. Check in at the **national park posts** (☎ 0434-22548; Jl AKD Mongkonai, Kotamobagu; ☺ 7.30am-noon & 1-4pm Mon-Fri) at either site for guides and information.

For Toraut, take a regular *angkot* (30,000Rp, 1½ hours) to Doloduo from the Serasi terminal in Kotamobagu, then hire an ojek for the 10km trip further west to the ranger station. Alternately, you can go direct to Doloduo on the southern road from Gorontalo.

For Tambun take an *angkot* to Imandi (25,000Rp, one hour) and from there get an ojek east to Tambun (20,000Rp, 20 minutes).

Because the school curriculum was taught in Dutch, the Minahasans had an early advantage in the competition for government jobs and positions in the colonial army.

The Minahasan sense of identity became an issue for the Indonesian government after independence. The Minahasan leaders declared their own autonomous state of North Sulawesi in June 1957. The Indonesian government then bombed Manado in February 1958 and, by June, Indonesian troops had landed in North Sulawesi. Rebel leaders retreated into the mountains, and the rebellion was finally put down in mid-1961.

Gorontalo

☎ 0435 / POP 186,000

Gorontalo has the feel of an overgrown country town, where all the locals seem to know each other. The compact city centre features some of the best-preserved Dutch houses in Sulawesi and retains a languid colonial feel, perhaps enhanced by the ruins of a Portuguese fort on a nearby hilltop. While most travellers come here because they are going somewhere else, consider taking a day to relax and explore the surrounds – especially in July and August when the whale sharks are in town.

The city has steadily modernised in recent years, with the landmark Gorontalo Mall dominating downtown, and several sleek new hotels opening close by.

◉ Sights & Activities

★ **Whale Shark Viewing**   WILDLIFE WATCHING
(Botubarani) Get to know the largest fish in the world: the gentle *hiu paus*, or whale shark. Members of this endangered species migrate near Gorontalo every year, hanging around between June and September. You can hire a boat and a bucket of prawns (125,000Rp, one hour) to float the 20m or so offshore and chum for new friends. The government regulates activity to protect the sharks, limiting how many boats or swimmers can be out at once. Report harassment.

It's 10km southeast of town.

Miguels Diving   DIVING
(☎ 0852 4004 7027; www.miguelsdiving.com; Jl Yos Sudarso 218) Professional school offering scuba diving along the northern coast of Tomini Bay to wrecks and reefs. A half-day of diving with two dives runs to 950,000Rp and equipment rental is 300,000Rp per day.

Lombongo Hot Springs   HOT SPRINGS
(Jl Taman Wisata; 8000Rp; ☺ 8am-5pm) At the western edge of Bogani Nani Wartabone Na-

tional Park, around 17km east of Gorontalo, this large swimming pool is filled with hot spring water. There's also a swimming hole at the foot of a 30m waterfall; it's a 3km walk past the springs.

Pantai Kurenai   BEACH
A sandy beach 10km south of town blissfully devoid of hawkers and warung.

🛏 Sleeping & Eating

New Melati Hotel   HOTEL $$
(📱 0813 4085 3322; www.facebook.com/newmelati hotelgorontalo; Jl Wolter Monginsidi 1; d incl breakfast 260,000-300,000Rp; ❉ 🛜) This long-time backpacker favourite has English-speaking staff who are very well informed about transport connections. It's based around a lovely home, built in the early 1900s for the harbour master. There are two classes of rooms, all clean with TV and aircon; the best are in a two-storey block overlooking the rear garden.

Grand Q Hotel   HOTEL $$
(📱 0435-822222; www.grandqhotelgorontalo.com; Jl Nani Wartabone 25; d incl breakfast 660,000-900,000Rp; ❉ 🛜 🏊) Classic hotel charm begins at the tiled driveway and extends up to the open-air rooftop swimming pool. Rooms have been renovated to great effect, making this your best option in Gorontalo above backpackers digs.

Amaris Hotel   HOTEL $$
(📱 0435-830988; www.amarishotel.com; Jl Sultan Botutihe 37; r incl breakfast 450,000Rp; ❉ 🛜) This well-managed hotel offers attractive, smallish rooms with clean lines and fast wi-fi that are (perhaps) short on character but big on cleanliness and comfort. It's a short walk from the Gorontalo Mall.

Ilabulo   INDONESIAN
(Jl Pandjaitan, north of roundabout; per piece 4000Rp) Follow the plumes of smoke north of the roundabout on Jl Pandjaitan to the roadside shacks grilling up the local delicacy of *ilabulo,* a savoury blend of pounded sago, eggs, spices and chicken liver rolled in banana leaves. Think of it as a really, really soft sausage.

Rumah Makan Sabar   INDONESIAN $
(Jl Sutoyo 31; mains from 15,000Rp; ⊙ 6am-6pm) Boasts an attractive colonial-style terrace and is renowned for its delicious *nasi kuning* (yellow rice) – an excellent way to start your day. Its soups and sambals also hit the spot.

ℹ Getting There & Away

AIR
There are daily flights to the major Sulawesi hubs, as well as Jakarta.

Djalaludin airport is 32km west of Gorontalo. At the time of research Damri was no longer operating, leaving you two options to get there: shared taxis (per person 70,000Rp) or walk 1km north to Jl Trans Sulawesi and catch an *oplet* (minibus; 20,000Rp) into town.

BOAT
The **ferry port** (Jl Laksamana Martadinata) for the Togean Islands is easily accessible by *mikrolet* (small taxis) along Jl Tantu, or by *ojek* or taxi. Tickets are sold at the port, starting three hours before departure.

Every two weeks the **Pelni** (📱 0435-821089; Jl 23 Januari; ⊙ 8am-5pm Mon-Fri, to 4pm Sat) liner *Tilongkabila* links Gorontalo with Bitung; the *Sangiang* tackles the same route monthly.

BUS
The main bus terminal, **Terminal 42 Andalas** (Jl Andalas), is 3km north of town and accessible by bemo or *ojek*. There are direct buses to Palu (150,000Rp, 18 hours, daily 5am) and Manado (100,000Rp, 11 hours, daily 9am). None of the Manado buses have air-con, so most people opt to make the trip by minibus or shared Kijang (150,000Rp to 200,000Rp); seats are sold by agents out front of the terminal.

Manado

📱 0431 / POP 458,500

Manado is a prosperous, well-serviced and friendly place, with a decent selection of comfortable hotels and excellent dining options. The waterfront is one nearly continuous mall, perhaps a testament to the city's relative affluence, and the streets are one nearly continuous traffic jam.

Most travellers blast through the city on their way between Pulau Bunaken and the Minahasa highlands, but if you find yourself waiting for a plane or a bus, give the metroplex a chance – you might just find Manado's hidden charm.

◎ Sights

Public Museum of
North Sulawesi   MUSEUM
(Museum Negeri Propinsi Sulawesi Utara; 📱 0431-870308; Jl Supratman 72; 5000Rp; ⊙ 8am-4pm Mon-Thu, to 11.30am Fri, 9am-2pm Sat) This museum features a large display of traditional costumes, and an exhibit illustrating

Manado

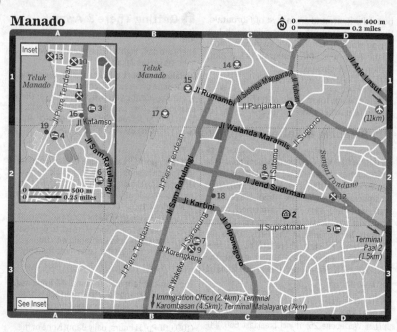

Manado

◉ Sights
1 Kienteng Ban Hian Kong	C1
2 Public Museum of North Sulawesi	C2

🛏 Sleeping
3 Hotel Minahasa	A1
4 Ibis City Center Boulevard	A2
5 Istanaku Guesthouse	D3
6 Libra Homestay	A2
7 Manado Green Hostel	B3
8 Sintesa Peninsula Hotel	C2

✖ Eating
9 Maminon	B3
10 Raja Sate	A1
11 Rumah Makan Green Garden	A1
12 Rumah Makan Raja Oci	D2
13 Tuna House	A1

🚌 Transport
14 Boats to Pulau Bunaken	C1
15 Ferry Terminal	B1
16 Garuda	A1
17 Majestic Kawanua	B1
18 Silk Air	C2
19 Sriwijaya Air	A2

traditional pottery-making. There are captions in English.

Kienteng Ban Hian Kong BUDDHIST TEMPLE
(Jl Panjaitan 70) The 19th-century Kienteng Ban Hian Kong is the oldest Buddhist temple in eastern Indonesia and it has been beautifully restored. The temple hosts a spectacular **festival** (⊙Feb) in February (dates vary according to the lunar calendar).

🎎 Festivals & Events

Pengucapan Syukur CULTURAL
A harvest festival that can take place any time from June to August.

🛏 Sleeping

Istanaku Guesthouse GUESTHOUSE $
(☑0431-851000; istanaku.guesthouse@yahoo.com; Jl Supratman 7; r from 240,000Rp; ❄☎) Colourful, whimsical, funky – it's nice to see a hotel in the city attempt a little personality. Of course underneath the cartoons, it's still just a bed in a box, but it's a clean one, the staff are super helpful and there's usually other hip young backpackers hanging around swapping stories. Istanaku 2 is a slightly newer, slightly more expensive expansion across the street.

Manado Green Hostel
HOSTEL **$**

(📞 0431-880 2967; Jl Sarapung 38; dm 150,000Rp) An actual hostel, with four-bed dorms (bunks) and lockers, clean shared bathrooms and a (tiny) communal kitchen. The best value for solo travellers at this price in Manado.

★ Libra Homestay
HOMESTAY **$$**

(📞 0821 9268 6320; librahomestay@gmail.com; Jl Pramuka XI 16; r 300,000-350,000Rp; 🕓🖥) This lovely private home occupies a spacious whitewashed villa on a quiet street, where the kindly Chinese family looks after guests well. There are five rooms, all with air-con, cable TVs, desks and private bathrooms with hot water. It's in the south of the city, a five-minute walk from restaurants and 15 minutes to the waterfront.

Ibis City Center Boulevard
HOTEL **$$**

(📞 0431-848800; www.accorhotels.com; Jl Piere Tendean 85; r 500,000Rp; 🕓🖥) Sometimes after a long day on a bus you just want a quality bed in a quiet, clean room run by professional staff. Doesn't hurt that it's got a great location across from the Manado Town Square Mall, which has lots of food options and a movie theatre.

Hotel Minahasa
HOTEL **$$**

(📞 0431-874871; www.hotelminahasa.com; Jl Sam Ratulangi 199; r with fan/air-con from 339,000/550,000Rp; 🕓🖥🏊) Stretching up to a hilltop villa, luxurious pool and fitness centre with city views, this place is all about stairs. Fan rooms are a little too basic – upgrade to the deluxe, especially the ones that have been renovated.

★ Lumbalumba Diving
RESORT **$$$**

(📞 0822 9291 9056; www.lumbalumbadiving.com; Jl Trans Sulawesi, Mokupa; bungalows per person €35-85; 🖥🏊) Consistently maintaining high standards, this serene, intimate resort is surrounded by gorgeous gardens and serves some of the best food in the region. Divers will love the small groups and knowledgeable staff, while nondivers can while their days away at the infinity pool with its marine-park view. The resort is 17km southwest of Manado.

Thalassa Manado
RESORT **$$$**

(www.thalassamanado.com; Jl Raya Molas; r per person incl meals €55-79; 🕓@🖥🏊) This resort 6km north of Manado has a warm, welcoming atmosphere with its recently upgraded facilities all spacious and well presented.

Chill by the lush pool when you're not using the service of the professionally run PADI five-star dive centre.

Sintesa Peninsula Hotel
HOTEL **$$$**

(📞 0431-855008; www.sintesapeninsulahotel.com; Jl Jend Sudirman; r from 900,000Rp; 🕓@🖥🏊) A gleaming white fortress on a hill in the middle of town, the Sintesa has all bases covered: a marble-clad lobby, spacious rooms with fine city views, a fitness centre, a big swimming pool and an excellent spa.

✗ Eating

Adventurous Minahasan cuisine can be found at its best in Manado. Get a taste for *rica-rica,* a spicy stir-fry made with *ayam* (chicken) or *babi* (pork). *Bubur tinotuan* (corn porridge), fresh seafood and *cakalang fufu* (smoked skipjack tuna) are other local specialities worth looking out for.

Little Jl Wakeke is the best-known eating street in town.

★ Maminon Kitchen
INDONESIAN **$**

(📞 0431-880 5777; Jl Sarapung 38; mains 35,000-55,000Rp; 🕙10am-10pm, closed 1st Sun of the month; 🖥) Sparkling cleanliness and true hospitality shine in this delightful contemporary Minahasan restaurant. Go for the *cakalang fufu* (local smoked tuna), perhaps with *sous rica tomat* (tomato chilli sambal), and you'll eat like royalty.

Tuna House
SEAFOOD **$**

(Jl Laksda John Lie; mains 30,000-50,000Rp; 🕚11am-11pm, from 4pm Sun) Of the *ikan bakar* huts stacked along this stretch of the waterfront – famous for their cheap dishes – Tuna House is our favourite. That's not to say the others aren't good, but they take it to the next level here. Look for it in front of the Whiz Prime hotel.

Rumah Makan Raja Oci
INDONESIAN **$**

(📞 0431-863946; Jl Jend Sudirman 85; mains 30,000-50,000Rp; 🕗8am-10pm) This authentic *rumah makan* packs in the locals for its *ikan oci* (barbecued small fish), which are served with a spicy Minahasan sauce known as *dabu-dabu* (made of tomatoes, shallots and fresh chilli).

★ Raja Sate
INDONESIAN **$**

(📞 0431-852398; www.rajasate.com; Jl Pierre Tendean 39; sate mains 30,000-55,000Rp; 🕦11.30am-11pm Mon-Sat, 6-10.30pm Sun; 🕓🖥) Rightly renowned for its *sate* (you can't go wrong

ⓘ DOG MEAT

Minhasan cuisine is known for its exotic meats, and you may come across r.w. (pronounced 'air weh'; dog) on some menus in Manado. Note there are significant animal-welfare issues associated with the dog-meat trade.

with a mixed plate that includes prawns, squid, chicken, beef and goat), Raja Sate also does great curries and even New Zealand steaks. Everything is excellent and there's cold Bintang.

Rumah Makan
Green Garden CHINESE, INDONESIAN $$
(☎ 0431-878650; Jl Sam Ratulangi 170; mains 47,000-65,000Rp; ☺ 9am-midnight) This popular Indo-Chinese restaurant does excellent pork dishes (try it barbecued or go for the pork belly) and seafood (perhaps crab, plucked live from the tank and served in corn soup, or grouper with salted mustard leaf). There's also fresh juice and cold beer.

🍸 Drinking & Nightlife

Corner Club CLUB
(Bahu Mall, Jl Monginsidi; ☺ 6pm-5am) Hosting DJs most nights, this thumping joint occupying the corner of Bahu Mall is the best place in town to get your groove on.

ⓘ Information

Immigration Office (Kantor Imigrasi; ☎ 0431-863491; www.imigrasi.go.id; Jl 17 Agustus; ☺ 7.30am-noon & 1.30-4.30pm Mon-Fri) Visa extensions can take up to five days with multiple visits.

ⓘ Getting There & Away

AIR

Direct international flights to Manado's **Sam Ratulangi Airport** include Singapore and a handful of Chinese cities, including Shenzhen Guangzhou and Shanghai. It's also fairly well connected to other Indonesian islands, with regular flights to Jakarta and Surabaya on Java, and one or two per day to Denpasar, Balikpapan, Sorong, Ambon and multiple airports on Maluku.

Airlines regularly flying into Manado:

Garuda & Citilink (☎ 0431-877737; Jl Sam Ratulangi 212; ☺ 8.30am-5pm Mon-Sat)

Lion & Wings Air (☎ 0431-847000; www.lionair.co.id; Jl Piere Tendean 19; ☺ 9am-5pm Mon-Fri, to 3pm Sat, to noon Sun)

Silk Air (☎ 0431-863744; Jl Sarapung; ☺ 9am-4pm Mon-Fri, to 1pm Sat)

Sriwijaya Air (☎ 0431-888 0988; www.sriwijayaair.co.id; Manado Town Sq 12A, Jl Piere Tendean; ☺ 8am-6.30pm)

BOAT

All Pelni boats use the deep-water port of Bitung, 44km from Manado on the island's east coast. There's no Pelni office in Manado but you can get information and purchase tickets from numerous travel agents around the harbour.

Ferries leave from the **main terminal** (Pelabuhan Manado; Jl Lembong) daily to Siau (200,000Rp, four hours) and on to Tahuna (220,000Rp, 6½ hours) in the Sangihe-Talaud Islands. Tickets and information are available from **Majestic Kawanua** (☎ 0851 0540 5499; majestickawanua@gmail.com; Komplek Marina Plaza, ground fl, Jl Piere Tendean; ☺ 8am-5pm).

There are also local boats to Maluku. Tickets are available from the stalls outside the port.

Boats to Pulau Bunaken (Dermaga Kalimas; Jl Veteran) leave from a harbour near the Pasar Jengki market. There's a once-daily ferry service leaving from 2pm, when full and depending on tides (one-way 50,000Rp). Otherwise, small fishing boats start the charter bids at 1,200,000Rp, but can be talked down to around 800,000Rp.

BUS

There are three reasonably orderly terminals for long-distance buses and the local *mikrolet*.

Terminal Karombasan (Jl Karombasan) Connections to Tomohon (10,000Rp) and other places south of Manado; 5km south of the city.

Terminal Malalayang (Jl Maruasey) Buses to Kotamobagu (60,000Rp) and Gorontalo (from 100,000Rp, 11 hours); far west of the city.

Terminal Paal 2 (Jl Rajawali) Varied public transport runs to Bitung (11,000Rp) and to the airport (10,000Rp); eastern end of Jl Martadinata.

ⓘ Getting Around

Mikrolet from Sam Ratulangi International Airport go to Terminal Paal 2 (10,000Rp), where you can change to a *mikrolet* (5000Rp) for elsewhere. There are also four daily air-conditioned buses (30,000Rp) to/from Jl Piere Tendean. Fixed-price taxis cost around 100,000Rp from the airport to the city (13km).

Ride-hailing app Grab works well in Manado. For a traditional taxi, call **Bluebird** (☎ 0431-861234; ☺ 24hr); cars all have meters. A 2km ride is about 15,000Rp.

Pulau Bunaken & Pulau Siladen

This tiny, coral-fringed isle is North Sulawesi's top tourist destination, yet it has managed to maintain a rootsy island soul. Accommodation is spread out along two beaches and beyond that, the isle belongs to the islanders. These friendly folk have a seemingly endless reserve of authentically warm smiles and there are no hassles here – just laid-back beachy bliss.

Most people come to Pulau Bunaken for the diving. The marine biodiversity is extraordinary, with more than 300 types of coral and 3000 species of fish, abundant sponges and phenomenally colourful life on vertical walls. The 808-hectare island is part of the 891-sq-km **Bunaken Manado Tua Marine National Park** (Taman Laut Bunaken Manado Tua), which includes Manado Tua (Old Manado), the dormant volcano that can be seen from Manado and climbed in about four hours; Nain and Mantehage islands; and Pulau Siladen, which also has a few fine resorts.

◎ Sights & Activities

Pantai Liang   BEACH
Suffering from erosion and rising sea levels, the beach at Liang has become a svelte, though pleasant, strip of white sand. At low tide, there's still plenty of room to toss a frisbee around. The beach is lined with resorts that crawl up the hillside behind.

Food stalls and trinket vendors seem out of place until the mobs of day-trippers arrive around 10am.

The beach just south of Pantai Liang is a protected turtle nesting ground, so keep off (even though it looks inviting).

Pantai Pangalisang   BEACH
Forming much of the east coast of Pulau Bunaken, Pantai Pangalisang is a long stretch of walkable soft white sand tucked between a thick wall of mangroves and the land. Just beyond the thicket is some outrageous snorkelling, and most lodges have cut paths for boats and swimmers. The beach all but disappears at high tide.

Pulau Siladen   ISLAND
Located 3km east of Pulau Bunaken and the smallest island of the archipelago, Siladen boasts wonderful white-sand beaches and a wall of gorgeous corals. All lodging is lined

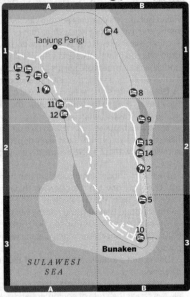

Pulau Bunaken

up on the island's west side, looking across at Bunaken.

Manado Tua   HIKING
Pulau Bunaken's western neighbour, Manado Tua, is a beautiful volcanic cone with some interesting hiking, including a stout route to the top. Guides can be found on the island. Check www.gunungbagging.com/manado-tua for useful, if a little old, information. Small outrigger fishing boats (return 200,000Rp) are happy to shuttle you to

DIVING & SNORKELLING AROUND PULAU BUNAKEN

Pulau Bunaken is uniquely surrounded by deep water, with strong, nutrient-laden currents, and a mangrove ecosystem that protects much of the beaches and corals from erosion; this makes it one of the best diving and snorkelling spots in the world. Beyond drop-offs you'll find caves and valleys full of brightly coloured sponges, thriving corals and biblical numbers of fish. It's very rare *not* to see several large hawksbill and green turtles on every dive, and you'll also encounter rays and sharks.

DIY snorkellers on the east coast will find that the front of Lorenso's Cottages is an easy place to get in the water. Over on the west side, look for Likuan, a spectacular coral wall just off Pantai Liang.

Most guesthouses, resorts and dive centres have maps of all the sites around Bunaken; where you go will most likely depend on the current conditions. If you're staying somewhere without a dive centre, it's easy to shop around for outings with a nearby place.

Well-worn snorkelling equipment can be rented from most homestays for about 50,000Rp per day, but it is often worth paying a little more to rent some quality equipment from one of the dive centres.

Trips around Bunaken and nearby islands, including two dives and equipment rental, will cost from 900,000Rp to 1,200,000Rp; PADI Open Water courses are about 6,000,000Rp. Snorkellers can go along with the dive boats for around 80,000Rp per person.

Divers and snorkellers pay a one-off 150,000Rp national park fee, usually collected by dive operators.

While there are no evidently dodgy dive schools operating in Bunaken, you should always check the state of equipment and ask about a centre's safety procedures before you commit.

Manado Tua, and can be arranged through your accommodation or at Bunaken village.

🛏 Sleeping

Some resorts discriminate against nondivers, either by charging higher room prices or by kicking them out when they find they're not diving.

Novita Homestay GUESTHOUSE $
(☑ 0812 443 0729; Bunaken Village; r per person incl meals 200,000-250,000Rp) Owned and operated by Vita, a terrific cook, Novita is a delightful old-fashioned homestay right in Bunaken village. Vita also organises tours, rents snorkelling gear and raises turtle hatchlings for release into the wild. Rooms with outside bathrooms are 50,000Rp cheaper and you can opt for breakfast-only for 150,000Rp.

Lorenso's Cottages GUESTHOUSE $
(☑ 0852 5697 3345; Pantai Pangalisang, Pulau Bunaken; r per person incl meals from 225,000Rp; 🕲) Lorenso's is an excellent choice for backpackers who like to pretend they've been shipwrecked. Rooms are very basic, and a bit run down, tucked around an empty grassy courtyard and makeshift bamboo common

area with no floor. The staff are very helpful, there's a good communal vibe (think impromptu jug band jams), and excellent snorkelling just beyond the mangroves.

★ Panorama Backpackers GUESTHOUSE $$
(☑ 0813 1804 5569; www.bunakenbackpackers. com; south of Pantai Liang, Pulau Bunaken; s/d incl meals garden view 375,000/700,000Rp, sea view 425,000/800,000Rp; 🕲) With a homestay atmosphere, excellent home-cooked meals and good-value huts terracing down the hillside above the beach, Panorama is the best budget stay on the western side of the island. Diving is accommodated through the more upmarket Panorama Dive Resort owned by relatives next door.

★ Living Colours BUNGALOW $$$
(☑ 0812 430 6401; www.livingcoloursdiving.com; Pantai Pangalisang, Pulau Bunaken; s/d cottages per person incl meals from €60/50; @🕲) This peaceful place enjoys a lovely hillside setting overlooking the mangroves. Its elegant wooden bungalows boast enormous terraces with hammocks, and spacious hot-water bathrooms. There's a little bar (the Safety Stop) by the shore, and meals are served in an open-sided restaurant above the bay.

Living Colours' five-star PADI dive school is particularly well organised.

Froggies
BUNGALOW **$$**

(📞 0812 430 1356; www.froggiesdivers.com; Pantai Liang, Pulau Bunaken; d bungalow per person incl meals €24-53, single surcharge €8; ✳🞉) This long-running dive centre and resort is run by a young and enthusiastic crew and is still one of the best midrange places on the island. It offers a fine beachfront location with views towards the sunset and the perfect cone of Manado Tua. Local boats can drop you at the jetty here and there's a small village market next door.

Two Fish
RESORT **$$**

(📞 0811 432 805; www.twofishdivers.com; Pantai Pangalisang, Pulau Bunaken; r/cottage per person incl meals from 375,000/675,000Rp; @🞉🞉) The birthplace of the extended Two Fish empire, this is still a well-run dive resort with attractive cottages dotted around manicured grounds and a pool – it has that tropical vacation vibe you've been looking for. The professional, eco-aware dive centre is one of the best in North Sulawesi, with a maximum of four divers per guide.

Happy Gecko
BUNGALOW **$$**

(📞 0852 9806 4906; www.happygeckoresort.com; Pantai Liang, Pulau Bunaken; s/d per person incl meals €36/28; 🞉) Tumbling down a hillside at the northern end of Pantai Liang, these cute but worn little cottages are a good deal for backpackers, with verandahs, bamboo furniture and private bathrooms. Dives cost just €25 each.

3Will Bunaken Dive Resort
RESORT **$$**

(📞 0823 4949 0270; www.bunaken.net; Pantai Pangalisang, Pulau Bunaken; s/d incl meals 600,000/800,000Rp; 🞉) Formerly Daniel's Homestay, this low-key dive resort has gone through an upgrade with well-constructed fan-cooled timber cottages in a rambling garden. Larger superior cottages were being added at the time of research. Fun dives start at 600,000Rp.

Panorama Dive Resort
BUNGALOW **$$**

(📞 0813 4021 7306, 0813 4021 7027; www.bunakendiving.co; Pantai Liang, Pulau Bunaken; cottage per person incl meals 350,000-450,000Rp; 🞉) A family-run place at the southern end of Pantai Liang, this large hillside complex high above a corner of sandy beach has wooden bungalows with grass roofs, decks and commanding views. There's a good dive shop here too; dives cost 450,000Rp.

★ Siladen Resort & Spa
RESORT **$$$**

(📞 0811 430 0641; www.siladen.com; Pulau Siladen; villa incl meals from €153-255; ✳🞉🞉) Luxurious airy resort with 17 sumptuously furnished villas that boast all mod cons; the older villas are directly on the beach. Facilities include a (saltwater) lagoon pool, an indulgent spa, pool table, and small army of blue-cushioned sofas and loungers spread

---

DIVE SITES AROUND BUNAKEN

Pulau Bunaken's profile is incredible: it rises abruptly out of the big blue and its underwater topography is of vertical walls of coral. Neighbouring islands are no less impressive. Off the mainland there is muck diving and a wreck. Of the 20-plus sites in the area, highlights include:

Likuan There are three dive sites on this remarkable coral wall, which plummets from the shallows into dark oblivion. Reef sharks and lots of turtles are typically encountered.

Fukui Point For sheer numbers of fish, this site is outstanding. It's something of a cleaning station for large fish and there are also garden eels and several giant clams.

Molas Wreck This is a huge Dutch cargo ship covered with soft corals and sponges. Because of its depth (24m to 40m), it's for advanced divers only.

Tanjung Kopi On the northern side of Manado Tua, with schools of barracudas, batfish and jacks; an advanced dive due to strong currents.

Celah Celah Great for macro life including ghost pipefish, nudibranchs and pygmy seahorses. Very popular with photographers.

Montehage Dramatic diving with barracuda, rays, Napoleon wrasse and schools of bumphead parrotfish. Hammerhead sharks are occasionally encountered, too.

Mandolin Huge gorgonians and a forest of whip corals; look out for Napoleon wrasse.

BANGKA ISLANDS

Strategically located between diving destinations of Pulau Bunaken and the Lembeh Strait, the Bangka Islands are part of what makes the region so diverse. This is where to go for pinnacle diving, and it's also a prime spot for big fauna: dolphins, manta rays and at least nine species of whale all migrate through these waters around March and April and again in August and September. At all times you're likely to see tuna, batfish, jacks and barracuda. There are often fairly strong currents but these make the plentiful soft corals bloom.

The main eponymous island has been threatened with large-scale mining, which locals fear could spell disaster for the environment. While the legal battles have been won for now, nothing is ever permanent in Indonesia. So visit while there's still something here to see.

Resorts will arrange your transport. We recommend the following:

Blue Bay Divers (☑0813 4028 6000; www.blue-bay-divers.de; Pulau Sahaung; dive packages per day from €105)

Mimpi Indah (☑0811 432264; www.mimpiindah.com; Pulau Bangka; per person incl all meals from 700,000Rp; 🛜)

out on the pristine white sand beach. There's also a top-notch PADI dive centre.

Bunaken Oasis RESORT $$$
(☑0821 4643 3393; www.bunakenoasis.com; Pantai Liang, Pulau Bunaken; per person incl meals US$530; ❄🛜🖥) This new addition to Bunaken is in a league entirely of its own. Each embarrassingly comfortable villa protruding from the lush gardens has commanding views and a breezy porch. The gleaming pool is what other infinity pools aspire to be. The staff is professional and attentive, and the dive shop immaculate.

Bobocha Cottages Siladen COTTAGE $$$
(☑0853 4161 5044; www.bobochasiladen.com; Pulau Siladen; cottage per person incl meals from €130; 🛜) These elegant, beautifully designed cottages in a lovely beachside setting don't offer diving, but do have Sarah – the owner and chef who whips up some of the finest home-cooked food in North Sulawesi. Oh, and diving is easily arranged at a neighbouring resort anyway.

Cha Cha RESORT $$$
(☑0813 569 30370; www.bunakenchacha.com; northeast coast, Pulau Bunaken; cottages/villas per person incl meals from US$110/140; ❄🛜) In splendid isolation on the northeastern tip of the island, Cha Cha has an intimate atmosphere and impressive attention to detail – like glass railings along the decks that don't impede your view. Accommodation (three-night minimum stay) has expanded

in recent years to include luxurious villas, and the food gets rave reviews.

Village Bunaken RESORT $$$
(☑0813 4075 7268; www.bunakenvillage.com; Pantai Pangalisang, Pulau Bunaken; cottages per person incl meals from €50; ❄🛜🖥) Catering to couples and a more mature crowd, this sophisticated Javanese-Balinese style resort is one of Bunaken's more refined options. Well-maintained cottages have stylish features and the spa is highly regarded.

Kuda Laut RESORT $$$
(☑0431-838876; www.celebesdivers.com; Pulau Siladen; r incl meals €142-314; ❄🛜🖥) Two resorts in one! Kuda Laut with its refined rooms, pool and beach bar command a premium, while its sister resort next door, Onong, is more basic, but no less comfortable. Both resorts are relatively good for extroverts, not so much for privacy.

ℹ Getting There & Away

Daily public boats (50,000Rp, one hour) leave at 2pm for Bunaken village and Pulau Siladen from Manado's Dermaga Kalimas (p712) – tides willing. They return at around 8am to 9am the next day.

Smaller speed boats leave throughout the day, and will happily take you if there is room and the price is right (usually around 50,000Rp to 75,000Rp, 30 minutes). The 'official' charter price for a speed boat is 1,200,000Rp, but in reality you can get one for around 350,000Rp.

When conditions are rough, the public boats stop running, but private boats may be willing to make the harrowing crossing to the closest point of mainland near Tongkaina.

ℹ️ Getting Around

From the boat landing in Bunaken village you can walk or hire an *ojek* (around 10,000Rp to 40,000Rp) to your lodge; or your hosts may arrange to collect you.

The island's two main beaches are 5km apart, connected by a strip of brick and concrete. It's only 8km from tip to tail – perfect for a day on a bicycle (or half day on a scooter if you're unreasonably impatient). Just about anyone will become an *ojek*.

A seat on a local boat between Bunaken and Siladen runs 40,000Rp to 60,000Rp (one way) for the 20-minute crossing. Small fishing boats can be chartered to putter around the islands for about 200,000Rp for a couple hours.

Tomohon

✍️ 0431 / POP 96,500

Guarded by two towering volcanic peaks, Tomohon consists of a number of small highland towns, surrounded by forests that have merged together into a lively market city. At 800m above sea level, the area provides a pleasant, cool respite from Manado and is popular with city folk on weekends. For travellers, it's an excellent base to explore the Minahasa region, which has ample opportunities for hiking, biking, trekking and birdwatching.

👁️ Sights

Muesum Pinawetengan   MUSEUM
(Pinabetengan; 20,000Rp; ⏱️8.30am-4.30pm Mon-Sat, 1-5pm Sun) Not just another roadside attraction, this complex is home to Minahasa houses, a history museum, a celebration of owls (the Minahasa Regency mascot), a weaving workshop, an anti-narcotics museum and a botanical garden. Also on display is the world's largest playable trumpet, the world's largest xylophone and the (formerly) world's longest silk sarong. It's all the work of Benny Mamoto, a Java-born police general who is passionate about Minahasa culture, and wants to put this region on the map. It's interesting, well-presented and definitely on our map.

Waruga Opo Worang   CEMETERY
(Jl Opo Worang) Minahasans traditionally interred their dead in a squatting position in *waruga* stone sarcophagi shaped like houses sitting above ground right near their settlement. During a particularly nasty outbreak of cholera, the Dutch government banned the practice, forcing Minahasans to bury their dead below ground some distance from the village. Waruga Opo Worang has a small collection in town.

Danau Linau   LAKE
(Lahendong) Danau Linau is a small, highly sulphurous lake that changes colours with the light, and is home to extensive birdlife. Take a *mikrolet* to Sonder, get off at Lahendong and walk 1.5km to the lake.

🏃 Activities

Gunung Lokon   TREKKING
Gunung Lokon (1580m) occasionally reminds residents it's an active volcano by sending out earthquakes or spewing ash high into the sky. The last major eruption was 2012, but it's occasionally closed to hikers due to increased seismic activity. You can hike to it from Tomohon in about three hours, with another hour to reach the peak.

Gunung Mahawu   SCENIC DRIVE
For lazy volcano thrills, you can drive almost all the way to the top of Gunung Mahawu, where you'll be rewarded with views over the whole region and into a 180m-wide, 140m-deep sulphuric crater lake, which you can walk around in less than an hour. There's no public transport to the volcano, and it's packed with locals on the weekends.

Pelangi   HOT SPRINGS
(Jl Kawangkoan; swimming 30,000-50,000Rp) Hot water from the spring below is pumped on-demand into small tubs (30,000Rp) in private rooms next to the clean, cold-water swimming pool (30,000Rp) on a hillside

> ### TOMAHON'S MACABRE MARKET
>
> It's said that the Minahasan people will eat anything on four legs, apart from the table and chairs, and nowhere is this more evident than at Tomohon's **daily market**. Visiting the market (which is right next to the *mikrolet* terminal) is a slaughterhouse-like experience, with dead and alive dogs, pigs, rats and bats all on display. Sadly the market is also known for displays of animal cruelty, and is likely to distress visitors with the slightest interest in animal welfare.

SULAWESI TOMOHON

above thermal mud pits. Get access to both for 50,000Rp.

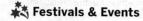 Festivals & Events

Tomohon International Flower Festival
FAIR

(www.tomohonflowerfestival.com; ⊙ early Aug) By far the most colourful time to visit Tomohon is when the city is decked out nearly head-to-toe with flowers and flower vendors. On the downside, traffic reaches near Manado-level gridlock; hire a bike. Book lodging well in advance.

🛏 Sleeping & Eating

⭐ Lanosa Guest House
GUESTHOUSE $$

(📞 0431-356926; www.facebook.com/Lanosa guesthouse1; Jl Raya Tomohon; r incl breakfast 506,000-870,000Rp; 📶) Conveniently located on the south end of town, this large guesthouse provides polished, clean and modern rooms arranged around impeccably manicured grounds and relaxing common areas. The guesthouse and attached cafe are both great places to hang out and enjoy the cool mountain air.

⭐ Highland Resort
RESORT $$

(📞 0431-353333; www.highlandresort.info; Jl Kali-Kinilow; r/ste incl breakfast from 340,000/750,000Rp; 📶) A collection of spacious, well-equipped wooden bungalows surround a green open courtyard and are run by a friendly owner who bends over backwards to help you fall in love with the Minahasa Highlands. The restaurant serves decent food, but it can take a while to prepare. Follow the signs from 'Kinilow', about 5km before Tomohon, on the road to Manado.

Mountain View Resort & Cekakak Hostel
COTTAGE $$

(📞 0431-315 8666; www.mountainviewtomohon.com; Jl Kali-Kinilow; hostel/cottage incl breakfast from 140,000/450,000Rp; @📶) You have two options: fine wooden cottages with slate bathrooms set around a pretty garden, or bunks in a dark room in the hostel across the road. Cottage dwellers get breakfast at the restaurant which serves international and local food, while hostel patrons will have to pay 20,000Rp. Note: Mountain View is a bit of a misnomer. Hillside view?

Follow the signs from 'Kinilow', 5km before Tomohon, on the road to Manado. It's on a side road off the highway.

Food Market
MARKET $

(Pusat Kuliner; Jl Nusantara; ⊙ noon-7pm) In the town centre, Tomohon's daily food market has stalls offering lots of local specialities.

Rumah Makan MTV
INDONESIAN $

(Jl Raya Tomohon; mains 7500-22,000Rp; ⊙ 7am-10pm; 📶) Half-way between Tomohon and Kinilow, this clean, busy dining hall has a long menu of local favourites including *bakso* (meatball soup) and noodles.

MINAHASA ACTIVITIES

A temperate climate and spectacular volcanic landscapes means the Minahasa region is rapidly developing as an adrenaline centre. Tomohon makes a perfect base for exploring. Possible activities include the following:

Gunung Lokon crater lake hike (half day) Follow an old lava flow to the rim of the crater.

Gunung Soputan volcano hike (full day) Walk to the highest peak in North Sulawesi, which is an active volcano.

Gunung Klabat volcano hike (two days) Take around five hours to ascend, with wonderful views of Manado city.

Whitewater rafting, Nimanga River (half day) Start near Tomohon; 25 rapids and a good chance to spot wildlife.

Exploring Tekaan Telu waterfall (half day) There are four separate drops of up to 60m; abseiling and canyoning is possible, too.

Birdwatching Gunung Mahawu (one day) Follow in the footsteps of Alfred Russel Wallace and spot flycatchers, and perhaps a scaly kingfisher.

Guesthouses can typically arrange guides, or check with Highland Resort.

🍸 Drinking & Nightlife

Kanzo CAFE
(📱0852 5670 0076; Jl Raya Tomohon; ⊙10am-
11pm; 🛜) Cold beer and live music are the
name of the game at this bamboo hangout
on the main drag. Also has a good selection
of tasty fried snacks.

ℹ️ Getting There & Around

Mikrolet travel regularly to Tomohon (10,000Rp,
one hour) from Terminal Karombasan (p712) in
Manado. From **Terminal Beriman** in Tomohon,
mikrolet head to Manado, and *mikrolet* and
buses go to Tondano, Tompaso and various
other towns. A good way to see local sights more
quickly is to charter a *mikrolet* or a (more comfortable, but expensive) taxi.

Hotels rent out motorcycles for around
150,000Rp per day (including the cost of petrol).

Bitung

📱0438 / POP 196,000

Bitung is the chief regional port in North
Sulawesi and home to many factories. Despite its spectacular setting, the town is
unattractive, so most travellers make for
Manado, nearby Pulau Lembeh, or the hills
of Tangkoko as soon as possible.

Regardless of what time you arrive by
boat in Bitung, there will be buses going to
Manado.

Botanica Nature Resort LODGE $$
(📱0438-223 0178; www.botanicaresort.com; Jl
Johan Pinontoan; r incl breakfast from 500,000Rp;
🛜) Tucked away on a hill above Bitung on
the other side of its own private river, Bo-
tanica's polished Minahasa-style lodges are
a beautiful place to escape from the city. It's
quiet – at least until your neighbours walk
through the creaky two-storey building
from their tiny room to the clean shared
bathroom.

ℹ️ Getting There & Away

Buses and shared cars leave regularly from
Terminal Paal 2 (p712) in Manado (10,000Rp, 1½
hours) to brand new **Terminal Tangkoko** (Jl Yos
Sudarso, Girian), just outside of Bitung. From
there you have to catch another *mikrolet* (10
minutes) into town or to the port.

Useful **Pelni ferries** (📱0438-36352; Jl Sam
Ratulangi; ⊙7am-noon & 1-4pm Mon-Fri) in-
clude the *Tilongkabila*, which sails up and down
the coast of Sulawesi to ports including Goronta-
lo, Luwuk, Kendari, Bau Bau and Makassar. The

WORTH A TRIP

TASIKOKI WILDLIFE RESCUE

About 9km southwest of Bitung,
Tasikoki Wildlife Rescue (📱0857
5747 1090; www.tasikoki.org; Jl Raya Tan-
jung Merah-Kema; ⊙tour by appointment
only 10am Mon-Fri) 🆓 is an entirely
volunteer-run organisation that rescues
and cares for animals confiscated from
smugglers. The aim is to rehabilitate
the animals and release them back into
the wild. You can make a day visit to the
centre (donations appreciated) or sign
on longer as a volunteer. Note: if you
turn up unannounced, you will be curtly
sent on your way.

There are more than 200 animals
of 40 different species (including sun
bears and sea eagles) at the centre,
and during a visit you'll learn about the
illegal animal trade and the animals
themselves.

Sangiang sails to Ternate and ports in Maluku
every two weeks.

Boats to Lembeh (charter 150,000Rp, 15 min-
utes) cross the strait from near the ferry port.

Pulau Lembeh & the Lembeh Strait

The Lembeh Strait between Bitung and
the large island of Pulau Lembeh is world
famous for its muck diving and now has
around a dozen scuba centres. There are
also some reefs, five wrecks, and fantastic
night dives lit by phosphorescence.

Lembeh attracts hardcore underwater
photographers and geeky types intent on
ticking off long lists of the bizarre sea crea-
tures that live here in profound, but dwin-
dling numbers. Whether it's the commercial
traffic, or near constant harassment by
groups of spotlight-wielding photogs, some
repeat visitors report a noticeable decrease
in critters.

NAD RESORT $$$
(📱0812 475 6661; www.nad-lembeh.com; Pulau
Lembeh; 3-night packages per person incl 5 dives
& meals from US$456; ❄🛜) This easygoing
place is very well set up for anyone with an
interest in dive photography, as one guide
is assigned per two divers. House reef dives
are free. Choose from stylish, attractive,

SULAWESI BITUNG

WEIRD & WILD CRITTERS OF THE LEMBEH STRAIT

For the uninitiated, welcome to an alien world on our very own planet. The wonderful creatures that inhabit these murky depths are much admired by underwater photographers and have probably inspired more than a few movie monsters. Here's just a sample of what you may find:

Hairy frogfish (*Antennarius striatus*) Camouflaged to look like a rock, covered in whispy-coral-like hairs and with a frown only the keenest diver could love, these guys are best known for the built-in appendage on their forehead, which they dangle like a worm to draw in prey. They don't swim like normal fish, but walk on their fins.

Mimic octopus (*Thaumoctopus mimicus*) This recently discovered underwater thespian can convincingly imitate more than 15 other animals including sea snakes, crabs, stingrays and jellyfish. It does this by contorting its body into a new shape, changing colours then mimicking the behaviour of said species.

Pygmy seahorse (*Hippocampus bargibanti*) Less than 2cm tall, these hard-to-spot cuties have the same texture and colour as the fan corals on which they live.

recently renovated rooms or sea-view bungalows. There's a small dark-sand beach out front.

Black Sand Dive Retreat
RESORT $$$

(☑0811 437 736; www.blacksanddive.com; Kasawari; 3-night packages per person incl 4 dives & meals from €553; ※🛜🏊) Enjoys a serene location on the mainland bay and is very well set up, including a Nitrox facility and a dedicated camera room. It's a boutique operation; you'll get plenty of personalised attention and the owner is particularly passionate about local wildlife.

VISITING TANGKOKO-BATUANGAS DUA SAUDARA NATURE RESERVE

Entrance to the park is 100,000Rp per person; guides (mandatory) cost between 75,000Rp to 200,000Rp per person, per half-day. Most people arrive at the park entrance at Batuputih in the afternoon, and take a guided afternoon/evening walk to see tarsiers (when sightings are nearly guaranteed). Morning walks are better for birdlife. Consider staying longer to enjoy the gorgeous beach setting at Batuputih and to take a variety of other tours available, including **dolphin-spotting**, **snorkelling**, **birdwatching** or **fishing** tours. All tours and walks can be arranged at your guesthouse, which will invariably be swarming with guides.

Lembeh Resort
RESORT $$$

(☑0438-550 3139; www.lembehresort.com; Pulau Lembeh; cottages per person incl meals from US$130; ※@🛜🏊) This Balinese-style resort gets top marks for service, and has many returning customers. The pool area, strewn with day beds and loungers, is gorgeous, and you'll find a spa and plenty of nondive tours on offer.

❶ Getting There & Away

Most resorts will pick you up at the airport, but if you're slumming it, you'll need to get to Bitung (10,000Rp) from Terminal Paal 2 (p712) in Manado, and hire a boat (30,000Rp to 50,000Rp) to your corner of the strait.

Tangkoko-Batuangas Dua Saudara Nature Reserve

With 88 sq km of forest bordered by a sandy coastline and offshore coral gardens, Tangkoko is one of the most impressive and accessible nature reserves in Indonesia. The park is home to black macaques, cuscuses and tarsiers, endemic maleo birds and red-knobbed hornbills, among other fauna, and rare types of rainforest flora. Tangkoko is also home to a plethora of midges, called *gonones*, which bite and leave victims scratching furiously for days afterwards. Always wear long trousers, tucked into thick socks, and covered shoes, and take plenty of insect repellent. Sadly, parts of the park are falling victim to encroachment by local communities, but money generated from visitors might help stave that off.

★**Tangkoko Hill** GUESTHOUSE **$$**
(☏0813 4030 2444; www.tangkokohill.com; Batu-putih; r incl meals from 400,000Rp; ❋ 🛜) About 1km inland from the village, this solid, comfortable, modern place is the best option in the area, with hyper-clean rooms, quality mattresses, desks and TVs. The genial owner, Franky, speaks good English and is super-helpful maximising your time here. Fine local food is served in the breezy dining room.

Tangkoko Lodge LODGE **$$**
(☏0813 4002 6980; www.tangkokolodge.com; Batuputih; r incl meals 300,000-500,000Rp; ❋ 🛜) With varying grades of room prices (and quality), this lodge – which feels more like a city hotel than a forest retreat – offers something for everyone. The indoor dining room resembles a function hall, but the food they serve is a hit.

❶ Information

Bring plenty of cash as there are no local ATMs.

❶ Getting There & Away

Pickup trucks leave from Girian outside of Bitung for Batuputih (15,000Rp, 45 minutes). Tangkoko package tours are possible from all over North Sulawesi, including Pulau Bunaken (a long, tiring day trip).

SOUTHEAST SULAWESI

Few visitors make it to Southeast Sulawesi, but if you're yearning to explore and have a passion for coral reefs and off-grid travel, you'll be richly rewarded here.

The top attraction is Wakatobi National Park, encompassing four main islands off the southern tip of the peninsula once known as the Tukangbesi Islands. They offer some of Indonesia's best and least-crowded snorkelling and diving. Meanwhile, the walls of the old *kraton* (walled city palace) at Bau Bau on Pulau Buton are some of the most well-preserved and impressive bulwarks in the country, worthy of a side trip in their own right.

❶ Getting There & Away

Kendari serves as the main hub of air transport, connecting Makassar with the rest of the peninsula. If you're arriving by boat, you'll likely be dropped in Bau Bau.

DON'T MISS

TARSIERS

If you're visiting Sulawesi's Tangkoko-Batuangas Dua Saudara Nature Reserve or Lore Lindu National Park (p697), keep your eyes peeled for something looking back at you: a tiny nocturnal primate known as a tarsier. These creatures are recognisable by their eyes, which are literally larger than their stomachs, so big in fact that they cannot rotate them within their sockets. Luckily, their heads can swivel nearly 360 degrees, so their range of vision isn't compromised. Tarsiers also have huge, sensitive ears, which can be retracted and unfurled, and disproportionately long legs, which they use to jump distances 10 times their body length. They use their anatomical anomalies and impressive speed to catch small insects. Tarsiers live in groups of up to eight, and communicate with what sounds like high-pitched singing. They are found only in some rainforests of Indonesia and the Philippines.

Kolaka

☑ 0405 / POP 37,000
The port of Kolaka connects to Bajoe in South Sulawesi and is the main thoroughfare between the two legs of the island. The centre of town is grouped around the bus terminal, about 500m north of the ferry terminal. There are ATMs but not many other facilities.

❶ Getting There & Away

All day and night, plenty of Kijangs, but few buses, travel between Kolaka and Kendari (80,000Rp, four hours).

Overnight **ferries** from Kolaka to Bajoe (deck/business class 75,000/116,000Rp, eight hours) leave at 5pm, 8pm and 11pm. Check www.indonesiaferry.co.id for occasionally updated information.

Kendari

☑ 0401 / POP 314,000
The capital of Southeast Sulawesi province has long been the key port for trade between the inland Tolaki people and seafaring Bugis and Bajau traders. During WWII it was a focal point of the Japanese advance as its

Kendari

```
Terminal
Puuwatu
(6km)
      Jl Sam Ratulangi  Jl Parman  Jl Sutoyo
Swiss-
Belhotel                      Jl Ir Haji Alala        Jl Diponegoro   Pasar    CENTRAL
Kendari                                                               Sentral  KENDARI
      Jl Edi Sabara                                    Hotel
Jl A Silondae                                          Benua
                                                            Pelabuhan  Pelni
(33 km)                          Teluk                       Nusantara
        Jl Masjid Al Alam        Kendari

Plaza Inn
Kendari (500m)
```

airstrip opened up the ability to bomb East Java and Timor. In 1942 they defeated the 400-man Dutch garrison.

Today Kendari is a bustling city with little to recommend it except its range of decent accommodation. It begins in a tangle of lanes in the old *kota* (city) precinct adjacent to the original port in the east, and becomes progressively more modern in the suburbs to the west. One very, very long main road has most of the facilities, except the bus terminal.

Hotel Benua　　　　　　　　　　　　HOTEL $
(☑ 0401-313 1154; Jl Diponegoro 75; r incl breakfast from 250,000Rp) Among the nicest of the budget places – which isn't saying much. If you can look past a few patches of peeling paint and less-than-sparkling bathrooms, you'll find a perfectly adequate place to spend a night.

★ Plaza Inn Kendari　　　　　　　HOTEL $$
(☑ 0401-313 1888; www.plazainn-kendari.com; Jl Antero Hamra 57-59; r incl breakfast 550,000-650,000Rp; ❄ ☀) Despite being the first 'luxury' hotel in Kendari, the Plaza is holding up well. Rooms have nice touches like clean carpets, artistic motifs on the walls, and modern bathrooms. It's located near the downtown action, and it rents bicycles (35,000Rp) for cruising down to the bay.

Swiss-Belhotel Kendari　　BUSINESS HOTEL $$
(☑ 0401-312 8777; www.swiss-belhotel.com; Jl Edi Sabara 88; r/ste from 500,000/1,200,000Rp; ❄ ☎ ☀) This is mainly a business hotel, but the relaxing outdoor garden pool is the best in town and staff are eager to please. Rooms and suites (in no less than six price categories) are in decent shape and spacious. It's

on the waterfront with good proximity to the mangrove boardwalk – a fine place for a sunrise stroll.

ⓘ Getting There & Away

AIR

Modern **Haluoleo Airport** is 24km southwest of town. Flights connect to Makassar, Surabaya and Jakarta, as well as to nearby islands. Both **Garuda** (☑ 0401-312 9777; Jl A Yani, next to Horison Inn; ⊗ 7.30am-3.30pm Mon-Fri, 9am-1pm Sat & Sun) and **Lion Air** (☑ 0401-313 1888; Plaza Inn Kendari, Jl Antero Hamra 57-59) have offices in town.

BOAT

Only one long-haul Pelni ship stops at Kendari: every fortnight the *Tilongkabila* heads to Kolonedale, Luwuk, Gorontalo and Bitung. In the other direction, the same boat goes to Raha, Bau Bau and Makassar (22 hours). You'll find the **Pelni** (☑ 0401-312 1935; Jl Lakidende 10; ⊗ 8am-5pm Mon-Fri, to noon Sat) office on top of a hill near the dock, **Pelabuhan Nusantara** (Ferry Terminal).

Two fast boats leave the Pelni dock heading to Raha (125,000Rp, 2½ hours) and then on to Bau Bau (185,000Rp, five hours). You can buy tickets by the dock. Pelni Jetliner goes to Bau Bau (95,000, 12 hours) and on to Wanci (Wakatobi; 152,000Rp, 23 hours) every Tuesday and Thursday.

Boats direct to Wanci (200,000Rp, 10 hours) leave at 11am on Monday, Tuesday, Thursday and Saturday.

BUS, BEMO & KIJANG

The bus terminal at **Puuwatu** (Jl Pattimura), about 10km west of town, is abandoned, but on the street out front Kijangs wait for passengers to Kolaka (80,000Rp, four hours).

Bau Bau

☑ 0402 / POP 149,000

With comfortable accommodation, great views from the well-preserved citadel walls and some decent beaches within easy *ojek* range, Pulau Buton's prosperous main town of Bau Bau is a perfectly acceptable place to await a boat connection to Maluku, North Sulawesi, or the diving paradise of the Wakatobi Islands.

The terminal, main mosque and market are about 500m west of the main Pelni port, along Jl Kartini, which diverges from the seafront esplanade, Jl Yos Sudarso. On the southwest side of town, the well-preserved walls of the *kraton* (walled city palace) snake around the hilltop, containing a quiet and friendly village within.

⊙ Sights

Kraton   PALACE
(Jl Sultan) FREE High above the town centre is the *kraton,* the Wolio royal citadel with impressively long and well-preserved 16th-century walls and battlements that offer great views over the town and its north-facing bay. Much of daily life once happened here as the coastal regions were too prone to sea pirate attacks. Even today, amid trees and flowers, within the walls villagers occupy evocative traditional homes and attend the old royal mosque. Look for the 400-year-old flagpole, still standing.

Pantai Nirwana   BEACH
(Jl Hayam Wuruk; parking 2000Rp) Nine kilometres southwest of Bau Bau, the nearest white-sand beach is the attractively palm-lined Pantai Nirwana, though like most beaches in the area, it gets absolutely mobbed on the weekends by locals and rubbish.

🛏 Sleeping & Eating

New Wisma Mulia   GUESTHOUSE $
(☑ 0402-282 1673; Jl Sutoyo 13; r incl breakfast 200,000-250,000Rp; ❋ 🛜) This utilitarian bed-in-a-box affair is leagues cleaner than other budget options nearby, though you'd be doing yourself a favour to bring your own sheet. And towel. And soap.

Villa Adios   HOTEL $$
(☑ 0402-282 2467; Jl Srikaya 17C; r incl breakfast 300,000-700,000Rp; ❋ 🛜) Just a touch ostentatious, this mansion was getting some much needed upgrades to bring the white tiled rooms back up to par when we last visited. It's on a hill above town off a side street that is quiet when the local kids are not playing football on the field next door. (If they are, it's a great opportunity to practice your high-five.)

Hotel Calista Beach   HOTEL $$
(☑ 0402-282 3088; hotelcalistabeach@yahoo.com; Jl Yos Sudarso 25; r incl breakfast from 350,000Rp; ❋ 🛜) Popular with expats and students, this dependable place may be basic, but it has a great location across from the waterfront

---

SANGIHE-TALAUD ISLANDS

Strewn across the sea between Indonesia and the southern Philippines are the volcanic island groups of Sangihe (also called Sangir) and Talaud. There are 77 islands, of which 56 are inhabited. Spice cultivation (vanilla, nutmeg and cloves) is a key industry. The two capitals are Tahuna, on Sangihe Besar, and Melonguane, in the Talaud group. Other major settlements are Lirung, on Pulau Salibabu, and Pulau Siau, which has a busy port.

The islands offer dozens of unspoilt sandy beaches, a few crumbling Portuguese forts, several volcanoes to climb, many caves and waterfalls to explore, and some superb diving and snorkelling (bring your own gear). Transport connections to the islands have improved in recent years, and there are hotels, guesthouses and simple beach resorts, as well as ATMs and internet cafes in the main towns.

Majestic Kawanua (p712) operates daily speed ferries that run from Manado to Tagulandang on Pulau Thulandang (150,000Rp, two hours), Siau on Pulau Ulu (170,000Rp, four hours) and Tahuna on Pulau Sangihe (180,000Rp, six hours).

Wings Air flies from Manado to Naha (474,000Rp, 50 minutes, daily) on Sangihe, and Melonguane (1,100,000Rp, one hour, daily) on Pulau Karakelong. An airport is also under construction in Siau.

Nirwana Sangihe (☑ 0821 9288 8039) is a good tour guide for the islands. Pak Nirwan speaks English and knows both of these archipelagos very well.

WORTH A TRIP

RAHA

The main settlement on Pulau Muna, Raha is fairly spread out between its quiet, tree-lined streets. The sleepy backwater is famous for its horse fighting, cave paintings and **Napabale**, a turquoise lagoon about 15km out of town. The lagoon is linked to the sea via a natural tunnel, so you can paddle through when the tide is low. It is a great area for hiking and swimming, and you can hire canoes (40,000Rp). An *ojek* to the lagoon from Raha costs around 30,000Rp.

Super-jet boats between Kendari and Bau Bau stop in Raha. These boats are scheduled to leave for Kendari (125,000Rp, 2½ hours) or Bau Bau (135,000Rp, 2½ hours) at about 9.30am and 3pm in either direction.

---

park which turns into a bustling night market every evening. The staff is very accommodating. If this place is full, try their budget offerings at Wisma Mulia (p723) out back.

RM Sambal Lado INDONESIAN $
(📱0813 4230 1295; Jl Yos Sudarso 5A; plates 15,000-23,000Rp; ⊙24hr) Being right across from the mosque and the ferry dock, this brightly lit *Padang* joint, with excellent green sambal, has a high turnover of food, which keeps dishes fresh.

⊙ Getting There & Away

AIR

Bau Bau's **Betoambari Airport** (Jl Hayam Wuruk) is 4km southwest of town. Between Wings Air and Garuda, there a five daily flights to Makassar (575,000Rp, one hour) and twice daily to Kendari (400,000Rp, 40 minutes). The Wings flight to Kendari continues from there on to Wangi-Wangi (often listed as Wakatobi) in the Wakatobi Islands (420,000Rp, 45 minutes) every day, while Garuda only adds the second leg on Tuesday, Thursday, Saturday and Sunday.

BOAT
To Raha & Kendari

The express **Super-jet** (Jl Yos Sudarso, across from port) leaves twice daily from Bau Bau at 7.30am and 12.30pm taking three hours to reach Raha (135,000Rp to 235,000Rp) and 5½ hours to Kendari (185,000Rp to 325,000Rp).

Pelni (Jl Pahlawan 1; ⊙8am-5pm Mon-Fri) runs a Jetliner boat that is slower, bigger, cheaper (and possibly safer) covering the same trip in 12 hours (95,000Rp) leaving at 7am on Monday and Thursday, and an even slower, bigger, cheaper ferry, the *Tilongkabila*, every two weeks.

To Wakatobi Islands

A slow overnight boat from Bau Bau to Wanci on Pulau Wangi Wangi (100,000Rp, nine to 11 hours) leaves at 9pm daily. The fancy Pelni Jetliner leaves Bau Bau to Wanci (85,000Rp, seven hours) at 10pm on Tuesday and Friday. Boats typically arrive in time to catch the daily water taxi from Wanci to the other islands.

A daily ASDP ferry to Wanci on Pulau Wangi Wangi (58,000Rp, six hours) also leaves at 7am from **Kamaru port** (www.indonesiaferry.co.id), a three-hour drive away on the other side of the island.

Direct boats to Kaledupa (130,000Rp, 12 hours) and Tomia (150,000, 14 hours) exist, but the schedule varies, typically running four to five times per week barring breakdowns.

To Elsewhere in Indonesia

Every few days a Pelni liner links Bau Bau to Makassar, and roughly every two weeks the *Tilongkabila* heads along the east coast of Sulawesi, stopping off at Kendari, Luwuk, Gorontalo and Bitung.

There are near-weekly connections to Ambon, and the *Ciremai* heads direct to Sorong every two weeks.

Wakatobi Islands

With over 50 named dive sites, one of the highest marine species diversity in Indonesia, and few visitors, Wakatobi is a diver's dream. Above water, it's not too shabby either: Bajau sea gypsies inhabit villages standing in the middle of the ocean, empty white sand beaches stretch between rocky outcrops, and boats thread between the maze-like channels of mangrove forests. Few visitors leave this remote island chain off the far southwest coast of Sulawesi disappointed.

The archipelago, formerly (and still occasionally) known as the Tukangbesi Islands, is now referred to as Wakatobi after the four main islands: Wangi-Wangi, Kaledupa, Tomia and Binongko. These form the heart of **Wakatobi National Park** (www.wakatobinationalpark.com), established in 2002 and declared a Unesco World Biosphere Reserve in 2012.

The islands may be difficult to reach, but that just makes it more likely you'll have this paradise all to yourself.

❶ Information

Outside of Wangi Wangi there are no banks or ATMs; bring cash.

❶ Getting There & Away

The easiest way to get to Wakatobi is by taking a daily flight on Garuda or Wings Air to Pulau Wangi Wangi, from Kendari (420,000Rp, one hour). From Wanci, the island's main town, there are daily boats to the other Wakatobi islands leaving in the morning.

Several direct boats between Bau Bau on Pulau Buton and Wangi Wangi, Kaledupa or Tomia depart four to five times per week. Enquire locally for the current schedule.

Once every four weeks the Pelni liner *Kelimutu* travels from Makassar to Bau Bau then on to Ambon via Wanci.

Pulau Wangi Wangi

Wangi Wangi is the first island in the Wakatobi chain and the archipelago's transport gateway. Despite that, it is still minimally inhabited and maximally peaceful. Cycling is a great way to get around this petite island, which is relatively flat and has good roads, with plenty of beaches and interesting caves to stop at.

Colourful **Wanci** is the main wooden-boat-clogged settlement on Pulau Wangi Wangi. It has a lively harbour, a sprawling Bajau village over the water and a night market with tasty treats, next to what must be the world's shortest divided highway – a halted government project of questionable value.

Further afield you'll find decent snorkelling and diving at places like **Sombu** or **Cemara Beach**, and lots of hidden nooks between folds in the coast. Several roads cut inland heading up to hilltop villages, some with sublime viewpoints.

Villa Nadila LODGE **$$**
(☑0821 8871 8355; villa-nadila@gmail.com; Jl Hoga Manugela, Wanci; r incl breakfast 300,000-550,000Rp; ❋ ☏) Wanci's newest, cleanest and quietest place to stay gets high marks for everything except location – it's about 2km out on the edge of town away from, well, everything. But, if you don't mind walking, it's a great option.

Patuno Resort Wakatobi RESORT **$$$**
(☑0811 400 2221; www.wakatobipatunoresort.com; r/bungalows incl breakfast from 540,000/890,000Rp; ❋ ☏) Patuno Resort Wakatobi is a sprawling dive resort on a long white-sand beach close to the northern tip of the island. Rooms in the hotel block are small but comfortable, though you'll want to spring for a bungalow if you're hoping to wow your partner. Free airport or harbour transfers.

Night Market MARKET
(☉ typically sundown to late) It's all smiles and good-natured jokes (usually at your expense) at the night market which typically hosts a few dozen ladies selling all kinds of grilled fish, stewed vegetables and fried... everything. Find it 2km north of Wanci's town centre near the waterfront.

Restoran Wisata Beach SEAFOOD **$**
(☑0812 4563 9300; Wisata Beach Hotel, Jl Ahmad Yani 59, Wanci; mains 25,000-40,000Rp; ☉9am-9pm; ☏) Enjoy your fish while the rest of its family swim beneath your feet at this breezy open-sided restaurant on stilts over the water. As ocean views go, this one is a bit rural, but the food is delicious and portions filling.

❶ Getting There & Away

Garuda or Wings Air fly daily to the **airport** (Wakatobi) on the east side of Pulau Wangi Wangi from Kendari (420,000Rp, one hour). Airport taxis start the bidding at 100,000Rp into Wanci, 18km away.

Once every four weeks the Pelni **ferry** (Wanci) *Kelimutu* travels from Makassar to Bau Bau then on to Ambon via Wanci.

SULAWESI WAKATOBI ISLANDS

BOATS FROM WANGI WANGI TO WAKATOBI ISLANDS

DESTINATION	FARE (RP)	DURATION (HR)	DEPARTS	RETURNS
Binongko	150,000	6+	9am	10am
Kaledupa	50,000	2	9am & 1pm	5am
Tomia	120,000	4-6	9am	6am
Tomia (speed)	150,000	2-3	8am or 3pm	6am

From Wanci, the island's main town, there are daily boats to the other Wakatobi islands leaving in the morning.

Pulau Kaledupa & Pulau Hoga

For most travellers, the Wakatobi Islands mean Pulau Hoga. This small desert island, 2km from the bigger Pulau Kaledupa, offers as close to a castaway existence as you could wish for. The water is turquoise; reefs are spectacular; and Bajau locals are superfriendly. When not diving or snorkelling, you can walk around parts of the island (best at low tide; some areas are only accessible by boat) and visit the fishing village at the northern end.

Nearby Pulau Kaledupa essentially has no tourist infrastructure on its beautiful, forested and beach-rich shores. In general the island is just a stopover for many travellers, albeit a rather stunning one. If you want to stay overnight, homestays are easy to arrange.

Sampela VILLAGE

Standing proud in the middle of the sea, this watery Bajau village is entirely built on stilts above the coral about 1km offshore from Ambeua pier. You're welcome to wander the boardwalks and bridges connecting the simple houses; the locals are generally friendly and forgiving.

★Hoga Island Dive Resort RESORT $$$

(Wakatobi Hoga Diving; www.hogaislanddiveresort.com; Pualu Hoga; bungalow 400,000Rp) Searching for that perfect barefoot vibe? Look no further: this relaxed place enjoys an idyllic location, with big, rustic wooden bungalows, a white-sand beach and hammocks galore. The ambience is warm thanks to the genial staff, food is fresh, plentiful and very tasty, and the dive shop is well managed, with excellent guides. All-inclusive dive packages are from 1,450,000Rp per person.

Pulau Tomia & Pulau Binongko

Pulau Tomia, the third island in the Wakatobi chain, hosts dozens of dive sites, two major towns, a handful of villages, an approachable 300m-tall mountain, and long stretches of empty beach. Accommodation is easy to come by here, but you'll need a little creativity to arrange adventures afield. **Pulau Tolandona** to the west houses Wakatobi's most exclusive dive resort.

South of Wakatobi, the somewhat more rugged Binongko island is ringed by villages famous for their blacksmiths. In fact the archipelago is sometimes called by its original name, Kepulauan Tukangbesi, meaning 'Islands of the Metal Workers'; look for them in **Popalia** village. In between the villages are numerous springs, caves and hidden beaches ripe for exploration.

Labore Homestay HOMESTAY $

(☎0813 4373 0361; Jl Pasar Waha, Pulau Tomia; r incl breakfast 150,000-200,000Rp) Clean and simple rooms right on the water within walking distance of the boat dock. The place is run by a helpful couple who can help arrange diving and excursions.

Wakatobi Dive Resort RESORT $$$

(www.wakatobi.com; Pulau Tolandona; per person incl meals from US$315; ❄@📶) Just west of Pulau Tomia, this ultra-exclusive hideaway offers beautiful bungalow accommodation and one of the most celebrated house reefs in Indonesia. Rates include full board; snorkel/dive packages start at US$110/150 per day. The resort is also the base for the elegant liveaboard *Pelagian*. Private charter flights direct to/from Bali (from US$725) are available.

Understand Indonesia

History

The story of how Indonesia became what it is today is a colourful dance of migrants and invaders, rebels and religions, kingdoms and empires, choreographed by Indonesia's island nature and its location on millennia-old Asian trade routes. It's a story full of heroes and villains, victors and victims, but the strangest part is how these 17,000-plus islands with over 300 spoken languages and diverse cultures ever came to be a nation at all.

The Trading Archipelago

Indonesians inhabit a diverse island world where a short sea voyage or journey inland can take a traveller into a whole new ecosystem providing a different set of useful commodities. Long ago, forest dwellers were collecting colourful bird feathers and tree resins and exchanging them for turtle shells or salt from people who lived by the sea. Some of these goods would find their way to nearby islands, from where they then reached more distant islands. By about 500 BC, routes sailed by Indonesian islanders began to overlap with those of sailors from mainland Asia. Thus, 2000 years ago, bird-of-paradise feathers from Papua could be depicted on beautiful bronze drums cast by the Dongson people of Vietnam, and some of the drums then ended up in Java, Sumatra and Bali.

Indonesia's main western islands – Sumatra, Kalimantan and Java – lie in the middle of the sea routes linking Arabia, India, China and Japan. Indonesia was destined to become a crossroads of Asia, and trade has been its lifeblood for at least 2000 years. It has brought with it nearly all the biggest changes the archipelago has seen through the centuries – new people, new ideas, new crops, new technologies, new religions, new wars, new rulers.

Simple iron tools, such as axes and plough tips, arrived from China around 200 BC, spurring Indonesians to find their own metal deposits and make their own knives, arrowheads, urns and jewellery.

Indian Influence & Sriwijaya

Pepper plants, originally from India, were spicing up western Indonesian food as early as 600 BC. Indonesian clothing got a lot smarter when boats from Indonesia reached India by the 2nd century BC and brought back cotton plants. In the early centuries AD, Indian Hindus based in

TIMELINE	60,000–40,000 BC	About 8000 BC	About 2000 BC
	Indonesia's western islands are still part of the Asian mainland. The first Homo sapiens arrive, probably ancestors of the Melanesians in today's population, who are now mainly in Papua.	Sea levels rise after the end of the last glacial period, separating Sumatra, Borneo, Java and Bali from the Asian mainland, and the island of New Guinea from Australia.	Austronesian people originating from Taiwan start to arrive in Indonesia, probably by sea routes. They absorb or displace Melanesians. The earliest evidence of settlement dates from the 6th century BC.

Southeast Asia began trading jewellery, fine cloth and pottery with early coastal trading settlements in Java, Sumatra and Kalimantan. The Indians brought Hindu and Buddhist culture with them as well.

From the 4th century AD, Chinese travellers arrived in Indonesian ports too. By the 7th century the Buddhist port state of Sriwijaya in southeast Sumatra was trading pepper, ivory, resins, feathers, turtle shells, mother of pearl and much more to ports around the Java Sea and on to China, from where they returned with from silk, ceramics and iron.

Traders from Arabia

The first Muslim traders from Arabia appeared in Indonesian ports within a few decades of the death of the Prophet Muhammad in AD 632. Arabian ships bound for China, carrying spices and rare woods or Indian cloth, would call in at Sumatra or other Indonesian islands to add local products such as aromatic woods, resins and camphor to their cargoes. By the 13th century, Arabs had established settlements in major Indonesian ports. Sulaiman bin Abdullah bin al-Basir, ruler of the small north Sumatran port of Lamreh in the early 13th century, was the first Indonesian ruler known to have adopted Islam and taken the title Sultan.

Majapahit

The first Indonesian sultanates came into being while the greatest of Indonesia's Hindu-Buddhist states, Majapahit, was flourishing in eastern Java. Like the earlier Sriwijaya, Majapahit's success was trade-based. Its powerful fleets exacted tribute from ports spread from Sumatra to Papua (disobedient states were 'wiped out completely' by the Majapahit navies, according to court poet Prapanca), and enabled its traders to dominate the lucrative commerce between Sumatran ports and China. Prapanca reported that traders in Majapahit ports came from Cambodia, Vietnam and Thailand. He also claimed, less credibly, that Majapahit ruled a hundred foreign countries. Majapahit was eventually conquered by one of the newly Islamic north Java ports, Demak, in 1478.

Spices & the Portuguese

As Islam continued to spread around the archipelago, another new breed of trader arrived – Europeans. In 1511 the Portuguese conquered Melaka, key to the vital Strait of Melaka between Sumatra and Malaya, and set up bases across Indonesia. They also established settlements in mainland ports from India to China and Japan.

Drawing the Portuguese to Indonesia were cloves, nutmeg and mace: three plant products long prized in Europe, China, the Islamic world and

The Majapahit kingdom reached its zenith during the reign of King Hayam Wuruk (r 1350–89), who was ably assisted by his prime minister and brilliant military commander Gajah Mada. Their names literally translate as Rotting Chicken and Rutting Elephant, respectively, but this had no ill-effect on the expansive kingdom.

500–1 BC	5th century AD	7th century	7th–13th centuries
Local trade routes mesh with mainland Asia's routes. Chinese iron tools, large Vietnamese bronze drums and Indian glass beads reach Indonesia. Local products such as spices reach India and China.	Under influence from India, some Indonesian trading ports have turned from animism to Hinduism or Buddhism. Indonesia's earliest-known inscriptions are carved in west Java and near Kutai, Kalimantan.	Muslim traders begin arriving in Indonesian ports bringing their religion as well as goods for trade. Over the next few centuries, thriving Muslim communities are established.	Buddhist Sriwijaya in southeast Sumatra dominates in western Indonesia. It may have been a collection of ports or a single state; its trade routes reached China and India.

THE CHINESE IN INDONESIA

As Indonesian trading states grew richer and more complex they came increasingly to rely on the growing numbers of Chinese settlers to oil the wheels of their economies. Indonesia's first recorded Chinese settlement was located at Pasai on Sumatra in the 11th century. By the 17th century, Chinese were filling a whole spectrum of roles as middlemen, artisans, labourers, tax-collectors, business-people, financiers, farmers and keepers of shops, brothels and opium dens. Today ethnic-Chinese Indonesians own many of the country's biggest and most profitable businesses. For centuries they have also been the subject of jealousy and hatred, and the victims of repeated outbreaks of violence, including during the shocking 1998 Jakarta riots.

Indonesia itself because they made food taste more interesting. All three plants were native to Maluku, the Spice Islands of eastern Indonesia. The sultans of the small Maluku islands of Ternate and Tidore controlled most of the already valuable trade in these spices.

Portuguese traders brought exotic new things to Maluku such as clocks, firearms, sweet potatoes and Christianity. Clove and nutmeg cultivation was stepped up to meet their demand. After they fell out with the Ternate sultan Babullah and were expelled in 1575, they headed south and set up on Pulau Ambon instead.

The Portuguese also traded at Aceh (north Sumatra) and Banten (northwest Java), where the principal product was pepper, which had also been used for many centuries to liven up taste buds in Europe, China and elsewhere.

In the 17th century the Portuguese were pushed out of the Indonesian spice business by the Dutch, a more determined, better-armed and better-financed rival.

From Animism to Islam

The earliest Indonesians were animists – they believed animate and inanimate objects had their own life force or spirit, and that events could be influenced by offerings, rituals or forms of magic. Indonesia's scattered prehistoric sites, and animist societies that have survived into modern times, provide evidence that there was often a belief in an afterlife and supernatural controlling powers, and that the spirits of the dead were believed to influence events. Megaliths, found from Pulau Nias to Sumba and Sulawesi's Lore Lindu National Park, are one manifestation of ancestor cults. Some megaliths may be 5000 years old, but in Sumba animist religion is still alive and well, and concrete versions of megalithic tombs are still being erected.

The British, keen to profit from the spice trade, kept control of the Maluku island of Run until 1667. Then they swapped it for a Dutch-controlled island in North America called Manhattan.

8th–9th centuries	1292	1294–1478	13th–15th centuries
The Buddhist Sailendra and Hindu Sanjaya (or Mataram) kingdoms flourish on Java's central plains, creating the huge – and still standing – Borobudur and Prambanan temple complexes respectively.	Marco Polo stops off in Sumatra on his way from China back to Persia, becoming the first of an all-star lineup of explorers to visit the islands.	The Hindu-Buddhist Majapahit kingdom, monopolises trade between Sumatra and China and exacts tribute from across Indonesia. The splendid Majapahit court is imitated by many later Indonesian states.	Influenced by Arab merchants, two north Sumatran towns adopt Islam, followed by Melaka on the Malay peninsula, the eastern island of Ternate and northern Java ports including Demak, which conquers Majapahit.

Hinduism & Buddhism

It was contact with the comparatively wealthy cultures of India in the first few centuries AD that first led Indonesians to adopt new belief systems. Indian traders who settled in Indonesia continued to practise Hinduism, or its offshoot Buddhism. Some built their own temples and brought in priests, monks, teachers or scribes. Impressed local Indonesian rulers started to use the Indian titles Raja or Maharaja or add the royal suffix *varman* to their names. It was a short step for them to cement their ties with the Indian world by adopting the Indians' religion or philosophy too. The earliest records of Indianised local rulers are 5th-century stone inscriptions in Sanskrit, found in west Java and near Kutai (now Tenggarong), Kalimantan. These record decrees and tales of the glorious deeds of the kings Purnavarman and Mulavarman, respectively.

The major Indonesian states from then until the 15th century were all Hindu or Buddhist. Sriwijaya, based in southern Sumatra, was predominantly Buddhist. In Central Java in the 8th and 9th centuries, the Buddhist Sailendra kingdom and the predominantly Hindu Sanjaya (or Mataram) kingdom constructed the great temple complexes of Borobudur and Prambanan respectively. They sought to re-create Indian civilisation in a Javanese landscape, and Indian gods such as Shiva and Vishnu were believed to inhabit the Javanese heavens, though this did not obliterate traditional beliefs in magical forces or nature spirits. In the 10th century, wealth and power on Java shifted to the east of the island, where a series of Hindu-Buddhist kingdoms dominated till the late 15th century. The greatest of these was Majapahit (1294–1478), based at Trowulan. Javanese Indian culture also spread to Bali (which remains Hindu to this day) and parts of Sumatra.

Central Java's unmissable Borobudur and Prambanan complexes are the finest ancient monuments in Indonesia, dating to the 8th century. The former is an iconic Buddhist monument built from two million stones while the latter has elaborate Hindu decoration.

Islam

Majapahit was eventually undone by the next major religion to reach Indonesia – Islam. Muslim Arab traders had appeared in Indonesia as early as the 7th century. By the 13th century Arabs had established settlements in major Indonesian ports, and it was then that the first local rulers, at Lamreh and Pasai in north Sumatra, adopted Islam. Gradually over the next two centuries, then more rapidly, other Indonesian ports with Muslim communities switched to Islam. Their rulers would become persuaded by Islamic teachings and, keen to join a successful international network, would usually take the title Sultan to proclaim their conversion. Melaka on the Malay Peninsula, controlling the strategic Strait of Melaka, switched to Islam in 1436 and became a model for other Muslim states to emulate.

In Java, Sumatra and Sulawesi, some Muslim states spread Islam by military conquest. The conversion of several north Java ports in the late

1505	1595	1602	1611–1700
Portuguese ships reach Indonesian waters. Interested in spices, the Portuguese go on to establish trading settlements across the archipelago, joining Indians, Arabs, Chinese, Malays and islanders in the sea trade.	Four small Dutch ships reach the pepper port Banten in northwest Java. Despite setbacks, the expedition returns home with enough spices to make a small profit.	Holland merges competing merchant companies into the VOC (United East India Company). It aims to drive other European nations out of Asian trade, especially in spices.	From its headquarters at Batavia (now Jakarta), the VOC expands its control through deals, alliances and battles. A chain of Dutch-controlled ports leads to the Spice Islands.

15th century meant that Hindu-Buddhist Majapahit was hemmed in by hostile states. One of these, Demak, conquered Majapahit in 1478.

The greatest of the Indonesian Muslim kingdoms, Mataram, was founded in 1581 in the area of Java where the Sailendra and Sanjaya kingdoms had flourished centuries earlier. Its second ruler, Senopati, was a descendant of Hindu princes and helped to incorporate some of the Hindu past, and older animist beliefs, into the new Muslim world.

Christianity

The last major religion to reach Indonesia was Christianity. The Catholic Portuguese made some conversions among Islamic communities in Maluku and Sulawesi in the 16th century, but most reverted to Islam. The Protestant Dutch, who gradually took control over the whole archipelago between the 17th and 20th centuries, made little effort to spread Christianity. Missionaries active in the 19th and 20th centuries were steered to regions where Islam was weak or nonexistent, such as the Minahasa and Toraja areas of Sulawesi, the Batak area of Sumatra and Dutch New Guinea (now Papua).

In 1292, Marco Polo on one of his forays east visited Aceh and noted that local inhabitants had already converted to Islam.

PANCASILA – THE FIVE PRINCIPLES

In government buildings and TV broadcasts and on highway markers and school uniforms you'll see the *garuda*, Indonesia's mythical bird and national symbol. On its breast are the five symbols of the philosophical doctrine of Indonesia's unitary state, Pancasila (which means Five Principles in Sanskrit and Pali, the sacred languages of Hinduism and Buddhism). Pancasila was first expounded by Sukarno in 1945 as a synthesis of Western democracy, Islam, Marxism and indigenous village traditions. Enshrined in the 1945 constitution, it was raised to the level of a mantra by Suharto's New Order regime. Suharto's successor BJ Habibie annulled the requirement that Pancasila must form the basic principle of all organisations, but it remains an important national creed. The five symbols are as follows.

Star Represents faith in God, through Islam, Christianity, Buddhism, Hinduism or any other religion.

Chain Represents humanitarianism within Indonesia and in relations with humankind as a whole.

Banyan Tree Represents nationalism and unity between Indonesia's many ethnic groups.

Buffalo Symbolises representative government.

Rice and Cotton Represents social justice.

1667	1670–1755	1795–1824	1800
The Dutch gain complete control of the Banda Islands and in return give the British a little island in their North America colony named Manhattan.	VOC exploits Mataram's internal turmoils to win control of the kingdom. In 1755 it splits Mataram into two kingdoms, with capitals at Yogyakarta and Surakarta (Solo) and now controls Java.	In the Napoleonic Wars, Britain seizes the possessions of the Dutch East Indies. An 1824 agreement divides the region between the Dutch and British; the borders are similar to modern Indonesia and Malaysia.	The now overstretched, corrupt and bankrupt VOC is wound up. Its territories pass to the Netherlands crown, converting a trading empire into a colonial one, the Netherlands East Indies.

Rajas & Sultans

The Hindu, Buddhist and Muslim states of Indonesia were mostly absolute monarchies or sultanates, whose rulers claimed to be at least partly divine. Their subjects were there to produce food or goods that they could pay as tribute to the ruler, or to do business from which they could pay taxes, or to fight in armies or navies, or to fill roles in the royal entourage from astrologer to poet, tax collector or concubine. Land was generally considered to belong to the ruler, who permitted subjects to use it in exchange for taxes and tribute. Slaves were an integral part of the scene well into the 19th century.

Other states could pay tribute too and the largest kingdoms or sultanates, such as the Java-based Hindu-Buddhist Majapahit (1294–1478) and Muslim Mataram (1581–1755), built trading empires based on tribute from other peoples whom they kept in line through the threat of military force.

In the 1650s and 1660s Banten's Sultan Ageng Tirtajasa decreed that all men aged 16 or over must tend 500 pepper plants.

European Influence

The coming of Europeans in the 16th and 17th centuries introduced new ways for Indonesian states and contenders to get one over on their rivals. They could use the Europeans as trading partners or mercenaries or allies, and if the Europeans became too powerful or demanding, they expected they could get rid of them. In Maluku the Muslim sultanate of Ternate, a small but wealthy clove-growing island, drove out its former trading partners, the Portuguese, in 1575. It later awarded the Dutch a monopoly on the sale of its spices and used the revenue to build up its war fleet and extract tribute from other statelets. Ternate eventually controlled 72 tax-paying tributaries around Maluku and Sulawesi.

Such agreements, and alliances and conquests, eventually gave the Dutch a hold over much Indonesian trade and territory. Their involvement in the endless internal feuds of the powerful Javanese Mataram kingdom won them such a stranglehold over the region that in 1749 the dying king Pakubuwono II willed them control over his kingdom. In 1755 the Dutch resolved yet another Mataram succession dispute by splitting it into two kingdoms, with capitals at Surakarta (Solo) and Yogyakarta. Both royal families later split again, so that by the early 19th century there were four rival royal houses in this tiny part of Central Java.

As long as local rulers and aristocrats cooperated, the Dutch were content to leave them in place, and these traditional rulers eventually became the top rank of the 'Native' branch of the colonial civil service, continuing to run their kingdoms under the supervision of a sprinkling of Dutch administrators.

The Dutch introduced coffee to Indonesia in 1696. United East India Company (VOC) officials got west Java nobles to instruct their farmers to grow coffee bushes, paying with cash and textiles for the harvested beans.

1815	1825–30	1820s–1910	1830
In the biggest explosion in modern history, Gunung Tambora on Sumbawa erupts. Tens of thousands die on the island; the ash cloud results in 1816 being dubbed 'the year without summer' across the northern hemisphere.	Prince Diponegoro, supported by many Muslims, the poor and some fellow Javanese aristocrats, rebels against the Dutch and their vassals. Some 200,000 Javanese die, most from famine and disease.	Holland takes control of nearly all the archipelago through economic expansion, agreements with local aristocrats and warfare. Many aristocrats become representatives of the Dutch administration.	Slavery, which had flourished among various kingdoms and sultanates, goes into final decline when the Balinese royalty renounce the practice. Proceeds had been used to finance wars and palaces.

Dutch Domination

When the Dutch first arrived at Banten in 1595 and then set up the United East India Company (Vereenigde Oost-Indische Compagnie; VOC) to conduct all their business in the East Indies in 1602, they did not plan to end up running the whole of Indonesia. They just wanted to drive other European powers out of the lucrative spice trade in Indonesia. Their strategy was to sign exclusive trade agreements with local rulers where possible, and to impose their will by military force where necessary. Their powerful fleets and effective soldiers made them a potent ally for local strongmen, and in return the Dutch could extract valuable trading rights.

Nathaniel's Nutmeg by Giles Milton offers a fascinating account of the battle to control trade from the Spice Islands. Now known as the Banda Islands, they still have many colonial-era sites and are well worth visiting.

Moving In

In the beginning the Dutch concentrated primarily on the spice trade. In 1605 they drove the Portuguese out of Ambon. They then set up their own chain of settlements in Muslim ports along the route to the Spice Islands, with their headquarters at Jayakarta, a small vassal port of Banten in northwest Java. When Banten, with English help, tried to expel them in 1619, the Dutch beat off the attack, rebuilt the town and renamed it Batavia. Today it's called Jakarta.

By varied means the Dutch took control of Banda in 1621, Melaka in 1641, Tidore in 1657, Makassar in 1669 and then several Javanese ports. In Banda they exterminated or expelled almost the whole population in the 1620s and replaced them with slave-worked nutmeg plantations.

The Javanese Mataram kingdom tried unsuccessfully to drive the Dutch out of Batavia in 1628 and again in 1629. In the 1640s, Mataram's King Amangkurat I, facing a host of internal challenges, decided it was

THE CULTIVATION SYSTEM

The seemingly intractable problems the Dutch had with their colony were made much worse by the devastating Diponegoro War in Java (1825–30). This conflict started when Prince Diponegoro got angry after the Dutch built a new road across land that contained his parents' memorial. Hostilities began and the prince received widespread support by others in Java who had grievances with the Dutch. To quell the conflict, the Dutch eventually needed to bring in troops from Sulawesi, Holland and even Dutch-African colonies at huge expense.

After the war, Holland desperately needed to make the East Indies profitable. Its answer was the new Cultivation (or Culture) System. Up to two million Javanese peasants were obliged to grow the export crops of coffee, tea, tobacco, indigo or sugar, and pay a proportion of their crop in tax, and sell the rest to the government at fixed prices. This saved Holland from bankruptcy, and while some villagers prospered, the cultivation system also resulted in famines, loss of rice-growing lands, poverty and corruption.

1830–70	1845–1900	1883	1901
The Cultivation System: two million Javanese peasants have to grow and pay tax on export crops (coffee, tea, tobacco, indigo, sugar). Holland is saved from bankruptcy, but most peasants suffer.	Private (European) enterprise is encouraged, forced cultivation is slowly wound down. Transportation infrastructure is greatly improved. Notoriously brutal rubber and tobacco plantations develop on Sumatra.	Mt Krakatau blows, almost completely destroying the namesake island in the Sumba Strait between Java and Sumatra. It's considered the loudest noise in recorded history.	The Ethical Policy is introduced to raise Indonesian welfare through better irrigation, education and health, but Europeans benefit most. The growth of cities spawns a new Indonesian middle class.

wiser to make peace with the VOC. He went further and gave it the sole licence to carry Mataram goods.

While Chinese, Arabs and Indians continued to trade in Indonesia in the 17th and 18th centuries, the VOC ended up with all the best business. Asian traders carried rice, fruit and coconuts from one part of the archipelago to another; Dutch ships carried spices, timber, textiles and metals to other Asian ports and Europe.

Trading successes brought the VOC an ever larger and costlier web of commitments around the archipelago. By 1800 it controlled most of Java and parts of Maluku, Sulawesi, Sumatra and Timor. Overstretched and corrupt, the VOC was also bankrupt. The Dutch crown took over the company's possessions but then lost them (first to France, then to Britain) during the Napoleonic Wars. Control was restored to the Dutch in 1816 following the Anglo-Dutch Treaty of 1814.

Commerce Rules

As the 19th century progressed, European private enterprise was encouraged to take over export agriculture. Privately owned rubber and tobacco plantations, both of which featured brutal working conditions, helped to extend Dutch control into eastern Sumatra. The colonial administration concentrated on creating a favourable investment climate by constructing railways, improving roads and shipping services, and quashing unrest. It also waged military campaigns to subjugate the last noncompliant local statelets.

The Banjarmasin sultanate in Kalimantan came under direct Dutch rule in 1863 after a four-year war; resource-rich Aceh in northern Sumatra was finally subdued in 1903 after 30 years of vicious warfare; southwest Sulawesi was occupied from 1900 to 1910; and Bali was brought to heel, after several attempts, in 1906. Some Balinese aristocrats killed their families and retainers and committed suicide rather than submit to the Dutch. In the late 19th century Holland, Britain and Germany all agreed to divide up the unexplored island of New Guinea.

The Ethical Policy

The end of the 19th century saw the rise of a new Dutch awareness of the problems and needs of the Indonesian people. The result was the Ethical Policy, launched in 1901, which aimed to raise Indonesians' welfare and purchasing power through better irrigation, education, health and credit, and with a decentralised government. The Ethical Policy's immediate effects were mixed, and its benefits often accrued to Europeans rather than Indonesians. An increase in private land ownership increased the number of locals without land. Local revolts and strikes were fairly frequent. But the colony's trade continued to grow. By the 1930s the Dutch East Indies

The name Indonesia was coined in the 1850s by Scotsman James Logan (editor of the Singapore-published *Journal of the Indian Archipelago and Eastern Asia*) as a shorter equivalent for the term Indian Archipelago.

Rimbaud in Java: The Lost Voyage by Jamie James (2011) re-creates poet Arthur Rimbaud's Java escape in 1876 when he first joined the Dutch army and then deserted, fleeing into the jungle.

HISTORY DUTCH DOMINATION

1912	1920	1927	1928
Sarekat Islam (Islamic Union) emerges as a Javanese Muslim economic assistance group, with anti-Christian and anti-Chinese tendencies. Linking with other groups, it grows into a million-member anticolonial movement.	The Indonesian Communist Party (PKI) is founded. A pro-independence party with support from urbanites, it is sidelined when uprisings in Java (1926) and Sumatra (1927) are suppressed by the Dutch.	The Indonesian National Party (PNI) emerges, led by a young engineer, Sukarno. It grows quickly into the most powerful pro-independence organisation. In 1930 its leaders are jailed.	Nationalism is given a boost when the All Indonesia Youth Congress proclaims its historic Youth Pledge, establishing goals of one national identity and one language (Bahasa Indonesia).

was providing most of the world's quinine and pepper, over one-third of its rubber and almost one-fifth of its tea, sugar, coffee and oil.

Breaking Free

The longer-term effects of the Ethical Policy were truly revolutionary. Wider education spawned a new class of Indonesians aware of colonial injustices, international political developments and the value of their own cultures. These people were soon starting up diverse new political and religious groups and publications, some of which were expressly dedicated to ending Dutch colonial rule.

The First Nationalists

Indonesians look back to 1908 as the year their independence movement began. This was when Budi Utomo (Glorious Endeavour) was founded. Led by upper-class, Dutch-educated, Indonesian men, Budi Utomo wanted to revive monarchy and modernise Javanese culture for the 20th century. It was soon followed by more radical groups. Sarekat Islam (Islamic Union), which emerged in 1912, began as a Javanese Muslim economic mutual-help group, with a strong anti-Christian and anti-Chinese streak. Linking with other groups, it grew steadily into a million-member anticolonial movement trying to connect villagers throughout the colony with the educated elite.

In 1920 the Indonesian Communist Party (PKI), which had operated within Sarekat Islam, split off on its own. A pro-independence party with support from urban workers, it launched uprisings in Java (1926) and Sumatra (1927) but was neutralised when these were quashed by the Dutch, who imprisoned and exiled thousands of communists.

A key moment in the growth of nationalist consciousness came in 1928 when the All Indonesia Youth Congress proclaimed its historic Youth Pledge, establishing goals of one national identity (Indonesian), one country (Indonesia) and one language (the version of Malay called Bahasa Indonesia). Meanwhile the Indonesian National Party (PNI), which emerged in 1927 from the Bandung Study Group led by a young engineer, Sukarno, was rapidly becoming the most powerful Indonesian nationalist organisation – with the result that in 1930 the Dutch jailed its leaders.

Nationalist sentiment remained high through the 1930s, but even when Germany invaded the Netherlands in 1940, the Dutch colonial government was determined to hold fast.

WWII

Everything changed when Japan invaded the Dutch East Indies in 1942 and swept aside Dutch and Allied resistance. Almost 200,000 Dutch and Chinese civilians and Allied military were put into prison camps, in

Clove-impregnated *kretek* cigarettes, popular throughout Indonesia today, were first marketed by Nitisemito, a man from Kudus, Java, in 1906. His Bal Tiga (Three Balls) brand grew into one of the biggest Indonesian-owned businesses in the Dutch East Indies.

1930s	1936	1942	1942–45
The Dutch East Indies provides most of the quinine used in the world's tonic water, to the delight of gin lovers everywhere. Pepper, rubber and oil are also major exports.	Americans Robert and Louise Koke build simple bamboo bungalows on Bali's otherwise deserted Kuta Beach. They also introduce a sport called surfing they had learned in Hawaii.	Japan invades Indonesia with little resistance. Europeans are sent to prison camps. Indonesians initially welcome the Japanese as liberators, but sentiment changes due to the harshness of the occupation.	The Japanese collaborate with nationalist leaders because of their anti-Dutch sentiments, and establish an Indonesian militia that later forms the backbone of the anti-Dutch resistance after WWII.

some of which 30% of the inmates would die. Many Indonesians at first welcomed the Japanese as liberators, but feelings changed as they were subjected to slave labour and starvation. The 3½-year Japanese occupation did, however, strengthen the Indonesian nationalist movement, as the Japanese used anti-Dutch nationalists to help them run things and allowed them limited political activity. Sukarno was permitted to travel around giving nationalist speeches. The Japanese also set up Indonesian home-defence militias, whose training proved useful in the Indonesians' later military struggle against the Dutch.

As defeat for Japan loomed in May 1945, the Investigating Agency for Preparation of Independence met in Jakarta. This Japanese-established committee of Indonesian nationalists proposed a constitution, philosophy (Pancasila) and extent (the whole Dutch East Indies) for a future Indonesian republic.

Anyone interested in the WWII campaigns in Indonesia, and the sites and relics that can be found there today, should check out the fascinating Pacific Wrecks (www.pacificwrecks.com).

HISTORY BREAKING FREE

The Revolution

When Japan announced its surrender on 15 August 1945, a group of *pemuda* (radical young nationalists) kidnapped Sukarno and his colleague Mohammed Hatta and pressured them to declare immediate Indonesian independence, which they did at Sukarno's Jakarta home on 17 August (you can see the text of their proclamation on the 100,000Rp banknote). A government was formed, with Sukarno president and Hatta the vice-president.

British and Australian forces arrived to disarm the Japanese and hold the Indonesian nationalists until the Dutch could send their own forces. But Indonesians wanted independence. Some, like Sukarno and Hatta, favoured a negotiated path to freedom; others wanted to fight to get it as fast as possible. The early months of the revolution were a particularly chaotic period, with massacres of Chinese, Dutch and Eurasian civilians and Indonesian aristocrats; attempted communist revolutions in some areas; and clashes between Indonesian struggle groups and the British and Japanese. In the bloody Battle of Surabaya in November 1945, thousands died, not just from British bombing and in street fighting with the British, but also in nationalist atrocities against local civilians. In December the nationalists managed to pull diverse struggle groups together into a republican army.

By 1946, 55,000 Dutch troops had arrived. They soon recaptured major cities on Java and Sumatra. Ruthless tactics by Captain Raymond Westerling in southern Sulawesi saw at least 6000 Indonesians executed (40,000 by some accounts). The first of two big Dutch offensives – called 'police actions' – reduced republican territory to limited areas of Java and Sumatra in August 1947, with its capital at Yogyakarta.

Aug 1945	Sep–Nov 1945	1946–49	1949
Japan surrenders. Indonesian nationalist students kidnap Sukarno and Hatta and pressure them to declare independence, which they do on 17 August. Sukarno becomes president and Hatta vice-president.	Allied troops suppress the nationalists. Sukarno wants independence through diplomacy, but other nationalists want to fight. The Battle of Surabaya between British and nationalists leaves thousands dead.	Dutch troops arrive to regain control; the nationalists form a Republican Army. Despite Dutch offensives and rifts between Sukarno's government, Muslim movements and the Communists, resistance continues.	Faced with an unwinnable war and hostile international opinion, the Netherlands transfers sovereignty over the Dutch East Indies (apart from Netherlands New Guinea) to the Indonesian republic.

Differences among the Indonesian forces erupted viciously. In Madiun, Java, the republican army and Muslim militias fought pro-communist forces in August 1948, leaving 8000 dead. The second Dutch 'police action' in December 1948 won the Dutch more territory, and they captured Sukarno, Hatta and their prime minister Sutan Syahrir. But the independence forces kept up a guerrilla struggle, and international (especially US) opinion turned against the Dutch. Realising that its cause was unwinnable, the Netherlands finally transferred sovereignty over the Dutch East Indies (apart from Dutch New Guinea) to the Indonesian republic on 27 December 1949. At least 70,000, possibly as many as 200,000, Indonesians had lost their lives in the revolution, along with 700 Dutch and British soldiers and some thousands of Japanese troops and European, Chinese and Eurasian civilians.

'Bung' Karno

Independent Indonesia had a troubled infancy. Tensions between Muslims and communists persisted, with the secular nationalists like Sukarno and Hatta trying to hold everything together. The economy was in a sorry state after almost a decade of conflict, and a drop in commodity prices in the early 1950s made things worse.

Early Divisions

There were some who wanted Indonesia to be an Islamic republic, and there were others who didn't want their home territories to be part of Indonesia at all. The western-Java-based Darul Islam (House of Islam) wanted a society under Islamic law. It linked up with similar organisations in Kalimantan, Aceh and south Sulawesi to wage guerrilla war against the republic, which lasted until 1962 in western Java. In Maluku, Ambonese former soldiers of the Dutch colonial army declared an independent South Moluccas Republic in 1950. They were defeated within a few months.

Guided Democracy

Coalition governments drawn from diverse parties and factions never lasted long, and when the much-postponed parliamentary elections were finally held in 1955, no party won more than a quarter of the vote. Sukarno responded with 'Guided Democracy', effectively an uneasy coalition between the military, religious groups and communists, with increasing power concentrated in the hands of the president (ie himself). In 1959 Sukarno also took on the job of prime minister for good measure. The elected legislature was dissolved in 1960, and of the political parties only the PKI continued to have any clout.

Sukarno's growing accumulation of power was one factor behind regional rebellions in Sumatra and Sulawesi in 1958, led by senior military

At the entrance to a neighbourhood or village you may see an arch with the words 'Dirgahayu RI' painted across it. This translates as 'Long live the Republic of Indonesia'. The arches celebrate Independence Day, 17 August.

1950–62	1955	1957	1961–63
Armed movements challenge the republic. Darul Islam (House of Islam) wages guerilla war on several islands, continuing until 1962 in western Java. Regionalist rebellions break out in Sumatra and Sulawesi.	The PNI, regarded as Sukarno's party, tops the polls in the parliamentary elections, but no clear winner emerges. Short-lived coalition governments continue. The economy struggles after commodity prices drop.	Sukarno proclaims 'Guided Democracy', in the village tradition of achieving consensus through discussion. A military-Muslim-communist coalition replaces Western-style democracy.	With the economy in the doldrums, Sukarno is aggressive towards Netherlands New Guinea. Indonesia takes control there in 1963. Subsequent opposition from the local Papuan people is brutally put down.

and civilian figures. The rebels, who had backing from the CIA, were also opposed to the increasing influence of the communists, the corruption and inefficiency in central government, and the use of export earnings from the outer islands to import rice and consumer goods for Java. The rebellions were smashed within a few months and in response Sukarno forged a new alliance with Indonesia's army.

Monuments & Confrontations

Unable to lift the economy from the doldrums, Sukarno built a series of ostentatious nationalist monuments as substitutes for real development – such as Jakarta's National Monument (Monas, also dubbed 'Sukarno's last erection') and Mesjid Istiqlal. He diverted Indonesians' attention outwards with a lot of bluster and aggression towards the supposedly threatening remnants of Western imperialism around Indonesia: Dutch New Guinea and Malaysia.

The New Guinea issue had already led Indonesia to seize all Dutch assets in the country and expel 50,000 Dutch people in 1957–58 after the UN rejected Indonesian claims to Dutch New Guinea. Bolstered by Soviet military backing, Indonesia finally took control of the territory in 1963 after a few military sorties and, more importantly, US pressure on the Netherlands. Subsequent opposition from the local Papuan population was brutally put down.

Coup & Anti-Communist Purge

Meanwhile back in the heartland, the PKI was encouraging peasants to seize land without waiting for official redistribution, leading to violent clashes in eastern Java and Bali. By 1965 the PKI claimed three million members, controlled the biggest trade union organisation and the biggest peasant grouping, and had penetrated the government apparatus extensively. Sukarno saw it as a potential counterweight to the army, whose increasing power now had him worried, and decided to arm the PKI by creating a new militia. This led to heightened tensions with the regular armed forces, and rumours started to circulate of a planned communist coup.

On 1 October 1965, military rebels shot dead six top generals in and near Jakarta. General Suharto, head of the army's Strategic Reserve, quickly mobilised forces against the rebels and by the next day it was clear the putsch had failed. Just who was behind it still remains a mystery, but there's no mystery about its consequences. The armed forces under Suharto, and armed anti-communist civilians, took it as a cue to ruthlessly target both communists and supposed communists. By March 1966, 500,000 or more people were killed, chiefly in Java, Bali and Sumatra. The anti-communist purge provided cover for settling all sorts of old scores.

HISTORY 'BUNG' KARNO

The Asia-Africa Conference staged at Bandung in 1955 launched the Non-Aligned Movement, comprising countries that wanted to align with neither the USA nor the USSR. It also gave birth to the term Third World, originally meaning countries that belonged to neither Cold War bloc.

1963–66	1964–65	1965	1965–66
Sukarno stages *konfrontasi* (confrontation) with the newly formed Malaysia. Fighting takes place along the Indonesia–Malaysia border in Borneo. The communist party (PKI) organises land seizures by hungry peasants.	Worried by the military's power, Sukarno decides to arm the communist party by creating a new militia, heightening tensions with the regular forces. Rumours of a planned communist coup circulate.	On 1 October, military rebels shoot dead six top generals in and near Jakarta. General Suharto mobilises forces against the rebels; the coup fails after only a day of fighting.	The armed forces and armed anti-communist civilians take the attempted coup as a cue to slaughter communists and supposed communists. More than 500,000 are killed, chiefly in Java, Bali and Sumatra.

Sukarno Pushed Aside

While Sukarno remained president, Suharto set about manoeuvring himself into supreme power. On 11 March 1966, Suharto's troops surrounded Sukarno's presidential palace, and Sukarno signed the 11 March Order, permitting Suharto to act on his own initiative to restore order. Sukarno loyalists in the forces and cabinet were soon arrested, and a new six-man inner cabinet including Suharto was established. After further anti-Sukarno purges and demonstrations, the People's Consultative Assembly (MPR) named Suharto acting president in March 1967. A year later, with Sukarno now under house arrest, the MPR appointed Suharto president.

Sukarno died of natural causes in 1970. An inspirational orator and charismatic leader, he is still held in great affection and esteem by many older Indonesians, who often refer to him as Bung Karno – *bung* meaning 'buddy' or 'brother'. He was a flamboyant, complicated and highly intelligent character with a Javanese father and Balinese mother, and was fluent in several languages. His influences, apart from Islam, included Marxism, Javanese and Balinese mysticism, a mainly Dutch education and the theosophy movement. He had at least eight wives (up to four at once) at a time when polygamy was no longer very common in Indonesia. Throughout his political career he strove to unite Indonesians and, more than anyone else, he was the architect and creator of Indonesia.

Peter Weir's gripping *The Year of Living Dangerously* (1982), based on the eponymous novel by Australian Christopher Koch (1978), stars a youthful Mel Gibson as an Australian reporter caught up in Indonesia's 1965 upheavals.

'Pak' Harto

Once the dust had settled on the killing of communists and supposed communists, and a million or so political prisoners had been put behind bars, the 31 years of Suharto's rule were really one of the duller periods of Indonesian history. Such a tight lid was kept on opposition, protest and freedom of speech that there was almost no public debate. Under the New Order, as Suharto's regime was known, everybody just had to do what he and his generals told them to, if they weren't already dead or imprisoned.

Career Soldier

Whereas Sukarno had led with charisma, Suharto's speeches seemed designed to stifle discussion rather than inspire. 'Enigmatic' was one of the kinder epithets used in his obituaries when he died in 2008. The normally restrained *Economist* magazine called him a 'kleptocrat' and 'a cold-war monster', behind whose 'pudgily smooth, benign-looking face lay ruthless cruelty'. Suharto wielded a supreme talent for manipulating events in his own interests and outwitting opponents of all kinds.

Born in Java in 1921, he was always a soldier, from the day he joined the Dutch colonial army in his late teens. He rose quickly up the ranks of the Indonesian army in the 1950s, and was involved in putting down

1966–68 >	1967 >	1975 >	1979–84 >
When Suharto's troops surround his palace, Sukarno signs the 11 March Order (1966), permitting Suharto to act independently. After anti-Sukarno purges, the MPR names Suharto president (March 1968).	Suharto's 'New Order', supported by the West, holds Indonesia together under military dictatorship for the next 30 years. The economy develops, dissent is crushed and corruption rages.	Indonesia invades and annexes former Portuguese colony East Timor, where left-wing party Fretilin has won a power struggle. A 20-year guerilla war begins; over 125,000 die in fighting, famines and repression.	The government's transmigration program reaches its peak with almost 2.5 million people moving to outer islands from overpopulated Java, Bali and Madura before the program ends in 2000.

the South Moluccas and Darul Islam rebellions. He was transferred to a staff college after being implicated in opium and sugar smuggling in 1959, but in 1962 Sukarno appointed him to lead the military campaign against Dutch New Guinea.

The New Order
The New Order did give Indonesia stability of a sort, and a longish period of pretty steady economic development. Whereas Indonesians had thought of Sukarno as Bung Karno, Suharto was never more than the more formal Pak (father) Harto, but he liked to be thought of as Bapak Pembangunan – the Father of Development. Authoritarianism was considered the necessary price for economic progress.

Suharto and his generals believed Indonesia had to be kept together at all costs, which meant minimising political activity and squashing any potentially divisive movements – be they Islamic radicals, communists or the separatist rebels of Aceh, Papua (former Dutch New Guinea) and East Timor.

Suharto Inc
Near absolute power allowed the forces and Suharto's family and business associates to get away with almost anything. The army was not just a security force, it ran hundreds of businesses, legal and illegal, supposedly to supplement its inadequate funding from the government. Corruption went hand-in-hand with secrecy and most notorious was the Suharto family itself. Suharto's wife Ibu Tien (nicknamed Madam Tien Per Cent) controlled the state monopoly on the import and milling of wheat; his daughter Tutut won the 1987 contract to build the Jakarta toll road; his son Tommy gained a monopoly on the cloves used in Indonesia's super-popular *kretek* cigarettes in 1989.

In 1995 Indonesia was ranked the most corrupt of all the 41 countries assessed in the first-ever Corruption Index published by Transparency International (TI). In 2004 TI placed Suharto at the top of its all-time world corruption table, with an alleged embezzlement figure of between US$15 billion and US$35 billion from his 32 years in power.

Extending Indonesia
Suharto's regime saw to it that the former Dutch New Guinea stayed in Indonesia by staging a travesty of a confirmatory vote in 1969. Just over 1000 selected Papuan 'representatives' were pressured into voting unanimously for continued integration with Indonesia, in what was named the Act of Free Choice.

In 1975 the left-wing party Fretilin won a power struggle within the newly independent former Portuguese colony of East Timor. The western

Breaking the Silence (2012) is a memoir by 15 people who survived the anti-communist purges of 1965–66 when over 500,000 were killed. The acclaimed films *The Act of Killing* (2012) and *The Look of Silence* (2014) cover this same era, although censorship has prevented their showing in Indonesia.

1989	1990s	1997–98	1998
The Free Aceh Movement (GAM), founded in 1976, reemerges as a guerilla force, fighting for independence for the conservatively Islamic Sumatran region. An estimated 15,000 people die in the subsequent violence.	NGOs, many of them started by young middle-class Indonesians, emerge as a focus of dissent, campaigning on issues from peasant dispossessions to destructive logging and restrictions on Islamic organisations.	The Asian currency crisis savages Indonesia's economy. After troops kill four at a Jakarta demonstration in May 1998, rioting and looting cause an estimated 1200 deaths. Suharto quits on 21 May.	Vice-president BJ Habibie becomes president. He releases political prisoners and relaxes censorship, but the army kills at least 12 in a Jakarta student protest. Christian/Muslim violence erupts in Jakarta and Maluku.

part of Timor island, a former Dutch possession, was Indonesian. Horrified at the prospect of a left-wing government in a neighbouring state, Indonesia invaded and annexed East Timor. Fretilin kept up a guerrilla

UNREST AT THE EXTREMES

Two regions at opposite ends of Indonesia, Papua and Sumatra's Aceh, have resisted efforts to create a unified state over the last several decades, although Aceh now seems to have found a way to coexist.

Aceh

The conservatively Islamic, resource-rich region of Aceh was only brought under Dutch rule by a 35-year war ending in 1908. After the Dutch departed, Aceh wasn't happy about Indonesian rule either. The Free Aceh Movement (Gerakan Aceh Merdeka; GAM), founded in 1976, gathered steam after 1989, waging a guerrilla struggle for Acehnese independence. The 1990s saw Aceh under something close to military rule, with the population suffering from abuses by both sides. Peace talks collapsed in 2003 and Aceh was placed under martial law.

Everything changed with the tsunami on 26 December 2004, which wrought its biggest devastation on Aceh, killing some 170,000 people. The government was forced to allow foreign aid organisations into Aceh and to restart negotiations with GAM. A deal in 2005 formally ended three decades of armed struggle, which had cost an estimated 15,000 lives. The peace has held since, even if 2016 research suggested that a majority of Aceh people still want independence. Aceh's regional government has also become ever-more fundamentalist while adhering to the sharia law that was introduced in 2005. Public canings for various offences are on the increase, with two men receiving 85 lashes in 2017 for having sex.

Papua

Papua wasn't brought into the Dutch East Indies until late in the colonial period. Papuan people are culturally distinct from other Indonesians, being of Melanesian heritage and having had very limited contact with the outside world until the 20th century. Today most of them are Christian. Resistance to Indonesian rule has continued ever since Sukarno's takeover in 1963, in the form of sporadic guerrilla attacks by the Free Papua Organisation (Organisasi Papua Merdeka; OPM). The Indonesian army keeps a large number of troops in the province and there are sporadic skirmishes with rebels and regular reports of human-rights abuses by international groups such as Human Rights Watch.

A resource-rich region, Papua is seen by many Indonesians as ripe for exploitation. About half the population is Indonesian – primarily migrants – and this adds to Jakarta's reasons for keeping Papua close. That the economy and administration are dominated by non-Papuans fuels indigenous people's grievances and makes an Aceh-type autonomy solution impossible. Pro-independence sentiment among Papuans is high.

1999	Jun–Oct 1999	1999–2001	2001
Some 78% vote for independence in East Timor. Militias backed by Indonesian military conduct a terror campaign before and after the vote. The region finally achieves independence in 2002.	Following Indonesia's first free election since 1955, Abdurrahman Wahid of the country's largest Islamic organisation, Nahdlatul Ulama (Rise of the Scholars), becomes president as leader of a multiparty coalition.	Wahid tries to reform government, tackle corruption, reduce military power, bring Suharto to justice and address the grievances of Aceh and Papua. But his efforts are hamstrung by opponents.	Violence erupts in Kalimantan between indigenous Dayaks and Madurese migrants. Over a million people are displaced by conflicts in Timor-Leste, Maluku, Kalimantan and elsewhere. Wahid is deposed.

struggle and at least 125,000 Timorese died in fighting, famines and repression over the next 2½ decades.

The End of the New Order

The end of the New Order was finally precipitated by the Asian currency crisis of 1997, which savaged Indonesia's economy. Millions lost their jobs and rising prices sparked riots. Suharto faced unprecedented widespread calls for his resignation. Anti-government rallies spread from universities to city streets, and when four students at Jakarta's Trisakti University were shot dead by troops in May 1998, the city erupted in rioting and looting, leaving an estimated 1200 people dead. Even Suharto's own ministers called for him to go, and Suharto finally resigned shortly after.

The Road to Democracy

Suharto's fall ushered in a period known as *reformasi* (reform), three tumultuous years in which elective democracy, free expression and human rights all advanced, and attempts were made to deal with the grievances of East Timor, Aceh and Papua. It was an era with many positives and some disasters and was ultimately a time when Indonesia's democracy emerged.

Of 18 people tried by an Indonesian human-rights court for abuses in East Timor in 1999, only militia leader Eurico Guterres was convicted. His conviction for a massacre of 12 people was quashed by the Indonesian Supreme Court in 2008.

The Habibie Presidency

Suharto's vice-president BJ Habibie stepped up as president when Suharto resigned. Habibie released political prisoners, relaxed censorship and promised elections, but he still tried to ban demonstrations and reaffirmed the political role of the unpopular army. Tensions between Christians and Muslims in some parts of Indonesia also erupted into violence – especially in Maluku, where thousands died in incidents between early 1999 and 2002.

The Wahid & Megawati Presidencies

Indonesia's first free parliamentary elections for 44 years took place in 1999. No party received a clear mandate, but the MPR elected Muslim preacher Abdurrahman Wahid president as leader of a coalition. The eccentric Wahid, from the country's largest Islamic organisation, Nahdlatul Ulama (Rise of the Scholars), was blind, had suffered two strokes and disliked formal dress and hierarchies. He embarked on an ambitious program to rein in the military, reform the legal and financial systems, promote religious tolerance, tackle corruption and resolve the problems of Aceh and Papua. Unsurprisingly, all this upset everybody who was anybody, and in July 2001 the MPR dismissed Wahid over alleged incompetence and corruption.

Vice-president Megawati of the Indonesian Democratic Party – Struggle (PDI-P) took over as president in Wahid's place. Supported by many

2001–04	2002–05	2004	Oct 2004
Vice-president Megawati Sukarnoputri, Sukarno's daughter, leading the PDI-P (Indonesian Democratic Party – Struggle) and supported by conservative elements, succeeds Wahid.	Terrorist bombs in Kuta, Bali, in 2002 kill over 200, mainly foreign tourists. The Islamic militant group Jemaah Islamiah is blamed. Another series of bombs in Bali in 2005 kills 20.	Anticorruption group Transparency International puts Suharto at the top of its all-time world corruption table, with an alleged embezzlement figure of between US$15 billion and US$35 billion from his 32 years in power.	In Indonesia's first direct presidential elections, Susilo Bambang Yudhoyono (SBY) of the new Democratic Party, a former general regarded as a liberal, wins a run-off vote against Megawati.

EAST TIMOR TROUBLES

Indonesia, under President Habibie, agreed to a UN-organised independence referendum in East Timor, where human-rights abuses, reported by Amnesty International among others, had blackened Indonesia's name internationally. In the 1999 vote, 78% of East Timorese chose independence. But the event was accompanied by a terror campaign by pro-Indonesia militia groups and Indonesian security forces, which according to Amnesty International killed an estimated 1300 people, and left much of East Timor's infrastructure ruined. The region finally gained full independence in 2002, and is now officially known as the Democratic Republic of Timor-Leste.

conservative, old-guard elements, Megawati – daughter of the legendary Sukarno – had none of her father's flair or vision and did little for reform in her three years in office.

The SBY Era

In 2004 Indonesia had its first-ever direct popular vote for president. Susilo Bambang Yudhoyono (SBY), leading the new Democratic Party (formed as his personal political vehicle), won in a run-off vote against Megawati. A popular and pragmatic politician, SBY quickly won favour by making sure foreign aid could get to tsunami-devastated Aceh and sealing a peace deal with Aceh's GAM rebels.

SBY's unspectacular but stable presidency saw the military forced to divest most of their business enterprises and edge away from politics (they lost their reserved seats in parliament in 2004). There was also progress against corruption. A former head of Indonesia's central bank, an MP, a governor of Aceh province and a mayor of Medan were all among those jailed thanks to the Corruption Eradication Commission, established in 2002, although no really big names were ensnared.

Fears of an upsurge in Islamic radicalism, especially after the Bali and Jakarta terrorist bombings of 2002–05, proved largely unfounded. The great majority of Indonesian Muslims are moderate and while Islamic parties receive a sizeable share of the vote in elections, they can only do so by remaining in the political mainstream.

Indonesians clearly appreciated the stability and nonconfrontational style of SBY's presidency, and his successful handling of the economy, for they reelected him in 2009 with over 60% of the vote. Interestingly neither religion nor ethnicity played a major part in determining how people voted, suggesting that many Indonesians valued democracy, peace and economic progress above sectarian or regional issues. Predictions that hard-line Islamist parties would make huge gains proved false when they received only 8% of the vote.

Dec 2004	2006	2009	2012
Over 200,000 Indonesians die in the 26 December tsunami that devastates large areas of Sumatra, especially Aceh. SBY restarts peace talks there, leading to a peace deal in 2005.	Bantul, near Yogyakarta, is hit by an earthquake on 27 May – 5800 die and 200,000 are left homeless across Central Java. Another 700 die in a 17 July quake.	SBY is reelected president with over 60% of the vote.	Bali's ancient rice terraces and irrigation system (subak) gain Unesco World Heritage status, the first such designation in Indonesia since 2004 and only the eighth overall.

Meanwhile, Indonesia's disasters – natural and otherwise – continued. In 2009, an earthquake killed over 1100 around Padang in West Sumatra. In 2010, an earthquake off the nearby coast killed 435 and spawned a tsunami that hit the Mentawai Islands. Over the same two-year period, there were eight fatal plane crashes (over 230 dead) and two ferries sank (over 275 dead). An SBY-ordered review of transport safety, begun in 2007, made little difference.

Joko Ascends

Given that destructive colonialism, revolution, mass slaughter, ethnic warfare, dictatorship and more have been part of daily life in Indonesia in just the past 100 years, it's remarkable that recent elections have been so peaceful. The 2009 national elections were a watershed. More than a dozen parties waged high-energy campaigns. Rallies throughout the myriad islands were passionate and vibrant. Yet what happened in the end? The incumbent, SBY and his Democratic Party, won; Indonesians chose to go with the status quo.

Not bad given that it wasn't that long ago, at the millennium, when there was blood in the streets from Lombok to the Malukus as religious and political factions settled scores and simply ran amok. Regional elections across the archipelago have also gone off without a hitch several times in recent years. All this set the stage in 2014 for Indonesia's most dramatic presidential election to date.

Representing Indonesia's old guard of wealth and the military was Prabowo Subianto, a former general who has long been dogged by allegations of human-rights abuses during his time in East Timor and during the 1998 riots that led to the resignation of Suharto. Running against him was Joko Widodo, the populist mayor of Jakarta and a man possibly overburdened with platitudes such as 'humble', 'man of the people' and 'Obama-like'.

The election was framed as old versus new, and it attracted huge interest not only across Indonesia but across the world. This would be the greatest test yet of Indonesia's status as the world's third-largest democracy (India is first followed by the US). Jokowi – as he's nearly universally known – captured the imagination of many voters fed up with the nation's endemic corruption and concentration of power among a tiny elite. There were even predictions of a Joko landslide; he won on 9 July with just over 53% of the vote to Prabowo's nearly 47%.

Despite rumblings from Prabowo's camp that they would challenge the results, the election was finally certified two weeks later. It seemed the old guard had been defeated in fair and peaceful elections, although this simple line doesn't necessarily hold up given that Joko's vice president is Jusuf Kalla, who held the same post under SBY from 2004–09,

> From 2000 several attacks in Indonesia (including the 2002 and 2005 Bali bombings) were blamed on Islamic terrorist group Jemaah Islamiah. Dozens of suspects were arrested or imprisoned. Abu Bakar Bashir, a radical cleric alleged to be the mastermind behind the attacks, received a 15-year jail sentence in 2011.

2014	Jul 2017	May 2018	Jun 2018
Joko Widodo is elected president with 53% of the vote.	President Joko Widodo signs a decree giving the government the power to ban or disband radical Islamic groups.	A group of suicide bombers, including two children, attack churches and the police headquarters in Surabaya, Java's second city, resulting in 28 fatalities.	An overloaded and unlicensed ferry sinks on Lake Toba in Sumatra with the loss of 167 lives, Indonesia's worst maritime disaster since 2009.

and many other old-guard stalwarts found their way into the administration. Interestingly, the coalition led by Prabowo won nearly 60% of the seats in the legislature, the People's Representative Council. At least at first they seemed content to work with Joko, although the long-term prospects of such cooperative spirit were by no means assured.

The Joko Era

Joko's record in power has been mixed, but there is little doubt that he remains popular among Indonesians. He has pushed through infrastructure projects in an effort to boost the economy and connect his far-flung nation, while also allocating funds for rural development and speeding up the distribution of land ownership certificates. But Joko has been accused of failing to address rising income inequality. The gap between the rich and poor in Indonesia is extreme, with 1% of the population owning 49% of all wealth, according to a 2017 report by Oxfam. Overseas, Joko has been criticised for his staunch defence of Indonesia's continuing use of capital punishment.

Regarded as a largely secular Muslim who has vowed to maintain Indonesia's multifaith society, Joko has also been targeted by hardliners for not being Islamic enough. The 2017 imprisonment for blasphemy of Joko ally and former Jakarta governor Basuki Tjahaja Purnama, an ethnic Chinese Christian, highlighted how Islamic conservatism is on the rise in Indonesia.

Joko burnished his Muslim credentials by announcing that his running mate in the April 2019 election would be 75-year-old cleric and Islamic scholar Ma'ruf Amin. As expected, Joko triumphed in the election over Prabowo Subianto, who Joko also defeated in the 2014 election. Joko won more votes – 85 million – than any previous single candidate in a democratic election in Indonesia.

Almost immediately, Joko revealed an ambitious US$32.7 billion plan to shift Indonesia's capital from Jakarta to a new city to be built in East Kalimantan Province on the island of Borneo. Civil servants are expected to start transferring to the as yet unnamed new capital in 2024, with the city set to be finished by 2028. The move is a response to Jakarta's unenviable status as the fastest-sinking city in the world, as well as fitting in with Joko's determination to address the striking economic imbalance between prosperous Java and the rest of Indonesia.

But Joko's efforts to create jobs and encourage more foreign investment ran into trouble in October 2020, when people across Indonesia took to the streets in sometimes violent protests against a new job creation law. Critics claim the new legislation will erode worker rights and further weaken Indonesia's already fragile environmental protection laws.

Joko Widodo is the seventh Indonesian president but the first not to be a member of the political or military elite.

The word *sembako* refers to Indonesia's nine essential culinary ingredients: rice, sugar, eggs, meat, flour, corn, fuel, cooking oil and salt. When any of these become unavailable or more costly, repercussions can be felt right through to the presidency.

Sep 2018	Apr 2019	Aug 2019	Oct 2020
An earthquake and subsequent tsunami in central Sulawesi kills over 2000 people and injures more than 10,000.	In a repeat of the 2014 general election, Joko Widodo defeats retired general Probowo Subianto to win a second term as president.	Indonesia announces that it will move its capital from Jakarta to a new city to be built in East Kalimantan Province on the island of Borneo by 2028.	Protests erupt across Indonesia in response to a controversial new job creation law that its opponents say will restrict worker rights.

Culture

Across Indonesia's 17,000-odd islands you can hear over 300 different languages spoken and find a range of people from hipsters in Jakarta to communities speaking tribal dialects and following animist traditions deep in the mountains of West Timor. And then there are the varied cultural expressions, from Bali's incredible richness to the buttoned-down conservatism of Aceh. Yet despite this diversity, almost everybody can speak one language: Bahasa Indonesia, the tongue that helps unify this sprawling collection of peoples.

National Identity

Indonesia comprises a massively diverse range of societies and cultures; the differences between, say, the Sumbanese and Sundanese are as marked as those between the Swedes and Sicilians. Even so, a strong national Indonesian identity has emerged, originally through the struggle for independence and, following that, through education programs and the promotion of Bahasa Indonesia as the national language. This is despite the fact that Indonesia continues to be stretched by opposing forces: 'strict' Islam versus 'moderate' Islam, Islam versus Christianity versus Hinduism, outer islands versus Java, country versus city, modern versus traditional, rich versus poor.

One Culture or Many?

The differences within Indonesian culture may challenge social cohesion and at times have been used as an excuse to incite conflict, but the nation still endures. And, with notable exceptions such as Papua, the bonds have grown stronger, with the notion of an Indonesian identity overlapping rather than supplanting the nation's many preexisting regional cultures. The national slogan *Bhinneka Tunggal Ika* (Unity in Diversity) – even though its words are old Javanese – has been adopted by Indonesians across widely varying ethnic and social standpoints.

Nationalism and Ethnic Conflict in Indonesia (2004) by Jacques Bertrand remains a solid primer on the reasons behind violence in areas such as Maluku and Kalimantan.

Religion as Culture

One cultural element that bridges both the regional and national is religion – the Pancasila principle of belief in a god holds firm. Though Indonesia is predominantly Islamic, in many places Islam is interwoven with traditional customs, giving it unique qualities and characteristics. Some areas are Christian or animist and, to leaven the mix, Bali has its own unique brand of Hinduism. Religion plays a role in the everyday:

THE POWER OF SMILES

A smile goes a very long way in Indonesia. It's said Indonesians have a smile for every emotion, and keeping one on your face even in a difficult situation helps to avoid giving offence. Indonesians generally seek consensus rather than disagreement, so maintaining a sense of accord, however tenuous, is a good idea in all dealings. Anger or aggressive behaviour is considered poor form and a loss of face.

mosques and *musholla* (prayer rooms) are in constant use, and the vibrant Hindu ceremonies of Bali are a daily occurrence, to the delight of visitors.

Trends & Traditions

Smartphones, huge malls, techno-driven nightclubs and other facets of international modernity are common in Indonesia. But while the main cities and tourist resorts can appear technologically rich, other areas remain untouched. And even where modernisation has taken hold, it's clear that Indonesians have a very traditionalist heart. As well as adhering to religious and ethnic traditions, Indonesians also maintain social customs. Politeness to strangers is a deeply ingrained habit throughout most of the archipelago. Elders are still accorded great respect. When visiting someone's home, elders are always greeted first, and often customary permission to depart is also offered. This can occur whether in a high-rise in Medan or a hut in the Baliem Valley.

Lifestyle

Daily life for Indonesians has changed rapidly in the last decade or two. These days, many people live away from their home region and the role of women has extended well beyond domestic duties to include careers and studies.

Family Life

The importance of the family remains high. This is evident during such festivals as Idul Fitri (Lebaran, the end of the Islamic fasting month), when highways become gridlocked, ferries get jammed and planes fill with those returning home to loved ones. Even at weekends, many travel for hours to spend a day with their relatives. In many ways, the notions of family and regional identity have become more pronounced: as people move away from small-scale communities and enter the milieu of the cities, the sense of belonging becomes more valued.

SMALL TALK
....

One thing that takes many visitors by surprise in Indonesia is what may seem like overinquisitiveness from complete strangers. Questions from them might include the following.

➤ *Dari mana?* (Where do you come from?)

➤ *Mau kemana?* (Where are you going?)

➤ *Tinggal dimana?* (Where are you staying?)

➤ *Jalan sendiri?* (Are you travelling alone?)

➤ *Sudah kawin?* (Are you married?)

➤ *Anak-anak ada?* (Do you have children?)

Visitors can find these questions intrusive or irritating, and in tourist areas they may just be a prelude to a sales pitch, but more often than not they are simply polite greetings and an expression of interest in a foreigner. A short answer or a Bahasa Indonesia greeting, with a smile, is a polite and adequate response. Try the following.

➤ *Jalan-jalan* (Walking around)

➤ *Saya pergi dulu* (literally 'I go first' nicely says that you can't pause for a pitch)

If you get into a slightly longer conversation, it's proper to ask some of the same questions in return. When you've had enough chatter, you can answer the question 'Where are you going?' even if it hasn't been asked.

Village Life
Beyond family, the main social unit is the village, whether it is in the country or manifests in the form of a suburb or neighbourhood in an urban area. Less than half the population still lives in rural areas (it was 80% in 1975), where labour in the fields, the home or the market is the basis of daily life, as is school for younger Indonesians – though not for as many as might be hoped. Nine out of 10 children complete the five years of primary schooling, but barely six out of 10 get through secondary school. Kids from poorer families have to start supplementing the family income at an early age.

The village spirit can be found on Jakarta's backstreets, which, for example, are home to tight-knit neighbourhoods where kids run from house to house and everyone knows who owns which chicken. A sense of community may also evolve in a *kos* (apartment with shared facilities), where tenants, far from their families, come together for meals and companionship.

Traditional Life
For the many Indonesians who still live in their home regions, customs and traditions remain a part of the everyday: the Toraja of Sulawesi continue to build traditional houses due to their social importance; the focus of a Sumbanese village remains the gravestones of their ancestors due to the influence they are believed to have in daily happenings. These aren't customs offered attention once a year – they are a part of life. And many Dayaks of Kalimantan still live in communal longhouses sheltering 20 families or more.

Although modernity has found purchase across much of the nation, age-old traditions still underpin life: Bali, for example, still scrupulously observes its annual day of silence, Nyepi (Balinese Lunar New Year), when literally all activity stops and everyone stays at home (or in their hotels) so that evil spirits will think the island uninhabited and leave it alone.

LGBT Life
Contradictions run through the status of the LGBT+ community in Indonesia. Indonesians of both sexes are actively gay and repression is mostly absent. But this isn't true across all the archipelago, especially in conservative Aceh where in 2017 two gay men were publicly flogged in Banda Aceh after being caught having sex in a private home.

Positive recognition of gay identity or gay rights is largely missing. *Waria* (transgender or transvestite) performers and prostitutes have quite a high profile. Otherwise gay behaviour is, by and large, accepted without being particularly approved of. Bali, with its big international scene, and some Javanese cities have the most open gay life – although a gay wedding ceremony at a resort on Bali in 2015 drew an official rebuke.

Multiculturalism
Indonesia is a country of literally hundreds of cultures. Every one of its 700-plus languages denotes, at least to some extent, a different culture. They range from the matrilineal Minangkabau of Sumatra and the artistic Hindu Balinese, to the seafaring Bugis and buffalo-sacrificing Toraja of Sulawesi and Papua's penis-gourd-wearing Dani, to name but a few. Indonesia's island nature and rugged, mountainous terrain has meant that groups of people often developed in near isolation from each other, resulting in an extraordinary differentiation of culture and language across the archipelago. Even in densely populated Java there are distinct groups, such as the Badui, who withdrew to the western

CULTURE MULTICULTURALISM

Riri Riza's *Gie* (2005), the story an ethnic Chinese anti-dictatorship activist, was submitted for consideration in the Best Foreign Film category of the Academy Awards. His *3 Hari Untuk Selamanya* (Three Days to Forever, 2007) is a classic road movie about a journey from Jakarta to Yogyakarta.

MIGRATION & HOMOGENISATION

Ethnic and cultural tensions in Indonesia have often been fuelled by *transmigrasi* (transmigration), the government-sponsored program of migration from more populated islands (Java, Bali and Madura) to less populated ones such as Kalimantan, Sumatra, Sulawesi and Papua. Over eight million people were relocated between 1950 and 2000. Local residents have often resented their marginalisation due to a sudden influx of people with little regard or use for local cultures and traditions. That the newcomers have the full sponsorship of the government adds to the dissatisfaction.

highlands as Islam spread through the island and have had little contact with outsiders.

One Nation, Many Cultures

The notion that Indonesia's diverse peoples could form one nation is a relatively young one, originating in the later part of the Dutch colonial era. Indonesia's 20th-century founding fathers knew that if a country of such diverse culture and religion was to hold together, it needed special handling. They fostered Indonesian nationalism and a national language (Bahasa Indonesia, spoken today by almost all Indonesians but the mother tongue for only about 20% of them). They rejected ideas that Indonesia should be a federal republic (potentially centrifugal), or a state subject to the law of Islam, even though this is the religion of the great majority. Today most Indonesian citizens (with the chief exceptions of many Papuans and Acehnese) are firmly committed to the idea of Indonesia, even if there is a lingering feeling that in some ways the country is a 'Javanese empire'.

Religion

Indonesia's constitution affirms that the state is based on a belief in 'the One and Only God'; yet it also, rather contradictorily, guarantees 'freedom of worship, each according to his/her own religion or belief'. In practice, this translates into a requirement to follow one of the officially accepted 'religions', of which there are now six: Islam, Catholicism, Protestantism, Hinduism, Buddhism and Confucianism.

In many Indonesian hotel rooms you'll notice a small arrow pointing in a seemingly random direction on the ceiling; it's actually indicating the direction of Mecca for Muslims who want to pray but can't get to a mosque.

Islam is the predominant religion, with followers making up about 88% of the population. In Java, pilgrims still visit hundreds of holy places where spiritual energy is believed to be concentrated. Christians make up about 10% of the population, in scattered areas spread across the archipelago. Bali's Hindus comprise about 1.5% of the population.

Nevertheless, old beliefs persist. The earliest Indonesians were animists who practised ancestor and spirit worship. When Hinduism and Buddhism and, later, Islam and Christianity spread into the archipelago, they were layered on top of this spiritual base.

Islam

Islam arrived in Indonesia with Muslim traders from the Arabian Peninsula and India as early as the 7th century AD, within decades of the Prophet Muhammad receiving the word of Allah (God) in Mecca. The first Indonesian rulers to convert to Islam were in the small North Sumatran ports of Lamreh and Pasai in the 13th century. Gradually over the following two centuries, then more rapidly, other Indonesian states adopted Islam. The religion initially spread along sea-trade routes, and the conversion of Demak, Tuban, Gresik and Cirebon, on Java's north coast, in the late 15th century was an important step in its progress.

The first Indonesian rulers to adopt Islam chose to do so from contact with foreign Muslim communities. Some other states were converted by conquest. Java's first Islamic leaders have long been venerated and mythologised as the nine *walis* (saints). Many legends are told about their feats of magic or war, and pilgrims visit their graves despite the official proscription of saint worship by Islam.

Customs

Today Indonesia has the largest Muslim population of any country in the world and the role Islam should play in its national life is constantly debated. Mainstream Indonesian Islam is moderate. Muslim women are not segregated nor, in most of the country, do they have to wear the *jilbab* (head covering), although this has recently become more common. Muslim men are allowed to marry two women but must have the consent of their first wife. Even so, polygamy in Indonesia is very rare. Many pre-Islamic traditions and customs remain in place. The Minangkabau society of Sumatra, for example, is strongly Islamic but remains matrilineal according to tradition.

Islam requires that all boys be circumcised, and in Indonesia this is usually done between the ages of six and 11. Muslims observe the fasting month of Ramadan. Friday afternoons are officially set aside for believers to worship, and all government offices and many businesses are closed as a result. In accordance with Islamic teaching, millions of Indonesians have made the pilgrimage to Mecca.

RAMADAN

One of the most important months of the Muslim calendar is the fasting month of Ramadan. As a profession of faith and spiritual discipline, Muslims abstain from food, drink, cigarettes and other worldly desires (including sex) from sunrise to sunset. However, many of the casually devout will find loopholes in the strictures.

Ramadan is often preceded by a cleansing ceremony, Padusan, to prepare for the coming fast (*puasa*). Traditionally, during Ramadan people get up at 3am or 4am to eat (this meal is called *sahur*) and then fast until sunset. Special prayers are said at mosques and at home.

The first day of the 10th month of the Muslim calendar is the end of Ramadan, called Idul Fitri or Lebaran. Mass prayers are held in the early morning, followed by two days of feasting. Extracts from the Koran are read and religious processions take place. During this time of mutual forgiveness, gifts are exchanged and pardon is asked for past wrongdoing.

During Ramadan, many restaurants and warungs are closed in Muslim regions of Indonesia. Those owned by non-Muslims will be open, but in deference to those fasting, they may have covered overhangs or will otherwise appear shut. In the big cities, many businesses are open and fasting is less strictly observed. Street stalls, mall food courts and warungs all come alive for the evening meal.

Though not all Muslims can keep to the privations of fasting, the overwhelming majority do, and you should respect their values. Do not eat, drink or smoke in public unless you see others doing so.

Note that for a week before and a week after the official two-day Idul Fitri holiday, transport is chaotic; don't even consider travelling during this time as roads and buses are jammed, flights full and ferries bursting. You will be better off in non-Muslim areas – such as Bali, east Nusa Tenggara, Maluku or Papua – but even these areas have significant Muslim populations. Plan well, find yourself an idyllic spot and stay put.

Ramadan and Idul Fitri move back 10 days or so every year, according to the Muslim calendar.

BELIEFS OUTSIDE THE OFFICIAL BOX

Fascinating elements of animism, mostly concerned with the spirits of the dead or fertility rituals, survive alongside the major religions all over Indonesia today – especially among peoples in fairly remote places. These belief systems often involve elaborate rituals, which have become tourist attractions in their own right, and include the following.

➡ Nusa Tenggara's Sumbanese (p405)

➡ Kalimantan's Dayaks (p609)

➡ Sumatra's Bataks (p532)

➡ Sumatra's Mentawaians (p569)

➡ Sumatra's Minangkabau (p560)

➡ Sumatra's Niassans (p536)

➡ Sulawesi's Toraja (p682)

➡ Papua's Dani (p501)

➡ Papua's Asmat (p508)

Islamic Laws

An attempt by some Islamic parties to make sharia (Islamic religious law) a constitutional obligation for all Indonesian Muslims was rejected by the national parliament in 2002. Sharia was firmly outlawed under the Suharto dictatorship, but elements of it have since been introduced in some cities and regions. Aceh was permitted to introduce strict sharia under its 2005 peace deal with the government. In Aceh gambling, alcohol and public affection between the sexes are banned, as are same-sex relationships. Some offenders receive corporal punishment. The *jilbab* is also compulsory for Muslim women. Public displays of intimacy, alcohol and 'prostitute-like appearance' are outlawed in the factory town of Tangerang on Jakarta's outskirts.

Recent elections have revealed that the great majority of Indonesia's Muslims are moderates and do not want an Islamic state. Neither of Indonesia's two biggest Muslim organisations, the traditionalist Nahdlatul Ulama (Rise of the Scholars) and the modernist Muhammadiyah, which have about 75 million members between them, now seeks an Islamic state.

Nevertheless, a more fundamentalist form of Islam is gaining some traction. While regions including Sumbawa, West Java and notably Aceh are quite conservative, changes are coming elsewhere. There are reports of mandatory Islamisation of young girls in some parts of West Papua and Sumatra, and in 2017 Jakarta's governor, a Christian of Chinese descent, was jailed for two years for blasphemy against Islam.

In the Shadow of Swords (2005) by Sally Neighbour investigates the rise of terrorism in Indonesia and beyond, from an Australian perspective.

Militant Islam

Militant Islamist groups that have made headlines with violent actions speak for only small minorities. Jemaah Islamiah was responsible for the 2002 Bali bombings and other acts of terror. The Indonesian government has captured or killed many of its principals, including cleric Abu Bakar Bashir who was jailed for 15 years in 2011. But suicide bomb attacks on churches in Surabaya in 2018 indicate that radical Islam retains a presence in Indonesia.

Christianity

The Portuguese introduced Roman Catholicism to Indonesia in the 16th century, but their influence was never strong. Protestantism arrived with the Dutch but missionary efforts came only after the Dutch set about establishing direct colonial rule throughout Indonesia in the 19th century.

Animist areas were targeted, and missionaries set about their work with zeal in parts of Nusa Tenggara, Maluku, Kalimantan, Papua, Sumatra and Sulawesi. A significant number of Chinese Indonesians converted to Christianity during the Suharto era.

Protestants (about 7% of the population) outnumber Catholics. The main Protestant populations are in the Batak area of Sumatra, the Minahasa and Toraja areas of Sulawesi, Timor and Sumba in Nusa Tenggara, Papua, parts of Maluku, and Dayak areas of Kalimantan. Catholics comprise 3% of the population and are most numerous in Papua and Flores.

Hinduism & Buddhism

These belief systems of Indian origin have a key place in Indonesian history but are now practised by relatively small numbers. Arriving with Indian traders by the 5th century AD, Hinduism and Buddhism came to be adopted by many kingdoms, especially in the western half of Indonesia. All the most powerful states in the archipelago until the 15th century – such as Sriwijaya, based in southeast Sumatra, and Majapahit, in eastern Java – were Hindu, Buddhist or a combination of the two, usually in fusion with earlier animist beliefs. Indonesian Hinduism tended to emphasise worship of the god Shiva, the destroyer, perhaps because this was closer to existing fertility worship and the appeasement of malevolent spirits. Buddhism, more a philosophy than a religion, shunned the Hindu pantheon of gods in its goal of escaping from suffering by overcoming desire.

Though Islam later replaced them almost everywhere in Indonesia, Hinduism and Buddhism left a powerful imprint on local culture and spirituality. This is most obvious today in the continued use of stories from the Hindu Ramayana and Mahabharata epics in Javanese and Balinese dance and theatre – as well as in major monuments such as the great Javanese temple complexes of Borobudur (Buddhist) and Prambanan (Hindu). Bali survived as a stronghold of Hinduism because nobles and intelligentsia of the Majapahit kingdom congregated there after the rest of their realm fell to Islam in the 15th century.

> Outside India, Hindus predominate only in Nepal and Bali. The Hinduism of Bali is literally far removed from that of India.

CULTURE RELIGION

ANTIPORN

One issue that continues to stir emotions in Indonesia is the 'antipornography' law introduced in 2008 after years of debate. Promoted by Islamic parties, the law has a very wide definition of pornography that can potentially be applied to every kind of visual, textual or sound communication or performance, and even conversations and gestures. Many traditional forms of behaviour across the archipelago are technically illegal – from wearing penis gourds on Papua to the modest gyrations of traditional Javanese dancers (to say nothing of the brazenly topless on Bali's beaches).

Exactly what the antiporn law means is ill-defined. Behaviour not sanctioned in some areas continues in others. And there have been assurances from the government that Balinese dance and other cultural forms of expression across the archipelago are safe from the law's ill-defined strictures. Opponents of the law include some secular political parties as well as women's, human-rights, regional, Christian, artists' and performers' groups and tourism-industry interests.

Many internet providers block a wide range of sites deemed immoral, and there has been a general chilling of freedom of expression. In 2011, the popular singer Ariel (aka Nazril Irham) was sentenced to more than three years in prison when a sex tape he made ended up on the internet, after his laptop was stolen.

Now it is members of Indonesia's LGBT community who are increasingly the victims of the antiporn law. Gay parties in Jakarta and Surabaya have been raided by police, and some men charged with violating the antiporn legislation.

Most Buddhists in Indonesia today are Chinese. Their numbers have been estimated at more than two million, although this may come down at the next count following the reinstatement of Confucianism as an official religion in 2006. Confucianism, the creed of many Chinese Indonesians, was delisted in the Suharto era, forcing many Chinese to convert to Buddhism or Christianity.

Women in Indonesia

For Indonesian women, the challenges of balancing traditional roles and the opportunities and responsibilities of the modern era are most pronounced. Many are well educated and in important jobs; women are widely represented in bureaucracy and business, although the general elections of 2009 and 2014 saw women win only about 18% of the seats, far below a goal of 30% professed by some of the parties. Two-income households are increasingly common and often a necessity; however, women typically still see roles such as housekeeping and child rearing as their domain.

As a predominantly Islamic society Indonesia remains male-oriented, though women are not cloistered or required to observe *purdah* (the practice of screening women from strangers by means of a curtain or all-enveloping clothes). The *jilbab* has become more common, but it does not necessarily mean that women who wear it have a subservient personality or even deep Islamic faith. It is often a means of deflecting unwanted male attention.

It's also increasingly common to see women in Muslim areas wearing headscarves even as the popular media typically shows women without.

Tenuous Gains?

Despite the social liberation of women visible in urban areas, there are those who see the advances made by conservative Islam in the past decade as a threat to women. Pressure on women to dress and behave conservatively comes from elements of sharia law that have been introduced in areas such as Aceh.

An attempt to reform family law in 2005 and give greater rights to women never even got to be debated in parliament after Islamic fundamentalists threatened those who were drafting it. Women still cannot legally be heads of households, which presents particular problems for Indonesia's estimated six million single mothers.

Sport

Soccer and badminton are the national sporting obsessions. Indonesian badminton players won the mixed-doubles gold medal at the 2016 Rio Olympics.

Although international success has eluded Indonesian soccer (football) teams, it is played with fervour on grassy verges across the archipelago.

Many regions, particularly those with a history of tribal warfare, stage traditional contests of various kinds to accompany weddings, harvest festivals and other ceremonial events. Mock battles are sometimes staged in Papua, *caci* whip fights are a speciality in Flores and men fight with sticks and shields in Lombok, but the most spectacular ceremonial fight is seen during Sumba's Pasola festival, where every February and March horse riders in traditional dress hurl spears at each other.

In Bali and other islands, the real sporting passion is reserved for cockfighting, which means the spectators (virtually all men) watch and bet while birds brawl. Although nominally illegal, many matches are held openly.

CULTURE WOMEN IN INDONESIA

Author Djenar Maesa Ayu shook up Indonesia's literary scene with her candid portrayal of the injustices tackled by women. Her books include *Mereka Bilang, Saya Monyet* (They Say I'm a Monkey, 2001), *Nayla* (2005) and *1 Perempuan, 14 Laki-laki* (1 Woman, 14 Men, 2011).

Jakartacasual (http://jakarta casual.blogspot. com) is a great English-language source for Indonesian soccer news.

Arts & Crafts

Indonesians are very artistic people. This is most obvious in Bali, where the creation of beauty is part of the fabric of daily life, but it's apparent throughout the archipelago in music, dance, theatre, painting and in handmade artisanry, of which every different island or area seems to have its own original form.

Arts

Theatre & Dance

Drama and dance in Indonesia are intimately connected in the hybrid form that is best known internationally: Balinese dancing. The colourful Balinese performances – at times supremely graceful, at others almost slapstick – are dances that tell stories, sometimes from the Indian Ramayana or Mahabharata epics. Balinese dance is performed both as entertainment and as a religious ritual, playing an important part in temple festivals.

Java's famed *wayang* (puppet) theatre also tells Ramayana and Mahabharata stories, through the use of shadow puppets, three-dimensional wooden puppets, or real people dancing the *wayang* roles. It too can still have ritual significance. Yogyakarta and Solo are centres of traditional Javanese culture where you can see a *wayang* performance.

Yogyakarta and Solo are also the centres of classical Javanese dance, a more refined, stylised manner of acting out the Hindu epics, performed most spectacularly in the Ramayana Ballet at Prambanan.

Many other colourful dance and drama traditions are alive and well around the archipelago. The Minangkabau people of West Sumatra have a strong tradition of Randai dance-drama at festivals and ceremonies, which incorporates *pencak silat* (a form of martial arts). The Batak Sigalegale puppet dance sees life-sized puppets dancing for weddings and funerals. Western Java's Jaipongan is a dynamic style that features swift movements to rhythms complicated enough to dumbfound an audience of musicologists. It was developed out of local dance and music traditions after Sukarno banned rock 'n' roll in 1961.

Central Kalimantan is home to the Manasai, a friendly dance in which tourists are welcome to participate. Kalimantan also has the Mandau, a dance performed with knives and shields. Papua is best known for its warrior dances, most easily seen at annual festivals at Danau Sentani and in the Baliem Valley and Asmat region.

Music

Traditional

Gamelan orchestras dominate traditional music in Java and Bali. Composed mainly of percussion instruments such as xylophones, gongs, drums and *angklung* (bamboo tubes shaken to produce a note), but also flutes, gamelan orchestras may have as many as 100 members. The sound produced by a gamelan can range from harmonious to eerie, with the tempo and intensity of sound undulating on a regular basis. Expect

The best bet for traditional dance? Ubud on Bali, where you can see several performances by talented troupes every night of the week.

Jalanan, a 2013 documentary by Daniel Ziv, provides a compelling look at the lives of three Jakarta street musicians as they try to keep pace with rapid societal change.

to hear powerful waves of music one minute and a single instrument holding court the next.

Balinese gamelan is more dramatic and varied than the refined Javanese forms, but all gamelan music has a hypnotic and haunting effect. It always accompanies Balinese and Javanese dance, and can also be heard in dedicated gamelan concerts, particularly in Solo and Yogyakarta in Java. Similar types of ensembles are also found elsewhere, such as the *telempong* of West Sumatra.

Another ethereal traditional music is West Java's serene *kacapi suling*, which features the *kacapi* (a harp-like instrument) and *suling* (a bamboo flute).

Contemporary

Indonesia has a massive contemporary music scene that spans all genres. The popular *dangdut* is a melange of traditional and modern, Indonesian and foreign musical styles that features instruments such as electric guitars and Indian tablas, and rhythms ranging from Middle Eastern pop to reggae or salsa. The result is sexy, love-drunk songs sung by heartbroken women or cheesy men, accompanied by straight-faced musicians in matching suits. The beats are gutsy, the emotion high, the singing evocative and the dancing often provocative.

The writhings of *dangdut* star Inul Daratista (whose adopted stage name means 'the girl with breasts') were one reason behind the passage of Indonesia's controversial 'antipornography' legislation. She continues to sell out large venues around the archipelago.

No discussion of modern Indonesian music is complete without mention of the punk band Superman Is Dead. From its start on Bali in 1995, the three-man group has gained fans across the country and the world. These days they're known for their environmental crusades.

Painting

Galleries in the wealthier neighbourhoods of Jakarta are the epicentre of Indonesia's contemporary art scene, which has flourished with a full panoply of installations, sculptures, performance art and more, and which can be either extremely original, eye-catching and thought-provoking, or the opposite. Jakarta (www.jakartabiennale.net) and Yogyakarta (www.biennalejogja.org) both hold big biennial art events.

Traditionally, painting was an art for decorating palaces and places of worship, typically with religious or legendary subject matter. Foreign artists in Bali in the 1930s inspired a revolution in painting: artists began to depict everyday scenes in new, more realistic, less crowded canvases. Others developed an attractive 'primitivist' style. Much Balinese art today is mass-produced tourist-market stuff, though there are also talented and original artists, especially in and around Ubud. Indonesia's most celebrated 20th-century painter was the Javanese expressionist Affandi (1907–90), who liked to paint by squeezing the paint straight out of the tube.

Architecture

Indonesia is home to a vast and spectacular variety of architecture, from religious and royal buildings to traditional styles of home building, which can differ hugely from one part of the archipelago to another. Indian, Chinese, Arabic and European influences have all added their mark to locally developed styles.

The great 8th- and 9th-century temples of Borobudur, Prambanan and the Dieng Plateau, in Central Java, all show the Indian influence that predominated in the Hindu-Buddhist period. Indian style, albeit with a distinctive local flavour, persists today in the Hindu temples of

Rock legend Iwan Fals has been around for decades but still packs stadiums. His anti-establishment bent has caused him to be arrested several times.

Cowboys in Paradise (2009), directed by Amit Virmani, made headlines for its unflinching portrait of real-life gigolos in Bali. Fixtures of Kuta Beach, these men are popular with some female tourists.

Bali, where the leaders of the Hindu-Buddhist Majapahit kingdom took refuge after being driven from Java in the 16th century.

Balinese Architecture

The basic feature of Balinese architecture is the *bale* (pronounced 'ba-lay'), a rectangular, open-sided pavilion with a steeply pitched roof of palm thatch. A family compound will have a number of *bale* for eating, sleeping and working. The focus of a community is the *bale banjar*, a large pavilion for meeting, debate, gamelan practice and so on. Buildings such as restaurants and the lobby areas of hotels are often modelled on the *bale* – they are airy, spacious and handsomely proportioned.

Like the other arts, architecture has traditionally served the religious life of Bali. Balinese houses, although attractive, have never been lavished with the architectural attention that is given to temples. Even Balinese palaces are modest compared with the more important temples. Temples are designed to fixed rules and formulas, with sculpture serving as an adjunct, a finishing touch to these design guidelines.

Mosques

Mosque interiors are normally empty except for five main features: the *mihrab* (a wall niche marking the direction of Mecca); the *mimbar* (a raised pulpit, often canopied, with a staircase); a stand to hold the Koran; a screen to provide privacy for important worshippers; and a water source for ablutions. There are no seats and if there is any ornamentation at all, it will be verses from the Koran, although Indonesia's growing economy has fuelled a construction boom of new and elaborately designed mosques.

Indonesia's most revered mosques tend to be those built in the 15th and 16th centuries in Javanese towns that were among the first to convert to Islam. The 'classical' architectural style of these mosques includes tiered roofs clearly influenced by the Hindu culture that Islam had then only recently supplanted. They are curiously reminiscent of the Hindu temples still seen on Bali today. During the Suharto era in the late 20th century, hundreds of standardised, prefabricated mosques were shipped and erected all around Indonesia in pale imitation of this classical Javanese style.

It's generally no problem for travellers to visit mosques, as long as appropriately modest clothing is worn.

Traditional Houses

Indonesians developed a range of eye-catching structures for their homes whose grandeur depended on the family that built them. Timber construction, often with stilts, and elaborate thatched roofs of palm leaves or grass are common to many traditional housing forms around the archipelago. The use of stilts helps to reduce heat and humidity and avoid mud, floods and pests. Tana Toraja in Sulawesi, Pulau Nias off Sumatra, and the Batak and Minangkabau areas of Sumatra exhibit some of the most spectacular vernacular architecture, with high, curved roofs.

Royal Palaces

Royal palaces around Indonesia are often developments of basic local housing styles, even if far more elaborate as in the case of Javanese *kraton* (walled palaces). Yogyakarta's *kraton* is effectively a city within a city and is inhabited by around 17,500 people. On Bali, where royal families still exist – even if they often lack power – the 'palaces' are much more humble. It's the same story for the sultans of Maluku, whose homes are mostly modest.

The glossy monthly English-language magazine *Jakarta Java Kini* contains interesting articles on what's hot in the arts and entertainment, with a Jakarta focus. Another good source of Jakarta and Bali cultural news is *The Beat* (https://thebeat bali.com).

Colonial Buildings

The Dutch colonists initially built poorly ventilated houses in the European style, but eventually a hybrid Indo-European style emerged, using elements such as the Javanese *pendopo* (open-sided pavilion) and *joglo* (a high-pitched roof). International styles such as art deco started to arrive in the late 19th century as large numbers of factories, train stations, hotels, hospitals and other public buildings went up in the later colonial period. Bandung in Java has one of the world's largest collections of 1920s art deco buildings.

The Banda Islands in Maluku are a fine place to spot Dutch colonial architecture, with some old forts still intact and streets lined with columned buildings sporting shady verandahs.

Modern Architecture

Newly independent Indonesia had little money to spare for major building projects, though President Sukarno did find the funds for a few prestige projects such as Jakarta's huge and resplendent Masjid Istiqlal. The economic progress of the Suharto years saw Indonesia's cities spawn their quota of standard international high-rise office blocks and uninspired government buildings, though tourism helped to foster original, even spectacular, hybrids of local and international styles in hotels and resorts. Bali in particular has some properties renowned for their architecture around the coast (especially on the Bukit Peninsula) and overlooking the river valleys near Ubud.

Bali Style (1995) by Barbara Walker and Rio Helmi is a lavishly photographed look at Balinese design, architecture and interior decoration. It captured a spare, tropical look that spawned oodles of copycat books and magazines and is today almost a cliche.

Crafts

History, religion, custom and modern styles are all reflected in Indonesia's vastly diverse range of crafts. Broadly speaking, there are three major influences: animism – traditions of animism and ancestor worship form the basis of many Indonesian crafts, particularly in Sumatra, Kalimantan, Sulawesi, Nusa Tenggara, Maluku and Papua; South Asian – the wave of Indian, and to a lesser extent Indo-Chinese, culture brought by extensive trading contacts created the Hindu-Buddhist techniques and styles reflected in Javanese and Balinese temple carvings, art forms, and crafts; and Islam – the third major influence only modified existing traditions.

Though the religious significance or practical function of many traditional objects is disappearing, the skill level remains high. driven by more discerning tourist tastes and by a booming export market. Javanese woodcarvers are turning out magnificent traditional panels and innovative furniture commissioned by large hotels, and Balinese jewellers influenced by Western designs are producing works of stunning quality.

Woodcarving

Woodcarving is often practised in conjunction with more practical activities such as house building. All traditional Indonesian dwellings have some provision for repelling unwanted spirits. The horned lion heads of Batak houses, the water-buffalo representations on Toraja houses and the serpent carvings on Dayak houses all serve to protect inhabitants from evil influences.

On the outer islands, woodcarvings and statues are crafted to represent the spirit world and the ancestors who live there. Woodcarving is an intrinsic part of the Toraja's famed funerals: the deceased is represented by a *tau tau* (a life-sized wooden statue), and the coffin is adorned with carved animal heads. In the Ngaju and Dusun Dayak villages in Kalimantan, *temadu* (giant carved ancestor totems) also depict the dead.

Top: Masjid Istiqlal (p67)

Bottom: *Tau tau* grave statues (p683), Tana Toraja

The most favoured and durable (and expensive) wood in Indonesia is *jati* (teak). Sandalwood is occasionally seen in Balinese carvings, as is mahogany and ebony (imported from Sulawesi and Kalimantan). Jackfruit is a common, cheap wood, though it tends to warp and split. Generally, local carvers use woods at hand: heavy ironwood and *meranti* (a hard wood) in Kalimantan, and *belalu* (a light wood) in Bali.

Regional Carving

Perhaps Indonesia's most famous woodcarvers are the Asmat of southwestern Papua. Shields, canoes, spears and drums are carved, but the most distinctive Asmat woodcarvings are *mbis* (ancestor poles). These poles show the dead, one above the other, and the open carved 'wing' at the top of the pole is a phallic symbol representing fertility and power. The poles are also an expression of revenge, and were traditionally carved to accompany a feast following a headhunting raid.

Balinese woodcarving is the most ornamental and elaborate in Indonesia. The gods and demons of Balinese cosmology populate statues, temple doors and relief panels throughout the island. Western influence and the demand for art and souvenirs has encouraged Balinese woodcarvers to reinvent their craft, echoing the 1930s revolution in Balinese painting by producing simpler, elongated statues of purely ornamental design with a natural finish.

On Java the centre for woodcarving, especially carved furniture, is Jepara. The intricate crafts share Bali's Hindu-Buddhist tradition, adjusted to reflect Islam's prohibition on human representation. Another Javanese woodcarving centre is Kudus, where elaborate panels for traditional houses are produced.

Textiles

Textiles are both practical and artistic in Indonesia. There is a long tradition of textile-making across the archipelago, with three major homegrown categories: ikat, *songket* and batik.

Ikat

The Indonesian word 'ikat', meaning 'to tie' or 'to bind', signifies the intricately patterned cloth of threads that are painstakingly tie-dyed before

---

EXQUISITE GIFTS
· ·

Amid the endless piles of tourist tat, Indonesia has truly extraordinary items that make perfect gifts. The secret is finding them. Here are a few ideas.

➡ West Timor in Nusa Tenggara is home to fab textile markets. Look for shops selling local ikat, antique masks, statues, and carved beams, reliefs and doors from old Timorese homes.

➡ In South Sumatra look for ceremonial *songket* sarongs that are used for marriages and other ceremonies near Palembang. They can take a month to make.

➡ Dayak rattan, *doyo* (bark beaten into cloth), carvings and other souvenirs from Kalimantan can be world-class.

➡ Street vendors in Bandaneira sell scrumptious *halua-kenari* (kenari-nut brittle), a treat found only in the Banda Islands in Maluku.

➡ On Bali, intricate and beautiful rattan items made in an ancient village are sold by Ashitaba, which has shops across the island full of exquisite and artful goods.

➡ Widely available in markets, look for *tikar* (woven palm-leaf mats) that show careful workmanship and can be rolled up for travel.

being woven together. Ikat is produced in many regions, most notably in Nusa Tenggara.

Ikat garments come in an incredible diversity of colours and patterns: the spectacular ikat of Sumba and the elaborately patterned work of Flores (including *kapita,* used to wrap the dead) are the best known.

Making Ikat

Traditionally, ikat is made of hand-spun cotton. The whole process of ikat production – from planting the cotton to folding the finished product – is performed by women. Once the cotton is harvested, it is spun with a spindle. The thread is strengthened by immersing it in baths of crushed cassava, rice or maize, then threaded on to a winder.

Traditional dyes are made from natural sources. The most complex processes result in a rusty colour known as *kombu* (produced from the bark and roots of the *kombu* tree). Blue dyes come from the indigo plant, and purple or brown can be produced by dyeing the cloth deep blue and then dyeing it again with *kombu.*

Any sections that are not coloured are bound together with dye-resistant fibre. Each colour requires a separate tying-and-dyeing process. The sequence of colouring takes into consideration the effect of each application of dye. This stage requires great skill, as the dyer has to work out – before the threads are woven – exactly which parts of the thread are to receive which colour in order to create the pattern of the final cloth. After the thread has been dyed, the cloth is woven on a simple hand loom.

Origins & Meaning of Ikat

Ikat technique was most probably introduced 2000 years ago by Dongson migrants from southern China and Vietnam.

Ikat styles vary according to the village and the gender of the wearer, and some styles are reserved for special purposes. In parts of Nusa Tenggara, high-quality ikat is part of a bride's dowry. Until recently on Sumba, only members of the highest clans could make and wear ikat textiles. Certain motifs were traditionally reserved for noble families (as on Sumba and Rote) or members of a specific tribe or clan (as on Sabu or among the Atoni of West Timor). The function of ikat as an indicator of social status has since declined.

Motifs & Patterns

Some experts believe that motifs found on Sumba, such as front views of people, animals and birds, stem from an artistic tradition even older than Dongson, whose influence was geometric motifs like diamond and key shapes (which often go together), meanders and spirals.

One strong influence was *patola* cloth from Gujarat in India. In the 16th and 17th centuries these became highly prized in Indonesia, and one characteristic motif – a hexagon framing a four-pronged star – was copied by local ikat weavers. On the best *patola* and geometric ikat, repeated small patterns combine to form larger patterns, like a mandala. Over the past century, European styles have influenced the motifs used in ikat.

Choosing Ikat

Unless you are looking for inexpensive machine-made ikat, shopping is best left to the experts. Even trekking out to an 'ikat village' may be in vain: the photogenic woman sitting at a wooden loom may be only for show. But here are some tips for recognising the traditional product.

In Tenganan (Bali), a cloth called *gringsing* is woven using a rare method of double ikat in which both warp and weft threads are predyed.

Made in Indonesia: A Tribute to the Country's Craftspeople (2005), by Warwick Purser with photos by the ubiquitous Rio Helmi, provides beautiful images and background information on the crafts of the country.

Thread Hand-spun cotton has a less perfect 'twist' to it than factory cloth.

Weave Hand-woven cloth, whether made from hand-spun or factory thread, feels rougher and, when new, stiffer than machine-woven cloth. It will probably have minor imperfections in the weave.

Dyes Until you've seen enough ikat to get a feel for whether colours are natural or chemical, you often have to rely on your instincts as to whether they are 'earthy' enough. Some cloths contain both natural and artificial dyes.

Dyeing method The patterns on cloths that have been individually tie-dyed using the traditional method are rarely perfectly defined, but they're unlikely to have the detached specks of colour that often appear on mass-dyed cloth.

Age No matter what anybody tells you, there are very few antique cloths around. There are several processes to make cloth look old.

A carefully curated list of books about art, culture and Indonesian writers, dancers and musicians can be found at www.ganesha booksbali.com, the website of the excellent Bali bookstore.

Songket

Songket is silk cloth interwoven with gold or silver threads, although imitation silver or gold is often used in modern pieces. *Songket* is most commonly found in heavily Islamic regions, such as Aceh, and among the coastal Malays, but Bali also has a strong *songket* tradition.

Batik

The technique of applying wax or other dye-resistant substances (like rice paste) to cloth to produce a design is found in many parts of the world, but none is as famous as the batik of Java, where the technique dates back to the 12th century. The most beautiful and distinctive batik has traditionally been created in Solo. The opinion is divided as to whether batik is an indigenous craft or imported from India along with Hindu religious and cultural traditions.

The word 'batik' is an old Javanese word meaning 'to dot'. Javanese batik was a major weapon in the competition for social status in the royal courts. The ability to devote extensive resources to the painstaking creation of fine batik demonstrated wealth and power. Certain designs indicated courtly rank, and a courtier risked public humiliation, or worse, by daring to wear the wrong sarong.

In 2009 Unesco added Indonesian batik to its Intangible Cultural Heritage list.

Making Batik

Batik painting, an odd blend of craft and art that all too often is neither, remains popular in Yogyakarta, where it was invented as a pastime for unemployed youth. Though most batik painting is tourist schlock, there are some talented artists working in the medium.

The finest batik is *batik tulis* (hand-painted or literally 'written' batik). Designs are first traced out on to cloth, then patterns are drawn in hot wax with a *canting,* a pen-like instrument. The wax-covered areas resist colour change when immersed in a dye bath. The waxing and dyeing, with increasingly darker shades, continues until the final colours are achieved. Wax is added to protect previously dyed areas or scraped off to expose new areas to the dye. Finally, all the wax is scraped off and the cloth is boiled to remove all traces of wax.

Topeng – Masks

Although carved masks exist throughout the archipelago, the most readily identifiable form of mask is the *topeng,* used in *wayang topeng,* the masked dance-dramas of Java and Bali. Dancers perform local tales or adaptations of Hindu epics such as the Mahabharata, with the masks used to represent different characters. Masks vary from the stylised but plain masks of Central and West Java to the heavily carved masks of East Java.

Balinese masks are less stylised and more naturalistic than in Java – the Balinese save their love of colour and detail for the masks of the Barong dance, starring a mythical lion-dog creature who fights tirelessly against evil. Look for masks in shops in and around Ubud, especially to the south in Mas.

Kris

No ordinary knife, the wavy-bladed traditional dagger known as a kris is a mandatory possession of a Javanese gentleman; it's said to be endowed with supernatural powers and is to be treated with the utmost respect. A kris owner ritually bathes and polishes his weapon, stores it in an auspicious location, and pays close attention to every rattle and scrape emanating from the blade and sheath in the dead of the night. The kris remains an integral part of men's ceremonial dress.

Distinctive features, the number of curves in the blade and the damascene design on the blade, are read to indicate good or bad fortune for its owner. The number of curves in the blade has symbolic meaning: five curves symbolise the five Pandava brothers of the Mahabharata epic; three represents fire, ardour and passion. Although the blade is the most important part of the kris, the hilt and scabbard are also beautifully decorated.

Although the kris is mostly associated with Java and Bali, larger and less ornate variations are found in Sumatra, Kalimantan and Sulawesi.

Puppets

The most famous puppets of Indonesia are the carved leather *wayang kulit* puppets. These intricate lace figures are cut from buffalo hide with a sharp, chisel-like stylus, and then painted. They are produced in Bali and Java, particularly in Central Java. The leaf-shaped *kayon* representing the 'tree' or 'mountain of life' is also made of leather and is used to end scenes during a performance.

Wayang golek are three-dimensional wooden puppets found in Central and West Java. The *wayang klitik* puppets are the rarer flat wooden puppets of East Java.

Jewellery

Gold and silverwork has a long history in Indonesia. Some of the best gold jewellery comes from Aceh, where fine filigree work is produced, while chunky bracelets and earrings are produced in the Batak region.

Balinese jewellery is nearly always handworked and rarely involves casting techniques; the work is innovative, employing both traditional designs and those adapted from jewellery presented by Western buyers.

Kota Gede in Yogyakarta is famous for its fine filigree work. Silverware from here tends to be more traditional, but new designs are also being adapted.

The popular annual Ubud Writers & Readers Festival (www. ubudwriters festival.com) in Bali, held in October, showcases both local and international writers and has an annual theme.

Food & Drink

When you eat in Indonesia you savour the essence of the country. The abundance of rice reflects Indonesia's fertile landscape, the spices recall a time of trade and invasion, and the fiery chilli echoes the passion of the people. Indonesian cuisine is really one big food swap. Chinese, Portuguese, colonists and traders have all influenced the ingredients that appear at the Indonesian table, and the cuisine has been further shaped over time by the archipelago's diverse landscape, people and culture.

Staples & Specialities

Indonesian cooking is not complex, and its ingredients maintain their distinct flavours. Coriander, cumin, chilli, lemon grass, coconut, soy sauce and palm sugar are all important flavourings; sambal, a hot chilli paste of Javanese origin, is a crucial condiment. Fish is a favourite and the seafood restaurants are often of a good standard. Indonesians traditionally eat with their fingers, hence the stickiness of the rice. *Sate* (skewered meat), nasi goreng (fried rice) and gado gado (vegetables with peanut sauce) are some of Indonesia's most famous dishes.

Jajanan (snacks) are sold everywhere – there are thousands of varieties of sweet and savoury snacks made from anything and everything: peanuts, coconuts, bananas, sweet potato and more.

Indonesia's national dish is *nasi campur*, which is essentially the plate of the day. Served in stalls, warungs and restaurants, it is always a combination of many dishes and flavours. At warungs you often choose your own combination from dozens of tasty items on offer.

Regional Variations

Just like sambal, Indonesia's flavours come in many, many forms.

Java

The cuisine of the Betawi (original inhabitants of the Jakarta region) is known for its richness. Gado gado is a Betawi original, as is *ketoprak* (noodles, bean sprouts and tofu with soy and peanut sauce; named after a musical style, as it resembles the sound of ingredients being chopped). *Soto Betawi* (beef soup) is made creamy with coconut milk. There's also *nasi uduk* (rice cooked in coconut milk, served with meat, tofu and/or vegetables).

In West Java, the Sundanese love their greens. Their specialities include *karedok* (salad of long beans, bean sprouts and cucumber with spicy sauce), *soto Bandung* (beef-and-vegetable soup with lemon grass) and *ketupat tahu* (pressed rice, bean sprouts and tofu with soy and peanut sauce). Sundanese sweet specialities include *colenak* (roasted cassava with coconut sauce) and *ulen* (roasted sticky rice with peanut sauce); both best

NO WIMPY SAMBAL!

Sambal, the spicy condiment, comes in myriad forms and can be the best part of a meal, but all too often, servers will assume you are a timid tourist who wants the tame stuff from a bottle. Insist on the real stuff (try saying '*sambal lokal?*' – 'local sambal?'), which will have been prepared fresh in the kitchen from some combination of ingredients that can include garlic, shallots, chilli peppers in many forms, fish sauce, tomatoes and more.

WE DARE YOU

Everyday eating in Indonesia can challenge your palate. Here are a few favourites.

➡ In Nusa Tenggara Timor (Alor and Flores in particular) there is a scintillating, spicy, oily, mildly astringent dish called *ikan kuah assam* (tamarind fish soup). It is absolutely sensational. It's basically a fish steak or half a fish (bones often included) steamed and swimming in spicy tamarind broth. It's simple, life affirming, bliss inducing and could easily be your favourite dish of the trip.

➡ The durian has a serious image problem. This fruit's spiky skin looks like a Spanish Inquisition torture tool, and opening it releases the fruit's odorous power. Most people form a lifelong passion – or aversion – on their first taste of this sulphury, custardy fruit.

➡ Balinese specialities are readily available; look for warungs advertising *siobak* (minced pig's head, stomach, tongue and skin cooked with spices).

➡ For avocado juice, take an avocado, blend with ice and condensed milk (or chocolate syrup) and serve. Indonesians don't consider this strange, as the avocado is just another sweet fruit.

eaten warm. Bandung's cooler hills are the place for *bandrek* (ginger tea with coconut and pepper) and *bajigur* (spiced coffee with coconut milk).

Central Javan food is sweet, including the curries such as *gudeg* (jackfruit curry). Yogyakarta specialities include *ayam goreng* (fried chicken) and *kelepon* (green rice-flour balls with a palm-sugar filling). In Solo, specialities include *nasi liwet* (rice with coconut milk, unripe papaya, garlic and shallots, served with chicken or egg) and *serabi* (coconut-milk pancakes topped with chocolate, banana or jackfruit).

There's a lot of crossover between Central and East Javan cuisine. Fish is popular, especially *pecel lele* (deep-fried catfish served with rice and *pecel*). The best *pecel* (peanut sauce) comes from the town of Madiun.

Two very popular Madurese dishes are *soto Madura* (beef soup with lime, pepper, peanuts, chilli and ginger) and *sate Madura* (skewered meat with sweet soy sauce).

Java's Cianjur region is famous for its sweet, spicy cuisine. Dishes include *lontong* (sticky rice with tofu in a delicious, sweet coconut sauce); the best beef *sate* in Java, locally known as *marangi*; and *pandan wangi*, fragrantly flavoured rice that's often cooked with lemon grass and spices.

Bali

Balinese specialities are easy to find, as visitor-friendly warungs offer high-quality Balinese dishes, with several options of spiciness. Many restaurants offer the hugely popular Balinese dish, *babi guling* (spit-roast pig stuffed with chilli, turmeric, garlic and ginger) on a day's notice, but look out for the many warungs that specialise in it. Look for the pig's head drawn on the sign or a real one in a display case. Also popular is *bebek betutu* (duck stuffed with spices, wrapped in banana leaves and coconut husks, and cooked in embers).

The local *sate, sate lilit,* is made with minced, spiced meat pressed on to skewers. Look for spicy dishes such as *lawar* (salad of chopped coconut, garlic and chilli with pork or chicken meat and blood).

Sumatra

In West Sumatra, beef is used in *rendang* (beef coconut curry). The region is the home of spicy Padang food, among the most famous of Indonesian cuisines. The market in Bukittinggi is a great place to sample *nasi Kapau* (cuisine from the village of Kapau) – it's similar to Padang food but uses more vegetables. There's also *bubur kampiun* (mung-bean porridge with banana and rice yoghurt).

In North Sumatra, the Acehnese love their *kare* or *gulai* (curry). The Bataks have a taste for pig and, to a lesser extent, dog. Pork features in *babi panggang* (pork boiled in vinegar and pig blood, and then roasted).

Sate pusut

Indonesia's food scene is better than ever. Bali has scores of world-class restaurants, and there are great eats in major cities and on Lombok, the Gilis and beyond. Remote areas once dismissed as culinary backwaters like Flores, West Timor and Sumba boast excellent restaurants, serving foods from Indonesia and beyond.

The culinary capital of South Sumatra is Palembang, famous for *pempek* (deep-fried fish and sago dumpling; also called *empek-empek*). South Sumatra is also home to *pindang* (spicy fish soup with soy and tamarind) and *ikan brengkes* (fish in a spicy, durian-based sauce). Palembang's sweetie is *srikaya* (green custard made from sticky rice, sugar, coconut milk and egg).

Nusa Tenggara

In dry east Nusa Tenggara you'll eat less rice (although much is imported) and more sago, corn, cassava and taro. Fish is popular and one local dish is Sumbawa's *sepat* (shredded fish in coconut and mango sauce).

The Sasak people of Lombok (and visitors!) like spicy *ayam Taliwang* (roasted chicken served with a peanut, tomato, chilli and lime dip) and *pelecing* sauce (made with chilli, shrimp paste and tomato). Also recommended is *sate pusut* (minced meat or fish satay, mixed with coconut, and grilled on sugar-cane skewers). Nonmeat dishes include *kelor* (soup with vegetables) and *timun urap* (cucumber with coconut, onion and garlic).

Kalimantan

Dayak food varies, but you may sample *rembang*, a sour fruit that's made into *sayur asem rembang* (sour vegetable soup). In Banjarmasin, the Banjar make *pepes ikan* (spiced fish cooked in banana leaves with tamarind and lemon grass). Kandangan town is famous for *ketupat Kandangan* (fish and pressed rice with lime-infused coconut sauce). The regional soup, *soto Banjar*, is a chicken broth made creamy by mashing boiled eggs into the stock. Chicken also goes into *ayam masak habang*, cooked with large red chillies.

There is a large Chinese population, and restaurants usually have specialities such as bird's-nest soup and jellyfish on the menus.

Ikan bakar served with *dabu-dabu*

Sulawesi

South Sulawesi locals love seafood, especially *ikan bakar* (grilled fish). Another popular local dish is *coto Makassar* (soup of beef innards, pepper, cumin and lemon grass). For sugar cravers, there's *es pallubutun* (coconut custard and banana in coconut milk and syrup).

The Toraja people have their own distinct cuisine with a heavy emphasis on indigenous ingredients, many of them odd to Western palates. You can easily find *pa'piong,* which is meat or fish cooked in bamboo tubes with spices. Also look for *pamarasan,* a spicy black sauce used to cook meat.

If a North Sulawesi dish has the name *rica-rica,* it's prepared with a paste of chilli, shallots, ginger and lime. Fish and chicken are two versions (also look out for dog). Things get very fishy with *bakasang* (flavouring paste made with fermented fish), sometimes used in *bubur tinotuan* (porridge made with corn, cassava, rice, pumpkin, fish paste and chilli).

Maluku

A typical Maluku meal is tuna and *dabu-dabu* (raw vegetables with a chilli and fish-paste sauce). Sometimes fish is made into *kohu-kohu* (fish salad with citrus fruit and chilli). Sago pith is used to make porridge, bread and *mutiara* (small, jelly-like 'beans' that are added to desserts and sweet drinks). Boiled cassava *(kasbi)* is a staple in Maluku homes as it's cheaper than rice.

In the Banda Islands you'll find nutmeg jelly on bread and pancakes, which is fitting as these were the original Spice Islands, where nutmeg was first cultivated.

Papua

Little rice is grown here: indigenous Papuans get their carbs from other sources, and the rice eaten by migrants from elsewhere in Indonesia is

At Banjarmasin's floating produce market in Kalimantan, you can sample exotic fruit to your heart's content. The range will include all manner of unfamiliar and unusual-looking treats such as the pungent, spiky durian.

mostly imported. In the highlands of Papua the sweet potato is king. The Dani people grow around 60 varieties, some of which can only be eaten by the elders.

In the lowlands the sago palm provides the starchy staple food: its pulped-up pith is turned into hard, moist sago cakes, to which water is added to make *papeda,* a kind of gluey paste usually eaten with fish in a yellow turmeric-and-lime sauce. You may find the fish tastier than the *papeda.* Some lowlanders also eat the sago beetle grubs found in rotting sago palms.

Cradle of Flavor (2006) by James Oseland (the editor of *Saveur* magazine) is a beautiful tome covering the foods of Indonesia and its neighbours.

Celebrations

Whether a marriage, funeral or party with friends, food – and lots of it – is essential. Celebratory meals can include any combination of dishes, but for special occasions a *tumpeng* is the centrepiece: a pyramid of yellow rice, the tip of which is cut off and offered to the VIP.

Muslims

For Muslims, the largest celebrations are Ramadan and Idul Adha. Each day of Ramadan, Muslims rise before sunrise to eat the only meal before sunset. It might sound like a bad time to be in Indonesia – you may have to plan meals and go without lunch – but when sunset comes, the locals' appreciation of a good meal is contagious.

The first thing Indonesians eat after fasting is *kolak* (fruit in coconut milk) as a gentle way to reacquaint the body with food. Then, after prayers, the evening meal begins with aplomb. In some areas, such as in Bukittinggi, cooks set out food on the street. People gather to savour and enjoy their food as a community. Foreign guests are always made welcome.

After Ramadan, much of the nation seems to hit the road to go home to their families and celebrate Idul Fitri (Lebaran) with their families. During this time, *ketupat* (rice steamed in packets of woven coconut fronds) are hung everywhere, like seasonal ornaments.

Seventy days after Lebaran is Idul Adha, marked by the sight of goats tethered to posts on both city streets and rural pathways throughout the archipelago. Individuals or community groups buy these unfortunate animals to sacrifice in commemoration of Abraham's willingness

---

FRUITY DELIGHTS

It's worth making a trip to Indonesia just to sample the tropical fruits.

➡ *Belimbing* (star fruit) is cool and crisp; slice one to see how it gets its name.

➡ Durian is the spiky, smelly fruit people either love or hate.

➡ *Jambu air* (water apple) is a pink bell-shaped fruit with crisp and refreshing flesh.

➡ *Manggis* (mangosteen) is a small purple fruit with white fleshy segments and fantastic flavour.

➡ *Nangka* (jackfruit) is an enormous, spiky fruit that can weigh over 20kg. Inside are segments of yellow, moist, sweet flesh with a slightly rubbery texture. The flesh can be eaten fresh or cooked in a curry.

➡ *Rambutan* is a bright-red fruit covered in soft spines; the name means 'hairy'. Break it open to reveal a delicious white fruit similar to lychee.

➡ *Salak* is recognisable by its brown 'snakeskin' covering. Peel it off to reveal segments that resemble something between an apple and a walnut.

➡ *Sirsak* (soursop or zurzak) is a warty, green-skinned fruit with a white, pulpy interior that has a slightly lemonish taste.

> ### QUICK EATS
>
> As many Indonesians can't afford fine service and surroundings, the most authentic food is found at street level. Even high rollers know this, so everyone dines at stalls or gets their noodle fix from roving vendors who carry their victuals in two bundles connected by a stick over their shoulders: a stove and wok on one side, and ready-to-fry ingredients on the other.
>
> Then there's *kaki lima* (roving vendors) whose carts hold a work bench, stove and cabinet. '*Kaki lima*' means 'five legs': two for the wheels of the cart, one for the stand and two for the legs of the vendor. You'll find any and every type of dish, drink and snack sold from a *kaki lima*. Some have a permanent spot; others roam the streets, calling out what they are selling or making a signature sound, such as the 'tock' of a wooden *bakso* bell. In some places, *sate* sellers operate from a boat-shaped cart, with bells jingling to attract the hungry.

to sacrifice his son at divine command. This is one of Indonesia's most anticipated festivals, as the sacrificial meat is distributed to the poor in each community.

Balinese

The Balinese calendar is peppered with festivals, and such celebrations are always observed with a communal meal, sometimes eaten together from one massive banana leaf piled with dishes.

Festivals aside, every day in Bali you'll see food used to symbolise devotion: rice in woven banana-leaf pockets are placed in doorways, beside rice fields, at bus terminals – wherever a god or spirit may reside. Larger offerings studded with whole chickens and produce are made to mark special occasions such as *odalan* (anniversary of a temple). You'll see processions of women gracefully balancing offerings on their heads as they make their way to the temple.

Where to Eat

Outside larger cities and tourist areas, there are limited choices for dining out in Indonesia. Warungs are simple, open-air eateries that provide a small range of dishes. Often their success comes from cooking one dish better than anyone else. *Rumah makan* (eating house) or *restoran* refers to anything that is a step above a warung. Offerings may be as simple as those from a warung but usually include a wider selection of meat and vegetable dishes, and spicy accompaniments.

As Indonesia's middle class grows, the warung is also going upmarket. In urban areas, a restaurant by any other name advertises itself as a 'warung', and serves good local dishes to customers who become more demanding by the year.

Indonesia's markets are wonderful examples of how food feeds both the soul and the stomach. There's no refrigeration, so freshness is dependent on quick turnover. You'll also find a huge range of sweet and savoury snacks. Supermarkets and convenience stores are common in cities and tourist areas.

Vegetarians & Vegans

Vegetarians will be pleased to know that tempeh and *tahu* (tofu) are available in abundance, sold as chunky slabs of *tempe penyet* (deep-fried tempeh), *tempe kering* (diced tempeh stir-fried with sweet soy sauce) and *tahu isi* (deep-fried stuffed tofu). Finding fresh veggies requires more effort. Look for Chinese establishments; they can whip up *cap cai* (mixed vegetables). Vegetarian fried rice or noodles can be found at many other eateries. And there's always the iconic gado gado.

A huge number of places, including Padang restaurants, offer what's essentially the national dish: *nasi campur* (rice with a variety of side

Meals of a Lifetime

Hujan Locale, Bali (p268)

Melati, Java (p182)

Historia, Jakarta (p75)

Sari Rasa, Nusa Tenggara (p384)

Ocean's Resto, Kalimantan (p643)

Coto Nusantara, Sulawesi (p669)

Top: *Nasi campur* (p773)

Bottom: Dragonfruit *es jus* (p772)

dishes). Here you can skip meat options and go for things such as tofu, tempeh, jackfruit dishes, egg dishes and leafy veggies.

And there's always fantastic fruit available at the local market.

Eating with Kids

There's always the fear that a hidden chilli is going to make your child explode, but proprietors will often warn you if a dish is spicy. In any case, you can always ask *'Pedas tidak?'* ('Is it spicy?') or *'Makanan tidak pedas ada?'* ('Are there nonspicy dishes?').

Children may enjoy nasi goreng, *mie goreng* (fried noodles), *bakso* (meatball soup), *mie rebus* (noodle soup), *perkedel* (fritters), *pisang goreng* (banana fritters), *sate, bubur* (rice porridge), fruit and fruit drinks. Indonesia's sugar-rich iced drinks are useful secret weapons for when energy levels are low. All of these are available at street stalls and restaurants. Not available, however, are highchairs and kiddie menus. That's not to say children aren't welcome; in fact, they'll probably get more attention than they can handle.

In touristy areas and cities you'll find plenty of familiar fast-food joints and convenience stores selling international snacks. A Magnum bar can quell the worst tantrum.

Rice in the field is called *padi;* rice grain at the market is called *beras;* cooked rice on your plate is called *nasi.*

Habits & Customs

With a population of over 260 million, you'd expect a little variety in Indonesia's culinary customs. There will be no surprises if you are eating at a restaurant, apart from the lack of a menu. However, if eating at someone's house, there are ways of fitting in – or at least not offending – especially if someone invites you into their home for a meal.

Dining Etiquette

In Indonesia hospitality is highly regarded. If you're invited to someone's home for a meal, you'll be treated warmly and social hiccups will be ignored. Nevertheless, here are some tips to make the experience more enjoyable for everyone.

MSG is widely used in Indonesia. In warungs, you can try asking the cook to hold off on the *ajinomoto.* If you get a look of blank incomprehension, well, the headache only lasts for a couple of hours.

➡ When food or drink is presented, wait until your host invites you to eat.

➡ Indonesians rarely eat at the table, preferring to sit on a mat or around the lounge room.

➡ Don't be surprised if, when invited to a home, you're the only one eating. This is your host's way of showing you're special, and you should have choice pickings. But don't eat huge amounts, as these dishes will feed others later. Fill up on rice and take a spoonful from each dish served.

➡ While chopsticks are available at Chinese-Indonesian eateries, and a fork and spoon in restaurants, most Indonesians prefer to eat with their hands. In a warung, it is acceptable to rinse your fingers with drinking water, letting the drops fall to the ground. Use only your right hand. If left-handed, ask for a spoon.

COOKING COURSES

If you want to carry on enjoying the tastes of Indonesia after you go home, Bali has several cooking schools where you can learn everything from how to shop in the markets and the basics of Indonesian cuisine to advanced cooking techniques. Best of all, though, is that you get to eat what you make! The following are two of the best.

Bumbu Bali Cooking School (p245) Long-time resident and cookbook author Heinz von Holzen runs a cooking school from his excellent South Bali restaurant.

Casa Luna Cooking School (p262) Half-day courses cover cooking techniques, ingredients and the cultural background of the Balinese kitchen.

➜ In Islamic areas, be sure not to eat and drink in public during Ramadan. Restaurants do stay open, though they usually cover the door so as not to cause offence.

➜ Though antismoking regulations are becoming common, smoking remains acceptable almost anywhere, anytime.

Drinks

First-time visitors encountering Jakarta and Bali's profusion of bars and clubs might wonder if Indonesia really is a predominantly Muslim country. But it is, and outside major cities and tourist destinations alcohol can be hard to find. Coffee shops abound though, some with live music, and you can always grab a fresh juice.

Tea

Indonesia's most popular brew is black tea with sugar. If you don't want sugar ask for *teh pahit* (bitter tea), and don't expect to be offered milk to go with it. Various forms of ginger tea are popular, including *bandrek* (ginger tea with coconut and pepper) and *wedang jahe* (ginger tea with peanuts and agar cubes slurped from a bowl).

Coffee

Indonesian coffee, especially from Sulawesi, is of exceptional quality, though most of the best stuff is exported. Warungs serve a chewy concoction called *kopi tubruk* (ground coffee with sugar and boiling water). Most urban cafes and restaurants offer quality coffee; beans from Sumatra and Bali are especially prized.

Ice & Fruit Drinks

A popular – and protein-filled – drink in Aceh is *kopi telor kocok*, one raw egg and sugar creamed together in a glass and topped up with coffee.

Indonesia's *es* (ice drinks) are not only refreshing, they are visually stimulating, made with syrups, fruit and jellies. There are plenty of places serving *es jus* (iced fruit juice) or cordial-spiked *kelapa muda* (young coconut juice). But beware of ice outside urban areas (ice in cities is made with filtered water).

Alcoholic Drinks

Islam is the predominant religion in Indonesia and restrictions on alcohol sales are increasing. In early 2015 a law was enacted that banned the sale of alcoholic beverages – including beer – in minimarkets and shops across Indonesia. Given that these are the very places most people buy their beer, the law *could* have severely limited the availability of beer and other drinks across the archipelago. But this being Indonesia, enforcement and compliance was spotty at best. After a few months of grumbling, the law was revised so that towns and regions could decide locally about beer sales as well as wine and some traditional drinks. With the exception of Aceh and parts of West Java, as well as regions in Sumbawa, Maluku, Papua and other conservative areas, you can still buy a beer – although many warungs are dry.

You will see traditional spirits for sale, including *tuak* (palm-sap wine), *arak* (rice or palm-sap wine) and Balinese *brem* (rice wine). Be careful when buying *arak*. Poisonous methanol is produced in its fermentation process, and sometimes it isn't burned off as it should be: there have been deaths from drinking *arak* in Bali and the Gilis especially.

Of the domestic breweries, iconic Bintang, a clean, slightly sweet lager, is the preferred choice for many.

Note that rapacious duties are added to imported alcohol sold in stores and restaurants, which means that you will be hard-pressed to find affordable Australian wine or British gin on Bali. Stock up on the duty-free. Elsewhere, it can be hard to find wine and spirits outside topend resorts, though most large towns have a clandestine liquor outlet, often stocking Indonesian-made spirits.

FOOD GLOSSARY

acar	pickle; cucumber or other vegetables in a mixture of vinegar, salt, sugar and water
air	water
arak	spirits distilled from palm sap or rice
ayam	chicken
ayam goreng	fried chicken
babi	pork; since most Indonesians are Muslim, pork is generally only found in market stalls and restaurants run by the Chinese, and in areas where there are non-Muslim populations, such as Bali, Papua and Tana Toraja on Sulawesi
bakar	barbecued, roasted
bakso/ba'so	meatball soup
bandrek	ginger tea with coconut and pepper
brem	rice wine
bubur	rice porridge
cassava	known as tapioca in English; a long, thin, dark-brown root that looks something like a shrivelled turnip
colenak	roasted cassava with coconut sauce
daging kambing	goat
daging sapi	beef
es buah	combination of crushed ice, condensed milk, shaved coconut, syrup, jelly and fruit
gado gado	very popular dish of steamed bean sprouts and various vegetables, served with a spicy peanut sauce
gudeg	jackfruit curry
ikan	fish
jajanan	snacks
karedok	salad of long beans, bean sprouts and cucumber with spicy sauce
kelepon	green rice-flour balls with a palm-sugar filling
ketoprak	noodles, bean sprouts and tofu with soy and peanut sauce
ketupat tahu	pressed rice, bean sprouts and tofu with soy and peanut sauce
kopi	coffee
krupuk	shrimp with cassava flour, or fish flakes with rice dough, cut into slices and fried to a crisp
lombok	chilli
lontong	rice steamed in a banana leaf
martabak	a pancake-like dish stuffed with meat, egg and vegetables
mie goreng	fried wheat-flour noodles, served with vegetables or meat
nasi	rice
nasi campur	steamed rice topped with a little bit of everything (some vegetables, some meat, a bit of fish, a *krupuk* or two; usually a tasty and filling meal)
nasi goreng	fried rice
nasi liwet	rice with coconut milk, unripe papaya, garlic and shallots, served with chicken or egg
nasi putih	white (putih) rice, usually steamed
nasi uduk	rice cooked in coconut milk, served with meat, tofu and/or vegetables
pecel	peanut sauce

pecel lele	deep-fried catfish served with rice and *pecel*
pempek (empek-empek)	deep-fried/grilled fish and sago balls (from Palembang)
pisang goreng	fried banana fritters
rica-rica	spice and pepper condiment added to meat or fish
rintek wuuk	dog meat
roti	bread; nearly always white and sweet
sambal	a hot, spicy chilli sauce served as an accompaniment with most meals
sate	small pieces of various types of meat grilled on a skewer and served with peanut sauce
sayur	vegetables
serabi	coconut-milk pancakes topped with chocolate, banana or jackfruit
soto	meat and vegetable broth; soup
soto Bandung	beef-and-vegetable soup with lemon grass
soto Betawi	beef soup
soto Madura	beef soup with lime, pepper, peanuts, chilli and ginger
tahu	tofu or soybean curd
teh	tea
teh pahit	tea without sugar
telur	egg
tuak	palm-sap wine
udang	prawns or shrimps
ulen	roasted sticky rice with peanut sauce

Environment

It makes sense that Indonesians call their country Tanah Air Kita (literally, 'Our Land and Water'), as it is the world's most expansive archipelago. Of its 17,500-plus islands, about 6000 are inhabited. These diverse lands and surrounding waters have an impressive collection of plant and animal life. Yet this very bounty is its own worst enemy, as resource exploitation threatens virtually every corner of Indonesia.

The Land

Just as the mash-up of cultures that form the political entity of Indonesia happened not too long ago, the mash-up of land that Indonesians call home also occurred relatively recently – geologically speaking. If Sulawesi looks a bit like an island caught in a blender, that is because it is where three major chunks of Earth converged in a vortex of tectonic chaos. About 30 million years ago, the Australian plate (carrying Papua and Maluku) careened into the Sunda Shelf (carrying Sumatra, Java and Borneo) from the south, while the twirling Philippine plate was pushed in from the east by the Pacific plate. The result: a landscape and ecology as diverse and dynamic as the people who live here.

British naturalist Alfred Russel Wallace was the first to notice Indonesia's duelling eco-zones during eight years of exploration, which he describes with gentlemanly prose in *The Malay Archipelago*.

Volcanoes

Much of Indonesia is defined by its 150 volcanoes, 127 of which are active: spectacular peaks towering above the forests, oceans and peoples below. Some hikers are drawn to their steaming summits, while others flock to their colourful lakes and bubbling mud pits. For the locals, nutrient-rich soils provide high crop yields allowing for higher population density – a benefit that comes with significant risk.

At least five million Indonesians live within the 'danger zone' of active volcanoes. Large and small eruptions are a near constant occurrence, and some have literally made history. Ash from the cataclysmic 1815 eruption of Gunung Tambora in Sumbawa killed 71,000 people and caused crop failures in Europe. The 1883 eruption of Krakatau between Java and Sumatra generated tsunamis that killed tens of thousands. Super-volcano Toba on Sumatra, which may have halved the world's human population 75,000 years ago, quietly reawakened in 2015. Gunung Sinabung, near Berastagi, erupted as recently as 2017 and continues to be on watch.

RING OF FIRE

Indonesia is stretched along part of the Pacific Ring of Fire. Tectonic forces cause the Indo-Australian and Pacific plates to plunge under the Eurasian plate, where they melt 150km beneath the surface. Some of this molten rock works its way upward where it can erupt in violent and deadly explosions.

Even more pernicious, as these plates slide past each other, they can cause devastating earthquakes and tsunamis. The 2004 tsunami in Sumatra was caused by an offshore earthquake, the third-largest ever recorded, and generated waves up to 10m tall. The tsunami killed 167,799 Indonesians and displaced half a million more.

Understandably, volcanoes play a pivotal role in most Indonesian cultures. In Bali and Java, major places of worship grace the slopes of prominent volcanic cones, and eruptions are taken as demonstrations of divine disappointment or anger.

Wildlife

From tiny tarsiers to enormous stinking flowers, Indonesia's natural diversity is astounding, and new species continue to be discovered, such as frizzy-haired orang-utans in Sumatra in 2017, a fanged frog in Sulawesi in 2015, an owl in Lombok in 2013, and three walking sharks since 2007 in Maluku. Papua's Pegunungan Foja (Foja Mountains) is a constant source of firsts, including the world's smallest wallaby, recorded in 2010. Sadly, habitat erosion means some animals will become extinct before even being discovered.

> Stick insects measuring over half a metre have been found in Kalimantan.

Animals

Great apes, tigers, elephants and monkeys – lots of monkeys – plus one mean lizard are just some of the more notable critters you may encounter in Indonesia. Here you can find an astonishing 12% of the world's mammal species and 17% of its bird species.

The diversity is partly a result of evolution occurring in two distinct ecozones, the Australian and Asian, which were later brought together by tectonic migration. This is why you won't find marsupials on the western islands, or tigers in the east.

Orang-utans

The world's largest arboreal mammal, Indonesia's orang-utans are an iconic part of the nation's image. Although they once swung through the forest canopy throughout all of Southeast Asia, they are now found only in Sumatra and Borneo. The shaggy orange great apes rarely come down from the trees. They spend most of their day searching for and eating forest fruit before building their characteristic nests for the night. Some populations use tools to raid termite colonies (for a rare protein-rich delicacy), and researchers have observed individuals learning new behaviour from others, suggesting an intelligence rare in the animal kingdom.

Orang-utans have long reproductive cycles, with mothers caring for their young for up to eight years. This makes them particularly susceptible to population decline, and less than 60,000 individuals remain in the wild. Researchers fear that the isolated populations will not survive the continued loss of habitat due to logging and agriculture.

Komodo Dragons

Tales of evil beasts with huge claws, menacing teeth and yellow forked tongues floated around the islands of Nusa Tenggara for centuries. This continued until around 100 years ago, when the first Westerners brought one out of its namesake island home near Flores.

> In 2011, the International Rhino Foundation declared the Javan rhino extinct in Vietnam, leaving the estimated 60 living on Java's Ujung Kulon Peninsula the only examples left in the wild.

As mean as these 3m-long 150kg lizards look, their disposition is worse. Scores of humans have perished after being attacked, and Komodos regularly stalk and eat small deer. One researcher compared the sound of a Komodo pounding across the ground in pursuit to that of a machine gun. They have also been known to follow bite victims for miles, waiting as the venom from glands located between their teeth slowly poisons and kills their prey within 24 hours.

Endangered Species

Despite lingering claims of sightings, the Javan tiger was declared extinct in 2003. The Sumatran tiger is literally fighting for survival with fewer than 500 individuals remaining in the wild. Leopards (the black leopard, or panther, is more common in Southeast Asia) are rare but still live in Sumatra and in Java's Ujung Kulon National Park. This park is also home to the 60 remaining one-horned Javan rhinoceroses. The two-horned variety, found in Sumatra and possibly Kalimantan, is also on the endangered list.

Perhaps the most famous endangered Indonesian animal is the orangutan. Also victims of the pet trade and habitat loss, Indonesian gibbon species are endangered.

Fewer than 2000 Sumatran elephants remain in the wild, and are being driven into conflict with people since 70% of their habitat has been cleared for plantations and farming. The pygmy elephants in North Kalimantan have been reduced to fewer than 100.

Birds of Paradise

Papua's glamorous birds of paradise are a product of extreme sexual selection. In a place where food is abundant, and predators scarce, the main factor deciding who gets to reproduce is the female's choice of mate – and, it turns out, the ladies love a flamboyant fella.

While the female tends to look unremarkable, male birds of paradise may be adorned with fancy plumage, perform elaborate dances, or develop bizarre calls, all in the hope of inspiring a lady to give him her number. The Wilson's bird of paradise, endemic to Indonesia, has both bright red and yellow feathers, as well as a curling tail like a handlebar moustache, while the Parotia dons a tutu and twirls for his potential mate.

Small Fry

Astrapias, sicklebills, rifle birds and manucodes are just a few of the 1600 species of exotic feathered creatures you'll see in the skies of Indonesia, 380 of which you'll only find here. On Papua alone, there isn't just one species called 'bird of paradise', but 30.

Birdwatching is popular in many of the national parks. On Sulawesi, Tangkoko-Batuangas Dua Saudara Nature Reserve has regular birdwatching tours. In Bali, you can go on guided bird walks in and around Ubud.

Plants

Indonesia's plant diversity rivals the Amazon, and its botanical riches have defined its history. Wars were fought over the archipelago's spices, while high-value timber extraction has opened the forests for settlement and further exploitation.

Many species are showy bloomers, though these are usually rare outside cultivated areas. Orchids are abundant (2500 different species at last count) and are best seen at Bali's excellent botanical gardens. You can expect a riot of fragrant frangipani, lotus and hibiscus blossoms as well as a festival of other blooms across the archipelago. Impossibly complex heliconias hang from vines in all their multifaceted crimson, orange and golden glory.

Look for coffee plantations, especially in the hills of Bali near Munduk. In Maluku – the original Spice Islands – you can still catch the scent of nutmeg, vanilla and cloves, the latter most often wafting off the glowing end of a sweet *kretek* cigarette.

But it wouldn't be Indonesia without some real characters. Consider *Rafflesia arnoldii,* the world's largest flower, and the *Amorphophallus titanum,* the world's tallest flower. Both can be found, usually by their smell, on Sumatra and parts of Kalimantan and Java.

Life Underwater

Indonesia's incredible range of life on land is easily matched beneath the waves. The waters around Komodo, Sulawesi, the north coast of Papua, and even some spots in Java, Bali and Kalimantan are home to a

For a stunning all-access look at the world's 39 birds of paradise, pick up the *National Geographic* coffee-table book, *Birds of Paradise: Revealing the World's Most Extraordinary Birds,* by Tim Lamen and Edwin Scholes.

The *Rafflesia arnoldii,* the world's largest flower, and the *Amorphophallus titanum,* the world's tallest flower, can both be found in Sumatra and smell like rotting flesh.

There are over 25,000 flowering plant species in Indonesia and an estimated 40% exist nowhere else on earth.

kaleidoscope of corals, reef dwellers and pelagic marine life. In the Raja Ampat region of Papua there are at least 450 species of coral, six times more than that found in the entire Caribbean. Thriving in that environment are over 1600 species of fish, with divers encountering up to 300 in a single dive. Manta rays are also found in abundance, along with 118 species of shark, including the endangered hammerhead and sawtooth.

Exit the oceans to head upriver, and the story continues: Irrawaddy dolphins and finless porpoises occupy many of Indonesia's bays; a single population of truly freshwater dolphins (called *pesut*) can be found in Kalimantan's Sungai Mahakam (Mahakam River); and the world's smallest fish (paedocypris progenetica, 7.9mm) occupies Sumatra's peat swamps.

National Parks & Protected Areas

Despite a constant nipping at the edges by illegal loggers and farmers, Indonesia still has large tracts of protected forest and parks, and many new protected areas have been gazetted in recent years. National parks receive greater international recognition and funding than nature, wildlife and marine reserves, of which there are also many in Indonesia.

TOP 10 NATIONAL PARKS & RESERVES

PARK	LOCATION	FEATURES	ACTIVITIES	BEST TIME TO VISIT	PAGE
Gunung Leuser	Sumatra	rivers, rainforest, mountains; tigers, rhinoceros, elephants, primates such as orang-utans, white-breasted Thomas's leaf monkeys	orang-utan viewing, wildlife spotting, birdwatching; trekking, rafting	Dec-Mar	p556
Tanjung Puting	Kalimantan	tropical rainforest, mangrove forest, wetlands; orang-utans, macaques, proboscis monkeys, diverse wildlife	orang-utan viewing, birdwatching	May-Sep	p625
Kelimutu	Nusa Tenggara	coloured lakes	volcanology, short walks	Apr-Sep	p385
Gunung Rinjani	Nusa Tenggara	volcano	volcano hiking	Apr-Sep	p327
Ujung Kulon	Java	lowland rainforest, scrub, grassy plains, swamps, sandy beaches; one-horned rhinoceros, otters, squirrels, white-breasted Thomas's leaf monkeys, gibbons	jungle walks; wildlife spotting	Apr-Oct	p88
Gunung Bromo	Java	volcanic landscape	crater climbing	Apr-Oct	p192
Pulau Bunaken	Sulawesi	coral-fringed islands	snorkelling, diving, island lazing	Jun-Jan	p713
Kerinci Seblat	Sumatra	mountainous rainforest, one of Sumatra's highest peaks	trekking; wildlife spotting, birdwatching	Dec-Mar	p582
Komodo	Nusa Tenggara	Komodo dragon	snorkelling, diving; being chased by wildlife	Apr-Sep	p366
Bali Barat	Bali	low hills, grasslands, coral-fringed coasts	snorkelling, diving; wildlife spotting	yr-round	p309

Environmental Issues

The side effects of deforestation and resource extraction are felt across the nation and beyond: floods and landslides wash away valuable topsoil, rivers become sluggish and fetid, and haze from clearing fires blankets western Indonesia and beyond most dry seasons. The carbon released from deforestation and fires is a significant contributor to global climate change, which in a vicious cycle creates a longer dry season, allowing for more fires.

The problems flow right through to Indonesia's coastline and seas, where more than 80% of reef habitat is considered to be at risk, in part from coral bleaching caused by rising sea temperatures. A long history of cyanide and dynamite fishing has left much of Indonesia's coral lifeless or crumbled. Shark finning and manta hunting have taken their toll on populations, while overfishing threatens to disrupt the marine ecosystem.

Meanwhile, the burgeoning middle class is straining the nation's infrastructure. Private vehicles clog urban streets, creating choking air pollution; waste-removal services have difficulty coping with household and industrial refuse; and a lack of sewage disposal makes water from most sources undrinkable without boiling, putting further pressure on kerosene and firewood supplies.

One hawksbill turtle that visited Bali was tracked for the following year. Its destinations: Java, Kalimantan, Australia (Perth and much of Queensland) and then back to Bali.

Local Action

As the environmental situation becomes more dire, more Indonesians are taking notice. Although international groups such as World Wildlife Fund and the Nature Conservancy have strong and effective presences in Indonesia, it is the burgeoning local environmental movements that will exact real and lasting change.

Profauna (www.profauna.net/en) Operates throughout Indonesia to protect turtles and combat wildlife trade.

Walhi (Indonesian Friends of the Earth; www.walhi.or.id) Works to protect the country's environment at many levels.

AMAN (Indigenous People's Alliance of the Archipelago; www.aman.or.id/en) Helps secure indigenous rights to the natural forests necessary for their livelihood.

JATAM (Mining Advocacy Network; https://english.jatam.org) Works towards environmental responsibility and human-rights protection in Indonesia's mining sector.

Local Issues

Java

As Indonesia's most densely populated island, it's not surprising that rampant development causes widespread flooding in Jakarta, Semarang and other cities every rainy season. This results in mass social upheaval and chokes surviving coastal mangroves. And while Jakarta has begun removing garbage from the city's rivers, around 300 tonnes of rubbish is still dumped each day in the Sungai Ciliwung (Ciliwung River) alone.

Java's longest river, the Cirtarum, is also one of the world's most polluted from both rubbish and chemical dumping by a growing industrial sector. A 15-year US$500 million loan from the Asian Development Bank, committed in 2008, is supposed to go towards its clean-up and rehabilitation.

Bali

The beautiful island of Bali is its own worst enemy: it can't help being popular. Walhi, the Indonesian Forum for Environment (www.walhi.or.id), estimates that the average hotel room uses 3000L of water. The typical golf course needs three million litres a day. Hence, a place fabled for its water is now running short. In addition, rice fields are being converted to commercial land at a rate of about 600 to 1000 hectares a year.

Sumatra

In July 2017, Unesco voted to keep the Tropical Rainforest Heritage of Sumatra on its list of world heritage sites in danger. The area listed includes three national parks that are the only places left in the world where tigers, elephants, rhinos and orang-utans co-exist in the wild. While ongoing deforestation by palm oil and logging companies, as well as new hydroelectric dams and mining projects, poses the greatest threat to what is left of Sumatra's rainforests, the Indonesian government has announced controversial plans to build roads through the Unesco-listed area. The scheme has been denounced by environmental activists because it will fragment the habitats of the animals in the area.

Harrison Ford (yes, *that* one) lambasts Indonesia's forestry minister about Sumatra's deforestation in the documentary series, *Years of Living Dangerously*.

Nusa Tenggara

On southern Lombok unprecedented new development in the previously untouched and beautiful beach area of Kuta will have untold environmental consequences. On West Sumbawa illegal gold-mining operations continue to dump a steady stream of mercury into the island's waterways, as well as releasing toxic fumes into the air, despite Indonesia ratifying the Minamata Convention in 2017, which is designed to limit the use of mercury across the world.

Elsewhere, dynamite fishing and poaching by locals is an ongoing concern in the Unesco-listed Komodo National Park. In 2018 Unesco highlighted the growing amounts of plastic waste within the park, something noticed by many visitors too.

More positively, the governor of East Nusa Tenggara announced in September 2018 that he plans to impose a moratorium on mining in the province, citing environmental damage and a lack of benefit to the locals. On the Gili Islands, the Gili Eco Trust continues to make great strides toward greening the islands.

Kalimantan

Deforestation and resource extraction occur in Kalimantan on a vast scale. In 2018 one coal-mining company was fined two billion rupiah for dumping nearly 4000 tonnes of hazardous waste in east Kalimantan.

Visit environmental news site www.mongabay. com for the latest information on Indonesia's conservation successes...and failures.

During the dry seasons of 2014 and 2015, smog from hundreds of unstoppable fires shut down airports and caused widespread respiratory illness. In 2015 Indonesia's government began cracking down for the first time, fining multiple companies for intentionally starting fires.

Meanwhile, several indigenous communities have secured official recognition of their rights to ancestral lands, and some are developing ecotourism initiatives to provide alternative income for their village.

Sulawesi

Uncontrolled and illegal logging continues on Sulawesi, along with increasing sand-mining operations in central Sulawesi, which are destroying mangrove forests, eroding the coastline, silting rivers and causing arable land to dry up. The World Wildlife Foundation estimates that over half of the island's forests have disappeared, with much of the rest fragmented. That threatens the habitat of some of the most unique animals on the planet, a blend of Asian and Australasian species such as cuscuses and pigs with tusks.

However, a 2017 survey revealed that Sulawesi's coral is in better shape than expected, despite the impact of coral bleaching caused by global warming.

Maluku

Ongoing efforts to carve sugar-cane plantations out of the remote Aru islands, one of Indonesia's biodiversity hot spots, continue despite extensive local opposition since the plans were first mooted in 2010. Indonesia's Minister of Agriculture said in 2018 that the Aru Islands were to be one of the sites for a series of sugar-cane factories and plantations across the archipelago.

The Maluku islands are also prime poaching ground for the wild-bird trade. Populations of endemic and rare species have plummeted in recent years, especially songbirds, which collectors buy to enter into lucrative singing contests.

Papua

Deforestation to make way for oil-palm plantations has increased fivefold in the last decade in Papua, according to a 2017 report. With Sumatra and Kalimantan's forests hugely depleted, Papua's vast rainforests – which help make the region uniquely biodiverse – are now being targeted by both palm-oil producers and logging companies.

Mining is also a big threat to the island viewed as Indonesia's final frontier. In 2018 a proposed new gold mine in West Papua, which will encroach into the Taman Nasional Teluk Cenderawasih, aroused fierce opposition among local rights groups and indigenous peoples.

> In 2011 Norway placed US$1 billion on the table to encourage Indonesia to get a handle on deforestation and climate change.

Deforestation

In September 2018 Indonesia announced a three-year ban on new oil-palm plantations. Along with illegal logging and mining, palm-oil production has led to the widespread deforestation of large parts of the country, with Sumatra and Kalimantan affected especially. Over 24 million hectares of forest was cleared in Indonesia between 2000 and 2017, according to Global Forest Watch, an area about the size of the United Kingdom. Around 1.3 million hectares of forest continues to disappear annually, with the vast rainforests of remote Papua the newest target for the loggers and plantation owners.

While the moratorium on new oil-palm developments is welcome news, enforcing it may prove difficult in such a far-flung nation, one where the diktats of the central government are often ignored by corrupt local officials. Indonesia has also shown a reluctance to crackdown on illegal logging, which is thought to account for over 70% of all timber clearance across the archipelago and is driven by overseas demand.

TRAVELLER TACT: ENVIRONMENTAL CONCERNS

You will still see plenty of animal exploitation in Indonesia, including performing monkeys on street corners in big cities and endangered birds in markets. Taking photos or paying the handlers money only encourages this behaviour.

Shops sell turtle-shell products, rare seashells, snakeskin, stuffed birds and framed butterflies. Avoid these. Not only are they illegal, but importing them into most countries is banned and items will probably be confiscated by customs. See the Convention on International Trade in Endangered Species (CITES; www.cites.org) for more information.

Some animal exploitation is more subtle. Consider the life of a cute civet locked in a cage in a warehouse and force fed coffee to 'naturally' process the beans, for example. It's a far cry from the happy story plantations sell to justify charging outrageous prices for *kopi luwak* (civet coffee).

Finally, garbage is an obvious problem. And while taking your biscuit wrapper away with you from some already rubbish-strewn waterfall may feel futile, your guides and other hikers will notice and might even join you. It is a small, but important step in the right direction.

Mineral Extraction

Coal, oil, gold, nickel, tin, aluminium, copper, iron ore, diamonds...what lies beneath Indonesia's forest is just as tempting for exploitation as what grows above. Although mining can be done in an ecologically responsible manner, a lack of oversight and poor enforcement of regulations has resulted in a legacy of environmental disaster. Vast swathes of land have been dug open with little regard for environmental impact and almost no reclamation.

Papua has become the front line in the battle between mining companies and local governments on one side and indigenous peoples and environmental activists on the other.

The Illegal Animal Trade

The thriving international trade in animals and animal parts is as much a threat to imperilled species in Indonesia as deforestation. Demand has been fuelled in part by the growing Chinese middle-class and their conspicuous consumption of exotic food and medicine. But the illegal wildlife trade is also driven by demand elsewhere in Asia and inside Indonesia itself.

Pangolins (or scaly anteater) – the world's most trafficked mammal – are close to extinction in Indonesia because of the demand for them in China and Vietnam. Tigers and sharks are also prized by the traffickers, with Indonesia thought to be the world's largest supplier of shark fins, regarded as a delicacy in Hong Kong and Singapore especially. Reptiles such as pythons and monitor lizards are sold online and often sent out of the country live by mail. Most recently turtles have become sought after, with two Chinese men arrested in Sulawesi in 2018 for being in possession of 200kg of turtle shells. Inside Indonesia, rare birds are frequently traded and several species are now severely endangered.

Indonesia's efforts to combat the illegal wildlife trade have been patchy at best. A draft bill to update the country's 1990 conservation law was sent to the government in April 2018, but has yet to be returned to parliament for ratification.

Its proximity to the Philippines makes the port at Bitung on Sulawesi an unfortunate epicentre for wildlife smuggling. Tasikoki (www.tasikoki. org) is an entirely volunteer-run organisation that rescues and cares for animals confiscated from smugglers.

Survival Guide

Directory A–Z

Accessible Travel

Despite enactment of a disability law in 2016 following the country's ratification of the CRPD (Convention on the Rights of Persons with Disabilities) in 2011 and increasing awareness of the needs of people with disabilities, Indonesia is a difficult destination for those with access issues, such as limited mobility, vision or hearing impairment.

Very few buildings have disabled access, and even international chain hotels may not have fully accessible facilities.

Pavements are riddled with potholes, loose manholes, parked motorcycles and all sorts of street life, and are very rarely level for long until the next set of steps. Even the able bodied walk on roads rather than negotiate the hassle of the pavement (sidewalk).

Public transport is entirely inaccessible for wheelchair users. Cars with a driver can be hired readily at cheap rates, but wheelchair-accessible vehicles can only be arranged through specialist accessible tour operators. Guides are easily found in tourist areas, and though it's not usual practice, they could be hired as helpers (eg as wheelchair-pushers) if needed.

At the same time, as in many developing countries, Indonesians are extremely helpful and welcoming, so no wheelchair-using traveller will wait for long in front of a step without someone coming to help.

Bali, with its wide range of tourist services and facilities, is the favoured destination for travellers with disabilities since it's much easier to find suitable amenities and adapted accommodation.

The owners of **Accessible Indonesia** (www.accessible indonesia.org) are knowledgeable and well connected and work with local organisations for the disabled. They offer tours principally to Java, Sulawesi and Bali, as well as day cruises, diving and snorkelling expeditions and wheelchair-accessible transfers. They are well used to problem-solving to overcome infrastructural barriers. There is access information for international airports and basic access information about the destinations they serve on their website.

Download Lonely Planet's free Accessible Travel guides from https://shop.lonely planet.com/categories/accessible-travel.com.

Accommodation

Accommodation in Indonesia ranges from the very basic to the super-luxurious. It's wise to reserve well in advance in the most touristed areas, especially if you're visiting during the peak months (July, August and December).

Hotels

Hotels in tourist areas can be excellent at any price range. But elsewhere standards quickly fall: slack maintenance and uneven service are common, although staff are usually pleasant. Costs vary considerably, but in general Indonesia is one of the better bargains in Southeast Asia.

Destinations frequented by travellers have plenty of reasonably priced accommodation. In Bali and other touristed areas such as the Gilis, Labuan Bajo on Flores, and Danau Toba on Sumatra, you'll have a wide range of sleeping choices. Options diminish quickly as you get off the beaten track, where you're often reliant on basic guesthouses and homestays, although lavish resorts, surf camps and idyllic yet mod-

---

PLAN YOUR STAY ONLINE

For more accommodation reviews by Lonely Planet authors, check out www.lonelyplanet.com. You'll find independent reviews, as well as recommendations on the best places to stay.

est getaways can be found across the archipelago.

➡ Accommodation attracts a combined tax and service charge (called 'plus plus') of 21%. In budget places, this is generally included in the price, but check first. Many midrange and top-end places will add it on, which can add substantially to your bill.

➡ Rates quoted include tax and are those that travellers are likely to pay during high season. Nailing down rates is difficult, as some establishments publish the rates they actually plan to charge, while others publish rates that are pure fantasy, fully expecting to discount by 50%.

➡ Shop online and contact hotels directly to find the best rates. There's no one formula that works across Indonesia.

BUDGET HOTELS & GUESTHOUSES

The cheapest accommodation is in hotels or guesthouses that are simple but usually reasonably clean and comfortable. Names often include the word losmen, homestay, inn, *penginapan* or *pondok*. Standards vary widely. You can expect the following:

➡ maybe air-con

➡ usually wi-fi

➡ maybe hot water

➡ sometimes no window

➡ private bathroom with shower and normally a Western-style toilet

➡ often a pool (on Bali)

➡ simple breakfast

MIDRANGE HOTELS

Many hotels have a range of rooms, from budget to midrange. The best may be called VIP, deluxe or some other moniker. In addition to what you'll get at a budget hotel, expect the following:

➡ balcony/porch/patio

➡ satellite TV

➡ small fridge

SLEEPING PRICE RANGES

Accommodation rates are for high season (May to September and Christmas/New Year).

The following price ranges refer to a double room with bathroom. Unless otherwise stated relevant taxes are included in the price.

Bali & Lombok

$ less than 450,000Rp

$$ 450,000–1,400,000Rp

$$$ more than 1,400,000Rp

Rest of Indonesia

$ less than 250,000Rp

$$ 250,000–800,000Rp

$$$ more than 800,000Rp

TOP-END HOTELS

Top-end hotels can range from international chains in Jakarta to beautiful resorts on Bali and lavish getaways elsewhere. You should expect the following:

➡ superb service

➡ views – ocean, lush valleys and rice fields or private gardens

➡ spa

➡ maybe a private pool

Hostels

Backpacker-style hostels with dormitories can be found in Jakarta, Bali, the Gilis and beyond, including Flores. Elsewhere, inexpensive guesthouses are more common.

Staying in Villages

In many places in Indonesia you'll often be welcome to stay in villages. If there is no hotel or guesthouse, speak to the *kepala desa* (village head) about finding a homestay that will usually include meals. Most village heads are generally very hospitable and friendly. Consider the following:

➡ You may not get a room of your own, just a bed.

➡ Payment is usually expected: 100,000Rp per night as a rule of thumb. The

kepala desa may suggest an amount, but often it is *terserah* (up to you), and you should always offer to pay.

➡ While the village head's house sometimes acts as an unofficial hotel, you are a guest and often an honoured one. Elaborate meals may be prepared just for you. It's also a good idea to have a gift or two to offer – cigarettes, photographs or small souvenirs from your country are popular.

➡ Homestays and village stays are a great way to socialise with families and neighbours, contribute to the local economy and experience Indonesian life up close.

➡ Villages on Baliem Valley trekking routes often have basic guesthouses for tourists.

Camping

Camping in national parks is popular among Indonesian youth, although formal camping grounds with power and other facilities are rare. Outside the parks, camping is unknown, and villagers will regard campers as a source of entertainment. Some Kalimantan and Papua treks may include camping as will some mountain treks such as Gunung Rinjani on Lombok.

Climate

Jakarta

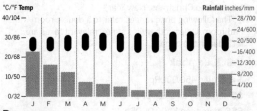

Denpasar

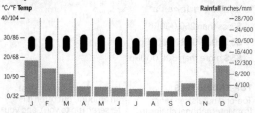

Padang

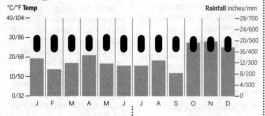

Guides or operators usually supply gear.

Villas & Long-Term Accommodation

Luxury villas are popular accommodation options on Bali, although they are not without their environmental costs in terms of water usage and placement amid once-pristine rice fields. Many come with pools, views, beaches and more. Often the houses are staffed and you have the services of a cook, driver etc.

Rates range from around US$200 per night for a modest villa to US$2000 per night and much more for your own tropical estate. There are often deals, especially in low season, and several couples sharing can make something grand affordable.

Enquire about the following when renting a villa:

➜ How far is the villa from the beach and nightlife?

➜ Is a driver or car service included?

➜ If there is a cook, is food included?

➜ Is laundry included?

For longer stays, look in the *Bali Advertiser* (www.baliadvertiser.biz) or search Facebook. If your tastes are simple, you can find basic bungalows for as little as US$300 a month.

Booking Services

Traveloka (www.traveloka.com) Indonesia-wide accommodation options.

Lonely Planet (www.lonelyplanet.com/indonesia/hotels) Recommendations and bookings.

Customs Regulations

Indonesia has the usual list of prohibited imports, including drugs, weapons, fresh fruit and anything remotely pornographic. Items allowed include the following:

➜ 200 cigarettes (or 25 cigars or 100g of tobacco)

➜ a 'reasonable amount' of perfume

➜ 1L of alcohol

Surfers with more than two or three boards may be charged a 'fee', and this could apply to other items if the officials suspect that you aim to sell them in Indonesia. If you have nothing to declare, customs clearance is usually quick.

Embassies & Consulates

It's important to know what your own embassy can and can't do to help you if you get into trouble. Generally speaking, it won't be much help if whatever trouble you're in is your own fault. Remember that you are bound by the laws of the country you are in. In genuine emergencies you might get some assistance, but only if other channels have been exhausted.

Foreign embassies are in Jakarta; Bali and Medan have a few consulates. There are also some in towns close to foreign borders.

Bali

Australian Consulate (☏0361-200 0100; www.bali.indonesia.embassy.gov.au; Jl Tantular 32, Denpasar; ◷8am-4pm Mon-Fri)

US Consulate (☏0361-233605; https://id.usembassy.gov; Jl Hayam Wuruk 310, Renon, Denpasar; ◷9am-noon & 1-3.30pm Mon-Fri)

Jakarta

Australian Embassy (☏021-2550 5555; www.indonesia.embassy.gov.au; Jl Patra Kuningan Raya Kav 1-4; ◷8am-4pm Mon-Fri)

Brunei Darussalam Embassy
(☎021-3190 6080; www.mofat.
gov.bn; Jl Patra Kuningan IX
3-5, Kuningan Timur; ◷8am-
4pm Mon-Fri)

Canadian Embassy (☎021-2550
7800; www.canadainternational.
gc.ca/indonesia-indonesie;
6th fl, World Trade Centre, Jl
Jenderal Sudirman Kav 29-31;
◷8am-4.30pm Mon-Thu, to
11.30am Fri)

Dutch Embassy (☎021-524
8200; www.netherlandsworld
wide.nl/countries/indonesia;
Jl HR Rasuna Said Kav S-3;
◷8am-4pm Mon-Thu, to
2pm Fri)

French Embassy (☎021-2355
7600; www.ambafrance-id.org;
Jl Thamrin 20, Menteng; ◷8am-
5pm Mon-Thu, to 1pm Fri)

German Embassy (☎021-3985
5000; www.jakarta.diplo.de; Jl
Thamrin 1, Menteng; ◷7.15am-
3.45pm Mon-Thu, to 1pm Fri)

Irish Embassy (☎021-2809
4300; World Trade Centre I, Jl
Jenderal Sudirman; ◷9am-
4pm Mon-Fri)

Malaysian Embassy (☎021-
522 4947; www.kln.gov.my/
web/idn_jakarta/home; Jl
HR Rasuna Said Kav X/6 1-3,
Kuningan; ◷8am-12.30pm &
2.30-4pm Mon-Fri)

New Zealand Embassy (☎021-
2995 5800; www.nzembassy.
com; 10th fl, Sentral Senayan
2, Jl Asia Afrika 8; ◷8am-4pm
Mon-Thu, to 1pm Fri)

Papua New Guinea Embassy
(☎021-725 1218; www.kundu
-jakarta.com; 6th fl, Panin Bank
Centre, Jl Jenderal Sudirman
1; ◷8am-4pm Mon-Thu, to
2pm Fri)

Singaporean Embassy (☎021-
2995 0400; www.mfa.gov.sg; Jl
HR Rasuna Said, Block X/4 Kav
2, Kuningan; ◷8.30am-noon &
1.30-5pm Mon-Fri)

UK Embassy (☎021-2356 5200;
http://ukinindonesia.fco.gov.
uk; Jl Patra Kuningan Raya Blok
L5-6; ◷7.30am-noon & 12.45-
4pm Mon-Thu, 7.30am-1pm Fri)

US Embassy (☎021-3435
9000; https://id.usembassy.
gov; Jl Merdeka Selatan 3-5;
◷7.30am-4pm Mon-Fri)

Kupang

Timor-Leste Consulate
(☎0380-855 4552; Jl Frans
Seda; ◷8-11.30am & 1.30-
3.30pm Mon-Thu, to 3pm Fri)
The visa office for Timor-Leste.

Medan

Malaysian Consulate (☎061-
453 1342; www.kln.gov.my/
web/idn_medan; Jl Diponegoro
43; ◷8am-4pm Mon-Fri)

Electricity

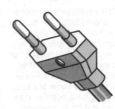

Type C
220V/50Hz

Type F
230V/50Hz

Insurance

A travel-insurance policy to
cover theft, loss and medical
problems is essential. There
are a wide variety of policies,
most sold online; make
certain your policy will cover
speedy medical evacuation
from anywhere in Indonesia.

Theft is a potential problem in Indonesia, so make
sure that your policy covers
expensive items adequately.
Many policies have restrictions on laptops and expensive camera gear, and refunds
are often for depreciated
value, not replacement value.

If you are diving, specialist
dive insurance is a wise investment.

Worldwide travel insur-
ance is available at www.
lonelyplanet.com/travel
-insurance. You can buy,
extend and claim online anytime – even if you're already
on the road.

Internet Access

Indonesia is increasingly
wired, although connection
speeds vary widely depending on where you are in the
archipelago.

➡ Wi-fi (pronounced
'wee-fee' in Indonesia) is
commonly available for
free in hotels, hostels and
guesthouses now, although it
doesn't always work in rural
areas.

➡ Many cafes and
restaurants in tourist areas
offer free wi-fi.

➡ Data through your
smartphone is often the
fastest way to connect to
the internet; 4G service
is spreading in Indonesia,
although download speeds
remain slow compared to
other countries.

Legal Matters

Drugs, gambling and por-
nography are illegal. Two
Australians were executed

for narcotics offences in 2015, and foreign nationals continue to receive death sentences for drug crimes.

➡ It is an offence to engage in paid work without a formal working permit.

➡ Visa length of stay is strictly enforced; many a careless tourist has seen the inside of an immigration detention facility or paid large fines.

➡ Corruption remains a fact of life. If you are pulled over for a dubious traffic infringement, be polite and respectful as the officer lectures you and then suggests an alternative to a trip to the police station and a courthouse date. Generally, 50,000Rp is plenty, but up to 500,000Rp may be demanded on Bali.

➡ In the case of an accident involving serious injury or death, drive straight to the nearest police station as 'mob rule' can prevail, with blame falling on the foreigner.

➡ If you need to report a crime, head to a police station in respectable dress with an Indonesian friend or interpreter in tow but don't expect much.

➡ If you find yourself in serious trouble with the law, contact your embassy or consulate immediately. They will not be able to arrange bail but will be able to provide you with an interpreter and may be able to suggest legal counsel.

LGBT+ Travellers

LGBT+ travellers in Indonesia should follow the same precautions as straight travellers: avoid public displays of affection. This is especially important in conservative areas such as Aceh, where locals of the same sex seen hugging have been sent for 'reeducation' by religious police.

➡ Gay men in Indonesia are referred to as *homo* or *gay*; lesbians are *lesbi*.

➡ Indonesia's community of transvestite/transsexual *waria* – from the words *wanita* (woman) and *pria* (man) – has always had a very public profile; it's also known by the less polite term *banci*.

➡ Islamic groups proscribe homosexuality, but violence against LGBT+ people is rare.

➡ Bali is especially friendly destination for LGBT+ travellers, with a large community of expats and people from elsewhere in Indonesia.

Indonesian LGBT+ organisations include the following:

GAYa Nusantara (www.gaya nusantara.or.id) Website for the Indonesian LGBT+ community.

Gaya Dewata (YGD; www. gayadewata.com) Bali's oldest and only community-run LGBT+ organisation.

Maps

Locally produced maps are often inaccurate. Periplus produces useful maps of most of the archipelago and the major cities, although the data for fast-changing areas such as Bali can be very out of date. Google maps has made extensive progress around the nation.

Hikers will have little chance of finding accurate maps of remote areas. It's far more useful (and wise) to employ the services of a local guide, who will be able to navigate seemingly uncharted territory.

Money
ATMs

➡ ATMs are common across Indonesia except in very rural areas. Most now accept cards affiliated with international networks, although they will not always work. Bank BNI, with ATMs across the nation, is reliable.

➡ ATMs in Indonesia have a maximum limit for withdrawals; sometimes it is 2,000,000Rp, but it can be as low as 500,000Rp, which is not much in foreign-currency terms.

➡ Many ATMs have a sticker that specifies whether the machine dispenses 50,000Rp or 100,000Rp notes.

➡ Always carry a sizeable amount of rupiah when you are travelling outside cities and tourist areas as ATM networks go down and/ or you can be on an island where the only ATM is broken or nonexistent.

Cash

The unit of currency used in Indonesia is the rupiah (Rp). Notes come in 2000Rp, 5000Rp, 10,000Rp, 20,000Rp, 50,000Rp and 100,000Rp denominations.

Coins of 50Rp, 100Rp, 200Rp, 500Rp and 1000Rp are also in circulation. For change in amounts below 50Rp, expect to receive a few sweets.

Try to carry a fair amount of money in bills 20,000Rp and under as getting change for larger bills is often a problem. ATMs dispense 50,000Rp or 100,000Rp bills only.

By government decree, all businesses are required to price goods and services in rupiah. Many tourist outfits such as hotels and dive shops try to price in dollars or euros to avoid currency fluctuations.

Credit Cards

➡ In cities and touristed areas (eg Bali), credit cards will be accepted at midrange and better hotels and resorts. More expensive shops as well as travel agents will also accept them, but often there will be a surcharge of around 3%.

➡ MasterCard and Visa are the most widely accepted credit cards. Cash advances are possible at many ATMs and banks.

➡ Before leaving home, inform your credit-card issuer that you will be travelling in Indonesia; otherwise your account may be frozen for suspected fraud the first time you try to use it.

➡ The skimming of credit cards at ATMs is a problem in Bali especially. It's best to use ATMs at a bank, rather than elsewhere.

Money Changers

➡ The US dollar is the most widely accepted foreign currency in Indonesia. Australian, British and Japanese currencies, as well as euros, are exchangeable only in the most touristed areas of Bali and Jakarta.

➡ Outside cities and tourist areas, banks may only be willing to exchange crisp, new US$100 bills. In many rural areas banks won't offer any exchange, or rates will be poor.

➡ Money changers range from the honest to dishonest. Signs bearing phrases such as 'official' and 'licensed' are meaningless. Follow these steps to avoid getting ripped off when exchanging money.

➡ Find out the going exchange rate online. Know that anyone offering a better rate will need to make a profit through other means.

➡ Stick to banks, exchange counters in airports or large and reputable storefront operations.

➡ Skip any place offering too-good exchange rates and claiming to charge no fees or commissions.

➡ Avoid exchange stalls down alleys or in otherwise dubious locations (that sounds obvious, but scores of tourists are taken in daily).

➡ Common exchange scams include rigged calculators, sleight-of-hand schemes, 'mistakes' on the posted rates and demands that you hand over your money before *you* have counted the money on offer.

➡ Use an ATM to obtain rupiah. Check with your bank about fees; if they are not outrageous, you'll avoid carrying large amounts of cash and get a decent exchange rate.

Rupiah Redenomination

Indonesia has plans to redenominate the rupiah by removing three digits from the currency. So, for example, the 20,000Rp note would become the 20Rp note. This could happen from 2020, although the old money will remain legal tender until at least 2025. Changing the national currency is likely to be a very complex process, with many implications for travellers. These include the following:

➡ New notes will be introduced that are identical to the current ones, except that the final three zeros missing. Long-term plans call for all-new designs.

➡ The government stresses that current banknotes will retain their value (eg the 100,000Rp note will be the same as the new 100Rp note); however, how this will play out is anyone's guess. In other nations, such as Russia, there has been widespread refusal to accept old notes, even after government guarantees of their value.

➡ It will likely take years for price lists and computer systems to be fully updated, so it will be up to customers to make certain that they are

---

EATING PRICE RANGES

The following ranges represent the average cost of a standard main course.

Bali & Lombok

$ less than 60,000Rp

$$ 60,000–250,000Rp

$$$ more than 250,000Rp

Rest of Indonesia

$ less than 50,000Rp

$$ 50,000–200,000Rp

$$$ more than 200,000Rp

being charged – and paying – appropriately.

➡ Introduction of the new denominations is likely to occur with little notice to avoid financial upheavals.

Photography

Indonesia and Indonesians can be very photogenic, but whatever you do, photograph with discretion and manners. It's always polite to ask first, and if the person says no, don't take the photo. A gesture, a smile and a nod are all that is usually necessary.

Post

Sending postcards and normal-sized letters (ie under 20g) by airmail is cheap but not really fast. For anything over 20g, the charge is based on weight. You can send parcels up to 20kg and have them properly wrapped and sealed at any post office (www.posindonesia.co.id).

Every substantial town has a *kantor pos* (post office). In tourist centres, there are also postal agencies. They are often open long hours and provide postal services. Many will also wrap and pack parcels.

Public Holidays

Following are the national public holidays in Indonesia. Unless stated, they vary from year to year. There are many regional holidays as well.

Tahun Baru Masehi (New Year's Day) 1 January

Tahun Baru Imlek (Chinese New Year) Late January to early February

Wafat Yesus Kristus (Good Friday) Late March or early April

Nyepi (Balinese New Year) Bali closes down for one day, usually in March, sometimes April

Hari Buruh (Labour Day) 1 May

Hari Waisak May

Kenaikan Yesus Kristus (Ascension of Christ) May

Hari Proklamasi Kemerdekaan (Independence Day) 17 August

Hari Natal (Christmas Day) 25 December

The following Islamic holidays have dates that change each year.

Muharram Islamic New Year: 1 September 2019, 20 August 2020, 10 August 2021

Maulud Nabi Muhammad Birthday of the Prophet Muhammad: 10 November 2019, 29 October 2020, 18 October 2021

Isra Miraj Nabi Muhammad Ascension of the Prophet Muhammad: 3 April 2019, 22 May 2020, March 11 2021

Idul Fitri Also known as Lebaran, this two-day national public holiday marks the end of Ramadan; avoid travel due to crowds: 5 June 2019, 24 May 2020, 15 May 2021

Idul Adha Islamic feast of the sacrifice: 12 August 2019, 31 July 2020, 20 July 2021

Safe Travel

Indonesia is fairly safe compared with many places in the world. There are some hassles from the avaricious, but most visitors face many more dangers at home. Petty theft occurs, but it is not prevalent.

RESPONSIBLE TRAVEL

To visit Indonesia responsibly, try to tread lightly as you go, with respect for both the land and the diverse cultures of its people.

Watch your use of water Water demand outstrips supply in much of Indonesia – even in seemingly green places like Bali. Take your hotel up on its offer to save water by not washing your sheets and towels every day. At the high end you can also forgo your own private plunge pool, or a pool altogether.

Don't hit the bottle Those bottles of Aqua (a top local brand of bottled water, owned by Danone) are convenient but they add up. The zillions of such bottles tossed away each year are a serious blight. Since tap water is unsafe, ask your hotel if you can refill from their huge containers of drinking water. Some businesses already offer this service.

Support environmentally aware businesses The number of businesses committed to good environmental practices is growing fast in Indonesia.

Conserve power Turn off lights and air-con when not using them.

Bag the bags Refuse plastic bags and say no to plastic straws too.

Leave the animals be Reconsider swimming with captive dolphins, riding elephants and patronising attractions where wild animals are made to perform for crowds, interactions that have been identified by animal-welfare experts as harmful to the animals. And don't try to pet, feed or otherwise interact with animals in the wild as it disrupts their natural behaviour and can make them sick.

Alcohol Poisoning

Outside of reputable bars and resorts, it's best to avoid buying *arak*, the locally produced booze made from rice or palm. It can contain poisonous methanol, which is produced during the fermentation process and is not always burned off. Deaths and injuries do happen – especially on Bali and the Gilis – when unscrupulous vendors substitute *arak* for other spirits like vodka, gin or whisky. If the price of drinks in a bar seems unnaturally low, pause to consider what you might be drinking.

Drugs

Indonesia has a zero-tolerance policy towards drugs and there have been many high-profile arrests and convictions. The execution by firing squad in 2015 of two Australians convicted of drug offences as part of the 'Bali Nine' should serve as a stark warning.

➡ Random raids of nightclubs in Jakarta and Bali and mandatory urine tests for anyone found with drugs occur regularly (entrapment schemes are not unknown: that dealer may be a cop).

➡ Private parties on Bali have been raided, and hotel owners are required by law to report offenders.

➡ The law does not provide for differentiation between substance types or amounts, whether a full bag of heroin or a few specks of marijuana dust in your pocket.

Pollution

➡ Avoid beaches in built-up areas, especially after storms flush sewage out to the surf. This is especially true of many beaches in south Bali.

➡ Air quality can be terrible in heavily populated areas and across Sumatra during annual land clearances for oil-palm plantations.

GOVERNMENT TRAVEL ADVICE

It is always worthwhile to check with official government sources before visiting Indonesia in order to check current travel conditions and the overall safety situation. But bear in mind that government sources generally take a conservative and overcautious view. Follow reputable news sources in order to get a more realistic picture.

Government travel advisories include the following:

Australia (www.smartraveller.gov.au)

Canada (www.travel.gc.ca)

New Zealand (www.safetravel.govt.nz)

UK (www.gov.uk/foreign-travel-advice)

US (www.travel.state.gov)

Safety

Security in touristed areas increased after the 2002 and 2005 Bali bombings but has since been relaxed. The odds you will be caught up in such a tragedy are low. Luxury hotels that are part of international chains tend to have the best security, though they also make the most tempting targets, as shown in Jakarta in 2003 and 2009. Suicide bombers did strike a bus terminal in East Jakarta in 2017, killing three policemen, and churches in Surabaya were targeted in May 2018 in attacks that killed 28 people, but such incidents remain rare.

Security issues in Indonesia are often exaggerated by foreign media, who portray rambunctious protest rallies and minor incidents of civil unrest as nationwide pandemonium. Foreign governments add to the hype with heavy-handed, blanket travel warnings. While it's true that small sections of Indonesia experience flashes of conflict, overall the archipelago is safe.

Scams

As in many developing countries, some people are out to relieve you of your money in one way or another. It's really hard to say when an 'accepted' practice like overcharging becomes an unacceptable rip-off, but plenty of instances of practised deceit occur.

➡ Credit-card fraud, especially the skimming of cards at ATMs and elsewhere, is widespread in Bali and Java. It's best to use ATMs attached to banks.

➡ Con artists exist. Some are smooth-talking guides seeking to lead you to a shop or hotel where they receive commission.

➡ Bali is the home of many scams. And there are continuing reports of short-changing money changers. As always, trust your common sense.

➡ Beggers (including children) are usually part of organised groups. Most Indonesians suffer in silence and would never ask for money; consider giving to aid programs if you want to help.

➡ Touts and hawkers are common in tourist areas. Ignore them.

Theft

Violent crime is uncommon, but bag-snatching from motorbikes, pickpocketing and theft from rooms and parked cars occurs. Take the same precautions you would in any urban area. Remember that other travellers will sometimes steal things. Other commonsense tips include the following:

➡ Secure money before leaving an ATM (and don't forget your card!).

➡ Don't leave valuables on a beach while swimming.

➡ Use front-desk/in-room safes.

Taxes & Refunds

Indonesia has a 10% sales tax for certain items. The tax is usually included in the purchase price.

Telephone Services

Mobile Phones

➡ Since April 2018 all new SIM cards bought in Indonesia must be registered. If you buy your card from an official store of a phone provider or at the airports in Jakarta or Bali, they will do it for you automatically.

➡ SIM cards start at 15,000Rp. They come with cheap rates for calling other countries, from around 5000Rp per minute.

➡ SIM cards are widely available and easily refilled with credit.

➡ Most official outlets offer deals where you pay 50,000Rp and up for a SIM card and credit.

➡ 4G networks are spreading across the nation, but speeds are slower than in other countries.

➡ Data plans average about 40,000Rp for 1GB of data.

➡ Mobile numbers start with a four-digit prefix that begins with 08 and have a total of 10 to 12 digits.

Internet Calling

Most hotel wi-fi will allow at least some form of internet calling such as Skype to work. Mobile carriers often have an access code so you can make international calls over the internet for about US$0.03 per minute,

or use a free app such as WhatsApp.

Time

There are three time zones in Indonesia.

➡ Java, Sumatra, and West and Central Kalimantan are on Western Indonesian Time (GMT/UTC plus seven hours).

➡ Bali, Nusa Tenggara, South and East Kalimantan, and Sulawesi are on Central Indonesian Time (GMT/UTC plus eight hours).

➡ Papua and Maluku are on Eastern Indonesian Time (GMT/UTC plus nine hours). In a country straddling the equator, there is no daylight-saving time.

Allowing for variations due to summer or daylight-saving time, when it is noon in Jakarta it is 9pm the previous day in San Francisco, midnight in New York, 5am in London, 1pm in Singapore, Bali and Makassar, 2pm in Jayapura and 3pm in Melbourne and Sydney.

Toilets

In much of Indonesia, the bathroom features a large water tank and a plastic scoop. *Kamar mandi* means bathroom and *mandi* means to bathe or wash.

➡ Don't go climbing into the water tank – it's your water supply and it's also the supply for every other guest that comes after you. Scoop water out of the tank and pour it over yourself.

➡ Most tourist hotels have showers now, many have hot water.

➡ Indonesian toilets are basically holes in the ground with footrests on either side, although Western-style toilets are common in tourist areas. To flush the toilet, reach for the plastic scoop, take water from the tank and

pour. Public toilets are rare; find a cafe and smile.

➡ Toilet paper is seldom supplied in public places, though you can easily buy it. Many Indonesians instead use their left hand and copious quantities of water – again, keep that scoop handy. Often there is a wastebasket next to the toilet where the toilet paper should go, as opposed to the easily clogged toilet.

➡ *Kamar kecil* is Bahasa Indonesia for toilet, but people usually understand 'way-say' (WC). *Wanita* means women and *pria* means men.

Tourist Information

Indonesia's Ministry of Tourism (www.indonesia.travel) has decent, basic information.

Most tourist offices in Indonesia offer little of value. Notable exceptions include tourist offices in Ubud, Bali; Yogyakarta, Java; and the Raja Ampat Tourism Management Office in Sorong, Papua.

Visas

Tourist Visas

The visa situation is constantly in flux. It is essential that you confirm current formalities before you arrive. Failure to meet all the entrance requirements can see you on the first flight out or subject to heavy fines. Overstaying your visa will result in a fine and can sometimes lead to you being detained.

No matter what type of visa you are going to use, your passport must be valid for at least six months from the date of your arrival.

At the time of research, the main visa options for visitors to Indonesia are as follows.

Visa in Advance Visitors can apply for a visa before they

STOPPING CHILD SEX-TOURISM

Indonesia has become a destination for foreigners seeking to sexually exploit local children. A range of socio-economic factors render many children and young people vulnerable to such abuse and some individuals prey upon this vulnerability. The sexual abuse and exploitation of children has serious, life-long and even life-threatening consequences for victims. Strong laws exist in Indonesia to prosecute offenders, and many countries have extraterritorial legislation that allows nationals to be prosecuted in their own country for these crimes.

Travellers can help stop child sex-tourism by reporting suspicious behaviour. Reports can be made to the Anti-Human Trafficking Unit (☑021 721 8098) of the Indonesian police. If you know the nationality of the individual, you can contact their embassy directly.

For more information, contact ECPAT (www.ecpat.net), a global network working on these issues, with over 70 affiliate organisations around the world. Child Wise (www.childwise.org.au) is the Australian member of ECPAT.

---

arrive in Indonesia. Typically this is a visitor's visa, which is usually valid for 60 days. Details vary by country; contact your nearest Indonesian embassy or consulate to determine processing fees and times. It is nearly always easiest to apply for this visa in your home country. Some Indonesian embassies are reluctant to grant these visas to non-nationals or non-residents of the country you are applying in. In Southeast Asia, Bangkok and Singapore are the most hassle-free places to apply for a 60-day visa. Note: this is the only way to obtain a 60-day visitor visa, even if you qualify for Visa on Arrival.

Visa Free Citizens of 169 countries can receive a 30-day visa for free upon arrival. But note that this visa cannot be extended and you may be limited to which airports and ports you can use to exit the country, eg the Timor-Leste visa run may not work with this visa.

Visa on Arrival This 30-day extendable visa is available at major airports and harbours (but not most land borders). The cost is US$35; be sure to have the exact amount in US currency. Eligible countries include Australia, Canada, much of the EU (including France, Germany, Ireland, the Netherlands and the UK), plus New Zealand and the USA. VOA renewals for 30 days are possible. If you don't qualify for VOA, you must get a visa in advance.

Fines for overstaying your visa expiration date are 300,000Rp per day for the first 60 days, although there are rumours that may be increased. Overstay more and you will be deported and blacklisted from entering Indonesia, but you don't have to pay a fine.

Study & Work Visas

You can arrange visas for study, short-term research, visiting family and similar purposes if you have a sponsor, such as an educational institution. These social/cultural (*sosial/budaya*) visas must be applied for at an Indonesian embassy or consulate overseas. Normally valid for three months on arrival, they can be extended every month after that for up to six months without leaving the country. Fees apply.

People wishing to study or work in Indonesia must apply directly to the **Central Immigration Office** (Direktorat Jenderal Imigrasi; ☑021-522 4658; www.imigrasi.go.id; Jl HR Rasuna Said 8 & 9; ◷8am-3pm Mon-Fri) in Jakarta for a Limited-Stay Visa (*Kartu Izin Tinggal Terbatas*, or *Kitas*). First, though, contact your nearest embassy for the most direct avenue and to find out what qualifies as 'study'. Those granted limited stay are issued a Kitas card, which is much prized among travellers.

If you're planning to work in Indonesia, your employer will need to organise your visa – it's a long and complicated process.

Travel Permits

Special permits are still technically required for travel in parts of Papua (p469).

Renewing Your Visa

You can renew a 30-day Visa on Arrival once (but not usually a Visa Free). The procedures are complex.

➡ At least seven days before your visa expires, go to an immigration office. These can usually be found in larger cities and regional capitals.

➡ Bring your passport, a photocopy of your passport and a copy of your ticket out of Indonesia (which should be for a date during the renewal period).

➡ Wear modest clothes, eg men may be required to wear long pants.

➡ Pay a fee of 350,000Rp. You may have to return to the office twice over a three- to five-day period.

One way to avoid the renewal hassle is to use a visa agent such as **ChannelOne** (☑0878 6204 3224; www.channel1.biz; Jl Sunset 100X) on Bali which, for a fee, will do the bureaucratic work for you.

Volunteering

There are excellent opportunities for aspiring volunteers in Indonesia, but Lonely Planet does not endorse any organisations that we do not work with directly, so it is essential that you do your own thorough research before agreeing to volunteer with or donate to any organisation. A three-month commitment is recommended for working with children.

For many groups, fundraising and cash donations are the best way to help. Some also can use skilled volunteers to work as English teachers and provide professional services such as medical care. A few offer paid volunteering, whereby volunteers pay for room and board and perform often menial tasks.

A good resource to find NGOs and volunteer opportunities on Bali is www.balispirit.com/ngos.

Alam Sehat Lestari (www.alamsehatlestari.org) Accepts skilled medical and conservation volunteers to help protect and restore Kalimantan's rainforest.

Borneo Orangutan Survival Foundation (www.orangutan.or.id) Accepts volunteers for its orang-utan and sun-bear rehabilitation and reforestation programs.

East Bali Poverty Project (www.eastbalipovertyproject.org) Works to help children in the impoverished mountain villages of east Bali. Uses English teachers and has a solid child-protection policy.

Friends of the National Parks Foundation (www.fnpf.org) Has volunteer programs on Nusa Penida off Bali and Kalimantan.

IDEP (www.idepfoundation.org) The Indonesian Development of Education & Permaculture has projects across Indonesia; works on environmental projects, disaster planning and community improvement.

ProFauna (www.profauna.net) A large nonprofit animal-protection organisation operating across Indonesia; has been active in protecting sea turtles.

Sea Sanctuaries Trust (www.seasanctuaries.org) Diving-based marine conservation volunteering in Raja Ampat.

Smile Foundation of Bali (www.senyumbali.org) Organises surgery to correct facial deformities; operates the Smile Shop in Ubud to raise money.

Yayasan Rama Sesana (www.yrsbali.org) Dedicated to improving reproductive health for women across Bali.

Yayasan Bumi Sehat (www.bumisehatfoundation.org) Operates an internationally recognised clinic and gives reproductive services to disadvantaged women in Ubud; accepts donated time from medical professionals. Founder Robin Lim has had international recognition.

International Organisations

The following agencies may have information about long-term paid or volunteer work in Indonesia:

Australian Volunteers International (www.australianvolunteers.com) Organises all manner of programs, with many in Indonesia.

Global Vision International (www.gviusa.com) Organises short-term volunteer opportunities; has offices in Australia, the UK and the US.

Global Volunteers (www.globalvolunteers.org) Arranges professional and paid volunteer work for US citizens.

Go Abroad (www.goabroad.com) Lists mostly paid volunteer work.

Voluntary Service Overseas (www.vso.org.uk) British overseas volunteer program that accepts qualified volunteers from other countries.

Volunteer Service Abroad (www.vsa.org.nz) Organises professional contracts for New Zealanders.

Women Travellers

Plenty of Western women travel in Indonesia either solo or in pairs, and most seem to travel through the country, especially on Bali, without major problems. However, women travelling solo or otherwise may receive unwanted attention.

➡ Dress modestly, especially in conservative Muslim areas. Even the tourist islands of the Gilis have signs asking women not to walk around off the beaches in bikinis. In Aceh, women are expected to wear head scarves and cover their arms, whether they are Muslim or not.

➡ Indonesian men are generally very courteous; however, there is a macho element that indulges in puerile behaviour – horn honking, lewd comments etc. Ignore them totally, as Indonesian women do.

➡ If you're a solo female and you hire a car with a driver for several days, it's not culturally appropriate for a male Muslim driver to be travelling alone with you. A third party will come along as a chaperone.

Work

A work permit is required to work legally in Indonesia. These are very difficult to procure and need to be arranged by your employer. Apart from expatriates employed by foreign companies and English teachers, most foreigners working in Indonesia are involved in the export business.

Transport

GETTING THERE & AWAY

There are many ways into Indonesia: by boat from Malaysia and Singapore, and overland to Kalimantan, Papua and West Timor. But most people will fly, landing at – or transiting through – Jakarta or Bali.

Flights, cars and tours can be booked online at lonely planet.com/bookings.

Entering the Country

Entering Indonesia by air is relatively simple and straightforward, once you navigate the complex visa options (p792). Numerous sea ports are similarly easy; if you're arriving by land, you'll have no problems as long as you have a valid visa in advance.

Passport

Your passport *must* be valid for six months after your date of arrival in Indonesia. It's no longer necessary to fill out a disembarkation card on arrival.

Air

Indonesia is well connected to the rest of the world by numerous airlines. Many international flights, especially those to Bali, stop first in Singapore or Kuala Lumpur due to runway restrictions at Bali.

Airports & Airlines

The principal gateways for entry to Indonesia are Jakarta's **Soekarno-Hatta International Airport** (CGK; http://soekarnohatta -airport.co.id; Tangerang City) and Bali's **Ngurah Rai International Airport** (http://bali -airport.com), which is sometimes shown as Denpasar in schedules.

Other airports with international links – albeit limited – include Balikpapan, Medan, Padang, Surabaya, Lombok and Manado.

Almost all major international airlines service Indonesia.

AirAsia (www.airasia.com) Budget airline serving a wide range of Indonesian destinations from Australia, Kuala Lumpur, Bangkok and Singapore.

Garuda Indonesia (www. garuda-indonesia.com) Indonesia's main national airline serves Bali and Jakarta from Australia, Asia and Amsterdam.

Tickets

Check websites to get an idea of airfares to Indonesia. Don't limit yourself to major sites either; search for 'Indonesian airfares' and you may well find sites belonging to small travel agencies that specialise in Indonesian travel. This can be particularly helpful when you are trying to book a complex itinerary to remote locations.

Land

Border Crossings

There are five possible land crossings into Indonesia.

➡ Regular buses between Pontianak (Kalimantan) and Kuching (Sarawak, eastern Malaysia) pass through the border post at Entikong. You can get a visa on arrival (p793) on this route.

➡ Cross between Lubok Antu (Sarawak) and Badau (West Kalimantan), provided you have a visa in advance (p792).

➡ Cross between Biawak (Sarawak), and PLBN Aruk (West Kalimantan), provided you have a visa in advance.

➡ The border crossing between West and East Timor (Timor-Leste) is open. Get a Timor-Leste visa in Kupang (p400); a visa is required when travelling from East to West Timor.

➡ The border from Jayapura or Sentani in Indonesia to Vanimo in Papua New Guinea can be

DEPARTURE TAX

Departure tax is now included in the price of the ticket.

crossed, depending on the current political situation. A visa is required if travelling into Indonesia.

Sea

There is currently no passenger sea travel between the Philippines, Papua New Guinea and Indonesia.

Australia

Major cruise lines often run cruise ships between Bali and Australia.

Timor-Leste

There are regular ferry services between Dili in Timor-Leste and Oecussi, which borders West Timor. If crossing into Indonesia from Oecussi, you will need to have organised your visa already in Dili.

Malaysia

Regular and comfortable high-speed ferries run the two-hour journey between Melaka (Malaysia) and Dumai (Sumatra). From Johor Bahru in southern Malaysia, daily ferries run to Pulau Bintan in Sumatra's Riau Islands.

Ferries and speedboats connect Tarakan and Nunukan in East Kalimantan with Tawau in Sabah. For these routes you'll need a visa in advance.

Singapore

From Batam, speedboats travel to Tanjung Buton

with minibus connections to Pekanbaru on the Sumatran mainland. Otherwise, Pelni ships pass through Batam to and from Belawan (the port for Medan) and Jakarta.

Boats also travel between Pulau Bintan and Singapore. Service includes Bintan Resort Ferries (www.brf. com.sg).

GETTING AROUND

Air

Air travel is the quickest and most convenient way of getting around Indonesia, and sometimes the only way to reach certain parts of the archipelago. There is an ever-changing number of domestic airlines, and flights are generally inexpensive. Bear in mind that flights to remote destinations are prone to cancellation, as well as delays, especially in periods of bad weather.

Airlines in Indonesia

Getting reliable information on Indonesian domestic flights can be a challenge – a few airlines on minor routes don't show up on travel websites, although www. traveloka.com and www.skyscanner.com are fairly complete. You can also check with local airline offices and travel agents; local hotel and tour operators are often the best sources of info.

➡ The domestic flight network continues to grow; schedules and rates are in a constant state of flux.

➡ Small carriers servicing remote routes often operate cramped and dated aircraft.

➡ With tiny regional airlines, reconfirm your ticket and hang around the check-in desk if the flight is full. Sometimes reservations are 'lost' when another passenger with more clout shows up.

Almost a dozen major airlines fly domestically.

Batik Air (www.batikair.com) Full-service subsidiary of Lion Air.

Citilink (www.citilink.co.id) Budget subsidiary to Garuda Indonesia that links major cities.

Dimonim Air (www.dimonim air.com) Flights in Papua.

Garuda Indonesia (www. garuda-indonesia.com) Serves major destinations across the archipelago. Tickets are easily bought online.

Indonesia AirAsia (www.air asia.com) Fast-growing budget carrier that is a subsidiary of its Malaysian-based parent.

Lion Air/Wings Air (www. lionair.co.id) Fast-growing Indonesian budget carrier (Wings Air operates prop planes to small destinations) with myriad flights.

Sriwijaya Air/NAM Air (www. sriwijayaair.co.id) Services across Indonesia.

CLIMATE CHANGE & TRAVEL

Every form of transport that relies on carbon-based fuel generates CO_2, the main cause of human-induced climate change. Modern travel is dependent on aeroplanes, which might use less fuel per kilometre per person than most cars but travel much greater distances. The altitude at which aircraft emit gases (including CO_2) and particles also contributes to their climate change impact. Many websites offer 'carbon calculators' that allow people to estimate the carbon emissions generated by their journey and, for those who wish to do so, to offset the impact of the greenhouse gases emitted with contributions to portfolios of climate-friendly initiatives throughout the world. Lonely Planet offsets the carbon footprint of all staff and author travel.

Susi Air (www.susiair.com) Routes across Indonesia.

Transnusa (www.transnusa. co.id) Good for flights within Nusa Tenggara and for flights from Denpasar to places like Labuan Bajo.

Tickets

The larger Indonesian-based carriers have websites listing fares; however, it can be difficult to purchase tickets over the internet using non-Indonesian credit cards. Consider the following methods.

Travel Agencies A good way to buy domestic tickets once you're in Indonesia. This is often the best way to get the lowest fares.

Travel websites Many general sites accept international cards.

Friends Get an Indonesian friend or guesthouse owner to buy you a ticket using their credit card, then pay them back.

Airport Some airlines will sell you a ticket at the airport, although travel agents and airline city offices are more reliable.

Indonesian Airline Safety

Indonesia's airlines do not have a good safety record, although the frequency of accidents has diminished in recent years. Flying conditions are often challenging (monsoons, volcanic eruptions etc), safety standards can be lax and the airlines themselves sometimes expand very rapidly, outpacing efforts to instil a safety culture.

Should you be worried? The odds of a fatal flight in Indonesia are very small, even if they are higher than elsewhere. When possible, pick a major airline over a smaller one, and in really remote locations, feel free to do your own inspection of the plane and crew before you fly.

Bicycle

With reasonable fitness, a bit of preparation and a ton of common sense, a cyclist will enjoy an incomparable travel experience almost anywhere in the archipelago. The well-maintained roads of Bali, Lombok, East Java and South Sulawesi are suitable for cyclists of all ability levels, while the adventurous can head for the hills along the length of Sumatra or Nusa Tenggara. Practical tips:

➡ Rest during the hottest hours of the day to avoid the tropical heat.

➡ Avoid most traffic problems by keeping to back roads or even jumping on a truck or bus to cover dangerous sections.

➡ Expect to be a constant focus of attention.

➡ You can rent bikes fairly easily in tourist centres; just ask at your accommodation. Rates range from 30,000Rp and up per day.

➡ Many tourist areas, particularly Bali, Lombok and Yogyakarta, offer organised, vehicle-supported bicycle tours.

➡ At major sights you can usually find a parking attendant to keep an eye on your bicycle for 5000Rp.

Cycling is gaining popularity among Indonesians, and bicycle clubs will be delighted to aid a foreign guest. Bike to Work (www.b2w-indonesia. or.id) has an extensive national network.

Boat

Sumatra, Java, Bali, Nusa Tenggara and Sulawesi are all connected by regular car ferries, and you can use them to island-hop all the way from Sumatra to West Timor. Local ferries run several times a week or daily (or even hourly on the busy Java–Bali–Lombok–Sumbawa routes). Check with shipping companies, the harbour office, travel agents or hotels for current schedules and fares.

Going to and between Kalimantan, Maluku and Papua, the main connections are provided by Pelni, the government-run passenger line.

Pelni

Pelni (www.pelni.co.id) has a fleet of large vessels linking all of Indonesia's major ports and the majority of the

TRAVELLING SAFELY BY BOAT

Boat safety is an important consideration across Indonesia, where boats that barely seem seaworthy may be your only option to travel between islands. In many cases these services are accidents waiting to happen, as safety regulation is lax at best. This is especially true on the busy routes linking Bali, Nusa Lembongan, Lombok and the Gilis, where both the fast tourist boats and the public car ferries have had accidents. Given Indonesia's poor record, it is essential that you take responsibility for your own safety, as no one else will.

Consider the following points for any boat travel in Indonesia.

Bigger is better It may take you 30 minutes or more longer, but a larger boat will simply deal with the open ocean better than the over-powered small speedboats.

Check for safety equipment Make certain your boat has life jackets and that you know how to locate and use them. In an emergency, don't expect a panicked crew to hand them out. Also, check for life rafts.

Avoid overcrowding Travellers report boats leaving with more people than seats and with aisles jammed with stacked luggage.

Look for exits Cabins may only have one narrow entrance making them death traps in an accident.

Avoid fly-by-nighters Taking a fishing boat and jamming too many engines on the rear in order to cash in on booming tourism is a recipe for disaster.

archipelago's outlying areas. Pelni's website is a good resource, showing arrivals and departures about a month in advance.

Its ships operate set routes around the islands, either on a fortnightly or monthly schedule. The ships usually stop for a few hours in each port, so there's time for a quick look around. Note that sailing times can be in flux until the last moment.

Economy fares can be quite cheap, but at higher levels of shipboard accommodation budget airlines are competitive if not cheaper.

Pelni ships range from modern, clean and well run to less modern, chaotic and dirty. Consider the following.

Booking Towns served by Pelni usually have a ticket office or agent. Book your ticket a few days in advance.

Classes Pelni ships have two to six classes. Economy class, which is the modern version of deck class, is a bare-bones experience. As you move up the price ladder, you exchange a seat on the deck for small accommodations until you reach a level that may give you your own private cabin with two beds (this is some variation of 1st class). These are functional at best and far from lavish.

Security There are no lockers, so you have to keep an eye on your gear if you are in any kind of group class. Beware of pickpockets when embarking and disembarking.

Crowding At busy times such as Idul Fitri, boats seem to have passengers crammed into every available space, including decks, passages and stairwells. Conditions can get grim.

Food Bring your own food and drink. Boats offer basic meals, or have shops offering instant noodles and snacks.

Boarding Getting aboard a Pelni ship can leave you bruised as it is truly every man, woman and child for him or herself as people try to get to scarce space first.

Other Vessels

There's a whole range of boats you can use to hop between islands, down rivers and across lakes. Just about any sort of vessel can be rented in Indonesia.

Fast Ferries When available, these are a great alternative to the slow car ferries that link many islands.

Fishing boats Small boats can be chartered to take you to small offshore islands.

Longbot The *longbot* is a long, narrow boat powered by a couple of outboard motors, with bench seats on either side of the hull for passengers to sit on. They are mainly used in Kalimantan where they are also called *klotok*.

Outrigger boats Used for some short interisland hops, such as the trip from Manado in North Sulawesi to the coral reefs surrounding nearby Pulau Bunaken. On Lombok they serve the Gilis while Komodo National Park is served from Labuan Bajo. On Bali they are called *jukung*.

River ferries Commonly found on Kalimantan, where the rivers *are* the roads. They're large, bulky vessels that carry passengers and cargo up and down the water network.

Tourist boats Often very fast speedboats outfitted to carry

40 or more passengers, most commonly used for quick trips between Bali, Nusa Lembongan, Lombok and the Gilis.

Bus

Buses are the mainstay of Indonesian transport (excepting Papua and Maluku). At any time of day, thousands of buses in all shapes and sizes move thousands of people throughout Indonesia. The 'leave-when-full' school of scheduling applies to almost every service, and 'full' sometimes means the aisles are occupied too. Consider the following.

➡ On major runs across Indonesia, air-con buses are at least tolerable.

➡ Crowded roads mean that buses are often stuck in traffic.

➡ On major routes, such as the 24-hour run from Bali to Jakarta, budget airlines are competitive price-wise.

➡ Buses on non-major routes are usually not air-conditioned.

➡ Bring as little luggage as possible – there is rarely any room for storage. Large bags will ride on your lap.

➡ Take precautions with your personal belongings and keep your passport, money and any other valuables secure and concealed.

Classes

➡ Economy-class (ekonomi) buses run set routes between towns. They can be hot, slow and crowded, but they're also ridiculously cheap and provide a never-ending parade of Indonesian life.

➡ Express (patas) buses look much the same as the economy buses, but stop only at selected bus terminals en route and (officially) don't pick up from the side of the road. Air-con patas buses are more comfortable and seating is often guaranteed.

➡ Air-con buses (or 'executive' buses) come in a variety of price categories, depending on whether facilities include reclining seats, toilets, TV, karaoke (usually very bad) or snacks. These buses should be booked in advance; ticket agents often have pictures of the buses and seating plans; check to see what you are paying for when you choose your seat.

Tickets

Bus tickets are cheap. For long-distance buses, you can buy your ticket from a travel agent or visit the bus terminal where you may find several companies competing for your business. Book longer trips in advance, especially on air-con buses.

Often, hotels will act as agents or buy a ticket for you and will arrange for the bus to pick you up at the hotel – they sometimes charge a few thousand rupiah for this service, but it's worth it.

Car & Motorcycle

Driving License

To drive in Indonesia, you officially need an International Driving Permit (IDP) from your local automobile association. This permit is rarely required as identification when hiring/driving a car in Indonesia, but police may ask to see it. Bring your home licence as well – it's supposed to be carried in conjunction with the IDP. If you also have a motorcycle licence at home, get your IDP endorsed for motorcycles too.

Fuel

Fuel prices are kept cheap by government subsidies. Unleaded petrol costs around 10,000Rp per litre. The opening of the domestic fuel market to foreign operators has spurred national oil company Pertamina to build petrol/gas stations (pompa

bensin) throughout the archipelago.

Hire

CAR HIRE

Small self-drive cars can be hired for as little as 300,000Rp a day with limited insurance in tourist areas.

It is very common for tourists to hire a car with a driver, and this can usually be arranged from 600,000Rp per day.

With a small group, a van and driver is not only economical but also allows maximum travel and touring freedom. Hotels can always arrange drivers.

MOTORCYCLE HIRE

Motorcycles are readily available for hire throughout Indonesia.

➡ Motorcycles and scooters can be hired for 50,000Rp to 100,000Rp per day.

➡ Wearing a helmet is required by law and essential given road conditions.

➡ In popular surfing areas, many motorbike rentals come with a surfboard rack.

➡ A licence is required by law, though you'll rarely need to show it unless stopped by the police, who may be looking for a 'tip'.

➡ Some travel-insurance policies do not cover you if you are involved in an accident while on a motorcycle and/or don't have a licence. Check the small print.

Insurance

Rental agencies and owners usually insist that the vehicle itself is insured, and minimal insurance should be included in the basic rental deal – often with an excess of as much as US$100 for a motorcycle and US$500 for a car (ie the customer pays the first US$100/500 of any claim). You can usually pay extra to reduce the excess.

Your travel insurance may provide some additional protection, although liability for motor accidents is specifically excluded from many policies.

A private owner renting out a motorcycle may not offer any insurance at all. Ensure that your personal travel insurance covers injuries incurred while motorcycling.

Road Conditions

➡ Relentless traffic congestion across many parts of Indonesia – including Bali – makes driving an exhausting activity.

➡ Delays due to roadworks, poor conditions and congestion are common.

➡ Finding your way around can be a challenge, as roads are only sometimes signposted and maps are often out of date.

➡ In much of the country, count on averaging only 35km per hour.

Road Rules

Indonesians drive on the left side of the road, as in Australia, Japan, the UK and most of Southeast Asia.

Considering the relatively small cost of a driver in relation to the total rental, it makes little sense to take the wheel yourself. Driving requires enormous amounts of concentration, and the legal implications of accidents can be a nightmare; as a foreigner, it's *your* fault.

Hitching

Hitching is not part of Indonesian culture, but if you put out your thumb, someone may give you a lift. On the back roads where no public transport exists, hitching may be the only alternative to walking, and passing motorists or trucks are often willing to help. You will increase your chances of a ride if you offer to pay.

Bear in mind that hitching is never entirely safe in any country, so we do not

recommend it. Travellers who decide to hitch should understand that they are taking a small but potentially serious risk.

Local Transport

Becak

These are three-wheeled carts, either pedal- or motor-powered. The becak is banned from the main streets of some large cities, but you'll still see them swarming the backstreets, moving anyone and anything.

Negotiate your fare *before* you get in; and if there are two passengers, make sure that it covers both people, otherwise you'll be in for an argument when you get to your destination. Becak drivers are hard bargainers, but they will usually settle on a reasonable fare, around 5000Rp per kilometre.

Bus

Large buses aren't used much as a means of city transport except on Java. There's an extensive system of buses in Jakarta, and these are universally cheap; beware of pickpockets.

Dokar

A *dokar* is the jingling, horse-drawn, two-wheeled cart found throughout the archipelago, including tourist areas. A typical *dokar* (known as *cidomo* in some areas such as the Gilis, or *bendi* in West Sumatra) has bench seating on either side, which can comfortably fit three or four people.

Given that many horses and ponies are mistreated, we can't recommend *dokars*.

Minibus

Public minibuses are used for local transport around cities and towns, short intercity runs and the furthest reaches of the transport network.

Minibuses are known as *bemos* or *angkot*, although they are called *taksi* in many parts of Papua, Kalimantan and East Java. Other names include *opelet*, *mikrolet*, *mobil*, *angkudes* and *pete-pete*.

➡ Most minibuses operate a standard route, picking up and dropping off people and goods anywhere along the way.

➡ Minibus drivers may try to overcharge foreigners and ask you for triple the normal fare. It's best to ask somebody, such as your hotel staff, about the *harga biasa* (normal price); otherwise, see what the other passengers are paying and offer the correct fare.

➡ Drivers wait until their vehicles are crammed to capacity before moving, or they may go *keliling* – driving endlessly around town looking for a full complement of passengers.

➡ Conditions can be extremely cramped, especially if you have luggage.

➡ On Bali, motorbikes are nearly universal and the *bemo* system is almost non-existent.

Ojek

Ojeks (or *ojegs*) are motorcycle riders who take pillion passengers for a bargainable price. They are found at bus terminals and markets, or just hanging around at crossroads. They will take you around town and go where no other public transport exists, or along roads that are impassable in any other vehicle. They are the preferred method for navigating Jakarta traffic. They can also be rented by the hour for sightseeing.

Go-Jek (www.go-jek.com) is an Uber-style service where you can order an *ojek* using a smartphone app at a fair price. It operates in major cities.

Private Car

Small air-con minivans carrying paying passengers

(known in some areas as *Taksi Gelap*) are common in some areas. They typically link major towns on main highways; the cost is more than a bus but they offer greater speed and door-to-door service. Hotels usually have info on these services and can arrange pickups.

However, these vehicles are unregulated and safety standards vary widely, if they exist at all.

Taxi

Metered taxis are readily available in major cities. If a taxi has a meter *(argo)*, make sure it is used. Where meters don't exist, you will have to bargain for the fare in advance. Offers of 'transport' are almost always more costly than using a metered taxi.

With services in major cities and tourist areas including south Bali, Bluebird Taxis (www.bluebirdgroup.com) is a good choice as drivers use the meter, speak some English and are honest. The smartphone app makes ordering a taxi a breeze.

The Southeast Asian ride-sharing app Grab (www.grab.com/id) has bought Uber's Indonesian operation and is active in larger cities and towns and tourist areas.

At airports, taxis sometimes operate on a prepaid system, payable at the relevant booth.

Train

Train travel in Indonesia is restricted to Java and a small network in Sumatra.

In Java, trains are among the most comfortable, fastest and easiest ways to travel. In the east, the railway service connects with the ferry to Bali, and in the west with the ferry to Sumatra. Sumatra's limited rail network runs in the south from Bandarlampung to Lubuklinggau, and in the north from Medan to Tanjung Balai and Rantau Prapat.

There are three classes; smoking is not allowed in any.

➡ Executive *(eksecutif)* – air-con with mandatory reservations.

➡ Business *(bisnis)* – no air-con but mandatory seat reservations.

➡ Economy *(ekonomi)* – no air-con, crowded and unreserved.

The railway's website (www.kai.id) has information on train schedules from individual stations.

TOURS

A wide range of trips can be booked from tour companies within Indonesia. Some of the best tours are with local guides, such as the ecotrips to Halimun National Park in Java with local guides in Bo-

gor. We recommend dozens of local options.

There are also specialist tour companies that use their in-depth knowledge of local dialects, culture and experience to create experiences you'd have a hard time equalling independently.

Finally there are numerous operators that can transport you around the archipelago in high style, say in a classic sailing ship.

Adventure Indonesia (www.adventureindonesia.com) Top Indonesian adventure-tourism firm.

Dewi Nusantara (www.dewi-nusantara.com) A 57m, three-masted traditional-style sailing ship that makes luxurious liveaboard diving journeys around the Malukus and Raja Ampat.

Laszlo Wagner (www.east-indonesia.info) An experienced Hungarian-born writer offers tailor-made trips around Maluku and Papua.

SeaTrek Sailing Adventures (www.seatrekbali.com) Runs itineraries on sailing ships from Bali to Flores, as well as Banda Islands and Papua trips.

Silolona Sojurns (www.silolona.com) This luxury yacht built in the style of classic Spice Islands trading vessels sails through Nusa Tenggara, Maluku and Papua.

Health

Treatment for minor injuries and common travellers' health problems is easily accessed in larger cities and on Bali, but the more remote the region the lower the standards. For serious conditions, you will need to leave Indonesia.

Travellers tend to worry about contracting exotic diseases when in the tropics, but they are a rare cause of serious illness or death in travellers. Pre-existing medical conditions, such as heart disease, and accidental injury (especially traffic accidents) account for most life-threatening problems.

If you are bringing your own medications, make sure they are packed in their original, clearly labelled containers. A signed and dated letter from your physician describing your medical conditions and medications (including generic names) is also a good idea. If you are carrying syringes or needles, be sure to have a physician's letter documenting their medical necessity.

If you happen to take any regular medication, bring double your needs in case of loss or theft. You can buy many medications over the counter without a doctor's prescription, but it can be difficult to find antidepressants, blood-pressure medications and contraceptive pills.

It's important to note what precautions you should take in Indonesia. On Bali your major concerns are rabies, mosquito bites and the tropical sun. Elsewhere in the country there are numerous important considerations.

The advice we give is a general guide only and does not replace the advice of a doctor trained in travel medicine.

BEFORE YOU GO

Health Insurance

Even if you are fit and healthy, don't travel without sufficient health insurance – accidents do happen. If you're uninsured, emergency evacuation is expensive – bills of more than US$100,000 are not uncommon.

Find out in advance if your insurance plan will make payments directly to providers or reimburse you later for overseas health expenditures.

If you're planning on scuba-diving, make sure your insurance covers that or get specialist dive insurance.

Medical Checklist

Recommended items for a convenient personal medical kit (more specific items can be obtained in Indonesia if needed):

➡ antibacterial cream

➡ antihistamine – there are many options

➡ antiseptic (eg Betadine)

➡ contraceptives

➡ DEET-based insect repellent

➡ first-aid items such as scissors, bandages, thermometer (but not a mercury one) and tweezers

➡ ibuprofen or another anti-inflammatory

➡ steroid cream for allergic/itchy rashes (eg 1% to 2% hydrocortisone)

➡ throat lozenges

➡ thrush (vaginal yeast infection) treatment

IN INDONESIA

Availability & Cost of Health Care

It is difficult to find reliable medical care in rural areas, but most major cities now have clinics catering specifically to travellers and expats. These clinics are usually more expensive than local medical facilities, but are worth utilising, as they will offer a superior standard of care. Additionally, they understand the local system and are aware of the safest local hospitals and best specialists. They can also liaise with insurance companies should you require evacuation.

If you think you may have a serious disease, especially malaria, do not waste time – travel immediately to the nearest quality facility to receive attention.

Local medical care in general is not yet up to international standards. Foreign doctors are not allowed to work in Indonesia, but some clinics (such as those in Bali and Jakarta) catering to foreigners have 'international advisors'. Almost all Indonesian doctors work at government hospitals during the day and in private practices at night. This means that private hospitals often don't have their best staff available during the day. Serious cases are evacuated to Australia, Bangkok or Singapore.

The cost of medical care in Indonesia remains cheap by international standards: a visit to the ER of a top hospital in a major city will start at around 500,000Rp for a minor treatment.

Pharmacies

In Jakarta, other large cities and Bali, pharmacies (apotik) are usually reliable. The Kimia Farma (www.kimiafarma.co.id) chain is good and has many locations nationwide. Be careful at small, local pharmacies, as fake medications and poorly stored or out-of-date drugs are common.

Infectious Diseases
Dengue Fever

This mosquito-borne disease is a major problem, and Indonesia has one of the world's highest infection rates. As there is no vaccine available, it can only be prevented by avoiding mosquito bites. The mosquito that carries dengue bites day and night, so use insect avoidance measures at all times. Symptoms include high fever, severe headache and body ache.

VACCINATIONS

Specialised travel-medicine clinics are your best source of information. The doctors will take into account factors such as past vaccination history, the length of your trip, activities you may be undertaking and underlying medical conditions, such as pregnancy.

Most vaccines don't provide immunity until at least two weeks after they're given, so visit a doctor four to eight weeks before departure. Ask your doctor for an International Certificate of Vaccination (otherwise known as the yellow booklet), which will list all the vaccinations you've received.

The only vaccine required by international regulations is yellow fever. Proof of vaccination will only be required if you have visited a country in the yellow-fever zone (primarily some parts of Africa and South America) within the six days prior to entering Southeast Asia.

Vaccination recommendations for Southeast Asia include the following for all travellers:

Tetanus Single booster recommended if none in the previous 10 years.

Hepatitis A Provides almost 100% protection for up to a year; a booster after 12 months provides at least another 20 years' protection. Mild side effects such as headache and sore arm occur in 5% to 10% of people.

Typhoid Recommended unless your trip is less than a week and only to developed cities. The vaccine offers around 70% protection, lasts for two to three years and comes as a single shot.

Rabies Three injections in all. A booster after one year will then provide 10 years' protection. Side effects are rare – occasionally headache and sore arm. Essential for Bali, where there has been a rabies epidemic for years.

These vaccines are recommended if you are travelling beyond major cities or outside Bali and Lombok:

Hepatitis B Now considered routine for most travellers. Given as three shots over six months. Lifetime protection occurs in 95% of people.

Cholera An oral vaccine recommended for very remote travel.

Japanese B Encephalitis Three injections in all. Booster recommended after two years. Sore arm and headache are the most common side effects.

Meningitis Single injection. Recommended for long-term backpackers aged under 25.

Some people develop a rash and experience diarrhoea. There is no specific treatment, just rest and paracetamol – do not take aspirin as it increases the likelihood of haemorrhaging. See a doctor to be diagnosed and monitored.

Hepatitis A

A problem throughout the region, this food- and water-borne virus infects the liver, causing jaundice (yellow skin and eyes), nausea and lethargy. There is no specific treatment; you just need to allow time for the liver to heal. All travellers to Southeast Asia should be vaccinated against hepatitis A.

Hepatitis B

The only sexually transmitted disease that can be prevented by vaccination, hepatitis B is spread by body fluids, including sexual contact. In some parts of Southeast Asia up to 20% of the population are carriers of hepatitis B.

HIV

HIV is a major problem in many Asian countries, and Bali has one of the highest rates of HIV infection in Indonesia. The main risk for most travellers is sexual contact with locals, sex workers and other travellers.

The risk of sexual transmission of the HIV virus can be dramatically reduced by the use of a *kondom* (condom). These are available from supermarkets, street stalls and drugstores in tourist areas, and from the *apotik* in almost any town.

Japanese B Encephalitis

While this is a rare disease in travellers, many locals are infected each year. This viral disease is transmitted by mosquitoes. Most cases occur in rural areas and vaccination is recommended for travellers spending more than one month outside cities. There is no treatment,

and a third of infected people will die while another third will suffer permanent brain damage.

Malaria

The risk of contracting malaria is greatest in rural areas of Indonesia, although only Java's main cities, Bali and the Gilis are considered malaria-free.

Two strategies should be combined to prevent malaria: mosquito avoidance and antimalarial medications.

Most people who contract malaria are taking inadequate precautions or no antimalarial medication.

Travellers are advised to prevent mosquito bites by taking these steps:

➡ Use a DEET-containing insect repellent on exposed skin. Insect sprays and lotions such as Off are only reliably found in the areas with the least risk of malaria (eg Bali). Bring small containers of highly concentrated DEET repellent from your home country and follow the label directions carefully.

➡ Sleep under a mosquito net impregnated with permethrin.

➡ Choose accommodation with screens and fans (if not air-conditioned).

➡ Impregnate clothing with permethrin in high-risk areas.

➡ Wear long sleeves and trousers in light colours.

➡ Use mosquito coils.

➡ Spray your room with insect repellent before going out for your evening meal.

There are a variety of medications available (note that Artesunate and Chloroquine are ineffective):

Doxycycline This daily tablet is a broad-spectrum antibiotic that has the added benefit of helping to prevent a variety of tropical diseases. Potential side effects include a tendency to sunburn, thrush in women, indigestion,

heartburn, nausea and interference with contraceptive pills.

Lariam (Mefloquine) Lariam has received much bad press, some of it justified, some not. This weekly tablet suits many people. Serious side effects are rare but include depression, anxiety, psychosis and having fits.

Malarone A combination of Atovaquone and Proguanil. Side effects, most commonly nausea and headache, are uncommon and mild. It is the best tablet for scuba divers and for those on short trips to high-risk areas. It must be taken for one week after leaving the risk area.

Rabies

Rabies is a disease spread by the bite or lick of an infected animal, most commonly a dog or monkey. Once you are exposed, it is uniformly fatal if you don't get the vaccine very promptly. Bali has a major outbreak that dates to 2008. Cases have been reported across Indonesia.

To minimise your risk, consider getting the rabies vaccine, which consists of three injections in all. A booster after one year will then provide 10 years' protection. The vaccines are often unavailable on Bali, so get them before you go.

Also, be careful to avoid animal bites. Especially watch children closely.

Having the pre-travel vaccination means the post-bite treatment is greatly simplified. If you are bitten or scratched, gently wash the wound with soap and water, and apply an iodine-based antiseptic then consult a doctor.

Those not vaccinated will need to receive rabies immunoglobulin as soon as possible. Clean the wound immediately and do not delay seeking medical attention. Note that Indonesia regularly runs out of rabies immunoglobulin, so be prepared to go to Singapore immediately for medical treatment.

Typhoid

This serious bacterial infection is spread via food and water. Its symptoms are a high and slowly progressive fever, headache and possibly a dry cough and stomach pain. It is diagnosed by blood tests and treated with antibiotics.

Bird Flu

Otherwise known as avian influenza, the H5N1 virus has claimed more than 100 victims in Indonesia. Most cases have been in Java. Treatment is difficult and every few years it reappears.

Traveller's Diarrhoea

Traveller's diarrhoea (aka Bali belly) is by far the most common problem affecting travellers – between 30% and 50% of people will suffer from it within two weeks of starting their trip. In over 80% of cases, traveller's diarrhoea is caused by bacteria (there are numerous potential culprits), and therefore responds promptly to treatment with antibiotics.

Traveller's diarrhoea is defined as the passage of more than three watery bowel actions within 24 hours, plus at least one other symptom such as fever, cramps, nausea, vomiting or feeling generally unwell.

Treatment

Loperamide (aka Imodium) is just a 'stopper' and doesn't get to the cause of the problem. However, it can be helpful, for example, if you have to go on a long bus ride. Don't take Loperamide if you have a fever or blood in your stools. Seek medical attention quickly if you do not respond to an appropriate antibiotic. Otherwise do the following:

➡ Stay well hydrated; rehydration solutions such as Gastrolyte are the best for this.

➡ Antibiotics such as Norfloxacin, Ciprofloxacin or Azithromycin will kill the bacteria quickly.

Environmental Hazards
Air Pollution

Air pollution, particularly vehicle pollution, is a problem in cities. In addition, smog from fires used to clear land for oil-palm plantations blankets Sumatra in the dry season. If you have severe respiratory problems, speak with your doctor before travelling. This pollution also causes minor respiratory problems such as sinusitis, dry throat and irritated eyes. Consider masks, which more and more Indonesians are wearing.

Diving

Divers and surfers should seek specialised advice before they travel to ensure their medical kit contains treatment for coral cuts and tropical ear infections, as well as the standard problems. Divers should ensure their insurance covers them for decompression illness.

Heat

Most parts of Indonesia are hot and humid throughout the year. For most people it takes at least two weeks to adapt to the hot climate. Swelling of the feet and ankles is common, as are muscle cramps caused by excessive sweating. Prevent these by avoiding dehydration and excessive activity in the heat. Be careful to avoid the following conditions:

Heat Exhaustion Symptoms include feeling weak; headache; irritability; nausea or vomiting; sweaty skin; a fast, weak pulse; and a normal or slightly elevated body temperature. Treatment involves getting out of the heat and/or sun, fanning the victim and applying cool wet cloths to the skin, laying the victim flat with their legs raised, and rehydrating with water containing one-quarter of a teaspoon of salt per litre. Recovery is usually rapid.

Heatstroke A serious medical emergency. Symptoms come on suddenly and include weakness, nausea, a hot dry body with a body temperature of over 41°C, dizziness, confusion, loss of coordination, fits and eventually collapse and loss of consciousness. Seek urgent medical help and commence cooling by getting the person out of the heat, removing their clothes, fanning them and applying cool wet cloths or ice to their body, especially to hot spots such as the groin and armpits.

Prickly Heat A common skin rash in the tropics, caused by sweat being trapped under the skin. The result is an itchy rash of tiny lumps. Treat by moving out of the heat into an air-conditioned area for a few hours and by having cool showers.

Insect Bites & Stings

During your time in Indonesia, you may make some unwanted friends.

Bedbugs These don't carry disease, but their bites are very itchy. They live in the cracks of furniture and walls and then migrate to the bed at night to feed on you as you sleep. You can treat the itch with an antihistamine.

Jellyfish Most are not dangerous, just irritating. Stings can be extremely painful but rarely fatal. First aid for jellyfish stings involves pouring vinegar onto the affected area to neutralise the poison. Anyone who feels ill in any way after being stung should seek medical advice.

Ticks Contracted after walking in rural areas, ticks are commonly found behind the ears, on the belly and in armpits. If you have had a tick bite and experience symptoms such as a rash at the site of the bite or elsewhere, fever or muscle aches, you should see a doctor.

Sunburn

Even on a cloudy day sunburn can occur rapidly, especially near the equator. Don't end up like the dopey tourists you see roasted pink on Bali's Kuta Beach.

➡ Use a strong sunscreen (at least factor 30).

➡ Reapply sunscreen after a swim.

➡ Wear a wide-brimmed hat and sunglasses.

➡ Avoid baking in the sun during the hottest part of the day (10am to 2pm).

Skin Problems

Fungal Rashes There are two common fungal rashes that affect travellers. The first occurs in moist areas that get less air such as the groin, armpits and between the toes. It starts as a red patch that slowly spreads and is usually itchy. Treatment involves keeping the skin dry, avoiding chafing and using an antifungal cream such as Clotrimazole or Lamisil.

Cuts & Scratches Take meticulous care of any cuts and scratches, which are easily infected in tropical climates. Immediately wash all wounds in clean water and apply antiseptic. If you develop signs of infection see a doctor. Divers and surfers should be careful with coral cuts as they become easily infected.

Drinking Water

➡ Never drink tap water in Indonesia.

➡ Widely available and cheap, bottled water is generally safe; however, check the seal is intact when purchasing. Look for places that allow you to refill containers, thus cutting down on landfill.

➡ Most ice in restaurants is fine if it is uniform in size and made at a central plant (standard for large cities and tourist areas). Avoid ice that is chipped off larger blocks (more common in rural areas).

➡ Fresh juices can be a risk outside of tourist restaurants and cafes.

Women's Health

In the tourist areas and large cities, sanitary products are easily found. This becomes more difficult the more rural you go. Tampons are especially hard to find.

Birth-control options may be limited, so bring adequate supplies of your own form of contraception.

Language

Indonesian, or Bahasa Indonesia as it is known to the locals, is the official language of Indonesia. It has approximately 220 million speakers, although it's the mother tongue for only about 20 million – most people also speak their own indigenous language. As a traveller you shouldn't worry too much about learning local languages, but it can be fun to learn a few words – we've included the basics for Balinese and Javanese in this chapter. For practical purposes, it probably makes better sense to concentrate your efforts on learning Bahasa Indonesia.

Indonesian pronunciation is easy to master. Each letter always represents the same sound and most letters are pronounced the same as their English counterparts. Just remember that c is pronounced as the 'ch' in 'chat' and sy as the 'sh' in 'ship'. Note also that kh is a throaty sound (like the 'ch' in the Scottish loch), and that the ng and ny combinations, which are also found in English at the end or in the middle of words such as 'ringing' and 'canyon' respectively, can also appear at the beginning of words in Indonesian. Syllables generally carry equal emphasis – the main exception is the unstressed e in words such as besar (big) – but the rule of thumb is to stress the second-last syllable.

In written Indonesian there are some inconsistent spellings of place names. Compound names are written as one word or two, eg Airsanih or Air Sanih, Padangbai or Padang Bai. Words starting with 'Ker' sometimes lose the e, eg Kerobokan/Krobokan. Some Dutch variant spellings also remain in use, with tj instead of

the modern c (eg Tjampuhan/Campuan), and oe instead of u (eg Soekarno/Sukarno).

Pronouns, particularly 'you', are rarely used in Indonesian. Anda is the egalitarian form used to overcome the plethora of words for 'you'.

BASICS

Hello.	Salam.
Goodbye. (if leaving)	Selamat tinggal.
Goodbye. (if staying)	Selamat jalan.
How are you?	Apa kabar?
I'm fine, and you?	Kabar baik, Anda bagaimana?
Excuse me.	Permisi.
Sorry.	Maaf.
Please.	Silahkan.
Thank you.	Terima kasih.
You're welcome.	Kembali.
Yes.	Ya.
No.	Tidak.
Mr/Sir	Bapak
Ms/Mrs/Madam	Ibu
Miss	Nona
What's your name?	Siapa nama Anda?
My name is ...	Nama saya ...
Do you speak English?	Bisa berbicara Bahasa Inggris?
I don't understand.	Saya tidak mengerti.

ACCOMMODATION

Do you have any rooms available?	Ada kamar kosong?
How much is it per night/person?	Berapa satu malam/ orang?
Is breakfast included?	Apakah harganya termasuk makan pagi?
I'd like to share a dorm.	Saya mau satu tempat tidur di asrama.

WANT MORE?

For in-depth language information and handy phrases, check out Lonely Planet's *Indonesian Phrasebook*. You'll find it at **shop.lonelyplanet.com**, or you can buy Lonely Planet's iPhone phrasebooks at the Apple App Store.

campsite	tempat kemah
guesthouse	losmen
hotel	hotel
youth hostel	hostel untuk pemuda
a ... room	kamar ...
single	untuk satu orang
double	untuk dua orang
air-conditioned	dengan AC
bathroom	kamar mandi
cot	pondok
window	jendela

DIRECTIONS

Where is ...?	Di mana ...?
What's the address?	Alamatnya di mana?
Could you write it down, please?	Anda bisa tolong tuliskan?
Can you show me (on the map)?	Anda bisa tolong tunjukkan pada saya (di peta)?
at the corner	di sudut
at the traffic lights	di lampu merah
behind	di belakang
in front of	di depan
far (from)	jauh (dari)
left	kiri
near (to)	dekat (dengan)
next to	di samping
opposite	di seberang
right	kanan
straight ahead	lurus

EATING & DRINKING

What would you recommend?	Apa yang Anda rekomendasikan?
What's in that dish?	Hidangan itu isinya apa?
That was delicious.	Ini enak sekali.
Cheers!	Bersulang!
Bring the bill/check, please.	Tolong bawa kuitansi.
I don't eat ...	Saya tidak makan ...
dairy products	susu dan keju
fish	ikan
(red) meat	daging (merah)
peanuts	kacang tanah
seafood	makanan laut

KEY PATTERNS

To get by in Indonesian, mix and match these simple patterns with words of your choice:

Where's (the station)?	Di mana (stasiun)?
When's (the next bus)?	Jam berapa (bis yang berikutnya)?
How much is it (per night)?	Berapa (satu malam)?
I'm looking for (a hotel).	Saya cari (hotel).
Do you have (a local map)?	Ada (peta daerah)?
Is there (a toilet)?	Ada (kamar kecil)?
Can I (enter)?	Boleh saya (masuk)?
Do I need (a visa)?	Saya harus pakai (visa)?
I have (a reservation).	Saya (sudah punya booking).
I need (assistance).	Saya perlu (dibantu).
I'd like (the menu).	Saya minta (daftar makanan).
I'd like to (hire a car).	Saya mau (sewa mobil).
Could you (help me)?	Bisa Anda (bantu saya?

a table ...	meja ...
at (eight) o'clock	pada jam (delapan)
for (two) people	untuk (dua) orang

Key Words

baby food (formula)	susu kaleng
bar	bar
bottle	botol
bowl	mangkuk
breakfast	sarapan
cafe	kafe
children's menu	menu untuk anak-anak
cold	dingin
dinner	makan malam
dish	piring
drink list	daftar minuman
food	makanan
food stall	warung
fork	garpu
glass	gelas

QUESTION WORDS

How?	Bagaimana?
What?	Apa?
When?	Kapan?
Where?	Di mana?
Which	Yang mana?
Who?	Siapa?
Why?	Kenapa?

highchair	kursi tinggi
hot (warm)	hangat
knife	pisau
lunch	makan siang
menu	daftar makanan
market	pasar
napkin	tisu
plate	piring
restaurant	rumah makan
salad	selada
soup	sop
spicy	pedas
spoon	sendok
vegetarian food	makanan tanpa daging
with	dengan
without	tanpa

Meat & Fish

beef	daging sapi
carp	ikan mas
chicken	ayam
duck	bebek
fish	ikan
lamb	daging anak domba
mackerel	tenggiri
meat	daging
pork	daging babi
shrimp/prawn	udang
tuna	cakalang
turkey	kalkun

Fruit & Vegetables

apple	apel
banana	pisang
beans	kacang
cabbage	kol
carrot	wortel
cauliflower	blumkol
cucumber	timun
dates	kurma
eggplant	terung
fruit	buah
grapes	buah anggur
lemon	jeruk asam
orange	jeruk manis
pineapple	nanas
potato	kentang
raisins	kismis
spinach	bayam
vegetable	sayur-mayur
watermelon	semangka

Other

bread	roti
butter	mentega
cheese	keju
chilli	cabai
chilli sauce	sambal
egg	telur
honey	madu
jam	selai
noodles	mie
oil	minyak
pepper	lada
rice	nasi
salt	garam
soy sauce	kecap
sugar	gula
vinegar	cuka

Drinks

beer	bir
coconut milk	santan

SIGNS

Buka	Open
Dilarang	Prohibited
Kamar Kecil	Toilets
Keluar	Exit
Masuk	Entrance
Pria	Men
Tutup	Closed
Wanita	Women

coffee	kopi
juice	jus
milk	susu
palm sap wine	tuak
red wine	anggur merah
soft drink	minuman ringan
tea	teh
water	air
white wine	anggur putih
yogurt	susu masam kental

EMERGENCIES

Help!	Tolong saya!
I'm lost.	Saya tersesat.
Leave me alone!	Jangan ganggu saya!
Call a doctor!	Panggil dokter!
Call the police!	Panggil polisi!
I'm ill.	Saya sakit.
It hurts here.	Sakitnya di sini.
I'm allergic to (antibiotics).	Saya alergi (antibiotik).

SHOPPING & SERVICES

| I'd like to buy ... | Saya mau beli ... |
| I'm just looking. | Saya lihat-lihat saja. |

NUMBERS	
1	satu
2	dua
3	tiga
4	empat
5	lima
6	enam
7	tujuh
8	delapan
9	sembilan
10	sepuluh
20	dua puluh
30	tiga puluh
40	empat puluh
50	lima puluh
60	enam puluh
70	tujuh puluh
80	delapan puluh
90	sembilan puluh
100	seratus
1000	seribu

May I look at it?	Boleh saya lihat?
I don't like it.	Saya tidak suka.
How much is it?	Berapa harganya?
It's too expensive.	Itu terlalu mahal.
Can you lower the price?	Boleh kurang?
There's a mistake in the bill.	Ada kesalahan dalam kuitansi ini.

credit card	kartu kredit
foreign exchange office	kantor penukaran mata uang asing
internet cafe	warnet
mobile/cell phone	henpon
post office	kantor pos
signature	tanda tangan
tourist office	kantor pariwisata

TIME & DATES

What time is it?	Jam berapa sekarang?
It's (10) o'clock.	Jam (sepuluh).
It's half to (seven; 6:30)	Setengah (tujuh).
in the morning	pagi
in the afternoon	siang
in the evening	malam
yesterday	kemarin
today	hari ini
tomorrow	besok

Monday	hari Senin
Tuesday	hari Selasa
Wednesday	hari Rabu
Thursday	hari Kamis
Friday	hari Jumat
Saturday	hari Sabtu
Sunday	hari Minggu

TRANSPORT

Public Transport

bicycle-rickshaw	becak
boat (general)	kapal
boat (local)	perahu
bus	bis
minibus	bemo
motorcycle-rickshaw	bajaj
motorcycle-taxi	ojek
plane	pesawat
taxi	taksi
train	kereta api

LOCAL LANGUAGES

Bahasa Indonesia is a second language for 90% of Indonesians. More than 700 *bahasa daerah* (local languages) rank Indonesia second only to Papua New Guinea in linguistic diversity. As a visitor, you'll never be expected to speak any local languages, but there's no doubt that locals will appreciate your extra effort.

Here are some useful basic phrases in Balinese (which has around four million speakers in Bali) and Javanese (spoken by about 80 million people in Java). Note that these languages don't have specific phrases for greetings like 'hello' or 'goodbye'. Also, there are three distinct language 'levels' – the differences are related to the social status of the speaker. We've provided the 'middle level' understood by all Balinese and Javanese speakers.

Balinese

How are you?	*Kenken kabare?*	Do you speak Balinese?	*Bisa ngomong Bali sing?*
Thank you.	*Matur suksma.*	What do you call this in Balinese?	*Ne ape adane di Bali?*
What's your name?	*Sire wastene?*		
My name is ...	*Adan tiange ...*	Which is the way to (Ubud)?	*Kije jalan lakar kel (Ubud)?*
I don't understand.	*Tiang sing ngerti.*		
How much is this?	*Ji kude niki?*		

Javanese

How are you?	*Piye kabare?*	Do you speak Javanese?	*Sampeyan saged basa Jawi?*
Thank you.	*Matur nuwun.*	What do you call this in Javanese?	*Napa namine ing basa Jawi?*
What's your name?	*Nami panjenengan sinten?*		
My name is ...	*Nami kula ...*	Which is the way to (Kaliurang)?	*Menawi bade dateng (Kaliurang) langkung pundi, nggih?*
I don't understand.	*Kula mboten mangertos.*		
How much is this?	*Pinten regine?*		

I want to go to ...	*Saya mau ke ...*
At what time does it leave?	*Jam berapa berangkat?*
At what time does it arrive at ...?	*Jam berapa sampai di ...?*
Does it stop at ...?	*Di ... berhenti?*
What's the next stop?	*Apa nama halte berikutnya?*
Please tell me when we get to ...	*Tolong, beritahu waktu kita sampai di ...*
Please stop here.	*Tolong, berhenti di sini.*
a ... ticket	*tiket ...*
1st-class	*kelas satu*
2nd-class	*kelas dua*
one-way	*sekali jalan*
return	*pulang pergi*
first/last	*pertama/terakhir*
platform	*peron*
ticket office	*loket tiket*
timetable	*jadwal*
train station	*stasiun kereta api*

Driving & Cycling

I'd like to hire a ...	*Saya mau sewa ...*
4WD	*gardan ganda*
bicycle	*sepeda*
car	*mobil*
motorcycle	*sepeda motor*
child seat	*kursi anak untuk di mobil*
helmet	*helem*
mechanic	*montir*
petrol	*bensin*
pump (bicycle)	*pompa sepeda*
service station	*pompa bensin*
Is this the road to ...?	*Apakah jalan ini ke ...?*
(How long) Can I park here?	*(Berapa lama) Saya boleh parkir di sini?*
The car/motocycle has broken down.	*Mobil/Motor mogok.*
I have a flat tyre.	*Ban saya kempes.*
I've run out of petrol.	*Saya kehabisan bensin.*

GLOSSARY

adat – traditional laws and regulations

air – water

air panas – hot water

air terjun – waterfall

AMA – Associated Mission Aviation; Catholic missionary air service operating in remote regions of Papua

anak – child

angklung – musical instrument made from different lengths and thicknesses of bamboo suspended in a frame

angkot – or *angkota;* short for *angkutan kota* (city transport); small minibuses covering city routes, like a *bemo*

angkudes – short for *angkutan pedesaan;* minibuses running to nearby villages from cities, or between villages

anjing – dog

arja – refined operatic form of Balinese theatre

Arjuna – hero of the *Mahabharata* epic and a popular temple gate guardian image

babi rusa – wild deer-like pig

bahasa – language; Bahasa Indonesia is the national language

bajaj – motorised three-wheeler taxi found in Jakarta

bak mandi – common Indonesian form of bath, consisting of a large water tank from which water is ladled over the body

bale – open-sided Balinese pavilion, house or shelter with steeply pitched roof; meeting place

balok – palm wine

bandar – harbour, port

bandara – airport

banjar – local division; a Balinese village consisting of married adult males

bapak – often shortened to *pak;* father; also a polite form of address to any older man

barat – west

Barong – mythical lion-dog creature

batik – cloth made by coating part of the fabric with wax, then dyeing it and melting the wax out

batik cap – stamped batik

batik tulis – hand-painted or literally 'written' batik

becak – bicycle-rickshaw

bemo – minibus

bendi – two-person horse-drawn cart; used in Sulawesi, Sumatra and Maluku

bensin – petrol

benteng – fort

bentor – motorised *becak*

Betawi – original name of Batavia (now Jakarta); ethnic group indigenous to Jakarta

bis – bus

bouraq – winged horselike creature with the head of a woman

Brahma – the creator; with Shiva and Vishnu part of the trinity of chief Hindu gods

bu – shortened form of *ibu*

bukit – hill

bule – common term for foreigner (Caucasian)

bupati – government official in charge of a *kabupaten*

caci – a ceremonial martial art in which participants duel with whips and shields

candi – shrine or temple; usually Hindu or Buddhist of ancient Javanese design

cenderawasih – bird of paradise

colt – minibus

dalang – puppeteer and storyteller of *wayang kulit*

danau – lake

dangdut – popular Indonesian music that is characterised by wailing vocals and a strong beat

desa – village

dinas pariwisata – tourist office

dokar – two-person, horse-drawn cart

dukun – faith healer and herbal doctor; mystic

Gajah Mada – famous Majapahit prime minister

gamelan – traditional Javanese and Balinese orchestra

gang – alley or footpath

Garuda – mythical man-bird, the vehicle of Vishnu and the modern symbol of Indonesia

gereja – church

gili – islet, atoll

Golkar – Golongan Karya (Functional Groupings) political party

gua – or *goa;* cave

gunung – mountain

gunung api – volcano; literally 'fire mountain'

harga touris – tourist price

hutan – forest, jungle

ibu – often shortened to *bu;* mother; also polite form of address to an older woman

ikat – cloth in which the pattern is produced by dyeing the individual threads before weaving

jadwal – schedule or timetable

jalan – abbreviated to Jl; street or road

jalan jalan – to go for a stroll

jalan pintas – short cut

jam karet – 'rubber time'; time is flexible

jamu – herbal medicine

jembatan – bridge

jilbab – Muslim head covering worn by women

kabupaten – regency

kain – cloth

kaki lima – mobile food carts; literally 'five feet' (the three feet of the cart and the two of the vendor)

kala – demonic face often seen over temple gateways

kamar kecil – toilet; literally 'small room'; also known as WC (pronounced way-say)

kampung – village, neighbourhood

kantor – office

Kantor Bupati – Governor's Office

karang – coral, coral reef, atoll

kav – lot, parcel of land

kepala desa – village head

kepulauan – archipelago

keraton – see kraton

ketoprak – popular Javanese folk theatre

Ketuktilu – traditional Sundanese (Java) dance in which professional female dancers perform for male spectators

kijang – a type of deer; also a popular Toyota 4WD vehicle, often used for public transport (Kijang)

kora-kora – canoe (Papua)

kramat – sacred

kraton – walled city palace

kretek – Indonesian clove cigarette

kris – wavy-bladed traditional dagger, often held to have spiritual or magical powers

krismon – monetary crisis

kulit – leather

lapangan – field, square

laut – sea, ocean

Legong – classic Balinese dance performed by young girls; Legong dancer

lontar – type of palm tree; traditional books were written on the dried leaves of the lontar palm

losmen – basic accommodation, usually cheaper than hotels and often family-run

MAF – Mission Aviation Fellowship; Protestant missionary air service that operates in remote regions

Mahabharata – venerated Hindu holy book, telling of the battle between the Pandavas and the Kauravas

Majapahit – last great Javanese Hindu dynasty, pushed out of Java into Bali by the rise of Islamic power

makam – grave

mandau – machete (Kalimantan)

marapu – term for all spiritual forces, including gods, spirits and ancestors

mata air panas – hot springs

menara – minaret, tower

meru – multiroofed shrines in Balinese temples; the same roof style also can be seen in ancient Javanese mosques

mesjid – *masjid* in Papua; mosque

mikrolet – small taxi; tiny *opelet*

moko – bronze drum from Pulau Alor (Nusa Tenggara)

muezzin – mosque official who calls the faithful to prayer five times a day

ngadhu – parasol-like thatched roof; ancestor totem of the Ngada people of Flores

nusa – island

Odalan – temple festival held every 210 days (duration of the Balinese year)

ojek – or *ojeg;* motorcycle taxi

oleh-oleh – souvenirs

opelet – small minibus, like a *bemo*

OPM – Organisasi Papua Merdeka; Free Papua Movement; main group that opposes Indonesian rule of Papua

orang kulit putih – white person, foreigner (Caucasian); *bule* is more commonly used

pak – shortened form of *bapak*

PAN – Partai Amanat Nasional; National Mandate Party

pantai – beach

pasar – market

pasar malam – night market

pasar terapung – floating market

pasir – sand

patas – express, express bus

patola – ikat motif of a hexagon framing a type of four-pronged star

PDI – Partai Demokrasi Indonesia; Indonesian Democratic Party

PDI-P – Partai Demokrasi Indonesia-Perjuangan; Indonesian Democratic Party for Struggle

pegunungan – mountain range

pelabuhan – harbour, port, dock

pelan pelan – slowly

pelawangan – gateway

Pelni – Pelayaran Nasional Indonesia; national shipping line with a fleet of passenger ships operating throughout the archipelago

pencak silat – form of martial arts originally from Sumatra, but now popular throughout Indonesia

pendopo – large, open-sided pavilion that serves as an audience hall; located in front of a Javanese palace

penginapan – simple lodging house

perahu – or *prahu;* boat or canoe

pesanggrahan – or *pasanggrahan;* lodge for government officials where travellers can usually stay

pete-pete – a type of *mikrolet* or *bemo* found in Sulawesi

PHKA – Perlindungan Hutan & Konservasi Alam; the Directorate General of Forest Protection & Nature Conservation; manages Indonesia's national parks; formerly PHPA

pinang – betel nut

pinisi – Makassar or Bugis schooner

PKB – Partai Kebangkitan Bangsa; National Awakening Party

pondok – or *pondok wisata;* guesthouse or lodge; hut

PPP – Partai Persatuan Pembangunan; Development Union Party

prahu – boat or canoe

prasada – shrine or temple; usually Hindu or Buddhist of ancient Javanese design

pulau – island

puputan – warrior's fight to the death; honourable, but suicidal, option when faced with an unbeatable enemy

pura – Balinese temple, shrine

pura dalem – Balinese temple of the dead

pura puseh – Balinese temple of origin

puri – palace

pusaka – sacred heirlooms of a royal family

puskesmas – short for *pusat kesehatan masyarakat;* community health centre

rafflesia – gigantic flower found in Sumatra and Kalimantan, with blooms spreading up to a metre

Ramadan – Muslim month of fasting, when devout Muslims refrain from eating, drinking and smoking during daylight hours

Ramayana – one of the great Hindu holy books; many Balinese and Javanese dances and tales are based on stories from the Ramayana

rangda – witch; evil black-magic spirit of Balinese tales and dances

rawa – swamp, marsh, wetlands

rebab – two-stringed bowed lute

reformasi – reform; refers to political reform after the repression of the Suharto years

RMS – Republik Maluku Selatan; South Maluku Republic; main group that opposed Indonesian rule of southern Maluku

rumah adat – traditional house

rumah makan – restaurant or *warung*

rumah sakit – hospital, literally 'sick house'

sarong – or *sarung*; all-purpose cloth, often sewn into a tube, and worn by women, men and children

Sasak – native of Lombok

sawah – an individual rice field; wet-rice method of cultivation

selat – strait

selatan – south

sembako – Indonesia's nine essential culinary ingredients: rice, sugar, eggs, meat, flour, corn, fuel, cooking oil and salt

semenanjung – peninsula

sirih pinang – betel nut, chewed as a mild narcotic

songket – silver- or gold-threaded cloth, hand woven using floating-weft technique

suling – bamboo flute

sungai – river

surat jalan – travel permit

taksi – common term for a public minibus; taxi

taman – ornamental garden, park, reserve

taman laut – marine park, marine reserve

taman nasional – national park

tanjung – peninsula, cape

tarling – musical style of the Cirebon (Java) area, featuring guitar, *suling* and voice

taxi – besides the Western definition which often applies, in some places this can be a small minibus like a *bemo*

taxi sungai – cargo-carrying river ferry with bunks on the upper level

telaga – lake

telepon kartu – telephone card

teluk – bay

timur – east

tirta – water (Bali)

TNI – Tentara Nasional Indonesia; Indonesian armed forces; formerly ABRI

toko mas – gold shop

tomate – Torajan funeral ceremony

tongkonan – traditional Torajan house with towering roof (Sulawesi)

topeng – wooden mask used in dance-dramas and funerary dances

tuak – homemade fermented coconut drink

uang – money

ular – snake

utara – north

wali songo – nine saints of Islam, who spread the religion throughout Java

Wallace Line – hypothetical line dividing Bali and Kalimantan from Lombok and Sulawesi; marks the end of Asian and the beginning of Australasian flora and fauna zones

waringin – banyan tree; large, shady tree with drooping branches that root and can produce new trees

warnet – short for *wartel internet;* internet stall or centre

warpostel – or *warpapostel;* wartel that also handles postal services

wartel – short for *warung telekomunikasi;* private telephone office

warung – simple eatery

wayang kulit – shadow-puppet play

wayang orang – or *wayang wong;* people theatre

wayang topeng – masked dance-drama

Wektu Telu – religion peculiar to Lombok that originated in Bayan and combines many tenets of Islam and aspects of other faiths

wisma – guesthouse or lodge

Behind the Scenes

SEND US YOUR FEEDBACK

We love to hear from travellers – your comments keep us on our toes and help make our books better. Our well-travelled team reads every word on what you loved or loathed about this book. Although we cannot reply individually to your submissions, we always guarantee that your feedback goes straight to the appropriate authors, in time for the next edition. Each person who sends us information is thanked in the next edition – the most useful submissions are rewarded with a selection of digital PDF chapters.

Visit **lonelyplanet.com/contact** to submit your updates and suggestions or to ask for help. Our award-winning website also features inspirational travel stories, news and discussions.

Note: We may edit, reproduce and incorporate your comments in Lonely Planet products such as guidebooks, websites and digital products, so let us know if you don't want your comments reproduced or your name acknowledged. For a copy of our privacy policy visit lonelyplanet.com/privacy.

AUTHOR THANKS

David Eimer

Special gratitude for their help to Aty in Ternate, Ere in Ambon, Alan in Bandaneira and Vicky in Kei Kecil. Thanks to Tanya Parker and the Lonely Planet crew in London. As ever, thanks to everyone who passed on tips along the way, whether knowingly or unwittingly.

Paul Harding

A big thanks to the many gracious and helpful Indonesians I encountered on the road in Kalimantan, including Denny in Pontianak, Agung, Kipli and Arly in Sintang, Bona Ventura, Liesa, Majid and the crew at Kumai, Tailah, Yayat and Wenny, Meiling in Balikpapan, Budiyono and Danielle. Most of all, thanks to Hannah and Layla for the regular phone calls and enduring patience.

Ashley Harrell

Thanks to editor Tanya Parker and my co-authors for their excellency, Katharine Krzyzanowski for hanging out, the Italians (Gianluca Affitti, Elena Rebeggiani, Maurizio Benedettini and Roberta Simoni) for admiring my recklessness and feeding me cheese, Antoni Sitepu for invaluable assistance and endless amusement, the Korowai people for their hospitality, Jon Clutton and Liz Morgan for their buoyancy tips, and Alex Harrell and Sarah Tosques for flying across the world to keep me company at 25m below sea level. I still can't believe you came.

Trent Holden

First up huge thanks to Tanya Parker at Lonely Planet for giving me this awesome gig to work on Sumatra. So good to be back! A big shout out to Gustri Tri Putra for all your hard work in helping me get around this beast of an island and the laughs and good tunes along the way. I'd also like to thank the following people for their assistance: Ling, Josh, Luke, Zacky, Brigitte, Mr Moon, Nella, Andrea, Timmy, Joseph, Ahmad, Linda, Mery and Abdy. Finally love to all of my family and my beautiful partner Kate.

Mark Johanson

Thanks to all the people on Lombok and Sumbawa who steered me in the right direction and helped me to navigate the post-earthquake islands, even when their personal lives were in shambles. I owe a debt of gratitude to Rudy Trekker, Gemma Marjaya, Kelly Goldie and Andy Wheatcroft for being fountains of knowledge along the way. A special thanks to my partner Felipe Bascuñán for tolerating my long absences and to my editor Niamh O'Brien for tirelessly ensuring I was OK!

BEHIND THE SCENES

MaSovaida Morgan

Deepest thanks to the wonderful souls who provided assistance, insight and companionship throughout my time on Bali: Rob, Margie, Max, Kristy and the Outsite crew; Gigi and Annette; Ty and Jeff; and especially to my dear brother Bayu for an efficient and unforgettable journey.

Jenny Walker

I first visited Indonesia 35 years ago and in a country where everything has changed, the sense of welcome has remained constant. A general thanks, then, to all who helped contribute to the information in the Central Java section of this country update. Specific thanks to Mr Dwi Cahyono of Akgkasa Trans for his wonderful dependability and gentle companionship. Biggest thanks are reserved as ever to beloved Sam (Owen) – husband, co-researcher and fellow traveller.

Ray Bartlett

Thanks first and foremost to Tanya, for the chance to work on this, and to each of the editors who will peek at it afterwards. Thanks as well to my family, friends, and to my incredible Indonesian contacts. In particular, huge thanks to Ms Tijo, the 'Buah Naga', to Sarah H, to Edy and to the rest of my Indonesian pals. Last, I want to send particular wishes to the people in Donggala, Palu and other regions so affected by the earthquake and tsunami. Words can't express my sorrow for your losses, and my admiration for your strength and recovery.

Loren Bell

The biggest thank you to Kari: for putting up with my long absences during these projects – both physical and mental – and for giving me a brief reprieve from dish duties as deadlines approached. Your love and support (and regular pupdates) are critical and felt even half way around the planet.

Jade Bremner

Thanks to Destination Editor Tanya Parker for her support, knowledge and quick-fire responses on Jakarta. Plus, the wider Indonesia team and everyone working behind the scenes on this project – Cheree Broughton, Neill Coen, Evan Godt and Helen Elfer. Last but not least, thanks to the friendly Jakarta locals, who always remain calm, polite and helpful despite the endlessly chaotic surroundings of the city.

Stuart Butler

The first people I must thank are my wife, Heather, and children, Jake and Grace, for their unending patience while I worked on this project (and for graciously accepting my only being able to take a week's holiday). In Java thank you to Dadang Supardi and Suwarna Adi as well as to all the many hotel and restaurant owners and other wonderful Indonesians who helped out. In Lonely Planet land thank you to Tanya for the chance to work on this project.

Sofia Levin

Erwin, Willy and Andy – thank you for your guidance on the road, but most of all, your friendship. To my husband, Matt, this job would be impossible without your constant support and encouragement, both when I'm away and by your side. And to my parents (aka my biggest fans), thank you for instilling me with curiosity, appetite and the travel bug from the moment I was born.

Virginia Maxwell

Thanks to Ryan Ver Berkmoes for the Bali briefing, Hanafi Dharma for the expert driving and navigation, and Niamh O'Brien for monitoring the safety situation. My support team of Peter and Max Handsaker stayed calm when they saw the earthquake reports and made regular Skype calls to check up on me. I couldn't work as a travel writer without them.

Ryan Ver Berkmoes

Thanks to an all-star cast of the Indonesian team: Amy and Romy and Charlie, Hanafi, Patticakes, Ibu Cat, Stuart, Suzanne, Eliot, Edwin, Ed and many more including the ever-productive Samuel L Bronkowitz. Love to Alexis Ver Berkmoes, who gave me Bali sunset memories of my dreams. And a dedication to David Averbuck, an indominable traveller and champion of the righteous.

ACKNOWLEDGMENTS

Climate map data adapted from Peel MC, Finlayson BL & McMahon TA (2007) 'Updated World Map of the Köppen-Geiger Climate Classification', *Hydrology and Earth System Sciences*, 11, 1633–44.

Cover photograph: Togean Islands, Sulawesi, Fabio Lamanna/Shutterstock ©.

THIS BOOK

This 13th edition of Lonely Planet's *Indonesia* guidebook was curated by David Eimer, Paul Harding, Ashley Harrell, Trent Holden, Mark Johanson, MaSovaida Morgan and Jenny Walker, who also researched and wrote it along with Ray Bartlett, Loren Bell, Jade Bremner, Stuart Butler, Sofia Levin, Virginia Maxwell and Ryan Ver Berkmoes. The previous edition was researched and written by Loren, Stuart, Trent, Ryan, Anna Kaminski, Hugh McNaughtan, Adam Skolnick and Iain Stewart. This guidebook was produced by the following:

Destination Editors Tanya Parker, Niamh O'Brien
Senior Product Editors Daniel Bolger, Kate Chapman
Product Editors Katie Connolly, Kathryn Rowan
Regional Senior Cartographers Corey Hutchison, Julie Sheridan
Book Designers Ania Bartoszek, Mazzy Prinsep
Assisting Editors Andrew Bain, James Bainbridge, Michelle Bennett, Heather Champion, Nigel Chin, Lucy Cowie, Kate Daly, Melanie Dankel, Samantha Forge, Carly Hall, Kate James,

Lou McGregor, Rosie Nicholson, Sarah Reid, Simon Williamson
Assisting Cartographers Hunor Csutoros, Julie Dodkins
Cover Researcher Ania Bartoszek
Thanks to Karin Biemel, Jennifer Carey, Barbara Delissen, Martin Heng, Evan Godt, Elizabeth Jones, Karen Henderson, Lauren Keith, Laszlo, Amy Lysen, Derry McCarthy, Catherine Naghten, Claire Naylor, Karyn Noble, Genna Patterson, Matt Phillips, Leslie Poulson, Rachel Rawling, Eleanor Simpson, James Smart, Angela Tinson, Colin Trainer.

BEHIND THE SCENES

Index

Map Legend

Sights

- Beach
- Bird Sanctuary
- Buddhist
- Castle/Palace
- Christian
- Confucian
- Hindu
- Islamic
- Jain
- Jewish
- Monument
- Museum/Gallery/Historic Building
- Ruin
- Shinto
- Sikh
- Taoist
- Winery/Vineyard
- Zoo/Wildlife Sanctuary
- Other Sight

Activities, Courses & Tours

- Bodysurfing
- Diving
- Canoeing/Kayaking
- Course/Tour
- Sento Hot Baths/Onsen
- Skiing
- Snorkelling
- Surfing
- Swimming/Pool
- Walking
- Windsurfing
- Other Activity

Sleeping

- Sleeping
- Camping
- Hut/Shelter

Eating

- Eating

Drinking & Nightlife

- Drinking & Nightlife
- Cafe

Entertainment

- Entertainment

Shopping

- Shopping

Information

- Bank
- Embassy/Consulate
- Hospital/Medical
- Internet
- Police
- Post Office
- Telephone
- Toilet
- Tourist Information
- Other Information

Geographic

- Beach
- Gate
- Hut/Shelter
- Lighthouse
- Lookout
- Mountain/Volcano
- Oasis
- Park
- Pass
- Picnic Area
- Waterfall

Population

- Capital (National)
- Capital (State/Province)
- City/Large Town
- Town/Village

Transport

- Airport
- Border crossing
- Bus
- Cable car/Funicular
- Cycling
- Ferry
- Metro/MTR/MRT station
- Monorail
- Parking
- Petrol station
- Skytrain/Subway station
- Taxi
- Train station/Railway
- Tram
- Underground station
- Other Transport

Routes

- Tollway
- Freeway
- Primary
- Secondary
- Tertiary
- Lane
- Unsealed road
- Road under construction
- Plaza/Mall
- Steps
- Tunnel
- Pedestrian overpass
- Walking Tour
- Walking Tour detour
- Path/Walking Trail

Boundaries

- International
- State/Province
- Disputed
- Regional/Suburb
- Marine Park
- Cliff
- Wall

Hydrography

- River, Creek
- Intermittent River
- Canal
- Water
- Dry/Salt/Intermittent Lake
- Reef

Areas

- Airport/Runway
- Beach/Desert
- Cemetery (Christian)
- Cemetery (Other)
- Glacier
- Mudflat
- Park/Forest
- Sight (Building)
- Sportsground
- Swamp/Mangrove

Note: Not all symbols displayed above appear on the maps in this book

Stuart Butler

East Java, West Java, Thousand Islands Stuart has been writing for Lonely Planet for a decade and during this time he's come eye to eye with gorillas in the Congolese jungles, met a man with horns on his head who could lie in fire, huffed and puffed over snow bound Himalayan mountain passes, interviewed a king who could turn into a tree, and had his fortune told by a parrot. And he's met more than his fair share of self-proclaimed gods. When not on the road for Lonely Planet he lives on the beautiful beaches of southwest France with his wife and two young children.

Sofia Levin

East Nusa Tenggara A Melbourne-based food and travel journalist, Sofia believes that eating in a country other than one's own is the simplest way to understand a culture. She has a stomach of steel and the ability to sniff out local haunts. Aside from trawling Melbourne as the Lonely Planet Local, she also co-authors guidebooks and writes for Fairfax newspapers and travel magazines. When she's not travelling or eating, Sofia runs copywriting and social media company Word Salad and spreads smiles with her Insta-famous poodle, @lifeofjinkee. Find her on Instagram and Twitter (@sofiaklevin).

Virginia Maxwell

Ubud, East Bali Although based in Australia, Virginia spends at least half of her year updating Lonely Planet destination coverage across the globe. The Mediterranean is her major area of interest – she has covered Spain, Italy, Turkey, Syria, Lebanon, Israel, Egypt, Morocco and Tunisia for Lonely Planet – but she also covers Finland, Bali, Armenia, the Netherlands, the US and Australia for Lonely Planet products. Follow her @maxwellvirginia on Instagram and Twitter.

Ryan Ver Berkmoes

Bali, Nusa Tenggara Ryan Ver Berkmoes has written more than 110 guidebooks for Lonely Planet. He grew up in Santa Cruz, CA, but now calls New York City home. He has been travelling the world, both for pleasure and for work, and has covered everything from wars to bars – definitely preferring the latter. His byline has appeared in scores of publications and he's talked travel on radio and TV. Read more at ryanverberkmoes.com and at @ryanvb. Ryan also contributed to the Understand and Survival Guide chapters.

Mark Johanson

Lombok, West Nusa Tenggara Mark Johanson grew up in Virginia and has called five different countries home over the last decade while circling the globe reporting for British newspapers (*The Guardian*), American magazines (*Men's Journal*) and global media outlets (CNN, BBC). When not on the road, you'll find him gazing at the Andes from his current home in Santiago, Chile. Follow his adventures at www.markjohanson.com.

MaSovaida Morgan

Bali MaSovaida is a travel journalist whose wayfaring tendencies have taken her to more than 55 countries across all seven continents. Previously, she was Lonely Planet's Destination Editor for South America and Antarctica for four years, and worked as an editor for newspapers and NGOs in the Middle East and the United Kingdom. Follow her on Instagram @MaSovaida.

Jenny Walker

Central Java A member of the British Guild of Travel Writers, Jenny Walker has travelled to more than 125 countries and has been writing for Lonely Planet for nearly 20 years. Currently working in Oman as Deputy CEO of Oman Academic Accreditation Authority, her MPhil thesis focused on the Arabic Orient in British Literature (Oxford University) and her PhD (nearing completion) is on the Arabian desert as trope.

Ray Bartlett

Sulawesi Ray Bartlett has been travel writing for nearly two decades, bringing Japan, Korea, Mexico, Tanzania, Guatemala, Indonesia and many parts of the United States to life in rich detail for top-industry publishers, newspapers and magazines. His acclaimed debut novel, *Sunsets of Tulum*, set in Yucatán, was a Midwest Book Review 2016 Fiction pick. Among other pursuits, he surfs regularly and is an accomplished Argentine tango dancer. Follow him on Facebook (@ Ray BartlettAuthor), Twitter and Instagram (@kaisoradotcom). Ray currently divides his time between homes in the USA, Japan and Mexico.

Loren Bell

Sulawesi When Loren first backpacked through Europe he was in the backpack. That memorable experience corrupted his six-month-old brain, ensuring he would never be happy sitting still. His penchant for peregrination has taken him from training dogsled teams in the Tetons to chasing gibbons in the jungles of Borneo – with only brief pauses for silly 'responsible' things like earning degrees. When he's not demystifying destinations for Lonely Planet, Loren writes about science and conservation news. He camps in the Rocky Mountains where he probably spends too much time on his mountain bike and skis.

Jade Bremner

Jakarta Jade has been a journalist for more than 15 years. She has lived in and reported on four different regions. Wherever she goes she finds action sports to try, the weirder the better, and it's no coincidence many of her favourite places have some of the best waves in the world. Jade has edited travel magazines and sections for *Time Out* and *Radio Times*, and has contributed to *The Times*, CNN and *The Independent*. She feels privileged to share tales from this wonderful planet we call home and is always looking for the next adventure. Follow her on Twitter @jadebremner.

OUR STORY

A beat-up old car, a few dollars in the pocket and a sense of adventure. In 1972 that's all Tony and Maureen Wheeler needed for the trip of a lifetime – across Europe and Asia overland to Australia. It took several months, and at the end – broke but inspired – they sat at their kitchen table writing and stapling together their first travel guide, *Across Asia on the Cheap*. Within a week they'd sold 1500 copies. Lonely Planet was born.

Today, Lonely Planet has offices in Tennessee, Dublin and Beijing, with a network of over 2000 contributors in every corner of the globe. We share Tony's belief that 'a great guidebook should do three things: inform, educate and amuse'.

OUR WRITERS

David Eimer

Maluku David has been a journalist and writer ever since abandoning the idea of a law career in 1990. After spells working in his native London and in Los Angeles, he moved to Beijing in 2005, where he contributed to a variety of newspapers and magazines in the UK. Since then, he has travelled and lived across China and in numerous cities in Southeast Asia, including Bangkok, Phnom Penh and Yangon. He has been covering China, Myanmar and Thailand for Lonely Planet since 2006. David also contributed to the Plan Your Trip, Understand and Survival Guide chapters.

Paul Harding

Kalimantan As a writer and photographer, Paul has been travelling the globe for the best part of two decades, with an interest in remote and offbeat places, islands and cultures. He's an author and contributor to more than 50 Lonely Planet guides to countries and regions as diverse as India, Belize, Vanuatu, Iran, Indonesia, New Zealand, Iceland, Finland, Philippines and – his home patch – Australia.

Ashley Harrell

Papua After a brief stint selling day spa coupons door-to-door in South Florida, Ashley decided she'd rather be a writer. She went to journalism grad school, convinced a newspaper to hire her, and starting covering wildlife, crime and tourism, sometimes all in the same story. Fueling her zest for storytelling and the unknown, she traveled widely and moved often, from a tiny NYC apartment to a vast California ranch to a jungle cabin in Costa Rica, where she started writing for Lonely Planet. From there her travels became more exotic and farther flung, and she still laughs when paycheques arrive.

Trent Holden

Sumatra A Geelong-based writer, located just outside Melbourne, Trent has worked for Lonely Planet since 2005. He's covered 30-plus guidebooks across Asia, Africa and Australia. With a penchant for megacities, Trent's in his element when assigned to cover a nation's capital – the more chaotic the better – to unearth cool bars, art, street food and underground subculture. On the flipside he also writes books to idyllic tropical islands across Asia, in between going on safari to national parks in Africa and the subcontinent. When not travelling, Trent works as a freelance editor and reviewer, and spends all his money catching live gigs. You can catch him on Twitter @hombreholden.

> **OVER PAGE** | **MORE WRITERS**

Published by Lonely Planet Global Limited
CRN 554153
13th edition – October 2021
ISBN 978 1 78868 436 1
© Lonely Planet 2021   Photographs © as indicated 2021
10 9 8 7 6 5 4 3 2 1
Printed in Singapore